The Editors

NICHOLAS HALMI is Assistant Professor of English at the University of Washington. He is the textual editor of the *Opus Maximum* in *The Collected Works of Samuel Taylor Coleridge*, a contributor to the *Encyclopedia of the Romantic Era*, and the author of numerous articles on Enlightenment and Romantic topics.

PAUL MAGNUSON is Professor of English at New York University. He is the author of *Coleridge's Nightmare Poetry, Coleridge and Wordsworth: A Lyrical Dialogue, Reading Public Romanticism*, and many articles and reviews in scholarly journals.

RAIMONDA MODIANO is Professor of English and Comparative Literature and Director of the Textual Studies Program at the University of Washington. She is the author of *Coleridge's Concept of Nature* and of articles and book chapters on Coleridge and British Romanticism. She co-edited the marginalia on German works for *Marginalia*, vols. 2–6, in *The Collected Works of Samuel Taylor Coleridge*, and (with Peter Shillingsburg and Leroy Searle) the collection *Voice, Text, and Hypertext: Emerging Practices in Textual Studies*. Her numerous grants and awards include the University of Washington's Distinguished Teaching Award.

W. W. NORTON & COMPANY, INC.
Also Publishes

THE NORTON ANTHOLOGY OF AFRICAN AMERICAN LITERATURE
edited by Henry Louis Gates Jr. and Nellie Y. McKay et al.

THE NORTON ANTHOLOGY OF AMERICAN LITERATURE
edited by Nina Baym et al.

THE NORTON ANTHOLOGY OF CHILDREN'S LITERATURE
edited by Jack Zipes et al.

THE NORTON ANTHOLOGY OF CONTEMPORARY FICTION
edited by R. V. Cassill and Joyce Carol Oates

THE NORTON ANTHOLOGY OF ENGLISH LITERATURE
edited by M. H. Abrams and Stephen Greenblatt et al.

THE NORTON ANTHOLOGY OF LITERATURE BY WOMEN
edited by Sandra M. Gilbert and Susan Gubar

THE NORTON ANTHOLOGY OF MODERN AND CONTEMPORARY POETRY
edited by Jahan Ramazani, Richard Ellmann, and Robert O'Clair

THE NORTON ANTHOLOGY OF POETRY
edited by Margaret Ferguson, Mary Jo Salter, and Jon Stallworthy

THE NORTON ANTHOLOGY OF SHORT FICTION
edited by R. V. Cassill and Richard Bausch

THE NORTON ANTHOLOGY OF THEORY AND CRITICISM
edited by Vincent B. Leitch et al.

THE NORTON ANTHOLOGY OF WORLD LITERATURE
edited by Sarah Lawall et al.

THE NORTON FACSIMILE OF THE FIRST FOLIO OF SHAKESPEARE
prepared by Charlton Hinman

THE NORTON INTRODUCTION TO LITERATURE
edited by Alison Booth, J. Paul Hunter, and Kelly J. Mays

THE NORTON INTRODUCTION TO THE SHORT NOVEL
edited by Jerome Beaty

THE NORTON READER
edited by Linda H. Peterson and John C. Brereton

THE NORTON SAMPLER
edited by Thomas Cooley

THE NORTON SHAKESPEARE, BASED ON THE OXFORD EDITION
edited by Stephen Greenblatt et al.

For a complete list of Norton Critical Editions, visit
www.wwnorton.com/college/english/nce_home.htm

A NORTON CRITICAL EDITION

COLERIDGE'S POETRY AND PROSE

AUTHORITATIVE TEXTS

CRITICISM

Selected and Edited by

Nicholas Halmi

UNIVERSITY OF WASHINGTON

Paul Magnuson

NEW YORK UNIVERSITY

Raimonda Modiano

UNIVERSITY OF WASHINGTON

W. W. NORTON & COMPANY

New York • London

In Memory of Karen Shabetai

Publication of this book has been aided by a grant from the Abraham and Rebecca Stein Faculty Publication Fund of New York University, Department of English.

W. W. Norton & Company has been independent since its founding in 1923, when William Warder Norton and Mary D. Herter Norton first published lectures delivered at the People's Institute, the adult education division of New York City's Cooper Union. The Nortons soon expanded their program beyond the Institute, publishing books by celebrated academics from America and abroad. By mid-century, the two major pillars of Norton's publishing program—trade books and college texts—were firmly established. In the 1950s, the Norton family transferred control of the company to its employees, and today—with a staff of four hundred and a comparable number of trade, college, and professional titles published each year—W. W. Norton & Company stands as the largest and oldest publishing house owned wholly by its employees.

Copyright © 2004 by W. W. Norton & Company, Inc.

Since this page cannot accommodate all the copyright notices, p. xxiv constitutes an extension of the copyright page.

All rights reserved.
Printed in the United States of America.
First Edition.

The text of this book is composed in Fairfield Medium with the display set in Bernhard Modern.
Composition by PennSet, Inc.
Manufacturing by the Courier Companies, Inc.
Book design by Antonina Krass.
Production manager: Benjamin Reynolds.

Library of Congress Cataloging-in-Publication Data

Coleridge, Samuel Taylor, 1772–1834.
  [Selections. 2002]
  Coleridge's poetry and prose : authoritative texts, criticism / selected and edited by
  p. cm. — (A Norton critical edition)
  Includes bibliographical references and index.

  ISBN 0-393-97904-0 (pbk.)

  1. Coleridge, Samuel Taylor, 1772–1834—Criticism and interpretation.
I. Halmi. Nicholas. II. Magnuson, Paul. III. Modiano, Raimonda. IV. Title.

PR4472 .H35 2002
821'.7—dc21

                                                                    2002026506

W. W. Norton & Company, Inc., 500 Fifth Avenue, New York, N.Y. 10110
www.wwnorton.com

W. W. Norton & Company Ltd., Castle House,
75/76 Wells Street, London W1T 3QT

2   3   4   5   6   7   8   9   0

Contents

The Texts of *Coleridge's Poetry and Prose*

Criticism

List of Illustrations

General Introduction

Coleridge was one of a handful of writers in English literature who combined the genius of a poet with the thought of a philosophical critic. He composed three or four of the finest poems in the language and created original lyric and narrative forms. His legacy includes not only the poems themselves but also the records he left of his attention to the craft of poetry, his obsessive revisions of his own poems, his comments on his and others' poetic style, and innumerable notebook entries on the craft of poetry. He pondered the philosophical and psychological bases of creativity and sought to develop a methodical criticism of literature (which he called *practical criticism*) in his lectures on Shakespeare and his close analysis of Wordsworth's poetry.

Coleridge was also among the best read of English writers, his reading extending from the Greek and Latin classics through philosophy and natural science to literature in seven languages, travel writing, history, and (as it was called in his day) political economy. He was, perhaps, one of the last thinkers to attempt to unify knowledge on a religious basis, to create a systematic, theoretical account of human knowledge and the processes of human thought. Although ultimately his efforts foundered, he left brilliant fragments of his engagement with the latest British and continental philosophy. Few of his contemporaries in Britain could claim as thorough a knowledge of the history of philosophy from Plato onward or as intimate a familiarity with the works of German idealist thinkers such as Immanuel Kant, J. G. Fichte, and F. W. J. Schelling. (Among the few in early-nineteenth-century Britain who shared Coleridge's interest in German philosophy and literature, the most notable—Thomas De Quincey, Thomas Carlyle, and Henry Crabb Robinson—were also personally acquainted with Coleridge.) Particularly interested in psychology, ethics, and theological matters in his later years, Coleridge had a profound influence on Anglican theology and the American Transcendentalist movement. By the end of his life, his erudition and eloquence had established him as a kind of cult figure, and numerous younger writers and artists made pilgrimages to visit him, including the American writers James Fenimore Cooper and Ralph Waldo Emerson.

Throughout his life, Coleridge was a publicly engaged figure. Initially a supporter of the revolution in France and of reform in Britain, he defended the principles of internationalism, equality, and liberty; later, when the excesses of the French Revolution became obvious, he defended British nationalism and the principle of private property. His outlets were lectures and pamphlets on politics in the 1790s, newspaper writing on various topics in the late-1790s and the first decade of the next century, lectures on literature and philosophy in the second decade of the nineteenth century, and books on theology and civil society in the 1820s. His role as a public man of letters inevitably made him controversial, the target of criticism and abuse. He entered debates early in life with a reckless devotion to reform and in later life with a determined defense of his character and thought. All of this he accomplished while enduring the personal—and sometimes humiliatingly public—agonies of his intense self-doubt, of his opium addiction (which became almost totally incapacitating in 1813–14), of his failed marriage, of his unrequited love for Sara Hutchinson, and of his financial and psychological dependence on the generosity and patronage of others.

This edition seeks, within the limits imposed by the series, to present a view of Coleridge's literary career as it unfolded before the eyes of his immediate contemporaries. Our selections from the poetry illustrate the development of his poetic style—the shift from the turgid, sentimental, and allegorical poetry of the mid-1790s to the meditative, conversational, blank-verse poetry of the late-1790s—as well as his collaboration with Wordsworth on *The Rime of the Ancient Mariner* and *Lyrical Ballads* and his poetic dialogue with Wordsworth in 1802. We also emphasize Coleridge's development of his poetic canon, as represented by his choice of poems in various volumes of his collected poetry, and by other forms of publication he chose. We comment on the locations of his publication, the printing of poems in newspapers, reviews, anthologies, and the like. For these purposes we have organized the poetry according to the volume in which a poem first appeared and the order in which the poems appeared in that volume. Printing early versions (with important later revisions indicated in footnotes) allows readers to see more clearly than alternative methods of presentation the transformations in Coleridge's style and its underlying aesthetic assumptions. Coleridge was as diligent an annotator of his own poetry as he was of others' books, and his comments, often quoted in criticism today, make more sense if readers can see the same version of the poem as that to which he refers.

In general, we have selected poems for this edition that Coleridge himself consistently reprinted and have omitted poems that he omitted or left uncollected. For each volume we include the important structural elements of prefaces, epigraphs, mottos, and footnotes to both the poems and the volume itself, all of which provided the frames in which Coleridge's first readers encountered his poems. Two volumes of poetry are printed in their entirety: *Fears in Solitude* and *Christabel, Kubla Khan, and The Pains of Sleep*; others are represented by selections. In addition, we have included "The Visions of the Maid of Orleans," originally published in the *Morning Post* and never before reprinted in its newspaper form, and a selection of the poems that he contributed to Robert Southey's *Annual Anthology*. We have printed *The Rime of the Ancient Mariner* in two versions, that of *Lyrical Ballads* (1798) and that of 1834, in parallel texts on facing pages. The first published version of "Dejection: An Ode" is printed immediately after the original version in a verse letter to Sara Hutchinson. Finally, we have included a category of uncollected poetry for poems that Coleridge did not print in any of his collected editions; these are taken from his notebooks or published sources such as newspapers.

Each volume or section is introduced by a headnote that describes the volume's development, its structure, and the circumstances of its publication. The headnotes detail the printing and sale of the volume, if known and significant; the roles played in their publication by publishers (like Joseph Cottle), patrons (like Lord Byron), and editors (like his nephew Henry Nelson Coleridge); and the contributions of others. The early collections included poems by Charles Lamb and Charles Lloyd; Wordsworth and Coleridge collaborated on *Lyrical Ballads*; and even *Sibylline Leaves* contained a poem by Coleridge's friend Washington Allston. Where it is relevant, the headnotes also describe the volume's historical context, as with *Fears in Solitude*, or the biographical context, as with the "Dejection" poems. The first footnote to each poem provides information about the poem's date and place of publication as well as, where relevant, about Coleridge's signature or pseudonym. Coleridge's annotations in presentation copies of his works—the first stage in the reception of those works—are frequently recorded in the footnotes. Notes to individual poems and lines contain Coleridge's manuscript annotations in presentation copies. We have noted Coleridge's comments made on proof sheets, when he was trying to ensure the accurate printing of his poems or responding to the printer's proposed changes to them, and we have cited Coleridge's comments on his poems in letters and notebooks. The footnotes present some of the more important revisions to the first published versions of texts, as well as some revisions entered in presentation copies but never printed. Our commentary extends beyond Coleridge's notes to include the observations of his close friends, the stylistic criticism of John Thelwall and Charles Lamb on the early poetry and the defense of his later poetry by John Morgan and James Gillman, all of whom could reasonably have had access to Coleridge's explanations. Throughout this edition, the level of annotation is higher than is customary in Norton Critical Editions, because Coleridge's allusiveness and linguistic range make demands that few modern-day readers are prepared to meet without the assistance of explanatory notes.

We have included a generous selection from Coleridge's political prose of 1795 and *The Watchman* of 1796, written at the same time that he was composing his first two volumes of poetry. Like many poets of his day, Coleridge printed extensive notes to his poetry, many of which refer to the political events and debates of his time. Later in life, under the pressure of attacks on both his political positions and his character, he tended to misrepresent his earlier radical years in attempts to defend his name. In spite of the efforts in his day and ours to label the youthful Coleridge a radical, Jacobin, or democrat and the mature Coleridge as a Tory, Conservative, or Apostate, we prefer to let him speak for himself and to illustrate his positions on those particular issues that animated his writing and constituted his public persona. *A Moral and Political Lecture* analyzes the diverse groups of radicals, or as they were called in Coleridge's day, both in France and Britain, the Friends of Freedom, to define a principled opposition to the government and to distinguish his position from that of groups carried away by the exasperated passion of hatred, which led to purposeless violence, or of those motivated merely by self-interest. *Conciones ad Populum* is a harangue against the war with France and the political and religious establishment that supports both the war and the empire. *The Plot Discovered* argues against the government's attempts to suppress free speech and political gatherings, and "On the Slave Trade" in *The Watchman* reflects Coleridge's active participation in the efforts to abolish the slave trade.

Coleridge's radical politics were deeply involved with his Unitarianism in 1795 and 1796, as his *Lectures on Revealed Religion* amply demonstrate. Lecture 2 and Lecture 5 draw on the history of the Jews to argue against the accumulation of wealth, luxury, and private property and for universal equality. These principles informed the idealistic and utterly impractical scheme developed by Coleridge, Southey, and a few other enthusiasts in 1795 to establish "pantisocracy," or government by all, in a small community in Pennsylvania. Lecture 5 reflects the Unitarian position, argued forcefully by Joseph Priestley, that the Christianity of the first few centuries, before the establishment of the doctrine of the Trinity and the alliance of the church with secular power, represented true Christianity. Woven into the fabric of Coleridge's rhetoric are the Unitarian rejections of Christ's atonement, the Trinity, and established priesthood. Atonement, for the Unitarians, was something one should enact for oneself, rather than rely on supernatural aid. In Coleridge's day, Unitarianism was regarded as a rational religion, but Coleridge's Unitarianism was prophetic and visionary, as reflected in "Religious Musings," and rejected much of the materialism, atheism, and purported immorality in the writings of John Thelwall and William Godwin. We include Coleridge's 1802 essay "Once a Jacobin Always a Jacobin" to mark his turn away from radical politics and toward support of the idea of a nation-state founded on inherited private property.

Coleridge's *Statesman's Manual*, addressed to the higher classes, combines philosophy, theology, and religion to argue against the utilitarian, practical, empirical, and materialistic ethos governing politics and for a philosophical idealism founded on a reading of the Bible. Our selections from Coleridge's central distinctions between reason and understanding and symbol and allegory reflect his consistent opposition to materialism in all its forms, as does his distinction between imagination and fancy in the *Biographia*. The distinction between reason and understanding is again his subject in our selections from the revised edition of *The Friend* (1818), which we have included along with selections from the "Essays in Method." Finally, we have included sections from *Aids to Reflection* on prudence and morality, in which Coleridge argues for a principled morality based on reason.

Our selections from Coleridge's literary criticism complement his philosophical writings. We include selections from his lectures of 1811–12, as recorded by John Payne Collier, to illustrate his understanding of psychology in *Romeo and Juliet* and *Hamlet* as well as his notions of the dramatic unities, genius, and the distinction between mechanical and organic form in art. Our selections from his 1818 lectures discuss his definitions of dramatic illusion and the distinction between an imitation and a copy. We also include generous selections from *Essays on the Principles of Genial Criticism*, in which he distinguishes the merely agreeable from beauty and defines the formal properties of beauty as unity. Coleridge's most important literary criticism is in the *Biographia Literaria*, where he defines genius by reference to Shakespeare and Milton, distinguishes between imagination and fancy, and applies these to practical criticism of Wordsworth's poetry. At the same time, he tries to ground his aesthetic distinctions in a philosophy that rejects his own earlier materialism and associationism for an idealism based on a philosophy of self consciousness that finds knowledge and aesthetic form originating in the mind, rather than in the external world. The philosophy is fragmentary and incomplete; the distinctions between imagination and fancy, fugitive; and the practical criticism, occasionally tendentious and self-serving; but the *Biographia*, his Shakespeare criticism, and his practical criticism remain classics of English literature.

At the end of the volume we have provided a necessarily limited selection of nineteenth- and twentieth-century criticism of Coleridge's poetry and prose, a selective bibliography of primary and secondary texts, a register of basic biographical information about persons mentioned frequently in the edition, a glossary of philosophical and political terms used frequently in Coleridge's texts and our notes, and a chronology of Coleridge's life. (Dates are not given in the notes for persons listed in the Biographical Register.) Information on editions cited frequently in the notes may be found in the list of abbreviations or in the notice of copyright permissions.

Paul Magnuson selected and edited the poetry and drafted notes for the second volume of the *Biographia*. Raimonda Modiano selected and edited *A Moral and Political Lecture, Conciones ad Populum, Lectures on Revealed Religion, The Plot Discovered, The Watchman*, "Once a Jacobin Always a Jacobin," the *Lay Sermons*, the first volume of the *Biographia*, and *On the Constitution of the Church and State*; she also selected the critical essays. Nicholas Halmi selected and edited the literary lectures, *Essays on the Principles of Genial Criticism, The Friend, Aids to Reflection*, the letters, and the miscellaneous prose; he also revised the notes for the second volume of the *Biographia* and compiled the bibliography, the biographical register, and the glossary. We read and revised each other's work in progress, so the volume is truly a collaborative effort.

Textual Introduction

Works published by Coleridge himself—both poetry and prose—are presented in this volume in their earliest published volumes. Where we have departed from this principle, as we have by printing two versions each of *The Rime of the Ancient Mariner* and "Dejection: An Ode," and in printing selections from Coleridge's revised editions of *The Friend* and *On the Constitution of the Church and State*, we have explained the reasons for the departure in the respective headnotes. Writings that remained unpublished in Coleridge's lifetime are either taken from the currently available standard editions of his *Collected Letters*, *Collected Works*, and *Notebooks*, or they have been transcribed afresh from the manuscripts; our notes indicate the sources of these and all other texts. Coleridge's annotations in presentation copies of his works have been recorded in footnotes (usually in our own transcriptions from the original volumes) when we judged them significant. Throughout the edition, we have retained the original spelling, capitalization, and punctuation of our printed or manuscript source-texts, with the following exceptions:

1. Obvious printer's errors, as opposed to variant spellings permitted in Coleridge's time, are silently corrected.
2. We have replaced the long *s*, used in editions of Coleridge's earliest poetry and prose, with a short *s*, and we have replaced large initial capitals with ordinary capital letters. We retain small capitals and italics as they appear in the original editions.
3. We have normalized the possessive forms *its*, *theirs*, and *ours* to conform to standard usage in Coleridge's time and ours.
4. We have removed the quotation marks originally surrounding block quotations in the prose writings, as they would now appear redundant and possibly cause confusion.
5. Deleted words and punctuation marks are omitted from texts derived from manuscript sources, such as the literary lectures, letters, and notebook entries quoted in the Miscellaneous Prose section and the footnotes.

Acknowledgments

Like all editors and readers of Coleridge, we owe an immense debt to the family editors, Henry Nelson Coleridge, Sara Coleridge, Derwent Coleridge, and Ernest Hartley Coleridge, who preserved, collected, arranged, and annotated their ancestor's writings. In the twentieth century, the late Kathleen Coburn began the modern editing of Coleridge's *Notebooks* and supervised the publication of his *Collected Works*, while the late Earl Leslie Griggs edited *The Collected Letters*. Our indebtedness to these editions, both for texts themselves and for material in our annotations, is immense, and gratefully acknowledged. We are also grateful for the assistance we have received from the staffs of the following libraries: the Beinecke Library, Yale University; the Berg Collection and Pforzheimer Library, New York Public Library; the Departments of Printed Books, Manuscripts, and Newspapers at The British Library, London; the Houghton Library, Harvard University; the Henry E. Huntington Library in San Marino; the J. Pierpont Morgan Library, New York; the Newberry Library, Chicago; the Osborne Collection of Early Children's Books, Toronto Public Library; the Princeton University Library; the Library of St. John's College, Cambridge; and the Victoria College Library (Coleridge Collection), University of Toronto.

We gratefully acknowledge support from the Royalty Research Fund at the University of Washington and the Arts Research Board at McMaster University. We thank those who have answered our queries or made suggestions for the edition: Brian Baker, Christopher Baptista, Patrick Bringley, James Butler, John Chioles, Jared Curtis, Michael Eberle-Sinatra, Doucet Fischer, Ernest Gilman, Bruce Graver, Dustin Griffin, Freda Gough, Heather Jackson, Robin Jackson, Beth Lord, Kimiko Nakabayashi, Lynda Pratt, Hugh Roberts, Laura Rotunno, Mary Seabey, James Staveley, Judith Thompson, George Thompson, Stephen Wagner, Todd Webb, Kurt Wildermuth, and Susan Wolfson. We particularly thank Jack Stillinger and Anthony Harding, who offered helpful advice at an early stage of our work; and Sarah Brophy, Jeff Hipolito, and Lance Rhoades, who provided invaluable research assistance. Finally, we owe gratitude to our editor, Carol Bemis, whose patience and clarity in answering our questions have been exemplary.

Permissions Acknowledgments

The editors and publisher gratefully acknowledge permission from the following editors, publishers, and institutions to publish materials in the text and notes of this edition:

Princeton University Press for texts from *The Collected Works of Samuel Taylor Coleridge*, gen. ed. Kathleen Coburn: vol. 1, © 1971 by Routledge & Kegan Paul Ltd.; vol. 2, © 1970 by Routledge & Kegan Paul Ltd.; vol. 3, © 1978 by Princeton University Press; vol. 4, © 1969 by Routledge & Kegan Paul Ltd.; vol. 5, © 1987 by Princeton University Press; vol. 6, © 1972 by Routledge & Kegan Paul Ltd.; vol. 7, © 1983 by Princeton University Press; vol. 8, © 2000 by Princeton University Press; vol. 9, © 1993 by Princeton University Press; vol. 10, © 1976 by Princeton University Press; vol. 11, © 1995 by Princeton University Press; vol. 12, parts 1, 2, 3, and 5, © 1980, 1984, 1992, and 2000 by Princeton University Press; vol. 13, © 1981 by Princeton University Press; vol. 14, © 1990 by Princeton University Press; vol. 16, © 2001 by Princeton University Press; and for texts from *The Notebooks of Samuel Taylor Coleridge*, ed. Kathleen Coburn: vol. 1, © 1957 by Bollingen Foundation, Inc., New York, N.Y.; vol. 2, © 1961 by Bollingen Foundation, Inc., New York, N.Y.; vol. 3, © 1973 by Princeton University Press; vol. 4, © 1990 by Princeton University Press.

Oxford University Press for texts from *The Collected Letters of Samuel Taylor Coleridge*, ed. Ernest Leslie Griggs: vols. 1 and 2, © Oxford University Press 1956; vols. 3 and 4, © Oxford University Press 1959; vols. 5 and 6, © Oxford University Press 1971; and for a quotation from *The Poetical Works of William Wordsworth*, ed. Ernest de Selincourt and Helen Darbishire, vol. 5 (Clarendon Press, 1949).

Victoria University Library (Dr. Robert Brandeis, Chief Librarian), University of Toronto, for manuscript texts from the Coleridge Collection.

Brown University Library for Charles Lamb's letter of December 1, 1796, to Coleridge.

Fairleigh Dickinson University Press for quotations from *The Poetical Works of Mark Akenside*, ed. Robin Dix, © 1996 by Associated University Presses, Inc.

Harvard University Press and the Trustees of the Loeb Classical Library for a quotation from *Aristophanes: Peace, Birds, Frogs*, trans. Benjamin Bickley Rogers, Loeb Classical Library, vol. L 179 (Harvard University Press, 1924). The Loeb Classical Library® is a registered trademark of the President and Fellows of Harvard College.

Houghton Mifflin Company for quotations from *The Riverside Milton*, ed. Roy Flannagan. Copyright © 1998 by Houghton Mifflin Company.

The Henry E. Huntington Library for Charles Lamb's letter of February 6, 1797, to Coleridge.

The J. Pierpont Morgan Library for Coleridge's holograph annotations to *Fears in Solitude* and *The Friend*.

Berg Collection of English and American Literature, The New York Public Library, Astor, Lenox and Tilden Foundations, for Charles Lamb's letter of January 30, 1801, to Coleridge.

W. W. Norton & Co. for quotations from William Wordsworth, *The Prelude: 1799, 1805, 1850*, ed. Jonathan Wordsworth, M. H. Abrams, and Stephen Gill (1979).

W. J. B. Owen for quotations from *The Prose Works of William Wordsworth*, ed. W. J. B. Owen and Jane Worthington Smyser, 3 vols. (Clarendon Press, 1974).

Princeton University Library for Coleridge's holograph annotations to *Christabel*.

The Master and Fellows of St. John's College, Cambridge, for Coleridge's holograph annotations to *Christabel* in the College Library.

University of Virginia Press for quotations from F. W. J. Schelling, *System of Transcendental Idealism*, trans. Peter Heath (1978).

The Wordsworth Trust for Coleridge's "A Letter to ———" and for quotations from William Wordsworth's Fenwick notes in Dove Cottage MS 153 and "Ode: Intimations of Immortality" in Dove Cottage MS 44.

Beinecke Rare Book and Manuscript Library, Yale University, for Coleridge's holograph annotations to *Poems* (1797) and *Sibylline Leaves*.

For permission to republish critical selections in the back of the book, we thank the authors, original publishers, or other copyright holders as specified in the bibliographical note to each selection.

Every effort has been made to contact the copyright holders of each selection. Rights holders of any selection not credited should contact W. W. Norton & Co., 500 Fifth Avenue, New York, N.Y. 10110, for a correction to be made in the next reprinting of our work.

Abbreviations

AA	Robert Southey, ed., *The Annual Anthology*, 2 vols. (Bristol, 1799–1800)
AR (1825)	S. T. Coleridge, *Aids to Reflection* (London, 1825)
AR (CC)	S. T. Coleridge, *Aids to Reflection*, ed. John Beer (1993) [= CC, vol. 9]
Ashley	Ashley MS 408, British Library
BL	The British Library, London
BL (1847)	S. T. Coleridge, *Biographia Literaria*, ed. Henry Nelson Coleridge and Sara Coleridge, 2 vols. (London, 1847)
BL (1907)	S. T. Coleridge, *Biographia Literaria*, ed. John Shawcross, 2 vols. (Oxford, 1907)
BL (1965)	S. T. Coleridge, *Biographia Literaria*, ed. George Watson (London, 1965)
BL (1997)	S. T. Coleridge, *Biographia Literaria*, ed. Nigel Leask (London, 1997)
BL (CC)	S. T. Coleridge, *Biographia Literaria*, ed. James Engell and W. J. Bate, 2 vols. (1983) [= CC, vol. 7]
BLJ	Lord Byron, *Byron's Letters and Journals*, ed. Leslie Marchand, 12 vols. (London, 1973–82)
Borrowings	George Whalley, "The Bristol Library Borrowings of Southey and Coleridge, 1793–8," *The Library* 4 (1949): 114–31
C	Samuel Taylor Coleridge (used in the notes)
C&S (CC)	S. T. Coleridge, *On the Constitution of the Church and State*, ed. John Colmer (1976) [= CC, vol. 10]
CC	*The Collected Works of Samuel Taylor Coleridge*, gen. ed. Kathleen Coburn (Princeton, 1969–2002)
CH	J. R. de J. Jackson, ed., *Coleridge: The Critical Heritage*, 2 vols. (London, 1970–91)
CL	*Collected Letters of Samuel Taylor Coleridge*, ed. E. L. Griggs, 6 vols. (Oxford, 1956–71)
Clarkson, *Impolicy*	Thomas Clarkson, *An Essay on the Impolicy of the African Trade*, 2nd ed. (London, 1788)
Clarkson, *Slavery*	Thomas Clarkson, *An Essay on the Slavery*

and Commerce of the Human Species, partic-
ularly the African, 2nd ed. (London, 1788)

CM (CC)   S. T. Coleridge, *Marginalia*, ed. George Whalley and H. J. Jackson, 6 vols. (1980–2001)
[= CC, vol. 12]

CN   *The Notebooks of Samuel Taylor Coleridge*,
ed. Kathleen Coburn, 5 vols. (in 10) (Lon-
don and Princeton, 1957–2002) (references
are to volume and entry number)

Colmer   John Colmer, *Coleridge: Critic of Society*
(Oxford, 1959)

CRB   Henry Crabb Robinson, *Henry Crabb Robin-*
son on Books and Their Writers, ed. Edith J.
Morley, 3 vols. (London, 1938)

CRD   Henry Crabb Robinson, *Diary, Reminis-*
cences, and Correspondence, ed. Thomas
Sadler, 3 vols. (London, 1869)

Davidson   F. W. J. Schelling, "Introduction to the Outlines of a System of Natural Philosophy,"
trans. Tom Davidson, *Journal of Speculative*
Philosophy 1 (1867): 193–220

De Q Works   *The Collected Writings of Thomas De*
Quincey, ed. David Masson, 14 vols. (Edinburgh, 1889–90)

Descartes,   René Descartes, *Philosophical Writings*, trans.
Philosophical Writings John Cottingham et al., 3 vols. (Cambridge,
1984–91)

DWJ   *Journals of Dorothy Wordsworth*, ed. Mary
Moorman (London, 1971)

EHC   Ernest Hartley Coleridge (C's grandson; used
in the notes)

EOT (CC)   S. T. Coleridge, *Essays on His Times*, ed. David
V. Erdman, 3 vols. (1978) [= CC, vol. 3]

Ellington   Immanuel Kant, *Metaphysical Foundations of*
Natural Science, trans. James Ellington (In-
dianapolis, 1970)

ER   Joseph Cottle, *Early Recollections, Chiefly*
Relating to the Late Samuel Taylor Coleridge,
2 vols. (London, 1837)

Erdmann   G. W. Leibniz, *Opera philosophica*, ed. J. E.
Erdmann (Berlin, 1840)

Facsimile   *Coleridge's Poems: A Facsimile Reproduction*
of the Proofs and MSS of Some of the Poems,
ed. James Dykes Campbell (London, 1899)

Fichte, *Grundlage*   J. G. Fichte, *Grundlage der gesamten Wis-*
senschaftlehre (Foundations of the Entire
Theory of Knowledge) (Jena, 1794)

Friend (CC)   S. T. Coleridge, *The Friend*, ed. Barbara
Rooke, 2 vols. (1969) [= CC, vol. 4]

Gregor	Immanuel Kant, *Groundwork of the Metaphysics of Morals*, trans. Mary Gregor (Cambridge, 1998)
Harris and Heath	F. W. J. Schelling, *Ideas for a Philosophy of Nature as Introduction to the Study of this Science*, ed. and trans. Errol Harris and Peter Heath (Cambridge, 1988)
Hatfield	Immanuel Kant, *Prolegomena to Any Future Metaphysics*, trans. Gary Hatfield (Cambridge, 1997)
Hartley	David Hartley, *Observations of Man, His Frame, His Duty, and His Expectations*, 3 vols. (London, 1791)
Heath	F. W. J. Schelling, *System of Transcendental Idealism*, trans. Peter Heath (Charlottesville, Va., 1978)
Heath and Lachs	J. G. Fichte, *Science of Knowledge (Wissenschaftslehre)*, ed. and trans. Peter Heath and John Lachs (New York, 1970)
HNC	Henry Nelson Coleridge (C's nephew and son-in-law; used in the notes)
Hume, *Treatise*	David Hume, *A Treatise of Human Nature*, ed. L. A. Selby-Bigge and P. H. Nidditch, 2nd ed. (Oxford, 1978)
Jacobi	F. H. Jacobi, *Ueber die Lehre des Spinoza in Briefen an Herrn Moses Mendelssohn* (On the Doctrine of Spinoza, in Letters to Mr. Moses Mendelssohn), 2nd ed. (Breslau, 1789)
JDC	*Coleridge's Poetical Works*, ed. James Dykes Campbell (London, 1893)
Jahrbücher	*Jahrbücher der Medizin als Wissenschaft* (Yearbook of Medicine as a Science)
Johnson	Mary Lynn Johnson, "How Rare Is a 'Unique Annotated Copy' of Coleridge's *Sibylline Leaves*?" *Bulletin of the New York Public Library* 78 (1975): 451–81
Johnson's *Dictionary*	Samuel Johnson, *A Dictionary of the English Language*, 2 vols. (London, 1755)
Kant, *Grundlegung*	Immanuel Kant, *Grundlegung zur Metaphysik der Sitten*, 4th ed. (Riga, 1797)
Kant, *Judgment*	Immanuel Kant, *Critique of the Power of Judgment*, trans. Paul Guyer and Eric Matthews (Cambridge, 2000)
Kant, *Practical Reason*	Immanuel Kant, *Critique of Practical Reason*, in *Practical Philosophy*, ed. and trans. Mary J. Gregor (Cambridge, 1996), 133–271
Kant, *Prolegomena*	Immanuel Kant, *Prolegomena zu einer jeden künftigen Metaphysik* (Prolegomena to Any Future Metaphysics) (Riga, 1783)

Kant, *Pure Reason*	Immanuel Kant, *Critique of Pure Reason*, ed. and trans. Paul Guyer and Allen W. Wood (Cambridge, 1997) (cited, as is conventional, by the page numbers of the first [1781] or second edition [1787], distinguished by the letters A and B: e.g., B242)
Kant, *Vermischte Schriften*	Immanuel Kant, *Vermischte Schriften*, 4 vols. (Halle, 1799–1807)
LB	William Wordsworth and S. T. Coleridge, *Lyrical Ballads*
LB (1798)	[William Wordsworth and S. T. Coleridge,] *Lyrical Ballads, With a Few Other Poems* (London, 1798)
LB (1800)	William Wordsworth [and S. T. Coleridge], *Lyrical Ballads, With Other Poems*, 2 vols. (London, 1800)
LB (1802)	William Wordsworth [and S. T. Coleridge], *Lyrical Ballads, With Pastoral and Other Poems*, 2 vols. (London, 1802)
LB (1992)	William Wordsworth, *Lyrical Ballads, and Other Poems, 1797–1800*, ed. James Butler and Karen Green (Ithaca, N.Y., 1992)
LCL	Loeb Classical Library (Cambridge, Mass., 1911–)
Lects 1795 (CC)	S. T. Coleridge, *Lectures 1795: On Politics and Religion*, ed. Lewis Patton and Peter Mann (1971) [= CC, vol. 1]
Lects 1808–19 (CC)	S. T. Coleridge, *Lectures 1808–1819: On Literature*, ed. R. A. Foakes, 2 vols. (1987) [= CC, vol. 5]
Lects 1818–19 (CC)	S. T. Coleridge, *Lectures 1818–1819: On the History of Philosophy*, ed. J. R. de J. Jackson (2000) [= CC, vol. 10]
Locke, *Essay*	John Locke, *An Essay concerning Human Understanding*, ed. P. H. Nidditch (Oxford, 1975)
LL	*The Letters of Charles and Mary Anne Lamb*, ed. Edwin W. Marrs Jr., 3 vols. (Ithaca, N.Y., 1975–78)
Logic (CC)	S. T. Coleridge, *Logic*, ed. J. R. de J. Jackson (1981) [= CC, vol. 13]
Lowes	John Livingston Lowes, *The Road to Xanadu: A Study in the Ways of the Imagination* (Boston, 1927)
LRR	S. T. Coleridge, *Lectures on Revealed Religion*
LS (CC)	S. T. Coleridge, *Lay Sermons*, ed. R. J. White (1972) [= CC, vol. 6]
Maass	J. G. E. Maass, *Versuch über die Einbil-*

	dungskraft (Essay on Imagination), rev. ed. (Halle, 1797)
Mendelssohn, *Morgenstuden*	Moses Mendelssohn, *Morgenstunden oder Vorlesungen über das Daseyn Gottes* (Morning Hours, or Lectures on the Existence of God), rev. ed. (Frankfurt, 1790)
MP	The *Morning Post*
N&Q	*Notes and Queries*
OED	The *Oxford English Dictionary*, 2nd ed. (1989)
Paley	Morton D. Paley, *Coleridge's Later Poetry* (Oxford, 1996)
Parl. Hist.	The *Parliamentary History of England*, ed. William Cobbet and John Wright, 36 vols. (London, 1806–20)
PGC	S. T. Coleridge, *Essays on the Principles of Genial Criticism*
PMLA	*Publications of the Modern Language Association of America*
PTV	William Wordsworth, *Poems in Two Volumes, and Other Poems, 1800–1807*, ed. Jared Curtis (Ithaca, N.Y., 1983)
PW	*The Complete Poetical Works of Samuel Taylor Coleridge*, ed. E. H. Coleridge (Oxford, 1912)
PW (CC)	S. T. Coleridge, *Poetical Works*, ed. J. C. C. Mays (Princeton, 2001) [= *CC*, vol. 16]
Remnant	G. W. Leibniz, *New Essays on Human Understanding*, trans. Peter Remnant and Jonathan Bennett (Cambridge, 1981)
RES	*Review of English Studies*
Rooke	Barbara E. Rooke, "An Annotated Copy of Coleridge's 'Christabel,'" *Studia Germanica Gandensia* 15 (1974): 174–92
SC	Sara Coleridge (C's daughter; used in the notes)
Schelling, *Abhandlungen*	F. W. J. Schelling, "Abhandlungen zur Erläuterung des Idealismus der Wissenschaftslehre" (Essays Elucidating the Idealism of the Doctrine of Knowledge), in *Philosophische Schriften* (Landshut, 1809), 341–96
Schelling, *Darlegung*	F. W. J. Schelling, *Darlegung des wahren Verhältniss der Naturphilosophie zu der verbesserten Fichte'schen Lehre* (Explanation of the True Relation of Natural Philosophy to the Improved Fichtean Doctrine) (Tübingen, 1806)
Schelling, *Einleitung*	F. W. J. Schelling, *Einleitung zu dem Entwurf eines Systems der Naturphilosophie* (Intro-

	duction to an Outline of a System of Natural Philosophy) (Jena, 1799)
Schelling, *Ideen*	F. W. J. Schelling, *Ideen zu einer Philosophie der Natur* (Ideas for a Philosophy of Nature) (Landshut, 1803)
Schelling, *PS*	F. W. J. Schelling, *Philosophische Schriften* (Philosophical Writings) (Landshut, 1809)
Schelling, *System*	F. W. J. Schelling, *System des transcendentalen Idealismus* (System of Transcendental Idealism) (Tübingen, 1800)
Schelling, *Vom Ich*	F. W. J. Schelling, *Vom Ich als Prinzip der Philosophie* (On the Self as a Principle of Philosophy), in *PS*
SIR	*Studies in Romanticism*
SM (CC)	S. T. Coleridge, *The Statesman's Manual*, in *Lay Sermons*, ed. R. J. White (1972) [= CC, vol. 6]
Stillinger	Jack Stillinger, *Coleridge and Textual Instability: The Multiple Versions of the Major Poems* (New York, 1994)
SW&F (CC)	S. T. Coleridge, *Shorter Works and Fragments*, ed. H. J. Jackson and J. R. de J. Jackson (1995) [= CC, vol. 11]
TLS	*The Times Literary Supplement*
TT (CC)	S. T. Coleridge, *Table Talk*, ed. Carl Woodring, 2 vols. (1990) [= CC, vol. 14]
var.	*variatim* ("variously"; used of quotations to indicate slight variations from the source text or a standard edition, or between different copies of a single text by Coleridge)
Walford	Immanuel Kant, *Theoretical Writings, 1755–1770*, ed. and trans. David Walford (Cambridge, 1992)
Watchman (CC)	S. T. Coleridge, *The Watchman*, ed. Lewis Patton (1970) [= CC, vol. 2]
WL	*The Letters of William and Dorothy Wordsworth*, rev. ed., ed. Chester Shaver, Mary Moorman, and Alan G. Hill, 8 vols. (Oxford, 1967–93)
Whalley	George Whalley, *Coleridge, Sara Hutchinson and the Asra Poems* (London, 1955)
Woodring	Carl Woodring, *Politics in the Poetry of Coleridge* (Madison, 1961)
W Prose	William Wordsworth, *Prose Works*, ed. W. J. B. Owen and Jane Worthington Smyser, 3 vols. (Oxford, 1974)
WPW	William Wordsworth, *Poetical Works*, ed. Ernest de Selincourt and Helen Darbishire, 5 vols. (Oxford, 1940–49)

The Bible is normally cited from the Authorized (or King James) Version; Shakespeare from *The Norton Shakespeare*, gen. ed. Stephen Greenblatt (New York, 1997); Milton from *The Riverside Milton*, ed. Roy Flannagan (Boston, 1998); and Gray and Collins from *The Poems of Gray, Collins, and Goldsmith*, ed. Roger Lonsdale (London, 1969). The bibliography contains the full publication information of works cited in brief form in the footnotes. Other frequently cited editions are listed in the permissions acknowledgments.

The Texts of
COLERIDGE'S POETRY
AND PROSE

FROM POEMS ON VARIOUS SUBJECTS (1796)

Coleridge assembled poems for his publisher, Joseph Cottle, in the summer of 1795. In October he thought of publishing two volumes with "none but large Poems in the second Volume," so he "crowded all" his "little pieces" in the first volume. The second volume never appeared, and the first was delayed to the following year while he completed "Religious Musings." The Preface and notes were written in late March 1796, and Coleridge called the volume "finished" on March 30 (*CL*, 1:157, 162, 195). It was published on April 16, 1796 (*CL*, 1:204), and contained four sonnets by Charles Lamb, one sonnet jointly authored by Coleridge and Samuel Favell (1775–1812), and another by Robert Southey and Coleridge, all omitted here. The title page listed the author as "S. T. Coleridge, / Late of Jesus College, Cambridge" and included a Latin motto adapted from Statius· "*Felix curarum, cui non Heliconia cordi / Serta, nec imbelles Parnassi e vertice laurus! / Sed viget ingenium, et magnos accinctus in usus / Fert animus quascunque vices.—Nos tristia vitæ / Solamur cantu*" (Happy thou in thy labours, who carest not for the chaplets of Helicon nor for unwarlike bays from Parnassus' summit, but thy intellect is keen, and thy mind girt up for mighty deeds endures whatever may befall; we beguile a mournful life with song) (Statius, *Silvae* 4.4.46–50, trans. J. H. Mozley [LCL, 1932]). Coleridge changed Statius' "*otia vitae*" (leisured life) to "*tristia vitae*" (mournful or melancholy life).

The volume opened with "Monody on the Death of Chatterton" and eight poems, of which only "To a Young Lady" is included here. A section of thirty-six "Effusions" with a separate title page and motto followed. Ten of the effusions were previously printed in the *Morning Chronicle* in December 1794 and January 1795 as "Sonnets on Eminent Characters," signed "S. T. C." Included here are the sonnets on William Lisle Bowles, Edmund Burke, William Pitt, Joseph Priestley, Thomas Erskine (1750–1823), and Richard Brinsley Sheridan (1751–1816). Coleridge's sonnets echo Milton's political sonnets, the sentimental sonnets by Bowles, and the elegiac sonnets by Charlotte Smith (1749–1806). "The Eolian Harp" was included in this series as "Effusion XXXV." The Effusions were followed by five "Poetical Epistles," also with their own title page and motto. The volume concluded with "Religious Musings," which interprets Revelation and the political events of the mid-1790s as foretelling that the final judgment is at hand when oppression will end and the millennium will arrive. "Religious Musings" is a prophecy and theodicy, which explains the presence of evil as part of a divine scheme of benevolence. Coleridge held the optimistic faith that "the perfectness of future Men is indeed a benevolent tenet, and may operate on a few Visionaries, whose studious habits supply them with employment, and seclude them from temptation" (*Lects 1795* [CC], 44).

Coleridge was pleased with the few reviews the volume received. The *Analytic Review* 23 (June 1796): 610, wrote that the volume displayed "splendour" rather than "simplicity" and judged that "the reader is left more strongly impressed with an idea of the strength of the writer's genius, than of the correctness of his taste." Similar notices in the *Critical Review* 17 (June 1796): 209–12, and the *Monthly Review* 20 (June 1796):

194–99, criticized Coleridge's meters, coined words, and double epithets but praised his genius, energy, and sublimity.

The poems here are printed from *Poems* (1796) in the order of the volume.

FROM POEMS ON VARIOUS SUBJECTS (1796)

Preface

Poems on various subjects written at different times and prompted by very different feelings; but which will be read at one time and under the influence of one set of feelings—this is an heavy disadvantage: for we love or admire a poet in proportion as he developes our own sentiments and emotions, or reminds us of our own knowledge.

Compositions resembling those of the present volume are not unfrequently condemned for their querulous egotism. But egotism is to be condemned then only when it offends against time and place, as in an History or an Epic Poem. To censure it in a Monody or Sonnet is almost as absurd as to dislike a circle for being round. Why then write Sonnets or Monodies? Because they give me pleasure when perhaps nothing else could. After the more violent emotions of Sorrow, the mind demands solace and can find it in employment alone; but full of its late sufferings it can endure no employment not connected with those sufferings. Forcibly to turn away our attention to other subjects is a painful and in general an unavailing effort.

> But O how grateful to a wounded heart
> The tale of misery to impart;
> From others eyes bid artless sorrows flow
> And raise esteem upon the base of woe![1]

The communicativeness of our nature leads us to describe our own sorrows; in the endeavor to describe them intellectual activity is exerted; and by a benevolent law of our nature from intellectual activity a pleasure results which is gradually associated and mingles as a corrective with the painful subject of the description. True! it may be answered, but how are the PUBLIC interested in your sorrows or your description? We are for ever attributing a personal unity to imaginary aggregates. What is the PUBLIC but a term for a number of scattered individuals of whom as many will be interested in these sorrows as have experienced the same or similar?

> Holy be the Lay,
> Which mourning soothes the mourner on his way![2]

---

1. Cuthbert Shaw (1738–1771), "An Evening Address to a Nightingale," lines 103–6, in Robert Anderson, *The Works of the British Poets* (1792–95), 11:565, which prints *For* in place of *But* in line 1 and *others'* in line 3.
2. Specific source untraced. Perhaps suggested by Bowles, "Sonnet XXI. To the River Cherwell" in *Sonnets written chiefly on Picturesque Spots During a Tour* (1789), lines 6–8: "that sad lay / Whose musick on my melancholy way / I woo'd."

There is one species of egotism which is truly disgusting; not that which leads us to communicate our feelings to others, but that which would reduce the feelings of others to an identity with our own. The Atheist, who exclaims "pshaw!" when he glances his eye on the praises of Deity, is an Egotist; an old man, when he speaks contemptuously of love-verses, is an Egotist; and your sleek favorites of Fortune are Egotists, when they condemn all "melancholy discontented" verses.

Surely it would be candid not merely to ask whether the Poem pleases ourselves, but to consider whether or no there may not be others to whom it is well-calculated to give an innocent pleasure. With what anxiety every fashionable author avoids the word *I!*—now he transforms himself into a third person,—"the present writer"—now multiplies himself and swells into "*we*"—and all this is the watchfulness of guilt. Conscious that this said *I* is perpetually intruding on his mind and that it monopolizes his heart, he is prudishly solicitous that it may not escape from his lips.

This disinterestedness of phrase is in general commensurate with selfishness of feeling: men old and hackneyed in the ways of the world are scrupulous avoiders of Egotism.

Of the following Poems a considerable number are styled "Effusions," in defiance of Churchill's line

Effusion on Effusion *pour* away.[3]

I could recollect no title more descriptive of the manner and matter of the Poems—I might indeed have called the majority of them Sonnets—but they do not posses that *oneness* of thought which I deem indispensible in a Sonnet—and (not a very honorable motive perhaps) I was fearful that the title "Sonnet" might have reminded my reader of the Poems of the Rev. W. L. Bowles—a comparison with whom would have sunk me below that mediocrity, on the surface of which I am at present enabled to float.

Some of the verses allude to an intended emigration to America on the scheme of an abandonment of individual property.

Monody
on the
Death of Chatterton[1]

When faint and sad o'er Sorrow's desert wild
Slow journeys onward poor Misfortune's child;
When fades each lovely form by Fancy drest,

3. Charles Churchill, "The Candidate," line 42. Churchill (1731–1764) satirizes John Langhorne, *Effusions of Friendship and Fancy* (1763). C may also have taken the word *effusion* from William Preston (1753–1807), who defined love poetry as a "spontaneous effusion of a mind wholly occupied by a single idea, careless of rules, little studious of poetic fame, and desirous only of expressing its emotions" (*Works*, 2 vols. [Dublin, 1793], I:xiii). C borrowed from Preston in his "Introduction to the Sonnets" in *Poems* (1797).
1. Thomas Chatterton died by drinking water and arsenic on August 24, 1770, either as an act of suicide or an attempt to cure a venereal infection. He wrote poems in a pseudo-medieval English and claimed that they were by a 15th-century Bristol monk named Thomas Rowley.

And inly pines the self-consuming breast;
No scourge of scorpions in thy right arm dread,   5
No helmed terrors nodding o'er thy head,
Assume, O DEATH! the cherub wings of PEACE,
And bid the heart-sick Wanderer's anguish cease!

Thee, CHATTERTON! yon unblest stones protect
From Want, and the bleak Freezings of neglect!   10
Escap'd the sore wounds of Affliction's rod²
Meek at the Throne of Mercy, and of God,

The poems were admired but started a controversy over their authenticity and Chatterton's ability to write them.

A "monody" is a poem spoken by one voice and in English is frequently an elegy. C wrote a ninety-line monody on Chatterton in 1790 at his school, Christ's Hospital, with an epigram adapted from Gray, "Elegy Written in a Country Churchyard": "Cold penury repress'd his noble rage, / And froze the genial current of his soul" (PW, 1:13–15). A later version of 107 lines, which retained only seventeen lines from the 1790 version, was printed as a preface to an edition of Chatterton's poems, Poems, supposed to have been written at Bristol, by Thomas Rowley and Others, in the Fifteenth Century (Cambridge, 1794). C's 1796 version adds thirty-six lines to the end of the 1794 version. The addition may have been written as early as September 1794. He revised the poem for his editions of 1797 and 1803; it was omitted from SL. In the editions of 1828 and later Coleridge placed it in the category of "Juvenile Poems" (I. A. Gordon, "The Case-History of Coleridge's 'Monody on the Death of Chatterton,' " RES 18 [1942]: 49–71; Arthur Freeman and Theodore Hofmann, "The Ghost of Coleridge's First Effort: 'A Monody on the Death of Chatterton,' " The Library 11 [1989]: 328–35). C had the following note set in type for Poems (1796) but deleted it:

> POOR CHATTERTON! HERBERT CROFT has written with feeling concerning him; and VICESIMUS KNOX has ATTEMPTED to write with feeling.——HAYLEY who (so future Antiquarians will inform our posterity) has written sundry things in the reign of King George the Third, describes the death of Chatterton in his Essay on Poetry—as tearing the strings of his lyre in the agonies of death! !—By far the best poem on this subject is "Neglected Genius or Tributary Stanzas to the memory of the unfortunate Chatterton," written by RUSHTON, a blind Sailor.
> WALPOLE writes thus. "All the house of Forgery are relations. Although it be but just to CHATTERTON'S Memory to say, that his poverty never made him claim kindred with the more enriching branches yet he who could so ingeniously counterfeit styles and (the asserter believes) hands, might easily have been led to the more facile imitation of prose promissory notes!" O ye, who honor the name of MAN, rejoice that this Walpole is called a LORD!
> Milles too, the Editor of his Poems—a Priest who though only a DEAN, in dullness and malignity was most episcopally eminent, foully calumniated him—An Owl mangling a poor dead Nightingale!— / Most inspired Bard! / To him alone in this benighted age / Was that divine Inspiration given, / Which glows in MILTON'S and in SHAKESPEARE'S page, / The pomp and prodigality of Heaven [Ashley, ff. 36–36v; Facsimile, 67–68].

C canceled the note when Joseph Cottle told him that "Captain Blake, whom he occasionally met, was the son-in-law of Dean Milles" (ER, 1:34–35). Herbert Croft (1751–1816) included "Letter on Chatterton" in Love and Madness, defending Chatterton against criticisms that he was a libertine and freethinker. Horace Walpole (1717–1797) wrote "A Letter to the Editor of the Miscellanies of Thomas Chatterton," privately printed at Strawberry Hill (1779) and reprinted in the Gentleman's Magazine (April–July 1782). Vicesimus Knox (1752–1821) included "On the Poems Attributed to Rowley" in Essays Moral and Literary (1780). William Hayley's (1745–1820) comment comes from his Essay on Epic Poetry (1782), 4:247. Edward Rushton (1756–1814) published Neglected Genius: or, Tributary Stanzas to the Memory of the Unfortunate Chatterton (1787). C's quotation from Walpole is copied from the Preface to Rushton's poem, which also supplied C with the figure of the owl mangling the dead nightingale. Jeremiah Milles (1714–1784), the dean of Exeter, edited Poems, Supposed to have been Written at Bristol in the Fifteenth Century by Thomas Rowley (1782) and argued that the poems were genuine 15th-century poetry because a young man sunk into sensuality and atheism could not recommend "precepts of benevolence, morality, and religion" found in the Rowley poems (23). C borrowed Milles's edition from the Jesus College library from January to May 1793 (J. C. C. Mays, "Coleridge's Borrowings from Jesus College Library, 1791–94," Transactions of the Cambridge Bibliographical Society 8 [1985]: 571).

2. For Thelwall's criticism of this and other lines in C's "Monody," see p. 21, n. 5 herein.

Perchance, thou raisest high th' enraptur'd hymn
   Amid the blaze of Seraphim!

Yet oft ('tis nature's bosom-startling call)   15
I weep, that heaven-born Genius *so* should fall;
And oft, in Fancy's saddest hour, my soul
Averted shudders at the poison'd bowl.
   Now groans my sickening heart, as still I view
      Thy corse of livid hue;   20
And now a flash of indignation high
Darts thro' the tear, that glistens in mine eye!

Is this the land of song-ennobled line?
Is this the land, where Genius ne'er in vain
      Pour'd forth his lofty strain?[3]   25
Ah me! yet SPENSER,[4] gentlest bard divine,
Beneath chill Disappointment's shade,
His weary limbs in lonely anguish lay'd
      And o'er her darling dead
      PITY hopeless hung her head,   30
While "mid the pelting of that merciless storm,"[5]
Sunk to the cold earth OTWAY'S[6] famish'd form!

Sublime of thought, and confident of fame,
From vales where Avon[7] winds the MINSTREL came.
      Light-hearted youth! aye, as he hastes along,   35
         He meditates the future song,
      How dauntless Ælla fray'd the Dacyan foes;[8]
         And, as floating high in air
         Glitter the sunny visions fair,
      His eyes dance rapture, and his bosom glows!   40
Friend to the friendless, to the sick man health,
With generous joy he views th' *ideal* wealth;
He hears the widow's heaven-breath'd prayer of praise;

---

3. Cf. "The Suicide" by Thomas Warton the younger (1728–1790), lines 37–39: " 'Is this,' mistaken Scorn will cry, / 'Is this the youth whose genius high / Could build the genuine rhyme?' "
   Warton's poem was published in 1777, but his editor, Richard Mant (1776–1848), said that
   its subject was not Chatterton (*Poetical Works of * * * Thomas Warton* [Oxford, 1802],
   1:146). By noting the neglect of poets in England, C challenges the nationalistic poetry of
   the 18th century, such as Gray's "The Progress of Poesy," which pointed with pride at England's care both for liberty and literature.
4. Ben Jonson spread the myth of Edmund Spenser's dying in poverty in London in 1599: "the
   Irish having robd Spensers goods, and burnt his house and a litle child new born, he and his
   wyfe escaped, and after, he died for lake of bread in King Street, and refused 20 pieces sent
   to him by my Lord of Essex, and said, He was sorrie he had no time to spend them" (*Ben
   Jonson's Conversations with William Drummond of Hawthornden*, ed. R. F. Patterson [Lon-
   don, 1923], 16–17).
5. *King Lear* 3.4.29–30: "Poor naked wretches, wheresoe'er you are, / That bide the pelting of
   this pitiless storm" and Charles Churchill, "The Prophecy of Famine" (1762), line 345:
   "Safe from the pelting of this perilous storm" (*The Poetical Works of Charles Churchill*, ed.
   Douglas Grant [Oxford, 1956]). In *Poems * * * by Thomas Rowley* (1794) C wrote "that pitiless storm" (*PW*, 1:126).
6. Thomas Otway (1652–1685), a popular dramatist, died in poverty. Theophilus Cibber
   (1703–1758) moralized "from the example of Mr. Otway, succeeding poets should learn not
   to place any confidence in the promises of patrons" (*Lives of the Poets* [1753], 2:334).
7. "Avon, a river near Bristol; the birth place of Chatterton." [C's 1796 note.]
8. C's phrase in *Poems * * * by Thomas Rowley* (1794) was *the Danish foes*, not *Dacyan foes*.

He marks the shelter'd orphan's tearful gaze;
Or, where the sorrow-shrivell'd captive lay,   45
Pours the bright blaze of Freedom's noon-tide ray:[9]
And now, indignant, "grasps the patriot steel,"[1]
And her own iron rod he makes Oppression feel.
  Clad in Nature's rich array,
  And bright in all her tender hues,   50
Sweet tree of Hope! thou loveliest child of Spring!
How fair didst thou disclose thine early bloom,
  Loading the west-winds with its soft perfume!
And Fancy, elfin form of gorgeous wing,
  On every blossom hung her fostering dews,   55
  That, changeful, wanton'd to the orient day!
But soon upon thy poor unsheltered head
Did Penury her sickly mildew[2] shed:
And soon the scathing Lightning bade thee stand
In frowning horror o'er the blighted land!   60

Ah! where are fled the charms of vernal Grace,
And Joy's wild gleams, that lighten'd o'er thy face?
YOUTH of tumultuous soul, and haggard eye![3]
Thy wasted form, thy hurried steps I view,
On thy cold forehead starts the anguish'd dew: 65
And dreadful was that bosom-rending sigh!

    Such were the struggles of the gloomy hour,
      When CARE, of wither'd brow,
      Prepar'd the poison's death-cold power:
    Already to thy lips was rais'd the bowl,   70
      When near thee stood AFFECTION meek
      (Her bosom bare, and wildly pale her cheek)
    Thy sullen gaze she bade thee roll
    On scenes that well might melt thy soul;
Thy native cot she flash'd upon thy view,   75
Thy native cot, where still, at close of day,
PEACE smiling sate, and listen'd to thy lay;
Thy Sister's shrieks she bade thee hear,
And mark thy Mother's thrilling tear;
      See, see her breast's convulsive throe,   80
      Her silent agony of woe!
  Ah! dash the poison'd chalice from thy hand!

9. Lines 41–46 were first drafted in July 1794 (*CL*, 1:87; *PW*, 1:57) and printed in the *Cambridge Intelligencer*, September 27, 1794, as part of "Lines written at the King's Arms, Ross, Formerly the House of the 'Man of Ross.' " The Man of Ross was John Kyrle (d. 1724) celebrated for his philanthropy in Pope, "Epistle to Bathurst," lines 250–98. The lines do not apply to Chatterton, as Lamb recognized: "the Man of Ross is scarce admissible as it now stands curtailed of its fairer half,—Reclaim its property from the Chatterton, which it does but encumber" (*LL*, 1:98). In subsequent printings C omitted these lines.
1. William Collins, "Ode to Fear," line 33 (var.).
2. A biblical plague that blights crops, e.g., 2 Chronicles 6.28.
3. Cf. Gray, "The Bard. A Pindaric Ode," lines 17–18: "Robed in the sable garb of woe, / With haggard eyes the poet stood," and Bowles, "Sonnet X. Written on a Cottage in Hampshire," lines 1–2 from *Sonnets written chiefly on Picturesque Spots* (1789): "O Poverty! though from thy haggard eye, / Thy cheerless mein, of every charm bereft." *Haggard*: a hawk caught as an adult, hence wild or untamed; it thus means wild as well as gaunt.

And thou had'st dash'd it, at her soft command,
But that DESPAIR and INDIGNATION rose,
And told again the story of thy woes; 85
Told the keen insult of th' unfeeling heart;
The dread dependence on the low-born mind;
Told every pang, with which thy soul must smart,
Neglect, and grinning Scorn, and Want combin'd!
Recoiling quick, thou bad'st the friend of pain 90
Roll the black tide of Death thro' every freezing vein!
Ye woods! that wave o'er Avon's rocky steep,[4]
To Fancy's ear sweet is your murm'ring deep!
For *here* she loves the cypress wreath to weave;
Watching, with wistful eye, the sad'ning tints of eve. 95
Here, far from men,[5] amid this pathless grove,
In solemn thought the Minstrel wont to rove,
Like star-beam on the slow sequester'd tide
Lone-glittering, thro' the high tree branching wide.
And here, in INSPIRATION'S eager hour, 100
When most the big soul feels the madning pow'r,
    These wilds, these caverns roaming o'er,
    Round which the screaming sea-gulls soar,
With wild unequal steps he pass'd along
Oft pouring on the winds a broken song: 105
Anon, upon some rough rock's fearful brow[6]
Would pause abrupt—and gaze upon the waves below.

Poor CHATTERTON! *he* sorrows for thy fate
Who would have prais'd and lov'd thee, ere too late.
Poor CHATTERTON! farewell! of darkest hues 110
This chaplet[7] cast I on thy unshap'd tomb;
But dare no longer on the sad theme muse,
Lest kindred woes persuade a kindred doom:
For oh! big gall-drops, shook from FOLLY'S wing,
Have blacken'd the fair promise of my spring; 115
And the stern FATE transpierc'd with viewless dart
The last pale Hope, that shiver'd at my heart!

Hence, gloomy thoughts![8] no more my soul shall dwell
On joys that were! No more endure to weigh
The shame and anguish of the evil day, 120
Wisely forgetful! O'er the ocean swell
Sublime of Hope I seek the cottag'd dell
Where VIRTUE calm with careless step may stray;

4. Cf. Gray, "The Progress of Poesy. A Pindaric Ode," lines 66–67: "Woods that wave o'er Delphi's steep, / Isles that crown the Aegean deep."
5. Cf. Gray, "Elegy Written in a Country Churchyard," line 73: "Far from the madding crowd's ignoble strife."
6. Cf. Gray, "The Bard," lines 15–16: "On a rock, whose haughty brow / Frowns o'er old Conway's foaming flood." In Gray's poem, a Welsh bard curses the English Edward I for killing the Welsh and their bards.
7. A wreath for the head.
8. Cf. Milton, "L'Allegro": "Hence loathed Melancholy" (line 1).

And, dancing to the moon-light roundelay,
The wizard PASSIONS weave an holy spell![9]   125

O, CHATTERTON! that thou wert yet alive!
Sure thou would'st spread the canvass to the gale,
And love, with us, the tinkling team to drive
O'er peaceful Freedom's UNDIVIDED dale;
And we, at sober eve, would round thee throng,   130
Hanging, enraptur'd, on thy stately song!
And greet with smiles the young-eyed POESY
All deftly mask'd, as hoar ANTIQUITY.

Alas vain Phantasies! the fleeting brood
Of Woe self-solac'd in her dreamy mood!   135
Yet will I love to follow the sweet dream,
Where Susquehannah[1] pours his untam'd stream;
And on some hill, whose forest-frowning side
Waves o'er the murmurs of his calmer tide,
Will raise a solemn CENOTAPH to thee,   140
Sweet Harper of time-shrouded MINSTRELSY!
And there, sooth'd sadly by the dirgeful wind,
Muse on the sore ills I had left behind.

To a
Young Lady
with
a Poem
on
the French Revolution[1]

Much on my early youth I love to dwell,
Ere yet I bade that friendly dome[2] farewell,
Where first, beneath the echoing cloisters pale,
I heard of guilt and wonder'd at the tale!
Yet tho' the hours flew by on careless wing,   5
Full heavily of Sorrow would I sing.

9. Originally lines 118–25 formed the first eight lines of a sonnet C sent to Southey in September 1794. C later told Southey, "I wrote the whole [of the sonnet] but the second & third Line" (*CL*, 1:104, 134). EHC gave the sonnet the title "Pantisocracy" (*PW*, 1:68–69), the idealistic plan referred to in the Preface to *Poems* (1796): "an intended emigration to America on the scheme of an abandonment of individual property." C quarreled with Southey, and by August 1795 pantisocracy was over as a practical scheme but remained a utopian ideal. SC wrote below line 125 in C's *Poetical Works* (1834), "Collins. The Manners. An Ode" (Derrick Woolf, "Sara Coleridge's Marginalia," *The Coleridge Bulletin* [Autumn 1993]: 5). Cf. Collins's ode, line 11: "At which the wizard Passions fly."
1. The proposed site for the Pantisocracy settlement in Pennsylvania.
1. In October 1794 the first version was inscribed in a copy of C's *The Fall of Robespierre* (1794) and sent to the actress Ann Brunton (*CL*, 1:117–18), but in 1796 the poem was addressed to his wife, Sara. Published in *The Watchman* for March 1, 1796 (*Watchman* [CC], 27–29).
2. C's school, Christ's Hospital.

Aye as the star of evening flung its beam
In broken radiance on the wavy stream,
My soul amid the pensive twilight gloom[3]
Mourn'd with the breeze, O Lee Boo![4] o'er thy tomb.   10
Where'er I wander'd, Pity still was near,
Breath'd from the heart and glisten'd in the tear:
No knell that toll'd, but fill'd my anxious eye,
And suff'ring Nature wept that *one* should die![5]

Thus to sad sympathies I sooth'd my breast   15
Calm, as the rainbow in the weeping West:
When slumb'ring Freedom rous'd by high Disdain
With giant fury burst her triple chain![6]
Fierce on her front the blasting Dog-star glow'd;
Her Banners, like a midnight Meteor, flow'd;   20
Amid the yelling of the storm-rent skies
She came, and scatter'd battles from her eyes!
Then Exultation wak'd the patriot fire
And swept with wilder hand th' Alcœan lyre:[7]
Red from the Tyrants' wound I shook the lance,   25
And strode in joy the reeking plains of France!

In ghastly horror lie th' Oppressors low,
And my heart akes, tho' Mercy struck the blow.
With wearied thought once more I seek the shade,
Where peaceful Virtue weaves the Myrtle braid.   30
And ô! if Eyes, whose holy glances roll,
The eloquent messengers of the pure soul;
If Smiles more winning, and a gentler Mien,
Than the love-wilder'd Maniac's brain hath seen
Shaping celestial forms in vacant air;   35
If these demand th' empassion'd Poet's care—

3. "Shadowy." [C's note in the letter to Southey (CL, 1:117).]
4. "Lee Boo, the son of Abba Thule, Prince of the Pelew Islands came over to England with Captain Wilson, died of the small-pox, and is buried in Greenwich Church-yard. See Keate's Account." [C's 1796 note.] The story is given in George Keate, *An Account of the Pelew Islands* (1788).
5. In a 1796 note C adapts Southey's "The Retrospect" from *Poems Containing The Retrospect, Odes, Elegies, Sonnets, &c* (Bath, 1795): "And suffering Nature weeps that *one* should die."
6. Lines 17–18 are from C's "The Destruction of the Bastile" [sic], possibly written in 1789, lines 7–8: "Yet Freedom rous'd by fierce Disdain / Has wildly broke thy triple chain" (PW, 1:10). Cf. Erasmus Darwin, *Botanic Garden* (1791), 1.2.377–82: "Long had the Giant-form on Gallia's plains lay, unconcious of his chains; / Round his large limbs were wound a thousand strings / By the weak hands of Confessors and Kings; / O'er his closed eyes a triple veil was bound, / And steely rivets lock'd him to the ground." *Triple chain*: king, church, and aristocracy.
7. Alcaeus of Lesbos (7th century B.C.E.), Greek poet. In a Christ's Hospital essay of November 26, 1790, C lamented the loss of much Greek literature since readers would "have admired the friend of Freedom in the noble Odes of Alcæus" (SW&F [CC], 1:9). C may have read of Alcaeus in Collins, "Ode to Liberty," lines 7–12. In a note Collins printed a Greek fragment he mistakenly attributed to Alcaeus, who promises to kill tyrants (Lonsdale, *The Poems of Thomas Gray, William Collins, and Oliver Goldsmith*, 442–43). C may also have read of Alcaeus as the "Lesbian patriot" in Akenside's "On Lyric Poetry" (line 24), whom Akenside identifies in a note to *Odes on Several Subjects* (1745) as a poet "of Mitylene, the capital of Lesbos, who fled from his native city to escape the oppression of those who had inslav'd it, and wrote against them in his exile those noble invectives which are so much applauded by the ancient Critics" (Akenside, *The Poetical Works*, ed. Robin Dix [1996], 285, 352).

If MIRTH, and soften'd SENSE, and WIT refin'd,
The blameless features of a lovely mind;
Then haply shall my trembling hand assign
No fading wreath to BEAUTY's saintly shrine.   40
Nor, SARA! thou these early flowers refuse——
Ne'er lurk'd the snake beneath their simple hues:
No purple bloom the Child of Nature brings
From Flatt'ry's night-shade: as he feels, he sings.

FROM EFFUSIONS

Content, as random Fancies might inspire,
If his weak harp at times or lonely lyre
He struck with desultory hand, and drew
Some soften'd tones to Nature not untrue.
                                    BOWLES[1]

Effusion I[1]

My heart has thank'd thee, BOWLES! for those soft strains
Whose sadness soothes me, like the murmuring
Of wild-bees in the sunny showers of spring!
For hence not callous to the mourner's pains
Thro' Youth's gay prime and thornless paths I went: 5
And when the *darker* day of life began,
And I did roam, a thought-bewilder'd man!
Their mild and manliest melancholy lent
A mingled charm, such as the pang consign'd
To slumber, tho' the big tear it renew'd;   10
Bidding a strange mysterious PLEASURE brood
Over the wavy and tumultuous mind,
As the great SPIRIT erst with plastic sweep
Mov'd on the darkness of the unform'd deep.[2]

1. Epigraph from Bowles, "Monody Written at Matlock, October 1791," lines 137–40, heavily influenced by Gray's "Elegy." In Bowles's poem the words are spoken about a "pensive poet," who died. Bowles wrote, "If his weak reed, at times, or lonely lyre, / He touch'd."
1. An earlier version published in the *Morning Chronicle*, December 26, 1794. William Lisle Bowles published *Fourteen Sonnets* (1789), reprinted often with additional sonnets, much admired by C and Southey (see the *Biographia*, p. 383 herein). In the *Morning Chronicle* version C translated a comment that he attributed to Maximus Tyrius (2nd-century minor Platonic philosopher) and applied it to Bowles: "I am not now treating of that poetry which is estimated by the pleasure it affords to the ear—the ear having been corrupted, and the judgment-seat of the perceptions; but of that which proceeds from the intellectual Helicon, that which is *dignified*, and appertaining to *human* feelings, and entering into the soul" (*PW*, 1:84).
2. Cf. Genesis. 1.2: "the Spirit of God moved upon the face of the waters."

Effusion II[1]

As late I lay in slumber's shadowy vale,
With wetted cheek and in a mourner's guise
I saw the sainted form of FREEDOM rise:
She spake! not sadder moans the autumnal gale.
"Great Son of Genius! sweet to me thy name,   5
"Ere in an evil hour with alter'd voice
"Thou badst Oppression's hireling crew rejoice
"Blasting with wizard spell my laurell'd fame.
"Yet never, BURKE! thou drank'st Corruption's bowl![2]
"Thee stormy Pity[3] and the cherish'd lure   10
"Of Pomp, and proud Precipitance of soul
"Wilder'd with meteor fires. Ah Spirit pure!
"That error's mist had left thy purged eye:
"So might I clasp thee with a Mother's joy!"

Effusion III[1]

Not always should the tear's ambrosial dew
Roll its soft anguish down thy furrow'd cheek!
Not always heaven-breath'd tones of suppliance meek
Beseem thee, MERCY! Yon dark Scowler view,
Who with proud words of dear-lov'd Freedom came—   5
More blasting, than the mildew from the South!
And kiss'd his country with Iscariot mouth

---

1. First published in the *Morning Chronicle*, December 9, 1794. Edmund Burke was a major Whig parliamentarian, who sympathized with the American colonies in the 1770s but opposed the French Revolution. His *Reflections on the Revolution in France* (1790) attacked the principles of the revolution as they were argued by British radicals and was the cause of his split from the Whigs and Charles James Fox in May 1791. On Burke's oratory, see *Conciones ad Populum* (p. 254 herein). In a review of Burke, *Letter to a Noble Lord* (1796), C described Burke's oratory as an appeal to the "imagination of his readers by a multitude and rapid succession of remote analogies" (*Watchman* [CC], 30–31).
2. "When I composed this line, I had not read the following paragraph in the Cambridge Intelligencer (of Saturday, November 21, 1795). 'When Mr. Burke first crossed over the House of Commons from the Opposition to the Ministry, he received a pension of 1200 l. a-year charged on the King's Privy Purse! When he had completed his labors, it was then a question of what recompence his service deserved. * * * a pension of 2500 l. per annum, for three lives on the 4½ West India Fund, the lives to be nominated by Mr. Burke, that he may accommodate the purchasers, is finally granted to this disinterested patriot! He has thus retir'd from the trade of politics, with pensions to the amount of 3700 l. a-year.' " [C's note in 1796.] A continuation of this note was set in type for *Poems* (1796) but canceled and printed as the last two paragraphs of C's review of Burke, *Letter to a Noble Lord*, March 1, 1796 (*Watchman* [CC], 38–39).
3. Cf. *Macbeth* 1.7.21–25: "pity, like a naked new-born babe, / Striding the blast or heaven's cherubin, horsed / Upon the sightless couriers of the air, / Shall blow the horrid deed in every eye / That tears shall drown the wind."
1. Published in the *Morning Chronicle*, December 23, 1794, as "Pitt" and in *The Watchman*, April 2, 1796, as "To Mercy." William Pitt changed his earlier liberal policies in the 1790s. C saw him as author of the war with France and repressive measures at home.

(Ah! foul apostate from his Father's fame!)[2]
Then fix'd her on the cross of deep distress,[3]
And at safe distance marks the thirsty lance   10
Pierce her big side! But ô! if some strange trance
The eye-lids of thy stern-brow'd Sister[4] press,
Seize, MERCY! thou more terrible the brand,
And hurl her thunderbolts with fiercer hand!

Effusion IV[1]

Tho' rous'd by that dark Vizir RIOT rude
Have driven our PRIESTLY o'er the ocean swell;[2]
Tho' SUPERSTITION and her wolfish brood
Bay his mild radiance, impotent and fell;
Calm in his halls of Brightness he shall dwell!   5
For lo! RELIGION at his strong behest
Starts with mild anger from the Papal spell,
And flings to Earth her tinsel-glittering vest,
Her mitred state and cumbrous pomp unholy;
And JUSTICE wakes to bid th' Oppressor wail   10
Insulting aye the wrongs of patient Folly;
And from her dark retreat by Wisdom won
Meek NATURE slowly lifts her matron veil
To smile with fondness on her gazing son!

Effusion V[1]

When British Freedom for an happier land
Spread her broad wings, that flutter'd with affright,

---

2. In *Conciones ad Populum* C quoted Pitt's speeches of June 1781 against the American war: "William Pitt exclaimed that '*our expences were enormous, while our victories were indecisive, and our defeats fatal—victories celebrated with short-lived triumph over men struggling in the holy cause of Freedom, and defeats which filled the Land with mourning.*' All this—O calumniated Judas Iscariot! all this WILLIAM PITT said!" (*Lects 1795* [CC], 64). Judas Iscariot's betrayal of Christ is in Luke 22.47–48. On the two bills, see *The Plot Discovered* (p. 274 herein). *Father's fame*: "Earl of Chatham" [C's note in the *Morning Chronicle*]. William Pitt (1708–1778), the first earl of Chatham, was the father of William Pitt the younger.
3. C wrote in the *MP* for December 3, 1801, in praise of political opposition in 1795: "when liberty was, as it were, fixed on the cross of shame and public abhorrence, amid the earthquake, that rent, and the darkness, that covered, the whole earth" (*EOT* [CC], 1:284).
4. "Justice." [C's note in the *Morning Chronicle*.]
1. First published in the *Morning Chronicle*, December 11, 1794. Joseph Priestley was a Unitarian theologian, political writer, and chemist, who discovered "dephlogisticated air," which Lavoisier (1743–1794) called oxygen. He emigrated to America in 1794. See p. 19, nn. 7 and 1 herein; p. 32, n. 9 herein; and p. 243, n. 8 herein.
2. Priestley's house and laboratory in Birmingham were burned by a "Church and King" crowd in 1791. *Dark Vizir*: Pitt; but the first line in the *Morning Chronicle* and in a copy sent to Southey December 17, 1794 (*CL*, 1:140), read, "Tho' king-bred Rage," implying that the king himself urged violence against dissent.
1. First published in the *Morning Chronicle*, December 1, 1794. Thomas Erskine (1750–1823) defended Thomas Paine, accused of seditious libel for publishing the second part of *The Rights of Man* in 1792; defended Thomas Hardy (1752–1832), Horne Tooke, and John Thelwall in the Treason Trials of 1794; and spoke in Parliament against the two bills in 1795.

ERSKINE! thy voice she heard, and paus'd her flight
Sublime of hope! For dreadless thou didst stand
(Thy censer glowing with the hallow'd flame)   5
And hireless Priest before th' insulted shrine,
And at her altar pourd'st the stream divine
Of unmatch'd eloquence. Therefore thy name
Her sons shall venerate, and cheer thy breast
With blessings heaven-ward breath'd. And when the doom   10
Of Nature bids thee die, beyond the tomb
Thy light shall shine: as sunk beneath the West
Tho' the great Summer Sun eludes our gaze,
Still burns wide Heaven with his distended blaze.

Effusion VI[1]

It was some spirit, SHERIDAN! that breath'd
O'er thy young mind such wildly-various power!
My soul hath mark'd thee in her shaping hour,
Thy temples with Hymettian flowrets[2] wreath'd:
And sweet thy voice, as when o'er Laura's bier   5
Sad music trembled thro' Vauclusa's glade;[3]
Sweet, as at dawn the love-lorn Serenade
That wafts soft dreams to Slumber's list'ning ear.
Now patriot Rage and Indignation high
Swell the full tones! And now thine eye-beams dance   10
Meanings of Scorn and Wit's quaint revelry![4]
Writhes inly from the bosom-probing glance
Th' Apostate[5] by the brainless rout ador'd,
As erst that elder Fiend beneath great Michael's sword.[6]

1. An early version was sent in a letter to Southey on December 17, 1794 (*CL*, 1:141–42). First published in the *Morning Chronicle,* January 29, 1795. Richard Brinsley Sheridan was a dramatist and Whig M.P.
2. "Hymettus a mountain near Athens, celebrated for its honey. This alludes to Mr. Sheridan's classical attainments, and the following four lines to the exquisite sweetness and almost *Italian* delicacy of his Poetry—In Shakespeare's 'Lover's Complaint' there is a fine stanza almost prophetically characteristic of Mr. Sheridan. 'So on the tip of his subduing tongue / All kind of argument and question deep, / All replication prompt and reason strong / For his advantage still did wake and sleep, / To make the weeper laugh, the laugher weep: / He had the dialect and different skill, / Catching all passions in his craft of will: / That he did in the general bosom reign / Of young and old.' " [C's note in 1796 quotes lines 120–28 (var.).]
3. Petrarch (1304–1374) wrote love lyrics to Laura. C read that "near to Avignon, was Valchiusa, the celebrated retreat of this divine poet" in William Preston, *Poetical Works,* 2 vols. (Dublin, 1793), 1:261.
4. In *Conciones ad Populum* C quoted Sheridan's ridicule of Pitt in Parliament and commented, "Fellow citizens! our laughter may be raised by the cause, but our indignation and sorrow must be excited by the consequences" (*Lects 1795* [CC], 61).
5. Satan in *Paradise Lost,* here applied to Pitt.
6. Cf. *Paradise Lost* 6.320–23: "the sword / Of *Michael* from the Armorie of God / Was giv'n him temper'd so, that neither keen / Nor solid might resist that edge."

Effusion XX
To the Author of the "Robbers"[1]

SCHILLER![2] that hour I would have wish'd to die,
If thro' the shudd'ring midnight I had sent
From the dark dungeon of the tower time-rent
That fearful voice, a famish'd Father's cry[3]——
Lest in some after moment aught more mean   5
Might stamp me mortal! A triumphant shout
Black HORROR scream'd, and all her *goblin* rout
Diminish'd shrunk from the more with'ring scene!
Ah Bard tremendous in sublimity!
Could I behold thee in thy loftier mood   10
Wand'ring at eve with finely-frenzied eye
Beneath some vast old tempest-swinging wood!
Awhile with mute awe gazing I would brood:
Then weep aloud in a wild extacy!

Effusion XXII
To
a Friend
together with
an Unfinished Poem[1]

Thus far my scanty brain hath built the rhyme
Elaborate and swelling: yet the heart
Not owns it. From thy spirit-breathing powers
I ask not now, my friend! the aiding verse,
Tedious to thee, and from thy anxious thought   5
Of dissonant mood. In fancy (well I know)
From business wand'ring far and local cares,
Thou creepest round a dear-lov'd Sister's bed
With noiseless step, and watchest the faint look,

1. C first read "The Robbers" in early November 1794 (*CL*, 1:122). Johann Christoph Friedrich von Schiller (1759–1805) wrote *Die Räuber* (1781), translated and adapted as *The Robbers* by A. F. Tytler in 1792 and parodied in the *Anti-Jacobin; or Weekly Examiner* as *The Rovers* in June 1798. Charles Moor, the elder son of a count, is disinherited by the plots of his brother, becomes an outlaw, and revenges himself upon all the institutions of society.
2. "One night in Winter, on leaving a College-friend's room, with whom I had supped, I carelessly took away with me 'The Robbers' a drama, the very name of which I had never before heard of:—A Winter midnight—the wind high—and 'The Robbers' for the first time!—The readers of SCHILLER will conceive what I felt. SCHILLER introduces no supernatural beings; yet his human beings agitate and astonish more than all the *goblin* rout—even of Shakespeare." [C's note in 1796.]
3. The count had been imprisoned by his younger son.
1. Included in letter to Southey, December 29, 1794, titled "To C. Lamb," with the following comment: "His Sister has lately been very unwell—confined to her Bed dangerously—She is all his Comfort—he her's. * * * Her illness preyed a good deal on his Spirits—though he bore it with an apparent equanimity, as beseemed him who like me is a Unitarian Christian and an Advocate for the Automatism of Man" (*CL*, 1:147). Later, on September 22, 1796, in a fit of madness Lamb's sister killed their mother. The unfinished poem is most likely "Religious Musings."

Soothing each pang with fond solicitude,   10
And tenderest tones medicinal of love.
I too a SISTER had,[2] an only Sister—
She lov'd me dearly, and I doted on her
To her I pour'd forth all my puny sorrows,
(As a sick Patient in his Nurse's arms)   15
And of the heart those hidden maladies
That shrink asham'd from even Friendship's eye.
O! I have woke at midnight, and have wept,
Because SHE WAS NOT!—Cheerily, dear CHARLES!
Thou thy best friend shalt cherish many a year: 20
Such warm presages feel I of high Hope.
For not uninterested the dear maid
I've view'd—her soul affectionate yet wise,
Her polish'd wit as mild as lambent glories,
That play around a sainted infant's head.   25
He knows (the SPIRIT that in secret sees,
Of whose omniscient and all-spreading Love
Aught to *implore* were impotence of mind)[3]
That my mute thoughts are sad before his throne,
Prepar'd, when he his healing ray vouchsafes,   30
To pour forth thanksgiving with lifted heart,
And praise Him Gracious with a BROTHER'S Joy!

Effusion XXXV
Composed
August 20th, 1795,
at Clevedon, Somersetshire[1]

My pensive SARA! thy soft cheek reclin'd
Thus on mine arm, most soothing sweet it is
To sit beside our cot, our cot o'er grown
With white-flower'd Jasmin, and the broad-leav'd Myrtle,[2]
(Meet emblems they of Innocence and Love!)   5
And watch the clouds, that late were rich with light,

2. C's sister Anne (d. 1791).
3. "I utterly recant the sentiment contained" in lines 27–28, "it being written in Scripture, 'Ask, and it shall be given you,' and my human reason being moreover convinced of the propriety of offering *petitions* as well as thanksgiving to Deity." [John 16.24; C's note, added in 1797.]
1. Drafted before his marriage on October 4, 1795, dated August 20, and completed before the end of the year. The title was slightly revised in the editions of 1797 and 1803 and changed to "The Eolian Harp. Composed at Clevedon, Somersetshire" in SL and subsequent editions. In a copy of *Poems* (1797) now at Yale, C wrote at the end of the poem, "This I think the most perfect Poem, I ever wrote. Bad may be the Best, perhaps. S. T. C." He also wrote a note at the end of the poem in a copy of SL, "Let me be excused, if it should seem to others too mere a trifle to justify my noticing it—but I have some claim to the thanks of no small number of the readers of poetry in having first introduced this species of short blank verse poems—of which Southey, Lamb, Wordsworth, and others have since produced so many exquisite specimens" (Johnson, 472).
2. In ancient Rome myrtle was associated with Venus. Cf. Eden in *Paradise Lost* 4.694–99: "Laurel and Mirtle, and what higher grew / Of firm and fragrant leaf * * * and Gessamin / Rear'd high thir flourisht heads."

Slow-sad'ning round, and mark the star of eve[3]
Serenely brilliant (such should Wisdom be)
Shine opposite! How exquisite the scents
Snatch'd from yon bean-field! and the world *so* hush'd!   10
The stilly murmur of the distant Sea
Tells us of Silence. And that simplest Lute[4]
Plac'd length-ways in the clasping casement, hark!
How by the desultory breeze caress'd,
Like some coy Maid half-yielding to her Lover,[5]   15
It pours such sweet upbraidings, as must needs
Tempt to repeat the wrong! And now its strings
Boldlier swept, the long sequacious notes
Over delicious surges sink and rise,
Such a soft floating witchery of sound   20
As twilight Elfins make, when they at eve
Voyage on gentle gales from Faery Land,
Where *Melodies* round honey-dropping flowers
Footless and wild, like birds of Paradise,
Nor pause nor perch, hov'ring on untam'd wing.[6]   25

And thus, my Love! as on the midway slope
Of yonder hill I stretch my limbs at noon
Whilst thro' my half-clos'd eyelids I behold
The sunbeams dance, like diamonds, on the main,
And tranquil muse upon tranquillity;   30
Full many a thought uncall'd and undetain'd,
And many idle flitting phantasies,
Traverse my indolent and passive brain
As wild and various, as the random gales
That swell or flutter on this subject Lute!   35
And what if all of animated nature

3. The planet Venus, also called Vesper or Hesperus.
4. The eolian harp is a stringed instrument that emits sounds when the wind blows over it. It was an emblem of nature's music, as described in James Thomson, *The Castle of Indolence* (1748), stanzas 39 and 40, and "An Ode on Æolus's Harp" (1748), lines 5–8: "Those tender notes, how kindly they upbraid / With what soft woe they thrill the lover's heart? / Sure from the hand of some unhappy maid / Who dy'd of love, these sweet complainings part" (*Liberty, The Castle of Indolence, and Other Poems*, ed. James Sambrook [Oxford, 1986], 315). In Romantic literature the harp is an emblem of the inspired mind.
5. Cf. Pope, "Windsor-Forest," lines 19–20: "As some coy Nymph her Lover's warm Address / Nor quite indulges, nor can quite repress."
6. In the errata of *SL* the following lines come after line 25, and they were included in subsequent printings: "O! the one Life, within us and abroad, / Which meets all Motion, and becomes its soul, / A Light in Sound, a sound-like power in Light, / Rhythm in all Thought, and Joyance every where— / Methinks, it should have been impossible / Not to love all things in a world so fill'd, / Where the breeze warbles and the mute still Air / Is Music slumbering on its instrument!" On July 4, 1817, C wrote to Ludwig Tieck (1773–1853), "I had adopted (probably from Behmen's Aurora, which I had *conjured over* at School) the idea, that Sound was = Light under the præpotence of Gravitation, and Color = Gravitation under the præpotence of Light" (*CL*, 4:751). C refers to Jakob Böhme (1575–1624), a German mystic, who wrote *Aurora* (1612). For C's early reading and later annotations of Böhme, see *CM* (*CC*, 1:553–696). For C's definition of the one life in poetry, see his letter to William Sotheby, September 10, 1802 (p. 630 herein). While the notion of the one life appealed to C's imagination and was useful for his poetry, C was skeptical of the materialists' claims that atoms had not only extension in space but also a life of their own. See the *Biographia*, chapter 8 (p. 435 herein).

Be but organic Harps diversly fram'd,
That tremble into thought, as o'er them sweeps,
Plastic and vast, one intellectual Breeze,
At once the Soul of each, and God of all?[7]   40
But thy more serious eye a mild reproof
Darts, O beloved Woman! nor such thoughts
Dim and unhallow'd dost thou not reject,
And biddest me walk humbly with my God.[8]

Meek Daughter in the Family of Christ,   45
Well hast thou said and holily disprais'd
These shapings of the unregenerate mind,
Bubbles that glitter as they rise and break
On vain Philosophy's aye-babbling spring.[9]
For never guiltless may I speak of Him,   50
Th' INCOMPREHENSIBLE! save when with awe[1]

---

7. C discusses definitions of "Life" in a letter to John Thelwall on December 31, 1796: "Monro believes in a plastic [i.e., shaping or forming] immaterial Nature—all-pervading." C then quotes lines 36–40 of "Effusion XXXV" and continues, "Now as to the Metaphysicians, Plato says," life "is Harmony—he might as well have said, a fiddle stick's end—but I love Plato—his dear *gorgeous* Nonsense! and *I, tho' last not least, I* do not know what to think about it—on the whole, I have rather made up my mind that I am a mere *apparition*—a naked Spirit!—And that Life is I myself I! which is a mighty clear account of it" (CL, 1:294–95).

   C read about Alexander Monro (1733–1817), *Observations on the Structure and Function of the Nervous System* (Edinburgh, 1783), in Dr. John Ferriar (1761–1815), "Observations concerning the Vital Principle," printed in the third volume of the *Memoirs of the Literary and Philosophical Society of Manchester* (1790): "Dr. Monro accounts for the commencement of the involuntary motions, and some other phænomena, on the supposition of a living principle, pervading the universe; similar, I apprehend, to the plastic nature of the Platonists" (222). Ferriar also refers to Ralph Cudworth (1617–1688), *True Intellectual System* (1678). C borrowed Thomas Birch's 1743 edition of Cudworth from the Bristol Library on May 15, 1795, and again on November 9, 1796 (*Borrowings*, 120, 124). A Cambridge Platonist, Cudworth argued against atheism, which accounted for life's origin in matter and its organization. He concluded that "there is a plastic nature under" God, "which, as an inferior and subordinate instrument, doth drudgingly execute that part of his providence, which consists in the regular and orderly motion of matter" (1:150). Cudworth likens the action of plastic nature to the arts, "particularly those musical ones of singing, playing on instruments, and dancing" (1:159), and refers to Plotinus, *Ennead* 3.2.16, where the universe is ruled by "a single rational principle; so that it would be better for one to compare it to the melody which results from conflicting sounds" (*Plotinus*, trans. A. H. Armstrong [LCL, 1993], 3:97).

   To Cudworth, plastic nature "is neither god nor goddess, but a low and imperfect creature * * * nor indeed is it expressly conscious of what it doth, it not knowing, but only doing, according to commands and laws impressed upon it" (1:164). C's phrases "intellectual Breeze" and "tremble into thought," however, seem to attribute a consciousness to Cudworth's "plastic nature" and Plotinus' "rational forming principle." His formulation is perhaps closer to Priestley's *Disquisitions Relating to Matter and Spirit* (1777), in which Priestley denied the common distinction among solid, impenetrable matter and spirit by arguing that matter was composed of "*physical points* only, endued with powers of attraction and repulsion" (19) and that nature and human consciousness were moved by God's energy. Later, in the *Biographia*, C expressed skepticism of the use of the breeze and harp analogy by materialists, including probably Priestley (see p. 427 herein).

8. Cf. Micah 6.8: "He hath shewed thee, O man, what is good; and what doth the Lord require of thee, but to do justly, and to love mercy, and to walk humbly with thy God?"

9. Cf. Pope, *Essay on Man* 3.19–20: the forms of nature "Like bubbles on the sea of Matter born, / They rise, they break, and to that sea return."

1. In a letter to the Reverend John Edwards on March 20, 1796, C asks "How is it that Dr Priestley is not an atheist?—He asserts in three different Places, that God not only *does*, but *is*, every thing.—But if God *be* every Thing, every Thing is God—: which is all, the Atheists assert—. An eating, drinking, lustful *God*—with no *unity* of *Consciousness*—these appear to me the unavoidable Inferences from his philosophy—Has not Dr Priestley forgotten that *Incomprehensibility* is as necessary an attribute of the First Cause, as Love, or Power, or Intelligence?" (CL, 1:192–93).

I praise him, and with Faith that inly *feels*;[2]
Who with his saving mercies healed me,
A sinful and most miserable man
Wilder'd and dark, and gave me to possess   55
PEACE, and this COT, and THEE, heart-honor'd Maid!

RELIGIOUS MUSINGS[1]

What tho' first,
In years unseason'd, I attun'd the Lay
To idle Passion and unreal Woe?
Yet serious Truth her empire o'er my song
Hath now asserted: Falshood's evil brood,

2. "*L'athée n'est point à mes yeux un faux esprit; je puis vivre avec lui aussi bien et mieux qu'avec le dévot, car il raisonne davantage, mais il lui manque un sens, et mon ame ne se fond point entièrement avec la sienne: il est froid au spectacle le plus ravissant, et il cherche un syllogisme lorsque je rends une action de grace.*" (The atheist is not in my eyes a soul in error. I am able to live with him as well or better than with the devout, because he reasons more, but he lacks judgment and my spirit does not blend with his. He is cold to the most ravishing spectacle and he searches for a syllogism when I offer thanksgiving.) C's 1796 note quotes *Appel a l'impartiale postérité, par la Citoyenne Roland* (Appeal to Impartial Posterity) (Paris, 1795), 2:66–67. Mme. Roland (1754–1793), a sympathizer with the Girondist Party, wrote her *Appel* in jail just before her execution by the more radical Jacobins.
1. Although C dates the poem Christmas 1794, it was not completed until 1796, just before *Poems* was published. His first reference to the poem, "on the Nativity" (*CL*, 1:147), on December 29, 1794, suggests its debt to Milton's "On the Morning of Christ's Nativity." By October 1795 it had reached almost 300 lines (*CL*, 1:162). Two sections from the poem were printed in *The Watchman*: lines 273–370 (var.) of the 1796 version, probably written after October 1795 (*Watchman* [CC], xlvii, 64–67), on March 9, 1796, with the title "The Present State of Society," and lines 220–38 (var.) of the 1796 version on March 25, 1796, in "On the Slave Trade" (p. 288 herein). C heavily annotated the poem in its versions of 1796 and 1797, a common practice among poets in the 1790s, and intended the notes to be an integral part of the work. Some of the inflammatory political notes were deleted in 1797. C's notes from 1796 and 1797 are included here.
    When the *Poems* (1796) was published, C sent a copy to the radical John Thelwall and confessed that "you will find much to blame in them—much effeminacy of sentiment, much faulty glitter of expression. I build all my poetic pretentions on the Religious Musings—which you will read with a POET'S EYE" (*CL*, 1:205). Thelwall responded with two letters, the second of which survives, in which he praised C's genius, but disagreed with his assessment of "Religious Musings": "I cannot admit that all your poetic pretensions rest on the Religious Musings." Thelwall disliked the religious sections of the poem: "They are the very acme of abstruse, metaphysical, mistical rant, & all ranting abstractions, metaphysic & mysticism are wider from true poetry than the equator from the poles. The whole poem also is infected with inflation & turgidity" (Warren E. Gibbs, "An Unpublished Letter from John Thelwall to S.T. Coleridge," *Modern Language Review* 25 [1930]: 86–87). Thelwall then cited lines from "Monody on the Death of Chatterton" and "Religious Musings" that he thought particularly weak. C responded to Thelwall:

    Why so violent against *metaphysics* in poetry? Is not Akenside's [*The Pleasures of the Imagination*] a metaphysical poem? Perhaps, you do not like Akenside—well—*but I do*—& so do a great many others—Why pass an act of *Uniformity* against Poets? * * * *my* religious poetry interests the *religious*, who read it with rapture—why? because it awakes in them all the associations connected with a love of future existence &c—. A very dear friend of mine, who is in my opinion the best poet of the age [Wordsworth] * * * thinks that the lines from 364 to 375 [356–67] & from 403 to 428 [395–419] the best in the Volume—indeed idea worth all the rest—And this man is a Republican & at least a *Semi*-atheist [*CL*, 1:215–16].

Similarly, Thomas Poole's brother Richard wrote C on May 3, 1796, that some parts of "*Religious Musings* are exquisitely sublime; I only regret that you write not more to the level of common understandings" (Mrs. Henry Sandford, *Thomas Poole and His Friends*, vol. 1 [1888], 137). C responded to Thomas Poole, "the Poem was not written for common Readers" (*CL*, 1:207).

Vice and deceitful Pleasure, She at once
Excluded, and my Fancy's careless toil
Drew to the better cause!²

Argument

Introduction. Person of Christ. His Prayer on the Cross. The process of his Doctrines on the mind of the Individual. Character of the Elect. Superstition. Digression to the present War. Origin and Uses of Government and Property. The present State of Society. French Revolution. Millenium. Universal Redemption. Conclusion.

Religious Musings
A Desultory Poem,
Written
on Christmas' Eve,
in the Year of Our Lord, 1794

This is the time, when most divine to hear,³
As with a Cherub's "loud uplifted"⁴ trump
The voice of Adoration my thrill'd heart⁵
Rouses! And with the rushing noise of wings
Transports my spirit to the favor'd fields   5
Of Bethlehem, there in shepherd's guise to sit
Sublime of extacy, and mark entranc'd

---

2. Adapted from Akenside, "The Pleasures of the Imagination" (1757), lines 49–59. C substituted "I attun'd the Lay / . . . / Hath now asserted" for Akenside's "haply ere the sports / Of childhood yet were o'er, the adventurous lay / With many splendid prospects, many charms, / Allur'd my heart, nor conscious whence they sprung, / Nor heedful of their end? yet serious truth / Her empire o'er the calm sequooter'd theme / Asserted soon." C borrowed the 1772 edition of Akenside's poems from the Bristol Library from December 24, 1795, to January 8, 1796 (*Borrowings*, 122).
3. Cf. the opening line of Milton, "On the Morning of Christ's Nativity": "This is the Month, and this the happy morn."
4. Milton, "At a Solemn Music," line 11, where the seraphim blow their "loud up-lifted Angel trumpets" before God's throne.
5. Thelwall criticized C's poetic accents: "I must notice an affectation of the Della Crusca school which blurs almost every one of your poems—I mean the frequent accent upon adjectives and weak words—'Escaped the *sore* wounds'—'Sunk to the *cold* earth'—'Love [C wrote *Lone*] glittering, thro' the *high* tree branching wide'—'When most the *big* soul feels'—'Anon upon some *rough* rock's fearful brow'—'But dare no longer on the *sad theme* muse'— ["Monody on the Death of Chatterton," lines 11, 32, 99, 101, 106, 112]. * * * Instances of this kind which give me, at least, the earache occur frequently also in the Religious Musings. 'The voice of Adoration my *thrill'd* heart rouses' [line 3]. 'Saw from her *dark* womb leap her *flamy* child!' flamy child! ! ! ! [line 14] 'For chiefly in the oppressed *good* Man's face' [line 18]" (Gibbs, 88). C responded to Thelwall, "Your remarks on the Della-crusca place of Emphasis are just in part—where we wish to point out the *thing*, & the *quality* is mentioned merely as a decoration, this mode of emphasis is indeed absurd—therefore I very patiently give up to critical vengeance *high* tree, *sore* wounds, & *rough* rock—but when you wish to dwell chiefly on the *quality* rather than the *thing*, then this mode is proper—& indeed is used in common conversation—who says Good *Man*—? therefore *big* soul, *cold* earth, *dark* womb, & *flamy* child are [quite] right—and introduce a variety into the versification— [which is] an advantage" (*CL*, 1:216).

The glory-streaming VISION throng the night.[6]
Ah not more radiant, nor loud harmonies
Hymning more unimaginably sweet   10
With choral songs around th' ETERNAL MIND,
The constellated company of WORLDS
Danc'd jubilant: what time the startling East
Saw from her dark womb leap her flamy Child!
Glory to God in the Highest! PEACE on Earth!   15

Yet Thou more bright than all that Angel Blaze,
Despised GALILÆAN! Man of Woes!
For chiefly in the oppressed Good Man's face
The Great Invisible (by symbols seen)
Shines with peculiar and concentred light,   20
When all of Self regardless the scourg'd Saint
Mourns for th' Oppressor. O thou meekest Man!
Meek Man and lowliest of the Sons of Men!
Who thee beheld thy imag'd Father saw.[7]
His Power and Wisdom from thy awful eye   25
Blended their beams, and loftier Love sate there
Musing on human weal, and that dread hour
When thy insulted Anguish wing'd the prayer
Harp'd by Archangels, when they sing of Mercy!
Which when th' ALMIGHTY heard, from forth his Throne   30
Diviner light flash'd extacy o'er Heaven!
Heav'n's hymnings paus'd: and Hell her yawning mouth
Clos'd a brief moment.

                    Lovely was the Death
Of Him, whose Life was Love! Holy with power
He on the thought-benighted Sceptic beam'd   35
Manifest Godhead, melting into day
What Mists dim-floating of Idolatry
Split and misshap'd the Omnipresent Sire:[8]
And first by TERROR, Mercy's startling prelude,
Uncharm'd the Spirit spell-bound with earthy lusts   40
Till of its nobler Nature it 'gan feel
Dim recollections; and thence soar'd to HOPE,
Strong to believe whate'er of mystic good
Th' ETERNAL dooms for his IMMORTAL Sons.

6. "And suddenly there was with the Angel a multitude of the heavenly Host, praising God and
saying glory to God in the highest and on earth peace." [Luke 2.13–14; C's 1796 note, omitted with lines 7–15 in 1797.]
7. "Philip saith unto him, Lord! shew us the Father and it sufficeth us. Jesus saith unto him,
Have I been so long time with you, and yet hast thou not known me, Philip? He that hath
seen me hath seen the Father." [John 14.8–9; C's 1796 note, omitted with line 24 in 1797.]
8. C included a note in Greek in 1797 that he translated in AR: "They *divided* the intelligible
into many and several individualities." C found the quotation from Damascius (b. c. 480
C.E.), a pagan Neoplatonist, in Thomas Birch's edition of Cudworth's *True Intellectual System* (1743), 1:461 (AR [CC], 33–34; Ian Wylie, *Young Coleridge and the Philosophers of Nature*, 12–13, 24), and mistakenly attributed it to a book actually written by Iamblicus
(c. 245–325), *De Mysteriis Ægyptiorum* (Of the Egyptian Mysteries). Thus cited, the sentence seems to refer to the proliferation of pagan gods, but the Unitarian C could have intended it to apply to the Christian Trinity.

From HOPE and stronger FAITH to perfect LOVE   45
Attracted and absorb'd: and center'd there
GOD only to behold, and know, and feel,
Till by exclusive Consciousness of GOD
All self-annihilated it shall make
GOD its Identity: God all in all![9]   50
We and our Father ONE!
              And blest are they,
Who in this fleshly World, the elect of Heaven,[1]
Their strong eye darting thro' the deeds of Men
Adore with stedfast unpresuming gaze
Him, Nature's Essence, Mind, and Energy!   55
And gazing, trembling, patiently ascend
Treading beneath their feet all visible things
As steps, that upward to their Father's Throne
Lead gradual—else nor glorified nor lov'd.
THEY nor Contempt imbosom nor Revenge: 60
For THEY dare know of what may seem deform
The SUPREME FAIR sole Operant:[2] in whose sight
All things are pure, his strong controlling Love
Alike from all educing perfect good.

Theirs too celestial courage, inly arm'd——   65
Dwarfing Earth's giant brood, what time they muse
On their great Father, great beyond compare!
And marching onwards view high o'er their heads
His waving Banners of Omnipotence.

---

9. "See this *demonstrated* by Hartley, vol. 1, p. 114, and vol. 2, p. 329. See it likewise proved, and freed from the charge of Mysticism, by Pistorius in his Notes and Additions to part second of Hartley on Man. Addition the 18th, 653d page of the third volume of Hartley, Octavo Edition." [C's 1797 note.] C refers to David Hartley, *Observations on Man* (1749): "Since God is the Source of all Good, and consequently must at last appear to be so, *i.e.* be associated with all our Pleasures, it seems to follow, even from this Proposition, that the Idea of God, and of the Ways by which his Goodness and Happiness are made manifest, must, at last, take place of, and absorb all other Ideas, and He himself become, according to the Language of the Scriptures, *All in All.*" C also cited, as a "demonstration," Hartley's calculation of the ratios of Love of the World (W), Fear of God (F), and Love of God (L) to conclude that "it follows from this Speculation concerning the Quantities W, F, and L, that W ought to be diminished, and F and L to be increased, as much as possible, that so W may be indefinitely less than F, and F indefinitely less than L; *i.e.* we ourselves indefinitely happy in the Love of God, by the previous Annihilation of Self and the World" (2:330).
      Pistorius' "On the Pure Love of God" explains that through the laws of association people will be led to love God: "As new gratifications incessantly arise from the divine benevolence, its love will never want food, and consequently the associations by which that love was generated will be continually renewed, refreshed, and strengthened. The consequence of this will be, that, to such minds, God, as our author expresses it in the words of scripture, will be all in all" (Herman Pistorius, *Observations on Man with Notes and Additions to Dr. Hartley's Observations* [1791], 3:663–64). Pistorius quotes 1 Corinthians 15.28: "And when all things shall be subdued unto him, then shall the Son also himself be subject unto him that put all things under him, that God may be all in all." Milton uses the phrase in *Paradise Lost*, 3:341. C's references to Hartley and Pistorius rely on reasoning and the laws of association to avoid mysticism and mystery.
1. C does not refer to the Calvinist doctrine of predestination, but, as he said in *A Moral and Political Lecture*, a "small but glorious band" (p. 245 herein). See a further description of this group in lines 97–113 of "Religious Musings."
2. In April 1814 C wrote to Cottle that " 'sole Operant' is indeed far too bold; may easily be misconstrued into Spinosism; and therefore * * * I should by no means now use such a phrase" (CL, 3:467). Baruch de Spinoza was regarded as a pantheist.

Who the Creator love, created might   70
Dread not: within their tents no Terrors walk.
For they are Holy Things before the Lord
Aye-unprofan'd, tho' Earth should league with Hell!
GOD's Altar grasping with an eager hand
FEAR, the wild-visag'd, pale, eye-starting wretch,   75
Sure-refug'd hears his hot pursuing fiends
Yell at vain distance. Soon refresh'd from Heaven
He calms the throb and tempest of his heart.
His countenance settles: a soft solemn bliss
Swims in his eye: his swimming eye uprais'd: 80
And Faith's whole armour glitters on his limbs!
And thus transfigured with a dreadless awe,
A solemn hush of soul, meek he beholds
All things of terrible seeming. Yea, and there,
Unshudder'd, unaghasted, he shall view[3]   85
E'en the SEVEN SPIRITS, who in the latter day[4]
Will shower hot pestilence on the sons of men.
For he shall know, his heart shall understand,
That kindling with intenser Deity
They from the MERCY-SEAT[5]—like rosy flames,   90
From God's celestial MERCY-SEAT will flash,
And at the wells of renovating LOVE
Fill their Seven Vials with salutary wrath,
To sickly Nature more medicinal
That what soft balm the weeping good man pours   95
Into the lone despoiled trav'ller's wounds![6]

Thus from th' Elect, regenerate thro' faith,
Pass the dark Passions and what thirsty Cares[7]
Drink up the spirit and the dim regards
Self-center. Lo they vanish! or acquire   100
New names, new features—by supernal grace
Enrob'd with Light, and naturaliz'd in Heaven.
As when a Shepherd on a vernal morn

3. Thelwall criticized lines 84–85, among others: "The whole poem also is infected with infla-
   tion & turgidity. * * * 'Yea, & there, Unshudder'd, *unaghasted*, he shall view E'en the Seven
   Spirits'—'Your pitiless rites *have floated* [with] *man's blood the skull-pil'd Temples*' [lines
   145–46]—'Thence voyage forth *Debauchments* [C wrote *Detachments*] *wild of seraph-
   warbled airs* And odors [lines 360–62]—'The odorous groves of *earth reparadis'd* Unbosom
   their glad *echoes*' [lines 380–81]—'A vision *shadowy* of truth' [line 414] * * * and a heap of
   like instances" (Gibbs, 87). On May 13, 1796, C responded to Thelwall, "Your remarks on
   my Poems are, I think, just in general—there is a rage, & affectation of double Epithets—
   'Unshuddered, unaghasted' is indeed truely ridiculous. * * * Why do you object to *shadowy
   of truth*? it is, I acknowlege, a Grecism—but, I think, an elegant one" (*CL,* 1:215–16). C
   changed *Unshuddered, unagahasted* to *unmov'd* in 1797.
4. "And I heard a great voice out of the Temple saying to the seven Angels, pour out the vials of
   the wrath of God upon the earth." [Revelation 16.1 (var.); C's 1796 note, omitted with
   line 86 in 1797.]
5. The covering of the ark of the covenant in Exodus 25.17. Generally, the throne of God
   (*OED*).
6. See the story of the Good Samaritan among the parables of Jesus (Luke 10.30–36).
7. "Our evil Passions under the influence of Religion, become innocent, and may be made to
   animate our virtue—in the same manner as the thick mist melted by the Sun, increases the
   light which it had before excluded. In the preceding paragraph, agreeably to this truth, we
   had allegorically narrated the transfiguration of Fear into holy Awe." [C's 1797 note.]

Thro' some thick fog creeps tim'rous with slow foot,
Darkling he fixes on th' immediate road   105
His downward eye: all else of fairest kind
Hid or deform'd. But lo, the bursting Sun!
Touch'd by th' enchantment of that sudden beam
Strait the black vapor melteth, and in globes
Of dewy glitter gems each plant and tree: 110
On every leaf, on every blade it hangs!
Dance glad the new-born intermingling rays,
And wide around the landscape streams with glory!

There is one Mind, one omnipresent Mind,
Omnific. His most holy name is LOVE.   115
Truth of subliming import! with the which
Who feeds and saturates his constant soul,
He from his small particular orbit flies
With blest outstarting![8] From HIMSELF he flies,
Stands in the Sun,[9] and with no partial gaze   120
Views all creation, and he loves it all,
And blesses it, and calls it very good![1]
This is indeed to dwell with the most High!
Cherubs and rapture-trembling Seraphim
Can press no nearer to th' Almighty's Throne.   125
But that we roam unconscious, or with hearts
Unfeeling of our universal Sire,
And that in his vast family no Cain[2]
Injures uninjur'd (in her best-aim'd blow
Victorious MURDER a blind Suicide)   130
Haply for this some younger Angel now
Looks down on Human Nature: and, behold!
A sea of blood bestrew'd with wrecks, where mad[3]
Embattling INTERESTS on each other rush
With unhelm'd Rage!

　　　　　　　　'Tis the sublime of man,   135
Our noontide Majesty, to know ourselves
Parts and proportions of one wond'rous whole:
This fraternizes man, this constitutes
Our charities and bearings. But 'tis God
Diffus'd thro' all, that doth make all one whole;   140
This the worst superstition, him except,[4]

8. Springing forth.
9. Cf. Revelation 19.17: "And I saw an angel standing in the sun."
1. Genesis 1.25: "God saw that it was good."
2. Cain killed his brother Abel (Genesis 4.1–15); see "Wanderings of Cain" (p. 211 herein).
3. Cf. Revelation 16.3: "And the second angel poured out his vial upon the sea; and it became
   as the blood of a dead man: and every living soul died in the sea."
4. "If to make aught but the Supreme Reality the object of final pursuit, be Superstition; if the
   attributing of sublime properties to things or persons, which those things or persons neither
   do or can possess, be Superstition; then Avarice and Ambition are Superstitions: and he,
   who wishes to estimate the evils of Superstition, should transport himself, not to the temple
   of the Mexican Deities, but to the plains of Flanders, or the coast of Africa—Such is the
   sentiment conveyed in this and subsequent lines." [C's 1797 note.]

Aught to desire, SUPREME REALITY!
The plenitude and permanence of bliss!
O Fiends of SUPERSTITION! not that oft
Your pitiless rites have floated with man's blood   145
The skull-pil'd Temple, not for this shall wrath[5]
Thunder against you from the Holy One!
But (whether ye th' unclimbing Bigot mock
With secondary Gods, or if more pleas'd
Ye petrify th' imbrothell'd Atheist's heart,   150
The Atheist your worst slave) I o'er some plain
Peopled with Death, and to the silent Sun
Steaming with tyrant-murder'd multitudes;
Or where mid groans and shrieks loud-laughing TRADE[6]
More hideous packs his bales of living anguish;   155
I will raise up a mourning, O ye Fiends!
And curse your spells, that film the eye of Faith;
Hiding the present God, whose presence lost,
The moral world's cohesion, we become
An Anarchy of Spirits! Toy-bewitch'd,   160
Made blind by lusts, disherited of soul,
No common center Man, no common sire
Knoweth! A sordid solitary thing,
Mid countless brethren with a lonely heart
Thro' courts and cities the smooth Savage roams   165
Feeling himself, his own low Self the whole,
When he by sacred sympathy might make
The whole ONE SELF! SELF, that no alien knows!
SELF, far diffus'd as Fancy's wing can travel!
SELF, spreading still! Oblivious of its own,   170
Yet all of all possessing! This is FAITH!
This the MESSIAH's destin'd victory!

But first offences needs must come! Even now[7]
(Black Hell laughs horrible—to hear the scoff!)
THEE to defend, meek Galilæan! THEE   175
And thy mild laws of Love unutterable,
Mistrust and Enmity have burst the bands
Of social Peace; and list'ning Treachery lurks
With *pious* fraud to snare a brother's life;
And childless widows o'er the groaning land   180
Wail numberless; and orphans weep for bread!
THEE to defend, dear Saviour of Mankind!

5. See A *Moral and Political Lecture* (p. 247 herein).
6. The slave trade.
7. "January 21st. 1794, in the debate on the Address to his Majesty, on the speech from the Throne, the Earl of Guildford [*sic*] moved an Amendment to the following effect: 'That the House hoped his Majesty would seize the earliest opportunity to conclude a peace with France, &c.' This motion was opposed by the Duke of Portland, who 'considered the war to be merely grounded on one principle—the preservation of the CHRISTIAN RELIGION'. May 30th, 1794, the Duke of Bedford moved a number of Resolutions, with a view to the Establishment of a Peace with France. He was opposed (among others) by Lord Abingdon in these remarkable words: 'The best road to Peace, my Lords, is WAR! and WAR carried on in the same manner in which we are taught to worship our CREATOR, namely, with all our souls, and with all our minds, and with all our hearts, and with all our strength.' " [C's 1797 note.]

THEE, Lamb of God! THEE, blameless Prince of Peace!
From all sides rush the thirsty brood of war!
AUSTRIA, and that foul WOMAN of the NORTH,   185
The lustful Murd'ress of her wedded Lord![8]
And he, connatural Mind! whom (in their songs[9]
So bards of elder time had haply feign'd)
Some Fury fondled in her hate to man,
Bidding her serpent hair in tortuous folds   190
Lick his young face, and at his mouth imbreathe
Horrible sympathy! And leagued with these
Each petty German Princeling, nurs'd in gore!
Soul-harden'd barterers of human blood![1]
Death's prime Slave-merchants! Scorpion-whips of Fate!   195
Nor least in savagery of holy zeal,
Apt for the yoke, the race degenerate,
Whom Britain erst had blush'd to call her sons!
THEE to defend the Moloch[2] Priest prefers
The prayer of hate, and bellows to the herd   200
That Deity, ACCOMPLICE Deity
In the fierce jealousy of waken'd wrath
Will go forth with our armies and our fleets
To scatter the red ruin on their foes!
O blasphemy! to mingle fiendish deeds   205
With blessedness! Lord of unsleeping Love,[3]
From everlasting Thou! We shall not die.
These, even these, in mercy didst thou form,
Teachers of Good thro' Evil, by brief wrong
Making Truth lovely, and her future might   210
Magnetic o'er the fix'd untrembling heart.

In the primeval age a dateless while
The vacant Shepherd wander'd with his flock
Pitching his tent where'er the green grass wav'd.
But soon Imagination conjur'd up   215

8. See *Conciones ad Populum* (p. 251 herein) and *A Moral and Political Lecture* (p. 242, n. 8 herein).
9. "That Despot who received the wages of an hireling that he might act the part of a swindler, and who skulked from his impotent attacks on the liberties of France to perpetrate more successful iniquity in the plains of *Poland*." [C's 1796 note, omitted 1797.] Poland was partitioned by Russia, Austria, and Prussia in October 1795. Frederick William of Prussia (1744–1797) accepted money from England to fight France, but spent it to invade Poland. See *A Moral and Political Lecture*, p. 251 herein.
1. "The Father of the present Prince of Hesse Cassell supported himself and his strumpets at Paris by the vast sums which he received from the British Government during the American war for the flesh of his subjects." [C's 1796 note, omitted 1797.] England paid Frederick II of Hesse-Cassel (1760–1785) over three million pounds for twenty-two thousand soldiers.
2. See *Paradise Lost* 2.43–45: "Moloc, Scepter'd King / Stood up, the strongest and the fiercest Spirit / That fought in Heav'n; now fiercer by despair."
3. "Art thou not from everlasting, O Lord, mine Holy One? We shall not die. O Lord! thou hast ordained them for judgment, &c." [C's 1796 note quotes Habakkuk 1.12.] C added to the note in 1797: "In this paragraph the Author recalls himself from his indignation against the instruments of Evil, to contemplate the *uses* of these Evils in the great process of divine Benevolence. In the first age, Men were innocent from ignorance of vice; they fell, that by the knowledge of consequences they might attain intellectual security, i. e. Virtue, which is a wise and strong-nerv'd Innocence."

An host of new desires: with busy aim,
Each for himself, Earth's eager children toil'd.
So PROPERTY began, twy-streaming fount,
Whence Vice and Virtue flow, honey and gall.
Hence the soft couch, and many-colour'd robe,   220
The timbrel, and arch'd dome and costly feast
With all th' inventive arts, that nurs'd the soul
To forms of beauty, and by sensual wants
Unsensualiz'd the mind, which in the means
Learnt to forget the grossness of the end,   225
Best-pleasur'd with its own activity.
And hence Disease that withers manhood's arm,
The dagger'd Envy, spirit-quenching Want,
Warriors, and Lords, and Priests—all the sore ills[4]
That vex and desolate our mortal life.   230
Wide-wasting ills! yet each th' immediate source
Of mightier good.[5] Their keen necessities
To ceaseless action goading human thought
Have made Earth's reasoning animal her Lord;
And the pale-featur'd Sage's trembling hand   235
Strong as an host of armed Deities!
From Avarice thus, from Luxury and War
Sprang heavenly Science: and from Science Freedom.
O'er waken'd realms Philosophers and Bards
Spread in concentric circles: they whose souls   240
Conscious of their high dignities from God
Brook not Wealth's rivalry; and they who long
Enamour'd with the charms of order hate
Th' unseemly disproportion; and whoe'er
Turn with mild sorrow from the victor's car   245
And the low puppetry of thrones, to muse
On that blest triumph, when the PATRIOT SAGE[6]
Call'd the red lightnings from th' o'er-rushing cloud
And dash'd the beauteous Terrors on the earth
Smiling majestic. Such a phalanx ne'er   250
Measur'd firm paces to the calming sound
Of Spartan flute! These on the fated day,

4. "I deem that the teaching of the gospel for hire is wrong; because it gives the teacher an improper bias in favor of particular opinions on a subject where it is of the last importance that
   the mind should be perfectly unbiased. Such is my private opinion; but I mean not to censure all hired teachers, many among whom I know, and venerate as the best and wisest
   of men—God forbid that I should think of these, when I use the word PRIEST, a name, after
   which any other term of abhorrence would appear an anti-climax. By a PRIEST I mean a man
   who holding the scourge of power in his right hand and a bible (translated by authority) in
   his left, doth necessarily cause the bible and the scourge to be associated ideas, and so produces that temper of mind that leads to Infidelity—Infidelity which judging of Revelation by
   the doctrines and practices of established Churches honors God by rejecting Christ. See
   'Addresses to the People.' " [C's 1796 note, omitted in 1797.] C refers to *Conciones ad Populum* (p. 255 herein).
5. Cf. C's theme in Lecture 1 of *LRR*: "But the greatest possible Evil is Moral Evil. Those Pains
   therefore that rouse us to the removal of it become Good" (*Lects 1795* [CC], 106)
6. "Dr. FRANKLIN." [C's 1796 note, omitted in 1797.] Benjamin Franklin (1706–1790) discovered the connection between electricity and lightning, which prompted further study of the
   elementary forces in nature and safety from destructive lightning.

When stung to rage by Pity eloquent men
Have rous'd with pealing voice th' unnumber'd tribes
That toil and groan and bleed, hungry and blind,   255
These hush'd awhile with patient eye serene
Shall watch the mad careering of the storm;
Then o'er the wild and wavy chaos rush
And tame th' outrageous mass, with plastic might
Moulding Confusion to such perfect forms,   260
As erst were wont, bright visions of the day!
To float before them, when, the Summer noon,
Beneath some arch'd romantic rock reclin'd
They felt the sea-breeze lift their youthful locks,
Or in the month of blossoms, at mild eve,   265
Wandering with desultory feet inhal'd
The wafted perfumes, and the flocks and woods
And many-tinted streams and setting Sun
With all his gorgeous company of clouds
Extatic gaz'd! then homeward as they stray'd   270
Cast the sad eye to earth, and inly mus'd
Why there was Misery in a world so fair.

Ah far remov'd from all that glads the sense,
From all that softens or ennobles Man,
The wretched Many! Bent beneath their loads   275
They gape at pageant Power, nor recognize
Their cots' transmuted plunder! From the tree
Of Knowledge, ere the vernal sap had risen,
Rudely disbranch'd! O *blest* Society!
Fitliest depictur'd by some sun-scorcht waste,   280
Where oft majestic thro' the tainted noon
The SIMOOM sails, before whose purple pomp[7]
Who falls not prostrate dies! And where, by night,
Fast by each precious fountain on green herbs
The lion couches; or hyæna dips   285
Deep in the lucid stream his bloody jaws;
Or serpent rolls his vast moon-glittering bulk,
Caught in whose monstrous twine Behemoth yells,[8]
His bones loud crashing!

7. "At eleven o'clock, while we contemplated with great pleasure the rugged top of Chiggre, to which we were fast approaching, and where we were to solace ourselves with plenty of good water, IDRIS cried out with a loud voice, 'Fall upon your faces, for here is the Simoom.' I saw from the S. E. an haze come on, in colour like the purple part of the rainbow, but not so compressed or thick.—It did not occupy twenty yards in breadth, and was about twelve feet high from the ground.—We all lay flat on the ground, as if dead, till IDRIS told us it was blown over. The meteor, or purple haze, which I saw, was indeed passed; but the light air that still blew was of heat to threaten suffocation." [C's 1796 note, omitted in 1797.] C cites James Bruce, *Travels to Discover the Source of the Nile* (1790), 4:557. In the proofs of *Poems* (1796), C added a sentence to the note, which, however, was never printed: "The Simoom is here introduced as emblematical of the pomp & powers of Despotism" (Ashley, f. 33; *Facsimile*, 63).
8. "Behemoth in Hebrew signifies wild beasts in general. Some believe it is the Elephant, some the Hippopotamus; some affirm it is the Wild-Bull. Poetically, it designates any large Quadruped." [C's 1797 expansion of a 1796 note.]

O ye numberless,
Whom foul Oppression's ruffian gluttony   290
Drives from life's plenteous feast! O thou poor Wretch,
Who nurs'd in darkness and made wild by want
Dost roam for prey, yea thy unnatural hand
Liftest to deeds of blood! O pale-eyed Form,
The victim of seduction, doom'd to know   295
Polluted nights and days of blasphemy;
Who in loath'd orgies with lewd wassailers
Must gaily laugh, while thy remember'd Home
Gnaws like a viper at thy secret heart!
O aged Women! ye who weekly catch   300
The morsel tost by law-forc'd Charity,
And die so slowly, that none call it murder!
O loathly-visag'd Suppliants! ye that oft
Rack'd with disease, from the unopen'd gate
Of the full Lazar-house,[9] heart-broken crawl!   305
O ye to scepter'd Glory's gore-drench'd field
Forc'd or ensnar'd, who swept by Slaughter's scythe,
(Stern nurse of Vultures!) steam in putrid heaps!
O thou poor Widow, who in dreams dost view
Thy Husband's mangled corse, and from short doze   310
Start'st with a shriek: or in thy half-thatch'd cot
Wak'd by the wintry night-storm, wet and cold,
Cow'rest o'er thy screaming baby! Rest awhile,
Children of Wretchedness! More groans must rise,
More blood must steam, or ere your wrongs be full.   315
Yet is the day of Retribution nigh:
The Lamb of God hath open'd the fifth seal:[1]
And upward rush on swiftest wing of fire
Th' innumerable multitude of Wrongs
By man on man inflicted! Rest awhile,   320
Children of Wretchedness! The hour is nigh:
And lo! the Great, the Rich, the Mighty Men,
The Kings and the Chief Captains of the World,
With all that fix'd on high like stars of Heaven
Shot baleful influence, shall be cast to earth,   325
Vile and down-trodden, as the untimely fruit
Shook from the fig-tree by a sudden storm.

9. A house for the diseased poor and lepers.
1. "See the sixth chapter of the Revelation of St. John the Divine.——And I looked and beheld
a pale horse; and his name that sat on him was Death, and Hell followed with him. And
power was given unto them over the FOURTH part of the Earth to kill with sword, and with
hunger, and with pestilence [the King James version has "death" for C's "pestilence"], and
with the beasts of the earth.—And when he had opened the fifth seal, I saw under the altar
the souls of them that were slain for the word of God, and for the testimony which they
held: and white robes were given unto every one of them; and it was said unto them, that
they should rest yet for a little season, until their fellow servants also, and their brethren,
that should be killed as they were should be fulfilled. And I beheld when he had opened the
sixth seal, the stars of Heaven fell unto the Earth, even as a fig tree casteth her untimely figs
when she is shaken of a mighty wind: And the Kings of the earth, and the great men, and the
rich men, and the chief captains, &c." [Revelation 6.8–15 with omissions; C's 1796 note,
omitted in 1797.] Verse 15 concludes, "hid themselves in the dens and in the rocks of the
mountains."

Ev'n now the storm begins: each gentle name,
Faith and meek Piety, with fearful joy
Tremble far-off—for lo! the Giant FRENZY[2]   330
Uprooting empires with his whirlwind arm
Mocketh high Heaven; burst hideous from the cell
Where the old Hag, unconquerable, huge,
Creation's eyeless drudge, black RUIN, sits
Nursing th' impatient earthquake.
                      O return![3]   335
Pure FAITH! meek PIETY! The abhorred Form
Whose scarlet robe was stiff with earthly pomp,
Who drank iniquity in cups of gold,
Whose names were many and all blasphemous,
Hath met the horrible judgement! Whence that cry?   340
The mighty army of foul Spirits shriek'd,
Disherited of earth! For She hath fallen
On whose black front was written MYSTERY;
She that reel'd heavily, whose wine was blood;
She that work'd whoredom with the DÆMON POWER   345
And from the dark embrace all evil things
Brought forth and nurtur'd: mitred ATHEISM;
And patient FOLLY who on bended knee
Gives back the steel that stabb'd him; and pale FEAR
Hunted by ghastlier terrors than surround   350
Moon-blasted Madness when he yells at midnight!
Return pure FAITH! return meek PIETY!
The kingdoms of the world are yours: each heart
Self-govern'd, the vast family of Love
Rais'd from the common earth by common toil   355
Enjoy the equal produce.[4] Such delights
As float to earth, permitted visitants!
When on some solemn jubilee of Saints
The sapphire-blazing gates of Paradise
Are thrown wide open, and thence voyage forth   360
Detachments wild of seraph-warbled airs,
And odors snatch'd from beds of amaranth,
And they, that from the chrystal river of life
Spring up on freshen'd wing, ambrosial gales!
The favor'd good man in his lonely walk   365
Perceives them, and his silent spirit drinks
Strange bliss which he shall recognize in heaven.
And such delights, such strange beatitude

2. "The French Revolution" [C's 1796 note.] C expanded the note in 1797: "This passage alludes to the French Revolution: And the subsequent paragraph to the downfall of Religious
Establishments. I am convinced that the Babylon of the Apocalypse does not apply to Rome
exclusively; but to the union of Religion with Power and Wealth, wherever it is found."
3. "And there came one of the seven Angels which had the seven vials and talked with me, saying unto me, come hither! I will shew unto thee the judgment of the great Whore, that sit-
teth upon many waters: with whom the Kings of the earth have committed fornication."
[Revelation 17.1–2 (var.); C's 1796 note, omitted in 1797.]
4. C's dream of pantisocracy, mentioned in the Preface to *Poems* (1796) and at the end of
"Monody on the Death of Chatterton," rested on the principle of the abandonment of private property. See *Lectures on Revealed Religion*, Lecture 6 (p. 269 herein).

Seize on my young anticipating heart
When that blest future rushes on my view!   370
For in his own and in his Father's might
The SAVIOUR comes! While as to solemn strains
The THOUSAND YEARS lead up their mystic dance,[5]
Old OCEAN claps his hands! the DESERT shouts!
And soft gales wafted from the haunts of Spring   375
Melt the primœval North! The mighty Dead
Rise to new life, whoe'er from earliest time
With conscious zeal had urg'd Love's wond'rous plan
Coadjutors of God. To MILTON'S[6] trump
The odorous groves of earth reparadis'd   380
Unbosom their glad echoes: inly hush'd
Adoring NEWTON[7] his serener eye
Raises to heaven: and he of mortal kind
Wisest, he[8] first who mark'd the ideal tribes
Down the fine fibres from the sentient brain   385
Roll subtly-surging. Pressing on his steps
Lo! Priestley there, Patriot, and Saint, and Sage,[9]
Whom that my fleshly eye hath never seen

5. "The Millenium:—in which I suppose, that Man will continue to enjoy the highest glory, of
which his human nature is capable.—That all who in past ages have endeavoured to amelio-
rate the state of man, will rise and enjoy the fruits and flowers, the imperceptible seeds of
which they had sown in their former Life: and that the wicked will during the same period,
be suffering the remedies adapted to their several bad habits. I suppose that this period will
be followed by the passing away of this Earth and by our entering the state of pure intellect;
when all Creation shall rest from its labours." [C's 1797 note.] Revelation (chapters 20, 21)
prophesies that Christ will return and rule on earth during a thousand years, the millennium, of peace, prosperity, and righteousness.
6. C includes Milton, Newton, and Priestley here because all opposed the Church of England
and hoped for the restoration of primitive Christianity that existed before the alliance of
church and state. In early 1796, when he was completing "Religious Musings," C copied
into his notebook a phrase from the following sentence of Milton, Of Reformation in England: "But he that will mould a modern Bishop into a primitive, must yield him to be
elected by the popular voice, undiocest, unrevenu'd, unlorded, and leave him nothing but
brotherly equality, matchless temperance, frequent fasting, incessant prayer and preaching,
continual watchings and labours in his ministry." CN, 1:106n. cites A Complete Collection of
the Historical, Political and Miscellaneous Works of Milton, ed. John Toland, 3 vols.
(1694–98), 1:255.
7. C praised Isaac Newton (1642–1727) in Lecture 4 of LRR, delivered June 2, 1795: "Sir
Isaac Newton employed his patient Industry and lynx-eyed Penetration in discovering how
the World had been constituted * * * The same temper of mind this great man manifested
in his Theological Studies, and to the comfort of the pious with equal success" (Lects 1795
[CC], 189–90). However, C rejected what he thought was Newton's materialism, and in a
note to Southey's Joan of Arc (1796) he commented: "It has been asserted that Sir Isaac
Newton's philosophy leads in its consequences to Atheism: perhaps not without reason. For
if matter, by any powers or properties given to it, can produce the order of the visible world
and even generate thought; why may it not have possessed such properties by inherent right?
and where is the necessity of a God? matter is according to the mechanic philosophy capable of acting most wisely and most beneficently without Wisdom or Benevolence" (PW,
2:1112–13). C's rejection of Newton was also based on the suspicion that Newton "worked
himself into a sort of Unitarianism" (TT [CC], 1:212). For C's own abandonment of Unitarianism, see p. 606, n. 1 herein.
8. "David Hartley." [C's 1796 note.] See p. 23, n. 9 herein and p. 423 herein.
9. See notes to "Effusion IV" (p. 17 herein). Shortly before he emigrated to America in 1794,
Priestley preached The Present State of Europe Compared with the Ancient Prophecies, in
which he interpreted the French Revolution as the fulfillment of the biblical prophecy of the
second coming of Christ and rule of the millennium. Priestley quoted William Whiston, Essay on the Revelation (1706): "Sir Isaac Newton had a very sagacious conjecture, which he
told Dr. Clarke, from whom I received it, that the overbearing tyranny and persecuting
power of the antichristian party, which hath so long corrupted Christianity, and enslaved the
Christian world, must be put a stop to, and broken to pieces by the prevalence of infidelity,

A childish pang of impotent regret
Hath thrill'd my heart. Him from his native land   390
Statesmen blood-stain'd and Priests idolatrous
By dark lies mad'ning the blind multitude
Drove with vain hate: calm, pitying he retir'd,
And mus'd expectant on these promis'd years.

O Years! the blest preeminence of Saints!   395
Sweeping before the rapt prophetic Gaze
Bright as what glories of the jasper throne[1]
Stream from the gorgeous and face-veiling plumes
Of Spirits adoring! Ye, blest Years! must end,
And all beyond is darkness! Heights most strange!   400
Whence Fancy falls, fluttering her idle wing.
For who of woman born may paint the hour,
When seiz'd in his mid course the Sun shall wane
Making noon ghastly! Who of woman born
May image in his wildly-working thought,   405
How the black-visag'd, red-eyed Fiend outstretcht[2]
Beneath th' unsteady feet of Nature groans
In feverish slumbers—destin'd then to wake,
When fiery whirlwinds thunder his dread name
And Angels shout, DESTRUCTION! How his arm   410
The mighty Spirit lifting high in air
Shall swear by Him, the ever-living ONE,
TIME IS NO MORE!

                    Believe thou, O my soul,[3]
Life is a vision shadowy of Truth,
And vice, and anguish, and the wormy grave,   415
Shapes of a dream! The veiling clouds retire,
And lo! the Throne of the redeeming God
Forth flashing unimaginable day
Wraps in one blaze earth, heaven, and deepest hell.

---

for some time, before primitive Christianity could be restored; which seems to be the very means that is now working in Europe, for the same good and great end of Providence" (24–25). Newton thus anticipated Priestley's *History of the Corruptions of Christianity* (1782), from which Priestley quoted for a note to his sermon: "the alliance of the kingdom of Christ with the kingdoms of this world (an alliance which our Lord himself expressly disclaimed) * * * supports the grossest corruptions of Christianity; and perhaps we must wait for the fall of the civil powers before this most unnatural alliance be broken. * * * May the kingdom of God, and of Christ * * * truly and fully come, though all the kingdoms of the world be removed in order to make way for it" (27). Southey took Priestley's *Corruptions of Christianity* from the Bristol Library March 27, 1795 (*Borrowings*, 119). Priestley added an appendix to his sermon with quotations from Hartley because he "got the leading ideas that are enlarged upon in the" sermon from Hartley (35).

1. "And immediately I was in the Spirit: and behold, a Throne was set in Heaven and one sat on the Throne. And he that sat was to look upon like a jasper and a sardine stone, &c." [Revelation 4.2–3 (var.); C's 1797 note.]
2. "The final Destruction impersonated." [C's 1797 note.]
3. "This paragraph is intelligible to those, who, like the Author, believe and feel the sublime system of Berkley [*sic*]; and the doctrine of the final Happiness of all men." This 1797 note indicates C's shift from Hartley's philosophy to that of George Berkeley beginning in November 1796, when he expressed his approval of Berkeley (*CL*, 1:245); C borrowed volume two of Berkeley's *Works* (1784) from the Bristol Library on March 10, 1796 (*Borrowings*, 122). See "This Lime-Tree Bower My Prison," p. 138, n. 7.

Contemplant Spirits! ye that hover o'er   420
With untir'd gaze th' immeasurable fount
Ebullient with creative Deity!
And ye of plastic power, that interfus'd
Roll thro' the grosser and material mass
In organizing surge! Holies of God!   425
(And what if Monads[4] of the infinite mind?)
I haply journeying my immortal course
Shall sometime join your mystic choir! Till then
I discipline my young noviciate thought
In ministeries of heart-stirring song,   430
And aye on Meditation's heaven-ward wing
Soaring aloft I breathe th' empyreal air
Of LOVE, omnific, omnipresent LOVE,
Whose day-spring rises glorious in my soul
As the great Sun, when he his influence   435
Sheds on the frost-bound waters—The glad stream
Flows to the ray and warbles as it flows.

FROM ODE ON THE DEPARTING YEAR (1796)

"Ode on the Departing Year" was published with a sonnet, "Lines Addressed to a Young Man of Fortune," omitted here, in a thin quarto dated December 26, 1796. A shorter version of the poem was printed in the *Cambridge Intelligencer*, December 31, as "Ode for the last day of the Year, 1796." Carl Woodring points out that its title was designed to contrast with optimistic laureate verse commonly titled "Ode for the New Year" and printed in newspapers on the last day of the year (Woodring, 174). "Ode on the Departing Year" was first in *Poems* (1797) and was reprinted in all subsequent editions. In *Poems* (1797) Coleridge included this note: "This Ode was written on the 24th, 25th, and 26th days of December, 1796; and published separately on the last day of the year." In the 1834 edition the title was changed to "Ode to the Departing Year."

The title page contained a quotation from Cassandra in *Agamemnon*, lines 1214–16 and 1240–41:

Ιου, ιου, ω ω κακα.
Υπ' αυ με δεινος ορθομαντειας πονος
Στροβει, ταρασσων φροιμιοις εφημιοις.
– – – – – – – – – – – – – – – – – – – –
Το μελλον ηξει· και συ μην ταχει παρων
Αγαν γ' αληθομαντιν μ' ερεις.

("Ha, ha! Oh, oh, the agony! Once more the dreadful throes of true prophecy whirl and distract me with their ill-boding onset. * * * What is to come, will come. Soon thou, present here thyself, shalt of thy pity pronounce me all too true a prophetess": Aeschylus, *Agamemnon*, trans. Her-

---

4. Although monads occupy a central place in the writings of Giordano Bruno (1548–1600) and Gottfried Leibniz (1646–1716), there is little evidence that C read either before 1801 (*CN*, 1:928; *CL*, 1:590). See C's "Destiny of Nations," lines 40–59, written for Southey, *Joan of Arc* (1796). C's use of the word "monad" probably came from Cudworth, who reported that for Pythagoras, "monads * * * were nothing else but corporeal atoms" (*True Intellectual System* [1743], 1:13). C adapted the term to designate an energy in nature.

bert Weir Smyth [LCL, 1992], 106–09). Coleridge wrote to John Prior Estlin (1747–1817), December 30, 1796: "You know, I am a *mottophilist*, and
almost a motto-*manist*—I love an apt motto to my Heart," and translated
"-ἐφημίοις φροιμίοις—" as "bloody Presages" (*CL*, 1:293). When the
motto was omitted from proofs of the 1797 version Coleridge wrote, "The
Motto—! where is the Motto—? I would not have lost the MOTTO for a
kingdom twas the best part of the ode," and on another set of proofs he
wrote, "Motto I beseech you, let the Motto be printed; and printed accurately (Ashley, ff. 58v, 66v; *Facsimile*, 84, 100). Cassandra, doomed to be
misunderstood and ignored, foretold the fall of Troy; in "Ode on the Departing Year" Coleridge fortells the fall of Britain, which he later recanted
in "France: An Ode." In the part of Cassandra's speech Coleridge omitted,
she foretold the death of Agamemnon, the king. He wrote to Bowles on
March 16, 1797, "My Ode you will read with a kindly forbearance as to its
political sentiments. * * * We both feel strongly for whomever our imaginations present to us in the attitude of suffering—I confess, that mine is
too often a '*stormy pity*' " (*CL*, 1:318). Coleridge quotes line 10 of "Effusion II" in *Poems* (1796). Coleridge's prophecy echoes Priestley's idea that
the fall of civil and ecclesiastical power must precede the restoration of
primitive Christianity (see p. 32, n. 9 herein).

In February 1797 Coleridge sent Cottle corrections to "Ode on the Departing Year" for *Poems* (1797), "which some people think superior to the
'Bard' of Gray, and which others think a rant of turgid obscurity; and the
latter are the more numerous class. It is not obscure. My 'Religious Musings' I know are, but not this 'Ode' " (*CL*, 1:309). Coleridge refers to
Thomas Gray, "The Bard. A Pindaric Ode." The Greek poet Pindar
(c. 522–442 B.C.E.) developed the ode, a poem divided into three sections:
a strophe and antistrophe, which use the same verse form, and an epode
in a different form. Thus in "Ode on the Departing Year" strophe I balances antistrophe I, and strophe II balances antistrophe II, while the two
epodes have unique forms. Coleridge added extensive notes to his ode,
most of which were political and removed in *Poems* (1797). The dedicatory letter to Thomas Poole identified this form as the "sublimer Ode,"
whose characteristics are abrupt transition and impassioned language,
characteristics that often prompted its readers to charge it with obscurity.

The text printed here is from the 1796 quarto, with the omission of final quotation marks at lines 41 and 110. A variant state of "Ode on the
Departing Year" is printed in *PW* (*CC*), 2:428.

To Thomas Poole, of Stowey

My Dear Friend,

Soon after the commencement of this month, the Editor of the Cambridge Intelligencer (a newspaper conducted with so much ability, and
such unmixed and fearless zeal for the interests of Piety and Freedom,
that I cannot but think my poetry honoured by being permitted to appear in it), requested me, by Letter, to furnish him with some Lines
for the last day of this Year. I promised him that I would make the attempt; but, almost immediately after, a rheumatic complaint seized on
my head, and continued to prevent the possibility of poetic composi-

tion till within the last three days. So in the course of the last three days the following Ode was produced. In general, when an Author informs the Public that his production was struck off in a great hurry, he offers an insult, not an excuse. But I trust that the present case is an exception, and that the peculiar circumstances, which obliged me to write with such unusual rapidity, give a propriety to my professions of it: nec nunc eam apud te jacto, sed et ceteris indico; ne quis asperiore limâ carmen examinet, et a confuso scriptum et quod frigidum erat ni statim traderem.[1] (I avail myself of the words of Statius, and hope that I shall likewise be able to say of any weightier publication, what *he* has declared of his Thebaid, that it had been tortured with a laborious Polish.)[2]

For me to discuss the *literary* merits of this hasty composition, were idle and presumptuous. If it be found to possess that Impetuosity of Transition, and that Precipitation of Fancy and Feeling, which are the *essential* excellencies of the sublimer Ode, its deficiency in less important respects will be easily pardoned by those, from whom alone praise could give me pleasure: and whose minuter criticisms will be disarmed by the reflection, that these Lines were conceived "not in the soft obscurities of Retirement, or under the Shelter of Academic Groves, but amidst inconvenience and distraction, in sickness and in sorrow."[3] I am more anxious, lest the *moral* spirit of the Ode should be mistaken. You, I am sure, will not fail to recollect, that among the Ancients, the Bard and the Prophet[4] were one and the same character; and you *know*, that although I prophesy curses, I pray fervently for blessings.

Farewell, Brother of my Soul!

──────────O ever found the same,
And trusted and belov'd![5]
Never without an emotion of honest pride do I subscribe myself
Your grateful and affectionate Friend,
BRISTOL,   S. T. COLERIDGE.
December 26, 1796.

1. Adapted from Statius' letter to his friend Melior prefacing book 2 of *Silvae*: "Nor am I boasting of it now to you but warning others not to criticize too sharply a poem written in distress and cold (or dull) unless issued quickly" (*Statius*, trans. J. H. Mozley [LCL, 1982], 1:73–75).
2. C refers to Statius, "Lyric Ode to Vibius Maximus," in *Silvae* 4.7.26, where Statius speaks of his "*Thebiad*, tortured by endless polishing."
3. Dr. Johnson's Preface to his *Dictionary* (var.) in *Samuel Johnson: Selected Writings*, ed. R. T. Davies (Evanston, Ill., 1965), 167.
4. On March 10, 1797, C wrote to Joseph Cottle, "Public affairs are in strange confusion—I am afraid that I shall prove at least as good a prophet as bard—O doom'd to fall, enslav'd & vile:—but may God make me a foreboder of evils never to come" (*CL*, 1:313). C quotes line 129 of "Ode on the Departing Year."
5. Mark Akenside, *The Pleasures of the Imagination* (1757), book I, 88–89 (var.).

Ode
on the
Departing Year[1]

Strophe I

SPIRIT, who sweepest the wild Harp of Time,
It is most hard with an untroubled Ear
Thy dark inwoven Harmonies to hear!
Yet, mine eye fixt on Heaven's unchanged clime,
Long had I listen'd, free from mortal fear,   5
With inward stillness and a bowed mind:
When lo! far onwards waving on the wind
I saw the skirts of the DEPARTING YEAR![2]
    Starting from my silent sadness
    Then with no unholy madness,   10
Ere yet the entered cloud forbade my sight,
I rais'd th' impetuous song, and solemnized his flight.

Strophe II

    Hither from the recent Tomb;
    From the Prison's direr gloom;
    From Poverty's heart-wasting languish: 15
    From Distemper's midnight anguish;
    Or where his two bright torches blending[3]
    Love illumines[4] Manhood's maze;
    Or where o'er cradled Infants bending
    Hope has fix'd her wishful gaze: 20
    Hither, in perplexed dance,
    Ye WOES, and young-eyed[5] JOYS, advance!
By Time's wild harp, and by the Hand
Whose indefatigable Sweep
Forbids its fateful strings to sleep,   25

1. In 1797 C added the "Argument": "The Ode commences with an Address to the Divine Providence, that regulates into one vast Harmony all the events of time however calamitous some of them may appear to mortals. The Second Strophe calls on men to suspend their private joys and sorrows, and devote them for awhile to the cause of human nature in general. The first Epode speaks of the Empress of Russia, who died of an Apoplexy on the 17th of November, 1796; having just concluded a subsidiary treaty with the Kings combined against France. The first and second Antistrophe describe the Image of the departing year, etc. as in a vision. The second Epode prophecies in anguish of spirit, the downfall of this Country."
2. Cf. Collins, "Ode to Evening," lines 5–8: "the bright-haired sun / Sits in yon western tent, whose cloudy skirts, / With brede ethereal wove, / O'erhang his wavy bed," and *Paradise Lost* 5.187: "Till the Sun paint your fleecie skirts with Gold." In *SL*, C changed the phrase to "the train of the Departing Year."
3. "The flames of two Candles joined give a much stronger Light than both of them separate—evid. by a person holding the two Candles near his Face, first separate, & then joined in one. Picture of Hymen" (CN, 1:13).
4. The printer for *Poems* (1797) set "illumine's" for "illumines" and C corrected the error: "illumine's! that villainous apostrophe ' belongs to the *Genitive case of Substantives* only—It should be illumines. O that Printers were wise! O that they would read Bishop Lowth" (Ashley, f. 60v; *Facsimile*, 88). Bishop Robert Lowth (1710–1787) published *A Short Introduction to English Grammar* (1762).
5. I.e., clear-sighted. Cf. *The Merchant of Venice* 5.1.61: "the young-eyed cherubins."

I bid you haste, a mixt tumultuous band!
   From every private bower,
   And each domestic hearth,
   Haste for one solemn hour;
And with a loud and yet a louder voice   30
O'er the sore travail of the common earth
      Weep and rejoice!
Seiz'd in sore travail and portentous birth
(Her eye-balls flashing a pernicious glare)
Sick NATURE struggles! Hark—her pangs increase!   35
Her groans are horrible! But ô! most fair
The promis'd Twins, she bears—EQUALITY and PEACE![6]

Epode

I mark'd Ambition in his war-array:
I heard the mailed Monarch's troublous cry—
   "Ah! whither does the Northern Conqueress[7] stay?   40
   "Groans not her Chariot o'er its onward way?
      Fly, mailed Monarch, fly!
   Stunn'd by Death's "twice mortal"[8] mace
   No more on MURDER'S lurid face
Th' insatiate Hag shall glote with drunken eye!   45
   Manes[9] of th' unnumbered Slain!
   Ye that gasp'd on WARSAW'S plain!
   Ye that erst at ISMAIL'S tower,
   When human Ruin chok'd the streams,

6. After Charles Lamb wrote to C on January 2, 1797, that "all that gradual description of the throes & pangs of nature in childbirth, I do not much like" (*LL*, 1:81), C wrote to John Thelwall on February 6, 1797, that "the whole Childbirth of Nature is at once ludicrous & disgusting—an epigram smart yet bombastic" (*CL*, 1:307). For the 1797 version C changed lines 33–37 to "Still echoes the dread Name that o'er the earth / Let slip the storm and woke the brood of Hell: / And now advance in saintly Jubilee / JUSTICE and TRUTH: they too have heard the spell, / They too obey thy Name, divinest LIBERTY!" In an 1803 note C explained that the "dread Name" was "The Name of Liberty, which at the commencement of the French Revolution was both the occasion and the pretext of unnumbered crimes and horrors" (*PW*, 1:161–62). C spoke about the Hebrew Jubilee, when lands were restored to their owners and debts cancelled, in Lecture 2 of his *LRR* (p. 260 and n. 4 herein).
7. "A Subsidiary Treaty had been just concluded; and Russia was to have furnished more effectual aid, than that of pious manifestoes, to the powers combined against France. I rejoice—not over the deceased Woman—(I never dared figure the Russian Sovereign to my imagination under the dear and venerable character of WOMAN—WOMAN, that complex term for Mother, Sister, Wife!) I rejoice, as at the disenshrining of a Dæmon! I rejoice, as at the extinction of the evil Principle impersonated! This very day, six years ago, the massacre of Ismail was perpetrated. THIRTY THOUSAND HUMAN BEINGS, MEN, WOMEN & CHILDREN, murdered in cold blood, for no other crime, than that their Garrison had defended the place with perseverance and bravery! Why should I recall the poisoning of her husband, her iniquities in Poland, or her late unmotivated attack on Persia; the desolating ambition of her public Life, or the libidinous excesses of her private Hours! I have no wish to qualify myself for the office of Historiographer to the King of Hell———! December 23, 1796." [C's 1796 note, omitted in 1797.] Catherine II died in 1796 at age sixty-seven. Her husband, Peter III (b. 1728), died in 1762 in suspicious circumstances after a rebellion of the palace guards. Count A. V. Suvorov (1729–1800) took Ismail, a Turkish outpost near the mouth of the Danube, in 1790.
8. Edward Young, *Night Thoughts* 4.763–65: "Thro' *Reason's* Wounds alone, thy *Faith* can die; / Which dying, tenfold Terror Gives to Death, / And dips in *Venom* his twice-mortal Sting" (*Night Thoughts*, ed. Stephen Cornford [Cambridge, 1989], 110).
9. Shades of the dead "as an object of reverence, or as demanding to be propitiated by vengeance" (*OED*).

Fell in Conquest's glutted hour 50
Mid Women's shrieks and Infant's screams;
Whose shrieks, whose screams were vain to stir
Loud-laughing, red-eyed Massacre!
Spirits of th' uncoffin'd Slain,
Sudden blasts of Triumph swelling 55
Oft at night, in misty train
Rush around her narrow Dwelling!
Th' exterminating Fiend is fled—
(Foul her Life and dark her Doom!)
Mighty Army of the Dead, 60
Dance, like Death-fires, round her Tomb!
Then with prophetic song relate
Each some scepter'd Murderer's fate!
When shall scepter'd SLAUGHTER cease?
Awhile He crouch'd, O Victor France! 65
Beneath the light'ning of thy Lance,
With treacherous dalliance wooing PEACE.[1]
But soon up-springing from his dastard trance
The boastful, bloody Son of Pride[2] betray'd
His Hatred of the blest and blessing Maid. 70
One cloud, O Freedom! cross'd thy orb of Light
And sure, he deem'd, that Orb was quench'd in night:
For still does MADNESS roam on GUILT's bleak dizzy height!

1. "With treacherous dalliance wooing Peace.—To juggle [i.e., deceive] this easily-juggled people into better humour with the supplies (and themselves, perhaps, affrighted by the successes of the French,) our Ministry sent an ambassador to Paris to sue for Peace. The
Supplies are granted: and in the mean time the Arch-duke Charles turns the scale of Victory
on the Rhine, and Buonaparte is checked before Mantua. Straightways, our courtly Messenger is commanded to *uncurl* his lips, and propose to the lofty Republic to *restore* all *its* con-
quests, and to suffer England to *retain* all *hers*, (at least all her *important* ones) as the only
terms of Peace, and the ultimatum of the negociation!
Θρασυνει γαρ αισχρομητις
Ταλαινα ΠΑΡΑΚΟΠΑ πρωτοπημων.
ÆSCHYL. AG. 230.
The friends of Freedom in this country are idle. Some are timid; some are selfish; and many
the torpedo touch of hopelessness has numbed into inactivity. We would fain hope, that (if
the above account be accurate—it is only the French account) this dreadful instance of
infatuation in our ministry will rouse them to one effort more; and that at one and the
same time in our different great towns the people will be called on to think solemnly, and
declare their thoughts fearlessly, by every method, which the *remnant* of the constitution
allows." [C's 1796 note, omitted in 1797 along with lines 64–73.] C quotes *Agamemnon*,
lines 222–23: "For mankind is emboldened by wretched delusion, counselor of ill, primal
source of woe" (Aeschylus, *Agamemnon*, trans. Herbert Weir Smyth [LCL, 1922], 22–23).
C wrote to John Prior Estlin on December 30, 1796, that "Παρακοπά * * * is a good
word—it is commonly, but loosely, rendered, *madness*—it means properly an *excision* of
mind—so that we see but *one* side, and are blind to noon day evidence on the other" (*CL*,
1:293). When Charles Louis of Austria (1771–1847) won victory on the Rhine (Woodring,
176), Pitt increased the terms for peace with France. Writing to Cottle, C proposed an alternative note for *Poems* (1797) that was never published: "At the time this Ode was being
composed, our Ambassador had returned from Paris, the French Directory professing to
consider his ultimatum, as an insult to the Republic—Surely, Cottle! no Aristocrat can be
angry at that note" (Peter Mann, "Two Autograph Letters of S. T. Coleridge," *RES* 25
[1974]: 313).
2. William Pitt, the prime minister (Woodring, 176).

Antistrophe I

DEPARTING YEAR! 'twas on no earthly shore[3]
My Soul beheld thy Vision.[4] Where, alone,   75
Voiceless and stern, before the Cloudy Throne
Aye MEMORY sits; there, garmented with gore,
With many an unimaginable groan
Thou storiedst thy sad Hours! Silence ensued:
Deep Silence o'er th' etherial Multitude,   80
Whose purple Locks with snow-white Glories shone.
    Then, his eye wild ardors glancing,
    From the choired Gods advancing,
The SPIRIT of the EARTH made reverence meet
And stood up beautiful before the Cloudy Seat![5]   85

Antistrophe II

On every Harp, on every Tongue
While the mute Enchantment hung;
Like Midnight from a thundercloud,
Spake the sudden SPIRIT loud—
"Thou in stormy Blackness throning   90
"Love and uncreated Light,
"By the Earth's unsolac'd groaning
"Seize thy terrors, Arm of Might!
"By Belgium's corse-impeded flood![6]
"By Vendee steaming Brother's blood!   95
"By PEACE with proffer'd insult scar'd,
"Masked hate, and envying scorn!
"By Years of Havoc yet unborn;
"And Hunger's bosom to the frost-winds bar'd!
    "But chief by Afric's wrongs   100
    "Strange, horrible, and foul!
    "By what deep Guilt belongs
"To the deaf Synod, "full of gifts and lies!"[7]

---

3. "The first Antistrophe describes the Image of the Departing Year, as in a vision; and concludes with introducing the Planetary Angel of the Earth preparing to address the Supreme Being" (*PW*, 1:164). [C's 1803 expansion of a shorter 1796 note.]
4. "Thy Image in a Vision." [C's 1796 note.]
5. Cf. Matthew 24.30: "the Son of man coming in the clouds of heaven"; Matthew 26.64: "the Son of man sitting on the right hand of power, and coming in the clouds of heaven"; and Ecclesiasticus 25.1: "In three things I was beautified, and stood up beautiful, both before God and men: the unity of brethren, the love of neighbors, a man and a wife that agree together" (*CN*, 1:265n.).
6. "The Rhine." [C's 1796 note.] Variants of lines 94–95 were included in C's untitled verses to the radical J. Horne Tooke (*CL*, 1:225; *PW*, 1:150–51) of July 4, 1796, where they are included in quotation marks as spoken by Tooke. In C's letter "Brother's" in line 95 is "brothers'." On July 9, 1796, C's poem to Tooke was published as "Poetical Address. Written for the Late Meeting of Mr. Tooke's Friends" in the *Telegraph* (*PW* [CC], 1:266–69, 2:365–67).
7. "Gifts used in Scripture for corruption." [C's note in the *Cambridge Intelligencer* (*PW*, 1:165).] For La Vendée, see "France: An Ode" (p. 118, n. 5 herein) and *Conciones ad Populum* (p. 252, n. 4 herein).

"By Wealth's insensate Laugh! By Torture's Howl!
    "Avenger, rise!   105
"For ever shall the bloody Island scowl?[8]
"For aye unbroken, shall her cruel Bow
"Shoot Famine's arrows o'er thy ravag'd World?
"Hark! how wide NATURE joins her groans below—
"Rise, God of Nature, rise! Why sleep thy Bolts unhurl'd?   110

Epode II

The Voice had ceas'd, the Phantoms fled,
Yet still I gasp'd and reel'd with dread.
And ever when the dream of night
Renews the vision to my sight,
Cold sweat-damps gather on my limbs,   115
My Ears throb hot, my eye-balls start,
My Brain with horrid tumult swims,
Wild is the Tempest of my Heart;
And my thick and struggling breath
Imitates the toil of Death!   120
No uglier agony confounds
The Soldier on the war-field spread,
When all foredone with toil and wounds
Death-like he dozes among heaps of Dead!
(The strife is o'er, the day-light fled,   125
And the Night-wind clamours hoarse;
See! the startful Wretch's head
Lies pillow'd on a Brother's Corse!)
O doom'd to fall, enslav'd and vile,[9]
O ALBION! O my mother Isle!   130
Thy valleys, fair as Eden's bowers,
Glitter green with sunny showers;
Thy grassy Upland's gentle Swells
Echo to the Bleat of Flocks;
(Those grassy Hills, those glitt'ring Dells   135
Proudly ramparted with rocks)
And Ocean 'mid his uproar wild
Speaks safety to his Island-child.
Hence for many a fearless age
Has social Quiet lov'd thy shore;   140
Nor ever sworded Foeman's rage
Or sack'd thy towers, or stain'd thy fields with gore.

---

8. C's 1796 note quotes *Conciones ad Populum* (p. 252 herein) on British crimes in Europe,
   Africa, Asia, and America.
9. Revised in *SL* to "Not yet enslav'd, not wholly vile." For C's recantation of line 129, see lines
   36–37 of "France: an Ode": "Yet still my voice unalter'd sang defeat / To all that brav'd the
   tyrant-quelling lance." Lines 129–42 (var.) were included in *On the Constitution of Church
   and State* (1830), where line 129 was changed to "O ne'er enchain'd nor wholly vile" (*C&S*
   [CC], 23–24).

Disclaim'd of Heaven![1] mad Av'rice at thy side,
At coward distance, yet with kindling pride—
Safe 'mid thy herds and corn-fields thou hast stood,   145
And join'd the yell of Famine and of Blood.
All nations curse thee: and with eager wond'ring
Shall hear DESTRUCTION, like a vulture, scream!
Strange-eyed DESTRUCTION, who with many a dream
Of central flames thro' nether seas upthund'ring   150
Soothes her fierce solitude, yet (as she lies
Stretch'd on the marge of some fire-flashing fount
In the black chamber of a sulphur'd mount,)
If ever to her lidless dragon eyes,
O ALBION! thy predestin'd ruins rise,   155
The Fiend-hag on her perilous couch doth leap,
Mutt'ring distemper'd triumph in her charmed sleep.

    Away, my soul, away!
In vain, in vain, the birds of warning sing—
And hark! I hear the famin'd brood of prey   160
Flap their lank pennons on the groaning wind![2]
    Away, my Soul, away!
I unpartaking of the evil thing,
With daily prayer, and daily toil
Soliciting my scant and blameless soil,   165
Have wail'd my country with a loud lament.
Now I recenter my immortal mind
In the long sabbath of high self-content;
Cleans'd from the fleshly Passions that bedim
God's Image, Sister of the Seraphim.[3]   170

1. "The Poet from having considered the peculiar advantages, which this Country has enjoyed, passes in rapid transition to the uses, which we have made of these advantages. We have been preserved by our insular situation, from suffering the actual horrors of War ourselves, and we have shewn our gratitude to Providence for this immunity by our eagerness to spread those horrors over nations less happily situated. In the midst of plenty and safety we have raised or joined the yell for famine and blood. Of the one hundred and seven last years, fifty have been years of war.—Such wickedness cannot pass unpunished. We have been proud and confident in our alliances and our fleets—but God has prepared the canker-worm, and will smite the *gourds* of our pride. 'Art thou better than populous No, that was situate among the rivers, that had the waters round about it, whose rampart was the Sea? Ethiopia and Egypt were her strength, and it was infinite: Put and Lubim were her helpers. Yet she was carried away, she went into captivity: and they cast lots for her honourable men, and all her great men were bound in chains. Thou also shalt be drunken: all thy strong-holds shall be like fig trees with the first ripe figs; if they be shaken, they shall ever fall into the mouth of the eater. Thou hast multiplied thy merchants above the stars of heaven. Thy crowned are as the locusts; and thy captains as the great grasshoppers which camp in the hedges in the cool-day; but when the Sun ariseth, they flee away, and their place is not known where they are. There is no healing of thy bruise; thy wound is grievous: all, that hear the report of thee, shall clap hands over thee: for upon whom hath not thy wickedness passed continually?' " [C's note, added in 1797; he quotes Nahum 3.8–19 with omissions.] In 1826 C connected the figure of destruction in the following lines to Revelation 9.15.
2. For *Poems* (1797) the printer set "dark pennons" for "lank pennons." C corrected it and wrote to Cottle in the margin: "I suspect, almost suspect, that the word 'dark' was *intentionally* substituted for 'lank'—if so, twas the most *tasteless* thing thou ever didst, dear Joseph!" Cottle responded "I cannot but think now that you gave me direction to alter this or I am unaccountably mistaken because I like lank so much better than dark myself J C" (Ashley, ff. 65, 72; *Facsimile*, 97, 111).
3. Cf. Crashaw, "The Flaming Heart," line 104: St. Teresa is "Fair sister of the SERAPHIM" (*Complete Poetry of Richard Crashaw*, ed. George Walton Williams [New York, 1970], 65). The Seraphim are the highest order of angels, who represent love.

FROM POEMS (1797)

Coleridge sent the list of contents for this volume to Joseph Cottle on January 6, 1797. The volume was to have begun with "The Progress of Liberty, or the Visions of the Maid of Orleans," an addition to Coleridge's contribution to Book 2 of Southey's *Joan of Arc* (1796), and was to conclude with "Ode on the Departing Year" and "Religious Musings" (*CL*, 1:298–99). Charles Lamb disliked the "Maid of Orleans," so that Coleridge had not the "heart to finish" it (*CL*, 1:309); see the headnote to the *Morning Post* and *The Annual Anthology* (p. 122 herein). Coleridge substituted "Ode on the Departing Year" as the first poem. The 1796 Preface was reprinted with some alterations, and a new Preface was added. The volume thus began with "Ode on the Departing Year," which prophesied ruin to England, and concluded with "Religious Musings," which looked with optimism upon an apocalyptic renewal led by a small band of the elect.

In re-organizing the second edition of his poems, Coleridge omitted nineteen of his poems, including the political sonnets, in *Poems on Various Subjects* (1796). Many of the poems omitted were reprinted in the third edition of 1803, published by Longman, who had purchased the copyright for *Poems* (1796) from Cottle. Charles Lamb arranged the poems in the third edition (*LL*, 2:111–15). Poems omitted in 1797 were also omitted in *Sibylline Leaves* (1817) and consigned to the category of "Juvenile Poems" in *Poetical Works* (1828) and later editions. Coleridge added twelve new poems, among them "Dedication. To the Reverend George Coleridge," "Ode on the Departing Year" (titled "Ode to the New Year" on the contents page), "To the River Otter," "On the Birth of a Son," "On First Seeing my Infant," and "Reflections on Having Left a Place of Retirement." The *Morning Post* announced that the volume was published on October 28, 1797. While *Poems on Various Subjects* (1796) included minor contributions by Southey and Lamb, *Poems* (1797) featured twenty-six poems by Charles Lloyd (1775–1839) and a sonnet by Coleridge to Lloyd under a separate title page, "Poems, by Charles Lloyd. Second Edition." It also included fifteen poems by Charles Lamb with a separate title page, "Poems, by Charles Lamb, of the India House." Lloyd's poems were added, as Coleridge said, to increase the sales among Lloyd's wealthy friends (*CL*, 1:313). The political sonnets were omitted to increase the audience. The title page contained the motto *"Duplex nobis vinculum, et amicitiæ similium junctarumque Camœnarum; quod utinam neque mors solvat, neque temporis longinquitas"* (We have a double bond: that of friendship and of our linked and kindred Muses: may neither death nor length of time dissolve it) (*CL*, 1:390; *PW*, 2:1142). The volume ended with the "Supplement," where Coleridge placed six poems that, as he explained in an advertisement to the "Supplement," he "excepted * * * from those, which I had determined to omit," with two poems by Lloyd and one by Lamb.

By the summer of 1797 Coleridge was simplifying his style at the urging of Richard Poole (d. 1798), Thelwall, and Lamb, who had written to him on November 8, 1796, "Cultivate simplicity, Coleridge, or rather, I should say, banish elaborateness; for simplicity springs spontaneous from the heart, and carries into daylight its own modest buds and genuine, sweet, and clear flowers of expression" (*LL*, 1:60–61). Coleridge wrote to Southey on July 17, 1797, that the "Monody on the Death of Chatterton" "*must not be reprinted.*" It would not "have been in the second Edition, but for dear Cottle's solicitous importunity. Excepting the last 18 lines of the Monody, which tho' deficient in chasteness & severity of diction, breathe a pleasing spirit of romantic feeling, there are not 5 lines * * * which might not have been written by a man who had lived & died in the self-same St Giles's Cellar. * * * on a life & death so full of heart-giving *realities*, as poor Chatterton's to find such shadowy nobodies, as cherub-winged DEATH, Trees of HOPE, bare-bosom'd AFFECTION, & simpering PEACE—makes one's blood circulate like ipecacacuanha [*sic*].—But so it is. A young man by strong feelings is impelled to write on a particular subject—and this is all, his feelings do for him. They set him upon the business & then they leave him" (*CL*, 1:333).

Within a few weeks of the publication of *Poems* (1797), Coleridge and Wordsworth began joint composition, which resulted in Coleridge's "The Rime of the Ancient Mariner" and *Lyrical Ballads*. The allegorical mode of "Ode on the Departing Year" and "Religious Musings," modeled on Milton, Collins, and Gray, was left behind. "The Eolian Harp," first published as "Effusion XXXV" in 1796, became the model of the Romantic meditative blank-verse poem, and "Reflections on Having Left a Place of Retirement" of 1796 and "This Lime-Tree Bower My Prison" written in July 1797, confirmed the new direction in style.

The poems printed here are from the 1797 edition in the order of the volume. On July 3 Coleridge sent Cottle a list of errata, but it arrived too late for corrections to be made. The errata are included in the notes herein (*CL*, 1:331).

FROM POEMS (1797)

Dedication.
To the Reverend George Coleridge,
of
Ottery St. Mary,
Devon[1]

Notus in fratres animi paterni.
Hor. Carm. Lib. II. 2.

A blessed Lot hath he, who having past
His youth and early manhood in the stir
And turmoil of the world, retreats at length,
With cares that move, not agitate the heart,
To the same Dwelling where his Father dwelt;   5
And haply views his tottering little ones
Embrace those aged knees and climb that lap,

---

1. C's older brother George followed his father as clergyman and headmaster of the King's School in Ottery St. Mary, C's birthplace. He became a surrogate father to C. C wrote in a copy of *Poems* (1797) now at Yale, "If this volume should ever be delivered according to its direction, *i.e.* to Posterity, let it be known that the Reverend George Coleridge was displeased and thought his character endangered by the Dedication. S. T. Coleridge" (*PW*, 1:173). The epigraph comes from Horace, *Odes* 2.2.6: "known for his fatherly spirit towards his brothers" (*Horace: Odes and Epodes*, trans. C. E. Bennett [LCL, 1914], 110–11).

On which first kneeling his own Infancy
Lisp'd its brief prayer. Such, O my earliest Friend!
Thy Lot, and such thy Brothers too enjoy.   10
At distance did ye climb Life's upland road,
Yet cheer'd and cheering: now fraternal Love
Hath drawn you to one centre. Be your days
Holy, and blest and blessing may ye live!

To me th' Eternal Wisdom hath dispens'd   15
A different fortune and more different mind—
Me from the spot where first I sprang to light,
Too soon transplanted, ere my soul had fix'd
Its first domestic loves; and hence through life
Chacing chance-started Friendships. A brief while   20
Some have preserv'd me from life's pelting ills;
But, like a Tree with leaves of feeble stem,
If the clouds lasted, or a sudden breeze
Ruffled the boughs, they on my head at once
Dropt the collected shower: and some most false,   25
False and fair-foliag'd as the Manchineel,[2]
Have tempted me to slumber in their shade
E'en mid the storm; then breathing subtlest damps,
Mix'd their own venom with the rain from heaven,
That I woke poison'd! But, all praise to Him   30
Who gives us all things, more have yielded me
Permanent shelter: and beside one Friend,[3]
Beneath th' impervious covert of one Oak,
I've rais'd a lowly shed, and know the names
Of Husband and of Father; nor unhearing   35
Of that divine and nightly-whispering VOICE,
Which from my childhood to maturer years
Spake to me of predestinated wreaths,
Bright with no fading colours!

                                Yet at times
My soul is sad, that I have roam'd through life   40
Still most a Stranger, most with naked heart
At mine own home and birth-place: chiefly then,
When I remember thee, my earliest Friend!
Thee, who didst watch my boy-hood and my youth;
Didst trace my wanderings with a father's eye;   45
And boding evil yet still hoping good

---

2. A West Indian tree with poisonous sap. C may also be thinking of the Upas tree of Java noted in Erasmus Darwin, *Botanic Garden* (1790): the tree "is said by its effluvia to have depopulated the country for 12 or 14 miles round the place of its growth" (2:115). C quarreled with Robert Southey in August 1795 over Southey's decision to leave the pantisocracy scheme.
3. "Mr. T. Poole, of Nether Stowey, near Bridgewater, Somerset." [C's annotation in *Poems* (1797), now at Yale.] Thomas Poole, a landowner, tanner, and passionate democrat, assisted Coleridge with grants of money and arranged for Coleridge to move into a small cottage in Nether Stowey, in December 1796.

Rebuk'd each fault and wept o'er all my woes.[4]
Who counts the beatings of the lonely heart,
That Being knows, how I have lov'd thee ever,
Lov'd as a Brother, as a Son rever'd thee!   50
O tis to me an ever-new delight,
My eager eye glist'ning with mem'ry's tear,
To talk of thee and thine; or when the blast
Of the shrill winter, ratt'ling our rude sash,
Endears the cleanly hearth and social bowl;   55
Or when, as now, on some delicious eve,
We in our sweet sequester'd Orchard-plot
Sit on the Tree crook'd earth-ward; whose old boughs,
That hang above us in an arborous roof,
Stirr'd by the faint gale of departing May   60
Send their loose blossoms slanting o'er our heads!

Nor dost not *thou* sometimes recall those hours,
When with the joy of hope thou gav'st thine ear
To my wild firstling lays. Since then my song
Hath sounded deeper notes, such as beseem   65
Or that sad wisdom, folly leaves behind;
Or the high raptures of prophetic Faith;
Or such, as tun'd to these tumultuous times
Cope with the tempest's swell!

              These various songs,
Which I have fram'd in many a various mood,   70
Accept my BROTHER! and (for some perchance
Will strike discordant on thy milder mind)
If aught of Error or intemperate Truth
Should meet thine ear, think thou that riper Age
Will calm it down, and let thy Love forgive it!   75

                    S. T. COLERIDGE.

May 26th, 1797.
Nether-Stowey, Somerset.

From Preface
to the Second Edition

I return my acknowledgments to the different Reviewers for the assistance, which they have afforded me, in detecting my poetic deficiencies. I have endeavoured to avail myself of their remarks: one third of

4. George paid some of C's college debts in February 1793 (*CL*, 1:55–56) and again in February 1794 after C left Cambridge in early December and enlisted in the army under the name Silas Tomkyn Comberbache. George, with the assistance of their brother James, then a captain in the army, arranged to have C discharged from service on April 10, 1794, on the grounds of insanity (*CL*, 1:75–76).

the former Volume I have omitted, and the imperfections of the re-published part must be considered as errors of taste, not faults of carelessness. My poems have been rightly charged with a profusion of double-epithets,[1] and a general turgidness. I have pruned the double-epithets with no sparing hand; and used my best efforts to tame the swell and glitter both of thought and diction. This latter fault however had insinuated itself into my Religious Musings with such intricacy of union, that sometimes I have omitted to disentangle the weed from the fear of snapping the flower. A third and heavier accusation has been brought against me, that of obscurity; but not, I think, with equal justice. An Author is obscure, when his conceptions are dim and imperfect, and his language incorrect, or unappropriate, or involved. A poem that abounds in allusions, like the Bard of Gray, or one that impersonates high and abstract truths, like Collins's Ode on the poetical character; claims not to be popular—but should be acquitted of obscurity. The deficiency is in the Reader. But this is a charge which every poet, whose imagination is warm and rapid, must expect from his *contemporaries*. Milton did not escape it; and it was adduced with virulence against Gray and Collins. We now hear no more of it; not that their poems are better understood at present, than they were at their first publication; but their fame is established; and a critic would accuse himself of frigidity or inattention, who should profess not to understand them. But a living writer is yet sub judice;[2] and if we cannot follow his conceptions or enter into his feelings, it is more consoling to our pride to consider him as lost beneath, than as soaring above, us. If any man expect from my poems the same easiness of style which he admires in a drinking-song, for him I have not written. Intelligibilia, non intellectum adfero.[3]

I expect neither profit or general fame by my writings; and I consider myself as having been amply repaid without either. Poetry has been to me its own "exceeding great reward:"[4] it has soothed my afflictions, it has multiplied and refined my enjoyments; it has endeared solitude; and it has given me the habit of wishing to discover the Good and the Beautiful in all that meets and surrounds me.

* * *

STOWEY,   S.T.C.
May, 1797.

---

1. See the *Biographia*, p. 378 herein and p. 24, n. 3 herein.
2. Under the consideration of a judge or court; i.e., undecided.
3. "I bring things to be understood, not things that are understood." C used the Latin phrase in *Essays on the Principles of Genial Criticism* (*SW&F* [CC], 1:378).
4. J. C. C. Mays identifies the source in Genesis 15.1 (*PW* [CC], 1:1233).

Introduction to the Sonnets[1]

The composition of the Sonnet has been regulated by Boileau in his Art of Poetry, and since Boileau, by William Preston,[2] in the elegant preface to his Amatory Poems: the rules, which they would establish, are founded on the practice of Petrarch.[3] I have never yet been able to discover either sense, nature, or poetic fancy in Petrarch's poems; they appear to me all one cold glitter of heavy conceits and metaphysical abstractions. However, Petrarch, although not the inventor of the Sonnet, was the first who made it popular; and his countrymen have taken *his* poems as the model. Charlotte Smith[4] and Bowles are they who first made the Sonnet popular among the present English: I am justified therefore by analogy in deducing its laws from *their* compositions.

The Sonnet then is a small poem, in which some lonely feeling is developed. It is limited to a *particular* number of lines, in order that the reader's mind having expected the close at the place in which he finds it, may rest satisfied; and that so the poem may acquire, as it were, a *Totality*,—in plainer phrase, may become a *Whole*. It is confined to fourteen lines, because as some particular number is necessary, and that particular number must be a small one, it may as well be fourteen as any other number. When no reason can be adduced

1. C originally used this as a preface to a collection of his and others' sonnets privately printed in 1796, which EHC titled "A Sheet of Sonnets." It included sonnets by Bowles, Lloyd, Lamb, Thomas Warton, Southey, Smith, and Anna Seward (1742–1809), among others (*PW*, 2:1138–41; *PW* [CC], 1:1199–1224). In *Poems* (1797) C's sonnets were introduced with a separate title page, "Sonnets, Attempted in the Manner of the Rev. W. L. Bowles" and included a motto from Lucretius, *De Rerum Natura* 3.5–6: "*Non ita certandi cupidus, quam propter amorem / Quod te* IMITARI *aveo*" (It's not in eager rivalry but rather for love that I long to imitate you). Lucretius (99–55 B.C.E.) praises things Greek, particularly Democritus (b. c. 460 B.C.E.).
2. Preston, *Poetical Works*, 2 vols. (Dublin, 1793), quotes eleven lines from Boileau's *L'Art poétique* (1674) (1:267), which read in translation:

> One says, regarding that topic, that once a strange God
> Trying to push all the French poetasters to the limit
> Invented for the sonnet the rigorous laws;
> Stated that in two quatrains of equal length,
> The rhyme with two sounds eight times strikes the ear,
> And that then six lines artistically sorted
> Were split by meaning in two tercets
> From that poem he especially forbade poetic license
> Himself measures the number of lines and syllables, and the rhythm
> Disallowed that one weak line may ever enter it,
> Or that one word already there be used again.

3. Francesco Petrarca (1304–1374), Italian poet who perfected the sonnet form. Coleridge later saw his comment as "a piece of petulant presumption, of which I should be more ashamed, if I did not flatter myself that it stands alone in my writings. The best of the Joke is, that at the time I wrote it, I did not understand a word of Italian, & could therefore judge of this divine poet only by bald Translations of some half a dozen of his Sonnets." [C's manuscript note in *Poems* (1797), now at Yale.]
4. Smith published *Elegiac Sonnets* (1784), which went through many editions with increased numbers of sonnets.

against a thing, Custom is a sufficient reason for it. Perhaps, if the Sonnet were comprized in less than fourteen lines, it would become a serious Epigram; if it extended to more, it would encroach on the province of the Elegy. Poems, in which no lonely feeling is developed, are not Sonnets because the Author has chosen to write them in fourteen lines: they should rather be entitled Odes, or Songs, or Inscriptions. The greater part of Warton's Sonnets are severe and masterly likenesses of the style of the Greek επιγραμματα.[5]

In a Sonnet then we require a developement of some lonely feeling, by whatever cause it may have been excited; but those Sonnets appear to me the most exquisite, in which moral Sentiments, Affections, or Feelings, are deduced from, and associated with, the scenery of Nature. Such compositions generate a habit of thought highly favourable to delicacy of character. They create a sweet and indissoluble union between the intellectual and the material world. Easily remembered from their briefness, and interesting alike to the eye and the affections, these are the poems which we can "lay up in our heart, and our soul," and repeat them "when we walk by the way, and when we lie down, and when we rise up."[6] Hence, the Sonnets of BOWLES derive their marked superiority over all other Sonnets; hence they domesticate with the heart, and become, as it were, a part of our identity.

Respecting the metre of a Sonnet, the Writer should consult his own convenience.—Rhymes, many or few, or no rhymes at all—whatever the chastity of his ear may prefer, whatever the rapid expression of his feelings will permit;—all these things are left at his own disposal. A sameness in the final sound of its words is the great and grevious defect of the Italian language. That rule therefore, which the Italians have established, of exactly *four* different sounds in the Sonnet, seems to have arisen from their wish to have *as many*, not from any dread of finding *more*. But surely it is ridiculous to make the *defect* of a foreign language a reason for our not availing ourselves of one of the marked excellencies of our own. "The Sonnet (says Preston) will ever be cultivated by those who write on tender pathetic subjects. It is peculiarly adapted to the state of a man violently agitated by a real passion, and wanting composure and vigor of mind to methodize his thought. It is fitted to express a momentary burst of passion," &c.[7] Now, if there be one species of composition more difficult and artificial than another, it is an English Sonnet on the Italian Model. Adapted to the agitations of a real passion! Express momentary bursts of feeling in it! I should sooner expect to write pathetic *Axes* or *pour*

---

5. "Epigrams." Thomas Warton's *Poems* (1777) was noted for its revival of the sonnet.
6. Deuteronomy 11.18–19.
7. Adapted from Preston, *Poetical Works*, 1:268

forth extempore Eggs and Altars![8] But the best confutation of such idle rules is to be found in the Sonnets of those who have observed them, in their inverted sentences, their quaint phrases, and incongruous mixture of obsolete and spenserian[9] words: and when, at last, the thing is toiled and hammered into fit shape, it is in general racked and tortured Prose rather than any thing resembling Poetry.

The Sonnet has been ever a favorite species of composition with me; but I am conscious that I have not succeeded in it. From a large number I have retained ten only, as not beneath mediocrity. Whatever more is said of them, *ponamus lucro.*[1]

S. T. COLERIDGE.

Sonnet IV

To the River Otter[1]

Dear native Brook! wild Streamlet of the West!
　How many various-fated Years have past,
　What blissful and what anguish'd hours, since last
I skimm'd the smooth thin stone along thy breast,
　Numbering its light leaps! Yet so deep imprest   5
Sink the sweet scenes of Childhood, that mine eyes
I never shut amid the sunny blaze,
　But strait with all their tints thy waters rise,
Thy crossing plank, thy margin's willowy maze,
　And bedded sand that vein'd with various dies   10
Gleam'd thro' thy bright transparence to the gaze!
　Visions of Childhood! oft have ye beguil'd
Lone Manhood's cares, yet waking fondest sighs,
　Ah! that once more I were a careless Child!

8. Arguing against the strictness of the Pindaric ode and in favor of the irregular ode, Preston writes, "If, in order to deter rash meddlers, the composition of an ode is to be rendered more difficult, by wantonly dividing it into strophe, antistrophe and epode, why rest there? Let the sanctuary of good writing be still more effectually secured from prophane intruders, by ordaining that lyric poems should be always written in the shape of a flute, a pair of wings, an egg, an axe, or an altar?" (*Poetical Works,* 2:8).
9. Edmund Spenser used archaic words to imitate Chaucer.
1. We count it as a gain. Cf. Horace, *Odes* 1.9.14–15 (trans. C. E. Bennett [LCL, 1914]): "*quem Fors dierum cumque dabit, lucro / appone*" (set down as gain each day that Fortune grants).
1. The river Otter flows through Ottery St. Mary, C's birthplace. EHC dates the poem 1793, but J. C. C. Mays suggests 1796 (*PW* [CC], 1:299). Lines 1–11 (var.) were first published in *The Watchman,* April 2, 1796, as part of "Recollection" (*Watchman* [CC], 167–68; *PW,* 2:1023–24). On July 3, 1797, C sent the following revisions to Cottle, too late for inclusion in *Poems* (1797), but entered finally in *SL* and later editions: line 3 "happy" for "blissful" and "mournful" for "anguish'd"; line 7 "ray" for "blaze"; line 9 "thy marge with willows grey"; line 11, a period after "transparence" and "on my way" for "to the gaze" (*CL,* 1:331).

Sonnet IX

Composed on a journey homeward; the Author having received intelligence of the Birth of a Son, September 20, 1796.[1]

Oft o'er my brain does that strange fancy roll
Which makes the present (while the flash doth last)
Seem a mere semblance of some unknown past,
Mix'd with such feelings, as perplex the soul
Self-question'd in her sleep: and some[2] have said   5
We liv'd, ere yet this fleshy robe we wore.[3]
O my sweet Baby! when I reach my door,
If heavy looks should tell me, thou wert dead
(As sometimes, thro' excess of hope, I fear)
I think, that I should struggle to believe   10
Thou wert a Spirit, to this nether sphere
Sentenc'd for some more venial crime to grieve;
Didst scream, then spring to meet Heaven's quick repricve,
While we wept idly o'er thy little bier!

1. David Hartley Coleridge, named after the philosopher David Hartley, was born September 19, 1796. C sent the sonnet to Thomas Poole on November 1, 1796, with the following opening lines in place of those printed here: "Oft of *some unknown Past* such Fancies roll / Swift o'er my brain, as make the Present seem, / For a brief moment, like a most strange dream / When, not unconscious that she dreamt, the Soul / Questions herself in sleep" and the comment that "the first four lines express a feeling which I have often had. The present has appeared like a vivid dream or exact similitude of some *past* circumstances" (CL, 1:246). On December 17, 1796, C defended his sonnet from Thewall's criticism that it was obscure, "you ought to distinguish between obscurity residing in the uncommonness of the thought, and that which proceeds from thoughts unconnected & language not adapted to the expression of them. * * * I *did* mean semblance of some unknown Past, like to a dream—and not 'a semblance *presented* in a dream.'—I meant to express, that oftimes, for a second or two, it flashed upon my mind, that the then company, conversation, & every thing, had occurred before, with all the precise circumstances; so as to make Reality appear a Semblance, and the Present like a dream in Sleep. Now this thought is obscure; because few people have experienced the same feeling" (CL, 1:277).
2. C added a note in Greek in *Poems* (1797): "Ἡν που ἡμων η ψυχη πριν εν τωδε τω ανθρω–πινω ειδει γενεσθαι" (This is impossible if our soul did not exist somewhere before being born in this human form) (Plato, *Phaedo* 73a, trans. Harold North Fowler [LCL, 1914]). C found the quotation in Thomas Birch's edition of Cudworth, *True Intellectual System* (1743) and copied it in a notebook in November 1796 (CN, 1:200).
3. "Alluding to Plato's doc[trine] of Pre-existence." [C's note, in the letter to Southey (CL, 1:261).] In SL C changed "fleshy robe" to "robe of Flesh." J. C. C. Mays suggests "fleshy" is a misprint for "fleshly."

Sonnet X[1]

*To a Friend, who asked how I felt, when the Nurse
first presented my Infant to me.*

CHARLES! my slow heart was only sad, when first
I scann'd that face of feeble infancy:
For dimly on my thoughtful spirit burst
All I had been, and all my babe might be!
But when I saw it on its Mother's arm,   5
And hanging at her bosom (she the while
Bent o'er its features with a tearful smile)
Then I was thrill'd and melted, and most warm
Impress'd a Father's kiss: and all beguil'd
Of dark remembrance, and presageful fear   10
I seem'd to see an Angel's form appear.—
'Twas even thine, beloved Woman mild!
So for the Mother's sake the Child was dear,
And dearer was the Mother for the Child.

Reflections[1]
on Having Left a Place of Retirement

Sermoni propriora.—HOR.[2]

Low was our pretty Cot: our tallest Rose
Peep'd at the chamber-window. We could hear
At silent noon, and eve, and early morn,
The Sea's faint murmur. In the open air
Our Myrtles blossom'd; and across the porch   5
Thick Jasmins twin'd: the little landscape round
Was green and woody and refresh'd the eye.
It was a spot, which you might aptly call
The VALLEY of SECLUSION![3] Once I saw
(Hallowing his Sabbath-day by quietness)   10

---

1. Charles is Charles Lloyd. Sent in a letter to Poole, November 1, 1796 (*CL*, 1:246–47). C's errata listed the omission of the period in line 11 (*CL*, 1:331).
1. Completed in March or April 1796 and first published in the *Monthly Magazine*, October 1796 as "Reflections on Entering into Active life. *A Poem, which affects Not To Be* POETRY," signed S. T. Coleridge. In 1797 the title on the contents page was "On leaving a Place of Residence." After his marriage on October 4, 1795, C and his wife moved into a cottage at Clevedon, near the Bristol Channel, but by the end of November he was lecturing in Bristol against the two bills. From January 9 to February 13 he was on a tour to gather subscribers for *The Watchman*. When he returned from the tour C lived in Bristol to produce *The Watchman*. When Charles Lamb read the version in the *Monthly Magazine*, he wrote to C, "write thus, & you most generally have written thus, & I shall never quarrel with you about" simplicity (*LL*, 1:65).
2. Horace, *Satires* 1.4.42. Horace's phrase is "sermoni propiora" ("nearer to prose"; from the Latin *propior*, "nearer"). C's misspelling may be a joke—"properer for a sermon" (from the Latin *proprius*, "proper")—as Charles Lamb translated it (*TT* [*CC*], 1:314). See C's translation of the phrase in his letter to William Sotheby, September 10, 1802 (p. 630 herein).
3. Clevedon.

A wealthy son of Commerce saunter by,
Bristowa's[4] citizen: Methought, it calm'd
His thirst of idle gold, and made him muse
With wiser feelings: for he paus'd, and look'd
With a pleas'd sadness, and gaz'd all around,   15
Then eyed our cottage, and gaz'd round again,
And sigh'd, and said, *it was a blessed place.*
And we *were* blessed. Oft with patient ear
Long-listening to the viewless sky-lark's note
(Viewless, or haply for a moment seen   20
Gleaming on sunny wing) in whisper'd tones
I've said to my Beloved, "Such, sweet Girl!
"The inobtrusive song of HAPPINESS—
"Unearthly minstrelsy! then only heard
"When the Soul seeks to hear; when all is hush'd   25
"And the Heart listens!"[5]

           But the time, when first
From that low Dell steep up the stony Mount
I climb'd with perilous toil and reach'd the top,
O what a goodly scene! *Here* the bleak Mount,
The bare bleak Mountain speckled thin with sheep;   30
Grey Clouds, that shadowing spot the sunny fields;
And River, now with bushy rocks o'erbrow'd
Now winding bright and full, with naked banks;
And Seats, and Lawns, the Abbey, and the Wood,
And Cots, and Hamlets, and faint City-spire: 35
The Channel *there*, the Islands and white Sails,
Dim Coasts, and cloud-like Hills, and shoreless Ocean—[6]
It seem'd like Omnipresence! God, methought,
Had built him there a Temple: the whole World
Seem'd *imag'd* in its vast circumference.   40
No *wish* profan'd my overwhelmed Heart.
Blest hour! It was a Luxury—to be!

    Ah quiet Dell! dear Cot! and Mount sublime!
I was constrain'd to quit you. Was it right,
While my unnumber'd Brethren toil'd and bled,   45
That I should dream away the trusted Hours
On rose-leaf Beds, pamp'ring the coward Heart
With feelings all too delicate for use?
Sweet is the Tear that from some Howard's[7] eye

---

4. Bristol's.
5. In a copy of *SL* now in the Berg Collection, someone, not C, has written "Dyer's Fleece" next to lines 25–26 in pencil. Cf. John Dyer, *The Fleece* (1757), 1.615–16: Nature's music is the "Music of paradise! which still is heard, / When the heart listens."
6. The view from the hill may be influenced by William Crowe, *Lewesdon Hill* (Oxford, 1788), which C borrowed from the Bristol Library in March 1795 (*Borrowings*, 119).
7. John Howard (1726–1790) a prison reformer and author of *The State of the Prisons in England and Wales* (1777), expanded in later reprintings, and *An Account of the Principal Lazarettos in Europe* (1789). A "lazaretto" is a refuge for the diseased poor and lepers. Bowles wrote two poems on Howard: "Verses to John Howard, F.R.S. on his State of Prisons and Lazarettos" (1789) and "On the Grave of Howard" (1790).

Drops on the cheek of One, he lifts from earth: 50
And He, that works me good with unmov'd face,
Does it but half: he chills me while he aids,
My Benefactor, not my Brother Man!
Yet even this, this cold Beneficence
Seizes my Praise, when I reflect on those,[8]   55
The sluggard Pity's vision-weaving Tribe!
Who sigh for Wretchedness, yet shun the Wretched,
Nursing in some delicious solitude
Their slothful loves and dainty Sympathies![9]
I therefore go, and join head, heart, and hand,   60
Active and firm, to fight the bloodless fight
Of Science, Freedom, and the Truth in CHRIST.

Yet oft when after honourable toil
Rests the tir'd mind, and waking loves to dream,
My Spirit shall revisit thee, dear Cot!   65
Thy Jasmin and thy window-peeping Rose,
And Myrtles fearless of the mild sea-air.
And I shall sigh fond wishes—sweet Abode!
Ah—had none greater! And that all had such!
    It might be so—but the time is not yet.   70
    Speed it, O FATHER! Let thy Kingdom come!

FROM LYRICAL BALLADS (1798, 1800)

At the end of May 1798 Joseph Cottle visited Coleridge and Wordsworth, and they settled the contents for *Lyrical Ballads* (1798). In addition to "The Ancient Mariner," the first poem in the volume, three more of Coleridge's poems were included: "The Foster-Mother's Tale," "Lewti," and "The Dungeon." The volume concluded with Wordsworth's "Lines Written a Few Miles above Tintern Abbey." Coleridge had published "Lewti" in the *Morning Post*, and since *Lyrical Ballads* was to be published anonymously to avoid attacks on Coleridge's reputation as a West Country radical, "Lewti" was removed after a few copies were printed. "The Nightingale" was substituted. When the volume was finished in late August or early September, Cottle distributed a few copies in Bristol and sold the printed copies, approximately five hundred (*ER*, 2:23), to the London firm of J. and A. Arch, because he thought the volume would be unsuccessful. Wordsworth prepared a second edition in two volumes published in 1800 under his own name. The first volume of 1800 opened with the Preface to *Lyrical Ballads*. Many reviewers of the 1798 volume thought "The Ancient Mariner" unintelligible nonsense, and Wordsworth believed the poem had hurt sales, so he moved it to the end of the first volume of 1800, just before "Tintern Abbey." The second volume of 1800 contained only Wordsworth's poems, among them "Heart-leap Well," "The Brothers," "Ruth," "Nutting," and "Michael."

8. See variant of line 55 in *AR* (CC), 59.
9. C distinguishes benevolence from mere sensibility, self-indulgent sentimentality, in "On the Slave Trade" (p. 298 herein).

Lyrical Ballads (1798) originated in efforts by Coleridge and Wordsworth at joint composition. In early November 1797 they began to write "Wanderings of Cain" (p. 211 herein); and within a week they attempted to compose "The Ancient Mariner," planned and partly written on a walking tour from November 12 to 20, 1797. They intended to send "The Ancient Mariner" to the *Monthly Magazine*, published by the radical bookseller Richard Phillips (1767–1840). Coleridge worked rapidly and by November 20 had composed 300 lines (*CL*, 1:357), but as Wordsworth said, "Our respective manners proved so widely different that it would have been quite presumptuous in me to do anything but separate from an undertaking upon which I could only have been a clog" (*LB* [1992], 348). On the same day, Dorothy Wordsworth wrote that the poets were "employing themselves in laying the plan of a ballad, to be published with some pieces of William's," the first indication of plans for *Lyrical Ballads* (*WL*, 1:194). In chapter 14 of the *Biographia* (p. 490 herein), Coleridge explained that Wordsworth's poems were to present an imaginative view of common life, while his poems were to concern the "dramatic truth" of the emotions of someone who believed himself affected by supernatural events, "supposing them real." Coleridge wrote little of "The Ancient Mariner" in December and January, since at the end of February he said that he had completed 340 lines (*CL*, 1:387). On March 23 Dorothy wrote in her journal that Coleridge visited with his ballad finished (*DWJ*, 11).

Wordsworth explained that "The Ancient Mariner" originated in a dream of Coleridge's friend John Cruikshank, who "fancied he saw a skeleton ship with figures in it" (*Reminiscences of Alexander Dyce*, ed. Richard J. Schrader [Columbus, Ohio, 1972], 185). Wordsworth told Thomas De Quincey that Coleridge "had meditated a poem on delirium, confounding its own dream-scenery with external things, and connected with the imagery of high latitudes" (*Recollections of the Lakes and the Lake Poets*, in *De Q Works*, 2:145). At the end of chapter 13 of the *Biographia*, Coleridge promised to preface "The Ancient Mariner" with an essay on the "uses of the Supernatural in poetry"; but that essay, if written, has not survived. However, in May 1830 Coleridge wrote in a notebook his idea of supernatural poetry: it should be "true *to Nature*—i.e. where the Poet of his free will and judgement does what the believing Narrator of a Supernatural Incident, Apparition or Charm does from ignorance & weakness of mind,—*i.e.* mistake a *Subjective* product (A saw the Ghost of Z) for an objective fact = the Ghost of Z was there to be seen" (*CN*, 5:6301).

Wordsworth contributed substantially to the poem. He suggested the killing of the albatross, the polar spirits' vengeance, and "the spectral persecution" as a result of the mariner's "crime and his own wanderings" (*LB* [1992], 347). Wordsworth told the Reverend Alexander Dyce (1798–1869), "I also suggested the re-animation of the dead bodies to work the ship" (185), and he told Crabb Robinson that he suggested "much of the plan" of the poem (*CRD*, 3:85). The plan resembles Wordsworth's narrative of a sailor in drafts for "Adventures on Salisbury Plain," a poem on crime and punishment, later published as "Guilt and Sorrow" (*The Salisbury Plain Poems of William Wordsworth*, ed. Stephen Gill [Ithaca, N.Y., 1975], 114–16). In "Adventures on Salisbury Plain" a sailor, exasperated by injustice, kills a stranger and spends his life in hopeless wandering. When "The Ancient Mariner" appeared in the second edition, Wordsworth added a note, which reads in part:

> The Poem of my Friend has indeed great defects; first, that the principal person has no distinct character, either in his profession of Mariner, or as a human being who having been long under the controul of supernatural impressions might be supposed himself to partake of something supernatural: secondly, that he does not act, but is continually acted upon: thirdly, that the events having no necessary connection do not produce each other; and lastly, that the imagery is somewhat too laboriously accumulated (*LB* [1992], 791).

Shortly after *Lyrical Ballads* (1800) was published, Charles Lamb defended the poem in a letter to Wordsworth (p. 648 herein).

In subsequent printings, Coleridge continuously revised "The Ancient Mariner." For *Lyrical Ballads* (1800), he removed many of the archaic words and spellings, most of which he had borrowed from "Sir Cauline" in Bishop Thomas Percy's *Reliques of Ancient English Poetry* (1765). When it was reprinted for the first time under his own name, in *Sibylline Leaves* (1817), Coleridge made the most substantial changes. He substituted the epigraph from Burnet for the original argument, added the marginal gloss, and revised several passages. The most important additions were the lines on the storm-blast (1834, lines 41–50), on the naming of Death (1834, lines 188–89), on the naming of the "Night-mare Life-in-Death" (1834, lines 193–94), and on fear drinking his life's blood (1834, lines 199–208). The major deletions were the passages on the ship's ghoulish mate (1798, lines 180–85 and 195–98), the Wedding Guest's interruption and the Mariner's response on his "sadder tale" (1798, lines 362–77), and the crews' standing before the mast in red torch light (1798, lines 481–502). The revised versions transformed the poem of 1798 from one that emphasized crime, punishment, and supernatural terror expressed by reveries and nightmares to one that, in the light of the epigraph from Burnet and the gloss, speculates on a spiritual and moral universe. It has been read as a psychological exploration of unanswerable moral questions in a dream world and as an archetypal pattern of spiritual death and rebirth as described in Robert Penn Warren's essay "A Poem of Pure Imagination" (p. 671 herein). The mariner's act of killing the albatross may be an act of satanic pride as Coleridge explains it in Appendix C of *The Statesman's Manual* (p. 364 herein). Coleridge was certainly aware of how complex a poem of pure imagination it was, because while he noted that both "The Eolian Harp" and "Christabel" were original models for poems by other poets, he remarked that "The Ancient Mariner" "cannot be imitated" (*TT* [CC], 2:359). It was, and is, unique.

The 1798 and 1834 versions of "The Ancient Mariner" are printed here in parallel texts on facing pages. The 1798 text includes the errata printed at the end of the volume, "fog-smoke white" for "fog smoke-white" (line 75), "these" for "those" (line 179), and the omissions of a comma after "loveth well" (line 645), but it leaves Coleridge's idiosyncratic use of quotation marks and inconsistent use of hyphens and capitals in "wedding-guest" and "cross-bow." Line 574 is printed without the initial quotation marks included in some copies (*PW* [CC], 2:539). Other errors and inconsistencies are mentioned in the notes. The 1834 text is also printed with Coleridge's inconsistent use of quotation marks and capitals on "wedding-guest." The 1834 version, the version commonly reprinted, differs little from the versions from 1817 through 1828, except that it removes the small capitals that called special attention to "the STORM-BLAST" (line 41), "the ALBATROSS" (line 82), "DEATH" (lines 188 and 189), and "the Night-Mair LIFE-IN-DEATH" (line 193). It is not clear whether Coleridge, his editor Henry Nelson Coleridge, or the printer removed the small capitals in the final printing. The other poems are printed from *Lyrical Ballads* 1798 and 1800.

THE RIME
OF THE
ANCYENT MARINERE,
IN
SEVEN PARTS (1798)[1]

Argument[1]

How a Ship having passed the Line was driven by Storms to the cold
Country towards the South Pole; and how from thence she made her
course to the tropical Latitude of the Great Pacific Ocean; and of the
strange things that befell; and in what manner the Ancyent Marinere
came back to his own Country.

---

1. The Advertisement to LB (1798) remarked that "The Rime of the Ancyent Marinere was
professedly written in imitation of the *style*, as well as of the spirit of the elder poets; but
with a few exceptions, the Author believes that the language adopted in it has been equally
intelligible for these three last centuries."
1. The Argument in LB (1800) reads, "How a Ship, having first sailed to the Equator, was
driven by Storms to the cold Country towards the South Pole; how the Ancient Mariner cruelly and in contempt of the laws of hospitality killed a Sea-bird and how he was followed by
many and strange Judgements: and in what manner he came back to his own Country" (PW,
1:186). In a copy of LB (1800) now in the state Library of Victoria in Melburne, C expanded
the clause "and in what manner he came back to his own country," some words of which are
now cropped by re-binding: "the Spirit, who loved the Sea-bird pursuing him & his Companions, & sh[ ] up against them two Spectres; and ho[w] all his Companions perished, &
he wa[s] left alone in the becalmed Vessel; ho[w] his guardian Saint took pity on him; &
[how] a choir of Angels descended, and entered into the bodies of the men who died; & in
what manner he ca[me] back to his own Country" (R. C. Bald, "The Ancient Mariner," TLS,
July 26, 1934: 528).

THE RIME
OF THE
ANCIENT MARINER (1834)

Facile credo, plures esse Naturas invisibiles quam visibiles in rerum universitate. Sed horum omnium familiam quis nobis enarrabit, et gradus et cognationes et discrimina et singulorum munera? Quid agunt? quæ loca habitant? Harum rerum notitiam semper ambivit ingenium humanum, nunquam attigit. Juvat, interea, non diffiteor, quandoque in animo, tanquam in tabulâ, majoris et melioris mundi imaginem contemplari: ne mens assuefacta hodiernæ vitæ minutiis se contrahat nimis, et tota subsidat in pusillas cogitationes. Sed veritati interea invigilandum est, modusque servandus, ut certa ab incertis, diem a nocte, distinguamus.

T: BURNET: *Archæol. Phil.* p. 68.[1]

---

1. C copied the epigraph in a notebook (CN, 1:1000H) sometime between the summer of 1801 and the summer of 1802. He quotes, with omissions and slight changes, from Thomas Burnet, *Archaeologiae Philosophicae* (1692):

   > I readily believe that there are more invisible than visible Natures in the Universe. But who will explain for us the family of all these beings, and the ranks and relations and distinguishing features and functions of each? What do they do? What places do they inhabit? The human mind has always desired the knowledge of these things, but never attained it. Meanwhile I do not deny that it is helpful sometimes to contemplate in the mind, as on a tablet, the image of the greater and better world; lest the intellect, habituated to the petty things of daily life, narrow itself and sink wholly into trivial thoughts. But at the same time we must be watchful for the truth and keep a sense of proportion, so that we may distinguish the certain from the uncertain, day from night.

   The major portion that C omitted comes after the fifth sentence in the translation above and reads in part:

   > The Heathen Divines have very much philosophised about the invisible World of Souls, Genii, Manes, Demons, Heroes, Minds, Deities, and Gods. * * * But of what Value are all these Things? Has this Seraphic Philosophy any Thing sincere or solid about it? I know that St. Paul speaks of the Angelic World, and has taken notice of many Orders and Distinctions among them; but this in general only; he does not philosophize about them; he disputes not, nor teaches anything in particular concerning them; nay, on the contrary, he reproves those as puft up with vain Science, who rashly thrust themselves forward to seek into these unknown and unsearchable Things [*Doctrina antiqua de rerum originibus, or, an Inquiry into the doctrine of the philosophers of all nations concerning the original of the World, by Thomas Burnet*, trans. Richard Mead and Thomas Foxton, (1736), 86–88].

   The Mead and Foxton translation cites St. Paul's warnings: "Beware lest any man spoil you through philosophy and vain deceit, after the tradition of men, after the rudiments of the world, and not after Christ," and "Let no man beguile you of your reward in a voluntary humility and worshipping of angels, intruding into those things which he hath not seen, vainly puffed up by his fleshly mind" (Colossians 2.8, 18) or a similar warning in Galatians 4.3: "Even so we, when we were children, were in bondage under the elements of the world." The quotation from Burnet is in chapter seven, "Of the Hebrews and their Cabala," in which Burnet rejects false knowledge and learning. The paragraph immediately preceding C's quotation is a stern warning: "We often fall into Errors. * * * Of this kind are the Speculations about the *Angelical World*, and its Furniture, into how many principal kinds, and subaltern Ranks the Celestial Hierarchy are distributed; what their employments are, and in what Mansions they dwell." It is not clear whether C omitted some parts of the quotation merely to shorten it or whether he wished to omit Burnet's strong admonition against excessive speculation.

The Rime
of the
Ancyent Marinere

I.

It is an ancyent Marinere,
  And he stoppeth one of three:
"By thy long grey beard and thy glittering eye[1]
"Now wherefore stoppest me?

"The Bridegroom's doors are open'd wide[2]   5
  "And I am next of kin;
"The Guests are met, the Feast is set,—
  "May'st hear the merry din.

But still he holds the wedding-guest—
  There was a Ship, quoth he—   10
"Nay, if thou'st got a laughsome tale,
  "Marinere! come with me."

He holds him with his skinny hand,
  Quoth he, there was a Ship—
"Now get thee hence, thou grey-beard Loon!   15
  "Or my Staff shall make thee skip.[3]

He holds him with his glittering eye—
  The wedding guest stood still
And listens like a three year's child;
  The Marinere hath his will.[4]   20

The wedding-guest sate on a stone,
  He cannot chuse but hear:
And thus spake on that ancyent man,
  The bright-eyed Marinere.

The Ship was cheer'd, the Harbour clear'd—   25
  Merrily did we drop
Below the Kirk,[5] below the Hill,
  Below the Light-house top.

---

1. The mariner's glittering eye suggests hypnotism or animal magnetism practiced by Friedrich
   Mesmer (1734–1815) to control a patient's will and nervous system. See lines 364–65 in the
   1798 version.
2. Cf. The translation of William Taylor (1765–1836) of Gottfried Bürger (1747–1794),
   "Lenore," in the *Monthly Magazine* (March 1796), lines 143–44: "The wedding guests thy
   coming waite, / The chamber dore is ope."
3. Cf. *King Lear* 5.3.275–76: "with my good biting falchion / I would have made them skip."
4. Wordsworth wrote lines 19–20 (*LB* [1992], 348).
5. Church.

Part I.

It is an ancient Mariner,
And he stoppeth one of three.
"By thy long grey beard and glittering eye,
Now wherefore stopp'st thou me?

*An ancient Mariner
meeteth three gal-
lants bidden to a
wedding-feast, and
detaineth one.*

5   "The Bridegroom's doors are opened wide,
And I am next of kin;
The guests are met, the feast is set:
May'st hear the merry din."

He holds him with his skinny hand,
10   "There was a ship," quoth he.
"Hold off! unhand me, grey-beard loon!"
Eftsoons his hand dropt he.

He holds him with his glittering eye—
The wedding-guest stood still,
15   And listens like a three years' child:
The Mariner hath his will.

*The wedding guest is
spell-bound by the
eye of the old sea-
faring man, and con-
strained to hear his
tale.*

The wedding-guest sat on a stone:
He cannot choose but hear;
And thus spake on that ancient man,
20   The bright-eyed Mariner.

The ship was cheered, the harbour cleared,
Merrily did we drop
Below the kirk, below the hill,
Below the light house top.

25   The sun came up upon the left,
Out of the sea came he!
And he shone bright, and on the right
Went down into the sea.

*The Mariner tells
how the ship sailed
southward with a
good wind and fair
weather, till it
reached the line.*

The Sun came up upon the left,
    Out of the Sea came he: 30
And he shone bright, and on the right
    Went down into the Sea.

Higher and higher every day,
    Till over the mast at noon—[6]
The wedding-guest here beat his breast,   35
    For he heard the loud bassoon.

The Bride hath pac'd into the Hall,
    Red as a rose is she;
Nodding their heads before her goes
    The merry Minstralsy.[7]   40

The wedding-guest he beat his breast,
    Yet he cannot chuse but hear:
And thus spake on that ancyent Man,
    The bright-eyed Marinere.

Listen, Stranger! Storm and Wind,   45
    A Wind and Tempest strong!
For days and weeks it play'd us freaks—
    Like Chaff we drove along.

Listen, Stranger! Mist and Snow,
    And it grew wond'rous cauld:
And Ice mast-high came floating by   50
    As green as Emerauld.

And thro' the drifts the snowy clifts[8]
    Did send a dismal sheen;
Ne shapes of men ne beasts we ken—   55
    The Ice was all between.

The Ice was here, the Ice was there,
    The Ice was all around:
It crack'd and growl'd, and roar'd and howl'd—
    Like noises of a swound.[9]   60

6. When the sun is directly overhead at noon, the ship has reached the equator.
7. In a copy of SL now in the Berg Library, someone, perhaps SC, has identified the source as
   line 268 of Chaucer, "Squire's Tale": "Toforn hym gooth the loude mynstralcye" (Johnson, 456).
8. Clefts, fissures. *Drifts*: floating ice.
9. A fainting fit. See lines 395–97 in the 1798 version.

Higher and higher every day,
30   Till over the mast at noon—
The Wedding-Guest here beat his breast,
For he heard the loud bassoon.

The bride hath paced into the hall,
Red as a rose is she;
35   Nodding their heads before her goes
The merry minstrelsy.

*The wedding guest
heareth the bridal
music; but the
mariner continueth
his tale.*

The Wedding-Guest he beat his breast,
Yet he cannot choose but hear;
And thus spake on that ancient man,
40   The bright-eyed Mariner.

And now the storm-blast came, and he
Was tyrannous and strong:
He struck with his o'ertaking wings,
And chased us south along.

*The ship drawn by a
storm toward the
south pole.*[2]

45   With sloping masts and dipping prow,
As who pursued with yell and blow
Still treads the shadow of his foe,
And forward bends his head,
The ship drove fast, loud roared the blast,
50   And southward aye we fled.[3]

And now there came both mist and snow,
And it grew wondrous cold:
And ice, mast-high, came floating by,
As green as emerald.

55   And through the drifts the snowy clifts
Did send a dismal sheen:
Nor shapes of men nor beasts we ken—
The ice was all between.

*The land of ice, and
of fearful sounds
where no living
thing was to be seen.*

The ice was here, the ice was there,
60   The ice was all around:
It cracked and growled, and roared and
    howled,
Like noises in a swound!

---

2. JDC changed "drawn" to "driven" on the supposition that "drawn" was a printer's error for
"driven" and that the ship is "chased" (line 44) south (597).
3. Lines 41–50 were added in *SL.* For C's use of the image of monarchs and ministers controlling the storm that kills mariners, see *Conciones ad Populum* (p. 257 herein). The storm was
commonly used in the 1790s to describe the French Revolution and the violence of the people, but Coleridge reverses the figure, blaming government for war and destruction.

At length did cross an Albatross,
   Thorough the Fog it came;
And an[1] it were a Christian Soul,
   We hail'd it in God's name.

The Marineres gave it biscuit-worms,   65
   And round and round it flew:
The Ice did split with a Thunder-fit;
   The Helmsman steer'd us thro'.

And a good south wind sprung up behind,
   The Albatross did follow;   · 70
And every day for food or play
   Came to the Marinere's hollo!

In mist or cloud on mast or shroud[2]
   It perch'd for vespers[3] nine,
Whiles all the night thro' fog-smoke white   75
   Glimmer'd the white moon-shine.

"God save thee, ancyent Marinere!
   "From the fiends that plague thee thus—
"Why look'st thou so?"—with my cross bow
   I shot the Albatross.[4]   80

II.

The Sun came up upon the right,
   Out of the Sea came he;
And broad as a weft[5] upon the left
   Went down into the Sea.

And the good south wind still blew behind,   85
   But no sweet Bird did follow
Ne any day for food or play
   Came to the Marinere's hollo!

---

1. And as.
2. Ropes supporting the mast.
3. Evening prayer service.
4. Wordsworth suggested the killing of the albatross: " 'Suppose,' I said, 'you represent him as having killed one of these birds on entering the South Sea, and that the tutelary Spirits of these regions take upon them to avenge the crime' " (*LB* [1992], 347). Wordsworth had been reading Captain George Shelvocke, *A Voyage Round the World* (1726). Shelvocke wrote that his ship sighted a black albatross, and "*Hatley*, (my second Captain) observing, in one of his melancholy fits, that this bird was always hovering near us, imagin'd, from his colour, that it might be some ill omen. * * * he, after some fruitless attempts, at length, shot the *Albitross*" (Lowes, 226). On his trip to Malta in May 1804 C observed sailors shooting at a hawk: "Poor Hawk! O Strange Lust of Murder in Man!—It is not cruelty / it is mere non-feeling from non-thinking" (*CN*, 2:2090).
5. Explained by Lowes (261–69) as a distress signal flag and by the *OED* as "a layer of smoke or mist."

At length did cross an Albatross,
Thorough the fog it came;
As if it had been a Christian soul,
We hailed it in God's name.

Till a great sea-bird, called the Albatross, came through the snow-fog and was received with great joy and hospitality.

It ate the food it ne'er had eat,
And round and round it flew.
The ice did split with a thunder-fit;
The helmsman steered us through!

And a good south wind sprung up behind;
The Albatross did follow,
And every day, for food or play,
Came to the mariner's hollo!

And lo! the Albatross proveth a bird of good omen, and followeth the ship as it returned northward through fog and floating ice.

In mist or cloud, on mast or shroud,
It perched for vespers nine;
Whiles all the night, through fog-smoke
    white,
Glimmered the white moon-shine.

"God save thee, ancient Mariner!
From the fiends, that plague thee thus!—
Why look'st thou so?"—With my cross-bow
I shot the Albatross.

The ancient Mariner inhospitably killeth the pious bird of good omen.

Part II

The Sun now rose upon the right:
Out of the sea came he,
Still hid in mist, and on the left
Went down into the sea.

And the good south wind still blew behind,
But no sweet bird did follow,
Nor any day for food or play
Came to the mariners' hollo!

65
70
75
80
85
90

And I had done an hellish thing
    And it would work 'em woe;   90
For all averr'd, I had kill'd the Bird
    That made the Breeze to blow.

Ne dim ne red, like God's own head,
    The glorious Sun[6] uprist:
Then all averr'd, I had kill'd the Bird   95
    That brought the fog and mist.
'Twas right, said they, such birds to slay
    That bring the fog and mist.

The breezes blew, the white foam flew,
    The furrow follow'd free:[7]   100
We were the first that ever burst
    Into that silent Sea.[8]

Down dropt the breeze, the Sails dropt down,
    'Twas sad as sad could be
And we did speak only to break   105
    The silence of the Sea.

All in a hot and copper sky
    The bloody sun at noon,
Right up above the mast did stand,
    No bigger than the moon.   110

Day after day, day after day,
    We stuck, ne breath ne motion,
As idle as a painted Ship
    Upon a painted Ocean.

Water, water, every where   115
    And all the boards did shrink;
Water, water, every where,
    Ne any drop to drink.

The very deeps did rot: O Christ!
    That ever this should be!   120
Yea, slimy things did crawl with legs
    Upon the slimy Sea.

6. The sun surrounded by a golden aureole of radiating light, different from the "bloody sun" in
   line 108. In December 1797 C copied in a notebook a passage from Robert South, "The
   Certainty of our Saviour's Resurrection" in *Sermons* (1737), 5:165: "Christ, the great Sun of
   Righteousness, & Saviour of the World, having by a glorious rising after a red & bloody setting, proclaimed his Deity to men & angels—& by a complete triumph over the two grand
   enemies of mankind sin & death set up the everlasting Gospel in the room of all false religions, has now (as it were) changed the Persian superstition into the Christian Devotion"
   (CN, 1:327, 327n.).
7. "I had not been long on board a ship, before I perceived that this was the image as seen by
   a spectator from the shore, or from another vessel. From the ship itself, the *Wake* appears
   like a brook flowing off from the stern." [C's note in SL.]
8. If the mariner was the first to enter the Pacific, his trip predates Magellan's circumnaviga-
   tion of the globe in 1519–22.

And I had done a hellish thing,
And it would work 'em woe:
For all averred, I had killed the bird
That made the breeze to blow.
95 Ah wretch! said they, the bird to slay,
That made the breeze to blow!

His ship-mates cry out against the ancient Mariner, for killing the bird of good luck.

Nor dim nor red, like God's own head,
The glorious Sun uprist:
Then all averred, I had killed the bird
100 That brought the fog and mist.
'Twas right, said they, such birds to slay,
That bring the fog and mist.

But when the fog cleared off, they justify the same, and thus make themselves accomplices in the crime.

The fair breeze blew, the white foam flew,
The furrow followed free;
105 We were the first that ever burst
Into that silent sea.

The fair breeze continues; the ship enters the Pacific Ocean, and sails northward, even till it reaches the Line.

Down dropt the breeze, the sails dropt down,
'Twas sad as sad could be;
And we did speak only to break
110 The silence of the sea!

The ship hath been suddenly becalmed.

All in a hot and copper sky,
The bloody Sun, at noon,
Right up above the mast did stand,
No bigger than the Moon.

115 Day after day, day after day,
We stuck, nor breath nor motion;
As idle as a painted ship
Upon a painted ocean.

Water, water, every where,
120 And all the boards did shrink;
Water, water, every where,
Nor any drop to drink.

And the Albatross begins to be avenged.

The very deep did rot: O Christ!
That ever this should be!
125 Yea, slimy things did crawl with legs
Upon the slimy sea.

About, about,[9] in reel and rout
   The Death-fires[1] danc'd at night;
The water, like a witch's oils,   125
   Burnt green and blue and white.

And some in dreams assured were
   Of the Spirit[2] that plagued us so:
Nine fathom deep he had follow'd us
   From the Land of Mist and Snow.   130

And every tongue thro' utter drouth[3]
   Was wither'd at the root;
We could not speak no more than if
   We had been choked with soot.

Ah wel-a-day! what evil looks   135
   Had I from old and young;
Instead of the Cross the Albatross
   About my neck was hung.

III.

I saw a something in the Sky
   No bigger than my fist;   140
At first it seem'd a little speck
   And then it seem'd a mist:
It mov'd and mov'd, and took at last
   A certain shape, I wist.

A speck, a mist, a shape, I wist![4]   145
   And still it ner'd and ner'd;[5]
And, an[6] it dodg'd a water-sprite,
   It plung'd and tack'd and veer'd.

---

9. From the witches song in *Macbeth* 1.3.30–32: "The weird sisters hand in hand, / Posters of the sea and land, / Thus do go about, about."
1. Ghostly luminous gas from decaying corpses reputedly seen in graveyards. See "Ode on the Departing Year," lines 60–61 (p. 39 herein). Also perhaps St. Elmo's fire, an electrostatic glow seen at the top of masts at sea. Robert Burton summarizes Michael Psellus's classifications of elemental spirits; the fiery spirits "counterfeit Sunnes and Moones, starres oftentimes, and sit on ship Masts. * * * Saint *Elmos* fires they commonly call them, & they doe likely appeare after a Sea storme" (*The Anatomy of Melancholy*, ed. Thomas C. Faulkner et. al., 6 vols. [Oxford, 1989–2000], 1:184).
2. A dæmon of the South Pole. See lines 131–34 of the 1834 version and p. 69, n. 4 herein.
3. Drought.
4. I knew.
5. Neared.
6. As if.

About, about, in reel and rout
The death-fires danced at night;
The water, like a witch's oils,
130　Burnt green, and blue and white.

And some in dreams assured were
Of the spirit that plagued us so;
Nine fathom deep he had followed us
From the land of mist and snow.

A spirit had followed them; one of the invisible inhabitants of this planet, neither departed souls nor angels; concerning

whom the learned Jew, Josephus, and the Platonic Constantinopolitan, Michael Psellus, may be consulted. They are very numerous, and there is no climate or element without one or more.[4]

135　And every tongue, through utter drought,
Was withered at the root;
We could not speak, no more than if
We had been choked with soot.

Ah! well a-day! what evil looks
140　Had I from old and young!
Instead of the cross, the Albatross
About my neck was hung

The ship-mates, in their sore distress, would fain throw the whole guilt on the ancient Mariner: in sign whereof they hang the dead sea-bird round his neck.

Part III.

There passed a weary time.   Each throat
Was parched, and glazed each eye.
145　A weary time! a weary time!
How glazed each weary eye,
When looking westward, I beheld
A something in the sky.

The ancient Mariner beholdeth a sign in the element afar off.

At first it seemed a little speck,
150　And then it seemed a mist;
It moved and moved, and took at last
A certain shape, I wist.

A speck, a mist, a shape, I wist!
And still it neared and neared:
155　As if it dodged a water-sprite,
It plunged and tacked and veered.

---

4. Lowes points out that the polar spirits are "dæmons," Neoplatonic intermediary beings between gods and men, not the Judeo-Christian "demons" or "devils" (234). Details of the dæmons and devils of the polar regions are given by Michael Psellus (1018–1105) in *De Dæmonibus* and in commentary on the *Chaldean Oracles* (CN, 1:180n.). Psellus comments that the spirits of water are able to appear as birds. Lowes argues that C's reference to Josephus is to Porphyry's "On the Abstinence of the Ancients" in which Porphyry reports that Josephus stated that the dead possess the realm of the air (235–37). Michael Mason points out (*Lyrical Ballads*, ed. Michael Mason [London, 1992], 185) that Burton mentions both Psellus and Josephus as describing fiery and aerial devils, who "cause whirlwinds on a sudden, and tempestuous stormes" (*The Anatomy of Melancholy*, ed. Thomas C. Faulkner et al., 1:184).

With throat unslack'd, with black lips bak'd
    Ne could we laugh, ne wail: 150
Then while thro' drouth all dumb they stood
I bit my arm and suck'd the blood
    And cry'd, A sail! a sail!

With throat unslack'd, with black lips bak'd
    Agape they hear'd me call: 155
Gramercy![7] they for joy did grin
And all at once their breath drew in
    As they were drinking all.

She doth not tack from side to side—
    Hither to work us weal   160
Withouten wind, withouten tide
    She steddies with upright keel.

The western wave was all a flame,
    The day was well nigh done!
Almost upon the western wave   165
    Rested the broad bright Sun;
When that strange shape drove suddenly
    Betwixt us and the Sun.

And strait the Sun was fleck'd with bars
    (Heaven's mother send us grace)   170
As if thro' a dungeon grate he peer'd
    With broad and burning face.

Alas! (thought I, and my heart beat loud)
    How fast she neres and neres!
Are those *her* Sails that glance in the Sun   175
    Like restless gossameres?[8]

Are those *her* naked ribs, which fleck'd
    The sun that did behind them peer?
And are these two all, all the crew,
    That woman and her fleshless Pheere?[9]   180

His bones were black with many a crack,
    All black and bare, I ween;
Jet-black and bare, save where with rust
Of mouldy damps and charnel crust
    They're patch'd with purple and green.   185

7. Grant mercy on us.
8. Cobwebs floating on the wind.
9. Mate in both the sexual and nautical senses.

With throats unslaked, with black lips baked,
We could nor laugh nor wail;
Through utter drought all dumb we stood!
160　I bit my arm, I sucked the blood,
And cried, A sail! a sail!

At its nearer approach, it seemeth him to be a ship; and at a dear ransom he freeth his speech from the bonds of thirst.

With throats unslaked, with black lips baked,
Agape they heard me call:
Gramercy! they for joy did grin,
165　And all at once their breath drew in,
As they were drinking all.

A flash of joy;

See! see! (I cried) she tacks no more!
Hither to work us weal;
Without a breeze, without a tide,
170　She steadies with upright keel!

And horror follows. For can it be a ship that comes onward without wind or tide?

The western wave was all a-flame.
The day was well nigh done!
Almost upon the western wave
Rested the broad bright Sun;
175　When that strange shape drove suddenly
Betwixt us and the Sun.

And straight the Sun was flecked with bars,
(Heaven's Mother send us grace!)
As if through a dungeon-grate he peered
180　With broad and burning face.

It seemeth him but the skeleton of a ship.

Alas! (thought I, and my heart beat loud)
How fast she nears and nears!
Are those her sails that glance in the Sun,
Like restless gossameres?

185　Are those her ribs through which the Sun
Did peer, as through a grate?
And is that Woman all her crew?
Is that a Death? and are there two?
Is Death that woman's mate?

And its ribs are seen as bars on the face of the setting Sun. The spectre-woman and her death-mate, and no other on board the skeleton-ship.

Her lips are red, *her* looks are free,
   Her locks are yellow as gold:
Her skin is as white as leprosy,
And she is far liker Death than he;
   Her flesh makes the still air cold.[1]   190

The naked Hulk alongside came
   And the Twain were playing dice;
"The Game is done! I've won, I've won!"
   Quoth she, and whistled thrice.[2]

A gust of wind sterte up behind   195
   And whistled thro' his bones;[3]
Thro' the holes of his eyes and the hole of his mouth
   Half-whistles and half-groans.

With never a whisper in the Sea
   Oft[4] darts the Spectre-ship;   200
While clombe above the Eastern bar
The horned Moon, with one bright Star
   Almost atween the tips.[5]

One after one by the horned Moon
   (Listen, O Stranger! to me)   205
Each turn'd his face with a ghastly pang
   And curs'd me with his ee.[6]

Four times fifty living men,
   With never a sigh or groan,
With heavy thump, a lifeless lump   210
   They dropp'd down one by one.

---

1. The women and her mate recall Sin and Death in Milton's *Paradise Lost*.
2. Lowes reports that a legend of the Netherlands concerns "one Falkenberg, who, for murder done, is doomed to wander forever on the sea, accompanied by two spectral forms, one white, one black. * * * And in a ship with all sails set, the two forms play at dice for the wanderer's soul" (277).
3. Cf. Wordsworth, "The Vale of Esthwaite" (c. 1787), lines 230–31: "sad and hollow moans / As if the wind sigh'd through his bones." (*Early Poems and Fragments, 1785–1797*, ed. Carol Landon and Jared Curtis [Ithaca, N.Y., 1997], 442).
4. C changed "Oft" to "Off" in 1800 (CL, 1:600).
5. C annotated these lines in a copy of *LB* (1798), now at Trinity College, Cambridge: "It is a common superstition among sailors, 'that something evil is about to happen, whenever a star dogs the moon' " (Lowes, 182).
6. Eye.

190 Her lips were red, her looks were free,
    Her locks were yellow as gold: *Like vessel, like*
    Her skin was as white as leprosy,   *crew!*
The Night-mare Life-in-Death was she,
    Who thicks man's blood with cold.

                                 Death and Life-in-
195 The naked hulk alongside came,   *death have diced for*
    And the twain were casting dice;   *the ship's crew, and*
"The game is done! I've, I've won!"   *she (the latter) win-*
    Quoth she, and whistles thrice.   *neth the ancient*
                                 Mariner.

    The Sun's rim dips; the stars rush out: *No twilight within*
200 At one stride comes the dark;   *the courts of the*
    With far-heard whisper, o'er the sea,   *sun.*[5]
Off shot the spectre-bark.

    We listened and looked sideways up!
    Fear at my heart, as at a cup,
205 My life-blood seemed to sip!
The stars were dim, and thick the night,
    The steersman's face by his lamp gleamed
        white;
From the sails the dew did drip—   *At the rising of the*
    Till clomb above the eastern bar   *Moon,*
210 The horned Moon, with one bright star
    Within the nether tip.[6]

    One after one, by the star-dogged Moon, *One after another,*
    Too quick for groan or sigh,
Each turned his face with a ghastly pang,
215 And cursed me with his eye.

    Four times fifty living men,   *His ship-mates drop*
    (And I heard nor sigh nor groan)   *down dead.*
With heavy thump, a lifeless lump,
    They dropped down one by one.

---

5. Not present when the rest of the gloss was added in 1817. An early draft in *SL* is clearer: "Between the Tropics there is no Twilight. As the Sun's last Segment dips down, and the evening Gun is fired, the Constellations appear arrayed" (Johnson, 469).

6. Lines 201–11 were first drafted in October 1806 (*CN*, 2:2880). In a letter of November 1796 C described Charles Lloyd's illness: "his distemper (which may with equal propriety be named either Somnambulism, or frightful Reverie, or *Epilepsy from accumulated feelings*) is alarming. He falls all at once into a kind of Night-mair: and all the Realities round him mingle with, and form a part of, the strange Dream. All his voluntary powers are suspended; but he perceives every thing & hears every thing, and whatever he perceives & hears he perverts into the substance of his delirious Vision" (*CL*, 1:257). For C's definition of the nightmare, see "Dreams and Sleep" (p. 590 herein). The title in *LB* 1800, 1802, and 1805 was "The Ancient Mariner, A Poet's Reverie." C may have thought of the nightmares in the paintings of Henry Fuseli (1741–1825). He wrote to Southey in December 1794: "Would not this be a fine subject for a *wild* Ode—'St Withold footed thrice the Oulds— / He met the Night Mare & her nine Foals— / He bade her alight and her troth plight— / And "aroynt thee, Witch["]—he said!' I shall set about one, when I am in a Humour to *abandon* myself to all the Diableries, that ever met the Eye of a Fuseli!" (*CL*, 1:135). C adapts Edgar's mad song in *King Lear* 3.4.110–14 (var.). See also C's definition of nightmares in *Lects 1808–19* (*CC*), 1:135–36.

Their souls did from their bodies fly,—
   They fled to bliss or woe;
And every soul it pass'd me by,
   Like the whiz of my Cross-bow.   215

IV.

"I fear thee, ancyent Marinere!
   "I fear thy skinny hand;
"And thou art long and lank and brown
   "As is the ribb'd Sea-sand.[7]

"I fear thee and thy glittering eye   220
   "And thy skinny hand so brown—
Fear not, fear not, thou wedding guest!
   This body dropt not down.

Alone, alone, all all alone
   Alone on the wide wide Sea;   225
And Christ would take no pity on
   My soul in agony.

The many men so beautiful,
   And they all dead did lie!
And a million million slimy things   230
   Liv'd on—and so did I.

I look'd upon the rotting Sea,
   And drew my eyes away;
I look'd upon the eldritch[8] deck,
   And there the dead men lay.   235

I look'd to Heaven, and try'd to pray;
   But or ever a prayer had gusht,
A wicked whisper came and made
   My heart as dry as dust.

I clos'd my lids and kept them close,   240
   Till the balls like pulses beat;
For the sky and the sea, and the sea and the sky
Lay like a load on my weary eye,
   And the dead were at my feet.

The cold sweat melted from their limbs,   245
   Ne rot, ne reek did they;
The look with which they look'd on me,
   Had never pass'd away.

---

7. "For the two last lines of this stanza, I am indebted to Mr. Wordsworth. It was on a delightful walk from Nether Stowey to Dulverton, with him and his sister, in the Autumn of 1797, that this Poem was planned, and in part composed." [C's note in SL.]
8. Ghostly.

220 The souls did from their bodies fly,—
They fled to bliss or woe!
And every soul, it passed me by,
Like the whizz of my cross-bow!

*But Life-in-Death
begins her work on
the ancient Mariner.*

Part IV.

"I fear thee, ancient Mariner!
225 I fear thy skinny hand!
And thou art long, and lank, and brown,
As is the ribbed sea-sand.

*The wedding guest
feareth that a spirit
is talking to him.*

I fear thee and thy glittering eye,
And thy skinny hand, so brown."—
230 Fear not, fear not, thou wedding-guest!
This body dropt not down.

*But the ancient
Mariner assureth
him of his bodily life,
and proceedeth to
relate his horrible
penance.*

Alone, alone, all, all alone,
Alone on a wide wide sea!
And never a saint took pity on
235 My soul in agony.

The many men, so beautiful!
And they all dead did lie:
And a thousand thousand slimy things
Lived on; and so did I.

*He despiseth the
creatures of the
calm.*

240 I looked upon the rotting sea,
And drew my eyes away;
I looked upon the rotting deck,
And there the dead men lay.

*And envieth that
they should live, and
so many lie dead.*

I looked to heaven, and tried to pray;
245 But or ever a prayer had gusht,
A wicked whisper came, and made
My heart as dry as dust.

I closed my lids, and kept them close,
And the balls like pulses beat;
250 For the sky and the sea, and the sea and the
    sky
Lay like a load on my weary eye,
And the dead were at my feet.

The cold sweat melted from their limbs,
Nor rot nor reek did they:
255 The look with which they looked on me
Had never passed away.

*But the curse liveth
for him in the eye of
the dead men.*

An orphan's curse would drag to Hell
    A spirit from on high: 250
But O! more horrible than that
    Is the curse in a dead man's eye!
Seven days, seven nights I saw that curse,
    And yet I could not die.

The moving Moon went up the sky   255
    And no where did abide:
Softly she was going up
    And a star or two beside—

Her beams bemock'd the sultry main
    Like morning frosts yspread;[9]   260
But where the ship's huge shadow lay,
The charmed water burnt alway
    A still and awful red.

Beyond the shadow of the ship
    I watch'd the water-snakes: 265
They mov'd in tracks of shining white;
And when they rear'd, the elfish light
    Fell off in hoary flakes.

Within the shadow of the ship
    I watch'd their rich attire: 270
Blue, glossy green, and velvet black
They coil'd and swam; and every track
    Was a flash of golden fire.[1]

O happy living things! no tongue
    Their beauty might declare: 275
A spring of love gusht from my heart,
    And I bless'd them unaware!
Sure my kind saint took pity on me,
    And I bless'd them unaware.

The self-same moment I could pray;   280
    And from my neck so free
The Albatross fell off, and sank
    Like lead into the sea.

9. Overspread.
1. The snakes' tracks are marked by phosphorescence from plankton in the water.

An orphan's curse would drag to hell
A spirit from on high;
But oh! more horrible than that
260　Is the curse in a dead man's eye!
Seven days, seven nights, I saw that curse,
And yet I could not die.

The moving Moon went up the sky, *In his loneliness and*
And no where did abide: *fixedness he yearneth*
265　Softly she was going up, *towards the journey-*
And a star or two beside— *ing Moon, and the*
stars that still so-
journ, yet still move

onward; and every where the blue sky belongs to them, and is their appointed rest, and their native country and their own natural homes, which they enter unannounced, as lords that are certainly expected and yet there is a silent joy at their arrival.

Her beams bemocked the sultry main,
Like April hoar-frost spread;
But where the ship's huge shadow lay,
270　The charmed water burnt alway
A still and awful red.

Beyond the shadow of the ship, *By the light of the*
I watched the water-snakes: *Moon he beholdeth*
They moved in tracks of shining white, *God's creatures of*
275　And when they reared, the elfish light *the great calm.*
Fell off in hoary flakes.

Within the shadow of the ship
I watched their rich attire:
Blue, glossy green, and velvet black,
280　They coiled and swam; and every track
Was a flash of golden fire.

O happy living things! no tongue *Their beauty and*
Their beauty might declare: *their happiness.*
A spring of love gushed from my heart,
285　And I blessed them unaware: *He blesseth them in*
Sure my kind saint took pity on me, *his heart.*
And I blessed them unaware.

The selfsame moment I could pray; *The spell begins to*
And from my neck so free *break.*
290　The Albatross fell off, and sank
Like lead into the sea.

V.

O sleep, it is a gentle thing
    Belov'd from pole to pole!   285
To Mary-queen the praise be yeven[2]
She sent the gentle sleep from heaven
    That slid into my soul.

The silly[3] buckets on the deck
    That had so long remain'd,   290
I dreamt that they were fill'd with dew
    And when I awoke it rain'd.

My lips were wet, my throat was cold,
    My garments all were dank;
Sure I had drunken in my dreams   295
    And still my body drank.

I mov'd and could not feel my limbs,
    I was so light, almost
I thought that I had died in sleep,
    And was a blessed Ghost.   300

The roaring wind! it roar'd far off,
    It did not come anear;
But with its sound it shook the sails
    That were so thin and sere.

The upper air bursts[4] into life,   305
    And a hundred fire-flags sheen[5]
To and fro they are hurried about;
And to and fro, and in and out
    The stars dance on between.

The coming wind doth roar more loud;   310
    The sails do sigh, like sedge:[6]
The rain pours down from one black cloud
    And the Moon is at its edge.[7]

---

2. Given. *Mary-queen*: the Virgin Mary.
3. Useless.
4. C changed "bursts" to "burst" in 1800 (*CL*, 1:600).
5. C imagines the aurora borealis of the Northern Hemisphere or the aurora australis of the
   Southern Hemisphere.
6. Like the wind through rushes or reeds.
7. Lowes quotes William Bartram, *Travels through North and South Carolina* (Philadelphia,
   1791): "The rain came down with such rapidity and fell in such quantities, that every object
   was totally obscured, excepting the *continuous streams or rivers of lightning* pouring from the
   clouds" and "the hurricane *comes on roaring* . . . *the dark cloud opens over my head, developing* [sic] *a vast river* of the etherial fire" (186, Lowes's italics).

Part V.

Oh sleep! it is a gentle thing,
Beloved from pole to pole!
To Mary Queen the praise be given!
295   She sent the gentle sleep from Heaven,
That slid into my soul.

The silly buckets on the deck,   *By grace of the holy*
That had so long remained,   *Mother, the ancient*
I dreamt that they were filled with dew; *Mariner is refreshed*
300   And when I awoke, it rained.   *with rain.*

My lips were wet, my throat was cold,
My garments all were dank;
Sure I had drunken in my dreams,
And still my body drank.

305   I moved, and could not feel my limbs:
I was so light—almost
I thought that I had died in sleep,
And was a blessed ghost.

And soon I heard a roaring wind: *He heareth sounds*
310   It did not come anear;   *and seeth strange*
But with its sound it shook the sails,   *sights and commo-*
That were so thin and sere.   *tions in the sky and*
                                              the element.

The upper air burst into life!
And a hundred fire-flags sheen,
315   To and fro they were hurried about!
And to and fro, and in and out,
The wan stars danced between.

And the coming wind did roar more loud,
And the sails did sigh like sedge;
320   And the rain poured down from one black
        cloud;
The Moon was at its edge.

Hark! hark! the thick black cloud is cleft,
    And the Moon is at its side: 315
Like waters shot from some high crag,
The lightning falls with never a jag
    A river steep and wide.

The strong wind reach'd the ship: it roar'd
    And dropp'd down, like a stone!   320
Beneath the lightning and the moon
    The dead men gave a groan.

They groan'd, they stirr'd, they all uprose,
    Ne spake, ne mov'd their eyes:
It had been strange, even in a dream   325
    To have seen those dead men rise.

The helmsman steer'd, the ship mov'd on;
    Yet never a breeze up-blew;
The Marineres all 'gan work the ropes,
    Where they were wont to do: 330
They rais'd their limbs like lifeless tools—
    We were a ghastly crew.

The body of my brother's son
    Stood by me knee to knee:
The body and I pull'd at one rope,   335
    But he said nought to me—
And I quak'd to think of my own voice
    How frightful it would be!

The day-light dawn'd—they dropp'd their arms,
    And cluster'd round the mast: 340
Sweet sounds rose slowly thro' their mouths
    And from their bodies pass'd.

Around, around, flew each sweet sound,
    Then darted to the sun:
Slowly the sounds came back again   345
    Now mix'd, now one by one.[8]

8. John Beer, *Coleridge the Visionary* (London, 1959), 161, cites lines 343–36 to counter Robert Penn Warren's thesis that the good things that happen to the mariner happen under the aegis of the moon or imagination and the bad things, under the aegis of the sun or reason: "the sun, in the poem as a whole, is not a symbol of wrath and retribution, but of God and the image of God in human reason."

The thick black cloud was cleft, and still
The Moon was at its side:
Like waters shot from some high crag,
325   The lightning fell with never a jag,
A river steep and wide.

The loud wind never reached the ship,   *The bodies of the*
Yet now the ship moved on!   *ship's crew are in-*
Beneath the lightning and the moon   *spired, and the ship*
330   The dead men gave a groan.   *moves on;*[7]

They groaned, they stirred, they all uprose,
Nor spake, nor moved their eyes;
It had been strange, even in a dream,
To have seen those dead men rise.

335   The helmsman steered, the ship moved on;
Yet never a breeze up blew;
The mariners all 'gan work the ropes,
Where they were wont to do;
They raised their limbs like lifeless tools—
340   We were a ghastly crew.

The body of my brother's son
Stood by me, knee to knee:
The body and I pulled at one rope,
But he said nought to me.   *But not by the souls*
                                                 of the men, nor by
345   "I fear thee, ancient Mariner!"   *demons of earth or*
Be calm, thou Wedding-Guest!   *middle air, but by a*
'Twas not those souls that fled in pain,   *blessed troop of an-*
Which to their corses came again,   *gelic spirits, sent*
But a troop of spirits blest:[8]   *down by the invoca-*
                                                 tion of the guardian
                                                 saint.
350   For when it dawned—they dropped their arms,
And clustered round the mast;
Sweet sounds rose slowly through their mouths,
And from their bodies passed.

Around, around, flew each sweet sound,
355   Then darted to the Sun;
Slowly the sounds came back again,
Now mixed, now one by one.

7. The word "inspired" was "inspirited" in *SL*, which accords with lines 347–49.
8. Lines 345–49 were added in 1800. C wrote next to them in a copy of *LB* (1800), now in the State Library of Victoria in Melbourne: "By the interception of his kind saint a choir of angels desc[ended] from Heaven, & entered into the dead bod[ies] using the bodies a[s] material Instrum[ents]" (R. C. Bald, "The Ancient Mariner," *TLS*, July 26, 1934: 528).

Sometimes a dropping from the sky
  I heard the Lavrock[9] sing;
Sometimes all little birds that are
How they seem'd to fill the sea and air   350
  With their sweet jargoning,[1]

And now 'twas like all instruments,
  Now like a lonely flute;
And now it is an angel's song
  That makes the heavens be mute.   355

It ceas'd: yet still the sails made on
  A pleasant noise till noon,
A noise like of a hidden brook
  In the leafy month of June,
That to the sleeping woods all night   360
  Singeth a quiet tune.

Listen, O listen, thou Wedding-guest!
  "Marinere! thou hast thy will:
"For that, which comes out of thine eye, doth make
  "My body and soul to be still."   365

Never sadder tale was told
  To a man of woman born:
Sadder and wiser thou wedding-guest!
  Thou'lt rise to morrow morn.

Never sadder tale was heard   370
  By a man of woman born:
The Marineres all return'd to work
  As silent as beforne.

The Marineres all 'gan pull the ropes,
  But look at me they n'old: 375
Thought I, I am as thin as air—
  They cannot me behold.

Till noon we silently sail'd on
  Yet never a breeze did breathe:
Slowly and smoothly went the ship   380
  Mov'd onward from beneath.

Under the keel nine fathom deep
  From the land of mist and snow
The spirit[2] slid: and it was He
  That made the Ship to go.   385
The sails at noon left off their tune
  And the Ship stood still also.

9. Lark.
1. Warbling.
2. The dæmonic polar spirit.

Sometimes a-dropping from the sky
I heard the sky-lark sing;
360   Sometimes all little birds that are,
How they seemed to fill the sea and air
With their sweet jargoning!

And now 'twas like all instruments,
Now like a lonely flute;
365   And now it is an angel's song,
That makes the heavens be mute.

It ceased; yet still the sails made on
A pleasant noise till noon,
A noise like of a hidden brook
370   In the leafy month of June,
That to the sleeping woods all night
Singeth a quiet tune.

Till noon we quietly sailed on,
Yet never a breeze did breathe:
375   Slowly and smoothly went the ship,
Moved onward from beneath.

Under the keel nine fathom deep,   *The lonesome spirit*
From the land of mist and snow,   *from the south-pole*
The spirit slid: and it was he   *carries on the ship as*
380   That made the ship to go.   *far as the line, in*
The sails at noon left off their tune,   *obedience to the an-*
And the ship stood still also.   *gelic troop, but still*
                                                    requireth vengeance.

The sun right up above the mast
   Had fix'd her to the ocean:
But in a minute she 'gan stir   390
   With a short uneasy motion—
Backwards and forwards half her length
   With a short uneasy motion.

Then, like a pawing horse let go,
   She made a sudden bound:[3]   395
It flung the blood into my head,
   And I fell into a swound.

How long in that same fit I lay,
   I have not[4] to declare;
But ere my living life return'd,   400
I heard and in my soul discern'd
   Two voices in the air,

"Is it he? quoth one, "Is this the man?
   "By him who died on cross,
"With his cruel bow he lay'd full low   405
   "The harmless Albatross.

"The spirit who bideth by himself
   "In the land of mist and snow,
"He lov'd the bird that lov'd the man
   "Who shot him with his bow.   410

The other was a softer voice,
   As soft as honey-dew:[5]
Quoth he the man hath penance done,
   And penance more will do.

VI.

FIRST VOICE.

"But tell me, tell me! speak again,   415
   "Thy soft response renewing—
"What makes that ship drive on so fast?
   "What is the Ocean doing?

---

3. Cf. Homer, *Odyssey*, trans. A. T. Murray and George E. Dimock (LCL, 1995), 13.80–83: "as on a plain four yoked stallions spring forward all together beneath the strokes of the lash, and leaping high swiftly accomplish their way, even so the stern of that ship leapt high."
4. I do not have the knowledge.
5. "A sweet sticky substance found on the leaves and stems of trees and plants" (*OED*).

The Sun, right up above the mast,
Had fixed her to the ocean:
385   But in a minute she 'gan stir,
With a short uneasy motion—
Backwards and forwards half her length
With a short uneasy motion.

Then like a pawing horse let go,
390   She made a sudden bound:
It flung the blood into my head,
And I fell down in a swound.

How long in that same fit I lay,   *The Polar Spirit's*
I have not to declare;   *fellow demons, the*
395   But ere my living life returned,   *invisible inhabitants*
I heard, and in my soul discerned   *of the element, take*
Two voices in the air.   *part in his wrong;*
                                         and two of them re-
"Is it he?" quoth one, "Is this the man?" *late, one to the*
By him who died on cross,   *other, that penance*
400   With his cruel bow he laid full low   *long and heavy for*
The harmless Albatross.   *the ancient Mariner*
                                         hath been accorded
"The spirit who bideth by himself   *to the Polar Spirit,*
In the land of mist and snow,   *who returneth south-*
He loved the bird that loved the man   *ward.*
405   Who shot him with his bow."

The other was a softer voice,
As soft as honey-dew:
Quoth he, "The man hath penance done;
And penance more will do."

Part VI.

FIRST VOICE.

410   But tell me, tell me! speak again,
Thy soft response renewing—
What makes that ship drive on so fast?
What is the ocean doing?

SECOND VOICE.

"Still as a Slave before his Lord,
    "The Ocean hath no blast: 420
"His great bright eye most silently
    "Up to the moon is cast—[6]

"If he may know which way to go,
    "For she guides him smooth or grim.
"See, brother, see! how graciously   425
    "She looketh down on him.

FIRST VOICE.

"But why drives on that ship so fast
    "Withouten wave or wind?

SECOND VOICE.

"The air is cut away before,
    "And closes from behind.   430

"Fly, brother, fly! more high, more high,
    "Or we shall be belated:
"For slow and slow that ship will go,
    "When the Marinere's trance is abated."

I woke, and we were sailing on   435
    As in a gentle weather:
'Twas night, calm night, the moon was high;
    The dead men stood together.

All stood together on the deck,
    For a charnel-dungeon fitter: 440
All fix'd on me their stony eyes
    That in the moon did glitter.

The pang, the curse, with which they died,
    Had never pass'd away:
I could not draw my een from theirs   445
    Ne turn them up to pray.

And in its time the spell was snapt,
    And I could move my een:
I look'd far-forth, but little saw
    Of what might else be seen.   450

6. Cf. John Davies, *Orchestra* (1596), stanza 49: "For loe the *Sea* that fleets about the Land, /
And like a girdle clips her solide wast, / Musick and measure both doth understand: / For his
great Christall eye is alwayes cast / Up to the Moone, and on her fixed fast" (*The Poems of
Sir John Davies*, ed. Robert Krueger [Oxford, 1975], 103).

SECOND VOICE.

Still as a slave before his lord,
415   The ocean hath no blast;
His great bright eye most silently
Up to the Moon is cast—

If he may know which way to go;
For she guides him smooth or grim.
420   See, brother, see! how graciously
She looketh down on him.

FIRST VOICE.

But why drives on that ship so fast,
Without or wave or wind?

SECOND VOICE.

The air is cut away before,
425   And closes from behind.

The Mariner hath
been cast into a
trance; for the an-
gelic power causeth
the vessel to drive
northward faster
than human life
could endure.

Fly, brother, fly! more high, more high!
Or we shall be belated:
For slow and slow that ship will go,
When the Mariner's trance is abated.

430   I woke, and we were sailing on
As in a gentle weather:
'Twas night, calm night, the moon was high;
The dead men stood together.

The supernatural
motion is retarded;
the Mariner awakes,
and his penance be-
gins anew.

All stood together on the deck,
435   For a charnel-dungeon fitter:
All fixed on me their stony eyes,
That in the Moon did glitter.

The pang, the curse, with which they died,
Had never passed away:
440   I could not draw my eyes from theirs,
Nor turn them up to pray.

And now this spell was snapt: once more
I viewed the ocean green,
And looked far forth, yet little saw
445   Of what had else been seen—

The curse is finally
expiated.

Like one, that on a lonely road
  Doth walk in fear and dread,
And having once turn'd round, walks on
  And turns no more his head:
Because he knows, a frightful fiend   455
  Doth close behind him tread.[7]

But soon there breath'd a wind on me,
  Ne sound ne motion made:
Its path was not upon the sea
  In ripple or in shade.   460

It rais'd my hair, it fann'd my cheek,
  Like a meadow-gale of spring—
It mingled strangely with my fears,
  Yet it felt like a welcoming.

Swiftly, swiftly flew the ship,   465
  Yet she sail'd softly too:
Sweetly, sweetly blew the breeze—
  On me alone it blew.

O dream of joy! is this indeed
  The light-house top I see?   470
Is this the Hill? Is this the Kirk?
  Is this mine own countrée?

We drifted o'er the Harbour-bar,
  And I with sobs did pray—
"O let me be awake, my God!   475
  "Or let me sleep alway!"

The harbour-bay was clear as glass,
  So smoothly it was strewn![8]
And on the bay the moon light lay,
  And the shadow of the moon.   480

---

7. Charles Lamb quoted lines 451–56 in his essay "Witches and Other Night Fears" to illustrate terror:

> These terrors are of older standing. They date beyond the body—or, without the body, they would have been the same. All the cruel, tormenting, defined devils in Dante—tearing, mangling, choking, stifling, scorching demons—are they one half so fearful to the spirit of a man, as the simple idea of a spirit unembodied following him [Lamb quotes lines 451–56] That the kind of fear here treated of is purely spiritual—that it is strong in proportion as it is objectless on earth—that it predominates in the period of sinless infancy—are difficulties, the solution of which might afford some probable insight into our ante-mundane condition [*Elia and The Last Essays of Elia*, ed. Jonathan Bate (New York, 1987), 78].

In a copy of *SL* now at Harvard, someone, perhaps James Gillman, has written "From Dante" next to these lines. Lowes (526) suggests the source is Dante, *Inferno* 21.25–30: "Then I turned round, like one who longs to see what he must shun, and who is dashed with sudden fear, so that he puts not off his flight to look; and behind us I saw a black Demon come running up the cliff."

8. Calmed (*OED*).

Like one, that on a lonesome road
Doth walk in fear and dread,
And having once turned round walks on,
And turns no more his head;
450 Because he knows, a frightful fiend
Doth close behind him tread.

But soon there breathed a wind on me,
Nor sound nor motion made:
Its path was not upon the sea,
455 In ripple or in shade.

It raised my hair, it fanned my cheek
Like a meadow-gale of spring—
It mingled strangely with my fears,
Yet it felt like a welcoming.

460 Swiftly, swiftly flew the ship,
Yet she sailed softly too:
Sweetly, sweetly blew the breeze—
On me alone it blew.

Oh! dream of joy! is this indeed
465 The light-house top I see?   *And the ancient*
Is this the hill? is this the kirk?   *Mariner beholdeth*
Is this mine own countree?   *his native country.*

We drifted o'er the harbour-bar,
And I with sobs did pray—
470 O let me be awake, my God!
Or let me sleep alway.

The harbour-bay was clear as glass,
So smoothly it was strewn!
And on the bay the moonlight lay,
475 And the shadow of the moon.

The moonlight bay was white all o'er,
   Till rising from the same,
Full many shapes, that shadows were,
   Like as of torches came.

A little distance from the prow   485
   Those dark-red shadows were;
But soon I saw that my own flesh
   Was red as in a glare.

I turn'd my head in fear and dread,
   And by the holy rood,   490
The bodies had advanc'd, and now
   Before the mast they stood.

They lifted up their stiff right arms,
   They held them strait and tight;
And each right-arm burnt like a torch,[9]   495
   A torch that's borne upright.
Their stony eye-balls glitter'd on
   In the red and smoky light.

I pray'd and turn'd my head away
   Forth looking as before.   500
There was no breeze upon the bay,
   No wave against the shore.

The rock shone bright, the kirk no less
   That stands above the rock:
The moonlight steep'd in silentness   505
   The steady weathercock.

And the bay was white with silent light,
   Till rising from the same
Full many shapes, that shadows were,
   In crimson colours came.   510

A little distance from the prow
   Those crimson shadows were:
I turn'd my eyes upon the deck—
   O Christ! what saw I there?

Each corse lay flat, lifeless and flat;   515
   And by the Holy rood
A man all light, a seraph-man,[1]
   On every corse there stood.

9. Lowes identifies the torch as the "Hand of Glory" (556). The hand of a hanged criminal, properly prepared, becomes a powerful burning talisman. On his trip to Malta in April 1804, C noted, "Edridge & his Warts cured by rubbing them with the hand of his Sister's dead Infant / knew a man who cured one on his Eye with the dead Hand of his Brother's—Comments on Ancient Mariner" (CN, 2:2048).
1. The seraphim, the highest order of angels, whose essence is love and whose color is red.

The rock shone bright, the kirk no less,
That stands above the rock:
The moonlight steeped in silentness
The steady weathercock.

480 And the bay was white with silent light,
Till rising from the same,
Full many shapes, that shadows were,   *The angelic spirits*
In crimson colours came.   *leave the dead bod-*
                                              ies,

A little distance from the prow   *And appear in their*
485 Those crimson shadows were: *own forms of light.*
I turned my eyes upon the deck—
Oh, Christ! what saw I there!

Each corse lay flat, lifeless and flat,
And, by the holy rood!
490 A man all light, a seraph-man,
On every corse there stood.

This seraph-band, each wav'd his hand:
    It was a heavenly sight: 520
They stood as signals to the land,
    Each one a lovely light:

This seraph-band, each wav'd his hand,
    No voice did they impart—
No voice; but O! the silence sank,   525
    Like music on my heart.

Eftsones[2] I heard the dash of oars,
    I heard the pilot's cheer:
My head was turn'd perforce away
    And I saw a boat appear.   530

Then vanish'd all the lovely lights;
    The bodies rose anew:
With silent pace, each to his place,
    Came back the ghastly crew.
The wind, that shade nor motion made,   535
    On me alone it blew.

The pilot, and the pilot's boy
    I heard them coming fast:
Dear Lord in Heaven! it was a joy,
    The dead men could not blast.   540

I saw a third—I heard his voice:
    It is the Hermit good!
He singeth loud his godly hymns
    That he makes in the wood.
He'll shrieve[3] my soul, he'll wash away   545
    The Albatross's blood.

VII.

This Hermit good lives in that wood
    Which slopes down to the Sea.
How loudly his sweet voice he rears!
He loves to talk with Marineres   550
    That come from a far Contrée.

He kneels at morn and noon and eve—
    He hath a cushion plump:
It is the moss, that wholly hides
    The rotted old Oak-stump.   555

2. Immediately.
3. Hear confession, give absolution, and set penance.

This seraph-band, each waved his hand:
It was a heavenly sight!
They stood as signals to the land,
495 Each one a lovely light;

This seraph-band, each waved his hand,
No voice did they impart—
No voice; but oh! the silence sank
Like music on my heart.

500 But soon I heard the dash of oars,
I heard the Pilot's cheer;
My head was turned perforce away,
And I saw a boat appear.

The Pilot and the Pilot's boy,
505 I heard them coming fast:
Dear Lord in Heaven! it was a joy
The dead men could not blast.

I saw a third—I heard his voice:
It is the Hermit good!
510 He singeth loud his godly hymns
That he makes in the wood.
He'll shrieve my soul, he'll wash away
The Albatross's blood.

Part VII.

This Hermit good lives in that wood   *The Hermit of the*
515 Which slopes down to the sea.   *wood,*
How loudly his sweet voice he rears!
He loves to talk with marineres
That come from a far countree.

He kneels at morn, and noon, and eve—
520 He hath a cushion plump:
It is the moss that wholly hides
The rotted old oak-stump.

The Skiff-boat ne'rd:[4] I heard them talk,
    "Why, this is strange, I trow!
"Where are those lights so many and fair
    "That signal made but now?

"Strange, by my faith! the Hermit said—   560
    "And they answer'd not our cheer.
"The planks look warp'd, and see those sails
    "How thin they are and sere!
"I never saw aught like to them
    "Unless perchance it were   565

"The skeletons of leaves that lag
    "My forest brook along:
"When the Ivy-tod[5] is heavy with snow,
"And the Owlet whoops to the wolf below
    "That eats the she-wolf's young.   570

"Dear Lord! it has a fiendish look—
    (The Pilot made reply)
"I am a-fear'd.—"Push on, push on!
    Said the Hermit cheerily.

The Boat came closer to the Ship,   575
    But I ne spake ne stirr'd!
The Boat came close beneath the Ship,
    And strait a sound was heard!

Under the water it rumbled on,
    Still louder and more dread: 580
It reach'd the Ship, it split the bay;
    The Ship went down like lead.

Stunn'd by that loud and dreadful sound,
    Which sky and ocean smote:
Like one that hath been seven days drown'd   585
    My body lay afloat:
But, swift as dreams, myself I found
    Within the Pilot's boat.

Upon the whirl, where sank the Ship,
    The boat spun round and round: 590
And all was still, save that the hill
    Was telling of the sound.

4. Corrected to "ner'd" in 1800 (CL, 1:601).
5. Ivy bush. Lamb wrote to C in June 1796 quoting from John Fletcher, *Bonduca* (1619),
    1.1.111–14, "Then did I see these valiant men of Britain, like boding owls creep into tods of
    ivy, and hoot their fears to one another nightly" (LL, 1:30).

The skiff-boat neared: I heard them talk,
"Why, this is strange, I trow!
525 Where are those lights so many and fair,
That signal made but now?"

"Strange, by my faith!" the Hermit said—   *Approacheth the ship*
"And they answered not our cheer!   *with wonder.*
The planks looked warped! and see those sails,
530 How thin they are and sere!
I never saw aught like to them,
Unless perchance it were

"Brown skeletons of leaves that lag
My forest-brook along;
535 When the ivy-tod is heavy with snow,
And the owlet whoops to the wolf below,
That eats the she-wolf's young."

"Dear Lord! it hath a fiendish look—
(The Pilot made reply)
540 I am a-feared"—"Push on, push on!"
Said the Hermit cheerily.

The boat came closer to the ship,
But I nor spake nor stirred;
The boat came close beneath the ship,
545 And straight a sound was heard.

Under the water it rumbled on,   *The ship suddenly*
Still louder and more dread: *sinketh.*
It reached the ship, it split the bay;
The ship went down like lead.

550 Stunned by that loud and dreadful sound,   *The ancient Mariner*
Which sky and ocean smote,   *is saved in the Pilot's*
Like one that hath been seven days   *boat.*
    drowned
My body lay afloat;
But swift as dreams, myself I found
555 Within the Pilot's boat.

Upon the whirl, where sank the ship,
The boat spun round and round;
And all was still, save that the hill
Was telling of the sound.

I mov'd my lips: the Pilot shriek'd
   And fell down in a fit.
The Holy Hermit rais'd his eyes   595
   And pray'd where he did sit.

I took the oars: the Pilot's boy,
   Who now doth crazy go,
Laugh'd loud and long, and all the while
   His eyes went to and fro,   600
"Ha! ha!" quoth he—"full plain I see,
   "The devil knows how to row."

And now all in mine own Countrée
   I stood on the firm land!
The Hermit stepp'd forth from the boat,   605
   And scarcely he could stand.

"O shrieve me, shrieve me, holy Man!
   The Hermit cross'd his brow—
"Say quick," quoth he, "I bid thee say
   "What manner man art thou?   610

Forthwith this frame of mine was wrench'd
   With a woeful agony,
Which forc'd me to begin my tale
   And then it left me free.

Since then at an uncertain hour,   615
   Now oftimes and now fewer,
That anguish comes and makes me tell
   My ghastly aventure.

I pass, like night, from land to land;[6]
   I have strange power of speech;   620
The moment that his face I see
I know the man that must hear me;
   To him my tale I teach.

6. In 1832 C said that the mariner "was in my mind the everlasting wandering Jew—had told this story ten thousand times since the voyage which was in early youth and fifty years before" (*TT* [CC], 1:273–74). The legend of the Wandering Jew, suggested by enigmatic passages in John 21.22 and Matthew 16.28, tells the story of a Jew who cursed Christ on the way to the Crucifixion and was therefore condemned to eternal wandering on earth until the Second Coming. He remains on earth as the last living witness to the Crucifixion and has become converted to Christianity. C referred to a work on the "Wandering Jew / a romance" in a notebook perhaps as early as 1795 (CN, 1:45), and read the story in Matthew Gregory Lewis's *The Monk* (1796), which he reviewed shortly before he wrote the poem (*SW&F* [CC], 1:57–65). See "Wanderings of Cain" (p. 211 herein). In his 1834 review of C's *Poetical Works* HNC wrote, "It was a sad mistake" of an artist who "has made the ancient mariner an old decrepit man. That is not the true image; no! he should have been a growthless, decayless being, impassive to time or season, a silent cloud—the wandering Jew. The curse of the dead men's eyes should not have passed away" (*Quarterly Review* 3 [August 1834]: 29; *CH*, 1:645).

560   I moved my lips—the Pilot shrieked
      And fell down in a fit;
      The holy Hermit raised his eyes,
      And prayed where he did sit.

      I took the oars: the Pilot's boy,
565   Who now doth crazy go,
      Laughed loud and long, and all the while
      His eyes went to and fro.
      "Ha! ha!" quoth he, "full plain I see,
      The Devil knows how to row."

570   And now, all in my own countree,
      I stood on the firm land!
      The Hermit stepped forth from the boat,
      And scarcely he could stand.

      "O shrieve me, shrieve me, holy man!"
575   The Hermit crossed his brow.
      "Say quick," quoth he, "I bid thee say—
      What manner of man art thou?"

The ancient Mariner earnestly entreateth the Hermit to shrieve him; and the penance of life falls on him.

      Forthwith this frame of mine was wrenched
      With a woful agony,
580   Which forced me to begin my tale;
      And then it left me free.

      Since then, at an uncertain hour,
      That agony returns:
      And till my ghastly tale is told,
585   This heart within me burns.

And ever and anon throughout his future life an agony constraineth him to travel from land to land;

      I pass, like night, from land to land;
      I have strange power of speech;
      That moment that his face I see,
      I know the man that must hear me:
590   To him my tale I teach.

What loud uproar bursts from that door!
    The Wedding-guests are there;   625
But in the Garden-bower the Bride
    And Bride-maids singing are:
And hark the little Vesper-bell
    Which biddeth me to prayer.

O Wedding-guest! this soul hath been   630
    Alone on a wide wide sea:
So lonely 'twas, that God himself
    Scarce seemed there to be.

O sweeter than the Marriage-feast,
    'Tis sweeter far to me   635
To walk together to the Kirk
    With a goodly company.

To walk together to the Kirk
    And all together pray,
While each to his great father bends,   640
Old men, and babes, and loving friends,
    And Youths, and Maidens gay.

Farewell, farewell! but this I tell
    To thee, thou wedding-guest!
He prayeth well who loveth well   645
    Both man and bird and beast.

He prayeth best who loveth best,
    All things both great and small:
For the dear God, who loveth us,
    He made and loveth all.[7]   650

The Marinere, whose eye is bright,
    Whose beard with age is hoar,
Is gone; and now the wedding-guest
    Turn'd from the bridegroom's door.

He went, like one that hath been stunn'd   655
    And is of sense forlorn:
A sadder and a wiser man
    He rose the morrow morn.

7. C made two comments that were combined into one entry in *Table Talk* (1835), frequently cited to explain the moral of the poem. The first dates from May 30, 1830: "The fault of the Ancient Mariner consists in making the moral sentiment too apparent and bringing it in too much as a principle or cause in a work of such pure Imagination." The second dates from March 3, 1832: "Mrs Barbauld told me that the only faults she found with the Ancient Mariner were—that it was improbable, and had no moral. As for the probability—to be sure that might admit some question—but I told her that in my judgment the chief fault of the poem was that it had too much moral, and that too openly obtruded on the reader. It ought to have had no more moral than the story [in *The Arabian Nights*] of the merchant sitting down to eat dates by the side of a well and throwing the shells aside, and the Genii starting up and saying he must kill the merchant, because a date shell had put out the eye of the Genii's son" (*TT* [CC], 1:149, 272–73; 2:100).

What loud uproar bursts from that door!
The wedding-guests are there:
But in the garden-bower the bride
And bride-maids singing are:
595 And hark the little vesper bell,
Which biddeth me to prayer!

O Wedding-Guest! this soul hath been
Alone on a wide wide sea:
So lonely 'twas, that God himself
600 Scarce seemed there to be.

O sweeter than the marriage-feast,
'Tis sweeter far to me,
To walk together to the kirk
With a goodly company!—

605 To walk together to the kirk,
And all together pray,
While each to his great Father bends,
Old men, and babes, and loving friends,
And youths and maidens gay!

610 Farewell, farewell! but this I tell   *And to teach, by his*
To thee, thou Wedding-Guest!   *own example, love*
He prayeth well, who loveth well   *and reverence to all*
Both man and bird and beast.   *things that God*
                                             made and loveth.

He prayeth best, who loveth best
615 All things both great and small;
For the dear God who loveth us,
He made and loveth all."

The Mariner, whose eye is bright,
Whose beard with age is hoar,
620 Is gone: and now the Wedding-Guest
Turned from the bridegroom's door.

He went like one that hath been stunned,
And is of sense forlorn:
A sadder and a wiser man,
625 He rose the morrow morn.

The
Foster-Mother's Tale,
A Dramatic Fragment[1]

FOSTER-MOTHER.

I never saw the man whom you describe.

MARIA

'Tis strange! he spake of you familiarly
As mine and Albert's common Foster-mother.

FOSTER-MOTHER

Now blessings on the man, whoe'er he be,
That joined your names with mine! O my sweet lady,   5
As often as I think of those dear times
When you two little ones would stand at eve
On each side of my chair, and make me learn
All you had learnt in the day; and how to talk
In gentle phrase, then bid me sing to you—   10
'Tis more like heaven to come than what *has* been.

MARIA

O my dear Mother! this strange man has left me
Troubled with wilder fancies, than the moon
Breeds in the love-sick maid who gazes at it,
Till lost in inward vision, with wet eye   15
She gazes idly!—But that entrance, Mother!

FOSTER-MOTHER

Can no one hear? It is a perilous tale!

MARIA.

No one.

FOSTER-MOTHER

My husband's father told it me,
Poor old Leoni!—Angels rest his soul!

---

1. From C's play *Osorio*, 4.154–234 (*PW*, 2:571–74), completed in October 1797 and revised
   as *Remorse*, staged and printed in 1813. In *Osorio* the scene was set in "the court before the
   Castle." The scene was omitted in *Remorse*, but was printed as a note to act 4. When "The
   Foster-Mother's Tale" was reprinted in *LB* (1800), the subtitle was changed to "A Narration
   in Dramatic Blank Verse" and the poem began with line 16, but in subsequent reprintings
   the original title and lines 1–15 were restored. In the second edition of *Remorse* (1813) C
   added a note: "The following scene as unfit for the stage was taken from the Tragedy in
   1797, and published in the *Lyrical Ballads*" (*PW*, 1:182).

He was a woodman, and could fell and saw   20
With lusty arm. You know that huge round beam
Which props the hanging wall of the old chapel?
Beneath that tree, while yet it was a tree
He found a baby wrapt in mosses, lined
With thistle-beards, and such small locks of wool   25
As hang on brambles. Well, he brought him home,
And reared him at the then Lord Velez' cost.
And so the babe grew up a pretty boy,
A pretty boy, but most unteachable—
And never learnt a prayer, nor told a bead,   30
But knew the names of birds, and mocked their notes,
And whistled, as he were a bird himself:
And all the autumn 'twas his only play
To get the seeds of wild flowers, and to plant them
With earth and water, on the stumps of trees.   35
A Friar, who gathered simples in the wood,
A grey-haired man—he loved this little boy,
The boy loved him—and, when the Friar taught him,
He soon could write with the pen: and from that time,
Lived chiefly at the Convent or the Castle.   40
So he became a very learned youth.
But Oh! poor wretch!—he read, and read, and read,
'Till his brain turned—and ere his twentieth year,
He had unlawful thoughts of many things:
And though he prayed, he never loved to pray   45
With holy men, nor in a holy place—
But yet his speech, it was so soft and sweet,
The late Lord Velez ne'er was wearied with him.
And once, as by the north side of the Chapel
They stood together, chained in deep discourse,   50
The earth heaved under them with such a groan,
That the wall tottered, and had well-nigh fallen
Right on their heads. My Lord was sorely frightened;
A fever seized him, and he made confession
Of all the heretical and lawless talk   55
Which brought this judgment: so the youth was seized
And cast into that hole. My husband's father
Sobbed like a child—it almost broke his heart:
And once as he was working in the cellar,
He heard a voice distinctly; 'twas the youth's,   60
Who sung a doleful song about green fields,
How sweet it were on lake or wild savannah,
To hunt for food, and be a naked man,
And wander up and down at liberty.
He always doted on the youth, and now   65
His love grew desperate; and defying death,
He made that cunning entrance I described:
And the young man escaped.

MARIA

'Tis a sweet tale:
Such as would lull a listening child to sleep,
His rosy face besoiled with unwiped tears.—   70
And what became of him?

FOSTER-MOTHER

He went on ship-board
With those bold voyagers, who made discovery
Of golden lands. Leoni's younger brother
Went likewise, and when he returned to Spain,
He told Leoni, that the poor mad youth,   75
Soon after they arrived in that new world,
In spite of his dissuasion, seized a boat,
And all alone, set sail by silent moonlight
Up a great river, great as any sea,
And ne'er was heard of more: but 'tis supposed,   80
He lived and died among the savage men.

The Nightingale;
A Conversational Poem, Written in April, 1798[1]

No cloud, no relique of the sunken day
Distinguishes the West, no long thin slip
Of sullen Light, no obscure trembling hues.
Come, we will rest on this old mossy Bridge!
You see the glimmer of the stream beneath,   5
But hear no murmuring: it flows silently
O'er its soft bed of verdure. All is still,
A balmy night! and tho' the stars be dim,
Yet let us think upon the vernal showers
That gladden the green earth, and we shall find   10
A pleasure in the dimness of the stars.
And hark! the Nightingale begins its song,
"Most musical, most melancholy"[2] Bird!

1. On May 10, 1798, C sent "The Nightingale" to Wordsworth with the following poem (CL, 1:406):

   In stale blank verse a subject stale / I send *per post* my *Nightingale*; / And like an honest bard, dear Wordsworth, / You'll tell me what you think, my Bird's worth. / My own opinion's briefly this— / His *bill* he opens not amiss; / And when he has sung a stave or so, / His breast, & some small space below, / So throbs & swells, that you might swear / No vulgar music's working there. / So far, so good; but then, 'od rot him! / There's something falls off at his bottom. / Yet, sure, no wonder it should breed. / That my Bird's Tail's a tail indeed / And makes its own inglorious harmony / AEolio crepitû, non carmine.

2. "This passage in Milton possesses an excellence far superior to that of mere description: it is spoken in the character of the melancholy Man, and has therefore a *dramatic* propriety. The author makes this remark, to rescue himself from the charge of having alluded with levity to a line in Milton: a charge than which none could be more painful to him, except perhaps that of having ridiculed his Bible." [C's 1798 note.] The quotation is from Milton, "Il Penseroso," lines 61–64: "Sweet Bird that shunn'st the noise of folly, / Most musicall, most melancholy! / Thee Chauntress oft the Woods among, / I woo to hear thy eeven-Song."

A melancholy Bird? O idle thought!
In nature there is nothing melancholy.   15
—But some night-wandering Man, whose heart was pierc'd
With the remembrance of a grievous wrong,
Or slow distemper or neglected love,
(And so, poor Wretch! fill'd all things with himself
And made all gentle sounds tell back the tale   20
Of his own sorrows) he and such as he
First nam'd these notes a melancholy strain;
And many a poet echoes the conceit,
Poet, who hath been building up the rhyme[3]
When he had better far have stretch'd his limbs   25
Beside a brook in mossy forest-dell
By sun or moonlight, to the influxes
Of shapes and sounds and shifting elements
Surrendering his whole spirit, of his song
And of his fame forgetful! so his fame   30
Should share in nature's immortality,
A venerable thing! and so his song
Should make all nature lovelier, and itself
Be lov'd, like nature!—But 'twill not be so;
And youths and maidens most poetical   35
Who lose the deep'ning twilights of the spring
In ball-rooms and hot theatres, they still
Full of meek sympathy must heave their sighs
O'er Philomela's pity-pleading strains.[4]
My Friend, and my Friend's Sister![5] we have learnt   40
A different lore: we may not thus profane
Nature's sweet voices always full of love
And joyance! 'Tis the merry Nightingale
That crowds, and hurries, and precipitates
With fast thick warble his delicious notes,   45
As he were fearful, that an April night
Would be too short for him to utter forth
His love-chant, and disburthen his full soul
Of all its music! And I know a grove
Of large extent, hard by a castle huge   50
Which the great lord inhabits not: and so
This grove is wild with tangling underwood,
And the trim walks are broken up, and grass,
Thin grass and king-cups grow within the paths.
But never elsewhere in one place I knew   55

---

3. Cf. Milton, "Lycidas," lines 10–11: Lycidas "knew / Himself to sing, and build the lofty rhyme."
4. "*Philomel*" in Greek means the "lover of song." Philomela was raped and her tongue was cut out so she could not reveal the crime. She was later changed into a nightingale. (See Ovid, *Metamorphoses*, book 6.) Contrast C's rejection of nature's melancholy here with his earlier enthusiasm for the nightingale's melancholy song in "To the Nightingale" (1795), lines 9–14: "But I *do* hear thee, and the high bough mark, / Within whose mild moon-mellow'd foliage hid / Thou warblest sad thy pity-pleading strains. / O! I have listen'd, till my working soul, / Waked by those strains to thousand phantasies, / Absord'd hath ceas'd to listen!" (*PW*, 1:93).
5. William and Dorothy Wordsworth.

So many Nightingales: and far and near
In wood and thicket over the wide grove
They answer and provoke each other's songs—
With skirmish and capricious passagings,
And murmurs musical and swift jug jug[6]   60
And one low piping sound more sweet than all—
Stirring the air with such an harmony,
That should you close your eyes, you might almost
Forget it was not day! On moonlight bushes,
Whose dewy leafits are but half disclos'd,   65
You may perchance behold them on the twigs,
Their bright, bright eyes, their eyes both bright and full,
Glistning, while many a glow-worm in the shade
Lights up her love-torch.

                                    A most gentle maid
Who dwelleth in her hospitable home   70
Hard by the Castle, and at latest eve,
(Even like a Lady vow'd and dedicate
To something more than nature in the grove)
Glides thro' the pathways; she knows all their notes,
That gentle Maid! and oft, a moment's space,   75
What time the moon was lost behind a cloud,
Hath heard a pause of silence: till the Moon
Emerging, hath awaken'd earth and sky
With one sensation, and those wakeful Birds
Have all burst forth in choral minstrelsy,   80
As if one quick and sudden Gale had swept
An hundred airy harps! And she hath watch'd
Many a Nightingale perch giddily
On blosmy[7] twig still swinging from the breeze,
And to that motion tune his wanton song,   85
Like tipsy Joy that reels with tossing head.

Farewell, O Warbler! till to-morrow eve,
And you, my friends! farewell, a short farewell!
We have been loitering long and pleasantly,
And now for our dear homes.—That strain again![8]   90
Full fain it would delay me!—My dear Babe,
Who, capable of no articulate sound,
Mars all things with his imitative lisp,
How he would place his hand beside his ear,
His little hand, the small forefinger up,   95
And bid us listen! And I deem it wise
To make him Nature's playmate. He knows well
The evening star: and once when he awoke
In most distressful mood (some inward pain

---

6. Common representation of one of the notes of the nightingale.
7. Blossomy.
8. Cf. *Twelfth Night* 1.1.1–4: "If music be the food of love, play on, / Give me excess of it that, surfeiting, / The appetite may sicken, and so die. / That strain again, it had a dying fall."

Had made up that strange thing, an infant's dream)   100
I hurried with him to our orchard plot,
And he beholds the moon, and hush'd at once
Suspends his sobs, and laughs most silently,
While his fair eyes that swam with undropt tears
Did glitter in the yellow moon-beam! Well—[9]   105
It is a father's tale. But if that Heaven
Should give me life, his childhood shall grow up
Familiar with these songs, that with the night
He may associate Joy! Once more farewell,
Sweet Nightingale! once more, my friends! farewell.   110

The Dungeon[1]

And this place our forefathers made for man!
This is the process of our love and wisdom,
To each poor brother who offends against us—
Most innocent, perhaps—and what if guilty?
Is this the only cure? Merciful God!   5
Each pore and natural outlet shrivell'd up
By ignorance and parching poverty,
His energies roll back upon his heart,
And stagnate and corrupt; till changed to poison,
They break out on him, like a loathsome plague-spot;   10
Then we call in our pamper'd mountebanks—
And this is their best cure! uncomforted
And friendless solitude, groaning and tears,
And savage faces, at the clanking hour
Seen through the steams and vapour of his dungeon,   15
By the lamp's dismal twilight! So he lies
Circled with evil, till his very soul
Unmoulds its essence, hopelessly deformed
By sights of ever more deformity!

With other ministrations thou, O nature!   20
Healest thy wandering and distempered child:
Thou pourest on him thy soft influences,
Thy sunny hues, fair forms, and breathing sweets,
Thy melodies of woods, and winds, and waters,
Till he relent, and can no more endure   25
To be a jarring and a dissonant thing,
Amid this general dance and minstrelsy;
But, bursting into tears, wins back his way,
His angry spirit healed and harmonized
By the benignant touch of love and beauty.   30

9. C entered the event in a notebook: "Hartley fell down & hurt himself—I caught him up crying & screaming—& ran out of doors with him.—The moon caught his eye—he ceased crying immediately—& his eyes & the tears in them, how they glittered in the Moonlight" (CN, 1:219, written perhaps as early as the fall of 1797).
1. From Osorio 5.107–36 (var.) and Remorse 5.1.1–30 (var.) (PW, 2:586–87, 871–72).

Love[1]

All Thoughts, all Passions, all Delights,
Whatever stirs this mortal Frame,
All are but Ministers of Love,
    And feed his sacred flame.

Oft in my waking dreams do I   5
Live o'er again that happy hour,
When midway on the Mount I lay
    Beside the Ruin'd Tower.

The Moonshine stealing o'er the scene
Had blended with the Lights of Eve;   10
And she was there, my Hope, my Joy,
    My own dear Genevieve!

She lean'd against the Armed Man,
The Statue of the Armed Knight:
She stood and listen'd to my Harp   15
    Amid the ling'ring Light.

Few Sorrows hath she of her own,
My Hope, my Joy, my Genevieve!
She loves me best, whene'er I sing
    The Songs, that make her grieve.   20

I play'd a soft and doleful Air,
I sang an old and moving Story—
An old rude Song that fitted well
    The Ruin wild and hoary.

She listen'd with a flitting Blush,   25
With downeast Eyes and modest Grace;
For well she knew, I could not choose
    But gaze upon her Face.

I told her of the Knight, that wore
Upon his Shield a burning Brand;   30
And that for ten long Years he woo'd
    The Lady of the Land.

1. Published in *LB* (1800) and probably written in November 1799 on a visit to the Hutchinsons at Stockburn (*PW* [CC], 1:604–05). Published with four additional stanzas at the beginning and three at the end in *MP* and the *Courier*, December 21, 1799, as "Introduction to the Tale of the Dark Ladie" with an introductory letter offering "a silly tale of old fashioned love" (*CL*, 1:551) in a time of turbulent revolution. The newspaper text is reproduced in *PW*, 2:1052–59. "The Ballad of the Dark Ladiè," first published in 1834, is fragmentary (*PW*, 1:293–95). The manuscript sent to the printer in July 1800 for *LB* (1800) is printed in *CL*, 1:595–97. C spoke of it as one of his most popular poems and linked it with "Christabel" (p. 162 herein) in the *Biographia* as two of his most admired poems.

I told her, how he pin'd: and, ah!
The low, the deep, the pleading tone,
With which I sang another's Love, 35
    Interpreted my own.

She listen'd with a flitting Blush,
With downcast Eyes and modest Grace;
And she forgave me, that I gaz'd
    Too fondly on her Face! 40

But when I told the cruel scorn
Which craz'd this bold and lovely Knight,
And that he cross'd the mountain woods
    Nor rested day nor night;

That sometimes from the savage Den, 45
And sometimes from the darksome Shade,
And sometimes starting up at once
    In green and sunny Glade,

There came, and look'd him in the face,
An Angel beautiful and bright; 50
And that he knew, it was a Fiend,
    This miserable Knight!

And that, unknowing what he did,
He leapt amid a murd'rous Band,
And sav'd from Outrage worse than Death 55
    The Lady of the Land;

And how she wept and clasp'd his knees
And how she tended him in vain—
And ever strove to expiate
    The Scorn, that craz'd his Brain. 60

And that she nurs'd him in a Cave;
And how his Madness went away
When on the yellow forest leaves
    A dying Man he lay;

His dying words—but when I reach'd 65
That tenderest strain of all the Ditty,
My falt'ring Voice and pausing Harp
    Disturb'd her Soul with Pity!

All Impulses of Soul and Sense
Had thrill'd my guileless Genevieve, 70
The Music, and the doleful Tale,
    The rich and balmy Eve;

And Hopes, and Fears that kindle Hope,
An undistinguishable Throng!
And gentle Wishes long subdued,   75
    Subdued and cherish'd long!

She wept with pity and delight,
She blush'd with love and maiden shame;
And, like the murmur of a dream,
    I heard her breathe my name.   80

Her Bosom heav'd—she stepp'd aside;
As conscious of my Look, she stepp'd—
Then suddenly with timorous eye
    She fled to me and wept.

She half inclosed me with her arms,   85
She press'd me with a meek embrace;
And bending back her head look'd up,
    And gaz'd upon my face.

'Twas partly Love, and partly Fear,
And partly 'twas a bashful Art   90
That I might rather feel than see
    The Swelling of her Heart.

I calm'd her fears; and she was calm,
And told her love with virgin Pride.
And so I won my Genevieve,   95
    My bright and beauteous Bride!

FEARS IN SOLITUDE (1798)

Early 1798 brought renewed fears of a French invasion of England and
dismay at the French invasion of Switzerland. The French had made a di-
versionary landing at Fishguard in Wales in February 1797 with 1,200 soldiers, mostly untrained men released from prisons, who immediately
surrendered to the local militia. In January 1798 the English ministers
raised fears of invasion, and the *Morning Post* circulated rumors that the
French were preparing an army of England and an invasion fleet at Brest.
On January 2 the "Ship News" in the *Morning Post* reported that a French
fleet put to sea with fifty thousand men to be landed on the Scilly Islands
and northern Ireland, but later reports found no such fleet. On January 15
the paper declared that "the alarm of an invasion has made a very deep
impression on the public mind within these last few days. The KING's message—the menacing language of the Directory, conveyed by the last Paris
Journals—the military preparations of this country—the ardent desire displayed in France for the attack; are circumstances which cannot fail of exciting anxiety and regret." Yet rumors of invasion were greeted with
skepticism. On January 20 the *Morning Post* judged that "we are not disposed to think the French fleet will yet proceed to sea." Contradictory reports continued through January and February. On February 15 a British

naval ship stationed outside Brest reported not a single French ship of the line in the harbor, yet two days later the *Morning Post* printed a report that two hundred ships were there. The British government continuously issued reports of an impending invasion, and the *Anti-Jacobin* claimed on March 12 "that an Invasion of this Country will be attempted, must appear probable to every man who considers the character of the persons who compose the French Directory." Finally on April 9 the *Morning Post* published a "Decree of the Directory of 11th Germinal": "1st General Buonaparte shall repair to Brest in the course of the present decade, to take upon himself the command of the Army of England. 2d. He is charged with the direction of all forces by both land and sea, destined for the expedition against England."

At about the same time there were uprisings against the oligarchy in Switzerland. France invaded portions of Switzerland in February, and on March 24 the *Morning Post* published the "Report to the Council of 500," which gloated over the defeat of the Swiss oligarchy and the frustration of English interests in Switzerland. Earlier, Coleridge and the *Morning Post* had little sympathy for the Swiss, speaking in an editorial of February 24, 1798, of the "dying convulsions of the Swiss Republics" (*EOT* [*CC*], 1:21), but after late March, the paper's sympathies changed to oppose French imperialism. Under pressure from the government, Daniel Stuart (1766–1846), the editor of the *Morning Post*, softened his editorial policy, and Coleridge's poetry followed the paper's change in policy.

Coleridge had been receiving copies of the *Morning Post* since the first of the year (*CL*, 1:360). On April 16, 1798, he published "The Recantation, An Ode," the original title of "France. An Ode," in the *Morning Post* with a headnote deploring the French action in Switzerland yet upholding the ideals of freedom. Coleridge also wrote "Frost at Midnight," in late February and "Fears in Solitude," which he dated "April 20th 1798." *Fears in Solitude* was composed as a volume in late August or early September, when, on his way to Germany with the Wordsworths, Coleridge met Joseph Johnson (1738–1809) (*CL*, 1:417–18, 420), a London publisher of Unitarian and dissenting tracts, the publisher of Priestley and Mary Wollstonecraft (1759–1797), and a friend of William Godwin and Thomas Paine. Like Daniel Stuart, Johnson was pressured by the government. He was tried on July 17 for selling a radical pamphlet by Gilbert Wakefield (1756–1801) and found guilty, but sentencing was postponed for months to prevent him from publishing more radical works. The poems in *Fears in Solitude*, first written to criticize the French and to claim loyalty to Britain, when collected became a public defense of both Johnson and Coleridge, who had been attacked in the Tory press. By December 1799, however, Coleridge reported that "not above two hundred" were sold (*CL*, 1:550).

In later years Coleridge used "Fears in Solitude" and "France. An Ode" for self-defense. He reprinted sections from "Fears in Solitude" in the *Morning Post*, October 14, 1802, and in *The Friend*, June 8, 1809. With similar purposes he reprinted a revised version of "France. An Ode" in both the *Morning Post* and the *Courier* October 14, 1802. He included lines from the final stanza of "France. An Ode" in chapter 10 of the *Biographia* (*BL* [*CC*], 1:199–200). Reprinted sections are indicated in the notes herein. The republication of the two poems in 1802 came a few days before Coleridge's article "Once a Jacobin Always a Jacobin" in the *Morning Post*. In 1807 or 1808 Coleridge made extensive annotations in a copy of *Fears in Solitude*—once in the possession of Sir George Beaumont

(1753–1827) and now in the J. Pierpont Morgan Library—which were published by B. Ifor Evans in "Coleridge's Copy of 'Fears in Solitude,' " *TLS*, April 18, 1935: 255. Some of these marginal comments are printed as notes herein.

The texts printed here are from *Fears in Solitude* (1798) in the order of the quarto.

Fears in Solitude[1]

Written, April 1798, During the Alarms of an Invasion

A green and silent spot amid the hills!
A small and silent dell!—O'er stiller place
No singing sky-lark ever pois'd himself!
The hills are heathy, save that swelling slope,
Which hath a gay and gorgeous covering on,   5
All golden with the never-bloomless furze,
Which now blooms most profusely; but the dell,
Bath'd by the mist, is fresh and delicate,
As vernal corn field, or the unripe flax,
When thro' its half-transparent stalks, at eve,   10
The level sunshine glimmers with green light.
O 'tis a quiet spirit-healing nook,
Which all, methinks, would love; but chiefly he,
The humble man, who in his youthful years
Knew just so much of folly as had made   15
His early manhood more securely wise:
Here he might lie on fern or wither'd heath,
While from the singing lark (that sings unseen
The minstrelsy which solitude loves best)
And from the sun, and from the breezy air,   20
Sweet influences trembled o'er his frame;
And he with many feelings, many thoughts,
Made up a meditative joy, and found
Religious meanings in the forms of nature!
And so, his senses gradually wrapp'd   25
In a half-sleep, he dreams of better worlds,
And dreaming hears thee still, O singing lark!
That singest like an angel in the clouds.

My God! it is a melancholy thing
For such a man, who would full fain preserve   30
His soul in calmness, yet perforce must feel
For all his human brethren—O my God,
It is indeed a melancholy thing,
And weighs upon the heart, that he must think

---

1. An early manuscript adds a note to the title: "The Scene, the Hills near Stowey." At the end of this manuscript, copied in 1799 (*PW* [CC], 1:469.), now in the Morgan Library, C wrote, "The above is perhaps not Poetry,—but a rather a sort of Middle thing between Poetry & Oratory—*sermoni propior.*—Some parts are, I am conscious, too tame even for animated prose" (*PW*, 1:257). *Sermoni propior*: see p. 52, n. 2 herein.

What uproar and what strife may now be stirring   35
This way or that way o'er these silent hills—
Invasion, and the thunder and the shout,
And all the crash of onset; fear and rage
And undetermined conflict—even now,
Ev'n now, perchance, and in his native Isle,   40
Carnage and screams beneath this blessed sun!
We have offended, O my countrymen!
We have offended very grievously,
And have been tyrannous. From east to west
A groan of accusation pierces heaven!   45
The wretched plead against us, multitudes
Countless and vehement, the sons of God,
Our brethren! like a cloud that travels on,
Steam'd up from Cairo's swamps of pestilence,
Ev'n so, my countrymen! have we gone forth   50
And borne to distant tribes slavery and pangs,
And, deadlier far, our vices, whose deep taint
With slow perdition murders the whole man,
His body and his soul! Meanwhile, at home,
We have been drinking with a riotous thirst   55
Pollutions from the brimming cup of wealth,
A selfish, lewd, effeminated[2] race,
Contemptuous of all honourable rule,
Yet bartering freedom, and the poor man's life,
For gold, as at a market! The sweet words   60
Of christian promise, words that even yet
Might stem destruction, were they wisely preach'd,
Are mutter'd o'er by men, whose tones proclaim,
How flat and wearisome they feel their trade.[3]
Rank scoffers some, but most too indolent,   65
To deem them falsehoods, or to *know* their truth.
O blasphemous! the book of life is made
A superstitious instrument, on which
We gabble o'er the oaths we mean to break,
For all must swear—all, and in every place,[4]   70
College and wharf, council and justice-court,
All, all must swear, the briber and the brib'd,
Merchant and lawyer, senator and priest,

2. William Godwin's *Political Justice* (1793) comments on the effects of wealth that are summarized in the margin as "Tendency of superfluity to inspire effeminacy." Prosperity invites
"our bodies to indolence, and our minds to lethargy," and in the case of nobles "deprives us
of all intercourse with our fellow men upon equal terms, and makes us prisoners of state,
gratified indeed with baubles and splendour" (2:385–86).
3. Cf. *Hamlet* 1.2.133–34: "How weary, stale, flat, and unprofitable / Seem to me all the uses
of this world."
4. In Lecture 3 of *LRR*, C quoted Jesus' Sermon on the Mount in Matthew 5.34–37 (*Lects 1795*
[CC], 165): "But I say unto you, Swear not at all; neither by heaven; for it is God's Throne.
* * * But let your communication be Yea, yea; Nay, nay: for whatsoever is more than these
cometh of evil." The Sermon on the Mount changes the law in Numbers 30.2: "If a man vow
a vow unto the Lord, or swear an oath to bind his soul with a bond, he shall not break his
word; he shall do according to all that proceedeth out of his mouth." The Test Act of 1673 required all who held offices of government to take oaths of allegiance, and the Corporation Act
of 1661 required all who held offices in corporations also to swear allegiance. Those who
wished repeal of these acts argued, as C did, by citing The Sermon on the Mount.

The rich, the poor, the old man, and the young,
All, all make up one scheme of perjury, 75
That faith doth reel; the very name of God
Sounds like a juggler's charm; and bold with joy,
Forth from his dark and lonely hiding-place
(Portentous sight) the owlet, ATHEISM,
Sailing on obscene wings athwart the noon, 80
Drops his blue-fringed lids, and holds them close,
And, hooting at the glorious sun in heaven,
Cries out, "where is it?"
                    Thankless too for peace,
(Peace long preserv'd by fleets and perilous seas)
Secure from actual warfare, we have lov'd 85
To swell the war-whoop, passionate for war!
Alas! for ages ignorant of all
Its ghastlier workings (famine or blue plague,
Battle, or siege, or flight thro' wintry snows)
We, this whole people, have been clamorous 90
For war and bloodshed, animating sports,
The which we pay for, as a thing to talk of,
Spectators and not combatants! no guess
Anticipative of a wrong unfelt,
No speculation on contingency, 95
However dim and vague, too vague and dim
To yield a justifying cause: and forth
(Stuff'd out with big preamble, holy names,
And adjurations of the God in heaven)
We send our mandates for the certain death 100
Of thousands and ten thousands! Boys and girls,
And women that would groan to see a child
Pull off an insect's leg, all read of war,
The best amusement for our morning meal!
The poor wretch, who has learnt his only prayers 105
From curses, who knows scarcely words enough
To ask a blessing of his heavenly Father,
Becomes a fluent phraseman, absolute
And technical in victories and defeats,
And all our dainty terms for fratricide, 110
Terms which we trundle smoothly o'er our tongues
Like mere abstractions, empty sounds to which
We join no feeling and attach no form,
As if the soldier died without a wound;
As if the fibres of this godlike frame 115
Were gor'd[5] without a pang: as if the wretch,
Who fell in battle doing bloody deeds,
Pass'd off to heaven, *translated*[6] and not kill'd;
As tho' he had no wife to pine for him,

5. The printer of *SL* suggested "rent" in place of "gor'd," and C responded on the proof sheets, now at Yale, "To *gore* is to wound so as at the same [time] to mangle—hence applied to a bull's horn."
6. Going to heaven without death. See Hebrews 11.5: "By faith Enoch was translated that he should not see death."

No God to judge him!—Therefore evil days   120
Are coming on us, O my countrymen!
And what if all-avenging Providence,
Strong and retributive, should make us know
The meaning of our words, force us to feel
The desolation and the agony   125
Of our fierce doings?—
                  Spare us yet a while,[7]
Father and God! O spare us yet a while!
O let not English women drag their flight
Fainting beneath the burden of their babes,
Of the sweet infants, that but yesterday   130
Laugh'd at the breast! Sons, brothers, husbands, all
Who ever gaz'd with fondness on the forms,
Which grew up with you round the same fire side,
And all who ever heard the sabbath bells
Without the infidel's scorn, make yourselves pure!   135
Stand forth! be men! repel an impious foe,
Impious and false, a light yet cruel race,
That laugh away all virtue, mingling mirth
With deeds of murder; and still promising
Freedom, themselves too sensual to be free,   140
Poison life's amities, and cheat the heart
Of Faith and quiet Hope, and all that soothes
And all that lifts the spirit! Stand we forth;[8]
Render them back upon th' insulted ocean,
And let them toss as idly on its waves,   145
As the vile sea-weeds, which some mountain blast
Swept from our shores! And O! may we return

---

7. Lines 126–94 (var.) were reprinted with revisions in the *MP*, October 14, 1802 (*PW*, 1:260–63; *EOT* [CC], 3:296). Lines 126–94 were reprinted with variants and the omission of lines 163–68 and retitled "Fears of Solitude" in *The Friend* June 8, 1809, with the following introduction:

> —will any man, who loves his Children and his Country, be slow to pardon me, if not in the spirit of vanity but of natural self-defence against yearly and monthly attacks on the very vitals of my character as an honest man and a loyal Subject, I prove the utter falsity of the charges by the only public means in my power, a citation from the last work published by me, in the close of the year 1798, and anterior to all the calumnies published to my dishonor. No one has charged me with seditious acts or conversation: if I have attempted to do harm, by my works it must have been effected. By my works therefore must I be judged: (if indeed one obscure volume of juvenile poems, and one slight verse pamphlet of twenty pages, can without irony be entitled *works*) [*Friend* (CC), 2:23].

    C refers to *Poems* (1796) and "Ode on the Departing Year" (1796) but omits reference to his radical Bristol lectures in 1795.

8. The Morgan copy has C's manuscript note that has been partially crossed out and is not all legible: "and at this very time, or rather immediately after the Publication I was declared in the 'Beauties of the Anti-Jacobin' * * * a runagate from his Country, who had denounced all patriotic feelings and to quote the very words 'become a Citizen of the world, & left my children fatherless & my wife destitute.' " "Runagate": fugitive. C refers to "New Morality" first printed in the *Anti-Jacobin or Weekly Examiner* on July 9, 1798, and reprinted in *The Beauties of the Anti-Jacobin* (1799), 306–07, with a note that concluded "He has since married, had children, and has now quitted the country, become a citizen of the world, left his little ones fatherless, and his wife destitute." The note implies that as a "citizen of the world" he is a Thomas Paine and that by abandoning his children he is a Rousseau, who abandoned his illegitimate children. C bought a copy of *The Beauties of the Anti-Jacobin* in December 1799 and thought of taking legal action against the authors, but nothing came of it (*CL*, 1:552).

Not with a drunken triumph, but with fear,
Repenting of the wrongs, with which we stung
So fierce a foe to frenzy!
        I have told,   150
O Britons! O my brethren! I have told
Most bitter truth, but without bitterness.
Nor deem my zeal or factious or mistim'd;
For never can true courage dwell with them,
Who, playing tricks with conscience, dare not look   155
At their own vices. We have been too long[9]
Dupes of a deep delusion! Some, belike,
Groaning with restless enmity, expect
All change from change of constituted power:
As if a government had been a robe,   160
On which our vice and wretchedness were tagg'd
Like fancy-points and fringes, with the robe
Pull'd off at pleasure. Fondly these attach
A radical causation to a few
Poor drudges of chastising Providence,   165
Who borrow all their hues and qualities
From our own folly and rank wickedness,
Which gave them birth, and nurse them. Others, meanwhile,
Dote with a mad idolatry;[1] and all,
Who will not fall before their images,   170
And yield them worship, they are enemies
Ev'n of their country!—Such have I been deem'd.[2]
But, O dear Britain! O my mother Isle!
Needs must thou prove a name most dear and holy
To me, a son, a brother, and a friend,   175
A husband and a father! who revere
All bonds of natural love, and find them all
Within the limits of thy rocky shores.
O native Britain! O my mother Isle!
How should'st thou prove aught else but dear and holy   180
To me, who from thy lakes and mountain-hills,
Thy clouds, thy quiet dales, thy rocks, and seas,

9. "All the Lines so marked [lines 156–72] convey, according to *my* conscience, sound good sense; but unfortunately they are neither poetry, nor any thing—as eloquence for instance— which approximates to it.—They are *Prose* that in a frolic has put on a masquerade Dress of metre & like most Masquerades, blundered in the assumed character.—What follows, I hope, will redeem it, for tho' in religion abhorring, yet in poetry, I cleave to the Catholic Doctrine of *supererogation*—& easily forgive many faults where I find any true beauty, when the faults are purely *literary*, not moral ones, and surely with reason—for such faults are merely *negative*—they do us *no harm*. * * * But the Good, that which is good to the Recipient is a positive gain—it either awakens him to new Thought or Feeling or both combined (as is *always* the case in Wordsworth's Poetry & forms perhaps an exampled Instance) or it recalls &—permit the word—*vivifies* the Thoughts & Feelings already acquired. S. T. Coleridge." [Morgan ms. annotation.] "Supererogation" is the performance of good works beyond what God requires to make up for others' deficiencies.
1. "They who affect to consider Idolatry as one of the harmless Absurdities shew a strange ignorance of History[.] * * * Atheism is a blessing compared with that state of mind in which men expect the blessings of Life not from the God of Purity and Love by being pure and benevolent; but from Jupiter the lustful Leader of the mythologic Banditti, from Mercury a thief; Bacchus a Drunkard, and Venus a harlot" (*Lects 1795* [CC], 142–43).
2. "Such have I been deem'd" emphasized by italics in *The Friend* (CC), 2:24.

Have drunk in all my intellectual life,
All sweet sensations, all ennobling thoughts,
All adoration of the God in nature,   185
All lovely and all honourable things,
Whatever makes this mortal spirit feel
The joy and greatness of its future being?
There lives nor form nor feeling in my soul
Unborrow'd from my country! O divine   190
And beauteous island, thou hast been my sole
And most magnificent temple, in the which
I walk with awe, and sing my stately songs,
Loving the God that made me!³—
                                    May my fears,
My filial fears, be vain! and may the vaunts   195
And menace of the vengeful enemy
Pass like the gust, that roar'd and died away
In the distant tree, which heard, and only heard;
In this low dell bow'd not the delicate grass.⁴
But now the gentle dew-fall sends abroad   200
The fruitlike perfume of the golden furze:
The light has left the summit of the hill,
Tho' still a sunny gleam lies beautiful
On the long-ivied beacon.—Now, farewell,
Farewell, awhile, O soft and silent spot!   205
On the green sheep-track, up the heathy hill,
Homeward I wind my way; and lo! recall'd
From bodings, that have well nigh wearied me,
I find myself upon the brow, and pause
Startled! And after lonely sojourning   210
In such a quiet and surrounded scene,⁵
This burst of prospect, here the shadowy main,
Dim-tinted, there the mighty majesty
Of that huge amphitheatre of rich
And elmy fields, seems like society,   215
Conversing with the mind, and giving it
A livelier impulse, and a dance of thought;
And now, beloved STOWEY! I behold⁶
Thy church-tower, and (methinks) the four huge elms

3. Lines 193–94 were drafted in the fall of 1796 when C was reading Ecclesiaticus 47.8: "In all his works he praised the Holy One most high with words of glory; and with his whole heart he sung songs, and loved him that made him" (*CN*, 1:268n.).
4. On October 30, 1819, C quoted lines 194–99 and commented: "I confess, that I read the Poem from which these lines are extracted * * * and now cite them with far other than an *Author's* Feelings—those, I *trust*, of a Patriot—I am *sure*, those of a Christian" (*CL*, 4:963).
5. C changed "scene" to "nook" with the following explanation to the printer in the proofs of *SL*, now at Yale: "*Scene* should never be used but either *properly* or by metaphorical allusion to the theatre. Mr. Pope was the first to introduce this with 500 other barbarisms in his Homer."
6. "My heart bids me say, after an interval of ten years, when the Poem is put the same to me as if it had been written by a man now dead—that he who can read these lines [lines 218–29] without some pleasure is—perhaps the Author of the Principles of Taste—: or one of his Brotherhood in the Family of Monkey-intellect." [Morgan ms. annotation.] The underlined words are crossed out. *Essays on the Nature and Principles of Taste* (1790) is by Archibald Alison (1757–1839). It is not clear whether C or someone else deleted the words.

Clust'ring, which mark the mansion of my friend;[7]   220
And close behind them, hidden from my view,
Is my own lowly cottage, where my babe
And my babe's mother dwell in peace! With light
And quicken'd footsteps thitherward I tend,
Rememb'ring thee, O green and silent dell!   225
And grateful, that by nature's quietness
And solitary musings all my heart
Is soften'd, and made worthy to indulge
Love, and the thoughts that yearn for[8] human kind.

Nether Stowey, April 20th, 1798.

France.
An Ode[1]

I

Ye Clouds, that far above me float and pause,
Whose pathless march no mortal may control!
Ye ocean waves, that, wheresoe'er ye roll,

7. Marginal note in *SL* in Thomas Poole's hand, now at Brown: "How little I merit this kindness."
8. To pity or sympathize with.
1. Although dated February 1798, it was perhaps not written until the end of March 1798 (*PW* [CC], 2:585). Introduced in the *MP*, April 16, 1798:

> The following excellent Ode will be in unison with the feelings of every friend to Liberty and foe to Oppression: of all who, admiring the French Revolution, detest and deplore the conduct of France towards Switzerland. It is very satisfactory to find so zealous and steady an advocate for Freedom as Mr. COLERIDGE concur with us in condemning the conduct of France towards the Swiss Cantons. Indeed his concurrence is not singular; we know of no Friend to Liberty who is not of his opinion. What we most admire, is the *avowal* of his sentiments, and public censure of the unprincipled and atrocious conduct of France. The Poem itself is written with great energy. The second, third, and fourth stanzas, contain some of the most vigorous lines we have ever read. The lines in the fourth stanza, "To scatter rage and trait'rous guilt / Where Peace her jealous home had built," to the end of the stanza, are particularly expressive and beautiful.

"France. An Ode" was reprinted in both the *MP* and the *Courier* on October 14, 1802, with the following headnote: "The following Ode was first published in this paper (in the beginning of the year 1798) in a less perfect state. The present state of France, and Switzerland, gives it so peculiar an interest at this present time, that we wished to re-publish it, and accordingly have procured from the Author, a corrected copy" (*EOT* [CC], 3:295–96).
    In September 1802 the French were again threatening the Helvetian Republic. The "Argument" followed in 1802:

> *First Stanza.* An invocation to those objects in Nature the contemplation of which had inspired the Poet with a devotional love of Liberty. *Second Stanza.* The exultation of the Poet at the commencement of the French Revolution, and his unqualified abhorrence of the Alliance against the Republic. *Third Stanza.* The blasphemies and horrors during the domination of the Terrorists regarded by the Poet as a transient storm, and as the natural consequence of the former despotism and of the foul superstition of Popery. Reason, indeed, began to suggest many apprehensions; yet still the Poet struggled to retain the hope that France would make conquests by no other means than by presenting to the observation of Europe, a people more happy and better instructed than under other forms of Government. *Fourth Stanza.* Switzerland, and the Poet's recantation. *Fifth Stanza.* An address to Liberty, in which the Poet expresses his conviction that those feelings and that great *ideal* of Freedom which the mind attains by its contemplation of its individual nature, and of the sublime surrounding objects (see Stanza the First) do not belong to men, as a society, nor can possibly be either gratified or realised, under any form of human government; but belong to the individual man, so far as he is pure, and inflamed with the love and adoration of God in Nature [*PW*, 1:244].

Yield homage only to eternal laws!
Ye woods, that listen to the night-bird's singing,   5
Midway the smooth and perilous steep reclin'd;
Save when your own imperious branches swinging
Have made a solemn music of the wind!
Where, like a man belov'd of God,
Thro' glooms, which never woodman trod,   10
How oft, pursuing fancies holy,
My moonlight way o'er flow'ring weeds I wound,
Inspir'd beyond the guess of folly,
By each rude shape, and wild unconquerable sound!
O, ye loud waves, and O, ye forests high,   15
And O, ye clouds, that far above me soar'd!
Thou rising sun! thou blue rejoicing sky!
Yea, every thing that is and will be free,
Bear witness for me wheresoe'er ye be,
With what deep worship I have still ador'd   20
The spirit of divinest liberty.

II

When France in wrath her giant limbs uprear'd,
And with that oath which smote earth, air, and sea,
Stamp'd her strong foot and said, she would be free,
Bear witness for me, how I hop'd and fear'd!   25
With what a joy my lofty gratulation
Unaw'd I sung amid a slavish band:
And when to whelm the disenchanted nation,
Like fiends embattled by a wizard's wand,
The monarchs march'd in evil day,   30
And Britain join'd the dire array;
Though dear her shores, and circling ocean,
Though many friendships, many youthful loves
Had swoln the patriot emotion,
And flung a magic light o'er all her hills and groves;   35
Yet still my voice unalter'd sang defeat
To all that brav'd the tyrant-quelling lance,[2]
And shame too long delay'd, and vain retreat!
For ne'er, O Liberty! with partial aim
I dimm'd thy light, or damp'd thy holy flame;   40
But blest the pæans of deliver'd France,
And hung my head, and wept at Britain's name!

2. Lines 36–37 refer to C's prophecy of ruin in "Ode on the Departing Year" (1796). In a copy of *SL*, C wrote at the end of that poem, "Let it not be forgotten during the perusal of this Ode that it was written many years before the abolition of the Slave Trade by the British Legislature, likewise before the invasion of Switzerland by the French Republic, which occasioned the Ode that follows ["France. An Ode"], a kind of Palinodia" (*PW*, 1:168). *Palinode*: recantation; i.e., "France. An Ode" is a recantation of "Ode on the Departing Year."

III

"And what (I said) tho' blasphemy's loud scream
"With that sweet music of deliv'rance strove;
"Tho' all the fierce and drunken passions wove   45
"A dance more wild than ever maniac's dream;
"Ye storms, that round the dawning east assembled,
"The sun was rising, tho' ye hid his light!"
And when to sooth my soul, that hop'd and trembled,
The dissonance ceas'd, and all seem'd calm and bright;   50
When France, her front deep-scar'd and gory,
Conceal'd with clust'ring wreaths of glory;
When insupportably advancing,[3]
Her arm made mock'ry of the warrior's ramp,[4]
While, timid looks of fury glancing,   55
Domestic treason, crush'd beneath her fatal stamp,[5]
Writh'd, like a wounded dragon in his gore;
Then I reproach'd my fears that would not flee,
"And soon (I said) shall wisdom teach her lore
"In the low huts of them that toil and groan!   60
"And conqu'ring by her happiness alone,
"Shall France compel the nations to be free,
"Till love and joy look round, and call the earth their own!"

IV

    Forgive me, Freedom! O forgive these dreams!
I hear thy voice, I hear thy loud lament,   65
From bleak Helvetia's icy caverns sent—
I hear thy groans upon her blood-stain'd streams!
Heroes, that for your peaceful country perish'd;
And ye, that fleeing spot the mountain snows
With bleeding wounds; forgive me, that I cherish'd   70
One thought, that ever bless'd your cruel foes!
To scatter rage and trait'rous guilt
Where Peace her jealous home had built;
A patriot race to disinherit
Of all that made their stormy wilds so dear,   75
And with inexpiable spirit
To taint the bloodless freedom of the mountaineer.—
O France! that mockest heav'n, adult'rous, blind,
And patriot[6] only in pernicious toils!

3. "Milton 'Samson Agonistes,' S. T. C." [Morgan ms. annotation.] Milton's lines 135–36 describe Samson: "safest he who stood aloof, / When insupportably his foot advanc't." The similarity to *Samson Agonistes* was noted in a review of *Fears in Solitude* in the *New London Review* 1 (January 1799): 99.
4. Of an animal, standing on its hind legs in threatening position, hence, to rage with violent gestures. Cf. *Samson Agonistes,* lines 138–39: "The bold *Ascalonite* / Fled from his Lion ramp."
5. In La Vendée, south of the Loire, peasants and priests resisted the French republicans in open rebellion from 1793 to 1795, with terrible carnage, reprisals, and executions. See *Conciones ad Populum* (p. 252 herein).
6. "I wrote it 'patient'—who altered it, I know not; but it seems to me an improvement." [Morgan ms. annotation.]

Are these thy boasts, champion of human kind: 80
To mix with kings in the low lust of sway,
Yell in the hunt, and share the murd'rous prey;
T' insult the shrine of liberty with spoils
From freemen torn; to tempt and to betray![7]

V

The sensual and the dark rebel in vain,[8]   85
Slaves by their own compulsion! In mad game
They burst their manacles, and wear the name
Of freedom graven on a heavier chain!
O Liberty! with profitless endeavour[9]
Have I pursued thee many a weary hour: 90
But thou nor swell'st the victor's strain, nor ever
Didst breathe thy soul in forms of human pow'r.
Alike from all, howe'er they praise thee,
(Nor pray'r, nor boastful name delays thee)
Alike from priesthood's harpy minions,   95
And factious blasphemy's obscener slaves,
Thou speedest on thy subtle pinions,
To live amid the winds, and move upon the waves![1]
And then I felt thee on that sea-cliff's verge,
Whose pines, scarce travell'd by the breeze above,   100
Had made one murmur with the distant surge!
Yes! while I stood and gaz'd, my temples bare,
And shot my being thro' earth, sea, and air,
Possessing all things with intensest love,
O Liberty, my spirit felt thee there!   105

February 1798.

7. "Alluding to Venice and Holland." [Morgan ms. annotation.]
8. "Southey in a review made some (me judice) *unfounded* objections to this last stanza—as if
   I had confounded moral with political Freedom—but surely the Object of the Stanza is to
   show that true political Freedom can only arise out of moral Freedom—what indeed is it but
   a *Dilatation* of those *golden* Lines of Milton:—'Licence they mean, when they cry—Liberty! /
   For who loves that must first be wise & good.' S. T. C." [Morgan ms. annotation.] C quotes
   lines 11–12 from Milton's Sonnet 12. Morton Paley suggests that C may be referring to the
   Critical Review 26 (1799): 474: "What does Mr. Coleridge mean by liberty in this passage?
   or what connexion has it with the subject of civil freedom?" (*Apocalypse and Millennium in
   English Romantic Poetry* [Oxford, 1999], 137).
9. The *MP* version of 1798 included a note before the present stanza V: "The fifth Stanza,
   which alluded to the African Slave-Trade, as conducted by this Country, and to the present
   Ministry and their supporters, has been omitted; and would have been omitted without remark if the commencing lines of the sixth Stanza had not referred to it." The "omitted" lines,
   if written, do not survive. The next stanza opened with the following lines in place of lines
   85–89: "Shall I with *these* my patriot zeal combine? / No, Afric, no! they stand before my
   ken, / Loath'd as th' Hyænas, that in murky den / Whine o'er their prey and mangle while
   they whine! / Divinest Liberty! with vain endeavour."
1. C quoted lines 85–98 (var.) in the *Biographia* with the following introductory comment: "In
   part from constitutional indolence, which in the very hey-day of hope had kept my enthusiasm in check, but still more from the habits and influences of a classical education and academic pursuits, scarcely had a year elapsed from the commencement of my literary and
   political adventures before my mind sunk into a state of thorough disgust and despondency,
   both with regard to the disputes and the parties disputant. With more than *poetic* feeling I
   exclaimed." In the *Biographia* C gave the title as "France, a Palinodia" (*BL* [CC],
   1:199–200).

Frost at Midnight[1]

The Frost performs its secret ministry,
Unhelp'd by any wind. The owlet's cry
Came loud—and hark, again! loud as before.
The inmates of my cottage, all at rest,
Have left me to that solitude, which suits   5
Abstruser musings: save that at my side
My cradled infant slumbers peacefully.
'Tis calm indeed! so calm, that it disturbs
And vexes meditation with its strange
And extreme silentness. Sea, hill, and wood,   10
This populous village! Sea, and hill, and wood,
With all the numberless goings on of life,
Inaudible as dreams! The thin blue flame
Lies on my low-burnt fire, and quivers not:
Only that film,[2] which flutter'd on the grate,   15
Still flutters there, the sole unquiet thing,
Methinks, its motion in this hush of nature
Gives it dim sympathies with me, who live,
Making it a companionable form,
With which I can hold commune. Idle thought!   20
But still the living spirit in our frame,
That loves not to behold a lifeless thing,
Transfuses into all its own delights
Its own volition, sometimes with deep faith,[3]
And sometimes with fantastic playfulness.   25
Ah me! amus'd by no such curious toys
Of the self-watching subtilizing mind,
How often in my early school-boy days,

1. Written after the snowstorm of February 17, 1798, as recorded in *DWJ* (see p. 123, n. 9 herein). While the private domestic scene of "Frost at Midnight" appears to contrast sharply with the two preceding political poems, its theme of domesticity and love of family resonate with the themes of nationalism and fear of invasion earlier in the volume. When the printer set copy for *SL*, it was first included in the category of "Poems Occasioned by Political Events or Feelings Connected with Them." C wrote on the proofs, now at Yale, "How comes this Poem here? What has it to do with Poems connected with Political Events?—I seem quite confident, that it will not be found in my arranged Catalogue of those sent to you.—It *must*, however, be deferred till it[s] proper place among my domestic & meditative Poems" (Stillinger, 55). Notes here include some changes listed in the errata of *SL*.
2. "In all parts of the kingdom these films are called *strangers*, and supposed to portend the arrival of some absent friend." [C's 1798 note.]
3. For lines 15–25, cf. Cowper, *The Task* 4.286–95:

> Me oft has fancy ludicrous and wild
> Sooth'd with a waking dream of houses, tow'rs,
> Trees, churches, and strange visages express'd
> In the red cinders, while with poring eye
> I gazed, myself creating what I saw.
> Nor less amused have I quiescent watch'd
> The sooty films that play upon the bars
> Pendulous, and foreboding in the view
> Of superstition prophesying still
> Though still deceived, some stranger's near approach.

(*The Poems of William Cowper*, ed. John D. Baird and Charles Ryskamp, 3 vols. [Oxford, 1980–95], 2:194). In a letter of December 17, 1796, C praised the "divine Chit chat of Cowper" (*CL*, 1:279).

With most believing superstitious wish
Presageful have I gaz'd upon the bars,   30
To watch the *stranger* there! and oft belike,
With unclos'd lids, already had I dreamt
Of my sweet birthplace, and the old church-tower,
Whose bells, the poor man's only music, rang
From morn to evening, all the hot fair-day,   35
So sweetly, that they stirr'd and haunted me
With a wild pleasure, falling on mine ear
Most like articulate sounds of things to come!
So gaz'd I, till the soothing things, I dreamt,
Lull'd me to sleep, and sleep prolong'd my dreams!   40
And so I brooded all the following morn,
Aw'd by the stern preceptor's face, mine eye
Fix'd with mock study on my swimming book:
Save if the door half-open'd, and I snatch'd
A hasty glance, and still my heart leapt up,   45
For still I hop'd to see the *stranger's* face,
Townsman, or aunt, or sister more belov'd,
My play-mate[4] when we both were cloth'd alike!

    Dear babe, that sleepest cradled by my side,
Whose gentle breathings, heard in this dead calm,[5]   50
Fill up the interspersed vacancies
And momentary pauses of the thought!
My babe so beautiful! it fills my heart
With tender gladness, thus to look at thee,
And think, that thou shalt learn far other lore,   55
And in far other scenes! For I was rear'd
In the great city, pent mid cloisters dim,[6]
And saw nought lovely but the sky and stars.
But *thou*, my babe! Shalt wander, like a breeze,
By lakes and sandy shores, beneath the crags   60
Of ancient mountain, and beneath the clouds,
Which image in their bulk both lakes and shores
And mountain crags: so shalt thou see and hear
The lovely shapes and sounds intelligible
Of that eternal language, which thy God   65
Utters, who from eternity doth teach
Himself in all, and all things in himself.
Great universal Teacher! he shall mould
Thy spirit, and by giving make it ask.

    Therefore all seasons shall be sweet to thee,   70
Whether the summer clothe the general earth[7]
With greenness, or the redbreasts sit and sing

---

4. C's sister Anne (d. 1791).
5. In the errata of *SL*, C changed "dead calm" to "deep calm" (line 50) and "fills" to "thrills" (line 53).
6. Cf. *Paradise Lost* 9.445–64: "As one who long in populous City pent, / Where Houses thick and Sewers annoy the Aire."
7. Generating earth, i.e., fertile.

Betwixt the tufts of snow on the bare branch
Of mossy apple-tree, while all the thatch
Smokes in the sun-thaw: whether the eave-drops fall   75
Heard only in the trances[8] of the blast,
Or whether the secret ministery of cold
Shall hang them up in silent icicles,

"Frost at Midnight" in *Fears in Solitude* (1798) with Coleridge's revisions (see p. 123, n. 1 herein). The verso prints an advertisement for "Poems / by W. Cowper."

---

8. In a copy of *SL* now at Harvard, the printer set "traces," and C corrected it to "trances" with the explanation "Trances—i.e. the brief moments of profound silence."

Quietly shining to the quiet moon,[9]
Like those, my babe! which, ere to-morrow's warmth   80
Have capp'd their sharp keen points with pendulous drops,
Will catch thine eye, and with their novelty
Suspend thy little soul; then make thee shout,
And stretch and flutter from thy mother's arms
As thou would'st fly for very eagerness.[1]   85

February 1798.

FROM THE MORNING POST AND THE ANNUAL ANTHOLOGY (1800)

Coleridge began writing for the *Morning Post* in December 1797 after James Mackintosh (1765–1832) introduced him to the editor, Daniel Stuart. Between December 1797 and the following summer he submitted nine short articles and a dozen poems, as well as three or four jointly authored with Wordsworth. After he returned from Germany, he contributed poems again from August 1799 to 1803, when Stuart sold the *Morning Post*. From December 1799 until the end of March 1800, he wrote articles weekly and sometimes daily, after which he submitted articles irregularly until 1803. He published in the *Morning Post* many of his political poems, including his addition to his earlier contribution to Robert Southey's *Joan of Arc* (1796), "The Visions of the Maid of Orleans," printed here from the *Morning Post*. He also published a shortened version of "Dejection: An Ode" in 1802 along with a number of minor poems and epigrams. After his return from Malta in 1806, he occasionally contributed minor poems to the *Courier*, partly owned by Stuart, and wrote articles frequently from May to September 1811 and irregularly until 1818.

In March 1800 Coleridge told Thomas Poole that Stuart offered him "half shares in the two Papers, the M.P. & Courier, if I would devote myself with him to them" (*CL*, 1:582), but Coleridge declined, content, he said, to accept a meager income from newspaper work and devote himself to literature and philosophy. In the *Biographia*, having explained his journalistic principles, he wrote that "the rapid and unusual increase in the

---

9. Dorothy Wordsworth wrote in her journal for February 17, 1798: "A deep snow upon the ground. * * * The sun shone bright and clear. A deep stillness in the thickest part of the wood, undisturbed except by the occasional dropping of the snow from the holly boughs; no other sound but that of the water, and the slender notes of a redbreast, which sang at intervals on the outskirts of the southern side of the wood" (*DWJ*, 7).

1. In the Morgan copy C crossed out lines 80–85 and wrote "The six last lines I omit because they destroy the rondo, and return upon itself of the Poem. Poems of this kind & length ought to be coiled with its tails round its head. S. T. C." See p. 122 for illustration. In 1815 C wrote to Joseph Cottle that "the common end of all *narrative*, nay, of *all*, Poems is to convert a *series* into a *Whole*: to make those events, which in real or imagined History move on in a *strait* Line, assume to our Understandings a *circular* motion—the snake with its Tail in its Mouth. Hence indeed the almost flattering and yet appropriate Term, Poesy—i.e. poiēsis = *making*" (*CL*, 4:545). In subsequent printings (e.g., in *SL*), the poem ended with line 79.

sale of the Morning Post is a sufficient pledge, that genuine impartiality with a respectable portion of literary talent will secure the success of a newspaper without the aid of party or ministerial patronage. * * * Yet in these labors I employed, and in the belief of partial friends wasted, the prime and manhood of my intellect. Most assuredly, they added nothing to my fortune or my reputation" (BL [CC], 1:214–15). After Coleridge's death, his nephew Henry Nelson Coleridge published Coleridge's Table Talk (1835), which recorded Coleridge as saying, "I raised the sale of the Morning Post from an inconsiderable number to 7000 a day, in the course of one year." (Specimens of the Table Talk of the Late Samuel Taylor Coleridge [1835], 1:173). Offended by Coleridge's suggestion that he was responsible for the success of the paper and that Coleridge was poorly paid while Stuart made a fortune, Stuart explained in the Gentleman's Magazine (May to August 1838) the growth of the Morning Post. When he bought the paper in 1795, it sold 350 copies a day, which rose, through Stuart's efforts, to 4,500 when he sold it in 1803, and when no other daily morning paper sold above 3,000 (May 1838: 490–91; June 1838: 579). Stuart belittled Coleridge's contributions to the paper's success and listed among Coleridge's failures his inability to meet deadlines. Stuart supported Coleridge financially for years, paying him for essays not delivered, loaning him money, and supporting The Friend, yet David Erdman's edition of Essays on His Times proves that Coleridge wrote many more articles for the two papers than Stuart credited.

In 1799 Robert Southey, who also contributed poetry to the Morning Post, edited the first of two volumes of The Annual Anthology, based, as its brief Advertisement said, on the anthologies "known in France and Germany, under the title of Almanacks of the Muses": "Of the poems contained in this volume, none have appeared in any regular form. Many have been printed in the Morning Post." Coleridge did not contribute to the first volume, but he had fifteen poems and twelve epigrams in the second volume, published in February 1800. Some appeared under his own name or anonymously, and others, under various pseudonyms. He was willing to give Southey the poems in Fears in Solitude, but Joseph Johnson held the copyright. He contributed "This Lime-Tree Bower My Prison," which had not appeared in the Morning Post. He offered "Christabel," "were it finished & finished as spiritedly as it commences." Coleridge complained that "the great & master fault" of the first volume of The Annual Anthology "was the want of arrangement / it is called a Collection, & meant to be continued annually; yet was distinguished in nothing from any other single volume of poems, equally good" (CL, 1:545). Southey thought of the anthology as a collection of his "lesser ballads" and saw no "advantage from method—mixed is best" (New Letters of Robert Southey, ed. Kenneth Curry [New York, 1965], 1:181, 207).

"The Visions of the Maid of Orleans" is here printed from the Morning Post, and the other poems are printed from The Annual Anthology (1800) in the order of the volume.

The Visions of the Maid of Orleans[1]

A Fragment, by S. T. Coleridge

If there be Beings of higher class than Man,
I deem no nobler province they possess
Than by disposal of apt circumstance
To rear up kingdoms: and the deeds they promp,
Distinguishing from mortal agency,   5
They chuse their servants from such mean estates
As still the Epic Song half fears to name,
Disdain'd by all the minstrelcies that strike
The palace roof, soothing the Monarch's pride.

And such perhaps the Spirit, who (if words   10
Witness'd by answering deeds may claim our faith,)
Held commune with that warrior-maid of France
Who scourg'd the invader. From her childish[2] days
With wisdom,[3] mother of retired thoughts,
Her soul had dwelt; and she was quick to mark   15
The good and evil thing, in human lore

1. C published this poem with his name in the title in *MP*, December 26, 1797. Southey began drafting *Joan of Arc* in the summer of 1793 and explained to a friend on Bastille Day, July 14, 1793, "Vive La Republique! my Joan is a great democrat or rather will be" (*New Letters of Robert Southey*, ed. Kenneth Curry [New York: 1965], 1:29). Southey revised the poem with C's assistance in the summer of 1795. C contributed scattered lines to books 1, 3, and 4 and about 360 of the first 450 lines of book 2, described in the argument as "Preternatural Agency" (*PW* [CC], 1:205–24). In a manuscript note at the end of book 4, Coleridge wrote, "All the preceding I gave my best advice in correcting. From this time Southey and I parted" (*CM* [CC], 5:119). The two quarreled over the failure of pantisocracy in August 1795. C added to his lines in book 2 the fragment printed here as "The Visions of the Maid of Orleans" and intended to expand it further as the opening work in *Poems* (1797) "entitled the progress of European Liberty, a vision," or "The Progress of Liberty—or the Visions of the maid of Orleans" (*CL*, 1:243, 285). He sent the expanded version to Charles Lamb, who complained in early February 1797, "You cannot surely mean to degrade the Joan of Arc into a pot girl; you are not going, I hope, to annex to that most splendid ornament of Southey's poem all this cock & a bull story of Joan the Publican's daughter of Neufchatel, with the lamentable episode of a waggoner, his wife & six children, the texture will be most lamentably disproportionate" (*LL*, 1:94). Joan was not canonized until 1908, so her cultural image was not fixed in the 1790s. Lamb preferred Southey's idealized Joan to C's innkeeper's daughter and included in his letter to C severe criticisms of C's style, some of which are noted here. C wrote his publisher on February 10, 1797, that "the lines which I added to my lines in the 'Joan of Arc,' have been so little approved by Charles Lamb, to whom I sent them, that although I differ from him in opinion, I have not heart to finish the poem" (*CL*, 1:309).
      In 1814, at William Hood's request, C read through a copy of the first version of *Joan of Arc* in order to identify his lines. He summarized Joan's character: "I was really astonished * * * at the transmogrification of the fanatic Virago into a modern novel-pawing Proselyte of the age of Reason, a Tom Paine in Petticoats, but *so* lovely" (*CL*, 3:510). At the same time, he toyed with the title "The National Independence or the Vision of the Maid of Orleans" (*CN*, 3:4202; *PW* [CC], 1:912), in which Joan was to be a symbol of justice and the resistance to conquerors like Napoleon. Finally, he constructed "The Destiny of Nations," printed as the last poem in *SL*, by placing the fragment printed here in the position in book 2 where Southey had described Joan's vision of the castle of Ambition, in a style that C called "school-boy wretched Allegoric Machinery" (*CL*, 3:510). Thus the narrative printed here took the place of Southey's allegorical house of horrors and is rather a prelude to Joan's visions than the visions themselves.
2. In "Destiny of Nations" C changed "childish" to "infant."
3. C may have in mind the feminine Wisdom in Ecclesiasticus 24. The line appears in a notebook entry in the fall of 1796 (*CN*, 1:180), at a time when C was reading Ecclesiasticus (*CN*, 1:265–69).

Undisciplined: for lowly was her birth,
And Heaven had doom'd her early years to toil,
That, pure from tyranny's least deed, herself
Unfear'd by fellow-natures, she might wait   20
On the poor lab'ring-man with kindly looks,
And minister refreshment to the tir'd
Way-wanderer, when along the rough-hewn bench
The sultry[4] man had stretch'd him, and aloft
Watch'd the gay sign-board on the mulberry bough   25
Swing to the pleasant breeze! Here too the Maid[5]
Learnt more than schools could teach, Man's shifting mind,
His vices and his sorrows; and full oft
At tales of cruel wrong, and strange distress,
Had wept and shiver'd. To the tott'ring Eld   30
Still as a daughter she would run; she plac'd
His cold limbs at the sunny door, and lov'd
To hear him story in his garrulous sort
Of his eventful years, all come and gone.—
So twenty summers pass'd. The Virgin's form   35
Active and tall, nor sloth nor luxury
Had sicklied o'er; her front sublime and broad;
Her flexile eye-brows wildly hair'd and low;
And her large eye, now bright, now unillum'd,
Spake more than woman's thought: and all her face   40
Was moulded to such features, as declar'd
That Pity there had oft and strongly work'd—
And sometimes Indignation! Bold her mien,
And like an haughty Huntress[6] of the woods
She mov'd: yet sure she was a gentle Maid!   45
And in each motion her most innocent soul
Out-beam'd so brightly, that who saw would say,
Guilt was a thing impossible in her.—[7]
Nor idly would have said, for she had liv'd
In this bad world, as in a place of tombs,   50
And touch'd not the pollutions of the dead.

'Twas the cold season, when the Rustic's eye
From the drear desolate whiteness of his fields
Rolls, for relief, to watch the skiey tints,
And clouds slow-varying their huge imagery;   55
When now, as she was wont, the healthful Maid

4. In "Destiny of Nations" C changed "sultry" to "sweltry."
5. Lamb wrote a letter to C on February 13, apologizing for his earlier harsh judgment and explaining that "I was only struck with [a] certain faulty disproportion in the matter and the
   style, which I still think I perceive, between these lines and the former ones." Lamb noted
   the version he read begins with speculations "into the sublimest mysteries of theory concerning man's nature and his noblest destination. * * * After all this cometh Joan, a *publican's* daughter, sitting on an ale-house *bench*, and marking the *swingings* of the *signboard*,
   finding a poor man, his wife and six children, starved to death with cold, and thence roused
   into a state of mind proper to receive visions emblematical of equality; which what the devil
   Joan had to do with, I don't know, or indeed with the French and American revolutions" (*LL*,
   1:101–02).
6. Artemis, the Greek goddess the Romans associated with Diana, was a virgin huntress.
7. C used lines 46–48 (var.) to describe Dorothy Wordsworth in July 1797 (*CL*, 1:330).

Had left her pallet, ere one beam of day
Slanted the fog-smoke. She went forth alone,
Urged by the indwelling Angel-guide, (that oft
With dim inexplicable sympathies,   60
Disquieting the heart, shapes out our course
To some predoom'd adventure) and the ascent
New pass'd of that steep upland (on whose top
Not seldom some poor nightly-roaming man
Shouts to himself, there first the cottage lights   65
Seen in Neufchatel's vale) she slop'd a-down
The bleak hill's further side, till at the base,
In the first entrance of the level road,
A waggon stay'd her speed. Its foremost horse
Lay with stretch'd limbs: the others yet alive,   70
But stiff with cold, stood motionless, their manes
Hoar with the frozen night-dews. Dismally
The dark-red dawn now glimmer'd; but its gleams
Disclosed no face of man. The Maiden paus'd,
And hail'd who might be near.[8] No voice reply'd.   75
At length she listen'd, from the vehicle
A voice so feeble, that it almost seem'd
Distant: and feebly with slow effort push'd
A miserable man crawl'd forth: his limbs
The silent Frost had eat, scathing like fire!   80
Faint on the shafts he rested: she meanwhile
Saw crowded close beneath the coverture
A mother and her children, lifeless all,
Yet lovely: not a lineament was marr'd,
Death had put on so slumberlike a form!   85
It was a piteous sight! and one, a babe,
Lay on the woman's arm, its little hand
Smooth on her bosom. Wildly pale the maid
Gaz'd at the living wretch, mute questioning.
He, his head feebly turning, on the group   90
Look'd with a vacant stare, and his eye spoke
The drowsy calm, that steals on worn out anguish.
She shudder'd; but each vainer pang subdu'd,
Quick disentangling from the foremost horse
The rustic bands, with difficulty and toil   95
The stiff cramp'd team forc'd homewards. There arriv'd,
Anxious she tended him with healing herbs
And wept and pray'd; but green putridity[9]
Spread o'er his limbs, and ere the noontide hour
The hov'ring spirits of his wife and babes   100
Hail'd him immortal![1]—Yet amid his pangs

8. Lamb enumerated "some woeful blemishes, some of 'em sad deviations from that simplicity which was your aim. 'haild who might be near.' (the canvas coverture moving by the bye is laughable)" (*LL*, 1:95). Lamb then listed many other blemishes, many of which C changed in the *MP* version. Lamb's other examples that C left unrevised are noted below.
9. Lamb disliked "green putridity," which C revised to "the numb power of Death" in "Destiny of Nations" (*LL*, 1:95).
1. Lamb commented, "hail'd him immortal (rather ludicrous again)" (*LL*, 1:95).

With interruptions strange from ghastly throes
His voice had falter'd out this simple tale.
The village where he dwelt, an husbandman,
By sudden foragers was seiz'd and fir'd   105
Late on the yester-evening, with his wife
And little ones he hurried his escape.
They saw the neighbouring hamlets flame: they heard
Uproar and shrieks: and terror-struck drove on
Thro' unfrequented roads, a weary way,   110
But saw nor house nor cottage: all had quench'd
Their evening hearthfires; for the alarm had spread.
The air clipp'd keen, the night was fang'd with frost,
And they provisionless; the weeping wife
Ill hush'd her children's cries—and still they cry'd,   115
Till fright, and cold, and hunger drank their life:
They clos'd their eyes in sleep, nor knew 'twas death!
He only, lashing his o'er wearied team,
Gain'd a sad respite, till beside the base
Of the high hill his foremost horse dropp'd dead.   120
Then hopeless, strengthless, sick for lack of food,
He crept beneath the coverture, and doz'd
Till waken'd by the maiden. Such his tale.[2]

Ah suffering to the height of what was suffer'd,[3]
Stung with too keen a sympathy, the maid   125
Brooded with moving lips, mute, startful, dark;
And now her flush'd tumultuous features shot
Such strange vivacity as fires the eye
Of misery fancy-craz'd; and now once more
Naked, and void, and fix'd—and all within   130
The unquiet silence of confused thought
And shapeless feelings. For a mighty hand
Was strong upon her, till in th' heat of soul
To the high hill top tracing back her steps
Aside the beacon, down whose moulder'd stones   135
The tender ivy-trails crept thinly, there
Unconscious of the driving element,
Yea, swallow'd up in th' ominous dream, she sate
Ghastly as broad-eyed slumber! a dim anguish
Breath'd from her look; and still with pant and sob   140
Inly she toil'd to fly, and still subdu'd,
Felt an inevitable presence near!

---

2. Lamb disliked "such his tale" (*LL*, 1:95). C's source for the story of the frozen family came
   from *An Accurate and Impartial Narrative of the War*, which related the campaigns of 1793
   to 1795, some paragraphs of which C printed in *The Watchman*, April 19, 1796 (*Watchman*
   [CC], 238–41).
3. Lamb also disliked this line (*LL*, 1:95). Cf. *The Tempest* 1.2.5–6: Miranda "suffered / With
   those that I saw suffer." See "[On Ancient and Modern Drama and *The Tempest*]" (p. 326
   herein).

Thus as she toil'd in troubled ecstacy,
An horror of great darkness wrapt her round,
And a voice utter'd forth unearthly tones   145
Calming her soul. "O thou of the Most High
Chosen, whom all the perfected in heaven
Behold expectant."

Recantation,
Illustrated in the Story of the Mad Ox[1]

By S. T. Coleridge.

I.

An Ox, long fed with musty hay,
    And work'd with yoke and chain,
Was turn'd out on an April day,
When fields are in their best array,
And growing grasses sparkle gay,   5
    At once with sun and rain.

II.

The grass was fine, the sun was bright,
    With truth I may aver it;
The Ox was glad, as well he might,
Thought a green meadow no bad sight,   10
And frisk'd to shew his huge delight,
    Much like a beast of spirit.

---

1. Published unsigned in *MP*, July 30, 1798, as "A Tale" with this headnote: "The following amusing Tale, gives a very humourous description of the French Revolution, which is represented as an Ox." Reprinted in *AA* with C's signature, minor alterations, and the important change in the final two lines noted herein. In a copy of *AA*, C entered a manuscript note: "Written when fears were entertained of an Invasion—& Mr Sheridan & Mr Tierney were absurdly represented as having *recanted*, because tho' [? opposed] to the war in its origin, they [. . .]" (*CM* [CC], 1:92). C's final words were cut away in re-binding. EHC speculates that C's sentence might have ended "changed their opinion when Revolutionists became unfaithful to their principles" (*PW*, 1:299). Peter Kitson suggests a source for the ox goaded to madness in James Burgh's *Political Disquisitions* ("Coleridge, James Burgh, and the Mad Ox: A Source for Coleridge's 'Recantation,' " *N&Q* 38 [September 1991]: 299–301). The final two lines in the *MP* version were "That TIERNEY's wounded Mr. PITT, / And his fine tongue enchanted?" Woodring explains that George Tierney (1761–1830) voted for Pitt's renewal of the suspension of the Habeas Corpus Act in April 1798, but an argument between them resulted in a bloodless duel on May 27. Pitt withdrew ill to Bath, and false rumors spread that Pitt had been wounded. Thus the *MP* version, which C thought mangled in publication, ends with Tierney overcoming Pitt. The *AA* version ends with Tierney's supporting Pitt on Habeas Corpus and allusions to Sheridan's insertion of patriotic speeches in his adaptation of Kotzebue's play *Pizarro*, performed in June 1799 (Woodring, 139–43). For Sheridan, see title note to "Effusion VI," p. 15 herein. In the *AA* version C's lines on recantation are ironic. As C's manuscript note may suggest, Sheridan and Tierney remained loyal to the principles, if not the events, of the French Revolution. C's ox may allude to the "Great Bedfordshire Ox," who runs amuck in St. James's Street, London, in James Gillray's cartoon "Promis'd Horrors of the French Invasion" (October 20, 1796). Gillray's ox is the duke of Bedford, a follower of Charles James Fox, who supported the French Revolution.

III.

"Stop, neighbours! stop! why these alarms?
    "The Ox is only glad."—
But still they pour from cots and farms—   15
Halloo! the Parish is up in arms
(A *hoaxing*[2] hunt has always charms)
    HALLOO! THE OX IS MAD.

IV.

The frighted beast scamper'd about,
    Plunge! thro' the hedge he drove—   20
The mob pursue with hideous rout,
A bull-dog fastens on his snout,
He gores the dog, his tongue hangs out—
    He's mad, he's mad, by Jove!

V.

"Stop, neighbours, stop!" aloud did call   25
    A sage of sober hue.
But all at once on him they fall,
And women squeak and children squall,
"What! would you have him toss us all!
    "And damme! who are you?"   30

VI.

Ah hapless sage! his ears they stun,
    And curse him o'er and o'er—
"You bloody-minded dog!" (cries one)
"To slit your windpipe were good fun—
" 'Od bl— you for an *impious*[3] son   35
    "Of a presbyterian[4] w——re!

VII.

"You'd have him gore the parish priest,
    "And run against the altar—
"You *Fiend!*"—The sage his warnings ceas'd,
And North, and South, and West, and East,   40
Halloo! they follow the poor beast,
    Mat, Dick, Tom, Bob, and Walter.

VIII.

Old Lewis, 'twas his evil day,
    Stood trembling in his shoes;
The Ox was his—what could he say?   45

2. The *OED* cites Francis Grose, *A Classical Dictionary of the Vulgar Tongue* (1785) as "bantering, ridiculing" and the *Gentleman's Magazine* 70 (1800): 947: "*Hoax, Hoxe, Goaxe*—a word much in vogue in political circles. It signifies to make any person the object of ridicule by a species of acclamation."
3. "One of the many *fine* words which the most uneducated had about this time a constant opportunity of acquiring from the sermons in the pulpit, and the proclamations on the——— corners." [C's note in *AA*.] The "bl—" here is "bl—st" in *MP*, i.e., "blast."
4. Presbyterians were dissenters and often supporters of the French Revolution.

His legs were stiffen'd with dismay,
The Ox ran o'er him mid the fray,
  And gave him his death's bruise.

IX.

The frighted beast ran on—but here,
  The gospel scarce more true is—   50
My muse stops short in mid career—
Nay! gentle reader! do not sneer,
I cannot chuse but drop a tear,
  A tear for good old Lewis.[5]

X.

The frighted beast ran thro' the town,   55
  All follow'd, boy and dad,
Bulldog, Parson, Shopman, Clown,
The Publicans rush'd from the Crown,
"Halloo! hamstring him! cut him down!"
  They drove the poor Ox mad.   60

XI.

Should you a Rat to madness teize,[6]
  Why even a Rat might plague you:
There's no Philosopher but sees,
That Rage and Fear are *one* disease—
Tho' that may burn and this may freeze,   65
  They're both alike the ague.

XII.

And so this Ox in frantic mood
  Faced round like any Bull—
The mob turn'd tail, and he pursued,
Till they with fright and fear were stew'd,   70
And not a chick of all this brood,
  But had his belly full.

XIII.

Old Nick's astride the beast, 'tis clear—
  Old Nicholas to a tittle!
But all agree, he'd disappear,   75
Would but the parson venture near,
And thro' his teeth[7] right o'er the steer,
  Squirt out some fasting spittle.

5. Louis XVI of France was executed on January 21, 1793.
6. To drive a hunted beast (*OED*).
7. "According to the superstition of the West Countries, if you meet the Devil, you may either cut him in half with a straw, or you may cause him instantly to disappear by spitting over his horns." [C's note in *AA*.]

XIV.

Achilles was a warrior fleet,
   The Trojans he could worry—   80
Our parson too was swift of feet,
But shew'd it chiefly in retreat!
The victor Ox scour'd down the street,
   The mob fled hurry-skurry.

XV.

Thro' gardens, lanes, and fields new-plough'd,   85
   Thro' *his* hedge and thro' *her* hedge,
He plung'd, and toss'd, and bellow'd loud,
Till in his madness he grew proud,
To see this helter skelter crowd,
   That had more wrath than courage.   90

XVI.

Alas! to mend the breaches wide
   He made for these poor ninnies,
They all must work, whate'er betide,
Both days and months, and pay beside,
(Sad news for Avarice and for Pride)   95
   A sight of golden guineas.

XVII.

But here once more to view did pop
   The man that kept his senses.
And now he cried—"Stop, neighbours! stop!
"The Ox is mad! I would not swop,   100
"No, not a school-boy's farthing top,
   "For all the parish fences.

XVIII.

"The Ox is mad! Ho! Dick, Bob, Mat!
   "What means this coward fuss?
"Ho! stretch this rope across the plat—   105
" 'Twill trip him up—or if not that,
"Why damme! we must lay him flat—
   "See, here's my blunderbuss!"

XIX.

"A lying dog! just now he said,
   "The Ox was only glad.   110
"Let's break his presbyterian head!"—
"Hush! (quoth the sage) you've been misled,
"No quarrels now—let's all make head—
   "*You drove the poor Ox mad!*"

XX.

As thus I sat in careless chat,   115
   With the morning's wet newspaper,
In eager haste, without his hat,
As blind and blundering as a bat,
In came that fierce aristocrat,[8]
   Our pursy Woollen-draper.   120

XXI.

And so my Muse perforce drew bit,
   And in he rush'd and panted—
"Well, have you heard?"—"No! not a whit."
"What, ha'nt you heard?"—"Come out with it—"
"That Tierney votes for Mister Pitt,   125
   "And Sheridan's *recanted*."

Lines
Written in the Album at Elbingerode,
in the Hartz Forest[1]

I stood on Brocken's[2] sovran height, and saw
Woods crowding upon woods, hills over hills,
A *surging* scene, and only limited
By the blue distance. Heavily my way
Homeward I dragg'd thro' fir-groves evermore,   5
Where bright green moss heaves in sepulchral forms,
Speckled with sunshine; and, but seldom heard,
The sweet bird's song became an hollow sound;
And the breeze murmuring indivisibly,
Preserv'd its solemn murmur most distinct   10
From many a note of many a waterfall,
And the brook's chatter; 'mid whose islet stones
The dingy kidling with its tinkling bell
Leapt frolicsome, or old romantic goat
Sat, his white beard slow waving. I mov'd on   15

8. Not a nobleman, but a conservative supporter of the nobility.
1. Published unsigned in *MP*, September 17, 1799, and in *AA* signed "C." C sent a version to
his wife on May 17, 1799, with the comment that, responding to a request to write in the album at the inn, "I wrote the follow[ing] Lines, which I send to you, not that they possess a
grain of merit as Poetry: but because they contain a true account of my journey from the
Brocken to Elbinrode [*sic*]." They arrived at "the foot of the Great Brocken / without a rival
the highest Mountain in all the north of Germany, & the seat of innumerable Superstitions.
On the first day of May all the Witches dance here at midnight. * * * We visited the Blocks-
berg, a sort of Bowling Green inclosed by huge Stones, something like those at Stonehenge;
& this is the Witches' Ball-room / thence proceeded to the house on the [hill] where we
dined / & now we descended. * * * I was really unwell" (*CL*, 1:504). Clement Carlyon
(1777–1864), who accompanied C on the walk, reported that they climbed to view the
specter of the Brocken, observable when the sun was on the horizon, and an individual's
shadow was projected on clouds (*Early Years and Late Reflections* [1856], 1:42–50, 170–74;
CN, 1:430–31n.). C used the image in "Constancy to an Ideal Object" (p. 210
herein). C's visit to the Brocken is the source of the "Witches' Home" in "A Letter to ——,"
line 192.
2. "The highest Mountain in the Hartz, and indeed in North Germany." [C's note in *AA*.]

In low and languid mood,[3] for I had found
That grandest scenes have but imperfect charms,
Where the sight vainly wanders, nor beholds
One spot with which the heart associates
Holy remembrances of Friend or Child,   20
Or gentle Maid, our first and early love,
Or Father, or the venerable name
Of our adored Country!—O thou Queen,
Thou delegated Deity of Earth,
O dear, dear, England! How my longing eye   25
Turn'd westward, shaping in the steady clouds
Thy sands and high white cliffs! O native Land,
Fill'd with the thought of Thee, this heart was proud,
Yea, mine eye swam with tears, that all the view
From sovran Brocken, woods, and woody hills,   30
Floated away, like a departing dream,
Feeble and dim!—Stranger, these impulses
Blame thou not lightly; nor will I profane
With hasty judgement or injurious doubt
That man's sublimer spirit, who can feel   35
That GOD is every where! the GOD who fram'd
Mankind to be one mighty Family,
Himself our Father, and the World our home.

C.

To a Friend[1]

Who Had Declared His Intention of Writing No More Poetry

Dear CHARLES! while yet thou wert a babe, I ween
That GENIUS plunged thee in that wizard fount,
Hight Castalie:[2] and (sureties for thy faith)
That PITY and SIMPLICITY stood by,
And promis'd for thee, that thou should'st renounce   5
The World's low cares and lying vanities,
Stedfast and rooted in the heavenly Muse,

---

3. " 'When I have gaz'd / From some high eminence on goodly vales, / And cots and villages em-
bower'd below, / The thought would rise that all to me was strange / Amid the scenes so fair,
nor one small spot / Where my tired mind might rest, and call it *home*.' Southey's *Hymn to
the Penates*." [C's note in *AA*; C quotes (var.) from the final poem in Southey's *Poems* (1797),
lines 250–55.]

1. Written to Charles Lamb. Cottle reported that C wrote the poem after the death of Robert
Burns, who died July 21, 1796, "to be inserted in a Bristol Paper," probably in September in
Sara Farley's Bristol Journal (*PW* [CC], 2:369) to raise money for Burns's family (*ER*, 1:244).
Signed "*ESTEESI. 1796*" in *AA* after the final line. In the letter announcing that his sister
in a fit of madness had murdered their mother on September 22, 1796, Lamb added a post
script, "mention nothing of poetry. I have destroyed every vestige of past vanities of that
kind" (*LL*, 1:45).

2. The Castalian spring sacred to the Muses on Mount Parnassus. C borrows from Spenser,
"The Ruines of Time," lines 428–31: "For not to haue been dipt in *Lethe* lake, / Could saue
the sonne of *Thetis* from to die; / But that blinde bard did him immortall make / With verses,
dipt in deaw of *Castalie*" (*Works of Edmund Spenser*, ed. Edwin Greenlaw et al. [Baltimore,
1947], 8:49).

And wash'd and sanctified to POESY.
Yes—thou wert plunged, but with forgetful hand
Held, as by Thetis[3] erst her warrior son: 10
And with those recreant[4] unbaptized heels
Thou'rt flying from thy bounden ministeries—
So sore it seems and burthensome a task
To weave unwithering flowers! But take thou heed:
For thou art vulnerable, wild-eyed Boy!   15
And I have arrows[5] mystically tipt,
Such as may stop thy speed. Is thy BURNS dead
And shall he die unwept and sink to earth
"Without the meed of one melodious tear?"[6]
Thy BURNS,[7] and Nature's own beloved Bard   20
Who to "the Illustrious[8] of his native land
So properly did look for patronage."
Ghost of Mæcenas![9] hide thy blushing face!
They snatch'd him from the sickle and the plough—
To gauge ale-firkins![1]
                       O for shame return!   25
On a bleak rock, midway the Aonian mount,[2]
There stands a lone and melancholy tree,
Whose aged branches to the midnight blast
Make solemn music: pluck its darkest bough,
Ere yet the unwholesome night-dew be exhal'd,   30
And weeping wreath it round thy poet's tomb.
Then in the outskirts, where pollutions grow,
Pick stinking hensbane, and the dusky flowers

---

3. The goddess Thetis, mother of Achilles, dipped him into the river Styx by the heel, which made him invulnerable, except at that heel.
4. Both faint hearted and unfaithful to duty.
5. C cites Pindar's Olympian Odes: "I have many swift arrows / * * * that speak to those who understand, but for the whole subject, they need / interpreters * * * Now aim the bow at the mark, come, my heart. At whom / do we shoot, and this time launch from a kindly spirit / our arrows of fame?" (*Pindar*, trans. William H. Race [LCL, 1997], 73).
6. From Milton, "Lycidas," line 14: "Without the meed of som melodious tear."
7. Lamb wrote to C December 10, 1796, "Burns was the god of my idolatry, as Bowles of yours" (*LL*, 1:78).
8. "Verbatim from Burns's Dedication of his Poem to the Nobility and Gentry of the Caledonian Hunt." [C's note in *AA*.] Burns's dedication of the 1787 Edinburgh edition of his poems "To the Noblemen and Gentlemen of the Caledonian Hunt" reads in part: "MY LORDS AND GENTLEMEN,—A Scottish Bard, proud of the name, and whose highest ambition is to sing in his Country's service—where shall he so properly look for patronage as to the illustrious Names of his native Land; those who bear the honours and inherit the virtues of their Ancestors? * * * Though much indebted to your goodness, I do not approach you, my Lords and Gentlemen, in the usual style of dedication, to thank you for past favours; that path is so hackneyed by prostituted Learning, that honest Rusticity is ashamed of it. Nor do I present this Address with the venal soul of a servile Author, looking for a continuation of those favours: I was bred to the Plough, and am independent." The Caledonian Hunt was "an association composed principally of noblemen and gentlemen of Scottish ancestry, whose chief tie was their common interest in field sports, as well as in races, balls, and assemblies for social and other purposes" (John D. Ross, *A Burns Handbook* [Stirling, 1931], 72–73).
9. Roman friend of the Emperor Augustus and patron of Virgil and Horace.
1. A small cask.
2. Aonia was the location of Mount Helicon and the fountains Aganippe and Hippocrene, sacred to Apollo and the Muses. Cf. *Paradise Lost* and Milton's "adventrous Song, / That with no middle flight intends to soar / Above th' *Aonian* Mount" (1.13–15).

Of night-shade,[3] or its red and tempting fruit.
These with stopp'd nostril and glove-guarded hand   35
Knit in nice intertexture, so to twine
The illustrious Brow of SCOTCH NOBILITY![4]

ESTEESI. 1796.

This Lime-Tree Bower My Prison,
A Poem,[1]

Addressed to Charles Lamb, of the India-House, London

ADVERTISEMENT.

In the June of 1797, some long-expected Friends paid a visit to the Author's Cottage; and on the morning of their arrival he met with an accident, which disabled him from walking during the whole time of their stay. One evening, when they had left him for a few hours, he composed the following lines, in the Garden Bower.

Well, they are gone, and here must I remain,
This lime-tree bower my prison! I have lost
Such beauties and such feelings, as had been
Most sweet to have remember'd, even when age
Had dimm'd my eyes to blindness! They, meanwhile,   5
My friends, whom I may never meet again,

---

3. Henbane and nightshade are poisonous plants.
4. Cottle reported that "in reading the Poem immediately after it was written, the rasping force which Mr. C. gave to" lines 17–37 "was inimitable." Cottle added that "Mr. Coleridge had often, in the keenest terms, expressed his contemptuous indignation at the Scotch patrons of the poet, in making him an exciseman! so that something biting was expected. It may here be noticed, that if Mr. C.'s nature had been less benevolent, and he had given full vent to the irascible and satirical; the restrained elements of which abounded in his spirit, he would have obtained the least enviable of all kinds of pre-eminence, and have become the undisputed Modern Juvenal" (*ER*, 1:244–5). *Exciseman*: tax collector.
1. Two early versions are contained in letters. The first is to Robert Southey, July 17, 1797, with the following introduction: "Charles Lamb has been with me for a week. * * * The second day after Wordsworth came to me, dear Sara accidently emptied a skillet of boiling milk on my foot, which confined me during the whole time of C. Lamb's stay & still prevents me from all *walks* longer than a furlong—While Wordsworth, his Sister, & C. Lamb were out one evening; / sitting in the arbour of T. Poole's garden, which communicates with mine, I wrote these lines, with which I am pleased" (*CL*, 1:334). The second letter, now in the Berg Collection in the New York Public Library, was sent to Charles Lloyd. "This Lime-Tree Bower" was first published in *AA* and signed at the end "ESTEESI," an echo of his initials, S. T. C., which C sometimes wrote in English letters and sometimes transliterated into the Greek ΕΣΤΗΣΕ. C explained it "signifies—*He hath stood*—which in these times of apostacy from the principles of Freedom, or of Religion in this country, & from both by the same persons in France, is no unmeaning Signature, if subscribed with humility, & in the remembrance of, Let him that stands take heed lest he fall—. However, it is in truth no more than S. T. C. written in Greek. Es tee see—" (*CL*, 2:867). C used the Greek as his motto. He paraphrases I Corinthians 10.12: "Wherefore let him that thinketh he standeth take heed lest he fall" and echoes God's words in *Paradise Lost*, "I made him just and right, / Sufficient to have stood, though free to fall" (3.98–99). See p. 226, n. 3 herein.

On springy[2] heath along the hill-top edge
Wander in gladness, and wind down, perchance
To that still roaring dell, of which I told;
The roaring dell,[3] o'erwooded, narrow, deep,   10
And only speckled by the mid-day sun;
Where its slim trunk the Ash from rock to rock
Flings arching like a bridge; that branchless Ash
Unsunn'd and damp, whose few poor yellow leaves
Ne'er tremble in the gale, yet tremble still   15
Fann'd by the water-fall! And there my friends,
Behold the dark-green file of long lank weeds,
That all at once (a most fantastic sight!)
Still nod and drip beneath the dripping edge
Of the dim clay-stone.
                              Now my friends emerge   20
Beneath the wide wide Heaven, and view again
The many-steepled track magnificent
Of hilly fields and meadows, and the sea
With some fair bark perhaps which lightly touches
The slip of smooth clear blue betwixt two isles   25
Of purple shadow! Yes! they wander on
In gladness all; but thou, methinks, most glad
My gentle-hearted CHARLES![4] for thou had'st pin'd
And hunger'd after nature many a year
In the great city pent, winning thy way   30
With sad yet patient soul, thro' evil and pain[5]
And strange calamity! Ah slowly sink
Behind the western ridge, thou glorious Sun!

---

2. "[E]lastic, I mean" [C's note in the letter to Southey (CL, 1:335).]
3. In Holford, near Alfoxden, where Wordsworth was living, or a stream valley in the Quan-
   tocks above Nether Stowey. Wordsworth described the scene in a note to his poem "Lines
   Written in Early Spring": "The brook fell down a sloping rock so as to make a waterfall considerable for that country, and, across the pool below had fallen a tree, an ash if I rightly remember, from which rose perpendicularly boughs in search of the light intercepted by the
   deep shade above. The boughs bore leaves of green that for want of sunshine had faded into
   almost lily-white; and, from the underside of this natural sylvan bridge depended long &
   beautiful tresses of ivy which waved gently in the breeze that might be poetically speaking be
   called the breath of the water-fall" (LB [1992], 349).
4. Lamb protested on August 6, 1800, "For God's sake (I never was more serious), don't make
   me ridiculous any more by terming me gentle-hearted in print, or do it in better verses. It did
   well enough five years ago when I came to see you, and was moral coxcomb enough at the
   time you wrote the lines, to feed upon such epithets; but, besides that, the meaning of gentle is equivocal at best, and almost always means poor-spirited, the very quality of gentleness
   is abhorrent to such vile trumpetings. My sentiment is long since vanished" (LL, 1:217–18).
   A week later he repeated his complaint, "In the next edition of the Anthology * * * please to
   blot out gentle hearted, and substitute drunken dog, ragged-head, seld-shaven, odd-ey'd,
   stuttering, or any other epithet which truly and properly belongs to the Gentleman in question" (LL, 1:224). In 1800 Lamb rejects sentiment and sensibility fashionable only a few
   years before. In one copy of AA in which C made extensive revisions to the poem, he did remove one instance of "gentle-hearted Charles," but these revisions never entered later printings of the poem (CM [CC], 1:95).
5. Cf. lines 30–31 with C's lines from Joan of Arc (1796) reprinted in "The Destiny of Nations,"
   lines 124–26: "from Bethabra northward, heavenly Truth / With gradual steps, winning her
   difficult way, / Transfer their rude Faith perfected and pure" (PW, 1:136). John baptized Jesus at Bethabara (John 1.26–28).

Shine in the slant beams of the sinking orb,
Ye purple heath-flowers! richlier burn, ye clouds!   35
Live in the yellow light, ye distant groves!
And kindle, thou blue ocean!—So my Friend
Struck with deep joy may stand, as I have stood,[6]
Silent with swimming sense; yea, gazing round
On the wide landscape,[7] gaze till all doth seem   40
Less gross than bodily, a living thing
Which *acts* upon the mind[8]—and with such hues
As cloath the Almighty Spirit, when he makes
Spirits perceive his presence.[9]
                              A delight
Comes sudden on my heart, and I am glad   45
As I myself were there! Nor in this bower,
This little lime-tree bower have I not mark'd
Much that has sooth'd me. Pale beneath the blaze
Hung the transparent foliage; and I watch'd
Some broad and sunny leaf, and lov'd to see   50
The shadow of the leaf and stem above
Dappling its sunshine! And that Wallnut tree
Was richly ting'd; and a deep radiance lay
Full on the ancient Ivy which *usurps*
Those fronting elms, and now with blackest mass   55
Makes their dark branches gleam a lighter hue
Thro' the late Twilight: and tho' now the Bat
Wheels silent by, and not a Swallow twitters,
Yet still the solitary humble Bee,
Sings in the bean-flower! Henceforth I shall know   60
That Nature ne'er deserts the wise and pure,
No scene so narrow but may well employ[1]
Each faculty of sense, and keep the heart
Awake to love and beauty! And sometimes
'Tis well to be bereft of promis'd good,   65
That we may lift the soul, and contemplate
With lively joy the joys we cannot share.

6. Echoes C's signature at the end of the poem.
7. The version sent to Southey contained the word "view" in place of "landscape." C explained,
   "You remember, I am a *Berkleian*" (*CL*, 1:335). C borrowed the second volume of Berkeley,
   Works (1784) from the Bristol Library from March 10 to 28, 1796 (*Borrowings*, 122).
8. In a copy of *AA*, C deleted "a living thing / Which *acts* upon the mind." C may have made
   this revision shortly after publication (*CM* [CC], 1:95).
9. Lamb complained that C ran "into the unintelligible abstraction-fit about the manner of the
   Deity's making Spirits perceive his presence. God, nor created thing alive, can receive any
   honor from such thin, shew-box, attributes" (*LL*, 1:224). *Show box*: a "box in which objects
   of curiosity are exhibited" (*OED*).
1. Cf. Cowper, *The Task* 5.771–74: The man who sees nature as God's creation "has wings that
   neither sickness, pain, / Nor penury, can cripple or confine. / No nook so narrow but he
   spreads them there / With ease, and is at large" (*Poems of William Cowper*, ed. John D. Baird
   and Charles Ryskamp [Oxford, 1980–95], 2:230).

My gentle-hearted CHARLES! when the last Rook
Beat its straight path along the dusky air
Homewards, I blest it! deeming its black wing[2]   70
(Now a dim speck, now vanishing in the light)
Had cross'd the mighty orb's dilated glory
While thou stood'st gazing; or when all was still
Flew *creeking*[3] o'er thy head, and had a charm
For thee, my gentle-hearted CHARLES! to whom   75
No sound is dissonant, which tells of Life.

ESTEESI.

Sonnet XII[1]

To W. L. Esq. while he sung a Song to Purcell's Music.

While my young cheek retains its healthful hues
    And I have many friends who hold me dear;
    L——! methinks, I would not often hear
Such melodies as thine, lest I should lose
All memory of the wrongs and sore distress,   5
    For which my miserable brethren weep!
    But should uncomforted misfortunes steep
My daily bread in tears and bitterness;
And if at Death's dread moment I should lie
    With no beloved face by my bed-side   10
To fix the last glance of my closing eye,
    O God! such strains breath'd by my angel guide
Would make me pass the cup of anguish by,
Mix with the blest, nor know that I had died!

2. Cf. Southey, "Elinor," lines 36–42 in *Poems* (1797): "thence at eve / When mildly fading
   sunk the summer sun, / Oft have I loved to mark the rook's slow course / And hear his hollow croak, what time he sought / The church-yard elm." C read Southey's *Poems* by December 27, 1796 (*CL*, 1:290).
3. "Some months after I had written this line, it gave me pleasure to observe that Bartram had
   observed the same circumstance of the Savannah Crane. 'When these birds move their
   wings in flight, their strokes are slow, moderate and regular; and even when at a considerable distance, or high above us, we plainly hear the quill feathers, their shafts and webs
   upon one another creek as the joints or working of a vessel in a tempestuous sea." [C's note
   in *AA* cites Bartram, *Travels in North and South Carolina* (Philadelphia, 1791), 221.]
1. First published unsigned in *AA*. A manuscript is dated September 12, 1797 (*PW* [CC],
   2:487). C met William Linley (1771–1835), Sheridan's brother-in-law, in September 1797.

Fire, Famine, & Slaughter.
A War Eclogue[1]

The SCENE, *a desolated Tract in La Vendee.*—FAMINE *is discovered
lying on the ground: to her enter* FIRE *and* SLAUGHTER.[2]

FAMINE.

Sisters! Sisters! who sent you here?

SLAUGHTER (TO FIRE)

I will whisper it in her ear.

FIRE.

No! no! no!
Spirits hear what Spirits tell,
'Twill make an holiday in Hell.   5
      No! no! no!
Myself I nam'd him once below,
And all the souls, that damned be,
Leapt up at once in anarchy,
Clapp'd their hands and danced for glee.   10
They no longer heeded ME;
But laugh'd to hear Hell's burning rafters
Unwillingly re-echo laughters!
      No! no! no!
Spirits hear what Spirits tell,   15
'Twill make an holiday in Hell!

FAMINE.

Whisper it, Sister! so and so!
In a dark hint, soft and low.

1. Although dated 1796 in *SL* and later editions, it was probably written in late 1797 (*PW*
[CC], 2:548–49). Published in *MP* January 8, 1798, with the signature "Laberius" and in
AA unsigned. It is close in spirit to "Ireland and La Vendee" in *MP*, January 17, 1798, which
David Erdman suggests may be by C (*EOT* [CC], 3:11–12). Reprinted in *SL* with a twenty-
page apologetic preface. A short extract follows: "Were I now to have read by myself for the
first time the Poem in question, my conclusion, I fully believe, would be, that the writer
must have been some man of warm feelings and active fancy; that he had painted to himself
the circumstances that accompany war in so many vivid and yet fantastic forms, as proved
that neither the images nor the feelings were the result of observation, or in any way derived
from realities. I should judge, that they were the product of his own seething imagination,
and therefore impregnated with that pleasurable exultation which is experienced in all energetic exertion of intellectual power; that in the same mood he had generalized the causes of
the war, and then personified the abstract and christened it by the name which he had been
accustomed to hear most often associated with its management and measures. * * * I concluded by observing, that the Poem was not calculated to excite *passion* in *any* mind, or to
make any impression except on *poetic* readers" (*PW*, 2:1100–01). C directly addresses the
government's fear of inciting the mob. English liberty permitted a wide latitude of political
discussion as long as it was not designed to incite the people.
    Ecologue: a short, pastoral poem, commonly in dialogue between rustics. Here C draws
upon the witches in *Macbeth* and alludes to the four horsemen in Revelation 6.
2. See *Conciones ad Populum* (p. 252 herein).

SLAUGHTER.

Letters four[3] do form his name—
And who sent you?

BOTH.

The same! the same!   20

SLAUGHTER.

He came by stealth, and unlock'd my den,
And I have drank the blood since then
Of thrice three hundred thousand men.

BOTH.

Who bade you do't?

SLAUGHTER.

The same! the same!
Letters four do form his name.   25
He let me loose, and cry'd Halloo!
To him alone the praise is due.

FAMINE.

Thanks, Sister! thanks! the men have bled,
Their wives and their children faint for bread.
I stood in a swampy field of battle;   30
With Bones and Skulls I made a rattle,
To frighten the wolf and the carrion crow
And the homeless dog—but they would not go:
So off I flew, for how could I bear
To see them gorge their dainty fare.   35
I heard a groan and a peevish squall,
And thro' the chink of a cottage wall—
Can you guess what I saw there?

BOTH.

Whisper it, Sister! in our ear.

---

3. Pitt financially supported a bloody royalist rebellion in France from 1793 to 1796. In an article in *MP* for January 2, 1798, C referred to "the treachery of that Minister, 'who purchases and pays La Vendee, who buys commotions, who excites revolts, who foments conspiracies and agitations, who scatters every where distrust and disquietude, who rears scaffolds, and inundates them with French blood.' " C may have borrowed the quotation from another opposition newspaper or may have written it himself (*EOT* [CC], 1:9). In *The Watchman* for April 11, 1796, C quotes a paragraph from the *Morning Chronicle* of April 2 on Pitt's involvement in La Vendée: "a War on which Mr. Pitt so confidently reckoned to increase the 'pressure' on the French Republic; and which, we are also free to add, was dreaded even more by its successive Rulers than all the combined efforts of their external enemies! It was in this Country the boast and the *resource* of the Ministers and their agents. * * * 40,000 Republicans bit the dust in La Vendee!" (*Watchman* [CC], 213).

FAMINE.

A baby beat its dying mother,   40
I had starv'd the one, and was starving the other!

BOTH.

Who bade you do't?

FAMINE.

            The same! the same!
Letters four do form his name.
He let me loose, and cry'd Halloo!
To him alone the praise is due.   45

FIRE.

Sisters! I from Ireland came
Hedge and corn-fields all on flame,[4]
Halloo! halloo! the work was done—
And on as I strode with my great strides,
I flung back my head and held my sides,   50
It was so rare a piece of fun
To see the swelter'd cattle run
With uncouth gallop thro' the night,
Scar'd by the red and noisy light.
By the light of his own blazing Cot   55
Was many a naked Rebel shot:
The house-stream met the flames, and hiss'd,
While crash! fell in the roof, I wist,
On some of those old bed-rid nurses,
That deal in discontent and curses.   60

BOTH.

Who bade you do't?

FIRE.

            The same! the same!
Letters four do form his name,
He let me loose and cry'd Halloo!
To him alone the praise is due.

ALL.

He let us loose and cry'd Halloo!   65
How shall we yield him honor due?

---

4. Woodring explains that the drunken soldiers under General Lake burned huts and cottages
in Ulster in March 1797 (129).

FAMINE.

Wisdom comes with lack of food,
I'll gnaw, I'll gnaw the multitude,
Till the cup of rage o'erbrim,
They shall seize him and his brood—   70

SLAUGHTER.

They shall tear him limb from limb!

FIRE.

O thankless Beldames and untrue,
And is this all that you can do
For him who did so much for you?
Ninety months[5] he, by my troth!   75
Hath richly cater'd for you both;
And in an hour would you repay
An eight year's work?—away! away!
I alone am faithful! I
Cling to him everlastingly.   80

Dejection: An Ode (1802)

In August 1794 in Bristol, Coleridge was introduced to Sara Fricker by Robert Southey, who was engaged to her sister, Edith, and there was an understanding that Coleridge and Sara would marry. The marriage of Coleridge and Southey to the Fricker sisters was part of their plans to emigrate to America and establish pantisocracy. After August, Coleridge went back to Cambridge and then London, ignoring Southey's requests that he return to Bristol. In December, submitting to Southey's remonstrance, Coleridge wrote from London, "Mark you, Southey!—*I will do my Duty*" (*CL*, 1:145). Southey went to London in January and brought Coleridge back to Bristol, where, on October 4, 1795, he married Sara Fricker. Their marriage began to fail in 1798, when in September, Coleridge, Wordsworth, and Dorothy Wordsworth went to Germany, leaving Coleridge's wife and sons, Hartley and Berkeley. Berkeley was born May 14, 1798, and died the following February.

Through 1799 Coleridge complained about his incompatibility with his wife. On a trip to visit Wordsworth in October and November, Coleridge met Sara Hutchinson, the sister of Mary Hutchinson, whom Wordsworth married on October 4, 1802. He fell into a tormented love for her, which lasted most of his life and which she, at times, discouraged. She never married. His hopes for their relationship ended in 1810 (see p. 232 herein). In December 1801 he portrayed himself in the privacy of a notebook: "A lively picture of a man, disappointed in marriage, & endeavoring to make a compensation to himself by virtuous & tender & brotherly friendship with an amiable Woman—the obstacles—the jealousies—the

---

5. Pitt became prime minister in 1783 with liberal policies and failed to see the threat of the French Revolution in 1789. If the poem was written just before publication in *MP*, Pitt's patronage of Slaughter and Famine began in the summer of 1791; if it was written earlier, it may date the beginning of Pitt's patronage earlier with the fall of the Bastille.

impossibility of it.—Best advice that he should as much as possible withdraw himself from pursuits of morals &c—& devote himself to abstract sciences" (*CN*, 1:1065). These thoughts were the origin of "Dejection: An Ode." In the spring of 1802 Coleridge left London to visit Wordsworth and stopped to see Sara Hutchinson on the way, which occasioned some anguish between them: "Friday, March 12th / '& wept aloud.'—you made me feel uncomfortable / Saturday, March, 13th, left Gallow Hill on the Mail, in a violent storm of snow & Wind" (*CN*, 1:1151).

On March 19 Coleridge arrived at Wordsworth's cottage for two days. Wordsworth's creative efforts had stagnated over the past year. He was busy with plans to wed Mary Hutchinson and to settle affairs with Annette Vallon, a French woman with whom he had had an illegitimate daughter in December 1792. On March 26 Wordsworth wrote "The Rainbow," which was later to preface to his "Ode: Intimations of Immortality." The following day Dorothy wrote in her journal "At Breakfast Wm wrote part of an ode" (*DWJ*, 106), a beginning of the first four stanzas of the "Ode," which were close to finished form by mid-July 1802. The next day he visited Coleridge. On April 4, in response to Wordsworth's drafts of the opening stanzas, Coleridge began the first version of "Dejection: An Ode," now referred to as "A Letter to ———— [Sara Hutchinson]," which alluded to Wordsworth's first four stanzas. Coleridge's "A Letter" was probably finished in the form printed here by mid-April. On April 21 Dorothy wrote, "Coleridge came to us and repeated the verses he wrote to Sara. I was affected with them and was on the whole, not being well, in miserable spirits" (*DWJ*, 113).

"A Letter" was probably finished by April 21 and was certainly completed by July 19, when he sent four fragments, addressed not to Sara but to Wordsworth (lines 76–93, 1–75, 135–39, and 94–125 of "Dejection: An Ode" with variants), in a letter to William Sotheby, in which he began to revise the personal verse letter into an ode that accounted for his failed creativity (*CL*, 2:815–19). Wordsworth responded to Coleridge's "A Letter," by beginning, on May 3, the first version of "Resolution and Independence." Coleridge published "Dejection: An Ode, Written April 4, 1802" in close to its final form, but with omission of lines 87–93 of the version printed here, addressed to an unidentified "Edmund" and signed ΕΣΤΗΣΕ in the *Morning Post* October 4, 1802, the day of Wordsworth's marriage to Mary Hutchinson and Coleridge's wedding anniversary. Coleridge sent an abbreviated version, again addressed to Wordsworth, in August 1803 to Sir George Beaumont (*CL*, 2:966–72) in a letter that also included a version of Wordsworth's "Resolution and Independence." He also included lines 21–38 and 47–75 in "Essays on the Principles of Genial Criticism" (*SW&F* [*CC*], 1:379–80).

The text of "A Letter" is here printed from Mary Hutchinson's transcript in Stephen Maxfield Parrish, *Coleridge's "Dejection": The Earliest Manuscripts and the Earliest Printings*, the reading text of the Cornell manuscript, "in the form it would have taken had it been published—that is, with ampersands expanded, lines doubled back for want of room restored, and scribal errors and idiosyncracies cleared away" (21). The first full version of "Dejection: An Ode" was printed in *Sibylline Leaves*, the version printed here. Subsequent reprintings made only minor changes.

A Letter to ———
[Sara Hutchinson][1]

1

Well! if the Bard was weather-wise who made
The dear old Ballad of Sir Patrick Spence,
This Night, so tranquil now, will not go hence
Unrous'd by Winds, that ply a busier trade
Than that, which moulds yon clouds in lazy flakes,   5
Or the dull sobbing Draft, that drones and rakes
Upon the strings of this Eolian Lute,
Which better far were mute.
For lo! the New-Moon, winter-bright!
And all suffus'd with phantom Light   10
(With swimming phantom Light o'erspread,
But rimm'd and circled with a silver Thread)
I see the Old Moon in her Lap foretelling
The coming-on of Rain and squally Blast.—
Ah Sara! That the gust ev'n now were swelling   15
And the slant Night-shower driving loud and fast.

2

A Grief without a Pang, void, dark, and drear,
A stifling, drowsy, unimpassioned Grief,
That finds no natural Outlet, no Relief
In word or sigh, or tear—[2]   20
This, Sara! well thou know'st,
Is that sore Evil which I dread the most
And oft'nest suffer. In this heartless Mood,
To other Thoughts by yonder Throstle[3] woo'd,
That pipes within the Larch-tree not unseen   25
(The Larch which pushes out in Tassels green
Its bundled Leafits) woo'd to mild Delights
By all the tender Sounds and gentle Sights
Of this sweet Primrose-month—and *vainly* woo'd!
O dearest Sara! in this heartless mood   30

---

1. Two early manuscripts survive of "A Letter," which are described along with all versions and variants in Parrish, *Coleridge's "Dejection"*; Stillinger; and *PW* (CC), 1:677–91, 2:861–76.
2. Thomas Allsop recorded C's 1821 comments on lines 17–20: "Oh! the sorrow, the bitterness of that grief which springs from love not participated, or not returned in the spirit in which it is bestowed. Fearful and enduring is that canker-worm of the soul" (*TT* [CC], 2:367). Lines 18–19 answer Wordsworth, Immortality Ode, lines 22–24: "To me alone there came a thought of grief / A timely utterance gave that thought relief / And I again am strong." Quotations from Wordsworth's ode here and below are taken from the earliest manuscript version printed in *PTV* (360–73).
3. Thrush.

3

All this long Eve so balmy and serene
Have I been gazing on the Western Sky
And its peculiar Tint of yellow Green:[4]
And still I gaze—and with how blank an eye!
And those thin Clouds above, in flakes and bars,　　　　35
That give away their motion to the Stars;
Those Stars, that glide behind them and between,
Now sparkling, now bedimm'd, but always seen;
Yon crescent Moon, as fixed as if it grew
In its own cloudless, starless Lake of Blue,　　　　40
A Boat becalm'd! dear William's Sky-Canoe![5]
I see them all, so excellently fair,
I *see*, not *feel*, how beautiful they are![6]

4

My genial Spirits fail—[7]
And what can these avail　　　　45
To lift the smoth'ring weight[8] from off my breast?
It were a vain Endeavour,
Tho' I should gaze for ever
On that green Light, that lingers in the West—
I may not hope from outward Forms to win　　　　50
The Passion and the Life, whose Fountains are within!
Those lifeless Shapes, around, below, above,
O dearest Sara! what can they impart?
Even when the gentle Thought, that thou, my Love,
Art gazing now, like me　　　　55
And see'st the Heaven, I see,
Sweet Thought it is—yet feebly stirs my Heart.

5

Feebly, o! feebly!—Yet
(I well remember it)
In my first dawn of Youth, that Fancy stole,　　　　60
With many gentle Yearnings, on my Soul!

---

4. Cf. lines from a 1797–99 draft of Southey, *Madoc*: "They fix their dwelling eyes; still on the light / The last green light that lingers in the west" (Lynda Pratt, "A Coleridge Borrowing from Southey," *N&Q* 41 [1994]: 336–38).
5. See the Prologue to Wordsworth, *Peter Bell* (1819), lines 6–8 and 16–17: "And now I *have* a little Boat, / In shape a very crescent-moon:— / Fast through the clouds my Boat can sail; * * * / Meanwhile I from the helm admire / The pointed horns of my canoe" (*Peter Bell*, ed. John E. Jordan [Ithaca, N.Y., 1985], 45).
6. Cf. Wordsworth, Immortality Ode, lines 37–38: "I see / The heavens laugh with you in your jubilee."
7. Cf. Milton, *Samson Agonistes*, lines 594–96: "So much I feel my genial spirits droop, / My hopes all flat, nature within me seems, / In all her functions weary of her self." *Genial*: both sexual generation in marriage and imaginative generation. C quoted Milton's lines in a letter to Cottle in April 1797 to describe "a depression too dreadful to be described. * * * A sort of calm hopelessness diffuses itself over my heart"; but C's worries in 1797 were over his ability to earn a living, not his sexual and creative crisis (*CL*, 1:319–20). In March 1802 he entered plans for a poem in a notebook: "Milton, a Monody in the metres of Samson's Choruses—only with more rhymes" (*CN*, 1:1155).
8. A symptom of nightmares.

At eve, Sky-gazing in "ecstatic fit"[9]
(Alas! far-cloister'd in a city school[1]
The Sky was all I knew of Beautiful)
At the barr'd window often did I sit,   65
And often on the leaded School-roof lay
    And to myself would say—
There does not live the Man so stripp'd of good Affections
As not to love to see a Maiden's quiet Eyes
Uprais'd and linking on sweet dreams by dim Connexions   70
To Moon, or Evening Star, or glorious Western Skies!
While yet a Boy, this thought would so pursue me,
That often it became a kind of Vision to me!

6

Sweet Thought! and dear of old
To Hearts of finer Mould!   75
Ten thousand times by Friends and Lovers blest!
    I spake with rash Despair
    And 'ere I was aware,
The weight was somewhat lifted from my Breast.
Dear Sara! in the weather-fended wood,   80
Thy lov'd Haunt, where the stock-doves coo at Noon,
    I guess that thou hast stood
And watch'd yon Crescent and that ghost-like Moon!
    And yet far rather, in my present mood,
I would that thou'dst been sitting all this while   85
Upon the sod-built seat[2] of Camomile—
And tho' thy Robin may have ceas'd to sing,
Yet needs for *my* sake must thou love to hear
  —The Bee-hive murmuring near,
That ever-busy and most quiet Thing   90
Which I have heard at Midnight murmuring![3]

7

    I feel my Spirit moved—
    And, wheresoe'er thou be,
    O Sister! O beloved!
    { Thy dear mild Eyes, that see   95
    { The very Heaven, *I* see,
    { There is a Prayer in them! It is for *me!*
And I dear Sara! *I* am blessing thee!

---

9. From Milton, "The Passion," lines 41–42: "There doth my soul in holy vision sit, / In pensive trance, and anguish, and ecstatick fit."
1. Christ's Hospital, C's school in London. See "Frost at Midnight," lines 56–58 (p. 121 herein).
2. Dorothy Wordsworth's journal entry for October 10, 1801, records the building of "Sara's seat" (*DWJ*, 55) at Dove Cottage, which C described: "First Stone layed by Sara on Thursday, March 26th, 1801. So it remained till Saturday noon, October 10th, 1801—when between the hours of 12 and 2, William Wordsworth, & his Sister, with S. T. Coleridge built it—to wit, all the stone-work, with the foot-stones." The final addition was the "Moss Cushion" (*CM* [*CC*], 3:837).
3. See "A Day Dream," line 35 (p. 208 herein). Lines 99–110 of "A Letter" describe the same scene.

8

It was as calm as this,—the happy Night
When Mary, Thou and I, together were,   100
The low-decaying Fire our only Light,
And listen'd to the stillness of the Air!
O that affectionate and blameless Maid,
Dear Mary!—on her Lap my Head she lay'd—
      Her Hand was on my Brow,   105
    Even as my own is now;
And on my Cheek I felt thy Eye-lash play—
Such joy I had that I may truly say,
My Spirit was awe-stricken with the Excess
And trance-like depth of its brief Happiness.   110

9

Ah fair Remembrances, that so revive
My Heart, and fill it with a living power,
Where were they Sara?—or did I not strive
To win them to me?—on the fretting Hour,
Then when I wrote thee that complaining Scroll   115
Which even to bodily sickness bruis'd thy Soul!
And yet thou blam'st thyself alone! and yet
      Forbidd'st me all Regret!

10

And must I not *regret*, that I distrest
Thee, Best-beloved! who lovest me the Best!   120
My better mind had fled, I know not whither—
For o! was this an absent Friend's Employ
To send from far both Pain and Sorrow thither,
Where still his Blessings should have call'd down Joy?
I read thy guileless Letter o'er again—   125
I hear thee of thy blameless Self complain—
And only this I learn—and this, alas! I know,
That thou art weak and pale with Sickness, Grief, and Pain,
And I—I made thee so!

11

O *for my own sake,* I regret, *perforce,*   130
Whatever turns *thee,* Sara! from the course
Of calm well-being and a heart at rest.
When thou, and with thee those, whom thou lov'sd best
Shall dwell together in one quiet Home,
One Home the sure *Abiding* Home of All![4]   135

---

4. In late February 1802 C knew of Wordsworth's plan to marry (*CL*, 2:788). C imagines Sara in a stable home with the Wordsworths. On the evening of April 3 Coleridge and Wordsworth sat up late talking of Wordsworth's marriage and of settling affairs with Annette Vallon, which C recalled in a notebook entry of May 1808: "O God! if it had been foretold me, when in my bed I—then ill—continued talking with [Wordsworth] the whole night till the Dawn of the Day, urging him to conclude on marrying" (*CN*, 3:3304 and 3304n.).

I too will crown me with a Coronal,[5]
Nor shall this Heart in idle wishes roam,
        Morbidly soft!
No! let me trust, that I shall wear away
In no inglorious Toils the manly Day;   140
And only now and then, and not too oft,
Some dear and memorable Eve shall bless.
Dreaming of all your Love and Happiness.

12

Be happy, and I need thee not in sight!
Peace in thy Heart and Quiet in thy dwelling.   145
Health in thy Limbs, and in thy Eyes the Light
Of Love, and Hope, and honourable Feeling,
Wheree'er I am, I needs must be content!
Not near thee, haply shall be more content!
To all things I prefer the Permanent;   150
And better seems it for a Heart like mine,
Always to *know* than sometimes to *behold*,
        Their Happiness and thine:
For change doth trouble me with Pangs untold!
To see thee, hear thee, feel thee, then to part—   155
        O! it weighs down the Heart!
To *visit* those, I love, as I love *thee*.
Mary, William and dear Dorothy,
It is but a temptation to repine!
The Transientness is Poison in the Wine,   160
Eats out the Pith of Joy, makes all Joy hollow!
All Pleasure a dim dream of Pain to follow!
My own peculiar Lot, my household Life
It is, and will remain Indifference or Strife—
While ye are well and happy, 'twould but wrong you,   165
If I should fondly yearn to be among you—
Wherefore, O! wherefore, should I wish to be
A wither'd Branch upon a blossoming Tree?

13

But,—(let me say it—for I vainly strive
To beat away the Thought) *but* if thou pin'd,   170
Whate'er the cause, in body or in mind,
I were the miserablest Man alive
To know it, and be absent! Thy Delights
Far off, or near, alike shall I partake—
But O! to mourn for thee, and to forsake   175
All power, all hope of giving comfort to thee!
To know that thou art weak and worn with pain,

---

5. Cf. Wordsworth, Immortality Ode, lines 39–40: "My heart is at your festival / My head hath
   its coronal."

And not to hear thee, Sara! not to view thee—
   Not sit beside thy Bed,
   Not press thy aking Head—   180
   Not bring thee Health again—
   (At least to hope, to try,)
By this Voice, which thou lov'st, and by this *earnest* Eye—

14

Nay—wherefore did I let it haunt my Mind,
   This dark distressful Dream!   185
I turn from it, and listen to the Wind,
Which long has howl'd unnoticed! What a Scream
Of Agony by Torture lengthen'd out
That Lute sent forth! O thou wild storm without!
Or Crag, or Tairn, or lightning-blasted Tree,   190
Or Pinegrove, whither Woodman never clomb,
Or lonely House long held the Witches' Home,[6]
Methinks were fitter Instruments for thee,
Mad Lutanist! That in this Month of Showers,
Or dark-brown Gardens, and of peeping Flowers   195
Mak'st Devil's Yule, with worse than wintry song
The blooms and Buds and timorous Leaves among!
Thou Actor perfect in all Tragic Sounds!
Thou mighty Poet, even to frenzy bold!
   What tell'st thou now about?   200
Tis of a rushing of an Host in rout,
And many Groans from Men with smarting wounds
That groan at once from Smart, and shudder with the cold!
But hush: there is a break of deepest silence—
Again!—but that dread sound as of a rushing Crowd,   205
With Groans and tremulous Shuddering, all are over—
And it has other Sounds, and all less deep, less loud!
   A Tale of less Affright,
   And tempered with delight,
As William's self had made the tender lay![7]   210
   Tis of a little Child
   Upon a heathy wild
Not far from home; but it has lost its way!
And now moans low in utter grief and fear,
And now screams loud and hopes to make its Mother hear![8]   215

---

6. On the Brocken in Germany, see "Lines Written in the Album at Elbingerode" (p. 133 herein).
7. Cf. Wordsworth, "Lucy Gray," lines 29–32: "The Storm came on before its time, / She wander'd up and down / And many a hill did Lucy climb / But never reach'd the Town" (*LB* [1992], 171).
8. On February 1, 1801, C wrote to Thomas Poole describing "the Tune of this Night Wind that pipes its thin doleful climbing sinking Notes like a child that has lost its way and is crying aloud, half in grief and half in the hope to be heard by its Mother" (*CL*, 2:669).

15

Tis midnight! and small thought have I of sleep!
Full seldom may my Friend such Vigils keep!
O breathe she softly in her gentle Sleep!
Cover her, gentle Sleep! with wings of Healing,
And be this Tempest but a mountain Birth! 220
May all the stars hang bright above her dwelling
Silent as tho' they watch'd the sleeping Earth,
Like elder Sisters, with love-twinkling Eyes!
Healthful, and light my Darling! may'st thou rise,
And of the same good Tidings to me send! 225
For O! beloved Friend!
I am not the buoyant Thing, I was of yore,
When like an own Child, I to Joy belong'd,
For others mourning oft, myself oft sorely wrong'd,
Yet bearing all things then, as if I nothing bore. 230

16

E'er I was wedded, tho' my path was rough,[9]
The joy within me dallied with distress.[1]
And all misfortunes were but as the Stuff
Whence Fancy made me Dreams of Happiness:
For Hope grew round me, like the climbing Vine, 235
And Leaves and Fruitage, not my own, seem'd mine!
But now Ill-tidings bow me down to Earth—
Nor care I, that they rob me of my Mirth;
  But O! each Visitation

9. In the Dove Cottage manuscript of "A Letter," line 231 is revised to two: "Yes, dearest Sara! Yes! / There *was* a time when tho' my path was rough" (Parrish, *Coleridge's Dejection,* 31). C's line recalls "The Voice from the Side of Etna; or, The Mad Monk. An Ode, in Mrs. Ratcliff's manner," published in the *MP,* October 13, 1800, and signed "Cassiani, jun.," perhaps a reference to Giuliano Cassiani (d. 1778), who "asserted a premonitory Italian nationalism" (Woodring, 230): "There was a time when earth, and sea, and skies, / The bright green vale and forest's dark recess, / When all things lay before my eyes / In steady loveliness / But now I feel on earth's uneasy scene / Such motions as will never cease! / I only ask for peace— / Then wherefore must I know, that such a time has been?" ("The Voice from the Side of Etna," lines 9–16). "The Mad Monk" may be by either or both C and Wordsworth (Stephen M. Parrish and David V. Erdman, "Who Wrote *The Mad Monk?* A Debate," *Bulletin of the New York Public Library* 64 [1960]: 209–37, which prints the *MP* version quoted above). Parrish argues that Wordsworth wrote it; Erdman, that it is Coleridge's parody of Wordsworth. Wordsworth's Immortality Ode begins "There was a time when meadow grove and stream / The earth and every common sight / To me did seem / Apparel'd in celestial light / The glory and the freshness of a dream / It is not now as it has been of yore."
1. On February 1, 1804, C wrote to Sir George Beaumont, "I was hardly used from infancy to Boyhood; & from Boyhood to Youth most, MOST cruelly / yet 'the Joy within me', which is indeed my own Life and my very Self, was creating me anew to the first purpose of Nature, when other & deeper Distress supervened—which many have guessed, but Wordsworth alone knows to the full extent of the Calamity" (*CL,* 2:1053). In his *Lectures on the History of Philosophy* C wrote that "all genius exists in a participation of a common spirit. In joy individuality is lost. * * * To have a genius is to live in the universal, to know no self but that which is reflected not only from the faces of all around us, our fellow creatures, but reflected from the flowers, the trees, the beasts. * * * A man of genius finds a reflex to himself, were it only in the mystery of being" (*Lects 1818–1819* [CC], 1:220).

Suspends, what Nature gave me at my Birth,   240
My shaping Spirit of Imagination!
I speak not now of those habitual Ills,
That wear out Life, when two unequal minds
Meet in one House, and two discordant Wills—
        This leaves me, where it finds,   245
Past cure and past Complaint! A fate Austere,
Too fixed and hopeless to partake of Fear!

17

But thou, DEAR Sara! (Dear indeed thou art)
My Comforter! A Heart within my Heart!
Thou and the Few, we love, tho' Few ye be,   250
Make up a world of Hopes and Fears for me.
And when Affliction, or distempering Pain,
Or wayward Chance befall you, I complain.
Not that I mourn—O Friends, most dear, most true,
        Methinks to weep with you   255
Were better far than to rejoice alone——
But that my coarse domestic life has known
No Griefs, but such as dull and deaden me,
No Habits of heart-nursing Sympathy,
No mutual mild enjoyments of its own,   260
No Hopes of its own Vintage, none, o! none—
Whence, when I mourn for you, my heart must borrow
Fair forms and living motions for its Sorrow,
For not to think of what I needs must feel,
But to be still and patient all I can;   265
And haply by abstruse Research to steal
From my own Nature all the Natural Man;
This was my sole Resource, my wisest Plan!
And that, which suits a part, infects the whole,
And now is almost grown the temper of my Soul![2]   270

---

2. C sent a version of lines 231–41 and 264–70 to William Sotheby, July 19, 1802, with the
following comment: "Sickness & some other & worse afflictions, first forced me into *downright metaphysics* / for I believe that by nature I have more of the Poet in me / In a poem written during that dejection to Wordsworth, & the greater part of a private nature—I thus
expressed the thought—in language more forcible than harmonious" (*CL*, 2:814–15). C
quoted lines 231–41 in a letter to Southey, July 29, 1802, with the comment, "As to myself,
all my poetic Genius, if ever I really possessed any *Genius*, & it was not rather a mere general
aptitude of Talent, & quickness in Imitation / is gone—and I have been fool enough to suffer
deeply in my mind, regretting the loss—which I attribute to my long & exceedingly severe
Metaphysical Investigations—& these partly to Ill-health, and partly to private afflictions
which rendered any subject, immediately connected with Feeling, a source of pain & disquiet
to me" (*CL*, 2:831). C quoted lines 264–70 in the same letter to Southey, "I so attentively
watch my own Nature, that my worst Self-delusion is, a compleat Self-knowledge, so mixed
with intellectual complacency, that my q[uick]ness to see & readiness to acknowledge my
faults is too often frustrated by the small pain, which the sight of them give[s] me, & the consequent slowness to amend them" (*CL*, 2:832). He also sent lines 264–70 to his brother
George on October 2, 1803, with the comment: "I have sometimes derived a comfort from
the notion, that possibly these horrid Dreams with all their mockery of Crimes, & Remorse,
& Shame, & Terror, might have been sent upon me to arouse me out of that proud & stoical
Apathy, into which I had fallen—it was Resignation indeed, for I was not an Atheist; but it
was Resignat[ion]—witho[ut] religion because it was without struggle, without d[iff]iculty—
because it originated in the Understanding & a stealing Sp[irit of] Contempt, not in the affections" (*CL*, 2:1008).

18

My little children are a Joy, a Love,
　　A good Gift from above!
But what is Bliss, that ever calls up Woe,
　　And makes it doubly keen?
Compelling me to feel what well I know,   275
What a most blessed Lot mine *might* have been!
Those little Angel children (woe is me!)
There have been hours, when feeling how they bind
And pluck out the wing-feathers of my mind,
Turning my Error to Necessity,   280
I have half-wished, they never had been born.
THAT—*seldom*; but sad Thought they always bring,
And like the Poet's Nightingale, I sing
My Love-song with my breast against a Thorn.

19

With no unthankful Spirit I confess,   285
This clinging Grief too in its turn awakes,
That Love and Father's Joy; but O! it makes
The Love the greater, and the Joy far less!
These Mountains too, these Vales, these Woods, these Lakes,
Scenes full of Beauty and of Loftiness   290
Where all my Life I fondly hope to live—
I were sunk low indeed, did they *no* solace give!
But oft I seem to feel, and evermore to fear,
They are not to me now the Things, which once they were.

20

O Sara! we receive but what we give   295
And in *our* Life alone does Nature live—
Ours is her Wedding-garment, ours her Shroud!
And would we aught behold of higher worth
Than that inanimate cold World allow'd
To the poor loveless, ever-anxious Crowd,   300
Ah! from the Soul itself must issue forth
A Light, a Glory, and a luminous Cloud,
　　Envelloping the Earth!
And from the Soul itself must there be sent
A sweet and potent Voice of its own Birth,   305
Of all sweet sounds the Life and Element.
O pure of Heart! thou need'st not ask of me,
What this strange music in the Soul may be,
What and wherein it doth exist,
This Light, this Glory, this fair luminous Mist,   310
This beautiful and beauty-making Power!
Joy, innocent Sara! Joy, that ne'er was given
Save to the pure and in their purest Hour,
JOY, Sara! is the Spirit and the Power

That wedding Nature to us gives in dower,   315
   A new Earth and new Heaven,[3]
Undreamt of by the Sensual and the Proud!
JOY is that sweet Voice, JOY that luminous cloud!
   We, we ourselves rejoice—
And thence flows all that charms or ear or sight,   320
All Melodies the Echoes of that Voice,
All Colors a *Suffusion* from that Light.[4]
Sister and Friend of my devoutest Choice!
Thou being innocent and full of Love,
And nested with the Darlings of thy Love,   325
And feeling in thy Soul, Heart, Lips, and Arms
Even what the conjugal and Mother Dove
That borrows genial warmth from these, she warms,
Feels in her thrill'd wings, blessedly outspread!
Thou, free'd awhile from Cares and human Dread   330
By the immenseness of the Good and Fair,
   Which thou see'st every where—
Thus, thus would'st thou rejoice!
To thee would all things *live* from pole to pole,
Their Life the Eddying of thy living Soul.   335
O dear! O Innocent! O full of Love!
Sara! thou Friend of my devoutest Choice!
As dear as Light and Impulse from above!
So may'st thou ever, evermore rejoice!

3. Cf. Revelation 21.1: "And I saw a new heaven and a new earth: for the first heaven and the first earth were passed away."
4. Lines 295–322 constitute C's answer to Wordsworth's question at the end of the fourth stanza of the Immortality Ode (lines 56–57): "Whither is fled the visionary gleam / Where is it gone the glory and the dream?" C responds that the "glory and the dream" are not properties of nature, but come from within the soul. C may have been influenced by Edward Young, "Night Thoughts" 6.429–34: "But for the magic Organ's powerful charm, / Earth were a rude, uncolour'd Chaos still. / *Objects* are but the Occasion; Ours, th' *Exploit*; / Ours is the Cloth, the Pencil, and the Paint, / Which Nature's admirable Picture draws; / And beautifies Creation's ample Dome" (Bjørn Tysdahl, "Edward Young in Coleridge's 'Dejection: An Ode,'" *N&Q* 42 [1995]: 179).

Dejection:
An Ode[1]

Late, late yestreen I saw the new Moon,
With the old Moon in her arms;
And I fear, I fear, my Master dear!
We shall have a deadly storm.
            Ballad of Sir PATRICK SPENCE[2]

I.

Well! If the Bard was weather-wise, who made
   The grand old ballad of Sir Patrick Spence,
   This night, so tranquil now, will not go hence
Unrous'd by winds, that ply a busier trade
Than those which mould yon clouds in lazy flakes,   5
Or the dull sobbing draft, that moans and rakes
      Upon the strings of this Æolian lute,
      Which better far were mute.
   For lo! the New-moon winter-bright!
   And overspread with phantom-light,   10
   (With swimming phantom-light o'erspread
   But rimm'd and circled by a silver thread)
I see the old Moon in her lap, foretelling
   The coming on of rain and squally blast.
And oh! that even now the gust were swelling,   15
   And the slant night-shower driving loud and fast!
Those sounds which oft have raised me, whilst they awed,
      And sent my soul abroad,
Might now perhaps their wonted impulse give,
Might startle this dull pain, and make it move and live!   20

II.

A grief without a pang, void, dark, and drear,
   A stifled, drowsy, unimpassion'd grief,
   Which finds no natural outlet, no relief,
      In word, or sigh, or tear—
O Lady! in this wan and heartless mood,   25

---

1. C began to transform "A Letter" into "Dejection: An Ode" in the summer of 1802. In transforming a poem of 339 lines to one of 139, C cut most of the personal references. The first three stanzas of "Dejection" follow the first four of "A Letter" with the addition of four lines at the end of the first stanza in "Dejection" and the omission of some lines from the second and fourth stanzas of "A Letter." The fourth and fifth stanzas of "Dejection" on the source of joy in the soul are taken with minor revisions from lines 295–322 of "A Letter," where they measure the joy Sara will experience. In their position in "Dejection," they describe an ideal creativity that C cannot enact and answer Wordsworth's questions at the end of the fourth stanza of the Immortality Ode. Stanza 6 of "Dejection" is formed from lines 231–41 and 264–70 of "A Letter" and attributes C's depression to vague "afflictions" (line 82) that substitutes for the "Ill-Tidings" in line 237 of "A Letter." Stanza 7 is taken from lines 184–215 of "A Letter," with minor changes that transform the "dark distressful Dream" (line 185) of Sara's pain to "Reality's dark dream" (line 95) of C's own self-analysis. The final stanza is composed from lines 216–22 and 334–39, with some variants and new lines.
2. First included in the draft sent to William Sotheby, July 19, 1802 (*CL*, 2:815). C found "Sir Patrick Spence" in Percy, *Reliques* (1765).

To other thoughts by yonder throstle woo'd,
　All this long eve, so balmy and serene,
Have I been gazing on the western sky,
　And its peculiar tint of yellow green:
And still I gaze—and with how blank an eye!   30
And those thin clouds above, in flakes and bars,
That give away their motion to the stars;
Those stars, that glide behind them or between,
Now sparkling, now bedimm'd, but always seen;
Yon crescent Moon, as fix'd as if it grew   35
In its own cloudless, starless lake of blue;
I see them all so excellently fair,
I see, not feel how beautiful they are!

III.

　My genial spirits fail,
　And what can these avail,   40
To lift the smoth'ring weight from off my breast?
　It were a vain endeavor,
　Though I should gaze for ever
On that green light that lingers in the west:
I may not hope from outward forms to win   45
The passion and the life, whose fountains are within.

IV.

O Lady! we receive but what we give,
And in our life alone does nature live:
Ours is her wedding-garment, ours her shroud!
　And would we aught behold, of higher worth,   50
Than that inanimate cold world allow'd
To the poor loveless ever-anxious crowd,
　Ah! from the soul itself must issue forth,
A light, a glory, a fair luminous cloud
　　Enveloping the Earth—   55
And from the soul itself must there be sent
　A sweet and potent voice, of its own birth,
Of all sweet sounds the life and element!

V.

O pure of heart! thou need'st not ask of me
What this strong music in the soul may be!   60
What, and wherein it doth exist,
This light, this glory, this fair luminous mist,
This beautiful, and beauty-making power.
　Joy, virtuous Lady! Joy that ne'er was given,
Save to the pure, and in their purest hour,   65
Life, and Life's Effluence, Cloud at once and Shower,[3]
Joy, Lady! is the spirit and the power,

---

3. Originally printed "effulgence, cloud at once and shower" in SL, corrected in the errata to
SL.

Which wedding Nature to us gives in dow'r
   A new Earth and new Heaven,
Undreamt of by the sensual and the proud—   70
Joy is the sweet voice, Joy the luminous cloud—
     We in ourselves rejoice!
And thence flows all that charms or ear or sight,
   All melodies the echoes of that voice,
All colours a suffusion from that light.[4]   75

VI.

There was a time when, though my path was rough,
   This joy within me dallied with distress,
And all misfortunes were but as the stuff
   Whence Fancy made me dreams of happiness:
For hope grew round me, like the twining vine,   80
And fruits, and foliage, not my own, seem'd mine.
But now afflictions bow me down to earth:
Nor care I that they rob me of my mirth,
     But oh! each visitation
Suspends what nature gave me at my birth,   85
   My shaping spirit of Imagination.
For not to think of what I needs must feel,
   But to be still and patient, all I can;
And haply by abstruse research to steal
   From my own nature all the natural Man—   90
   This was my sole resource, my only plan:
Till that which suits a part infects the whole,
And now is almost grown the habit of my Soul.[5]

VII.

Hence, viper thoughts, that coil around my mind,
     Reality's dark dream!   95
I turn from you, and listen to the wind,
   Which long has rav'd unnotic'd. What a scream
Of agony by torture lengthen'd out
That lute sent forth! Thou Wind, that rav'st without,
   Bare crag, or mountain-tairn,[6] or blasted tree,   100
Or pine-grove whither woodman never clomb,
Or lonely house, long held the witches' home,
   Methinks were fitter instruments for thee,
Mad Lutanist! who in this month of show'rs,
Of dark brown gardens, and of peeping flow'rs,   105
Mak'st Devils' yule, with worse than wint'ry song,

---

4. Following line 75 in the version sent to Sotheby, C addressed Wordsworth: "Calm stedfast Spirit, guided from above, / O Wordsworth! friend of my devoutest choice, / Great Son of Genius! full of Light & Love! / Thus, thus dost thou rejoice" (CL, 2:817).
5. Lines 87–93 omitted in MP. The version sent to Sir George Beaumont in August 1803 ends with line 86 and the comment: "I am so weary of this doleful Poem that I must leave off" (CL, 2:973).
6. "Tairn is a small lake, generally if not always applied to the lakes up in the mountains and which are the feeders of those in the valleys. This address to the Storm-wind will not appear extravagant to those who have heard it at night and in a mountainous country." [C's note; first printed in MP (PW, 1:367) and corrected in the errata to SL.]

The blossoms, buds, and tim'rous leaves among.
 Thou Actor, perfect in all tragic sounds!
Thou mighty Poet, e'en to Frenzy bold!
  What tell'st thou now about?   110
   'Tis of the Rushing of an Host in rout,
 With groans of trampled men, with smarting wounds—
At once they groan with pain, and shudder with the cold!
But hush! there is a pause of deepest silence!
  And all that noise, as of a rushing crowd,   115
With groans, and tremulous shudderings—all is over—
 It tells another tale, with sounds less deep and loud!
   A tale of less affright,
   And temper'd with delight,
As Otway's[7] self had fram'd the tender lay—   120
   'Tis of a little child
   Upon a lonesome wild,
Not far from home, but she hath lost her way:
And now moans low in bitter grief and fear,
And now screams loud, and hopes to make her mother hear.   125

                          VIII.

'Tis midnight, but small thoughts have I of sleep:
Full seldom may my friend such vigils keep!
Visit her, gentle Sleep! with wings of healing,
 And may this storm be but a mountain-birth,[8]
May all the stars hang bright above her dwelling,   130
 Silent as though they watch'd the sleeping Earth!
   With light heart may she rise,
    Gay fancy, cheerful eyes,
 Joy lift her spirit, joy attune her voice:
To her may all things live, from Pole to Pole,   135
Their life the eddying of her living soul!
  O simple spirit, guided from above,
Dear Lady! friend devoutest of my choice,
Thus may'st thou ever, evermore rejoice.

CHRISTABEL, KUBLA KHAN, AND THE PAINS OF SLEEP (1816)

Part 1 of "Christabel" was written in the spring of 1798, not, as Coleridge said in the Preface, in 1797. Part 2 was written in August 1800, and it was to be the concluding poem in *Lyrical Ballads* (1800), but Dorothy Wordsworth wrote in her journal on October 6 that they decided to omit "Christabel." Wordsworth wrote "Michael" to take its place. On October 9 Coleridge wrote that "Christabel" was excluded because it contradicted

7. The "Letter" refers to Wordsworth, "Lucy Gray." C changed the reference to Otway, perhaps thinking of Otway's play *The Orphan* (1680), widely regarded for its treatment of love and pathos, as reflected in Collins, "Ode to Pity" (lines 22–23), which refers to Otway's singing "the female heart, / With youth's soft notes unspoiled by art."
8. Cf. Horace, *Ars Poetica*, line 139: "Mountains will labour, to birth will come a laughter-rousing mouse" (trans. H. Ruston Fairclough [LCL, 1929], 463).

the purpose of *Lyrical Ballads*, "an experiment to see how far those passions, which alone give any value to extraordinary Incidents, were capable of interesting, in & for themselves, in the incidents of common Life" (*CL*, 1:631). Coleridge planned to publish "Christabel" with Wordsworth's "The Pedlar," but nothing came of this and other plans to publish "Christabel," which, although it circulated widely in manuscript and was much admired, remained unpublished until 1816.

In March 1815 Coleridge asked Byron's help in publishing his poems. Byron responded with a gift of one hundred pounds (*CL*, 4:622) and warm praise for "Christabel," which he described in a note to his *Siege of Corinth* (1816) as a "wild and singularly original and beautiful poem." In April 1816 Byron heard Coleridge recite "Kubla Khan," which deeply impressed him (*CL*, 4:636n. 4), and he convinced John Murray (1778–1843) to publish "Christabel," along with "Kubla Khan" and "The Pains of Sleep." Murray gave Coleridge seventy guineas for the copyright to "Christabel," as long as it remained unfinished, and twenty pounds for "Kubla Khan" (*CL*, 4:634n. 1; *A Publisher and His Friends: Memoir and Correspondence of the Late John Murray*, ed. Samuel Smiles [1891], 1:303). In 1816 *Christabel* went through three editions. When it was published on May 25, 1816, reviewers attacked it. William Hazlitt wrote in the *Examiner* for June 2 that "there is something disgusting at the bottom of his subject, which is but ill glossed over by a veil of Della Cruscan sentiment and fine writing—like moon-beams playing on a charnel-house, or flowers strewed on a dead body" (*CH*, 1:207). The *Edinburgh Review* (September 1816), in a notice Coleridge thought by Hazlitt, suggested that the baron thought Christabel was seduced. Coleridge responded privately with bitterness at Hazlitt's attacks: "Some Genius in a pamphlet entitled Hypocrisy unveiled * * * has pronounced poor Christabel 'the most obscene poem in the English Lange [*sic*].' It seems that Hazlitt from pure malignity had spread about the Report that Geraldine was a man in disguise" (*CL*, 4:917–18; for Coleridge's characterization of Hazlitt, see his September 16, 1803, letter to Thomas Wedgwood [p. 633 herein]). Coleridge wrote in chapter 24 of the *Biographia* (p. 546 herein) that, after it was published, "Christabel" received "nothing but abuse, and this too in a spirit of bitterness" over a poem that "pretended to be nothing more than a common Faery Tale." Other reviewers questioned the character of Geraldine. The *Critical Review* (May 1816) associated Christabel and Geraldine with Una and Duessa in book 1 of Spenser's *Faerie Queene*. The *Champion* (May 26, 1816) asked, "What is it all about? What is the idea? Is *Lady Geraldine* a sorceress? or a vampire? or a man? or what is she, or he, or it?" (*CH*, 2:251). It also hinted that the poem's horrors resembled those in Matthew Gregory Lewis (1775–1818), *The Monk* (1796), which Coleridge reviewed in February 1797 (*SW&F* [*CC*], 1:57–65). Hazlitt had called her a witch, perhaps on the basis of her quotation from the witches in *Macbeth* in line 199, and she may also be a lamia, a monster with a woman's body.

After publication, most of Coleridge's revisions, annotations, and accounts of the poem responded to the reviews. He gave contradictory explanations of Geraldine to defend the poem from charges of indecency. In 1819 he wrote in Derwent Coleridge's presentation copy, now at St. John's College, Cambridge, that "Geraldine is *not* a Witch, in any proper sense of that word—That she is a man in disguise, is a wicked rumor sent abroad with malice prepense, and against his own belief and knowledge, by poor Hazlitt" (John Beer, "Coleridge, Hazlitt, and 'Christabel,'" *RES* 37

[1986]: 40). In the "Introductory Essay" in his edition of Coleridge's *Poems* (1870), Derwent, following Coleridge's comments in the presentation copy, stated that "the sufferings of Christabel were to have been presented as vicarious, endured for 'her lover far away' " and that Geraldine was "no witch or goblin, or malignant being of any kind, but a spirit executing her appointed task with the best good will" (xlii). While some of Coleridge's revisions and accounts of the poem suggest that Geraldine was struggling against demonic possession, others suggest that Geraldine was simply an evil being. James Gillman (*The Life of Coleridge* [1838], 283) reported that the moral of the tale was that "the virtuous of this world save the wicked. The pious and good Christabel suffers and prays for 'The weal of her lover that is far away,' exposed to various temptations in a foreign land," and she "defeats the power of evil represented in the person of Geraldine." An unpublished defense of "Christabel," probably by John Morgan, with whom Coleridge frequently stayed from 1810 to 1816, described Geraldine as a "supernatural and malignant being" (Earl Leslie Griggs, "An Early Defense of *Christabel*," *Wordsworth and Coleridge*, ed. E. L. Griggs [Princeton, 1939], 176).

In 1824 Coleridge annotated a presentation copy, now at Princeton, with nine marginal notes, like those for "The Ancient Mariner," which depict the struggle between an evil Geraldine and innocent Christabel. Coleridge's annotations may respond to a review of "Christabel" in the *Academic* (September 15, 1821), which complained of the poem's "extravagance and absurdity. If it had been furnished, like his 'Rime of the Ancient Mariner,' with marginal annotations, to explain the incidents and fill up the vacancies of the poem, we might have attempted to extract the substance of its story" (*CH*, 2:282). Coleridge's 1824 marginal annotations written at Ramsgate in Rooke, Stillinger (190–215), and *PW* (*CC*) 2:657–62, and are included here as notes.

It is not clear whether Coleridge had any or all of these readings in mind in 1798 and 1800. "Christabel" was begun shortly after "The Ancient Mariner," and Coleridge linked them as poems of the supernatural in chapter 14 of the *Biographia*. While the 1816 Preface presented "Christabel" as a case of failed creativity, in 1798 "Christabel" was a poem of supernatural and psychological horror derived from Coleridge's observations of his own dreams and from his reading of Andrew Baxter, *Enquiry into the Nature of the Human Soul* (1733), and Erasmus Darwin, *Zoonomia* (1794–96) (*CN*, 1:188n). Observing the terror of lightning during the day, Coleridge wrote in a notebook in October 1804, "A ghost by day time / Geraldine" (*CN*, 2:2207), which reflects the themes of part 2. Coleridge told Henry Nelson Coleridge in July 1833 that "the reason of my not finishing Christabel is not that I don't know how to do it; for I have, as I always had, the whole plan entire from beginning to end in my mind; but I fear I could not carry on with equal success the execution of the Idea— the most difficult, I think, that can be attempted to Romantic Poetry—I mean witchery by daylight. I venture to think that Geraldine, so far as she goes, is successful" (*TT* [*CC*], 1:409–10). Wordsworth disputed Coleridge's claim that he knew how to finish the poem (*TT* [*CC*], 1:576–77), and it is doubtful that Coleridge had a clear plan when he began. "Christabel" is a narrative fragment about the initiation of innocence into evil, a dream poem of doubles and echoes that was, as Hartley Coleridge reported, his "Father's favourite child—the fondling of his genius, the child in which he recognized himself most and finest" (Earl Leslie Griggs, "Hartley Coleridge on His Father," *PMLA* 46 [1931]: 1252).

The 1816 version is printed here with stanza breaks at lines 56, 123, 189, and 310, where the 1816 text is ambiguous and later versions omit the breaks (*PW* [*CC*], 1:481). Coleridge began revisions of "Christabel" by November 1816. His major revisions were all to part 1. Selected marginal annotations in presentation copies are here printed as notes along with the comments from Morgan's unpublished review and Gillman's *Life*.

CHRISTABEL

Preface

The first part of the following poem was written in the year one thousand seven hundred and ninety seven, at Stowey in the county of Somerset. The second part, after my return from Germany, in the year one thousand eight hundred, at Keswick, Cumberland. Since the latter date, my poetic powers have been, till very lately, in a state of suspended animation.[1] But as, in my very first conception of the tale, I had the whole present to my mind, with the wholeness, no less than with the liveliness of a vision; I trust that I shall be able to embody in verse the three parts yet to come, in the course of the present year.

It is probable, that if the poem had been finished at either of the former periods, or if even the first and second part had been published in the year 1800, the impression of its originality would have been much greater than I dare at present expect. But for this, I have only my own indolence to blame. The dates are mentioned for the exclusive purpose of precluding charges of plagiarism or servile imitation from myself.[2] For there is among us a set of critics, who seem to hold, that every possible thought and image is traditional; who have no notion that there are such things as fountains in the world, small as well as great; and who would therefore charitably derive every rill, they behold flowing, from a perforation made in some other man's tank. I am confident however, that as far as the present poem is concerned, the celebrated poets whose writings I might be suspected of having imitated, either in particular passages, or in the tone and the spirit of the whole, would be among the first to vindicate me from the charge, and who,

---

1. In 1810 C confided in a notebook that a quarrel with Charles Lloyd and Lloyd's caricaturing him in his novel *Edmund Oliver*, published in April 1798, prevented him from finishing "Christabel" and prompted him to take opium (*CN*, 3:4006). In November 1800 he blamed the labor of translating Schiller's *Wallenstein* the previous spring for the trouble he had in working on the poem (*CL*, 1:643). The struggle of joint publication with Wordsworth for the second volume of *LB* (1800) also discouraged him. C admitted that a delay in publication was "owing in part to me, as the writer of Christabel—Every line has been produced with labor-pangs. I abandon Poetry altogether—I leave the higher & deeper Kinds to Wordsworth, the delightful, popular & simply dignified to Southey; & reserve for myself the honorable attempt to make others feel and understand their writings" (*CL*, 1:623). In October 1823 C noted, "Were I free to do so, I feel as if I could compose the third part of Christabel, or the song of her desolation" (*CN*, 4:5032). Although in 1800 he claimed to have written more than 1,300 lines of the poem (*CL*, 1:631), no record of further work beyond the first two parts is known.
2. Sir Walter Scott, *Lay of the Last Minstrel* (1805) and later metrical tales; Byron, *Giaour* (1813) and some of his other Oriental tales; and Wordsworth, *White Doe of Rylstone* (1815), all published before "Christabel," used metrical patterns similar to that in "Christabel." C's defense against charges of plagiarism is also a claim for originality.

on any striking coincidence, would permit me to address them in this doggrel version of two monkish Latin hexameters:

> 'Tis mine and it is likewise yours,
> But an if this will not do;
> Let it be mine, good friend! for I
> Am the poorer of the two.

I have only to add, that the metre of the Christabel is not, properly speaking, irregular, though it may seem so from its being founded on a new principle: namely, that of counting in each line the accents, not the syllables. Though the latter may vary from seven to twelve, yet in each line the accents will be found to be only four. Nevertheless this occasional variation in the number of syllables is not introduced wantonly, or for the mere ends of convenience, but in correspondence with some transition in the nature of the imagery or passion.[3]

Christabel

Part I

'Tis the middle of night by the castle clock,
And the owls have awaken'd the crowing cock;
Tu—whit!——Tu—whoo![1]
And hark, again! the crowing cock,
How drowsily it crew.   5

Sir Leoline, the Baron rich,
Hath a toothless mastiff bitch;
From her kennel beneath the rock
She makes answer to the clock,
Four for the quarters, and twelve for the hour;   10
Ever and aye, moonshine or shower,
Sixteen short howls, not over loud;
Some say, she sees my lady's shroud.

Is the night chilly and dark?
The night is chilly, but not dark.   15
The thin gray cloud is spread on high,
It covers but not hides the sky.
The moon is behind, and at the full;

3. Commentators have noted a resemblance between C's explanation of the meter of "Christabel" and Old English meter, which counts only the number of accents in a line. In a draft of the Preface C offers more detail: his meter "is the common 8 syllable verse, in technical phrase, the tetrameter Iambic acatalectic [without the omission of a syllable in the final foot of a line]—the liberties besides that of using a double rhyme, ad libitum are that of substituting an anapest or dactyl followed by a trochee instead of two Iambics, either in the first or latter half of the verse & sometimes of giving four anapests, sometimes four trochees, instead of the four Iambics—in brief, having no other *law* of metre, except that of confining myself to four *strokes*, or accentuated syllables" (SW&F [CC], 1:442). However, the entry "Christabel Meter" in the *New Princeton Encyclopedia of Poetry and Poetics* (1993) points out that approximately 80 percent of the lines are regular four-stress iambic lines.
1. Cf. *Love's Labors Lost* 5.2.892–93: "Then nightly sings the staring owl: / Tu-whit, tu-whoo— a merry note."

And yet she looks both small and dull.[2]
The night is chill, the cloud is gray: 20
'Tis a month before the month of May,
And the Spring comes slowly up this way.[3]

The lovely lady, Christabel,[4]
Whom her father loves so well,
What makes her in the wood so late,   25
A furlong from the castle gate?
She had dreams all yesternight
Of her own betrothed knight;
Dreams, that made her moan and leap,
As on her bed she lay in sleep;[5]   30
And she in the midnight wood will pray
For the weal of her lover that's far away.

She stole along, she nothing spoke,
The breezes they were still also;
And nought was green upon the oak,   35
But moss and rarest misletoe:[6]
She kneels beneath the huge oak tree,
And in silence prayeth she.

The lady leaps up suddenly,
The lovely lady, Christabel!   40
It moan'd as near, as near can be,
But what it is, she cannot tell,—
On the other side it seems to be,
Of the huge, broad-breasted, old oak tree.

The night is chill; the forest bare;   45
Is it the wind that moaneth bleak?
There is not wind enough in the air
To move away the ringlet curl
From the lovely lady's cheek—
There is not wind enough to twirl   50
The one red leaf, the last of its clan,
That dances as often as dance it can,
Hanging so light, and hanging so high,
On the topmost twig that looks up at the sky.[7]

2. Cf. *DWJ*, 3, for January 31, 1798: "the moon immensely large, the sky scattered over with clouds. These soon closed in, contracting the dimensions of the moon without concealing her."
3. Cf. *DWJ*, 11, for March 24, 1798: "The spring continues to advance very slowly, no green trees, the hedges leafless; nothing green but the brambles that still retain their old leaves, the evergreens, and the palms, which indeed are not absolutely green."
4. The name "Christabel" came from the ballad "Sir Cauline" in Bishop Thomas Percy (1729–1811), *Reliques of Ancient English Poetry* (1765), which C mentions in January 1798 (*CL*, 1:379) and which was the source of much of the archaic diction in "The Ancient Mariner."
5. Lines 29–30 exist in no other version.
6. In Britain mistletoe grows mainly on apple trees, rarely on oaks. On oaks it was venerated by Druids (*OED*).
7. Cf. *DWJ*, 9, for March 7, 1798: "One only leaf upon the top of a tree—the sole remaining leaf—danced round and round like a rag blown by the wind."

Hush, beating heart of Christabel!   55
Jesu,[8] Maria, shield her well!

She folded her arms beneath her cloak,
And stole to the other side of the oak.
   What sees she there?

There she sees a damsel bright,   60
Drest in a silken robe of white;
Her neck, her feet, her arms were bare,
And the jewels disorder'd in her hair.[9]
I guess, 'twas frightful there to see
A lady so richly clad as she—   65
Beautiful exceedingly!

Mary mother, save me now!
(Said Christabel,) And who art thou?

The lady strange made answer meet,
And her voice was faint and sweet:—   70
Have pity on my sore distress,
I scarce can speak for weariness.
Stretch forth thy hand, and have no fear,
Said Christabel, How cam'st thou here?
And the lady, whose voice was faint and sweet,   75
Did thus pursue her answer meet:—

My sire is of a noble line,
And my name is Geraldine.
Five warriors seiz'd me yestermorn,
Me, even me, a maid forlorn: 80
They chok'd my cries with force and fright,
And tied me on a palfrey white.
The palfrey was as fleet as wind,
And they rode furiously behind.
They spurr'd amain, their steeds were white;   85
And once we cross'd the shade of night.
As sure as Heaven shall rescue me,

8. The shortened form of "Jesus" in both Spanish and Portuguese. C may have borrowed the
   exclamation either from *Romeo and Juliet* 2.2.69 or from Matthew G. Lewis, *The Castle
   Spectre* (1797), 3.3 (*Seven Gothic Dramas*, ed. Jeffrey N. Cox [Athens, Ohio, 1992], 192),
   which C criticized harshly in January 1798 (*CL*, 1:378–79). Walter Scott borrowed this line
   for *The Lay Of the Last Minstrel* (1805), 1.1.5. C noted in 1811 that the phrase "might have
   occurred to a score of Writers who had been previously familiar with Poems & Romances
   written before the Reformation or translated from the Spanish" (*CL*, 3:357). Mays argues
   from manuscript evidence that the printer changed some of C's punctuation and capitalization and that there should be no comma after "Jesu" (J. C. C. Mays, "*Christabel* as Example," *Imprints & Re-visions*, ed. Peter Hughes and Robert Rehder [Tübingen, 1995], 134–35;
   PW [*CC*], 2:654–55).
9. C revised lines 62–63 in November 1816 to read, "That shadowy in the moonlight shone: /
   The neck, that made that white robe wan, / Her stately neck, and arms were bare; / Her
   blue-veined feet unsandal'd were; / And wildly glitter'd here and there / The Gems entangled
   in her hair." The revision was entered in a copy presented to David Hinves described in
   Rooke (183–84) and *PW* (1:214). Here, as at lines 107, 117, and 249, the text of C's revisions comes from Rooke's transcription of C's 1816 revisions.

I have no thought what men they be;
Nor do I know how long it is
(For I have lain in fits, I wis)   90
Since one, the tallest of the five,
Took me from the palfrey's back,
A weary woman, scarce alive.
Some mutter'd words his comrades spoke:
He plac'd me underneath this oak,   95
He swore they would return with haste;
Whither they went I cannot tell—
I thought I heard, some minutes past,
Sounds as of a castle bell.
Stretch forth thy hand (thus ended she),   100
And help a wretched maid to flee.[1]

Then Christabel stretch'd forth her hand
And comforted fair Geraldine,
Saying, that she should command
The service of Sir Leoline,   105
And straight be convoy'd, free from thrall,
Back to her noble father's hall.[2]

So up she rose, and forth they pass'd,
With hurrying steps, yet nothing fast;
Her lucky stars the lady blest,   110
And Christabel she sweetly said—
All our household are at rest,
Each one sleeping in his bed;
Sir Leoline is weak in health,
And may not well awaken'd be;   115
So to my room we'll creep in stealth,
And you to-night must sleep with me.[3]

1. In the Derwent Coleridge presentation copy (1819) C noted next to lines 79–101: "This
   paragraph I purpose to re-write, with the exception of two or perhaps three Lines. As it
   stands, it might be placed in any one's mouth, appropriately therefore in no one's, and in
   Geraldine's it falls flat" (Beer, "Coleridge, Hazlitt, and Christabel," 53). In later versions C
   did not revise the passage.
2. In November 1816 C replaced lines 104–07 with the following: "O well, bright dame! may
   you command / The Service of Sir Leoline: / And gladly our stout Chivilray / Will He send
   forth, and Friends withal, / To guide and guard you, safe and free, / Home to your noble Father's Hall" (Rooke, 186, without C's deletions; PW, 1:219).
3. C revised lines 108–17 in November 1816 and transcribed the revisions with some variants
   in 1824, where they accompanied the first marginal gloss. The 1816 revision was

> She rose: and forth with steps they pass'd,
> That strove to be, yet were not, fast:
> Her gracious stars the lady blest,
> And thus spake on sweet Christabel—
> All our household are at rest,
> The Hall as silent as the Cell;
> Sir Leoline is weak in health,
> And may not well awaken'd be;
> But we will move, as if in stealth,
> And I beseech your courtesy
> This night to share your bed with me.   [Rooke, 186; PW, 1:219–20]

C added in the margin in 1824: "The Strange Lady cannot rise, without the touch of
Christabel's Hand: and now she blesses her *Stars*. She will not praise the *Creator* of the
Heavens, or name the Saints."

They cross'd the moat, and Christabel
Took the key that fitted well;
A little door she open'd straight,   120
All in the middle of the gate;
The gate that was iron'd within and without,
Where an army in battle array had march'd out.

The lady sank, belike thro' pain,
And Christabel with might and main   125
Lifted her up, a weary weight,
Over the threshold of the gate:
Then the lady rose again,
And mov'd, as she were not in pain.[4]

So free from danger, free from fear,   130
They cross'd the court: right glad they were.
And Christabel devoutly cried,
To the lady by her side,
Praise we the Virgin all divine
Who hath rescued thee from thy distress!   135
Alas, alas! said Geraldine,
I cannot speak for weariness.[5]
So free from danger, free from fear,
They cross'd the court: right glad they were.

Outside her kennel, the mastiff old   140
Lay fast asleep, in moonshine cold.
The mastiff old did not awake,
Yet she an angry moan did make!
And what can ail the mastiff bitch?
Never till now she utter'd yell   145
Beneath the eye of Christabel.
Perhaps it is the owlet's scritch:
For what can ail the mastiff bitch?

They pass'd the hall, that echoes still,
Pass as lightly as you will!   150
The brands were flat, the brands were dying,
Amid their own white ashes lying;
But when the lady pass'd, there came
A tongue of light, a fit of flame;
And Christabel saw the lady's eye,   155
And nothing else saw she thereby,
Save the boss of the shield of Sir Leoline tall,

---

4. C annotated lines 124–29 in the margin in 1824: "The strange Lady may not pass the threshold without Christabel's help and will," a common superstition that an evil being cannot enter a sanctified place unaided. Morgan wrote that "here is given the first indication of Geraldine's supernatural character" (178). Other signs C took from folklore include the mastiff's moan in line 143 and the "flit of flame" in line 154.
5. C annotated lines 136–37 in the margin in 1824: "The strange Lady makes an excuse, not to praise the Holy Virgin."

Which hung in a murky old nitch in the wall.
O softly tread, said Christabel,
My father seldom sleepeth well.   160

Sweet Christabel her feet she bares,
And they are creeping up the stairs;[6]
Now in glimmer, and now in gloom,
And now they pass the Baron's room,
As still as death with stifled breath!   165
And now have reach'd her chamber door;
And now with eager feet press down
The rushes of her chamber floor.

The moon shines dim in the open air,
And not a moonbeam enters here: 170
But they without its light can see
The chamber carv'd so curiously,
Carv'd with figures strange and sweet,
All made out of the carver's brain,
For a lady's chamber meet: 175
The lamp with twofold silver chain
Is fasten'd to an angel's feet.

The silver lamp burns dead and dim;
But Christabel the lamp will trim.
She trimm'd the lamp, and made it bright,   180
And left it swinging to and fro,
While Geraldine, in wretched plight,
Sank down upon the floor below.

O weary lady, Geraldine,
I pray you, drink this cordial wine!   185
It is a wine of virtuous powers;
My mother made it of wild flowers.

And will your mother pity me,
Who am a maiden most forlorn?

Christabel answer'd—Woe is me!   190
She died the hour that I was born.
I have heard the gray-hair'd friar tell,
How on her death-bed she did say,
That she should hear the castle bell
Strike twelve upon my wedding day.   195
O mother dear! that thou wert here!
I would, said Geraldine, she were!

6. As early as November 1816 C tried several revisions of line 162 and in *Poetical Works* (1828)
replaced them with "And, jealous of the listening air, / They steal their way from stair to
stair" (Stillinger, 198).

But soon with alter'd voice, said she—
"Off, wandering mother! Peak and pine!
"I have power to bid thee flee."   200
Alas! what ails poor Geraldine?
Why stares she with unsettled eye?
Can she the bodiless dead espy?[7]
And why with hollow voice cries she,
"Off, woman, off! this hour is mine—   205
"Though thou her guardian spirit be,
"Off, woman, off! 'tis given to me."[8]

Then Christabel knelt by the lady's side,
And rais'd to heaven her eyes so blue—
Alas! said she, this ghastly ride—   210
Dear lady! it hath wilder'd you!
The lady wip'd her moist cold brow,
And faintly said, " 'Tis over now!"

Again the wild-flower wine she drank:
Her fair large eyes 'gan glitter bright,   215
And from the floor whereon she sank,
The lofty lady stood upright:
She was most beautiful to see,
Like a lady of a far countrée.

And thus the lofty lady spake—   220
All they, who live in the upper sky,
Do love you, holy Christabel!
And you love them, and for their sake
And for the good which me befel,
Even I in my degree will try,   225
Fair maiden, to requite you well.
But now unrobe yourself; for I
Must pray, ere yet in bed I lie.[9]

Quoth Christabel, so let it be!
And as the lady bade, did she.   230
Her gentle limbs did she undress,
And lay down in her loveliness.

But thro' her brain of weal and woe
So many thoughts mov'd to and fro,
That vain it were her lids to close;   235

7. C annotated lines 198–203 in the margin in 1824: "The Mother of Christabel, who is now
   her Guardian Spirit, appears to Geraldine, as in answer to her wish. Geraldine fears the
   Spirit, but yet has power over it for a time." Cf. the witches' song in Macbeth 1.3.21–22:
   "Weary sennights nine times nine / Shall he dwindle, peak, and pine."
8. Gillman explained that "the mother instantly appears, though she is invisible to her daughter" (Life, 290).
9. In the Derwent Coleridge presentation copy C noted that lines 223–28 "must likewise be
   changed, for the same reason" as lines 81–98 (Beer, "Coleridge, Hazlitt, and Christabel,"
   53). C did not revise them.

So half-way from the bed she rose,
And on her elbow did recline
To look at the lady Geraldine.

Beneath the lamp the lady bow'd,
And slowly roll'd her eyes around;   240
Then drawing in her breath aloud,
Like one that shudder'd, she unbound
The cincture from beneath her breast:
Her silken robe, and inner vest,
Dropt to her feet, and full in view,   245
Behold! her bosom and half her side——
A sight to dream of, not to tell!¹
And she is to sleep by Christabel.²

She took two paces, and a stride,³
And lay down by the maiden's side: 250
And in her arms the maid she took,
                    Ah wel-a-day!
And with low voice and doleful look
These words did say:
In the touch of this bosom there worketh a spell,⁴   255
Which is lord of thy utterance, Christabel!
Thou knowest to-night, and wilt know to-morrow
This mark of my shame, this seal of my sorrow;
          But vainly thou warrest,
                    For this is alone in   260
          Thy power to declare,
                    That in the dim forest
                    Thou heard'st a low moaning,
And found'st a bright lady, surpassingly fair:
And didst bring her home with thee in love and in charity,   265
To shield her and shelter her from the damp air.

1. Hazlitt's review in the *Examiner* (June 2, 1816) mistakenly reported that originally this line
was "Hideous, deformed, and pale of hue" (*CH*, 1:207). A manuscript copied by Hazlitt's future wife, Sarah Stoddart (d. 1842), now in the Berg Collection, had "Are lean and old and
foul of hue," as it was in other early manuscripts (*PW*, 1:224). C may have had in mind the
disrobing of Duessa in Spenser, *Faerie Queene* 1.8.46–48.
2. By July 1817 C had substituted "O shield her! shield sweet Christabel" for line 248 (Stillinger, 201).
3. By November 1816 C deleted lines 249–50 and substituted the following: "She gaz'd upon
the maid, she sigh'd! / Then lay down by the maiden's side: / Deep from within she seems
half-way / To lift some weight, with sick assay, / And eyes the Maid, and seeks delay: / Then
suddenly as one defied / Collects herself in scorn and pride / And lay down by the Maiden's
side" (Rooke, 189–90). In the Derwent Coleridge presentation copy C deleted line 249 and
wrote, "Two or more Lines, by which the pronoun 'She' is made to refer to Geraldine." He
drafted two lines: "A woman she: and in her mood / Still wrought the soul of womanhood"
(Beer, "Coleridge, Hazlitt, and *Christabel*," 50). These drafted lines exist in no other version
but suggest, along with the lines substituted for line 249, that Geraldine is a woman struggling against demonic possession.
4. C annotated lines 249–55 in the margin in 1824: "As soon as the wicked Bosom, with the
mysterious sign of Evil stamped thereby, touches Christabel, she is deprived of the power of
disclosing what has occurred."

The Conclusion
to
Part the First

It was a lovely sight to see
The lady Christabel, when she
Was praying at the old oak tree.
    Amid the jagged shadows   270
    Of mossy leafless boughs,
    Kneeling in the moonlight,
    To make her gentle vows;
Her slender palms together prest,
Heaving sometimes on her breast;   275
Her face resign'd to bliss or bale—
Her face, oh call it fair not pale;
And both blue eyes more bright than clear,
Each about to have a tear.

With open eyes (ah woe is me!)   280
Asleep, and dreaming fearfully,
Fearfully dreaming, yet I wis,
Dreaming that alone, which is——
O sorrow and shame! Can this be she,
The lady, who knelt at the old oak tree?   285
And lo! the worker of these harms,
That holds the maiden in her arms,
Seems to slumber still and mild,
As a mother with her child.

A star hath set, a star hath risen,   290
O Geraldine! since arms of thine
Have been the lovely lady's prison.
O Geraldine! one hour was thine—
Thou'st had thy will! By tairn and rill,
The night-birds all that hour were still.[5]   295
But now they are jubilant anew,
    From cliff and tower, tu—whoo! tu—whoo!
Tu—whoo! tu—whoo! from wood and fell!

And see! the lady Christabel
Gathers herself from out her trance;   300
Her limbs relax, her countenance
Grows sad and soft; the smooth thin lids
Close o'er her eyes; and tears she sheds—
Large tears that leave the lashes bright!
And oft the while she seems to smile   305
As infants at a sudden light!

5. Gillman commented at line 295 that "During this rest (her mother) the guardian angel is supposed to have been watching over her. But these passages could not escape coarse minded critics, who put a construction on them which never entered the mind of the author of Christabel, whose poems are marked by delicacy" (*Life*, 293–94).

Yea, she doth smile, and she doth weep,
Like a youthful hermitess,
Beauteous in a wilderness,
Who, praying always, prays in sleep.   310

And, if she move unquietly,
Perchance, 'tis but the blood so free,
Comes back and tingles in her feet.
No doubt, she hath a vision sweet.
What if her guardian spirit 'twere   315
What if she knew her mother near?
But this she knows, in joys and woes,
That saints will aid if men will call:
For the blue sky bends over all!⁶

Part II⁷

Each matin bell, the Baron saith,   320
Knells us back to a world of death.
These words Sir Leoline first said,
When he rose and found his lady dead:
These words Sir Leoline will say
Many a morn to his dying day.   325

And hence the custom and law began,
That still at dawn the sacristan,
Who duly pulls the heavy bell,
Five and forty beads must tell
Between each stroke—a warning knell,   330
Which not a soul can choose but hear
From Bratha Head to Wyn'dermere.

Saith Bracy the bard, So let it knell!
And let the drowsy sacristan
Still count as slowly as he can!   335
There is no lack of such, I ween
As well fill up the space between.
In Langdale Pike and Witch's Lair,
And Dungeon-ghyll so foully rent,
With ropes of rock and bells of air   340
Three sinful sextons' ghosts are pent,

6. C wrote in a notebook in 1810: "Christabel—My first cries mingled with my Mother's Death-groan / —and she beheld the vision of Glory ere I the earthly Sun—when I first looked up to Heaven, consciously, it was to look up after or for my Mother" (CN, 3:3720).
7. In May 1821 C quoted to Thomas Allsop (1795–1880) the following lines from Richard Crashaw, "A Hymn to the Name and Honour of the Admirable Saint Teresa," as printed in Robert Anderson, Works of the British Poets (1792–95), where in 1807 or later C annotated Crashaw's poem: "Since 'tis not to be had at home, / She'll travel for a martyrdom. / No home for her's confesses she, / But where she may a martyr be. / * * * Farewell house, and farewell home, / She's for the Moors and martyrdom" (CM [CC], 1:66–67). C commented that "these verses were ever present to my mind whilst writing the second part of Christabel; if, indeed, by some subtle process of the mind they did not suggest the first thought of the whole poem" (TT [CC], 2:369). For C's view of St. Teresa see CN, 3:3911 and Lects 1818–19 [CC], 2:462–66.

Who all give back, one after t'other,
The death-note to their living brother;
And oft too, by the knell offended,
Just as their one! two! three! is ended,   345
The devil mocks the doleful tale
With a merry peal from Borrowdale.

The air is still! thro' mist and cloud
That merry peal comes ringing loud;
And Geraldine shakes off her dread,   350
And rises lightly from the bed;
Puts on her silken vestments white,
And tricks her hair in lovely plight,
And nothing doubting of her spell
Awakens the lady Christabel.   355
"Sleep you, sweet lady Christabel?
"I trust that you have rested well."

And Christabel awoke and spied
The same who lay down by her side—
O rather say, the same whom she   360
Rais'd up beneath the old oak tree!
Nay, fairer yet! and yet more fair!
For she belike hath drunken deep
Of all the blessedness of sleep!
And while she spake, her looks, her air   365
Such gentle thankfulness declare,
That (so it seem'd) her girded vests
Grew tight beneath her heaving breasts.
"Sure I have sinn'd!" said Christabel,
"Now heaven be prais'd if all be well!"   370
And in low faltering tones, yet sweet,
Did she the lofty lady grect
With such perplexity of mind
As dreams too lively leave behind.[8]

So quickly she rose, and quickly array'd   375
Her maiden limbs, and having pray'd
That He, who on the cross did groan,
Might wash away her sins unknown,
She forthwith led fair Geraldine
To meet her sire, Sir Leoline.   380

The lovely maid and the lady tall
Are pacing both into the hall,
And pacing on thro' page and groom
Enter the Baron's presence room.

8. C annotated lines 371–74 in the margin in 1824: "Christabel is made to believe, that the
fearful Sight had taken place only in a Dream."

The Baron rose, and while he prest   385
His gentle daughter to his breast,
With cheerful wonder in his eyes
The lady Geraldine espies,
And gave such welcome to the same,
As might beseem so bright a dame!   390

But when he heard the lady's tale,
And when she told her father's name,
Why wax'd Sir Leoline so pale,
Murmuring o'er the name again,
Lord Roland de Vaux of Tryermaine?[9]   395

Alas! they had been friends in youth;[1]
But whispering tongues can poison truth;
And constancy lives in realms above;
And life is thorny; and youth is vain;
And to be wroth with one we love,   400
Doth work like madness in the brain.
And thus it chanc'd, as I divine,
With Roland and Sir Leoline.
Each spake words of high disdain
And insult to his heart's best brother: 405
They parted—ne'er to meet again!
But never either found another
To free the hollow heart from paining—
They stood aloof, the scars remaining,
Like cliffs which had been rent asunder;   410
A dreary sea now flows between,
But neither heat, nor frost, nor thunder,
Shall wholly do away, I ween,
The marks of that which once hath been.

Sir Leoline, a moment's space,   415
Stood gazing on the damsel's face;
And the youthful Lord of Tryermaine
Came back upon his heart again.

O then the Baron forgot his age,
His noble heart swell'd high with rage;   420

9. The place names in part 2 come from the Lake District in northwest England. C found the
manor of Tryermaine in William Hutchinson, *History of Cumberland* (Carlisle, 1794),
99–100. The manor contained "Irthing flood," "Knorren Moor," and Halegarth Wood," mentioned in lines 481–85.
1. C may allude to the split with Southey in 1795. Byron used lines 396–401 and 407–14 as
an epigraph for "Fare Thee Well," when Murray published it in July 1816. Written on
March 18, 1816, on Byron's separation from his wife, it was privately printed and circulated
along with "A Sketch from Private Life," an intemperate attack on his wife's maid, Mary Jane
Clermont. Both poems were printed without authorization on April 14, 1816, in the *Cham-
pion*, a Tory newspaper, along with an attack on Byron and his politics (*Lord Byron: The
Complete Poetical Works*, ed. Jerome J. McGann [Oxford, 1981], 3:380–83, 493–95; David
Erdman, "Byron, Fare Thee Well," *Shelley and His Circle* [Cambridge, Mass., 1970], 4:664).
Byron's patronage, praise of "Christabel," and quotation from it, along with C's allusion to
Byron in the Preface to "Kubla Khan," may have influenced the reception of "Christabel."

He swore by the wounds in Jesu's side,
He would proclaim it far and wide
With trump and solemn heraldry,
That they, who thus had wrong'd the dame,
Were base as spotted infamy!   425
"And if they dare deny the same,
"My herald shall appoint a week,
"And let the recreant traitors seek
"My tournay court—that there and then
"I may dislodge their reptile souls   430
"From the bodies and forms of men!"
He spake: his eye in lightning rolls!
For the lady was ruthlessly seiz'd; and he kenn'd
In the beautiful lady the child of his friend!

And now the tears were on his face,   435
And fondly in his arms he took
Fair Geraldine, who met th' embrace,
Prolonging it with joyous look.
Which when she view'd, a vision fell
Upon the soul of Christabel,   440
The vision of fear, the touch and pain!
She shrunk and shudder'd, and saw again
(Ah, woe is me! Was it for thee,
Thou gentle maid! such sights to see?)[2]

Again she saw that bosom old,   445
Again she felt that bosom cold,
And drew in her breath with a hissing sound:
Whereat the Knight turn'd wildly round,
And nothing saw, but his own sweet maid
With eyes uprais'd, as one that pray'd.   450

The touch, the sight, had pass'd away,
And in its stead that vision blest,
Which comforted her after-rest,
While in the lady's arms she lay,
Had put a rapture in her breast,   455
And on her lips and o'er her eyes
Spread smiles like light![3]
                              With new surprise,
"What ails then my beloved child?"
The Baron said—His daughter mild
Made answer, "All will yet be well!"   460
I ween, she had no power to tell

2. C annotated lines 439–44 in the margin in 1824: "Christabel then recollects the whole, and
   knows that it was not a Dream; but yet cannot disclose the fact, that the strange Lady is a
   supernatural Being with the stamp of the Evil Ones on her." Gillman explains that "Geraldine then appears to her in her real character (*half* human only,) the sight of which alarms
   Christabel" (*Life*, 296).
3. C annotated lines 451–57 in the margin in 1824: "Christabel for a moment sees her
   Mother's Spirit."

Aught else: so mighty was the spell.
Yet he, who saw this Geraldine,
Had deem'd her sure a thing divine,
Such sorrow with such grace she blended,   465
As if she fear'd, she had offended
Sweet Christabel, that gentle maid!
And with such lowly tones she pray'd,
She might be sent without delay
Home to her father's mansion.
                                    "Nay!   470
"Nay, by my soul!" said Leoline.
"Ho! Bracy the bard, the charge be thine!
"Go thou, with music sweet and loud,
"And take two steeds with trappings proud,
"And take the youth whom thou lov'st best   475
"To bear thy harp, and learn thy song,
"And clothe you both in solemn vest,
"And over the mountains haste along,
"Lest wand'ring folk, that are abroad
"Detain you on the valley road.   480

"And when he has cross'd the Irthing flood,
"My merry bard! he hastes, he hastes
"Up Knorren Moor, thro' Halegarth Wood,
"And reaches soon that castle good
"Which stands and threatens Scotland's wastes.   485

"Bard Bracy! bard Bracy! your horses are fleet,[4]
"Ye must ride up the hall, your music so sweet,
"More loud than your horses' echoing feet!
"And loud and loud to Lord Roland call,
"Thy daughter is safe in Langdale hall!   490
"Thy beautiful daughter is safe and free—
"Sir Leoline greets thee thus thro' me.
"He bids thee come without delay
"With all thy numerous array;
"And take thy lovely daughter home,   495
"And he will meet thee on the way
"With all his numerous array
"White with their panting palfreys' foam,
"And, by mine honour! I will say,
"That I repent me of the day   500
"When I spake words of fierce disdain
"To Roland de Vaux of Tryermaine!—
"—For since that evil hour hath flown,
"Many a summer's sun have shone;
"Yet ne'er found I a friend again   505
"Like Roland de Vaux of Tryermaine."

4. C annotated lines 482–86 at the bottom of the page in 1824: "How gladly Sir Leoline repeats the names and shews, how familiarly he had once been acquainted with all the spots
& paths in the neighborhood of his former Friend's Castle & Residence."

The lady fell, and clasped his knees,
Her face uprais'd, her eyes o'erflowing;
And Bracy replied, with faltering voice,
His gracious hail on all bestowing:—   510
Thy words, thou sire of Christabel,
Are sweeter than my harp can tell;
Yet might I gain a boon of thee,
This day my journey should not be,
So strange a dream hath come to me: 515
That I had vow'd with music loud
To clear yon wood from thing unblest,
Warn'd by a vision in my rest!
For in my sleep I saw that dove,
That gentle bird, whom thou dost love,   520
And call'st by thy own daughter's name—
Sir Leoline! I saw the same,
Fluttering, and uttering fearful moan,
Among the green herbs in the forest alone.
Which when I saw and when I heard,   525
I wonder'd what might ail the bird:
For nothing near it could I see,
Save the grass and green herbs underneath the old tree.

And in my dream, methought, I went
To search out what might there be found;   530
And what the sweet bird's trouble meant,
That thus lay fluttering on the ground.
I went and peer'd, and could descry
No cause for her distressful cry;
But yet for her dear lady's sake   535
I stoop'd, methought the dove to take,
When lo! I saw a bright green snake
Coil'd around its wings and neck.
Green as the herbs on which it couch'd,
Close by the dove's its head it crouch'd;   540
And with the dove it heaves and stirs,
Swelling its neck as she swell'd hers!
I woke; it was the midnight hour,
The clock was echoing in the tower;
But tho' my slumber was gone by,   545
This dream it would not pass away—
It seems to live upon my eye!
And thence I vow'd this self-same day,
With music strong and saintly song
To wander thro' the forest bare,   550
Lest aught unholy loiter there.

Thus Bracy said: the Baron, the while,
Half-listening heard him with a smile;
Then turn'd to Lady Geraldine,
His eyes made up of wonder and love;   555

And said in courtly accents fine,
Sweet maid, Lord Roland's beauteous dove,
With arms more strong than harp or song,
Thy sire and I will crush the snake!
He kiss'd her forehead as he spake,   560
And Geraldine in maiden wise,
Casting down her large bright eyes,
With blushing cheek and courtesy fine
She turn'd her from Sir Leoline;
Softly gathering up her train,   565
That o'er her right arm fell again;
And folded her arms across her chest,
And couch'd her head upon her breast,
And look'd askance at Christabel——
Jesu, Maria, shield her well!   570

A snake's small eye blinks dull and shy,
And the lady's eyes they shrunk in her head,
Each shrunk up to a serpent's eye,
And with somewhat of malice, and more of dread
At Christabel she look'd askance!——   575
One moment—and the sight was fled!
But Christabel in dizzy trance,
Stumbling on the unsteady ground—
Shudder'd aloud, with a hissing sound;
And Geraldine again turn'd round,   580
And like a thing, that sought relief,
Full of wonder and full of grief,
She roll'd her large bright eyes divine
Wildly on Sir Leoline.[5]

The maid, alas! her thoughts are gone,   585
She nothing sees—no sight but one!
The maid, devoid of guile and sin,
I know not how, in fearful wise
So deeply had she drunken in
That look, those shrunken serpent eyes,   590
That all her features were resign'd
To this sole image in her mind:
And passively did imitate
That look of dull and treacherous hate.
And thus she stood, in dizzy trance,   595
Still picturing that look askance,
With forc'd unconscious sympathy

5. In 1828 C was shown Thomas Stothard's (1755–1834) sketch of this scene for *The Bijou*
(1829). An anonymous correspondent informed Stothard that when asked whether Sir Leoline was to marry Geraldine, C replied that his affection for Geraldine "was merely
parental—He said that Leoline was an aged man,—hurried by his chivalrous feelings back to
the days of his youth, so much so, that if you remember he declared he would himself encounter in a tilt the wretches who had run away with Geraldine. * * * Geraldines character
is that of *apparent* innocence but of real *malice*" (G. E. Bentley, Jr., "Coleridge, Stothard,
and the First Illustration of 'Christabel,' " *SIR* 20 [1981]: 114).

Full before her father's view——
As far as such a look could be,
In eyes so innocent and blue!   600

But when the trance was o'er, the maid
Paus'd awhile, and inly pray'd,
Then falling at her father's feet,
"By my mother's soul do I entreat
"That thou this woman send away!"   605
She said; and more she could not say,
For what she knew she could not tell,
O'er-master'd by the mighty spell.

Why is thy cheek so wan and wild,
Sir Leoline? Thy only child   610
Lies at thy feet, thy joy, thy pride,
So fair, so innocent, so mild;
The same, for whom thy lady died!
O by the pangs of her dear mother
Think thou no evil of thy child!   615
For her, and thee, and for no other,
She pray'd the moment, ere she died;
Pray'd that the babe for whom she died,
Might prove her dear lord's joy and pride!
    That prayer her deadly pangs beguil'd,   620
            Sir Leoline!
    And would'st thou wrong thy only child,
            Her child and thine?
Within the Baron's heart and brain
If thoughts, like these, had any share,   625
They only swell'd his rage and pain,
And did but work confusion there.
His heart was cleft with pain and rage,
His cheeks they quiver'd, his eyes were wild,
Dishonour'd thus in his old age;   630
Dishonour'd by his only child,
And all his hospitality
To th'insulted daughter of his friend
By more than woman's jealousy,
Brought thus to a disgraceful end—   635
He roll'd his eye with stern regard
Upon the gentle minstrel bard,
And said in tones abrupt, austere—
Why, Bracy! dost thou loiter here?
I bade thee hence! The bard obey'd;   640
And turning from his own sweet maid,
The aged knight, Sir Leoline,
Led forth the lady Geraldine!

The Conclusion
to
Part the Second[6]

A little child, a limber elf,
Singing, dancing to itself, 645
A fairy thing with red round cheeks
That always finds, and never seeks,
Makes such a vision to the sight
As fills a father's eyes with light;
And pleasures flow in so thick and fast 650
Upon his heart, that he at last
Must needs express his love's excess
With words of unmeant bitterness.
Perhaps 'tis pretty to force together
Thoughts so all unlike each other; 655
To mutter and mock a broken charm,
To dally with wrong that does no harm.
Perhaps 'tis tender too and pretty
At each wild word to feel within,
A sweet recoil of love and pity. 660
And what, if in a world of sin
(O sorrow and shame should this be true!)
Such giddiness of heart and brain
Comes seldom save from rage and pain,
So talks as it's most used to do.[7] 665

6. Not in any surviving manuscript of the poem. The conclusion to part 2 was first drafted in a letter to Southey of May 6, 1801, and described by his son Hartley. C thought it "a very metaphysical account of Fathers calling their children rogues, rascals, & little varlets" (CL, 2:729).

7. In August 1820 C told Thomas Allsop, "If I should finish 'Christabel,' I shall certainly extend it, and give it new characters, and a greater number of incidents. This the 'reading public' require, and this is the reason that Sir Walter Scott's poems, though so loosely written, are pleasing, and interest us by their picturesqueness. * * * [C]ertainly the first canto is more perfect, has more of the true wild weird spirit than the last" (TT [CC], 2:359). Perhaps C's comment to Allsop explains Gillman's account of C's plans for the rest of the poem:

> Over the mountains, the Bard, as directed by Sir Leoline, 'hastes' with his disciple; but in consequence of one of those inundations supposed to be common to this country, the spot only where the castle once stood is discovered,—the edifice itself being washed away. He determines to return. Geraldine being acquainted with all that is passing, like the Weird Sisters in Macbeth, vanishes. Re-appearing, she waits the return of the Bard, exciting in the mean time, by her wily arts, all the anger she could rouse in the Baron's breast, as well as that jealousy of which he is described to have been susceptible. The old Bard and the youth at length arrive, and therefore she can no longer personate the character of Geraldine, the daughter of Lord Roland de Vaux, but changes her appearance to that of the accepted though absent lover of Christabel. Next ensues a courtship most distressing to Christabel, who feels—she knows not why— great disgust for her once favoured knight. This coldness is very painful to the Baron, who has no more conception than herself of the supernatural transformation. She at last yields to her father's entreaties, and consents to approach the altar with this hated suitor. The real lover returning, enters at this moment, and produces the ring which she had once given him in sign of her betrothment. Thus defeated, the supernatural being Geraldine disappears. As predicted, the castle bell tolls, the mother's voice is heard, and to the exceeding great joy of the parties, the rightful marriage takes place, after which follows a reconciliation and explanation between father and daughter [Life, 301–02].

KUBLA KHAN:

OR

A VISION IN A DREAM[1]

Of the
Fragment of Kubla Khan

The following fragment is here published at the request of a poet of great and deserved celebrity,[2] and as far as the Author's own opinions are concerned, rather as a psychological curiosity, than on the ground of any supposed *poetic* merits.[3]

In the summer of the year 1797, the Author, then in ill health, had retired to a lonely farmhouse between Porlock and Linton, on the Exmoor confines of Somerset and Devonshire. In consequence of a slight indisposition, an anodyne had been prescribed, from the effects of which he fell asleep in his chair at the moment that he was reading the following sentence, or words of the same substance, in "Purchas's Pilgrimage:" "Here the Khan Kubla commanded a palace to be built, and a stately garden thereunto. And thus ten miles of fertile ground were inclosed with a wall."[4] The author continued for about three

---

1. On the only manuscript of the poem, known as the Crewe manuscript, now in the British Library, C wrote at the bottom, "This fragment with a good deal more, not recoverable, composed, in a sort of Reverie brought on by two grains of Opium, taken to check a dysentery, at a Farm House between Porlock and Linton, a quarter of a mile from Culbone Church, in the fall of the year, 1797." A penciled notation on the manuscript says that it was "sent by Mr. Southey, as an Autograph of Coleridge" to Elizabeth Smith (1770–1859), a friend of Southey and collector of autographs, on February 2, 1804, so the latest date of the manuscript is the middle of January when C left for London and Malta (Hilton Kelliher, "The *Kubla Khan* Manuscript and Its First Collector," *The British Library Journal* 20 [1994]: 189–92). The earliest reference to the poem is in Dorothy Wordsworth's journal for October 1798, when in Germany she took "Kubla to a fountain," a pun on *Kübel*, the German word for bucket or can (*Journals of Dorothy Wordsworth*, ed. E. de Selincourt [New York, 1941], 1:34). It may have been written, not in the summer as C said in the Preface, but in the fall of 1797, since C wrote Thelwall on October 14 that he had been "absent a day or two" (*CL*, 1:349). It might also have been written in November 1797 when C and the Wordsworths were on a walk to the Valley of the Rocks, described in "Wanderings of Cain." Another possible date is May 16 or 17, 1798, since Dorothy Wordsworth notes a walking tour to the same area (*DWJ*, 14), and in a notebook entry of 1810 C linked his failure to finish "Christabel" and his "retirement between Linton & Porlock" with taking opium and the distress over Lloyd's publishing *Edmund Oliver* (*CN*, 3:4006 and n.). Culbone is on the south coast of the Bristol Channel, west of Porlock, and is set in a landscape of hills falling sharply into the ocean. "Kubla Khan" may reflect C's letter of March 10, 1798, to his brother George, which described his taking opium for a painful tooth. He described repose, "a spot of inchantment, a green spot of fountains, & flowers & trees, in the very heart of a waste of Sands" (*CL*, 1:394). The Crewe manuscript has some variants, noted here, and is divided into only two verse paragraphs between lines 36 and 37, whereas the version in *Christabel* is divided into four stanzas with divisions after lines 11, 30, and 36. In *Poetical Works* (1828, 1834) it is printed in three stanzas, with divisions after lines 11 and 30; most modern editions, following EHC, divide the poem after lines 11 and 36 (Stillinger, 75–76).
2. Byron.
3. This paragraph was included in *Poetical Works* (1828 and 1829) but omitted in 1834, whether by C or HNC is unclear. See the headnote to *Poetical Works* (p. 203 herein).
4. It is not clear which edition of *Purchas his Pilgrimage* by Samuel Purchas (?1577–1626) C was reading. EHC quotes the edition of 1626, 4.13.418: "In Xamdu did Cublai Can build a stately Palace, encompassing Sixteene miles of plaine ground with a wall, wherein are fertile Meddowes, pleasant Springs, delightfull streams, and all sorts of beasts of chase and game, and in the middest thereof a sumptuous house of pleasure" (*PW*, 1:296). *Purchas his Pilgrimage* was first published in 1613. Wordsworth owned a copy of the third edition of 1617, and C may have been reading that edition (Lowes, 360).

hours in a profound sleep, at least of the external senses, during which
time he has the most vivid confidence, that he could not have composed less than from two to three hundred lines; if that indeed can be
called composition in which all the images rose up before him as
things, with a parallel production of the correspondent expressions,
without any sensation or consciousness of effort. On awaking he appeared to himself to have a distinct recollection of the whole, and taking his pen, ink, and paper, instantly and eagerly wrote down the lines
that are here preserved. At this moment he was unfortunately called
out by a person on business from Porlock, and detained by him above
an hour, and on his return to his room, found to his no small surprise
and mortification, that though he still retained some vague and dim
recollection of the general purpose of the vision, yet, with the exception
of some eight or ten scattered lines and images, all the rest had passed
away like the images on the surface of a stream into which a stone has
been cast, but, alas! without the after restoration of the latter:[5]

> Then all the charm
> Is broken—all that phantom-world so fair
> Vanishes, and a thousand circlets spread,
> And each mis-shape the other.   Stay awhile,
> Poor youth! who scarcely dar'st lift up thine eyes—
> The stream will soon renew its smoothness, soon
> The visions will return! And lo, he stays,
> And soon the fragments dim of lovely forms
> Come trembling back, unite, and now once more
> The pool becomes a mirror.[6]

Yet from the still surviving recollections in his mind, the Author has
frequently purposed to finish for himself what had been originally, as
it were, given to him. Σαμερον αδιον ασω:[7] but the to-morrow is yet
to come.

As a contrast to this vision, I have annexed a fragment of a very different character, describing with equal fidelity the dream of pain and
disease.[8]

---

5. There are no other lines for "Kubla Khan." The poem has been read either as a fragment of
   a longer narrative or, more often, as a completed poem.
6. From C's "The Picture, or the Lover's Resolution," lines 90–99 in *SL*.
7. "I will sing something sweeter today." C's source is Theocritus, "Idylls," line 145, in *The
   Greek Bucolic Poets*, trans. J. M. Edmonds (LCL, 1912), 22–23: "I'll e'en sing you a sweeter
   song another day," which in 1834 C or HNC changed to "I'll sing a sweeter song a later day."
8. "The Pains of Sleep"

Kubla Khan

In Xanadu did KUBLA KHAN
A stately pleasure-dome decree:
Where ALPH,[9] the sacred river, ran
Through caverns measureless to man
   Down to a sunless sea.   5
So twice five miles[1] of fertile ground
With walls and towers were girdled[2] round;
And here were gardens bright with sinuous rills
Where blossom'd many an incense-bearing tree;
And here were forests ancient as the hills,[3]   10
And folding[4] sunny spots of greenery.

But oh that deep romantic chasm which slanted
Down the green hill athwart a cedarn cover!
A savage place! as holy and inchanted
As e'er beneath a waning moon was haunted   15
By woman wailing[5] for her demon-lover!
And from this chasm, with ceaseless[6] turmoil seething,
As if this earth in fast thick pants were breathing,
A mighty fountain momently was forced:
Amid whose swift half-intermitted Burst   20
Huge fragments vaulted like rebounding hail,
Or chaffy grain beneath the thresher's flail:
And mid these dancing rocks at once and ever
It flung up momently the sacred river.
Five miles meandering with a mazy motion[7]   25
Through wood and dale the sacred river ran,
Then reached the caverns measureless to man,
And sank in tumult to a lifeless ocean:
And 'mid this tumult Kubla heard from far
Ancestral voices prophesying war!   30

9. Alpheus is a river in Greece. As told by Ovid in the *Metamorphoses* 5.574–641, the nymph Arethusa bathed in the river, and the river god, Alpheus, fell in love with her. She became a river and then a fountain in Ortygia, an island near Syracuse. Alpheus flowed under the sea to be united with the fountain. Milton used the myth in "Lycidas," lines 85 and 132 and in "Arcades," lines 30–31: "Divine *Alpheus*, who by secret sluse, / Stole under Seas to meet his *Arethuse*."
1. In the Crewe manuscript "twice six miles."
2. In the Crewe manuscript "compass'd."
3. The landscape recalls Eden in *Paradise Lost* 4.132–35: "*Eden*, where delicious Paradise, / Now nearer, Crowns with her enclosure green, / As with a rural mound the champain head / Of a steep wilderness"; 4:216–17: "Out of the fertil ground he caus'd to grow / All Trees of noblest kind for sight, smell, taste"; 4.223–25: "Southward through *Eden* went a River large, / Nor chang'd his course, but through the shaggie hill / Pass'd underneath ingulft"; and 4.229–331: "many a rill / Waterd the Garden; thence united fell / Down the steep glade, and met the nether Flood."
4. Most likely a printer's error for "Enfolding," as in the Crewe manuscript and later printings.
5. Perhaps Κυβέλα, or Cybele, the Asiatic goddess of wild nature, the great mother or earth mother, whose original shrine was a cave, whose symbol was a stone, and who wailed the loss of her lover Attis. See Richard Gerber, "Keys to 'Kubla Khan,'" *English Studies* (Amsterdam) 44 (1963): 321–41.
6. In the Crewe manuscript "hideous."
7. Cf. *Paradise Lost* 4.239: the streams in Eden run with "mazie error" and Gray's "Progress of Poesy," line 4: "A thousand rills their mazy progress take," from the springs of Helicon.

The shadow of the dome of pleasure
Floated midway on the waves;
Where was heard the mingled measure[8]
From the fountain and the caves.
It was a miracle of rare device,   35
A sunny pleasure-dome with caves of ice![9]

A damsel with a dulcimer
In a vision once I saw:
It was an Abyssinian maid
And on her dulcimer she play'd,   40
Singing of Mount Abora.[1]
Could I revive within me
Her symphony and song,
To such a deep delight 'twould win me,
That with music loud and long,   45
I would build that dome in air,
That sunny dome! those caves of ice!
And all who heard should see them there,
And all should cry, Beware! Beware!
His flashing eyes, his floating hair![2]   50
Weave a circle round him thrice,
And close your eyes with holy dread:
For he on honey-dew hath fed,
And drank the milk of Paradise.[3]

8. Cf. Collins, "The Passions. An Ode for Music," line 64: "Through glades and glooms the mingled measure stole."
9. Probably before the summer of 1797 C copied in a notebook a passage from Thomas Maurice, *The History of Hindostan* (1795), 1:106–07: "In a cave in the mountains of Cashmere an Image of Ice, which makes its appearance thus—[']two days before the new *moon* there appears a bubble of Ice which increases in size every day till the 15ᵗʰ day, at which it is an ell or more in height: then as the moon decreases, the Image['] does also till it vanishes" (*CN*, 1:240). C could also be thinking of the Russian ice palace described in Cowper, *The Task* 5.127–76.
1. In the Crewe manuscript the name was written Amora and then changed to Amara. In *Paradise Lost* 4.280–83, the Abyssinian "Kings thir issue Guard, / Mount *Amara*, though this by some suppos'd / True Paradise under the *Ethiop* Line / By *Nilus* head." James Bruce, *Travels to Discover the Source of the Nile* (1790), describes a tributary of the Nile, the river Abola (Lowes, 373).
2. Cf. *The Aeneid* 4.147–48, where Apollo is described with "flowing locks" (*Virgil: Eclogues, Georgics, Aeneid 1–VI*, trans. H. Rushton Fairclough, rev. G. P. Goold [LCL, 1999], 433), and Horace, *Odes* 3.4.62, where Apollo has "flowing locks" (*Horace: Odes and Epodes*, trans. C. E. Bennett [LCL, 1914], 190–91).
3. C draws on the portrait of the inspired, lyric poets in Plato, *Ion*, 534, whose songs "are the sweets they cull from honey-dropping founts in certain gardens and glades of the Muses" (*Plato: Ion*, trans. W. R. M. Lamb [LCL, 1925], 423.)

The Pains of Sleep[1]

Ere on my bed my limbs I lay,
It hath not been my use to pray
With moving lips or bended knees;
But silently, by slow degrees,
My spirit I to Love compose,   5
In humble Trust mine eye-lids close,
With reverential resignation,
No wish conceived, no thought expressed!
Only a *sense* of supplication,
A sense o'er all my soul imprest   10
That I am weak, yet not unblest,
Since in me, round me, every where
Eternal Strength and Wisdom are.

But yester-night I pray'd aloud
In anguish and in agony,   15
Up-starting from the fiendish crowd
Of shapes and thoughts that tortured me:
A lurid light, a trampling throng,
Sense of intolerable wrong,
And whom I scorn'd, those only strong!   20
Thirst of revenge, the powerless will
Still baffled, and yet burning still![2]
Desire with loathing strangely mixed
On wild or hateful objects fixed.
Fantastic passions! mad'ning brawl![3]   25
And shame and terror over all!
Deeds to be hid which were not hid,
Which all confused I could not know,
Whether I suffered, or I did:
For all seemed guilt, remorse or woe,   30
My own or others still the same
Life-stifling fear, soul-stifling shame!

So two nights passed: the night's dismay
Sadden'd and stunn'd the coming day.

1. Sent in a letter to Southey, September 11, 1803, upon his return from a walking tour in Scotland, which began with the Wordsworths but ended in their going their separate ways, with the introductory comment as a "true portrait of my nights": "I have walked 263 miles in eight Days—so I must have strength somewhere / but my spirits are dreadful, owing entirely to the Horrors of every night—I truly dread to sleep / it is no shadow with me, but substantial Misery foot-thick, that makes me sit by my bedside of a morning, & *cry*—. I have abandoned all opiates except Ether be one; & that only in *fits*—& that is a blessed medicine!—& when you see me drink a glass of Spirit & Water, except by prescription of a physician, you shall despise me—but still I can not get quiet rest" (*CL*, 2:982–84). On October 3 he sent a version of lines 18–32 to Poole with the description of his "own loud Screams that had awakened me * * * till my repeated Night-yells had made me a Nuisance in my own House. As I live & am a man, this is an unexaggerated Tale—my Dreams became the Substances of my Life" (*CL*, 2:1009).
2. In the letter to Poole C added two lines following line 22: "Tempestuous pride, vain-glorious Vaunting, / Base Men my vices justly taunting" (*CL*, 2:1009).
3. In the letter to Southey this line was "Rage, sensual Passion, mad'ning Brawl" (*CL*, 2:983).

Sleep, the wide blessing, seemed to me   35
Distemper's worst calamity.
The third night, when my own loud scream
Had waked me from the fiendish dream,
O'ercome with sufferings strange and wild,
I wept as I had been a child;   40
And having thus by tears subdued
My anguish to a milder mood,
Such punishments, I said, were due
To natures deepliest stain'd with sin:
For aye entempesting anew   45
Th'unfathomable hell within
The horror of their deeds to view,
To know and loathe, yet wish and do!
Such griefs with such men well agree,
But wherefore, wherefore fall on me?   50
To be beloved is all I need,
And whom I love, I love indeed.[4]

FROM SIBYLLINE LEAVES (1817)

In March 1815 Coleridge asked Byron for help in obtaining a publisher
for a two-volume edition of his poetry, which would contain a preface on
"the Principles of philosophic and genial criticism" (CL, 4:561). On October 15 Coleridge told Byron that "a few Friends at Bristol undertook the
risk of printing two volumes for me," which had been sent to the printer.
Coleridge's school friend John Gutch (1776–1861) supervised the printer,
John Evans (1774–1828), in Bristol, before they contracted with a publisher. The preface projected in March had expanded into a full volume,
"Biographical Sketches of my own literary Life and Opinions, on Politics,
Religion, Philosophy and the Theory of Poetry," and the projected two volumes of poetry became one volume, "a collection of all the Poems, that
are my own property, which I wish to have preserved" (CL, 6:1037). John
Murray held the copyright to "Christabel" until it was finished. Joseph
Cottle had sold the copyright for Poems (1796) to Longman (1771–1842),
but Coleridge retained the rights to the poems added in 1797 (CL,
6:1006n., 1034n.). As a result, Sibylline Leaves did not contain the poems
in Christabel and Poems (1796), with the exception of "The Eolian Harp."
   The printing of Sibylline Leaves began late in November 1815 with "The
Ancient Mariner," and continued through June 1816 (CL, 4:618n.). Since
Coleridge had not obtained a publisher, the title page and preface were
not printed first. John Evans sent proofs to Coleridge with corrections entered in ink and a few queries and suggestions for revision, some of which,

4. On May 19, 1814, C sent a variant of lines 50–53 to Henry Daniel, whom C had consulted
   on his attempts to free himself from opium as "an exact and most faithful portraiture of the
   state of my mind under influences of incipient bodily derangement from the use of Opium,
   at the time that I yet remained ignorant of the cause": "O, if for such sufferings be, / Yet why,
   O God, yet why for me? / From low desires my Heart hath fled, / On Beauty hath my Fancy
   fed; / To be beloved is all I need, / And whom I love, I love indeed. / My waking thoughts
   with scorn repell / Loveless Lust, Revenge[ful] spell:— / O why should Sleep be made my
   Hell" (CL, 3:495). C was probably not aware of the addictive power of opium when he wrote
   the poem, and his pains were most likely from withdrawal.

along with Coleridge's responses, are included here in the notes from the proofs now at Yale. Coleridge corrected each set of proofs as it was sent to him, and then the sheets for 750 copies were printed. Since Murray had published *Christabel* and had advised him on the publication of the *Biographia*, Coleridge assumed that Murray would publish *Sibylline Leaves*; but Murray declined, disappointed with the reviews of *Christabel* and wary of the metaphysics in the *Biographia*. Coleridge negotiated with Rest Fenner, but disputes over printing bills and the final transmission of the printed sheets to London delayed publication until July 1817.

As Coleridge says in the Preface, the title "*Sibylline Leaves*" refers to the legend of the Sibyl's scattered prophecies. In the *Aeneid* 3.443–52 Virgil describes the Sibyl as an inspired prophetess, who writes prophecies on leaves that she hangs in her cave. When any breeze disturbs their order and scatters them, the Sibyl does not bother to restore order, and those who wish to consult the prophecies depart frustrated, being unable to understand the signs and symbols of prophecy. *Sibylline Leaves* collects poems originally scattered in many different publications. It contains sixty-one poems by Coleridge and one by the American painter Washington Allston (see headnote to *Essays on The Principles of Genial Criticism* on p. 338 herein). Thirty-two poems were first published in whole or in part in various newspapers or magazines. Of the other twenty-nine poems, "The Eolian Harp" first appeared in *Poems* (1796); six, in *Poems* (1797); three, in *Fears in Solitude* (1798); three, in *Lyrical Ballads* (1798 and 1800); four, in *The Annual Anthology* (1800); and two, in *The Friend* (1809). Ten poems had not been published before. A second legend of the Sibyl is relevant to "The Ancient Mariner." In *Metamorphoses* 14.130–53 Ovid tells the Sibyl's story. Apollo granted her one wish. She asked for as many years of life as grains of sand she held in her hand but forgot to ask for eternal youth. When Aeneas meets her, she has shriveled to almost nothing. Only her voice remains. *Sibylline Leaves* begins with "The Ancient Mariner," whose soul is won by the "Night-mare Life-in-Death," lines first printed in *Sibylline Leaves*.

"The Ancient Mariner" is followed by "The Foster-Mother's Tale," which is in turn followed by four categories of poems: "Poems Occasioned by Political Events or Feelings Connected with Them"; "Love-Poems"; "Meditative Poems in Blank Verse," followed by "The Three Graves"; and "Odes and Miscellaneous Poems," which ends with "The Destiny of Nations." "The Destiny of Nations" concludes with ten pages introduced with a note that "the following fragments were intended to form part of the Poem when finished." *Sibylline Leaves*, like the Sibyl's prophecies, ends in scattered fragments. The contents of each category are described in the notes.

The poems are printed here in the order of the volume, with the errata entered.

Preface[1]

The following collection has been entitled SIBYLLINE LEAVES; in allusion to the fragmentary and widely scattered state in which they have

1. When C agreed with Rest Fenner in London to publish *SL*, Samuel Curtis printed the front pages. They included the Preface, three poems, and a two-page errata list. The poems were "Time, Real and Imaginary"; "The Raven"; and "Mutual Passion," a close imitation of Ben Jonson, "A Nymph's Passion." All are omitted here, as is the final paragraph of the Preface, which describes these poems.

been long suffered to remain. It contains the whole of the author's poetical compositions, from 1793 to the present date, with the exception
of a few works not yet finished, and those published in the first edition
of his juvenile poems, over which he has no controul. They may be divided into three classes: First, A selection from the Poems added to
the second and third editions, together with those originally published
in the LYRICAL BALLADS, which after having remained many years out
of print, have been omitted by Mr. Wordsworth in the recent collection of all his minor poems,[2] and of course revert to the author. Second, Poems published at very different periods, in various obscure or
perishable journals, &c. some with, some without the writer's consent;
many imperfect, all incorrect. The third and last class is formed of Poems which have hitherto remained in manuscript. The whole is now
presented to the reader collectively, with considerable additions and
alterations, and as perfect as the author's judgment and powers could
render them.

In my Literary Life, it has been mentioned that, with the exception
of this preface, the SIBYLLINE LEAVES have been printed almost two
years;[3] and the necessity of troubling the reader with the list of errata,
which follows this preface, alone induces me to refer again to the circumstance, at the risk of ungenial feelings, from the recollection of its
worthless causes. A few corrections of later date have been added.—
Henceforward the author must be occupied by studies of a very different kind.

> Ite hinc, CAMŒNÆ! Vos quoque ite, suaves,
> Dulces CAMŒNÆ! Nam (fatebimur verum)
> Dulces fuistis!—Et tamen meas chartas
> Revisitote: sed pudenter et raro!
> VIRGIL. Catalect. vii.[4]

*   *   *

2. *Poems by William Wordsworth: Including Lyrical Ballads, and the Miscellaneous Pieces of the Author* was published in April 1815.
3. The last proofs of *SL* printed in Bristol were sent to C in June 1816. The volume was pub-
lished in July 1817 (*CL*, 4:618n., 754n.).
4. C quotes Virgil, "Catalepton" 5.11–14 (var.): "Get ye hence, ye Muses! yea, away now even
with you, ye sweet Muses! For the truth we must avow—ye have been sweet. And yet, come
ye back to my pages, though with modesty and but seldom!" (*Aeneid VII–XII, The Minor Poems*, trans. H. Ruston Fairclough [LCL, 1934]). C copied the quotation into a notebook
sometime in 1807 or 1808 (*CN*, 2:3200) and used it in the first number of *The Friend*
[*Friend* [CC], 2:15]).

LOVE-POEMS[1]

The Picture,
or
The Lover's Resolution[1]

Through weeds and thorns, and matted underwood
I force my way; now climb, and now descend
O'er rocks, or bare or mossy, with wild foot
Crushing the purple whorts; while oft unseen,
Hurrying along the drifted forest-leaves,   5
The scared snake rustles. Onward still I toil,
I know not, ask not whither! A new joy,
Lovely as light, sudden as summer-gust,
And gladsome as the first-born of the spring,
Beckons me on, or follows from behind,   10
Playmate, or guide! The master-passion quell'd,
I feel that I am free. With dun-red bark
The fir-trees, and th' unfrequent slender oak,
Forth from this tangle wild of bush and brake
Soar up, and form a melancholy vault   15
High o'er me, murmuring like a distant sea.

Here Wisdom might resort, and here Remorse;
Here too the love-lorn Man who, sick in soul
And of this busy human heart aweary,

1. The category of love poems contains seventeen poems, most of them connected with Sara
Hutchinson. The section begins with "Love," first printed in *LB* (1800), and "Lewti," printed
in *AA*. The category is prefaced by lines in Latin from Petrarch, "Epistola Barbato Sulmonensi" (Letter to Barbato da Sulmona), lines 42–49, 63–65, which Coleridge copied in a
notebook in 1813: you read what "once in my tender youth my humble pen poured forth.
You read here of tears and how the quivered boy wounded me, a boy, with piercing barb. Advancing time devours all things by degrees, and as we live we die, and as we rest we are hurried onward. For if I am compared with myself I shall not seem the same. My face is
changed, my ways are changed, I have a new kind of understanding, my voice sounds otherwise. With cold heart now I pity hot Lovers, and am ashamed that I myself burned. The
peaceful mind shudders at past tumults, and reading again thinks that some other wrote
those words" (*CN*, 3:4178n.). For another use of this quotation, see the *Biographia*, chapter
10 (p. 461 herein).
1. Composed August 1802 and first published in *MP*, September 6, 1802, signed ΕΣΤΗΣΕ
(*EOT* [*CC*], 3:293). The theme of a failed resolution may have been suggested by "Der feste
Vorsatz" (The Fixed Resolution) by Salomon Gessner (1730–1788), whom C was reading in
July 1802 (*CL*, 2:808). The theme of lines 117–18 is stated in a notebook entry of March or
April 1802: "A Poem on the endeavor to emancipate the soul from day-dreams & note the
different attempts & the vain ones" (*CN*, 1:1153). The poem describes C's walking tour in
the Lake District in early August 1802 recorded in his notebooks. C wrote a note at the beginning of the poem in a copy of *SL*: "I do not recollect any number of lines under the name
of a Poem, that more strikingly illustrates the nature and necessity of some *one Spirit*, a
Unity beside and beyond mere connection, a Life in and over all, as the Light at once hidden and revealed in all the Colours that are the component Integers of the Vision.—In this
poem there is no defect of *Connection*. The thoughts pass into each other without a saltus
[a leap], the Imagery is sufficiently homogeneous, and the Feelings harmonize with both,
and plainly produce or modify both. But there is no under-current that 'moves onward from
within'—the *one Spirit* is absent, '*and it is he, That makes the ship to go*.' S.T.C." (Johnson,
471). C quotes "The Ancient Mariner" (1834), lines 379–80. The text printed here includes
the errata printed in *SL*.

Worships the spirit of unconscious life 20
In tree or wild-flower.—Gentle Lunatic!
If so he might not wholly cease to be,
He would far rather not be that, he is;
But would be something, that he knows not of,
In winds or waters, or among the rocks![2] 25

But hence, fond wretch! breathe not contagion here!
No myrtle-walks are these: these are no groves
Where Love dare loiter! If in sullen mood
He should stray hither, the low stumps shall gore
His dainty feet, the briar and the thorn 30
Make his plumes haggard. Like a wounded bird
Easily caught, ensnare him, O ye Nymphs,
Ye Oreads chaste, ye dusky Dryades!
And you, ye EARTH-WINDS! you that make at morn
The dew-drops quiver on the spiders' webs! 35
You, O ye wingless AIRS! that creep between
The rigid stems of heath and bitten furze,
Within whose scanty shade, at summer-noon,
The mother-sheep hath worn a hollow bed—
Ye, that now cool her fleece with dropless Damp, 40
Now pant and murmur with her feeding lamb.
Chase, chase him, all ye Fays, and elfin Gnomes!
With prickles sharper than his darts bemock
His little Godship, making him perforce
Creep through a thorn-bush on yon hedgehog's back. 45

This is my hour of triumph! I can now
With my own fancies play the merry fool,
And laugh away worse folly, being free.
Here will I seat myself, beside this old,
Hollow, and weedy oak, which ivy-twine 50
Cloaths as with net-work: here will couch my limbs,
Close by this river, in this silent shade,
As safe and sacred from the step of man
As an invisible world—unheard, unseen,
And listening only to the pebbly brook 55
That murmurs with a dead, yet bell-like sound
Tinkling, or bees, that in the neighbouring trunk
Make honey-hoards. This breeze, that visits me,
Was never Love's accomplice, never rais'd
The tendril ringlets from the maiden's brow, 60
And the blue, delicate veins above her cheek;
Ne'er play'd the wanton—never half disclosed
The maiden's snowy bosom, scattering thence

2. C quoted lines 17–25 (var.) in a letter to Cottle, May 27, 1814, as "descriptive of a gloomy
solitude" in which "I disguised my own sensations" (CL, 3:499). On February 8, 1826, C
quoted lines 20–25 (var.) in a letter to Edward Coleridge (1800–1883) with the remark that
"My state of mind was too often in too close a neighbourhood to the relaxing Malaria of the
Mystic Divinity, which affects to languish after an extinction of individual Consciousness—
the sickly state which I had myself described" (CL, 6:555).

Eye-poisons for some love-distempered youth,
Who ne'er henceforth may see an aspen-grove   65
Shiver in sunshine, but his feeble heart
Shall flow away like a dissolving thing.

   Sweet breeze! thou only, if I guess aright,
Liftest the feathers of the robin's breast,
Who swells his little breast, so full of song,   70
Singing above me, on the mountain-ash.
And thou too, desert Stream! no pool of thine,
Though clear as lake in latest summer-eve,
Did e'er reflect the stately virgin's robe,
Her face, her form divine, her downcast look   75
Contemplative! Ah see! her open palm
Presses her cheek and brow! her elbow rests
On the bare branch of half-uprooted tree,
That leans towards its mirror! He, meanwhile,
Who from her countenance turn'd, or look'd by stealth,   80
(For fear is true love's cruel nurse,) he now,
With stedfast gaze and unoffending eye,
Worships the watery idol, dreaming hopes
Delicious to the soul, but fleeting, vain,
E'en as that phantom-world on which he gazed.   85
She, sportive tyrant! with her left hand plucks[3]
The heads of tall flowers that behind her grow,
Lychnis, and willow-herb, and fox-glove bells;
And suddenly, as one that toys with time,
Scatters them on the pool! Then all the charm   90
Is broken—all that phantom-world so fair
Vanishes, and a thousand circlets spread,
And each mis-shape the other. Stay awhile,
Poor youth, who scarcely dar'st lift up thine eyes!
The stream will soon renew its smoothness, soon   95
The visions will return! And lo! he stays:
And soon the fragments dim of lovely forms
Come trembling back, unite, and now once more
The pool becomes a mirror, and behold[4]
Each wildflower on the marge inverted there,   100
And there the half-uprooted tree—but where,
O where the virgin's snowy arm, that lean'd
On its bare branch? He turns, and she is gone!
Homeward she steals through many a woodland maze
Which he shall seek in vain. Ill-fated youth!   105
Go, day by day, and waste thy manly prime
In mad Love-yearning by the vacant brook,
Till sickly thoughts bewitch thine eyes, and thou

---

3. JDC (628) reports that in a copy of *SL*, C drew a line down the margin of lines 76–86 and
added the comment: "These lines I hope to fuse into a more continuous flow, at least to articulate more organically." No major revisions survive.
4. Lines 90–99 were quoted in the preface to "Kubla Khan" (p. 181 herein).

Behold'st her shadow still abiding there,
The Naiad of the Mirror!

                    Not to thee,   110
O wild and desert Stream! belongs this tale:
Gloomy and dark art thou—the crowded firs
Tower from thy shores, and stretch across thy bed,
Making thee doleful as a cavern-well:
Save when the shy king-fishers build their nest   115
On thy steep banks, no loves hast thou, wild stream!

   This be my chosen haunt—emancipate
From passion's dreams, a freeman, and alone,
I rise and trace its devious course. O lead,
Lead me to deeper shades and lonelier glooms.   120
Lo! stealing through the canopy of firs
How fair the sunshine spots that mossy rock,
Isle of the river, whose disparted waters
Dart off asunder with an angry sound,
How soon to re-unite! And see! they meet,   125
Each in the other lost and found: and, see!
Placeless, as spirits, one soft Water-sun
Throbbing within them, Heart at once and Eye!
With its soft neighbourhood of filmy Clouds,
The Stains and Shadings of forgotten Tears,   130
Dimness o'erswum with lustre!—Such the hour
Of deep enjoyment, following Love's brief feuds!
But hark, the noise of a near waterfall!
I come out into light—I find myself
Beneath a weeping birch (most beautiful   135
Of forest-trees, the Lady of the woods),
Hard by the brink of a tall weedy rock
That overbrows the cataract. How bursts
The landscape on my sight! Two crescent hills
Fold in behind each other, and so make   140
A circular vale, and land-lock'd, as might seem,
With brook and bridge, and grey stone cottages,
Half hid by rocks and fruit-trees.   At my feet,
The whortle-berries are bedewed with spray,
Dashed upwards by the furious waterfall.   145
How solemnly the pendent ivy-mass
Swings in its winnow!   All the air is calm.
The smoke from cottage-chimnies, ting'd with light,
Rises in columns: from this house alone,
Close by the waterfall, the column slants,   150
And feels its ceaseless breeze.   But what is THIS?
That cottage, with its slanting chimney-smoke,
And close beside its porch a sleeping child,
His dear head pillowed on a sleeping dog—
One arm between its fore legs, and the hand   155
Holds loosely its small handful of wild-flowers,

Unfilletted, and of unequal lengths.
A curious picture, with a master's haste
Sketch'd on a strip of pinky-silver skin,
Peel'd from the birchen bark!   Divinest maid!   160
Yon bark her canvas, and those purple berries
Her pencil! See, the juice is scarcely dried
On the fine skin! She has been newly here;
And lo! yon patch of heath has been her couch—
The pressure still remains!   O blessed couch!   165
For this may'st thou flower early, and the Sun,
Slanting at eve, rest bright, and linger long
Upon thy purple bells!   O Isabel!
Daughter of genius! stateliest of our maids!
More beautiful than whom Alcæus woo'd   170
The Lesbian woman of immortal song![5]
O child of genius! stately, beautiful,
And full of love to all, save only me,
And not ungentle e'en to me!   My heart,
Why beats it thus?   Through yonder coppice-wood   175
Needs must the pathway turn, that leads straightway
On to her father's house.   She is alone!
The night draws on—such ways are hard to hit—
And fit it is I should restore this sketch,
Dropt unawares no doubt.   Why should I yearn   180
To keep the relique? 'twill but idly feed
The passion that consumes me.   Let me haste!
The picture in my hand which she has left;
She cannot blame me that I follow'd her:
And I may be her guide the long wood through.   185

The Visionary Hope[1]

Sad lot, to have no Hope! Tho' lowly kneeling,
He fain would frame a prayer within his breast;
Would fain intreat for some sweet breath of healing,
That his sick body might have ease and rest;
He strove in vain! the dull sighs from his chest   5
Against his will the stifling load revealing.

---

5. The only line on Sappho that modern scholarship attributes to Alcaeus is commonly translated "violet-haired, holy, sweetly smiling Sappho" and comes from Hephaestion, *Handbook
on Metres* (*Greek Lyric I, Sappho and Alcaeus*, trans. David A. Campbell [LCL, 1990], 405;
Denys Page, *Sappho and Alcaeus* [Oxford, 1955], 295–96). The poem printed by EHC as C's
"Alcaeus to Sappho" (*PW*, 1:353) and in *MP*, November 24, 1800, where Mary Robinson
(1758–1800) signed her poems "Sappho," was written by Wordsworth between October 6
and December 28, 1798, although C probably added the title (*LB* [1992], 296, 457–58).

1. No manuscript exists and dating is speculative. The "breath of healing" (line 3) echoes
"wings of healing" in "Dejection: An Ode" (line 128) and the troubled sleep echoes "The
Pains of Sleep," written in the fall of 1803. EHC dates it 1810 without explanation. If it was
written in 1810, it may reflect Wordsworth's comment that he had given up hope for C. See
headnote to "To a Gentleman" (p. 200 herein). In *SL* the erratum to line 7 says "omit the
full stop after *guest*," but the line actually ends with a comma. C may have intended to remove the period at the end of line 6 (*PW* [CC], 2:1086).

Tho' Nature forc'd; tho' like some captive guest,
Some royal prisoner at his conqueror's feast,
An alien's restless mood but half concealing,
The sternness on his gentle brow confest   10
Sickness within and miserable feeling:
Tho' obscure pangs made curses of his dreams,
And dreaded sleep, each night repell'd in vain,
Each night was scatter'd by its own loud screams:
Yet never could his heart command, tho' fain,   15
One deep full wish to be no more in pain.

That HOPE, which was his inward bliss and boast,
Which wan'd and died, yet ever near him stood,
Tho' chang'd in nature, wander where he wou'd—
For Love's Despair is but Hope's pining Ghost!   20
For this one hope he makes his hourly moan,
He wishes and *can* wish for this alone!
Pierc'd, as with light from Heaven, before its gleams
(So the love-stricken visionary deems)
Disease would vanish, like a summer shower,   25
Whose dews fling sunshine from the noon-tide bower!
Or let it stay! yet this one Hope should give
Such strength that he would bless his pains and live.

Recollections of Love[1]

I.

How warm this woodland wild Recess!
  LOVE surely hath been breathing here.
  And this sweet bed of heath, my dear!
Swells up, then sinks with faint caress,
  As if to have you yet more near.   5

II.

Eight springs have flown, since last I lay
  On sea-ward Quantock's heathy hills,
  Where quiet sounds from hidden rills
Float here and there, like things astray,
  And high o'er head the sky-lark shrills.   10

1. Stanzas 1–4 were drafted as metrical experiments, which Kathleen Coburn dates October 1804, but the dating of the notebook entry is difficult (CN, 2:2224). The opening lines of the second stanza suggest a date of 1807, during C's final visit to Nether Stowey after an eight-year absence. The Greta River (line 25) flows through Kendal in the Lake District, where C moved his family in July 1800. A later draft of stanza 3 is in an 1810 notebook and headed "Questions and Answers in the court of Love" (PW, 2:1109; CN, 3:4036). The final stanzas may have been written when Coleridge was preparing copy for SL in 1814–15. An annotation in HNC's copy of SL, now at Harvard, reads "The most *musical* of S.T.C.'s poems" (PW [CC], 2:983).

III.

No voice as yet had made the air
  Be music with your name: yet why
  That asking look? That yearning sigh?
That sense of promise every where?
  Beloved! flew your spirit by?   15

IV.

As when a mother doth explore
  The rose-mark on her long lost child,
  I met, I lov'd you, maiden mild!
As whom I long had lov'd before—
  So deeply had I been beguil'd.   20

V.

You stood before me like a thought,
  A dream remember'd in a dream.
  But when those meek eyes first did seem
To tell me, Love within you wrought—
  O Greta, dear domestic stream!   25

VI.

Has not, since then, Love's prompture deep,
  Has not Love's whisper evermore,
  Been ceaseless, as thy gentle roar?
Sole voice, when other voices sleep,
  Dear under-song in Clamor's hour.   30

MEDITATIVE POEMS
IN
BLANK VERSE

Yea, he deserves to find himself deceived,
Who seeks a Heart in the unthinking Man.
Like shadows on a stream, the forms of life
Impress their characters on the smooth forehead:
Nought sinks into the Bosom's silent depth.
Quick sensibility of Pain and Pleasure
Moves the light fluids lightly; but no Soul
Warmeth the inner frame.
                                    SCHILLER.[1]

---

1. The epigraph comes from Coleridges's translation of Schiller, *The Death of Wallenstein* (1800) 1.7.42–9 (*PW*, 2:738). In addition to the poems printed here, this category includes "Lines Written in the Album at Elbingerode," "On Observing a Blossom on the 1st of February, 1796" (omitted in this edition), "The Eolian Harp," "Reflections on Having Left a Place of Retirement," "To the Reverend George Coleridge," "This Lime-Tree Bower My Prison," "To a Friend, Who Had Declared his Intention of Writing No More Poetry," "The Nightingale," and "Frost at Midnight." The major poems in this category are called the "conversation poems," a term coined by G. M. Harper ("Coleridge's Conversation Poems," *Spirit of Delight* [New York, 1928], 3–27), and form the basis of M. H. Abrams's definition of the "greater romantic lyric" (p. 682 herein).

Hymn
Before Sun-rise, in the Vale of Chamouny[1]

Besides the Rivers, Arve and Arveiron, which have their sources in the
foot of Mount Blanc, five conspicuous torrents rush down its sides;
and within a few paces of the Glaciers, the Gentiana Major grows in
immense numbers, with its "flowers of loveliest blue."

Hast thou a charm to stay the Morning-Star
In his steep course? So long he seems to pause
On thy bald awful head, O sovran BLANC!
The Arve and Arveiron at thy base
Rave ceaselessly; but thou, most awful Form!   5
Risest from forth thy silent Sea of Pines,
How silently! Around thee and above
Deep is the air and dark, substantial, black,
An ebon mass: methinks thou piercest it,
As with a wedge! But when I look again,   10
It is thine own calm home, thy crystal shrine,
Thy habitation from eternity!
O dread and silent Mount! I gaz'd upon thee,
Till thou, still present to the bodily sense,
Did'st vanish from my thought: entranc'd in prayer   15
I worshipped the Invisible alone.

Yet, like some sweet beguiling melody,
So sweet, we know not we are listening to it,
Thou, the meanwhile, wast blending with my Thought,
Yea, with my Life and Life's own secret Joy: 20
Till the dilating Soul, enrapt, transfus'd,

---

1. First printed as "Chamouni: The Hour before Sun-Rise. A Hymn" in *MP*, September 11,
1802, with a long headnote signed ΕΣΤΗΣΕ and reprinted in *The Friend*, October 26, 1809
(*Friend* [CC], 2:156–58). Printed here with the errata in *SL*. C never visited Chamounix in
France. He wrote to William Sotheby (1757–1833) on September 10, 1802, that when he
was on Scafell, a mountain in the English Lake District, "I involuntarily poured forth a
Hymn in the manner of the *Psalms*, tho' afterwards I thought the Ideas &c disproportionate
to our humble mountains—& accidentally lighting on a short Note in some swiss Poems,
concerning the Vale of Chamouny, & its Mountain, I transferred myself thither, in the Spirit,
& adapted my former feelings to these grander external objects" (*CL*, 2:864–65).
    Thomas De Quincey was the first to raise the issue of C's plagiarisms in 1834 in *Tait's Ed-
inburgh Magazine*. He pointed out that C plagiarized a poem by Friederike Brun
(1765–1835). HNC responded to De Quincey in his Preface to *Table Talk* (1835) by calling
De Quincey's observation "just" but refused to believe that C used Brun's poem with an intention to deceive. HNC printed a "very bald English translation" of Brun's twenty-line
poem (*TT* [CC], 2:21–22). Brun wrote "Chamounix beym Sonnenaufgange" in May 1791.
EHC prints her poem in *PW*, 2:1131 as does Mays in *PW* (CC), 1:718. A. P. Rossiter points
out that C also used Brun's notes to the poem (*TLS*, September 28 and October 26, 1951:
613, 677; *CL*, 2:865).

Into the mighty Vision passing—there
As in her natural form, swell'd vast to Heaven![2]

Awake, my soul! not only passive praise
Thou owest! not alone these swelling tears,   25
Mute thanks and secret extacy! Awake,
Voice of sweet song! Awake, my Heart, awake!
Green Vales and icy Cliffs, all join my Hymn.

Thou first and chief, sole Sovran of the Vale!
O struggling with the Darkness all the night,[3]   30
And visited all night by troops of stars,
Or when they climb the sky or when they sink:
Companion of the Morning-Star at Dawn,
Thyself Earth's ROSY STAR, and of the Dawn
Co-herald! wake, O wake, and utter praise!   35
Who sank thy sunless pillars deep in Earth?
Who fill'd thy Countenance with rosy light?
Who made thee Parent of perpetual streams?

And you, ye five wild torrents fiercely glad!
Who call'd you forth from night and utter death,   40
From dark and icy caverns call'd you forth,
Down those precipitous, black, jagged Rocks
For ever shattered and the same for ever?[4]
Who gave you your invulnerable life,
Your strength, your speed, your fury, and your joy,   45
Unceasing thunder and eternal foam?
And who commanded (and the silence came),
Here let the Billows stiffen, and have Rest?

2. In a letter to an unknown correspondent that may date from November 1819, C commented
on the poem: "I described myself under the influence of strong devotional feelings gazing on
the Mountain till as if it had been a Shape emanating from and sensibly representing her
own essence, my Soul had become diffused thro' 'the mighty Vision.' " C then quotes line 23
and continues:

> Mr. Wordsworth, I remember, censured the passage as strained and unnatural, and con-
> demned the Hymn in toto * * * as a specimen of the Mock Sublime. It may be so for
> others; but it is impossible that I should myself find it unnatural, being conscious that
> it was the image and utterance of Thoughts and Emotions in which there was no Mock-
> ery. Yet on the other hand I could readily believe that the mood and Habit of mind out
> of which the Hymn rose—that differs from Milton's and Thomson's and from the
> Psalms, the source of all three, in the Author's addressing himself to *individual* Objects
> actually present to his Senses, while his great Predecessors apostrophized *classes* of
> Things, presented by the Memory and generalized by the understanding—I can readily
> believe, I say, that in this there may be too much of what our learned Med'ciners call
> the *Idiosyncratic* for true Poetry. From my very childhood I have been accustomed to *ab-
> stract* and as it were unrealize whatever of more than common interest my eyes dwelt
> on; and then by a sort of transfusion and transmission of my consciousness to identify
> myself with the Object [*CL*, 4:974–75].

3. In 1803 C sent a copy of the "Hymn" to Sir George Beaumont and noted of this line: "I had
written a much finer Line when Sca' Fell was in my Thoughts—viz—O blacker than the
Darkness all the Night" (*CL*, 2:996).

4. In October 1814 C introduced a variation of line 43, "For ever changing, and the same for
ever," with the comment, "It is the sole prerogative * * * of that Omniscience, which is one
with Omnipotence, to number, to sustain, and to actuate, each drop of each billow in the
mighty torrent of MATERIAL CREATION" (*EOT* [CC], 2:387).

Ye Ice-falls! ye that from the Mountain's brow
Adown enormous Ravines slope amain—[5]   50
Torrents, methinks, that heard a mighty Voice,
And stopp'd at once amid their maddest plunge!
Motionless Torrents! silent Cataracts!
Who made you glorious as the Gates of Heaven
Beneath the keen full Moon?   Who bade the Sun   55
Cloath you with Rainbows?   Who, with living flowers
Of loveliest blue, spread garlands at your feet?—[6]
GOD! let the Torrents, like a Shout of Nations
Answer! and let the Ice-plains echo, GOD!
GOD! sing ye meadow-streams with gladsome voice!   60
Ye Pine-groves, with your soft and soul-like sounds!
And they too have a voice, yon piles of Snow,
And in their perilous fall shall thunder, GOD!

   Ye living flowers that skirt th' eternal Frost!
Ye wild goats sporting round the Eagle's nest!   65
Ye Eagles, play-mates of the Mountain-Storm!
Ye Lightnings, the dread arrows of the Clouds!
Ye signs and wonders of the element!
Utter forth GOD, and fill the Hills with Praise!

   Thou too, hoar Mount! with thy sky-pointing Peaks,   70
Oft from whose feet the Avalanche, unheard,
Shoots downward, glittering thro' the pure Serene,[7]
Into the depth of Clouds that veil thy breast—
Thou too again, stupendous Mountain! thou
That as I raise my head, awhile bow'd low   75
In adoration, upward from thy Base
Slow-travelling with dim eyes suffus'd with tears,
Solemnly seemest, like a vapoury cloud,
To rise before me—Rise, O ever rise,
Rise like a cloud of Incense, from the Earth!   80
Thou kingly Spirit throned among the hills,
Thou dread Ambassador from Earth to Heaven,
Great Hierarch![8] tell thou the silent Sky,
And tell the Stars, and tell yon rising Sun,
Earth, with her thousand voices, praises GOD.   85

---

5. In the MP version and a copy sent to Beaumont in 1803, C ended line 50 with "*steeply slope*" in place of "slope amain" and said "*a bad line*; & I hope to be able to alter it" (*CL*, 2:996).
6. The MP headnote explains that "The beautiful *Gentiana major*, or greater gentian, with blossoms of the brightest blue, grows in large companies a few steps from the never-melted ice of the glaciers. I thought it an affecting emblem of the boldness of human hope, venturing near, and, as it were, leaning over the brink of the grave" (*PW*, 1:377). The source of C's headnote is Brun's note: "*Ich pflückte * * * wenige Schritte vom ewigen Eise, die Schöne Gentiana major in grosser Menge*" (I picked * * * a few steps from the eternal ice, the beautiful gentiana major in great quantity) (*TLS*, September 28, 1951: 613).
7. Clear, bright sky. From the Latin *serenum*, "fair weather."
8. Both high priest and angel. The word "angel" means messenger, hence "Ambassador" in line 82. In *Paradise Lost* 5.468 Raphael is the "winged Hierarch."

Inscription
for a Fountain on a Heath[1]

This Sycamore, oft musical with Bees,—
Such Tents the Patriarchs lov'd! O long unharm'd
May all its aged Boughs o'er-canopy
The small round Basin, which this jutting stone
Keeps pure from falling leaves! Long may the Spring,   5
Quietly as a sleeping Infant's breath,
Send up cold waters to the Traveller
With soft and even Pulse! Nor ever cease[2]
Yon tiny Cone of Sand its soundless Dance,[3]
Which at the Bottom, like a Fairy's Page,   10
As merry and no taller, dances still,
Nor wrinkles the smooth Surface of the Fount.
Here Twilight is and Coolness: here is Moss,
A soft Seat, and a deep and ample Shade.
Thou may'st toil far and find no second Tree.   15
Drink, Pilgrim, here! Here rest! and if thy Heart
Be innocent, here too shalt thou refresh
Thy Spirit, list'ning to some gentle Sound,
Or passing Gale or Hum of murmuring Bees![4]

A Tombless Epitaph[1]

'Tis true, Idoloclastes Satyrane!
(So call him, for so mingling Blame with Praise
And smiles with anxious looks, his earliest friends,
Masking his birth-name, wont to character

---

1. First published in *MP*, September 24, 1802, as "Inscription on a Jutting Stone, Over a Spring," signed ΕΣΤΗΣΕ and entered (var.) in "Sara Hutchinson's Poets" in late 1801 (Whalley, 11). "Sara Hutchinson's Poets" is a notebook kept by C and Wordsworth in which she copied poems by C and Wordsworth.
2. In March 1805 C wrote in a notebook: "O best reward of Virtue! to feel pleasure made more pleasurable, in legs, knees, chests, arms, cheek—all in a deep quiet, a fountain with un-wrinkled surface yet still the living motion at the bottom that 'with soft and even pulse' keeps it full—& yet to know that this pleasure so impleasured is making us more *good*, is preparing virtue and pleasure for many known and many unknown to us" (*CN*, 2:2495).
3. C wrote in a notebook in September 1801: "The spring with the little tiny cone of loose sand ever rising & sinking at the bottom, but its surface without a wrinkle.—W.W. M.H. D.W. S.H." The initials are those of William Wordsworth, Mary Hutchinson (who married Wordsworth in 1802), Dorothy Wordsworth, and Sara Hutchinson. Kathleen Coburn remarks that C's initials are omitted, indicating that the image reflects the Wordsworth circle, from which C was excluded (*CN*, 1:980).
4. Cf. lines 14–19 with "A Letter to ———," lines 85–91.
1. First published in *The Friend*, November 23, 1809 (var.), with the note "Imitated, though in the movements rather than the thoughts, from the VIIth. of Gli Epitafi of *Chiabrera*," where C introduces a portrait of Satyrane and defines Idoloclast as the "breaker of Idols" (*Friend* [CC], 2:184–85); printed here with errata in SL. Satyrane is a character in Spenser's *Faerie Queene* 1.6.28, who is the son of a satyr and faithful to Una, or Truth. C often referred to himself as Satyrane, as in "Satyrane's Letters" first published in *The Friend* and subsequently used to fill volume 2 of the *Biographia*. In December 1803 C jotted in a notebook, "Motto for my Idoloclastes 'It is ambition enough to be employed as an under-labourer in clearing

His wild-wood fancy and impetuous zeal,)   5
'Tis true that, passionate for ancient truths
And honoring with religious love the Great
Of elder times, he hated to excess,
With an unquiet and intolerant scorn,
The hollow puppets of an hollow Age,   10
Ever idolatrous, and changing ever
Its worthless Idols!   Learning, Power, and Time,
(Too much of all) thus wasting in vain war
Of fervid colloquy.   Sickness, tis true,
Whole years of weary days, besieged him close,   15
Even to the gates and inlets of his life!
But it is true, no less, that strenuous, firm,
And with a natural gladness, he maintained
The Citadel unconquer'd, and in joy
Was strong to follow the delightful Muse.   20
For not a hidden Path, that to the Shades
Of the belov'd Parnassian forest leads,
Lurk'd undiscover'd by him; not a rill
There issues from the fount of Hippocrene,
But he had trac'd it upward to its source,[2]   25
Thro' open glade, dark glen, and secret dell,
Knew the gay wild flowers on its banks, and cull'd
Its med'cinable herbs. Yea, oft alone,
Piercing the long-neglected holy cave,
The haunt obscure of old Philosophy,   30
He bade with lifted torch its starry walls
Sparkle, as erst they sparkled to the flame
Of od'rous Lamps tended by Saint and Sage.
O fram'd for calmer times and nobler hearts!
O studious Poet, eloquent for truth!   35
Philosopher! contemning wealth and death,

---

the Ground a little, and removing some of the Rubbish that lies in the way to Knowledge' "
(CN, 1:1729). C quotes John Locke, "Epistle to the Reader" (Essay Concerning Human Understanding, ed. Peter H. Nidditch [Oxford, 1975], 10). For C's breaking of idols, see "Fears
in Solitude" (p. 114, n. 1 herein) and his letter to John Prior Estlin, December 7, 1802:
"Surely, religious Deism is infinitely nearer the religion of our Saviour, than the gross Idolatry of Popery, or the more decorous, but not less genuine, Idolatry of a vast majority of
Protestants.—If there be meaning in words, it appears to me that the Quakers & Unitarians
are the only Christians, altogether pure from Idolatry" (CL, 2:893). When C turned from
Unitarianism after 1805, his attacks on idolatry were on superstition of various kinds, but he
wrote to Southey in early 1809, "You will grin at my modest account of Satyrane, the Idoloclast, in No. 14 [of The Friend]—but what can I do? I must wear a mask" (CL, 3:261).
2. Cf. lines 20–25 with Wordsworth's translation of the same epitaph by Gabriello Chiabrera
(1552–1637), "Per il Signor Ambrosio Salinero," lines 8–13: "And he was strong to follow in
the steps / Of the fair Muses. Not a covert path / Leads to the dear Parnassian forest's shade,
/ That might from him be hidden; not a track / Mounts to pellucid Hippocrene, but he / Had
traced its windings" (Wordsworth, Shorter Poems, 1807–1820, ed. Carl H. Ketcham [Ithaca,
N.Y., 1989], 60). Ketcham comments that "WW's translation and STC's * * * originated
about the same time" (504). On March 16, 1840, Wordsworth wrote to Henry Crabb Robinson about C's plagiarism, "Compare Chiabrera's epitaph upon Ambrosio Salinero, which I
have translated, with Coleridge's tombless epitaph upon one he calls Satyrane and you will
have another instance how unadvised was his way in these little matters. I used to beg he
would take the trouble of noting his obligations, but half his time was passed in dreams, so
that such hints were thrown away" (WL, 7.50–51).

Yet docile, childlike, full of Life and Love!
Here, rather than on monumental stone,
This record of thy worth thy Friend inscribes,
Thoughtful, with quiet tears upon his cheek.   40

To a Gentleman[1]

Composed on the night after his recitation of a Poem on the Growth
of an Individual Mind.

Friend of the Wise! and Teacher of the Good!
Into my heart have I received that Lay
More than historic, that prophetic Lay
Wherein (high theme by thee first sung aright)
Of the foundations and the building up   5
Of the Human Spirit, thou hast dared to tell
What may be told, to th' understanding mind
Revealable; and what within the mind
By vital Breathings, like the secret soul
Of vernal growth, oft quickens in the Heart   10
Thoughts all too deep for words!—
                            Theme hard as high!
Of smiles spontaneous, and mysterious fears
(The first-born they of Reason and twin-birth)
Of tides obedient to external force,
And currents self-determined, as might seem,   15
Or by some inner Power; of moments awful,
Now in thy inner life, and now abroad,
When Power stream'd from thee, and thy soul received

1. An early manuscript, dated January 1807, is at Dove Cottage and has been printed in *The Prelude,* ed. Jonathan Wordsworth, M. H. Abrams, and Stephen Gill (New York, 1979), 542–45, where it is titled "To William Wordsworth. Lines Composed, For the greater part on the night, on which he finished the recitation of his Poem (in thirteen books) concerning the growth and history of his own Mind." A second early manuscript, printed by JDC (525–26), is now at the Morgan Library (*CL,* 4:572n.). C titled the poem "To a Gentleman" after Wordsworth asked him in May 1815 not to publish the poem: "the commendation would be injurious to us both, and my work when it appears, would labour under a great disadvantage in consequence of such a precursorship of Praise" (*WL,* 3:238). The title "To William Wordsworth" was not used until *Poetical Works* (1834).
   There had been a serious split between the Wordsworths and C in the fall of 1810 that cooled their relationship for years and effectively ended C's relationship with Sara Hutchinson, who often lived with the Wordsworths. In October 1810 Basil Montagu (1770–1851) traveled with C from the Lake District to London, where Montagu was to provide a home for C. Montagu thoughtlessly told C that Wordsworth had warned Montagu of C's use of opium and alcohol. Coleridge was deeply wounded when he arrived in London and wrote in a notebook "W. authorized M. to tell me, he had no Hope of me!—O God! What good reason for saying this?" A few days later he wrote "No hope of me! absol. Nuisance! God's Mercy is it a Dream" (*CN,* 3:3991, 3997). For eighteen months there was no communication between C and the Wordsworths, although their friends openly discussed the matter. C complained of Wordsworth's callousness, and the Wordsworths resented being blamed for C's anguish. A reconciliation of sorts was arranged through Henry Crabb Robinson in May 1812. Wordsworth denied to Robinson that he had commissioned Montagu to speak to C, denied he used the phrase "*rotten drunkard,*" and denied that he said C "*had been a nuisance in his family.*" Wordsworth "did not deny having said he had no hopes of Coleridge. And with respect to the phrase 'rotting out his entrails by intemperance,' he does not think he used such an expression, but the idea might be conveyed in what he said, and Montagu might give that as the conclusion from all he said" (*CRB,* 1:74–75).

The light reflected, as a light bestow'd—
Of Fancies fair, and milder hours of youth,   20
Hyblean[2] murmurs of Poetic Thought
Industrious in its Joy, in Vales and Glens
Native or outland, Lakes and famous Hills!
Or on the lonely High-road, when the Stars
Were rising; or by secret Mountain-streams,   25
The Guides and the Companions of thy way!

    Of more than Fancy, of the Social Sense
Distending wide, and Man belov'd as Man,
Where France in all her Towns lay vibrating
Even as a Bark becalm'd beneath the Burst   30
Of Heaven's immediate Thunder, when no cloud
Is visible, or shadow on the Main.
For thou wert there, thine own brows garlanded,
Amid the tremor of a realm aglow,
Amid a mighty nation jubilant,   35
When from the general Heart of Human kind
Hope sprang forth like a full-born Deity!
—— Of that dear Hope afflicted and struck down,
So summon'd homeward, thenceforth calm and sure
From the dread[3] Watch-Tower of man's absolute Self,   40
With light unwaning on her eyes, to look
Far on—herself a glory to behold,
The Angel of the vision![4] Then (last strain)
Of Duty, chosen Laws controlling choice,
Action and Joy!—An orphic[5] song indeed,   45
A song divine of high and passionate thoughts,
To their own Music chaunted![6]

                 O great Bard!
Ere yet that last strain dying awed the air,
With stedfast eye I view'd thee in the choir
Of ever-enduring men. The truly Great   50
Have all one age, and from one visible space
Shed influence! They, both in power and act,
Are permanent, and Time is not with *them*,

2. From Hybla, in Sicily, famous for its honey.
3. Inspiring awe.
4. Cf. Milton, "Lycidas," lines 161–63, where the angel is Michael.
5. Refers to the Orphic mysteries, which emphasized individual guilt, punishment, and the purification of souls.
6. C included lines 12–47 (var.) in a May 30, 1815, letter in response to Wordsworth's request that C not publish this poem and in explanation of his disappointment in Wordsworth's *Excursion* (1814): "I never once thought of printing ["To a Gentleman"] without having consulted you. * * * I wanted no additional reason for its not being published in my Life Time, than its *personality* respecting myself. * * * It is for the Biographer, not the Poet, to give the *accidents* of *individual* Life. * * * [T]here is nothing in the Lines as far [as] your Powers are concerned, which I have not as fully expressed elsewhere" (*CL*, 4:572–74). C quoted lines 45–47 in *The Friend* to introduce lines 428–89 of book 1 of *The Prelude* (1805), with the title "Growth of Genius from the Influences of Natural Objects, on the Imagination in Boyhood, and Early Youth" (*Friend* [CC], 2:258–59). The lines include what is now called the skating episode, which Wordsworth published in *Poems* (1815). In chapter 13 of the *Biographia* (p. 486 herein) C applied variants of lines 45–47 to himself.

Save as it worketh *for* them, they *in* it.
Nor less a sacred Roll, than those of old,   55
And to be placed, as they, with gradual fame
Among the Archives of Mankind, thy work
Makes audible a linked lay of Truth,
Of Truth profound a sweet continuous lay,
Not learnt, but native, her own natural notes![7]   60
Ah! as I listen'd with a heart forlorn
The pulses of my Being beat anew:
And even as Life returns upon the Drown'd,
Life's joy rekindling rous'd a throng of Pains—
Keen Pangs of Love, awakening as a babe   65
Turbulent, with an outcry in the heart;
And Fears self-will'd, that shunn'd the eye of Hope;
And Hope that scarce would know itself from Fear;
Sense of past Youth, and Manhood come in vain,
And Genius given, and Knowledge won in vain;   70
And all which I had cull'd in Wood-walks wild,
And all which patient toil had rear'd, and all,
Commune with *thee* had open'd out—but Flowers
Strew'd on my corse, and borne upon my Bier,
In the same Coffin, for the self-same Grave![8]   75

That way no more! and ill beseems it me,
Who came a welcomer in Herald's Guise,
Singing of Glory, and Futurity,
To wander back on such unhealthful road,
Plucking the poisons of self-harm! And ill   80
Such Intertwine beseems triumphal wreaths
Strew'd before *thy* advancing!

Nor do thou,
Sage Bard! impair the memory of that hour
Of thy communion with my nobler mind
By Pity or Grief, already felt too long!   85

7. After line 60 the following lines were set in type in *SL*:

> Dear shall it be to every human heart,
> To me how more than dearest! me on whom
> Comfort from thee, and utterance of thy Love
> Came with such Height and Depth of Harmony,
> Such sense of Wings uplifting, that its might
> Scatter'd and quell'd me, till my thoughts became
> A bodily tumult; and thy faithful Hopes,
> Thy Hopes of me, dear Friend! by me unfelt!
> Were troublous to me, almost as a voice
> Familiar once and more than musical,
> As a dear Woman's voice—
> To one cast off, whose Hope had seem'd to die,
> A wanderer with a worn-out heart forlorn
> Mid strangers pining with untended wounds.

These lines are close to the early version printed in full by JDC (525–26) and by EHC, who recorded the variants (*PW*, 1:406–07n.). In the middle of February 1816 C cut these lines from the proofs, perhaps because they acknowledge Wordsworth's "hopes of me" betrayed by Wordsworth's warnings and Montagu's insensitivity.

8. C included lines 65–75 at the end of chapter 10 of the *Biographia* (p. 460 herein).

Nor let my words import more blame than needs.
The tumult rose and ceas'd: for Peace is nigh
Where wisdom's voice has found a listening heart.
Amid the howl of more than wintry storms,
The Halcyon hears the voice of vernal Hours   90
Already on the wing!

          Eve following Eve,[9]
Dear tranquil time, when the sweet sense of Home
Is sweetest! moments for their own sake hail'd
And more desired, more precious for thy song,
In silence listening, like a devout child,   95
My soul lay passive, by thy various strain
Driven, as in surges now beneath the stars,
With momentary Stars of my own birth,
Fair constellated Foam, still darting off[1]
Into the darkness; now a tranquil sea,   100
Outspread and bright, yet swelling to the Moon.

          And when—O Friend! my comforter and guide!
Strong in thy self, and powerful to give strength!—
Thy long sustained Song finally closed,
And thy deep voice had ceased—yet thou thyself   105
Wert still before my eyes, and round us both
That happy vision of beloved Faces—
Scarce conscious, and yet conscious of its close[2]
I sate, my being blended in one thought
(Thought was it? or Aspiration? or Resolve?)   110
Absorb'd, yet hanging still upon the sound—
And when I rose, I found myself in prayer.

FROM POETICAL WORKS (1828, 1829, 1834)

In Coleridge's final years William Pickering (1796–1854) published three editions of his collected poetry: *The Poetical Works of S. T. Coleridge, Including the Dramas of Wallenstein, Remorse, and Zapolya* in 1828 and 1829 and *The Poetical Works of S. T. Coleridge* in 1834, all in three volumes. Not one of these editions completely reflects Coleridge's intentions for a collected edition, and later editors disagree about which, if any, edition should be considered authoritative. The three editions were collabo-

9. Evenings when Wordsworth read *The Prelude* to C.
1. "A beautiful white cloud of Foam at momentary intervals coursed by the side of the Vessel with a Roar, and little stars of flame danced and sparkled and went out in it: and every now and then light detachments of this white cloud-like foam darted off from the vessel's side, each with its own small constellation, over the Sea and scoured out of sight like a Tartar Troop over a Wilderness." [C's note in *SL*, taken from his description of his 1798 voyage to Germany in Satyrane's Letters (*CN*, 1:335; *Friend* [CC], 2:193).]
2. C wrote between lines 107 and 108, "All whom I deepliest love—in one room all!" (*PW*, 1:408n.). Wordsworth and his wife and wife's sister, Sara Hutchinson, and C with his son Hartley were staying at Hall Farm in Coleorton loaned to the Wordsworths by Sir George Beaumont; C's wife and other children, Derwent and Sara, were absent.

rative efforts by Coleridge, Pickering, and various friends and relatives. Coleridge favored editions of his best, or published, poems rather than editions that included his minor or juvenile poems. After *Poems* (1796), he excluded many of his early poems, and *Sibylline Leaves* excluded many of his minor poems. In August 1827 he wrote, "Another vexatious thing is about the Edition of my poems by Pickering—against my will and judgement from the beginning. Tho' it was expressly bargained to be only the Poems already published, yet under various pretences * * * all I had to publish, and much that had far better in their present state have remained unpublished, has been forced from me" (*CL*, 6:699–700).

Coleridge left the supervision of the edition to James Gillman and Robert Jameson (d. 1854), a friend of Coleridge's son Hartley (*CL*, 6:672). Pickering persuaded Gillman to obtain more poems, and after persistent requests from Gillman, Coleridge agreed to add unpublished poems. The edition was published in August 1828. In September Coleridge complained in a letter to Alaric Watts (1797–1864) that "to this hour I have had not a single Copy of my Poems, except an imperfect one that had been brought up to our house by Mr. B. Montagu, to prove to Mr G. that the Volumes were really on the eve of being finished" (*CL*, 6:760), so Coleridge may not have read proofs. In the same letter he further complained that only three hundred copies were printed, so that sales covered only the costs of printing without any profits to him.

The first volume began with the category "Juvenile Poems," which contained thirty-seven of Coleridge's forty-seven poems in *Poems* (1796), including the political sonnets and "Religious Musings." "Juvenile Poems" was followed by poems from *Sibylline Leaves* in the categories and order of that volume. The first volume concluded with "Kubla Khan," "The Pains of Sleep," and the "Apologetic Preface to 'Fire, Famine, and Slaughter.' " The second volume began with "The Ancient Mariner" and "Christabel," followed by the section "Prose in Rhyme: Or, Epigrams, Moralities, and Things Without a Name," which included six poems printed here. It concluded with two dramas, *Remorse* and *Zapolya*. The third volume included Coleridge's translations from Schiller's dramas, *The Piccolomini* and *The Death of Wallenstein*.

The edition was sold out by October 1828. Coleridge prepared a second edition with the same organization. By January 1829 he had corrected the 1828 edition. He also added three new poems, "The Garden of Boccaccio" (printed here), and "The Allegoric Vision" and "The Improvisatore" (omitted here). For her edition of *The Poems of Samuel Taylor Coleridge* (1852) Coleridge's daughter, Sara, chose the 1828 edition as "the last upon which he was able to bestow personal care and attention" (*PW*, 2:1170), although later editors have speculated that 1828 may have been a slip for 1829. James Dykes Campbell (1838–1895) used Sara Coleridge's exact words to describe the 1829 volume as the last Coleridge supervised. Campbell used the 1829 edition as the standard for the texts of the poems in his 1893 edition of *The Poetical Works*, but he printed the poems in chronological order of composition, not in Coleridge's categories, basing his decision on Coleridge's comment of January 1, 1834: "I still think the chronological order the best for arranging a poet's works. All your divisions are in particular instances inadequate, and they destroy the interest which arises from watching the progress, maturity, and even the decay of genius" (*TT* [*CC*], 2:271), which reflects a difference in Coleridge's conception of his poetic canon from the organization of these three editions.

Sara Coleridge noted that the 1834 edition "was arranged mainly, if not entirely, at the discretion of his earliest Editor," Henry Nelson Coleridge, her husband and Coleridge's nephew (*PW*, 2:1170). Its three volumes were published in March, April, and July 1834, before Coleridge died on July 25 (*CL*, 6:981n.). Henry Nelson Coleridge retained the arrangement of the two earlier editions, but added nineteen unpublished or uncollected poems to the category "Juvenile Poems." In the second volume he or Coleridge changed the 1828 to 1829 category "Prose in Rhyme" to "Miscellaneous Poems," awkwardly echoing the category of "Odes and Miscellaneous Poems" in the first volume. Henry Nelson Coleridge added forty-one unpublished or uncollected poems to "Miscellaneous Poems," the category of the poems printed here. In a review of the 1834 edition in the *Quarterly Review* for August 1834, Henry Nelson Coleridge boasted that Coleridge's poems were "for the first time completely collected" (*CH*, 1:620). In August 1832 Coleridge reported to Henry Nelson Coleridge that he was "setting about the corrections of the Poems in good earnest" (*CL*, 6:923). In comparing the 1829 and 1834 editions, Arthur Turnbull noted revisions in twenty-three poems (*Biographia Epistolaris* [London, 1911], 297, 324–25), only one of which is printed here, "Lines Suggested by the Last Words of Berengarius." For his edition of *Poetical Works* (1912), Ernest Hartley Coleridge chose the 1834 edition for his texts because "the existence of conclusive proof that, here and there, Coleridge altered and emended the text of 1829." While acknowledging Henry Nelson Coleridge's role in selecting and arranging the poems, Ernest Hartley Coleridge argued that the texts of 1834 differ from those of 1829 "and that Coleridge himself," and not Henry Nelson Coleridge "was responsible for that difference" (*PW*, 1:iii). Yet Henry Nelson Coleridge or Pickering may have had a hand in the design of the poems as well as the selection and arrangement, since a comparison of either 1828 or 1829 with 1834 shows a greatly reduced use of capitals, small capitals, and italics, yet Coleridge wrote in August 1833, "I sadly quarrel with our modern Printers for their levelling spirit of antipathy to all initial Capitals. * * * I greatly approve of the German Rule of distinguishing all Noun-Substantives by a Capital: & at least, all *Personifications* shall be in small Capitals" (*CL*, 6:955). J. C. C. Mays concludes that Coleridge's final three collections often possess less authority than earlier editions and manuscripts (*PW* [*CC*], 1:1254).

While preparing these editions Coleridge also contributed to annual gift books designed for the Christmas book trade: *The Bijou*, *The Keepsake*, *The Literary Souvenir*, and *Friendship's Offering*. Several of the poems included here were also printed in these gift books, and important variants and prose commentary from the gift books are included here in the notes. Morton D. Paley gives a full account of Coleridge's involvement with gift books in "Coleridge and the Annuals," *The Huntington Library Quarterly* 57 (1994): 1–24.

The texts printed here are from *Poetical Works* (1828, 1829, and 1834) in the categories and order of each volume.

206

FROM POETICAL WORKS (1828)

PROSE IN RHYME:
OR,
EPIGRAMS, MORALITIES, AND THINGS WITHOUT A NAME

"Ἔρως ἀεὶ λάληθρος ἑταῖρος.

In many ways does the full heart reveal
The presence of the love it would conceal;
But in far more th' estranged heart lets know,
The absence of the love, which yet it fain would shew.[1]

Phantom or Fact?
A Dialogue in Verse[1]

AUTHOR.

A lovely form there sate beside my bed,
And such a feeding calm its presence shed,
A tender Love so pure from earthly leaven
That I unnethe[2] the fancy might control,
Twas my own spirit newly come from heaven   5
Wooing its gentle way into my soul!
But ah! the change—It had not stirr'd, and yet
Alas! that change how fain would I forget?
That shrinking back, like one that had mistook!
That weary, wandering, disavowing Look!   10
Twas all another, feature, look, and frame,
And still, methought, I knew, it was the same!

FRIEND.

This riddling Tale, to what does it belong?
Is't History? Vision? or an idle Song?
Or rather say at once, within what space   15
Of Time this wild disastrous change took place?

AUTHOR.

Call it a *moment's* work (and such it seems)
This Tale's a Fragment from the Life of Dreams;
But say, that years matur'd the silent strife,
And 'tis a Record from the Dream of Life.   20

---

1. The Greek is "Love is ever a talkative companion." This quatrain was used as a motto for the category "Prose in Rhyme" in the 1828 and 1829 editions and for the corresponding category, "Miscellaneous Poems," in the 1834 edition. The poems printed here come from "Prose in Rhyme."
1. The date of composition is uncertain, probably no later than fall 1827.
2. Hardly.

Work Without Hope[1]

Lines Composed 21st. February, 1827

All Nature seems at work. Stags[2] leave their lair—
The bees are stirring—birds are on the wing
And WINTER slumbering in the open air,
Wears on his smiling face a dream of Spring!
And I, the while, the sole unbusy thing,   5
Nor honey make, nor pair, nor build, nor sing.[3]

Yet well I ken the banks where Amaranths[4] blow,
Have traced the fount whence streams of nectar flow.
Bloom, O ye Amaranths! bloom for whom ye may,
For me ye bloom not! Glide, rich streams, away!   10
With lips unbrightened, wreathless brow, I stroll:

---

1. Published in *The Bijou* (1828). First drafted in a notebook entry of February 21, 1825, as a letter to an anonymous addressee, introduced by the following comment: "Strain in the manner of G. HERBERT—: which might be entitled, THE ALONE MOST DEAR: a Complaint of Jacob to Rachel as in the tenth year of his Service he saw in her or *fancied* that he saw Symptoms of Alienation." C applied the story of Jacob and Rachel in Genesis 29 to himself and Mrs. Gillman. The tenth year of his service roughly marks the ten years C lived with the Gillmans. Next to this note Mrs. Gillman wrote in pencil, "It was fancy." Following the lines printed here as "Work Without Hope," C wrote the following lines in several rough drafts:

   > I speak in figures, inward thoughts and woes
   > Interpreting by Shapes and outward Shews.
   > Call the World Spider, and at fancy's touch
   > Thought becomes image and I see it such.
   > With viscous masonry of films and threads
   > Tough as the nets in Indian Forests found
   > It blends the Waller's and the Weaver's trade
   > And soon the tent-like Hangings touch the ground
   > A dusky Chamber that excludes the Day—
   > But cease the prelude & resume the lay.

   > Where daily nearer me, with magic Ties,
   > What time and where (Wove close with
   > Line over line & thickning as they rise)
   > The World her spidery thread on all sides spun
   > Side answ'ring Side with narrow interspace.
   > My faith (say, I: I and my Faith are one)
   > Hung, as a Mirror there! And face to face
   > (For nothing else there was, between or near)
   > One Sister Mirror had the dreary Wall.
   > But *That* is broke! And with that bright Compeer
   > I lost my Object and my inmost All—
   > Faith *in* the Faith of THE ALONE MOST DEAR!

   C signed these drafts "Jacob Hodiernus," or the modern Jacob (*CN*, 4:5192; *CL*, 5:415–16).
2. In the notebook, *The Bijou*, and later printings the word is "slugs." C caught the misprint in 1832 and complained that "Stags" "is really so much grander that I grieve, it should be senseless" (*CL*, 6:904). "Slugs" was restored in 1834.
3. In a copy of the 1834 edition now at the Coleridge Cottage, Somerset, Sara Coleridge annotated this line "Herbert's Employment" (Derrick Woolf, "Sara Coleridge's Marginalia," *The Coleridge Bulletin* [Autumn 1993]: 11). Lines 17–20 of Herbert's "Employment" read "All things are busie; only I / Neither bring Honey with the Bees, / Nor flowres to make that, nor the husbandry / To water these." C annotated Herbert, *The Temple*, 10th edition (1674), quoted here, in 1824 (*CM* [*CC*], 2:1032–47).
4. C explained in his notebook, "*Literally* rendered is Flower Fadeless, or never-fading—from the Greek a *not* and marainō, to whither" (*CN*, 4:5192). Cf. *Paradise Lost* 3.353–55: "Immortal Amarant, a Flour which once, / In Paradise, fast by the Tree of Life / Began to bloom."

And would you learn the spells that drowse my soul?
WORK WITHOUT HOPE draws nectar in a sieve,
And HOPE without an object cannot live.

A Day Dream[1]

My eyes make pictures, when they are shut:—
    I see a Fountain, large and fair,
A Willow and a ruined Hut,
    And thee, and me and Mary[2] there.
O Mary! make thy gentle lap our pillow!   5
Bend o'er us, like a bower, my beautiful green Willow!

A wild-rose roofs the ruined shed,
    And that and summer well agree:
And, lo! where Mary leans her head,
    Two dear names carved upon the tree!   10
And Mary's tears, they are not tears of sorrow:
Our sister and our friend[3] will both be here to-morrow.

'Twas Day! But now few, large, and bright
    The stars are round the crescent moon!
And now it is a dark warm Night,   15
    The balmiest of the month of June!
A glow-worm fallen, and on the marge remounting
Shines and its shadow shines, fit stars for our sweet fountain.

O ever—ever be thou blest!
    For dearly, ASRA![4] love I thee!   20
This brooding warmth across my breast,
    This depth of tranquil bliss—ah me!
Fount, Tree and Shed are gone, I know not whither,
But in one quiet room we three are still together.

The shadows dance upon the wall,   25
    By the still dancing fire-flames made;
And now they slumber, moveless all!
    And now they melt to one deep shade!
But not from me shall this mild darkness steal thee:
I dream thee with mine eyes, and at my heart I feel thee!   30

1. Published in *The Bijou* (1828). Probably composed in early March 1802 before "A Letter to ———," as Whalley argues, since C refers to the episode in "A Letter to ———," lines 91, 99–110 (125), but Mays suggests 1826–28 (*PW* [CC], 1:1070). C visited the Hutchinsons at Gallow Hill from March 2 to 13, 1802 (*CN*, 1:1150, 1151).
2. Mary Hutchinson.
3. Probably William and Dorothy Wordsworth, although the exact dates of the June scene in lines 1–18 are uncertain.
4. Sara Hutchinson.

Thine eyelash on my cheek doth play—
'Tis Mary's hand upon my brow!
But let me check this tender lay
    Which none may hear but she and thou!
Like the still hive at quiet midnight humming,   35
Murmur it to yourselves, ye two beloved women!

Lines Suggested by the Last Words of Berengarius[1]

Ob. Anno Dom. 1088

No more 'twixt conscience staggering and the Pope
Soon shall I now before my God appear,
By him to be acquitted, as I hope;
By him to be condemned, as I fear.—[2]

REFLECTION ON THE ABOVE.

Lynx amid moles! had I stood by thy bed,   5
Be of good cheer, meek soul! I would have said:
I see a hope spring from that humble fear.
All are not strong alike through storms to steer
Right onward. What? though dread of threatened death
And dungeon torture made thy hand and breath   10
Inconstant to the truth within thy heart?
That truth, from which, through fear, thou twice didst start,
Fear haply told thee, was a learned strife,
Or not so vital as to claim thy life:
And myriads had reached Heaven, who never knew   15
Where lay the difference 'twixt the false and true!

Ye, who secure 'mid trophies not your own,
Judge him who won them when he stood alone,
And proudly talk of *recreant* BERENGARE—
O first the age, and then the man compare!   20
That age how dark! congenial minds how rare!

1. First published in *The Literary Souvenir* (1827), with the following as a note to the title: "Τὸ τοῦ ΕΣΤΗΣΕ τοῦ ἐπιθανοῦς Epitaphium testamentarium αὐτόγραφον. Quae linquam, aut nihil, aut nihili, aut vix sunt mea. Sordes Do Morti: reddo caetera, Christe! tibi." (The testamentary epitaph of the dying STC, written by himself. The things that I shall leave behind are either nothing, or worthless, or scarcely mine. Dust I give to Death. I return the rest, Christ, to you.) C's note identifies himself with Berengarius of Tours (c. 1000–1088), a French theologian, tried twice for his denial of transubstantiation, the change of the bread and wine of the Eucharist into the body and blood of Christ. At each trial he recanted his claim that transubstantiation was contrary to reason, the last in 1079. In a long notebook meditation on sacraments and symbols C wrote, "Berengarius asserts and vindicates the real Presence (and in the same words as our Church Catechism) as earnestly as he rejects the total changes of the corporeal Elements" (CN, 4:4831). "The real Presence" is "the actual presence of Christ's body and blood in the sacrament of the Eucharist" (OED).
2. Mays identifies C's source in Thomas Fuller (1608–1661), *Abel Redevivus* (1652) (PW [CC], 1:1064).

No host of friends with kindred zeal did burn![3]
No throbbing hearts awaited his return!
Prostrate alike when prince and peasant fell,
He only disenchanted from the spell,   25
Like the weak worm that gems the starless night,
Moved in the scanty circlet of his light:
And was it strange if he withdrew the ray
That did but guide the night-birds to their prey?

The ascending Day-star with a bolder eye   30
Hath lit each dew-drop on our trimmer lawn!
Yet not for this, if wise, will we decry
The spots and struggles of the timid DAWN;
Lest so we tempt th' approaching NOON to scorn
The mists and painted vapours of our MORN.   35

Constancy to an Ideal Object[1]

Since all, that beat about in Nature's range,
Or veer or vanish; why should'st thou remain
The only constant in a world of change,
O yearning THOUGHT, that liv'st but in the brain?
Call to the HOURS, that in the distance play,   5
The faery people of the future day—
Fond THOUGHT! not one of all that shining swarm
Will breathe on *thee* with life-enkindling breath,
Till when, like strangers shelt'ring from a storm,
Hope and Despair meet in the porch of Death![2]   10
Yet still thou haunt'st me: and though well I see,
She is not thou, and only thou art she,
Still, still as though some dear *embodied* Good,
Some *living* Love before my eyes there stood
With answering look a ready ear to lend,   15
I mourn to thee and say—"Ah! loveliest Friend!
"That this the meed of all my toils might be,
"To have a home, an English home, and thee![3]
"Vain repetition! Home and Thou are one.
"The peacefull'st cot, the moon shall shine upon,   20
"Lulled by the Thrush and wakened by the Lark

---

3. In a notebook entry of 1823–24 C wrote, "The learning and Genius that existed in a succession of Individuals during the tenth, 11th, and 12 centuries, have been much under
rated—The names indeed are few; but each must have had friends, and admirers—" (CN,
4:5062). C names Berengarius among others.
1. Date of composition uncertain. C wrote to J. H. Green (1791–1863) in June 1825, "Could
you procure me a Copy of those Lines which a long time ago I sent to Mrs Green by you, on
constancy to the *Idea* of a beloved Object—ending, I remember, with a Simile of a Woodman
following his own projected Shadow" (CL, 5:467).
2. Cf. C's "Allegoric Vision" in LS (CC), 133: "like two strangers that have fled to the same
shelter from the same storm, not seldom do Despair and Hope meet for the first time in the
porch of Death."
3. Only lines 16–18 are enclosed in quotation marks in *Poetical Works* of 1829 and 1834.

"Without thee were but a becalmed Bark,
"Whose Helmsman on an Ocean waste and wide
"Sits mute and pale his mouldering helm beside."

And art thou nothing? Such thou art, as when   25
The woodman winding westward up the glen
At wintry dawn, where o'er the sheep-track's maze
The viewless snow-mist weaves a glist'ning haze,
Sees full before him, gliding without tread,
An image with a glory round its head![4]   30
The enamoured rustic worships its fair hues,
Nor knows, he *makes* the shadow, he pursues!

Prefatory Note
to The Wanderings of Cain[1]

A prose composition, one not in metre at least, seems *prime facie* to
require explanation or apology. It was written in the year 1798, near
Nether Stowey in Somersetshire, at which place (*sanctum et amabile*

---

4. "This phœnomenon, which the Author has himself experienced, and of which the reader
   may find a description in one of the earlier volumes of the Manchester Philosophical Transactions, is applied figuratively in the following passage of the AIDS to REFLECTION: 'Pindar's
   fine remark respecting the different effects of music, on different characters, holds equally
   true of Genius: as many as are not delighted by it are disturbed, perplexed, irritated. The be-
   holder either recognizes it *as a projected form of his own Being, that moves before him with a
   Glory round its head,* or recoils from it as a spectre.' " [C's 1828 note; see *AR* (CC), 227.] C
   refers to John Haygarth (1740–1827), "Description of a Glory," in the third volume of the
   Memoirs of the Manchester Literary and Philosophical Society (1790). Haygarth describes his
   shadow projected on a low cloud: "The head of my shadow * * * was surrounded, at some
   distance, by a circle of various colours, whose centre appeared to be near the situation of the
   eye, and whose circumference extended to the shoulders. * * * It exhibited the most vivid
   colours, red being outermost * * * all the colours appeared in the same order and proportion
   that the rain-bow presents to our view. It resembled, very exactly, what in pictures is termed
   a *glory*, around the head of our Saviour" (463–64). C refers to Pindar, *Pythian Ode* 1.1–17,
   where Apollo's song delights some gods and terrifies others (*Pindar: Olympian Odes, Pythian
   Odes*, trans. William H. Race [LCL, 1997], 210–15).
1. The story of Cain and Abel is told in Genesis 4. The verses in the Preface were first published in *AR*, where C says that they were written in the "same year in which I wrote the Ancient Mariner and the first book of Christabel" (*AR* [CC], 390). The prose without the
   preface or verses was published in *The Bijou* (1828). The final paragraph of the "Prefatory
   Note" was omitted in 1834. The collaboration C describes in the Preface took place not in
   1798 but in early November 1797, before collaboration on "The Ancient Mariner," when C
   and Wordsworth visited Linton and the Valley of Rocks on the south coast of the Bristol
   Channel, which provides the setting for "The Wanderings of Cain." EHC prints a continuation or alternative version from a British Museum manuscript (Egerton 2800, ff 1–1v):

   > He falls down in a trance—when he awakes he sees a luminous body coming before
   > him. It stands before him an orb of fire. It goes on, he moves not. It returns to him
   > again, again retires as if wishing him to follow it. It then goes on and he follows: they
   > are led to near the bottom of the wild woods, brooks, forests etc. etc. The Fire gradually
   > shapes itself, retaining its luminous appearance, into the lineaments of a man. A dia-
   > logue between the fiery shape and Cain, in which the being presses upon him the enor-
   > mity of his guilt and that he must make some expiation to the true deity, who is a severe
   > God, and persuades him to burn out his eyes. Cain opposes this idea, and says that God
   > himself who had inflicted this punishment upon him, had done it because he neglected
   > to make a proper use of his senses, etc. The evil spirit answers him that God is indeed
   > a God of mercy, and an example must be given to mankind, that this end will be
   > answered by his terrible appearance, at the same time he will be gratified with the
   > most delicious sights and feelings. Cain, over-persuaded, consents to do it, but wishes
   > to go to the top of the rocks to take a farewell of the earth. His farewell speech con-

nomen![2] rich by so many associations and recollections) the Author
had taken up his residence in order to enjoy the society and close
neighbourhood of a dear and honoured friend, T. Poole, Esq. The
work was to have been written in concert with another,[3] whose name
is too venerable within the precincts of genius to be unnecessarily
brought into connection with such a trifle, and who was then residing
at a small distance from Nether Stowey. The title and subject were
suggested by myself, who likewise drew out the scheme and the contents for each of the three books or cantos, of which the work was to
consist, and which, the reader is to be informed, was to have been finished in one night! My partner undertook the first canto; I the second:
and which ever had *done first,* was to set about the third. Almost thirty
years have passed by; yet at this moment I cannot without something
more than a smile moot the question which of the two things was the
more impracticable, for a mind so eminently original to compose another man's thoughts and fancies, or for a taste so austerely pure and
simple to imitate the Death of Abel?[4] Methinks I see his grand and no-

cluding with an abrupt address to the promised redeemer, and he abandons the idea on
which the being had accompanied him, and turning round to declare this to the being
he sees him dancing from rock to rock in his former shape down those interminable
precipices.

Child affeared by his father's ravings, goes out to pluck the fruits in the moonlight
wildness. Cain's soliloquy. Child returns with a pitcher of water and a cake. Cain wonders what kind of beings dwell in that place—whether any created since man or
whether this world had any beings rescued from the Chaos, wandering like shipwrecked
beings from another world etc.

Midnight on the Euphrates. Cedars, palms, pines. Cain discovered sitting on the upper part of the ragged rock, where is cavern overlooking the Euphrates, the moon rising
on the horizon. His soliloquy. The Beasts are out on the ramp—he hears the screams of
a woman and children surrounded by tigers. Cain makes a soliloquy debating whether he
shall save the woman. Cain advances, wishing death, and the tigers rush off. It proves to
be Cain's wife with her two children, determined to follow her husband. She prevails
upon him at last to tell his story. Cain's wife tells him that her son Enoch was placed
suddenly by her side. Cain addresses all the elements to cease for a while to persecute
him, while he tells his story. He begins with telling her that he had first after his leaving
her found out a dwelling in the desart under a juniper tree, etc., etc., how he meets in
the desart a young man whom upon nearer approach he perceives to be Abel, on whose
countenance appears marks of the greatest misery . . . of another being who had power
after this life, greater than Jehovah. He is going to offer sacrifices to this being, and persuades Cain to follow him—he comes to an immense gulph filled with water, whither
they descend followed by alligators etc. They go till they come to an immense meadow so
surrounded as to be inaccessible, and from its depth so vast that you could not see it
from above. Abel offers sacrifice from the blood of his arm. A gleam of light illumines the
meadow—the countenance of Abel becomes more beautiful, and his arms glistering—he
then persuades Cain to offer sacrifice, for himself and his son Enoch by cutting his
child's arm and letting the blood fall from it. Cain is about to do it when Abel himself in
his angelic appearance, attended by Michael, is seen in the heavens, whence they sail
slowly down. Abel addresses Cain with terror, warning him not to offer up his innocent
child. The evil spirit throws off the countenance of Abel, assumes its own shape, flies off
pursuing a flying battle with Michael. Abel carries off the child [*PW,* 1:285–86].

Another transcription, which includes deletions and variations in wording and punctuation,
is in *PW* [CC], 2:495–96, 503–04. EHC dates this continuation in 1798, when C was reading in Bartram's *Travels* (1791) passages referring to alligators; but Kathleen Coburn cites an
1804 notebook entry, describing a gulf, "*full of alligators*" (CN, 2:2257), which may be C's
source.

2. Holy name worthy of love.
3. Wordsworth.
4. The Swiss poet Salomon Gessner (1730–1788), *Der Tod Abels* (1758), translated by Mary
   Collyer as *The Death of Abel* (1761). Collyer describes Gessner's style as "a kind of loose poetry, unshackled by the tagging of rhymes, or counting of syllables. This method of writing
   seems perfectly suited to the German language, and is of a middle species between verse and
   prose: It has the beauties of the first, with the ease of the last" (Lowes, 255–56).

ble countenance as at the moment when having dispatched my own portion of the task at full finger-speed, I hastened to him with my manuscript—that look of humourous despondency fixed on his almost blank sheet of paper, and then its silent mock-piteous admission of failure struggling with the sense of the exceeding ridiculousness of the whole scheme—which broke up in a laugh: and the Ancient Mariner was written instead.

Years afterward, however, the draft of the Plan and proposed Incidents, and the portion executed, obtained favor in the eyes of more than one person, whose judgment on a poetic work could not but have weighed with me, even though no parental partiality had been thrown into the same scale, as a make-weight: and I determined on commencing anew, and composing the whole in stanzas, and made some progress in realizing this intention, when adverse gales drove my bark off the "Fortunate Isles"[5] of the Muses; and then other and more momentous interests prompted a different voyage, to firmer anchorage and a securer port. I have in vain tried to recover the lines from the Palimpsest tablet of my memory: and I can only offer the introductory stanza, which had been committed to writing for the purpose of procuring a friend's judgment on the metre, as a specimen.

> Encinctured with a twine of leaves,
> That leafy twine his only dress!
> A lovely Boy was plucking fruits,
> By moonlight, in a wilderness.
> The morn[6] was bright, the air was free,
> And fruits and flowers together grew
> On many a shrub and many a tree:
> And all put on a gentle hue,
> Hanging in the shadowy air
> Like a picture rich and rare.
> It was a climate where, they say,
> The night is more belov'd than day.
> But who that beauteous Boy beguil'd,
> That beauteous Boy to linger here?
> Alone, by night, a little child,
> In place so silent and so wild—
> Has he no friend, no loving Mother near?[7]

---

5. C alludes to Ben Jonson's masque *The Fortunate Isles, and their Union* (1625) and draws on the Renaissance commonplace that Britain was one of the Fortunate Isles, or the Isles of the Blest, or the Elysium of the Greeks (Josephine Waters Bennett, "Britain among the Fortunate Isles," *Studies in Philology* 53 [1956]: 114–40).
6. In a letter to Byron, October 22, 1815 (*CL*, 4:602), *AR*, and *PW* (1834), "morn" was "Moon."
7. Kathleen Coburn dates the following notebook entry (*CN*, 2:2780) sometime between 1805 and 1819, but she speculates that it may have been written as a continuation of "The Wanderings of Cain" in 1815–16, when C was preparing *Christabel* for publication, but Mays suggests a date of 1807 (*PW* [CC], 2:492). The ellipsis in brackets indicates an illegible word:

   The Child is born, the Child must die / Among the desert Sands / And we too all must die of Thirst / for not a Drop remains. But whither do we retire / to Heaven or possibility of Heaven / But this to darkness, Cold, & tho' not positive Torment, yet positive Evil—Eternal Absence from Communion with the Creator. O how often have the [. . .] Sands at night roar'd & whitened like a burst of waters / O that indeed they were! Then

I have here given the birth, parentage, and premature decease of the "Wanderings of Cain, a poem,"—intreating, however, my Readers not to think so meanly of my judgment as to suppose that I either regard or offer it as any excuse for the publication of the following fragment, (and I may add, of one or two others in its neighbourhood) in its primitive crudity. But I should find still greater difficulty in forgiving myself, were I to record pro *tædio* publico[8] a set of petty mishaps and annoyances which I myself wish to forget. I must be content therefore with assuring the friendly Reader, that the less he attributes its appearance to the Author's will, choice, or judgment, the nearer to the truth he will be.

S. T. Coleridge.

The Wanderings of Cain

Canto II

"A little further, O my father, yet a little further, and we shall come into the open moonlight:"[1] Their road was through a forest of fir-trees; at its entrance the trees stood at distances from each other, and the path was broad, and the moonlight, and the moonlight shadows reposed upon it, and appeared quietly to inhabit that solitude. But soon the path winded and became narrow; the sun at high noon sometimes speckled, but never illumined it, and now it was dark as a cavern.

"It is dark, O my father!" said Enos, "but the path under our feet is smooth and soft, and we shall soon come out into the open moonlight."

"Lead on, my child!" said Cain: "guide me, little child!" And the innocent little child clasped a finger of the hand which had murdered

full of enthusiastic faith kneels & prays, & in holy frenzy covers the child with sand. In the name of the Father &c &c / —Twas done / the Infant died / the blessed Sand retired, each particle to itself, conglomerating, & shrinking from the profane sand / the Sands shrank away from it, & left a pit / still hardening & hardening, at length shot up a fountain large & mighty / How wide around its Spray, the rain-bow played upon the Stream & the Spray—but lo! another brighter, O far far more bright / it hangs over the head of a glorious Child like a floating veil (vide Raphael's God)—the Soul arises / they drink, & fill their Skins, & depart rejoicing—O Blessed the day when that good man & all his Company came to Heaven Gate & the Child—then an angel—rushed out to receive them.

8. For the boredom of the public, a play on the common phrase "pro bono publico" (for the public good).
1. Cf. Wordsworth, "A Little Onward" (1816), lines 1–4: "*A little onward lend thy guiding hand / To these dark steps, a little further on!* / —What trick of memory to *my* voice hath brought / This mournful iteration?" Wordsworth's first two lines quote the opening lines of Milton, *Samson Agonistes*, and his poem alludes to Antigone's leading Oedipus in Sophocles, *Oedipus at Colonus* (Wordsworth, *Shorter Poems, 1807–1820*, ed. Carl H. Ketcham [Ithaca, N.Y., 1989], 222–25, 542–43).

the righteous Abel, and he guided his father. "The fir branches drip upon thee, my son." "Yea, pleasantly, father, for I ran fast and eagerly to bring thee the pitcher and the cake, and my body is not yet cool. How happy the squirrels are that feed on these fir trees! they leap from bough to bough, and the old squirrels play round their young ones in the nest. I clomb a tree yesterday at noon, O my father, that I might play with them, but they leapt away from the branches, even to the slender twigs did they leap, and in a moment I beheld them on another tree. Why, O my father, would they not play with me? I would be good to them as thou art good to me: and I groaned to them even as thou groanest when thou givest me to eat, and when thou coverest me at evening, and as often as I stand at thy knee and thine eyes look at me?" Then Cain stopped, and stifling his groans he sank to the earth, and the child Enos stood in the darkness beside him.

And Cain lifted up his voice and cried bitterly, and said, "The Mighty One that persecuteth me is on this side and on that; he pursueth my soul like the wind, like the sand-blast he passeth through me; he is around me even as the air! O that I might be utterly no more! I desire to die—yea, the things that never had life, neither move they upon the earth—behold! they seem precious to mine eyes. O that a man might live without the breath of his nostrils. So I might abide in darkness, and blackness, and an empty space! Yea, I would lie down, I would not rise, neither would I stir my limbs till I became as the rock in the den of the lion, on which the young lion resteth his head whilst he sleepeth. For the torrent that roareth far off hath a voice; and the clouds in heaven look terribly on me; the mighty one who is against me speaketh in the wind of the cedar grove; and in silence am I dried up." Then Enos spake to his father, "Arise my father, arise, we are but a little way from the place where I found the cake and the pitcher." And Cain said, "How knowest thou?" and the child answered—"Behold the bare rocks are a few of thy strides distant from the forest; and while even now thou wert lifting up thy voice, I heard the echo." Then the child took hold of his father, as if he would raise him: and Cain being faint and feeble rose slowly on his knees and pressed himself against the trunk of a fir, and stood upright and followed the child.

The path was dark till within three strides' length of its termination, when it turned suddenly; the thick black trees formed a low arch, and the moonlight appeared for a moment like a dazzling portal. Enos ran before and stood in the open air; and when Cain, his father, emerged from the darkness, the child was affrighted. For the mighty limbs of Cain were wasted as by fire; his hair was as the matted curls on the Bison's forehead, and so glared his fierce and sullen eye beneath: and the black abundant locks on either side, a rank and tangled mass, were stained and scorched, as though the grasp of a burning iron hand had striven to rend them; and his countenance told in a strange and terrible language of agonies that had been, and were, and were still to continue to be.

The scene around was desolate; as far as the eye could reach it was desolate: the bare rocks faced each other, and left a long and wide interval of thin white sand. You might wander on and look round and round, and peep into the crevices of the rocks and discover nothing that acknowledged the influence of the seasons. There was no spring, no summer, no autumn: and the winter's snow, that would have been lovely, fell not on these hot rocks and scorching sands. Never morning lark had poised himself over this desert; but the huge serpent often hissed there beneath the talons of the vulture, and the vulture screamed, his wings imprisoned within the coils of the serpent. The pointed and shattered summits of the ridges of the rocks made a rude mimicry of human concerns, and seemed to prophecy mutely of things that then were not; steeples, and battlements, and ships with naked masts. As far from the wood as a boy might sling a pebble of the brook, there was one rock by itself at a small distance from the main ridge. It had been precipitated there perhaps by the groan which the Earth uttered when our first father fell. Before you approached, it appeared to lie flat on the ground, but its base slanted from its point, and between its point and the sands a tall man might stand up-right. It was here that Enos had found the pitcher and cake, and to this place he led his father. But ere they had reached the rock they beheld a human shape: his back was towards them, and they were advancing unperceived, when they heard him smite his breast and cry aloud, "Wo, is me! wo, is me! I must never die again, and yet I am perishing with thirst and hunger."

Pallid, as the reflection of the sheeted lightning on the heavy-sailing Night-cloud, became the face of Cain; but the child Enos took hold of the shaggy skin, his Father's robe, and raised his eyes to his Father, and listening whispered, "Ere yet I could speak, I am sure, O my father, that I heard that voice. Have not I often said that I remembered a sweet voice. O my father! this is it:" and Cain trembled exceedingly. The voice was sweet indeed, but it was thin and querulous like that of a feeble slave in misery, who despairs altogether, yet can not refrain himself from weeping and lamentation. And, behold! Enos glided forward, and creeping softly round the base of the rock, stood before the stranger, and looked up into his face. And the Shape shrieked, and turned round, and Cain beheld him, that his limbs and his face were those of his brother ABEL whom he had killed! And Cain stood like one who struggles in his sleep because of the exceeding terribleness of a dream.

Thus as he stood in silence and darkness of Soul, the SHAPE fell at his feet, and embraced his knees, and cried out with a bitter outcry, "Thou eldest born of Adam, whom Eve, my mother, brought forth, cease to torment me! I was feeding my flocks in green pastures by the side of quiet rivers, and thou killedst me; and now I am in misery." Then Cain closed his eyes, and hid them with his hands; and again he opened his eyes, and looked around him, and said to Enos, "What beholdest thou? Didst thou hear a voice my son?" "Yes, my father, I beheld man in unclean garments, and he uttered a sweet voice, full of lamentation." Then Cain raised up the Shape that was like Abel, and said, "The Creator of our father, who had respect unto thee, and unto thy offering, wherefore hath he forsaken thee?" Then the Shape shrieked a second time, and rent his garment, and his naked skin was like the white sands beneath their feet; and he shrieked yet a third time, and threw himself on his face upon the sand that was black with the shadow of the rock, and Cain and Enos sate beside him; the child by his right hand, and Cain by his left. They were all three under the rock, and within the shadow. The Shape that was like Abel raised himself up, and spake to the child; "I know where the cold waters are but I may not drink, wherefore didst thou then take away my pitcher?" But Cain said, "Didst thou not find favour in the sight of the Lord thy God?" The Shape answered, "The Lord is God of the living only, the dead have another God." Then the child Enos lifted up his eyes and prayed; but Cain rejoiced secretly in his heart. "Wretched shall they be all the days of their mortal life," exclaimed the Shape, "who sacrifice worthy and acceptable sacrifices to the God of the dead; but after death their toil ceaseth. Woe is me, for I was well beloved by the God of the living, and cruel wert thou, O my brother, who didst snatch me away from his power and his dominion." Having uttered these words, he rose suddenly, and fled over the sands; and Cain said in his heart, "The curse of the Lord is on me; but who is the God of the dead!" and he ran after the Shape, and the Shape fled shrieking over the sands, and the sands rose like white mists behind the steps of Cain, but the feet of him that was like Abel disturbed not the sands. He greatly outran Cain, and turning short, he wheeled round, and came again to the rock where they had been sitting, and where Enos still stood; and the child caught hold of his garment as he passed by, and he fell upon the ground. And Cain stopped, and beholding him not, said, "he has passed into the dark woods," and he walked slowly back to the rocks and when he reached it the child told him that he had caught hold of his garment as he passed by, and that the man had fallen upon the ground; and Cain once more sat beside him, and said, "Abel, my brother, I would lament for thee, but that the spirit within me is withered, and burnt up with extreme agony. Now, I pray thee, by thy flocks, and by thy pastures, and by the quiet rivers which thou lovedst, that thou tell me all that thou knowest. Who is the God of the dead? where doth he make his dwelling? what sacrifices are acceptable unto him? for I have offered, but have not been received; I have prayed, and have not been heard; and how can I be afflicted more than I already am?" The Shape arose and answered, "O that thou hadst had pity on me as I will have pity on thee. Follow me, Son of Adam! and bring thy child with thee!"

And they three passed over the white sands between the rocks, silent as the shadows.

FROM POETICAL WORKS (1829)

The Garden of Boccaccio[1]

Of late, in one of those most weary hours,
When life seems emptied of all genial powers,
A dreary mood, which he who ne'er has known
May bless his happy lot, I sate alone;
And, from the numbing spell to win relief,   5
Call'd on the PAST for thought of glee or grief.
In vain! bereft alike of grief and glee,
I sate and cow'r'd o'er my own vacancy!
And as I watch'd the dull continuous ache,
Which, all else slumb'ring, seem'd alone to wake;   10
O Friend! long wont to notice yet conceal,
And soothe by silence what words cannot heal,
I but half saw that quiet hand of thine
Place on my desk this exquisite design,[2]
Boccaccio's Garden and its faery,   15
The love, the joyaunce, and the gallantry!
An IDYLL, with Boccaccio's spirit warm,
Framed in the silent poesy of form.
Like flocks adown a newly-bathed steep
  Emerging from a mist: or like a stream   20
Of music soft that not dispels the sleep,
  But casts in happier moulds the slumberer's dream,
Gazed by an idle eye with silent might
The picture stole upon my inward sight.
A tremulous warmth crept gradual[3] o'er my chest,   25
As though an infant's finger touch'd my breast.
And one by one (I know not whence) were brought
All spirits of power that most had stirr'd my thought
In selfless boyhood, on a new world tost
Of wonder, and in its own fancies lost;   30
Or charm'd my youth, that, kindled from above,
Loved ere it loved, and sought a form for love;
Or lent a lustre to the earnest scan
Of manhood, musing what and whence is man!
Wild strain of Scalds,[4] that in the sea-worn caves   35
Rehearsed their war-spell to the winds and waves;
Or fateful hymn of those prophetic maids,

---

1. First published in *The Keepsake* (1829) preceded by an engraving by F. Englehart (1775–1849) of a watercolor by Thomas Stothard (1755–1834) titled *A Fête Champetre* [sic], an illustration of the scene of the third day of Boccaccio's *Decameron* (1349–51). In *Poetical Works* (1829) it followed "The Wanderings of Cain" in volume two.
2. In 1828, perhaps at the urging of Frederic Reynolds (d. 1850), the editor of *The Keepsake*, Mrs. Gillman placed the engraving on C's desk (Lucy E. Watson, *Coleridge at Highgate* [London, 1925], 137).
3. Cf. Keats, *Hyperion* 1.259–60, published in 1820: "an agony / crept gradual, from the feet unto the crown."
4. Early Norse poets.

That call'd on Hertha[5] in deep forest glades;
Or minstrel lay, that cheer'd the baron's feast;
Or rhyme of city pomp, of monk and priest,   40
Judge, mayor, and many a guild in long array,
To high-church pacing on the great saint's day.
And many a verse which to myself I sang,
That woke the tear yet stole away the pang,
Of hopes which in lamenting I renew'd.   45
And last, a matron now, of sober mien
Yet radiant still and with no earthly sheen,
Whom as a faery child my childhood woo'd
Even in my dawn of thought—PHILOSOPHY.
Though then unconscious of herself, pardie,   50
She bore no other name than POESY;
And, like a gift from heaven, in lifeful glee,
That had but newly left a mother's knee,
Prattled and play'd with bird and flower, and stone,
As if with elfin playfellows well known,   55
And life reveal'd to innocence alone.[6]

Thanks, gentle artist! now I can descry
Thy fair creation with a mastering eye.
And all awake! And now in fix'd gaze stand,
Now wander through the Eden of thy hand;   60
Praise the green arches, on the fountain clear
See fragment shadows of the crossing deer,
And with that serviceable nymph I stoop
The crystal from its restless pool to scoop.
I see no longer! I myself am there,   65
Sit on the ground-sward, and the banquet share.
'Tis I, that sweep that lute's love-echoing strings,
And gaze upon the maid who gazing sings:
Or pause and listen to the tinkling bells
From the high tower, and think that there she dwells.   70
With old Boccaccio's soul I stand possest,
And breathe an air like life, that swells my chest.

The brightness of the world, O thou once free,
And always fair, rare land of courtesy!
O Florence! with the Tuscan fields and hills,   75

5. Teutonic fertility goddess worshiped by the Lombards with mysterious rites described by the Roman historian Tacitus (d. c. 117) in *Germania* 40, trans. M. Hutton and E. H. Warmington (LCL, 1970), 197.
6. Lines 49–56 were drafted in a notebook in October 1819, followed by "Exerts the power excited in her as passive or negative subject by the Mother & becoming in her turn positive acts upon her Toys, like Light, that meeting eyeless things falls back & so reflects the image of her inward self. / Yet what she now attributes in her play, / She shall here after, armed / With stedfast stronger will, *awake* and *find*— / For Metaphor and Simile / Are notes of lisping prophecy— / New creation—'fell not out in man & by man must arise'—St. Paul— / Then Poesy shall rise into Philosophy / When Philosophy hath known herself as Poesy" (CN, 4:4623). C is not quoting directly from St. Paul, but his words resemble Romans 6.3–4: "Know ye not, that so many of us as were baptized into Jesus Christ were baptized into his death? Therefore we are buried with him by baptism into death: that like as Christ was raised up from the dead by the glory of the Father, even so we also should walk in newness of life."

And famous Arno, fed with all their rills;
Thou brightest star of star-bright Italy!
Rich, ornate, populous, all treasures thine,
The golden corn, the olive, and the vine.
Fair cities, gallant mansions, castles old,   80
And forests, where beside his leafy hold
The sullen boar hath heard the distant horn,
And whets his tusks against the gnarled thorn;
Palladian[7] palace with its storied halls;
Fountains,[8] where LOVE lies listening to their falls;   85
Gardens, where flings the bridge its airy span,
And Nature makes her happy home with man;
Where many a gorgeous flower is duly fed
With its own rill, on its own spangled bed,
And wreathes the marble urn, or leans its head,   90
A mimic mourner, that with veil withdrawn
Weeps liquid gems, the presents of the dawn;
Thine all delights, and every muse is thine;
And more than all, the embrace and intertwine
Of all with all in gay and twinkling dance!   95
Mid gods of Greece and warriors of romance,
See! BOCCACE[9] sits, unfolding on his knees
The new-found roll of old Mæonides;[1]
But from his mantle's fold, and near the heart,
Peers Ovid's HOLY BOOK of Love's sweet smart![2]   100

O all-enjoying and all-blending sage,
Long be it mine to con thy mazy page,
Where, half conceal'd, the eye of fancy views
Fauns, nymphs, and winged saints, all gracious to thy muse!

7. In the style of the Italian architect Andrea Palladio (1518–1580), who adapted Roman architecture, but also suggests Pallas, goddess of wisdom (*OED*).
8. The engraving depicts the scene of the third day, a walled garden where "a stream of water * * * gushed high into the air and then with a delightful sound, descended again into the crystal-clear water. The water which overflowed from the fountain ran through some hidden path through the lawn and then became visible again through finely constructed artificial channels which completely surrounded the lawn" (Giovanni Boccaccio, *The Decameron*, trans. Mark Musa and Peter Bondanella [New York, 1983], 163–64).
9. Boccaccio's presence in the picture is C's invention.
1. "Boccaccio claimed for himself the glory of having first introduced the works of Homer to his countrymen." [C's note in *The Keepsake* and *Poetical Works* (1829).] Homer is called Maeonides because his father was Maeon or because Homer was said to be born in Maeonia, or Lydia.
2. "I know few more striking or more interesting proofs of the overwhelming influence which the study of the Greek and Roman classics exercised on the judgments, feelings, and imaginations of the literati of Europe at the commencement of the restoration of literature, than the passage in the Filocopo of Boccaccio: where the sage instructor, Racheo, as soon as the young prince and the beautiful girl Biancofiore had learned their letters, sets them to study the HOLY BOOK, Ovid's ART OF LOVE: 'Incominciò Racheo a mettere il suo officio in esecuzione con intera sollecitudine. E loro, in breve tempo, insegnato a conoscer le lettere, *fece leggere il santo libro d'Ovvidio, nel quale il sommo poeta mostra, come i santi fuochi di Venere si debbano ne' freddi cuori accendere.*' " [C's note in *The Keepsake* and *Poetical Works* (1829).] The Italian reads: "Immediately Racheo began his office with entire thoughtfulness. And having in short time taught them to read, he made them read the holy book of Ovid, in which the great poet shows how the sacred fires of Venus can speedily be kindled in cold hearts." C annotated this passage in Il Filocopo: "The *holy* Book, Ovid's Art of Love!!—This is not the result of mere Immorality. / Multum, Multum / Hic jacet sepultum" (Much, Much, Here lies buried) (*CM* [*CC*], 1:544).

Still in thy garden let me watch their pranks,   105
And see in Dian's vest between the ranks
Of the trim vines, some maid that half believes
The *vestal* fires, of which her lover grieves,
With that sly satyr peeping through the leaves!

FROM POETICAL WORKS (1834)

MISCELLANEOUS POEMS

Phantom[1]

All look and likeness caught from earth,
All accident of kin and birth,
Had pass'd away.   There was no trace
Of aught on that illumined face,
Uprais'd beneath the rifted stone   5
But of one spirit all her own;—
She, she herself, and only she,
Shone thro' her body visibly.

Youth and Age[1]

Verse, a breeze mid blossoms straying,
Where Hope clung feeding, like a bee—
Both were mine! Life went a maying
      With Nature, Hope, and Poesy,
            When I was young!   5

1. "Phantom" and the following poems were published in the category of "Miscellaneous Poems" in volume two of 1834. C wrote in a notebook in April 1804, "My Dreams *now* always connected in some way or other with Isulia, all their forms in a state of fusion with some Feeling or other, that is the distorted Reflection of my Day Feelings respecting her / but the more distressful my Sleep, & alas! how seldom is it otherwise, the more distant, & Xst's Hospitalized the forms & incidents—& in one or two sweet Sleeps the Feeling has grown distinct & true, & at length has created its appropriate form, the very Isulia / or as I well described it in those Lines, 'All Look' &c" (*CN*, 2:2055). This note suggests a date of composition before 1804. Sara Hutchinson is Isulia, a name C found in Samuel Daniel's *Hymen's Triumph* (1615), parts of which Lamb later printed in *Specimens of English Dramatic Poets* (1808). "Xst's Hospital" is Christ's Hospital, C's school in London. Later he wrote, "On Friday Night, 8th Feb / 1805, my feeling, in sleep, of exceeding great Love for my Infant / seen by me in the Dream / yet so as that it might be Sara, Derwent or Berkley / and still *it was an individual Babe and mine.* Of Love in Sleep, the seldomness of the Feeling, scarcely ever in short absences, or except after very long Absence / a certain indistinctness, a sort of *universal-in-particularness* of Form, seems necessary—vide the note preceding, and my Lines," and then C quotes "Phantom." After the poem, C comments, "This abstract Self is indeed in its nature a Universal personified—as Life, Soul, Spirit, &c. Will not this prove it to be a *deeper* Feeling, & of such intimate affinity with ideas, so to modify them & become one with them, whereas the appetites and the feelings of Revenge and Anger co-exist with the Ideas, not combine with them; and alter the apparent effect of the Forms not the Forms themselves. / Certain modifications of Fear seem to approach nearest to this Love-sense, in its manner of acting" (*CN*, 2:2441).
1. First published in this complete form in 1834. Lines 1–43 were drafted in a notebook in 1823 (*CN*, 4:4994, 4996; *PW*, 2:1084–87). Kathleen Coburn speculates that the poem's mood reflects C's visit with Sara Hutchinson in October 1823 (*CN*, 4:4994n.) and suggests a possible date of late 1823. Lines 1–38 were published in *Poetical Works* (1828) in the cate-

When I was young?—Ah, woful when!
Ah! for the change 'twixt Now and Then!
This breathing house not built with hands,[2]
This body that does me grievous wrong,
O'er aery cliffs and glittering sands,   10
How lightly then it flashed along:—
Like those trim skiffs, unknown of yore,
On winding lakes and rivers wide,
That ask no aid of sail or oar,
That fear no spite of wind or tide!   15
Nought cared this body for wind or weather
When Youth and I liv'd in't together.

Flowers are lovely; Love is flower-like;
Friendship is a sheltering tree;
O! the joys, that came down shower-like,   20
Of Friendship, Love, and Liberty,
                              Ere I was old!
Ere I was old?   Ah woful Ere,
Which tells me, Youth's no longer here!
O Youth! for years so many and sweet,   25
'Tis known, that Thou and I were one,
I'll think it but a fond conceit—
It cannot be, that Thou art gone!
Thy vesper-bell hath not yet toll'd:—
And thou wert aye a masker bold!   30
What strange disguise hast now put on,
To make believe, that Thou art gone?
I see these locks in silvery slips,
This drooping gait, this altered size:
But springtide blossoms on thy lips,   35
And tears take sunshine from thine eyes!
Life is but thought: so think I will
That Youth and I are house-mates still.

Dew-drops are the gems of morning,
But the tears of mournful eve!   40
Where no hope is, life's a warning
That only serves to make us grieve,
                              When we are old:[3]
That only serves to make us grieve

gory of "Prose in Rhyme," in *The Literary Souvenir* (1828) with C's permission, and in *The Bijou* (1828) without his permission. William Pickering, the publisher of C's *Poetical Works*, also published *The Bijou*, whose editor took "Youth and Age," "The Wanderings of Cain," "A Day Dream," and "Work Without Hope" for Pickering's gift book without C's knowledge (*CL*, 6:710–11n.). Lines 39–49 were published as "The Old Man's Sigh. A Sonnet" in *Blackwood's Magazine* (June 1832). Paley questions whether C or EHC added the lines in 1834 (72). When C sent the poem to Alaric Watts for *The Literary Souvenir*, he called it the best of his new poems (*CL*, 6:700).
2. Paley identifies C's source as 2 Corinthians 5.1: "For we know that if our earthly house of this tabernacle were dissolved, we have a building of God, an house not made with hands, eternal in the heavens" (67).
3. C applied lines 39–43, the final ones in the first draft, to an imagined "estrangement" from Mrs. Gillman and the "indifference" of the Wordsworth circle (*CN*, 4:5184).

With oft and tedious taking-leave,   45
Like some poor nigh-related guest,
That may not rudely be dismist.
Yet hath outstay'd his welcome while,
And tells the jest without the smile.[4]

Love's Apparition and Evanishment[1]

An Allegoric Romance

Like a lone Arab, old and blind
Some caravan had left behind
Who sits beside a ruin'd well,
Where the shy sand-asps bask and swell;
And now he hangs his aged head aslant,   5
And listens for a human sound—in vain!
And now the aid, which Heaven alone can grant,
Upturns his eyeless face from Heaven to gain;—
Even thus, in vacant mood, one sultry hour,
Resting my eye upon a drooping plant,   10
With brow low bent, within my garden bower,
I sate upon the couch of camomile;
And—whether 'twas a transient sleep, perchance,
Flitted across the idle brain, the while
I watch'd the sickly calm with aimless scope,   15
In my own heart; or that, indeed a trance,
Turn'd my eye inward—thee, O genial Hope,
Love's elder sister! thee did I behold,
Drest as a bridesmaid, but all pale and cold,
With roseless cheek, all pale and cold and dim   20
    Lie lifeless at my feet!
And then came Love, a sylph in bridal trim,
    And stood beside my seat;
She bent, and kissed her sister's lips,
    As she was wont to do;—   25
Alas! 'twas but a chilling breath
Woke just enough of life in death
    To make Hope die anew.

4. Lines 39–49 in *Blackwood's* included an additional line after line 43, "Whose bruised wings quarrel with the bars of the still narrowing cage," and two final lines: "O! might Life cease! and Selfless Mind, / Whose total *Being* is Act, alone remain behind!" In *Blackwood's* the sonnet was introduced as an "Out-slough, or hypertrophic Stanza, of a certain poem, called 'Youth and Age,' having, by a judicial Ligature of the Versemaker's own tying, detached itself, and dropt off from the poem aforesaid" (956).
1. First published in *Friendship's Offering* (1834) signed and dated "August 1833." The original subtitle, sent to Thomas Pringle (1789–1834) for *Friendship's Offering*, was "a Madrigal" (*CL*, 6:954); for C's reading of Italian madrigals, see *BL* [*CC*], 2:34–39. On August 18, 1833, C wrote that he composed the verses "some three or four mornings ago" (*CL*, 6:956). EHC prints a "first draft" that begins with four lines, originally drafted in April 1824 (*CN*, 4:5146; *CL*, 5:360), but excluded from printed versions in C's lifetime, which Sara and Derwent Coleridge added to the end of the poem as "L'envoy" in 1852 and which EHC printed with the poem: "In vain we supplicate the Powers above; / There is no resurrection for the Love / That, nursed in tenderest care, yet fades away / In the chill'd heart by gradual self-decay" (*PW*, 1:489; 2:1087–88).

A Character[1]

A bird, who[2] for his other sins
Had liv'd amongst the Jacobins;
Tho' like a kitten amid rats,
Or callow tit in nest of bats,
He much abhorr'd all democrats;   5
Yet nathless stood in ill report
Of wishing ill to Church and Court,
Tho' he'd nor claw, nor tooth, nor sting,
And learnt to pipe God save the King;
Tho' each day did new feathers bring,   10
All swore he had a leathern wing;
Nor polish'd wing, nor feather'd tail,
Nor down-clad thigh would aught avail;
And tho'—his tongue devoid of gall—
He civilly assur'd them all:—   15
"A bird am I of Phœbus' breed,
And on the sunflower cling and feed;
My name, good Sirs, is Thomas Tit!"[3]
The bats would hail him brother cit,[4]
Or, at the furthest, cousin-german.[5]   20
At length the matter to determine,
He publicly denounced the vermin;
He spared the mouse, he prais'd the owl;

1. First published in 1834, when HNC changed its title from C's original "A Trifle" to "A Character" (Earl Leslie Griggs, *Coleridge Fille: A Biography of Sara Coleridge* [London, 1940], 89). An undated manuscript is in the British Library (Add. Ms. 34,225 ff10–13). EHC speculates that the poem may have been a response to Hazlitt's portrait of C in *The Spirit of the Age* (1825), but similar attacks on C and Southey as apostates from liberty were frequent from the time Southey was appointed poet laureate in 1813, so the date of composition is uncertain. It may have been drafted in the wake of the *Wat Tyler* episode in 1817 (see p. 226, n. 4 herein).
2. In the manuscript "A Bard who."
3. Several collections of poetry were published in the 18th century with the title *Tom Tit* as listed in the British Library Catalogue, a *Tom Tit's Song Book* (c. 1790) is listed in the *Oxford Companion to Children's Literature*, and *The Eagle's Masque* by Tom Tit (1808) is held in the Osborne Collection of Early Children's Books in the Toronto Public Library. In the *Eagle's Masque* the queen eagle hosts a masque at court, where the jay is a chattering critic; the goldfinch, a petty lord vain of his gold feathers; and the bat, a "leathery, feathery mongrel," who is excluded (9). It is not clear which, if any, of these C had in mind. Lines 17–18 resemble C's marginal annotation of George Stanley Faber, *Mysteries of the Cabiri* (Oxford, 1803), in which Faber (1773–1854) offers a fanciful derivation of Greek mythical names from the Hebrew narrative of the Flood. Sometime after 1817–19 C parodied these derivations, and in early February 1828 repeated his annotation in a notebook: "The Sun-flower in its broadest Disk with the seedy area within the circle of Florets a symbol of Chaos in the moment of bring[ing] forth Light. At this time you will be sure almost of seeing a Tom Tit clinging to the Flower. * * * How obvious then the true etymology of the Bird's name. T'goinah Tit, the Dove of Chaos!" (*CM* [*CC*], 2:580–81). C's derivation from the Hebrew is as fanciful as Faber's derivations.
4. Short for "citizen," a term used for London radicals and Jacobins. See "Modern Patriotism" (p. 285 herein).
5. In *Lectures on the English Poets* (1818) Hazlitt wrote that the Lake School of poets—Wordsworth, Coleridge, and Southey—"had its origin in the French revolution, or rather in those sentiments and opinions which * * * were indirectly imported into this country in translations from the German about that period" (*The Selected Writings of William Hazlitt*, ed. Duncan Wu, 9 vols. [London, 1998], 2:314). Hazlitt alludes to the radical German dramas of Schiller and August von Kotzebue (1761–1819) and to the Illumanti, a secret society, led by Adam Weishaupt (1748–1830), thought to have plotted the French Revolution. *Cousin-german*: first cousin once removed (*OED*).

But bats were neither flesh nor fowl.
Blood-sucker, vampire, harpy, goul,   25
Came in full clatter from his throat,
Till his old nest-mates chang'd their note
To hireling, traitor, and turncoat,—
A base apostate who had sold
His very teeth and claws for gold;—   30
And then his feathers!—sharp the jest—
No doubt he feather'd well his nest!
A Tit indeed! aye, tit for tat—[6]
With place and title, brother Bat,
We soon shall see how well he'll play   35
Count Goldfinch, or Sir Joseph Jay!"[7]
    Alas, poor Bird! and ill-bestarred—
Or rather let us say, poor Bard!
And henceforth quit the allegoric
    With metaphor and simile,   40
For simple facts and style historic:—
Alas, poor Bard! no gold had he.
Behind another's team he stept,
And plough'd and sow'd, while others reapt;
The work was his, but theirs the glory,[8]   45
Sic vos non vobis,[9] his whole story.
Besides, whate'er he wrote or said
Came from his heart as well as head;
And tho' he never left in lurch
His king, his country, or his church,   50
'Twas but to humour his own cynical
Contempt of doctrines Jacobinical;
To his own conscience only hearty,
'Twas but by chance he serv'd the party;—
The self-same things had said and writ,   55
Had Pitt been Fox, and Fox been Pitt;
Content his own applause to win,
Would never dash thro' thick and thin,
And he can make, so say the wise,
No claim who makes no sacrifice;—   60
And bard still less:—what claim had he,
Who swore it vex'd his soul to see
So grand a cause, so proud a realm
With Goose and Goody at the helm;
Who long ago had fall'n asunder   65
But for their rivals, baser blunder,[1]
The coward whine and Frenchified

---

6. EHC follows this text and omits quotation marks at the beginning of line 33, where later editors have placed them. Mays omits them at lines 33 and 36 (*PW* [CC], 1:971).
7. In the manuscript "Judas Jay."
8. C refers to his newspaper work for Daniel Stuart (see headnote *The Morning Post*, p. 123
herein).
9. Adaption of a line attributed to Virgil by Aelius Donatus (4th century C.E.) in his commentary on Virgil: "*Sic vos non vobis mellificatis apes*" (So you bees make honey, but not for yourselves). See the *Biographia*, chapter 2 (p. 398 herein).
1. JDC changed line 66 to "rivals' baser blunder," which EHC printed.

Slaver and slang of the other side?—[2]
　Thus, his own whim his only bribe,
Our bard pursued his old A. B. C.　　　　　　　　　70
Contented if he could subscribe
In fullest sense his name Ἔστησε;
('Tis Punic Greek, 'for he hath stood!')[3]
Whate'er the men, the cause was good;
And therefore with a right good will,　　　　　　75
Poor fool, he fights their battles still.
Tush! squeak'd the Bats;—a mere bravado
To whitewash that base renegado;[4]
'Tis plain unless you're blind or mad,
His conscience for the bays[5] he barters;—　　　80
And true it is—as true as sad—
These circlets of green baize[6] he had—
But then, alas! they were his garters!
　Ah! silly Bard, unfed, untended,
His lamp but glimmer'd in its socket;　　　　　85
He liv'd unhonor'd and unfriended
With scarce a penny in his pocket;—
Nay—tho' he hid it from the many—
With scarce a pocket for his penny!

—E cœlo descendit γνῶθι σεαυτόν.—Juvenal.[1]

Γνῶθι σεαυτὸν!—and is this the prime
And heaven-sprung adage of the olden time!—
Say, canst thou make thyself?—Learn first that trade;—
Haply thou mayst know what thyself had made.
What hast thou, Man, that thou dar'st call thine own?—　　5
What is there in thee, Man, that can be known?—
Dark fluxion, all unfixable by thought,
A phantom dim of past and future wrought,
Vain sister of the worm,—life, death, soul, clod—
Ignore thyself, and strive to know thy God!　　　10

2. C's *Table Talk* quotes lines 62–68 with C's introductory comment: "Fox's Gallicism * * * was a treasury of weapons to Pitt. He could never conceive the French right without making the English wrong. Ah! I remember" (*TT* [CC], 2:168). Fox and Pitt split over the French Revolution, Fox supporting it.
3. The literal translation should be the transitive "he hath placed" or "he hath made to stand" (*CN*, 4:4946n). C puns on "Punic" to mean "punning Greek" (see title note to "This Lime-Tree Bower," p. 136, n. 1 herein). In a notebook entry of December 1829 C referred to one of his early poems as "Ode on Punning, inspired by the Punic Muse" (*CN*, 5:6213).
4. Southey's radical play *Wat Tyler*, composed in 1794, was published in 1817 much to his embarrassment. In the House of Commons on March 14, 1817, William Smith, a Unitarian M.P. from Norwich, read from *Wat Tyler* and Southey's conservative journalism and said that Southey's journalism reflected the "malignity of a renegado" (T. C. Hansard, *Parliamentary Debates from the Year 1803*, 35:1090–91). C wrote four letters to the *Courier* in March and April defending Southey (*EOT* [CC], 2:449–60, 466–78).
5. I.e., bay leaves, the sign of Southey's position as poet laureate.
6. Coarse woolen cloth.
1. The only manuscript is dated January 1834 (*PW* [CC], 2:1368). The title comes from Juvenal, Satire 11, line 27: "The maxim 'Know Thyself' comes down to us from the skies" (*Juvenal and Persius*, trans. G. G. Ramsay [LCL, 1924], 222–23). The title "Self-Knowledge" was added by JDC in 1893 (see the *Biographia*, chapter 12, p. 466 herein).

Epitaph[1]

Stop, Christian Passer-by![2]—Stop, child of God,
And read with gentle breast. Beneath this sod
A poet lies, or that which once seem'd he.—
O, lift one thought in prayer for S. T. C.;
That he who many a year with toil of breath   5
Found death in life, may here find life in death![3]
Mercy for[4] praise—to be forgiven for fame
He ask'd, and hoped, through Christ. Do thou the same!

9th November, 1833

UNCOLLECTED POETRY

William Pickering and Henry Nelson Coleridge, who collaborated in constructing the 1834 edition of Coleridge's poetry, persuaded Coleridge to
enlarge his canon by adding previously unpublished poems. Subsequent
editors, James Dykes Campbell and Ernest Hartley Coleridge, expanded
the canon further by adding poems from notebooks and manuscripts.
They often selected parts of poems drafted in manuscripts, rearranged
lines, changed punctuation and paragraphing, and added titles. They
printed some poems in their chronological arrangement alongside poems
Coleridge chose to publish; they placed others in separate categories as
fragments from notebooks or other sources. Some later editors of selected
editions and anthologies printed Coleridge's poems in one chronological
sequence, so that the distinction between poems he considered finished
and wanted to publish and those he did not wish to publish in his collected edition was obscured. The poems printed here are among those that
Coleridge did not publish in any of his volumes, with the exceptions of
"Limbo" and "Ne Plus Ultra," which were published in *Poetical Works*
(1834), but which are printed here from Coleridge's notebook for reasons
explained in the notes. Some were printed in his lifetime in newspapers or
in gift books and are printed here from those sources; others unpublished
in his lifetime, which have found their way into selected editions, are

1. C first drafted a version of lines 3–6 in Thomas Poole's copy of *Toden Tanz* (Dance of Death)
   in *La Danse des Morts* (Basle, 1789), first printed in Mrs. Henry Sandford (d. 1903), *Thomas
   Poole and His Friends* (1888), 2: 301, to which two lines from the final version were added
   by another hand. A manuscript note to this version says that it was written in "Thomas
   Poole's Library at Nether Stowey." If this note is accurate, C must have written the first version in 1807, during his last visit to Nether Stowey (*PW*, 2:1089). Two subsequent versions,
   which expand the poem to six lines and then eight, were drafted about October 26, 1833
   (*PW*, 2:1088–89; *CM* [CC], 2:880, 903–06). C also sent three copies of the full eight lines
   in letters dated at the end of October and beginning of November 1833 (*CL*, 6:963, 969–70,
   973). In the letter version of October 28 he introduced the poem with the following comment: "I send you the Epitaph * * * on an Author not wholly unknown; but better known by
   the initials of his Name than by the Name itself—which he fondly Graecized—ἔστησε.
   ἔστησε: κεῖται· ἀναστήσει—. Hic Jacet, qui stetit, restat, resurget." [He hath stood; he lies
   at rest; he will rise again. Here lies one who hath stood, awaits, will rise again] (*CL*, 6:963;
   CM [CC] 2:905).
2. An echo of the Latin, *siste viator* (stop, traveler), a convention of classical epitaphs in which
   the deceased speaks.
3. Paley compares John 12.25: "He that loveth his life shall lose it; and he that hateth his life
   in this world shall keep it unto life eternal" (124).
4. " 'For' in the sense of 'instead of.' " [C's ms. note (*CL*, 6:973).]

printed here from his notebooks without the later editors' alterations but with the removal of words and lines Coleridge deleted. Two other poems that Coleridge did not publish in his volumes of poetry are included elsewhere in this edition: "The Visions of the Maid of Orleans" (p. 125 herein), first printed in the *Morning Post* and later incorporated in "The Destiny of Nations," printed in *Sibylline Leaves*, and "A Letter to ———— [Sara Hutchinson]," printed here with "Dejection: An Ode" (p. 145 herein).

[Apologia pro vita sua][1]

The poet in his lone yet genial hour
Gives to his eye a magnifying power:
Or rather he emancipates his eyes
From the black shapeless accidents of size—[2]
In unctuous cones of kindling coal,   5
Or smoke upwreathing from the pipe's trim bole,
       His gifted ken can see
       Phantoms of sublimity.

The Day Dream[1]

From an Emigrant to His Absent Wife

If thou wert here, these tears were tears of light!
    But from as sweet a vision did I start
As ever made these eyes grow idly bright!
    And tho' I weep yet still around my heart
A sweet and playful tenderness doth linger,   5
Touching my heart, as with an infant's finger.

My mouth half-open, like a witless man,
    I saw our couch, I saw our quiet room,
    Its shadows heaving by the fire-light gloom:
And o'er my lips a subtle feeling ran,   10

---

1. Drafted in a notebook, August 1800. First printed without a title in C's "The Historie and Gests of Maxilian" in *Blackwood's Magazine* 11 (January 1822): 12, the text printed here (*SW&F* [CC], 2:983–84). The title "Apologia Pro Vita Sua" (Defense of His Life) was first given by EHC (*PW*, 1:345n). The notebook entry begins: "11 o'clock at night—that conical Volcano of coal, half an inch high, ejaculating its inverted cone of smoke—the smoke in what a furious wind, this way, that way—& what a noise!" (*CN*, 1:791). In January 1805 in a notebook meditation on substance, magnitude, and spaciousness, C asked, "why do I seek for mountains when in the flattest countries the Clouds present so many so much more romantic & *spacious* forms, & the coal-fire so many so much more varied & lovely forms? * * * so by this factitious scale make them mountains, my pleasure being consequently playful, a voluntary poem in *hieroglyphics* or picture-writing—'*phantoms* of Sublimity' which I continue to know to be *phantoms*?" (*CN*, 2:2402).
2. The notebook draft began, "The poet's eye in his tipsy hour / Hath a magnifying power / Or rather his soul emancipates his eyes / Of the accidents of size" (*CN*, 1:791).
1. The text printed here was published in *MP*, October 19, 1802, signed ΕΣΤΗΣΕ, and never reprinted in C's lifetime. A manuscript of "A Letter to ————," discovered in 1977, included "The Day Dream." Stephen Parrish dates the manuscript before mid-July 1802 (*Coleridge's Dejection*, 14–15). "The Day Dream" is closely related to "A Letter to ————" and "A Day Dream."

And o'er my lips a soft and breeze-like feeling—
I know not what—but had the same been stealing

Upon a sleeping mother's lips, I guess
   It would have made the loving mother dream
That she was softly bending down to kiss   15
Her babe, that something more than babe did seem,
A floating presence of its darling father,
And yet its own dear baby self far rather!

Across my chest there lay a weight, so warm!
   As if some bird had taken shelter there: 20
And lo! I seem'd to see a woman's form—
   Thine, Sara? thine? O joy, if thine it were!
I gaz'd with stifled breath, and fear'd to stir it,
No deeper trance e'er wrapt a yearning spirit!

And now, when I seem'd sure thy face to see,   25
   Thy own dear self in our own quiet home;
There came an elfish laugh, and waken'd me.
   'Twas FREDERIC,[2] who behind my chair had clomb,
And with his bright eyes at my face was peeping—
I bless'd him, tried to laugh, and fell a weeping!   30

ΕΣΤΗΣΕ.

[Metrical Experiments, 1805][1]

Upon the mountain's Edge all lightly resting
There a brief while the Globe of splendor sits,
And seems a creature of this earth; but soon
   More changeful than the Moon
To Wane fantastic his great orb submits,   5
Or cone or mow of Fire, till sinking slowly
Even to a Star at length he lessens wholly.

Abrupt, as Spirits vanish, he is sunk
A soul-like breeze possesses all the wood;
   The Boughs, the Sprays have stood   10
As motionless, as stands the ancient Trunk,
But every leaf thro' all the forest flutters,
And deep the Cavern of the Fountain mutters

2. In the manuscript "Hartley," C's son.
1. Drafted in a long notebook sequence of metrical experiments and sample stanzas from German and Italian poetry (CN, 2:2224, f25–25v) and printed here with C's corrections and without his deletions. JDC published the first two stanzas in 1893 and gave them the title "A Sunset" (172, 632). C sent these two stanzas in a letter of April 22, 1819, with the title "Description of the Sun setting in a mountainous Country: a Fragment from an unpublished Poem" (CL, 4:937). Lines 14–15 may originally have been intended as alternatives for the last two lines of the second stanza above it. However, the final eight lines were published in The Literary Souvenir (1829) with the title "What is Life?" (PW, 1:394).

These lines I wrote as nonsense verses merely to try a metre; but they are by no means contemptible—at least, on reading them over I am surprised at finding them so good/ 16 Aug. 1805—Malta.

Now will it be a more English Music if the first & fourth are double rhymes; & the 5 & 6ᵗʰ single?—or all single; or the second & 3ʳᵈ double? Try

> Resembles Life, what once was held of Light,
> Too simple in itself for human Sight?   15
>
> An absolute Self? an Element ungrounded?
> All, that we see, all colors of all shade
>   By incroach of Darkness made?
> Is Life itself by consciousness unbounded,
> And all the Thoughts, Pains, Joys of mortal Breath   20
> A War-embrace of wrestling Life and Death?

Written in the same manner, and for the same purpose, but of course with more conscious Effort than the two stanzas in the preceding Leaf—16 Aug. 1805—the day of the Valetta Horse-racing—Bells jangling, & stupefying music playing all Day—

A Thought Suggested by a View of Saddleback in Cumberland[1]

> On stern Blencartha's perilous height
>   The winds are tyrannous and strong;[2]
> And flashing forth unsteady light,
> From stern Blencartha's skiey height,
>   As loud the torrents throng!   5
> Beneath the moon, in gentle weather,
> They bind the earth and sky together.
> But oh! The sky, and all its forms, how quiet!
> The things that seek the earth, how full of noise and riot!

---

1. First published in *The Amulet* (1833), the text printed here, and reprinted in *Friendship's Offering* (1834) with the title "A Versified Reflection" and a note: "The following stanza (it may not arrogate the name of poem) or versified reflection was composed while the author was gazing on three parallel *Forces* on a moonlight night, at the foot of the Saddleback Fell. S.T.C." (*PW*, 1:347). *Forces*: waterfalls. It was written in a notebook in February or March 1806 (*CN*, 2:2798n.) but may have been composed in 1800. Lowes points out that the first two lines come from a poem by Isaac Ritson (1761–1789) in William Hutchinson (1732–1814), *The History of the County of Cumberland* (Carlisle, 1794), 1:336, which C was reading when he wrote the second part of "Christabel": "The winds upon *Blenkarthur's* head, / Are often loud and strong" (Lowes, 604k). Mays dates it 1802 (*PW* [CC], 2:901).
2. C used the phrase "tyrannous and strong" in line 42 of "The Ancient Mariner" in 1834 but not in the 1798 version. The phrase occurs in Wordsworth's "The Waterfall and the Eglantine," line 15 in *LB* (1800). C first mentions Saddleback in November 1799 (*CN*, 1:542); he first climbed it in August 1800 (*CN*, 1:784). If C drafted the poem in 1799 or 1800, it is difficult to determine whether C or Wordsworth was the first to use the phrase.

[Notebook Fragment, 1806][1]

I know tis but a Dream, yet feel more anguish
Than if 'twere Truth. It has been often so,
Must I die under it? Is no one near?
Will no one hear these stifled groans, & wake me?

[Notebook Fragment, 1807][1]

Life wakeful over all knew no gradation
That Bliss in its excess became a Dream;
For every sense, each thought, & each sensation
Lived in my eye, transfigured not supprest.[2]
And Time drew out his subtle threads so quick,   5
And with such Spirit-speed & silentness,
That only in the web, of space like Time,
On the still spreading web I still diffused
Lay still commensurate—[3]

What never is but only is to be   10
This is not Life—
O Hopeless Hope, and Death's Hypocrisy!
And with perpetual Promise, breaks its Promises.—

The Stars that wont to start, as on a chase,
And twinkling insult on Heaven's darkened Face,   15
Like a conven'd Conspiracy of Spies
Wink at each other with confiding eyes,
Turn from the portent, all is blank on high,
No constellations alphabet the Sky—
The Heavens one large black Letter only shews,   20
And as a Child beneath its master's Blows
Shrills out at once its Task and its Affright,
The groaning world now learns to read aright,
And with its Voice of Voices cries out, O![4]

1. Written in a notebook immediately following "A Thought Suggested by a View of Saddle-back" in February or March 1806 (*CN*, 2:2799). First published by EHC in *PW*, 2:998, with the title "The Night-mare Death in Life." Osorio speaks the final line (*Osorio* 5.2.260 [*PW*, 2:594]. *Osorio* was completed in October 1797.
1. Drafted in 1807 in a notebook, and printed here without C's deletions. Lines 14–24 (var.) were first published by EHC as "Coeli Enarrant" (The heavens speak, or tell a tale) (*PW*, 1:486). After the notebook draft C commented, "I wrote these Lines, as an imitation of Du Bartas, as translated by our Sylvester" (*CN*, 2:3107). C refers to Joshua Sylvester's (1563–1618) translation, *Bartas: His Devine Weekes and Works* (1605).
2. Cf. Sylvester's "God, of himselfe incapable to sence, / In's Works reueales him t'our intelligence: / There—in our fingers feele, our nostrils smell, / Our Palats taste his vertues that excell: / He shewes him to our eyes, talkes to our eares, / In th'ord'red motions of the spangled Spheares" (6).
3. An earlier draft of line 9 in the same notebook entry was "A Space on which I lay commensurate."
4. Cf. lines 14–24 with Sylvester's "The World's a Booke in *Folio*, printed all / With God's great Workes in Letters Capitall: / Each Creature, is a Page, and each effect, / A faire Caracter, void of all defect" (7). Since C's surrounding notebook entries refer to Richard Crashaw

[Notebook Fragment, 1810][1]

When absent soon to meet again That morning & that last Employ[2]
Had only so much Pain, As the fears of Hope detract from certain
Joy—And now—O then I am least opprest When with the cleansing
Stream I mix my tears—and oft I'd fain neglect myself—Such anguish
& such sinking down of Heart comes o'er me—yet never can I—

> For neither death, nor absence, nor demerit
> Can free the love-enchanted spirit—
> And I seem always in her eye,
> And she will never more appear to mine.

> I have experience'd   5
> The worst, the World can wreak on me; the worst
> That can make Life indifferent, yet disturb
> With whisper'd Discontents the dying prayer.
> I have beheld the whole of all, wherein
> My Heart had any interest in this Life,   10
> To be disrent and torn from off my Hopes,
> That nothing now is left. Why then live on?
> That Hostage, which the world had in its keeping
> Given by me as a Pledge that I would live,
> That Hope of Her, say rather, that pure Faith   15
> In her fix'd Love, which held me to keep truce
> With the Tyranny of Life—is gone ah whither?
> What boots it to reply?—" 'tis gone! and now
> Well may I break this Pact, this League, of Blood
> That ties me to myself—and break I shall"—   20

(1612–1649), Kathleen Coburn suggests a comparison with Crashaw, "In the Glorious
Epiphanie of our Lord God, a Hymn," lines 183–88: "It was their Weaknes woo'd his beauty;
/ But it shall be / Their wisdome now, as well as duty, / To'injoy his Blott; and as a large black
letter / Use it to spell Thy beautyes better / And make the night it self their torch to thee"
(*Complete Poetry of Richard Crashaw*, ed. George Walton Williams [New York, 1970],
44–45; CN, 2:3107n.).

1. Lines 5–20 were first published by JDC in 1893 as Fragment 76 (462) and later by EHC as
Fragment 35 in *PW*, 2:1004–05. They were drafted in a notebook between March and May
1810, which provides the text printed here (CN, 3:3795, 3796). The first line of the notebook entry is heavily inked out and illegible; and the lines that follow, although written as
prose, resemble lines of poetry.

2. Kathleen Coburn notes that C refers to the middle of March 1810, when Sara Hutchinson,
who had been assisting C as an amanuensis for *The Friend*, left to live with her brother Tom
(1773–1849) and cousin John Monkhouse (1782–1866), who had taken a farmhouse in
Wales. C's note suggests tension between them in work on *The Friend* (CN, 3:3795n.).
Shortly after her departure *The Friend* ceased publication, and C's hope for affection from
her diminished greatly, to end finally with the split with the Wordsworths later in the year
(see title note to "To a Gentleman," p. 200, n. 1 herein).

[Notebook Fragments, 1811][1]

Crathmocraulo's[2] Thoughts like Lice—They don't *run* in his Head, as in other men's; but he scratches it—that wakens them—& then they begin to *crawl*—and this increases his *Itching* (to be witty) & so he scratches it again.—At most, his Lice & his Sense, which I suppose is what he means by his "poetic Licence," differ only as the note of a Cat & a Hawk—the one *mews*, & the other *pews*—the Lice crawl & the Thoughts drawl.—Hence when he murders some dull Jest which he has caught from some other man, he aptly calls it cracking a Joke— His own are too sluggish, even to change their Quarters—Tungstic Acid's[3] Wit is of the Flea kind—skips & bites—& his Jokes Flea-skips & Flea-bites—but they leave a mark behind them, much of the same depth & duration—

Copioso deems his genius mercurial[4]—and truly it *is* very like a Salivation—it flows from him without effort; but it is but Dribble after all—

1. Three sections from two notebook entries of April to May 1811 were published in C's lifetime (CN, 3:4073, 4074): "Limbo" (lines 35–59, 91–94) in *Poetical Works* (1834); "Ne Plus Ultra" (lines 63–83) in *Poetical Works* (1834); and lines 30–34 in *The Friend* as a satire on materialists (*Friend* [CC], 1:494), later titled "Moles" in *Poetical Works* (1834). A version of lines 35–59, 91–94, with additional lines (PW, 1:430–1), was copied into SC's album on October 15, 1827. In September 1828 in a letter to Alaric Watts, the editor of *The Literary Souvenir*, C referred to a version of "Limbo," which he left for Watts, as "containing some of the most forcible Lines & with the most original imagery that my niggard Muse ever made me a present of" (CL, 6:758). C feared Watts did not receive the copy, so he sent him a fragment in December 1828 consisting of only lines 35–54, shorter than that in SC's album and that published in *Poetical Works* (1834) (CL, 6:779–80), but Watts did not publish it. In 1893 JDC constructed another version of "Limbo," consisting of lines 25–59 (including "Moles") and 91–94 (189–90). EHC reprinted JDC's "Limbo" (PW, 1:429–30) and lines 9–20 under the title "On Donne's Poem 'To a Flea' " in the category of "Jeux d'Esprit" (PW, 2:980–81). Both JDC and EHC printed "Ne Plus Ultra" as it appeared in *Poetical Works* (1834). Since the degree of C's supervision of his edition of 1834 is uncertain, it is unclear whether he authorized these printings. Because "Limbo" exists in different versions, the notebook entries from which these poems come are printed here without deleted lines and words.
  The printing here presents the two notebook entries in one continuous sequence as they actually appear in the notebooks. The continuous sequence exemplifies the complexity of C's mind, the velocity with which it begins in satire and moves to serious philosophical and theological musings. The entry begins, as John Hodgson has noted, with an allusion to a remark by Dr. Johnson. On being asked whether he thought Derrick or Smart the better poet, Dr. Johnson replied, "Sir, there is no settling the point of precedency between a louse and a flea" (CN, 3:4104n.; John A. Hodgson, "Coleridge, Puns, and 'Donne's First Poem': The Limbo of Rhetoric and the Conception of Wit," *John Donne Journal* 4 [1985]: 183). C appears to be caricaturing personalities of his age, but the identifications of specific individuals are uncertain and are mentioned in the notes below.
2. Caricature unidentified. C wrote to Mrs. J. J. Morgan on November 20, 1813, "The longer I live, the more I do loathe in stomach, & deprecate in Judgement all, *all* Bluestockingism. The least possible of it implies at least two *Nits*, in one egg a male, in t'other a female—& if not killed, O the sense of the Lady will be *Licence*! Crathmocrawlo!" (CL, 3:459). *Nit*: the egg of a louse; hence Crathmocraulo is a "nit-wit." C may recall *The Taming of the Shrew* 4.3.108: "Thou flea, thou nit, thou winter-cricket." *Bluestocking*: slang term for educated literary women. C expresses dislike of them to comfort Mrs. Morgan, who was neither well educated nor literary.
3. Charles Lamb, who stuttered, i.e., tongue-stuck. Cf. "Tungstic Acid—applied to Lamb stammer'd Sarhaha," i.e., Sara (CN, 1:977).
4. The medicinal use of mercury produced excessive saliva. *Copioso*: unidentified.

(As when the Tempest *scours* the Heaven bright.)
Huge Tungtubig[5] has such a *hungry* Wit
That his Mouth waters at a lucky Hit.
But the stream passing o'er a poison'd ground,
The poor dead Jests, like Gudgeons[6] drugg'd and drown'd,   5
Float, wrong side up, in a full Flow of Dribble:
While Crawl, *whose earth-worm Wit* lives under ground,
Slow wriggles up to Light in some laborious Quibble[7]—

On Donne's first Poem.[8]

Be proud, as Spaniards! and Leap for Pride, ye Fleas
Henceforth in Nature's *Minim* World Grandees,[9]   10
In Phœbus' Archives registered are ye—
And this your Patent[1] of Nobility.
No Skip-Jacks[2] now, nor civiller Skip-Johns,
Dread Anthropophagi![3] Specks of living Bronze,
I hail you one & all, sans Pros or Cons,   15
Descendents from a noble Race of *Dons*.[4]

What tho' that great ancestral Flea be gone
Immortal with immortalizing Donne—
His earthly Spots bleach'd off as Papists gloze,
In purgatory fire on Bardolph's Nose,[5]   20
Or else starved out, his aery tread defied
By the dry Potticary's[6] bladdery Hide,
Which cross'd unchang'd and still keeps in ghost-Light
Of lank Half-nothings his, the thinnest Sprite
The sole true *Something* this in Limbo Den   25
It frightens Ghosts as Ghosts here frighten men—
Thence cross'd unraz'd and shall, some fated Hour,
Be pulverized by Demogorgon's Power[7]
And given as poison, to annilate Souls—
Even now it shrinks them! they shrink in, as Moles   30
(Nature's mute Monks, live Mandrakes[8] of the ground)

5. Tongue too big; unidentified.
6. Small fish used for bait, and figuratively a person who will swallow anything, gullible (*OED*).
7. A pun.
8. C annotated Lamb's copy of Donne's *Poems* in May 1811. "The Flea" was the first poem in "Songs and Sonnets," where C entered variants of lines 9–13 and 16 (*CM* [CC], 2:217)
9. Spanish noblemen of the highest rank.
1. A letter from a sovereign granting special privilege.
2. Fish that jump out of water, hence "a pert, shallow brained fellow; a puppy; a conceited fop" (*OED*).
3. Cannibals. Cf. *Othello* 1.3.142–43: "the cannibals that each other eat, / The Anthropophagi."
4. Spanish titles of nobility and a pun on Donne.
5. In *Henry V*, after Falstaff's death, a boy remembers him seeing "a flea stick upon Bardolph's nose." Falstaff "said it was a black soul burning in hell-fire" (2.3.34–35).
6. Apothecary's. In *Romeo and Juliet* the impoverished Apothecary's shop contains "an alligator stuffed, and other skins / Of ill-shaped fishes; and about his shelves / A beggarly account of empty boxes, / Green earthen pots, bladders, and musty seeds" (5.1.43–46).
7. In Plato, *Timaeus*, Demiourgos is the creator, but in Boccaccio, *De Genealogia Deorum*, he is a primeval god as in Spenser, *Faerie Queene* 1.1.37: "Great *Gorgon* Prince of Darknesse and dead night, / At which *Cocytus* quakes, and *Styx* is put to flight," and *Paradise Lost* 2.965.
8. A plant with forked roots resembling a human figure reputed in legend to cry when pulled from the ground.

Creep back from Light, then listen for its Sound—
See but to dread, and dread they know not why
The natural Alien of their negative Eye.

Tis a strange Place, this Limbo! not a Place,   35
Yet name it so—where Time & weary Space
Fetter'd from flight, with night-mair sense of Fleeing
Strive for their last crepuscular Half-being—
Lank Space, and scytheless Time with branny Hands
Barren and soundless as the measuring Sands,   40
Mark'd but by Flit of Shades—unmeaning they[9]
As Moonlight on the Dial of the Day—
But that is lovely—looks like Human Time,
An old Man with a steady Look sublime
That stops his earthly Task to watch the Skies—   45
But he is blind—a statue hath such Eyes—
Yet having moon-ward turn'd his face by chance—
Gazes the orb with moon-like Countenance
With scant white hairs, with fore-top bald & high
He gazes still, his eyeless Face all Eye—   50
As twere an Organ full of silent Sight[1]
His whole Face seemeth to rejoice in Light/
Lip touching Lip, all moveless, Bust and Limb,
He seems to gaze at that which seems to gaze on Him!

No such sweet Sights doth Limbo Den immure,   55
Wall'd round and made a Spirit-jail secure
By the mere Horror of blank Nought at all—
Whose circumambience doth these Ghosts enthrall.
A lurid Thought is growthless dull ~~Nega~~ Privation,[2]
But the Hag, Madness, scalds the Fiends of Hell   60
With frenzy-dreams, all incompassible[3]
Of aye-unepithetable ~~Priv~~ Negation.

    Sole Positive of Night!
      Antipathist of Light!
Fate's only Essence! Primal Scorpion Rod!   65
  The one permitted Opposite of God!
  Condensed Blackness, and Abysmal Storm
    Compacted to one Sceptre
    Arms the Grasp enorm,
      The Intercepter!   70
The Substance, that still casts the Shadow, Death!
    The Dragon foul and fell!
    The unrevealable
And hidden one, whose Breath

---

9. In *Poetical Works* (1834) this line was "Not mark'd by flit of Shades."
1. In the letter to Watts C wrote "actual Sight" and explained that it meant "imperfectly recollected" (*CL*, 6:779).
2. C's deletions are retained here and lines 62, 91, and 94 to emphasize his contrasting privation and negation.
3. Incompatible.

Gives Wind and Fuel to the fires of Hell!   75
   A sole Despair
Of both th' Eternities in Heaven!
Sole Interdict of all-bedewing Prayer,
   The All-compassionate!
Save to the Lampads seven   80
Revealed to none of all th' Angelic State,
   Save to the Lampads seven[4]
That watch the Throne of Heaven!

For skimming in the wake, it mock'd the care[5]
Of the Old Boat-God[6] for his Farthing Fare,   85
Tho' Irus'[7] Ghost itself he neer frown'd blacker on,
The skin and skin-pent Druggist crost the Acheron,
Styx and with Puriphlegethon Cocytus:[8]
The very names, methinks, might thither fright us—
Unchang'd it cross'd & shall &c[9]   90

A lurid thought is growthless dull ~~Negation~~ Privation
Yet that is but a Purgatory Curse
Hell knows a fear far worse,
A fear, a future fate. Tis *positive* ~~Privation~~ *Negation!*

A Specimen of the Sublime dashed to pieces by cutting too close with
her fiery Four in Hand round the corner of Non-sense.

A MORAL AND POLITICAL LECTURE (1795)

In 1795 Coleridge delivered a series of lectures in Bristol in order to raise
funds for his projected pantisocratic plan of setting up an ideal society in
America that fulfilled the perennial human aspirations for freedom, peace,
justice, and equality. For Coleridge, as for many of his contemporaries,
these aspirations had been severely undermined by oppressive government

---

4. Cf. lines 74–78 first printed in "Ode on the Departing Year" in *SL*: "Throughout the blissful
   throng, / Hushed were harp and song: / Till wheeling round the throne the LAMPADS seven, /
   (The mystic Words Of Heaven) / Permissive signal make." In his *Lectures on the History of
   Philosophy* C spoke of the Cabala, which made "no essential distinction between God and
   his creation but that of the manifested and the manifestation." For the cabalists the manifestation was "represented as the seven spirits or the [Sephiroth]. The last, which was to be
   the Messiah or the Shekinah, was to be the same as the second person of the triad and to be
   in the Shekinah a concentration of all the seven spirits of the manifestation, a doctrine
   which must have been very early indeed in the Church because we find a clear reference to
   it in the beginning of [the] Apocalypse" (*Lects 1818–19* [CC], 1:435–36).
5. C may have intended lines 84–90 as a substitute for or addition to lines 20–27. Line 90 appears to repeat line 27. EHC places these lines after line 26, as a note (*PW*, 1:429).
6. Charon ferried the dead to Hades and collected coins left in the mouths of the dead for their
   fare.
7. A voracious beggar of Ithaca, in books 17 and 18 of the *Odyssey*, with whom Odysseus fights.
   C wrote an allegory of Napoleon using Irus (*Friend* [CC], 1:363–65).
8. Rivers in the underworld.
9. Since line 91 repeats line 59, C may have intended lines 91–94 to substitute for lines
   59–62.

A

MORAL AND POLITICAL

LECTURE,

DELIVERED AT

BRISTOL.

BY

S. T. COLERIDGE,

OF

Jesus College, Cambridge.

——— To calm and guide
The fwelling democratic tide;
To watch the ftate's *uncertain* frame;
To baffle Faction's *partial* aim;
But chiefly with determin'd zeal
To quell the fervile Band that kneel
To Freedom's jealous foes;
And lafh that Monfter, who is daily found
Expert and bold our country's peace to wound,
Yet dreads to handle arms, nor manly counfel knows.

. AKENSIDE.

Bristol:
PRINTED BY GEORGE ROUTH, IN CORN-STREET.

PRICE, SIX-PENCE.

measures in the aftermath of the French Revolution, including the suspension of the Habeas Corpus Act and the subsequent State Trials of British reformists in 1794; the ongoing war with France; the continuation of the slave trade; and the so-called gagging bills of 1795 that threatened the freedom of speech, of the press, and of political meetings. In his lectures Coleridge exposed the corrupt policies of the ministry of William Pitt and church officials, condemned the war with France, advocated the abolition of private property, called attention to the scandal of the slave trade, and insisted on the necessity of enlightenment and reform to be implemented by a select group of disinterested patriots. The lectures are an important document of Coleridge's participation in the radical reformist movement of his time, as represented (among others) by William Godwin, John Thelwall, William Frend (1757–1841), and Thomas Holcroft (1745–1809). Although Coleridge did not belong to active political organizations such as the London Corresponding Society and criticized the professed atheism of Thelwall and Holcroft, his concerns were in large measure congruent with those of prominent radicals of his time, as well as of Whig politicians such as Charles James Fox. (For the view that Coleridge, far from being isolated from the reformist movement of his time, sustained his allegiance to radical politics longer than other contemporaries, see Roe, pp. 722–31 herein and Morrow, 17–19.)

Coleridge gave a total of eleven lectures, six of which were devoted to revealed religion. The lectures had a modest attendance compared to the large crowd who came to hear Thelwall's lectures for the same price of admission (one shilling). According to Joseph Cottle, they were "enthusiastically applauded" (*ER*, 1:20), and gained him the support of middle-class rational Dissenters such as the merchant Josiah Wade (fl. 1795–1836) and the tanner Thomas Poole, who became one of Coleridge's closest friends. But the lectures also contributed to Coleridge's designation as a "Jacobin" from which he tried hard to exculpate himself in later years (see "Once a Jacobin Always a Jacobin," pp. 301–06 herein). A letter to George Dyer (1755–1841) on February 1795 indicates that Coleridge's lectures exposed him to the threat of persecution and attack: "But the opposition of the Aristocrats is so furious and determined, that I begin to fear, that the Good I do is not proportionate to the Evil I occasion—Mobs and Mayors, Blockheads and Brickbats, Placards and Press gangs have leagued in horrible Conspiracy against me * * * and * * * were scarcely restrained from attacking the house in which the 'damn'd Jacobine was jawing away' " (*CL*, 1:152).

A Moral and Political Lecture was the first lecture given by Coleridge in late January or February 1795. It was published soon afterward, as Coleridge felt "*obliged*" to print it, "it having been confidently asserted that there was Treason in it. * * * The reasons which compelled me to publish it forbad me to correct it * * *" (*CL*, 1:152). The lecture in a revised and expanded form was reissued under a new title ("Introductory Address") in the pamphlet *Conciones ad Populum* published in December 1795, which included a second piece titled "On the Present War" (p. 250 herein). Coleridge made a number of substantial changes to *A Moral and Political Lecture* for *Conciones ad Populum*, some of which reveal his worries about the potentially seditious implications of his statements in the original lecture. For example, Coleridge added passages that strengthened his critique of false patriots, which now included the "majority of Democrats"; defined the role of reformers as that of pleading "*for* the Oppressed, not *to* them"; and stressed the importance of religion as a means of moral im-

provement and enlightenment of the lower classes (*Lects 1795* [CC], 37,
43–45). A third revised version of *A Moral and Political Lecture* appeared
in the 1818 *The Friend* with a misleading headnote referring to its earlier
delivery (misdated as 1794–95) and its closeness to the original lecture
except for the omission of names of persons (*Friend* [CC], 1:326). But
Coleridge in fact deleted about 250 lines from *A Moral and Political Lecture* and "Introductory Address" in places where he wanted to soften his
earlier radical positions. He omitted, for example, the statement that, as a
result of the French Revolution, "There was not a Tyrant in Europe, who
did not tremble on his Throne. Freedom herself heard the Crash
aghast!——" He also deleted an entire section that contained a scathing
critique of Pitt whose policies instigated the 1791 Birmingham riots, during which Dissenters, among them Joseph Priestley, were attacked and
their houses burned (see p. 243, n. 8 herein; and *Friend* [CC], 1:327, 331).
For other textual omissions, see the editorial notes in *Friend* (CC),
1:326–38.

A *Moral and Political Lecture* shows distinct traces of Godwin's influence, particularly the view that vice is error caused by circumstances. In
the revised version ("Introductory Address") Coleridge attempts to distance himself from radicals such as Godwin, even as he still retained Godwinian passages from the original lecture. He also omits a passage from *A
Moral and Political Lecture* in which he alluded to John Horne Tooke, one
of several British reformers charged with high treason in the 1794 State
Trials, but retains references to the 1793 trials and sentencing of Scottish
reformers such as Joseph Gerrald (1763–1796). On this inconsistency, see
Colmer (12–14). (For the view that passages that sound Godwinian in *A
Moral and Political Lecture* actually stem from David Hartley and Priestley, who unlike Godwin, suited Coleridge's Christian beliefs, see *Lects
1795* [CC], lviii–lxvii, lxxv.)

The text printed here is from *A Moral and Political Lecture* (Bristol,
1795). The citation on the title page, adapted from Mark Akenside
(1721–1770), "To the Right Honourable Francis Earl of Huntingdon,"
Ode xviii (*Poems* [1772], 302–03), highlights some of the themes of the
lecture, and appeared to Coleridge to be an adequate reflection of the
threat posed by Pitt's "monstrous" ministry. On the next page appeared the
following advertisement drawing on biblical references from Acts 17.13,
21.27, and 24.5:

> They, who in these days of jealousy and Party rage dare publicly ex-
> plain the Principles of Freedom, must expect to have their Intentions
> misrepresented, and to be entitled like the Apostles of Jesus, "stirrers up
> of the People, and men accused of Sedition." The following Lecture is
> therefore printed as it was delivered, the Author choosing that it should
> be published with all the inaccuracies and inelegant colloquialisms of
> an hasty composition, rather than that he should be the Object of possi-
> ble Calumny as one who had rashly uttered sentiments which he after-
> wards timidly qualified.

From A Moral and Political Lecture

—————To calm and guide
The swelling democratic tide;
To watch the state's *uncertain* frame;
To baffle Faction's *partial* aim;
But chiefly with determin'd zeal
To quell the servile Band that kneel
To Freedom's jealous foes;
And lash that Monster, who is daily found
Expert and bold our country's peace to wound,
Yet dreads to handle arms, nor manly counsel knows.
                                        AKENSIDE.

When the Wind is fair and the Planks of the Vessel sound, we may safely trust every thing to the management of professional Mariners; but in a Tempest and on board a crazy Bark, all must contribute their Quota of Exertion. The Stripling is not exempted from it by his Youth, nor the Passenger by his Inexperience. Even so in the present agitations of the public mind, every one ought to consider his intellectual faculties as in a state of immediate requisition. All may benefit Society in some degree. The exigences of the Times do not permit us to stay for the maturest years, lest the opportunity be lost, while we are waiting for an increase of power. Omitting therefore the disgusting Egotisms of an affected Humility, we shall briefly explain the design, and possible benefit, of the proposed political disquisitions.

Companies resembling the present will from a variety of circumstances consist *chiefly* of the zealous Advocates for Freedom. It will be therefore our endeavour, not so much to excite the torpid, as to regulate the feelings of the ardent: and above all, to evince the necessity of *bottoming* on fixed Principles,[1] that so we may not be the unstable Patriots of Passion or Accident, or hurried away by names of which we have not sifted the meaning, and by tenets of which we have not examined the consequences. The Times are trying: and in order to be prepared against their difficulties, we should have acquired a prompt facility of adverting in all our doubts to some grand and comprehensive Truth. In a deep and strong Soil must that Blessing fix its Roots, the height of which, like that of the Tree in Daniel, is to "reach to Heaven, and the Sight of it to the ends of all the Earth."[2]

The Example of France is indeed a "Warning to Britain."[3] A nation

---

1. Edmund Burke (1729–1797) in *Reflections on the Revolution in France* (1790) used a similar phrase in a passage in which he defended the hereditary succession of the crown against both those who supported popular elections and those "fanatics" who considered the monarchy to have "more of a divine sanction than any other mode of government * * *." He pointed out that "an absurd opinion concerning the king's hereditary right to the crown does not prejudice one that is rational, and bottomed upon solid principles of law and policy" (36–37).
2. An adaptation from Daniel 4.11.
3. C refers to the influential pamphlet *The Example of France, a Warning to Britain*, 4th ed. (1794), by the distinguished agriculturist Arthur Young (1741–1820). In this work Young launched a vituperative attack against the French Revolution, admonishing his contemporaries to oppose radical reformists at home and support the British constitution "uncontam-

wading to their Rights through Blood, and marking the track of Freedom by Devastation! Yet let us not embattle our Feelings against our Reason. Let us not indulge our malignant Passions under the mask of Humanity. Instead of railing with infuriate declamation against these excesses, we shall be more profitably employed in developing the sources of them. French Freedom is the Beacon, that while it guides us to Equality should shew us the Dangers, that throng the road.

The annals of the French Revolution have recorded in Letters of Blood, that the Knowledge of the Few cannot counteract the Ignorance of the Many;[4] that the Light of Philosophy, when it is confined to a small Minority, points out the Possessors as the Victims, rather than the Illuminators, of the Multitude.[5] The Patriots of France either hastened into the dangerous and gigantic Error of making certain Evil the means of contingent Good, or were sacrificed by the Mob, with whose prejudices and ferocity their unbending Virtue forbade them to assimilate. Like Sampson, the People were strong—like Sampson, the People were blind. Those two massy Pillars of Oppression's Temple, Monarchy and Aristocracy

> With horrible convulsion to and fro
> They tugg'd, they shook—till down they came and drew
> The whole Roof after them with burst of Thunder
> Upon the heads of all who sat beneath,
> Lords, Ladies, Captains, Counsellors, and Priests,
> Their choice Nobility!
>
> MILTON, SAM. AGON.[6]

---

inated by *reforms*" (144), since "ruin and reform are synonymous" (213). His hope was that "With the example of France in full display, propositions of reform, which in that kingdom produced conflagration and massacre, will, in this, have the effect of putting the nation on guard against men, who so openly profess a readiness to stake all we enjoy, on the desperate throw of a new Revolution" (144). C admired Young's earlier work *Travels, during the Years 1787, 1788, 1789 * * * [in] France* (Bury St. Edmund's, 1792), which gave a favorable representation of the French Revolution but viewed *The Example of France* as a form of "recantation" that secured for the author a plump job at four hundred pounds a year as secretary of the Board of Agriculture. In his review of Young's pamphlet *The Question of Scarcity Plainly Stated* (*EOT* [CC], 1:233–38), C suggests that the "horror against the excesses of the French Revolution" expressed in *The Example of France* was an indication of Young's awareness "that some portion of this horror would attach to all those who, like himself, had blown the trump of gratulation on the first approach of that Revolution" (233).

4. Cf. Young's different use of the relationship between "the many" and "the few" in *The Example of France*. Citing Joseph Priestley's statement (in *Letters to the Right Honourable Edmund Burke Occasioned by His Reflections on the Revolution in France*, 2nd ed. [Birmingham, 1791]) that "The generality of governments * * * have hitherto been little more than a combination of *the few* against *the many*," Young argues that, as proven by the events in France, "the combination of the *many* against the *few*, can also deluge a nation in blood, with a cruelty more accused, because unnecessary to the many * * *" (27).

5. On the importance of enlightenment of the masses as a prerequisite for a successful revolution, cf. a passage added in the revised version of this lecture ("Introductory Address") in *Conciones ad Populum*: "That general Illumination should precede Revolution, is a truth as obvious, as that the Vessel should be cleansed before we fill it with a pure Liquor." C believed that this task could be accomplished by a small group of genuine patriots, constituting an intellectual and moral rather than social elite, who would "plead *for* the Oppressed, not *to* them," and "teach them their *Duties*" so as to "render them susceptible of their *Rights*" (*Lects 1795* [CC], 43). Cf. Godwin's view that the "complete reformation" of society consists in "an universal illumination" (*Political Justice* [1793], 1:222) and that the "public mind must first be enlightened" before reforms can be carried out (*Considerations on Lord Grenville's and Mr. Pitt's Bills, Concerning Treasonable and Seditious Practices and Unlawful Assemblies* [1795], 17).

6. Milton, *Samson Agonistes*, lines 1649–54 (var.).

There was not a Tyrant in Europe, that did not tremble on his Throne. Freedom herself heard the Crash aghast[7]—yet shall she not have heard it unbenefited, if haply the Horrors of that Day shall have made other nations timely wise—if a great people shall from hence become adequately illuminated for a Revolution bloodless, like Poland's, but not, like Poland's assassinated by the foul Treason of Tyrants against Liberty.[8]

Revolutions are sudden to the unthinking only. Political Disturbances happen not without their warning Harbingers. Strange Rumblings and confused Noises still precede these earthquakes and hurricanes of the moral World. In the eventful years previous to a Revolution, the Philosopher as he passes up and down the walks of Life, examines with an anxious eye the motives and manners, that characterise those who seem destined to be the Actors in it. To delineate with a free hand the different Classes of our present Oppositionists to "Things as they are,"[9]—may be a delicate, but it is a necessary Task—in order that we may enlighten, or at least beware of, the misguided men who have enlisted themselves under the banners of Freedom from no Principles or from bad ones—whether they be those, "Who extol things vulgar"—and

> admire they know not what,
> And know not whom, but as one leads the other[1]—

or whether those,

> Whose end is private Hate, not help to Freedom,
> In *her* way to *Virtue* adverse and turbulent.[2]

The first Class among the professed Friends of Liberty is composed of Men, who unaccustomed to the labor of thorough Investigation and not particularly oppressed by the Burthen of State, are yet impelled by their feelings to disapprove of its grosser depravities, and prepared to give an indolent Vote in favor of Reform. Their sensibilities unbraced by the co-operation of fixed principles, they offer no sacrifices to the divinity of active Virtue. Their political Opinions depend with weather-

---

7. In "Introductory Address" of *Conciones ad Populum* C stopped the sentence here and instead of the subsequent reference to Poland, added two long paragraphs that include vivid portraits of the Girondist leader Jean-Pierre Brissot (1754–1793) and of the visionary yet unscrupulous, passionate yet intolerant Maximilien-François-Marie-Isidore de Robespierre (1758–1794), a veritable "Caligula with the Cap of Liberty on his head" to whom C had devoted the drama *The Fall of Robespierre* (1794), composed with Southey (*Lects 1795* [CC] 34–36).

8. In 1794 the Polish commander Thaddeus Kosciusko (1746–1817), who had distinguished himself in the American War of Independence, led a rebellion against Prussia and Russia, which had twice partitioned his country and were to do so again in October 1795. C celebrated Kosciusko in a sonnet published in the *Morning Chronicle* in 1794 (*PW*, 1:82–83) and printed a sketch of his life in *Watchman* (CC), 367–69. The "Tyrants against Freedom" are Catherine II, the Great, empress of Russia (1729–1795); Francis II of Austria, Holy Roman emperor (1768–1835); and Frederick William II, king of Prussia (1744–1797). For C's attack on his government's alliance with the "MERCIFUL Catherine" and "the HONEST King of Prussia," see p. 251, n. 5 herein. The Russian Empress's "inequities to Poland" and "libidinous excesses" are also exposed in "Ode on the Departing Year," lines 40–61 and C's note (p. 38 and n. 7 herein).

9. An allusion to Godwin's novel *Things as They Are; or, the Adventures of Caleb Williams*, 3 vols. (1794), which in turn alludes to *Man as He Is* (1792) by Robert Bage (1728–1801).

1. Milton, *Paradise Regained* 3.52–53.

2. C adapts two passages from Milton, *Samson Agonistes*, lines 1265–66 and 1039–40.

cock uncertainty on the winds of Rumor, that blow from France. On the report of French Victories they blaze into Republicanism, at a tale of French Excesses they darken into Aristocrats;[3] and seek for shelter among those despicable adherents to Fraud and Tyranny, who ironically style themselves Constitutionalists.[4] These *dough-baked*[5] *Patriots* may not however be without their use. This Oscillation of political Opinion, while it retards the Day of Revolution, may operate as a preventative to its Excesses. Indecision of Character, though the effect of Timidity, is almost always associated with benevolence.

Wilder Features characterize the second Class. Sufficiently possessed of natural Sense to despise the Priest, and of natural Feeling to hate the Oppressor, they listen only to the inflammatory harangues of some mad-headed Enthusiast, and imbibe from them Poison, not Food, Rage not Liberty. Unillumined by Philosophy and stimulated to a lust of Revenge by aggravated wrongs, they would make the Altar of Freedom stream with blood, while the grass grew in the desolated Halls of Justice. These men are the rude Materials from which a detestable Minister[6] manufactures Conspiracies. Among these men he sends a brood of sly political Monsters, in the character of sanguinary Demagogues, and like Satan of Old, "The Tempter ere the Accuser"[7] ensnares a few into Treason, that he may alarm the whole into Slavery. He, who has dark purposes to serve, must use dark means—Light would discover, reason would expose him: He must endeavour to shut out both—or if this prove impracticable, make them appear frightful by giving them frightful Names: For farther than Names the Vulgar enquire not. Religion and Reason are but poor Substitutes for "Church and Constitution;" and the sable-vested Instigators of the Birmingham Riots[8] well knew, that a Syllogism could not disarm a drunken Incendiary of his Firebrand, or a demonstration *helmet* a Philosopher's Head against a Brickbat. But in the principles, which this Apostate has, by his emissaries, sown among a few blind zealots for Freedom, he has digged a pit into which he himself may perhaps be doomed to fall.[9] We contemplate those principles with horror. Yet they possess a kind of wild Justice well calculated to spread them among the grossly ignorant. To uninlightened minds, there are terrible charms in the idea of Retribution, however savagely it be inculcated.

3. In the *Annual Register* for 1794, 2nd ed. (1809), 179–80, an "Aristocrat" is defined as one "who opposed all changes in the constitution," as opposed to a "Democrat," who "demanded these, together with an immediate peace with France, and an acknowledgment of the French republic" (*Lects 1795* [CC], 8n. 3).
4. Those who, like Edmund Burke, admired the British constitution and regarded it as superior to the French constitution.
5. Signifies "imperfect, badly finished; deficient" (*OED*); also used by C in the version of the lecture included in *Friend* (CC), 1:331, and in a letter to Godwin of October 13, 1800, with reference to "dough-baked Democrats of Fortune" (*CL*, 1:636).
6. I.e., William Pitt.
7. Milton, *Paradise Lost* 4.10. C refers here to the widespread use of government spies to trap reformers and charge them with treason. Cf. his "Spy Nozy" story in the *Biographia*, pp. 453–55 herein.
8. C refers to the 1791 Birmingham riots during which the houses of Dissenters, among them Priestley's, were burned. C's allusion to "Sable-vested" figures implicates the Anglican clergy in the instigation of these attacks.
9. Another reference to Pitt with an allusion to Ecclesiastes 10.8: "He that diggeth a pit shall fall into it * * *."

The Groans of the Oppressors make fearful yet pleasant music to the ear of him, whose mind is darkness, and into whose soul the iron has entered.

This class, at present, is comparatively small—Yet soon to form an overwhelming majority, unless great and immediate efforts are used to lessen the intolerable grievances of our poorer brethren, and infuse into their sorely wounded hearts the healing qualities of knowledge. For can we wonder that men should want humanity, who want all the circumstances of life that humanize? Can we wonder that with the ignorance of Brutes they should unite their ferocity? peace and comfort be with these! But let us shudder to hear from men of dissimilar opportunities sentiments of similar revengefulness. The purifying alchemy of Education may transmute the [fi]erceness of an ignorant man into virtuous energy—but what remedy shall we apply to him, whom Plenty has not softened, whom Knowledge has not taught Benevolence? This is one among the many fatal effects which result from the want of fixed principles. Convinced that vice is error,[1] we shall entertain sentiments of Pity for the vicious, not of Indignation— and even with respect to that bad man, to whom we have before alluded,[2] altho' we are now groaning beneath the burthen of his misconduct, we shall harbour no sentiments of revenge; but rather condole with him that his chaotic Iniquities have exhibited such a complication of Extravagance, Inconsistency, and rashness, as may alarm him with apprehensions of approaching lunacy!

There are a third class among the friends of Freedom who possess not the wavering character of the first description, nor the ferocity last delineated.[3] They pursue the interests of Freedom steadily, but with narrow and self-centering views: they anticipate with exultation the abolition of priviledged orders, and of acts that persecute by exclusion from the right of citizenship:[4] they are prepared to join in digging up the rubbish of mouldering establishments and stripping off the taudry pageantry of Governments. Whatever is above them they are most willing to drag down; but alas! they use not the pulley! Whatever tends to improve and elevate the ranks of our poorer brethren, they regard with suspicious jealousy, as the dreams of the visionary; as if there were any thing in the superiority of Lord to Gentleman, so mortifying

1. A view derived from Godwin: "All vice is nothing more than error and mistake reduced into practice, and adopted as the principle of our conduct" (*Political Justice*, 1:31).
2. In spite of C's apparent attempt here to plead that Pitt deserves pity rather than revenge, his mockery of Pitt hardly diminishes, as the reference to the minister's "approaching lunacy" indicates.
3. On the four classes of "Friends of Liberty," see Morrow, 13–15; Roe, 8–9; and Colmer, 11. In his speech to the London Corresponding Society at its meeting of October 26, 1795, Thelwall, possibly under C's influence, also divided false patriots into three classes. Thelwall's first class, which includes government spies and treacherous conspirators, reflects quite closely the second class in C's analysis (*The Speech of John Thelwall, at the General Meeting of the Friends of Parliamentary Reform Called by the London Corresponding Society, and Held in the Neighbourhood of Copenhagen-House; On Monday, October 26, 1795* [1795], 3–5). For C and Thelwall, see headnote to *The Plot Discovered* (p. 274 herein); p. 276, n. 8 herein; p. 278, n. 7 herein.
4. A reference to the Test and Corporation Acts of 1673 and 1661 (not repealed until 1828), which required allegiance to the rites of the Church of England, effectively excluding Catholics and Dissenters from holding public offices.

in the barrier, so fatal to happiness in the consequences, as the more real distinction of master and servant, of rich man and of poor. Wherein am I made worse by my ennobled neighbour? do the childish titles of aristocracy detract from my domestic comforts, or prevent my intellectual acquisitions? but those institutions of society which should condemn me to the necessity of twelve hours daily toil, would make my *soul* a slave, and sink *the rational* being in the mere animal. It is a mockery of our fellow creatures' wrongs to call them equal in rights, when by the bitter compulsion of their wants we make them inferior to us in all that can soften the heart, or dignify the understanding. Let us not say that this is the work of time—that it is impracticable at present, unless we each in our individual capacities do strenuously and perseveringly endeavour to diffuse among our domestics those comforts and that illumination which far beyond all political ordinances are the true equalizers of men. But of the propriety and utility of holding up the distant mark of attainable perfection, we shall enter more fully towards the close of this address;[5] we aim with pleasure to the contemplation of that small but glorious band, whom we may truly distinguish by the name of thinking and disinterested Patriots:[6] these are the men who have encouraged the sympathetic passions till they have become irresistable habits, and made their duty a necessary part of their self interest, by the long continued cultivation of that moral taste which derives our most exquisite pleasures from the contemplation of possible perfection, and proportionate pain from the perception of existing *depravation*.[7] Accustomed to regard all the affairs of man as a process, they never hurry and they never pause; theirs is not that twilight of political knowledge which gives us just light enough to place one foot before the other; as they advance, the scene still opens upon them, and they press right onward with a vast

---

5. C did not embark on this subject at the end of the lecture and deleted this statement in the revised "Introductory Address" in *Conciones ad Populum*.

6. Embedded here is C's idea of "clerisy," which he was to develop later in *Church and State* (p. 583, n. 9 herein; p. 585, and n. herein; and p. 586 herein; cf. *Lectures on Revealed Religion*, p. 269, n. 4 herein). For other instances of this emerging doctrine in 1795, see *Lects 1795* (CC), 137, 218, and nn.; and "Religious Musings," line 97 (p. 24 herein). Critics disagree as to which contemporaries C had in mind as belonging to the fourth category of true patriots. According to Colmer, the class of "disinterested patriots" includes the followers of Godwin, even as Godwin is not directly mentioned (11). Roe argues that the patriots with whom C indentified himself were specifically Joseph Gerrald and Maurice Margarot (d. 1815), leading members of the London Corresponding Society; the lawyer Thomas Muir (1765–1798), founder of the Whig society Friends of the People in Edinburgh; and the Unitarian minister Thomas Fysshe Palmer (1747–1802), who was also a member of the Friends of the People. All four were charged with sedition in 1793 and 1794 and transported to Botany Bay, from where only Margarot survived and returned to England (Roe, 8–9). On the other hand, Lewis Patton and Peter Mann argue that the account of the true patriots betrays the influence of Hartley and Priestley rather than Godwin and his disciples. C retained this section in "Introductory Address" "precisely because it was not and had never been conceived as a 'panegyric in favour of Godwinism,'" as Colmer contended (14; *Lects 1795* [CC], lxxv).

7. C draws here on Hartley's discussion of the development of "sympathetic passions" and the coincidence of duty and self-interest in *Observations on Man* (see p. 289, n. 5 herein). On the relationship between morality and the contemplation of perfection, cf. Godwin, *Political Justice*, 2:894: "It is a well known principle of morality, that he who proposes perfection to himself, though he will inevitably fall short of what he pursues, will make a more rapid progress, than he who is contented to aim only at what is imperfect. * * * Such a view * * * will impress us with a just apprehension of what it is of which man is capable and in which his perfection consists; and will fix our ambition and activity upon the worthiest objects."

and various landscape of existence around them. Calmness and energy mark all their actions, benevolence is the silken thread that runs through the pearl chain of all their virtues.[8] Believing that vice originates not in the man, but in the surrounding circumstances;[9] not in the heart, but in the understanding; he is hopeless concerning no one— to correct a vice or generate a virtuous conduct he pollutes not his hands with the scourge of coercion; but by endeavouring to alter the circumstances removes, or by strengthening the intellect disarms, the temptation. The unhappy children of vice and folly, whose tempers are adverse to their own happiness as well as to the happiness of others, will at times awaken a natural pang; but he looks forward with gladdened heart to that glorious period when Justice shall have established the universal fraternity of Love. These soul ennobling views bestow the virtues which they anticipate. He whose mind is habitually imprest with them soars above the present state of humanity, and may be justly said to dwell in the presence of the most high. Regarding every event even as he that ordains it, evil vanishes from before him, and he views with naked eye the eternal form of universal beauty.

*　　*　　*

To accomplish the great object in which we are anxiously engaged to place Liberty on her seat with bloodless hands, we have shewn the necessity of forming some fixed and determinate principles of action to which the familiarized mind may at all times advert. We now proceed to that most important point, namely, to shew what those principles must be. In times of tumult firmness and consistency are peculiarly needful, because the passions and prejudice of mankind are then more powerfully excited: we have shewn in the example of France that to its want of general information, its miseries and its horrors may be attributed. We have reason to believe that a revolution in other parts of Europe is not far distant. Oppression is grievous—the oppressed feel and complain. Let us profit by the example of others; devastation has marked the course of most revolutions, and the timid assertors of Freedom equally with its clamorous enemies, have so closely associ-

8. In an added passage in the revised version of the lecture in "Introductory Address" of *Conciones ad Populum*, C stressed the importance of benevolence for "the searcher after Truth" and claimed that "The intensity of private attachments encourages, not prevents, universal Benevolence" (*Lects 1795* [CC], 46), objecting to Godwin's much disputed contention that private attachments to friends and family conflict with the principles of impartial justice and universal benevolence (*Political Justice*, 2:848, 852). Cf. "Modern Patriotism" (p. 285, n. 4 herein). Godwin did change his view on private attachments, as reflected in the second edition of *Political Justice* (1796) and *The Enquirer* (1797). (See Chris Jones, *Radical Sensibility* [London, 1993], 120–22.)

9. Citing Jean-Jacques Rousseau and Hartley as precursors, Godwin noted that we do not have "an original propensity to evil," vice being "nothing more than error" (*Political Justice*, 1:16–18, 28–32), a view also shared by Thelwall (*The Speech of John Thelwall at the Second Meeting of the London Corresponding Society * * * November 12, 1795* [1795], 23). C did not always maintain the view of the socially determined origin of vice and evil. From 1798 on, he represented evil as "distinct from Error" and "not derived from circumstances" but from original sin and a "diseased" will. For C on the origin of evil, see *Lects 1795* (CC), 107n. 1.

ated the ideas, that they are unable to contemplate the one, disunited from the other. The evil is great, but it may be averted—it has been a general, but it is not therefore a necessary consequence. In order to avert it, we should teach ourselves and others habitually to consider, that truth wields no weapon, but that of investigation, we should be cautious how we indulge even the feelings of virtuous indignation. Indignatio is the handsome brother of Anger and Hatred—Benevolence alone beseems the Philosopher. Let us not grasp even Despotism with too abrupt a hand, lest like the envenomed insect of Peru,* it infect with its poison, the hand that removes it harshly. Let us beware that we continue not the evils of tyranny, when the monster shall be driven from the earth. Its temple is founded on the ruins of mankind. Like the fane of Tescalipoca the Mexican Deity; it is erected with human skulls and cemented with human blood,[2]—let us beware that we be not transported into revenge while we are levelling the loathsome pile with the ground, lest when we erect the temple of Freedom we but vary the stile of architecture, not change the materials. Our object is to destroy pernicious systems not their misguided adherents. Philosophy imputes not the great evil to the corrupted but to the system which presents the temptation to corruption. The evil must cease when the cause is removed, and the courtier who is enabled by State Machinations to embroil or enslave a nation when levelled to the standard of men will be impotent of evil, as he is now unconscious of good. Humane from principle, not fear, the disciple of liberty shrinks not from his duty. He will not court persecution by the ill-timed obtrusion of Truth, still less will he seek to avoid it by concealment or dereliction. J. H. Tooke on the morning of his trial wrote to a fellow sufferer in these words "Nothing will so much serve the cause of freedom as our *acquittal*, except our *execution*."[3] He meant I presume to

---

* The COYA, an insect of so thin a skin, that on being incautiously touched, it bursts, and of so subtle a poison that it is immediately absorbed into the body, and proves fatal.[1]

---

1. Antonio de Ulloa in A *Voyage to South-America*, 2 vols. (1758), 1:358–59 describes this bright, red, small insect, "shaped like a spider," as having such a powerful venom that when any of it falls on the skin of people or animals, "it immediately penetrates into the flesh, and causes large tumors which are soon succeeded by death." The only known remedy for it, as used by Native Americans, was to singe the entire body of the afflicted person with "the flame of a straw or long grass growing in those plains."

2. C highlights here the similarity between contemporary forms of violence and oppression and ancient rites of human sacrifice, a common strategy in the period's political literature on wars, the slave trade, or the French Revolution. In Francesco Saverio Clavigero's *The History of Mexico*, trans. Charles Cullen, 2 vols. (1787), Tezcatlipoca is described as "the greatest god adored" by the Aztecs, "after the invisible God, or supreme Being" (1:244), to whom thousands of victims were sacrificed, their skulls providing the decoration for the temple and buildings nearby. In "Religious Musings" C referred to the "skull-pil'd Temple" (line 146), which refers most likely not to the temple of Tezcatlipoca but to a nearby building called *Huitzompan*, a "prodigious rampart of earth * * * in the form of a half pyramid," which could be ascended by means of staircase of thirty steps with a skull "betwixt every stone." Spanish conquerors counted a total of 136,000 heads preserved on the structure of this building (266–67). Clavigero's controversial and widely reviewed book, which featured a defense of Aztec rites as being less "barbarous" than the rites of ancient Romans and Greeks (2:436–63), caught the attention of Southey who copied passages from it (*Southey's Common-Place Book*, ed J. W. Warter, 4 vols. [1849–51], 4:144–47).

3. Horne Tooke was one among twelve radicals arrested in 1794 on charges of high treason and, together with Thomas Hardy (1752–1832) and Thelwall, was acquitted during the State Trials (see p. 276, n. 8 herein). The source of Tooke's remark cited by C might be

imply that whatever contributes to increase discussion must accelerate
the progress of liberty. Let activity and perseverance and moderation
supply the want of numbers. Convinced of the justice of our principles, let neither scorn nor oppression prevent us from disseminating
them. By the gradual deposition of time, error has been piled upon error and prejudice on prejudice, till few men are tall enough to look
over them, and they whose intellects surpass the common stature, and
who describe the green vales and pleasant prospects beyond them, will
be thought to have created images in vacancy and be honoured with
the name of madman; but

> It is the motive strong the conscience pure
> That bids us firmly act or meek endure:
> 'Tis this will shield us when the storm beats hard
> Content tho' poor had we no other guard!
>   BOWLES.[4]

FINIS.

FROM CONCIONES AD POPULUM
OR ADDRESSES TO THE PEOPLE (1795)

Conciones ad Populum was published on December 3, 1795, and consisted of two essays originally given as lectures in late January and February 1795. The first, called "Introductory Address," is an expanded version
of *A Moral and Political Lecture*. The excerpts printed here are from the
second address, "On the Present War," drawn from two lectures delivered
in February 1795. Here Coleridge lends strong support to Whig leaders
and radicals who opposed the war with France and blamed the British
ministry for the worst atrocities committed during the French Revolution.
He also evokes shattering spectacles of the misery and destruction of
millions of people as a result of British war policies endorsed by Prime
Minister Pitt and Anglican bishops. Coleridge paints a bleak picture of
"four Quarters of the Globe" that "groan under the intolerable iniquity" of
the British government, and of a generation afflicted by the horrors of war,
national guilt, loss of civil liberties, and a deteriorating "social confidence."

The text printed here is from *Conciones ad Populum* (Bristol, 1795).

Thomas Holcroft, *A Narrative of Facts, Relating to a Prosecution for High Treason* * * *
(1795), 87: "Conversing with Mr. Horne Tooke on the morning of our arraignment, he told
me that the best thing our prosecutors could have done, for the cause of freedom, was that
which they had done; imprison and indict us; except the still better thing which they had yet
to do; namely, to hang us" (quoted in *Lects 1795* [CC], 19n. 1).

4. William Lisle Bowles, *Verses to the Right Honourable Edmund Burke, on His Reflections on
the Revolution in France*, lines 165–68 (var.), in *Sonnets, with Other Poems*, 3rd ed. (1794),
117–18: " 'Tis the unshaken mind, the conscience pure, / That bids us firmly act, or meek
endure; / 'Tis this might shield us when the storm beat hard, / Content, though poor, had we
no other guard!" In the considerably revised ending of "Introductory Address," a biblical passage adapted from St. Paul replaces Bowles's poem: "Watch ye! Stand fast in the principles
of which ye have been convinced! Quit yourselves like Men! Be strong! Yet let all things be
done in the spirit of Love" (*Lects 1795* [CC], 49).

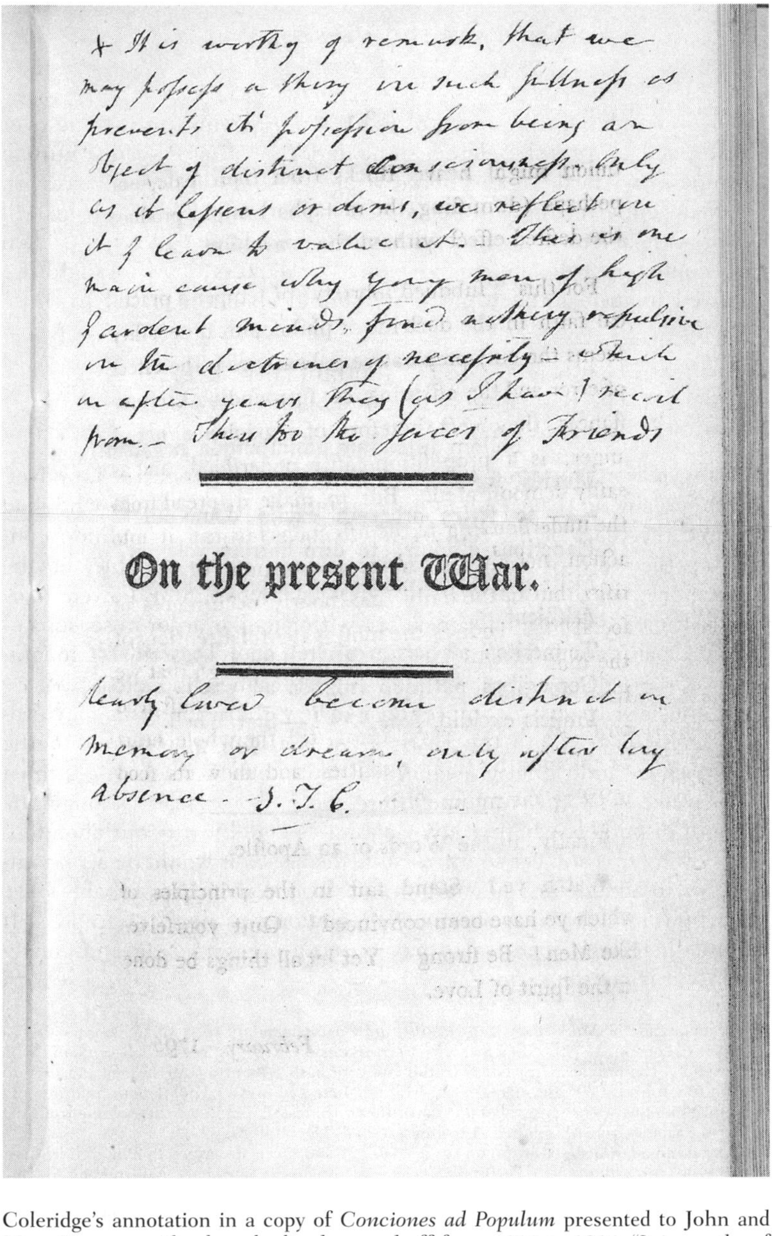

+ It is worthy of remark, that we
may possess a thing in such fullness as
prevents its possession from being an
object of distinct Consciousness. Only
as it lessens or dims, we reflect on
it & learn to value it. This is one
main cause why young men of high
& ardent minds find nothing repulsive
in the doctrines of necessity—which
in after years they (as I have) recoil
from.— Thus too the faces of Friends

On the present War.

dearly loved become distinct in
memory or dreams, only after long
absence. S.T.C.

Coleridge's annotation in a copy of *Conciones ad Populum* presented to John and Mary Morgan, with whom he lived on and off from 1811 to 1816: "It is worthy of remark, that we may possess a thing in such fullness as presents its possession from being an object of distinct Conciousness. Only as it lessens or dims, we reflect on it & learn to value it. This is one main cause why young men of high & ardent minds find nothing repulsive in the doctrines of necessity—which in after years they (as I have) recoil from. Thus too the faces of Friends dearly loved become distinct in memory or dreams, only after long absence. S.T.C."

From On the Present War

* * *

He, who wanders in the maze of POLITICAL ENQUIRY, must tread over Corses, and at every step detect some dark Conspirator against human happiness, or startle at the fierce visage of some imperial Murderer. Every ungentle feeling will be excited in his bosom, and now he will shiver with horror, and now glow with indignation, and now sicken with contempt. I delight not to paint Wickedness or Misery and if I followed Impulse rather than Duty should abandon myself to those Pursuits

> That heighten to the youthful Poet's Eye
> The Bloom of Nature, and before him place
> The gayest happiest Attitude of Things.[1]

But my reason confirms the regulation of the Athenian Lawgiver, which ordained, that it should be infamous for a Man, who had reached the years of discretion, not to have formed an opinion concerning the state of affairs in his country, and treasonable, having formed one, not to propagate it by every legal mean in his power.[2] This Duty we should exert at all times, but with peculiar ardor in seasons of public Calamity, when there exists an Evil of such incalculable magnitude as the PRESENT WAR. Of its peculiar crimes and distresses we shall endeavor to give a comprehensive view, that each of us may proportion his energies to the vastness of the general evil, not to the weight of his individual grievances. But its total Causelessness must be proved:—as if the War had been just and necessary, it might be thought disputable whether any Calamities could justify our abandonment of it. On a subject so universally discussed it would be a vain endeavour to adduce any new argument. The War might probably have been prevented by Negociation: Negociation was never attempted. It cannot therefore be *proved* to have been a *necessary* war, and consequently it is not a just one.[3]

1. An adaptation of Mark Akenside, *The Pleasures of Imagination* (first version), lines 28–30 (*Poems* [London, 1772], 12). Lines 25–30 in Akenside read: "Be present all ye Genii, who conduct / The wandering footsteps of the youthful bard, / New to your springs and shades: who touch his ear / With finer sounds: who heighten to his eye / The bloom of nature, and before him turn / The gayest, happiest attitude of things." C borrowed this volume from the Bristol Library from December 24 to January 8, 1795 (*Borrowings*, 122).
2. C refers to a law decreed by Solon (c. 640–c. 558 B.C.E.), as described by Plutarch in *Lives* (11 vols., trans. Bernadette Perrin [LCL, 1967], 1:457), that "he shall be disfranchised who, in time of faction, takes neither side. He wishes, probably, that a man should not be insensible or indifferent to the common weal, * * * but should rather espouse promptly the better and more righteous cause, share its perils and give it his aid, instead of waiting in safety to see which cause prevails."
3. In his message concerning the declaration of war with France of February 11, 1793, King George III (1738–1820) indicated that he relied "on the firm and effectual support of the House of Commons, and on the zealous exertion of a brave and loyal people, in prosecuting a just and necessary war * * *" (*Parl. Hist.*, 30:344). In the subsequent debate on the king's message, Pitt made a motion to present an address to the king, reassuring him that he "may rely on the firm and effectual support of the representatives of a brave and loyal people, in the prosecution of a just and necessary war" (*Parl. Hist.*, 30:360). In accordance with Article 37 of the thirty-nine Articles of the Church of England (1563), Christians were allowed to engage in a "just war" exclusively (*Lects 1795*, 54n. 3).

It has been repeatedly said, that we could not honorably negociate with men so stained with atrocious guilt, so avowedly the enemies of Religion, as the popular Leaders in France.[4] Admire, I pray you, the cautions Delicacy of our Government! that will profess itself the Ally of the Immaculate only—of the MERCIFUL Catharine, the HONEST King of Prussia,[5] and that most CHRISTIAN Arch-pirate, the Dey of Algiers![6]

* * *

French Principles are widely different from those of the British Constitution:[7] French Excesses are disgraceful to Humanity: it is therefore impossible to treat with the French. But might not the American States refuse to negotiate with us on the same foundation? The principles industriously propagated by the friends of our Government are opposite to the American Constitution—and indeed to Liberty every where; and in order to form a just estimate of our excesses, let us recollect that prominent feature of the late War—*Scalping!*

What the wisdom of Agur wished, the inhabitants of Wyoming enjoyed—they had neither Riches or Poverty: their climate was soft and salubrious, and their fertile soil asked of these blissful Settlers as much labor only for their sustenance, as would have been otherwise convenient for their health. The Fiend, whose crime was Ambition, leapt over into this Paradise—Hell-hounds laid it waste.[8] *English* Generals invited the Indians "to banquet on blood:" the savage Indians headed by an Englishman attacked it. Universal massacre ensued. The Houses were destroyed: the Corn Fields burnt: and where under the broad Maple trees innocent Children used to play at noontide, there the Drinkers of human Blood, and the Feasters on human Flesh were seen in horrid circles, counting their scalps and anticipating their gains.[9]

* * *

Such were our hideous excesses during that holy Rebellion:—yet who among the Americans considered them as precluding a treaty of Peace? Nor has their aversion from War been less exemplary since the

4. A common sentiment expressed by supporters of the war against France, particularly in the wake of the execution of King Louis XVI on January 21, 1793. See, e.g., Pitt's speech in the House of Commons of June 17, 1793: "What could be the effect of any negotiation for peace in the present moment? * * * A band of leaders had swayed the mob in constant succession, all resembling in guilt, but each striving to improve upon the crime of his predecessor * * *" (*Parl. Hist.*, 30:1017–18).

5. On C's indictment of Catherine the Great and Frederick William II of Prussia, see p. 242 and n. 8 herein. On Catherine the Great, see also lines 185–86 of "Religious Musings" (p. 27 and n. 9 herein). C is in line with Fox's argument in the debate of June 17, 1793, on reestablishing peace with France, that the conduct of Russia and Prussia concerning Poland was more "dangerous to Europe" and "equal in infamy to any thing that France was ever guilty of" (*Parl. Hist.*, 30:997–98, 1005). On Fox, see p. 253, n. 2 herein and p. 254, n. 6 herein.

6. A 1795 treaty with Hassan-Baba, Dey of Algiers (fl. 1805), gave free hand to Algerian pirates to sell their appropriated goods in Corsica (*Lects 1795* [CC], 55n. 1).

7. Pitt pointed out the clash between French revolutionary principles and the British constitution in his February 1, 1793, speech (*Parl. Hist.*, 30:272–73), as did William Windham (1750–1819) on many occasions. For Windham on the danger of French principles, see p. 304, n. 9 herein and p. 305, nn. 1–4 herein.

8. An allusion to Satan, referred to as the "Fiend" by Milton in *Paradise Lost* 4.166–83. Disdaining the proper entry into Paradise through the eastern gate, Satan lept into it over the "Hill or highest Wall" (cf. p. 428, n. 5 herein).

9. C refers to the scandalous incident in 1778 of the invasion and brutal devastation of Wyoming (in Western Pennsylvania) by Major John Butler, who enlisted 500 Indians in this attack and collected 227 scalps. C's source might have been Robert Macfarlane, *The History*

Revolution. Lord Dorchester had roused the War-whoop among the Savages: instigated by his Agents the merciless Tribes poured in on the back settlements[1]; and the Algerines[2] were incited against their Commerce. The conduct of the English was every where insolent, and through all the Union detested. The lower classes of the People cried aloud for War. But the Legislature well knew, that the evils even of a *just* war were not to be calculated, and that no war could be just, unless it had been preceded by *sincere* negociations for the permanence of Peace. They knew the English Nation to be practical Atheists, professing to believe a God, yet acting as if there were none. In Europe the smoaking Villages of Flanders,[3] and the putrified Fields of La Vendee[4]—from Africa the unnumbered Victims of a detestable Slave-trade[5]—in Asia the desolated plains of Indostan and the Million whom a rice-contracting Governor caused to perish[6]—in America the recent enormities of their Scalp Merchants—the four Quarters of the Globe groan beneath the intolerable iniquity of this nation![7] Yet these high-minded Republicans did not refuse to negociate with us. They thought it criminal folly to make themselves miserable because their Enemies were wicked.—But a lying Spirit hath descended upon us, "which hath made the heart of this People fat and shut their eyes"—and "therefore Hell hath enlarged itself and opened her mouth without measure."[8]

---

of the Second Ten Years of the Reign of George the Third (1782), as noted in Lects 1795 (CC), 56n. 3. A more likely source, however, was A Convention the Only Means of Saving Us from Ruin (1793) by Joseph Gerrald, who describes this incident (22–27), using the same image of a demon leaping into and spoiling "this Eden of the new world, where every man possessed an abundance, which was the fruit of moderate labour and industry; where no man was very rich, nor very great" and where "the inhabitants exhibited such a picture of primeval happiness as has seldom been equalled * * *" (22–23). Gerrald's essay, in its outspoken opposition to war and anti-Pittite sentiments, has marked affinities with C's Conciones ad Populum, although it is more inflamatory in its advocacy of radical electoral reforms. On Gerrald, see p. 245, n. 6 herein.

1. Guy Carleton, Lord Dorchester (1724–1808), governor of Canada, promised a delegation of Indians that they would gain new territories in exchange for their support of the war against the United States (Lects 1795 [CC], 58n. 1).
2. Inhabitants of Algeria. Algerian pirates were allowed a free hand by Britain after a treaty with the Dey of Algiers in 1795.
3. The retreat of the defeated and diminished British troops through Flanders in 1795 was used by C as one of the most compelling and heart-rending testimonies of the miseries caused by the war. See Lects 1795 (CC), 58n. 2, and 59n. 3; Watchman (CC), 238–41, 282–84.
4. C refers to the 1793 peasant uprising against the French revolutionary government in La Vendée, led by royalist commanders François-Athannase Charette de la Contrie (1763–1796) and Jean-Nicolas Stofflet (1741–1796), which ended in the bloody slaughter of many Vendeans and the execution of their two leaders in 1796. In Watchman (CC), 213 C blamed the British government for encouraging this revolt and for using it as a way of diverting attention from the losses incurred by the British forces in the unnecessary war against France. La Vendée is used by C as the setting for his poem "Fire, Famine, & Slaughter. A War Eclogue" (p. 140 herein), which contains one of his most virulent attacks on Pitt.
5. See C's essay "On the Slave Trade" (p. 287 herein).
6. Warren Hastings (1732–1818), governor general of India (1772–85), accused by Burke of numerous high crimes and misdemeanors, including "ravaging countries, depopulating kingdoms, reducing the gardens of the universe to a desert, plundering opulent towns, and consigning to atrocious cruelty and destruction the innocent and industrious inhabitants of whole empires * * *" (Parl. Hist., 24:1254). Hastings was impeached in 1788 and, after a lengthy and costly trial, acquitted on April 23, 1795.
7. The passage from "In Europe" to "nation" was reprinted as a footnote to line 106 of C's poem "Ode on the Departing Year" (p. 41 and n. 8 herein; PW, 1:165n.).
8. Isaiah 6.10 and 5.14 (var.).

*   *   *

We will now take a rapid survey of the consequences of this unjust because unnecessary War. I mean not to describe the distressful stagnation of Trade and Commerce: I direct not your attention to the wretches that sadden every street in this City, the pale and meagre Troop, who in the bitterness of reluctant Pride, are forced to beg the Morsel, for which they would be willing to "work their fingers to the bone" in honest Industry: I will not frighten you by relating the distresses of that brave Army, which has been melted away on the Continent, nor picture to your imaginations the loathsome pestilence that has mocked our Victories in the West-Indies:[9] I bid you not hear the screams of the deluded Citizens of Toulon[1]—I will not press on your recollection the awful Truth, that in the course of this calamitous Contest more than a Million of men have perished—a* MILLION of men, of each one of whom the mangled corse terrifies the dreams of her that loved him, and makes some mother, some sister, some widow start from slumber with a shriek! These arguments have been urged even to satiety—a British Senator has sneeringly styled them mere *common-place* against wars.[2] I could weep for the criminal Patience of Humanity! These arguments are *hacknied*; yet *Wars* continue!

*   *   *

Who is this Minister, to whom we have thus implicitly trusted every blessing? Are his Qualities commensurate with the giant evils, which he has occasioned? My mind may be jaundiced by my abhorrence of the man's actions—but whether Truth or Prejudice be the source of my failure I must acknowledge that having investigated attentively the

---

*   By the internal disturbances of France in La Vendee and other places, disturbances excited by English agents, and rendered obstinate by our Ministers' promises, more than *Three Hundred Thousand* have been butchered.

---

9. The British successes in the occupation of West Indies colonies from 1793 to 1796 caused the death of thousands of men due to yellow fever and other diseases (see *Lects* 1795 [CC], 59n. 4, and 379n. 3). In *Watchman* (CC), 332 C reported the return from the West Indies of only seventy out of the original seven hundred constituting the Twentieth Regiment. For a brief history of the war in the West Indies betwen 1793 and 1794, see Bryan Edwards, *The History, Civil and Commercial, of the British Colonies in the West Indies*, 3 vols. (1793–1801), 3:405–443. Edwards reveals the high mortality rate among British soldiers during this campaign due to pestilence (esp. 3:430–31).

1. Toulon was occupied by British, Spanish, and French royalist forces in August 1793 and recaptured by the French in December 1793. In a declaration published in the king's name on November 20, 1793, by Admiral Samuel Hood (1724–1816) and Sir Gilbert Elliott (1751–1814), the king promised to return Toulon to the French, provided that a hereditary monarchy was re-established and the inhabitants of Toulon were protected against all attacks (*Parl. Hist.*, 30:1060–61). In the ensuing debate about the king's declaration in 1794, Richard Brinsley Sheridan (1751–1816) pointed out that in the occupation of Toulon "we had seen nothing but incapacity and blunder in the execution, as well as disaster in the event" (*Parl. Hist.*, 30:1243), a sentiment voiced by C here. In an article published in *MP* on January 4, 1800, C argued that the British occupation of Toulon was one of the factors that caused the replacement of the more humane party led by the Girondist Jean-Pierre Brissot with "the faction of Robespierre, and the furies of Jacobinism" (*EOT* [CC], 1:74).

2. A remark made by Edmund Burke in response to Thomas Erskine (1750–1823) in the debate of December 15, 1792, on Charles James Fox's motion to send a minister to Paris (*Parl. Hist.*, 30:109). In the debate in the Commons of February 12, 1793, on the king's declaration of war with France, Fox alluded to Burke's phrase: "He would not enter into any of the common-place arguments on the miseries and calamities inseparable from war. He did not mean to call them common-place arguments in the bad sense of the words * * *" (*Parl. Hist.*, 30:366).

Speeches and Measures of William Pitt, I am as little able to discover
Genius in the one, as Virtue in the other. I think of Edmund Burke's
declamatory Invectives with emotion; yet while I shudder at the excesses, I must admire the strength, of this Hercules Furens of Oratory.[3]
But our Premier's Harangues!—Mystery concealing Meanness, as
steam-clouds invelope a dunghill. To rouse the fears of the Wealthy,
and the prejudices of the Ignorant is an easy task for one, who possesses the privilege of manufacturing Royal Eloquence and sticking up
Royal Hand-bills.[4] But what Question proposed to him by his great political Adversary[5] has he ever directly answered? His speeches, which
seemed so swoln with meaning, alas! what did they mean?[6]

*   *   *

If they, who mingled the cup of bitterness, drank its contents, we
might look with a calm compassion on the wickedness of great Men.
But alas! the storm which they raise, falls heaviest on the unprotected
Innocent: and the Cottage of the poor Man is stripped of every Comfort, before the Oppressors, who send forth the mandate of Death, are
amerced in one Luxury or one Vice. If a series of calamities succeed
each, they deprecate the anger of Heaven by a FAST![7]—A word that
implies, Prayers of Hate to the God of Love—and after these, a Turbot
Feast for the rich, and their usual scanty Morsel to the poor, if indeed
debarred from their usual labor they can procure even this. But if Victory be the event,

> They o'er the ravag'd Earth,
> As at an Altar wet with human Blood
> And flaming with the Fires of Cities burnt,
> Sing their mad Hymns of Triumph, Hymns to God
> O'er the destruction of his gracious Works,
> Hymns to the Father o'er his slaughter'd Sons![8]

3. Cf. C's review of Burke's "Letter to a Noble Lord" in *Watchman* (CC), 30–31: "Mr. Burke
   always appeared to me to have displayed great vigor of intellect, and an almost prophetic
   keenness of penetration; nor can I think his merit diminished, because he has secured the
   aids of sympathy to his cause by the warmth of his own emotions, and delighted the imagination of his readers by a multitude and rapid succession of remote analogies." While C admired the "manner" of Burke's rhetoric, he often disagreed with its content, a reaction well
   captured in his notebook description of Burke's *Reflections on the Revolution in France*
   (1790) as "a web wrought with admirable beauty from a black bag of Poison!" (CN, 1:24).
   Cf. also C's sonnet on Burke (p. 13 herein).
4. For C's attack on Pitt, see p. 276 and n. 1 herein and p. 278 and n. 5 herein.
5. Pitt's adversary was the leading Whig statesman Charles James Fox, a staunch admirer of
   the French Revolution and persistent opponent of the war with France. C was one among
   "many souls" who were "converted * * * to the Foxite Faith" while he was a student at
   Cambridge (CL, 1:51); but later on he made a public denunciation of Fox and in the *Biographia* disavowed having ever been a partisan of the Foxite party. See his letters to Fox
   published in *MP* on November 4 and 9, 1802 (*EOT* [CC], 1:376–90, 391–402) and p. 453,
   n. 8 herein.
6. In the section omitted here C goes over Pitt's record as an opponent of the war with America to point out his apostasy once he became prime minister. See *Lects 1795* (CC), 63–65.
   The same strategy is used by Fox in his speech of February 12, 1793 (*Parl. Hist.*,
   30:363–64).
7. The king proclaimed fast days to secure God's help in the war with France. In his "Essay on
   Fasts" C attacked this practice on both religious and political grounds, showing that it served
   the interests of the government's "harangues against the French" and was an insult to the
   poor who "already eat neither fish, flesh, or fowl at any time" (*Watchman* [CC], 51–55).
8. A quotation (var.) from lines 32–38 of the poem "Verses Intended to Have Been Addressed
   to His Grace the Duke of Portland * * *" by William Crowe (1745–1829), published anony-

It is recorded in the shuddering hearts of Christians, that while Europe is reeking with Blood, and smoaking with unextinguished Fires, in a contest of unexampled crimes and unexampled calamities, every Bishop but one voted for the continuance of the War.[9] They deemed the fate of their Religion to be involved in the contest!—Not the Religion of Peace, my Brethren, not the Religion of the meek and lowly Jesus, which forbids to his Disciples all alliance with the powers of this World—but the Religion of Mitres and Mysteries, the Religion of Pluralities and Persecution, the Eighteen-Thousand-Pound-a-Year[1] Religion* of Episcopacy. Instead of the Ministers of the Gospel, a Roman

---

* Wherever Mens' temporal interests depend on the general belief of disputed tenets, we must expect to find hypocrisy and a persecuting Spirit, a jealousy of investigation, and an endeavor to hold the minds of the people in submissive Ignorance. That pattern of Christian meekness, Bishop Horsley, has declared it to be the vice of the age and government that it has suffered a free and general investigation of the most solemn Truths that regard Society[2]—and there is a remark in the last charge of the disinterested Bishop Prettyman, that the same busy spirit which inclines men to be Unitarians in Religion, drives them into Republicanism in Politics.[3] And truly, the most exalted Forms of Society are cemented and preserved by the purest Notions of Religion.[4] But whatever I may deem of the justice of their Lordship's observations, the prudence and policy of them have gained my immediate assent. Alas! what room would there be for Bishops or for Priests in a Religion where Deity is the only object of Reverence, and our Immortality the only article of Faith—Immortality made probable to us by the Light of Nature, and proved to us by the Resurrection of Jesus. Him the High Priests crucified; but he has left us a Religion, which shall prove fatal to every HIGH PRIEST—a Religion, of which every true Christian is the Priest, his own Heart the Altar, the Universe its Temple, and Errors and Vices its only Sacrifices.[5] Ride on, mighty Jesus! because of thy words of Truth, of Love, and EQUALITY! The age of Priesthood will soon be no more—that of Philosophers and of Christians will succeed, and the torch of Superstition be extinguished for ever. Never, never more shall we behold that generous Loyalty to rank,

---

mously in the *European Magazine* 27 (1795): 418–19. The poem denounces the ravages of war and the poets who sing "Of arms and combats" (line 4). C changes "desolated earth" (line 33) to "ravag'd earth," among other variants.

9. Richard Watson, bishop of Llandaff (1737–1816), supported the duke of Bedford's motion in the House of Lords on January 27, 1795, that "any particular form of government which may prevail in France, should not preclude negotiation or prevent peace * * *" (*Parl. Hist.*, 31:1252). Like C, Watson attacked the assumption that the war with France was "a just and necessary war" and expressed doubts that sufficient efforts of negotiation were made to prevent the war. He saw no connection between "the establishment of a republic in France, and the subversion of the English constitution" and argued that "a perseverance in shutting the door of negotiation, in prosecuting an expensive war, will shake the stability of the throne, and endanger the independence of the nation" (*Parl. Hist.*, 31:1257–68). By contrast, Shute Barrington, the bishop of Durham, argued that the war was "justifiable on Christian principles" and that any negotiation with the French at this time would be perceived by the enemy as a weakness and lead to an invasion by the French that will cost the British nation "torrents" of blood (*Parl. Hist.*, 31:1277–79).

1. A fairly accurate estimate by C of the income of the sees of Canterbury and Durham (*Lects 1795* [CC], 68n. 2).

2. In *A Sermon, Preached before the Lords Spiritual and Temporal, in the Abbey Church of St. Peter, Westminster, on Wednesday, January 30, 1793 * * * (1793), Samuel Horsley (1733–1806) complained about the "freedom of dispute, in which, for several years past, it hath been the folly in this country to indulge, upon matters of such high importance as the origin of Government, and the authority of Sovereigns * * *" (1). For Horsley the solemn principles challenged by radical reformists of his time involved the absolute submission of individuals to the government and "the will of God" (6–7). On Samuel Horsley, see p. 275 and n. 3 herein.

3. C refers to *A Charge Delivered to the Clergy of the Diocese of Lincoln* (1794), in which Sir George Pretyman (1750–1827), bishop of Lincoln, argued that in keeping with the "natural alliance" between religious and political opinions, the subversion by Unitarians of the main tenets of the Church of England went hand in hand with their attack on the British constitution under the influence of the French Revolution: "Our ancestors of the last century had frequent opportunities of observing the close alliance between Popery and Despotism; and we, who live at the end of the eighteenth century, have seen the Disciples of Socinus amongst the most zealous abettors of Republican Principles" (14).

4. C may draw again on Pretyman, who discusses the dependence of society on religion (8–12): e.g., "if we look into the history of the whole human race, we shall in vain seek for a civilized nation, in which some notion of a Deity has not prevailed * * *."

might recognize in these Dignitaries the High-priests of Mars—with this difference, that the Ancients fatted their Victims for the Altar, we prepare ours for sacrifice by leanness.[8] War ruins our Manufactures; the ruin of our Manufactures throws Thousands out of employ; men cannot starve: they must either pick their countrymen's Pockets—or cut the throats of their fellow-creatures, because they are Jacobins. If they chuse the latter, the chances are that their own lives are sacrificed: if the former, they are hung or transported to Botany Bay.[9] And here we cannot but admire the deep and comprehensive Views of Ministers, who having starved the wretch into Vice send him to the barren shores of new Holland to be starved back again into Virtue. It must surely charm the eye of humanity to behold Men reclaimed from stealing by being banished to a Coast, where there is nothing to steal, and helpless Women, who had been

> Bold from despair and prostitute for Bread,[1]

find motives to Reformation in the sources of their Depravity, refined by Ignorance, and famine-bitten into Chastity. Yet even these poor unfortunates, these disinherited ones of Happiness, appear to me more eligibly situated than the wretched Soldier—because more innocently! Father of Mercies! if we pluck a wing from the back of a Fly, not all

which is prodigal of its own virtue and its own happiness to invest a few with unholy Splendors;—that subordination of the Heart, which keeps alive the spirit of Servitude amid the empty forms of boasted Liberty! This dear-bought Grace of Cathedrals, this costly defence of Despotism, this nurse of grovelling sentiment and cold-hearted Lip-worship, will be gone——it will be gone, that sensibility to Interest, that jealous tenacity of Honors, which suspects in every argument a mortal wound; which inspires Oppression, while it prompts Servility;—which stains indelibly whatever it touches; and under which supple Dullness loses half its shame by wearing a Mitre where reason would have placed a Fool's-Cap![6] The age of Priesthood will be no more—Peace to its departing spirit! With delighted ears should I listen to some fierce Orator from St. Omers[7] or from Bedlam, who should weep over its Pageantries rent and faded, and pour forth eloquent Nonsense in a funeral Oration.

---

5. C articulates here sentiments often expressed by Unitarian and Dissenting ministers who rejected the view of Christ's sacrifice as a sin offering; defended enlightenment, a rational religion, and individual worship of the deity unmediated by priests; and exposed the superstitious rites of the established Church as ways to keep people in a state of servility and oppression. Cf. *A Discourse on the Love of Our Country*, 3rd ed. (1790), by Richard Price (1723–1791), in which he proposed enlightenment and a rational religion "consisting not in any rites and ceremonies, but in worshipping God with a pure heart" as an antidote to "that gloomy and cruel superstition * * * which has hitherto gone under the name of religion, and to the support of which civil government has been perverted" (12–13). Cf. also Joseph Priestley: "Religion I consider as a thing that requires no civil establishment whatever, and that its beneficial operation is injured by such establishment, and the more in proportion to its riches" (Letter 6 in *Letters to the Right Honourable Edmund Burke, Occasioned by his Reflections on the Revolution in France*, 2nd ed. [Birmingham, 1791], 53).
6. In the Norton Perkins copy of *Conciones ad Populum* (at Harvard), C wrote a marginal note on this passage: "Parody on Burke's celebrated passage in 'Letter on the French Revolution' " (*Lects 1795* [CC], 68n. 1). C refers to the notorious passage in Burke's *Reflections on the Revolution in France* (1790) in which he pronounced that "the age of chivalry is gone," being succeeded by one of "sophisters, œconomists, and calculators" advocating a "barbarous philosophy * * * destitute of all taste and elegance" (113–15).
7. A seminary in France used by Irish Jesuits. C implies that Burke himself was a Jesuit (*Lects 1795* [CC], 68n. 2).
8. On C's use of analogies between contemporary and ancient sacrificial rites, see p. 247, n. 2 herein.
9. Death or transportation was the penalty for picking pockets in England. On Botany Bay—located south of Sydney, Australia (a continent known in C's time as New Holland)—see *Lects 1795* (CC), 68n. 3.
1. Mathew Prior, "Henry and Emma," line 453 (*Poetical Works*, 2 vols. [1779], 1:252): "Made bold by want, and prostitute for bread."

the Ministers and Monarchs in Europe can restore it—yet they dare to send forth their mandates for the Death of Thousands, and if they succeed call the Massacre Victory. They with all that majestic serenity, which the sense of personal safety fails not to inspire, can "Ride in the whirl-wind and direct the storm,"[2] or rather like the gloomy Spirits in Ossian, "sit on their distant clouds and enjoy the Death of the Mariner."[3]

In former wars the victims of Ambition had crowded to the standard from the influence of national Antipathies; but this powerful stimulant has been so unceasingly applied, as to have well nigh produced an exhaustion. What remains? Hunger. Over a recruiting place in this city I have seen pieces of Beef hung up to attract the half-famished Mechanic.[4] It has been said,[5] that GOVERNMENT, though not the best preceptor of Virtue, procures us security from the attack of the lower Orders.—Alas! why should the lower Orders attack us, but because they are brutalized by Ignorance and rendered desperate by Want? And does Government remove this Ignorance by Education? And does not GOVERNMENT increase their want by Taxes?—Taxes rendered necessary by those national assassinations called Wars, and by that worst Corruption and Perjury, which a reverend Moralist has justified under the soft title of "Secret Influence!"[6] The poor Infant born in an English or Irish Hovel breathes indeed the air and partakes of the light of Heaven; but of its other Bounties he is disinherited. The powers of Intellect are given him in vain: to make him work like a brute Beast he is kept as ignorant as a brute Beast. It is not possible that this despised and oppressed Man should behold the rich and idle without malignant envy. And if in the bitter cravings of Hunger the dark Tide of Passions should swell, and the poor Wretch rush from despair into guilt, then the GOVERNMENT indeed assumes the right of Punishment though it had neglected the duty of Instruction, and hangs the victim for crimes, to which its own wide-wasting follies and its own

2. Joseph Addison, line 292 of *The Campaign* (1705): "Rides in the Whirl-wind, and directs the Storm."

3. In Ossian, *Fingal*, Swaran "sits dim, on the clouds of the north, and enjoys the death of the mariner" (*The Poems of Ossian*, trans. James Macpherson, 2 vols. [1773], 1:234). The lines describe Swaran, king of Lochlin, after the battle with the army led by Cuthullin, general of the Irish tribes.

4. Cf. CN, 1:42: "People starved into War—over an enlisting place in Bristol a quarter of Lamb and piece of Beef hung up—."

5. With this sentence to the end of the paragraph, C uses a passage from Lecture 6 of *LRR* (see *Lects 1795* [CC], 221–23).

6. The "reverend Moralist" is William Paley, who in *The Principles of Moral and Political Philosophy*, 2 vols., 10th ed. (1794), defended strongly the influence of the Crown in parliamentary representation (2:223–25). Paley also traces the change in British history from a "government by force" before the reign of James I (1566–1625), during which kings instituted policies in the Parliament "by *intimidation*," to the "more successful expedient of *influence*" practiced after the Restoration (2:226–27). The collocation "secret Influence" does not appear as such in this section of *Principles*, though the terms "influence" and "secret" appear separately in a passage in which Paley discusses the importance of the "influence" of the Crown in counteracting various suspicious motives goading members of the House of Commons, including the "secret pleasure of mortifying the great, or the hope of dispossessing them" (2:225–26). Paley, however, explicitly rejects secret negotiations by the king or "any clandestine reward or solicitation whatever" (2:228). On Paley's "qualified defence of influence," see *Lects 1795* (CC), 222n. 1.

most sinful omissions had supplied the cause and the temptation. And yet how often have the fierce Bigots of Despotism told me, that the Poor are not to be pitied, however great their necessities: for if they be out of employ, the KING wants men!—They may be shipped off to the Slaughter-house abroad, if they wish to escape a Prison at home!—Fools! to commit ROBBERIES, and get hung, when they might MURDER with impunity—yea, and have Sixpence a day into the bargain![7]

* * *

Lastly, in this inventory of guilt as the immediate and peculiar effect of the present War, and justly attributable to our Ministry, we must place the EXCESSES OF THE FRENCH, their massacres and blasphemies, all their crimes and all their distresses. This effect the War produced by a two-fold operation of terror:—First, on the people of France, secondly, on their Rulers.[8]

* * *

Such in addition to the evils attending all wars, are the peculiar horrors of the present. Our national faith has been impaired; our social confidence hath been weakened, or made unsafe; our liberties have suffered a perilous breach, and even now are being (still more perilously) undermined;[9] the Dearth, which would otherwise have been scarcely visible, hath enlarged its terrible features into the threatening face of Famine; and finally, of us will justice require a dreadful account of whatever guilt France has perpetrated, of whatever miseries France has endured. Are we men? Freemen? rational men? And shall we carry on this wild and priestly War against reason, against freedom, against human nature? If there be one among you, who departs from me without feeling it his immediate duty to petition or remonstrate against the continuance of it, I envy that man neither his head or his heart!

February, 1795.

FROM LECTURES ON REVEALED RELIGION (1795)

In May and June 1795 Coleridge delivered six lectures on revealed religion at the Assembly Coffeehouse in Bristol. In these lectures Coleridge continued the critique of despotism, inequality, and depraved government and church officials he had formulated in his earlier political lectures; and unlike many prominent radicals of the time, including the French Jacobins, he advocated the abolition of private property, rather than its mere redistribution. While Coleridge admired the Jewish state under Moses, which by equalizing property and eliminating debts became "the only Republic" other than Sparta with a legitimate right to "boast of Liberty and Equality" (Lec-

---

7. In the errata list at the end of *Conciones* C, evidently sensing the seditious language here, changed "murder" to "Fight for his King and Country."
8. In the passage omitted here C shows how the determination of his government to pursue a "war of *extermination*" against France led to the Jacobin reign of terror (*Lects 1795* [CC], 72–74).
9. A reference to the Two Bills (see *The Plot Discovered*, p. 274 herein).

ture 2, p. 260 herein), he found in the teachings of Jesus a much more thoroughgoing exposure of individual possessions as the root of moral degeneration. Private property, Coleridge claimed, feeds "selfish Passions" and leads to the evils of commerce, which in turn "make a government neccessary." For Coleridge "Emperor and King are but the lord lieutenants of conquered Souls—secondaries and vicegerents who govern not with their own right but with power delegated to them by our Avarice and appetites" (Lecture 6, p. 273 herein), a statement for which Coleridge could have been charged with treason. The lectures demonstrate the extent to which Coleridge's political views were shaped by his contact at Cambridge University with dissenting Unitarians such as William Frend, who became zealous advocates for democratic reforms and opponents of the Church of England. In line with Unitarian doctrines, as espoused by, among others, Joseph Priestley, a major presence in these lectures, Coleridge denounced the corruption of the Anglican Church and rejected the belief in the Trinity and atonement (Lecture 5). Coleridge regarded the Christian doctrine of atonement (i.e., the view that the sacrifice of Christ was required to satisfy God's sense of justice and redeem the world from sin) as an "irrational" and degrading "Superstition." Late in life (1834) Coleridge admitted that it was his "strong sense of the repugnancy of the doctrine of vicarious atonement to the moral being" that dictated his conversion to Unitarianism (TT [CC], 1:489).

The lectures provide a telling point of contrast to Coleridge's later defense of private property, his denunciation of Unitarianism, and his adoption of Trinitarian religion (see p. 264, n. 1 herein; p. 306, n. 5 herein; p. 451, n. 2 herein; p. 580, n. 9 herein).

The text printed here is from Victoria College Library BT5, Theological Lectures, ff. 3–154, a volume of lectures transcribed by Ernest Hartley Coleridge from original manuscripts now lost.

From Lecture 2[1]

* * *

The Jewish Government was founded on an original Contract. The Constitution was presented to the whole nation by Moses, and each Individual solemnly assented to it. By this Constitution the Jews became a federal Republic consisting of twelve Tribes. The Country contained 15 millions of acres, which were equally divided among the People, 25 acres to each man, the number of the People being about 700,000.[2] To preserve this equal division it became necessary to prevent Alienation[3]—To this end interest for money was forbidden and an act of grace for the abolition of all debts passed every 6th year. Thus the lending of money was made unadvantageous and insecure—and where there were no Creditors there could be no debtors. But as

1. For this lecture C draws primarily on Moses Lowman's *A Dissertation on the Civil Government of the Hebrews* (1740; 2nd ed. 1795), a popular book among Unitarians, which offered an eloquent eulogy of the religious and political institutions of the Jews against their misrepresentation by others "not only as unwise and unequal, but as most unjust, tyrannical, and cruel" (3). Lowman notes that the Constitution of the Jews arose from "the Covenant of *Jehovah* with the *Hebrew* People," a "solemn Transaction" that "may be called the *original Contract* of the *Hebrew* Government * * *" (9–10).
2. C derives these figures from Lowman (39).
3. Lowman discusses the inalienability of property in the Jewish state (41, 46, 236–37).

Abuses might gradually creep in, and as all Constitutions require to be frequently brought back to their first principles, on every 50th year a solemn Jubilee was appointed, in which all Lands were restored, and the Estate of every Family discharged from all incumbrances returned to the Family again.[4] ["]Ye shall hallow the 50th year, and proclaim Liberty throughout all the Land, unto[5] all the Inhabitants thereof—it shall be a Jubilee unto you, and ye shall return every man to his Possession, and ye shall return every man to his Family—For the Land shall not be sold for ever for the Land is mine, saith the Lord God, and ye are strangers and sojourners with me.["][6] The terms of this Law are beautiful and so replete with practical Wisdom and Benevolence that it would be almost criminal to leave any part of it unobserved. Liberty was proclaimed through the whole nation—the whole nation were informed by divine authority that it was unlawful to acknowledge any human superior. Every Hebrew was thus the Subject of God alone. Nor was an end proposed without means established. The Lands were restored. Property is Power and equal Property equal Power. A Poor Man is necessarily more or less a Slave. Poverty is the Death of public Freedom—it virtually enslaves Individuals, and generates those Vices, which make necessary a dangerous concentration of power in the executive branch.[7] If we except the Spartan, the Jewish has been the only Republic that can consistently boast of Liberty and Equality.[8] * * * ["]The Land shall not be sold, for the Land is mine, saith the Lord, and ye are strangers and sojourners with me.["][9] There is nothing more pernicious than the notion that any one possesses an absolute right to the Soil, which he appropriates—to the system of accumulation which flows from this supposed right we are indebted for nine-tenth of our Vices and Miseries. The Land is no one's—the Produce belongs equally to all, who contribute their due proportion of Labour.[1] Nature seems to say to us, I have invited you to sojourn with me awhile[,] I have prepared you a bountiful Feast, but he is ungrateful and a thief who takes what he cannot use and hides what his Brethren want.[2] An abolition of all individual Property is perhaps the

---

4. On the law of the Jubilee C draws on Lowman (46). At the end of this sentence is a cancelled passage: "The terms of this Law are beautiful and replete with political wisdom."
5. The manuscript has a textual variant here, "with" written under "unto."
6. EHC indicated in the margin the source of this passage in Leviticus 25.10, 23. The passage is also cited in Lowman (47).
7. C summarizes a passage from Lowman that begins with the statement "Property is the natural Foundation of Power, and so of Authority * * *" (33–34). The full passage is cited in *Lects 1795* (CC), 126n. 2.
8. Lowman asserts the superiority of the Jewish constitution to the Spartan in instituting equality and preventing "the Temptations of *Luxury, Pride* and *Envy*," which in turn lead to civic unrest (240).
9. Leviticus 25.23 (var.).
1. C's interest in a society based on equal labor, property, and distribution of produce was influenced by his reading of John Locke, *Two Treatises of Government* (1690), esp. book 2, chapter 5 ("Of Property," 243–70); Godwin, *Political Justice* (1793), 2:788–95; Jean-Jacques Rousseau, *A Discourse upon the Origin and Foundation of Inequality among Mankind* (1761); and possibly Robert Wallace, *Various Prospects of Mankind, Nature, and Providence* (1761), esp. 9, 26–27, 40 (see *Lects 1795* [CC], 127n. 1; p. 269, n. 5 herein and p. 271, n. 9 herein).
2. The manuscript has a cancelled passage here: "Every other mode was adopted by Divine Wisdom—but the Jews were too ignorant a people, too leavenend with the Vices of Ægypt, to be capable of so exalted a state of society."

only infallible Preventative against accumulation,[3] but the Jews were too ignorant a people[,] too deeply leavened with the vices of Ægypt to be capable of so exalted a state of Society—Every other mode was adopted by divine Wisdom—Property was equalized Debts periodically liquidated—Estates rendered unalienable. * * *

Thus, I trust, the Wisdom and Benevolence of the civil Government of the Jews as established by a Moses has been sufficiently proved—and to a man who accurately contemplates the power of the human mind in different circumstances this alone would be a miracle sufficient to prove the divinity of his Legation.[4] For the Jews seem to have been grossly ignorant of every thing, and disposed to the grossest Idolatry. And though Moses is said to have been learned in all the learning of the Ægyptians, yet the Ægyptian Government was an absolute Monarchy—and the people never admitted into any share of the Government.[5] So that where Moses in that infant state of the World could have gained the model of so perfect a government I cannot conceive, unless we allow [it] to have come from God.[6]

* * *

I here mention only the mildest superstitions, and such as took place among the most civilized of the gentile World. Father of Mercies! how sunk indeed must be thy creature[s] when the Temples of Religion float with human blood and Murder, and unnatural Lusts are made rites of Piety! But the Canaanites were especially abominable—It was a common and meritorious rite of Religion among them to burn their children as sacrifices to Moloch. We shiver at these—but we sicken with intense loathing at the horrible pollutions and unspeakable lasciviousness that pervade and almost constitute the rest of their Religion! Such Idolatry cannot be tolerated, it is not consistent with the peace of Society, you might as well tolerate a Band of armed Bedlamites because they do not know themselves to be wrong—No Conscience or pretence of Conscience can make Murder and the crime that may not be named, innocent.[7] How can such minds be convinced of their Errors? By philosophical arguments? or even

---

3. According to C, the abolition rather than the "Equalization of Property" was the goal of the teachings of Jesus Christ (see Lecture 6, p. 273 herein).

4. C continues here his discussion of the authenticity and divine origin of the books and laws of Moses, which he had tackled in his first lecture (see Lects 1795 [CC], 114–19). The view that the government of Moses derived its legitimacy from God is the informing premise of Lowman's treatise: "The *Hebrew* Commonwealth is, without question, one of the most ancient of the World, and justly looked upon as a Model of Government of divine Original * * *" (1; see also p. 259 and n. 1 herein). The same view was maintained by William Warburton in *The Divine Legation of Moses Demonstrated*, 2 vols. (1738–41), and Joseph Priestley in *Discourses on the Evidence of Revealed Religion* (1794). See Lects 1795 (CC), 135–36n. 2.

5. In *The Divine Legation of Moses* (2:346) Warburton dwells on the contrast between the Egyptian monarchic state and the Jewish government: "Again, it was the civil Policy of *Egypt* to prefer an hereditary despotic *Monarchy* to all other Forms of Government. *Moses*, on the contrary, erects a *Theocracy* on the free Choice of the People * * *." A longer passage from Warburton is cited in *Lects 1795* (CC), 136n. 2.

6. In *Discourses* Priestley repeatedly makes the point that the Jews had as much a propensity to idolatry and superstition as the surrounding heathen nations, so that the only explanation that accounts for their superiority in matters of religion and morality was "an actual interposition of Divine Providence in favour of the Israelitish nation" (119–20; see also 46–47).

7. A close paraphrase of Lowman (27–28, 232–33; see *Lects 1795* [CC], 143n. 3, and 144n. 1). It is unclear what crime C has in mind that "may not be named." Lowman includes among the vices that originate from idolatry "Intemperance, Uncleanness * * * Sodomy, Bestiality, or the frequent Murder of innocent Children * * *," as well as the "most unnatu-

Miracles? No! not even by Miracles! The mind-annihilated Canaanites would have answered. Ah! I'll worship your God, but my own is as great— Moloch and Astoreth are they that make me work wonders in battle. The only mode of meliorating idolatrous Nations seems to be that adopted by Providence. To choose out one Nation, and make them by repeated Miracles wavering Believers in his Unity—While these remained faithful, to make them all powerful in Battle and the means of extirpating the tribes most enormous in their Idolatry. When they fell off and adopted the rites of the surrounding nations to render them weak and contemptible to those whom with miraculous success they had so recently subdued! And on their return to God again to renew their arms in Battle! This is the only reasoning which these Idolaters were capable of understanding. Surely, they said—This is indeed a great God, our Gods shrink before him in Fight—Thus, tho' probably they would not elevate their minds to the belief or conception of the divine Unity and Perfections, yet from a principle of Fear they would omit the detestable ceremonies which, it appeared, were most hateful to this great and terrible God, resolving to hazard the anger of the inferior Deities rather than his consuming Vengeance. From the operation of these and similar causes, I doubt not, more human Lives were saved by the amelioration of Superstition,[8] than were lost by the destruction of the Canaanites—so that even by this, the secondary End of the Mosaic Dispensation[,] its extirpating Spirit might be justified. But if we join to this its primary view, and consider the necessity on the account of Christianity for preserving [the] Israelites themselves, I trust that in the course of these Lectures I shall be able to prove the final End so vast and benevolent as to justify any means that were necessary to it.[9] In this view the devastations of the Hebrews were highly useful as rousing against them the deeply-rooted abhorrence of the surrounding Nations, and thus exciting national antipathy—I might add too that the Belief of one God and his Perfections were necessary to preserve them a Free State since the Superstitions that surrounded [them] disposed the mind to imbecility and unmanly Terrors—which would soon bring in political Slavery, whereas they who accustomed themselves to contemplate the infinite Love of the true Deity, that by the comparison they do so dwarf the giant Sons of Earth[1] as to become incapable of not yielding Obedience to God by Rebellion to Tyrants—[2]

---

ral Sins," such as "the Use of that obscene Ceremony the *Phalli*" which "ow'd its Original to the Memory of the Sin against Nature, and to the History of a God hallowing it by his own Act." It is probably this ceremony that constitutes the unmentionable crime for C.

8. Cf. "The Destiny of Nations," lines 87–88: "Till Superstition with unconscious hand / Seat Reason on her throne" (*PW*, 1:134).

9. C draws on Lowman (esp. 23–31, 220–33). Priestley also considered the question as to whether the destruction of the Canaanites was inconsistent with divine benevolence and justice, concluding that it was actually an appropriate measure, showing "great wisdom" and a necessary means of instruction by setting a "striking example of a nation so far sunk into idolatry, and corruptions of all kinds, as all the inhabitants of Canaan are said to have been * * *" (*Institutes of Natural and Revealed Religion*, 2 vols., 2nd ed. [Birmingham, 1782], 2:18–31).

1. I.e., the biblical giants (Genesis 6.4, Numbers 13.33). Cf. Milton, *Paradise Lost* 1.777–81: "Behold a wonder! they but now who seemd / In bigness to surpass Earths Giant Sons / Now less than smallest Dwarfs, in narrow room / Throng numberless, like that Pigmean Race / Beyond the *Indian* Mount * * *." For other instances where C used the giant/dwarf image, see *Lects 1795* (CC), 145n. 1.

2. This slogan, attributed to Benjamin Franklin (1706–1790) and used by Thomas Jefferson (1743–1826) on his seal, was cited by C in *The Watchman* as evidence of the British minis-

From Lecture 5

That there is one God infinitely wise, powerful and good, and that a future state of Retribution is made certain by the Resurrection of Jesus who is the Messiah—are all the *doctrines* of the Gospel. That Christians must behave towards the majority with loving kindness and submission preserving among themselves a perfect Equality is a Synopsis of its Precepts.[1]

Go, preach the Gospel to the Poor.[2] The disciples of Christ were commanded to proclaim good Tidings to All Men; but their zeal was directed more particularly to the Poor, because being oppressed they wanted comfort, being ignorant they wanted knowledge, and being simple in lowliness they were likely to receive the Gospel and preserve it in purity. Their hearts were not bloated by the self confidence of the Philosopher, nor their understanding distorted by the vanity of Genius. Add to this that almost in all Countries, the poor are the most numerous Class. The dispensation was adapted to the Objects. By the benevolence of its precepts it would soften their affections, by the sublimity of its doctrines elevate their understanding and by its simplicity ensure to itself their conviction. If we did not recollect, that every event however calamitous is the necessary mean of the best possible end, we might regret the æra in which the Greek and the Philosopher became converts. For a while they rejected Christianity, their minds being made impervious to Truth by the Incrustation of favorite systems and learned Prejudices—and when they could no longer resist its evidences they leavened with human phantasies what they had received from divine Wisdom.[3] The first men of learning, who embraced the doctrines of Christ, were from among the Gnostics, a sect against which St John and the Apostle Paul employ severe reprehension and prophetic Warnings.[4] Their opinions were wild and fanciful yet peculiarly fascinating to the taste of a vitiated age, in which intellectual Brilliance received the honors due only to patient investi-

---

ters' failure to absorb the important lessons taught by the American Revolution (*Watchman* [CC], 241n. 1). The slogan had also been used by Joseph Gerrald in the pamphlet *A Convention the Only Means of Saving Us from Ruin* (1793), 59. On Gerrald, see p. 251, n. 9 herein.

1. A similar description of the essential constituents of the Christian faith appears in C's letter to Thelwall of December 17, 1796: "You say the Christian is a *mean* Religion: now the Religion, which Christ taught, is simply 1 that there is an Omnipresent Father of infinite power, wisdom, & Goodness, in whom we all of us move, & have our being & 2. That when we appear to men to die, we do not utterly perish; but after this Life shall continue to enjoy or suffer the consequences & [natur]al effects of the Habits, we have formed here, whether good or evil.—This is the Christian *Religion* & all of the Christian *Religion*" (CL, 1:280).
2. Cf. Luke 4.18, 7.22; Mark 16.15.
3. C draws on Priestley's *An History of Early Opinions Concerning Jesus Christ*, 4 vols. (Birmingham, 1786), 1:139–41, the main source for this lecture.
4. C follows closely Priestley's analysis of various tenets of the Gnostics that led to the corruption of Christianity (*Early Opinions*, 1:139–60). Later in the lecture, again drawing on Priestley, C documents the rejection of the Gnostics in the Gospel of St. John and St. Paul's Epistles (*Lects 1795* [CC], 199–200 and nn.). Priestley divided the Gnostics into two groups—the Jews and the Gentiles—and argued that it was the Jews who opposed the apostles and that Paul's allusions to the Gnostics pertain only to the Jews (142–49). Priestley's main attack on the Gnostics concerned their doctrine of the divinity of Christ (see p. 264, n. 8 herein). On Gnosticism, see Glossary.

gation, and the Philosopher invading the province of the Poet endeavoured to strike and dazzle by bold Fiction, and allegoric Personification. They held that matter was self-existent and its intractability the Cause of Evil. From God, or the supreme mind they supposed a derivation of Æons or Intelligences by efflux or emanation. The genealogy or pedigrees of Intelligences male and female formed the greater part of their baseless system.[5] These Intelligences, different in rank & dignity they supposed occasionally to assume the form of man in order to instruct the world. Such they imagined Christ to have been, and Simon Magus pretended to be one of these great Powers.[6] Among the lowest of these Emanations they classed the human Soul, which they held to be imprisoned in the Body; and that these Souls were divided into Classes, the one good and the other bad, which difference they received from their nature and would retain to all Eternity.[7] Their opinions concerning Christ were these—the Earlier Gnostics held the Christ to be a Spirit distinct from the man Jesus, entering into him at his Baptism, and quitting him before his Agony.[8] To this Christ or superangelic Being they affirmed that the Man Jesus addressed himself on the Cross, when he exclaimed, My God! My God! why hast thou forsaken me?[9] Some of them believed that even the Body which he assumed was not a body of flesh & blood, but a phantom—that it was not born of Mary, but only exhibited by her—and in confirmation they feigned that Mary after the Delivery was found to be a Virgin. This was not however the universal Opinion.[1] However they all of them en-

5. In *Early Opinions* (1:154–55) Priestley cites the philosopher Valentinus for the view that evil derived from matter and discusses the Gnostic concept of the emanation of intelligences or *aeons* from God. The passage from Priestley that serves as C's source is cited in *Lects 1795* (CC), 197n. 1. For Priestley's view that Valentinus had the "most complicated system of aeons" and regarded Christ as "one of the *aeons*," see *Early Opinions*, 156, 179–80.
6. C reproduces nearly verbatim a passage from *Early Opinions* (1:156; cited in *Lects 1795* [CC], 197n. 2) in which Priestley mentions Simon Magus.
7. C adapts a passage from *Early Opinions* (1:161–62; cited in *Lects 1795* [CC], 197n. 3) where Priestley reviews the Gnostic doctrine of the soul and refers to the opinion held by Saturninus (fl. 2nd century), as reported by Theodoret (c. 393–c. 458), that " 'there were two kinds of souls, the one good, and the other bad; and that they had this difference from nature, and that as the evil daemon assisted the bad, so the Saviour came to assist the good.' "
8. In *Early Opinions* (1:144–45) Priestley discusses the Gnostic view of the divinity of Christ, which C reproduces here.
9. Matthew 27.46; Mark 15.34.
1. C summarizes a passage from *Early Opinions* (1:175–77; *Lects 1795* [CC], 198n. 3). Unitarians were strongly opposed to the view that Christ was divine, arguing on the basis of scriptural evidence that he was merely human. For Priestley the Gnostic belief in the divinity of Christ was one of the most deplorable departures from the "pristine purity" of primitive Christianity, a position Priestley elaborated in *A History of the Corruptions of Christianity*, 2 vols. (Birmingham, 1782), vol. 1, part 1, esp. 6–87. Cf. *Early Opinions*, 1:22, in which Priestley notes that Christ always referred to himself as a man, as did the apostles and evangelists, who said "nothing that can be construed into a declaration of his divinity or pre-existence." For this view Priestley was bitterly attacked by Samuel Horsley in *Tracts in Controversy with Dr. Priestley upon the Historical Question of the Belief of the First Ages in Our Lord's Divinity* (Gloucester, 1789), where he took issue with Priestley's strategy of building his argument "upon a pretended silence of St. John, about the error of those who maintained the meer humanity of Christ" (14). On C's interest in Priestley's controversy with Horsley, which included Priestley's ten letters to Horsley, see *Defences of Unitarianism for the Years 1788 & 1789. Containing Letters to Dr. Horsley* (1790), 1–74 and *Lects 1795* (CC), 200n. 4. In the 1790s C did not deny the divinity of Christ as explicitly as he endorsed other reactions against orthodox doctrines by Unitarians, such as their rejection of atonement and the Trinity. Nonetheless, letters written by C between 1796 and 1798 and his third lecture on revealed religion suggest that he thought of Jesus primarily as a teacher and founder of a religious system rather than the Son of God. C's refusal to adopt the sacraments, as ex-

tertained so mean an opinion of matter that they denied the Resurrection,[2] affirming that the Body was indeed miraculously conveyed away from the Sepulchre, but that the Christ who appeared to the disciples was a Spirit, who assumed the form of the crucified Jesus and impressed the idea of reality on their senses by a miracle.

Their genealogy of Christ is amusing from its absurdity. Christ and the Holy Spirit were the twin offspring of Monogenes. What this Monogenes is I cannot discover, or of what attribute he is the Personification; however he proceeds from Logos and Zoe, in plain English from Wisdom & Life. Logos and Zoe were the offspring of Nous & Αληθεια, that is, of pure Intelligence and Truth, and Nous and Aletheia were the offspring of Bythus and Sigè, or Abyss and Silence.[3] I have been thus particular in my account of the gnostic Sect, because their doctrine in its consequences produced all the Mysteries, Impostures, and Persecutions, that have disgraced the Christian Community * * *.[4]

The next Corruption which took place among Christians is the doctrine of Redemption. While the Jewish Ceremonies were still existing, or fresh in the memory of men, the scriptural allusions to them and figures of Speech built upon them escaped misinterpretation. But when their City and Sanctuary were destroyed, and the study of the Jewish Antiquities, had become less and less fashionable, the Similes of the New Testament were made to signify the thing assimilated, and Metaphors consolidated into realities.[5] In order to understand the expressions in Scripture that relate to Atonement, we must examine the meaning and use of the Sacrifices and Victims. In a moral Sense a Sacrifice is nowhere considered by the Prophets as a cause operating on Deity, but merely as the means of meliorating our own Hearts. The feelings are increased and made permanent by the frequent outward expression of them. In the earlier ages Victims were the universal Language of Gratitude and Dependence and their uses were precisely the same as those of Prayer and Thanksgiving in the present day—to warm and purify the weak Mortal, not to work a change in the im-

---

pressed in his letter to the Unitarian minister and friend John Prior Estlin (1747–1817) of July 23, 1797 (CL, 1:337–38), also indicates that C had difficulties with the idea of Christ's divinity. C began to defend the divinity of Christ in late 1803 (see CN, 1:1445), a change that went along with his gradual adoption of Trinitarianism (see J. Robert Barth, *Coleridge and Christian Doctrine*, 3–13; McFarland, *Coleridge and the Pantheist Tradition*, 178–84; and p. 451, n. 2 herein).

2. Cf. *Early Opinions*, 1:123: "They had too bad an opinion of *matter*, and consequently of the *body*, which was composed of it, to think the resurrection a desirable thing."

3. Another adaptation from *Early Opinions* 1:179–80 (*Lects 1795* [CC], 199n. 1). Zoe: being; Nous: mind; Αληθεια: truth.

4. A view established by Priestley in chapter 3 of *Early Opinions*, 1:139–236 ("Of the Principles of the Christian Gnostics").

5. In part 2 of *Corruptions* Priestley formulates the Unitarian rejection of redemption and atonement that C reproduces here. Priestley denies that the death of Christ was a sacrifice demanded by God as a "*display of his justice*, and of his *abhorence of sin*, to the subjects of his government" (1:155). He contends that the mistaken doctrine of the divinity of Christ was directly responsible for the corrupt notion of atonement, "because it is said, that sin, as an offence against an *infinite being*, requires an *infinite satisfaction*, which can only be made by an *infinite person* [Christ], that is, one who is no less than God himself" (153). Priestley also shows how figurative representations of the death of Christ in the Scriptures have "unfortunately misled many christians" into conceiving it as a sin offering (181–86).

mutable God.[6] Whenever the superstitious Jews addicted to Vice yet afraid of Deity offered sacrifices in the real sense of atonement, and converted the Thing signifying into the Thing signified, they are reproved for it. "To what purpose is the multitude of your Sacrifices unto me, saith the Lord. I delight not in the Blood of Bullocks, or of Lambs, or of Goats."[7] Wherever therefore whether in the Prophets or in S[t] Paul the Messiah is represented as having sacrificed himself for us it must be understood—as a necessary means relative to man not a motive influencing the Almighty. To awaken Gratitude, to confirm Purity, to evidence sincerity the pious Jew for himself offered a part of his property, the first fruits of his Flock—to effect the same ends in others Christ offered himself, i.e. he evidenced his sincerity by voluntarily submitting to a cruel Death, in order that he might confirm the Faith or awaken the Gratitude of Men. Such is the moral sense of Atonement in Scriptures. There is likewise a ceremonial Sense. Both among the Jews and Gentiles no one was allowed to make prayer and thanksgiving in the temple until a sacrifice had been offered. Our Saviour who exposed himself to Death in the promulgation of that spiritual Law, which doing away all rites and ceremonies gave to us the Liberty of worshipping God in all times and places, may be figuratively yet truly styled a universal Sacrifice. Such seems the fair interpretation of the Scriptural Passages that relate the Doctrine of Atonement which as it is now held, is perhaps the most irrational and gloomy Superstition that ever degraded the human mind.[8] * * * The Being who made both the mind and the motive, who ordained both the man and the circumstance, must at least have permitted Sin, but no proposition can approach more nearly to an axiom than that maxim in common Law. That he who permits what he might have prevented, orders and is the actual cause of it. To assert therefore with Bishop Butler that Sin is of so heinous a nature that God cannot pardon it without an adequate Satisfaction being made to his justice, and the honour of his Laws and Governments, appears to me not to be Blasphemy only because it is nonsense.[9] He who foresees and permits what he might have prevented predestines. And is this the all-loving Parent of the Uni-

---

6. In *Corruptions* (1:188) Priestley defines sacrifices as "a method which men themselves thought of * * * of expressing their gratitude to God, for his favours to them" and suggests that they fall in the category of gifts "or the more particular one of *entertainments*, furnished at the expence of the person who was dependant and obliged" (188). Cf. also the closely related analogy between sacrifice and prayer in Priestley's *Institutes of Natural and Revealed Religion*, 2:323: "If, as it is possible, sacrifices were not originally of divine appointment, we may suppose, that the natural foundation, or original of them, was the same, in general, with that of prayer, viz. a method which mankind thought of, to express the sense they had of their gratitude and obligation to God for the gifts and protection of his providence * * *."

7. Isaiah 1.11 (var.).

8. A parenthesis in the text ("+ add something—Rep. and Ref. Turn you to me") suggests that C may have intended to draw on Psalms 25.16 ("Turn thee unto me, and have mercy upon me") to discuss the doctrine of atonement (*Lects 1795* [CC], 204n. 2).

9. The statement that sin "is of so heinous a nature, that God cannot pardon it without an adequate satisfaction being made to his justice, and the honour of his laws and government" appears in Priestley (*Corruptions*, 1:155) but is not attributed to Joseph Butler (1692–1752) and no such citation can be found in Butler's *The Analogy of Religion* (1736). In chapter 5 (284–313) Butler does formulate the traditional doctrine of atonement that is reflected in Priestley's citation. Priestley either summarizes Butler's position in *The Analogy of Religion* or cites from a different source, as yet untraced.

verse, who mocks the Victims of his Government with a semblance of Justice and predestines to Guilt whom he had doomed to Damnation—And what is Justice? [Is it] not[1] "the best means of producing the greatest Happiness?["] And is this effected by infinite Punishment and eternal Reprobation? Or by retrieving a few of unnumbered Victims from this dire necessity by substituting the pangs of the Innocent? Such are the ideas of Deity which the doctrines of Orthodoxy instill.[2]

*   *   *

A mysterious Doctrine is never more keenly ridiculed, than when a man of sense, who professes it from interested motives, endeavours to make it appear consistent with Reason. By the happy chemistry of explanation, so common among men of abilities who think a good Living a more substantial thing than a good Conscience, he volatilizes absurdity into nothingness, and escapes from the charge of self-contradiction by professing a solemn Belief in the great Mystery of[3]—what every man believes without profession or solemnity. Thus have I heard a very vehement Trinitarian explain himself away into a perfect Humanist![4] and the thrice strange Union of Father, Son and Holy Ghost in one God, each Person full and perfect God transmuted into the simple notion that God is Love, and Intelligence and Life, and that Love, Intelligence and Life are God! a Trinity in Unity equally applicable to Man or Beast! Thus you are told of the wondrous Power of the Cross, yet you find that this wonder working Sacrifice possesses no efficacy unless there be added to it everything that, if God be benevolent, must be sufficient without it. This is the mysterious cookery of the Orthodox—which promises to make Broth out of a Flint, but when you are congratulating yourself on the cheapness of your proposed Diet, requires as necessary ingredients, Beef, Salt and Turnips! But the Layman might say—I can make Broth out of Beef, Salt and Turnips myself. Most true! but the Cook would have no plea

---

1. The original manuscript has "It is not."
2. C draws on Priestley here (*Corruptions*, 1:168–69). At stake in the rejection of the doctrine of vicarious atonement is the view, favored by Priestley and other Unitarians, of a benevolent rather than stern deity, who desires the happiness of his subjects, dispensing grace freely, and requiring from them no more than "repentance and and reformation": "Every degree of severity therefore, that is so circumstanced as not to have this tendency, viz. to promote repentance and the practice of virtue, must be inconsistent with the fundamental principle of the moral government of God, and even with justice itself, if it have the same end with divine goodness, the happiness of God's creatures." Priestley also upheld the principle of happiness as the "great standard by which every thing * * * must finally be determined" in *An Essay on the First Principles of Government* (1768), 17.
3. In *Early Opinions* Priestley exposed the doctrine of the Trinity as resting on the fundamental contradiction of asserting at once the equality of the three Gods (The Father, the Son, and the Holy Ghost) and declaring that there is "only *one God*" (1:48). He maintained that while the doctrine of the unity of God is clearly stated in the Scripture, the doctrine of the Trinity is shrouded in "*inexplicable mysteries*" (1:89). Cf. *Corruptions*, 1:104: "By this happy device, and that of declaring the doctrine to be *incomprehensible*, the Trinitarians imagine that they sufficiently screen themselves from the charge of *Polytheism*, and *Idolatry*." In *Corruptions*, Priestley provided a brief historical overview of the controversies engendered by the introduction of the doctrine of the Trinity (1:102–51), contending that it has been the main stumbling block in the spread of Christianity among Jews and Mahometans, and envisioning "*the perfect day*" after "so long a season of darkness," when the unity and supremacy of God will "be uniformly professed by all that bear the christian name * * *" (1:151).
4. Lewis Patton and Peter Mann speculate that the "vehement Trinitarian" might be John Hey (1734–1815), professor of divinity at Cambridge (*Lects 1795* [CC], 207n. 2).

for demanding his wages were it not for his merit in dropping in the Flint.

* * *

To Priests we speak not, but it were to be wished that those who are desired by two or three to communicate stated Instruction should confine themselves to the reading and expounding of Scriptures—the Scriptures once understood, every man becomes his own Teacher. But these principles which I hope and trust, begin to spread among true Christians are so obnoxious to our spiritual Noblemen, that Bishop Horsley has declared to his Clergy, that Papists are more their Brethren than Protestant Dissenters.[5] God forbid it should be otherwise. He who sees any real difference between the Church of Rome and the Church of England possesses optics which I do not possess— the mark of antichrist is on both of them. Have not both an intimate alliance with the powers of this World, which Jesus positively forbids? Are they not both decked with gold and precious stones? Is there not written on both their Foreheads Mystery![6] Do they not both SELL the Gospel—Nay, nay, they neither sell, nor is it the Gospel—they forcibly exchange Blasphemy for the first fruits, and snatching the scanty Bread from the poor Man's Mouth they cram their lying Legends down his Throat! The Right Reverend Priest did wisely in recommending to his Clergy a fraternizing spirit. It has been the fashion for the English Church to heap abuses on the Church of Rome and apply to her exclusively the prophetic Title of Babylon, the Mother of Abomination.[7] D[r] Horsley has attempted to reform this intemperance, and exclaim in the words of Holy Writ—"Ye be Brethren, fall not out by the Way"—[8]

* * *

5. In a notorious Circular Letter of 1793 often attacked by Unitarian Dissenters, Samuel Horsley stated that the French Catholic priests who were forced to emigrate to England due to their opposition to the French Revolution were more "near, and dear to us in truth by far, than some, who affecting to be called our Protestant brethren, have no other title to the name of Protestant, than a Jew or a Pagan" (*The Welsh Freeholder's Farewell Epistles to the Right Rev. Samuel Lord Bishop * * * of Rochester; in which the Unitarian Dissenters, and the Dissenters in General, Are Vindicated from Charges Advanced against Them in His Lordship's Circular Letter, on the Case of the Emigrant French Clergy: with a Copy of That Letter* [1794], viii; a longer passage from this document is cited in *Lects 1795* [CC], 210n. 1). The Preface includes letters written in response to Horsley's Circular Letter of 1793 that take special notice of his offensive preference for the French Catholic priests over dissenting Protestants (see, e.g., Letter 1 [4–6], which alleges the moral degeneracy of the French priests, and Letter 2 [10–11], which mocks Horsley's implicit declaration of the unity between the churches of Rome and England).
6. A similar condemnation of the Church of England as aligned with mystery and political despotism appears in a "Letter from Liberty to Her Dear Friend Famine," which introduces C's *Conciones ad Populum*. There C describes religion as an "old Harlot * * * decked with precious stones and pearls, and upon her Forehead was written 'MYSTERY' " (*Lects 1795* [CC], 30). Cf. Revelation 17.5 ("And upon her forehead *was* a name written, MYSTERY") and lines 342–43 of "Religious Musings" ("* * * For She hath fallen / On whose black front was written Mystery") (p. 31 herein).
7. Cf. Letter 2 of *The Welsh Freeholder* (11): "Between your Lordship, and the emigrant clergy, the French fraternity exists in perfection. While the poor Unitarian is rudely repulsed, you admit them into close embrace. How fondly do you hug them! Your professions on this head somewhat surprised me. It seemed to me, not consistent with episcopal maxims of prudence, openly to state, even if there did exist, such nearness between your church and the Roman church, especially, if, as a host of commentators of your communion have maintained, that church be the *mother of harlots* spoken of in the Revelations."
8. Cf. Genesis 45.24; Acts 7.26.

When Christians had permitted themselves to receive as Gospel the idolatrous doctrine of the Trinity, and the more pernicious dogma of Redemption, is it not wonderful, that an Episcopal Church should be raised, fit superstructure for such foundations![9]

* * *

From Lecture 6[1]

* * *

In the moral world there is a constant Alternation of Cause and Effect—and Vice and Inequality mutually produce each other. Hence the necessity of Governments[2] and the frequency of Wars—Jesus Christ therefore commanded his disciples to preserve a strict equality—and enforced his command by the only thing capable of giving it effect. He proved to them the certainty of an Hereafter—and by the vastness of the Future diminished the Tyranny of the Present.[3] If not with hereditary faith but from the effect of our examination and reflection we are really convinced of a state after Death, then and then only will Self-interest be wedded to Virtue—Universal Equality is the object of the Mess[iah's] mission not to be procured by the tumultuous uprising of an indignant multitude but this final result of an unresisting yet deeply principled Minority,[4] which gradually absorbing kindred minds shall at last become the whole. To appreciate justly the value of this Panacea, we should behold the dreadful effects of the disease which it removes. Inequality originated in the institution of landed Property[5]—In the early ages of the World the right of landed Property must have been none or transient—a man was proprietor of the Land only while his Flocks were feeding on it. * * * As Manufactures improved and the artificial Want[s] of Life increased, inequality

9. The manuscript may be missing a section as marked by EHC here, even though "The End," written by either C or EHC, seems to indicate the closure of the lecture.
1. The lecture begins with an abbreviated version of the fable of the maddening rain, which C published later in an expanded form in *Friend* (CC), 2:11–12. The fable tells of a wise prophet who was unsuccessful in convincing his people to take shelter from rain that was going to make them mad. When the prophet became prey to ridicule and violence from people who deemed him to be the mad one, he rolled into a puddle of rain to become as mad as the rest. The fable addresses the situation of patriotic reformers who have to abandon their principles in the face of stubborn opposition from their countrymen.
2. C, like Godwin and other radicals, shared the view of Thomas Paine that vice generated the institution of government, which, in counterdistinction to the "blessing" of society, was "but a necessary evil" (*Common Sense* [1791], 5). Godwin, who cited Paine's statement in *Political Justice* (1:79), might have been the source of C's use of it here as well as in *Conciones ad Populum* (see Colmer [15n. 3] and *Lects 1795* [CC], 219–20n. 1).
3. Cf. "Introductory Address" of *Conciones ad Populum*, where C emphasized the beneficial effects of this aspect of Christian faith to the situation of the poor: "In a man so circumstanced [by poverty and hunger] the Tyranny of the *Present* can be overpowered only by the tenfold mightiness of the *Future*" (*Lects 1795* [CC], 45).
4. This is another earlier articulation in a more democratic vein of C's notion of the clerisy developed in chapter 5 of *Church and State* (see p. 585 and its n. 5 herein and p. 586 herein); cf. *A Moral and Political Lecture*, p. 245 and its n. 6 herein.
5. C's discussion of the root of inequality in private property was indebted to works of Locke, Godwin, and Wallace. For specific references, see p. 260, n. 1 herein. In the opposite camp, C would have found a defense of the institution of private property in Paley, *The Principles of Moral and Political Philosophy* (1794), 1:105–22. On Paley, see p. 257, n. 6 herein.

of Life became more mark'd and enviable and the motives to mutual Injury numerous. From their undisciplined Passions as Individuals and as Communities, private Vices and public Wars became frequent—and the influence of Kings and Chieftains increased with Despotism. Thus the jarring Interests of Individuals rendered Governments necessary and governments have operated like quack Medicines; they have produced new diseases, and only checked the old ones—and the evils which they check, they perpetuate. I will paint to you the despotism of Moroco or Sĕrīngăpătām[6]—they are avowed Tyrannies, and we bless ourselves that we live under the free Constitution of England—let us examine this free Constitution—this happy mixture of the excellencies of all Governments—this well poised Balance of Interests and powers—and examine it by the only fair Criterion; its Effects. Since the Revolution[7] we have been engaged in perpetual Wars—in the course of which it has been calculated that more [than] ten million Lives have been lost—Yet for no one of these Wars could any cause be assigned which would have justified the Death of one Individual—they every one have originated in the Folly and Prejudices of our Monarchs and the wretched compliance of Ministers, and through them we are a bloodstained People. Such has been the price which Human Nature has payed for the advantages of Government—but what are these advantages? Has Government educated me? Has it ploughed for me? Has it cloathed me? Has it built me a house? No! these things we do as Individuals—and with them the Government interferes not except to make them more difficult to be procured. But perhaps it possesses virtues of a negative Class—it has prevented us from being vicious. The very contrary is the Truth. What, that can deprave the understanding and subvert the integrity of the People, does it not employ? It has spread among us almost an universal contagion of depravity—The Minister is bribed by his Offices, the Senator by the Minister—the corporation Elector by the Senator, and the citizen by the corporation elector—Selfishness is planted in every bosom, and prepares us for Slavery which it introduces. There is scarcely a Vice which Government does not teach us—criminal prodigality and an unholy Splendor surrounds it—disregard of solemn Promises marks its conduct—and more than half the business of Ministers is to find inducements to Perjury! Nay of late it has become the fashion to keep wicked and needy men in regular Pay, who without scruple take the most awful oaths in order to gain the confidence which it is their Trade to betray.[8] The very officers of Religion are con-

---

6. The capital of Mysore, a state in southwest India.
7. The Glorious Revolution of 1688, during which King James II (1633–1701), who tried to restore Roman Catholicism in England, was ousted by William, prince of Orange (1650–1702), and his wife, Mary (1662–1694), who came from the Netherlands to rule as king and queen. British writers and politicians often contrasted this "bloodless" revolution, during which James II escaped to France unharmed, with the violence of the French Revolution, during which King Louis XVI (1754–1793) and Queen Marie Antoinette (1755–1793) were executed.
8. C refers here to the "system of Spies and Informers" used by the government to infiltrate radical circles, a practice that, as he argued in Conciones ad Populum, led to the "depravation of private morals" and undermined the very foundation of love and trust that holds society together. C had his own direct experience of this system when he resided near Nether

verted into machines of Despotism; and if a Clergyman hunts after
Preferment, it will be better for him to have procured five votes at a
contested Election, than to have written the most learned Commentary on the 15 Prophets.

*   *   *

Such are the effects of our Government which is allowed to be the
best which has been yet tried excepting the American; but I confess
that while this is a commercial and manufacturing nation, some kind
of Government is necessary! But what is Commerce? these manufactures? Are the good which they occasion proportioned to the vast evils
which they make necessary? When I consider my own wants which of
them might I not obtain though Commerce were now unknown? Does
Commerce bring me Corn, or Bricks or Wool? The true advantages of
Commerce consist in debauching the field Labourer with impropor-
tionable toil by exciting in him artificial Wants. The necessaries of
twenty men are raised by one man, who works ten hours a day exclusive of his meals. How then are the other nineteen employed? Some of
them are mechanics and merchants who collect and prepare those
things which urge this field Labourer to unnatural Toil by unnatural
Luxuries—others are Princes and Nobles and Gentlemen who stimulate his exertions by exciting his envy, and others are Lawyers and
Priests and Hangmen who seduce or terrify him into passive submission—Now if instead of this one man the whole Twenty were to divide
the labor and dismiss all unnecessary Wants it is evident that none of
us would work more than two hours a day of necessity, and that all of
us might be learned from the advantages of opportunities, and innocent from the absence of Temptations.[9] Commerce then is useless except to continue Imposture and Oppression. Its Evils are vast and
various—and first, [in] Cities Drunkenness, Prostitution, Rapine, Beggary and Diseases—Can we walk the Streets of a City without observing them in all their most loathsome forms? Add to these Irreligion.
The smoakes that rise from our crowded Towns hide from us the face
of Heaven. In the country, the Love and Power of the great Invisible
are everywhere perspicuous, and by degrees we become partakers of
that which we are accustomed to contemplate. The Beautiful and the
Good are miniatured on the Heart of the Contemplator as the surrounding Landscape on a Convex Mirror. But in Cities God is every-

Stowey with Wordsworth and his sister and was suspected of being an agent for the French
government. This became the basis for the amusing "Spy Nozy" story, which C narrates in
chapter 10 of *Biographia* (pp. 453–55 herein).
9. Godwin argued that it is "unjust, if one man labour to the destruction of his health or his
life, that another man may abound in luxuries. It is unjust, if one man be deprived of leisure
to cultivate his rational powers, while another man contributes not a single effort to add to
the common stock" (*Political Justice*, 2:791). He calculated that "half an hour a day, seriously employed in manual labor by every member of the community, would sufficiently supply the whole with necessaries" (2:823). In *Various Prospects of Mankind*, Wallace estimated
that three to six hours a day were sufficient to secure provisions for everyone and allow all
time "for improving their minds in knowledge and virtue" (40). On Wallace and and his importance to both C and Godwin, see p. 260, n. 1 herein and p. 269, n. 5 herein and *Lects
1795* (CC), 127n. 1 and 223n. 3. The idea of reduced hours of labor was essential to C's and
Southey's projected Pantisocratic scheme. According to Poole, the men in the Pantisocratic
community were to work two to three hours each day (*Thomas Poole and His Friends*, 2 vols.
[London, 1888], 1:97–98, and cf. *CL*, 1:114). On Pantisocracy, see Glossary.

where removed from our Sight and Man obtruded upon us—not Man, the work of God, but the debased offspring of Luxury and Want. At every step some Instance of bloated Depravity, or squallid wretchedness meets us till at last we have doubts of providential Benevolence—and selfish Man accuses God for Miseries, which, if he had been employing himself as God and Nature ordained, he would not have been present to behold.

I address myself to those who acknowledge the Scriptures as their rule of Life and depend for eternal happiness on their obedience to them. In these Scriptures Christians are ordered to keep themselves unspotted from the World. Now can a conscientious man make himself the Instrument of upholding and increasing those Enormities, which make the World a contradistinction to the kingdom of God? If he be a commercial Man, can he be always sincere? Can he always prevent a spirit of selfishness? and is [he] not guilty of tempting God by placing himself in a situation so full of danger? Let him look around his shop? Does nothing in it come from the desolate plains of Indostan? From what motives did Lord Clive murder his million and justify it to all but his own Conscience? From what motives did the late rice-contracting Governor famish a million and gain from the Company the Title of Saviour of India?[1] Was it not that wicked as they were they increased and preserved the commercial Intercourse? It has been openly asserted that our commercial intercourse with the East Indies has been the occasion of the loss of eight million Lives—in return for which most foul and heart-inslaving Guilt we receive gold, diamonds, silks, muslins & callicoes for fine Ladies and Prostitutes—Tea to make a pernicious Beverage, Porcelain to drink it from, and salt-petre for the making of gunpowder with which we may murder the poor Inhabitants who supply all these things. Not one thing necessary or even useful do we receive in return for the horrible guilt in which we have involved ourselves. Africa and the West India Islands, on these fearful subjects I shall observe nothing at present. I hang my head when I think of them, they leave an indelible stain on our national character—all the waters of the Ocean cannot purify, all the perfumes of Araby cannot sweeten it. But the continuance of these abominations depends on the will of those who consume the produce of the Trade. And is not he more particularly the Consumer who administers to others the means of providing themselves with these pestilent Luxuries?[2] And can a Christian

---

1. In the 1760s the East India Company came under sharp scrutiny by the British Parliament and public sentiment rose against the corruption of its officers and the atrocities to which natives had been subjected. The near bankrupcy of the company in 1772 led to an investigation (by a Select Committee of the House of Commons) of Robert Clive (1725–1774), governor of Bengal and founder of the British Empire in India. Clive was acquitted by the House of the various crimes revealed by the Select Committee, but his case prepared the way for the more dramatic indictment of the affairs of the company in the 1780s and the impeachment of Warren Hastings in 1788. (On Hastings, see p. 252, n. 6 herein.) In his speech to the House of Commons of July 30, 1784, Burke accused Hastings of transforming India from a luxurious paradise into a pitiful wasteland and causing a famine of unprecedented proportions. He also contended that Hastings, far from being the "savior, protector and champion" of "many millions of people," as his friends described him, was in fact "the scourge of India" (*Parl. Hist.*, 24:1252–71).
2. C was to address these subjects in detail in "On the Slave-Trade" (p. 288 herein).

justify himself? God is not to be mocked! Family connections, and the necessity of a maintenance are no excuses! "He that loveth Father or Mother more than me is not worthy of me, and he that loveth Son or Daughter more than me is not worthy of me—and taketh not his Cross, is not worthy of me."[3] I appeal to common sense whether or no every motive by which these men excuse themselves might not have been urged by the Apostles—and with much greater reason!

I have asserted that Jesus Christ forbids to his disciples all property—and teaches us that accumulation was incompatible with their Salvation! * * * Our Saviour by no means authorizes an Equalization of Property—which in the first place is impracticable for how are we to equalize? Measuring will not do it—one soil is better than another—and where is the scale to adjust the differences, and balance Quality with Quantity? and secondly—if it were practicable—it would answer no end, for this Equalization could not continue for a year, and while it continued, it would only narrow the Theatre, and exclude the actors. While I possess anything exclusively mine, the selfish Passions will have full play—and our Hearts will never learn that great Truth that the good of the Whole etc.[4] We find in the twelfth of Luke that our Lord refused to authorize a division of Inheritance, and in the subsequent verses forbids all property, and orders men to depend for their subsistence upon their Labor.[5] And in Luke the 20th 21.22, they asked Jesus—"Is it lawful for us to give Tribute unto Cæsar or no? And he said unto them—Shew me a penny whose Image and Superscription hath it? They answered and said Cæsar's[.] And he said unto them—render unto Cæsar the Things that are Cæsar[']s, and unto God the Things that are God's.["][6] A wise Sentence—That we use money is a proof that we possess individual property, and Commerce and Manufactures—and while these evils continue, your own vices will make a government necessary—and it is fit that you maintain that government. Emperor and King are but the lord lieutenants of conquered Souls—secondaries and viceregents who govern not with their own right but with power delegated to them by our Avarice and appetites! Let us exert over our own hearts a virtuous despotism, and lead our own Passions in triumph, and then we shall want neither Monarch nor General. If we would have no Nero[7] without, we must place a Cæsar within us, and that Cæsar must be Religion!

*   *   *

---

3. Matthew 10.37–38 (var.).
4. For the common use in political writings of the equation between the "good of the whole" and the good of "each individual," see p. 286, n. 1 herein.
5. Luke 12.13–23.
6. Luke 20.22–25 (var.).
7. Claudius Caesar Drusus Germanicus Nero (37–68 C.E.), emperor of Rome.

FROM THE PLOT DISCOVERED (1795)

In the fall of 1795 a series of repressive measures were instituted by the British parliament that caused intense consternation and protest among politicians, writers, and ordinary citizens. The attack on the carriage of King George III by a mob on October 29, 1795, an ominous event in view of the execution in 1793 of Louis XVI in revolutionary France, led to the introduction of two Bills that severely threatened the freedom of speech, of the press, and of political gatherings. The first Bill (Lord Grenville's Bill, or the Treason Bill), presented by Lord Grenville (1759–1834) in the House of Lords on November 6, redefined treason as including any speeches or writings that showed "hatred or dislike of his Majesty," his "successors," and his government. The second Bill (Pitt's Bill, or the Convention Bill), presented by William Pitt in the House of Commons on November 10, stipulated prior approval by a magistrate for all meetings of fifty or more people. The second Bill was aimed at the London Corresponding Society, which organized a mass meeting on October 26, 1795, during which the leading radical John Thelwall spoke against fictitious conspiracies attributed to "friends of freedom" by a despotic government and in support of the "universal diffusion of equal rights and equal laws." The government linked this meeting to the attack on the king, a connection disputed in the parliament by Whig leaders and passionately denied by Thelwall in the Preface to the published version of his October 26 speech and in his address to the London Corresponding Society at its meeting of November 12, 1795.

Coleridge became an active and most eloquent opponent of the two Bills. On November 17 and 20, 1795, he attended two meetings in Bristol that resulted in a petition by the inhabitants of Bristol sent to the parliament against the two Bills. The London newspaper *Star*, which published the proceedings of the meetings, singled out Coleridge's speech as "the most elegant, the most pathetic, and the most sublime Address that was ever heard, perhaps, within the walls of that building [Guildhall]" (*Lects 1795* (CC), 361). On November 26, 1795, Coleridge delivered a lecture on the two Bills at the Pelican Inn, Bristol, which was published in an expanded version as *The Plot Discovered* sometime before December 10. Its title, which is derived from Thomas Otway's 1682 play *Venice Preserv'd, or, A Plot Discover'd* performed in Bristol in July 1795, highlights the sentiments often expressed by Thelwall and other reformers that the real conspirators who "fabricate plots of violence" are in fact the advocates of Pitt's corrupt administration who "project impracticable crimes, that they may saddle them upon those friends of liberty, who abhor alike both them and their abominations" (*The Speech of John Thelwall, at the General Meeting of the Friends of Parliamentary Reform Called by the London Corresponding Society, and Held in the Neighbourhood of Copenhagen-House; On Monday, October 26, 1795* [1795], 4; cf. *A Moral and Political Lecture*, p. 244, n. 3 herein).

The text printed here is from *The Plot Discovered* (Bristol, 1795).

FROM THE PLOT DISCOVERED; OR AN ADDRESS TO THE PEOPLE, AGAINST MINISTERIAL TREASON[1]

We have entrusted to Parliament the guardianship of our liberties, not the power of surrendering them. Shame fall on the mitred mufti, who aims to persuade us, that it is the Almighty's will that the greatest part of mankind should come into the world with saddles on their backs and bridles in their mouths, and the remaning few ready booted and spurred for the purpose of riding them.[2]

"THE MASS OF THE PEOPLE HAVE NOTHING TO DO WITH THE LAWS, BUT TO OBEY THEM!"[3]——Ere yet this foul treason against the majesty of man, ere yet this blasphemy against the goodness of God be registered among our statutes, I enter my protest! Ere yet our laws as well as our religion be muffled up in mysteries, as a CHRISTIAN I protest against this worse than Pagan darkness! Ere yet the sword descends, the two-edged sword that is now waving over the head of Freedom, as a BRITON, I protest against slavery! Ere yet it be made legal for Ministers to act with vigour beyond law,[4] as a CHILD OF PEACE, I protest against civil war. This is the brief moment, in which Freedom pleads on her knees: we will join her pleadings, ere yet she rises terrible to wrench the sword from the hand of her merciless enemy! We will join the still small voice of reason, ere yet it be overwhelmed in the great and strong wind, in the earthquake, and in the fire![5] These detestable Bills I shall examine in their undiminished proportions, as they first dared shew themselves to the light, disregarding and despising all subse-

1. On the page opposite to the first page of text, C lists a citation from book 7 of Lucan, *De bello civile* (On the Civil War), lines 58–59: "Hoc placet, O Superi, cum vobis vertere cuncta / Propositum" ("Does this please You, O Gods Above, when You plan / universal doom [to compound our crimes with guilt]?"). Trans. Jane Wilson Joyce (Lucan, *Pharsalia* [Ithaca, N.Y., 1993], 172).
2. From "it is the Almighty's will" to the end, C cites from the dying speech of Richard Rumbold (who had tried to assasinate Charles II [1630–1685]), which appears in *History of My Own Time* by Gilbert Burnett, bishop of Salsbury (1643–1715), cited by James Burgh (1714–1775) in *Political Disquisitions*, 3 vols. (1774–75), 1:3 (*Lects 1795* [CC], 285n. 1). *Mitred mufti:* alludes to Samuel Horsley's remark cited in the opening sentence of C's pamphlet and the retort by James Maitland, earl of Lauderdale (1759–1839), that if he "had been in Turkey, and had heard such a declaration from the mouth of a Mufti, he should have attributed it to his ignorance, the despotic government of his country, or the bias of his religious opinions; but to hear a British prelate, in a British house of parliament, declare that he did not know what the people had to do with the laws but to obey them, filled him with wonder and astonishment" (*Parl. Hist.*, 32:258). Cf. the reference to "mitred ATHEISM" in line 347 of *Religious Musings* (p. 31 herein).
3. A provocative remark by Samuel Horsley, bishop of Rochester (from 1793 to 1802), during a debate on the wording of the Treason Bill in the House of Lords on November 11, 1795, and boldly reaffirmed on November 13: "My lords, it is a maxim which I ever will maintain,—I will maintain it to the death,—I will maintain it under the axe of the guillotine * * * " (*Parl. Hist.*, 32:258, 268). In *Considerations on Lord Grenville's and Mr. Pitt's Bills* * * * (32; see p. 241, n. 5 herein). Godwin also highlights this offensive statement by Horsley. On Horsley, cf. C's remark in a letter to Southey of September 11, 1794: "Horsley, the Bishop, is believed in the higher Circles and by all the World of Authors to be—a determined *Deist.*—What a villain, if it is true!—" (*CL*, 1:102).
4. In an often-cited statement made in response to Fox's speech against the two bills on November 23, 1795, William Windham, secretary-at war, indicated that "ministers * * * were ready to exert a vigour beyond the law, as exercised in ordinary times and under ordinary circumstances" (*Parl. Hist.*, 32:386). For C on Windham, see p. 251, n. 7 herein; p. 304, nn. 8–9 herein; p. 305, nn. 1–4 herein.
5. 1 Kings 19.11–12 (var.).

quent palliatives and modifications.[6] From their first state it is made evident beyond all power of doubt, what are the wishes and intentions of the present Ministers; and their wishes and intentions having been so evidenced, if the legislature authorize, if the people endure one sentence of such Bills from such manifest conspirators against the Constitution, that legislature will by degrees authorize the whole, and the people endure the whole—yea, that legislature will be capable of authorising even worse, and the people will be unworthy of better.

The first of these Bills is an attempt to assassinate the Liberty of the Press: the second, to smother the Liberty of Speech.[7]

*   *   *

In all ministerial measures there are two reasons, the real, and the ostensible. The ostensible reason of the present Bill we have heard; the real reason will not elude the search of common sagacity. The existing laws of Treason were too clear, too unequivocal. Judges indeed (what will not Judges do?) Judges might endeavour to transfer to these laws their own flexibility; Judges might make strange interpretations. But English Juries could not, would not understand them. Hence instead of eight hecatombs of condemned traitors behold eight triumphant acquitted felons![8] Hinc illae lacrymae[9]—The present Bills were conceived and laid in the dunghill of despotism among the other yet unhatched eggs of the old Serpent.[1] In due time and in fit opportunity they crawled into light. Genius of Britain! crush them!

The old Treason Laws are superseded by the exploded commentaries of obsequious Crown lawyers, the commentary has conspired against the text: a vile and useless slave has conspired to dethrone its venerable master. "If any person within the realm or without shall compass, imagine, invent, devise, or intend death or destruction, or any bodily harm tending to death or destruction, maim or wounding,

---

6. In his speech in the House of Commons of November 23, 1795, Fox stated twice that he preferred the two Bills to be presented without amendments and alterations so that their poison should not thus "be made more palatable" to the people (*Parl. Hist.*, 32:382–83).

7. In the section omitted here (*Lects 1795* [CC], 286–88) C cites from the Treason Bill and explains that the official (or, as he puts it below, "ostensible") reason given for it was the attack on the king's carriage, which was linked to the wide dissemination of seditious literature. C attributes the attack to the hunger and ravages caused by the ongoing war with France, a common claim among the opponents of the Bills (see, e.g., the speeches of November 1795 by the earl of Lauderdale and Richard Brinsley Sheridan [*Parl. Hist.*, 32:250, 335]).

8. C refers to the State Trials of 1794, during which leading members of of the parliamentary reform movement were arrested and charged with treason. Among them were John Horne Tooke, Thomas Hardy, and Thelwall, who were tried and acquitted (see p. 247, n. 3 herein). On December 30, 1794, Windham said with reference to those acquitted during the State Trials that "He wished them joy of the innocence of an acquitted felon" (*Parl. Hist.*, 31:1029), an offensive remark for which Windham was often attacked. Thelwall, in his October 26 speech, used this remark for rhetorical purposes ("Remember, Citizens, you are in very bad Company. You are listening to AN ACQUITTED FELON" [21]).

9. "Hence these tears." From Terence's *Andria* 1.1.125 and often cited by Burgh (e.g., *Political Disquisitions* 1:368, 469) (*Lects 1795* [CC], 288n. 3).

1. I.e., Pitt, ridiculed by C in his political prose and poetry and often associated with a snake (see "Fire, Famine & Slaughter," p. 140 herein; *Conciones ad Populum*, p. 254, nn. 4–6 herein; and *EOT* [CC], 1:221).

imprisonment or restraint of the person of our sovereign Lord, the King, or if he levy war against his Majesty, or move or stir any foreigner or stranger to invasion—he shall be adjudged a traitor." We object not. But "whoever by printing, writing, preaching, or malicious and advised speaking, shall compass, or imagine, or devise to deprive or depose the King, or his heirs and successors from the style, power, and kingly name, of the imperial crown of this realm, he shall be adjudged a traitor."[2] Here lurks the snake. To promulge what we believe to be truth is indeed a law beyond law; but now if any man should publish, nay, if even in a friendly letter or in social conversation any should assert a Republic to be the most perfect form of government, and endeavour by all argument to prove it so, he is guilty of High Treason: for what he declares to be the more perfect, and the most productive of happiness, he recommends; and to recommend a Republic is to recommend an abolition of the kingly name. By the existing treason laws a man so accused would plead, It is the privilege of an Englishman to entertain what speculative opinions he pleases, provided he stir up to no present action. Let my reasonings have been monarchical or republican, whilst I act as a royalist, I am free from guilt. Soon, I fear, such excuse will be of no avail. It will be in vain to alledge, that such opinions were not wished to be realized, except as the result of progressive reformation and ameliorated manners; that the author or speaker never dreamed of *seeing* them realized; though he should expressly set forth, that they neither could be, nor would be, nor ought to be, realized in the present or the following reign; still he would be guilty of high Treason: for though he recommends not an attempt to depose his present Majesty from the kingly name, yet he evidently recommends the denial of it to some one of his distant successors. All political controversy is at an end. Those sudden breezes and noisy gusts, which purified the atmosphere they disturbed, are hushed to deathlike silence. The cadaverous tranquillity of despotism will succeed the generous order and graceful indiscretions of freedom—the black moveless pestilential vapour of slavery will be inhaled at every pore. But, beware, O ye rulers of the earth! For it was ordained at the foundation of the world by the King of kings, that all corruption should conceal within its bosom that which will purify; and THEY WHO SOW PESTILENCE MUST REAP WIRLWINDS.[3]

2. C paraphrases from the Treason Bill, which was printed in parliamentary documents and newspapers, including *MP*. His point is that while under the old treason laws only an overt action against the king could qualify as treasonable, the new bill extends the charge of treason to mere political opinions, even when no action against the king is in evidence. Cf. Godwin's point that Lord Grenville's bill puts "the author of every speculative and philosophical disquisition" at risk and "at the mercy" of the ministers (*Considerations on Lord Grenville's and Mr. Pitt's Bills*, 39). On the treason laws, see John Barrell, "Imaginary Treason, Imaginary Law: The State Trials of 1794" in *The Birth of Pandora and the Division of Knowledge* (Philadelphia, 1992), 119–43.

3. Hosea 8.7: "For they have sown the wind, and they shall reap the whirlwind! * * *." In the section omitted here (*Lects 1795* [CC], 289–95) C takes a closer look at the consequences of the Treason Bill, arguing that it affects not only present but also past generations and would result in censorship of books and an inquest into private and public libraries. C stresses the danger of admitting words rather than actions as evidence of treasonable intent and shows that the Bill would in effect render the king immune to censure and deprived of the benefit of proper advice or truth from anyone.

*   *   *

We proceed to the second Bill, for more effectually preventing seditious meetings and assemblies. At my first glance over it, it recalled to
me by force of contrast the stern simplicity and perspicuous briefness
of the Athenian laws. But our minister's meaning generally bears an
inverse proportion to the multitude of his words. If his declaration
consist of fifty lines, it may be compressed into ten; if it extend to five
hundred, it may be compressed into five. His style is infinitely porous:
deprived of their vacuities the το πᾶν,[4] the universe of his bills and
speeches would take up less room than a nutshell.[5] The Bill now
pending is indeed as full-foliaged, as the Manchineel tree; (and like
the manchineel, will poison those who are fools enough to slumber
beneath it)[6] but its import is briefly this—first, that the people of England should possess no unrestrained right of consulting in common on
common grievances: and secondly, that Mr. Thelwall should no longer
give political lectures.[7]

*   *   *

But we will take a nearer view of the subject. These Bills are levelled against all who excite hatred or contempt of the Constitution
and Government:[8] that is, all who endeavour to prove the Constitution
and Government defective, corrupt, or fraudulent. (For it has been before observed, that all detection of weakness, imposture, or abuse,
necessarily tend to excite hatred or contempt.)[9] Now the Constitution
and Government are defective and corrupt, or they are not. If the former, the Bills are iniquitous, since they would *kill off* all who promulge truths necessary to the progression of human happiness: of[1] the
latter, (that is, if the Constitution and Government are perfect) the
Bills are still iniquitous, for they destroy the sole boundary which divides that Government from Despotism, and *change* that Constitution,
from whose present perfectness they derive their only possible justification. In order to prove these assertions, we must briefly examine the
British Constitution, or mode of Government.

*   *   *

Hitherto nothing has been adduced that truly distinguishes our
Government from Despotism: it seems to be a Government *over*, not

4. "The whole."
5. For similar attacks on Pitt's swelling rhetorical style abounding in abstractions, see pp.
   253–54 herein. In an essay on Pitt published in *MP* of March 19, 1800 (*EOT* [CC],
   1:219–26), C uncovered in Pitt's childhood the source of his excessive interest in "combination of words" at the expense of "present objects" or "genuine feelings."
6. The manchineel fruit had been used by Reverend James Boyer, C's teacher at Christ's Hospital, as an example of inflated and imprecise use of language (see p. 381, n. 8 herein).
7. Thelwall's political lectures and his journal *The Tribune* had been linked by the government
   with the spread of seditious views and the unrest that led to the attack on the king's carriage.
   C's defense of Thelwall here, though misunderstood by Thelwall as a covert attack, prepared
   the way for an active correspondence between them in 1796 and a strong though short-lived
   friendship, from which C withdrew after 1797 and which he never mentioned in the *Biographia* (see Nicholas Roe, "Coleridge and John Thelwall: The Road to Nether Stowey" in
   The Coleridge Connection, 60–80; see also, Roe, 117, 148–50).
8. The Treason and Convention Bills both stipulated punishments of those who incited the
   people to "Hatred or Contempt" not only of the king and his heirs but also of "the established Government and Constitution of this realm" (*Lects 1795* [CC], 305n. 3).
9. In an earlier passage (not included here) C mentioned that "censure tends to excite *dislike*"
   (*Lects 1795* [CC], 293).
1. Printer's error for "if"?

by, or *with* the people. But this conclusion we disavow. The Liberty of the Press, (a power resident in the people) gives us an *influential* sovereignty. By books necessary information may be dispersed; and by information the public will may be formed; and by the right of petitioning that will may be expressed; first, perhaps, in low and distant tones such as beseem the children of peace; but if corruption deafen power, gradually increasing till they swell into a deep and awful thunder, the VOICE OF GOD, which his vicegerents must hear, and hearing dare not disobey.[2] This unrestricted right of over-awing the Oligarchy of Parliament by constitutional expression of the general will forms our liberty: it is the sole boundary that divides us from Despotism.

> Τουλευθερον δ' ἐκεινο, τις θελει πολει
> Χρηστον τι Βουλευμ' εις μεσον φερειν, εχων.
> Και ταυθ' ο χρηζων, λαμπρος εσθ', ο μη θελων
> Σιγα· τι τουτων εστιν ισαιτερον πολει;
>   EURIP. SUPPLIC. 440.[3]

By the almost winged communication of the Press, the whole nation becomes one grand Senate, fervent yet untumultuous. By the right of meeting together to petition (which, Milton says, is good old english for *requiring*)[4] the determinations of this Senate are embodied into legal form, and conveyed to the *executive* branch of Government, the Parliament. The present Bills annihilate this right. The *forms* of it indeed will remain; (the *forms* of the Roman republic were preserved under Tiberius and Nero)[5] but the reality will have flown. No political information from the Press can previously enlighten the people; and if they meet, the deliberation must be engrossed by the hireling defenders of that scheme of cruelty and imposture, which the ministry chuse to call our Constitution. We can no longer consult in common on common grievances. Our assemblies will resemble a silent and sullen mob of discontented slaves who have surrounded the palace of some eastern tyrant. By the operation of Lord Grenville's Bill, the Press is made useless. Every town is insulated; the vast conductors are destroyed by the which the electric fluid of truth was conveyed from man to man, and nation to nation. A French Gentleman in the reign of Lewis the fourteenth[6] was comparing the French and English writers with all the boastfulness of national pre-possession. Moniseur (replied an Englishman better versed in the principles of freedom than the canons of criticism) there are but two subjects worthy the human

---

2. The equation of the voice of the people with the voice of God (*vox populi vox Dei*) is commonplace in political discourse and was used by Willloughby Bertie, fourth earl of Abingdon (1740–1799), in an attack on Horsley's offensive statement cited earlier (*Lects 1795* [CC], 312n. 4).
3. Euripides, *The Suppliant Women*, lines 438–41 (trans. Frank Jones, in *Euripides IV* [Chicago, 1958], 74): "This is the call of freedom: / 'What man has good advice to give the city, / And wishes to make it known?' He who responds / Gains glory; the reluctant hold their peace."
4. Burgh 3:438–39.
5. Julius Caesar Augustus Tiberius (42 B.C.E.–37 C.E.) and Nero (37–68 C.E.), Roman emperors. C referred to Tiberius earlier in the pamphlet (*Lect 1795* [CC], 295) and discussed Nero in Lecture 4 of *LRR* (see *Lects 1795* [CC], 169–71).
6. Louis XIV (1638–1715), king of France.

intellect—Politics and Religion, our state here, and our state here-after: and on neither of these *dare* you write![7] This spirited reproof may now be retorted on us. By Mr. Pitt's Bill Britons are allowed to pe-tition—with Justices of Peace at their elbow! Justices of Peace in-vested with absolute censorial power over the individuals, and the chance-right of military domination over the assembly. British Liberty leaves her cell by permission, and walks abroad to take the air between two jailors; fettered, and handcuffed, and with a gagg in her mouth!!![8]

*   *   *

THE WATCHMAN (1796)

In late December 1795 Coleridge attended a meeting at the Rummer Tav-ern in Bristol, where, as he later told the story in *Biographia Literaria*, he "was persuaded" to start "a periodical work, entitled THE WATCHMAN, that (according to the general motto of the work) *all might know the truth, and that the truth might make us free!*" (*BL* [CC]), 1:179; the motto, which headed each issue, was derived from John 8.32). The plan was attractive to Coleridge in that it provided an opportunity for disseminating his polit-ical views in a form other than lectures and with some prospect, however modest, of financial profit. On January 9 Coleridge left Bristol on a tour of the Midlands and the north, in order to secure subscribers. For a descrip-tion of the tour, see his letters to Josiah Wade (*CL*, 1:175–78, 180–81, 184]) and his later account in chapter 10 of the *Biograhia* (*BL* [CC], 1:180–84). Due to the length of the trip (Coleridge returned to Bristol on February 13), the first issue of *The Watchman* did not appear on Friday, February 5, as previously announced, but on March 1, 1796. Subsequent issues were published every eighth day in an octavo form, so as to be bound at the end of the year and become, as Coleridge hoped, "an annual Register." Each issue was made up of thirty-two pages and sold at the low price of four pence. Although Coleridge, with the help of many zealous friends, obtained many subscribers (*BL* [CC], 1:184 and *ER*, 1:155), the paper had a run of only ten issues, and left Coleridge in debt to his printer Nathaniel Biggs (fl. 1796–1810). In the closing address to the reader in the last issue of *The Watchman*, which appeared on May 13, 1796, Cole-ridge stated that he discontinued the paper because "the Work does not pay its expenses," and he could not see a way of reconciling the contradic-tory expectations of readers, some desiring more "original composition," and others complaining that "it contained too much" at the expense of lo-cal news. The last words of *The Watchman*, an adaptation from the proph-esies of Ezekiel, convey Coleridge's sense of frustration and defeat: "O Watchman! thou hast watched in vain!" (*Watchman* [CC], 374–75).

7. Source untraced. C used the same anecdote in *Friend* (CC), 2:208.
8. The two Bills came to be known as "gagging bills" after the title of a pamphlet by Thomas Beddoes (1760–1808) called *A Word in Defence of the Bill of Rights, against Gagging Bills* (Bristol, 1795), an extract of which C printed in the last number of *The Watchman* (see *Watchman* [CC], 344–46; 344n. 1 for the remark by Joseph Jekyll [1754–1837] in the House of Commons that Pitt's Bill "gaggs the mouth of every British subject." Beddoes's pamphlet is reproduced in *Lects 1795* [CC], 371–84). Godwin also attacked the two Bills, but unlike C or Beddoes, he blamed the London Corresponding Society and political associ-ations in general for alarming the ministers and misunderstanding the process whereby gen-uine social reforms can take place. In the end, however, Godwin placed far greater blame on "the king's ministers, and the opulent and titled alarmists" than on the "friends of freedom," for their intemperate behavior and provocative calls "for blood" (*Considerations on Lord Grenville's and Mr. Pitt's Bills*, esp. 75–82). Cf. p. 277 and n. 2 herein, and Roe, 148–56.

Coleridge began *The Watchman* with the hope that it would provide an alternative to the "weekly provincial Newspapers" subsidized by the government and expected to promote the government's views. The paper was also to be distinct from others by including, in addition to news about current domestic and foreign events, original essays, poetry and reviews of publications. *The Watchman*, as London advertisements claimed, was to "supply at once the places of a Review, Newspaper, and Annual Register" (*Watchman* [CC], 380). But as the difficulties of being at once "the editor, chief contributor, and private distributor" for the paper increased (Colmer, 32), Coleridge was unable to ensure for each issue the balanced content that he projected in the "Prospectus." Lacking a sufficient number of contributors, he was often forced to fill the pages of the paper with reports of parliamentary debates and domestic and foreign affairs taken directly from London newspapers. While original contributions by Coleridge dominate the first number of *The Watchman*, they decrease in subsequent issues, fulfilling the uncharitable prediction of Coleridge's Cambridge friend G. L. Tuckett (b. c. 1771) that, given Coleridge's "fits of idleness," it was not surprising that "after three or four numbers the sheets will contain nothing but Parliamentary Debates, and Coleridge will add a note at the bottom of the page: 'I should think myself deficient in my duty to the Public if I did not give these *interesting* Debates at *full* length' " (*CL*, 1:192n.). For the distribution of original and reprinted material in each issue, see *Watchman* (CC), li–liv.

In *The Watchman* Coleridge tackled some of the main lines of radical opposition to the policies of his government that concerned him in his political lectures of 1795. The affairs of France and England's ongoing war against it continued to preoccupy Coleridge, inspiring one of his finest essays ("Remonstrance to the French Legislators," *Watchman* [CC], 269–273) and inflamatory anti-Pitt pronouncements (e.g., *Watchman* [CC], 39, 41). Coleridge followed closely the abolitionist debates of that year and reworked his 1795 lecture on the slave trade into a polished essay that does credit to his rhetorical skills and what he considered to be his life-long opposition to this inhumane trade. He also attacked the Church of England, ridiculed the rich for their insensitivity to the poor ("Essay on Fasts," *Watchman* [CC], 51–55, which lost Coleridge many subscribers to the journal), and prophesied the overthrow of kings (65–66). But Coleridge's opposition to Lord Grenville's and Pitt's Bills, which curtailed the freedom of political associations and discusion, was no longer as virulent as in the days when he produced the pamphlet *The Plot Discovered* (p. 274 herein). Although the Prospectus indicated that the main object of the *The Watchman* was to aid the Whig Club "in procuring a repeal of Lord Grenville's and Mr. Pitt's bills" (p. 283 herein), the first number noted that the two Bills "will not have been useless if they should render the language of political publications more cool and guarded, or even confine us for a while to the teaching of first principles, or the diffusion of that general knowledge which should be the basis or substratum of politics" (*Watchman* [CC], 14). In the *Biographia* Coleridge reproduced this comment on the two Bills as a strategy of disavowing his early involvement in radical politics (pp. 452–53 herein). For the same purpose, he also drew attention to his attack on Jacobin and democratic advocates of "French morals" in his essay "Modern Patriotism." But as Colmer points out, by alienating "the sympathies of the democrats, dissenters, and the Godwinites alike," Coleridge created the very conditions that led to the failure of *The Watchman*," since "it was from these three groups that he had to look for subscribers" (49–50). On the failure of this work, see also *Watchman* (CC), xliii, liv–lv.

The copy text for selections from the *The Watchman* is Ashley 2842, British Library. This is one of two copies annotated by Coleridge that has come to light. The other, which originally belonged to the bookseller A. E. Dobell, is now in the Spencer Library of the University of Kansas (Spencer C5959). Ashley 2842 has nine annotations, which appear in numbers 2, 3, 4, and 8, one of which is dated February 17, 1813 (235–36 of the original). All alterations of substantives and of punctuation made by Coleridge in his annotations to the essay "On the Slave Trade" are indicated in the notes. For a description of the annotations, see William P. Albrecht, "An Annotated Copy of *The Watchman*," *The Wordsworth Circle* 9 (1978): 106–07. *The Watchman* appeared in a single edition, and only the first number went through two printings. Ashley 2842 and Spencer C5959 give the first printing of number 1. The second printing is reproduced in *Watchman* (CC), 9–50.

Prospectus: The copy text for the Prospectus to *The Watchman* is Ashley 406, British Library. An article attached to this copy by George B. Winship from Harvard University specifies that there were two or possibly three issues of the Prospectus and two surviving copies of the third issue, both of which were in Joseph Cottle's possession. But as Lewis Patton indicates, Cottle's version of the Prospectus (*ER*, 1:151–52) actually reproduces in a slightly altered form the handbills advertising the first number of *The Watchman*. There are three known copies of the original Prospectus: Ashley 406, H. Buxton Forman's copy at Harvard University Library, and the C. B. Tinker copy at Yale University Library (see *Watchman* [CC], 379–81).

Prospectus

IN AN ENSLAVED STATE THE RULERS FORM AND SUPPLY THE OPINIONS OF THE PEOPLE. This is the mark by which Despotism is distinguished: for it is the power, by which Despotism is begun and continued.————"*The abuses, that are rooted in all the old Governments of Europe, give such numbers of men such a direct interest in supporting, cherishing, and defending abuses, that no wonder advocates for tyranny of every species are found in every country, and almost in every company. What a mass of People in every part of England are some way or other interested in the present representation of the people, in tythes, charters, corporations, monopolies, and taxation ! and not merely in the things themselves, but in all the abuses attending them; and how many are there who derive their profit or their consideration in life, not merely from such institutions, but from the evils they engender!*"

ARTHUR YOUNG'S TRAVELS.[1]

Among the most powerful advocates and auxiliaries of abuses we must class (with a few honorable exceptions) the weekly provincial Newspapers, the Editors of which receive the Treasury Prints gratis,

---

1. Arthur Young, *Travels, during the Years 1787, 1788, 1789 * * * [in] France* (Bury St. Edmund's, 1792), 540n. (var.). For C on Young, see p. 240, n. 3 herein.

and in some instances *with particular paragraphs marked out for their insertion.*——These Papers form the chief, and sometimes the only, reading of that large and important body of men, who living out of towns and cities have no opportunity of hearing calumnies exposed and false statements detected. Thus are Administrations enabled to steal away their Rights and Liberties, either so gradually as to undermine their Freedom without alarming them; or if it be necessary to carry any great point suddenly, to overthrow their Freedom by alarming them against themselves.

A PEOPLE ARE FREE IN PROPORTION AS THEY FORM THEIR OWN OPINIONS. In the strictest sense of the word KNOWLEDGE IS POWER.[2] Without previous illumination a change in the *forms* of Government will be of no avail.[3] These are but the shadows, the virtue and rationality of the People at large are the substance, of Freedom: and where Corruption and Ignorance are prevalent, the best *forms* of Government are but the "Shadows of a Shade!"[4] We actually transfer the Sovereignty to the People, when we make them susceptible of it. In the present perilous state of our Constitution the Friends of Freedom, of Reason, and of Human Nature, must feel it their duty by every mean in their power to supply or circulate political information. We ask not their patronage: It will be obtained in proportion as we shall be found to deserve it.——Our Miscellany will be comprized in two sheets, or thirty-two pages, closely printed, the size and type the same as of this PROSPECTUS.——The contents will be

I.—An History of the domestic and foreign Occurrences of the preceding days.

II.—The Speeches in both Houses of Parliament: and during the Recess, select Parliamentary Speeches, from the commencement of the reign of Charles the First to the present æra, with Notes historical and biographical.

III.—Original Essays and Poetry, chiefly or altogether political.

Its chief objects are to co-operate (1) with the WHIG CLUB in procuring a repeal of Lord Grenville's and Mr. Pitt's bills, now passed into laws,[5] and (2) with the PATRIOTIC SOCIETIES, for obtaining a Right of Suffrage general and frequent.[6]

2. The phrase, derived from Francis Bacon's *De Haeresibus* (On Heresies) in *Meditationes sacrae* (Sacred Meditations), is quoted by Priestley in *An Essay on the First Principles of Government* (1768), 7 (*Watchman* [CC], 4n. 2).
3. That individual illumination rather than government is the source of progress in society is a Godwinian notion. See p. 241, n. 5 herein.
4. Edward Young, *A Paraphrase on Part of the Book of Job* (Dublin, 1719), line 187 (var.). Cf. lines 187–88: "Fond Man! the Vision of a Moment made! / Dream of a Dream! and Shadow of a Shade!" (14).
5. For C's attack on Lord Grenville's and Pitt's Bills, see *The Plot Discovered* (p. 274 herein). The Whig Club was very active in organizing opposition to the two Bills in 1795 and January 1796; but by February 1796 the Whigs no longer fought for the repeal of the two Bills, focusing instead on negotiations of peace with France. C's statement in n. 1 of *The Watchman* that the Bills had the positive effect of making "the language of political publications more cool and guarded" reflects a trend in Whig politics (*Watchman* (CC), xxxvii–viii, 385–90).
6. Patriotic societies, such as the London Corresponding Society, fought for parliamentary reforms, including annual parliaments and universal suffrage. In *The Watchman* C does not, as the Prospectus promises, take up the issue of parliamentary reform, given his Godwinian belief that social progress will be effected by general illumination rather than changes of government (see Colmer, 33).

In the cities of London, Bristol,   ,   , and   ,
it will appear as regularly as a Newspaper, over which it will have these
advantages:

I.—There being no advertisement, a greater quantity of original
matter must be given.

II.—From its form, it may be bound up at the end of the year, and
become an Annual Register.

III.—This last circumstance may induce Men of Letters to prefer
this Miscellany to more perishable publications, as the vehicle of their
effusions.

It remains to say, that whatever powers or acquirements the Editor
possesses, he will dedicate *entirely* to this work; and (which is of more
importance to the Public) he has received promises of occasional assistance from literary men of eminence and established reputation.
With such encouragement he offers himself to the Public as a faithful

WATCHMAN,

to proclaim the State of the Political Atmosphere, and preserve Freedom and her Friends from the attacks of Robbers and Assassins!!

MODERN PATRIOTISM

The title of the essay is derived from George Berkeley's "Maxims Concerning Patriotism," *Works*, 2 vols. (1784), 2:346, maxim 21: "I have no opinion of your bumper patriots. Some eat, some drink, some quarrel for their
country. MODERN PATRIOTISM." Coleridge borrowed the second volume of
Works from the Bristol Library in March 1796 (*Borrowings*, 122) and drew
on several of Berkeley's maxims for his satire on false patriots. As John
Colmer points out, Coleridge's satire is directed at "various types of reformers: the tavern demagogue, the uncritical disciple of Godwin, the
middle class radical whose chief activity seemed to be attending public
dinners, the rich Whig aristocrat with a taste for gaming, and the opponent of slavery who complacently enjoyed the benefits of the vile trade
* * *" (41). Coleridge's main target, however, was Godwin whose influence on radical reformists he tried to counteract. Although Coleridge acknowledged Godwin's "holy guidance" in the sonnet "To William Godwin"
published in the *Morning Post* on January 10, 1795, he did not, like
Wordsworth, go through a phase of uncritical conversion that he had to
outgrow. He met Godwin on January 21, 1794, at the house of Thomas
Holcroft, a radical reformist, notorious for his atheism, who was imprisoned for high treason in October 1794 but released without a trial in December (For Coleridge's negative opinion of him, see *CL*, 1:138–39). Even
before that meeting Coleridge was predisposed to take a critical stance toward Godwin's atheism (see his letter to Southey of September 11, 1794
[*CL*, 1:102]). Coleridge's main disagreement with Godwin concerned his
disregard for private attachments in the name of an abstract principle of
justice and his licentious views on marriage, the intercourse of the sexes,
and religion (see *Lects 1795* [*CC*], 46, 163–64; *Watchman* [*CC*], 196–97,
and p. 285, n. 4 herein).

According to Lewis Patton and Peter Mann, "Coleridge's response to Godwin was one of the most important single factors in his early political thinking," forcing him to develop a "Christian alternative to Godwin's atheistic radicalism" and to dissociate himself from radical reformers such as Thomas Paine, John Thelwall, and Holcroft (*Lects 1795* [*CC*], lxvii–lxxx). But cf. Nicholas Roe's diverging opinion that it was precisely Coleridge's "wish to counter Godwin's intellectual influence among other reformists" that did not isolate him from, but brought Coleridge to the very "epicentre of British radical life" (pp. 726–31 herein). For Coleridge's relationship with Godwin from 1800 to 1812 and his "remorse" expressed in marginalia and letters at having "spoken unkindly of such a Man," see *CM* (*CC*), 2:847 and n. 4; *Watchman* (*CC*), 197n. 1.

"Modern Patriotism" was responsible for inciting a highly critical review of *The Watchman* in the *Bristol Gazette* and a defense of Godwin against Coleridge's prejudicial treatment of him. Coleridge reproduced the review and his response to it in no. 5 of *The Watchman* (*Watchman* [*CC*], 194–98). Coleridge received a similar reaction to "Modern Patriotism" from Thelwall, an ardent Godwinian who helped disseminate Godwin's philosophy through his political lectures. Thelwall, as Coleridge's letter to him of May 13, 1796, shows, must have felt directly implicated in Coleridge's attack on false patriots in this essay (*CL*, 1:212–16).

Modern Patriotism

It is advisable that men should not deceive themselves, or their neighbours, by assuming titles which do not belong to them. Good Citizen——! why do you call yourself a PATRIOT?[1] You talk loudly and rapidly; but powers of vociferation do not constitute a PATRIOT.[2] You wish to be distinguished from the herd; you like victory in an argument; you are the tongue-major of every company: therefore you love a Tavern better than your own fire-side. Alas! you hate power in others, because you love power yourself![3] You are not a PATRIOT! You have studied Mr. Godwin's Essay on Political Justice; but to think filial affection folly, gratitude a crime, marriage injustice, and the promiscuous intercourse of the sexes right and wise, may class you among the despisers of vulgar prejudices,[4] but cannot increase the probability that you are a PATRIOT.

1. The reference is most likely to Thelwall, the leading spokesman of the London Corresponding Society, whose political lectures and his journal *The Tribune* were viewed by the government as responsible for the attack on the king's carriage on October 29, 1795, which precipitated the passing of the two Bills (see headnote to *The Plot Discovered*, p. 274 herein). The term "citizen" was a common form of address among members of radical political associations such as the London Corresponding Society. See p. 276, n. 8 herein and the following anecdote about Thelwall from *TT* (*CC*), 1:180–81: "We were once sitting in Somersetshire in a beautiful recess. I said to him—'Citizen John, this is a fine place to talk treason in!' 'Nay! Citizen Samuel!' replied he, 'it is rather a place to make a man forget that there is any necessity for treason!'" See also p. 278, n. 7 herein.
2. In Maxims 2 and 23 Berkeley mentions that "loud and vehement" outbursts against or for a court are "no proof of patriotism" (*Works*, 2:345–46). Cf. also Maxim 39: "A man rages, rails and raves; I suspect his patriotism" (2:348).
3. In Maxim 3 Berkeley contends that passion for money and an "appetite * * * for power" are at odds with the qualities that make a patriot (*Works*, 2:345).
4. C articulated the same indictment of Godwin in Lecture 3 of *LRR* (*Lects 1795* [*CC*], 164–65), as well as in a letter to Thelwall of May 18, 1796 (*CL*, 1:213). In *Political Justice* Godwin declared all attachments to family, friends, or benefactors as detrimental to justice and universal benevolence, which is secured by a rational assessment of individual merit and

But you act up to your principles.—So much the worse! Your principles
are villainous ones! I would not entrust my wife or sister to you—Think
you, I would entrust my country?[5] The PATRIOT indulges himself in no
comfort, which, if society were properly constituted, all men might not
enjoy; but you get drunk on claret, and you frequent public dinners,
where whole joints are stewed down into essences—and all for your
country! You are a Gamester—*you* a Patriot![6]——A very poor man was
lately hovering round a Butcher's shop—he wanted to buy a sheep's
liver; but your footman in livery outbid him, and your spaniel had it![7] I
doubt your Patriotism. You harangue against the Slave-Trade; you attribute the present scarcity to the war—yet you wear powder, and eat
pies and sugar![8] Your patriotism and philanthrophy cost you very little.
If I might presume so far, I would inform *how* you might become a Patriot. Your *heart* must believe,[9] that the good of the whole is the greatest possible good of each individual: that *therefore* it is your *duty* to be
just, because it is your *interest*.[1] In the present state of society, taking
away Hope and Fear, you cannot believe this—for it is not true; yet you
cannot be a Patriot unless you do believe it. How shall we reconcile
this apparent contradiction? You must give up your sensuality and your
philosophy, the pimp of your sensuality;[2] you must condescend to believe in a God, and in the existence of a Future State![3]

"the good of the whole." For Godwin's view of gratitude as having "no part either of justice
or virtue," causing one "to prefer one man to another, from some other consideration than
that of his superior usefulness or worth," see *Political Justice*, 1:83–84. For his views of co-
habitation as "an evil" that "checks the independent progress of mind," of "the institution of
marriage" as "a system of fraud," and of "the intercourse of the sexes" in a society without
marriage in which it may not be known "who is the father of each individual child," see *Political Justice*, 2:848–52. C consistently opposed Godwin's position that domestic affections
interfere with universal benevolence. But see p. 246, n. 8 herein for Godwin's later moderation of his views on private attachments.
5. C draws on Berkeley, Maxim 9: "A man who hath no sense of God or conscience: would you
make such a one guardian to your child? if not, why guardian to the state?" (*Works*, 2:345).
6. Berkeley points out that true patriots do not indulge in sensual pleasures in Maxim 5 ("It is
impossible an epicure should be a patriot") and in Maxim 11 ("A fop or man of pleasure
makes but a scurvy patriot"). He refers to "gamesters" in Maxim 25: "Gamesters, fops, rakes,
bullies, stock-jobbers: alas! what patriots?" (*Works*, 2:345–47). Colmer speculates that the
reference in this section to the Whig "taste for gaming" includes "a veiled attack on Fox; nor
would it have required much ingenuity to associate Horne Tooke with the democrat who appeared at all public dinners" (41). On Fox, who lost his whole fortune by indulging his passion for gaming, see *Lects 1795* (CC), 312n. 3.
7. Cf. CN, 1:67: "Reason for a Tax upon Dogs—Poor man—sheepsheads &c" (*Watchman*
[CC], 99n. 5).
8. Cf. C's essay "On the Slave Trade," where he exposed the hypocrisy of those who presumably oppose the slave trade without giving up food "sweetened with human blood"
(pp. 296–98 herein).
9. Cf. Berkeley, Maxim 1 ("Every man, by consulting his own heart, may easily know whether
he is or is not a patriot") and Maxim 32 ("Where the heart is right, there is true patriotism")
(*Works*, 2:345, 347).
1. The emphasis on "the good of the whole" to which individuals must be responsible is a commonplace in writings of this period, voiced among others by Priestley (*An Essay on the First
Principles of Government* [1761], 38, 41–42, 59), and Berkeley in Maxims 24 and 27
(*Works*, 2:347). C's target here is Godwin, whose commitment to this principle (e.g., *Political Justice*, 1:81; 2:856) appeared to C to be overly rationalistic and heartless, purchased at
the expense of private attachments. C found Hartley's definition of the coincidence of self-
interest and duty toward others more acceptable than Godwin's, because it did not rule out
the "pleasures of sympathy" and attachments to family and friends (see p. 289, n. 5 herein).
2. This is yet another attack on Godwin, whose philosophy C associated with sensuality and
atheism. See *Watchman* (CC), 196: "I do consider Mr. Godwin's Principles as vicious; and
his book as a Pandar to Sensuality."
3. Berkeley and Hartley are in the background of C's claim that a belief in God and a future
state are essential to true patriotism. Cf. Maxim 9 (cited p. 286, n. 5 herein); Maxim 4,

ON THE SLAVE TRADE

This essay appeared in the fourth issue of *The Watchman* (March 25, 1796) and is an abbreviated revised version of Coleridge's lecture on the slave trade delivered on June 16, 1795, at the Assembly Coffee-house in Bristol (see *Lects 1795* [CC], 232–51). In the 1790s Coleridge was a vehement opponent of the slave trade, supporting the efforts of Thomas Clarkson (1760–1846) and William Wilberforce (1759–1833), founders of the Society for the Suppression of the Slave Trade (1787), to put a stop to this inhumane practice. In the late 1780s the opposition against the slave trade grew rapidly in England, the parliament receiving numerous petitions requesting its prohibition. In response to this demand the parliament began a lengthy investigation of the slave trade, calling in many witnesses to testify about their knowledge of the methods used in acquiring slaves, the conditions of their transportation on ships and the treatment they received at the hands of the traders. In spite of shocking revelations of the crimes perpetrated against the slaves that surfaced during this investigation, Wilberforce's abolition bills introduced in the parliament from 1788 on failed repeatedly. An abolition bill was finally passed in 1807 under the Fox-Grenville Ministry, but it did not prevent the supply of slaves to British colonies by Spanish and Portuguese traders paid by British merchants. It was not until 1833 that slavery was abolished by an act of parliament throughout the British colonies.

In 1833, close to the end of his life, Coleridge wrote in a letter to the Scottish poet Thomas Pringle (1789–1834), who became secretary of the Anti-Slavery Society in 1827, that he had been "an ardent & almost lifelong Denouncer of Slavery" (*CL*, 6:940). His record as an abolitionist did indeed contain a number of outspoken denunciations of the slave trade, including his 1792 Greek poem "Ode on the Slave Trade," which won a gold medal from Cambridge University; his 1795 lecture on the slave trade; this essay from *The Watchman*; and his 1808 review in the *Edinburgh Review* of Clarkson's *The History of the Rise, Progress, and Accomplishment of the Abolition of the African Slave-Trade by the British Parliament*, 2 vols. (1808) (see *SW&F* [CC], 1:216–43). References to the slave trade also appear frequently in Coleridge's poetry of the 1790s. In later years, however, Coleridge did articulate views that are not in tune with the position on the slave trade he presented in this essay and other writings of the 1790s, expressing, for example, serious misgivings about accomplishing the abolition of the slave trade through acts of parliament and liberating slaves before they had been properly christianized (see Patrick J. Keane, *Coleridge's Submerged Politics*, 66–81).

---

which states that "a believer" has a "better chance" of being regarded as a patriot than "an infidel"; and Maxim 16, which notes that "he who hath no religion or no home makes a suspected patriot" (*Works*, 2:345, 346). Cf. Hartley's claim that "self-love is only to be destroyed by, and for the sake of, the love of God, and of our neighbour. Now the ultimate prevalency of these is a still stronger argument for a future life, in which we may first love God, and then our neighbour in and through him" (2:385–86).

On the Slave Trade

Whence arise our Miseries? Whence arise our Vices? From *imaginary* Wants. No man is wicked without temptation, no man is wretched without a cause. But if each among us confined his wishes to the actual necessaries and real comforts of Life, we should preclude all the causes of Complaint and all the motives to Iniquity. What Nature demands, she will supply, asking for it that portion only of *Toil*, which would otherwise have been necessary as *Exercise*.[1] But Providence, which has distinguished Man from the lower orders of Being by the progressiveness of his nature, forbids him to be contented. It has given us the restless faculty of *Imagination*.[2]

> *Hence* the soft Couch and many-colour'd Robe,
> The Timbrel and arch'd Dome and costly Feast
> With all th' inventive Arts that nurse the Soul
> To forms of Beauty; and by sensual wants
> Unsensualize the mind, which in the *Means*
> Learns to forget the grossness of the *End*,
> Best-pleasur'd with its own activity.
> And *hence* DISEASE that withers manhood's arm,
> The dagger'd ENVY, spirit-quenching WANT,
> WARRIORS, and LORDS, and PRIESTS—all the fore ills
> That vex and desolate our mortal life.
> Wide-wasting ills! yet each th' immediate source
> Of mightier good! Their keen necessities
> To ceaseless action, goading human thought
> Have made Earth's reasoning Animal her Lord,
> And the pale-featur'd SAGE's trembling hand
> Strong as an Host of armed Deities!
> From Avarice thus, from Luxury, and War
> Sprang heavenly SCIENCE, and from Science FREEDOM![3]
>   RELIGIOUS MUSINGS.

1. See Southey's letter to Horace Walpole Bedford of August 22, 1794, which details the pantisocracy project: "Whence arise the various vices and misfortunes that disgrace human nature and destroy human happiness?" Southey's answer to the origin of vice is "individual property" rather than "imaginary wants," and he refers to the minimal "daily toil" of half an hour that would be required to satisfy all "necessaries and comforts of life" if all people worked (*New Letters of Robert Southey*, ed. Kenneth Curry, 2 vols. [New York and London, 1965], 1:70). A closer source is Carl Bernhard Wadström, *An Essay on Colonization* (1794), a work C borrowed from the Bristol Library on June 15, 1795, a day before his lecture on the slave trade (*Borrowings*, 121; *Lects 1795* (CC), 235, n. 3). Wadström opposed the view that natives of Africa were "incurably stupid and indolent," arguing that "All men are idle till incited to industry, by their natural or artificial wants." He further noted that while their "soil easily supplies their natural necessities," European slave traders commonly incited them to develop artificial wants such as brandy "to intoxicate and amuse their chiefs, and to afford them the means of laying waste their country" (14–15). C exposes this practice of slave traders in a later passage that is indebted to Wadström (see p. 292, n. 7 herein).
2. In his "Lecture on the Slave Trade" C gives the imagination a much more expansive role than here, assigning it a divine origin and the "noble end" of focusing the mind on ever higher sights of "*real* excellence." But C also makes clear that the divine gift of imagination can be misused, leading to the formation of "unreal Wants," as exemplified "so dreadfully" by "the Slave Trade & the West India Commerce" (*Lects 1795* [CC], 235–36).
3. C reworks lines 220–38 of "Religious Musings" (p. 28 herein) by adding italics and capitals for greater emphasis, changing the punctuation, and changing two verbs from the past to the present tense.

I have the firmest Faith, that the final cause of all evils in the moral and natural world is to awaken intellectual activity. Man, a vicious and discontented *Animal*, by his vices and his discontent is urged to develope the powers of the Creator, and by new combinations of those powers to imitate his creativeness. And from such enlargement of mind Benevolence will necessarily follow;[4] Benevolence which may be defined "Natural Sympathy made permanent by an acquired Conviction, that the Interests of each and of all are one and the same," or in fewer words, "Natural Sympathy made permanent by enlightened Selfishness."[5] In my calmer moments I have the firmest Faith that all things work together for Good. But alas! it seems a long and a dark Process.

> The early Year's fast-flying Vapours stray
> In shadowing Trains across the orb of Day:
> And we, poor Insects of a few short Hours,
>   Deem it a world of Gloom.
> Were it not better hope a nobler doom
> Proud to believe, that with more active powers
> On rapid many-coloured Wing
> We thro' one bright perpetual Spring
> Shall hover round the Fruits and Flowers
> Screen'd by those Clouds & cherish'd by those Showers!
>   *From an unpublished Poem.*[6]

I have dwelt anxiously on this subject, with a particular view, to the Slave-trade, which, I knew, has insinuated in the minds of many, uneasy doubts respecting the existence of a beneficient[7] Deity. And indeed the evils arising from the formation of *imaginary* Wants, have in no instance been so dreadfully exemplified, as in this inhuman Traffic. We receive from the West-India Islands, Sugars, Rum, Cotton, Logwood,[8] Cocoa, Coffee, Pimento, Ginger, Indigo, Mahogany, and Conserves. Not one of these articles are necessary; indeed with the exception of Cotton and Mahogany we cannot truly call them even useful: and not one of them is at present attainable by the poor and labouring part of Society. In return we export vast

---

4. Cf. Hartley (2:292): "All meditations upon the attributes of God, and particularly upon his infinite benevolence to all his creatures, have a strong tendency to refine and augment our benevolent affections." Hartley's influence is already in evidence in the passage cited from "Religious Musings" in which all evil is seen as a necessary step in the ultimate perfectibility of mankind. For the influence of Hartley as well as Priestley on C's adoption of notions such as human perfectibility and the progressive annihilation of evil, see *Lects 1795* (CC), lviii–lxvii.

5. Hartley discusses the relationship among sympathy, benevolence, and self-interest and the progress from interested to disinterested benevolence. He divides self-interest into three classes—gross, refined and rational—and although recommending benevolence rather than any type of self-interest as the desired goal of life, establishes the superiority of rational self-interest (what C might refer to as "enlightened Selfishness"?) over the former two (1:458–70, 471–74). The subject of benevolence is given extensive coverage in 2:271–82, 283–308, where the coincidence between benevolence and self-interest is often noted, e.g., "As refined self-interest arises from benevolence, piety, and the moral sense; so, conversely, it promotes them in various ways. * * * And thus benevolence to a single person may ultimately become equal to self-interest, by this tendency of self-interest to increase benevolence, and reciprocally of benevolence to lessen self-interest * * *" (2:281, 286). For the related connection of duty and self-interest, see p. 286, n. 1 herein.

6. This poem, which did not appear again in collections published during C's life, was included in *PW*, 1:148 and given the title *Ver Perpetuum* (perpetual spring) by EHC.

7. In the BL copy of *The Watchman* (Ashley 2842) C corrected "beneficient" to "beneficent."

8. The heart of a West Indian tree used for dyeing fabrics.

quantities of necessary Tools, Raiment, and defensive Weapons, with great stores of Provision. So that in this Trade as in most others the Poor are employed with unceasing toil first to raise, and then to send away the Comforts, which they themselves absolutely want, in order to procure idle super-fluities for their Masters. If this Trade had never existed, no one human being would have been less comfortably cloathed, housed, or nourished. Such is its value—they who would estimate the price which we pay for it, may consult the evidence delivered before the House of Commons.[9] I will not mangle the feelings of my readers by detailing enormities, which the gloomy Imagination of Dante would scarcely have dared attribute to the Inhabitants of Hell.[1] For the honour of our common nature, I would fain hope that these accounts have been exaggerated. But, by the confession of all, these enormities might have been perpetrated and with impunity: and when was power possessed and not exercised? By the confession of all parties great cruelties have been inflicted: and therefore before I can suspect exaggeration, I must disbelieve the oaths of the humane and disinterested in compliment to the assertions of men from whose shoulders though I should take mountains of guilt, enough would remain to sink them to perdition.—These Facts have been pressed on the Public even to satiety. It is my present purpose to consider the objections to the Abolition of this Commerce—which may be reduced to the five following—First, that the Abolition would be useless, since though *we* should not carry it on, other nations would. II. That the Africans are better treated and more happy in the Plantations than in their native Country. III. That the Revenue would be greatly injured. IV. That the Right of Property would be invaded. V. That this is not a fit opportunity.

I. That if England abolish the Slave-trade, other nations will carry it on.[2] The same argument has been adduced by the* French Planters: a

---

* "Very soon this society of Friends to the Negroes require an abolition of the slave-trade: that is to say, that the profits which may result from it to the French commerce should be transferred to foreigners. For never will their romantic philosophy persuade the other European Powers &c." See the address of the Planters of St. Domingo to the French Legislature.[3]

9. See *An Abstract of the Evidence Delivered before a Select Committee of the House of Commons, in the Years 1790, and 1791* (1791), which contains the testimonies of various witnesses called in by the parliament for its investigation of the slave trade, including vivid details about the horrid conditions in which slaves were carried in ships and the countless atrocities to which they were subjected.

1. In "Lecture on the Slave Trade" C did not spare the feelings of his audience, documenting in greater detail than here the indignities and cruelties inflicted on slaves (*Lects 1795* [CC], 241–43). C refers to Dante's *Inferno*, a copy of which (in Henry Boyd's translation, 2 vols. [1785]) Southey had borrowed from the Bristol Library in September and October 1794 (*Borowings*, 118, and cf. CN, 1:170 and n.).

2. Thomas Clarkson, in *An Essay on the Impolicy of the African Trade*, 2nd ed. (1788), 129–32, considered and refuted this contention: "That the French would take it up, if the English abolished it, is, like most of the assertions of the advocates for slavery, but a bare conjecture; notwithstanding that it is assumed and delivered with as much confidence as if it were a fact." On the opposite side, Bryan Edwards, in *The History, Civil and Commercial, of the British Colonies in the West Indies*, 3 vols. (1703–1801), argued that if the English were to abolish the slave trade, other nations would simply increase their share in the trade, "or, having the choice and refusal of 38,000 more than they have at present, will become more difficult to please; confining their purchases to such only as are called prime slaves. Thus the old, and the very young, the sickly and the feeble, will be scornfully rejected; and perhaps *twenty* poor wretches be considered as unsaleable then, and sacrificed accordingly, to *one* that is so considered and sacrificed now" (2:108–09). C borrowed Clarkson's *Impolicy* from the Bristol Library in June 15–25, 1795, and volume 2 of Edwards's *History* from July 14 to August 7, 1795 (*Borrowings*, 121).

3. C cites variatim and shortens the following passage from *A Particular Account of the Commencement and Progress of the Insurrection of the Negroes in St. Domingo * * *, 2nd ed.

sufficient proof of its fallacy. Somebody must *begin*; and there is little reason to fear, that a wise and politic example will not be followed.[4] As Society is constituted, there will be always highway robberies: it is useless therefore to prevent any *one* man from committing them. Fortunately for Travellers this logic will not hold good in law. But although it cannot operate in favour of little Rogues, it appears to possess wonderful power in the higher circles of Villany. Assuming the universal depravity of Mankind as an axiom, a corrupt member of Parliament lulls his Conscience to sleep with "to be sure these bills are subversive of the Constitution; but with such immense treasures to bestow, Ministry *will* secure a majority in the House: my opposition will therefore be useless to my Country; and if I vote for them, I shall only assist to do what would be otherwise done without me—and why should I not have this contract, or this sinecure, as well as another man, who perhaps would make a worse use of it?" &c.

II. That the Slaves are more humanely treated and live more happily in the Plantations than in their native Country[5]—If any incredulous person should entertain a doubt of this, the slave-merchants, slave-holders, and slave-drivers together with the manufacturers of neck-collars and thumb-screws, are ready and willing to take their bible oaths of it!!—When treated with tolerable humanity the human race

---

(1792): "On a sudden this society demands *an Abolition of the Slave-Trade*; that is to say, that the profits, which may result from it to the French commerce, should be transferred to foreigners; for, never will their romantic philosophy persuade all the European powers, that it is incumbent upon them to abandon the culture of their colonies, and to leave the natives of Africa a prey to the barbarity of their native tyrants, rather than employ them elsewhere, and under more humane masters, in cultivating a soil, which, without them, must remain uncultivated, and whose valuable productions are, to the nation which possesses them, a fertile source of industry and prosperity" (19). The reference is to the *Societé des Amis des Noirs*, a group that promoted the abolition of the slave trade in France. Under its influence the French National Assembly issued a decree in May 1791 that gave citizenship to free-born people of color in French colonies. The resistance to this decree by white planters in the island of St. Domingo led to a ferocious uprising by black slaves and mulattos. The planters, after an unsuccessful appeal to the French Assembly, asked the British for help, who sent troops to stop the uprising (*Lects 1795* [CC], 239n. 4). *A Particular Account* is a translation of the speech made by the French Planters to the National Assembly on November 3, 1791, requesting the repeal of the decree of May 1791 and describing the enormous atrocities committed against the planters by the slaves. A survey of the history of the French colony of St. Domingo, including a detailed account of the uprising against the planters is provided by Edwards (*History*, 3:3–258).

4. C draws on Clarkson who argued that, if the English abolished the slave trade, the French would do so as well, not out of humanitarian reasons but because they "are well aware that nations are guided by motives, that are termed *political*; that if we were to put a stop to the trade, it would be probably from the consideration of its *impolicy*; and that if it were *politick* in us to abolish it, it would be *equally so* in them" (*Impolicy*, 129).

5. This argument is advanced in *A Particular Account*: "The situation of the negroes, in Africa, without property, without political or civil existence, continually a prey to the weak capricious fury of tyrants, who divide among them that vast uncivilized country, is changed in our colonies for a condition of comfort and enjoyment" (16). This was a claim often made by slave traders who tried to defend their occupation during the inquiry initiated by the British Parliament about the trade. Excerpts from their statements appear in a telling fourteen-page tract by a citizen from Derby who originally signed a petition in favor of the abolition of the slave trade but regretted it when he was informed by a parson who had been in Jamaica that the condition of the slaves in colonies was far better than that of poor laborers in England (*The True State of the Question. Addressed to the Petitioners for the Abolition of the Slave Trade* [1792]). Cf. Clarkson, *Slavery* (1788): "It is affirmed that the punishments, which the Africans undergo, are less severe than the military; that their life is happier than that of the English peasant; * * * that they have their little spots of ground, their holy-days, their dances; in short, that their life is a scene of festivity and mirth, and that they are much happier in the colonies than in their own country" (147). Clarkson goes on to refute these claims (147–57).

as well as other animals, multiply.—The Negroes multiply in their native country:—They do *not* multiply in the West-India Islands;[6] for if they did, the slave-trade would have been abolished long ago by its inutility.—This is a fact which no perjury can overwhelm, which no sophistry can undermine.

The tyranny of the African Chiefs is in a great measure owing to the agency of Europeans, who flock to their Courts, and seduce them by bribery, and madden them by intoxication.[7] The Africans are not slaves in their native Country;[8] Slavery is their highest punishment for the greatest crimes, which their Chiefs now wantonly impute to the innocent for the sole purpose of making them slaves in order to sell them to the European Merchants: and with the same views the Chiefs make war with each other. Wadestrom, a disinterested and religious man, who has travelled into the interior parts of Africa, informs us, that the Africans who are situated beyond the contagion of European Vice, are innocent and happy. The peaceful Inhabitants of a fertile soil, they cultivate their fields in common, and reap the crop as the common property of all. Each Family, like the Peasants in some parts of Europe, spins, weaves, sews, hunts, fishes, and makes baskets, fishing-tackle, and the implements of agriculture: and this variety of employment gives an acuteness of intellect to the Negro which the Mechanic whom the division of labor condemns to one simple operation is precluded from attaining.[9]

III. That the Revenue would be injured.—To the friends of humanity this is indeed a cogent argument against the abolition. They will doubtless reflect, how worthily this Revenue has been employed for these last hundred years—they will review with delight waste-lands cultivated, sciences publickly protected and rewarded, population in-

---

6. Clarkson notes that slaves multiply in their own country but decrease dramatically in colonies. He gives the example of a colony in Europe in which 650,000 imported slaves decreased to 140,000 within a hundred years, arguing that under normal conditions 10,000 people would in their own country produce more descendants during the same time, that is, about 160,000. "This is the proportion in which the Americans increased; and the Africans in their own country increase in the same, if not in a greater proportion" (*Slavery*, 156, 157n.). Cf. also *Impolicy*, 87, where Clarkson shows that slaves increased in number on plantations where they were treated with greater humanity.
7. For this section of the essay C draws on Wadström, 1:12–18. Wadström exposes "the infamous arts of the Europeans" who customarily intoxicate African chiefs in order to obtain slaves: "So very successful, indeed, have the European slave-dealers been, in exciting in them a thirst for spirits, that it is now become one of the principal pillars of their trade; for the chiefs, intoxicated by the liquor with which they are purposely bribed by the whites, often make bargains and give orders fatal to their subjects, and which, when sober, they would gladly retract" (12).
8. Cf. Clarkson, *Cries of Africa* (1822), 40: "The fact is, that there are but few slaves in Africa at all. Nineteen out of twenty of the population there are freemen; and it is this circumstance which renders the fate of most of them so peculiarly distressing."
9. Wadström, 1:14–8. In answer to common allegations that the Africans are "indolent," Wadström produces proof of their varied manufactures "some of which equal any articles of the kind fabricated in Europe" (14). C reproduces parts of Wadström's text almost verbatim, e.g., "Each individual or family, like the peasants in some parts of Europe, spins, weaves, sews, hunts, fishes, and makes baskets, fishing-tackle and implements of agriculture * * *" (16). Wadström notes the practice among Africans of cultivating the fields and reaping the crop "which is considered as the common property of the inhabitants" (17) and the fact that variety of employment sharpens their intellect: "* * * as the situation of the Africans approaches much nearer to that of intelligent peasants than that of stupid mechanics, I am inclined to think that their intellects may have been improved by being so variously exercised * * *" (17–18).

creased, and the peasantry of England and *Ireland* instructed in useful learning, and humanized. The universal plenty, which this Revenue has been applied to scatter and secure, they will recognize in every lane, hamlet, and cottage—REVENUE, the grand preventive against that fiendish composition of Murder and Suicide, called WAR REVENUE! that so completely precludes Intoxication in the lower classes, Luxury in the higher ranks, and Bribery in all!—The friends of humanity may mourn that so excellent an end could not be effected by less calamitous means; but they will stifle their feelings, and lose the miseries of the West-Indies in the contemplation of that paradisiacal state of their native country—for which it is indebted to this well-raised, well-applied REVENUE, which while it remains in such *pure* hands, no friend of Freedom and Virtue can possibly wish diminished!!—If to start a doubt were practicable, it might perhaps be hinted, that the Revenue must be always in proportion to the wealth of the nation, and that it seems to have been proved, that the West-India trade is more often a losing than a winning trade[1]—a Lottery with more blanks than prizes in it. It is likewise asserted to be the grave of our Seamen.[2] This argument therefore, however cogent it would otherwise have been, ought not to have been adduced, till these doubts had been cleared up, and this assertion satisfactorily disproved.

IV. That the Right of Property would be injured.[3]—Yes perhaps, if immediate emancipation had been the object of Mr. Wilberforce's bill.[4] But how would the right of property be invaded by a law which should leave the estate and every thing on it untouched, and only prevent the owner from *forcing* men to work for him? from *forcing* men to leave their friends and country, and live slaves in a climate so unwholesome or beneath a usage so unnatural, that contrary to the universal law of life they annually diminish? Can a man possess a right to commit actual and virtual murder? to shorten and prevent existence? It is a well-known and incontrovertible fact, that in some few planta-

1. See Clarkson, *Impolicy*, esp. 103–11. The "patrons of the slave trade," Clarkson notes, "assert first, that if such an event were to take place, it would *annihilate a considerable branch of the revenue*" (103). Clarkson goes on to document the loss of duty on items exported to Africa or imported into England and concludes that "the revenue could not possibly be diminished, in consequence of the abolition of the slave trade, till the rising generation were put into employ. It is probable that it would be increased: and it is certain that it *could* be made, under proper regulations, to receive a greater augmentation in this, than in any former period of an equal length" (111). Specific losses incurred in the West India trade are addressed by Clarkson in *Impolicy* (54–58).
2. Cf. Clarkson, *Impolicy* (49–50): "I come now to the argument, upon which so great a stress has been laid, that *the slave trade is a nursery for our seamen*. The truth of this argument I deny in the most explicit and unequivocal manner. I assert, on the other hand, that it is a *grave* for our seamen, and that it destroys more in *one* year, than *all the other* trades of Great Britain, when put together, destroy in *two*."
3. The fear that the abolition of the slave trade would injure property rights was often voiced in debates in the Parliament and was one of the factors that caused the repeated failures of abolition bills introduced by Wilberforce. See, e.g., W. Young's objection to Wilberforce's bill (in the March 15, 1796, debate) that it would bring ruin to West India merchants and planters and deprive him of his own property (*Parl. Hist.*, 32:866).
4. In the debate of April 2, 1792, in the House of Commons, Wilberforce explicitly denied allegations that immediate emancipation was the intent of his motion for the abolition of the slave trade: "It was pretty generally, and he believed rather industriously, rumoured abroad, that it was his design, and that of his friends, to propose, besides an abolition of the trade, the immediate emancipation of the negroes. This, however, was an intention he could never have entertained for a moment" (*Parl. Hist.*, 29:1057).

tions in which tyranny has been instructed by an enlightened selfishness to relax and soften her features, there have been no slaves bought for a series of years.[5] By whomever therefore they have been bought yearly, yearly murders must have been committed!

V. This is not the time—This not the time?[6] "The French (says Abbe Sieyes)[7] hear with delight of the numerous armaments which England sends to certain death in the West-India Islands. We make war there more effectually as well as economically by sending over a few adventurous officers to preach the rights of man to the negroes, and furnish them with weapons to assert those rights."—What can prevent the success of these intrigues among the slaves, but the most active humanity on the part of their present masters?

Such have been the cosmetics with which our parliamentary orators have endeavoured to conceal the deformities of a commerce, which is blotched all over with one leprosy of evil. In the year 1786 its enormities became the subject of general conversation, and in the following years petitions poured into parliament from various parts of the kingdom, requesting its abolition. The bill for that purpose passed the House of Commons mangled and mutilated by the *amendments* of Mr. Dundas, and it has been dying ever since of a slow decline in the House of Lords.[8] The jealous spirit of liberty placed the Elector of Hanover on the throne of Great Britain: and the Duke of Clarence, one of his illustrious descendants, made his maiden speech in favour of the slave trade![9] For the last unsuccessful attempt to expedite the abolition in the House of Commons, see the proceedings in the

---

5. As pointed out by Clarkson (see p. 292, n. 6 herein). "Enlightened selfishness" is a phrase C used earlier in the essay in a different context (see p. 289, n. 5 herein).

6. A frequent statement made in debates in the parliament. See, e.g., the speech by Home Secretary Henry Dundas (1742–1811) in the debate of February 26, 1795 ("The propriety of abolishing the slave trade he thought no man could doubt; and he thought it equally clear, that this was not the period for its abolition" [*Parl. Hist.*, 31:1340]) and again in the debate of March 15, 1796 ("he thought that the African slave trade was contrary to justice and humanity, and that it ought to be abolished; but he had no hesitation in saying, that it was not possible for parliament to give effect to the bill at the present moment" [*Parl. Hist.*, 32:877]).

7. Emmanuel-Joseph, abbé Sieyès (1748–1836), proponent of new constitutions for France and author of a pamphlet on the third estate that was highly influential in the early phase of the French Revolution. For C's references to Sieyès in contributions to the *MP* on the French constitution, see *EOT* (CC) 1:31n. 2; 33n. 8; 47–49; 52–53; 100. C reproduces variatim a citation from the *Morning Chronicle* of January 6, 1796 (*Watchman* [CC], 136n. 1).

8. In 1792 Wilberforce's motion of April 2 for the abolition of the slave trade was amended by Henry Dundas in favor of gradual abolition and the amendment succeeded in the debate of April 23 (see *Parl. Hist.*, 29:1055–158; 1203–93). At that time the House of Commons also resolved to abolish the slave trade by January 1, 1796, but it was not until 1807 that the abolition of the slave trade became law. On February 26, 1795, Wilberforce once again introduced a motion to abolish the slave trade, and Dundas proposed that "it should be done gradually, and with such an allowance of time as would not make it felt very severely" (*Parl. Hist.*, 31:1340).

9. In the BL copy C changed the last part of the sentence to: "IN FAVOUR OF THE SLAVE TRADE!!" Prince William Henry (1765–1837), duke of Clarence, gave his maiden speech on May 3, 1792, opposing the abolition of the slave trade on the ground that he had information that the slaves were "far from being miserable," enjoying a "state of humble happiness." He also voiced concern about the effect of the abolition on "the great property and the immense commerce which was intimately connected with this trade" (*Parl. Hist.*, 29:1349–50). For another vituperative reaction to this speech, see Benjamin Flower (1755–1829), editor of *The Cambridge Intelligencer*, in *The French Constitution; with Remarks on Some of the Principal Articles*, 2nd ed. (1792), 450–51.

British Legislature in this Number.[1] Gracious God! enormities, at which a Caligula might have turned pale, are authorised by our laws, and jocosely defended by our Princes; and yet we have the impudence to call the French a Nation of *Atheists!*[2] They, who believe a God, believe him to the loving Parent of all men,—And is it possible that they who really believe and fear the Father, should fearlessly authorize the oppression of his Children?[3] The Slavery and Tortures, and most horrible Murder of tens of thousands of his Children!

Yes! the wicked and malignant can believe a God—they need not the solutions, which the enlarged views of the Optimist prompt; their own hearts teach them, that an intelligent being may be malevolent; and what they themselves are, they impiously imagine of the Deity. These men are are not Atheists, they are the causes of Atheism.— There are some who think Mr. Pitt sincere in his zeal for the abolition of this Trade; and I must certainly applaud their charity: but charity itself will allow that there are suspicious circumstances.[4] Several violent and unpopular bills have lately been carried through both Houses[5]— how came this bill, (certainly not an unpopular measure) to fail? It has been generally supposed, that a majority is always at the command of the existing minister; indeed that in the present state of the Constitution he could not guide the machine of government without an arranged majority. In answer to this objection, it has been confidently asserted by the advocates for Mr. Pitt, that the cabinet was divided on the subject; and at length agreed that the friends of the minister should be left, each individual to his own opinion. The cabinet therefore, we may suppose, were unanimous with regard to the late sedition

1. C refers to the debate of March 15, 1796, on Wilberforce's motion to abolish the slave trade (for his summary of this debate, see *Watchman* [CC], 155–58). For a similar indignant review of the fate of various abolition bills, cf. Flower, *The French Constitution*, 449–52.
2. C alludes to the fact that the French, so often branded as atheists by opponents of the French Revolution, in fact had abolished the slave trade (in 1794 under Robespierre), whereas the English, who prided themselves on their Christian faith, continued this criminal activity. Cf. C's related indictment of English war crimes, which far outweigh the excesses of the French, those "enemies of Religion," in *Conciones ad Populum* (pp. 251–52 herein). Cf. also Anthony Benezet's indictment of the English in *A Short Account of That Part of Africa Inhabited by the Negroes* (Philadelphia, 1762): "Were we to hear or read of any other Nation in the World that did destroy every Year, in some other Way, or on some other Account, as many human Creatures as are destroyed by this Trade, we should look upon them as a very bloody, cruel, barbarous People" (39–40).
3. The incompatibility between Christianity and the slave trade is often stressed in anti-abolitionist literature (see Clarkson, *Slavery*, 85–86, 160–67). As Clarkson contends, the primary doctrine of Christianity "is that of brotherly love. It commands good will towards men. It enjoins us to love our neighbours as ourselves, and to do unto all men, as we would that they should do unto us. And how can any man fulfil this scheme of universal benevolence, who reduces an unfortunate person *against his will*, to the *most insupportable* of all human conditions. * * * These doctrines therefore are sufficient to shew, that slavery is incompatible with the Christian system" (162–63). Granville Sharp, in *The Just Limitation of Slavery in the Laws of God, Compared with the Unbounded Claims of the African Traders and British American Slaveholders* (1776), argued that slavery is inconsistent with the Jewish law or God's promises in the New Testament made to all mankind without any exception. Cf. also Flower, *The French Constitution*, 450: "What were those Lords who call themselves SPIRITUAL—THE SUCCESSORS OF THE APOSTLES—THE BISHOPS—about? Where was their christianity, or even their humanity, when they suffered the accursed traffic to continue, without making a single effort to abolish it?"
4. Although Pitt opposed the slave trade on many occasions, his failure to influence the passing of the abolition bills made C suspect him to be disingenuous. A similar suspicion was voiced by Flower in *The French Constitution*, 451 (*Lects 1795* [CC], 245n. 3).
5. Such as, e.g., the renewal in February 1795 of the 1794 Habeas Corpus Suspension Act.

and treason bills; and to this unanimity we may attribute the speed
with which they were precipitated into laws.[6] But it may be answered,
that to unloose the fetters from the limbs of their brethren was a perfectly novel employment, and that therefore we ought not to wonder,
if the minister and his friends are slow and aukward and finally unsuccessful. But to fasten them on is an old job, and difficult as it appears to the inexperienced, they executed it with an ease and rapidity
which might have astonished the oldest turnkey in Newgate.[7]

The Abbe Raynal computes that at the time of his writing,[8] nine
millions of slaves had been consumed by the Europeans—add one
million since, (for it is near thirty years since his book was first published) and recollect, that for one procured ten at least are slaugh-
tered, that a fifth die in the passage, and a third in the seasoning;[9] and
the calculation will amount to ONE HUNDRED and EIGHTY MILLION! Ye
who have joined in this confederacy, ask of yourselves this fearful
question—"if the God of Justice inflict on us that mass only of anguish which we have wantonly heaped on our brethren, what must a
state of retribution be["]?[1] But who are they who have joined in this
tartarean confederacy? Who are these kidnappers, and assassins?[2] In
all reasonings neglecting the intermediate links we attribute the final
effect to the first cause. And what is the first and constantly acting
cause of the Slave-trade? That cause, by which it exists and deprived
of which it would immediately cease? Is it not self-evidently the consumption of its products? And does not then the guilt rest on the con-
sumers? And is it not an allowed axiom in morality, that wickedness
may be multiplied, but cannot be divided; and that the guilt of all, at-
taches to each one who is knowingly an accomplice.[3] Think not of the

6. On the sedition and treason Bills, see *The Plot Discovered* (p. 274 herein).
7. The infamous prison in London.
8. In *A Philosophical and Political History of the Settlement and Trade of the Europeans in the
East and West Indies,* trans. J. O. Justamond, 8 vols. (1783 [originally published in 1770]),
Guillaume-Thomas-François Raynal showed that of the eight or nine million slaves sent to
European colonies, only fourteen or fifteen hundred thousand survived (5:274). He attributed this high rate of mortality to the cruel manner in which the slaves were treated in
colonies, suggesting that measures such as "lessening labour, alleviating punishments and
rendering to man part of his rights" would alleviate this situation (5:274–76).
9. In the first edition of *Slavery* (1786) Clarkson estimated that "at least one fifth of the exported negroes perish in the passage," i.e., "not less than *twenty thousand*" (129 and n.). In
the second edition (1788) Clarkson admitted to have been mistaken about this estimate and
found the number of slaves lost in the Middle Passage to be higher, i.e., one fourth (103–04
and n.). On the mortality rate of slaves during "seasoning" in colonies, C again draws on
Clarkson: "One third of the whole number imported, is often computed to be lost in the seasoning, which, in round numbers, will be 25,000" (*Slavery* [1788], 104 and n.). Cf. Flower,
The French Constitution, 449: "It appears, on a moderate computation, that between 40 and
50,000 slaves are annually imported into our islands * * * and that one third of this number, 14,000, are annually murdered by the methods taken to procure them, or by the cruelties committed in the middle passage, and in what is called the *seasoning* in the West
Indies."
1. The text omits closing quotation marks, and it is not clear whether they should be placed
here or elsewhere in the passage.
2. Kidnapping was a common method of procuring slaves and was a focus of the investigation
of the slave trade in the parliament. See, e.g., the testimony of Alex Falconbridge (who
served as surgeon on voyages to Africa and West Indies) supporting this idea (*Abridgment of
the Minutes of the Evidence, Taken before a Committee of the Whole House, to Whom it Was
Referred to Consider of the Slave-Trade* [1789–91], no. 2 [1790]: 225–44). Clarkson also argued that nearly half of the one hundred thousand slaves transported to colonies were acquired through kidnapping (*Slavery* [1788], 33–39).
3. In the BL copy C changed the period to a question mark at the end of the sentence.

slave-captains and slave-holders—these very men, their darkened minds, and brutalized hearts, will prove one part of the dreadful charge against you.[4] They are more to be pitied than the slaves; because more depraved. I address myself to you who independently of all political distinctions, profess yourself Christians! As you hope to live with Christ hereafter, you are commanded to do unto others as ye would that others should do unto you. Would you[5] choose, that a slave merchant should incite an intoxicated Chieftain to make war on your Country, and murder your Wife and Children before your face, or drag them with yourself to the Market? Would you choose to be sold,[6] to have the hot iron hiss upon your breasts, after having been crammed into the hold of a Ship with so many fellow-victims, that the heat and stench[7] arising from your diseased bodies, should rot the very planks? Would you[8] that others should do this unto you?[9] and if you shudder with selfish horror at the bare idea, do you yet dare be the occasion of it to others?—The application to the Legislature was altogether wrong. I am not convinced that on any occasion a Christian is justified in calling for the interference of secular power; but on the present occasion it was superfluous. If only one tenth part among you who profess yourselves Christians, if one half only of the Petitioners,[1] instead of bustling about with ostentatious sensibility, were to leave off—not *all* the West-India commodities—but only Sugar and Rum, the one useless and the other pernicious—all this misery might be stopped.[2] Gracious Heaven![3] At your meals you rise up, and pressing your hands to your bosoms, you lift up your eyes to God, and say, "O Lord! bless the food which thou hast given us!" A part of that food among most of you, is sweetened with Brother's Blood.[4] "Lord! bless the food which thou hast given us!" O Blasphemy! Did God give food mingled with the blood of the Murdered? Will God bless the food which is polluted with the Blood of his own innocent children? Surely if the inspired Philanthropist[5] of

---

4. In the BL copy C changed the period to an exclamation mark at the end of the sentence.
5. In the BL copy C italicized "you."
6. In the BL copy C changed the comma to a question mark.
7. In the BL copy C added a comma after "stench."
8. In the BL copy C italicized "you."
9. In the BL copy C italicized "you."
1. In the BL copy C placed a comma after "Christians" and a semicolon after "Petitioners."
2. In the BL copy C changed "stopped" to "ended."
3. Cf. Flower, *The French Constitution*, 452: "The most pathetic and powerful appeals have been repeatedly made to the honour, to the justice, to the humanity, and to the christianity of our Slave Merchants and West India Planters. These have produced no other effect, than to draw forth a new specimen of the hardness of the human heart * * *." Flower also indicates, like C, that given the futility of petitions to the Parliament or appeals to slave traders, the best way to subvert the slave trade is to abstain from consuming sugar and other products of the trade. Flower recommends to ladies in particular two treatises that have dealt with this subject, one by William Fox (*An Address to the People of Great Britain, on the Propriety of Abstaining from West India Sugar and Rum* [1791]), which showed that 38,000 people who abstained from sugar and rum could bring the slave trade to a standstill (3); the other by Samuel Bradburn (*An Address, to the People Called Methodists; Concerning the Wickedness of Encouraging Slavery* [1792]), which recommended abstention from sugar and rum as one of three measures meant to promote the abolition of the slave trade, the other two being petitioning to the parliament and praying to God (see esp. 12, 17–23).
4. Cf. Flower, *The French Constitution*, 453: "Let them [the ladies], if they can, when reflecting on this subject, continue morning and evening, to sweeten their tea, and the tea of their families and visitors, with the blood of their fellow creatures * * *."
5. In the BL copy C changed "inspired Philanthropist" to "redeeming Theanthropist."

Gallilee were to revisit Earth, and be among the Feasters as at Cana, he would not now change water into wine, but convert the produce into the things producing, the occasion into the things occasioned. Then with our fleshly eye should we behold what even now Imagination ought to paint to us; instead of conserves, tears and blood, and for music, groanings and the loud peals of the lash.

There is observable among the Many a false and bastard sensibility[6] that prompts them to remove those evils and those evils alone, which by hideous spectacle or clamorous outcry are present to their senses, and disturb their selfish enjoyments. Other miseries, though equally certain and far more horrible, they not only do not endeavour to remedy—they support, they fatten on them. Provided the dunghill be not before their parlour window, they are well content to know that it exists, and that it is the hot-bed of their pestilent luxuries.—To this grievous failing we must attribute the frequency of wars, and the continuance of the Slave-trade. The merchant finds no argument against it in his ledger: the citizen at the crouded feast is not nauseated by the stench and filth of the slave-vessel—the fine lady's nerves are not shattered by the shrieks! She sips a beverage sweetened with human blood, even while she is weeping over the refined sorrows of Werter or[7] of Clementina.[8] Sensibility is not Benevolence.[9] Nay, by making us tremblingly alive to trifling misfortunes, it frequently prevents it, and induces effeminate and cowardly selfishness. Our own sorrows, like the Princes of Hell in Milton's Pandemonium, sit enthroned "bulky and vast:"[1] while the miseries of our fellow-creatures dwindle into pigmy forms, and are crouded, an innumerable multitude, into some dark corner of the heart. There is one criterion by which we may always distinguish benevolence from mere sensibility—Benevolence impels to action, and is accompanied by self-denial.[2]

---

6. This paragraph was reprinted in *Omniana*, ed. Robert Southey, 2 vols. (1812), 2:2–4, with a number of alterations that improve the prose in some instances. Compare, e.g., the opening sentence of the paragraph here with the following version in *Omniana*: "There is observable among the many, a false and bastard sensibility, prompting them to remove those evils and those alone, which disturb their enjoyments by being present to their senses." See also the version that appeared in AR (1825), 51–54, under the heading "Reflections Respecting Morality." See also "On Sensibility" (AR [CC], 57–61).

7. Johann Wolfgang von Goethe, *Die Leiden des jungen Werthers* (The Sorrows of Young Werther), originally published in Germany in 1774 and available in several English translations. The impact of the novel was powerful enough to cause a series of suicides in Germany in imitation of its hero (see CN, 1:398n.).

8. A character in the novel *History of Sir Charles Grandison* by Samuel Richardson (1689–1761). She suffers a bout of madness because she cannot marry Sir Charles.

9. Cf. Flower, *The French Constitution*, 453: "but should they [the ladies] continue such a practice [of sweetening their tea with blood of slaves], they must be not surprised, if some persons should presume to think, that the pretensions of the present age to exalted sentiments, refined feelings, and exquisite sensibility, are little more than pretensions; and that pure sterling excellence and goodness are not so often found in real life, as in the imagination of the poet and the novelist."

1. C recollects a passage from Milton, *Paradise Lost*, on Satan ("in bulk as huge / As whom the Fables name of monstrous size," 1.196–97) and a passage from *Samsom Agonistes* ("Though in these chains, bulk without spirit vast," line 1238). *Watchman* (CC), 139n. 6.

2. In "Lecture on the Slave Trade" C's discussion of benevolence included an attack not just on the ladies but also on Godwin in terms that anticipate his essay on "Modern Patriotism": "True Benevolence is the only possible Basis of Patriotism, and I am afraid, that what with sensuality and Vanity, and yet more disgusting Pride—true Benevolence is a rare Quality among us" (*Lects 1795* [CC], 249).

P. S.[3] It has been objected, that if we leave off sugar and rum, why not the other West-India commodities, as cotton and mahogany? To this we answer, First, that if the reasons adduced against the use of sugar and rum be valid and irresistible, and the same reasons apply to cotton and mahogany, why should we not disuse them? Surely no impossibility, no insurmountable inconvenience is implied. The whole objection resolves itself into this—If sugar and rum were the only West-India commodities, I could be honest and act like a Christian; but because I like cotton better than linen, and think mahogany genteeler furniture than oak, it is impossible. Secondly, the disuse of sugar and rum only would in a certain number of years prove the adequate means of abolishing the whole of the trade. And there is reason to believe that the additional disuse of cotton, mahogany, &c. would not accelerate the time; for when we might proselyte fifty to the disuse of sugar, we could not perhaps make five persons converts to the disuse of *all* the West-India commodities. So that what we should gain in point of time by the greater quantity of commodities disused, we should more than lose by the smaller number of persons disusing them. This the very objection makes probable. For they, who start it, do not start it in favour of a severe consistency, but in the hope of keeping themselves in countenance by the multitude of their accomplices. But thirdly, the other West-India commodities do not require such intense labor in their growth and preparation, as the Sugar and Rum. They might be raised by European Labourers. The Sugar plantations make Africans necessary, and their slavery intolerable.

I have read and heard one argument in favour of the slave-trade, which I mention chiefly on account of its seditious and treasonable tendency. It has been asserted by more than one Writer on the subject, that the plantation slaves are at least as well off as the peasantry in England. Now I appeal to common sense, whether to affirm that the slaves are as well off as our peasantry, be not the same as to assert that our peasantry are as bad off as negro-slaves? And whether if our peasantry believed it, they would not be inclined to rebel?[4]

ONCE A JACOBIN ALWAYS A JACOBIN (1802)

The Jacobins were a political group, originally associated with Club Breton in Versaille, which gained increasing influence during the French Revolution. The Jacobins evolved rapidly with the political conflicts and power shifts of the period, from the first founding of the Jacobin Clubs in 1789 to the legislated closing of those clubs in August 1795. In 1793 the Jacobins became instrumental in the overthrow of the monarchy, the elim-

---

3. A vertical line across the postscript in the BL copy suggests that C intended to delete the concluding two paragraphs of the essay.
4. Cf. Flowers, *The French Constitution*, 450–51, on Prince William Henry's maiden speech in favor of the slave trade: "How could a ROYAL DUKE be so inattentive to that respect due to himself, and to the ILLUSTRIOUS FAMILY to which he belongs, as to make his *Maiden* speech in defence of *Slavery!*—To intimate, that the miserable slaves in the West Indies, are as happy as the poor (a large class of his Father's subjects) in this kingdom! (*Lects 1795* [CC], 244n. 5).

ination of the more moderate Girondists led by Jean Jacques-Pierre Brissot (1754–1793) and the subsequent reign of Terror, during which about forty thousand "counter-revolutionaries" were guillotined. (On the rapid changes that took place among Jacobins from the original middle-class reformers of 1789 to the "Jacobin Dictatorship" of 1793–94, see Isser Woloch, *Jacobin Legacy: The Democratic Movement Under the Directory* [Princeton, 1970]). Although the Jacobins lost their power after the fall of Robespierre in 1794, in England their principles were perceived as having "infected" numerous radicals, and the term "Jacobin" was generally attached to anyone who approved of revolutionary violence, professed atheism, criticized the monarchy and the church, and became an advocate for liberty, equality, and democratic reforms. Coleridge was well aware that his political and religious lectures of 1795 made him an easy target for accusations of harboring Jacobinic sentiments. This essay represents Coleridge's concerted effort to contain the fanatic reaction against Jacobinism in England and clear himself from the suspicion that he supported "the system of French politics."

The essay was published in the *Morning Post* on October 21, 1802. Its title refers to Pitt's "Security" speech of February 17, 1800, on the importance of refusing Napoleon's overtures of peace negotiations with England. In that speech Pitt argued that "a vigorous prosecution of the war" was necessary in order to counteract the threat of Jacobinism, which remained just as serious as during the time of Robespierre, for "a mind once tainted with that infection, never recovers its healthful state. I am afraid that no purification is sufficient to eradicate the poison of that foul distemper" (*Parl. Hist.*, 34:1443). As a reporter for the *Morning Post* under Daniel Stuart, Coleridge attended the debates in the House of Commons on the continuation of the war with France and published detailed transcriptions of Pitt's memorable speeches of February 3 and 17, 1800 (see *EOT* [CC], 1:152–62; 184–95). Coleridge's variant rendition of Pitt's statement that inspired the title of his essay is "The mind once tainted with Jacobinism can never be wholly free from the taint" (*EOT* [CC], 1:186), but Coleridge used the association of Jacobinism with an infectious disease both in this essay and in his attack on Charles Fox published in the *Morning Post* in November 1802 (*EOT* [CC], 1:381–82).

Coleridge reprinted parts of the essay in *The Friend* and drew attention to it in the *Biographia* as proof that he had offered "the first fair and philosophical * * * definition of Jacobinism" and, moreover, that he had never himself been a "Convert" to Jacobinism (*The Friend* [CC], 2:144–46; and p. 452, n. 4 herein). His contemporaries, however, including Robert Southey, John Thelwall, and William Hazlitt, and a number of modern critics, most notably E. P. Thompson, have castigated Coleridge's defense against Jacobinism as disingenuous and charged him with apostasy. (See E. P. Thompson, "Disenchantment or Default? A Lay Sermon" in *Power and Consciousness*, ed. Conor Cruise O'Brien and William Dean Vanech [London, 1969], 149–81, and Norman Fruman, "Review Essays: Aids to Reflection on the New *Biographia*," *Studies in Romanticism* 24 [1985]: 152–54). Others have challenged the view that Coleridge was a "committed Jacobin" in the 1790s "who then became an apostate Tory" (Thomas McFarland, "Coleridge and the Charge of Political Apostasy," in *Coleridge's "Biographia Literaria": Text and Meaning*, ed. Frederick Burwick, 191–232, 294–306), arguing that his political positions were typically inclusive of rival points of view, "always both Jacobin and anti-Jacobin, Radical and Tory" (David Erdman, *EOT* [CC], 1: lxv).

The text printed here is from the *Morning Post*, October 21, 1802.

Once a Jacobin Always a Jacobin

This charitable adage was at one time fashionable in the ministerial circles; and Mr. Pitt himself, in one of his most powerful speeches, gave it every advantage, that is derivable from stately diction. What he thus condescended to decorate, it were well, if he had attempted to prove. But no! he found it a blank assertion, and a blank assertion he suffered it to remain. What *is* a Jacobin? Perhaps the best answer to this question would be, that it is a term of abuse, the convenient watch-word of a faction. Of course, it has either no meaning, or a very vague one: for definite terms are unmanageable things, and the passions of men do not readily gather round them. Party rage, and fanatical aversion, have their birth place, and natural abode, in floating and obscure generalities, and seldom or never burst forth, except from clouds and vapours.[1] Thunder and lightning from a clear blue sky has been deemed a miracle in all ages. But though we should find it difficult to determine, what a Jacobin *is*, we may however easily conjecture, what the different sects of Anti-Jacobins have meant by the word. The base and venal creatures, and the blind and furious bigots, of the late Ministry, comprehended under that word all, who from whatever cause opposed the late war, and the late Ministry, and whom they hate for this opposition with such mortal hatred,[2] as is usual with bigots alarmed, and detected culprits. "*Once a Jacobin, always a Jacobin,*" signifies no more in the minds of these men, than "*such a one is a man, whom I shall never cease to hate.*" With other men, honest and less violent Anti-Jacobins, the word implies a man, whose affections have been warmly and deeply interested in the cause of general freedom, who has hoped all good and honourable things both *of*, and *for*, mankind. In this sense of the word, Jacobin, the adage would affirm, that no man can ever become altogether an apostate to Liberty, who has at any time been sincerely and fervently attached to it. His hopes will burn like the Greek fire, hard to be extinguished, and easily rekin-

1. Cf. C's closely related argument in *Conciones ad Populum* that a strongly prejudiced man is liable to fall under the spell of an "unmeaning term" or obscure "Watch-word": "The indistinctness of the Ideas associated with it increases its effect, as 'objects look gigantic thro' a mist'. The favorite phrases of the present Day are—'It may be very well in *Theory*'—and the 'effects of Jacobine Principles' " (*Lects 1795* [CC], 52–53). C is in line with Edmund Burke's popular treatise *A Philosophical Enquiry into the Origin of Our Ideas of the Sublime and the Beautiful* (1757) in stressing the effect of indistinct objects or concepts on "the passions of men," but here C links this psychological mechanism to political fanaticism rather than the uplifting experience of sublimity.

2. Pitt's resolve to continue the war with France and reject Napoleon's proposal of peace sent to King George III in December 1799 attracted a great deal of criticism from numerous opponents. In his speech of February 3, 1800, Pitt addressed all the charges in a comprehensive way and was attacked in the House of Commons by Thomas Erskine, Samuel Whitbread (1758–1815), and finally Fox who made a sensational return to the Parliament (*Parl. Hist.*, 34:1301–97). Cf. C's summary of the substance of the debate in *EOT* (CC), 1:162–71.

dling. Even when he despairs of the cause, he will yet *wish*, that it had been successful. And even when private interests have warped his public character, his convictions will remain, and his wishes often rise up in rebellion against his outward actions and public avowals. Thus interpreted, the assertion, "*Once a Jacobin, always a Jacobin*," is so favourable a representation of human nature, that we are willing, too willing perhaps, to admit it even without proof.[3] There is yet a third class of Anti-jacobins, and of this class we profess ourselves to be, who use the word, *Jacobin*, as they use the word, *Whig*, and both words only for want of better; who confess, that Jacobin is too often a word of vague abuse, but believe, that there are certain definite ideas, hitherto not expressed in any single word, which may be attached to this word; and who in consequence uniformly use the word, Jacobin, with certain definite ideas attached to it, those ideas, and no other. A Jacobin, in *our* sense of the term, is one who believes, and is disposed to act on the belief, that all, or the greater part of, the happiness or misery, virtue or vice, of mankind, depends on forms of government; who admits no form of government as either good or rightful, which does not flow directly and formally from the persons governed; who, considering life, health, moral and intellectual improvement, and liberty both of person and conscience, as blessings which governments are bound as far as possible to increase and secure to every inhabitant, whether he has or has not any fixed property, and moreover as blessings of infinitely greater value to each individual, than the preservation of property can be to any individual—does consequently and consistently hold, that every inhabitant, who has attained the age of reason, has a natural and inalienable right to an *equal* share of power in the choice of the governors. In other words, the Jacobin affirms, no legislature can be rightful or good, which did not proceed from universal suffrage. In the power, and under the controul, of a legislature so chosen, he places all and every thing, with the exception of the natural rights of man, and the means appointed for the preservation and exercise of these rights, by a direct vote of the nation itself—that is to say, by a CONSTITUTION. Finally, the Jacobin deems it both justifiable and expedient to effect these requisite changes in faulty governments, by absolute revolutions, and considers no violences as properly rebellious or criminal, which are the *means* of giving to a nation the power of declaring and enforcing its sovereign will.[4] In brief, therefore, a Jacobin's Creed is this: 1. A government is the organ, by which form and publicity are given to the sovereign will of the people; and by which that will is enforced and exercised. 2. A government is likewise the instrument and means of purifying and regulating the national will by its

---

3. C has implicated himself in the first and second classes of Jacobins since he had opposed the war with France (see *Conciones ad Populum*, p. 248 herein, and *EOT* [CC], 1:72–79) and had demonstrated his fervent attachment to liberty in his 1795 political lectures.
4. According to Thomas McFarland, this paragraph offers an "accurate" and "eminently fair" representation of the "aspirations of Jacobins," who appear here "more like bourgeois liberals in the Jeffersonian mold than architects of terror" ("Coleridge and the Charge of Political Apostasy," in *Coleridge's "Biographia Literaria": Text and Meaning*, ed. Frederick Burwick, 224–25).

public discussions, and by direct institutions for the comforts and instruction of the people. 3. Every native of a country has an equal right to that quantity of property, which is necessary for the sustenance of his life, and health. 4. All property beyond this, not being itself a right, can confer no right. Superior wisdom, with superior virtue, would indeed confer a right of superior power; but who is to decide on the possession? Not the person himself, who makes the claim: and if the people, then the right is given, and not inherent. Votes, therefore, *cannot be weighed* in this way, and they *must not* be weighed in any other way, and nothing remains possible, but that they must be *numbered*. No form of electing representatives is rightful, but that of universal suffrage. Every individual has a *right* to elect, and a capability of being elected. 5. The legislature has an absolute power over all other property, but that of article 3: unless the people shall have declared otherwise in the constitution. 6. All governments not constituted on these principles are unjust Governments. 7. The people have a right to overturn them, in whatever way it is possible; and any means necessary to this end become, *ipso facto*, right means. 8. It is the right and duty of each individual, living under that Government, as far as in him lies, to impel and enable the people to exercise these rights. The man who subscribes to *all* these articles is a complete Jacobin; to many, but not to all of them, a Semi-Jacobin, and the man who subscribes to any one article (excepting the second, which the Jacobin professes only in common with every other political sect not directly an advocate of despotism), may be fairly said to have a *shade* of Jacobinism in his character. If we are not greatly deceived we could point out more than one or two celebrated Anti-Jacobins, who are not slightly infected with some of the worst symptoms of the madness against which they are raving;[5] and one or two acts of parliament which are justifiable only upon Jacobin principles. These are the ideas which we attach to the word Jacobin; and no other single word expresses them. Not Republican; Milton was a pure Republican; and yet his notions of government were highly aristocratic, Brutus was a Republican, but he perished in consequence of having killed the Jacobin, Caesar.[6] Neither does Demagogue express that which we have detailed; nor yet Democrat. The former word implies simply a mode of conduct, and has no reference to principles; and the latter does of *necessity* convey no more than that a man prefers in any country a form of government, without monarchy or aristocracy, which in any country he *may* do, and yet be no Jacobin, and which in some countries he can do without any impeachment of good sense or honesty; for instance, in the purely pastoral and agricultural districts of Switzerland, where there is no other property but that of land and cattle, and that property very

5. Cf. *Friend* (CC), 2:140–44, where C demonstrated how anti-Jacobins in opposing Jacobinism "imitated it in its worst features; in personal slander, in illegal violence, and even in the thirst for Blood" (2:141).

6. Cf. C's essay on France and Rome published in *MP* on October 2, 1802: "We have so long connected the names of Brutus and Cassius with the word, Liberty, that we have forgotten that, by the Roman populace, they were considered as the leaders of the senatorian aristocracy—Caesar was the child and champion of Jacobinism" (*EOT* [CC], 1:335).

nearly equalised.[7] Whoever builds a Government on personal and natural rights, is so far a Jacobin. Whoever builds on social rights, that is, hereditary rank, property, and long prescription, is an Anti-Jacobin, even though he should nevertheless be a Republican, or even a Democrat.

If we have been prolix, let the importance of the subject induce our readers to consider it as a venial fault. Concerning a term, which nine-tenths of the nation have been in the habit of using, either as a name of glory, or a name of reproach and abhorrence, it is not only our advantage but even our duty to have clear, correct, and definite conceptions. In the sense of the word, Jacobin, which we have here detailed (and, we dare be confident, that no other sense can be given which belongs exclusively to this word), the truth of the adage, "ONCE A JA-COBIN, AND ALWAYS A JACOBIN," ought to be proved, before it can be used otherwise than wickedly and uncharitably. To prove its falsehood is rendered difficult by this circumstance alone, that there is no pretence, no shadow of an argument in support of its truth—no pretended facts, which we might invalidate—no train of reasoning, of which we might detect the sophistry. It is a blank assertion, the truth of which would be strange, inexplicable, monstrous; a fact standing by itself, without companion or analogy. An *assertion* therefore of its utter falsehood would be a complete overthrow of the *assertion* of its truth; and the only confutation, which it merits. It is an assertion that is consistent and pardonable only in the mouth of a thorough Jacobin, who held his principles to be of such undeniable, obvious, and eternal truth, and that a man who had once understood could abandon them, no more than the elements of geometry; and indeed we must admit, that the whole faction of Re-alarmists,[8] from whose manufactory this precious adage proceeded, have both talked and acted precisely as if they believed in their hearts that Jacobinism presented arguments which were not answerable except by the sword,[9] and charms, and an appearance of happiness, which were not to be withstood except by turning away our eyes from them. Whence, but from these convic-

---

7. William Coxe, *Sketches of the Natural, Civil, and Political State of Swisserland: In a Series of Letters to William Melmoth, Esq.*, 2nd ed. (1780), praised the original simplicity of the pastoral life of Switzerland, and the happiness, spirit of freedom and equality that distinguished its people from other nations in Europe: "If I had never seen these little democratical states, I could have formed no idea of the general equality and indistinction that prevails among the inhabitants" (61). Wordsworth was familiar with this work, which he read in 1790–91 and used in *Descriptive Sketches*.

8. Such "Re-alarmists" include Pitt, described in *An Answer to "A Letter to Edward Long Fox, MD"* as relying on "alarming bustle" to influence the "diseased fancy of Englishmen" (*Lects 1795* [CC], 328), and William Windham, who supported Pitt and Burke and whom C often attacked in his political writings. In *Watchman* (CC), 38, C grouped Windham with other zealous anti-Jacobins such as John Reeves (c. 1752–1829); and in an article published in *MP* on January 25, 1800, C referred to him as one of Pitt's friends "who are so panic-struck from Jacobinism and Atheism, that they do not *think* at all" (*EOT* [CC], 1:130). In the Parliament, Windham was often portrayed by his opponents as a "panick-struck" alarmist who participated in the hysteria of alleged Jacobin inspired plots and conspiracies in England instigated by the government as a justification for the war with France (see, e.g., *Parl. Hist.*, 30:528). On Windham, see p. 275, n. 4 herein.

9. Cf. Windham's speech of February 1, 1793, referring to "the great danger of the propagation of French principles" in which he stated that "opinions and principles, supported and propagated by arms, ought to be opposed by arms" (*Parl. Hist.*, 30:314).

tions, acting *unconsciously*, perhaps, did certain speeches proceed; speeches containing such sentiments concerning the press and the public journals, as beseemed only the private conclave of an Inquisition, where every inquisitor was an Atheist, and yet bent to suppress Atheism?[1] Whence that notable sentiment from the orator, that those, who could not be made *dumb*, ought to be so; and where this could not be, that the others were to be made *deaf*?[2] From what other source that alarm concerning peace, because we should flock to Paris, and all come back *Jacobins*?[3] In the name of all that is sacred, of all that is great and honourable, in the name of Briton, unless this alarmist and his faction believe the truth of Jacobinism, although from self-interest they oppose it, what do they imagine we have done with our common sense and common feelings? Is Jacobinism an absurdity—and have we no reason to detect it with? Is it productive of all misery, and all horrors! and have we no natural humanity to make us turn away with indignation and loathing from it? Uproar and confusion, personal insecurity, insecurity of property, the tyranny of mobs, or the domination of a soldiery; private houses changed to brothels, the very ceremony of marriage itself only an initiation to harlotry, while marriage itself is degraded to mere concubinage—these, Mr. W[indham] and his friends, have said, and truly said, are the effects of Jacobinism! An insufferable licentiousness in their houses, and abroad an insufferable despotism! These are the effects of Jacobinism; and these, the whole English nation was to be clapped under hatches, lest they should see and fall in love with! "Once a Jacobin, always a Jacobin!"[4] And why? Is it because the creed which we have stated, is dazzling at first sight to the young, the innocent, the disinterested, and to those who, judging of men in general, from their own uncorrupted hearts, judge erroneously, and expect unwisely? Is it because it de-

1. The view as expressed by Windham in 1801 that revolutionary France was "founded upon a declared atheism, and filled with all the abominations and pollutions certain to result from such an origin" (*Parl. Hist.*, 36:128) was common among politicians strongly opposed to Jacobinism and to British reformists suspected of treasonable activities under the influence of French ideology.
2. In his speech in the House of Commons of April 8, 1796, Windham supported the buildings of barracks for soldiers, partly on the ground that British soldiers would be protected from the influence of seditious views. He suggested as an antidote to "advocates for free discussion" the "cure prescribed in a French comedy [Molière's *Le Médicine malgré lui*]—'If I cannot make him dumb, I will make you deaf' " (*Parl. Hist.*, 32:935). C cited this remark in *Watchman* (CC), 259.
3. Windham warned that peace with France would inevitably open the "intercourse between the two countries" with the result that "the French would pour in their emissaries, and all the English infected with French principles * * * would return to disseminate their abominable tenets among our people" (*Parl. Hist.*, 31:1030 [December 30, 1794]). In his speech of November 4, 1801, Windham also argued that under conditions of peace the "infection" of French "principles and morals" would spread "without let or hindrance, with nothing to limit their extent, or to control their influence" (*Parl. Hist.*, 36:124).
4. C draws on Windham's speech of November 4, 1801 (*Parl. Hist.*, 36:86–140). Windham, like Pitt in his "Security" speech, argued that nothing can eradicate the infection of Jacobinism "out of any community, in which it has taken once root." With reference to the danger of French morals, Windham stated: "What are we to think of a country, that having struck out of men's minds * * * all sense of religion, and all belief of a future life, has struck out of its system of civil polity, the institution of marriage? That has formally, professedly, and by law, established the connexion of the sexes, upon the footing of an unrestrained concubinage? That has turned the whole country into one universal brothel?" (*Parl. Hist.*, 36:126).

ceives the mind in its purest and most flexible period? Is it because it is an error that every day's experience aids to detect? an error against which all history is full of warning examples? Or, is it because the experiment has been tried before our eyes, and the error made palpable? From what source are we to derive this strange phaenomenon, that the young, and the inexperienced, who, we know by regular experience, are deceived in their religious antipathies, and grow wiser; in their friendships, and grow wiser; in their modes of pleasure, and grow wiser; should, if once deceived in a question of abstract politics, cling to the error for ever and ever! though, in addition to the natural growth of judgment and information with increase of years, they live in the age, in which the tenets had been unfortunately acted upon, and the consequences, deformities, at which every good man's heart sickens, and head turns giddy? We were never at any period of our life converts to the system of French politics. As far back as our memory reaches, it was an axiom in politics with us, that in every country in which property prevailed, property must be the grand basis of the government; and that that government was the best, in which the power was the most exactly proportioned to the property.[5] Yet we do not feel the less shocked by those who would turn an error in speculative politics into a sort of sin against the Holy Ghost, which in some miraculous and inexplicable manner shuts out not only mercy but even repentance!—and who now, that religious bigotry is dying away, would substitute in its place dogmas of *election* and *reprobation* in politics.

We were led to these considerations by the questions which we stated, and attempted in part to answer, in our last—and to which we shall again return, on the first open day[6]—namely, what are the circumstances that more especially favor the restoration of the Bourbons at the present time?[7] What are the difficulties? And is there any possible point of junction between the Royalists and Jacobins?—The last of the three questions recalled to our memory the sentence, which we have been examining; and which we therefore examined, because we were unwilling that any of our readers should stumble at the threshold.

FROM LECTURES ON LITERATURE (1811–12, 1818)

Shortly after returning to England from Malta and Italy in August 1806, Coleridge was invited to give a series of lectures at the Royal Institution, a London scientific and philanthropic society at which his old friend

---

5. C's statement is not accurate. In the 1790s he had strongly opposed private property as the root of many social evils, including the slave trade (see Lecture 6 in *Lectures on Revealed Religion* (pp. 269–70 herein). C began to defend private property from about 1799 on, and this trend became dominant by the time he published *The Friend*. See *Friend* (CC), 2:131–33; C&S (CC), 24n. 6 and 87–88. For an analysis of C's changing views on property, see Morrow, passim.
6. C did not revisit this subject as promised here.
7. The restoration of the Bourbon dynasty did not occur until 1814 after Napoleon's abdication at Fontainebleau. Louis XVIII (1755–1824), son of the the the ill-fated Louis XVI (1754–1793) executed during the French Revolution, returned to rule France.

Humphry Davy was a celebrated lecturer. Being desperately short of money and wanting to avoid journalistic work, Coleridge at first agreed to lecture on "the Principles common to the Fine Arts" (*CL*, 2:1188, 1190–91); but illness, marital discord, and pressure from Robert Southey and William Wordsworth soon led him to withdraw. When the offer was renewed in August 1807, he again accepted it but changed the proposed subject to "the Principles of Poetry" (*CL*, 3:29). After further delays, Coleridge began lecturing in January 1808 and managed to give about twenty of the scheduled twenty-five lectures (principally on Shakespeare and Milton) by June, when, suffering from loneliness and from the effects of his opium addiction, he canceled the remainder of the series (see *CL*, 3:117).

In the 1808 series Coleridge formed the habit of speaking extemporaneously and digressing frequently from his stated theme, and he maintained that habit in his next series, undertaken at his own initiative and advertised as "A Course of Lectures on Shakespeare and Milton in Illustration of the Principles of Poetry." Speaking to paying audiences in a rented hall at the London Philosophical Society, he gave seventeen lectures between November 1811 and January 1812. The first three lectures in the selections printed here are taken from this series, which was recorded in shorthand by two hired notetakers, one of whom, John Payne Collier, much later published an edited version of his transcripts under the title *Seven Lectures on Shakespeare and Milton, by the Late Samuel Taylor Coleridge* (1856). (Coleridge's own notes for these lectures do not survive.) According to Henry Crabb Robinson, the average attendance at the early lectures in the 1811–12 series was 150, of which the majority were subscribers to the whole series (*Lects 1808–19* [*CC*], 1:xlii). In addition to such regulars as Robinson and John Morgan, the audience at this series included, at various times, the American politician Aaron Burr (1756–1836), Lord Byron, William Hazlitt, Charles Lamb, the essayist Mary Russell Mitford (1787–1855), and the poet Samuel Rogers (1763–1855).

The relative success of these lectures encouraged Coleridge to give two further series in 1812–13 in London and another two in 1813–14 in Bristol, where he lectured not only on Shakespeare and Milton, as he had done before, but also on Cervantes's *Don Quixote*. Illness and severe depression prevented him, however, from fulfilling a plan to devote four lectures to the French Revolution. He did not return to lecturing until 1818, when he gave fourteen talks on European literature between January and March at the London Philosophical Society, and it is from this series that the last lecture printed here is taken. This series was even better attended than that of 1811–12, despite the rival attraction of concurrent lectures by Hazlitt on English poets—including Coleridge himself. Coleridge's final series dates from the winter of 1818–19, when he lectured twice a week at the Crown and Anchor Tavern in London, alternating between literature and the history of philosophy.

In February 1812, just after the series of 1811–12 had ended, Crabb Robinson noticed that "Coleridge did not disdain to borrow observations" from the German critic and translator August Wilhelm Schlegel (1767–1845), whose own lectures on Shakespeare and other dramatists, delivered in Vienna in 1808, had been published in 1809–11 under the title *Ueber dramatische Kunst und Litteratur, Vorlesungen* (On Dramatic Art and Literature, Lectures) (*CRB*, 1:63). Coleridge had told Robinson three months earlier that he was "very anxious to see Schlegel's Werke [Works]," but there is no reason to doubt his claim, in a draft letter of about December 1811 to an unidentified correspondent, that he did not actually see the *Vorlesungen* until after his eighth lecture (December 9), when a "German Gentleman" who had attended the lecture gave him a copy of the book (*CL*, 3:359–60; cf. 4:831). Coleridge told his correspondent that he was more "far more flattered, or * * * more confirmed, than sur-prize[d]" by the extent of the agreement between Schlegel and himself, for both had studied the philosophy of Immanuel Kant (*CL*, 3:360). Both Coleridge and Schlegel were also familiar with and indebted to eighteenth-century Shakespearean criticism, particularly by G. W. Less-ing, J. G. Herder, and Friedrich Schiller in Germany and by Samuel John-son in England. (The relation of Schlegel and Coleridge to earlier critics and philosophers is examined by René Wellek in *A History of Modern Crit-icism, 1750–1950* [New Haven, Conn., 1955], 2:36–73, 151–87; and by Thomas McFarland in *Coleridge and the Pantheist Tradition*, 256–61.)

Coleridge's defensiveness in regard to Schlegel increased after 1815, when an English translation of Schlegel's lectures was published and prompted some reviewers (notably Hazlitt) to give Schlegel sole credit for ideas that Coleridge too had expressed, and other reviewers to accuse Coleridge of having plagiarized Schlegel in 1808 (see *CL*, 4:898 and n. 3; *Lects 1808–19* [*CC*], 1:lx–lxi, 173–74). In his 1818 lectures Coleridge responded to these slights of his originality by insisting not merely on his independence of Schlegel—that much seems to have been perfectly true—but also and more dubiously on his priority over Schlegel, for in-stance in pronouncing Shakespeare's judgment equal to his genius and in demonstrating the organic unity of his plays (*Lects 1808–19* [*CC*], 2:263–64, 274, 278–79, 293–94). Coleridge did make direct use of Schlegel in the ninth and subsequent lectures of the 1811–12 series and again in various lectures of 1812–13, sometimes borrowing his examples, sometimes paraphrasing his general points, less often translating him word for word. In his lecture of December 16, 1811 (p. 320 herein), Cole-ridge spoke of having just received "a Work by a German Writer" whose view of Shakespeare agreed remarkably with his own, and a letter of Octo-ber 25, 1813, reveals that he took Schlegel's book into the lecture hall during his 1812–13 lectures. But there is no indication in the surviving records that Coleridge ever explicitly acknowledged his use of Schlegel.

Despite the controversy generated by his apparent failure to state the degree of his indebtedness to Schlegel, Coleridge's lectures are widely ac-cepted as a major body of criticism, in particular of Shakespearean criti-cism. This is due less to his attempts to provide a consistent theoretical basis for criticism—for these remained tentative and derivative—than to his analyses of individual literary works, or what Coleridge called "practi-cal criticism." Rejecting the eighteenth-century practice of judging works by their conformity to external criteria of decorum or morality, Coleridge approached works on their own terms, relating them to their historical contexts and identifying their internal organizing principles. (One could not, he maintained, criticize Shakespeare for failing to adhere to the prin-ciples of ancient Greek drama, because the conditions of the Elizabethan stage were fundamentally different from those of the classical Athenian stage.) Coleridge's particular interest as a Shakespearean critic was in the psychology of drama, both that of the characters in the plays and that of the audience in relation to the plays. And his most distinctive and influen-tial contributions to Shakespearean criticism consist in his character analyses, representative examples of which are included here. (Fuller ac-

counts of Coleridge's lecturing can be found in the R. A. Foakes's introduction to *Lects 1808–19* [CC], vol. 1, and in Richard Holmes, *Coleridge:
Darker Reflections*, 107–41, 221–87, 343–45, 465–68.)

The texts included here are taken from *Lects 1808–19* (CC). With the
exception of the lecture of December 17, 1818, for which Coleridge's
notes survive, these texts derive from Collier's longhand transcripts of his
original shorthand notes.

[On *Romeo and Juliet*]¹

* * *

Coleridge now proceeded to Romeo & Juliet, not because it was the
earliest or among the earliest of Shakespeare's works but because in it
were to be found all his excellencies such as they afterwards appeared
in his more perfect Dramas but differing from them in being less happily combined: all the parts were present but they were not united with
the same harmony: there were many passages where the whole of his
excellence was discovered and nothing superior could be found in the
productions of his after years. The distinction between this play & others was that the parts were less happily combined or to borrow a phraze
from the Painter the whole work was less in keeping:² there was the
production of grand portions: there were the limbs of what was excellent; but the production of a whole in which each part gave delight for
itself and where the whole gave more intellectual delight was the effect
of judgment and taste not to be obtained but by painful study & in
which we gave up the stronger pleasures, derived from the dazzling light
which a man of genius throws over every circumstance and where we
were chiefly struck by vivid and strong images: taste was a subsequent
attainment, after the Poet had been disciplined by experience and adds
to genius that talent by which he knows what part of his genius he can
make intelligible to that part of mankind for whom he writes.³

It would be a hopeless symptom in Coleridge's mind if he found a
young man with perfect taste. In the early works of Shakespeare a profusion of double epithets would be found⁴ and sometimes the coarsest

---

1. After attending this lecture of December 9, 1811, the seventh in the 1811–12 series at the
   London Philosophical Society, C's friend Henry Crabb Robinson noted in his diary that the
   lecturer had "declaimed with great eloquence on love, without wandering from his subject,
   Romeo and Juliet. He was spirited for the greater part, intelligible though profound, and he
   was methodical" (*CRB*, 1:54). C used this lecture to elaborate his conception of Shakespeare as a dramatist who seemed to disappear into his characters, subordinating his personality to theirs, and he criticized those passages in *Romeo and Juliet* in which the
   playwright seemed to be speaking in his own person. The text printed here follows that in
   Lects 1808–19 (CC), 1:303–18, except for the correction of misspellings and the omission
   of canceled words.
2. An 18th-century phrase meaning "the maintenance of harmony of composition" in paintings, specifically in the "relation between the representations of nearer and more distant objects" (*OED*, s.v. "keeping").
3. Like others in his time, C distinguished between "genius" and "talent," defining the former
   as "originality in intellectual construction" and the latter as "the comparative facility of acquiring, arranging, and applying the stock furnished by others and already existing in books
   or other conservatories of intellect" (*Friend* [CC], 1:419; see also *BL* [CC], 1:31–32).
4. In the *Biographia* C noted the profusion of double epithets in Milton's and his own youthful
   verse (e.g., "skull-pil'd" and "seraph-warbled") as well as in Shakespeare's, see also pp.
   378–79 herein and p. 24, n. 3 herein).

words were used if they conveyed a more vivid image but by degrees the associations are connected with the image they are to impress and the Poet descends from the ideal into the real world so far as to conjoin both, to give a sphere of active operations to the ideal to elevate & refine the real.

In Romeo and Juliet the principal characters might be divided into those in which passion is drawn and drawn truly but not individualized further than as the actor appears on the Stage. It was a very just description and developement of the passion without giving, if he might so express himself the philosophical history of it; without knowing how such a man became acted upon by that particular passion but leading it thro' all the incidents and making it predominant.

Such was the character of Tybalt which in itself was a common character: And here there was a great distinction between Shakespeare and all those who wrote in imitation of him, that Coleridge knew no character in Shakespeare, unless indeed his Pistol,[5] which could be called mere Portraits of Individuals: while the reader felt all the delight arising from the individual there was a sort of class character which made Shakespeare the Poet of all ages.

Of this kind was the character of Tybalt a man abandoned to his passions & with all the pride of family only because he thought it belonged to him as of such a family and valuing himself highly simply because he did not care for Death. This perhaps was a more common feeling than any other. Men were apt to consider themselves very great and flattered themselves highly because they possessed that which it was a disgrace not to have but which a wise man never brought forward but when it was required.

Bishop Jeremy Taylor[6] in some part of his voluminous works speaking of a great man says "that he was in his ordinary feelings a Coward, as indeed most men are, knowing the value of life but the power of his reason enabled him when necessary to conduct himself with uniform courage and fortitude"[7]—The good Bishop perhaps had in his mind a story told of one of the ancients. A Philosopher was on board a ship in a storm and gave strong marks of fear. A Coxcomb who was on board stepped up to him and with the greatest impudence reviled him and said "Why are you so frightened: I am not afraid of being drowned: I don't care a farthing"—"You are perfectly in the right (replied the Sage) your life is not worth a farthing."[8]—

In all cases Shakespeare never made his characters win your esteem but left it to the general command of the passion and poetic justice. It was most beautiful in the Tragedy of Romeo & Juliet that the great characters he had principally in view are preserved innocent from all that could do them injury in our feelings concerning them and yet the other characters which deserve little interest themselves, derive it

5. A braggart and associate of Falstaff in *The Merry Wives of Windsor*, *2 Henry IV*, and *Henry V*.
6. An Anglican bishop and theologian (1613–1667) whom C admired both for his thought and for his prose style.
7. Quotation untraced.
8. C paraphrases the anecdote from Diogenes Laertius, *Lives of the Eminent Philosophers* 2.8.71. The philosopher in question was Aristippus (c. 435–350 B.C.E.).

from being instrumental in those situations in which the most important personages develope their thoughts & passions.

Another character of this kind was Capulet: a worthy noble minded
old man of high rank with all the impatience of character which is
likely to accompany it. It is delightful to see the sensibilities of nature
always so exquisitely called forth as if the Poet had the 100 arms of
the Polypus,[9] thrown out in all directions to catch the predominant
feeling. We might see in Capulet the way in which Anger seizes hold
of every thing that comes in its way as in the lines where Capulet is
reproving Tybalt for his fierceness of behaviour which led him to wish
to insult a Montague and disturb the merryment:

> ————————Go to, go to
> You are a saucy boy. Ist so indeed?
> This trick may chance to scathe you—I know what.—
> You must contrary me: marry tis time
> Well said my hearts! You are a princox; go.—
> Be quiet or—More light more light, for shame!
> I'll make you quiet: What? Cheerly my hearts'[1]

The Line—"This trick may [chance to] scathe you:—I know what—"
was in allusion to the Legacy Tybalt might expect: & then seeing the
lights burn dimly Capulet turns his anger ag[ains]t the servants: so
that no one passion is too predominant but that it always includes all
the parts of the character so that the reader never had a mere abstract
of a passion as of anger or ambition but the whole man was presented:
the one predominant passion acting as the leader of the band to the
rest.—

It would not do to introduce into every piece such characters as
Hamlet; but even in the subordinate personages the passion is made
instructive at least even if it have not been an individual and it has
made the reader look with a keener eye into human nature than if it
had not been pointed out to us.

It was one of the great advantages of Shakespeare that he availed
himself of his psychological genius to develope all the minutiae of the
human heart;—that he shewing us the thing makes visible what we
should otherwise not have seen: just as after looking at distant objects
through a Telescope when we behold them afterwards with the naked
eye we see them with greater distinctness than we should otherwise
have done.

Mercutio was the next character and here begins one of the truly
Shakesperian characters, for throughout the Plays of Shakespeare especially those of the highest order it is plain that the characters were
drawn rather from meditation than from observation, or rather by observation which was the child of meditation. There was a vast difference between a man going about the world with his Pocket book,
noting down what he hears and observes and by practice obtains a fa-

9. An aquatic invertebrate with tentacles, such as a jellyfish or hydra (an 18th-century use of
   the word).
1. *Romeo and Juliet* 1.5.79–85.

cility of representing what he has heard & observed—himself frequently unconscious of its bearings. This was entirely different from the observation of that mind which having formed a theory & a system in its own nature has remarked all things as examples of the truth and confirming him in that truth and above all enabling him to convey the truths of philosophy as mere effects derived from the outward watchings of life.

Hence it was that Shakespeare's favourite characters are full of such lively intellect. Mercutio was a man possessing all the elements of a Poet: high fancy; rapid thoughts: the whole world was as it were subject to his law of association: whenever he wished to impress anything, all things became his servants: all things told the same tale, and sound as it were in unison: this was combined with a perfect gentleman himself unconscious of his powers. It was by his Death contrived to bring about the whole catastrophe of the Play. It endears him to Romeo and gives to Mercutio's death an importance which it otherwise could not have acquired.—

Coleridge mentioned this circumstance in answer to an observation made he believed by Dryden, to which indeed Dr Johnson had fully replied, that Shakespeare had carried on the character of Mercutio as far as he could, till his genius was exhausted and then killed him to get him out of the way.[2]—In truth on the Death of Mercutio the catastrophe depended and it was produced by it; it served to shew how indifference and aversion to activity in Romeo may be overcome, & roused, by any deep feeling that is called forth, to the most determined actions. Had not Mercutio been made so amiable and so interesting an object to every reader we could not have felt so strongly as we do the necessity of Romeo's interference or connecting it so passionately with the future fortunes of the lover & the Mistress.

But what should he say of the Nurse? that he was told was the product of mere observation, that it was like Swift's "polite Conversation"[3] which was certainly the most stupendous work of human memory and of unceasingly active attention that exists in human records. The Nurse in Romeo & Juliet was compared sometimes to a Portrait by Gerard Dow[4] in which every hair was so exquisitely painted that it would bear the test even of the microscope. He appealed to his auditors whether the observation of one or two old nurses would have enabled Shakespeare to draw this character of admirable generalization?—No surely not: Were any man to attempt to paint in his mind all the qualities that could possibly belong to a nurse he would find

---

2. C refers to a remark made by John Dryden in *Defence of the Epilogue; or, An Essay on Dramatic Poetry of the Last Age* (1672): "Shakespeare showed the best of his skill in his Mercutio; and he said himself, that he was forced to kill him in the third act, to prevent being killed by him" (*Essays*, vol. 1, ed. W. P. Kerr [Oxford, 1926], 174). Samuel Johnson, in his edition of Shakespeare (1765), defended Mercutio's death on the grounds that it occurs when "he has lived out the time allotted him in the construction of the play" (*The Yale Edition of the Works of Samuel Johnson*, vol. 8, ed. Arthur Sherbo [New Haven, Conn., 1968], 957).
3. Jonathan Swift's *Complete Collection of Genteel and Ingenious Conversation* (1738), better known as *Polite Conversation*, was a collection of common expressions assembled over many years. Juliet's devoted nurse generally speaks in colloquial prose.
4. Gerard Dou or Douw (1613–1675), a Dutch portrait painter.

them there. It was an effect produced not by mere observation. The great prerogative of genius (& Shakespeare had felt and availed himself of it) is now to swell itself into the dignity of a god and now to keep dormant some part of that nature, to descend to the lowest characters; to become anything in fact but the vicious.[5]

Thus in the Nurse you had all the garrulity of old age and all its fondness which was one of the greatest consolations of humanity. He had often thought what a melancholly world it would be without children and what an inhuman world without the aged.

You had likewise the arrogance of ignorance with the pride of real meanness at being connected with a great family; the grossness too which that situation never removes though it sometimes suspends, & arising from that grossness the little low vices belonging to it which indeed in their minds were scarcely vices. Romeo at one time was the delightful man and she was most willing to assist him but it soon turned in favour of Paris of whom she professed the same feelings: how admirably too was this contrasted with a young & pure mind educated in other circumstances.

Another circumstance which ought to be mentioned was truly characteristic of the ignorance of the Nurse, which was that in all her recollections she entirely assists herself by a remembrance of visual circumstances. The great difference between the cultivated and uncultivated mind[6] was this, that the cultivated mind would be found to recal the past by certain regular trains of cause & effect whereas with the uncultivated it was wholly done by a coincidence of images or circumstances which happened at the same time—This position was exemplified in the following passage which was put into the mouth of the ignorant Nurse.—It is found in Act I. Sc. 3 beginning with the lines

> Even or odd of all the days in the year
> Come Lammas eve at night she shall be fourteen

and concluding

> And since that time it is eleven years
> For then she could stand alone.—[7]

Still going on added Coleridge with visual images which was true to the character.[8] More in fact was brought into one portrait here than any single observation could have given & nothing incongruous to the whole was introduced—

* * *

5. Cf. C's lecture of November 25, 1811: "In the meanest characters it was still Shakespeare, it was not the mere Nurse in Romeo & Juliet * * * but it was this great & mighty being changing himself into the Nurse * * * that gave delight" (*Lectures 1808–19* [CC], 1:225). This quality had already been noticed by Friedrich Schiller (1759–1805) in his essay *Über naive und sentimentalische Dichtung* (On Naive and Sentimental Poetry) (1795), which C had read in 1803 (CN, 1:1705n.): "Like the deity behind the structure of the world, so [the poet] stands behind his work; he is the work, and the work is he" (*Sämtliche Werke*, vol. 5, ed. Gerhard Fricke and Herbert G. Göpfert [Munich, 1959], 713).
6. C referred again to the nurse as a character with an "uncultivated understanding," in *The Friend* (p. 562 herein).
7. *Romeo and Juliet* 1.3.18–38 (var.).
8. The syntax is muddled in the transcript.

But Shakespeare would ever be found to speak the language of nature. Where did he learn the dialogue of generals: where was he to have learnt by observation only such language as the following where Othello is speaking to Iago regarding Brabantio (Act 1. Sc: 2.)

————Let him do his spite &c

and concluding

> I would not my unhoused free condition
> Put into circumscription and confine
> For the Sea's worth.—[9]

I ask (said the Lecturer) where did Shakespeare observe this? If he did observe it, it was with the inward eye of meditation on his own nature. He became Othello and spoke therefore as Othello would have spoken.—

Another remark he would make on this play was that in it the Poet is not entirely blended with the Dramatist at least not in that degree which is afterwards noticed in Lear, Hamlet, Othello & Macbeth.— For instance Capulet and Montague frequently talked language only belonging to the Poet and not so much characteristic of passion as of a faculty;[1] a mistake or rather an indistinctness which many of our later Poets have carried [through] the whole of their work.

When Coleridge read the song of Deborah he never supposed that she was a Poet, altho he thought the song itself a sublime Poem. It was as simple a dytherambic[2] Poem as exists but it was the proper effusion of a woman, highly elevated by triumph, by the natural hatred to oppressors resulting from a sense of wrongs: it was an exultation on deliverance from them and this too accomplished by herself. When she commenced

> I Deborah the mother of Israel[3]

It was poetry in the highest sense; but he had no reason to suppose that if she had not been agitated by the same passion she would have been able to talk in the same way—or that if she had been placed under different circumstances, which she was not likely to be placed in she would still have spoken the language of truth.—

On the other hand there was a language which was not descriptive of passion and yet was poetic and shewed a high and active fancy; as when Capulet says

> Such comfort as do lusty young men feel
> When well apparelled April on the heel
> Of limping Winter treads, even such delight
> Among fresh female buds shall you this night
> Inherit at my house—[4]

---

9. *Othello* 1.2.17–28. At this point in the play Brabanzio, Desdemona's father, wants to retrieve his daughter from Othello, whom she has secretly married.
1. I.e., a mental faculty.
2. An effusive song or poem. In a note to "The Thorn" in *LB* (1800), Wordsworth cited Deborah's song for the beauty of its repetitions.
3. Judges 5.7: "The inhabitants of the villages ceased, they ceased in Israel until that I Deborah arose, that I arose a mother in Israel."
4. *Romeo and Juliet* 1.2.24–28.

Other passages, more happy in illustrating this might be adduced where the Poet forgets the character & speaks in his own person—

In other parts Shakespeare's conceits were, in Coleridge's mind, highly justifiable as belonging to the state of age or passion of the person using them. In other parts where they could not be so justified they might be excused from the taste of his own and the preceding age; as for instance

> Here's much to do with hate but more with love:
> Why then oh brawling love! Oh loving hate!
> Oh anything of nothing first created!
> Oh heavy lightness! Serious vanity!
> Misshapen Chaos of wellseeming forms!
> Feather of lead! bright smoke, cold fire, sick health!
> Still waking sleep that is not what it is!—[5]

Such passages as these Coleridge dared not declare to be absolutely unnatural because there is an effort in the mind when it would describe what it cannot satisfy itself with the description of, to reconcile opposites and to leave a middle state of mind more strictly appropriate to the imagination than any other when it is hovering between two images: as soon as it is fixed on one it becomes understanding and when it is waving between them attaching itself to neither it is imagination.—Such was the fine description of Death in Milton "Of Shadow like but called Substance" &c.[6]

These were the grandest effects where the imagination was called forth, not to produce a distinct form but a strong working of the mind still producing what it still repels & again calling forth what it again negatives and the result is what the Poet wishes to impress, to substitute a grand feeling of the unimaginable for a mere image—Coleridge sometimes thought that the passage from Milton might be quoted as exhibiting a certain limit between the Poet & the Painter—Sundry painters had not so thought and had made pictures of the meeting between Satan & Death at Hell Gate and how was the latter represented? By the most defined thing that could be conceived in nature—A Skeleton, perhaps the dryest image that could be discovered which reduced the mind to a mere state of inactivity & passivity & compared with which a Square or a triangle was a luxuriant fancy.

After noticing the general and mistaken notion that because certain forms of writing & combinations of thought were not in common and daily use they were unnatural, he observed that there was no form of language that might not be introduced by a great Poet with great effect in particular situations because they were true to nature and without an original they never could have existed. Take Punning for instance which was the most harmless of all kinds of wit because it

---

5. *Romeo and Juliet* 1.1.168–74 (Romeo speaking).
6. *Paradise Lost* 2.666–70: "The other shape, / If shape it might be call'd that shape had none / Distinguishable in member, joynt, or limb, / Or substance might be call'd that shadow seem'd, / For each seem'd either." Death was usually represented as a skeleton in illustrations of this episode of *Paradise Lost* (*Lects 1808–19* [CC], 1:312n. 23, citing Marcia Pointon, *Milton and English Art* [Toronto, 1970]).

never excited envy. It might be the necessary consequence of association; as if one man were attempting to shew something resisted by another that other when agitated by passion might employ a term used by his adversary in one sense to a directly contrary meaning: it came into his mind to do it as one way & sometimes the best of replying. It generally arose from a mixture of anger and contempt which punning was a natural mode of expressing.

It was Coleridge's intention not to pass any of the important conceits in Shakespeare some of which were introduced in his after productions with great propriety—It would be recollected that at the time this great Poet lived there was an attempt at and an affectation of quaintness wch emanated even from the Court and to which satire had been directed by Osrick[7] in Hamlet. Among the Schoolmen of that age nothing was more common than such conceits as he had employed and it was aided after the restoration of letters & the bias thus given was very generally felt.

The Lecturer had in his possession a Dictionary of Phrazes in which those applied to Love Hate jealousy and such abstract terms consisted entirely of phrazes taken from Seneca or his imitators, or from the Schoolmen themselves composed of perpetual antitheses and describing those passions by conjunction and combination of things absolutely irreconcileable.[8] But he was only palliating Shakespeare as a man because he did not write for his own but for all ages, & so far he admitted it to be a defect.

If in these lectures we were able to find what were the peculiar faults as well as the peculiar beauties of Shakespeare it would be an additional mode of deciding what authority was to be attached to parts of what were called his works. If we discovered a Play in which there were neither Shakespeare's defects or his excellencies, or defects or excellencies incompatible with his, or individual scenes so circumstanced, we should have strong reason to believe that it was not Shakespeare's & that they were taken either from the old plays which in some instances he reformed & altered; that they were inserted by some underhand to please the mob, and that they were written and played because such a part of Shakespeare's original was too heavy, where the mob called for the Clown to lighten the scene. If we found such to be the case we might conclude that the Play or the Scene was not Shakespeare's.

It remained now for him to speak of the Hero & Heroine of the Play Romeo & Juliet themselves & he should do it with unaffected diffidence, not only from the delicacy but from the great importance of the subject: because it was impossible to defend Shakespeare from the most cruel of all charges against him, viz: that he was an immoral writer, without entering fully into his mode of displaying female char-

---

7. An affected courtier whom Hamlet mocks.
8. C's dictionary has not been identified. Lucius Annaeus Seneca (c. 4 B.C.E.–65 C.E.) was the author of moral treatises and nine tragedies that strongly influenced English and Italian playwrights of the Renaissance. The nurse in *Romeo and Juliet* is an adaptation of a stock character in Seneca.

acters and Love which he had done with greater perfection than any
other writer with the single exception perhaps of Milton in his delin-
eation of the character of Eve.—

*   *   *

Perhaps there was no one more sure criterion of the degree of refinement in a moral character and the purity of the intellectual intention & the deep conviction & sense of what our own nature is in all its
combinations than the different definitions men would give of love,
supposing them to be perfectly serious. He would not state the various
definitions that had been given; they were probably well known to
many & it would be better not to repeat them. He would rather give
one of his own equally free from extravagance & pretended Platonism,
which like all other things which super-moralize are sure to demoral-
ize and yet he had kept it distinct from the grosser opposite—

Considering himself and his fellow men as it were a link between
heaven & earth as composed of the body & of the soul: to reason & to
will & the perpetual aspiration which tells us that this is ours for a
while but it is not ourselves. Considering man in this twofold character, & yet united in one person he conceived that there could be no
correct definition of love which did not correspond with the being and
with that subordination of one part to another which constitutes our
perfection. He w^d say therefore that

"*Love is a perfect desire of the whole being to be united to some thing
or some being which is felt necessary to its perfection by the most perfect
means that nature permits & reason dictates.*"[9]

It is inevitable to every noble mind whether man or woman to feel
itself of itself imperfect and insufficient, not as an animal merely but
altogether as a moral being. How wonderfully therefore has providence provided for us to make that which is necessary for us a step of
that exaltation to a higher and nobler state.—The Creator had ordained that one should possess what the other does not and the union
of both is the most complete ideal of the human character that can be
conceived—In everything blending the similar with the dissimilar is
the secret of all pure delight—Who should dare then to stand alone
and vaunt himself in himself sufficient? In poetry Coleridge had
shewn that it was the blending of passion with order & still more in
morals & more than all was it (which woe be to us if we did not at
some time contemplate in a moral view solely) the exclusive attachment of the Sexes to each other.

It was true that the world and its business might be carried on without marriage but it is so evident that Providence meant man to be the
master of the world; he was the only animal of all climates, & his reason was so preeminent over instinct whose place it supplied & marriage or the knitting together of society by the tenderest ties rendered
him able to maintain his superiority over the brutes. Man alone was
privileged to clothe himself and to do all things so as to make him as it

---

9. A paraphrase of *The Siedge; or Love's Convert* 2.6.85–88 by William Cartwright
(1611–1643), copied from a notebook entry of 1809 (CN, 3:3514 and n.).

were a secondary creator of himself & of his own happiness or misery and in this as in all the image of his Maker was impressed upon him.

Providence then has not left us to Prudence only for the power of calculation which prudence impels cannot have existed but in a state which pre-supposes the Marriage State. If God has done this shall we suppose that he has given us no moral sense, no yearning, which is something more than animal, to secure that without which man might be a herd but could not be a Society: the very idea seems to breathe absurdity—

From this union arose the filial maternal brotherly and sisterly relations of life and every State is but a family magnified: all the operations of the mind—all that distinguished us from mere brute animals arises from the more perfect state of domestic life. One certain criterion in forming an opinion of man was the reverence in wch he held woman. Plato had said that by this we rose from sensuality to affection, from affection to love, & from love to pure intellectual delight & by which we became worthy to conceive that infinite in ourselves without which it were impossible for man to have believed in a God.[1] In short to sum up all, the most delightful of all promises was expressed to us by this practical state, namely our marriage with the Redeemer of Mankind.

He might safely appeal to every gentleman in the room whether when a young man who had been accustomed to abandon himself to his passions and to have lived with freedom, fell in love the first symptom is not a complete change in his manners—a contempt & hatred of himself for having asserted that he acted by the dictates of nature, & that they were the inevitable consequences of his youth, & that it was impossible they could be conquered—The surest friend of Chastity is love it lead men not to sink the mind in the body but to draw the body to the mind, the immortal part of our nature. Contrast this feeling with the works of those writers who have done the direct contrary even by the ebullitions of comic humour while in other parts of the same work from the vile confusion, great purity is displayed, such as the purity of love which above all other qualities rendered us most lovely.

Love was not like hunger: Love was an associative quality: the hungry savage is a mere animal thinking of nothing but the satisfaction of his appetite.—What was the first effect of love, but to associate the feeling with every object in nature: the trees whisper the roses exhale their perfumes the nightingales sing the very sky seems in unison with the feeling of love: it gives to every object in nature a power of the heart without which it would indeed be spiritless; a mere dead copy.

Shakespeare had described this passion in various states & he had begun as was most natural with love in the young mind. Did he begin with making Romeo & Juliet in love at the first glimpse as a common and ordinary thinker would do?—No—he knew what he was about, he

---

1. In Plato, *Symposium* 210–11, Socrates advocates a progression from the love of physical beauty to the love of knowledge.

was to develope the whole passion and he takes it in its first elements: that sense of imperfection, that yearning to combine itself with something lovely.—Romeo became enamoured of the ideal he formed in his own mind & then as it were christened the first real being as that which he desired. He appeared to be in love with Rosaline, but in truth he was in love only with his own idea.[2] He felt the necessity of being beloved which no noble mind can be without: Shakespeare then introduces Romeo to Juliet and makes it not only a violent but permanent love at first sight which had been so often ridiculed in Shakespeare.

This called upon Coleridge to remark one characteristic of Shakespeare which he thought belonged truly to a man of profound thought & genius—It had been too much the custom when we could not explain anything that happened by the few words that were employed to explain everything; we passed it over as beyond our reach: they were looked upon as hints which Philosophy could not explain: as the terra incognita for future discoveries; the great ocean of unknown things to be afterward explored, or the sacred fragments of a ruined temple, every part of which in itself was beautiful but the particular relation of which parts was unknown. In Shakespeare they were every where introduced with respect & he had acted upon them and had drawn his characters as seriously influenced by them.

As he might not again have an opportunity he would here compare the different manner in which Shakespeare had treated the priestly character [and] other writers. In Beaumont and Fletcher they are described as a vulgar mockery;[3] as in other characters the errors of a few were mistaken for the character of the many but in Shakespeare they always brought with them your love and respect: he made no abstracts, no copies from the bad parts of human nature; his characters of priests were drawn from the general.

It was remarkable too that throughout all his works Shakespeare had never introduced the passion of Avarice. I[t] belonged only to particular parts of our nature: it was only prevalent in particular states of society and could not be permanent. The Miser of Molière & Plautus[4] was now looked upon as a sort of madman. Elves was a peculiar individual[5] that partook of insanity but as a passion it had disappeared & how admirably did Shakespeare forsee that such characters could not be permanent in as much as the passion on which they were founded would soon be lost depending only on accidental circumstances.

None of the Plays of Shakespeare were built upon anything but

2. Rosaline does not appear in the play but is named by Benvolio as the object of Romeo's affection before he meets Juliet (1.2.82–87). In 1.1.164–76 Romeo speaks wittily of his frustrated love for Rosaline, but without naming her.
3. C was perhaps thinking of Lopez in Fletcher, *The Spanish Curate*. The play is included in Beaumont and Fletcher, *Fifty Comedies and Tragedies* (1679), which C had borrowed from Charles Lamb in October 1811 (*Lects 1808–19* [CC], 1:317n. 34; *CM* [CC], 1:362–72).
4. The character of Harpagon in *L'Avare* (The Miser) by the French playwright Molière (Jean-Baptiste Poquelin, 1622–1673) is based on that of Euclio in *Aurulalia* (The Pot of Gold) by the Roman playwright Plautus (c. 254–184 B.C.E.).
5. I.e., John Elwes (1714–1789), the subject of a popular biography by Edward Topham, *The Life of Mr. Elwes, the Celebrated Miser* (1795).

what was absolutely necessary for our existence and consequently must be permanent while we continue men. Take the admirable Tragedy of Orestes or the husband of Jocasta[6] yet whatever might be the genius of Sophocles they had a fault. There we see a man oppressed by fate for an action of wch he was not morally guilty: the crime is taken from the moral [actor][7] and given to the action; we are obliged to say to ourselves that in those days they considered things without reference to the real guilt of the persons—

There was no one character in which Envy was pourtrayed excepting in Cassius in Julius Caesar; yet even there it is not hateful to you but he has counterbalanced it by a number of excellent feelings.[8] He leads the reader to suppose that it is rather something constitutional, something derived from his mother which he cannot avoid: throwing the blame from the will of the man to some unavoidable circumstance, rather than fix the attention of the reader on one of those passions which actually debase the mind.

Wherever love is described as of a serious nature & much more when it is to lead to a tragical end it depends on a law of the mind which Coleridge believed he should make intelligible and which would not only justify Shakespeare but shew an analogy to all his other characters. This subject he reserved to his next lecture.—

[On Ancient and Modern Drama and *The Tempest*][1]

He observed that it is a known and unexplained phenomenon that among the ancients Statuary rose to such a degree of perfection as to leave almost the hope of imitating it baffled, & mingled with despair of excelling it; while Painting at the same time, notwithstanding the admiration bestowed upon the ancient paintings of Apelles by Pliny & others had been proved to be an excellence of much later growth and to have fallen far short of Statuary.[2]

*   *   *

Something of the same kind appears to have been the case with regard to their dramas. Early in the lectures the Greek Stage had been noticed which had been imitated by the French and by the writers of

6. Sophocles, *Electra* and *Oedipus Rex*.
7. Collier's transcript has "act."
8. Cassius reveals his envy of Caesar in two diatribes against him (1.2.137–62 and 1.3.103–14).
1. This lecture, the ninth of the 1811–12 series, was given at the London Philosophical Society on December 16, 1811. Lord Byron probably attended it (see *BLJ*, 2:147); Henry Crabb Robinson certainly did, and he noted afterward that "Coleridge was again very desultory during half the lecture * * * [b]ut at length he bethought himself of Shakespeare * * * and treated beautifully of *The Tempest*, and especially Prospero, Miranda, Ariel, and Caliban. This part most excellent" (*CRB*, 1:56). This was the first of C's lectures to show the influence of August Wilhelm Schlegel's *Lectures on Dramatic Art and Literature*, particularly in the contrasts between ancient and modern drama and between mechanical and organic form. While acknowledging his agreement on these points with Schlegel—whom, however, he apparently did not name—C insisted that he had reached his conclusions independently. The text printed here follows that in *Lects 1808–19* (CC), 1:347–68, but omits the cancellations.
2. Apelles (4th century B.C.E.), a Greek painter, is discussed at length by the Roman soldier and encyclopedist Pliny the Elder (23–79 C.E.) in his *Natural History*, book 35.

England since the reign of Charles II.[3] Their scheme[4] allowed nothing more than a variation of the same note and admitted nothing of that which is the true principle of life, the attaining of the same end by an infinite variety of means.

It is true that the writings of Shakespeare are not likenesses of the Greek: they are analogies because by very different means they produce the same end; whereas the greater part of the French Tragedies and the English plays on the same plan cannot be called likenesses, but may be called the failing of the same end by adopting the same means under most unappropriate circumstances.[5]

This had led Coleridge to consider that the ancient drama, meaning the works of Aeschylus, Eurypedes & Sophocles (for the miserable rhetorical works by the Romans are scarcely to be mentioned as dramatic poems) might be contrasted with the Shakespearian Drama: he had called it Shakespearian, because he knew no other writer who had realized the same idea altho' he had been told that the Spanish Poet Calderon[6] had been as successful—The Shakespearian drama and the Greek drama might be compared to painting & statuary.[7] In the latter as in the Greek drama the characters must be few because the very essence of statuary was a high degree of abstraction which would prevent a great many figures from being combined into the same effects. In a grand groupe of Niobe[8] or any other ancient heroic subject how disgusting it would appear were an old nurse introduced. The numbers must be circumscribed & nothing undignified must be brought into company with what is dignified: no one personage must be brought in but what is abstraction: all must not be presented to the eye but the effect of multitude must be produced without the introduction of anything discordant.

*   *   *

The advantage is indeed vastly on the side of the modern: he appeals to the imagination, to the reason and to the noblest powers of the human heart: he is above the iron compulsion of space & time: he

3. I.e., since 1660, when Charles II (1630–1685), having returned from exile to take the throne, lifted the ban that had been imposed on theatrical productions eighteen years earlier. In his lecture of November 25, 1811, C had argued that the observance of the "unities" in Greek drama—that is, the confinement of the dramatic action to a single time and place—was accidental and dictated by the conditions of the ancient theaters (*Lects 1808–19* [CC], 1:225–27). See also p. 337, n. 4, herein.
4. The unities (see the preceding note).
5. Neither in this lecture nor in that of November 25 did C specify which French and English plays he had mind, but in conversation with John Payne Collier in 1811 he criticized the domestic tragedies of Thomas Southerne (1660–1746) and Edward Moore (1712–1757) (see *Lects 1808–19* [CC], 2:361n. 1). Schlegel contrasted French drama of the 17th and 18th centuries, generally unfavorably, with classical Greek and Roman drama in his tenth and eleventh lectures (*A Course of Lectures on Dramatic Art and Literature*, trans. John Black [London, 1815], 2:1–90).
6. Pedro Calderón de la Barca (1600–1681), Spanish playwright and priest. Schlegel ranked Shakespeare and Calderón as the greatest modern dramatists. C's sweep from Greek to Roman to English and Spanish drama follows the opening of Schlegel's twelfth lecture (*Lectures*, 2:91–94).
7. This comparison of Shakespearean drama with painting and of Greek drama with sculpture is almost certainly derived from Schlegel (*Lectures*, 2:99–101).
8. A group of statues of Niobe and her seven sons and seven daughters, installed in the Uffizi Gallery in Florence in 1775. C had probably seen the group when he visited the Uffizi in May or June 1806.

appeals to that which we most wish to be when we are most worthy of being while the ancient drama binds us down to the meanest part of our nature and its chief compensation is a simple acquiescence of the mind that what the Poet has represented might possibly have taken place—a poor compliment to a Poet who is to be a creator, to tell him that he has all the excellencies of a historian!—In dramatic composition the Unities of Time & Place so narrowed the space of action & so impoverishes the sources of pleasure that of all the Athenian dramas there is scarcely one wch has not fallen into absurdity by aiming at an object & failing or which has not incurred greater absurdity by bringing events into a space of time in which it is impossible for them to have happened: not to mention that the grandest effect of the Dramatist to be the mirror of life is completely lost.—

The limit allowed by the Greeks was 24 hours but we might as well take 24 months because it has already become an object of imagination. The mind is then acted upon by such strong stimulants that the one & the other are indifferent: when once the limit of possibility is passed there are no bounds which can be assigned to imagination. We soon find that such effects may arise from such causes.—Above all in reading Shakespeare we should first consider in what plays he means to appeal to the reason or imagination faculties which have no relation to time & place excepting as in the one case they imply a succession of cause & effect and as in the other they form a harmonious picture so that the impulse given by reason is carried on by the imagination.

Shakespeare was often spoken of as a Child of Nature[9] and many had been his imitators and attempted to copy real incidents and some of them had not even genius enough to copy nature, but still they produced a sort of phenomenon of modern times neither tragic nor comic nor tragicomic but the Sentimental.[1] This sort of writing consisted in taking some very affecting incidents, which in its highest excellence only aspired to the genius of an onion, the power of drawing tears and in which the Author acting like a Ventriloquist distributed his own insipidity.[2] Coleridge had seen plays some translated and some the growth of our own soil so well acted & so ill written that if the auditor could have produced an artificial deafness he would have been much pleased with the performance as a pantomime.

Shakespeare's characters from Othello or Macbeth down to Dogberry are ideal:[3] they are not the things but the abstracts of the things which a great mind may take into itself and naturalize to its own

---

9. It was a critical commonplace from the Restoration on that Shakespeare had been a natural, untutored genius who faithfully represented what he observed in life: see, e.g., John Dryden's essay *Of Dramatick Poesy* (1668); Joseph Addison's *Spectator*, No. 160 (September 3, 1711); Alexander Pope's preface to his edition of Shakespeare (1725); and Thomas Gray's ode "The Progress of Poetry" (1757), lines 83–88.

1. C mocks the "novels of sensibility," popular in the late 18th century for their portrayal of characters of extreme emotional sensitivity, sympathy toward others, and moral virtue.

2. C was fond of the image of the ventriloquist, applying it not only (as here and on p. 531 herein) to writers who used their characters as mouthpieces for themselves, but also to truth as the voice through which God speaks (p. 448 herein). Cf. also *SM* (CC), 80.

3. I.e., Shakespeare's characters are embodiments of specific traits or states of mind and are not naturalistic representations of persons.

heaven. In the character of Dogberry[4] itself some important truths are conveyed or some admirable allusion is made to some folly reigning at the time & which the Poet saw must forever reign.—The enlightened readers of Shakespeare may be divided into two classes.

1. Those who read with feeling and understanding
2. Those who without affecting to understand or criticise merely feel and are recipients of the poet's power.—[5]

Between the two no medium could be endured.—The reader often feels that some ideal trait of our own is caught or some nerve has been touched of which we were not before aware and it is proved that it has been touched by the vibration that we feel a sort of thrilling which tells us that we know ourselves the better for it. In the plays of Shakespeare every man sees himself without knowing that he sees himself as in the phenomena of nature, in the mist of the mountain a traveller beholds his own figure but the glory round the head distinguishes it from a mere vulgar copy, or as a man traversing the Brocken in the north of Germany at sunrise when the glorious beams are shot ascance the mountain:[6] he sees before him a figure of gigantic proportions; & of such elevated dignity, that he only knows it to be himself by the similarity of action—Or as the [Fata Morgana] at Messina[7] in which all forms at determined distances are presented in an invisible mist dressed in all the gorgeous colors of prismatic imagination and with magic harmony uniting them and producing a beautiful whole in the mind of the Spectator.

*   *   *

Yesterday afternoon a friend had left for him a Work by a German writer of which Coleridge had had time only to read a small part but what he had read he approved & he should praise the book much more highly were it not that in truth it would be praising himself, as the sentiments contained in it were so coincident with those Coleridge had expressed at the Royal Institution.[8] It was not a little wonderful that so many ages had elapsed since the time of Shakespeare and that

---

4. The bumbling, long-winded constable in *Much Ado about Nothing*, who accidentally exposes Don John's plot to prevent the marriage of Hero and Claudio.

5. In his lecture of November 21, 1811, C identified four classes of readers: "sponges," who retain everything but do not reflect on it critically; "sand-glasses" (i.e., hourglasses), who retain nothing; "strain-bags" (i.e., sieves), who "retained only the dregs of what they received"; and "Great Mogul Diamonds," who identify what is valuable and retain only that (*Lects 1808–19* [CC], 1:203–04).

6. C climbed the Brocken, the highest peak of the Harz mountains near Göttingen, in May and again in June 1799 in the hope of seeing the "Brocken specter," as the phenomenon he describes here was known. He continued to be fascinated by the phenomenon—which he did not succeed in experiencing himself—and he included a description of something very like it in his "Constancy to an Ideal Object," lines 25–32 (pp. 210–11 herein). See also "Lines Written in the Album at Elbingerode" (p. 133 herein).

7. The *fata morgana*—the name of which appears in Collier's shorthand notes but not in his longhand transcript (*Lects 1808–19* [CC], 1:352n. 21)—is a mirage commonly seen in the Strait of Messina between Sicily and mainland Italy. In May 1799 C copied out a description of this phenomenon (along with one of the Brocken specter) from a German scientific periodical (*CN*, 1:430–31 and nn.).

8. C had given his 1808 series of lectures at the Royal Institution in London. The work he refers to is the original edition of August Wilhelm Schlegel's lectures on drama, *Ueber dramatische Kunst und Litteratur: Vorlesungen*, 3 vols. (Heidelberg, 1809–11), a copy of which had been presented to him after his lecture of December 12, 1811 (*CL*, 3:359). See the headnote (p. 307 herein).

it should remain for foreigners first to feel truly & to appreciate properly his mighty genius. The solution of this fact must be sought in the history of the nation. The English had become a busy commercial people and had unquestionably derived from it many advantages moral and physical: we had grown into a mighty nation: one of the gyant nations of the world whom moral superiority still enables to struggle with the other, the evil genius of the Planet.[9]—

The German nations on the other hand, unable to act at all have been driven into speculation: all the feelings have been forced back into the thinking and reasoning mind. To do was impossible for them but in determining what ought to be done they perhaps exceeded every people of the globe. Incapable of acting outwardly they have acted internally: They first rationally recalled the ancient philosophy: they acted upon their own spirits with an energy of which England produced no paralel since those truly heroic times in body & in soul the days of Elizabeth.—

* * *

It is a mistake Coleridge maintained to suppose that any of Shakespeare's characters strike us as Portraits. They have the union of reason perceiving, & the judgment recording actual facts and the imagination diffusing over all a magic glory and while it records the past projects in a wonderful degree to the future & makes us feel however slightly & see however dimly that state of being in which there is neither past nor future but which is permanent, & is the energy of nature.

Though Coleridge had affirmed & truly that all Shakespeare's characters were ideal yet a just division may be made, of those in which the ideal is more prominent to the mind; where it is brought forward more intentionally where we were made more conscious of the ideal tho' in truth they possessed no more or less reality, and secondly of those w[ch] tho' equally idealized the delusion upon the mind is that of their being real.—Shakespeare's plays might be separated into those where the real is disguised in the ideal & those where the ideal is hidden from us in the real.—The difference is made by the powers of the mind which the Poet chiefly appeals to.—

* * *

Among the ideal Plays was the Tempest which he wo[d] take as an example. Many other might be mentioned but it was impossible to go through every separate piece and what was said on the Tempest would apply to all.—

In this Play Shakespeare has appealed to the imagination and he constructed a plan according to it: the scheme of his drama did not appeal to any sensuous impression (the word sensuous was authorized by Milton)[1] of time & space but to the imagination and it would be recollected that his works were rather recited than acted.

9. Napoleon, with whom Britain was still at war in 1811.
1. *Sensuous*: pertaining to the senses. Milton used the word in this sense in *Of Education* (1644), defending poetry as "simple; sensuous and passionate" (*Complete Prose Works*, vol. 2, ed. Ernest Sirluck [New Haven, Conn., 1959], 403). See also *Biographia* (p. 449 herein).

In the first scene was introduced a mere confusion on board a ship: the lowest characters were brought together with the highest and with what excellence.—A great part of the Genius of Shakespeare consisted of these happy combinations of the highest & lowest, and of the gayest and the sadest. He was not droll in one scene and mellancholly in the other but both the one & the other in the same scene: laughter is made to swell the tear of sorrow and to throw as it were a poetic light upon it, & the tear mixes a tenderness with the laughter that succeeds. In the same scene Shakespeare has shewn that power which above all other men, he possessed that of introducing the profoundest sentiments of wisdom just where they would be least expected and yet where they are truly natural and the admirable secret of his drama was that the separate speeches do not appear to be produced the one by the former but to arise out of the peculiar character of the speaker—

Coleridge here explained the difference between what he called mechanic and organic regularity.[2] In the former the copy must be made as if it had been formed in the same mould with the original—In the latter there is a law which all the parts obey conforming themselves to the outward symbols & manifestations of the essential principle. He illustrated this distinction by referring to the growth of Trees, which from peculiar circumstances of soil, air or position differed in shape even from trees of the same kind but every man was able to decide at first sight which was an ash or a poplar.—

This was the case in Shakespeare: he shewed the life and principle of the being, with organic regularity.—Thus the Boatswain in the storm when a sense of danger impresses all and the bonds of reverence are thrown off and he gives a loose to his feelings and thus to the old Counsellor pours forth his vulgar mind.

"Hence! What care these roarers for the name of King? To cabin—Silence! trouble us not." Gonzalo observes—"Good: yet remember whom thou hast aboard!"

The Boatswain replies, "None that I more love than myself.—You are a Counsellor if you can command these elements to silence and work the peace of the present we will not handle a rope more; use your authority: If you cannot give thanks you have lived so long and make yourself ready in your Cabin for the mischance of the hour, if it so hap.—Cheerly good hearts!—Out of our way I say"[3]—

An ordinary dramatist would after this speech have introduced Gonzalo moralizing or saying something connected with it: for common dramatists are not men of genius: they connect their ideas by associa-

---

2. A distinction derived from Schlegel:

> Form is mechanical when, through, external influence, it is communicated to any material merely as an accidental addition * * * as, for example, when we give a particular shape to a soft mass. * * * Organical form, again, is innate; it unfolds itself from within, and acquires its determination along with the complete development of the germ. We every where discover such forms in nature * * * from the crystallization of salts and minerals to plants and flowers, and from them to the human figure. In the fine arts, as well as in the province of nature, all genuine forms are organical, that is, determined by the quality [i.e., nature] of the work [*Lectures*, 2:94–95].

3. *The Tempest* 1.1.15–24 (var.).

tion or logical connection, but the vital writer in a moment transports himself into the very being of each character and instead of making artificial puppets he brings the real being before you.—Gonzalo replies therefore

"I have great comfort from this fellow: methinks he hath no drowning mark upon him, his complexion is perfect gallows. Stand fast good fate to his hanging; make the rope of his destiny our cable for our own doth little advantage. If he be not born to be hanged our case is miserable."[4]

Here is the true sailor proud of his contempt of danger and the high feeling of the old man who instead of condescending to reply to the words addressed to him, turns off and meditates with himself and draws some feeling of comfort to his own mind by trifling with his face founding upon it a hope of safety.

Shakespeare had determined to make the plot of this play such as to involve a certain number of low characters and at the beginning of the piece pitched the note of the whole. It was evidently brought in as a lively mode of telling a story and the reader is prepared for something to be developed and in the next scene he brings forward *Prospero & Miranda*—

How was it done? By first introducing his favourite character Miranda by a sentence which at once expresses the vehemence and violence of the storm such as it might appear to a witness from the land and at the same time displays the tenderness of her feelings; the exquisite feelings of a female brought up in a desert yet with all the advantages of education, all that could be given by a wise, learned & affectionate father: with all the powers of mind not weakened by the combats of life, Miranda says—

> —Oh I have suffered
> With those [that] I saw suffer! a brave vessel
> Which had *no doubt* some noble creatures in her
> Dashed all to pieces—[5]

The Doubt here expressed could have occurred to no mind but to that of Miranda who had been bred up with her father and a Monster only: she did not know as others do what sort of creatures were in a ship: they never would have introduced it as a conjecture.—This shows that while Shakespeare is displaying his vast excellence he never fails to introduce some touch or other wch not only makes [the scene] characteristic of the peculiar person but combines two things, the person and the circumstances that acted upon the person. She proceeds

> —Oh the cry did knock
> Against my very heart—Poor souls they perished.
> Had I been any God of power I would
> Have sunk the sea within the earth or ere
> It should the good ship so have swallowed &
> The freighting souls within her—[6]

4. *The Tempest* 1.1.25–29.
5. *The Tempest* 1.2.5–8 (C's emphasis).
6. *The Tempest* 1.2.8–13.

Still dwelling on that which was most wanting in her nature: these fellow creatures from whom she appeared banished with only one relict to keep them alive not in her memory but in her imagination.—

Another instance of excellent judgment (for Coleridge was principally speaking of that) was the preparation. Prospero is introduced first in his magic robes which with the assistance of his daughter he removes & it is the first time the reader knows him as a being possessing supernatural powers. Then he instructs his daughter in the story of their arrival in that Island and it is done in such a manner that no reader [ever][7] conjectures the technical use the poet has made of the relation, viz; informing the audience of the story—[8]

The next step is that Prospero gives warning that he means for particular purposes to lull Miranda to sleep and thus he exhibits his first & mildest proof of his magical power. It was not as in vulgar plays where a person is introduced that nobody knows or cares anything about merely to let the audience into the secret.—Prospero then lulls his Daughter asleep & by the sleep stops the relation at the very moment when it was necessary to break it off in order to excite curiosity and yet to give the memory & understanding sufficient to carry on the progress of the fable uninterruptedly—[9]

Coleridge could not help here noticing a fine touch of Shakespeare's knowledge of human nature, & generally of the great laws of the mind: he meant Miranda's infant remembrance. Prospero asks her

> —Canst thou remember
> A time before we came unto this cell?
> I do not think thou canst; for then thou wast not
> But three years old.—
> > *Miranda answers*
> Certainly sir, I can—
> > *Prospero enquires*
> By what?—By any other house or person?
> Of anything the image tell me that
> Hath kept with thy remembrance.
> > *Miranda replies*
> Tis far off—
> And rather like a dream than an assurance
> That my remembrance warrants. Had I not
> Four or five women, once that tended me?[1]

This is exquisite.—In general our early remembrances of life arise from vivid colours especially if we have seen them in motion: persons when grown up for instance will remember a bright green door seen when they were young: but in Miranda, who was somewhat older it was by 4 or 5 women. She might know men from her father & her remembrance of the past might be worn out by the present object but women she only knew by herself, the contemplation of her own figure

7. Collier's transcript has "never."
8. C refers to act 1, scene 2 of *The Tempest*.
9. *The Tempest* 1.2.185–87.
1. *The Tempest* 1.2.38–47 (var.).

in the fountain and yet she recalled to her mind what had been. It is not that she saw such and such Grandees, or such & such peeresses but she remembered to have seen something like a reflection of herself but it was not herself and it brought back to her mind what she had seen most like herself: it was a constant yearning of fancy reproducing the past, of what she had only seen in herself & could only see in herself.

* * *

The power of Poetry is by a single word to produce that energy in the mind as compells the imagination to produce the picture. Thus when Prospero says

> one midnight
> Fated to his purpose did Antonio open
> The gates of Milan & i' the dead of darkness
> The Ministers for his purpose hurried thence
> Me & thy crying self.[2]

Thus by introducing the simple happy epithet *crying* in the last line a complete picture is present to the mind & in this the power of true poetry consists.

Coleridge would next mention the preparation of the reader first by the storm as before mentioned. The introduction of all that preceded the tale, as well as the tale itself served completely to develope the main character and the intention of Prospero. The fact of Miranda being charmed asleep fits us for what goes beyond our ordinary belief and gradually leads us to the appearance and disclosure of a being gifted with supernatural powers.—

Before the introduction of Ariel too the reader was prepared by what preceded: the moral feeling called forth by the sweet words of Miranda "Alack what trouble was I then to you"[3]—in which she considered only the sufferings & sorrows of her parent; the reader was prepared to exert his imagination for an object so interesting. The Poet made him wish that if supernatural agency were employed it should be used for a being so lovely.—"The wish was father to the thought"—[4]

In this state of mind was comprehended what is called Poetic Faith[5] before which our common notions of philosophy give way: This feeling was much stronger than historic faith in as much as by the former the mind was prepared to exercise it.

* * *

Coleridge now returned to the introduction of Ariel prepared as he had explained—If ever there could be a doubt that Shakespeare was a great Poet acting by laws arising out of his own nature and not acting without law as had been asserted it would be removed by the character

2. *The Tempest* 1.2.128–32 (var.).
3. *The Tempest* 1.2.151–52: "Alack, what trouble / Was I then to you!"
4. C adapts King Henry's remark to Prince Harry in *2 Henry IV* 4.3.220 (4.5.92 in some editions): "Thy wish was father, Harry, to that thought."
5. See *Biographia Literaria* (p. 490 herein) for further discussion of what C there calls "that willing suspension of disbelief for the moment, which constitutes poetic faith."

of Ariel. The very first words spoken by Ariel[6] introduced him not as an Angel above men, not as a Gnome or a Fiend but while the Poet gives him all the advantages all the faculties of reason he divests him of all moral character not positively but negatively. In air he lives, and from air he derives his being. In air he acts and all his colours & properties seem to be derived from the clouds.—There is nothing in Ariel that cannot be conceived to exist in the atmosphere at sunrise or sunset: hence all that belongs to Ariel is all that belongs to the delight the mind can receive from external appearances abstracted from any inborn or [individual][7] purpose. His answers to Prospero are either directly to the question and nothing beyond, or if he expatiates which he does frequently it is upon his own delights, & the unnatural situation in which he is placed tho' under a good power and employed to good ends. Hence Shakespeare has made his very first demand characteristic of him. He is introduced discontented from his confinement, & from being bound to obey any thing that he is commanded: we feel it almost unnatural to him & yet it is delightful that he is so employed. It is as if we were to command one of the winds to blow otherwise than nature dictates or one of the waves, now sinking away and now rising, to recede before it bursts upon the shore—This is the sort of feeling we experience.

But when Shakespeare contrasts the treatment of Prospero with that of Sycorax instead of producing curses and discontent, Ariel feels his obligation, he immediately assumes the airy being with a mind in which when one feeling is past not a trace is left behind—

If there be anything in nature from which Shakespeare caught the idea of Ariel [it is] from the child to whom supernatural powers are given: he is neither born of Heaven nor of earth but between both: it is like a May blossom kept by the fanning breeze from falling to the ground suspended in air, and only by violence of compulsion touching the earth. This aversion of the Sylph is kept up through the whole and Shakespeare in his admirable judgment has availed himself of this circumstance to give Ariel an interest in the event looking forward to that moment when he was to gain his last and only reward simple liberty—

Another instance of admirable judgment and preparation is the being contrasted with Ariel, Caliban, who is described in such a manner by Prospero as to lead the Reader to expect & look for a monstrous unnatural creature. You do not see Caliban at once—you first hear his voice: it was a sort of preparation because in nature we do not receive so much disgust from sound as from sight—Still Caliban does not appear but Ariel enters as a Water Nymph:[8] all the strength of contrast is thus acquired without any of the shock of abruptness or of the unpleasant feeling which surprize awakes when the object is a being in any way hateful to our senses.

The character of Caliban is wonderfully conceived: he is a sort of

---

6. The lines suggest both Ariel's incorporeality and his powers: "All hail, great master, grave sir, I come / To answer thy best pleasure. Be't to fly, / To swim, to dive into the fire, to ride / On the curled clowds, to thy strong bidding task / Ariel" (*The Tempest* 1.2.190–94).
7. This word appears in Collier's shorthand notes but not in his longhand transcript (*Lects 1808–19* [CC], 1:363n. 42).
8. C refers to the stage direction after 1.2.319: "Enter Ariel, like a water-nymph."

creature of the earth partaking of the qualities of the brute and distinguished from them in two ways, 1. by having mere understanding without moral reason, 2. by not having the instincts which belong to mere animals.—Still Caliban is a noble being: a man in the sense of the imagination, all the images he utters are drawn from nature & are all highly poetical; they fit in with the images of Ariel: Caliban gives you images from the Earth—Ariel images from the air.[9] Caliban talks of the difficulty of finding fresh water, the situation of Morasses & other circumstances which the brute instinct not possessing reason could comprehend.[1] No mean image is brought forward and no mean passion but animal passions & the sense of repugnance at being commanded.

The manner in which the Lovers are introduced is equally excellent and the last point the Lecturer would mention in this wonderful play: In every scene the same judgment might be pointed out, still preparing and still recalling like a lively piece of music. One thing however, he wished to notice before he concluded & that was the subject of the Conspiracy against the life of Alonzo & how our Poet had so well prepared the feelings of his readers for their plot, which was to execute the most detestable of all crimes & which in another play Shakespeare had called "the murder of sleep"—[2]

These men at first had no such notion: it was suggested only by the magical sleep cast on Alonzo & Gonzalo: but they are previously introduced as scoffing & scorning at what was said without any regard to situation or age:[3] without any feelings of admiration of the excellent truths but giving themselves up entirely to the malignant & unsocial feeling that of listening to everything that is said not to understand and to profit by the learning & experience of others but to find something that may gratify vanity by making them believe that the person speaking is inferior to themselves—

*   *   *

Before he terminated however he would take notice of one passage which had fallen under the very severe censure of Pope & Arbuthnot who had declared it to be a piece of the grossest bombast—It was this Prospero addressing himself to his Daughter directing her attention to Ferdinand—

> The fringed curtains of thine eye advance
> And say, what thou seest yond?—[4]

9. Schlegel observed this as well, though only in passing (Lectures, 2:180).
1. In 1.2.340–41 Caliban expresses regret at having shown Prospero "all the qualities o'th' isle, / The fresh springs, brine-pits, barren place and fertile." In The Friend (p. 556 herein) C emphasizes that both animals and humans possess understanding, but only humans possess reason.
2. Conspiracy: C refers to the shipwrecked party of Alonso, king of Naples, in act 2, scene 1, of The Tempest: while the king and his counselor Gonzalo sleep, Prospero's brother Antonio and Alonso's brother Sebastian plot to kill the sleeping men, but are prevented from doing so by Ariel. Another play: Macbeth, in which Macbeth, having just killed Duncan, tells Lady Macbeth that he has heard a voice crying, "Sleep no more, / Macbeth does murder sleep" (2.2.33–34).
3. I.e., Antonio and Sebastian do not consider killing Alonso and Gonzalo before they are presented with an opportunity to do so, but they are arrogant and sarcastic from the play's beginning.
4. The Tempest 1.2.412–13, Prospero intending Miranda to fall in love with Alonso's son Ferdinand, who is the first man she has seen besides her father and Caliban. The lines are quoted, as an example of "cumbrous" style, in Peri Bathous: or, Of the Art of Sinking in Poetry (1728)—a work in which Pope probably had a much larger share than did his friend John Arbuthnot (1667–1735).

Putting this passage as a paraphraze of "Look what is coming," it certainly did appear ridiculous and seemed to fall under the rule Coleridge had laid down that whatever without injury could be translated into a foreign language in simple terms ought to be so in the original or it is not good—[5]

But the different modes of expression it should be remembered frequently arose from dif[ference] of situation & education: a blackguard would use very different words to express the same thing, to those a gentleman would employ and both would be natural & proper: the difference arose from the feeling: the gentleman would speak with all the polished language and regard to his own dignity which belonged to his rank, while the blackguard who must be considered almost a half brute and would speak like a half brute having respect neither for himself or others.—

*   *   *

This solemnity of phraseology was in Coleridge's opinion completely in character with Prospero who was assuming the Magician whose very art seems to consider all the objects of nature in a mysterious point of view and who wishes to produce a strong impression on Miranda at the first view of Ferdinand—

It is much easier to find fault with a writer merely by reference to former notions & experience than to sit down & read him and to connect the one feeling with the other & to judge of words & phrazes in proportion as they convey those feelings together.

Miranda possessed in herself all the ideal beauties that could be conceived by the greatest Poet altho' it was not Coleridge's object so much to point out the high Poetic powers of Shakespeare as his exquisite judgment. But to describe one of the female characters of Shakespeare was almost to describe the whole for each possessed all the excellences with which they could be invested.—

Coleridge concluded by a panegyric upon Shakespeare whom he declared to be the wonder of the ignorant part of mankind but much more the wonder of the learned who at the same time that he possessed profundity of thought could be looked upon as no less than a Prophet—Yet at the same time with all his wonderful powers making us feel as if [he] were unconscious of himself & of his mighty abilities: disguising the half-god in the simplicity of a child or the affection of a dear companion—[6]

---

5. C restates this "rule" in *Biographia Literaria* (p. 389 herein).
6. This conclusion recalls Schegel's extravagant praise of Shakespeare: "The world of spirits and nature have laid all their treasures at his feet: in strength a demi-god, in profoundity of view a prophet, in all-seeing wisdom a protecting spirit of a higher order, he lowers himself to mortals, as if unconscious of his superiority, and is as open and unassuming as a child" (*Lectures*, 2:138).

[On *Hamlet*]¹

* * *

The Lecturer then passed to Hamlet, in order, as he said, to obviate some of the general prejudices against Shakespeare in reference to the character of the hero.² Much had been objected to, which ought to have been praised, and many beauties of the highest kind had been neglected, because they were somewhat hidden.

The first question was—What did Shakespeare mean when he drew the character of Hamlet? Coleridge's belief was that the poet regarded his story before he began to write much in the same light that a painter looked at his canvas before he began to paint. What was the point to which Shakespeare directed himself? He meant to pourtray a person in whose view the external world and all its incidents and objects were comparatively dim, and of no interest in themselves, and which began to interest only when they were reflected in the mirror of his mind. Hamlet beheld external objects in the same way that a man of vivid imagination who shuts his eyes, sees what has previously made an impression upon his organs.

Shakespeare places him in the most stimulating circumstances that a human being can be placed in: he is the heir apparent of the throne: his father dies suspiciously: his mother excludes him from the throne by marrying his uncle. This was not enough but the Ghost of the murdered father is introduced to assure the son that he was put to death by his own brother. What is the result? Endless reasoning and urging—perpetual solicitation of the mind to act, but as constant an escape from action—ceaseless reproaches of himself for his sloth, while the whole energy of his resolution passes away in those reproaches. This, too, not from cowardice, for he is made one of the bravest of his time—not from want of forethought or quickness of apprehension, for he sees through the very souls of all who surround him, but merely from that aversion to action which prevails among such as have a world within themselves.³

---

1. This discussion of the character of Hamlet comes from the second half of the twelfth lecture of the 1811–12 series, given on January 2, 1812, at the London Philosophical Society; the first half of the lecture was devoted to *Richard II*. Henry Crabb Robinson who considered this lecture the best he had heard thus far in the series, noted in C's discussion of Hamlet "striking observations on the virtue of action and the futility of talents that divert from rather than lead to action. I doubt whether he did not design that an application should be made to himself" (*CRB*, 1:57). The text printed here follows that in *Lects 1808–19* (CC), 1:385–90, but omits the cancellations and silently incorporates Collier's manuscript insertions into the text.
2. C would have been familiar with the criticisms by, among others, Samuel Johnson and August Wilhelm Schlegel. In his edition of Shakespeare (1765) Johnson accused the playwright "of having shewn little regard to poetical justice" and suggested that he "may be charged with equal neglect of poetical probability" (*The Yale Edition of the Works of Samuel Johnson*, vol. 8, ed. Arthur Sherbo [New Haven, Conn., 1968], 1011). In one of his 1808 lectures on drama Schlegel complained that Hamlet is hypocritical, malicious, and "has no firm belief in himself or in any thing else" (*A Course of Lectures on Dramatic Art and Literature*, vol. 2, trans. John Black [London, 1815], 195). On Schlegel, see also the headnote, p. 307 herein.
3. C expands on this point later (p. 334 herein).

How admirable is the judgment of the poet! Hamlet's own fancy has not conjured up the Ghost of his father: it has been seen by others: he is by them prepared to witness its appearance, & when he does see it he is not brought forward as having long brooded on the subject. The moment before the Ghost enters Hamlet speaks of other matters in order to relieve the weight on his mind: he speaks of the coldness of the night, and observes that he has not heard the clock strike, adding, in reference to the custom of drinking that it is

> More honour'd in the breach, than the observance.[4]

From the tranquil state of his mind he indulges in moral reflections. Afterwards the Ghost suddenly enters

> Hor.   Look, my lord, it comes.
> Ham. Angels & Ministers of grace defend us![5]

The same thing occurs in Macbeth: in the dagger scene, the moment before he sees it he has his mind drawn to some indifferent matters;[6] thus the appearance has all the effect of abruptness, and the reader is totally divested of the notion that the vision is a figure in the highly wrought imagination.

Here Shakespeare adapts himself to the situation so admirably and as it were put himself into the situation that though poetry, his language is the language of nature: no words, associated with such feeling, can occur to us but those which he has employed especially on the highest, the most august & the most awful subject that can interest a human being in this sentient world. That this is no mere fancy Coleridge undertook to shew from Shakespeare himself.[7] No character he has drawn could so properly express himself as in the language put into his mouth.

There was no indecision about Hamlet: he knew well what he ought to do & over & over again he made up his mind to do it: the moment the Players and the two spies set upon him have withdrawn of whom he takes leave with the line, so expressive of his contempt

> Ay so; good bye you.—Now I am alone,[8]

he breaks out into a delirium of rage against himself for neglecting to perform the solemn duty he had undertaken, and contrasts the artificial feelings of the players with his own apparent indifference.

> What's Hecuba to him, or he to Hecuba
> That he should weep for her?[9]

4. *Hamlet* 1.4.18.
5. *Hamlet* 1.4.19–20.
6. Before murdering Duncan, the king of Scotland, Macbeth has a vision of a bloody dagger. *Indifferent matters*: C refers to Macbeth's instructions to a servant immediately preceding his vision (*Macbeth* 2.1.31–32).
7. The remainder of this sentence, which is canceled in the manuscript, runs: "as among other instances Hamlet, not long after the Players come in, where he speaks of a drama 'well digested in the scenes, & set down with as much modesty as cunning.' " The quotation is from *Hamlet* 2.2.421–22.
8. *Hamlet* 2.2.526 (Hamlet speaking to Rosencrantz, Guildenstern, and Polonius). C modernizes Hamlet's "God b' wi' ye" into "good bye you."
9. *Hamlet* 2.2.536–37.

Yet the player did weep for her, and was in an agony of grief at her sufferings, while Hamlet could not rouse himself to action that he might
do the bidding of his Father, who had come from the grave to incite
him to revenge:

> This is most brave,
> That I, the son of a dear father murdered,
> Prompted to my revenge by heaven and hell,
> Must like a whore, unpack my heart with words
> And fall a cursing, like a very drab,
> A scullion.[1]

It is the same feeling—the same conviction of what is his duty, that
makes Hamlet exclaim in a subsequent part of the tragedy

> How all occasions do inform against me,
> And spur my dull revenge! What is a man,
> If his chief good & market of his time
> *Be but to sleep and feed?* A beast, no more.
> ————————I do not know
> Why yet live I to say—this thing's to do
> Sith I have cause, & will & strength and means
> To do't.[2]

Yet with all this sense of duty, this resolution arising out of conviction nothing is done: this admirable & consistent character, deeply acquainted with his own feelings, painting them with such wonderful
power & accuracy, and just as strongly convinced of the fitness of executing the solemn charge committed to him, still yields to the same re-
tiring from all reality, which is the result of having what we express by
the terms a world within himself.

Such a mind as this is near akin to madness: Dryden has said

> Great wit to madness, *nearly* is allied[3]

and he was right; for he means by wit that greatness of genius, which
led Hamlet to the perfect knowledge of his own character, which with
all strength of motive was so weak as to be unable to carry into effect
his most obvious duty.

Still, with all this he has a sense of imperfectness, which becomes
obvious while he is moralising on the skull in the churchyard[4] something is wanted to make it complete—something is deficient and he is
therefore described as attached to Ophelia. His madness is assumed
when he discovers that witnesses have been placed behind the arras to
listen to what passes, & when the heroine has been thrown in his way
as a decoy.

Another objection has been taken by Dr Johnson, and has been

---

1. *Hamlet* 2.2.560–65 (var.).
2. *Hamlet* 4.4.9.22–25, 9.33–36 (a passage from the Second Quarto of the play; see *The Norton Shakespeare*, pp. 1666–67, on the differences between the quarto and folio texts).
3. *Absalom and Achitophel: A Poem* (1691), line 163: "Great Wits are sure to Madness near ally'd." See also p. 397, n. 6 herein.
4. *Hamlet* 5.1.170–80.

treated by him very severely. I refer to the scene in the third act where Hamlet enters and finds his Uncle praying, and refuses to assail him excepting when he is in the height of his iniquity: to take the King's life at such a moment of repentance & confession Hamlet declares

Why this is hire & salary, not revenge.[5]

He therefore forbears and postpones his Uncle's death until he can take him in some act

That has no relish of salvation in't.[6]

This sentiment D[r] Johnson has pronounced to be so atrocious & horrible as to be unfit to be put into the mouth of a human being.[7] The fact is that the determination to allow the King to escape at such a moment was only part of the same irresoluteness of character. Hamlet seizes hold of a pretext for not acting, when he might have acted so effectually. Therefore he again defers the revenge he sought, and declares his resolution to accomplish it at some time

When he is drunk, asleep, or in his rage,
Or in th'incestuous pleasures of his bed.[8]

This, as Coleridge repeated, was merely the excuse Hamlet made to himself for not taking advantage of this particular moment to accomplish his revenge.

D[r] Johnson further states that in the voyage to England Shakespeare merely followed the novel as he found it, as if he had no other motive for adhering to his original:[9] but Shakespeare never followed a novel but where he saw the story contributed to tell or explain some great & general truth inherent in human nature. It was unquestionably an incident in the old story & there it is used merely as an incident, but Shakespeare saw how it could be applied to his own great purpose, and how it was consistent with the character of Hamlet, that after still resolving and still refusing, still determining to execute and still postponing the execution, he should finally give himself up to his destiny, and in the infirmity of his nature at last hopelessly place himself in the power and at the mercy of his enemies.

Even after the scene with Osrick,[1] we see Hamlet still indulging in

5. *Hamlet* 3.3.79 (var.).
6. *Hamlet* 3.3.92.
7. Johnson objected to this scene in his edition of Shakespeare: "This speech, in which Hamlet, represented as a virtuous character, is not content with taking blood for blood, but contrives damnation for the man that he would punish, is too horrible to be read or to be uttered" (*The Yale Edition of the Works*, 8:990).
8. *Hamlet* 3.3.89–90 (var.).
9. As *Lects 1808–19* (CC), 1:390n. 38 points out, Johnson did not make the statement C attributes to him, but it does appear in an edition known to C, *The Plays of William Shakespeare*, vol. 18, ed. Isaac Reed (London, 1803), 270: "The circumstances mentioned as inducing the king to send the prince to England, rather than elsewhere, are likewise found in *The Hystory of Hamblet*." In *Hamlet* 4.3.39–45 Claudius tells Hamlet, who has just killed Polonius, that he must go to England for his own safety. This part of the play was indirectly derived from the account of Amleth, a Danish nobleman, in Saxo Grammaticus's *Historiae Danicae* (Danish History), written in the late 12th century but first printed in 1519.
1. Act 5, scene 2, in which Hamlet mocks Osric, the courtier sent to request that he fence with Laertes.

reflection, and thinking little of the new task he has just undertaken; he is all meditation, all resolution as far as words are concerned, but all hesitation & irresolution when called upon to act; so that resolving to do everything he in fact does nothing. He is full of purpose, but void of that quality of mind wch wo^d lead him at the proper time to carry his purpose into effect.

Anything finer than this conception & working out of a character is merely impossible: Shakespeare wished to impress upon us the truth that action is the great end of existence—that no faculties of intellect however brilliant can be considered valuable, or otherwise than as misfortunes, if they withdraw us from or render us repugnant to action, and lead us to think and think of doing, until the time has escaped when we ought to have acted.[2] In enforcing this truth Shakespeare has shewn the fulness, and force of his powers: all that is amiable and excellent in nature is combined in Hamlet, with the exception of this one quality: he is a man living in meditation, called upon to act by every motive human & divine but the great purpose of life defeated by continually resolving to do, yet doing nothing but resolve.

[On Dramatic Illusion][1]

We commence with the Tempest, as a specimen of the Romantic Drama.[2] But Whatever Play of Shakespere's we had selected, there is one preliminary point to be first settled, as the indispensable Condition not only of just and genial criticism,[3] but of all consistency in our opinions.—This point is contained in the words, probable, natural. We are all in the habit of praising Shakespear, or of hearing him extolled for his fidelity to Nature. Now what are we to understand by these words, in their application to the Drama? Assuredly, not the ordinary meaning of them. Farquar the most ably and if we except a few sentences in one of Dryden's Prefaces (written for a partic[ular] purp[ose] and in contrad[iction] to the opinions elsewhere supported by him)

2. The day after the lecture Crabb Robinson quoted this sentence in a letter and noted that its applicability to C himself had occurred to the audience: "Somebody said to me, this is a Satire on himself; No, said I, it is an elegy. A great many of his remarks on Hamlet were capable of a like application" (quoted in *Lects 1808–19* [CC], 1:391). T. S. Eliot, probably referring to this lecture, insisted that C "had made of Hamlet a Coleridge" ("Hamlet," in *Selected Essays*, 3rd ed. [London, 1951], 141); and C himself is supposed to have said on June 24, 1827, "I have a smack of Hamlet myself, if I may say so" (*Table Talk*, ed. HNC [London, 1835], 1:69). For further discussion of *Hamlet*, see "Essays on the Principle of Method" (pp. 563–64 herein).

1. C's notes for this lecture of December 17, 1818, on dramatic illusion and *The Tempest* are divided between three blank leaves in his interleaved copy of *The Dramatic Works of William Shakespeare*, vol. 1, ed. Samuel Ayscough (London, 1807), which he took with him into the lecture hall, and two leaves now gathered in BL MS Egerton 2800. The text printed here, which omits cancellations and silently incorporates C's corrections and additions, is taken from *Lects 1808–19* (CC), 2:264–66, though a few words have been altered in accordance with the text printed more recently in *CM* (CC), 4:779–81.

2. Later in his lecture notes C, following the German critic August Wilhelm Schlegel, defined "Romantic drama" as "a Drama, the interests of which are independent of all historical facts and associations, and arise from their fitness to that faculty of our nature, the Imagination I mean, which owes no allegiance to Time and Place" (*Lects 1808–19* [CC], 2:268).

3. See the headnote to *Essays on the Principles of Genial Criticism* (p. 339 herein).

first exposed the ludicrous absurdities involved in the supposition, and demolished as with the single sweep of a careless hand the whole Edifice of French Criticism respecting the so called Unities of Time and Place.[4]—But a moment's reflection suffices to make every man conscious of what every man must have before felt, that the Drama is an *imitation* of reality not a *Copy*—and that Imitation is contradistinguished from Copy by this, that a certain quantum is Difference is essential to the former, and an indispensable condition and cause of the pleasure, we derive from it; while in a Copy it is a defect, contravening its name and purpose.[5] If illustration were needed, it would be sufficient to ask—why we prefer a Fruit View of Vanuysen's to a marble Peach on a mantle-piece—or why we prefer an historical picture of West's to Mrs Salmon's Wax-figure Gallery.[6] Not only that we ought, but that we actually do, all of us judge of the Drama under this impression, we need no other proof than the impassive Slumber of our Sense of Probability when we hear a Actor announce himself a Greek, Roman, Venetian or Persian in good Mother English. And how little our great Dramatist feared awakening on it, we have a lively instance in proof in Portia's Answer to Neæra's question, What say you then to Falconbridge, the young Baron of England?—to which she replies—You know, I say nothing to him: for he understands not me nor I him. He hath neither Latin, French or Italian: and you will come into the Court and swear that I have a poor Penny-worth in the English.[7]

Still, however, there is a sort of Improbab[ilit]y with which we are shocked in dramatic repres[entatio]n no less than in the narration of real Life—Consequently, there must be Rules respecting it, and as Rules are nothing but Means to an end previously ascertained (the inattention to which simple truth has been the occasion of all the pedantry of the French School) we must first ascertain what the immediate End or Object of the Drama is—Here I find two extremes in critical decision—The French, which evidently presupposes that a perfect Delusion is to be aimed at—an Opinion which now needs no fresh confutation—The opposite, supported by Dr Johnson, supposes the auditors throughout as in the full and positive reflective knowlege[8]

---

4. The importance of the unities (see p. 321, n. 3 herein) had been asserted by French writers such as François Hédelin d'Aubignac (1604–1676), Pierre Corneille (1606–1684), and Voltaire. George Farquhar (?1677–1707), an Irish-born comic and satirical playwright, wrote disparagingly of the unities in *A Discourse upon Comedy* (1701). John Dryden (1631–1700), English poet, encouraged flexibility in adhering to the unities, advising that "better a mechanic rule were stretched or broken, than a great beauty were omitted" (*Essays*, ed. W. P. Ker [Oxford, 1926], 2:158, quoted in *Lects 1808–19* [CC], 2:264n. 2).

5. A favorite distinction of C's: whereas an imitation, which does not pretend to replicate the form or material of what it imitates, captures the essence of the original, a copy captures only the form, and thus calls attention to its difference in essence from the original. See also p. 497, n. 1 herein.

6. Mrs. Salmon's gallery of wax figures, a popular London attraction (like Madame Tussaud's today) from the end of the 17th century to 1831. Jan van Huysum (1683–1749), Dutch still-life painter (cf. *CL* 3:511). Benjamin West (1738–1820), American-born English historical painter.

7. C quotes *The Merchant of Venice* 1.2.55–60, in which Portia, a rich heiress, discusses Lord Falconbridge, one of her suitors, with her maid Nerissa (and not, as C has, Neaera, who is a maiden in Virgil's third *Eclogue* and is also mentioned in Milton's *Lycidas*, line 69).

8. C's habitual spelling of this word.

of the contrary. In evincing the impossibility of Delusion he makes no sufficient Allowance for an intermediate State, which we distinguish by the term, Illusion.[9] In what this consists, I cannot better explain, than by referring you to the highest degree of it, namely, Dreaming. It is laxly said, that during Sleep we take our Dreams for Realities; but this is irreconcilable with the nature of Sleep, which consists in a suspension of the voluntary and therefore of the comparative power.[1] The fact is, that we pass no judgement either way—we simply do *not* judge them to be unreal—in conseq[uence] of which Images act on our minds, as far as they act at all, by their own force as images. Our state while we are dreaming differs from that in which we are in the perusal of a deeply interesting Novel, in the degree rather than the Kind, and from three causes—First, from the exclusion of all outward impressions on our senses the images in Sleep become proportionally more vivid, than they can be when the organs of Sense are in their active state. Secondly, in sleep the Sensations, and with these the Emotions & Passions which they counterfeit, are the causes of our Dream-images, while in our waking hours our emotions are the effects of the Images presented to us—(*apparitions so detectible*). Lastly, in sleep we pass at once by a sudden collapse into this suspension of Will and the Comparative power: whereas in an interesting Play, read or represented, we are brought up to this point, as far as it is requisite or desirable gradually, by the Art of the Poet and the Actors, and with the consent and positive Aidance of our own will. We *chuse* to be deceived.—The rule therefore may be easily inferred. What ever tends to prevent the mind from placing it or from being gradually placed, in this state in which the Images have a negative reality, must be a defect, and consequently any thing that must force itself on the Auditors' minds as improbable—not because it *is* improbable (for that the whole play is foreknown to be) but because it can not but *appear* as such.

*   *   *

From ESSAYS ON THE PRINCIPLES OF GENIAL CRITICISM (1814)

On August 6, 1814, *Felix Farley's Bristol Journal*, a weekly newspaper whose editor, John Gutch, had known Coleridge from his Christ's Hospital days, announced a series of essays: "The termination of the calamities

9. In the preface to his edition of Shakespeare (1765), Johnson, making no distinction between delusion and illusion, insisted merely that the audience of a play never mistakes the play for reality and knows "from the first act to the last, that the stage is only a stage, and that the players are only players. * * * [The drama] is credited with all the credit due to a drama. It is credited * * * as a just picture of a real original; as representing to the auditor what he would himself feel, if he were to do or suffer what is there feigned to be suffered or to be done" (*The Yale Edition of the Works of Samuel Johnson*, vol. 7, ed. Arthur Sherbo [New Haven, Conn., 1968], 77–78). For C illusion, unlike delusion, is a consciously and voluntarily accepted state, requiring what he famously called in the *Biographia* "that willing suspension of disbelief for the moment, which constitutes poetic faith" (p. 490 herein).
1. C adheres to the dominant 18th-century understanding of dreams as combinations of remembered images formed randomly when the powers of judgment and will are weakened or suspended by sleep. See also "Dreams and Sleep" (p. 589 herein).

of war [with France] having at length furnished us with more vacant room, than we for years have been accustomed to find unoccupied, it is our intention, next week, to diversify our columns by the commencement of a series of Essays upon the FINE ARTS, particularly upon that of Painting, illustrated by Criticisms upon the Pictures now exhibiting by *Mr. Allston.* * * * The pleasure to be derived from their perusal will readily be anticipated, when we inform our readers, that they are furnished us by the pen of *Mr. Coleridge.*" Three essays and an appendix were published in the issues of August 13, 20, and 27, and September 10 and 24, 1814.

As the advertisement indicates, the essays were written to accompany an exhibition of paintings by Washington Allston (1799–1843), an American painter and writer best known for his large canvasses of religious scenes. Coleridge had met Allston in Rome in 1805, and resumed their friendship when Allston moved to London in 1811 (details of their friendship are given in CN, 2:2784n). In October 1813 both Coleridge and Allston moved to Bristol, and the following summer Allston exhibited some of his paintings there at the Merchant Taylor's Hall. (He also painted a portrait of Coleridge, now in the National Portrait Gallery, London.) Coleridge claimed on September 12, 1814, that his purpose in writing the essays was to draw favorable attention to Allston, who at the time was in poor health and financial difficulty (CL, 3:354), but a letter of July 1814 revealed his broader purpose of laying down the fundamental principles of criticism of the fine arts: "I thought, that a bold Avowal of *my* sentiments on the fine Arts, as divided into—Poetry—1 of language—2 of the ear— and 3 of the eye—& the last subdivided into the *plastic* (statuary) & the graphic (painting), connected (& as it were *isthmused*) with common Life by the Link of Architecture—& exemplifying my principles by continual reference to Allston's Pictures—would * * * answer our friend's *pecuniary* interests best" (CL, 3:520). In particular, Coleridge is concerned with distinguishing between beauty and pleasure: while many things that give pleasure are not beautiful (Coleridge's example is a haunch of venison), beautiful things give pleasure precisely because they are beautiful. And beauty, he maintains, consists in the appearance of a unified form within a diversity of elements—"Multëity in Unity" (Essay 2). Like Immanuel Kant, to whose *Critique of Judgment* (1790) he is heavily indebted in formulating his argument, Coleridge insists that the judgment of something as beautiful can claim universal validity. But unlike Kant, he tries to explain that validity by proposing an innate harmony between the perceiving subject and the perceived object. (The complicated relation of Coleridge's essays to the *Critique of Judgment* is examined by Wellek, *Immanuel Kant in England* [Princeton, 1931], 111–14, and by Orsini, *Coleridge and German Idealism*, 167–71.) In September 1814 Coleridge declared the essays "the best compositions, *I* have ever written" (CL, 3:535), but he did not republish them and at the end of his life regretted that he had no copy of them (TT [CC], 1:453).

The first essay appeared under the general title "On the PRINCIPLES OF SOUND CRITICISM," but the second and third essays substituted "GENIAL" for "SOUND." What Coleridge meant by "genial" was clearly not "jovial," "kindly," or "sociable"—the usual meanings of the word at the time (OED)—but perhaps closer to "generative" or "creative" (cf. "Dejection: An Ode," line 39, p. 156 herein). The meanings of the German word *genial*—"intelligent," "gifted," "brilliant"—may also have been in his mind. Orsini interprets "genial criticism" as meaning "sympathetically evaluating

Genius" (168), and notes the relevance of one of Coleridge's annotations of Milton: "the genial Judgement is to distinguish accurately the characters & characteristics of each poem, praising them according to their force & vivacity in their own kind—& to reserve Reprehension for such as have no *character*" (*CM* [*CC*], 3:886). But Coleridge's own explanation of his goal might be the best gloss on the term: "to judge in the same spirit in which the Artist produced, or ought to have produced" (Preliminary Essay). In an 1815 letter to Byron, Coleridge referred to the work that was to grow into the *Biographia* as a "general Preface * * * on the Principles of philosophic and genial criticism relatively to the Fine Arts in general; but especially to Poetry" (*CL*, 4:561).

The text is taken from *Felix Farley's Bristol Journal*, August 20 and 27, and September 10, 1814.

From Essay 2

On the principles of Genial Criticism *concerning the* Fine Arts, *more especially those of* Statuary *and* Painting, *deduced from the laws and impulses which guide the true* Artist *in the production of his works.*

In Mathematics the definitions, of necessity, precede not only the demonstrations, but likewise the postulates and axioms: they are the rock, which at once forms the foundation and supplies the materials of the edifice. Philosophy, on the contrary, concludes with the definition: it is the result, the compendium, the remembrancer of all the preceding facts and inferences.[1] Whenever, therefore, it appears in the front, it ought to be considered as a faint outline, which answers all its intended purposes, if only it circumscribe the subject and direct the reader's anticipation toward the one road, on which he is to travel.

Examined from this point of view, the definition of Poetry, in the preliminary Essay, as the regulative idea of all the Fine Arts, appears to me after many experimental applications of it to general illustrations and to individual instances, liable to no just *logical* reversion, or complaint: "the excitement of emotion for the purpose of *immediate* pleasure, through the medium of beauty."[2]—But like all previous statements in Philosophy (as distinguished from Mathematics) it has the inconvenience of presuming conceptions, which do not perhaps consciously or distinctly exist. Thus, the former part of my definition might appear equally applicable to any object of our animal appetites, till by after-reasonings the attention has been directed to the full force of the word "*immediate;*" and till the mind, by being led to refer discriminatingly to its own experience, has become conscious that all objects of mere desire constitute an *interest* (i.e. aliquid quod *est inter*

---

1. As René Wellek notes (*Immanuel Kant in England*, 111), the first two sentences of this essay loosely paraphrase the second section of Kant's *Inquiry Concerning the Distinctness of the Principles of Natural Theology and Morality* (1763; see Walford, 250–51).
2. The quotation marks are used to mark off the definition, not to indicate a quotation from another text.

hoc et aliud, or that which *is between* the agent and his motive) and which is therefore valued only as the means to the end.[3] To take a trivial but unexceptionable instance, the venison is aggreable because it gives pleasure; while the Apollo Belvidere[4] is not beautiful because it pleases, but it pleases us because it is beautiful. The term, pleasure, is unfortunately so comprehensive, as frequently to become equivocal: and yet it is hard to discover a substitute. *Complacency*, which would indeed better express the intellectual nature of the enjoyment essentially involved in the sense of the beautiful, yet seems to preclude all emotion: and *delight*, on the other hand, conveys a comparative *degree* of pleasurable emotion, and is therefore unfit for a *general* definition, the object of which is to abstract the *kind*.[5] For this reason, we added the words "through the medium of beauty." But here the same difficulty recurs from the promiscuous use of the term, Beauty. Many years ago the writer in company with an accidental party of travellers was gazing on a cataract of great height, breadth, and impetuosity, the summit of which appeared to blend with the sky and clouds, while the lower part was hidden by rocks and trees; and on his observing, that it was in the strictest sense of the word, a sublime object, a lady present assented with warmth to the remark, adding—"Yes! and it is not only sublime, but beautiful and absolutely *pretty*."[6]

And let not these distinctions be charged on the writer, as obscurity and needless subtlety; for it is in the nature of all disquisitions on matters of taste, that the reasoner must appeal for his very premises to facts of feeling and of inner sense, which all men do not possess, and which many, who do possess and even act upon them, yet have never reflectively adverted to, have never made them objects of a full and distinct consciousness. The Geometrician refers to certain figures in space, and to the power of describing certain lines, which are intuitive to all men, as men; & therefore his demonstrations are throughout *compulsory*. The Moralist and the Philosophic Critic lay claim to no *positive*, but only to a *conditional* necessity. It is not necessary, that A or B should judge *at all* concerning poetry; but *if* he does, in order to a just taste such and such faculties *must have* been developed in his mind.[7] If a man upon questioning his own experience can detect no

---

3. C here draws on Kant's definition of the beautiful as an object of disinterested contemplation—i.e., as something necessarily pleasing to the mind, without reference to a prior knowledge of the object and without regard for its actual existence (Kant, *Judgment*, section 5). *Immediate*: equivalent to "disinterested." The Latin phrase means "something that *is between* this thing and another."
4. See p. 343, n. 5 herein.
5. C's distinction between "complacency" and "delight" corresponds to Kant's distinction between "satisfaction" (*Wohlgefallen*), a feeling derived from "the agreeable," and "gratification" (*Vergnügen*), a feeling derived from "the beautiful" (Kant, *Judgment*, section 5).
6. C liked using this anecdote to illustrate the imprecise use of philosophical terms and told slightly different versions of it in his literary lectures of January 15, 1808, and November 18, 11 (*Lects 1808–19* [CC], 1:34, 193). The incident had occurred on August 21, 1803, at the Falls of the Clyde in Scotland, during a trip with the Wordsworths.
7. Cf. Kant, *Judgment*, section 19: "A judgment of taste ascribes assent to everyone, and whoever declares something to be beautiful wishes that everyone *should* approve of the object in question and similarly declare it to be beautiful. The *should* in aesthetic judgments is thus pronounced only conditionally. * * * One solicits assent from everyone else because one has a ground for it that is common to all."

difference in *kind* between the enjoyment derived from the eating of turtle, and that from the perception of a new truth; if in *his* feelings a taste *for* Milton is essentially the same as the taste *of* mutton, he may still be a sensible and a valuable member of Society; but it would be desacration[8] to argue with him on the Fine Arts; and should he himself dispute on them, or even publish a book (and such books *have* been perpetrated within the memory of man), we can answer him only by silence or a courteous waiving of the subject. To tell a blind man declaiming concerning light and color, "you should wait till you have got eyes to see with" would indeed be telling the truth, but at the same time be acting a useless as well as an inhuman part. An English critic, who assumes and proceeds on the identity in kind of the pleasures derived from the palate and from the intellect, and who literally considers *taste* to mean one and the same thing, whether it be the taste of venison, or a taste for Virgil, and who in strict consistence with his principles passes sentence on Milton as a tiresome poet, because he finds nothing *amusing* in the Paradise Lost (i.e. damnat *Musas*, quia animum *a musis* non divertunt)[9]—this taste-meter to the fashionable world gives a ludicrous portrait of an African Belle, and concludes with a triumphant exclamation "such is the ideal of beauty in Dahoma!"[1] Now it is curious, that a very intelligent traveller,[2] describing the low state of the human mind in this very country, gives as an instance, that in their whole language they have no word for Beauty or the beautiful; but say either it is nice, or it is good; doubtless, says he, because this very sense is as yet dormant, and the idea of beauty as little developed in their minds as in that of an infant.—I give the substance of the meaning, not the words; as I quote both writers from memory.

There are few mental exertions more instructive, or which are capable of being rendered more entertaining, than the attempt to establish and exemplify the distinct meaning of terms, often confounded in common use, and considered as mere synonymes.[3] Such are the words, Agreeable, Beautiful, Picturesque, Grand, Sublime: and to at-

---

8. C's usual spelling of this word.
9. "He condemns the *Muses* because they do not divert his mind *from the muses*" (i.e., from his studies, in this case of the poem itself). A variant of this bilingual pun on the word "amusing" appears in *BL* (CC), 1:48. Samuel Johnson complained in his *Life of Milton* that "We read Milton for instruction, retire harassed and overburdened, and look elsewhere for recreation" (*Lives of the Poets*, ed. G. B. Hill [Oxford, 1905], 1:183–84); but the critic that C means here is the associationist Richard Payne Knight (1750–1824), who quoted Johnson's complaint approvingly in *An Analytical Inquiry into the Principles of Taste*, 2nd ed. (London, 1805), 116–17.
1. I.e., Dahomey, the West African kingdom where the slave trade was centered. Not a quotation but a murky recollection of Knight's comparison of European and African ideals of beauty in the *Analytical Inquiry* (13–15). Knight's point, with which C disagrees, is that ideals of beauty are not universally shared but culturally specific. *SW&F* (CC), 364n. 1 refers to a notebook entry of 1804 in which C interpreted the supposed attractiveness of whiteness to black people as an argument "in favor of permanent Principles of *Beauty* as distinguishable from Association or the Agreeable" (*CN*, 2:2604).
2. Unidentified.
3. This is what C elsewhere calls "desynonymizing" (see p. 417, n. 7 herein).

tach a distinct and separate sense to each of these is a previous step of indispensable necessity to a writer, who would reason intelligibly, either to himself or to his readers, concerning the works of poetic genius, and the sources and the nature of the pleasure derived from them.[4] But more especially on the essential difference of the Beautiful and the Agreeable rests fundamentally the whole question, which assuredly must possess no vulgar or feeble interest for all who regard the dignity of their own nature: whether the noblest productions of human genius (such as the Iliad, the Works of Shakespear and Milton, the Pantheon, Rafael's Gallery, and Michael Angelo's Sestine Chapel, the Venus de Medici and the Apollo Belvidere,[5] involving of course the human forms that approximate to them in actual life) delight us merely by chance, from accidents of local associations—in short, please us because they please us (in which case it would be impossible either to praise or to condemn any man's taste, however opposite to our own, and we could be no more justified in assigning a corruption or absence of just taste to a man, who should prefer Blackmore to Homer or Milton, or the Castle Spectre to Othello,[6] than to the same man for preferring a black-pudding to a sirloin of beef: or whether there exists in the constitution of the human Soul a sense, and a regulative principle, which may indeed be stifled and latent in some, and be perverted and denaturalized in others, yet is nevertheless universal in a given state of intellectual and moral culture; which is independent of local and temporary circumstances, and dependent only on the degree in which the faculties of the mind are developed; and which, consequently, it is our duty to cultivate and improve, as soon as the sense of its actual existence dawns upon us.* * * TASTE is the intermediate faculty which connects the active with the passive powers of our nature, the intellect with the senses; and its appointed function is to elevate the *images* of the latter, while it realizes the *ideas* of the former. We must therefore have learnt what is peculiar to each, before we can understand that "Third something,"[7] which is formed by an harmony of both.

4. Shortly before composing the present essays on "genial criticism," C had defined "the beautiful" as the "*distinct* Perception of a Whole arising out of a *clear* simultaneous Perception of the constituent Parts"; "the picturesque," as the distinct perception of the parts and clear perception of the whole; "the grand," as the vivid perception of the parts without a perception of the whole; and "the sublime," as the suspension of "the Comparative Power" with respect to both parts and whole (SW&F [CC], 350–51).

5. A conventional list, in C's time and ours, of examples of artistic greatness. The Pantheon is a 2nd-century domed temple in Rome. Raphael painted frescoes in the papal apartments (1509–17). Michelangelo painted the ceiling (1508–12) and altar (1536–41) of the Sistine Chapel. The *Venus de' Medici* and *Apollo Belvedere*, both ancient copies of older Greek statues (although thought in C's time to be originals), were regarded in the 18th century and later to be the epitomes of female and male beauty, respectively.

6. Matthew Gregory ("Monk") Lewis's play *The Castle Spectre* (1797), which C had read in January 1798 and described contemptuously to Wordsworth (CL, 1:378–79), was a popular Gothic melodrama. Sir Richard Blackmore (1654–1729), author of *Prince Arthur: An Heroic Poem* and five other epics, was regarded even in his own lifetime as a failed epic poet.

7. The English translation of the Latin *tertium aliquid*, which C used frequently (e.g., p. 485 herein, where he applied it to the imagination as a synthesis of mind and nature). Here he means that taste depends on the senses and the intellect acting in concert.

From Essay 3

On the PRINCIPLES *of* GENIAL CRITICISM concerning the
FINE ARTS, especially those of STATUARY and PAINTING.

* * *

AGREEABLE.—We use this word in two senses, in the first for whatever agrees with our nature, for that which is congruous with the primary constitution of our senses.[1] Thus green is naturally agreeable to the eye. In this sense the word expresses, at least involves, a pre-established harmony[2] between the organs and their appointed objects. In the second sense, we convey by the word agreeable, that the thing has by force of habit (thence called a second nature) been *made* to agree with us; or that it has become agreeable to us by its recalling to our minds some one or more things that were dear and pleasing to us; or lastly, on account of some after pleasure or advantage, of which it has been the constant cause or occasion. Thus by force of custom men *make* the taste of tobacco, which was at first hateful to the palate, agreeable to them; thus too, as our Shakespear observes,

> Things base and vile, holding no quantity,
> Love can transpose to form and dignity—[3]

the crutch that had supported a revered parent, after the first anguish of regret, becomes agreeable to the affectionate child; and I once knew a very sensible and accomplished Dutch gentleman, who spite of his own sense of the ludicrous nature of the feeling, was more delighted by the first grand concert of frogs he heard in this country, than he had been by Catalani singing the compositions of Cimarosa.[4] The last clause needs no illustrations, as it comprizes all the objects that are agreeable to us, only because they are the means by which we gratify our smell, touch, palate, and mere bodily feeling.

The BEAUTIFUL, contemplated in its essentials, that is, in *kind* and not in *degree*, is that in which *the many*, still seen as many, becomes *one*. Take a familiar instance, one of a thousand. The frost on a window-pane has by accident chrystallized into a striking resemblance of a tree or a sea-weed. With what pleasure we trace the parts, and their relations to each other, and to the whole! Here is the stalk or trunk, and here the branches or sprays—sometimes even the buds or flowers. Nor will our pleasure be less, should the caprice of chrystallization represent some object disagreeable to us, provided only we can

1. Cf. Kant, *Judgment*, section 3: "*The agreeable is that which pleases the senses in sensation.* Now here there is an immediate opportunity to reprove and draw attention to a quite common confusion of the double meaning that the word 'sensation' can have." The first meaning to which Kant refers is the act of perception; the second, the act of associating a feeling with a perceived object. He explains the latter by referring to a green meadow: while its greenness belongs to "*objective* sensation," its agreeableness belongs to "*subjective* sensation" (92).
2. A term associated with the German philosopher G. W. Leibniz (1646–1716), who used it to explain how the individual entities ("monads") of which he thought the universe to be composed were related to each other.
3. *A Midsummer Night's Dream* 1.1.232–33.
4. Domenico Cimarosa (1749–1801), an Italian composer of comic operas, one of C's favorite composers. Angelica Catalani (1780–1849), a celebrated Italian soprano whom C admired.

see or fancy the component parts each in relation to each, and all forming a whole. A lady would see an admirably painted tiger with pleasure, and at once pronounce it beautiful,—nay, an owl, a frog, or a toad, who would have shrieked or shuddered at the sight of the things themselves. So far is the Beautiful from depending wholly on association, that it is frequently produced by the mere removal of associations. Many a sincere convert to the beauty of various insects, as of the dragon-fly, the fangless snake, &c. has Natural History made by exploding the terror or aversion, that had been connected with them.

The most general definition of Beauty, therefore, is—that I may fulfil my threat of plaguing my readers with hard words—Multëity in Unity.[5] Now it will be always found, that whatever is the definition of the *kind*, independent of degree, becomes likewise the definition of the highest degree of that kind. An old coach-wheel lies in the coach maker's yard, disfigured with tar and dirt—(I purposely take the most trivial instances)—if I turn away my attention from these, and regard the *Figure* abstractedly, "still," I might say to my companion, "there is Beauty in that wheel, and you yourself would not only admit, but would feel it, had you never seen a wheel before. See how the rays proceed from the centre to the circumferences, and how many different images are distinctly comprehended at one glance, as forming one whole, and each part in some harmonious relation to each and to all." But imagine the polished golden wheel of the chariot of the Sun,[6] as the Poets have described it: then the figure, and the real thing so figured, exactly coincide. There is nothing heterogeneous, nothing to abstract from: by its perfect smoothness and circularity in width, each part is (if I may borrow a metaphor from a sister sense) as perfect a melody, as the whole is a compleat harmony. This, we should say, is beautiful throughout. Of all "the many," which I actually see, each and all are really reconciled into unity: while the effulgence from the whole coincides with, and seems to represent, the effluence of delight from my own mind in the intuition of it.

It seems evident then, 1st. that Beauty is harmony, and subsists only in composition; & 2dly, that the first species of the Agreeable can alone be a component part of the beautiful, that namely which is naturally consonant with our senses by the pre-established harmony between nature & the human mind; and 3dly, that even of this species, those objects only can be admitted (according to rule the first) which belong to the eye and ear, because they alone are susceptible of distinction of parts. Should an Englishman gazing on a mass of cloud rich with the rays of the rising sun exclaim, even without distinction of or reference to its form, or its relation to other objects, how beautiful! I should have no quarrel with him. First, because by the law of association there is in all visual beholdings at least an indistinct subsumption of form and re-

---

5. A favorite expression of C's, which he elaborates as "reducing multitude to unity" (*BL* [CC], 2:23) and even uses as a definition of life itself (see p. 596, n. 5 herein). See Orsini, *Coleridge and German Idealism* (170–71) for the background of this formula.
6. In Greek myth the chariot of Helios, the sun god (see Ovid, *Metamorphoses* 2.107–10, and Dante, *Purgatorio* 29.115–20).

lation, and 2ndly, because even in the coincidence between the sight and the object there is an approximation to the reduction of *the many* into one.[7] But who, that heard a Frenchman call the flavour of a leg of mutton a *beautiful* taste, would not immediately recognize him for a Frenchman, even tho' there should be neither grimace or characteristic nasal twang?[8] The result then of the whole is that the shapely (i.e. *formosus*) joined with the *naturally* agreeable, constitutes what speaking accurately we mean by the word Beautiful (i.e. *Pulcher.*)[9]

But we are conscious of faculties far superior to the highest impressions of sense: we have life and free-will.—What then will be the result, when the Beautiful arising from regular form is so modified by the perception of life and spontaneous action, as that the latter only shall be the object of our conscious *perception*, while the former merely acts, and yet does effectively act, on our *feelings?* With pride and pleasure I reply by referring my reader to the groupe in Mr. Allston's grand Picture of the Dead Man reviving from the touch of the bones of the Prophet Elisha,[1] beginning with the Slave at the head of the reviving body, then proceeding to the daughter clasping her swooning mother; to the mother, the wife of the reviving man; then to the soldier behind who supports her; to the two figures eagerly conversing; and lastly, to the exquisitely graceful girl who is bending downward, and whose hand nearly touches the thumb of the slave! You will find, what you had not suspected, that you have here before you a circular groupe. But by what variety of life, motion, and passion, is all the stiffness, that would result from an obvious regular figure swallowed up, and the figure of the groupe as much concealed by the action and passion, as the skeleton which gives the form of the human body, is hidden by the flesh and its endless outlines!

> Si tenebris sibilet Criticus sine dente malignus,
>   Stultorum adrudat si invidiosa Cohors;
> Fac, fugias! Si nulla tibi sit Copia eundi,
>   Contemnas tacitè, scommata quaeque ferens.
> Frendeat, allatret, vacuas gannitibus auras
>   Impleat, haud cures: his placuisse nefas!
>   BURTON, *Anat. of Melanch.*[2]

---

7. I.e., to the extent that some elements in the contemplated scene appear more vivid or distinct than others, and are therefore retained by the mind while the others are forgotten, the act of perception involves an approximation to what C defines as beauty. C's own law of association is expressed a little more clearly in *CM* (*CC*), 3:791–92 and *Biographia*, chapter 7 (pp. 432–33 herein.)
8. A manifestation of C's personal disapproval of the French, but likely to resonate with the anti-Napoleonic feelings of his audience.
9. *Formosus* and *Pulcher* are both Latin words meaning "beautiful."
1. C refers to Washington Allston, *The Dead Man Restored to Life by Touching the Bones of Prophet Elisha* (1811–13), which he had seen at the beginning and end of its execution and admired greatly (*CL*, 3:352, 517).
2. Adapted from "Democritus Junior ad Librum suum" (Democritus Junior to His Book), lines 63–70, the prefatory verses to the third (1628) and later editions of Robert Burton's *Anatomy of Melancholy*, Democritus Junior being Burton's pseudonym: "If a malicious critic should hiss toothlessly in the dark, if a crowd of fools should bray with envy, then flee! If you have no means of leaving, disdain them in silence, enduring all their taunts. They may gnash their teeth, bark, fill the empty air with snarls—don't trouble yourself about it. To please such people would be a crime!" C has rewritten the first two lines to make them more relevant to himself and Allston.

In Rafael's admirable Galatea[3] (the print of which is doubtless familiar to most of my readers) the circle is perceived at first sight; but with what multiplicity of rays and chords within the area of the circular group, with what elevations and depressions of the circumference, with what an endless variety, and sportive wildness in the component figures and in the junctions of the figures, is the balance, the perfect reconciliation, effected between these two conflicting principles of the FREE LIFE, and of the confining FORM! How entirely is the stiffness that would have resulted from the obvious regularity of the latter, *fused* and (if I may hazard so bold a metaphor) almost *volatilized* by the interpenetration and electrical flashes of the former.

But I shall recur to this consummate work for more specific illustrations hereafter: and have indeed in some measure offended already against the laws of method, by anticipating materials which rather belong to a more advanced stage of the disquisition. It is time to recapitulate, as briefly as possible, the arguments already advanced, and having summed up the result, to leave behind me this, the only portion of these essays, which, as far as the subject itself is concerned, will demand any *effort* of attention from a reflecting and intelligent reader. And let me be permitted to remind him, that the distinctions, which it is my object to prove and elucidate, have not merely a foundation in nature and the noblest faculties of the human mind, but are likewise the very ground-work, nay, an indispensable condition, of all *rational* enquiry concerning the Arts. * * *

RECAPITULATION. *Principle the 1st.* That which has *become*, or which has been *made* agreeable to us from causes not contained in its own nature, or in its original conformity to the human organs and faculties; that which is not pleasing for its own sake, but by connection or association with some other thing separate or separable from it; is neither beautiful, nor capable of being a component part of Beauty: though it may greatly increase the sum of our pleasure, when it does not interfere with the beauty of the object, nay, even when it detracts from it. A moss-rose, with a sprig of myrtle and Jasmine, is not more *beautiful* from having been plucked from the garden, or presented to us by the hand, of the woman we love, but is abundantly more delightful. The total pleasure received from one of Mr. Bird's[4] finest pictures may, without any impeachment of our taste, be the greater from his having introduced into it the portrait of one of our friends, or from our pride in him as our townsman, or from our knowledge of his personal qualities; but the amiable artist would rightly consider it a coarse compliment were it affirmed, that the *beauty* of the piece, or its merit as a work of genius, was the more perfect on this account. I am conscious that I look with a stronger and more pleasurable emotion at Mr. Allston's large Landscape in the spirit of Swiss scenery,[5] from its having

3. In 1806 C and Allston had together visited the Villa Farnesina in Rome and seen this fresco (1511), which depicts the sea nymph Galatea riding two dolphins and surrounded by satyrs (CL, 3:520–21).
4. Edward Bird (1772–1819), English painter resident in Bristol, where C approached him on Allston's behalf (CL, 3:492).
5. Allston, *Diana in the Chase*, which C had first seen in 1806 (CN, 2:2796, 2831, and plate 5).

been the occasion of my first acquaintance with him in Rome. This may or may not be a compliment to *him*; but the true compliment to the picture was made by a lady of high rank and cultivated taste, who declared, in my hearing, that she never stood before that landscape without seeming to feel the breeze blow out of it upon her. But the most striking instance is afforded by the portrait of a departed or absent friend or parent, which is endeared to us, and more delightful from some awkward position of the limbs, which had defied the contrivances of art to render it picturesque, but which was the characteristic habit of the original.

Principle the 2nd. That which is naturally agreeable and consonant to human nature, so that the exceptions may be attributed to disease or defect; that, the pleasure from which is contained in the immediate impression; cannot indeed with strict propriety be called beautiful, exclusive of its relations, but one among the component parts of beauty, in whatever instance it is susceptible of existing as a part of a whole. This of course excludes the mere objects of the taste, smell, and feeling, though the sensations from these, especially from the latter when organized into touch, may secretly & without our consciousness enrich and vivify the perceptions and images of the eye and ear; which alone are true organs of sense, their sensations in a healthy or uninjured state being too faint to be noticed by the mind. We may indeed in common conversation call purple a beautiful color, or the tone of a single note on an excellent piano-forte a beautiful tone; but if we were questioned, we should agree that a rich or delightful color; a rich, or sweet, or clear tone; would have been more appropriate—and this with less hesitation in the latter instance than in the former, because the single tone is more manifestly of the nature of a *sensation*, while color is the medium which seems to blend sensation and perception so as to hide, as it were, the former in the latter; the direct opposite of which takes place in the lower sense of feeling, smell, and taste. (In strictness, there is even in these an ascending scale. The smell is less sensual and more sentient, than *mere* feeling, the taste than the smell, and the eye than the ear: but between the ear and the taste exists the chasm or break which divides the beautiful and the elements of beauty from the merely agreeable.) When I reflect on the manner in which smoothness, richness of sound, &c. enter into the formation of the beautiful, I am induced to suspect that they act negatively rather than positively. Something there must be to realize the form, something in and by which the forma informans[6] reveals itself: and these, less than any that could be substituted, and in the least possible degree, distract the attention, in the least possible degree obscure the idea, of which they (composed into outline and surface) are the symbol. An illustrative hint may be taken from a pure chrystal, as compared with an opaque, semi-opaque, or clouded mass on the one hand, and with a perfectly transparent body, such as the air is, on the other. The chrystal is lost in the light, which yet it contains, embodies,

---

6. "Informing form," a variant of C's usual term *"forma formans,"* "forming form," as in *Logic* (CC), 232n., 242.

and gives a shape to; but which passes shapeless through the air, and in the ruder body is either quenched or dissipated.

Principle the 3rd. The safest definition then of BEAUTY, as well as the oldest, is that of Pythagoras:[7] THE REDUCTION OF MANY TO ONE—or, as finely expressed by the sublime Disciple of Ammonius, το αμερες ον, εν πολλοις φανταζομενον,[8] of which the following may be offered as both paraphrase and corollary. *The sense[9] of Beauty subsists in simultaneous [intuition][1] of the relation of parts, each to each, and of all to a whole: exciting an immediate and absolute complacency, without intervenience therefore of any interest sensual or intellectual.* The BEAUTIFUL is thus at once distinguished both from the AGREEABLE, which is beneath it, and from the GOOD, which is above it:[2] for both these have an interest necessarily attached to them; both act on the WILL, and excite a desire for the actual existence of the image or idea contemplated: while the sense of beauty rests gratified in the mere contemplation or [intuition] regardless whether it be a fictitious Apollo, or a real Antinous.[3]

SCHOLIUM. We have sufficiently distinguished the beautiful from the agreeable by the sure criterion, that when we find an object agreeable, the *sensation* of pleasure always precedes the judgement, and is its determining cause. We *find* it agreeable. But when we declare an object beautiful, the contemplation or intuition of its beauty precedes the *feeling* of complacency, in order of nature at least: nay, in great depression of spirits may even exist without sensibly producing it.—[4]

*   *   *

Now the least reflection convinces us, that our sensations, whether of pleasure or of pain, are the incommunicable parts of our nature; such as can be reduced to no universal rule; and in which therefore we have no right to expect that others should agree with us, or to blame them for disagreement. That the Greenlander prefers train oil[5] to olive oil, and even to wine, we explain at once by our knowledge of the climate and productions to which he has been habituated. Were the man as enlightened as Plato, his palate would still find that most agreeable to which it had been most accustomed. But when the Iroquois Sachem after having been led to the most perfect specimens of Architecture in Paris said, that he saw nothing so beautiful as the cook's shops,[6] we at-

---

7. Actually Plotinus, in the passage from which C proceeds immediately to quote. He refers to Plotinus, obliquely but correctly, as a disciple of the Alexandrian philosopher Ammonius Saccas (early 3rd century).
8. Plotinus, *Enneads* 1.6.3.9: "the undivided appearing in the many."
9. A lengthy footnote by C is omitted here.
1. *Felix Farley's Bristol Journal* has "intuitive."
2. As Orsini notes, C's hierarchical arrangement of the beautiful, the agreeable, and the good follows Kant's (*Coleridge and German Idealism*, 169).
3. Antinous (c. 110–130), a youth beloved by the Roman emperor Hadrian, drowned in the Nile and by Hadrian's order was commemorated across the empire with statues and festivals. His name subsequently became synonymous with male beauty. *Felix Farley's Bristol Journal* has "intuitive" instead of "intuition" in this sentence.
4. Cf. Kant, *Judgment*, section 9: "Now this merely subjective (aesthetic) judging of the object, or of the representation through which the object is given, precedes the pleasure in it and is the ground of this pleasure in the harmony of the faculties of cognition." C proceeds to quote stanza 2 of his own "Dejection: An Ode."
5. Cod-liver oil, popularly supposed to have been a staple of the diet of Greenlanders.
6. The anecdote is taken from Kant, *Judgment*, section 2.

tribute this without hesitation to savagery of intellect, and infer with certainty that the sense of the beautiful was either altogether dormant in his mind, or at best very imperfect. The beautiful, therefore, not originating in the sensations, must belong to the intellect: and therefore we *declare* an object beautiful, and feel an inward right to *expect*, that others should coincide with us. But we feel no right to *demand* it:[7] and this leads us to that, which hitherto we have barely touched upon, and which we shall now attempt to illustrate more fully, namely, to the distinction of the BEAUTIFUL from the GOOD.

Let us suppose Milton in company with some stern and prejudiced Puritan contemplating the front of York Cathedral, and at length expressing his admiration of its beauty. We will suppose it too at that time of his life, when his religious opinions, feelings, and prejudices most nearly coincided with those of the rigid Anti-prelatists.[8]—P. Beauty! I am sure, it is not the beauty of holiness.—M. True! but yet it is beautiful.—P. It delights not me. What is it good for? Is it of any use but to be stared at?—M. Perhaps not! but still it is beautiful.—P. But call to mind the pride and wanton vanity of those cruel shavelings, that wasted the labor and substance of so many thousand poor creatures in the erection of this haughty pile.—M. I do. But still it is very beautiful.—P. Think how many score of places of worship incomparably better suited both for prayer and preaching, and how many faithful ministers might have been maintained, to the blessing of tens of thousands, to them and their children's children, with the treasures lavished on this worthless mass of stone and cement.—M. Too true! but nevertheless it is *very* beautiful.—P. And it is not merely useless; but it feeds the pride of the Prelates, and keeps alive the popish and carnal spirit among the people.—M. Even so! and I presume not to question the wisdom, nor detract from the pious zeal, of the first Reformers of Scotland, who for these reasons destroyed so many fabrics, scarce inferior in beauty to this now before our eyes.[9] But I did not call it *good*, nor have I told thee, Brother! that if this were levelled with the ground, and existed only in the works of the modeller or engraver that I should desire to reconstruct it. The GOOD consists in the congruity of a thing with the laws of the reason and the nature of the will, and in its fitness to determine the latter to actualize the former: and it is always discursive. The BEAUTIFUL arises from the perceived harmony of an object, whether sight or sound, with the inborn and constitutive rules of the judgement and imagination: and it is always intuitive.[1] As light to the eye, even such is beauty to the mind, which cannot but have complacency in whatever is perceived as pre-configured to its living faculties. Hence the Greeks called a beautiful object καλον, quasi

---

7. A Kantian qualification (see p. 341, n. 7 herein).
8. The years 1641–42, when Milton wrote five tracts concerning prelacy, the governance of the Church of England by bishops (*SW&F* [CC], 382n. 1).
9. Churches in Scotland, notably St. Andrews Cathedral, were ransacked as a result of agitation by such Reformers as George Wishart (c. 1513–1546) and John Knox (c. 1513–1572) against the Catholic hierarchy.
1. The definitions of "the good" and "the beautiful" are close to Kant's (*Judgment*, sections 4 and 17, respectively).

καλοῦν,[2] i.e. *calling on* the soul, which receives instantly and welcomes it as something connatural.[3]

* * *

LAY SERMONS (1816–17)

Lay Sermons originated from a request made by the Gale and Fenner publishing house, commisioning Coleridge to write "a small Tract on the present Distresses in the form of a Lay-sermon." The subject absorbed Coleridge to such an extent that he found himself "writing a Volume not a Tract of a single sheet" (*CL*, 4:672). By September 17, 1816, Coleridge announced the prospective publication of three Lay Sermons (*CL*, 4:670), but he completed only two of them. The first lay sermon (with the title *The Statesman's Manual; or the Bible the Best Guide to Political Skill and Foresight: A Lay Sermon, Addressed to the Higher Classes of Society, with an Appendix, Containing Comments and Essays Connected with the Study of the Inspired Writings*) appeared in 1816, and the second in 1817. The second sermon is often listed under the title *Blessed are ye that sow beside all Waters*, which is actually the motto (from Isaiah 32.20) above the title (*A Lay Sermon, Addressed to the Higher and Middle Classes, on the Existing Distresses and Discontents*) with which the sermon also concludes. Coleridge was dissatisfied with the titles of both sermons. He had evidently pleaded with the publishers without success to change part of the title of *The Statesman's Manual* to "addressed to the Learned and Reflecting of all Ranks and Professions, especially among the Higher Class" (*CL*, 4:695), and wrote to the publisher John Murray that the "second Lay-sermon" had a "most unfortunate name" (*CL*, 4:706). The third projected sermon, which was advertised on the back wrapper of *The Statesman's Manual*, was to be addressed "to the Lower and Labouring Classes of Society," but no evidence exists that Coleridge ever wrote it.

Lay Sermons were written during a period of deep economic crisis and social unrest following the end of the war after the defeat of Napoleon at Waterloo in 1815. Dissatisfaction with high prices, especially grain prices, which rose sharply in 1816–17, and the low demand for labor due to the availability of discharged servicemen, led to riots and increased political activities among the working classes (Morrow, 100–01). As John Colmer notes, Coleridge was highly aware that "the nation that had so recently triumphed over France by force of arms was in danger of being overcome by revolutionary forces in her midst" (152). Coleridge's solution to the postwar crisis was the education of the upper classes through a critique of the materialist philosophy of the dominant school of political economists (as represented by Adam Smith [1723–1790], David Ricardo [1772–1823], or contemporaries such as Thomas Robert Malthus [1766–1834] and Jeremy Bentham [1748–1832]), and a defense of a philosophy of history and po-

2. "Beautiful, as if it were summoning." C is drawing on a speculative etymology (not accepted by scholars today) in Plato, *Cratylus* 416b–c, where Socrates links the mind's beauty to its function of calling things by name.
3. C concludes by quoting Plotinus, *Enneads* 1.6.2.1–8 in the original Greek. In translation the passage reads, "So let us resume and state what beauty in bodies really is. First, it is something that is perceived at first glance, and the soul speaks of it as if it were familiar with it, recognizes and welcomes and, so to speak, adapts itself to it. But when it confronts the ugly it shrinks back, rejects it, and turns away from it, being out of harmony with it and alienated from it."

litical economy based on the metaphysics of ideas, on universal principles derived from the Bible. While in his early political writings Coleridge emphasized the need for general illumination among the lower classes, urging patriots to involve themselves personally with the poor (*Lects 1795* [*CC*], 43), he now targeted the upper classes as in need of reformation. Coleridge's main object in writing *Lay Sermons* was "first, the Old Testament considered as a Code of true political Economy, and a specimen of bonâ fide *philosophical* History; and secondly, a defence of ancient Metaphysics (principally the Pythagorean, Heraclitic and Platonic)" in contrast to modern philosophy (*LS* [*CC*], 244). As Coleridge wrote in a letter to Robert Banks Jenkinson, 2nd earl of Liverpool (1770–1828), on July 28, 1817, as long as the "principles of our Gentry and Clergy are grounded in a false Philosophy, which retains but the name of *Logic*, and has succeeded in rendering Metaphysics a word of opprobrium, all the Sunday and National schools in the world will not preclude Schism in the lower & middle Classes" (*CL*, 4:762; on Liverpool's response to this letter, see *CL*, 4:757).

There is a considerable difference between the first and the second Lay Sermon, of which Coleridge was keenly aware. *The Statesman's Manual* is more of a philosophical treatise directed at a learned audience who was predisposed to "philosophic thought." Grounded in the distinction between the understanding and reason and the metaphysics of ideas further elaborated in its appendices (see pp. 362–69 herein), the work has few references to contemporary events and, according to some commentators, is unsuccessful in demonstrating the relationship of the Bible to contemporary politics. Coleridge had few illusions about its chances of popularity and thought that it would not "be understood (except in fragments) by the general Reader" (*CL*, 4:713). Even as sympathetic a reader as Dorothy Wordsworth complained that it was "ten times more obscure than the darkest parts of the Friend" (*WL*, 3:373).

On the other hand, *A Lay Sermon* focused largely on the actual ailments of the country during the postwar crisis and, according to Coleridge, was "meant to be *popular*" (*LS* [*CC*], 245), written in a style that was accessible to "any man of common education and information" (*CL*, 4:713). Here Coleridge attacked materialist economic philosophers of his time for their indifference to the distinction between persons and things, their focus on demand rather than supply, production rather than distribution, and their assumption that scarcity was "the inevitable condition of modern economies" (see Calleo, 13, 16–17). Coleridge also criticized reformers such as William Cobbett (1762–1835) both for their disreputable characters and for their uninformed attacks on taxation and commerce. Contrary to popular opinion, Coleridge claimed that the Napoleonic wars were a "stimulant" to British economy, whereas the peace following it naturally led to reduced expenditures and economic depression (*LS* [*CC*], 158–59). Coleridge exhibited a far better grasp than his contemporaries of the recurrent cycles of growth and depression and the "periodical Revolutions of Credit" that marked capitalist economy (*LS* [*CC*], 158–67; 202–03). As David Calleo notes, "Coleridge's attitude toward economic processes was surprisingly modern. He was among the first to grasp the possibly beneficial effects of taxation and national debt and to have some comprehension of the role of credit" (14). Coleridge's main contribution to the contemporary debate about England's postwar distresses was his argument that they were caused not by commerce as such, but by an "OVERBALANCE OF THE

COMMERCIAL SPIRIT," which invaded the three spheres that in a healthy society were meant to provide an adequate counterbalance: the aristocracy,
religion and philosophy (see also Calleo, chapter 1; Colmer, 141–43; and
Morrow, 100–25). Coleridge's view in *Lay Sermons* that a society needed a
learned class preoccupied with moral, religious and intellectual rather than
material values anticipates his fuller analysis of the clerisy in *On the Constitution of the Church and State* (pp. 582–86 herein) and of the necessary
balance between the interests of the landed and commercial classes.

Lay Sermons met with a particularly hostile reception among Coleridge's
contemporaries. William Hazlitt wrote a vicious review of *The Statesman's
Manual* in the *Examiner* of September 8, 1816, based on an advertisement before the work's publication, and two further reviews in the *Examiner* and the *Edinburgh Review* after the work appeared (see *CH*, 1:248–77
and *CL*, 4:669n.; for a detailed analysis of the reviews, see Robert Keith
Lapp, *Contest for Cultural Authority: Hazlitt, Coleridge and the Distresses
of the Regency* [Detroit, 1999], 49–66, 87–111). The short notice in the
Monthly Magazine focused on the lack of an audience for Coleridge's obscure treatise, as did Henry Crabb Robinson in his more detailed and
moderate review in the *Critical Review*, in which he predicted that the
work would be misunderstood and unpopular due to Coleridge's reliance
on metaphysics and his attack on John Locke, the prevailing influence on
British philosophy. *A Lay Sermon* fared poorly in the *Monthly Magazine*
(in which Coleridge was declared to be a lunatic as well as a fool) and the
Monthly Repository (focused entirely on Coleridge's unfavorable remarks
on Unitarianism), but received an appreciative review from Henry Crabb
Robinson in the *Critical Review* (*CH*, 1:278–94).

The texts printed here are from *The Statesman's Manual* (London,
1816) and *A Lay Sermon* (London, 1817). Textual variants from annotated
presentation copies are quoted selectively from *LS* (*CC*). The following
abbreviations have been used for the annotated copies: Copy A (John
Aster's copy); Copy B (R. H. Brabant's copy); Copy C (Coleridge's annotated copy); Copy CL (John Gibson Lockhart's copy); Copy G (James Gillman's copy); Copy R (William Lorance Rogers's copy); Copy SC (Sara
Coleridge's copy).

From The
Statesman's Manual;
or
The Bible the Best Guide to Political
Skill and Foresight:
A Lay Sermon, Addressed to
the Higher Classes of Society,
with an Appendix, Containing
Comments and Essays
Connected with
the Study of the Inspired Writings

Ad ist hæc quæso vos, qualia cunque primo videantur aspectu, adten-
dite, ut qui vobis forsan insanire videar, saltem quibus insaniam ra-
tionibus cognoscatis.[1]

*   *   *

To the immense majority of men, even in civilized countries, speculative philosophy has ever been, and must ever remain, a terra incognita.
Yet it is not the less true, that all the *epoch-forming* Revolutions of the
Christian world, the revolutions of religion and with them the civil,
social, and domestic habits of the nations concerned, have coincided
with the rise and fall of metaphysical systems. So few are the minds
that really govern the machine of society, and so incomparably more
numerous and more important are the indirect consequences of things
than their foreseen and direct effects.[2]

*   *   *

A calm and detailed examination of the facts justifies me to my own
mind in hazarding the bold assertion, that the fearful blunders of the
late dread revolution, and all the calamitous mistakes of its opponents
from its commencement even to the æra of loftier principles and wiser
measures (an æra, that began with, and ought to be named from, the
war of the Spanish and Portuguese insurgents)[3] every failure with all its
gloomy results may be unanswerably deduced from the neglect of some

---

1. From Giordano Bruno (1548–1600), *De immenso et innumerabilibus* (on the Immense
   and the Innumerable) (Frankfurt 1591), 154–55 (var.): "I beg you, pay attention to these
   things, however they appear at first sight, in order that, though you perhaps may think
   me mad, you may at least discover the rational principles behind my madness" (*SM* [CC],
   4n. 2).
2. An anticipation of C's view of the *clerisy*, that "small but glorious band" of priviliged intellectuals and patriots who are fit to lead a nation (see p. 245, n. 6 herein and pp. 582–86
   herein).
3. In 1807, after the treaty of Tilsit, Napoleon secured the cooperation of Russia, Prussia, and
   Austria to forbid the import of all British goods and ordered Denmark and Portugal to join
   the Continental System. When Portugal refused, Napoleon invaded it, sending an army of
   about twenty thousand soldiers led by General Andoche Junot (1771–1813). In 1808 he en-
   gineered the abdication of Charles IV (1748–1819) and his son Ferdinand (1784–1833)
   and installed his brother Joseph Bonaparte (1768–1844) as king of Spain, leaving a large
   French army to support his reign. This led to fierce revolts against the French in Portugal
   and Spain, which inspired wars of liberation in some European nations. In his "Letters on
   the Spaniards" written for the *Courier* in 1809, C—like Wordsworth in *The Convention of
   Cintra* (1809)—expressed strong sympathy for the Spanish cause, arguing that "it was the

maxim or other that had been established by clear reasoning and plain facts in the writings of Thucydides,[4] Tacitus,[5] Machiavel,[6] Bacon,[7] or Harrington.[8] These are red-letter names even in the almanacks of worldly wisdom: and yet I dare challenge all the critical benches of infidelity to point out any one important truth, any one efficient, practical direction or warning, which did not pre-exist, and for the most part in a sounder, more intelligible, and more comprehensive form in the Bible.

In addition to this, the Hebrew legislator, and the other inspired poets, prophets, historians and moralists of the Jewish church have two immense advantages in their favor. First, their particular rules and prescripts flow directly and visibly from universal principles, as from a fountain: they flow from principles and ideas that are not so properly said to be confirmed by reason as to be reason itself![9] Principles, in act and procession, disjoined from which, and from the emotions that inevitably accompany the actual intuition of their truth, the widest maxims of prudence are like arms without hearts,[1] muscles without nerves. Secondly, from the very nature of these principles, as taught in the Bible, they are understood in exact proportion as they are believed and felt. The regulator is never separated from the main spring. For the words of the apostle are literally and philosophically true: WE (that is, the human race) LIVE BY FAITH.[2] Whatever we do or know, that in

---

noble efforts of Spanish Patriotism, that first restored us, without distinction of party, to our characteristic enthusiasm for *liberty*" (*EOT* [CC], 2·38). For the full text of C's "Letters on the Spaniards" and its connection to *The Convention of Cintra*, see *EOT* (CC), 1:cxxxiv–cxli, 2:37–100, 3:98–103.

4. Thucydides (c. 464–c. 401 B.C.E.), distinguished Greek historian, participated in the Peloponnesian War between Athens and Sparta and was banished after the loss of Amphipolis, for which he was held unduly responsible. During his years of exile he wrote a painstakingly detailed history of the first twenty years of the Peloponnesian War, a history that has been often compared with Herodotus's. C himself compared Thucydides with Herodotus, arguing that while Herodotus is merely focused on narrative events, having "as little subjectivity as Homer," in Thucydides it is his subjectivity that dominates a narrative where events are "of minor importance" (*TT* [CC], 1:417).

5. Cornelius Tacitus (c. 55–c. 120), Roman historian and senator, and author of two major works on imperial history from the death of Augustus (14 C.E.) to that of Domitian (96 C.E.). For a later reference to Thucydides' and Tacitus' histories, see *TT* (CC), 1:193–94.

6. Niccolò Machiavelli (1469–1527), famous Florentine political philosopher and author of the controversial *The Prince* (1513), was exiled by the Medici family on the grounds of conspiracy.

7. On Francis Bacon, see p. 769 herein.

8. James Harrington (1611–1677), influential political theorist advocating republican principles and the author of *The Commonwealth of Oceana* (1656), is cited by C in *The Plot Discovered* in the distinguished company of Milton, Locke, and Sydney (see *Lects 1795* [CC], 290). It is, however, unlikely that C read *Oceana* before 1800, when he came into the possession of the John Toland's 1700 edition of this work (see *CN*, 1:639–42, 934 and nn.; and *C & S* [CC], 65n. 3). In 1795 C might have absorbed Harringtonian philosophy through Moses Lowman's *A Dissertation on the Civil Government of the Hebrews* (1740), a work he used for *Lectures on Revealed Religion* (see pp. 259–62 herein, and *Lects 1795* [CC], 126n. 2. Cf. also *CN*, 2:2223; *BL* [CC], 1:54n. 2).

9. From "itself!" to "truth," Copies B and CL read: "itself, reason, in act and procession; they originate in truths disjoined from which, and from the emotions that inevitably accompany their actual intuition," and then continue as printed here.

1. C reworks here a section from *Friend* (CC), 2:85, which also contains the statement that ruin might have been prevented in recent European history if the maxims of great minds would have been heeded. But in *The Friend* Thucydides and Tacitus are missing from "the red-letter names" of "the almanach of worldly wisdom," leaving Machiavelli, Bacon, and Harrington as the only contenders for that distinction. The same company of Bacon, Machiavelli, Harrington with the addition of Spinoza appears in *BL* (CC), 1:54.

2. Paul's exact words in Romans 1.17, Galatians. 3.11, and Hebrews 10.38 are "The just shall live by faith" (cf. *Friend* [CC], 1:97; *CM* [CC], 4:348).

kind is different from the brute creation, has its origin in a determination of the reason to have faith and trust in itself. This, its first act of faith is scarcely less than identical with its own being. *Implicitè*, it is the COPULA— it contains the *possibility*—of every position, to which there exists any correspondence in reality. It is itself, therefore, the realizing principle, the spiritual substratum of the whole complex body of truths.[3] This primal act of faith is enunciated in the word, GOD: a faith not derived from experience, but its ground and source,[4] and without which the fleeting *chaos of facts* would no more form experience, than the dust of the grave can of itself make a living man.[5] The imperative and oracular form of the inspired Scripture is the form of reason itself in all things purely rational and moral.

If it be the word of Divine Wisdom, we might anticipate that it would in all things be distinguished from other books,[6] as the Supreme Reason, whose knowledge is creative, and antecedent to the things known, is distinguished from the understanding,[7] or creaturely mind of the individual, the acts of which are posterior to the things, it records and arranges. Man alone was created in the image of God: a position groundless and inexplicable, if the reason in man do not differ from the understanding. For this the inferior animals, (many at least) possess *in degree*: and assuredly the divine image or idea is not a thing of degrees.[8]

*   *   *

This then is the prerogative of the Bible; this is the privilege of its believing students. With them the principle of knowledge is likewise a

3. For this discussion of the copula, C is indebted to Schelling's "Aphorismen zur Einleitung in die Naturphilosophie" (Aphorisms concerning an Introduction to Natural Philosophy) in *Jahrbücher*, 1.2:11–13, and 1.2:34. Here Schelling argues that productive nature ("die schaffende Natur") is "the absolute identity, or eternal *copula*" of substance. He further defines the copula as "the *eternal*" in every individual thing (12), and as "the absolute identity of the infinite and the finite" (34). Cf. C's statement in *Logic* (CC), 132 that the copula represents the reality principle of every proposition. In C's dynamic model of philosophical grammar the copula occupies the place of the "verb substantive," expressing "the identity or coinherence of being and act" (p. 595 herein).
4. Copy G has a longer version here: "which is itself the ground and source of all true experience;."
5. Although C talks about faith here, his logic is identical to that of Kant's analysis of *a priori* forms of sensible intuition (space and time) or the categories of the understanding which, by virtue of making experience possible, cannot therefore be derived from experience. The following note in Copy G makes plain C's appropriation of this basic Kantian premise in *Pure Reason* for his definition of faith: "The *Sense* can only say, It seems: that 'it *is*', is a decision of the Reason, judging, by the instrument of the Understanding, or the phaenomena acording to their participation of its own constituent attributes. The Rules of *Certificates* (as it were) of Reality granted to the outward Appearances are what the elder Logicians name the Categories—without which there can be no Experience. For Experience is—the Reduction of the notices of the Senses to the a priori Forms of the Understanding" (*SM* [CC], 18n. 2).
6. Copy B replaces "other books" with "every work of the mere reflex understanding."
7. Copies B and CL read: "understanding itself or the."
8. C regarded the crucial distinction between reason and understanding, which he adapted from Kant, as the cornerstone of his philosophy and insisted that the difference in kind between the two faculties defines the hierarchical status of man over animal (see pp. 555–60 herein and p. 362 and its n. 2 herein). In a note on this passage in Copy A, C showed that the understanding differs only in degree from other drives, such as "vital power" or "instinct" possessed by animals, but a wide gap separates it from reason, which pertains only to man and to permanent and universal truths rather than, as in the case of the understanding, to the adaptation of means to an end (*SM* [CC], 19n. 1). On the recurrent distinction in C between differences in kind and degree, see p. 420 herein; p. 463, n. 5 herein; pp. 479–80 herein; and CL, 4:575.

spring and principle of action.[9] And as it is the only *certain* knowledge, so are the actions that flow with it the only ones on which a secure reliance can be placed. The understanding may suggest motives, may avail itself of motives,[1] and make judicious conjectures respecting the probable consequences of actions. But the knowledge taught in the Scriptures *produces* the motives, *involves* the consequences; and its highest formula is still: As sure as God liveth, so will it be unto thee!

* * *

Notions, the depthless abstractions of fleeting phenomena, the shadows of sailing vapors, the colorless repetitions of rain-bows, have effected their utmost when they have added to the *distinctness* of our knowledge. For this very cause they are of themselves adverse to lofty emotion, and it requires the influence of a light and warmth, not their own, to make them chrystallize into a semblance of growth. But every principle is actualized by an idea; and every idea is living, productive, partaketh of infinity,[2] and (as Bacon has sublimely observed) containeth an endless power of semination.[3] Hence it is, that science, which consists wholly in ideas and principles, is power. Scientia et potentia (saith the same philosopher) in idem coincidunt.[4] Hence too it is, that notions, linked arguments, reference to particular facts and calculations of prudence, influence only the comparatively few, the men of leisurely minds who have been trained up to them: and even these few they influence but faintly. But for the reverse, I appeal to the general character of the doctrines which have collected the most numerous sects, and acted upon the moral being of the converts with a force that might well seem supernatural![5] The great PRINCIPLES of our religion, the sublime IDEAS spoken out everywhere in the Old and New Testament, resemble the fixed stars, which appear of the same size to the naked as to the armed eye;[6] the magnitude of which the telescope may rather seem to diminish than to increase. At the annunciation of *principles*, of *ideas*, the soul of man awakes, and starts up, as an exile in a far distant land at the unexpected sounds of his native language, when after long years of absence, and almost of oblivion, he

9. Cf. *Friend* (CC), 2:70–71 for C's argument that the Bible is singular among scriptures of other religions in its encouragement of knowledge as a basis for faith and actions.
1. Copy G replaces "motives" with "consequences."
2. C defines once again the difference between the faculties of the understanding and reason by dwelling on the distinction between notions and ideas. In Appendix E of this work C offers a glossary of terms used in speculative philosophy in which he defines a "notion" as "a purely mental" conception "abstracted from the forms of the Understanding itself" and an "Idea" as "an educt of the Imagination actuated by the pure Reason, to which there neither is or can be an adequate correspondent in the world of the senses" (SM [CC], 113–14). For this definition of ideas, C may have been indebted to Kant, *Judgment*, "Analytic of the Sublime," section 49, where he defines aesthetical ideas as being produced by the imagination, which activates the reason, engendering more thought than can be represented by any determinate concept. On the connection between ideas, lofty feelings and the sublime, see *Friend* (CC), 2:72.
3. Source in Bacon is untraced.
4. "Knowledge and power meet in one." From Bacon, *Novum organum*, book 1, section 3 (var.) (*Works*, 4 vols. [1740], 1:274).
5. Copies B and CL add a sentence here: "The efficiency of the main scriptural truths does not, of necessity, suppose either dialectic skill, or more than ordinary penetration, in those who receive them."
6. I.e., an eye armed with a telescope, an image often used by C (see SM [CC], 24n. 3 and p. 428 herein).

is suddenly addressed in his own mother-tongue. He weeps for joy, and embraces the speaker as his brother. How else can we explain the fact so honorable to Great Britain, that the poorest[7] amongst us will contend with as much enthusiasm as the richest for the rights of property?[8] These rights are the spheres and necessary conditions of free agency. But free agency contains the idea of the free will; and in this he intuitively knows the sublimity, and the infinite hopes, fears, and capabilities of his own nature. On what other ground but the cognateness of ideas and principles to man as man, does the nameless soldier rush to the combat in defence of the liberties or the honor of his country?—Even men wofully neglectful of the precepts of religion will shed their blood for its truth.

*   *   *

But do you require some one or more particular passage from the Bible, that may at once illustrate and exemplify its applicability to the changes and fortunes of empires? Of the numerous chapters that relate to the Jewish tribes, their enemies and allies, before and after their division into two kingdoms, it would be more difficult to state a single one, from which some guiding light might *not* be struck. And in nothing is Scriptural history more strongly contrasted with the histories of highest note in the present age,[9] than in its freedom from the hollowness of abstractions.[1] While the latter present a shadow-fight of Things and Quantities, the former gives us the history of Men, and balances the important influence of individual Minds with the previous state of the national morals and manners, in which, as constituting a specific susceptibility, it presents to us the true cause both of the Influence itself, and of the Weal or Woe that were its Consequents. How should it be otherwise? The histories and political economy of the present and preceding century partake in the general contagion of its mechanic philosophy,[2] and are the *product* of an unenlivened gen-

---

7. C has a footnote not included here, referring to an anecdote in an essay by Oliver Goldsmith (1728–1774), in which a soldier who suffered numerous calamities, including losing a limb, and was reduced to beggary, nonetheless blessed God for granting him good health and the enjoyment of liberty. *Essays and Criticisms*, 3 vols. (London, 1798), 1:201–10.

8. While in his political lectures of 1795 C opposed private property, from 1799 on he became a staunch defender of it (see pp. 269–70 herein; p. 306 and its note 5 herein; p. 580 and its note 9 herein).

9. Among the distinguished histories C alludes to here are David Hume, *History of England*, 6 vols. (1754–62), and Edward Gibbon, *History of the Decline and Fall of the Roman Empire*, 6 vols., 3rd ed. (1777–88). Earlier in this work C argued that Hume's history, devoted as it was to "the undermining of the Christian religion," revealed in essence the "inadequacy of the mere understanding," a faculty yielding exclusively abstractions that were unfit to represent the "moral greatness" of an individual subject (*SM* [CC], 22–23). C used Gibbon extensively, as, e.g., for Lecture 4 of *LRR* (*Lects 1795* [CC], 169–71) and articles for *MP* and the *Courier* (*EOT* [CC], 1:23–26; 2:349–55). He did, however, express considerable reservations concerning Gibbon's style (which he found "detestable") and his view that the corruption of Christianity was a cause of the downfall of the Roman Empire (see *CN*, 3:3814–18). While in a notebook entry of May 10, 1810, after listing the numerous defects of Gibbon's history, C could still recommend that he should be "canonized" when compared to Hume (*CN*, 3:3823), later on he could find little to salvage in Gibbon, considering even the title of his history "a gross misnomer" (*TT* [CC], 1:418–19 and n. 15).

1. C repeatedly differentiated Christian religion and scriptural history from abstract knowledge produced by the mere faculty of the understanding, aligning them with the faculties of reason, intuition, imagination and with faith, that "*total* act of the soul" (*Friend* [CC], 2:314). Cf. p. 367, n. 8 herein.

2. On mechanical philosophy, see p. 775 herein.

eralizing Understanding. In the Scriptures they are the living *educts* of the Imagination;[3] of that reconciling and mediatory power, which incorporating the Reason in Images of the Sense, and organizing (as it were) the flux of the Senses by the permanence and self-circling energies of the Reason, gives birth to a system of symbols,[4] harmonious in themselves, and consubstantial[5] with the truths, of which they are the *conductors*. These are the Wheels which Ezekiel beheld, when the hand of the Lord was upon him, and he saw visions of God as he sate among the captives by the river of Chebar. *Whithersoever the Spirit was to go, the wheels went, and thither was their spirit to go: for the spirit of the living creature was in the wheels also.*[6] The truths and the symbols that represent them move in conjunction and form the living chariot that bears up (for *us*) the throne of the Divine Humanity. Hence, by a derivative, indeed, but not a divided, influence, and though in a secondary yet in more than a metaphorical sense, the Sacred Book is worthily intitled *the* WORD OF GOD. Hence too, its contents present to us the stream of time continuous as Life and a symbol of Eternity, inasmuch as the Past and the Future are virtually contained in the Present. According therefore to our relative position on its banks the Sacred History becomes prophetic, the Sacred Prophecies historical, while the power and substance of both inhere in its Laws, its Promises, and its Comminations. In the Scriptures therefore both Facts and Persons must of necessity have a two-fold significance,

3. Copy G has *"Produce"* and Copy R has "Growth" for *"educts."* The terms "educt" and "educing" are often used by C in his theory of education. Cf. "Education" (p. 591 herein) and *SM* (*CC*), 40. The Latin term *"educare"* (to educate), a derivative of *"educere"* (to educe), means "to draw forth" or "bring out." It refers both to an inner process of natural growth and to a "process of *educing* from without," similar to the way in which the sun or rain would stimulate the maturation of plants or the way a teacher would "draw forth" the natural predispositions and talents of a student (*Logic* [*CC*], 9–10). In Copy G, C has a note further exploring the distinction between the products of the understanding and a different product inseparable from the act of production called *"Produce"*—or Growths," which belongs to "imaginative Reason" (*SM* [*CC*], 29n. 1). C would have found in Schelling's philosophy of nature a dynamic model that shows the inseparability of products from the power of productivity that engenders them. Franz Baader (1765–1841) also draws a distinction between "educts" and "products" in his essays "Ueber die Analogie des Erkenntniss-und des Zeugungs-Triebes" (On the Analogy of the Knowledge Instinct and the Procreative Instinct), where he defines "haughtiness" (*Uebermuth*) and "meanness" (*Niederträchtigkeit*) not as *"educts"* of love" but as "products" of the transformation of loftiness (*Erhabenheit*) and humility (*Demuth*) when love wanes; and in "Ueber Starres und Fliessendes" (On Solids and Fluids), where he regards these not as *"educts* of a living substance" but as *"products* of its extinguished life" (*Jahrbücher*, 3.1:123n., 3.2:201).
4. While using a Kantean schema of the faculties of reason and imagination, C narrows the gap between the sensory world and the ideas of reason that for Kant admit of no sensory representation. He also merges imagination with reason, a move that makes possible his theory of symbols as "consubstantial" with the reality they represent. Cf. C's note in Derwent Coleridge's copy of *The Friend*: "It is wonderful, how closely Reason and Imagination are connected, and Religion the union of the two" (*Friend* [*CC*], 1:203n. 1). In this departure from Kant, C was influenced by Schelling, who regarded the imagination as a power that could bridge the distance between transcendental ideas and the empirical world (see *BL* [*CC*], 1:156n. 1).
5. The term adopted by the Western Church in the Nicene Creed (325 C.E.) to characterize the relation between the Father and Son in the Trinity. The term is paraphrased as "of one substance with the Father" in the Second Article of Religion of the Church of England. The term was also applied to the Eucharist by Martin Luther (1483–1546), who insisted that the substances of the bread and wine co-exist with the body and blood of Christ. C repeatedly rejected Luther's conception of the Eucharist (see, e.g., *CN*, 3:3847 and *CM* [*CC*], 1:862–63).
6. Ezekiel 1.20 (var.).

a past and a future, a temporary and a perpetual, a particular and a universal application. They must be at once Portraits and Ideals.[7]

Eheu! paupertina philosophia in paupertinam religionem ducit:[8]—A hunger-bitten and idea-less philosophy naturally produces a starveling and comfortless religion. It is among the miseries of the present age that if recognizes no medium between *Literal* and *Metaphorical*. Faith is either to be buried in the dead letter, or its name and honors usurped by a counterfeit product of the mechanical understanding, which in the blindness of self-complacency confounds SYMBOLS with ALLEGORIES.[9] Now an Allegory is but a translation of abstract notions into a picture-language which is itself nothing but an abstraction from objects of the senses; the principal being more worthless even than its phantom proxy, both alike unsubstantial, and the former shapeless to boot. On the other hand a Symbol (ὁ ἔστιν ἀεὶ ταυτηγόρικον)[1] is characterized by a translucence of the Special in the Individual or of the General in the Especial or of the Universal in the General. Above all by the translucence of the Eternal through and in the Temporal. It always partakes of the Reality which it renders intelligible; and while it enunciates the whole, abides itself as a living part in that Unity, of which it is the representative. The other are but empty echoes which the fancy arbitrarily associates with apparitions of matter, less beautiful but not less shadowy than the sloping orchard or hill-side pasture-field seen in the transparent lake below. Alas! for the flocks that are to be led forth to such pastures! *"It shall even be as when the hungry dreameth, and behold! he eateth; but he waketh and his soul is empty: or as when the thirsty dreameth, and behold he drinketh; but he awaketh*

---

7. Cf. *BL* (CC), 2:215, on the application of the union of the individual with the universal, the *"portrait"* and *"the ideal,"* to a reader's experience of a work of art.

8. "Eheu! poverty-stricken philosophy leads to poverty-stricken religion." C draws on the essay "Des Andreas Wissowatius Einwürfe wider die Dreieinigkeit" (Andreas Wissowatius's Objections to the Trinity) in which Gotthold Ephraim Lessing (1729–1781) quotes the statement by Leibniz that "Locke inclined to the Socinians, whose philosophy on God and the mind was always poverty-stricken" (*Sämmtliche Schriften*, 30 vols. [Berlin, 1784–96], 7:95; *SM* [CC], 30n. 1).

9. The distinction between symbol and allegory is a cornerstone of C's religious and aesthetic philosophy and parallels the other crucial distinction between fancy and imagination (see chapter 4 of the *Biographia*, pp. 416–20 herein). C represents the imagination as the "mediating power" that makes possible the "reconciliation" of "the general, with the concrete; the idea, with the image; the individual, with the representative * * *" (p. 495 herein). The imagination is described in the *Biographia* as accomplishing the same function as the symbol in this work and can be viewed, therefore, as the faculty that is associated with the production of symbols, while fancy can produce only allegories. For C's view (indebted to Schelling, *Abhandlungen*) that "An IDEA, in the *highest* sense of that word, cannot be conveyed but by a *symbol*" and involves a contradiction," see p. 445, n. 1 herein. C consistently maintained that the symbol (which for him could exist in nature as well as in art) was an inherent part of what it represented, whereas allegory (which was a strictly human creation and confined to art) arbitrarily related concrete imagery to abstract conceptions.

1. "Which is always tautegorical." The term "tautegorical" is C's coinage, according to *OED*, and means "expressing the *same* subject but with a *difference*" as opposed to "metaphors and similitudes, that are always allegorical." See p. 576 herein. Schelling acknowledged C's distinction in a late lecture on mythology (*Sämmtliche Werke*, 14 vols. [Stuttgart, 1856–61], 11:196n). Cf. a notebook entry of September 1820 where C repeated his view that the symbol, instead "of being *allegorical*" is "necessarily *tautegorical*" (*CN*, 4:4711). See also "On the Prometheus of Aeschylus" (*SW&F* [CC], 2:1268, 1280). For a detailed definition of the terms "symbol," "simile," "metaphor," "allegory," and "fable," see *CN*, 4:4832; and for the view that in spite of privileging the symbol, C was not as hostile to allegory as his statements might indicate, see John Gatta, "Coleridge and Allegory," 62–77.

and is faint!" (ISAIAH xxix. 8.)[2] O! that we would seek for the bread which was given from heaven, that we should eat thereof and be strengthened! O that we would draw at the well at which the flocks of our fore-fathers had living water drawn for them,[3] even that water which, instead of mocking the thirst of him to whom it is given, becomes a well within himself springing up to life ever-lasting!

When we reflect how large a part of our present knowledge and civilization is owing, directly or indirectly, to the Bible; when we are compelled to admit, as a fact of history, that the Bible has been the main Lever by which the moral and intellectual character of Europe has been raised to its present comparative height; we should be struck, me thinks, by the marked and prominent difference of this Book from the works which it is now the fashion to quote as guides and authorities in morals, politics and history.[4] I will point out a few of the excellencies by which the one is distinguished, and shall leave it to your own judgment and recollection to perceive and apply the contrast to the productions of highest name in these latter days.[5] In the Bible every agent appears and acts as a self-subsisting individual: each has a life of its own, and yet all are one life.[6] The elements of necessity and free-will are reconciled in the higher power of an omnipresent Providence, that predestinates the whole in the moral freedom of the integral parts. Of this the Bible never suffers us to lose sight. The root is never detached from the ground. It is God everywhere: and all creatures conform to his decrees, the righteous by performance of the law, the disobedient by the sufferance of the penalty.

*   *   *

O what a mine of undiscovered treasures, what a new world of Power and Truth would the Bible promise to our future meditation, if in some gracious moment one solitary text of all its inspired contents should but dawn upon us in the pure untroubled brightness of an IDEA, that most glorious birth of the God-like within us, which even as the Light, its material symbol, reflects itself from a thousand surfaces, and flies homeward to its Parent Mind enriched with a thousand forms, itself above form and still remaining in its own simplicity and identity! O for a flash of that same Light, in which the first position of geometric science that ever loosed itself from the generalizations of a groping and insecure experience, did for the first time reveal itself to a human intellect in all its evidence and all its fruitfulness, Transparence without Vacuum, and Plenitude without Opacity! O that a single gleam of our own inward experience would make comprehensible to us the rapturous EUREKA, and the grateful Hecatomb, of the

---

2. Isaiah 29. 8 (var.).
3. Cf., e.g., John 4.10, 4.11, and 7.38.
4. C alludes to *Principles of Moral and Political Philosophy*, 2 vols. (1794), by William Paley, to whom he often referred disparagingly as the "reverend Moralist." For his attacks on Paley, see p. 257, n. 6 herein, and *Lects 1795* (CC), 131, 222 and n. 1, 310.
5. Copy G deletes this sentence.
6. This echoes lines 36–40 of "Effusion XXXV" (pp. 18–19 herein), which formulates the pantheistic "one life" philosophy. Cf. also C's letter to Sotheby of September 10, 1802 (p. 630 herein).

philosopher of Samos![7] or that Vision which from the contemplation of an arithmetical harmony rose to the eye of KEPLER, presenting the planetary world, and all their orbits in the divine order of their ranks and distances: or which, in the falling of an Apple, revealed to the ethereal intuition of our own Newton the constructive principle of the material Universe.[8] The promises which I have ventured to hold forth concerning the hidden treasures of the Law and the Prophets will neither be condemned as paradox or as exaggeration, by the mind that has learnt to understand the possibility, that the reduction of the sands of the Sea to number should be found a less stupendous problem by Archimedes than the simple conception of the Parmenidean ONE.[9]

* * *

From Appendix C of The Statesman's Manual

Reason and Religion differ only as a two-fold application of the same power.[1] But if we are obliged to distinguish, we must *ideally* separate. In this sense I affirm, that Reason is the knowledge of the laws of the WHOLE considered as ONE: and as such it is contradistinguished from the Understanding, which concerns itself exclusively with the quantities, qualities, and relations of *particulars* in time and space. The UNDERSTANDING, therefore, is the science of phænomena, and their subsumption under distinct kinds and sorts, (*genus* and *species*.) Its functions supply the rules and constitute the possibility of EXPERIENCE; but remain mere logical *forms*, except as far as *materials* are given by the senses or sensations. The REASON, on the other hand, is the science of the *universal*, having the ideas of ONENESS and ALL-NESS as its two elements or primary factors.[2]

7. It was Archimedes (c. 287–212 B.C.E.) who exclaimed "Eureka!" when he was able to identify the baser metal in Hieron's gold crown. According to Plutarch (*Moralia* 1094B–C), the philosopher Pythagoras (6th century B.C.E.) from the Island of Samos offered a hecatomb to the Muses when he discovered the property of right-angled triangles (*SM* [CC], 50n. 4).

8. Cf. C's statement in the 1822 essay "The Science and System of Logic" that the "sublime discoveries of Kepler" were "perfected" by Newton "with no less fruitful than wonderful application of the higher mathesis to the movement of the celestial bodies, and to the laws of light" (*SW&F* [CC], 2:1019). Johannes Kepler (1571–1630), distinguished mathematician and astronomer and successor of Tycho Brahe (1546–1603), discovered the laws of planetary motion. C had a great deal of admiration for Kepler, who, in spite of his poverty, rose to scientific eminence, proving that "true genius can overpower all obstacles" (*Friend* [CC], 1:485–86). Cf. a late statement of October 8, 1830, that "Galileo was a great genius, and so was Newton; but it would take two or three Galileos and Newtons to make one Kepler" (*TT* [CC], 1:210). On C's varied opinions on Kepler and Newton, see *TT* (CC), 2:210n. 1; 211n. 4.

9. In *Arenarius* Archimedes calculated the total number of grains of sands in the world. Parmenides (6th century B.C.E.) believed in the existence of a single infinite and indivisible being, which he pictured as a sphere (*SM* [CC], 51n. 3).

1. An earlier passage in *The Statesman's Manual* on the interrelationship of reason and religion incurred the charge of infidelity from William Hazlitt (who reviewed the work in the *Edinburgh Review* 27 [1816]: 444–59; see *CH*, 1:269–71), which prompted a response from C in chapter 24 of the *Biographia*. Cf. C's point that "Religion passes out of the ken of Reason only where the eye of Reason has reached its own Horizon; and that Faith is then but its continuation" (*BL* [CC], 2:247). See also his marginal note to Böhme (*CM* [CC], 1:576) from which the *Biographia* passage is derived.

2. On the recurrent distinction in C, based on Kant, between reason and understanding, see p. 356, n. 8 herein and p. 357, n. 2 herein. See also C's long note on this distinction on the front fly-leaf of Copy G reproduced in *SM* (CC), 60n. 2. Cf. p. 450, n. 1 herein. The view that the under-

*   *   *

The comprehension, impartiality, and far-sightedness of Reason, (the LEGISLATIVE of our nature) taken singly and exclusively, becomes mere visionariness in *intellect*, and indolence or hard-heartedness in *morals*. It is the science of cosmopolitism without country, of philanthropy without neighbourliness or consanguinity,[3] in short, of all the impostures of that philosophy of the French revolution, which would sacrifice each to the shadowy idol of ALL. For Jacobinism is *monstrum hybridum*,[4] made up in part of despotism, and in part of abstract reason misapplied to objects that belong entirely to experience and the understanding. Its instincts and mode of action are in strict correspondence with its origin. In all places, Jacobinism betrays its mixt parentage and nature, by applying to the brute passions and physical force of the multitude (that is, to man as a mere animal,) in order to build up government and the frame of society on natural rights instead of social privileges, on the universals of abstract reason instead of positive institutions, the lights of specific experience, and the modifications of existing circumstances.[5] RIGHT in its most proper sense is the creature of law and statute, and only in the technical language of the courts has it any substantial and independent sense. In morals, Right is a word without meaning except as the correlative of Duty.[6]

From all this it follows, that Reason as the science of All as the Whole, must be interpenetrated by a Power, that represents the concentration of All in Each—a Power that acts by a contraction of universal truths into individual duties, as[7] the only form in which those truths can attain life and reality. Now this is RELIGION, which is the EXECUTIVE of our nature, and on this account the name of highest dignity, and the symbol of sovereignty.

*   *   *

But neither can reason or religion exist or co-exist as reason and religion, except as far as they are actuated by the WILL[8] (the platonic

---

standing provides mere forms to which the senses lend the material see Kant (*Pure Reason* B75–76): "Without sensibility no object would be given to us, and without understanding none would be thought. Thoughts without content are empty, intuitions without concepts are blind. It is thus just as necessary to make the mind's concepts sensible (i.e., to add an object to them in intuition) as it is to make its intuitions understandable (i.e., to bring them under concepts)."

3. Cf. C's critique in *Friend* (CC), 2:323–24 of a cosmopolitism that is severed from nationality or the sphere of "human affections" and his sense that true cosmopolitism is "at once the Nursling and the Nurse of patriotic affection!"

4. "Hybrid monster." On C's position on Jacobinism, see "Once a Jacobin Always a Jacobin" (p. 299 herein). The "hybrid monster" of Jacobinism, with "its fang resting on a bag of the old venom" is described by C in "To Mr. Justice Fletcher. III" (*EOT* [CC], 2:389).

5. From "brute passions" to here, Copies B and CL list the following variants: "blind passions and animal force of the Multitude (that is, to the materials of *Despotism*) in order to substitute the universals of *abstract* Reason, for positive In[s]titutions, the Lights of specific Experience, and the modifications of existing circumstances: in other words, to build up Government and the Frame of society on (pretended) natural Rights instead of social privileges. But."

6. The interrelationship of rights and duties is a recurrent emphasis in C's political writings. See *Lects 1795* (CC), 43; *Watchman* (CC), 122n.; and *Friend* (CC), 2:98, 126, 131.

7. Copy G replaces "as" with "such contraction being."

8. C explored the relationship of reason and the will in a series of notebook entries of 1803, stimulated by his reading of Kant, *Groundwork*. See CN, 1:1705, 1:1710, 1717. In a note in Copy G, C referred to "the Primacy of the Will, as deeper than, and (in the order of *thought*) antecedent to, Reason" (SM [CC], 67n. 2). On the importance of the will for C, see p. 427, n. 1 herein; pp. 432–33 herein; p. 477, n. 4 herein.

Θυμὸς,[9]) which is the sustaining, coercive and ministerial power, the functions of which in the individual correspond to the officers of war and police in the ideal Republic of Plato. In its state of immanence (or indwelling) in reason and religion, the WILL appears indifferently, as wisdom or as love: two names of the same power, the former more intelligential, the latter more spiritual, the former more frequent in the Old, the latter in the New Testament. But in its utmost abstraction and consequent state of reprobation, the Will becomes satanic pride and rebellious self-idolatry in the relations of the spirit to itself, and remorseless despotism relatively to others; the more hopeless as the more obdurate by its subjugation of sensual impulses, by its superiority to toil and pain and pleasure; in short, by the fearful resolve to find in itself alone the one absolute motive of action, under which all other motives from within and from without must be either subordinated or crushed.

This is the character which Milton has so philosophically as well as sublimely embodied in the Satan of his Paradise Lost. Alas! too often has it been embodied in *real* life! Too often has it given a dark and savage grandeur to the historic page! And wherever it has appeared, under whatever circumstances of time and country, the same ingredients have gone to its composition; and it has been identified by the same attributes. Hope in which there is no Chearfulness; Stedfastness within and immovable Resolve, with outward Restlessness and whirling Activity; Violence with Guile; Temerity with Cunning; and, as the result of all, Interminableness of Object with perfect Indifference of Means; these are the qualities that have constituted the COMMANDING GENIUS![1] these are the Marks, that have characterized the Masters of Mischief, the Liberticides, and mighty Hunters of Mankind, from NIMROD[2] to NAPOLEON. And from inattention to the possibility of such a character as well as from ignorance of its elements, even men of honest intentions too frequently become fascinated. Nay, whole nations have been so far duped by this want of insight and reflection as to regard with palliative admiration, instead of wonder and abhorrence, the Molocks of human nature, who are indebted, for the far larger portion of their meteoric success, to their total want of principle, and who surpass the generality of their fellow creatures in one act of courage only, that of daring to say with their whole heart, "Evil, be thou my good!"—[3] All *system* so far is power; and a *systematic* criminal, self-consistent and entire in wickedness, who entrenches villainy within villainy, and barricadoes crime by crime, has removed a world

9. "Spirit." In Plato's *Republic*, book 4 (440B), spirit is the mediating principle of the soul between reason and appetite, siding with the former.
1. According to Woodring, C derived the concept of "commanding genius" from Schiller's *Wallenstein* (87, 199–200). Cf. C's distinction between absolute and commanding genius and his sense that the latter is dangerously destructive during "times of tumult" in chapter 2 of the *Biographia* (BL [CC], 1:31–33 and 32n. 1). See also *EOT* (CC), 1:222 and n. 6.
2. Biblical figure described in Genesis 10.8–12 as "a mighty hunter." As noted in CN, 1:280n. C's early interest in Nimrod, as an example of a despotic ruler, may have been derived from Thomas Hyde, *Historia religionis veterum Persarum* (History of the Religion of the Ancient Persians) (Oxford, 1700) and Thomas Maurice, *History of Hindostan,* 2 vols. (1795).
3. Milton, *Paradise Lost* 4.110. Cf. *Friend* (CC), 2:84, which quotes this line in a paragraph that also includes a variant and expansion of the following sentence.

of obstacles by the mere decision, that he will have no obstacles, but those of force and brute matter.

I have only to add a few sentences, in completion of this note, on the CONSCIENCE and on the UNDERSTANDING. The conscience is neither reason, religion, or will, but an *experience* (sui generis)[4] of the coincidence of the human will with reason and religion. It might, perhaps, be called a *spiritual sensation*; but that there lurks a contradiction in the terms, and that it is often deceptive to give a common or generic name to that, which being unique, can have no fair analogy.[5] Strictly speaking, therefore, the conscience is neither a sensation or a sense; but a testifying state, best described in the words of our liturgy, as THE PEACE OF GOD THAT PASSETH ALL UNDERSTANDING:[6]

                           *   *   *

Of the *discursive* understanding, which forms for itself general notions and terms of classification for the purpose of comparing and arranging phænomena, the Characteristic is Clearness without Depth. It contemplates the unity of things in their *limits* only, and is consequently a knowledge of superficies without substance. So much so indeed, that it entangles itself in contradictions in the very effort of comprehending the *idea* of substance. The completing power which unites clearness with depth, the plenitude of the sense with the comprehensibility of the understanding, is the IMAGINATION, impregnated with which the understanding itself becomes intuitive, and a living power.[7] The REASON, (not the abstract reason, not the reason as the mere *organ* of science, or as the faculty of scientific principles and schemes a priori; but reason) as the integral *spirit* of the regenerated man, reason substantiated and vital, "one only, yet manifold, overseeing all, and going through all understanding; the breath of the power of God, and a pure influence from the glory of the Almighty; which remaining in itself regenerateth all other powers, and in all ages entering into holy souls maketh them friends of God and prophets;" (Wisdom of Solomon, c. vii.)[8] the REASON without being either the SENSE, the UNDERSTANDING or the IMAGINATION contains all three within itself, even as the mind contains its thoughts, and is present in and through them all; or as the expression pervades the different features of an intelligent countenance. Each individual must bear witness of it to his own mind, even as he describes life and light: and with the silence of light it describes itself, and dwells in *us* only as far as we dwell in *it*. It cannot in strict language be called a faculty, much less a personal property, of any human mind! He, with whom it is present, can as little appropriate it, whether, totally or by partition, as he can

4. "Of its own kind."
5. Cf. C's definition of conscience as "that inward something * * * which being absolutely *unique* no man can *describe*, because every man is bound to *know*" (*Friend* [CC], 1:150). For the view that morality is "grounded in Conscience or the *selfless* Reason," see *Friend* (CC), 1:425n. 2.
6. Philippians 4.7 (var.).
7. Cf. *Friend* (CC), 1:203n. 1: "It is wonderful, how closely Reason and Imagination are connected, and Religion the union of the two."
8. Wisdom of Solomon 7.22–23, 25, 27 (var.).

claim ownership in the breathing air or make an inclosure in the cope of heaven.[9]

The object of the preceding discourse was to recommend the Bible, as the end and center of our reading and meditation. I can truly affirm of myself, that my studies have been profitable and availing to me only so far, as I have endeavoured to use all my other knowledge as a glass enabling me to receive more light in a wider field of vision from the word of God. If you have accompanied me thus far, thoughtful reader! Let it not weary you if I digress for a few moments to another book, likewise a revelation of God—the great book of his servant Nature.[1] That in its obvious sense and literal interpretation it declares the being and attributes of the Almighty Father, none but the *fool in heart* has ever dared gainsay.[2] But it has been the music of gentle and pious minds in all ages, it is the *poetry* of all human nature, to read it likewise in a figurative sense, and to find therein correspondencies and symbols of the spiritual world.[3]

I have at this moment before me, in the flowery meadow[4] on which my eye is now reposing, one of its most soothing chapters, in which there is no lamenting word, no one character of guilt or anguish. For never can I look and meditate on the vegetable creation without a feeling similar to that with which we gaze at a beautiful infant that has fed itself asleep at its mother's bosom, and smiles in its strange dream of obscure yet happy sensations.[5] The same tender and genial pleasure takes possession of me, and this pleasure is checked and drawn inward by the like aching melancholy, by the same whispered remonstrance, and made restless by a similar impulse of aspiration. It seems as if the soul said to herself: from this state hast *thou* fallen! Such shouldst thou still become, thy Self all permeable to a holier power! thy Self at once hidden and glorified by its own transparency, as the accidental and dividuous[6] in this quiet and harmonious object is subjected to the life and light of nature which shines in it,[7] even as the transmitted power, love and wisdom, of God over all fills, and shines through, na-

---

9. This view of reason as a faculty that we cannot claim as a possession may have been derived from Aphorism 46 of Schelling's "Aphorismen" (*Jahrbücher* 1:15): "Reason is no faculty, no instrument and does not lend itself to use. In general, there is no such thing as a reason which we possess, but only a reason which possesses us." For C's use of this work by Schelling, see p. 356, n. 3 herein.

1. Cf. Lecture 12 of *Lects 1818–19* (CC), 2:541, where C refers to "the other great Bible of God, the book of nature," which becomes "transparent to us when we regard the forms of matter as words, as symbols valuable only for the meaning which they convey to us, only for the life which they speak of, and venerable only as being the expression, an unrolled but yet glorious fragment, of the wisdom of the Supreme Being."

2. Psalms 14.1 (var.).

3. Cf. the closely related passage in Lecture 3 of *LRR* (*Lects 1795* [CC], 158): "to the pious man all Nature is thus beautiful because its every Feature is the Symbol and all its Parts the written Language of infinite Goodness and all powerful Intelligence."

4. C was at this time residing with the Gillmans at Moreton House, Highgate.

5. A familiar image in C's poems. See, e.g., "To an Infant," lines 12–15 and "Epitaph to an Infant," lines 1–4 (*PW*, 1:91, 417).

6. C's coinage, meaning "separable" (*OED*).

7. From "the accidental" to here, variants are "whatever seems accidental and individualized in this quiet and harmonious Object is subjected to universal Nature,—to that life and light of Nature, which shine in *it*," (Copies B and CL); "—to that life and light, of Nature, which work and shine forth in every plant and flower" (Copy G).

ture! But what the plant *is*, by an act not its own and unconsciously—
that must thou *make* thyself to *become!* must by prayer[8] and by a
watchful and unresisting spirit, *join* at least with the preventive and
assisting grace to *make* thyself, in that light of conscience which in-
flameth not, and with that knowledge which puffeth not up.[9]

But further, and with particular reference to that undivided Reason,
neither merely speculative or merely practical, but both in one,[1] which
I have in this annotation endeavoured to contra-distinguish from the
Understanding, I seem to myself to behold in the quiet objects, on
which I am gazing, more than an arbitrary illustration, more than a
mere *simile*, the work of my own Fancy! I feel an awe, as if there were
before my eyes the same Power, as that of the REASON—the same
Power in a lower dignity, and therefore a symbol established in the
truth of things. I feel it alike, whether I contemplate a single tree or
flower, or meditate on vegetation throughout the world, as one of the
great organs of the life of nature. Lo!—with the rising sun it commences its outward life and enters into open communion with all the
elements, at once assimilating them to itself and to each other. At the
same moment it strikes its roots and unfolds its leaves, absorbs and
respires, steams forth its cooling vapour and finer fragrance, and
breathes a repairing spirit, at once the food and tone of the atmosphere, into the atmosphere that feeds *it*. Lo!—at the touch of light
how it returns an air akin to light, and yet with the same pulse effec-
tuates its own secret growth, still contracting to fix what expanding it
had refined. Lo!—how upholding the ceaseless plastic[2] motion of the
parts in the profoundest rest of the whole it becomes the visible or-
ganismus of the whole *silent* or *elementary* life of nature[3] and, therefore, in incorporating the one extreme becomes the symbol of the
other; the natural symbol of that higher life of reason, in which the
whole series (known to us in our present state of being) is perfected,

---

8. For C on the necessity of prayer and its connection with faith, see CN, 3:3355, 4017, 4183
   and Appendix A of SM (CC), 55 and n. 3.
9. In Copy G, C expressed his embarrassment about his "imperfect" conception of nature in
   the latter part of this paragraph, noting that its erasure "would be the best amendment" (SM
   [CC], 71n. 6).
1. C has in mind Kant's distinction between the merely speculative reason that in theoretical
   philosophy cannot prove the existence of supersensibile ideas such as of God and freedom,
   and practical reason that in the sphere of ethics takes such ideas as postulates of the moral
   law (see p. 441, n. 6 herein and p. 444, n. 3 herein). C follows Schelling in asserting the
   unity of theoretic and practical philosophy (see Schelling, *System*, 64): "We should proceed
   forthwith to the establishment of theoretical and practical philosophy as such, were it not
   that this division itself requires prior deduction by the science of knowledge, which is by nature neither theoretical nor practical, but both of these at once" (Heath, 34). On Schelling's
   critique of Kant's view of theoretic reason and C's response to it, see CM (CC), 4:409–10
   and BL (CC), 1:154n. 2.
2. Cf. C's vision of an "animated nature" brought to unity by a divine power "Plastic and vast" in
   lines 36–40 of "Effusion XXXV" (pp. 18–19 herein). On the term "plastic" and its relationship
   to the unifying power of the imagination, see p. 19, n. 7 herein and p. 449, n. 6 herein.
3. In Copy G, C has the following note to this on the fitness of the natural world of supplying
   metaphors for spiritual and moral values: "It is worth noticing that in the Scriptures, and indeed in the elder poesy of all nations, the metaphors for our noblest and tenderest relations,
   for all the Affections and Duties that arise out of the Reason, the Ground of our proper Humanity, are almost wholly taken from Plants, Trees, Flowers, and their functions and accidents" (SM [CC], 72n. 2).

in which, therefore, all the subordinate gradations recur, and are re-ordained *"in more abundant honor."* We had seen each in its own cast, and we now recognize them all as co-existing in the unity of a higher form, the Crown and Completion of the Earthly, and the Mediator of a new and heavenly series. Thus finally, the vegetable creation, in the simplicity and uniformity of its *internal* structure symbolizing the unity of nature, while it represents the omniformity of her delegated functions in its *external* variety and manifoldness, becomes the record and chronicle of her ministerial acts, and inchases the vast unfolded volume of the earth with the hieroglyphics of her history.

*   *   *

That, which we find in ourselves, is (gradu mutato)[4] the substance and the life of *all* our knowledge. Without this latent presence of the "I am," all modes of existence in the external world would flit before us as colored shadows, with no greater depth, root, or fixture, than the image of a rock hath in a gliding stream or the rain-bow on a fast-sailing rain-storm.[5] The human mind is the compass, in which the laws and actuations of all outward essences are revealed as the dips and declinations. (The application of Geometry to the forces and movements of the material world is both proof and instance.) The fact therefore, that the mind of man in its own primary and constituent forms represents the laws of nature, is a mystery which of itself should suffice to make us religious: for it is a problem of which God is the only solution,[6] God, the one before all, and of all, and through all!— True natural philosophy is comprized in the study of the science and language of *symbols*. The power delegated to nature is all in every part: and by a symbol I mean, not a metaphor or allegory or any other figure of speech or form of fancy, but an actual and essential part of that, the whole of which it represents.[7] Thus our Lord speaks symbolically when he says that "the eye is the light of the body."[8] The genuine naturalist is a dramatic poet in his own line: and such as our myriad-minded[9] Shakespear is, compared with the Racines and Metastasios,[1] such and by a similar process of self-transformation would the man

---

4. "On a different level."

5. On the "I AM" as a grounding principle of philosophy and religion and its German sources, see the notes to Thesis 6 in chapter 12 of the *Biographia* (p. 475 and its nn. 4–7 herein and p. 476 herein).

6. The view that the constitutive forms of the mind "prescribe laws *a priori* * * * to nature as the sum total of all appearances" is a Kantian position (*Pure Reason*, B162–65), which here, as elsewhere in C, culminates in a theistic resolution. Whereas Kant makes the object dependent on the subject, C wants to reconcile subject and object by grounding both in God. See the *Biographia*, chapter 12, Thesis 9 (p. 478 herein): "We begin with I KNOW MYSELF, in order to end with the absolute I AM. We proceed from the SELF; in order to lose and find all self in GOD." See also p. 441, n. 6 herein.

7. On the symbol, as distinct from allegory and as being a "living part" of the whole which it represents, p. 360 and its nn. 9–1 herein.

8. Matthew 6.22 (var.); Luke 11.34 (var.).

9. On this phrase, which C derived from Naucratius's eulogy of St. Theodorus Studita (759–826), cited by the English divine William Cave (1637–1713), see *BL* (CC), 2:19n. 3.

1. Jean Baptiste Racine (1639–1699), major French dramatist, often compared with Shakespeare, author of popular tragedies such as *Britannicus* (1669), *Bérénice* (1670), *Iphigénie* (1674), and *Phédre* (1677). C himself joined the names of Racine and Shakespeare, but not without doing "violence to" his "own feelings," in *Friend* (CC), 2:216 (see also *BL* [CC], 2:184). Pietro Metastasio (1698–1782), prolific Italian poet, librettist and drama theorist. C copied some of his verses in a notebook entry of 1804 (*CN*, 2:2224) and referred to "the melodious Metastasio" in *Friend* (CC), 2:9.

be, compared with the Doctors of the mechanic school, who should construct his physiology on the heaven-descended, Know Thyself.[2]

* * *

Join with me, Reader! in the fervent prayer, that we may seek within us, what we can never find elsewhere, that we may find within us what no words can put there, that one only true religion, which elevateth Knowing into Being, which is at once the Science of Being, the Being and the Life of all genuine Science.

From A Lay Sermon ("*Blessed are ye that sow beside all Waters!*")

Addressed to the Higher and Middle Classes, on the Existing Distresses and Discontents

Ἐὰν μὴ ἐλπιζητε, ἀνέλπιστον οὐχ εὑρήσετε, ἀνεξερεύνητον ὄν καὶ ἄπορον.

HERACLITUS *apud Theodoret*, Vol. iv. p. 716.[1]

If ye do not hope, ye will not find: for in despairing ye block up the mine at its mouth! ye extinguish the torch, even when ye are already in the shaft.

* * *

The immediate occasions of the existing distress may be correctly given with no greater difficulty than would attend any other series of known historic facts; but toward the discovery of its true seat and sources, I can but offer a humble contribution. They appear to me, however, resolvable into the OVERBALANCE[*] OF THE COMMERCIAL

---

[*] I entreat attention to the word, *over*-balance. My opinions would be greatly misinterpreted if I were supposed to think hostilely of the spirit of commerce to which I attribute the largest proportion of our actual freedom (i.e. as *Englishmen*, and not merely as *Landowners*) and at least as large a share of our virtues as of our vices. Still more anxiously would I guard against the suspicion of a design to inculpate any number or class of individuals. It is not in the power of a minister or of a cabinet to say to the current of national tendency, stay here! or flow there! The excess can only be remedied by the slow progress of intellect, the influences of religion, and irresistible events guided by Providence. In the points even, which I have presumed to blame,[2] by the word Government I intend all the directors of political power, that is, the great estates of the Realm,[3] temporal and spiritual, and not only the Parliament, but all the elements of Parliament.

---

2. On this favorite maxim of C's, derived from Juvenal, *Satires* 11.27, see p. 466, n. 8 herein and cf. "—E coelo descendit" (p. 226 and its n. 1 herein).
1. C combines two versions of an aphorism attributed to Heraclitus by Titus Flavius Clemens (c. 150–c. 220) and Theodoret of Cyrrhus (c. 390–c. 457). Both versions are cited by Friedrich Daniel Schleiermacher in his article "Herakleitos" (see *LS* [CC], 119n. 2, which also gives a literal translation of the aphorism).
2. Copy L adds "the *Government*" after "blame."
3. The three estates of the realm were the clergy, the nobility, and the commons (see p. 582, n. 3 herein).

SPIRIT IN CONSEQUENCE OF THE ABSENCE OR WEAKNESS OF THE COUNTER-WEIGHTS; this overbalance considered as displaying itself, 1. In the COMMERCIAL WORLD itself: 2. In the Agricultural: 3. In the Government: and, 4. In the combined Influence of all three on the more numerous and labouring Classes.

Of the natural counter-forces to the impetus of trade the first, that presents itself to my mind, is the ancient feeling of rank and ancestry, compared with our present self-complacent triumph over these supposed prejudices. Not that titles and the rights of precedence are pursued by us with less eagerness than by our Forefathers. The contrary is the case; and for this very cause, because they inspire less reverence. In the old times they were valued by the possessors and revered by the people as distinctions of *Nature*, which the crown itself could only ornament, but not give. Like the stars in Heaven, their influence was wider and more general, because for the mass of mankind there was no hope of reaching, and therefore no desire to appropriate, them. That many evils as well as advantages accompanied this state of things I am well aware: and likewise that many of the latter have become incompatible with far more important blessings. It would therefore be sickly affectation to suspend the thankfulness due for our immunity from the one in an idle regret for the loss of the other. But however true this may be, and whether the good or the evil preponderated, still it[4] acted as a counterpoise to the grosser superstition for wealth.

*　*　*

Thus then, of the three most approved antagonists to the Spirit of Barter, and the accompanying disposition to overvalue Riches with all the Means and Tokens thereof—of the three fittest and most likely checks to this tendency, namely, the feeling of ancient birth and the respect paid to it by the community at large; a genuine intellectual Philosophy with an accredited, learned, and philosophic *Class*;[5] and lastly, Religion; we have found the first declining, the second not existing, and the third efficient, indeed, in many respects and to many excellent purposes, only not in this particular direction: the Religion here spoken of, having long since parted company with that inquisitive and bookish Theology which tends to defraud the student of his worldly wisdom, inasmuch as it diverts his mind from the accumulation of wealth by pre-occupying his thoughts in the acquisition of knowledge. For the Religion of best repute among us holds all the truths of Scripture and all the doctrines of Christianity so very transcendent, or so very easy, as to make study and research either vain or needless.[6] It professes, therefore, to hunger and thirst after Righteousness alone, and the rewards of the Righteous; and thus habitually *taking for granted* all truths of spiritual import leaves the understanding vacant and at leisure for a thorough insight into present and temporal

---

4. In several annotated copies C replaced "it" with the more specific "this reverence for *ancientry* in families" (Copies G and SC) or "the Influence of Rank and Ancestry" (Copy C).
5. This is what C was to call "the clerisy" in *Church and State* (pp. 582–86 herein).
6. C refers to Evangelicalism as a religion inefficient in counteracting the commercial spirit because he believed that, like the religion of Quakers (see *LS* [CC], 191), it relinquished the spirit of inquiry and relied on "feelings and motives" and unexamined truths.

interests: which, doubtless, is the true reason why its followers are in general such shrewd, knowing, wary, well-informed, thrifty and thriving men of business. But this is likewise the reason, why it neither does or can check or circumscribe the Spirit of Barter; and to the consequent *monopoly* which this commercial Spirit possesses, must its over-balance be attributed, not to the extent or magnitude of the Commerce itself.[7]

* * *

What then is the remedy? Who the physicians? The reply may be anticipated. An evil, which has come on gradually, and in the growth of which all men have more or less conspired, cannot be removed otherwise than gradually, and by the joint efforts of all. If we are a christian nation, we must learn to act nationally as well as individually, as Christians. We must remove half-truths, the most dangerous of errors (as those of the poor visionaries called SPENCEANS)[8] by the whole Truth. The Government is employed already in retrenchments; but he who expects immediate relief from these, or who does not even know that if they do any thing at all, they must for the time tend to aggravate the distress, cannot have studied the operation of public expenditure.

I am persuaded that more good would be done, not only ultimate and permanent, but immediate, good, by the abolition of the Lotteries accompanied with a public and parliamentary declaration of the moral and religious grounds that had determined the Legislature to this act; of their humble confidence in the blessing of God on the measure; and of their hopes that this sacrifice to principle, as being more exemplary from the present pressure on the Revenue of the State, would be the more effective in restoring confidence between man and man—I am deeply convinced, that more sterling and visible benefits would be derived from this one solemn proof and pledge of moral fortitude and national faith, than from retrenchments to a tenfold greater amount.[9] Still more, if our Legislators should pledge themselves at the same time, that they would hereafter take council for the gradual removal or counteraction of all similar encouragements and temptations to Vice and Folly, that had alas! been tolerated hitherto, as the easiest way of supplying the exchequer. And truly, the financial motives would be strong indeed, if the Revenue Laws in question were but half as productive of money to the State as they are of guilt and wretchedness to the people.

Our manufacturers must consent to regulations; our gentry must concern themselves in the *education* as well as in the *instruction*[1] of

7. Cf. C's footnote (p. 369 herein) in which he emphasized that he did not oppose "the spirit of commerce" to which he attributed "the largest proportion of our actual freedom." As Morrow argues, "Coleridge's acceptance of commercialism distinguished his position from that taken by many popular proponents of political and social reform, and provided an important element in his critique of contemporary radicalism" (107).
8. I.e., those belonging to the Society of Spencean Philanthropists, founded in 1814 after the death of Thomas Spence (1750–1814), a schoolmaster of Newcastle who believed that the land should be returned to the people (see LS [CC], 228n. 2).
9. State lotteries had been denounced as immoral by various politicians and reformists and were abolished by parliament in 1823.
1. For C on the distinction between education and instruction, see C&S (CC), 48 and n. 2, 62, 216.

their natural clients and dependents, must regard their estates as secured indeed from all human interference by every principle of law,
and policy, but yet as offices of trust,[2] with duties to be performed, in
the sight of God and their Country. Let us become a better people,
and the reform of all the public (real or supposed) grievances, which
we use as pegs whereon to hang our own errors and defects, will follow of itself. In short, let every man measure his efforts by his power
and his sphere of action, and do all he can do! Let him contribute
money where he cannot act personally; *but let him act personally and
in detail* wherever it is practicable.[3] Let us palliate where we cannot
cure, comfort where we cannot relieve; and for the rest rely upon the
promise of the King of Kings by the mouth of his Prophet, "BLESSED
ARE YE THAT SOW BESIDE ALL WATERS."[4]

FINIS.

BIOGRAPHIA LITERARIA (1817)

Biographia Literaria, Coleridge's most influential and controversial work,
holds a unique place in the history of literary criticism. It is an unusual
book, challenging conventional generic expectations, by mixing autobiography, satire, philosophy and literary criticism. The *Biographia* has been a
seminal text for the New Critics, whose views dominated American acade-
mia from the 1930s through the 1960s, but it has also attracted virulent
criticisms and heated controversies, which center on the following issues: its
compositional history, specifically the dating of the philosophical chapters
(chapters 5–13); its plagiarisms from Schelling and other German philosophers, first disclosed by Thomas De Quincey shortly after Coleridge's death; the question of genre; and its structure, unity, or inchoateness.
    Although Coleridge did not begin the composition of the *Biographia* un-
til 1815, its origins go as far back as 1800, the time when, at Coleridge's
request, Wordsworth wrote a Preface to the second edition of the *Lyrical
Ballads*. By 1802 Coleridge's objection to "a daring Humbleness of
Language & Versification, and a strict adherence to matter of fact"
in Wordsworth's recent poetry, led him to acknowledge "a radical Difference" in their "theoretical opinions respecting Poetry" and to establish
"some plain, & perspicuous, tho' not superficial, Canons of Criticism respecting Poetry" (*CL*, 2:830). In 1803 Coleridge had evidently settled on
autobiography as the form most conducive to the presentation of his
philosophical views: "Seem to have made up my mind to write my metaphysical works, as *my Life & in* my Life—intermixed with all the other
events / or history of the mind & fortunes of S. T. Coleridge" (*CN*,
1:1515). But even as the germ of the *Biographia* is in evidence in these
early plans, and Coleridge continued to develop his critical principles in
lectures, maginalia, reviews, and his "Essays on the Principles of Genial
Criticism," it was not until 1815 that Coleridge sat down to compose this

2. In *Church and State* C developed the points raised here regarding the necessary security of
the property owned by the landed classes as well as the perspective that they were mere
trustees of the land (see esp. *C&S* [CC], 40–41 and 41n. 4).
3. C had formulated the same advice to patriots in *Conciones ad Populum* (*Lects 1795* [CC],
43).
4. Isaiah 32.20.

work, which he completed in the record time of about three and a half months.

In March 1815, after years of deteriorating health, increased opium addiction, and depression over the meager size of his publications, Coleridge moved in with his friend John James Morgan with whom he had been living on and off since 1810. To secure money, Coleridge planned to publish a collected edition of his poems (which became the *Sibylline Leaves*; pp. 185–88 herein) with a preface. Thanks to the support of his friend William Hood, he obtained several sponsors, among them John Matthew Gutch (1776–1861), a former schoolfellow at Christ's Hospital, who offered to supervise the printing of the work contracted with the Bristol firm of John Evans & Co. By March 30, when Coleridge, seeking a London publisher, approached Lord Byron, he projected the first week in June as a date for sending the collection to press, now envisioned as two volumes with an attached preface "on the Principles of philosophic and genial criticism relatively to the Fine Arts in general; but especially to Poetry: and a Particular Preface to the Ancient Mariner and the Ballads, on the employment of the Supernatural in Poetry * * *" (*CL*, 4:561).

Meanwhile, the appearance of the edition of Wordsworth's collected poems (1815), which Coleridge received in May, deeply affected him and was to change considerably the shape and size of Coleridge's projected collection. So obsessed was Coleridge with this edition, especially its Preface, that in late May or early June, he began to work feverishly on his own preface, giving instructions to the printer to set it in the exact size and type as Wordsworth's Preface (see Morgan's letter to Hood of August 14 and 17 (*BL* [*CC*], 2:284–86). There were good reasons for Coleridge's anxious reaction to Wordsworth's new volume. Coleridge had long been troubled by Wordsworth's 1800 preface (its inadequacy as criticism and its effect on the reception of Wordsworth's poems and Coleridge's own works) and troubled even more by what he took to be the appropriation of his own critical concepts in Wordsworth's 1815 Preface (e.g., the distinction between fancy and imagination). Coleridge, who in his own estimate had already given up poetry for the sake of Wordsworth (see *CL*, 1:656, 658), was not willing to be dispossessed once more. He mobilized all available material from previous notebook jottings, his lectures on literature, and his extensive arsenal of German philosophy; and by the end of July 1815, he managed to dictate to Morgan a sizable manuscript, which turned from a preface into "an Autobiographia literaria" (*CL*, 4:578–79). By September 19, 1815, the completed manuscript was sent by Morgan to Gutch at Bristol.

Unfortunately, in spite of Coleridge's extraordinary feat of speedy composition, the *Biographia* was not published until 1817, even though the printing of the work began almost immediately (October 1815). There were two major setbacks that confronted Coleridge with difficult decisions. In April 1816 after the printing of the *Biographia* was almost two-thirds done, the Bristol printers realized that the prose volume was going to be considerably longer than the poetry volume. To redress this disproportion, Coleridge, following the advice of Morgan and the London publisher John Murray (1778–1843), agreed to split the material into two volumes. Thus there were to be three volumes of equal length, the first two volumes containing the *Biographia* and the third volume Coleridge's poems. On May 6, 1816, Morgan transmitted to Gutch the decision by Coleridge to end the first volume with chapter 13 on "the distinction between Fancy & the Imagination," adding that this way the three volumes

"will be of nearly equal size." But a further and more severe disappointment awaited Coleridge just as he was reviewing the proofs of the first
fourteen pages of what he then regarded as the final chapter of the *Biographia* (chapter 22).

In July 1816 Gutch informed Coleridge that the second volume of the
Biographia was too short compared to the first, and 150 additional pages
were needed to correct this imbalance. This severely strained Coleridge's
relationship with Gutch and led to his decision to transfer the printing of
the *Biographia* to the London publishers Gale & Fenner. The Bristol printing thus stopped at page 144 of Volume 2. During this troubled period,
which involved difficult financial negotiations with Gutch, Coleridge had
to make agonizing decisions about the new material that was to be added
to the second volume of the *Biographia*, briefly entertaining the plan of
using his tragedy *Zapolya*, for this purpose. Eventually Coleridge decided
to expand chapter 22 on the "defects" and "beauties" of Wordsworth's poetry by inserting lengthy quotations; republishing "Satyrane's Letters," a
series of letters written during his trip to Germany in 1798–99 that appeared in numbers 14, 16, and 18 of the 1809 *The Friend*; and using an
adaptation of his critique of the popular tragedy *Bertram* by Charles
Robert Marturin (1782–1824), which he had previously published anonymously in the *Courier* in 1816. His final revisions dealt with the conclusion to the manuscript (the version Gutch received in September 1815),
introducing a defense of the much maligned "Christabel," which had appeared in 1816; of *Zapolya*, which had been rejected by Covent Garden
and Drury Lane; and of *The Statesman's Manual*, published in 1816,
which had incurred vicious attacks from William Hazlitt. At long last, in
July 1817, the *Biographia* was published.

As difficult as the publication history was for Coleridge, for critics it presents fewer problems than the history of the composition of the manuscript
between May or June and September 19, 1815, when it was sent to Gutch.
Nothing definitive can be said about the composition of the *Biographia* because no manuscript survives, and Coleridge's letters about its composition
are contradictory and unreliable as evidence, since he was prone to exaggeration and inaccuracy in correspondence concerning his publications.
Nonetheless, two divergent views about the composition history of the *Biographia* have been proposed. On the one hand, following Earl Leslie
Griggs, several critics (e.g., Daniel Fogel, James Engell, and W. J. Bate) have
argued that Coleridge wrote the critique of Wordsworth first and the philosophical chapters after August 10, possibly writing part of chapter 12 and
chapter 13 between September 16 and 19 under considerable pressure (*BL*
[*CC*], 1:li–lviii), giving weight to Morgan's description of the manuscript in
a letter to Hood of August 10, 1815 (*CL*, 4:585n. 2) and Coleridge's letter of
September 17, 1815 (*CL*, 4:584–87) in which he assigned a later date for
these chapters. On the other hand, other critics have suggested that Coleridge wrote the philosophical chapters by July 29, as indicated by his letter
to R. H. Brabant (*CL*, 4:578–79), and spent the last month and a half correcting Morgan's transcription (Norman Fruman) or writing mainly the
chapters "of an anecdotal, autobiographical or polemical (rather than philo-
sophical/critical character," e.g., chapters 10 and 11 of volume 1 and chapters 15 and 16 of volume 2 (Nigel Leask, *BL* [1997], xlvi–xlvii).

Such speculations have been motivated by the desire to account for the
most troubling aspect of the book—its plagiarisms, which Thomas De
Quincey first pointed out in articles published in *Tait's Magazine* (1834).
If Coleridge wrote the "philosophical chapters" last, then the plagiarisms

can be attributed to the rushed writing during difficult circumstances when Coleridge had to meet the printer's deadlines, was immensely fatigued, was afflicted by opium addiction, and likely to confuse quotations in his notebooks with his own work. But if those chapters were written earlier and at greater leisure, then Coleridge's plagiarisms can be seen simply as a result of his need to project an aggrandized image of his philosophical accomplishments for the sake of which he was willing to resort to unscrupulous stealing from works of German contemporaries. Again, there is no solid evidence to support either theory of the time when the "philosophical chapters" were written. What we know for certain is that Coleridge did translate passages without acknowledgment mainly from Schelling, Kant, Maass, and Jacobi, and that he betrayed an awareness of the practice by warning readers in chapter 9 that they might detect "a genial coincidence" between his writings and Schelling's. The borrowings provided Coleridge with the philosophical basis for his theory of imagination, even though he gave it a more overtly theistic coloring than did Kant or Schelling.

The question of the genre of the *Biographia*, though not as charged as that of Coleridge's plagiarisms, has nonetheless been debated in Coleridge criticism ever since Hazlitt, in his review of the book after its publication, deplored the fact that Coleridge did not produce a proper autobiography, as the title indicated, there being "only two or three passages in the work which relate to the details of the author's life" (*CH*, 1:295). Coleridge himself introduced several disclaimers, strategically placed in the opening page and the concluding chapter of the *Biographia*, asking the reader not to mistake his work as an autobiography, as "the least" in it concerned him "personally." He explained that he used an autobiographical narrative purely as a convenience, "for the purpose of giving continuity to the work," and as a preliminary introduction to the book's real concerns, namely an explanation of his "principles in Politics, Religion, and Philosophy"; the application of rules "deduced from philosophical principles, to poetry and criticism"; and the "settlement" of the controversy with Wordsworth over the issue of poetic diction and the "real *poetic* character of the poet" (pp. 377–78 herein). In the same spirit, Coleridge changed the title of the work from the originally intended *Autobiographia Literaria* (see his letter to Brabant of July 29, 1815 [*CL*, 4:578–79]) to *Biographia Literaria*.

Following Coleridge's own directions, numerous critics have contested the book's status as autobiography, regarding it primarily as a masterpiece of literary criticism and theory, or as too eccentric to be subsumed within a given genre (e.g., Jerome Christensen). Others have argued that the book was an autobiography proper and Coleridge's reasons for ultimately choosing the "biography" over "autobiography" had to do with the uncommonness of the latter term (Southey was the first to use it in 1809), the identity between "biography" and "self-biography" in the period, and his desire to avoid the egotistical implications of the term "autobiography" (e.g., H. J. Jackson). Several critics have also drawn attention to the importance of the autobiographical elements in Coleridge's philosophical chapters and to the hybridity that characterizes this text, which fuses autobiography, philosophy and literary criticism, poetry and prose. The *Biographia* is not a memoir, but it has autobiographical elements; it is not a novel or satire, but its subtitle clearly points to Laurence Sterne's satiric masterpiece *The Life and Opinions of Tristram Shandy, Gent.*; it is not a philosophical treatise, but it includes sustained philosophic discussion in line with the most advanced developments in continental philosophy; it is not a study of Wordsworth, but it includes detailed criticism of his works.

More importantly, the *Biographia* is primarily apologia, as Hazlitt assessed—that is, "not so properly an account of his Life and Opinions, as an Apology for them" (*CH*, 1:295). "Apologia" means both a public defense of a person, or an admission of offense and regret of having caused it (originally the term meant a speech made by a defendant at a trial). Much of the *Biographia* is concerned with a defense of the man of letters (primarily himself, Southey, and Wordsworth) against the unprincipled and ignorant attacks of anonymous reviewers and the establishment of an authoritative countermodel of literary review based on impartial judgments grounded in philosophical principles. It is the biography of a public literary figure who has been involved in a great number of literary and political battles and not a biography of an interior life, like Wordsworth's *The Prelude*, which must have been on Coleridge's mind. (Although *The Prelude* was not published until 1850, Coleridge took with him a manuscript of this work in the 1804 version on his journey to Malta and heard the poem recited by Wordsworth after his return from Malta in 1806.)

The question of genre is intimately linked with the controversy over whether the *Biographia* has any unity or is an "immethodical * * * miscellany," as Coleridge himself described it (p. 420 herein). The haste with which the work was composed, its flagrant plagiarisms and overtly digressive narrative have fostered the view that Coleridge neither planned nor achieved a cohesive work. And yet many critics with very different theoretical orientations have offered passionate defenses of the work's "integrity" and unity, revealing the underlying "method" in Coleridge's deceptively "immethodical" work. (For a review of arguments on both sides of this divide, see Max F. Schulz's chapter on Coleridge in *The English Romantic Poets: A Review of Research* [1985], 427–32.) As Jerome McGann has shown, Coleridge's main purpose is clearly and coherently formulated throughout his work, namely to distinguish himself from the anonymous reviewers who heaped indiscriminate abuse on men of letters by developing "fixed canons of criticism." Coleridge spends the bulk of the first volume of the *Biographia* building a formidably impressive intellectual biography to show that he derived the foundation for his critical opinions from German transcendentalist thought, after a careful examination of the flaws of empirical philosophy, particularly Hartley's associationist doctrines, Cartesian dualism (chapters 5–8) and the contributions of Kant, Fichte, and Schelling toward the development of a systematic science of knowledge (chapters 9, 12, and 13). Volume 1 thus sets into play all the conceptual arsenal Coleridge needed (especially the distinction between fancy and imagination) to impart authority to his theory of poetry and criticism of Wordsworth's poetry. There are then important links between volumes 1 and 2 of the *Biographia*, and this text is best understood by adopting, as Katherine Wallace suggests, a bifocal vision, reading each chapter "both as a stage in the speaker's intellectual development, and as a stage in the effort" to settle the controversy with Wordsworth on poetic diction and the character of the poet (*The Design of the "Biographia Literaria,"* 15).

Biographia Literaria was published only once during Coleridge's lifetime in 1817 and is therefore the version printed here. The work was not reprinted until 1847, when Henry Nelson Coleridge and Sara Coleridge brought out a heavily annotated edition that documented Coleridge's plagiarisms while downplaying their significance.

FROM BIOGRAPHIA LITERARIA
OR
BIOGRAPHICAL SKETCHES
OF
MY LITERARY LIFE
AND
OPINIONS

So wenig er auch bestimmt seyn mag andere zu belehren, so wünscht er dock sich denen mitzutheilen, die er sieh glcichgesinnt weiss oder hofft, deren Anzahl aber in der Breite der Welt zerstreut ist: er wünscht sein Verhältniss zu den ältesten Freunden wieder anzuknüpfen, mit neuen es fortzusetzen, und in der letzen Generation sich wieder andere für sein übrige Lebenszeit zu geiwinnen. Er wünscht der Jugend die Umwege zu ersparen, auf denen er sich selbst verirrte.

GOETHE.[1]

TRANSLATION. Little call as he may have to instruct others, he wishes nevertheless to open out his heart to such as he either knows or hopes to be of like mind with himself, but who are widely scattered in the world: he wishes to knit anew his connections with his oldest friends, to continue those recently formed, and to win other friends among the rising generation for the remaining course of his life. He wishes to spare the young those circuitous paths, on which he himself had lost his way.

From Volume I

CHAPTER I

The motives of the present work—Reception of the Author's first publication—The discipline of his taste at school—The effect of contemporary writers on youthful minds— Bowles's sonnets—Comparison between the Poets before and since Mr. Pope.

It has been my lot to have had my name introduced both in conversation, and in print, more frequently than I find it easy to explain, whether I consider the fewness, unimportance, and limited circulation of my writings, or the retirement and distance, in which I have lived, both from the literary and political world. Most often it has been connected with some charge, which I could not acknowledge, or some principle which I had never entertained. Nevertheless, had I had no other motive, or incitement, the reader would not have been troubled with this exculpation. What my additional purposes were, will be seen in the following pages. It will be found, that the least of what I have written concerns myself personally. I have used the narration chiefly for the purpose of giving a continuity to the work, in part for the sake of the miscellaneous

1. C's motto is taken from Johann Wolfgang von Goethe's introduction to the periodical *Propyläen* (Tübingen, 1798), 1.1.viii–ix (var.). For a longer passage from this introduction, copied by C in a notebook entry of 1807–08 along with a literal translation, see *CN*, 2:3221 and n.

reflections suggested to me by particular events, but still more as introductory to the statement of my principles in Politics, Religion, and Philosophy, and the application of the rules, deduced from philosophical
principles, to poetry and criticism. But of the objects, which I proposed
to myself, it was not the least important to effect, as far as possible, a
settlement of the long continued controversy concerning the true nature
of poetic diction: and at the same time to define with the utmost impartiality the real *poetic* character of the poet, by whose writings this controversy was first kindled, and has been since fuelled and fanned.

In 1794, when I had barely passed the verge of manhood, I published a small volume of juvenile poems.[2] They were received with a
degree of favor, which, young as I was, I well knew, was bestowed on
them not so much for any positive merit, as because they were considered buds of hope, and promises of better works to come. The critics
of that day, the most flattering, equally with the severest, concurred in
objecting to them, obscurity, a general turgidness of diction, and a
profusion of new coined double epithets.[*3] The first is the fault which
a writer is the least able to detect in his own compositions: and my
mind was not then sufficiently disciplined to receive the authority of

---

*   The authority of Milton and Shakespeare may be usefully pointed out to young authors. In
     the Comus, and earlier Poems of Milton there is a superfluity of double epithets; while in
     the Paradise Lost we find very few, in the Paradise Regained scarce any. The same remark
     holds almost equally true, of the Love's Labour Lost, Romeo and Juliet, Venus and Adonis,
     and Lucrece compared with the Lear, Macbeth, Othello, and Hamlet of our great Drama-
     tist.[4] The rule for the admission of double epithets seems to be this: either that they should
     be already denizens of our Language, such as blood-stained, terror-stricken, self-applauding:
     or when a new epithet, or one found in books only, is hazarded, that it, at least, be one word,
     not two words made one by mere virtue of the printer's hyphen. A language which, like the
     English, is almost without cases, is indeed in its very genius unfitted for compounds. If a
     writer, every time a compounded word suggests itself to him, would seek for some other
     mode of expressing the same sense, the chances are always greatly in favor of his finding a
     better word. "Tanquam scopulum sic vites insolens verbum," is the wise advice of Cæsar to
     the Roman Orators, and the precept applies with double force to the writers in our own lan-
     guage.[5] But it must not be forgotten, that the same Cæsar wrote a grammatical treatise for
     the purpose of reforming the ordinary language by bringing it to a greater accordance with
     the principles of Logic or universal Grammar.[6]

---

2.   C misdates the appearance of his first volume of collected poems by two years. *Poems on
     Various Subjects*, which included contributions by Charles Lamb and Robert Southey, was
     published in 1796 (see p. 3 herein).
3.   C summarizes accurately the opinions of reviewers of *Poems on Various Subjects* published
     in the *Monthly Review* 20 (1796): 194–95, the *Critical Review* 17 (1796): 209–12; and the
     Analytical Review 13 (1796): 610–12, among other periodicals. Reviewers generally praised
     the author's "lively imagination," "boldness and novelty of conception," and his "ardor of
     passion," but found fault with his uneven versification and extravagant diction. See *CH*,
     1:32–38 and pp. 3–4 herein. See also Preface to *Poems* (1797) (pp. 46–47 herein) for C's
     comments on these reviews and his defense against the charge of obscurity.
4.   Cf. C's lecture on Shakespeare in *Lects 1808–19* (CC), 1:304, where he comments on the
     "profusion of double epithets" in early Shakespeare and remarks that it is unusual to find in
     a young man of genius "perfect taste," taste being a "subsequent attainment, after the Poet
     had been disciplined by experience." By placing himself in the company of Shakespeare and
     Milton, C assumes the identity of a self-improving genius, who can correct the shortcomings
     of his early works. Cf. the assessment in the *Critical Review* that "Mr. Coleridge's blemishes
     are such as are incident to young men of luxuriant imaginations, which time and experience
     will, we doubt not, enable him to correct. His beauties are those of a very superior genius
     * * *" (CH, 1:35).
5.   An abbreviated version of the following remark attributed to Caesar (book 1 of *De Analogia*
     [On Analogy]) by Aulus Gellius (2nd century C.E.) in *Noctes Atticae* (Attic Nights), 1.10.4
     (*BL* [1907], 1:204n.): "You should avoid an unusual word as if it were a rock." C used this
     maxim in CN, 1:384 and *Friend* (CC), 1:449.
6.   Only a few fragments survive of Caesar's grammatical treatise *On Analogy*.

others, as a substitute for my own conviction. Satisfied that the thoughts, such as they were, could not have been expressed otherwise, or at least more perspicuously, I forgot to enquire, whether the thoughts themselves did not demand a degree of attention unsuitable to the nature and objects of poetry. This remark however applies chiefly, though not exclusively to the *Religious Musings*. The remainder of the charge I admitted to its full extent, and not without sincere acknowledgments to both my private and public censors for their friendly admonitions. In the after editions, I pruned the double epithets with no sparing hand, and used my best efforts to tame the swell and glitter both of thought and diction; though in truth, these parasite plants of youthful poetry had insinuated themselves into my longer poems with such intricacy of union, that I was often obliged to omit disentangling the weed, from the fear of snapping the flower.[7] From that period to the date of the present work I have published nothing, with my name, which could by any possibility have come before the board of anonymous criticism.[8] Even the three or four poems, printed with the works of a friend,[9] as far as they were censured at all, were charged with the same or similar defects, though I am persuaded not with equal justice: with an EXCESS OF ORNAMENT, in addition to STRAINED AND ELABORATE DICTION. (*Vide the criticisms on the* "Ancient Mariner," *in the Monthly and Critical Reviews of the first volume of the Lyrical Ballads.*)[1] May I be permitted to add, that, even at the early period of my juvenile poems, I saw and admitted the superiority of an austerer, and more natural style, with an insight not less clear, than I at present possess. My judgment was stronger, than were my powers of realizing its dictates; and the faults of my language, though indeed partly owing to a wrong choice of subjects, and the desire of giving a poetic colouring to abstract and metaphysical truths, in which a new world then seemed to open upon me, did yet, in part likewise, originate in unfeigned diffidence of my own comparative talent.—During several years of my youth and early manhood, I reverenced those, who had re-introduced the manly simplicity of the Grecian, and of our own elder poets, with such enthusiasm, as made the hope seem presumptuous of writing successfully in the same style. Perhaps a similar process has happened to others; but my earliest poems were marked

---

7. From "The remainder of the charge" to here, C draws on his Preface to *Poems* (1797) (p. 47 herein). C did not, as he claims, get rid of many double epithets.
8. Actually C's publications before 1815 included *Fears in Solitude* (1798); the translation of Schiller, *Wallenstein* (1800); *The Friend* (1809–10); and the drama *Remorse* (1813). "Ode on the Departing Year" had appeared in 1796 and was included in the 1797 volume.
9. C contributed four poems to the first edition of the *LB* (1798), which appeared anonymously: "The Rime of the Ancyent Marinere," "The Foster-Mother's Tale," "The Nightingale," and "The Dungeon."
1. C is correct that criticisms of his contributions to *Lyrical Ballads* were similar to those leveled against his *Poems* (1796). The reviewer of *Poems* (1796) for the *Analytical Review* described C's compositions as lacking simplicity, while the reviewer of *Lyrical Ballads* for the *Analytical Review* 28 (1798): 583–85 wrote that "The Ancient Mariner" had "more of the extravagance of a mad german poet, than of the simplicity of our ancient ballad writers." To Robert Southey, the reviewer for the *Critical Review* 24 (1798): 197–204, "The Ancient Mariner" appeared to be unintelligible, a "Dutch attempt at German sublimity," an opinion shared by the reviewer of the *Monthly Review* 29 (1799): 202–10, who described the poem as "a rhapsody of unintelligible wildness and incoherence" (*CH*, 1:33, 52, 53, 56).

by an ease and simplicity, which I have studied, perhaps with inferior success, to impress on my later compositions.

At school I enjoyed the inestimable advantage of a very sensible, though at the same time, a very severe master.[2] He* early moulded my taste to the preference of Demosthenes to Cicero, of Homer and Theocritus to Virgil, and again of Virgil to Ovid. He habituated me to compare Lucretius, (in such extracts as I then read) Terence, and above all the chaster poems of Catullus,[3] not only with the Roman poets of the, so called, silver and brazen ages;[4] but with even those of the Augustan era: and on grounds of plain sense and universal logic to see and assert the superiority of the former, in the truth and nativeness, both of their thoughts and diction. At the same time that we were studying the Greek Tragic Poets, he made us read Shakspeare and Milton as lessons: and they were the lessons too, which required most time and trouble to *bring up*, so as to escape his censure. I learnt from him, that Poetry, even that of the loftiest, and, seemingly, that of the wildest odes, had a logic of its own, as severe as that of science;[5] and more difficult, because more subtle, more complex, and dependent on more, and more fugitive causes. In the truly great poets, he would say, there is a reason assignable, not only for every word, but for the position of every word; and I well remember, that availing himself of the synonimes to the Homer of Didymus,[6] he made us attempt to show, with regard to each, *why* it would not have answered the same purpose; and

---

* The Rev. James Bowyer, many years Head Master of the Grammar-School, Christ Hospital.

---

2. James Boyer (1736–1814), C's teacher and Upper Grammar Master at Christ's Hospital, known for his floggings and intransigence, and vividly described by Lamb in his essay "Christ's Hospital Five and Thirty Years Ago," which also includes a memorable evocation of C (p. 647 herein). In 1782 C was admitted to Christ's Hospital, a charity institution, where he remained until 1791, when he went to Jesus College, Cambridge.
3. Demosthenes (c. 385–322 B.C.E.), prestigious Greek orator and politician, who mobilized the Greeks against Macedonian rule. Cicero (106–43 B.C.E.), one of the greatest orators and statesmen of ancient Rome, allied with the Republican cause, and author of the philosophical treatises De oratore (On the Orator) and De republica (On the Republic). Homer, the presumed author of the earliest epic poems, the Iliad and the Odyssey. Theocritus (c. 310–c. 250 B.C.E.), author of the Idylls, which influenced the emergence of pastoral literature. Virgil (70–19 B.C.E.), influential Roman poet and author of the Eclogues, the Georgics and the epic poem the Aeneid. Ovid (43 B.C.E.–c. 17 C.E.), Roman poet of the Golden Age and author of the Art of Love and Metamorphosis. Lucretius (c. 96–c. 55 B.C.E.), Roman philosopher-poet and author of the influential didactic poem De rerum natura (Of the Nature of Things). Terence (c. 185–c. 159 B.C.E.), popular Roman playwright. Catullus, (c. 84–c. 54 B.C.E.), Roman poet known for his widely admired poems to his mistress Lesbia.
4. The Silver Age of Latin literature extends from the death of the Roman emperor Augustus (14 C.E.) to the death of Trajan (117 C.E.). The Bronze Age began in 117 C.E. and ended with the sacking of Rome by the Goths in 410 C.E.
5. In a letter to William Sotheby (1757–1833) of September 10, 1802, C identified Edward Young (1683–1765) as the author of the view that poetry had a logic of its own. In his essay "On Lyric Poetry," Young claimed that there was as much logic in Pindar as in Aristotle or Euclid (Works, 6 vols. [1774–78], 6:130). See p. 631, n. 7 herein. C jotted down notes from Young's essay in 1795 (CN, 1:33–36 and nn.).
6. Didymus Chalcenterus (1st century B.C.E.), Greek scholar, who taught in Alexandria and Rome, reputed to have written over 3,500 books, among them a treatise on Homer and numerous commentaries on grammar and Greek poets and prose writers. Boyer might have used Homer, Ilias et Odyssea et in easdem scholia sive interpretatio Didymi (Iliad and Odyssey and the Scholia on Them with the Commentary of Didymus), ed. Cornelius Schrevelius (Amsterdam, 1655–56), a copy of which was housed in the library of Christ's Hospital (BL [CC], 1:9n. 3).

wherein consisted the peculiar fitness of the word in the original text.

In our own English compositions (at least for the last three years of our school education) he showed no mercy to phrase, metaphor, or image, unsupported by a sound sense, or where the same sense might have been conveyed with equal force and dignity in plainer words. Lute, harp, and lyre, muse, muses, and inspirations, Pegasus, Parnassus, and Hipocrene,[7] were all an abomination to him. In fancy I can almost hear him now, exclaiming "*Harp? Harp? Lyre? Pen and ink, boy, you mean! Muse, boy, Muse? your Nurse's daughter, you mean! Pierian spring? Oh 'aye! the cloister-pump, I suppose!*" Nay certain introductions, similies, and examples, were placed by name on a list of interdiction. Among the similies, there was, I remember, that of the Manchineel fruit, as suiting equally well with too many subjects;[8] in which however it yielded the palm at once to the example of Alexander and Clytus, which was equally good and apt, whatever might be the theme. Was it ambition? Alexander and Clytus!—Flattery? Alexander and Clytus!—Anger? Drunkenness? Pride? Friendship? Ingratitude? Late repentance? Still, still Alexander and Clytus![9] At length, the praises of agriculture having been exemplified in the sagacious observation, that had Alexander been holding the plough, he would not have run his friend Clytus through with a spear, this tried, and serviceable old friend was banished by public edict in secula seculorum.[1] I have sometimes ventured to think, that a list of this kind, or an index expurgatorius of certain well known and ever returning phrases, both introductory, and transitional, including the large assortment of modest egotisms, and flattering illeisms,[2] &c. &c. might be hung up in our law-courts, and both houses of parliament, with great advantage to the public, as an important saving of national time, an incalculable relief to his Majesty's ministers, but above all, as insuring the thanks of country attornies, and their clients, who have private bills to carry through the house.

Be this as it may, there was one custom of our master's, which I cannot pass over in silence, because I think it imitable and worthy of imitation. He would often permit our theme exercises, under some pretext of want of time, to accumulate, till each lad had four or five to be looked over. Then placing the whole number *abreast* on his desk, he would ask the writer, why this or that sentence might not have found as appropriate a place under this or that other thesis: and if no satisfying answer could be returned, and two faults of the same kind were found in one exercise, the irrevocable verdict followed, the exercise was torn up, and another on the same subject to be produced, in addition to the tasks of

7. Pegasus, a winged horse in Greek mythology who created the fountain of Hippocrene (regarded as sacred to the Muses and the source of poetic inspiration) on Mount Helicon with a kick from his hoof. Parnassus was a mountain in ancient Greece associated with Apollo, the Muses, and poetry.
8. For C's political use of the image of the poisonous West Indian manchineel tree, see p. 278, n. 6 herein. C had also used the image in the poem "To the Reverend George Coleridge," line 26 (p. 45 and n. 2 herein).
9. As narrated by Plutarch in *Lives* 50–52, Alexander killed his friend Clytus during a banquet when both were drunk.
1. "For ever and ever."
2. C coins this term from the Latin *ille* (that).

the day. The reader will, I trust, excuse this tribute of recollection to a man, whose severities, even now, not seldom furnish the dreams, by which the blind fancy would fain interpret to the mind the painful sensations of distempered sleep; but neither lessen nor dim the deep sense of my moral and intellectual obligations. He sent us to the University excellent Latin and Greek scholars,[3] and tolerable Hebraists. Yet our classical knowledge was the least of the good gifts, which we derived from his zealous and conscientious tutorage. He is now gone to his final reward, full of years, and full of honors, even of those honors, which were dearest to his heart, as gratefully bestowed by that school, and still binding him to the interests of that school, in which he had been himself educated, and to which during his whole life he was a dedicated thing.

From causes, which this is not the place to investigate, no models of past times, however perfect, can have the same vivid effect on the youthful mind, as the productions of contemporary genius. The Discipline, my mind had undergone, "Ne falleretur rotundo sono et versuum cursu, cincinnis et floribus; sed ut inspiceret quidnam subesset, quæ sedes, quod firmamentum, quis fundus verbis; an figuræ essent mera ornatura et orationis fucus: vel sanguinis e materiæ ipsius corde effluentis rubor quidam nativus et incalescentia genuina;"[4] removed all obstacles to the appreciation of excellence in style without diminishing my delight. That I was thus prepared for the perusal of Mr. Bowles's sonnets and earlier poems, at once increased *their* influence, and *my* enthusiasm.[5] The great works of past ages seem to a young man things of another race, in respect to which his faculties must remain passive and submiss[ive], even as to the stars and mountains. But the writings of a contemporary, perhaps not many years elder than himself, surrounded by the same circumstances, and disciplined by the same manners, possess a *reality* for him, and inspire an actual friendship as of a man for a man. His very admiration is the wind which fans and feeds his hope. The poems themselves assume the properties of flesh and blood. To recite, to extol, to contend for them is but the payment of a debt due to one, who exists to receive it.

There are indeed modes of teaching which have produced, and are producing, youths of a very different stamp; modes of teaching, in comparison with which we have been called on to despise our great public schools, and universities

In whose halls are hung
Armoury of the invincible knights of old—[6]

3. C's "excellent" Greek bore fruit at Cambridge, where he won the Sir William Browne gold medal for his Greek ode on the slave trade (see p. 287 herein).
4. "So that it [i.e. my mind] was not misled by the smooth sound and flow of the verses, their ringlets and flowers, but examined what lay beneath them, what was their ground, their firmament, their foundation; whether the figures were mere ornamentation and the paint of rhetoric, or a natural flush and genuine warmth of the blood flowing from the heart of the matter itself." Source untraced. Previous editors have speculated that the Latin was C's or came from a Renaissance treatise on rhetoric (*BL* [CC], 1:12n. 1).
5. William Lisle Bowles (1762–1850), the author of *Sonnets, Written Chiefly on Picturesque Spots, During a Tour* (Bath, 1789), reprinted in many expanded editions.
6. William Wordsworth, *Sonnets Dedicated to Liberty*, Sonnet 16, lines 9–10: "In our Halls is hung / Armoury of the invincible Knights of old" (*Poems* [1815], 2:214).

modes, by which children are to be metamorphosed into prodigies. And prodigies with a vengeance have I known thus produced! Prodigies of self-conceit, shallowness, arrogance, and infidelity! Instead of storing the memory, during the period when the memory is the predominant faculty, with facts for the after exercise of the judgement; and instead of awakening by the noblest models the fond and unmixed LOVE and ADMIRATION, which is the natural and graceful temper of early youth; *these* nurselings of improved pedagogy are taught to dispute and decide;[7] to suspect all, but their own and their lecturer's wisdom; and to hold nothing sacred from their contempt, but their own contemptible arrogance: boy-graduates in all the technicals, and in all the dirty passions and impudence, of anonymous criticism. To such dispositions alone can the admonition of Pliny be requisite, "Neque enim debet operibus ejus obesse, quod vivit. An si inter eos, quos nunquam vidimus, floruisset, non solum libros ejus, verum etiam imagines conquireremus, ejusdem nunc honor præsentis, et gratia quasi satietate languescet? At hoc pravum, malignumque est, non admirari hominem admiratione dignissimum, quia videre, complecti, nec laudare tantum, verum etiam amare contingit." *Plin. Epist. Lib. I.*[8]

I had just entered on my seventeenth year when the sonnets of Mr. Bowles, twenty in number,[9] and just then published in a quarto pamphlet, were first made known and presented to me, by a school-fellow who had quitted us for the University, and who, during the whole time that he was in our first form (or in our school language a GRECIAN) had been my patron and protector. I refer to Dr. Middleton, the truly learned, and every way excellent Bishop of Calcutta:[1]

> Qui laudibus amplis
> Ingenium celebrare meum, calamumque solebat,
> Calcar agens animo validum. Non omnia terræ

7. According to C's philosophy of education, "little is taught or communicated by contest or dispute, but everything by sympathy and love" (*Lects* 1808–19 [CC], 1:106). See also his literary lecture of March 2, 1818, in which he claimed that in "the education of children, love is first to be instilled," whereas the "comparing power, the judgement * * * ought not to be forcibly excited, as is too frequently and mistakenly done in the modern systems of education, which can only lead to selfish views" and "an inflated sense of merit" (2:192–93). See also entry on "Education" (pp. 591–92 herein).

8. Pliny, *Letters*, 1. 16 (var.), trans. William Melmoth, rev. W. M. L. Hutchinson (LCL, 1915), 57–58: "[Let it not be] any prejudice to his merit that he is a contemporary writer. Had he flourished in some distant age, not only his works, but the very pictures and statues of him would have been passionately inquired after; and shall we then, from a sort of satiety, and merely because he is present among us, suffer his talents to languish and fade away unhonoured and unadmired? It is surely a very perverse and envious disposition, to look with indifference upon a man worthy of the highest approbation, for no other reason but because we have it in our power to see him and to converse familiarly with him, and not only to give him our applause, but to receive him into our friendship." This passage with two additional sentences appears in a notebook entry of 1804 (*CN*, 2:1944) and was used with reference to Wordsworth in *Friend* (CC), 2:108n. (*BL* [CC], 1:13n. 2).

9. The second edition of Bowles's *Sonnets* (Bath, 1789) had twenty-one poems (the first had fourteen sonnets).

1. Thomas Fanshaw Middleton (1769–1822), friend of C's at Christ's Hospital until 1788, when Middleton left for Cambridge, and at Cambridge in 1791, when C entered the university. Middleton left Cambridge in 1792 and was bishop of Calcutta from 1814 till his death. *Grecian*: the designation given to the most academically gifted pupils at Christ's Hospital, i.e., the handful who were expected to go on to Oxford or Cambridge, as opposed to the navy or trades.

Obruta! Vivit amor, vivit dolor! Ora negatur
Dulcia conspicere; at flere et meminisse* relictum est.
                                           Petr. Ep. Lib. I. Ep. I.[2]

It was a double pleasure to me, and still remains a tender recollection, that I should have received from a friend so revered the first knowledge of a poet, by whose works, year after year, I was so enthusiastically delighted and inspired. My earliest acquaintances will not have forgotten the undisciplined eagerness and impetuous zeal, with which I laboured to make proselytes, not only of my companions, but of all with whom I conversed, of whatever rank, and in whatever place. As my school finances did not permit me to purchase copies, I made, within less than a year and an half, more than forty transcriptions, as the best presents I could offer to those, who had in any way won my regard.[3] And with almost equal delight did I receive the three or four following publications of the same author.[4]

Though I have seen and known enough of mankind to be well aware, that I shall perhaps stand alone in my creed, and that it will be well, if I subject myself to no worse charge than that of singularity; I am not therefore deterred from avowing, that I regard, and ever have regarded the obligations of intellect among the most sacred of the claims of gratitude. A valuable thought, or a particular train of thoughts, gives me additional pleasure, when I can safely refer and attribute it to the conversation or correspondence of another. My obligations to Mr. Bowles were indeed important, and for radical good.[5] At

---

* I am most happy to have the necessity of informing the reader, that since this passage was written, the report of Dr. Middleton's death on his voyage to India has been proved erroneous. He lives and long may he live; for I dare prophecy, that with his life only will his exertions for the temporal and spiritual welfare of his fellow men be limited.

---

2. "Who, with lavish praises, was wont to celebrate my genius and my pen, setting a sharp spur to my spirit. Not everything is buried in the earth. Love lives, grief lives on! We are denied now the sight of those sweet features; but it is left for us to weep and to remember." Petrarch, "Epistola Barbato Sulmonensi" (Letter to Barbato da Sulmona), lines 12–16 (var.) in *Opera*, 4 vols. (Basle, 1581), 3:76. (*BL* [CC], 1:14n. 1). C replaced Petrarch's *"Regia"* (royal) with *"Dulcia"* (sweet). For C's use of William Sotheby's copy of this edition of Petrarch, see *CN*, 3:3360n. C greatly appreciated this letter, which he thought should be read and translated (see *CN*, 3:4178) and used it again in chapters 10 (p. 461 and its n. 6 herein) and 14 (p. 495 and its n. 3 herein). The extract in chapter 10 was also used as an epigram for "Love-Poems" in *Sibylline Leaves* (p. 188 and its n. 1 herein).
3. C did not actually offer Bowles's *Sonnets* as gifts to his friends, but, for the price of sixpence each, sold two hundred copies of a collection of twenty-eight sonnets entitled *Sonnets from Various Authors* (1796), which included, among others, sonnets by Lamb, Southey, Lloyd, and Charlotte Smith (1749–1806), and four by C. This collection was bound with Bowles's *Sonnets*. Among the several surviving copies of this combined volume, the ones at the Huntington Library and the Victoria and Albert Museum feature the third (1794) and fourth (1796) edition of Bowles's *Sonnets*, respectively (see *CL*, 1:252 and n. 1). Most of the sonnets in the collection had already been published, but C altered some considerably, compressing and leaving out lines in order to get them into the fourteen line format required for a sonnet. On the content of the volume, see *Coleridge's "Sonnets from Various Authors,"* ed. Paul M. Zall (Glendale, Calif., 1968), 11–24.
4. Bowles's subsequent publications, in addition to the third, fourth, and fifth edition of his *Sonnets* in 1796, include *The Grave of Howard* (1790); *Verses on the Benevolent Institution of the Philanthropic Society* (1790); *Monody, Written at Matlock, October 1791* (1791); *Hope, an Allegorical Sketch, on Recovering Slowly from Sickness* (1796); and *Elegiac Stanzas* (1796).
5. Although early on C expressed enthusiasm for "the exquisite Bowles" (*CL*, 1:29), whom he regarded as "with the exception of Burns, the only *always-natural* poet in our Language" (*CL*, 1:278), his view of Bowles began to change after 1797, when the two poets met. In a letter to William Sotheby of 1802, C complained that Bowles "has indeed the *sensibility* of a

a very premature age, even before my fifteenth year, I had bewildered myself in metaphysicks, and in theological controversy. Nothing else pleased me.[6] History, and particular facts, lost all interest in my mind. Poetry (though for a school-boy of that age, I was above par in English versification, and had already produced two or three compositions which, I may venture to say, without reference to my age, were somewhat above mediocrity, and which had gained me more credit, than the sound, good sense of my old master was at all pleased with)[7] poetry itself, yea novels and romances, became insipid to me. In my friendless wanderings on our *leave-* days*, (for I was an orphan,[8] and had scarce any connections in London) highly was I delighted, if any passenger, especially if he were drest in black, would enter into conversation with me. For I soon found the means of directing it to my favorite subjects

> Of providence, fore-knowledge, will, and fate,
> Fix'd fate, free will, fore-knowledge absolute,
> And found no end in wandering mazes lost.[9]

This preposterous pursuit was, beyond doubt, injurious, both to my natural powers, and to the progress of my education. It would perhaps have been destructive, had it been continued; but from this I was auspiciously withdrawn, partly indeed by an accidental introduction to an amiable family,[1] chiefly however, by the genial influence of a style of poetry, so tender, and yet so manly, so natural and real, and yet so dignified, and harmonious, as the sonnets, &c. of Mr. Bowles! Well were it for me perhaps, had I never relapsed into the same mental disease; if I had continued to pluck the flower and reap the harvest from the cultivated surface, instead of delving in the unwholesome quicksilver mines of metaphysic depths. But if in after time I have sought a refuge from bodily pain and mismanaged sensibility in abstruse researches,[2]

---

* The Christ Hospital phrase, not for holidays altogether, but for those on which the boys are permitted to go beyond the precincts of the school.

---

poet; but he has not the *Passion* of a great Poet. His latter Writings all want *native* Passion * * * because he is not a Thinker * * *" (see p. 360 and its n. 4 herein). Cf. C's opinion (later in this chapter, p. 391 herein) that Bowles was "the first * * * who reconciled the heart with the head," which conflicts with that expressed to Sotheby that Bowles failed to unite sensibility with thought.

6. As Lamb remembered him, C was steeped in metaphysical pursuits as a young student at Christ's Hospital (see p. 380 and n. 2 herein and p. 647 herein). Early on C did not view metaphysics as injurious to, but as an indispensable ingredient in all good poetry (see, e.g., his letter to John Thelwall of May 13, 1796 [CL, 1:215]). C's apologetic stance toward metaphysics developed in the wake of Wordsworth's rejection of "Christabel" for the second edition of the *Lyrical Ballads*, which left C feeling displaced as a poet and occupying the inferior role of a "kind of a Metaphysician" (CL, 1:658). In "Dejection: An Ode" C claimed that metaphysics incapacitated his imaginative powers, a view also given currency by Wordsworth in book 6 of *The Prelude* (p. 646 herein).
7. Boyer included five of C's poems—"Nil Pejus est Caelibe Vitâ" (The Single Life Is by No Means the Worst), "Julia," "Quae Nocent Docent" (Those Things that Hurt Teach), "Progress of Vice," and "Monody on the Death of Chatterton"—in *Liber Aureus* (Golden Book), which listed his students' best work (*BL* [CC], 1:16n. 1).
8. C's mother was still alive when C was as Christ's Hospital. She died in 1809. C's father had died in 1781.
9. Milton, *Paradise Lost* 2.559–61 (var.).
1. In 1788 C was introduced to the Evans family by his school mate William Evans. During his visits, C fell in love with one of William's three sisters, Mary Evans, who did not reciprocate his sentiments.
2. Cf. lines 87–93 of "Dejection: An Ode" (p. 157 herein).

which exercised the strength and subtlety of the understanding without awakening the feelings of the heart; still there was a long and
blessed interval, during which my natural faculties were allowed
to expand, and my original tendencies to develope themselves: my
fancy, and the love of nature, and the sense of beauty in forms and
sounds.

The second advantage, which I owe to my early perusal, and admiration of these poems (to which let me add, though known to me at a
somewhat later period, the Lewsdon Hill of Mr. Crow)[3] bears more
immediately on my present subject. Among those with whom I conversed, there were, of course, very many who had formed their taste,
and their notions of poetry, from the writings of Mr. Pope and his followers: or to speak more generally, in that school of French poetry,
condensed and invigorated by English understanding, which had pre-
dominated from the last century. I was not blind to the merits of this
school, yet as from inexperience of the world, and consequent want of
sympathy with the general subjects of these poems, they gave me little
pleasure, I doubtless undervalued the *kind*, and with the presumption
of youth withheld from its masters the legitimate name of poets. I saw,
that the excellence of this kind consisted in just and acute observations on men and manners in an artificial state of society, as its matter
and substance: and in the logic of wit, conveyed in smooth and strong
epigramatic couplets, as its *form*. Even when the subject was addressed to the fancy, or the intellect, as in the Rape of the Lock, or the
Essay on Man; nay, when it was a consecutive narration, as in that as-
tonishing product of matchless talent and ingenuity, Pope's Translation of the Iliad;[4] still a *point* was looked for at the end of each second
line, and the whole was as it were a sorites,[5] or, if I may exchange a
logical for a grammatical metaphor, a *conjunction disjunctive*, of epigrams.[6] Meantime the matter and diction seemed to me characterized
not so much by poetic thoughts, as by thoughts *translated* into the language of poetry. On this last point, I had occasion to render my own
thoughts gradually more and more plain to myself, by frequent amica-

3. C borrowed a copy of *Lewesdon Hill* (1788) by William Crowe (1745–1829) from the Bristol Library from March 2 to 10, 1795 (*Borrowings*, 119). The poem shares with Bowles an
interest in a natural setting and style of writing but also Bowles's "trick of *moralizing* every
thing," to which C objected in a letter of 1802 (*CL*, 2:864).
4. In a letter to Humprey Davy of September 9, 1807, C listed in his outline of a series of
lectures on literature one on "Dryden, & Pope, including the origin, & after history of
poetry of witty logic" (*CL*, 3:30, 42), a subject he might have addressed in one or several
lectures of 1808 (see *Lects 1808–19* [CC], 1:119–21). In a later lecture of October 28,
1813, C questioned whether one could confer upon Alexander Pope the status of poet
(1:515). C was especially critical of Pope's translation of the *Iliad*, published between
1715 and 1720 (see p. 396, n. 1 herein), an opinion also shared by Wordsworth (*W Prose*
3:73).
5. A term used in logic, referring to syllogisms in which the conclusion of a syllogism becomes
the starting point of the following one.
6. In a notebook entry of 1804, using examples from Wordsworth's "The Mad Mother" and
Hudibras (1663–80) by Samuel Butler, C sets up a distinction between "continuous minds,"
who function by means of passion and imagination and can blend opposite qualities, and
"discontinuous minds," who juxtapose diverse elements for the sake of wit. To the first group
he assigns the category "disjunction conjunctive" and to the second "conjunction disjunctive" (*CN*, 2:2112 and n.). C implies that Pope is a writer of fancy and not of imagination,
creating according to a principle superimposed mechanically from the outside rather than
one arising naturally from within the artist.

ble disputes concerning Darwin's BOTANIC GARDEN,[7] which, for some
years, was greatly extolled, not only by the *reading* public in general,
but even by those, whose genius and natural robustness of understanding enabled them afterwards to act foremost in dissipating these
"painted mists" that occasionally rise from the marshes at the foot of
Parnassus. During my first Cambridge vacation, I assisted a friend in a
contribution for a literary society in Devonshire:[8] and in this I remember to have compared Darwin's work to the Russian palace of ice, glittering, cold and transitory.[9] In the same essay too, I assigned sundry
reasons, chiefly drawn from a comparison of passages in the Latin poets with the original Greek, from which they were borrowed, for the
preference of Collins's odes to those of Gray;[1] and of the simile in
Shakspeare

> How like a younker or a prodigal,
> The skarfed bark puts from her native bay
> Hugg'd and embraced by the strumpet wind!
> How like a prodigal doth she return,
> With over-weather'd ribs and ragged sails,
> Lean, rent, and beggar'd by the strumpet wind![2]

to the imitation in the bard;

> Fair laughs the morn, and soft the zephyr blows
> While proudly riding o'er the azure realm
> In gallant trim the gilded vessel goes,
> YOUTH at the prow and PLEASURE at the helm,
> Regardless of the sweeping whirlwinds sway,
> That hush'd in grim repose, expects its evening prey.[3]

(In which, by the bye, the words "realm" and "sway" are rhymes dearly
purchased.) I preferred the original on the ground, that in the imitation it depended wholly in the compositor's putting, or not putting a
small Capital, both in this, and in many other passages of the same

---

7. Written in heroic couplets in the tradition of Pope, *The Botanic Garden* (1789–91) by Eras-
    mus Darwin was a popular work, which attempted to make natural science the subject of
    poetry. The second part ("The Loves of the Plants"), which dealt with the sexuality of plants,
    was sufficiently provocative to elicit dispute.
8. Possibly the "Society of Gentlemen at Exeter" founded by Dr. Hugh Downman
    (1740–1809), which remained active from about 1790 to 1808. In 1796 it published a vol-
    ume titled *Essays by a Society of Gentlemen, at Exeter*. C's essay is not in the volume and has
    not been traced (*BL* [*CC*], 1:19n. 4).
9. The ice palace built by Empress Anna in St. Petersburg in winter 1739–40, which melted
    the following spring. For a possible source of this reference, see William Cowper's *The Task*
    (1785), 5.127–76 (*BL* [1997], 367n.).
1. For C's preference for William Collins (1721–1759) over Thomas Gray (1716–1771), see
    the entry of April 21, 1811 in *TT* (*CC*), 1:12. In 1796 C had planned to publish an edition
    of Collins and Gray, to which he was to attach a "preliminary Dissertation" (*CN*, 1:161,
    174), and he wrote to Thelwall that Collins's "Ode on a Poetical Character" had inspired
    him more than "the most *impassioned* Scene in Schiller or Shakspere" (*CL*, 1:279; cf. *CN*,
    1:383). Early on C also held Gray in high esteem, but by 1799, his enthusiasm for Gray be-
    gan to wane. "*The Bard*," C wrote, "once intoxicated me, & now I read it without pleasure"
    (*CN*, 1:383). For his later view that Gray's lyrics and especially *The Bard* were "frigid and ar-
    tificial," see, e.g., the entry of October 23, 1833 in *TT* (*CC*), 1:447.
2. *The Merchant of Venice* 2.6.14–19 (var.).
3. Gray, *The Bard* (1757), lines 71–76 (var.).

poet, whether the words should be personifications,[4] or mere abstracts. I mention this, because in referring various lines in Gray to their original in Shakspeare and Milton; and in the clear perception how completely all the propriety was lost in the transfer; I was, at that early period, led to a conjecture, which, many years afterwards was recalled to me from the same thought having been started in conversation, but far more ably, and developed more fully, by Mr. WORDSWORTH;[5] namely, that this style of poetry, which I have characterised above, as translations of prose thoughts into poetic language, had been kept up by, if it did not wholly arise from, the custom of writing Latin verses, and the great importance attached to these exercises, in our public schools. Whatever might have been the case in the fifteenth century, when the use of the Latin tongue was so general among learned men, that Erasmus[6] is said to have forgotten his native language; yet in the present day it is not to be supposed, that a youth can *think* in Latin, or that he can have any other reliance on the force or fitness of his phrases, but the authority of the author from whence he has adopted them. Consequently he must first prepare his thoughts, and then pick out, from Virgil, Horace, Ovid, or perhaps more compendiously from his* Gradus, halves and quarters of lines, in which to embody them.

I never object to a certain degree of disputatiousness in a young man from the age of seventeen to that of four or five and twenty, provided I find him always arguing on one side of the question. The controversies, occasioned by my unfeigned zeal for the honor of a favorite contemporary, then known to me only by his works, were of great ad-

---

* In the Nutricia of Politian there occurs this line:[7]
    Pura coloratos interstrepit unda lapillos.
Casting my eye on a University prize-poem, I met this line,
    Lactea purpureos interstrepit unda lapillos.[8]

Now look out in the Gradus for *Purus*, and you find as the first synonime, *lacteus*; for *coloratus*, and the first synonime is *purpureus*.[9] I mention this by way of elucidating one of the most ordinary processes in the *ferrumination*[1] of these centos.

---

4. Cf. entry of April 21, 1811, in *TT* (CC), 1:12: "Gray's personifications, he said, were mere printer's devils' personifications—persons with a capital letter, abstract qualities with a small one."
5. In chapter 2 of the *Biographia* C again refers to a conversation with Wordsworth in connection with his developing critical sense of Gray's poetry, arguing that he was led by Wordsworth to examine Gray's "Elegy Written in a Country Church-yard" more critically than at an earlier time when he had viewed it as "proof against all fair attacks." C admits that this poem, as well as *The Bard*, gave him great delight, in spite of his awareness of "faults in certain passages" (*BL* [CC], 1:40–41n.). In his Preface to *Lyrical Ballads* Wordsworth cites Gray's "Sonnet on the Death of Richard West" to advance his argument that the best lines of the sonnet and the only valuable ones did not differ from the language of prose (*W Prose*, 1:132–34). C comments on this passage from the Preface in chapter 18 of the *Biographia* (*BL* [CC], 2:63).
6. C considered the classicist, biblical scholar, and satirist Desiderius Erasmus (c. 1469–1536) to be the witty "Pioneer of the Reformation" (*Friend* [CC], 2:112).
7. Angelo Ambrogini (1454–94), known as Poliziano or Politianus. The line cited by C comes from *Rusticus* rather than *Nutricia*: "The clear [stream] murmurs on amid the little coloured stones" (*BL* [CC], 1:21 n1).
8. "The milky [stream] murmurs on among the little purple stones."
9. C refers to *Gradus ad Parnassum* (Steps to Parnassus) (1687), a book of Latin prosody by Paul Aler (1656–1727) commonly used in English schools. *Purus*: "pure"; *lacteus*: "milky"; *coloratus*: "colored"; *purpureus*: "purple." In *Gradus*, *lacteus* and *purpureus* do not appear as synonyms for *purus* and *coloratus* (*BL* [CC], 1:21n. 2).
1. "Cementing."

vantage in the formation and establishment of my taste and critical opinions. In my defence of the lines running into each other, instead of closing at each couplet; and of natural language, neither bookish, nor vulgar, neither redolent of the lamp, or of the kennel, such as *I will remember thee;*[2] instead of the same thought tricked up in the rag-fair finery of,

> ——Thy image on her wing
> Before my FANCY's eye shall MEMORY bring,[3]

I had continually to adduce the metre and diction of the Greek Poets from Homer to Theocritus inclusive; and still more of our elder English poets from Chaucer to Milton. Nor was this all. But as it was my constant reply to authorities brought against me from later poets of great name, that no authority could avail in opposition to TRUTH, NATURE, LOGIC, and the LAWS of UNIVERSAL GRAMMAR; actuated too by my former passion for metaphysical investigations; I labored at a solid foundation, on which permanently to ground my opinions, in the component faculties of the human mind itself, and their comparative dignity and importance.[4] According to the faculty or source, from which the pleasure given by any poem or passage was derived, I estimated the merit of such poem or passage. As the result of all my reading and meditation, I abstracted two critical aphorisms, deeming them to comprize the conditions and criteria of poetic style; first, that not the poem which we have *read*, but that to which we *return*, with the greatest pleasure, possesses the genuine power, and claims the name of *essential poetry*. Second, that whatever lines can be translated into other words of the same language, without diminution of their significance, either in sense, or association, or in any worthy feeling, are so far vicious in their diction.[5] Be it however observed, that I excluded from the list of worthy feelings, the pleasure derived from mere novelty, in the reader, and the desire of exciting wonderment at his powers in the author. Oftentimes since then, in perusing French tragedies, I have fancied two marks of admiration at the end of each line, as hieroglyphics of the author's own admiration at his own cleverness.[6] Our genuine admiration

---

2. As in Bowles, Sonnet 3 ("To the River Wensbeck"), line 14: "* * * he will remember you") (*Sonnets*, 3rd ed. [1794], 6; *BL* [CC], 1:22n. 1).
3. A self-critical reference to an image ("Memory's Wing[s]") that C himself used in several early poems (*PW*, 1:29, 49; 2:497).
4. C is responding here to Wordsworth's 1815 Preface to *Poems* (1815), in which he explained the arrangement of his poems according to the faculties of the mind (*W Prose*, 3:28–29). C is right to claim priority over Wordsworth in advocating the importance of understanding the specific functions of mental faculties, which he developed in the course of studying Kant and other German philosophers. Cf. C's Lecture of November 11, 1813: "The only nomenclature of criticism should be the classification of the faculties of the mind, how they are placed, how they are subordinate, whether they do or do not appeal to the worthy feelings of our nature" (*Lects 1808–19* [CC], 1:564).
5. C is enunciating here one of the fundamental principles of an organic view of art according to which a work, once brought into the existence by the creative power of imagination, has a unity that is as impervious to alteration, as the pyramids of Egypt. This means that poems in which synonyms could be provided for words in any line are by definition defective. Cf. also the stress C placed on "desynonymizing" later in chapter 4 (pp. 417–18 herein).
6. For C's poor opinion of French tragedies, cf. the statement in a lecture of April 1, 1808, that they are "the natural Produce of the Hot-bed of Vanity, namely an Author's Closet, who is actuated originally by a desire to excite Surprize & Wonderment at *his* superiority to other Men" (*Lects 1808–19* [CC], 1:86).

of a great poet is a continuous *under-current* of feeling; it is every where present, but seldom any where as a separate excitement. I was wont boldly to affirm, that it would be scarcely more difficult to push a stone out from the pyramids with the bare hand, than to alter a word, or the position of a word, in Milton or Shakspeare, (in their most important works at least) without making the author say something else, or something worse, than he does say. One great distinction, I appeared to myself to see plainly, between, even the characteristic faults of our elder poets, and the false beauty of the moderns. In the former, from Donne to Cowley,[7] we find the most fantastic out-of-the-way thoughts, but in the most pure and genuine mother English; in the latter, the most obvious thoughts, in language the most fantastic and arbitrary. Our faulty elder poets sacrificed the passion, and passionate flow of poetry, to the subtleties of intellect, and to the starts of wit; the moderns to the glare and glitter of a perpetual, yet broken and heterogeneous imagery, or rather to an amphibious something, made up, half of image, and half of abstract* meaning. The one sacrificed the heart to the head; the other both heart and head to point and drapery.

The reader must make himself acquainted with the general style of composition that was at that time deemed poetry, in order to understand and account for the effect produced on me by the Sonnets, the Monody at Matlock, and the Hope, of Mr. Bowles;[8] for it is peculiar to original genius to become less and less *striking*, in proportion to its success in improving the taste and judgement of its contemporaries.[9] The poems of West indeed had the merit of chaste and manly diction, but they were cold, and, if I may so express it, only *dead-coloured;*[1] while in the best of Warton's there is a stiffness, which too often gives them the appearance of imitations from the Greek.[2] Whatever relation therefore of cause or impulse Percy's collection of Ballads may bear to

---

* I remember a ludicrous instance in the poem of a young tradesman:

> No more will I endure love's pleasing pain,
> Or round my *heart's leg* tie his galling chain.

---

7. C became acquainted with Donne's poetry as early as 1796 in the version published in vol. 4 of *The Works of the British Poets*, ed. Robert Anderson, 13 vols. (Edinburgh, 1792–95) (see *CM* [CC], 1:43–4). Subsequently, he read and annotated Lamb's copy of Donne's *Poems* (1669) and two copies of Donne, *Sermons* (1640). The marginalia often reveal his great admiration for Donne's creative powers (*CM* [CC], 2:213–338). See also ["Notebook Fragments, 1811"] (p. 233 herein). C also admired "the elegant simplicity" of Abraham Cowley (1618–1667), regarding him as a legitimate heir of Donne (*Lects 1808–19* [CC], 2:240; *CM* [CC], 2:219), but he also thought that Cowley was inferior to Donne in poetic "vigor" (*CM* [CC], 2:219–20), and unlike Milton, who was a poet of imagination, Cowley was a poet of fancy (p. 418 herein).

8. For Bowles, *Sonnets, Hope,* and *Monody. Written at Matlock,* see p. 382, n. 5 herein and p. 384, n. 4 herein. C used lines 137–40 of *Monody* for an epigram to "Effusions" in *Poems* (1796) (see p. 12 herein).

9. Wordsworth acknowledged C as the author of the view that he shared, that genius creates "the taste by which he is to be enjoyed" ("Essay Supplementary to the Preface," *Poems* [1815]; *W Prose*, 3:80, 102n.).

1. Gilbert West (1703–1756), author of imitations of Spenser and translations of Pindar and Euripides. For opinions about West's work among his contemporaries, ranging from lavish praise to censure, see *BL* (1907), 1:210n.

2. Thomas Warton (1728–1790), poet laureate (in 1785) and author of the prestigious *The History of English Poetry,* 3 vols. (1774–81). Shawcross suggested a direct link between Warton's "To the River Lodon," Bowles's "To the Itchin," and C's "To the River Otter," pointing out that C did not acknowledge his debt to Warton or to Akenside (*BL* [1907], 1:210n.).

the most *popular* poems of the present day;[3] yet in the more sustained and elevated style, of the then living poets Bowles and Cowper* were, to the best of my knowledge, the first who combined natural thoughts with natural diction; the first who reconciled the heart with the head.[6]

It is true, as I have before mentioned, that from diffidence in my own powers, I for a short time adopted a laborious and florid diction, which I myself deemed, if not absolutely vicious, yet of very inferior worth. Gradually, however, my practice conformed to my better judgement; and the compositions of my twenty-fourth and twenty-fifth year (*ex. gr.* the shorter blank verse poems,[7] the lines which are now adopted in the introductory part of the VISION in the present collection in Mr. Southey's Joan of Arc, 2nd book, 1st edition,[8] and the Tragedy of RE-MORSE)[9] are not more below my present ideal in respect of the general tissue of the style, than those of the latest date. Their faults were at least a remnant of the former leaven, and among the many who have done me the honor of putting my poems in the same class with those of my betters, the one or two, who have pretended to bring examples of affected simplicity from my volume, have been able to adduce but one instance, and that out of a copy of verses half ludicrous, half splenetic, which I intended, and had myself characterized, as *sermoni propriora.*[1]

---

* Cowper's task was published some time before the sonnets of Mr. Bowles;[4] but I was not familiar with it till many years afterwards. The vein of Satire which runs through that excellent poem, together with the sombre hue of its religious opinions, would probably, *at that time*, have prevented its laying any strong hold on my affections. The love of nature seems to have led Thompson to a chearful religion;[5] and a gloomy religion to have led Cowper to a love of nature. The one would carry his fellow-men along with him into nature; the other flies to nature from his fellow-men. In chastity of diction however, and the harmony of blank verse, Cowper leaves Thompson unmeasureably below him; yet still I feel the latter to have been the *born* poet.

---

3. The *Reliques of Ancient English Poetry* (1765) by Thomas Percy (1729–1811) was a popular collection of ballads, which cast its spell on C, Wordsworth, and Walter Scott (1771–1832), among others. Wordsworth openly acknowledged his debt to the *Reliques* in the "Essay, Supplementary to the Preface," *Poems* (1815) (*W Prose*, 3:78). On the influence of the *Reliques* on "The Ancient Mariner," see Lowes, 244, 249.

4. *The Task* by William Cowper (1731–1800) was published in 1785, four years before Bowles's *Sonnets*. C expressed his admiration for Cowper in a letter to Thelwall of December 17, 1796, in which he also conveyed his equal admiration for "the *head* and fancy of Akenside," "the *heart* and fancy of Bowles," and the "solemn Lordliness of Milton" (*CL*, 1:279). On Cowper's influence on C's early poetry, see p. 120, n. 3 herein and House, *Coleridge*, 71–73.

5. C hailed James Thomson (1700–1748) as the "Honor, yea, the Redeemer of Scotland" (*CM* [CC], 1:74) and praised the *Castle of Indolence* as a "lovely Poem" (*CL*, 1:154). According to Hazlitt, C admired Thomson's *Seasons* and thought of its author as "a great poet, rather than a good one" (William Hazlitt, *Complete Works*, ed. P. P. Howe, 21 vols. [1930–34], 5:88; 7:125; 17:120; 20:216).

6. For C's opposite opinion that Bowles did not reconcile the heart with the head, see p. 384, n. 5 herein.

7. I.e, poems published in his 1796 and 1797 collections, such as "Effusion XXXV," "Reflections on Having Left a Place of Retirement," and "This Lime-Tree Bower My Prison."

8. On C's contribution to Southey's *Joan of Arc* (1796), see p. 125, n. 1 herein.

9. In 1797 C wrote the tragedy *Osorio* at the request of Richard Brinsley Sheridan (1751–1816), who finally rejected it. In 1812 C produced a revised version of it, under the title *Remorse*, that ran for twenty days at Drury Lane in January 1813.

1. According to Shawcross (*BL* [1907], 1:211n.), C refers to the poem "Address to a Young Jackass and Its Tethered Mother," published originally on December 30, 1794, in the *Morning Chronicle* and included as "Effusion XXX" in *Poems* (1796) with the changed title "To a Young Ass, Its Mother Being Tethered Near It" (*PW*, 1:74–76). The motto *Sermoni Propriora*, translated by Lamb as "properer for a sermon" (*TT* [CC], 2:180), was attached, however, to a different poem, "Reflections on Having Left a Place of Retirement" (p. 52 and its n. 2 herein), which appeared in *Poems* (1797).

Every reform, however necessary, will by weak minds be carried to an excess, that itself will need reforming.[2] The reader will excuse me for noticing, that I myself was the first to expose *risu honesto*[3] the three sins of poetry, one or the other of which is the most likely to beset a young writer. So long ago as the publication of the second number of the monthly magazine, under the name of NEHEMIAH HIGGENBOTTOM I contributed three sonnets, the first of which had for its object to excite a good-natured laugh at the spirit of *doleful egotism*, and at the recurrence of favorite phrases, with the double defect of being at once trite, and licentious. The second, on low, creeping language and thoughts, under the pretence of *simplicity*. And the third, the phrases of which were borrowed entirely from my own poems, on the indiscriminate use of elaborate and swelling language and imagery.[4] The reader will find them in the note* below, and will I trust

*SONNET I

PENSIVE at eve, on the *hard* world I mused,
And *my poor* heart was sad; so at the MOON
I gazed, and sighed, and sighed; for ah how soon
Eve saddens into night! mine eyes perused
With tearful vacancy the *dampy* grass
That wept and glitter'd in the *paly* ray:
And I *did pause me*, on my lonely way
And *mused me*, on the *wretched ones* that pass
O'er the bleak health of sorrow. But alas!
Most of *myself* I thought! when it befel,
That the *soothe* spirit of the *breezy* wood
Breath'd in mine ear: "All this is very well,
But much of ONE thing, is for NO thing good."
Oh *my poor heart's* INEXPLICABLE SWELL!

SONNET II

OH I do love thee, meek SIMPLICITY!
For of thy lays the lulling simpleness
Goes to my heart, and soothes each small distress,
Distress tho' small, yet haply great to me,
'Tis true on Lady Fortune's gentlest pad
I amble on; and yet I know not why
So sad I am! but should a friend and I
Frown, pout and part, then I am *very* sad.
And then with sonnets and with sympathy
My dreamy bosom's mystic woes I pall;
Now of my false friend plaining plaintively,
Now raving at mankind in general;

2. This comment may have been derived from Edmund Burke, "Speech of the Œconomical Reform," of February 11, 1780 (*Works*, 16 vols. [1803–27], 3:248). There Burke defended the need for "temperate reform" and denounced "hot reformations" that are "so contrary to the whole course of human nature, and human institutions, that, the very people who are most eager for it, are among the first to grow disgusted at what they have done. Then some part of the abdicated grievance is recalled from its exile in order to become a corrective of the correction." Godwin also argued that reforms should "be carried on by slow, almost insensible steps, and by just degrees" (*Considerations on Lord Grenville's and Mr. Pitt's Bills*, pp. 17–18; see p. 275, n. 3 herein; p. 277, n. 2 herein; and p. 280, n. 8 herein).
3. "With honest laughter."
4. Cf. C's letter to Joseph Cottle of November 1797 (*CL*, 1:357–58): "I sent three mock Sonnets in ridicule of my own, & Charles Lloyd's, & Lamb's, &c &c—in ridicule of that affectation of unaffectedness, of jumping & misplaced accent on common-place epithets, flat lines forced into poetry by Italics * * *—the instances are almost all taken from mine & Lloyd's poems——I signed them Nehemiah Higginbottom." The sonnets appeared in a slightly altered form in the *Monthly Magazine* in November 1797 under the title *Sonnets Attempted in the Manner of Contemporary Writers*. The sonnets caused friction between C and Lamb as well as between C and Southey, who thought that the second sonnet on simplicity was a direct attack on his poetry (*CL*, 1:358–59, 404). Southey later published four sonnets as a parody of C's style and signed them "Abel Shufflebottom" (*BL* [*CC*], 1:28n. 2).

regard them as reprinted for biographical purposes, and not for their poetic merits. So general at that time, and so decided was the opinion concerning the characteristic vices of my style, that a celebrated physician (now, alas! no more)[6] speaking of me in other respects with his usual kindness to a gentleman, who was about to meet me at a dinner party, could not however resist giving him a hint not to mention the "*House that Jack built*" in my presence, for "that I was *as sore as a boil* about that sonnet;" he not knowing, that I was myself the author of it.

FROM CHAPTER II

Supposed irritability of men of Genius—Brought to the test of Facts— Causes and Occasions of the charge—Its Injustice.

* * *

The men of the greatest genius,[7] as far as we can judge from their own works or from the accounts of their contemporaries, appear to

---

But whether sad or fierce, 'tis simple all,
All very simple, meek SIMPLICITY!

SONNET III

AND this reft house is that, the which he built,
Lamented Jack! and here his malt he pil'd,
Cautious in vain! these rats, that squeak so wild,
Squeak not unconscious of their father's guilt.
Did he not see her gleaming thro' the glade!
Belike 'twas she, the maiden all forlorn.
What tho' she milk no cow with crumpled horn,
Yet, *aye* she haunts the dale where *erst* she stray'd:
And *aye*, beside her stalks her amorous knight!
Still on his thighs their wonted brogues are worn,
And thro' those brogues, still tatter'd and betorn,
His hindward charms glean an unearthly white.
Ah! thus thro' broken clouds at night's high Noon
Peeps in fair fragments forth the full-orb'd harvest-moon!

The following anecdote will not be wholly out of place here, and may perhaps amuse the reader. An amateur performer in verse expressed to a common friend, a strong desire to be introduced to me, but hesitated in accepting my friend's immediate offer, on the score that "he was, he must acknowledge the author of a confounded severe epigram on my *ancient mariner*, which had given me great pain.["] I assured my friend that if the epigram was a good one, it would only increase my desire to become acquainted with the author, and begg'd to hear it recited: when, to my no less surprise than amusement, it proved to be one which I had myself some time before written and inserted in the Morning Post.

To the author of the Ancient Mariner

Your poem must eternal be,
Dear sir! it cannot fail,
For 'tis incomprehensible
And without head or tail.[5]

---

5. These lines appeared in a slightly altered form in the *MP* of January 24, 1800, and were addressed not to "the author of the Ancient Mariner" but to the poet laureate Henry James Pye (1745–1813) with the subtitle *Carmen Seculare* ("a title which has by various persons who have heard it, been thus translated, 'A Poem *an age long*' " [*PW*, 2:959]). The lines, indebted to Lessing's "Die Ewigkeit gewisser Gedichte" (The Eternity of Certain Poems) were copied by C in one of his notebooks (*CN*, 1:625 and n.; *BL* [*CC*], 1:28n. 1).
6. The reference might be to C's physician friend Thomas Beddoes (1760–1808) (*BL* [*CC*], 1:29n. 1).
7. In the opening pages of this chapter (omitted here) C refutes Horace's claim that men of genius are irritable, diagnosing the cause of anger, superstition, and fanaticism as residing in a "debility and dimness of the imaginative power" and a "reliance on the immediate impressions of the senses" (*BL* [*CC*], 1:30–33).

have been of calm and tranquil temper, in all that related to themselves. In the inward assurance of permanent fame, they seem to have been either indifferent or resigned, with regard to immediate reputation.[8] Through all the works of Chaucer there reigns a chearfulness, a manly hilarity, which makes it almost impossible to doubt a correspondent habit of feeling in the author himself.[9] Shakspeare's evenness and sweetness of temper were almost proverbial in his own age.

* * *

The same calmness, and even greater self-possession, may be affirmed of Milton, as far as his poems, and poetic character are concerned. He reserved his anger, for the enemies of religion, freedom, and his country.[1] My mind is not capable of forming a more august conception, than arises from the contemplation of this great man in his latter days: poor, sick, old, blind, slandered, persecuted,[2]

Darkness before, and danger's voice behind,[3]

in an age in which he was as little understood by the party, *for* whom, as by that, *against* whom he had contended; and among men before whom he strode so far as to *dwarf*[4] himself by the distance; yet still listening to the music of his own thoughts, or if additionally cheered, yet cheered only by the prophetic faith of two or three solitary individuals, he did nevertheless

————Argue not
Against Heaven's hand or will, nor bate a jot
Of heart or hope; but still bore up and steer'd
Right onward.[5]

From others only do we derive our knowledge that Milton, in his latter day, had his scorners and detractors; and even in his day of youth and

---

8. Cf. *CN*, 3:3291, in which C defines fame as "any thing rather than 'Reputation,' " namely as "the desire of working on the good & great permanently, thro' indefinite ages * * *"; and *CN*, 3:3325, in which he refers to Wordsworth (in cypher) as one among those who were driven by "the pursuit of literary Reputation" rather than "an honorable Love of *Fame*," with the consequence of becoming vulnerable to attacks by contemporaries and responding to them "with undue Irritation & vehemence of Language."
9. On the "manly cheerfulness" and tenderness of Chaucer, see entry of March 15, 1834, in *TT* (CC), 1:466.
1. Cf. a long discussion of Milton in contrast to Jeremy Taylor (1613–1667), in which C castigates Milton's detractors and justifies his stern condemnation of "such men [who,] as from motives of selfish ambition and the lust of personal aggrandizement should, against their own light, persecute truth and the true religion, and willfully abuse the powers and gifts entrusted to them, to bring vice, blindness, misery and slavery, on their native country * * *" ("Apologetic Preface to *Fire, Famine, & Slaughter*" [*PW*, 2:1103–07]).
2. Milton was frequently attacked in print on account of his pamphlets denouncing episcopacy (governance of the Church of England by bishops) in the early 1640s, his pamphlets defending divorce in 1643–44, his defense of the freedom of the press (*Aeropagitica*, 1644), and his defense of the Commonwealth in the face of the restauration of Charles II (*The Readie and Easie Way to Establish a Free Commonwealth*, 1660). In 1649 Milton was appointed Latin secretary to the Council of State under Cromwell, and commissioned to write a defense of the execution of Charles I (*Eikonoklastes*). After the Restoration he was temporarily imprisoned and spent his old age, as C described him, blind (since 1652), poor, and infirm (from gout).
3. Wordsworth, *The Prelude* (1805), 3.286.
4. Cf. C's political use of the "dwarf" image in *Lects 1795* (CC), 145 and n. 1.
5. Milton, "To Mr. Cyriack Skinner. Upon his Blindness," lines 6–9 (var.).

hope, that he had enemies would have been unknown to us, had they not been likewise the enemies of his country.[6]

I am well aware, that in advanced stages of literature, when there exist many and excellent models, a high degree of talent, combined with taste and judgement, and employed in works of imagination, will acquire for a man the *name* of a great genius; though even that *analogon*[7] of genius, which, in certain states of society, may even render his writings more popular than the absolute reality could have done, would be sought for in vain in the mind and temper of the author himself. Yet even in instances of this kind, a close examination will often detect, that the irritability, which has been attributed to the author's *genius* as its cause, did really originate in an ill conformation of body, obtuse pain, or constitutional defect of pleasurable sensation. What is charged to the *author*, belongs to the *man*, who would probably have been still more impatient, but for the humanizing influences of the very pursuit, which yet bears the blame of his irritability.

How then are we to explain the easy credence generally given to this charge, if the charge itself be not, as we have endeavoured to show, supported by experience? This seems to me of no very difficult solution. In whatever country literature is widely diffused, there will be many who mistake an intense desire to possess the reputation of poetic genius, for the actual powers, and original tendencies which constitute it. But men, whose dearest wishes are fixed on objects wholly out of their own power, become in all cases more or less impatient and prone to anger. Besides, though it may be paradoxical to assert, that a man can know one thing, and believe the opposite, yet assuredly, a vain person may have so habitually indulged the wish, and persevered in the attempt to appear, what he is not, as to become himself one of his own proselytes. Still, as this counterfeit and artificial persuasion must differ, even in the person's own feelings, from a real sense of inward power, what can be more natural, than that this difference should betray itself in suspicious and jealous irritability?[8] Even as the flowery sod, which covers a hollow, may be often detected by its shaking and trembling.

But, alas! the multitude of books, and the general diffusion of literature, have produced other, and more lamentable effects in the world

6. In his early years C did not admire Milton as much as this passage indicates. C considered Milton to be inferior to Schiller (*CL*, 1:122), "barely tolerable" compared to the Bible (*CL*, 1:281), and on a par with poets such as Akenside, Bowles, and Cowper (*CL*, 1:279). Of note is the fact that Milton became especially important to C during the years of his disenchantment with Wordsworth after the publication of the second edition of *Lyrical Ballads*. In a letter to Southey of 1802 C began to use Milton as a way of articulating the "radical Difference" in his and Wordsworth's views on poetry (*CL*, 2:830).

7. The Greek word for "analogue." The *OED* attributes to C the first use of "analogon" in the 1810 *Friend*, but C used the term in a related notebook entry of 1808, in which he reflected that he "must have some *analogon* of Genius," because in the company of men he felt otherwordly (*CN*, 3:3324).

8. For an earlier refutation of the opinion that genius is predisposed to irritability, see C's letter to Sotheby of September 10, 1802 (p. 630 herein). Cf. also a notebook entry focused on Sarah Fricker in which C linked irritability with a deficiency of tactual sensibility and the propensity to "hang upon the opinions of others" (*CN*, 1:979), rather than rely on inward powers.

of letters, and such as are abundant to explain, tho' by no means to justify, the contempt with which the best grounded complaints of injured genius are rejected as frivolous, or entertained as matter of merriment.[9]

*　*　*

Now it is no less remarkable than true, with how little examination works of polite literature are commonly perused, not only by the mass of readers, but by men of first rate ability, till some accident or chance[1] discussion have roused their attention, and put them on their guard. And hence individuals below mediocrity not less in natural power than in acquired knowledge; nay, bunglers that had failed in the lowest mechanic crafts,[2] and whose presumption is in due proportion to their want of sense and sensibility; men, who being first scriblers from idleness and ignorance next become libellers from envy and malevolence; have been able to drive a successful trade in the employment of the book-sellers, nay have raised themselves into temporary name and reputation with the public at large, by that most powerful of all adulation, the appeal to the bad and malignant passions of mankind.[3] But as it is the nature of scorn, envy, and all malignant propensities to require a quick change of objects, such writers are sure, sooner or later to awake from their dream of vanity to disappointment and neglect with embittered and envenomed feelings.

*　*　*

Sensibility indeed, both quick and deep, is not only a characteristic feature, but may be deemed a component part, of genius. But it is no less an essential mark of true genius, that its sensibility is excited by any other cause more powerfully, than by its own personal interests; for this plain reason, that the man of genius lives most in the ideal world,[4] in which the present is still constituted by the future or the past; and because his feelings have been habitually associated with thoughts and images, to the number, clearness, and vivacity of which the sensation of *self* is always in an inverse proportion. And yet, should

---

9. In the passage omitted here C describes the evolution of poetic language from the time of Chaucer and John Gower (c. 1325–1408) to his own time, in which it had become "mechanized as it were into a barrel-organ," making it possible for many to produce poems with "the least talent or information" (*BL* [CC], 1:38–40).

1. C has a note (omitted here) in which he quotes examples from Pope's translation of Homer's *Iliad* to demonstrate that unlike Pope's "original compositions," the translation is "the main source of our pseudo-poetic diction." He adds that under Wordsworth's influence, he discovered defects in individual passages of Gray's "The Bard" and his "Elegy Written in a Country Churchyard," but these did not spoil the "delight" he experienced every time he read them (*BL* [CC], 1:39–41). For C on Pope, cf. p. 386, n. 4 herein.

2. Possibly an allusion to William Gifford (1756–1826), editor of the *Quarterly Review*, who was once a shoemaker (*BL* [CC], 1:41n. 2).

3. In a footnote (omitted here) taken from *Friend* (CC), 2:138, C labels his age as the "AGE OF PERSONALITY" and "political GOSSIPING," which encouraged the circulation of "the most vapid satires" (*BL* [CC], 1:41–42).

4. Cf. *CL*, 2:863: "Men of great Genius have indeed, as an essential of their composition, great sensibility * * *." C emphasized repeatedly that the true genius remains detached from "private interests" or immediate circumstances and lives in an ideal world (see *BL* [CC], 2:20–22 and *CN*, 3:3324). This very standard was used to praise Wordworth's achievement in "Salisbury Plain" and to denigrate his experimental poetry in *Lyrical Ballads* (see pp. 413–15 herein).

he perchance have occasion to repel some false charge, or to rectify some erroneous censure, nothing is more common, than for the many to mistake the general liveliness of his manner and language *whatever* is the subject, for the effects of peculiar irritation from its accidental relation to himself.*

For myself, if from my own feelings, or from the less suspicious test of the observations of others, I had been made aware of any literary testiness or jealousy; I trust, that I should have been, however, neither silly or arrogant enough, to have burthened the imperfection on GENIUS. But an experience (and I should not need documents in abundance to prove my words, if I added) a tried experience of twenty years, has taught me, that the original sin of my character consists in a careless indifference to public opinion, and to the attacks of those who influence it; that praise and admiration have become yearly, less and less desirable, except as marks of sympathy; nay that it is difficult and distressing to me, to think with any interest even about the sale and profit of my works, important, as in my present circumstances, such considerations must needs be. Yet it never occurred to me to believe or fancy, that the quantum of intellectual power bestowed on me by nature or education was in any way connected with this habit of my feelings; or that it needed any other parents or fosterers, than constitutional indolence, aggravated into languor by ill-health;[7] the accumulating embarrassments of procrastination; the mental cowardice, which is the inseparable companion of procrastination, and which makes us anxious to think and converse on any thing rather than on what concerns ourselves; in fine, all those close vexations, whether chargeable on my faults or my fortunes which leave me but little grief to spare for evils comparatively distant and alien.

Indignation at literary wrongs, I leave to men born under happier stars. I cannot *afford it.* But so far from condemning those who can, I deem it a writer's duty, and think it creditable to his heart, to feel and express a resentment proportioned to the grossness of the provocation,

---

* This is one instance among many of deception, by the telling the half of a fact, and omitting the other half, when it is from their mutual counteraction and neutralization, that the *whole* truth arises, as a tertiam aliquid[5] different from either. Thus in Dryden's famous line "Great wit" (which here means genius) "to madness sure is near allied."[6] Now as far as the profound sensibility, which is doubtless *one* of the components of genius, were alone considered, single and unbalanced, it might be fairly described as exposing the individual to a greater chance of mental derangement; but then a more than usual rapidity of association, a more than usual power of passing from thought to thought, and image to image, is a component equally essential; and in the due modification of each by the other the GENIUS itself consists; so that it would be as just as fair to describe the earth, as in imminent danger of exorbitating, or of falling into the sun, according as the assertor of the absurdity *confined* his attention either to the projectile or to the attractive force exclusively.

5. A slip for "tertium." *Tertium aliquid*: a term in philosophy indicating a third entity (see p. 485, n. 1 herein).
6. *Absalom and Architophel* (1681), lines 163–64: "Great Wits are sure to Madness near alli'd / And thin Partitions do their Bounds divide." Cf. C's use of Dryden's "famous line" in *TT* (CC), 2:221 and CL, 6:729 to demonstrate the unusually intense activity of thought and imaginative association in genius, which nonetheless, he insisted, "is most alien to Madness, divided from it by an impassable Mountain." See also "[On *Hamlet*]" (p. 334 herein).
7. In the 1809–10 *Friend* (CC), 2:16, 36, C presents a similar portrait of himself as constitutionally indolent and in bad health.

and the importance of the object. There is no profession on earth, which requires an attention so early, so long, or so unintermitting as that of poetry; and indeed as that of literary composition in general, if it be such, as at all satisfies the demands both of taste and of sound logic.[8] How difficult and delicate a task even the mere mechanism of verse is, may be conjectured from the failure of those, who have attempted poetry late in life. Where then a man has, from his earliest youth, devoted his whole being to an object, which by the admission of all civilized nations in all ages is honorable as a pursuit, and glorious as an attainment; what of all that relates to himself and his family, if only we except his moral character, can have fairer claims to his protection, or more authorise acts of self-defence, than the elaborate products of his intellect, and intellectual industry? Prudence itself would command us to *show*, even if defect or diversion of natural sensibility had prevented us from *feeling*, a due interest and qualified anxiety for the offspring and representatives of our nobler being. I know it, alas! by woeful experience! I have laid too many eggs in the hot sands of this wilderness the world, with ostrich carelessness and ostrich oblivion. The greater part indeed have been trod under foot, and are forgotten; but yet no small number have crept forth into life, some to furnish feathers for the caps of others, and still more to plume the shafts in the quivers of my enemies, of them that unprovoked have lain in wait against my soul.[9]

"Sic vos, non vobis mellificatis, apes!"[1]

* * *

FROM CHAPTER III

*The author's obligations to critics, and the probable
Occasion—Principles of modern criticism—Mr. Southey's
works and character.*

To anonymous critics in reviews, magazines, and news-journals of various name and rank, and to satirists with or without a name, in verse or prose, or in verse-text aided by prose-comment, I do seriously believe and profess, that I owe full two thirds of whatever reputation and publicity I happen to possess. For when the name of an individual has occurred so frequently, in so many works, for so great a length of time, the readers of these works (which with a shelf or two of Beau-

8. On C's view that logic, "as severe as that of science," pertains to poetry, see chapter 1 (p. 380 and its n. 5 herein).
9. One of C's favorite images, which appears with few variations in a notebook entry of 1802 (*CN*, 1:1248) and letters to Thomas Poole, Francis Jeffrey, and Sir George Beaumont of 1803 and 1808 (*CL*, 2:1011; 3:126, 145).
1. "So you, but not for yourselves, produce honey, O Bees." From a poem by Virgil written after the poet Bathyllus claimed as his own a couplet composed by Virgil anonymously for the emperor Augustus (63 B.C.E.–14 C.E.): "I made these verses, Another took the honor. / So you, but not for yourselves, build nests, Birds; / So you, but not for yourselves, bear fleeces, Sheep; / So you, but not for yourselves, produce honey, Bees; / So you, but not for yourselves, pull the plough, Cattle" (*BL* [CC], 1:46n. 2). C ends this chapter with a footnote in which he disputes Thomas Seward's reading of a passage from Beaumont and Fletcher, *The Faithful Shepherdess* (*BL* [CC], 1:46–47).

TIES, ELEGANT EXTRACTS[2] and ANAS,[3] form nine-tenths of the reading of the reading public*) cannot but be familiar with the name, without distinctly remembering whether it was introduced for an eulogy or for censure. And this becomes the more likely, if (as I believe) the habit of perusing periodical works may be properly added to Averrhoe's[9] catalogue of ANTI-MNEMONICS, or weakeners of the memory. But where this has not been the case, yet the reader will be apt to suspect, that there must be something more than usually strong and extensive in a reputation, that could either require or stand so merciless and long-continued a cannonading. Without any feeling of *anger* therefore (for which indeed, on my own account, I have no pretext) I may yet be allowed to express some degree of *surprize*, that after having run the critical gauntlet for a certain class of faults which I *had*, nothing having come before the judgement-seat in the interim, I should, year after year, quarter after quarter, month after month (not to mention sundry petty periodicals of still quicker revolution, "or weekly or diurnal") have been for at least 17 years consecutively dragged forth by them into the foremost ranks of the *proscribed*, and forced to abide the brunt of abuse, for faults directly opposite, and which I certainly had not.[1] How shall I explain this?

---

*   For as to the devotees of the circulating libraries, I dare not compliment their *pass-time*, or rather *kill-time*, with the name of *reading*.[4] Call it rather a sort of beggarly day-dreaming, during which the mind of the dreamer furnishes for itself nothing but laziness and a little mawkish sensibility; while the whole *materiel* and imagery of the doze is supplied *ab extra*[5] by a sort of mental *camera obscura*[6] manufactured at the printing office, which *pro tempore*[7] fixes, reflects and transmits the moving phantasms of one man's delirium, so as to people the barrenness of an hundred other brains afflicted with the same trance or suspension of all common sense and all definite purpose. We should therefore transfer this species of *amusement*, (if indeed those can be said to retire *a musis*,[8] who were never in their company, or relaxation be attributable to those, whose bows are never bent) from the genus, *reading*, to that comprehensive class characterized by the power of reconciling the two contrary yet co-existing propensities of human nature, namely; indulgence of sloth, and hatred of vacancy. In addition to novels and tales of chivalry in prose or rhyme, (by which last I mean neither rhythm nor metre) this genus comprizes as its species, gaming, swinging, or swaying on a chair or gate; spitting over a bridge; smoking; snuff-taking; tete a tete quarrels after dinner between husband and wife; conning word by word all the advertisements of the daily advertizer in a public house on a rainy day, &c. &c. &c.

---

2. C refers to the collection of Vicesimus Knox (1752–1821), *Elegant Extracts; or Useful and Entertaining Passages* * * * (1784) and *The Beauties of the Anti-Jacobin* (1799). C copied a passage from *Elegant Extracts* in a notebook entry (CN, 1:531) and used it in his *Treatise on Method* (SW&F [CC], 1:663) and *Friend* (CC), 1:484n. The passage offers what must have seemed to C a superficial recipe for acquiring general knowledge of all things "ancient and modern," "natural, civil, and religious," and sets off C's diatribe against circulating libraries and a fickle public, for whom education is mistaken for a species of amusement no different from other self-indulgent activities. On *The Beauties of the Anti-Jacobin*, see p. 113, n. 8 herein and the end of this chapter (p. 406 and n. 7).
3. A collection of memorable quotations.
4. For C's attack on circulating libraries, see *SM* (CC), 36n. 3 and 38n. 3.
5. "From without."
6. "Dark room."
7. "For a time."
8. "From the muses." C is punning on "amusement."
9. In a footnote (omitted here) C lists various causes of loss of memory, drawing on a similar list in the *Kabbalistische Briefe* (Kabbalistic Letters) (1773–77) of Jean Baptiste de Boyer, marquis d'Argens (1704–1771). Contrary to C's contention, d'Argens's list does not derive from the Aristotelian philosopher Averroes (c. 1126–1198) (*BL* [CC], 1:49n. 3).
1. C is careful not to convey anger in addressing the unfair charges against him so as to qualify as a genius, who, as he argued in chapter 2, is not prone to irritability. Cf. his letter to Mathilda Betham of April 3, 1808, where he also spoke of his "surprise" rather than anger at being the target of so much unfavorable critical notice (*CL*, 3:84). According to *BL* (CC),

Whatever may have been the case with others, I certainly cannot attribute this persecution to personal dislike, or to envy, or to feelings of vindictive animosity. Not to the former, for, with the exception of a very few who are my intimate friends, and were so before they were known as authors, I have had little other acquaintance with literary characters, than what may be implied in an accidental introduction, or casual meeting in a mixt company. And, as far as words and looks can be trusted, I must believe that, even in these instances, I had excited no unfriendly disposition.* Neither by letter, or in conversation, have

---

* Some years ago, a gentleman, the chief writer and conductor of a celebrated review, distinguished by its hostility to Mr. Southey, spent a day or two at Keswick.[2] That he was, without diminution on this account, treated with every hospitable attention by Mr. Southey and myself, I trust I need not say. But one thing I may venture to notice; that at no period of my life do I remember to have received so many, and such high coloured compliments in so short a space of time. He was likewise circumstantially informed by what series of accidents it had happened, that Mr. Wordsworth, Mr. Southey, and I had become neighbours; and how utterly unfounded was the supposition, that we considered ourselves, as belonging to any common school,[3] but that of good sense confirmed by the long-established models of the best times of Greece, Rome, Italy, and England; and still more groundless the notion, that Mr. Southey (for as to myself I have published so little, and that little, of so little importance, as to make it almost ludicrous to mention my name at all)[4] could have been concerned in the formation of a poetic sect with Mr. Wordsworth, when so many of his works had been published not only previously to any acquaintance between them;[5] but before Mr. Wordsworth himself had written any thing but in a diction ornate, and uniformly sustained; when too the slightest examination will make it evident, that between those and the after writings of Mr. Southey, there exists no other difference than that of a progressive degree of excellence from progressive developement of power, and progressive facility from habit and increase of experience. Yet among the first articles which this man wrote after his return from Keswick, we were characterized as "the School of whining and hypochondriacal poets that haunt the Lakes."[6] In reply to a letter from the same gentleman, in which he had asked me, whether I was in earnest in preferring the style of Hooker to that of Dr. Johnson;[7] and Jeremy Taylor to Burke;[8] I stated, somewhat at large, the comparative excellences and defects which characterized our best prose writers, from the reformation, to the first half of Charles 2nd; and that of those who had flourished during the present reign, and the preceding one. About twelve months afterwards, a review appeared on the same subject, in the concluding paragraph of which the reviewer asserts, that his chief motive for entering into the discussion was to separate a rational and qualified admiration of our elder writers, from the indiscriminate enthusiasm of a recent school, who praised what they did not understand, and caricatured what they were unable to imitate. And, that no doubt might be left concerning the persons alluded to, the writer annexes the names of Miss BAILIE,[9] W. SOUTHEY, WORDSWORTH and COLERIDGE. For that which follows, I have only ear-sal[1] evidence; but yet such as demands my belief; viz. that on being questioned concerning this apparently wanton attack, more especially with reference to Miss Bailie, the writer had stated as his motives, that this lady when at Edinburgh had declined a proposal of introducing him to her; that Mr. Southey had written against him; and Mr. Wordsworth had talked contemptuously of him; but that as to Coleridge he had noticed him merely because the names of Southey and Wordsworth and Coleridge always went together. But if it were worth while to mix together, as ingredients, half the anecdotes which I either myself know to be true, or which I have received from men incapable of intentional falsehood, concerning the characters, qualifications, and motives of our anonymous critics, whose decisions are oracles for our reading public; I might safely borrow the words of the apocryphal Daniel; "*Give me leave, O* SOVEREIGN PUBLIC, *and I shall slay this dragon without sword or staff.*" For the compound would be as the "*Pitch, and fat, and hair, which Daniel took, and did seethe them together, and made lumps thereof, and put into the dragon's mouth, and so the dragon burst in sunder; and Daniel said* LO; THESE ARE THE GODS YE WORSHIP."[2]

1:50n. 1, C exaggerates the extent to which his publications (which, since the *Lyrical Ballads*, included only the 1809–10 *Friend* and the 1813 *Remorse*) met with adverse criticism. But C was responding to the new style of attack and ridicule in periodicals such as the *Anti-Jacobin Review*, the *Edinburgh Review*, and the *Examiner*, in which his name was frequently mentioned in association with writers such as Southey and Wordsworth. From 1802 on the *Edinburgh Review* was engaged in a campaign against any poets who abided by the standards enunciated in the Preface to the *Lyrical Ballads* (see David Erdman and Paul Zall, "Coleridge and Jeffrey in Controversy," *SIR* 14 [1975]: 75–83). C may, therefore, as the two critics contend, have "had ample grounds for complaining" here "about twenty years of gratuitous abuse in the public journals" (75).

I ever had dispute or controversy beyond the common social interchange of opinions. Nay, where I had reason to suppose my convictions fundamentally different, it has been my habit, and I may add, the impulse of my nature, to assign the grounds of my belief, rather than

2. Francis Jeffrey (1773–1850), editor of the *Edinburgh Review*, began his attack on the Lake School poets in the first issue of the periodical (1 [1802]: 63–72) in his review of Southey's *Thalaba* (1801). Jeffrey came to visit C in 1810 at Keswick, where C was living in Southey's residence. He was received with hospitality, according to SC (*BL* [1847], 1:clix), and apparently was "dazzled" by C's conversation (see Thomas Moore's letter of October 21, 1810, cited in *BL* [*CC*], 1:51n. 1). After the visit Jeffrey's direct attack on C subsided (see Erdman and Zall, "Coleridge and Jeffrey," 80–83).

3. C was particularly sensitive to being lumped together (by Jeffrey and other reviewers) with Southey and Wordsworth into a single school of poetry. During their meeting in 1810 C had evidently mentioned to Jeffrey the unfairness of being charged with affected simplicity "in every Review & Magazine" on account of his association with Southey and Wordsworth (*CL*, 3:203), and Jeffrey promised not to couple his name with those of his friends, a promise which he kept (see *CH*, 1:316; Erdman and Zall, "Coleridge and Jeffrey," 80).

4. A frequent complaint, for which see the opening of chapter 1 (p. 377 herein) and *CL*, 3:84, 116.

5. Southey met Wordsworth in Bristol in September 1795. Wordsworth was on his way to Racedown where he was to commence residence with his sister Dorothy. Before this meeting, Southey had published the second and third act of *The Fall of Robespierre* (Cambridge, 1794), the first having been written by C. The poems by Wordsworth featuring an "ornate diction" that predate *LB* (1798) are "An Evening Walk" and "Descriptive Sketches," written in heroic couplets and published in 1793, and the "Salisbury Plain" poems, written in Spenserian stanzas, which were not published until 1842. C reviews these poems in chapter 4 (pp. 412–15 herein).

6. In a note appended to Hazlitt's review of the *Biographia* (the *Edinburgh Review* 28 [1817]: 507–12), Jeffrey acknowledged (in response to this note of C's) that he regarded the Lake Poets as "whining and hypochondriacal" (*CH*, 1:315).

7. C's letter has not been found. On Jeffrey's statement to C that "it was hopeless to persuade men to prefer Hooker and Jeremy Taylor to Johnson and Gibbon," see *TT* (*CC*), 2:383. Richard Hooker (c. 1554–1600), Anglican theologian, frequently cited by C, earned C's admiration as early as 1801 for his prose style (*CN*, 1:1052, 1655). In *Friend* (*CC*), 2:150 C praised the "eloquence of Hooker" and placed him in the company of "Bacon, Milton and Jeremy Taylor." On Hooker, cf. also *TT* (*CC*), 1:92nn. 3 and 4 and *CM* (*CC*), 2:1131–67. C would most likely have preferred Hooker to Samuel Johnson, about whom he made disparaging remarks, considering him to have done great injury to mankind on account of his lack of genius and faulty critical judgment of writers such as Shakespeare and Milton (see, e.g., *CN*, 3:3321 and n.; *Lects 1808–19* [*CC*], 1:138 and n. 44). In a late *TT* entry of July 1, 1833, Johnson is shown to compare poorly with Burke and, as Burke claimed, to have been "greater in talking than in writing" (*TT* [*CC*], 1:405–06 and nn. 26, 27).

8. C admired Burke's rhetorical style, even as he disagreed with some of his political views (see p. 254, n. 3 herein and *Poems* [1796], p. 13 herein). As late as 1833 he still thought of Burke as "a great man," who read history more philosophically than any other man (*TT* [*CC*], 1:358). According to Hazlitt, C had a "much higher opinion of Burke as an orator and politician, than of Fox or Pitt," but still "thought him very inferior in riches of style and imagery to some of our elder prose-writers, particularly Jeremy Taylor" (*TT* [*CC*], 1:359n. 23). Jeremy Taylor (1613–1667), Bishop of Down and Connor and chaplain to archbishop William Laud (1573–1645) and Charles I (1600–1649), provided C with "many remarkable passages," which he cited freely in his work (see *Friend* [*CC*], 1:52n. 1; 282n. 1; 347n.). C regarded him as one of the four great models of prose style in English (together with Milton, Bacon, and Hooker) who "tho' writing in prose might be considered one of the first of our Poets" (*Lects 1808–19* [*CC*], 2:233; 1:190). He also admired the "impetuous, thought-agglomerating, flood" of Taylor's prose (*Lects 1808–19* [*CC*], 2:235–36), which he described in the vivid comparison of Taylor with Milton in the "Apologetic Preface" to "Fire, Famine, & Slaughter" (*PW*, 2:1103–07).

9. C paraphrases quite accurately the charge made by Jeffrey in his review of *The Dramatic Works of John Ford* in the *Edinburgh Review* 18 (1811): 283. For Jeffrey's complaint that C cites these statements out of context, omitting the flattering remarks he made about him and his company of poets, see his note to Hazlitt's review of the *Biographia* (*CH*, 1:316–17). Joanna Baillie (1762–1851) was a poet and playwright of Scottish origin and author of the popular collection *Plays on the Passions*, 3 vols. (1798, 1802, 1812). C thought well of the printed version of her play *De Montfort*, which had a short run in London in December 1800 (*CL*, 1:621).

1. Shawcross corrects this as "hearsay" (*BL* [1907], 1:37), but C may have intended it as a pun.

2. Apocrypha: Bel and the Dragon, verses 26–27 (var.; C substitutes "Sovereign Public" for "king") (*BL* [*CC*], 1:52n. 4).

the belief itself; and not to express dissent, till I could establish some points of complete sympathy, some grounds common to both sides, from which to commence its explanation.

Still less can I place these attacks to the charge of envy. The few pages, which I have published, are of too distant a date; and the extent of their sale a proof too conclusive against their having been popular at any time; to render probable, I had almost said possible, the excitement of envy on *their* account; and the man who should envy me on any *other*, verily he must be *envy-mad!*

Lastly, with as little semblance of reason, could I suspect any animosity towards me from vindictive feelings as the cause. I have before said, that my acquaintance with literary men has been limited and distant; and that I have had neither dispute nor controversy. From my first entrance into life, I have, with few and short intervals, lived either abroad or in retirement.[3] My different essays on subjects of national interest, published at different times, first in the Morning Post and then in the Courier,[4] with my courses of lectures on the principles of criticism as applied to Shakspeare and Milton, constitute my whole publicity; the only occasions on which I *could* offend any member of the republic of letters. With one solitary exception in which my words were first misstated and then wantonly applied to an individual, I could never learn, that I had excited the displeasure of any among my literary contemporaries.[5]

*   *   *

How then, dismissing, as I do, these three causes, am I to account for attacks, the long continuance and inveteracy of which it would require all three to explain. The solution may seem to have been given, or at least suggested, in a note to a preceding page. *I was in habits of intimacy with Mr. Wordsworth and Mr. Southey!* This, however, transfers, rather than removes, the difficulty. Be it, that by an unconscionable extension of the old adage, "noscitur a socio"[6] my literary friends are never under the water-fall of criticism, but I must be wet through with the spray; yet how came the torrent to descend upon *them?*

First then, with regard to Mr. Southey. I well remember the general reception of his earlier publications: viz. the poems published with Mr. Lovell under the names of Moschus and Bion;[7] the two volumes of poems under his own name, and the Joan of Arc.[8] The censures of the

---

3. C went to Germany from September 1798 to July 1799 and to Malta and Italy from April 1804 to August 1806. He was active in London during several periods, e.g., as a reporter for *MP* (1797–1803) and lecturer at the Royal Institution and London Philosophical Society (1808; 1811–12), but he lived mostly in the west and north of England.
4. C contributed to *MP* (1797–1803) and the *Courier* (1804–14) and lectured on criticism and literature (see pp. 306–38 herein). But C once again gives an inaccurate account of his publicity, which included several other works (see p. 379 and its n. 8 herein).
5. Possibly the comment made by C during a lecture of 1811 about Samuel Rogers (1763–1855) while the author was in the audience, describing his work *The Pleasures of Hope* (1799) as "made up by heaping together a certain number of images, & a certain number of thoughts" (*Lects 1808–19* [CC], 1:272 and *BL* [CC], 1:53n. 3).
6. "He is known by the company he keeps."
7. In his first volume of poetry *Poems* (Bath, 1795), published by Southey and Robert Lovell (c. 1770–1796), the names "Bion" (for Southey) and "Moschus" (for Lovell) are used to identify the authors of individual poems in the collection.
8. I.e., *Poems*, 2 vols. (Bristol, 1797–99) and *Joan of Arc* (Bristol, 1796). See also p. 401, n. 5 herein.

critics by profession are extant, and may be easily referred to:—careless lines, inequality in the merit of the different poems, and (in the lighter works) a predilection for the strange and whimsical; in short, such faults as might have been anticipated in a young and rapid writer, were indeed sufficiently enforced. Nor was there at that time wanting a party spirit to aggravate the defects of a poet, who with all the courage of uncorrupted youth had avowed his zeal for a cause, which he deemed that of liberty, and his abhorrence of oppression by whatever name consecrated. But it was as little objected by others, as dreamt of by the poet himself, that he *preferred* careless and prosaic lines on rule and of forethought, or indeed that he pretended to any other art or theory of poetic diction, besides that which we may all learn from Horace, Quintilian, the admirable dialogue de Causis Corruptæ Eloquentiæ, or Strada's Prolusions;[9] if indeed natural good sense and the early study of the best models in his own language had not infused the same maxims more securely, and, if I may venture the expression, more vitally. All that could have been fairly deduced was, that in his taste and estimation of writers Mr. Southey agreed far more with Warton,[1] than with Johnson. Nor do I mean to deny, that at all times Mr. Southey was of the same mind with Sir Philip Sidney in preferring an excellent ballad in the *humblest* style of poetry to twenty indifferent poems that strutted in the *highest*.[2] And by what have his works, published since then, been characterized, each more strikingly than the preceding, but by greater splendor, a deeper pathos, profounder reflections, and a more sustained dignity of language and of metre?[3] Distant may the period be, but whenever the time shall come, when all his works shall be collected by some editor worthy to be his biographer, I trust that an excerpta of all the passages, in which his writings, name, and character have been attacked, from the pamphlets and periodical works of the last twenty years, may be an accompaniment. Yet that it would prove medicinal in after times, I dare not hope; for as long as there are readers to be delighted with calumny, there will be found reviewers to calumniate. And such readers will become in all

9. Horace (65–8 B.C.E.), the great lyric poet of imperial Rome and author of *Satires, Epodes* and *Odes,* frequently cited by C. C has in mind *Dialogus de Oratoribus* (Dialogue on Oratory) by Tacitus, believed to be the lost *De Causis corruptae eloquentiae* (On the Cause of Corrupt Eloquence) by Quintilian (fl. 68 C.E.). *Prolusiones academicae oratoriae, historicae, poeticae* (Academic Essays on Oratory, History, and Poetics) (1617, with several later editions) by Famiano Strada (1572–1649), Italian Jesuit historian and author of a history covering the wars in Flanders from 1555 to 1590 (*De bello belgico* [Of the Belgian War, 1632–47). His *Prolusiones* included a series of dissertations on literary subjects, which, as Kathleen Coburn notes, "may be worth study as background to some of Coleridge's critical views" (CN, 3:3276n.).
1. Probably Thomas Warton, the Younger (1728–1790), author of *History of English Poetry* (1774–81), which C might have used as a source for his lectures on criticism and literature. Cf. a late *Table Talk* entry of 1833 in which C compared Southey with Warton: "With more than Warton's learning, he possesses an eloquence and refinement of imagination to which that amiable writer has no pretensions" (*TT* [CC], 2:464).
2. Sir Philip Sidney (1554–1586) mentions being moved by the "old song of Percy and Douglas" even as it is "sung but by some blind crowder, with no rougher voice than rude style" ("Defence of Poetry," in *Miscellaneous Prose*, ed. Katherine Duncan-Jones and Jan van Dorsten [Oxford, 1973], 97).
3. Southey's works published after his early poems include *Thalaba the Destroyer*, 2 vols. (1801), *Madoc: A Poem* (1805), *The Curse of Kehama* (1810), and *Roderick: the Last of the Goths* (1814).

probability more numerous, in proportion as a still greater diffusion of literature shall produce an increase of sciolists; and sciolism bring with it petulance and presumption.[4] In times of old, books were as religious oracles; as literature advanced, they next became venerable preceptors; they then descended to the rank of instructive friends; and as their numbers increased, they sunk still lower to that of entertaining companions; and at present they seem degraded into culprits to hold up their hands at the bar of every self-elected, yet not the less peremptory, judge,[5] who chuses to write from humour or interest, from enmity or arrogance, and to abide the decision (in the words of Jeremy Taylor) "of him that reads in malice, or him that reads after dinner."[6]

* * *

But till reviews are conducted on far other principles, and with far other motives; till in the place of arbitrary dictation and petulant sneers, the reviewers support their decisions by reference to fixed canons of criticism, previously established and deduced from the nature of man; reflecting minds will pronounce it arrogance in them thus to announce themselves to men of letters, as the guides of their taste and judgment. To the purchaser and mere reader it is, at all events, an injustice. He who tells me that there are *defects* in a new work, tells me nothing which I should not have taken for granted without his information. But he, who points out and elucidates the *beauties* of an original work, does indeed give me interesting information, such as experience would not have authorised me in anticipating. And as to compositions which the authors themselves announce with "Hæc ipsi novimus esse nihil,"[7] why should we judge by a different rule two printed works; only because the one author was alive, and the other in his grave? What literary man has not regretted the prudery of Spratt in refusing to let his friend Cowley appear in his slippers and dressing gown?[8] I am not perhaps the only one who has derived an innocent amusement from the riddles, conundrums, tri-syllable lines,[9] &c. &c. of Swift and his correspondents, in hours of languor when to have read his more finished works would have been useless to myself,

4. "Sciolism" (superficial knowledge) is a term first used by C (*OED*); see *SM* (CC), 94, 168.
5. C draws from material used in Lecture 1 of the November 18, 1811, where he expressed the same lament about the public's changing attitude toward authors—from regarding them as "intermediary beings between Angels & men" to considering itself as their "Judge & therefore" their "Superior" (*Lects 1808–19* [CC], 1:189, 187).
6. C adapts and quotes from the dedicatory letter to Lord Hatton in Jeremy Taylor, *Polemicall Discourses* (1674): "* * * and men with their understandings or with their no understandings give their sentence upon Books, not only before they understand all, not only before they read all, but before they read three Pages, receiving their information from humour or interest, from chance or mistake, from him that reads in malice, or from him that reads after dinner * * *."
7. A motto Southey used for his *Minor Poems*, 3 vols. (1815), at C's advice (*CL*, 1:549), derived from Martial 13.2.8: "Nos haec novimus esse nihil" (We ourselves know these things to be nothing) (*BL* [CC], 1:62n. 1).
8. A remark made by Thomas Sprat (1635–1713) in his "Account of the Life and Writings of Mr. Abraham Cowley" to justify his exclusion of Cowley's private letters from his edition of Cowley's *Works*. Sprat argued that letters "can only affect the humour of those to whom they were intended" and that in such documents, "the Souls of Men" appear "undress'd: And in that negligent habit, they may be fit to be seen by one or two in a Chamber, but not to go abroad into the Streets" (*Works*, 7th ed. [1681], sig. c1). On Cowley and C's annotations of this edition of *Works*, see p. 390 and n. 7 herein.
9. I.e., three-syllable rhymes (rather than lines), as used by Swift and others.

and, in some sort, an act of injustice to the author. But I am at a loss to conceive by what perversity of judgement, these relaxations of his genius could be employed to diminish his fame as the writer of "Gulliver's travels," and the "Tale of a Tub."[1] Had Mr. Southey written twice as many poems of inferior merit, or partial interest, as have enlivened the journals of the day, they would have added to his honour with good and wise men, not merely or principally as proving the versatility of his talents, but as evidences of the purity of that mind, which even in its levities never wrote a line, which it need regret on any moral account.

I have in imagination transferred to the future biographer the duty of contrasting Southey's fixed and well-earned fame,[2] with the abuse and indefatigable hostility of his anonymous critics from his early youth to his ripest manhood. But I cannot think so ill of human nature as not to believe, that these critics have already taken shame to themselves, whether they consider the object of their abuse in his moral or his literary character. For reflect but on the variety and extent of his acquirements! He stands second to no man, either as an historian or as a bibliographer; and when I regard him, as a popular essayist, (for the articles of his compositions in the reviews are for the greater part essays on subjects of deep or curious interest rather than criticisms on particular works*) I look in vain for any writer, who has conveyed so much information, from so many and such recondite sources, with so many just and original reflections, in a style so lively and poignant, yet so uniformly classical and perspicuous; no one in short who has combined so much wisdom with so much wit; so much truth and knowledge with so much life and fancy.[4]

*   *   *

But still more striking to those, who by biography or by their own experience are familiar with the general habits of genius, will appear the poet's matchless industry and perseverance in his pursuits; the worthi-

---

* See the articles on Methodism, in the Quarterly Review; the small volume on the New System of Education, &c.[3]

1. Two of Swift's most famous satires: *A Tale of a Tub* (1704), a religious allegory, and *Gulliver's Travels* (1726).
2. Cf. C's opposite opinion, that Southey's poetry, like that of Walter Scott and Thomas Campbell (1777–1844), would not survive "beyond their day" (*TT* [CC], 2:333).
3. Southey wrote a single article ("On Evangelical Sects") for the *Quarterly Review* 4 (1810): 480–515. C may also have in mind his earlier review of William Myles's *History of the Methodists* in the *Annual Review* (1803), 1:210–13 (*BL* [CC], 1:63n. 2). The "small volume" is Southey's *The Origin, Nature, and Object, of the New System of Education* (1812), in which he offered a detailed account of the educational experiments of Andrew Bell and Joseph Lancaster. On Southey's treatise and the systems of Bell and Lancaster, see *SM* (*CC*), 40–42 and nn., p. 591 and its n. 1 herein. According to C, Southey's treatise was a "dilution" of his lecture of May 3, 1808, on education at the Royal Institution (*CL*, 3:474), in which C praised Bell's system of education and spoke with indignation against the humiliating punishments of pupils recommended by Lancaster (*Lects 1808–19* [CC], 1:96–109). For C's use of Southey's treatise for his 1813 lectures on Shakespeare and education, see *Lects 1808–19* (CC), 1:504–05.
4. In the passage omitted here C goes on to praise Southey's prose and the versatility of his poetic compositions, expressing his outrage at the public vilification of a writer who possesses "the best gifts of talent and genius free from all their characteristic defects" (*BL* [CC], 1:64–65). For the contrast between C's eulogy here and his more critical views of Southey as poet, see *BL* (CC), 1:65n. 1.

ness and dignity of those pursuits; his generous submission to tasks of transitory interest, or such as *his* genius alone could make otherwise; and that having thus more than satisfied the claims of affection or prudence, he should yet have made for himself time and power, to achieve more, and in more various departments than almost any other writer has done, though employed wholly on subjects of his own choice and ambition. But as Southey possesses, and is not possessed by, his genius,[5] even so is he the master even of his virtues. The regular and methodical tenor of his daily labours, which would be deemed rare in the most mechanical pursuits, and might be envied by the mere man of business, loses all semblance of formality in the dignified simplicity of his manners, in the spring and healthful chearfulness of his spirits. Always employed, his friends find him always at leisure. No less punctual in trifles, than stedfast in the performance of highest duties, he inflicts none of those small pains and discomforts which irregular men scatter about them, and which in the aggregate so often become formidable obstacles both to happiness and utility; while on the contrary he bestows all the pleasures, and inspires all that ease of mind on those around him or connected with him, which perfect consistency, and (if such a word might be framed) absolute *reliability*, equally in small as in great concerns, cannot but inspire and bestow: when this too is softened without being weakened by kindness and gentleness. I know few men who so well deserve the character which an antient attributes to Marcus Cato,[6] namely, that he was likest virtue, in as much as he seemed to act aright, not in obedience to any law or outward motive, but by the necessity of a happy nature, which could not act otherwise. As son, brother, husband, father, master, friend, he moves with firm yet light steps, alike unostentatious, and alike exemplary.[7] As a writer, he has uniformly made his talents subservient to the best interests of humanity, of public virtue, and domestic piety; his cause has ever been the cause of pure religion and of liberty, of national independence and of national illumination.

5. C made the same claim about Shakespeare in Lecture 4 of November 28, 1811 (*Lects. 1808–19* [CC], 1:244) and chapter 15 (*BL* [CC], 2:26–27).
6. Marcus Porcius Cato, the Elder (234–149 B.C.E.), Roman statesman and orator and author of *Origins* (the first history of Rome in Latin), was well known for his opposition to Hellenistic culture and his stern morality. C's source appears to be the Roman historian Marcus Velleius Paterculus (c. 19 B.C.E.–30 C.E.), who claimed that Cato "resembled Virtue herself, and in all his acts he revealed a character nearer to that of gods than of men. He never did a right action solely for the sake of seeming to do the right, but because he could not do otherwise" (*Compendium of Roman History* 2.35.2, trans. Frederick Shipley [LCL, 1924]; *BL* [CC], 1:66n. 4).
7. Cf. C's memorable remark in a letter to George Dyer of February 1795 that Southey was "a man of *perpendicular Virtue*" (*CL*, 1:152). C paints here an idealized version of a man who, in the opinion of many contemporaries and his own painful self-reflection, would have appeared to be the complete opposite of C. C was often perceived as a man of irregular habits of writing, wasteful of his genius, and unreliable in his duties to friends and family. In his final note, not included here, C attempts to redress this image, first by acknowledging that he had absorbed Southey's moral influence since his days at Cambridge and then by pointing out the irony of being slandered as negligent of religious and domestic duties in *The Anti-Jacobin* while being associated with Lamb and Southey, known to be "exemplary in their domestic affections" (*BL* (CC), 1:67–68 and nn.). In her comment on this note SC enhanced the eulogy of her uncle Southey, by showing how his impeccable purity was free from all traces of "puritanism" and mentioned additional laudatory remarks by C on Lamb's character (*BL* [1847], 1:66–67).

When future critics shall weigh out his guerdon of praise and censure, it will be Southey the poet only, that will supply them with the scanty materials for the latter. They will likewise not fail to record, that as no man was ever a more constant friend, never had poet more friends and honorers among the good of all parties; and that quacks in education, quacks in politics, and quacks in criticism were his only enemies.

* * *

CHAPTER IV

The lyrical ballads with the preface—Mr. Wordsworth's earlier poems—
On fancy and imagination—The investigation of the
distinction important to the fine arts.

I have wandered far from the object in view, but as I fancied to my-self readers who would respect the feelings that had tempted me from the main road; so I dare calculate on not a few, who will warmly sym-pathize with them. At present it will be sufficient for my purpose, if I have proved, that Mr. Southey's writings no more than my own, fur-nished the original occasion to this fiction of a *new school* of poetry, and of clamors against its supposed founders and proselytes.

As little do I believe that "Mr. WORDSWORTH's Lyrical Ballads" were in *themselves* the cause. I speak exclusively of the two volumes so en-titled.[8] A careful and repeated examination of these confirms me in the belief, that the omission of less than an hundred lines would have precluded nine-tenths of the criticism on this work. I hazard this dec-laration, however, on the supposition, that the reader had taken it up, as he would have done any other collection of poems purporting to de-rive their subjects or interests from the incidents of domestic or ordi-nary life, intermingled with higher strains of meditation which the poet utters in his own person and character; with the proviso, that they were perused without knowledge of, or reference to, the author's peculiar opinions, and that the reader had not had his attention previ-ously directed to those peculiarities.[9] In these, as was actually the case with Mr. Southey's earlier works, the lines and passages which might have offended the general taste, would have been considered as mere inequalities, and attributed to inattention, not to perversity of judge-ment. The men of business who had passed their lives chiefly in cities, and who might therefore be expected to derive the highest pleasure from acute notices of men and manners[1] conveyed in easy, yet correct and pointed language; and all those who, reading but little poetry, are most stimulated with that species of it, which seems most distant from

8. I.e., the second edition of *LB* (1800), published under Wordsworth's name. Volume 1 in-cluded the poems C contributed to *LB* (1798) and "Love"; volume 2 had new poems by Wordsworth and excluded the projected "Christabel."

9. C refers to the critical opinions Wordsworth formulated in the Preface to *LB* (1800), which he had once regarded as "half a child of" his "own Brain" (*CL*, 2:830). For C's view that the Preface hurt the critical reception of Wordsworth's poems and an analysis of its pecularities, see pp. 408–09 herein and volume 2 (pp. 491, 496–523 herein).

1. In chapter 1 (p. 386 herein) C attributes the type of poetry concerned with "observations on men and manners" to Alexander Pope.

prose, would probably have passed by the volume altogether. Others more catholic in their taste, and yet habituated to be most pleased when most excited, would have contented themselves with deciding, that the author had been successful in proportion to the elevation of his style and subject. Not a few perhaps, might by their admiration of "the lines written near Tintern Abbey," those "left upon a Seat under a Yew Tree," the "old Cumberland beggar," and "Ruth," have been gradually led to peruse with kindred feeling the "Brothers," the "Hart leap well," and whatever other poems in that collection may be described as holding a middle place between those written in the highest and those in the humblest style; as for instance between the "Tintern Abbey," and "the Thorn," or the "Simon Lee."[2] Should their taste submit to no further change, and still remain unreconciled to the colloquial phrases, or the imitations of them, that are, more or less, scattered through the class last mentioned; yet even from the small number of the latter, they would have deemed them but an inconsiderable subtraction from the merit of the whole work; or, what is sometimes not unpleasing in the publication of a new writer, as serving to ascertain the natural tendency, and consequently the proper direction of the author's genius.

In the critical remarks therefore, prefixed and annexed to the "Lyrical Ballads," I believe, that we may safely rest, as the true origin of the unexampled opposition which Mr. Wordsworth's writings have been since doomed to encounter.[3] The humbler passages in the poems themselves were dwelt on and cited to justify the rejection of the theory. What in and for themselves would have been either forgotten or forgiven as imperfections, or at least comparative failures, provoked direct hostility when announced as intentional, as the result of choice after full deliberation. Thus the poems, admitted by *all* as excellent, joined with those which had pleased the far *greater* number, though they formed two-thirds of the whole work, instead of being deemed (as in all right they should have been, even if we take for granted that the reader judged aright) an atonement for the few exceptions, gave wind and fuel to the animosity against both the poems and the poet. In all perplexity there is a portion of fear, which predisposes the mind to anger. Not able to deny that the author possessed both genius and a powerful intellect, they felt *very positive*, but were not *quite certain*, that he might not be in the right, and they themselves in the wrong; an unquiet state of mind, which seeks alleviation by quarrelling with

2. Cf. chapter 17 (p. 501 herein) and chapter 20 (p. 518 herein) for further instances of C's praise for poems written by Wordsworth in his own voice. By contrast, C found poems such as "Simon Lee" and "The Thorn" flawed by Wordsworth's adherence to the language of rustic people, in accordance with the principles put forward in his Preface to *LB* (1800) (*W. Prose*, 1:118–58). Of "Ruth" C wrote that it is "the finest poem in the collection" and that he would have rather written this poem than "Christabel" (*CL*, 1:623, 632).

3. This is confirmed by Jeffrey's reaction to Wordsworth's program of imitating the "ordinary language" of the middle and lower classes, as announced in his Preface. But C himself embraced Jeffrey's view that Wordsworth was most successful when he abandoned his system. See Jeffrey's review of Southey's *Thalaba* and of Wordsworth's *Poems in Two Volumes* (1807) in the *Edinburgh Review* 1 (1802): 64–67; 11 (1807): 214–31, and chapters 17, 18, and 20.

the occasion of it,[4] and by wondering at the perverseness of the man, who had written a long and argumentative essay to persuade them, that

Fair is foul, and foul is fair;[5]

in other words, that they had been all their lives admiring without judgement, and were now about to censure without reason.*

That this conjecture is not wide from the mark, I am induced to believe from the noticeable fact, which I can state on my own knowledge, that the same general censure should have been grounded almost by each different person on some different poem. Among those, whose candour and judgement I estimate highly, I distinctly remember six who expressed their objections to the "Lyrical Ballads" almost in the same words, and altogether to the same purport, at the same time admitting, that several of the poems had given them great pleasure; and, strange as it might seem, the composition which one had cited as execrable, another had quoted as his favorite.[8] I

---

* In opinions of long continuance, and in which we had never before been molested by a single doubt, to be suddenly *convinced* of an *error*, is almost like being *convicted* of a fault. There is a state of mind, which is the direct antithesis of that, which takes place when we *make a bull*. The *bull* namely consists in the bringing together two incompatible thoughts, with the *sensation*, but without the *sense*, of their connection. The psychological condition, or that which constitutes the possibility of this state, being such disproportionate vividness of two distant thoughts, as extinguishes or obscures the consciousness of the intermediate images or conceptions, or wholly abstracts the attention from them.[6] Thus in the well known bull, "*I was a fine child, but they changed me;*" the first conception expressed in the word "*I*," is that of personal identity—*Ego contemplans*: the second expressed in the word "*me*," is the visual image or object by which the mind represents to itself its past condition, or rather, its personal identity under the form in which it imagined itself previously to have existed,—Ego contemplatus.[7] Now the change of one visual image for another involves in itself no absurdity, and becomes absurd only by its immediate juxta-position with the first thought, which is rendered possible by the whole attention being successively absorbed in each singly, so as not to notice the interjacent notion, "changed" which by its incongruity with the first thought, "*I*," constitutes the bull. Add only, that this process is facilitated by the circumstance of the words "*I*," and "*me*," being sometimes equivalent, and sometimes having a distinct meaning; sometimes, namely, signifying the act of self-consciousness, sometimes the external image in and by which the mind represents that act to itself, the result and symbol of its individuality. Now suppose the direct contrary state, and you will have a distinct sense of the connection between two conceptions, without that *sensation* of such connection which is supplied by habit. The man *feels*, as if he were standing on his head, though he cannot but *see*, that he is truly standing on his feet. This, as a painful sensation, will of course have a tendency to associate itself with the person who occasions it; even as persons, who have been by painful means restored from derangement, are known to feel an involuntary dislike towards their physician.

---

4. See chapter 2 (pp. 393–98 herein and *BL* [CC], 1:30–31), where C diagnoses the state of irritability as belonging to the class of people who, unlike true geniuses, are uncertain about their powers and hence experience fear that gets vented in anger. On C's frequent distinction between genuine certainty and pretended positiveness, see, e.g., *Friend* (CC), 2:7, where C vows to prove how "different the sensation of positiveness is from the sense of certainty," and *Lects 1818–19* (CC), 1:260, where he warns that "feverish positiveness * * * deludes minds under the best impulses into the worst actions." For an application of this distinction to love, see *CN*, 2:3095.
5. Shakespeare, *Macbeth* 1.1.10.
6. C was fascinated by the psychological phenomenon of "bulls" whereby the mind under the influence of passions connects two ideas that are incongruous (see, e.g., *CN*, 1:915, 1620, 1643, 1645; *LS* [CC], 153 and n. 2). The subject was also addressed by Richard and Maria Edgeworth in *Essays on Irish Bulls* (1802).
7. The distinction between the "I contemplating" and the "I contemplated" refers to the self as the experiencing subject and the self as object of experience. C indicates that it is precisely the conflation of these two distinct states that accounts for the phenomenon of "bulls."
8. Christopher Wordsworth, in *Memoirs of William Wordsworth* (1851), 1:174–75, cites such contradictory opinions of Wordsworth's poems (*BL* [CC], 1:73n. 1).

am indeed convinced in my own mind, that could the same experiment have been tried with these volumes, as was made in the well known story of the picture, the result would have been the same; the parts which had been covered by the number of the *black* spots on the one day, would be found equally *albo* lapide notatæ on the succeeding.[9]

However this may be, it is assuredly hard and unjust to fix the attention on a few separate and insulated poems with as much aversion, as if they had been so many plague-spots on the whole work, instead of passing them over in silence, as so much blank paper, or leaves of bookseller's catalogue;[1] especially, as no one pretends to have found immorality or indelicacy;[2] and the poems therefore, at the worst, could only be regarded as so many light or inferior coins in a roleau of gold, not as so much alloy in a weight of bullion. A friend whose *talents* I hold in the highest respect, but whose *judgement* and strong sound sense I have had almost continued occasion to *revere*, making the usual complaints to me concerning both the style and subjects of Mr. Wordsworth's minor poems;[3] I admitted that there were some few of the tales and incidents, in which I could not myself find a sufficient cause for their having been recorded in metre. I mentioned the "Alice Fell" as an instance;[4] "nay," replied my friend with more than usual quickness of manner, "I cannot agree with you *there!* that I own *does* seem to me a remarkably pleasing poem." In the "Lyrical Ballads" (for my experience does not enable me to extend the remark equally unqualified to the two subsequent volumes) I have heard at different times, and from different individuals every single poem *extolled* and *reprobated*, with the exception of those of loftier kind, which as was before observed, seem to have won universal praise. This fact of itself would have made me diffident in my censures, had not a still stronger ground been furnished by the strange contrast of the heat and long continuance of the opposition, with the nature of the faults stated as justifying it. The seductive faults, the dulcia vitia[5] of Cowley, Marini, or Darwin[6] might reasonably be thought capable of corrupting the

9. "Marked with a *white* stone." The story is untraced. White and black pebbles were used by Cretans to differentiate good from bad days, and by the Romans to cast yes or no votes.
1. C raises the same point in connection with Southey, complaining about the undue attention paid by reviewers to minor poems or passages they found "especially worthless" "(*BL* [CC], 1:60–61). He thus exposes the dubious taste of reviewers, while at the same time acknowledging that writers produce inferior poems that would best remain unmentioned. In selecting poems for his own collected editions, C preferred to leave out those he considered to be minor. See pp. 203–04 herein.
2. Cf. the same statement about Southey, that, even if he had written "twice as many poems of inferior merit," they would remain "evidences of the purity of that mind, which even in its levities never wrote a line, which it need regret on any moral ground" (p. 405 herein).
3. Possibly Thomas Poole or Charles Lamb.
4. In chapter 18 (*BL* [CC], 2:68) C includes Wordsworth's "Alice Fell" in a group of poems that "would have been more delightful" in prose. The poem, written in 1802, first appeared in *Poems in Two Volumes* (1807), to which C refers here.
5. "Charming faults."
6. On Cowley and Darwin, see pp. 387, 390, 418 herein. Giambattista Marino (1569–1625), Italian poet, widely imitated, founder of the style known as "Marinism," which dominated 17th-century poetry and was characterized by abundant imagery, word play, sensuality, and mythological themes. C transcribed and commented at length on some of his sonnets in a notebook entry of 1805 (*CN*, 2:2625 and n.).

public judgement for half a century, and require a twenty years war, campaign after campaign, in order to dethrone the usurper and re-establish the legitimate taste. But that a downright simpleness, under the affectation of simplicity, prosaic words in feeble metre, silly thoughts in childish phrases, and a preference of mean, degrading, or at best trivial associations and characters, should succeed in forming a school of imitators, a company of almost *religious* admirers, and this too among young men of ardent minds, liberal education, and not

with academic laurels unbestowed;[7]

and that this bare and bald *counterfeit* of poetry, which is characterized as *below* criticism, should for nearly twenty years have well-nigh *engrossed* criticism, as the main, if not the only, *butt* of review, magazine, pamphlets, poem, and paragraph;—this is indeed matter of wonder![8] Of yet greater is it, that the contest should still continue as* undecided as that between Bacchus and the frogs in Aristophanes; when the former descended to the realms of the departed to bring back the spirit of old and genuine poesy.

---

* Without however the apprehensions attributed to the *Pagan* reformer of the poetic republic. If we may judge from the preface to the recent collection of his poems,[9] Mr. W. would have answered with Xanthias—

Συ δ' ουκ εδεισας τον ψοφον των ρηματων,
Και τας απειλας; ΞΑΝ. ουμα Δι', ουδ' εφροντισα.[1]

And here let me dare hint to the authors of the numerous parodies, and pretended imitations of Mr. Wordsworth's style,[2] that at once to conceal and convey wit and wisdom in the semblance of folly and dulness, as is done in the clowns and fools, nay even in the Dogberry, of our Shakespear,[3] is doubtless a proof of genius, or at all events, of satiric talent; but that the attempt to ridicule a silly and childish poem, by writing another still sillier and still more childish, can only prove (if it prove any thing at all) that the parodist is a still greater block-head than the original writer, and what is far worse, a *malignant* coxcomb to boot. The talent for mimicry seems strongest where the human race are most degraded. The poor, naked, half human savages of New Holland were found excellent mimics:[4] and in civilized society, minds of the very lowest stamp alone satirize by *copying*. At least the difference, which must blend with and balance the likeness, in order to constitute a just imitation,[5] existing here merely in caricature, detracts from the libeller's heart, without adding an iota to the credit of his understanding.

---

7. A misquotation of the last line of the sonnet "To the River Lodon" by Thomas Warton (1728–1790): "Nor with the Muse's laurel unbestow'd" (*Poems* [1777], 83 [Sonnet 9]).
8. Cf. chapter 1, where C ridicules "affectations of simplicity" in the second sonnet under the name of Nehemiah Higginbottom and establishes his preference for a different type of simplicity based on the "elevated style" of Bowles and Cowper (pp. 390–92 herein).
9. C refers to Wordsworth's Preface to his two-volume *Poems* (1815), where he confronts the insults "heaped upon" his writings by "the ignorant, the incapable, and the presumptuous reviewers" (*W Prose*, 3:35).
1. Aristophanes, *Frogs*, lines 492–93 (trans. B. B. Rogers [LCL, 1924], 341): "DIONYSUS: But weren't *you* frightened at those dreadful threats / And shoutings? / XANTIAS: Frightened? Not a bit. I cared not."
2. As, e.g., Peter Bayley's parody of "The Idiot Boy" in the poem "The Fisherman's Wife" (*Poems* [1803], 215–28). For Wordsworth's reaction to this parody, see *WL*, 1:413, 455.
3. On Dogberry, the head constable of Messina in Shakespeare's *Much Ado About Nothing*, see p. 323, n. 4 herein and p. 453, n. 1 herein.
4. In Lecture 2 (February 5, 1808) C uses the same example of the Aborigines of New Holland, Australia, to show the connection between mimicry and a degraded culture (*Lects 1808–19* [CC], 1:46).
5. This distinction between copy and imitation is a cornerstone of C's aesthetic theories and in its most developed form is drawn from Schelling's *Über das Verhältniss der bildenden Künste zu der Natur* (On the Relationship of the Plastic Arts to Nature), in *PS*, 341–96 (see *CN*, 3:4397). For other instances and the sources of this distinction in Aristotle, Kant, and Schiller, as well as 18th-century British philosophers and aestheticians, see *BL* (CC), 2:72n. 4. See also "[On Dramatic Illusion]" (p. 337 and its n. 5 herein).

Χορος Βατραχων; Διονυσος

Χ. βρεκεκεκεξ, κοαξ, κοαξ!

Δ. αλλ' εξολοισθ' αυτω κοαξ.
ουδεν γαρ εοτι, ἤ κόαξ.
οιμωζετ : ου μοι μελει.

Χ. αλλα μην κεκραξομεσθα
γ'οποσον η φυρυγξ αν ημων
χανδανῃ δὶ ημερας
βρεκεκεκεξ, κοαξ, κοαξ!

Δ. τουτῳ γαρ ου νικησετε.

Χ. ουδε μεν ημας συ παντως.

Δ. ουδε μεν υμεις γε δη με
ουδεποτε· κεκραξομαι γαρ
κἄν με δει δι' ημερας,
εως ἄν ὑμῶν ἐπικρατήσοω τῳ Κοαξ!

Χ. βρεκεκεκεξ, ΚΟΑΞ, ΚΟΑΞ![6]

During the last year of my residence at Cambridge, I became acquainted with Mr. Wordsworth's first publication entitled "Descriptive Sketches;"[7] and seldom, if ever, was the emergence of an original poetic genius above the literary horizon more evidently announced. In the form, style, and manner of the whole poem, and in the structure of the particular lines and periods, there is an harshness and acerbity connected and combined with words and images all a-glow, which might recall those products of the vegetable world, where gorgeous blossoms rise out of the hard and thorny rind and shell, within which the rich fruit was elaborating. The language was not only peculiar and strong, but at times knotty and contorted, as by its own impatient strength; while the novelty and struggling crowd of images acting in conjunction with the difficulties of the style, demanded always a greater closeness of attention, than poetry, (at all events, than descriptive poetry) has a right to claim.[8] It not seldom therefore justified the

6. Aristophanes, Frogs, lines 227–29, 256–68 (trans. Rogers, 319, 321): "FROGS: Brekekex, ko-ax, ko-ax. / DIONYSUS: Hang you, and your ko-axing too! / There's nothing but ko-ax with you. * * * / Go hang yourseves, for what care I? / FROGS: All the same we'll shout and cry, / Brekekex, ko-ax, ko-ax. / DIONYSUS: In this you'll never, never win. / FROGS: This you shall not beat us in. / DIONYSUS: No, nor ye prevail o'er me. / Never! never! I'll my song / Shout, if need be, all day long, / Until I've learned to master your ko-ax. / Brekekex, ko-ax, ko-ax." (Copyright 1924 by the President and Fellows, Harvard College. Reprinted by permission.)

7. C's last year in Cambridge was 1794. Wordsworth's first publication was actually An Evening Walk (1793), which was followed by Descriptive Sketches in Verse, Taken During a Pedestrian Tour in the Italian, Grison, Swiss, and Savoyard Alps, published in the same year. C discussed Wordsworth's poems with Wordsworth's brother Christopher at Cambridge on November 4, 1793 (Christopher Wordsworth, Social Life at the English Universities [Cambridge, 1874], 589).

8. In chapter 1 (p. 379 herein) C makes a similar remark about his early poetry, but locates the difficulty for readers of poems such as "Religious Musings" in the "thoughts themselves" rather than, as in Wordsworth, in a stylistic overabundance of images. But in that self-description C may be echoing the charge in the Monthly Review, 2nd series, 12 (October 1793): 216–18, about the defects of Wordsworth's Descriptive Sketches: "How often shall we in vain advise those, who are so delighted with their own thoughts that they cannot forbear from putting them into rhyme, to examine those thoughts till they themselves understand them? No man will ever be a poet, till his mind be sufficiently powerful to sus-

complaint of obscurity.[9] In the following extract I have sometimes fancied, that I saw an emblem of the poem itself, and of the author's genius as it was then displayed.

> 'Tis storm; and hid in mist from hour to hour,
> All day the floods a deepening murmur pour;
> The sky is veiled, and every cheerful sight:
> Dark is the region as with coming night;
> And yet what frequent bursts of overpowering light!
> Triumphant on the bosom of the storm,
> Glances the fire-clad eagle's wheeling form;
> Eastward, in long perspective glittering, shine
> The wood-crowned cliffs that o'er the lake recline;
> Wide o'er the Alps a hundred streams unfold,
> At once to pillars turn'd that flame with gold;
> Behind his sail the peasant strives to shun
> The West, that burns like one dilated sun,
> Where in a mighty crucible expire
> The mountains, glowing hot, like coals of fire.[1]

The poetic PSYCHE, in its process to full developement, undergoes as many changes as its Greek name-sake, the* butterfly. And it is remark-

---

* The fact, that in Greek Psyche is the common name for the soul, and the butterfly, is thus alluded to in the following stanza from an unpublished poem of the author:

> The butterfly the ancient Grecians made
> The soul's fair emblem, and its only name—
> But of the soul, escaped the slavish trade
> Of mortal life! For in this earthly frame
> Our's is the reptile's lot, much toil, much blame,
> Manifold motions making little speed,
> And to deform and kill the things, whereon we feed.
> S. T. C.[2]

---

tain this labour" (218). The review began with a general complaint about the abundance of descriptive poetry and cited images from the poem that were contrived and incomprehensible.

9. In a letter of February 16, 1793, Dorothy Wordsworth singles out obscurity as the "chief" of the poem's "many Faults," and Wordsworth himself admits in a letter of April 9, 1801, that the poem was "inflated and obscure" (WL, 1:89, 327). C's opinion is also in line with contemporary reviews. The *Analytical Review* 15 (March 1793): 294–96 stated that the poem was marred by "a certain laboured and artificial cast of expression, which often involves the poet's meaning in obscurity"; the *Critical Review*, 2nd series, 8 (August 1793): 472–74, complained that Wordsworth's lines are "often harsh and prosaic; his images ill-chosen," and the "Introduction is almost unintelligible"; and the *Monthly Review* ridiculed nonsensical images and the obscure thoughts behind them (p. 412, n. 8 herein). See Stephen E. Sharp, "The Unmerited Contempt of Reviewers: Wordsworth's Response to Contemporary Reviews of *Descriptive Sketches*," *The Wordsworth Circle* 8 (1977): 25–31.
1. C quotes from the version of *Descriptive Sketches* that appeared in *Poems* (1815), 1:79–80, which included selections from lines 332–47 of the original version (1793), 25–26. C introduces a number of variants of his own, the most significant being "And yet what frequent bursts of overpowering light!" for "But what a sudden burst of overpowering light!" in the 1815 version.
2. Composed in 1808, this poem was published for the first time in the *Biographia* and subsequently in *The Amulet* in 1833 (PW, 1:412). C was greatly fascinated by the "convulsive agonies of the Caterpillar in its laborious" transformation into a butterfly (CN, 3:3362). In a notebook entry of 1803 C took copious notes about this process from Moses Harris's *The Aurelian: or, Natural History of British Insects: namely, Moths and Butterflies * * * * (1766) (CN 1:1378 and n). Cf. also CN, 3:3264. For the association between the metamorphosis of the caterpillar and disease, cf. CN, 3:3474: "* * * doubtless the state of a Caterpillar during the fœtal quickening of the Psyche would appear & for the Caterpillar would be, a Disease * * *."

able how soon genius clears and purifies itself from the faults and errors of its earliest products; faults which, in its earliest compositions,
are the more obtrusive and confluent, because as heterogeneous elements, which had only a temporary use, they constitute the very *ferment*, by which themselves are carried off. Or we may compare them to
some diseases, which must work on the humours, and be thrown out
on the surface, in order to secure the patient from their future recurrence. I was in my twenty-fourth year, when I had the happiness of
knowing Mr. Wordsworth personally,[3] and while memory lasts, I shall
hardly forget the sudden effect produced on my mind, by his recitation
of a manuscript poem, which still remains unpublished, but of which
the stanza, and tone of style, were the same as those of the "Female Vagrant" as originally printed in the first volume of the "Lyrical Ballads."[4]
There was here, no mark of strained thought, or forced diction, no
crowd or turbulence of imagery, and, as the poet hath himself well described in his lines "on re-visiting the Wye,"[5] manly reflection, and human associations had given both variety, and an additional interest to
natural objects, which in the passion and appetite of the first love they
had seemed to him neither to need or permit. The occasional obscurities, which had risen from an imperfect controul over the resources of
his native language, had almost wholly disappeared, together with that
worse defect of arbitary and illogical phrases, at once hackneyed, and
fantastic, which hold so distinguished a place in the *technique* of ordinary poetry, and will, more or less, alloy the earlier poems of the truest
genius, unless the attention has been specifically directed to their
worthlessness and incongruity.* I did not perceive any thing particular

---

* Mr. Wordsworth, even in his two earliest "the Evening Walk and the Descriptive Sketches,"
is more free from this latter defect than most of the young poets his contemporaries. It may
however be exemplified, together with the harsh and obscure construction, in which he
more often offended, in the following lines:—

---

3. C first met Wordsworth in early September 1795 in Bristol, at the house of the West Indian
sugar merchant John Pinney. By 1796 C identified Wordsworth as "a very dear friend"
and "the best poet of the age," and Wordsworth had read C's *Poems* (1796) (*CL*, 1:215 and
n. 2).

4. In 1795 Wordsworth would have recited to C the poem "Salisbury Plain," composed in
1793, the earliest version of *Guilt and Sorrow; or Incidents upon Salisbury Plain*, which was
eventually published in 1842. This poem was inspired by Wordsworth's lonesome journey
across Salisbury Plain in 1793, after his trip to revolutionary France. It features two destitute and traumatized travelers, a man and a woman, who meet in a stark and terrifying landscape, haunted by the cries of ancestral victims of Druid rites of sacrifice. The focus of the
poem is on the female vagrant's loss of home and family through the ravages of war and social injustice. Wordsworth published a revised version of the vagrant's story in *LB* (1798) under the title "The Female Vagrant" to which C refers. But C suppresses the fact that he was
well acquainted with the much revised and expanded second version of the poem ("Adventures on Salisbury Plain"), which was sent to him in March 1796 for comment by the publisher Joseph Cottle. In this version, the focus falls on the suffering and eventual execution
of a sailor who commits a crime as sudden and senseless as the killing of the albatross in C's
"The Rime of the Ancient Mariner." On the connection between Wordsworth's sailor and C's
Mariner, see Magnuson, *Coleridge and Wordsworth*, 84, and Eilenberg, *Strange Power of
Speech*, 47–49.

5. I.e., "Lines: Composed a Few Miles above Tintern Abbey, on Revisiting the Banks of the Wye
During a Tour, July 13, 1798." The association between "Salisbury Plain" and "Tintern
Abbey" (to which Wordsworth himself alluded in book 12 of *The Prelude*) obfuscates the
poem's representation of Druid sacrifices; the Gothic visitation of ghosts upon the characters; and its bleak, inhospitable natural world, which, unlike that of "Tintern Abbey," wors-
ens rather than ameliorates the travelers' alienated state. See Modiano, "Recollection and

in the mere style of the poem alluded to during its recitation, except indeed such difference as was not separable from the thought and manner; and the Spencerian stanza,[7] which always, more or less, recalls to the reader's mind Spencer's own style, would doubtless have authorized in my then opinion a more frequent descent to the phrases of ordinary life, than could without an ill effect have been hazarded in the heroic couplet. It was not however the freedom from false taste, whether as to common defects, or to those more properly his own, which made so unusual an impression on my feelings immediately, and subsequently on my judgement. It was the union of deep feeling with profound thought; the fine balance of truth in observing with the imaginative faculty in modifying the objects observed; and above all the original gift of spreading the tone, the *atmosphere*, and with it the depth and height of the ideal world around forms, incidents, and situations, of which, for the common view, custom had bedimmed all the lustre, had dried up the sparkle and the dew drops.[8] "To find no contradiction in the union of old and new; to contemplate the ANCIENT of days and all his works with feelings as fresh, as if all had then sprang forth at the first creative fiat; characterizes the mind that feels the riddle of the world, and may help to unravel it.[9] To carry on the feelings of childhood into the powers of manhood; to combine the child's sense of wonder and novelty with the appearances, which every day for perhaps forty years had rendered familiar;

> With sun and moon and stars throughout the year,
> And man and woman;[1]

this is the character and privilege of genius, and one of the marks which distinguish genius from talents.[2] And therefore is it the prime

---

'Mid stormy vapours ever driving by,
Where ospreys, cormorants, and herons cry;
Where hardly given the hopeless waste to cheer,
Denied the bread of life the foodful ear,
Dwindles the pear on autumn's latest spray,
And *apple sickens* pale in summer's ray;
Ev'n here content has fixed her smiling reign
With independence, child of high disdain.[6]

I hope, I need not say, that I have quoted these lines for no other purpose than to make my meaning fully understood. It is to be regretted that Mr. Wordsworth has not republished these two poems entire.

Misrecognition: Coleridge's and Wordsworth's Reading of the 'Salisbury Plain' Poems," *The Wordsworth Circle* 28 (1997): 74–82.

6. *Descriptive Sketches*, lines 317–24 (C's italics). Ever sensitive to C's criticisms, Wordsworth revised these lines in 1849. For the 1849 version (lines 254–61), see *WPW*, 1:61.
7. A stanza of eight lines of iambic pentameter and an alexandrine (a twelve-syllable line of six iambic pentameters with the caesura after the third), with the rhyme scheme *ababbcbcc*.
8. Cf. *The Prelude* (1805), 12.356–65, in which Wordsworth recalls C's delight in finding that in "Salisbury Plain" he "excercised / Upon the vulgar forms of present things / And actual world of our familiar days, / A higher power * * *."
9. This sentence is extracted from a notebook entry of 1803 (*CN*, 1:1622). Cf. also *SM* (*CC*), 25. The full passage in quotation marks is adapted with some deletions and other variants from the 1809–10 *The Friend* (*Friend* [*CC*], 2:73–74).
1. Milton, "To Mr. Cyriack Skinner. Upon his Blindness," lines 5–6 (var.): "Or sun, or Moon, or Star, throughout the Year; / Or Man, or Woman * * *."
2. Cf. *Friend* (*CC*), 1:419: "In short, I define GENIUS, as originality of intellectual construction: the moral accompaniment, and actuating principle of which consists, perhaps, in the carry-

merit of genius and its most unequivocal mode of manifestation, so to represent familiar objects as to awaken in the minds of others a kindred feeling concerning them and that freshness of sensation which is the constant accompaniment of mental, no less than of bodily, convalescence. Who has not a thousand times seen snow fall on water? Who has not watched it with a new feeling, from the time that he has read Burn's comparison of sensual pleasure

> To snow that falls upon a river
> A moment white—then gone for ever![3]

In poems, equally as in philosophic disquisitions, genius produces the strongest impressions of novelty, while it rescues the most admitted truths from the impotence caused by the very circumstance of their universal admission. Truths of all others the most awful and mysterious, yet being at the same time of universal interest, are too often considered as *so* true, that they lose all the life and efficiency of truth, and lie bed-ridden in the dormitory of the soul, side by side, with the most despised and exploded errors." THE FRIEND,* page 76, No. 5.

This excellence, which in all Mr. Wordsworth's writings is more or less predominant, and which constitutes the character of his mind, I no sooner felt, than I sought to understand. Repeated meditations led me first to suspect, (and a more intimate analysis of the human faculties, their appropriate marks, functions, and effects matured my conjecture into full conviction) that fancy and imagination were two distinct and widely different faculties, instead of being, according to the general belief, either two names with one meaning, or at furthest, the lower and higher degree of one and the same power.[5] It is not,

---

* As "the Friend" was printed on stampt sheets, and sent only by the post to a very limited number of subscribers,[4] the author has felt less objection to quote from it, though a work of his own. To the public at large indeed it is the same as a volume in manuscript.

---

ing on of the freshness and feelings of childhood into the powers of manhood. By TALENT, on the other hand, I mean the comparative facility of acquiring, arranging, and applying the stock furnished by others and already existing in books or other conservatories of intellect." For this familiar distinction, a cornerstone of C's aesthetic theories, see p. 309, n. 3 herein, and *Lects 1808–19* (CC), 1:287n. 7 and 2:362. For other uses of this distinction in the *Biographia*, see p. 462 herein and p. 485 and its n. 9 herein; and for sources of this distinction in British and German philosophers, see BL (CC), 1:32n. 5.

3. A reference to Robert Burns, "Tam O'Shanter," lines 59–62: "But pleasures are like poppies spread, / You seize the flow'r, its bloom is shed; / Or like the snow falls in the river, / A moment white,—then melts for ever" (*Poems*, 2 vols. [Edinburgh, 1811], 2:6).

4. Although the full record of subscribers to *The Friend* is not available, a fairly substantial list of 398 subscribers, some taking several copies, appears in one of Sara Hutchinson's notebooks. For the list of subscribers in 1809–10, see *Friend* (CC), 2:407–67. On the reception of *The Friend*, see reviews in *CH*, 1:73–110. For the view that *The Friend* "went virtually unnoticed, leading Coleridge to speak of it in later life as a well-kept 'secret,' " see Coleman, *Coleridge and "The Friend"* (1809–1818), 1.

5. C developed the distinction between fancy as the "*aggregating* power" and imagination as the "*modifying*, and co-*adunating* Faculty" in letters of 1802–03 (CL, 2:865–66, 1034) and subsequently in his 1808 and 1811–12 lectures (see *Lects 1808–19* [CC], 1:68n. 17; 81n. 20; 217; 220; and 245). This distinction, which dominates the rest of the chapter—between a faculty that mechanically assembles images supplied by the senses that have no natural connection to each other and a synthesizing power that creates unity out of "opposite or discordant qualities"—provides a major conceptual thread in the *Biographia*, which culminates in chapter 13 (pp. 488–89 herein). It is not surprising that C introduces this distinction in the chapter in which he discusses Wordsworth's poetry. What preoccupies him here is actually Wordsworth's Preface to *Poems* (1815), in which Wordsworth employed concepts borrowed from Coleridge, including the distinction between fancy and imagination. C's state-

I own, easy to conceive a more opposite translation of the Greek *Phantasia*, than the Latin Imaginatio;[6] but it is equally true that in all societies there exists an instinct of growth, a certain collective, unconscious good sense working progressively to desynonymize*[7] those words originally of the same meaning, which the conflux of dialects had supplied to the more homogeneous languages, as the Greek and German: and which the same cause, joined with accidents of translation from original works of different countries, occasion in mixt languages like our own. The first and most important point to

---

* This is effected either by giving to the one word a general, and to the other an exclusive use; as "to put on the back" and "to indorse;"[8] or by an actual distinction of meanings as "naturalist," and "physician;" or by difference of relation as "I" and "Me;" (each of which the rustics of our different provinces still use in all the cases singular of the first personal pronoun). Even the mere difference, or corruption, in the *pronunciation* of the same word, if it have become general, will produce a new word with a distinct signification; thus "property" and "propriety;" the latter of which, even to the time of Charles II.[9] was the *written* word for all the senses of both. Thus too "mister" and "master" both hasty pronunciations of the same word "magister," "mistress," and "miss," "if," and "give," &c. &c. There is a sort of *minim immortal* among the animalcula infusoria[1] which has not naturally either birth, or death, absolute beginning, or absolute end: for at a certain period a small point appears on its back, which deepens and lengthens till the creature divides into two, and the same process recommences in each of the halves now become integral. This may be a fanciful, but it is by no means a bad emblem of the formation of words, and may facilitate the conception, how immense a nomenclature may be organized from a few simple sounds by rational beings in a social state. For each new application, or excitement of the same sound, will call forth a different sensation, which cannot but affect the pronunciation. The after recollection of the sound, without the same vivid sensation, will modify it still further; till at length all trace of the original likeness is worn away.

---

ment later in the chapter that he "had been the first" of "his countrymen, who had pointed out the diverse meaning" of fancy and imagination, though not accurate, betrays his eagerness to claim priority over Wordsworth for the accurate use of these terms (see p. 418 herein).

6. In classical and medieval thought the Greek term *"phantasia"* was used to designate a creative power, whereas the Latin *"imaginatio"* was linked with the senses and relegated to an inferior role. Cf. C's reference to the survival of this view in Juan Ludovicus Vives (1492–1540) in chapter 5: "Phantasia, it is to be noticed, is employed by Vives to express the mental power of comprehension, or the *active* function of the mind; and imaginatio for the receptivity (vis receptiva) of impressions, or for the *passive* perception" (*BL* [CC], 1:99). Gradually, *phantasia* became associated with a lower faculty, just as imagination acquired a more esteemed function. In Germany, beginning with Ernst Platner (1744–1818), the term *"Phantasie"* is used for "fancy," as understood by C, i.e., as a faculty that mechanically "yoked together" images. For a late formulation, see *TT* (CC), 1:489–90. Imagination as a creative faculty that unifies "the many into one" is generally designated by the term *"Einbildungskraft."* For a summary of the complicated history of the differentiation of fancy and imagination in British and German aesthetics, see *BL* [CC], 1:xcvii–civ.

7. C's coinage. On the importance of this linguistic function for C—determining "the whole process of human intellect"—see *Lects 1818–19* (CC), 1:212. Cf. C's statement in *CN*, 3:4397 (an entry drawing on this chapter and later used for Lecture 13 of the 1818 series) that "all Languages perfect themselves by a gradual process of desynonymizing words originally equivalent." See also *CN*, 3:4422 and n., and *Lects 1808–19* (CC), 1:294 and n. 28; 295n. 31; and 2:219n. 6.

8. From the Latin *in-dorsum* (on the back of). In Lecture 2 of November 21, 1811, C uses the term as an example of "the laxity of expression" by which words acquire new meanings, and "general terms" become "confined to one individual sense" (*Lects 1808–19* [CC], 1:201–03n. 10).

9. Charles II (1630–1685) became king of England, Scotland, and Ireland after the defeat of Richard Cromwell in 1660. In Johnson's *Dictionary* the term "propriety" still retained "property" as one of its meanings, being defined as "Peculiarity of possession; exclusive right." In a marginal note to his copy of the *Biographia* Thelwall attributes all of C's linguistic reasoning here to Horne Tooke's *Diversions of Purley*, 2 vols. (1798, 1805) (*BL* [CC], 1:83). For C's use and view of Tooke's work, see *Aids to Reflection* (pp. 571–72 herein) and "Language" (p. 595 and n. 1 herein).

1. The "minimum immortality" of one-cell organisms that multiply by continuous division. Shawcross speculates that an early version of the theory of the immortality of the Protozoon, first established in 1881, must have been circulating at the time (*BL* [1907], 1:225).

be proved is, that two conceptions perfectly distinct are confused under one and the same word, and (this done) to appropriate that word exclusively to one meaning, and the synonyme (should there be one) to the other. But if (as will be often the case in the arts and sciences) no synonyme exists, we must either invent or borrow a word. In the present instance the appropriation had already begun, and been legitimated in the derivative adjective: Milton had a highly *imaginative*, Cowley a very *fanciful* mind.[2] If therefore I should succeed in establishing the actual existences of two faculties generally different, the nomenclature would be at once determined. To the faculty by which I had characterized Milton, we should confine the term *imagination*; while the other would be contra-distinguished as *fancy*. Now were it once fully ascertained, that this division is no less grounded in nature, than that of delirium from mania,[3] or Otway's

Lutes, lobsters, seas of milk, and ships of amber,[4]

from Shakespear's

What! have his daughters brought him to this pass?[5]

or from the preceding apostrophe to the elements;[6] the theory of the fine arts, and of poetry in particular, could not, I thought, but derive some additional and important light. It would in its immediate effects furnish a torch of guidance to the philosophical critic; and ultimately to the poet himself. In energetic minds, truth soon changes by domestication into power; and from directing in the discrimination and appraisal of the product, becomes influencive in the production. To admire on principle, is the only way to imitate without loss of originality.

It has been already hinted, that metaphysics and psychology have long been my hobby-horse. But to have a hobby-horse, and to be vain of it, are so commonly found together, that they pass almost for the same. I trust therefore, that there will be more good humour than contempt, in the smile with which the reader chastises my self-complacency, if I confess myself uncertain, whether the satisfaction from the perception of a truth new to myself may not have been rendered more poignant by the conceit, that it would be equally so to the public. There was a time, certainly, in which I took some little credit to myself, in the belief that I had been the first of my countrymen, who had pointed out the diverse meaning of which the two terms were capable, and analyzed the faculties to which they should be appropri-

2. On Milton and Cowley, see p. 390 and n. 7 herein.
3. The distinction between delirium and mania is a corrolary of that between fancy and imagination. According to Henry Crabb Robinson, C associated delirium with "the excess of fancy" and mania with "the excess of imagination" (*CRD*, 1:306). A succinct formulation of this distinction appears in an entry of June 23, 1834, *TT* (CC), 1:489: "You may conceive the difference in kind between Fancy and Imagination in this way—that if the check of the senses and the reason were withdrawn, the first would become delirium, and the second mania." On mania, cf. *AR* (CC), 271n. 28.
4. Thomas Otway (1652–1685), *Venice Preserv'd* (1682), 5.369: "Lutes, Laurells, Seas of Milk, and ships of Amber."
5. *King Lear* 3.4.61 (var.).
6. *King Lear* 3.2.13–17.

ated.[7] Mr. W. Taylor's recent volume of synonimes[8] I have not yet seen;* but his specification of the terms in question has been clearly shown to be both insufficient and erroneous by Mr. Wordsworth in the preface added to the late collection of his "Lyrical Ballads and other poems." The explanation which Mr. Wordsworth has himself given, will be found to differ from mine, chiefly perhaps, as our objects are different. It could scarcely indeed happen otherwise, from the advantage I have enjoyed of frequent conversation with him on a subject to

---

* I ought to have added, with the exception of a single sheet which I accidentally met with at the printers. Even from this scanty specimen, I found it impossible to doubt the talent, or not to admire the ingenuity of the author. That his distinctions were for the greater part unsatisfactory to *my* mind, proves nothing against their accuracy; but it may possibly be serviceable to him in case of a second edition, if I take this opportunity of suggesting the query; whether he may not have been occasionally misled, by having assumed, as to me he appeared to have done, the non-existence of *any* absolute synonimes in our language? Now I cannot but think, that there are many which remain for our posterity to distinguish and appropriate, and which I regard as so much reversionary wealth in our mother-tongue. When two distinct meanings are confounded under one or more words, (and such must be the case, as sure as our knowledge is progressive and of course imperfect) erroneous consequences will be drawn, and what is true in one sense of the word, will be affirmed as true in toto. Men of research startled by the consequences, seek in the things themselves (whether in or out of the mind) for a knowledge of the fact, and having discovered the difference, remove the equivocation either by the substitution of a new word, or by the appropriation of one of the two or more words, that had before been used promiscuously. When this distinction has been so naturalized and of such general currency, that the language itself does as it were *think* for us (like the sliding rule which is the mechanic's safe substitute for arithmetical knowledge) we then say, that it is evident to *common sense*.[9] Common sense, therefore, differs in different ages. What was born and christened in the schools passes by degrees into the world at large, and becomes the property of the market and the tea-table. At least I can discover no other meaning of the term, *common sense*, if it is to convey any specific difference from *sense* and judgement in genere, and where it is not used scholastically for the *universal reason*. Thus in the reign of Charles II. the philosophic world was called to arms by the moral sophisms of Hobbs, and the ablest writers exerted themselves in the detection of an error, which a school-boy would now be able to confute by the mere recollection, that *compulsion* and *obligation* conveyed two ideas perfectly disparate, and that what appertained to the one, had been falsely transferred to the other by a mere confusion of terms.[1]

---

7. On the fancy-imagination distinction, see pp. 416–17 and nn. 5–7 herein; p. 449 and n. 6 herein; pp. 488–89 herein.
8. C refers to *English Synonyms Discriminated* (London, 1813) by William Taylor (1765–1836), in which Taylor upholds the older meaning of fancy as a higher faculty connected with originality and "ideal representations of absent objects" and relegates the imagination to a faculty that merely reproduces sense impressions. In his Preface to *Poems* (1815) Wordsworth criticizes Taylor's use of the terms and presents imagination as a faculty that modifies images and is creative (*W Prose*, 3:30–33). C must have felt that Wordsworth appropriated C's definition of the imagination as a "modifying power," as developed in his 1808 and 1811 lectures (see p. 416, n. 5 herein), and ungenerously criticized C's conception of fancy as "too general," which prompted him to offer yet another Coleridgean assessment of the imagination as the faculty that "recoils from every thing but the plastic, the pliant, and the indefinite" (*W Prose*, 3:36). In a letter of February 1799 (*CL*, 1:465–66) C associates imagination with indefiniteness while distinguishing between Greek and Christian religion (as did Wordsworth in the Preface to *Poems* [1815]; *W Prose*, 3:34–35). The emphasis on the "plastic power" of the imagination informs his definition of this faculty at the start of chapter 10 (p. 449 herein).
9. A closely related definition of common sense appears in *CN*, 3:3549: "What is common sense?—It is when the Language has been so determined in its meanings by great men (being in itself mere arbitrary counters, or physical equivalents, as compulsion & obligation &c) that the very words of a language as used in common Life carry with them the confutation of an error or establishment of a Truth, then we call convictions so received common sense, bearing to the original reason the same relations as operations by an Arithmetical Rules to those by universal Arithmetic."
1. Cf. *Lects 1818–19* (CC), 1:213n. 10, for an expanded version of C's reference to Hobbes's use of "compulsion" and "obligation" as synonymous, which might have been indebted to Moses Mendelssohn (1729–1786). For instances in Hobbes's equation of compulsion with obligation, see *BL* (CC), 1:87n. 1.

which a poem of his own first directed my attention,[2] and my conclusions concerning which, he had made more lucid to myself by many happy instances drawn from the operation of natural objects on the mind. But it was Mr. Wordsworth's purpose to consider the influences of fancy and imagination as they are manifested in poetry, and from the different effects to conclude their diversity in kind; while it is my object to investigate the seminal principle, and then from the kind to deduce the degree. My friend has drawn a masterly sketch of the branches with their *poetic* fruitage. I wish to add the trunk, and even the roots as far as they lift themselves above ground, and are visible to the naked eye of our common consciousness.

Yet even in this attempt I am aware, that I shall be obliged to draw more largely on the reader's attention, than so immethodical a miscellany can authorize; when in such a work (*the Ecclesiastical Policy*) of such a mind as Hooker's, the judicious author, though no less admirable for the perspicuity than for the port and dignity of his language; and though he wrote for men of learning in a learned age; saw nevertheless occasion to anticipate and guard against "complaints of obscurity," as often as he was to trace his subject "to the highest wellspring and fountain." Which, (continues he) "because men are not accustomed to, the pains we take are more needful a great deal, than acceptable; and the matters we handle, seem by reason of newness (till the mind grow better acquainted with them) dark and intricate."[3] I would gladly therefore spare both myself and others this labor, if I knew how without it to present an intelligible statement of my poetic creed; not as my *opinions*, which weigh for nothing, but as deductions from established premises[4] conveyed in such a form, as is calculated either to effect a fundamental conviction, or to receive a fundamental confutation. If I may dare once more adopt the words of Hooker, "they, unto whom we shall seem tedious, are in no wise injured by us, because it is in their own hands to spare that labour, which they are not willing to endure." Those at least, let me be permitted to add, who have taken so much pains to render me ridiculous for a perversion of taste, and have supported the charge by attributing strange notions to me on no other authority than their own conjectures, owe it to themselves as well as to me not to refuse their attention to my own statement of the theory, which I *do* acknowledge; or shrink from the trouble of examining the grounds on which I rest it, or the arguments which I offer in its justification.

---

2. Wordsworth's definition of the "modifying power of imagination" is different from C's in that imagination is represented not just as "consolidating numbers into unity" (what C would call making the *"many into one"* [*CN*, 3:3290]), but also as "separating unity into number" (*W Prose*, 3:33).
3. This and the next quotation are from Richard Hooker, *Of the Laws of Ecclesiastical Polity*, in *Works* (1682), 70 (var.). C reverses the order of the two passages and introduces the variants "because men are not accustomed to" for Hooker's "because we are not oftentimes accustomed to do, when we do it"; "the matters we handle" for "and the Matters which we handle"; and "dark and intricate" for "dark, intricate and unfamiliar." For C's marginalia to this work, see *CM* (CC), 2:1135–59. On Hooker, see p. 401, n. 7 herein.
4. Cf. *LS* (CC), 121, for C's view that opinions should be referred to *"ultimate principles,"* a recurrent theme in *The Friend*.

FROM CHAPTER V

*On the law of association—Its history traced
from Aristotle to Hartley.*[5]

* * *

The *general law* of association, or more accurately, the *common condition* under which all exciting causes act, and in which they may be
generalized, according to Aristotle is this. Ideas by having been together
acquire a power of recalling each other; or every partial representation
awakes the total representation of which it had been a part.[6] In the
practical determination of this common principle to particular recollections, he admits five agents or occasioning causes: 1st, connection in
time, whether simultaneous, preceding or successive; 2nd, vicinity or
connection in space; 3rd, interdependence or necessary connection, as
cause and effect; 4th, likeness; and 5th, contrast.[7] As an additional solution of the occasional seeming chasms in the continuity of reproduction he proves, that movements or ideas possessing one or the other of
these five characters had passed through the mind as intermediate
links, sufficiently clear to recal other parts of the same total impressions with which they had co-existed, though not vivid enough to excite
that degree of attention which is requisite for distinct recollection, or
as we may aptly express it, *after-consciousness*.[8] In association then
consists the whole mechanism of the reproduction of impressions, in

5. In this and the next four chapters C offers a critique of associationist materialistic philosophy—as represented, among others, by David Hartley, Thomas Hobbes, David Hume, and
Étienne Bonnot de Condillac (1715–1780)—with the view of grounding the distinction between fancy and imagination presented in chapter 4 and of "laying the foundation Stones of
the Constructive or Dynamic Philosophy in opposition to the merely mechanic" (*CL*, 4:579).
C's main source for his critique of associationist philosophy was Johann Gebhard Ehren-
reich Maass (1766–1823), whose work he annotated (*CM* [*CC*], 3:789–93). C's plagiarisms
from Maass were first exposed by Sir William Hamilton (1788–1856) in his "Supplementary
Dissertation" to his edition of *The Works of Thomas Reid* (1846). See McFarland, *Coleridge
and the Pantheist Tradition*, 6.
6. C draws here from Maass (324–26), who attributes to Aristotle the correct view of the general law of association: "* * * Representations, by having been together, recall each other,
or: every partial representation awakens its total representation." Maass had defined this law
in similar terms earlier in his treatise (28–29) in section 13, which was annotated by C (*CM*
[*CC*], 3:791–92).
7. In *On Memory*, chapter 2, Aristotle examines the process of association connected with recollection and singles out four cases: contiguity in time, contiguity in space, similarity and
contrast (*Complete Works* [Princeton, 1984], 717–20). Maass (327–28) lists these four cases
as proof of Aristotle's thorough grasp of the rules of association and their dependence on the
higher general law that only ideas that have coexisted in the mind partially or totally can become associated with one another. C's additional category ("interdependence or necessary
connection, as cause and effect"), which is third in his schema, is derived from Hume, who
lists it as one among three principles of association, the other two being resemblance and
contiguity in time and place (Hume, *Treatise*, 11). Hume modified the Aristotelian theory by
lumping time and space into one category, adding cause and effect, and leaving out the relation of contrast. But in the next section Hume introduces contrast (which he calls "contrariety") among seven qualities that make objects comparable (Hume, *Treatise*, 15).
8. The passage, as pointed out in *BL* (1847), 1:107, is derived from Maass (27), where he
shows how a given idea (A) becomes associated with another (B) by means of an intermediary (C), which co-existed with both but remains too dim to be recorded by consciousness.
This leads to the misrecognition that idea A is directly linked with idea B. McFarland argues
(*Originality and Imagination*, 104n. 43) that C's term "after-consciousness" is indebted to
the word "*Nachempfindung*" (after-perception), as used by the German philosopher Johann
Nicolaus Tetens (1736–1807).

the Aristolelian Psychology.[9] It is the universal law of the *passive* fancy and *mechanical* memory; that which supplies to all other faculties their objects, to all thought the elements of its materials.

In consulting the excellent commentary of St. Thomas Aquinas on the Parva Naturalia of Aristotle, I was struck at once with its close resemblance to Hume's essay on association. The main thoughts were the same in both, the *order* of the thoughts was the same, and even the illustrations differed only by Hume's occasional substitution of more modern examples. I mentioned the circumstance to several of my literary acquaintances, who admitted the closeness of the resemblance, and that it seemed too great to be explained by mere coincidence; but they thought it improbable that Hume should have held the pages of the angelic Doctor worth turning over.[1] But some time after Mr. Payne, of the King's mews, shewed Sir James Mackintosh some odd volumes of St. Thomas Aquinas, partly perhaps from having heard that Sir James (then Mr.) Mackintosh had in his lectures past a high encomium on this canonized philosopher, but chiefly from the fact, that the volumes had belonged to Mr. Hume, and had here and there marginal marks and notes of reference in his own hand writing. Among these volumes was that which contains the *Parva Naturalia*, in the old latin version, swathed and swaddled in the commentary afore mentioned![2]

It remains then for me, first to state wherein Hartley differs from Aristotle; then, to exhibit the grounds of my conviction, that he differed only to err; and next as the result, to shew, by what influences of the choice and judgment the associative power becomes either memory or fancy; and, in conclusion, to appropriate the remaining offices

---

9. C follows Maass (329) for the view that Aristotle had developed a psychological rather than a physiological theory of association. In the paragraph preceding the excerpt printed here, C praised Aristotle for avoiding the pitfalls of those modern philosophers who explained the phenomena of association on the basis of a material substance, be it particles, animal spirits, or the ever-present ether (*BL* [CC], 1:100–02).

1. The view that Hume was closely indebted to Thomas Aquinas (c. 1225–1274) was sharply criticized by the reviewer of the *Biographia* in *Blackwood's Edinburgh Magazine* 3 (September 1818): 653–57, who argued that there is a single short passage in the whole of Aquinas's commentary on Aristotle that bears any similarity with Hume; and even in this passage Aquinas's doctrine of association of ideas differs considerably from Hume's. See CN, 1:973An., for the passage from Aquinas's commentary on Aristotle's *On Memory* copied by Sara Hutchinson for C from the 1612 edition of *Opera Omnia*, which C borrowed from the library of Durham Cathedral in 1801.

2. Sir James Mackintosh (1765–1832) offered a series of lectures in January–March 1800, five of which C attended (see CN, 1:634 and n., for C's notes from these lectures). C's negative reaction to the lectures is vividly expressed in a letter to Poole of February 13, 1801: "I attended 5 of his Lectures—such a wretched patch work of plagiarisms from Condilliac—of contradictions, and blunders in matter of fact, I never heard from any man's mouth before. *Their* opinion weighs as nothing with me" (*CL*, 2:675). Mackintosh later claimed in response to the *Biographia* that the work given to him by the bookseller Thomas Payne (1752–1843) was not Aquinas's commentary on Aristotle, *Parva Naturalia* ([Short Writings on Nature], the title given in the 13th century to a collection of short treatises by Aristotle, including *On Memory*), but *Secunda Secundae* (The Second of the Second), a title that refers to the second volume of the second part of Aquinas's *Summa theologiae* (The Sum of Theology), and that the marginal annotations were not in Hume's handwriting. C developed an antipathy to Mackintosh on philosophical as well as political grounds (of which Mackintosh was fully aware). In his philosophical letters to Josiah Wedgwood (1769–1843) of February 1801, C revealed that his attack on Locke was triggered by Mackintosh's statement that Locke overthrew Descartes's doctrine of innate ideas (*CL*, 2:681–703). Mackintosh replaced C as the writer for *MP*, endorsed the policies of the ministry, and was knighted in 1803. For C's relationship with Mackintosh see *BL* (CC), 1:91n. 1, 93n. 1, and 104n. 3; see also *EOT* (CC), 1:cxv–vii.

of the mind to the reason, and the imagination. With my best efforts
to be as perspicuous as the nature of language will permit on such a
subject, I earnestly solicit the good wishes and friendly patience of my
readers, while I thus go "sounding on my dim and perilous way."[3]

FROM CHAPTER VI

That Hartley's system, as far as it differs from that of Aristotle, is neither
tenable in theory, nor founded in facts.

Of Hartley's hypothetical vibrations in his hypothetical oscillating
ether of the nerves, which is the first and most obvious distinction between his system and that of Aristotle, I shall say little.[4] This, with all
other similar attempts to render *that* an object of the sight which has
no relation to sight, has been already sufficiently exposed by the
younger Reimarus,[5] Maasse, &c. as outraging the very axioms of mechanics in a scheme, the merit of which consists in its being mechanical. Whether any other philosophy be possible, but the mechanical;
and again, whether the mechanical system can have any claim to be
called philosophy;[6] are questions for another place. It is, however,
certain, that as long as we deny the former, and affirm the latter, we
must bewilder ourselves, whenever we would pierce into the *adyta*[7]
of causation; and all that laborious conjecture can do, is to fill up

3. Cf. Wordsworth, *The Excursion* (1814), 3.700–01: "The intellectual Power, through words
   and things, / Went sounding on, a dim and perilous way!"
4. Hartley's doctrine of association is an attempt to synthesize Locke's theory of the sensory
   origin of ideas and their association (in Locke, *Essay*, 104–401, esp. 394–401) and Newton's
   theory of vibrations and ether, that subtle and elastic substance diffused throughout solid
   bodies and outer space, by means of which Newton explained the phenomena of attraction
   between bodies, electricity, the action of light, as well as sensation and motion in animal
   bodies. On Newton's view of ether, see *Opticks*, 3rd ed. (London, 1721; the edition owned
   by C), 323–28, 338–45 (Querries 18–24, 28). According to Hartley (*Observations on Man*,
   1:11–34), the brain and the sensory nerves are filled with a uniform white medullary substance that is made of "infinitesimal" particles and the ubiquitous ether spread among them.
   When external bodies act upon sense organs, they cause vibrations in the ether and particles
   of the nerves, which are then propagated to other contiguous particles in the brain. Through
   repetition, these original sensations leave fainter copies of themselves in the mind and cause
   "diminutive Vibrations," or what Hartley calls "Vibratiuncles." These are simple ideas, which
   form complex ideas through processes of association as vivid as the former (58–84). C annotated the 1791 two-volume edition of *Observations on Man*, to which was added a third
   volume with interpretative notes by Herman Andrew Pistorius, translated from German (see
   CM [*CC*], 2:959–62).
5. C refers to *Ueber die Gründe der menchlichen Erkenntniss und der natürlichen Religion* (On
   the Foundations of Human Knowledge and of Natural Religion) (Hamburg, 1787) by the
   German physician and philosopher Johann Albert Heinrich Reimarus (1729–1814), which
   he annotated sometime between 1811 and 1815 (*CM* [*CC*], 4:215–31). C may be referring
   to Reimarus's critique of materialism in sections 3–7 (*BL* [1847], 1:330n.), but he may also
   have in mind Maass's summary of Reimarus's theory of association (433–34). There Maass
   points out that Reimarus understood clearly that specific rules of association, such as resemblance or contrast, are subordinated to the general law according to which only those
   ideas that had been previously linked in the mind can recall each other. Reimarus's conception thus reinforces Maass's own formulation of the general law of association (see p. 421,
   n. 6 herein).
6. C is indebted here to Maass, who showed the "impossibility of a mechanical type of explanation of association" based on physiological grounds, such as the hypothesis of vibrations
   in the nerves and animal spirits (30–50). See also his critique of the contradictions in Hartley's system (Maass, 382–96).
7. "Innermost sanctuaries" or "shrines." For other uses of this term in C, see *CN*, 3:4166
   and n.

the gaps of fancy.[8] Under that despotism of the eye[9] (the emancipation from which Pythagoras by his *numeral*, and Plato by his *musical*,
symbols,[1] and both by geometric discipline, aimed at, as the first
προπαιδευτικον[2] of the mind)—under this strong sensuous influence,
we are restless because invisible things are not the objects of vision;
and metaphysical systems, for the most part, become popular, not
for their truth, but in proportion as they attribute to causes a susceptibility of being *seen*, if only our visual organs were sufficiently powerful.

From a hundred possible confutations let one suffice. According to
this system the idea or vibration *a* from the external object A becomes
associable with the idea or vibration *m* from the external object M, because the oscillation *a* propagated itself so as to re-produce the oscillation *m*. But the original impression from M was essentially different
from the impression A: unless therefore different causes may produce
the same effect, the vibration *a* could never produce the vibration *m*:
and this therefore could never be the means, by which *a* and *m* are associated.[3] To understand this, the attentive reader need only be reminded, that the ideas are themselves, in Hartley's system, nothing
more than their appropriate configurative vibrations. It is a mere delusion of the fancy to conceive the pre-existence of the ideas,[4] in any
chain of association, as so many differently colored billiard-balls in
contact, so that when an object, the billiard-stick, strikes the first or
white ball, the same motion propagates itself through the red, green,
blue, black, &c. and sets the whole in motion.[5] No! we must suppose
the very same force, which *constitutes* the white ball, to *constitute* the
red or black; or the idea of a circle to *constitute* the idea of a triangle;
which is impossible.

But it may be said, that, by the sensations from the objects A and M,
the nerves have acquired a disposition to the vibrations *a* and *m*, and

8. For his discussion of mechanical philosophy here to the end of the paragraph, C reproduces
a note (var.) he wrote to line 34 of book 2 of Southey's *Joan of Arc* ([1796], 41–42), to which
he contributed 360 lines. See p. 125, n. 1 herein and p. 391 herein.
9. C was not alone in regarding sight as despotic, reacting to the ascendancy of empirical philosophy and optics at this time (of which Newton's *Opticks* is but one example), which gave
prominence to this sense. Cf. Wordsworth, *The Prelude* (1805), 12.171–76, in which he regretted the period in his life when the eye, that "most despotic of our senses," held his mind
in "absolute dominion."
1. Cf. *CN*, 3:4436: "The more I reflect, the more important do both the Pythagorean or arithmetical, and the Platonic or harmonical Schemes of Nature present themselves to my
mind." C regarded the theory of numbers by Pythagoras (6th century B.C.E.), developed to
explain the essence of the universe, as "the best symbol * * * of the representation of the
laws of nature considered as homogeneous with the pure reason in man" (Lecture 2 of *Lects
1818–19* [CC], 1:78). On Plato's view of musical symbols, see *Republic* 398–403, 443D–E,
522–32 and *Timaeus* 35B–36B.
2. "Preparatory education"; as used by Plato, e.g., *Republic* 536D.
3. Adapted from Maass (32–33). For the passage in Maass, see *BL* (*CC*), 1:108n. 1.
4. Cf. Hartley (1:56–57), in which an allusion to fancy appears in a paragraph that also reveals
Hartley's view of ideas, as C correctly renders it: "* * * ideas are copies and offsprings of the
impressions made on the eye and ear, in which the same orders were observed respectively.
And though it happens, that trains of visible and audible ideas are presented in sallies of the
fancy, and in dreams, in which the order of time and place is different from that of any former impressions, yet the small component parts of these trains are copies of former impressions * * *."
5. The image of the billiard balls is derived from Hume, *An Enquiry concerning Human Understanding* (28–30), where he uses it to document the arbitrary connection between cause
and effect and the view that "every effect is a distinct event from its cause," and Hume, *Treatise* (164). In chapter 5 C mistakenly attributes this image to Hobbes (*BL* [CC], 1:101n. 2).

therefore *a* need only be repeated in order to re-produce *m*.[6] Now we will grant, for a moment, the possibility of such a disposition in a material nerve, which yet seems scarcely less absurd than to say, that a weather-cock had acquired a *habit* of turning to the east, from the wind having been so long in that quarter: for if it be replied, that we must take in the circumstance of *life*, what then becomes of the mechanical philosophy? And what is the *nerve*, but the flint which the wag placed in the pot as the first ingredient of his stone-broth, requiring only salt, turnips and mutton, for the remainder![7] But if we waive this, and presuppose the actual existence of such a disposition; two cases are possible.[8] Either, every idea has its own nerve and correspondent oscillation, or this is not the case. If the latter be the truth, we should gain nothing by these dispositions; for then, every nerve having several dispositions, when the motion of any other nerve is propagated into it, there will be no ground or cause present, why exactly the oscillation *m* should arise, rather than any other to which it was equally pre-disposed. But if we take the former, and let every idea have a nerve of its own, then every nerve must be capable of propagating its motion into many other nerves; and again, there is no reason assignable, why the vibration *m* should arise, rather than any other ad libitum.

It is fashionable to smile at Hartley's vibrations and vibratiuncles;[9] and his work has been re-edited by Priestley, with the omission of the *material* hypothesis.[1] But Hartley was too great a man, too coherent a thinker, for this to have been done, either consistently or to any wise purpose.[2] For all other parts of his system, as far as they are peculiar to that system, once removed from their mechanical basis, not only lose their main support, but the very motive which led to their adoption. Thus the principle of *contemporaneity*, which Aristotle had made the common *condition* of all the laws of association, Hartley was constrained to represent as being itself the sole *law*.[3] For to what law can

6. Adapted from Maass (33); *BL* (*CC*), 1:108 n. 4.
7. An allusion to the European folk tale "The Soup Stone Sold" *BL* (*CC*), 1:109n. 1.
8. This sentence to the end of the paragraph is a direct translation of Maass (33–34 [var.]) with one addition ("rather than any other to which it was equally pre-disposed").
9. Vibrations are "motions backwards and forwards" like the swing of a pendulum, transmitted through the ether to the particles of the sensory nerves and brain (Hartley, 11). *Vibratiuncles*: "diminutive vibrations" caused by repeated sensory impressions with which they agree "in kind, place, and line of direction" but differ in intensity (Hartley, 58–64). See p. 423, n. 4 herein.
1. C refers to Joseph Priestley's *Hartley's Theory of the Human Mind, on the Principle of Association of Ideas*, 2nd ed. (1790), in which he published selections from Hartley's *Observations on Man*, which did indeed, as C assesses, strip the work of its material basis. Priestley thought that he could make Hartley "more intelligible" by presenting his theory of association without recourse to "the doctrine of *vibrations* and the *anatomical disquisitions* which are connected with it" (iii). Consequently, he either omitted sections in which the theory of vibration is discussed, or found synonyms for the terms "vibration" and "vibrantiuncle." Priestley did, however, give a summary of Hartley's theory of vibration in the first of the three introductory essays on Hartley (vii–xxi).
2. Cf. C's suspicion, however, articulated in a marginal note, that "Hartley himself must have *felt* that association was not of itself capable of explaining all the phaenomen[a] of the human mind * * *" (*CM* [*CC*], 2:961).
3. Hartley: "SENSATIONS may be said to be associated together, when their impressions are either made precisely at the same instant of time, or in the contiguous successive instants" (65). Cf. C's marginal note to Maass (28–29), in which he states that contemporaneity is the condition which makes association possible, "rather than itself the effective Law" (*CM* [*CC*], 3:792). On the related confusion of the "*conditions* of a thing for its *causes* and *essence*," see chapter 7 (p. 431 herein).

the action of *material* atoms be subject, but that of proximity in *place?* And to what law can their *motions* be subjected, but that of *time?*[4] Again, from this results inevitably, that the will, the reason, the judgment, and the understanding, instead of being the determining causes of association, must needs be represented as its *creatures*, and among its mechanical *effects.* Conceive, for instance, a broad stream, winding through a mountainous country with an indefinite number of currents, varying and running into each other according as the gusts chance to blow from the opening of the mountains. The temporary union of several currents in one, so as to form the main current of the moment, would present an accurate image of Hartley's theory of the will.[5]

Had this been really the case, the consequence would have been, that our whole life would be divided between the despotism of outward impressions, and that of senseless and passive memory. Take his law in its highest abstraction and most philosophical form, viz. that every partial representation recalls the total representation of which it was a part;[6] and the law becomes nugatory, were it only from its universality.[7] In practice it would indeed be mere lawlessness. Consider, how immense must be the sphere of a total impression from the top of St. Paul's church; and how rapid and continuous the series of such total impressions. If therefore we suppose the absence of all interference of the will, reason, and judgement, one or other of two consequences must result. Either the ideas (or relicts of such impression) will exactly imitate the order of the impression itself, which would be absolute *delirium:*[8] or any one part of that impression might recal any other part, and (as from the law of continuity, there must exist in every total impression some one or more parts, which are components of some other following total impression, and so on ad infinitum) *any* part of *any* impression might recal *any* part of any *other*, without a cause present to determine *what* it should be. For to bring in the will, or reason, as causes of their own cause, that is, as at once causes and effects, can satisfy those only who in their pretended evidences of a God having first demanded organization, as the sole cause and ground of intellect, will then coolly demand the preexistence of intellect, as the cause and ground-work of organization. There is in truth but one state to which this theory applies at all, namely, that of complete light-headedness; and even to this it applies

4. See chapter 5 (p. 421, n. 7 herein) for these laws.
5. C articulates here his main objection to Hartley, which he takes up again in chapter 7 (pp. 427–28 herein), namely his representation of the faculties of the mind and of the will in particular, as mere results of the mechanical processes of association. For Hartley the will is primarily a faculty that controls the functions of memory, fancy, and bodily motions (e.g., speaking or walking). Hartley defines the will as a "set of compound vibratiuncles" (1:103), an opinion that is congruent with his overall thesis that all "sensation, thought, and motion, must all be performed by vibrations" (1:88), but at complete odds with C's elevated conception of the will (see p. 427, n. 1 herein).
6. For this general law, drawn from Maass, see chapter 5 (p. 421, n. 6 herein).
7. C uses a marginal note to Maass (29) where he articulates the objection that the general law of association (as summarized by Maass) is "nugatory by its universality" (i.e., explains nothing by trying to explain everything), giving the same example of a view from the top of St. Paul's cathedral (*CM* [CC], 3:792).
8. Cf. C's notion of the delirium generated by the excess of fancy (p. 418, n. 3 herein).

but partially, because the will, and reason are perhaps never wholly suspended.

⋎ ⁂ ⊁

FROM CHAPTER VII

Of the necessary consequences of the Hartleian theory—Of the original mistake or equivocation which procured admission for the theory— Memoria Technica.

We will pass by the utter incompatibility of such a law (if law it may be called, which would itself be the slave of chances) with even that *appearance* of rationality forced upon us by the outward phænomena of human conduct, abstracted from our own consciousness. We will agree to forget this for the moment, in order to fix our attention on that subordination of final to efficient causes in the human being,[9] which flows of necessity from the assumption, that the will, and with the will all acts of thought and attention, are parts and products of this blind mechanism, instead of being distinct powers,[1] whose function it is to controul, determine, and modify the phantasma chaos of association.[2] The soul becomes a mere ens logicum;[3] for as a real separable being, it would be more worthless and ludicrous, than the Grimalkins in the Cat-harpsichord, described in the Spectator.[4] For these did form a part of the process; but in Hartley's scheme the soul is present only to be pinched or *stroked*, while the very squeals or purring are produced by an agency wholly independent and alien. It involves all the difficulties, all the incomprehensibility (if it be not in-

---

9. Aristotle classified causes into four categories. Material causes refer to the substance from which a thing originates and is maintained (e.g., bronze would be the material cause of a statue made out of it). Formal causes pertain to the form or archetype that defines the essence of a thing. Efficient causes identify the source of movement and change. Final causes represent the telos, end or goal "for the sake of which a thing is done" (*Physics*, book 2, 194b–195a).

1. Maass, after his critique of mechanical systems of association (see p. 423, n. 6 herein), takes up the question of the will as a faculty that controls the process of association (50–51, 61–62). For his view that the will can either enable or prevent certain representations to become associated with one another, see Maass (163–68). Under the influence of Maass as well as other German philosophers (especially Kant, Fichte, and Schelling), C developed a view of the will that was not, as it was for Hartley or Priestley, "the mere result and aggregate of fibres, motions, and sensations" but a "real, distinct, correspondent power" (*CM* [CC],2:801), the highest faculty not only in human but also in divine consciousness (see p. 426, n. 5 herein). For Kant's view of the "absolute worth" of the will regarded as "the highest good and the condition of every other, even of all demands for happiness," see Kant, *Grundlegung*, 4, 7 (Gregor 8, 10). C objected, however, to Kant's definition of the will as "nothing other than practical reason" (*Grundlegung*, 36 [Gregor, 24]; *CN*, 1:1717), considering the will to be "deeper than, and (in order of *thought*) antecedent to, Reason" (*SM* [CC], 67n. 2). On the will, see p. 477, n. 4 herein.

2. Cf. *CN*, 3:3909 on the "importance of any *act* in restoring the mind from its wanderings, the servitude of mere association, by streghtening & re-enlivening the *Will*."

3. "Logical entity." I.e., a "product of the mind" derived from the understanding, as C defines the term in *Logic* (CC), 68–69, 176, 239.

4. *Spectator*, no. 361 (April 24, 1712). In that issue Joseph Addison (1672–1719) responded to an inquiry about the provenance of the "strange Instrument" called *catcall*, which was heard during the performance of a play. He suggested that the instrument, which imitates the sound of a cat, was of ancient origin and might have been used by Orpheus to attract animals around him. He also argued that it was well suited to the British theater, as it "very much improves the Sound of Nonsense, and often goes along with the Voice of the Actor who pronounces it, as the Violin or Harpsichord accompanies the *Italian* Recitativo * * *."

deed, ὡς ἐμοιγε δοκεῖ,[5] the absurdity) of intercommunion between substances that have no one property in common, without any of the convenient consequences that bribed the judgement to the admission of the
dualistic hypothesis.[6] Accordingly, this caput mortuum[7] of the Hartleian
process has been rejected by his followers,[8] and the consciousness considered as a *result*, as a *tune*, the common product of the breeze and the
harp:[9] tho' this again is the mere remotion of one absurdity to make way
for another, equally preposterous. For what is harmony but a mode of
relation, the very *esse* of which is *percipi*?[1] An ens rationale,[2] which presupposes the power, that by perceiving creates it? The razor's edge becomes a saw to the armed vision;[3] and the delicious melodies of Purcell
or Cimarosa[4] might be disjointed stammerings to a hearer, whose partition of time should be a thousand times subtler than ours. But this obstacle too let us imagine ourselves to have surmounted, and "at one
bound high overleap all bound!"[5] Yet according to this hypothesis the
disquisition, to which I am at present soliciting the reader's attention,
may be as truly said to be written by Saint Paul's church, as by *me*: for it
is the mere motion of my muscles and nerves;[6] and these again are set
in motion from external causes equally passive, which external causes
stand themselves in interdependent connection with every thing that exists or has existed. Thus the whole universe co-operates to produce the
minutest stroke of every letter, save only that I myself, and I alone, have
nothing to do with it, but merely the causeless and *effectless* beholding
of it when it is done. Yet scarcely can it be called a beholding;[7] for it is

5. "As it seems to me, at least."
6. On dualism, see chapter 8 (pp. 433–34 herein).
7. "Death's head"; a term designating the leftover residue after the distillation of a substance.
8. According to *BL* (*CC*), 1:117n. 5, C refers to Priestley here. Priestley did indeed strip Hartley's system of its material basis (see p. 425, n. 1 herein), but C regarded Priestley as committing the same error as Hartley in representing the will as "mere result and aggregate of
   fibres, motions and sensations" (*CM* [*CC*]), 2:801). See also p. 426, n. 5 herein.
9. C uses the image of the Eolian harp to highlight the error of interpreting consciousness as
   the result of sensory associative processes. See p. 426, n. 5 herein. On the Eolian harp, see
   "Effusion XXXV" ["The Eolian Harp"], pp. 17–20 and nn. herein.
1. C refers to the idealism of Berkeley, according to which objects exist only in so far as they
   are perceived by the mind: "Their *esse* [being] is *percipi* [perceiving] * * *" (*A Treatise Concerning the Principles of Human Knowledge* [1734], *Works*, 1:24). For C's reaction to Berkeley, see p. 138, n. 7 herein and p. 439, n. 5 herein.
2. "Rational entity."
3. I.e., vision aided by an instrument such as a telescope, for which see p. 357, n. 6 herein.
4. Henry Purcell (c. 1658–1695), one of the English composers most celebrated in C's time,
   for whom C had a special fondness. Domenico Cimarosa (1749–1801), Italian composer of
   many operas and seven symphonies. C described the experience of listening to a symphony
   by Cimarosa in *Friend* (*CC*), 2:111 and Lecture 10 of *Lects 1818–19* (*CC*), 1:445n. 78. See
   also *PGC* (p. 344, n. 4 herein).
5. A reference to Satan's avoidance of the proper entrance into Paradise through the eastern
   gate and his leap into it over "Hill or highest Wall" (Milton, *Paradise Lost* 4.181 [var.]). C
   also used this Miltonic passage in *Conciones ad Populum* (p. 251, n. 8 herein).
6. Friedrich Heinrich Jacobi (1743–1819), who may be the source of this passage, reproduces
   in French, with German translation, a letter he wrote to Frans Hemsterhuis (1721–1790):
   "What you adopt from the doctrine of fatalism is enough for me; since one needs no more
   than to establish that St. Peter's in Rome built itself; that Newton's discoveries were made by
   his body; and that in all such instances the soul is occupied only with looking on" (143–44;
   BL [*CC*], 1:118n. 6).
7. C uses the term for an act of intuition that combines activity and passivity and is the "indispensable Condition of all Consciousness." For this notion, derived mainly from Fichte and
   Schelling, see *CN*, 3:4186 and C's marginal annotations to Fichte (*CM* [*CC*], 2:602,
   623–24, and nn.). For the source of the definition of intuition as "immediate beholding" in
   Richard Hooker (1554–1600), see p. 449, n. 8 herein and p. 450, n. 2 herein.

neither an act nor an effect; but an impossible creation of a *something—nothing* out of its very contrary! It is the mere quick-silver plating behind a looking-glass; and in this alone consists the poor worthless I! The sum total of my moral and intellectual intercourse dissolved into its elements are reduced to *extension, motion, degrees of velocity*, and those diminished *copies* of configurative motion,[8] which form what we call notions, and notions of notions. Of such philosophy well might Butler say—

> The metaphysics but a puppet motion
> That goes with screws, the notion of a notion;
> The copy of a copy and lame draught
> Unnaturally taken from a thought:
> That counterfeits all pantomimic tricks,
> And turns the eyes, like an old crucifix;
> That counterchanges whatsoe'er it calls
> B' another name, and makes it true or false;
> Turns truth to falsehood, falsehood into truth,
> By virtue of the Babylonian's tooth.
> MISCELLANEOUS THOUGHTS.[9]

The inventor of the watch did not in reality invent it; he only look'd on, while the blind causes, the only true artists, were unfolding themselves. So must it have been too with my friend ALLSTON, when he sketched his picture of the dead man revived by the bones of the prophet Elijah.[1] So must it have been with Mr. SOUTHEY and LORD BYRON, when the one *fancied* himself composing his "RODERICK," and the other his "CHILD HAROLD."[2] The same must hold good of all systems of philosophy; of all arts, governments, wars by sea and by land; in short, of all things that ever have been or that ever will be produced. For according to this system it is not the affections and passions that are at work, in as far as they are *sensations* or *thoughts*. We only *fancy*, that we act from rational resolves, or prudent motives, or from impulses of anger, love, or generosity. In all these cases the real agent is a *something—nothing—every-thing*, which does all of which we know, and knows nothing of all that itself does.

The existence of an infinite spirit, of an intelligent and holy will, must on this system be mere articulated motions of the air.[3] For as the function of the human understanding is no other than merely (to appear to itself) to combine and to apply the phænomena of the association; and as these derive all their reality from the primary sensations;

---

8. C most likely refers to Hartley's "vibratiuncles" (see p. 423, n. 4 herein and p. 425, n. 9 herein).
9. Samuel Butler (1612–1680), "Miscellaneous Thoughts," lines 93–102 (*Poetical Works*, 3 vols. [Edinburgh, 1777], 3:176–77).
1. For C's friendship with the American painter Washington Allston, whom he met in Rome in 1805, see p. 346, n. 1 herein. The painting C refers to is actually called *The Dead Man Touching Elisha's Bones* (1810–11).
2. Southey, *Roderick, the Last of the Goths* (1814). C thought that in *Roderick* Southey "surpassed himself in language and metre, in the construction of the whole, and in the splendor of particular passages" (*BL* [CC], 1:64). The first two cantos of Byron's *Childe Harold's Pilgrimage* were published in 1812, with the last two appearing in 1816 and 1818.
3. I.e., mere sounds of words, rather than "living powers," as spirit, will, and language itself ought to be, according to C (see *EOT* [CC], 2:249 and n. 4).

and the sensations again all *their* reality from the impressions ab extra; a God not visible, audible, or tangible, can exist only in the sounds and letters that form his name and attributes. If in *ourselves* there be no such faculties as those of the will, and the scientific reason, we must either have an *innate* idea of them, which would overthrow the whole system; or we can have no idea at all. The process, by which Hume degraded the notion of cause and effect into a blind product of delusion and habit,[4] into the mere sensation of *proceeding* life (nisus vitalis)[5] associated with the images of the memory; this same process must be repeated to the equal degradation of every *fundamental* idea in ethics or theology.[6]

Far, very far am I from burthening with the odium of these consequences the moral characters of those who first formed, or have since adopted the system! It is most noticeable of the excellent and pious Hartley, that in the proofs of the existence and attributes of God, with which his second volume commences, he makes no reference to the principles or results of the first.[7] Nay, he assumes, as his foundations, ideas which, if we embrace the doctrines of his first volume, can exist no where but in the vibrations of the ethereal medium common to the nerves and to the atmosphere. Indeed the whole of the second volume is, with the fewest possible exceptions, independent of his peculiar system. So true is it, that the faith, which saves and sanctifies, is a collective energy, a total act of the whole moral being;[8] that its living sensorium is in the *heart*; and that no errors of the understanding can be morally arraigned unless they have proceeded from the heart.—[9] But whether they be such, no man can be certain in the case of another, scarcely perhaps even in his own. Hence it follows by inevitable consequence, that man may perchance determine,

---

4. Hume (*Treatise*, 155–76), like Locke, denied the existence of innate ideas, showing that since all ideas are derived from sense impressions, "the idea of a deity proceeds from the same origin" (160). He showed, moreover, that the mind cannot form an idea of the necessary connection between two objects as that of cause and effect. Such a perception was a delusion brought about by custom, which causes the imagination to connect the idea of one object with another that has repeatedly been discovered to follow it. Hence "all our reasonings concerning causation are deriv'd from the experienc'd conjunction of objects, not from any reasoning or reflexion * * *" (*Treatise*, 172).
5. "Vital impulse." C derived this from two terms: *nisus formativus* and the German *Bildungstrieb*, both meaning "formative impulse." In *Friend* (CC), 1:493–94, C wrote with reference to *nisus formativus*: "So our medical writers commonly translate Professor Blumenbach's *Bildungstrieb*, the vis plastica [plastic force], or vis vitae formatrix [formative vital force] of the elder physiologists, and the life or living principle of JOHN HUNTER * * *." For C and John Hunter (1728–1793), see Levere, *Poetry Realized in Nature*, 46–52, 92–94, 205–10, and for C and Johann Friedrich Blumenbach (1752–1840), see CN (3:3744n.) and BL (CC) (1:207n. 1).
6. In a notebook entry of 1809 C stated that "Atheism is the necessary Consequence or Corrolary of the Hartleian Theory of the Will * * *" (CN, 3:3587). For Hartley's conception of the will, see p. 426, n. 5 herein.
7. Volume 2 of *Observations on Man* is devoted to religion and ethics, e.g., the attributes of God, the belief in an afterlife, the "terms of Salvation," and the principles of honor. Priestley, who thought that the work would have been better received if it had not been "clogged with a whole system of moral and religious knowledge," included very little from it. See *Hartley's Theory of the Mind* (iii, 347–64). For C's sense of the marked difference between the two volumes, see CN, 3:3907.
8. For C's view of faith as "a *total* act of the soul," see *Friend* (CC), 2:314.
9. For C's view of the heart as a corrective of the understanding, see BL (CC), 1:217 and his letter to Southey of August 7, 1803: "Believe me, Southey! a metaphysical Solution, that does not instantly *tell* for something in the Heart, is grievously to be suspected as apocry[p]hal" (CL, 2:961).

what is an heresy; but God only can know, *who* is a heretic. It does not, however, by any means follow, that opinions fundamentally false are harmless. An hundred causes may co-exist to form one complex antidote. Yet the sting of the adder remains venemous, though there are many who have taken up the evil thing; and it hurted them not![1] Some indeed there seem to have been, in an unfortunate neighbour-nation at least,[2] who have embraced this system with a full view of all its moral and religious consequences; some—

> ————who deem themselves most free,
> When they within this gross and visible sphere
> Chain down the winged thought, scoffing assent,
> Proud in their meanness; and themselves they cheat
> With noisy emptiness of learned phrase,
> Their subtle fluids, impacts, essences,
> Self-working tools, uncaus'd effects, and all
> Those blind omniscients, those Almighty slaves,
> Untenanting Creation of its God![3]

Such men need discipline, not argument; they must be made better men, before they can become wiser.

The attention will be more profitably employed in attempting to discover and expose the paralogisms, by the magic of which such a faith could find admission into minds framed for a nobler creed. These, it appears to me, may be all reduced to one sophism as their common genus; the mistaking the *conditions* of a thing for its *causes* and *essence*; and the process by which we arrive at the knowledge of a faculty, for the faculty itself.[4] The air I breathe, is the *condition* of my life, not its cause. We could never have learnt that we had eyes but by the process of seeing; yet having seen we know that the eyes must have pre-existed in order to render the process of sight possible. Let us cross-examine Hartley's scheme under the guidance of this distinction; and we shall discover, that contemporaneity (Leibnitz's *Lex Continui*)[5] is the *limit and condition* of the laws of mind, itself being rather a law of matter, at least of phænomena considered as material. At the utmost, it is *to thought* the

---

1. A paraphrase from Mark 16.18: "They shall take up serpents; and if they drink any deadly thing, it shall not hurt them * * *."
2. France. The reference here might to the French philosopher Étienne Bonnot de Condillac (1715–1780), follower of Locke and author of the influential *Traite de sensations* (Treatise on Sensations) (1754). For C Condillac embodied the typical sins of empirical philosophy, in which ideas, including moral ideas, are derived from the senses. C thought that Condillac in his *Logique* (Logic) (1781) plagiarized from Hartley (*CL*, 2:947) and that, according to his theory, one might define virtue by the color of a coat worn by a man (*Lects 1818–19* [CC], 2:536n. 84; *SM* [CC], 102n. 4; *Logic* [CC], 237n. 2).
3. "The Destiny of Nations," lines 27–35, which C contributed to Southey, *Joan of Arc* (p. 125, n. 1 herein and p. 391 herein).
4. Cf. C's related argument that Hartley misinterpreted the principle of "contemporaneity" (p. 425, n. 3 herein).
5. Leibniz first formulated the *lex continui* (law of continuity) in his 1687 "Lettre à Mr. Bayle sur un principe général, utile a l'explication des loix de la nature" (Letter to Mr. Bayle on a General Principle, Useful for an Explanation of the Laws of Nature), where he defined it as a relationship of cause and effect, according to the principle that "If there is order in the grounds there will also be order in the consequents" (Erdmann, 1:104–06). In the Preface to *Nouveaux essais sur l'entendement humaine* (New Essays on Human Understanding) (1703), the law of continuity is contained in the maxim that "*nature never makes leaps*" (Erdmann, 198; Remnant, 56).

same, as the law of gravitation is to loco-motion. In every voluntary movement we first counteract gravitation, in order to avail ourselves of it. It must exist, that there may be a something to be counteracted, and which by its re-action, aids the force that is exerted to resist it. Let us consider, what we do when we leap. We first resist the gravitating power by an act purely voluntary, and then by another act, voluntary in part, we yield to it in order to light on the spot, which we had previously proposed to ourselves. Now let a man watch his mind while he is composing; or, to take a still more common case, while he is trying to recollect a name; and he will find the process completely analogous. Most of my readers will have observed a small water-insect on the surface of rivulets, which throws a cinque-spotted shadow fringed with prismatic colours on the sunny bottom of the brook; and will have noticed, how the little animal *wins* its way up against the stream, by alternate pulses of active and passive motion, now resisting the current, and now yielding to it in order to gather strength and a momentary *fulcrum* for a further propulsion. This is no unapt emblem of the mind's self-experience in the act of thinking. There are evidently two powers at work, which relatively to each other are active and passive; and this is not possible without an intermediate faculty, which is at once both active and passive.[6] (In philosophical language, we must denominate this intermediate faculty in all its degrees and determinations, the IMAGINATION. But in common language, and especially on the subject of poetry, we appropriate the name to a superior degree of the faculty, joined to a superior voluntary controul over it.)

*   *   *

* * * [T]he true practical general law of association is this; that whatever makes certain parts of a total impression more vivid or distinct than the rest, will determine the mind to recall these in preference to others equally linked together by the common condition of contemporaneity, or (what I deem a more appropriate and philosophical term) of *continuity*.[7] But the will itself by confining and intensifying* the attention may arbi-

---

* I am aware, that this word occurs neither in Johnson's Dictionary or in any classical writer. But the word, "*to intend*," which Newton and others before him employ in this sense, is now so completely appropriated to another meaning, that I could not use it without ambiguity:[8] while to paraphrase the sense, as by *render intense*, would often break up the sentence and destroy that harmony of the position of the words with the logical position of the thoughts, which is a beauty in all composition, and more especially desirable in a close philosophical investigation. I have therefore hazarded the word, *intensify*; though, I confess, it sounds uncouth to my own ear.

---

6. The conception of an active and passive principle at work in consciousness and of a faculty that unites both is largely derived from C's readings of German transcendentalist philosophy, especially Fichte and Schelling. These philosophers explain how the self (for Fichte) or self-consciousness (for Schelling), which are originally unbounded and infinite, create finitude and thus represent themselves in an object. Both demonstrate the coexistence of opposite principles—one unlimited and active, the other limited and passive—in an absolute identity available to intuition or self-consciousness. Cf. C's exposition of this fundamental tenet in CN, 3:4186: "The Spirit then is no other than this activity * * * and this limitation, both conceived as co-instantaneous. * * * The Spirit is at once active & passive, and this is a conditio sine quâ non of our Consciousness. * * * Again, an Intuition, or * * * Present Beholding, combines actively, Activity & Passivity * * *."
7. See p. 421, n. 6 herein.
8. Attributed to C by the OED as the first use of the word, and possibly derived from Maass's use of "intensiv grösser sein" (to be of greater intensity) with regard to objects that become associated with one another (387). Johnson's Dictionary includes "to enforce" as a definition of "intend" (BL [CC], 1:127n. 1).

trarily give vividness or distinctness to any object whatsoever;[9] and from hence we may deduce the uselessness if not the absurdity of certain recent schemes which *promise* an artificial *memory*,[1] but which in reality can only produce a confusion and debasement of the *fancy*. Sound logic, as the habitual subordination of the individual to the species, and of the species to the genus; philosophical knowledge of facts under the relation of cause and effect; a chearful and communicative temper that disposes us to notice the similarities and contrasts of things, that we may be able to illustrate the one by the other; a quiet conscience; a condition free from anxieties; sound health, and above all (as far as relates to passive remembrance) a healthy digestion; *these* are the best, these are the only ARTS OF MEMORY.

CHAPTER VIII

The system of Dualism introduced by Des Cartes—Refined first by
Spinoza and afterwards by Leibnitz into the doctrine of Harmonia
præstabilita—Hylozoism—Materialism—Neither of these systems on
any possible theory of association, supplies or supersedes a theory
of perception, or explains the formation of the associable.

To the best of my knowledge Des Cartes was the first philosopher, who introduced the absolute and essential heterogeneity of the soul as intelligence, and the body as matter.[2] The assumption, and the form of speaking, have remained, though the denial of all other properties to matter but that of extension, on which denial the whole system of dualism is grounded, has been long exploded. For since impenetrability is intelligible only as a mode of resistance; its admission places the essence of *matter* in an act or power,[3] which it possesses in common with *spirit*;[4] and body and spirit are therefore no longer absolutely het-

9. See p. 427, n. 1 herein.
1. For contemporary works that C might have known on the subject of artificial memory, see *BL* (CC), 1:127n. 2.
2. For René Descartes (1596–1650) the mind and body are sharply differentiated, the former being an indivisible substance constituted by thought, the latter a divisible corporeal substance constituted by extension. For C the major flaw in Descartes's system was the "utter disanimation of Body" placed in a relation of "contrariety * * * to Soul" (*CM* [CC], 2:170–71). But C also regarded Descartes as a "truly great man" (*Lects 1818–19* [CC], 2:566).
3. C repeats the passage (var.) beginning with this sentence to the end of the fourth paragraph in Lecture 12 of *Lects 1818–19* (CC), 2:519–23. Descartes defines "extension" as the constituent property of matter in *Principles of Philosophy* (*Philosophical Writings*, 1:210–11). In his "Lettre sur la question, si l'essence du corps consiste dans l'étendue" (Letter on the Question as to whether the Essence of the Body Consists in Extension) (1691), Leibniz argued that, although there can be no matter without extension, matter also has in addition to extension a force of resistance, a "natural inertia," by means of which it opposes movement and penetrability (Erdmann, 1:112–13). For the discussion of matter C also draws on Kant's *Metaphysische Anfangsgründe der Naturwissenschaft* (Metaphysical Foundations of Natural Science), 2nd. ed. (Riga, 1787), where Kant established that matter is constituted by the interaction of two forces: attraction and repulsion. For Kant impenetrability is linked with the force of repulsion, which is its ground. In chapter 2, proposition 3, explication 4, Kant also argues that relative impenetrability rests "on resistance, which increases proportionally to the degree of compression" (40; Ellington, 47). C's disatisfaction with Kant's analysis of the interaction of the two primary forces of matter and the "barren Dualism" of his system is expressed in a number of marginal notes to this work (*CM* [CC], 3:269–303).
4. C may be drawing here on Schelling, who in *Ideen* argued that force (*Kraft*) does not provide the ultimate explanation of the constitution of matter, as the dynamic interaction of opposite forces itself presupposes a third higher principle, which is Mind (*Geist*) or Soul (55–57; Harris and Heath, 37–38).

erogeneous, but *may* without any *absurdity* be supposed to be different modes, or degrees in perfection, of a common substratum.[5] To this possibility, however, it was not the fashion to advert. The soul was a *thinking* substance; and body a *space-filling* substance.[6] Yet the apparent action of each on the other pressed heavy on the philosopher on the one hand; and no less heavily on the other hand pressed the evident truth, that the law of causality holds only between homogeneous things, i. e. things having some common property; and cannot extend from one world into another, its opposite.[7] A close analysis evinced it to be no less absurd, than the question whether a man's affection for his wife, lay North-east, or South-west of the love he bore towards his child?[8] Leibnitz's doctrine of a pre-established harmony,[9] which he certainly borrowed from Spinoza,[1] who had himself taken the hint from Des Cartes's animal machines,[2] was in its *common* interpretation too strange to survive the inventor—too repugnant to our *common sense* (which is not indeed entitled to a judicial voice in the courts of scientific philosophy; but whose whispers still exert a strong secret influence.) Even Wolf the admirer, and illustrious systematizer of the Leibnitzian doctrine, contents himself with defending the possibility of the idea, but does not adopt it as a part of the edifice.[3]

5. A fundamental principle of Schelling's philosophy of the identity of body and spirit, object and subject, in a third principle partaking of both. The term "substratum" is common in philosophic texts, and Schelling uses it in *Abhandlungen* (220–21) with reference to sensory objects conceived as a substratum to all explanations of external events, as does Fichte in *Grundlage* (12; Heath and Lachs, 98), with reference to the self as a substrate of consciousness. For C's variant use of "substrate" in chapter 9, see p. 441, n. 6 herein.
6. As formulated by Descartes in *Principles of Philosophy* (*Philosophical Writings*, 1:195, 210–11, 215–16, 224) and in *Meditiations* (*Philosophical Writings*, 2:16–23, 50–62).
7. A paraphrase from Schelling, *System* (112–13; Heath, 57).
8. For this common illustration, see C's marginal note to John Petvin (*CM* [CC], 4:108 and *Lects 1818–19* [CC], 2:520).
9. Leibniz's view that the universe is constituted by an infinity of monads, each different from and unable to affect any other, presupposes the doctrine of pre-established harmony, which was needed to provide unity to what would otherwise appear to be a series of disparate, noninteractive powers. Leibniz formulated the doctrine in his first, second, and third "Éclaircissement du nouveau systeme de la communication des substances" (Explanation of the New System of Communication between Substances) (1696; Erdmann, 1:131–36) and further developed it in later works, including *Theodicy* (1710), a copy of which C annotated (*CM* [CC], 3:503–06), and *Monadology* (1714).
1. The view that Leibniz borrowed the doctrine of pre-established harmony from Spinoza was put forward by Moses Mendelssohn (1729–1786) in *Philosophische Gespräche* (Philosophical Conversations) (Berlin, 1755), which opened with the question as to whether Leibnitz was the originator of this view. Jacobi cited Mendelssohn's view and established broad connections between Leibniz's and Spinoza's systems (31–38, 361–97). In *Ideen* Schelling discussed Spinoza's and Leibniz's systems as two partially successful attempts to overcome the dualism of mind and matter, and to explain cognition on the basis of the unity of subject and object. Schelling favored Leibniz's solution of locating the source of knowledge inside the activity of the self rather than in an external substance, but he argued that, by resorting to the concept of a pre-established harmony of divine origin, Leibniz in effect contradicted his previous claims, locating the source of knowledge, as did Spinoza, in an external agency (35–41; Harris and Heath, 27–30).
2. Descartes maintained that animals lack consciousness, reason, or the capacity for language and can, therefore, be regarded as machines, nature's own automata (*Discourse on Method*, *Philosophical Writings*, 1:139–41). This controversial view was opposed by Descartes's English correspondent Henry More (1614–1687), the Cambridge Platonist, and led Descartes to restate his position in a more qualified manner (Letter to More of February 5, 1649, *Philosophical Writings*, 3:365–67). C doubted that Descartes degraded animals to mere machines, as Schelling claimed (*CM* [CC], 4:389).
3. The German philosopher Christian Wolff (1679–1754) popularized Leibniz's system but also altered it by introducing a Cartesian distinction between physical and spiritual monads, which entailed the abandonment of the doctrine of pre-established harmony. See also p. 483, n. 7 herein.

The hypothesis of Hylozoism on the other side, is the death of all rational physiology, and indeed of all physical science;[4] for that requires a limitation of terms, and cannot consist with the arbitrary power of multiplying attributes by occult qualities. Besides, it answers no purpose; unless indeed a difficulty can be solved by multiplying it, or that we can acquire a clearer notion of our soul, by being told that we have a million souls, and that every atom of our bodies has a soul of its own. Far more prudent is it to admit the difficulty once for all, and then let it lie at rest. There is a sediment indeed at the bottom of the vessel, but all the water above it is clear and transparent. The Hylozoist only shakes it up, and renders the whole turbid.

But it is not either the nature of man, or the duty of the philosopher[5] to despair concerning any important problem until, as in the squaring of the circle, the impossibility of a solution has been demonstrated. How the *esse* assumed as originally distinct from the *scire*, can ever unite itself with it; how *being* can transform itself into a *knowing*, becomes conceivable on one only condition; namely, if it can be shown that the vis representativa, or the Sentient, is itself a species of being; i.e. either as a property or attribute, or as an hypostasis or self subsistence. The former is indeed the assumption of materialism; a system which could not but be patronized by the philosopher, if only it actually performed what it promises. But how any affection from without can metamorphose itself into perception or will; the materialist has hitherto left, not only as incomprehensible as he found it, but has aggravated it into a comprehensible absurdity. For, grant that an object from without could act upon the conscious *self*, as on a consubstantial object; yet such an affection could only engender something homogeneous with itself.[6] Motion could only propagate motion. Matter has no

4. Hylozoism is an ancient philosophy, according to which matter is considered to possess life and intelligence. C found discussions of hylozoism in Cudworth's *The True Intellectual System of the Universe*, 2 vols., 2nd. ed. (1743), under the heading "Hylozoic Atheism" (1:104–10). Here Cudworth distinguishes hylozoism from that "most notorious form of atheism in particular, that is called *Atomical*," which does not attribute life to matter, and argues that while not every hylozoist can be regarded an atheist, nonetheless, the hylozoist, by deriving everything from a nonsensical nature at once animate and wise, yet without any self-consciousness, "is really an Atheist, though carrying more the semblance and disguise of a Theist, than other Atheists * * *" (1:104, 106–07). On Cudworth, see p. 19, n. 7 herein. Schelling, in *System*, calls hylozoism a nonsensical system in that it either "supposes *matter itself* to be intelligent" or "as merely the mode of intuition of an intelligent being" (447–48; Heath, 216). The source of C's statement that hylozoism is the "death" of "all physical science" is Kant's similar remark in *Metaphysical Foundations* (121; Ellington, 106) that hylozoism is "the death of all natural philosophy" (see *CM* [*CC*], 3:298–99; McFarland, *Coleridge and the Pantheist Tradition*, 159n. 7; 356n. 36). The image of sediment stirred up from the bottom of a vessel filled with transparent water was used by C in a notebook entry in an attack on materialism (*CN*, 1:920).
5. From this paragraph through the end of the chapter, C draws extensively on Schelling's discussion (mostly in *System* and *Abhandlungen*) concerning the failure of materialism to account for the process of cognition, specifically the correspondence between our representations of reality and reality itself. Materialism, by assuming the independent existence of objects as the cause of our representations, ends up separating matter from spirit and making the process of cognition unintelligible.
6. The passage from the second sentence of this paragraph to here is an approximate translation from Schelling, *System* (112–13; Heath, 57), with several additions and modifications. C adds the specification "either as a property or attribute, or as an hypostasis or self subsistence," and leaves out Schelling's claim that materialism, "when it becomes intelligible, no longer differs, in fact, from transcendental idealism." (C's less precise version is that

Inward.[7] We remove one surface, but to meet with another. We can but divide a particle into particles; and each atom comprehends in itself the properties of the material universe. Let any reflecting mind make the experiment of explaining to itself the evidence of our sensuous intuitions, from the hypothesis that in any given perception there is a something which has been communicated to it by an impact or an impression ab extra.[8] In the first place, by the impact on the percipient or ens representans not the object itself, but only its action or effect, will pass into the same.[9] Not the iron tongue, but its vibrations, pass into the metal of the bell. Now in our immediate perception, it is not the mere power or act of the object, but the object itself, which is immediately present.[1] We might indeed attempt to explain this result by a chain of *deductions* and *conclusions*; but that, first, the very faculty of deducing and concluding would equally demand an explanation; and secondly, that there exists in fact no such intermediation by logical notions, such as those of cause and effect. It is the object itself, not the product of a syllogism, which is present to our consciousness. Or would we explain this supervention of the object to the sensation, by a productive faculty set in motion by an impulse; still the transition, into the percipient, of the object itself, from which the impulse proceeded, assumes a power that can permeate and wholly possess the soul,

> And like a God by spiritual art,
> Be all in all, and all in every part.
>   Cowley.[2]

And how came the *percepient* here? And what is become of the wonder-promising MATTER, that was to perform all these marvels by force of mere figure, weight, and motion?[3] The most consistent proceeding of the dogmatic materialist is to fall back into the common rank of *soul-and-bodyists*; to affect the mysterious, and declare the whole process a revelation *given*, and not to be *understood*, which it would be prophane to examine too closely. Datur non intelligitur.[4] But a revelation unconfirmed by miracles,

---

materialism has turned into a "comprehensible absurdity" the incomprehensible problem of how the action of an external object on the self can become perception or will; see also p. 437, n. 7 herein.) C also reverses the order of statements in Schelling's text, which starts with the claim that the impact of an external object on the self "could only engender something homogenous."

7. For this, the next sentence, and part of the third up to "a particle into particles," C draws on Schelling, *Abhandlungen* (240). C again reverses the order of Schelling's arguments. See also *Ideen* (16–17, 22; Harris and Heath, 17, 20), where Schelling contests the view that matter has an inside, arguing that one can divide it endlessly in "infinitely many parts" without coming "farther than to the surfaces of bodies."
8. "From without."
9. Translated from Schelling, *System* (149; Heath, 73). *Ens representans*: being that forms representations of objects, or the percipient.
1. Translated from Schelling, *System* (149; Heath, 73). With the next sentence, up to the quotation from Cowley, C provides a condensed approximate translation of a passage from *System* (149–50; Heath, 73–74).
2. A modified version of "All-over Love," lines 9–10: "But like a *God* by pow'rful Art, / 'Twas *all* in *all*, and *all* in *every part*" (*The Mistress, or Several Copies of Love-Verses* in *Works*, 2 parts in 1 vol., 7th ed. [1681], 1:25). On Cowley, see p. 390, n. 7 herein.
3. The following sentence up to *Datur non intelligitur* is translated and adapted from Schelling, *System* (150; Heath, 74).
4. "It is given, not understood."

and a faith not commanded by the conscience, a philosopher may venture to pass by, without suspecting himself of any irreligious tendency.

Thus as materialism has been generally taught, it is utterly unintelligible,[5] and owes all its proselytes to the propensity so common among men, to mistake distinct images for clear conceptions;[6] and vice versa, to reject as inconceivable whatever from its own nature is unimaginable. But as soon as it becomes intelligible, it ceases to be materialism.[7] In order to explain *thinking*, as a material phænomenon, it is necessary to refine matter into a mere modification of intelligence, with the two-fold function of *appearing* and *perceiving*. Even so did Priestley in his controversy with Price![8] He stript matter of all its material properties; substituted spiritual powers; and when we expected to find a body, behold! we had nothing but its ghost! the *apparition* of a defunct substance!

I shall not dilate further on this subject; because it will (if God grant health and permission) be treated of at large and systematically in a work, which I have many years been preparing, on the PRODUCTIVE LOGOS human and divine; with, and as the introduction to, a full commentary on the Gospel of St. John.[9] To make myself intelligible as far as my present subject requires, it will be sufficient briefly to observe—1. That all association demands and presupposes the existence of the thoughts and images to be associated.—2. The hypothesis of an external world exactly correspondent to those images or modifications of our own being, which alone (according to this system) we actually behold, is as thorough idealism as Berkeley's, inasmuch as it equally (perhaps, in a more perfect degree) removes all reality and immediate-

5. Translated from Schelling, *System* (113; Heath, 57). See p. 435, n. 6 herein, where the same passage from Schelling is used.
6. On the confusion between clear images and distinct conceptions, see C's letter to Wordsworth of May 30, 1815, in which he attributes this error to the "philosophy of mechanism" (*CL*, 4:575).
7. This and the next sentence are a loose translation from Schelling, *System* (113; Heath, 57). C modifies Schelling's statement that materialism "when it becomes intelligible, no longer differs, in fact from transcendental idealism" to "it ceases to be materialism" (see p. 435, n. 6 herein) and also changes Schelling's "thought and matter" to "*perceiving* and *appearing*." Schelling's statement that "To explain thinking as a material phenomenon is possible only by turning matter into a phantom, a mere modification of intelligence" is captured by C in his reference to Priestley's controversy with Richard Price (1723–1791) in the next sentence.
8. The controversy appeared in *A Free Discussion of the Doctrines of Materialism, and Philosophical Necessity, in a Correspondence between Dr. Price and Dr. Priestley* (1778). C probably refers to the first part of this work ("Remarks Concerning the Penetrability of Matter," 3–47, esp. 10–25), in which Price argued that by departing from the Newtonic conception of matter as constituted by "solid particles or atoms" occupying space, and by reducing matter to the powers of attraction and repulsion, Priestley turned matter into a "*non-entity*," a mere "*nothing*" (13–14), and also have in mind Priestley's replies to Price that "the term *thing* or *substance*, signifies nothing more than that to which properties are ascribed, and is itself absolutely unknown, and incapable of suggesting any idea whatever." Stripped of all properties, such as length or breadth, the substance of a mass of gold, for example, vanishes and there is "nothing left to contemplate" (17). Schelling's point that materialists turn matter into a "phantom, a mere modification of intelligence" resonates in these claims made by Price and Priestley.
9. A reference to C's never-completed *Logosophia*, which was to include five or six treatises on "the Logos, or communicative Intelligence, Natural, Human and Divine" and provide a comprehensive history of philosophy from Pythagoras to pantheist, mystical, and contemporary dynamic philosophy. In addition to a treatise on logic and on "the Causes & Consequences of modern Unitarianism," C also projected a separate treatise, consisting of a "full Commentary on the Gospel of St John." See *CL*, 3:533–34, 4:589–90; *CN*, 3:4300 and n.; and p. 471, n. 5 herein.

ness of perception, and places us in a dream-world of phantoms and spectres, the inexplicable swarm and equivocal generation of motions in our own brains.[1]—3. That this hypothesis neither involves the explanation, nor precludes the necessity, of a mechanism and co-adequate forces in the percepient, which at the more than magic touch of the impulse from without is to create anew for itself the correspondent object. The formation of a copy is not solved by the mere pre-existence of an original;[2] the copyist of Raphael's Transfiguration must repeat more or less perfectly the process of Raphael.[3] It would be easy to explain a thought from the image on the retina, and that from the geometry of light, if this very light did not present the very same difficulty.[4] We might as rationally chant the Brahmin creed of the tortoise that supported the bear, that supported the elephant, that supported the world, to the tune of "This is the house that Jack built."[5] The *sic Deo placitum est*[6] we all admit as the sufficient cause, and the divine goodness as the sufficient reason; but an answer to the whence? and why? is no answer to the how? which alone is the physiologist's concern. It is a mere sophisma pigrum,[7] and (as Bacon hath said) the arrogance of pusillanimity,[8] which lifts up the idol of a mortal's fancy and commands us to fall down and worship it, as a work of divine wisdom, an ancile or palladium fallen from heaven.[9] By the very same argument the supporters of the Ptolemaic system might have rebuffed the Newtonian, and pointing to the sky with self-complacent*

* "And Coxcombs vanquish Berkeley with a grin." *Pope.*[1]

1. In *Abhandlungen* (217) Schelling points out that the idealist lives in a world "surrounded on all sides by phantoms"; but the context in which he makes this statement is a critique of Kant's brand of idealism, not Berkeley's. Schelling argues that Kant and his followers inhabit a world of mere appearances because they separate objects from their representations, and concepts from intuitions. For them the immediacy of intuition in which subject and object coalesce does not exist, and the world changes into a phantomatic appearance before their very eyes. See p. 471, n. 1 herein.
2. C uses a passage from Schelling, *Abhandlungen* (218 and n.), in which Schelling, after his critique of Kant's idealism, argues that, since representations are separated from reality, they cannot be regarded as "copies of things in themselves." In a footnote Schelling points out that "Kant denied that representations are copies of things in themselves" even as he "ascribed to representations reality." For Schelling this meant that in fact there can be no things in themselves and "no *original*" outside of our representations (218).
3. A painting by Raphael (1483–1520), which had been commissioned by Giulio de' Medici (1478–1534) in 1517.
4. Schelling, *Abhandlungen* (254n.) uses the same illustration to show the inadequacy of systems that try to explain how representations arise in consciousness through the action of external objects: "We see only because the light strikes our eyes, etc.—But what then is light itself? Again an object!"
5. The Hindu legend of the tortoise supporting the world was a common reference in philosophic texts. Locke in *Essay* (175) and Leibniz in *New Essays* (Erdmann, 1:272; Remnant 218) used it as an illustration of the difficulties of defining the concept of substance.
6. "Thus it is pleasing to God."
7. "Slothful sophism." In *Logic* (CC), 119 C translates this phrase as "sophistry of indolence."
8. Bacon, *Novum Organum*, book 1, aphorism 88, in *Works* (1740), 1:295: "And what is worst of all, this very littleness of spirit [*pusillanimitas*] comes with a certain air of arrogance and superiority" (*BL* [CC], 1:138n. 4). C copied this sentence in *CN*, 1:913 and used it in chapter 12 (*BL* [CC] 1:293n. 1).
9. The ancile (shield) and the palladium (statue of Pallas Athena) were symbols of the preservation of Rome.
1. C mistakenly attributes to Pope this line from John Brown, *An Essay on Satire: Occasioned by the Death of Mr. Pope* (1745), possibly because his source might have been the version of the poem published by Bishop Warburton in volume 3 of Pope's *Works*, 9 vols. (1751), where the poem was listed before Pope's *Essay on Man*: "Truth's sacred Fort th'exploded laugh shall win; / And Coxcombs vanquish Berkley by a grin" (xix, lines 223–24).

grin have appealed to *common sense*, whether the sun did not move and the earth stand still.[2]

FROM CHAPTER IX

Is philosophy possible as a science, and what are its conditions?[3]—*Giordano Bruno—Literary aristocracy, or the existence of a tacit compact among the learned as a privileged order—The author's obligations to the Mystics;—to Emanuel Kant—The difference between the letter and the spirit of Kant's writings,*[4] *and a vindication of prudence in the teaching of philosophy—Fichte's attempt to complete the critical system—Its partial success and ultimate failure—Obligations to Schelling; and among English writers to Saumarez.*

After I had successively studied in the schools of Locke, Berkeley, Leibnitz, and Hartley,[5] and could find in neither of them an abiding place for my reason, I began to ask myself; is a system of philosophy, as different from mere history and historic classification possible?[6] If possible, what are its necessary conditions? I was for a while disposed to answer the first question in the negative, and to admit that the sole practicable employment for the human mind was to observe, to collect, and to classify. But I soon felt, that human nature itself fought up against this wilful resignation of intellect; and as soon did I find, that the scheme taken with all its consequences and cleared of all inconsis-

2. A related point is made by Kant, *Pure Reason* (Bxxii), that the Newtonian force of attraction, which Copernicus formulated as a hypothesis from the laws of the motions of planets, "would have remained forever undiscovered if Copernicus had not ventured, in a manner contradictory to the senses yet true, to seek for the observed movements not in the objects of the heavens but in the observer."

3. C's question echoes the problems Kant set out to resolve in *Prolegomena*, e.g., "1. How is pure mathematics possible? 2. How is pure natural science possible? 3. How is metaphysics in general possible? 4. How is metaphysics as science possible?" (48; Hatfield, 31). See also Kant, *Pure Reason* (B20–23).

4. The distinction between "letter" and "spirit" (Romans 7.6) was current in debates about interpretations of the Bible and pervades the writings of German transcendentalists. See, e.g., Fichte, *Ueber Geist und Buchstab in der Philosophie* * * * (Concerning the Difference between the Spirit and the Letter within Philosophy * * *) (*Early Philosophical Writings*, 185–215). Both Schiller (in *On the Aesthetic Education of Man*, ed. and trans. Elisabeth M. Wilkinson and L. A. Willoughby [Oxford, 1967], 86n. 2) and Schelling (in *Abhandlungen*, 275–76) invoke this distinction to defend Kant's system against possible misrepresentations, but Kant himself expressed a preference for reading a text, his own work included, according to its letter. See p. 446, n. 4 herein.

5. For C on Hartley, see chapter 5. C read Berkeley attentively as early as 1796, when he borrowed the second volume of his *Works* (1784) from the Bristol Library (*Borrowings*, 122). His early infatuation with Berkeley led him to name his second son after the philosopher. Although C viewed Berkeley as one of the "only three *great* Metaphysicians which this Country *has* produced" (*CL*, 2:703), his developing interest in Kant, Schelling, and other German philosophers, who often pitted their brand of transcendental idealism against Berkeley's subjective idealism, dictated a turn away from Berkeley. See McFarland, *Coleridge and the Pantheist Tradition*, 158–59. Berkeley continued, however, to supply C with philosophical concepts such as "outness" (see p. 594, n. 5 herein) and citations for his later works. On C's reaction to Berkeley's subjective idealism, see *Lects 1818–19* (CC), 2:557–58; *CM* (CC), 4:447–48; and p. 428, n. 1 herein. For a discussion of Berkeley in relation to Locke and Descartes, see his philosophical letters of February 1801 (*CL*, 2:677–703) and CN, 3:3605 and n.; and for C's sense that Berkeley's, Locke's, and Leibniz's systems are inconsistent, see CN, 3:3757 and n. On C's view of Leibniz, see p. 431, n. 5 herein; p. 433, n. 3 herein; p. 434, nn. 9–1 herein; and *Lects 1818–19* (CC), 2:574–77.

6. In *Prolegomena* (3; Hatfield, 5) Kant notes that his work is not written for those "for whom the history of philosophy (ancient as well as modern) is itself their philosophy."

tencies was not less impracticable, than contra-natural. Assume in its full extent the position, *nihil in intellectu quod non prius in sensu*, without Leibnitz's qualifying *præter ipsum intellectum*,[7] and in the same sense, in which it was understood by Hartley and Condilliac:[8] and what Hume had demonstratively deduced from this concession concerning cause and effect,[9] will apply with equal and crushing force to all the* other eleven categorical forms, and the logical functions corresponding to them. How can we make bricks without straw? Or build without cement? We learn all things indeed by *occasion* of experience; but the very facts so learnt force us inward on the antecedents, that must be pre-supposed in order to render experience itself possible.[2] The first book of Locke's Essays (if the supposed error, which it labours to subvert,[3] be not a mere thing of straw, an absurdity which, no man ever did, or indeed ever could believe) is formed on a Σόφισμα Ετεροζητη–σέως, and involves the old mistake of *cum hoc: ergo, propter hoc.*[4]

The term, Philosophy, defines itself as an affectionate seeking after the truth; but Truth is the correlative of Being.[5] This again is no way

---

* Videlicet; quantity, quality, relation, and mode, each consisting of three subdivisions. Vide Kritik der reinen Vernunft, p. 95, and 106. See too the judicious remarks in Locke and Hume.[1]

---

7. Leibniz, in *New Essays*, book 2, chapter 1, makes this statement ("*Nihil est in intellectu, quod non fuerit in sensu, excipe: nisi ipse intellectus*" [There is nothing in the mind that was not before in the senses, except the mind itself]) in the context of a critique of Locke's theory of the mind as originally a *tabula rasa* (Erdmann, 223; Remnant, 111). For Locke's view that "there appear not to be any Ideas in the Mind, before the Senses have conveyed any in," see Locke, *Essay* (117). Cf. *CL*, 2:680–81; *Lects 1818–19* (CC), 2:574–75.
8. For Hartley's Lockean view that all ideas originate from sense impressions, see p. 423, n. 4 herein and p. 424, n. 4 herein. For C on Condillac, a name he typically misspells as "Condilliac," see p. 431, n. 2 herein.
9. C refers to Hume's acceptance of the empirical premises of Locke on the basis of which he argued that the presumed notion of necessary causality was nothing but a delusion brought about by the repeated experience of a given sequence of phenomena (see p. 430, n. 4 herein). Kant in *Prolegomena* (7–18; Hatfield, 7–12) discusses Locke and Leibniz and devotes a long section to Hume. There he praises Hume as a great thinker, largely misunderstood by his followers, whose demonstration that reason was deluded in thinking that it could prove the existence of causality, though ultimately misguided, awakened Kant from "his dogmatic slumber," and gave new direction to his philosophical investigations. In *Pure Reason* (B19–20) Kant has a less appreciative take on Hume.
1. In *Critik der reinen Vernunft*, 2nd ed. (1787), Kant presents a table with the four logical categories of the understanding (quantity, quality, relation, and modality), each with three subdivisions that represent "the pure concepts of synthesis that the understanding contains within itself *a priori*" (*Pure Reason* [A70/B95, B106]). Cf. also *Prolegomena* (86; Hatfield, 56–57). C probably refers to the "judicious remarks" not in but on Locke and Hume by Kant (*Pure Reason* [B127–28]). There Kant exposed Locke's error of first deriving the concepts of the understanding from experience and then attempting to obtain by this means knowledge that exceeds the limits of experience, as well as Hume's similar empirical bias, which led him to reject the possibility of determining causality. Kant saw his project as negotiating between the two extremes of an uncritical faith in the capabilities of reason, which, as in Locke, led to "enthusiasm" (*Schwärmerai*), and of a complete scepticism regarding reason's ability to cast aside the "deceptions of our faculty of cognition."
2. A reference to Kant's notion of *a priori* concepts of the understanding and forms of sensible intuition that alone make experience possible and are, therefore, independent of sense objects. See Kant, *Pure Reason* (esp. Bxvi–xxvii).
3. I.e., book 1 of Locke, *Essay* (43–103), in which he denied the existence of innate ideas.
4. "The sophism of looking for something else," which involves the erroneous reasoning "with this, therefore because of this." Another instance of confusing the condition for the cause of a given phenomenon (see p. 431 herein). As indicated in *BL* (1847), 1:144n. 3, C's reflection and the term "sophisma heterozeteseos" are indebted to Maass (366), who charged Locke with this fallacy of reasoning.
5. For Aquinas's view that "truth is exactly the same as being," see *BL* (CC), 1:142n. 4. For the coincidence of the principles of being and knowledge, C was indebted to Schelling, *Vom Ich* (1–3) and *System* (48: Heath, 26), which he also used in chapter 12 (p. 472, n. 9 herein).

conceivable, but by assuming as a postulate, that both are ab initio, identical and co-inherent; that intelligence and being are reciprocally each others Substrate.[6] I presumed that this was a possible conception (*i.e.* that it involved no logical inconsonance) from the length of time during which the scholastic definition of the *Supreme Being*, as actus purissimus sine ullâ potentialitate,[7] was received in the schools of Theology, both by the Pontifician and the Reformed divines. The early study of Plato and Plotinus, with the commentaries and the THEOLOGIA PLATONICA, of the illustrious Florentine;[8] of Proclus,[9] and Gemistius Pletho;[1] and at a later period of the "De Immenso et Innumerabili," and the *"De la causa, principio et uno,"* of the philosopher of Nola, who could boast of a Sir Philip Sidney, and Fulke Greville among his patrons, and whom the idolaters of Rome burnt as an athe-

---

See also Schelling, *Aphorismen zur Einleitung in die Naturphilosophie* (Aphorisms concerning an Introduction to Natural Philosophy) in *Jahrbücher*, 1:21 (aphorism no. 61).

6. C was the first to use "substrate" as a derivative of "substratum" (OED). In *Pure Reason* (A 575–76 / B603–04) Kant shows that reason employs as an ideal "a transcendental substratum, which contains as it were the entire storehouse of material from which all possible predicates of things can be taken" and is none other than the idea of God. Kant goes on to demonstrate that while the existence of God cannot be proven by merely speculative reason, it cannot be denied either: "Thus the highest being remains for the merely speculative use of reason a mere but nevertheless *faultless ideal*, a concept which concludes and crowns the whole of human cognition, whose objective reality cannot of course be proven on this path, but also cannot be refuted * * *" (A641 / B669). It is precisely such a window (as well as Kant's claim that in moral philosophy the existence of God must be assumed as a postulate of practical reason; see p. 444, n. 3 herein) that allowed C to build a bridge between transcendental philosophy and Christian theism, though, according to René Wellek, at the expense of distorting the most radical implications of German philosophy (*Immanuel Kant in England 1793–1838*, esp. 114–16, 123–24). For C's accurate understanding of this section of *Pure Reason*, namely that while one cannot "theoretically *demonstrate* the existence of God * * * not a word of *Sense* ever was or ever can be brought against it," see his marginal note to Schelling, PS 122 (CM [CC], 4:409). See also his later statement in 1820 that in Kant "you have a firm faith in God, the responsible Will of Man, and Immortality—& Kant will demonstrate to you, that this Faith is acquiesced in, indeed, nay, confirmed by the Reason & Understanding, but grounded on Postulates authorized & substantiated solely by the *Moral* Being" (CL, 5:14). Coleridge thought that Kant's *Critique of Pure Reason*, Bacon's *Novum Organum*, and Spinoza's *Ethics* constituted "the three greatest Works since the introduct[ion] of Christianity" (CM [CC], 4:403).
7. "Purest act without any potentiality." C often referred to this scholastic definition of God of Aristotelian provenance (Aristotle, *Metaphysics*, books 12 and 13), for which see, e.g., CL, 2:1195 and his marginalia to Baxter (CM [CC], 1:232).
8. Marsilio Ficino (1433–1499), philosopher and theologian of the Italian Renaissance and president of the Platonic Academy in Florence, was the author of influential Latin translations of and extensive commentaries on Plato and Plotinus. C admired greatly Ficino's Latin translation of Plato, predicting a time when his name would "once more be pronounced with honor and open reverence" (CN, 3:3861). He also owned and annotated Ficino's important work *Platonica theologica de imortalitate animorum* (Platonic Theology on the Immortality of Souls) (1525), for which see CM (CC), 2:647–48.
9. Proclus (c. 412–485), distinguished Neoplatonist who succeeded Syrianus (5th century) as head of the Platonic Academy in Athens, and author of commentaries on Plato's dialogues and Euclid's *Elements* (on C's early interest in Proclus, see CN, 1:1727, 1728 and nn. and Appendix B). C's "hunt for Proclus" (CN, 3:3276) accelerated between 1808 and 1810. See his marginalia to Thomas Taylor's translation of *The Philosophical and Mathematical Commentaries of Proclus * * * on the First Book of Euclid's Elements * * *,* 2 vols. (1792) (CM [CC], 4:154–60). C thought that Proclus' *Platonic Theology* and *Elements of Theology* were crucial for the education of the clergy (CN, 3:3934); and in a letter to Lady Beaumont on January 21, 1810, he expressed his great admiration for Proclus' *Platonic Theology* as well as his reservations concerning Taylor's translation of it (CL, 3:279). On Proclus as "a complete pantheist," see McFarland, *Coleridge and the Pantheist Tradition*, 356–57, n. 37.
1. Georgius Gemistus Pletho (c. 1355–1452), influential commentator on Plato who settled in Mistra, Greece, credited with introducing Plato to the Western world. In Florence, where his lectures on Plato led to the establishment of the Platonic Academy by Cosimo de' Medici (1389–1464), he was known as "the second Plato."

ist in the year 1660;[2] had all contributed to prepare my mind for the reception and welcoming of the Cogito quia sum, et sum quia Cogito;[3] a philosophy of seeming hardihood, but certainly the most ancient, and therefore presumptively the most natural.

Why need I be afraid? Say rather how dare I be ashamed of the Teutonic theosophist, Jacob Behmen? Many indeed, and gross were his delusions; and such as furnish frequent and ample occasion for the triumph of the learned over the poor ignorant *shoemaker*, who had dared think for himself.[4] But while we remember that these delusions were such, as might be anticipated from his utter want of all intellectual discipline, and from his ignorance of rational psychology, let it not be forgotten that the latter defect he had in common with the most learned theologians of his age. Neither with books, nor with booklearned men was he conversant. A meek and shy quietist, his intellectual powers were never stimulated into fev'rous energy by crowds of proselytes, or by the ambition of proselyting. JACOB BEHMEN was an enthusiast, in the strictest sense, as not merely distinguished, but as contra-distinguished, from a fanatic.[5] While I in part translate the following observations from a contemporary writer of the Continent, let me be permitted to premise, that I might have transcribed the substance from memoranda of my own, which were written many years before his pamphlet was given to the world; and that I prefer another's words to my own, partly as a tribute due to priority of publication; but still more from the pleasure of sympathy in a case where *coincidence* only was possible.[6]

2. Giordano Bruno (c. 1548–1600), Italian philosopher and teacher of mnemonic techniques who opposed Aristotelianism and believed that God, as an infinite being, must have created an infinite universe with an infinite number of inhabited worlds. He was ordained as a Domenican priest, but his unorthodox views forced him into exile. He was eventually arrested, tried, and burnt at the stake by the Inquisition. Stimulated by the treatment of Bruno in Jacobi (261–306) and in Schelling's *Bruno* (1802), C made a concerted effort to find and read Bruno's scarce works (see CN, 1:927–29 and nn.; McFarland, *Coleridge and the Pantheist Tradition*, 245–51, 381–82), and he praised Bruno highly in his philosophical lecture of March 8, 1819 (*Lects 1818–19* [CC], 2:477–81).

3. Descartes's famous definition *cogito, ergo sum* (I think, therefore I am), formulated in *Principles of Philosophy* (*Philosophical Writings*, 1:194–96), drew forth ample discussion and criticisms among subsequent philosophers. C joined Kant, Fichte, and Schelling, among others, in identifying the pitfalls of this definition. See Kant, *Pure Reason* (B422–23); Fichte, *Grundlage* (15; Heath and Lachs, 100–01); Schelling, *System* (17; Heath, 25–26); and p. 476 herein.

4. Jacob Böhme (1575–1624), the learned shoemaker of Görlitz and mystical German philosopher. His main work, *Aurora, oder die Morgenröte im Aufgang* (Aurora, or the Rising of Dawn) (1612), which derived the evolution of all powers of nature and of the Trinity from an original ground, the divine Abyss (*Ungrund*), engaged much of C's thinking on natural philosophy and theology. C, who may have read *Aurora* while still in school, wrote copious marginalia on it and several other works by Böhme in the four-volume edition of William Law, which was given to him by Thomas De Quincey (see *CM* [CC], 1:553–696). For C's plan to write on Böhme, see CN, 1:174, 1646, and for his debt to Böhme, see McFarland, *Coleridge and the Pantheist Tradition*, 249–51, 325–32. C repeats the passage from "Why need I be afraid" to "fanatic" in Lecture 11 of *Lects 1818–19* (CC), 2:481.

5. On the distinction between "enthusiasm" and "fanaticism," see chapter 2 (*BL* [CC], 1:30–31).

6. C refers to Schelling, *Darlegung* (1806), from which he translates the next paragraph. Later in the chapter C points out the improperly acknowledged "coincidence of SCHELLING's system with certain general ideas of Behmen" compared to his own deeply felt debt and gratitude to Böhme (see p. 447 herein). In the following section, omitted here, C points out that throughout history learned men have not felt free to practice speculative science and philosophy outside certain authorized boundaries, and the task of original investigation was taken up by powerfully imaginative but uneducated men like Böhme, who were exposed to scorn and persecution.

* * *

The feeling of gratitude, which I cherish towards these men, has caused me to digress further than I had foreseen or proposed; but to have passed them over in an historical sketch of my literary life and opinions, would have seemed to me like the denial of a debt, the concealment of a boon. For the writings of these mystics acted in no slight degree to prevent my mind from being imprisoned within the outline of any single dogmatic system. They contributed to keep alive the *heart* in the *head*; gave me an indistinct, yet stirring and working presentment, that all the products of the mere *reflective* faculty partook of DEATH, and were as the rattling twigs and sprays in winter, into which a sap was yet to be propelled, from some root to which I had not penetrated, if they were to afford my soul either food or shelter.[7] If they were too often a moving cloud of smoke to me by day, yet they were always a pillar of fire throughout the night,[8] during my wanderings through the wilderness of doubt, and enabled me to skirt, without crossing, the sandy deserts of utter unbelief. That the system is capable of being converted into an irreligious PANTHEISM, I well know. The ETHICS of SPINOZA, may, or may not, be an instance.[9] But at no time could I believe, that *in itself* and *essentially* it is incompatible with religion, natural, or revealed: and now I am most thoroughly persuaded of the contrary. The writings of the illustrious sage of Königsberg, the founder of the Critical Philosophy, more than any other work, at once invigorated and disciplined my understanding. The originality, the depth, and the compression of the thoughts; the novelty and subtlety, yet solidity and importance, of the distinctions; the adamantine chain of the logic; and I will venture to add (paradox as it will appear to those who have taken their notion of IMMANUEL KANT, from Reviewers and Frenchmen) the *clearness* and *evidence*, of the "CRITIQUE OF THE PURE REASON;" of the JUDGMENT; of the "METAPHISICAL ELEMENTS OF NATURAL PHILOSOPHY," and of his "RELIGION WITHIN THE BOUNDS OF PURE REASON," took possession of me as with a giant's hand.[1] After fifteen years

7. On the importance of the heart as a counterbalance to metaphysics, see p. 430, n. 9 herein. On the reconciliation of the head with the heart in Bowles, see p. 391, n. 6 herein. The danger of engaging only the reflective faculty is emphasized by Schelling in a passage from *Ideen*, which is echoed by C here and appears to have affinities as well with stanza 4 of "Dejection: An Ode": "*Mere* reflection, therefore, is a spiritual sickness in mankind, the more so where it imposes itself in domination over the whole of man, and kills at the root what in germ is his highest being, his spiritual life, which issues only from Identity" (Harris and Heath, 11).
8. Cf. Exodus 13.21.
9. C was critical of Spinoza's pantheistic view of substance and his lack of recognition that God has "the Ground of his own Existence within himself, and the originating Principle of all dependent Existence in his Will and World" (*CL*, 4:548n.; letter of March 10, 1815), but thought that his *Ethics* (1677, published posthumously) "would never, could never, have brought on him the charge of *atheism*," an allegation made, for example, by Jacobi (223), which C rejected: "I do not believe, that Spinoza would have acknowledged the system attributed to him by Jacobi. * * * Spinoza does not in my opinion, deny the Intelligence of God other than as the word implies Choice and Deliberation—or in short, *passivity* in any sense. His God is severely actus purrissimus—Esse absolutum sine ullâ *Potentialitate* [purest act—absolute being without any *Potentiality*]" (*CM* [CC], 3:78–79). For C on Spinoza, see p. 579 and n. 4 herein; p. 603, n. 8 herein; p. 607, n. 3 herein.
1. Kant, *Pure Reason* 2nd ed. (1787; C read the 1799 reprint of the 2nd edition); Kant, *Judgment* (1790); Kant, *Metaphysical Foundations of Natural Science* (1786; C had the 1787 edition); Kant, *Religion within the Bounds of Mere Reason* (1793; C had the 1794 edition). For C's annotations of these works, see *CM* (CC), 3:241–51, 269–313.

familiarity with them, I still read these and all his other productions with undiminished delight and increasing admiration. The few passages that remained obscure to me, after due efforts of thought, (as the chapter on *original apperception*,)[2] and the apparent contradictions which occur, I soon found were hints and insinuations referring to ideas, which KANT either did not think it prudent to avow, or which he considered as consistently *left behind* in a pure analysis, not of human nature in toto, but of the speculative intellect alone. Here therefore he was constrained to commence at the point of *reflection*, or natural consciousness: while in his *moral* system he was permitted to assume a higher ground (the autonomy of the will) as a POSTULATE[3] deducible from the unconditional command, or (in the technical language of his school) the categorical imperative, of the conscience.[4] He had been in imminent danger of persecution during the reign of the late king of Prussia, that strange compound of lawless debauchery, and priest-ridden superstition:[5] and it is probable that he had little inclination, in his old age, to act over again the fortunes, and hair-breadth escapes of Wolf.[6] The expulsion of the first among Kant's disciples, who attempted to complete his system, from the university of Jena, with the confiscation and prohibition of the obnoxious work by the joint efforts of the courts of Saxony and Hanover, supplied experimental proof, that the venerable old man's caution was not groundless.[7] In spite therefore of his own declarations, I could never believe, it was possible for him to have meant no more by his *Noumenon*, or THING IN ITSELF, than his mere words ex-

2. I.e., the chapter in which Kant grounds the unity of all experience in the "I am" (*Ich bin*), the pure "*original* apperception" or "transcendental unity of self-consciousness," which involves the synthesis of the understanding and the imagination (*Pure Reason*, B132–36). In his marginalia to Kant C singled out pages 129–69 (of which section 16 on "apperception" is a part) as "the most difficult and obscure passages of this Critique" (*CM* [*CC*], 3:242).
3. "Postulate" is a term that in Kant designates a necessary hypothesis that determines the subjective possibility and necessity of moral laws. Kant showed that in moral philosophy (the domain of practical reason), the existence of God, or supersensible ideas such as freedom or immortality of the soul (which are not objects of theoretical knowledge), must be assumed as postulates of moral laws (*Pure Reason*, A633–34/B661–62).
4. For Kant on the "categorical imperative" (the principle according to which one should act in such a way that one's action "should become a univeral law"), see *Groundwork* (esp. 14–16, 24–31, 39–41, 47) and C's marginalia to this work in *CM* (*CC*), 3:252–55. For Kant the categorical imperative is intrinsically connected with the autonomy of the will. The will remains subject to the moral law without giving up its autonomy because it is the author of the law, establishing for itself the very law it must obey.
5. Kant ran the risk of persecution after the publication of the first part of his *Religion within the Bounds of Mere Reason*, which was published in *Berlinische Monatsschrift* in 1792. Kant published the rest in Köningsberg in 1793 against his government's injuction not to do so, after which he was forced to promise not to write anything on a religious subject, a promise he kept until the death of Frederick William II (1744–1797). For C's indictment of the polygamous and notoriously licentious King of Prussia for his actions during the French Revolution, see *A Moral and Political Lecture* (p. 242, n. 8 herein) and *Conciones ad Populum* (p. 251, n. 5 herein).
6. Christian Wolff's troubles with German pietists at Halle due to his rationalistic views on religion led to his expulsion by order of King Frederick William I (1688–1740) from Halle (in 1723), where he was a professor of mathematics and philosophy. Wolff went to Marburg and eventually returned triumphantly to Halle in 1740 at the invitation of Frederick II the Great (1712–1786). Wolff's expulsion served his interests in the long run, attracting attention to his works, a point made in the "Life of Baron Wolfius," abstracted from Gottsched of Leipsic, which precedes the English translation of Wolff's *Logic* (1770), xx–xxi.
7. Fichte held a professorship in philosophy in Jena in 1794 but was expelled in 1798 on charges of atheism.

press;[8] or that in his own conception he confined the whole *plastic* power to the forms of the intellect, leaving for the external cause, for the *materiale* of our sensations, a matter without form, which is doubtless inconceivable. I entertained doubts likewise, whether in his own mind, he even laid *all* the stress, which he appears to do on the moral postulates.[9]

An IDEA, in the *highest* sense of that word, cannot be conveyed but by a *symbol*; and, except in geometry, all symbols of necessity involve an apparent contradiction.[1] Φώνησε Συνέτοισεν:[2] and for those who could not pierce through this symbolic husk, his writings were not intended. Questions which can not be fully answered without exposing the respondent to personal danger, are not entitled to a fair answer; and yet to say this openly, would in many cases furnish the very advantage, which the adversary is insidiously seeking after. Veracity does not consist in *saying*, but in the intention of *communicating* truth;[3] and the philosopher who can not utter the whole truth without conveying falsehood, and at the same time, perhaps, exciting the most malignant passions, is

8. One of the fundamental premises of Kant's system is that "objects in themselves are not known to us at all and what we call outer objects are nothing other than mere representations of our sensibility" (*Pure Reason* [B45]). On the related distinction between "noumenon" (defined by Kant as "a thing so far as it is *not an object of sensible intuition*") and phenomenon, see *Pure Reason* (A235–60/B294–15). C, along with Fichte and Schelling, questioned this distinction: "Why then make the opposition between Phænomena and Things in themselves?" (*CM* [CC], 3:249). He also draws on Schelling's argument in *Abhandlungen* (275–76) that there is a deeper meaning in Kant's notion of the unknowable "*Ding-an-sich*" (thing-in-itself) than is available to those who stick to the "letter" of his philosophy, i.e., to "what his mere words express," as C writes here. On the distinction between "letter" and "spirit," see p. 439, n. 4 herein.

9. From "or that" to the end of this paragraph, C uses two passages from different works by Schelling. The first is from Schelling, *System* (114; Heath, 57), in which he discusses the impossibility of explaining thought as a material appearance. If one supposes, Schelling writes, "that only stuff pertains to things, then before it reaches the self this stuff must be without form, at least in the transition from the thing to presentation, which is assuredly inconceivable" (*System*, 114; Heath, 57). For the last sentence C draws on *Philosophische Briefe über Dogmatismus und Kriticismus* (Philosophical Letters on Dogmatism and Criticism) (*PS*, 119–25), in which Schelling challenges Kant's view that only in practical reason is the idea of God realized by means of a postulate, showing that, according to both the letter and the spirit of Kant's philosophy, God cannot be viewed as the author of the moral law. Hence, Kant's moral system is "so constructed that the moral law comes first and God last" (124). See C's marginal note to this passage in Schelling, in which C claims that "God is the originator of the moral Law" (*CM* [CC], 4:410).

1. C continues to draw on Schelling, *Abhandlungen* (276–77), the passage where Schelling advised against a literal reading of Kant's notion of the "*Ding-an-sich*" (see p. 439, n. 4 herein). He explained that Kant expressed himself symbolically, having the contradictory task of representing that which lies beyond all representation, i.e., a supersensible idea: "Now Kant *symbolized* this supersensible ground of all that is sensible by the expression *things in themselves*, which, like *all* other symbolic expression, contains in itself a *contradiction*, because it seeks to represent the unconditioned through the conditioned [element] and to make the infinite finite. But such contradictory (absurd) expressions are the only ones by which *ideas* can be generally represented." For C's view of an idea as "an educt of the Imagination actuated by the pure Reason, to which there neither is nor can be an adequate correspondent in the world of the senses," see p. 357, n. 2 herein. For his view of the symbol, see p. 360 and nn. 9–1 herein.

2. "He spoke to the wise." Pindar, *Olympian Odes* 2.85 (var.).

3. An extended discussion of the relationship of veracity to truth appears in *Friend* (CC), 2:40–43. There C distinguishes between merely "*verbal* truth," by which "we mean no more than the correspondence of a given fact to given words," and "*moral* truth," which involves veracity and the intentions of the speaker: "Veracity therefore, not mere accuracy; to convey truth, not merely to say it; is the point of Duty in Dispute: and the only difficulty in the mind of an honest man arises from the doubt, whether more than *veracity* (i.e., the truth and nothing but the truth) is not demanded of him by the Law of Conscience, namely *Simplicity*; that is, the truth only, and the whole truth." Cf. also *CN*, 3:3592.

constrained to express himself either *mythically* or equivocally. When Kant therefore was importuned to settle the disputes of his commentators himself, by declaring what he meant, how could he decline the honours of martyrdom with less offence, than by simply replying. "I meant what I said, and at the age of near four score, I have something else, and more important to do, than to write a commentary on my own works."[4]

Fichte's Wissenschaftslehre, or *Lore* of Ultimate Science,[5] was to add the key-stone of the arch: and by commencing with an *act*, instead of a *thing* or *substance*,[6] Fichte assuredly gave the first mortal blow to Spinozism, as taught by Spinoza himself;[7] and supplied the *idea* of a system truly metaphysical, and of a *metaphysique* truly systematic: (i.e. having its spring and principle within itself.) But this fundamental idea he overbuilt with a heavy mass of mere *notions*, and psychological acts of arbitrary reflection. Thus his theory degenerated into a crude[8] egoismus, a boastful and hyperstoic hostility to Nature, as lifeless, godless, and altogether unholy: while his *religion* consisted in the assumption of a mere ordo ordinans, which we were permitted *exotericé*[9] to call God; and his *ethics* in an ascetic, and almost monkish, mortification of the natural passions and desires.

4. C may (as mentioned in *BL* [CC], 1:157n. 2) refer to Kant's "Erklärung in Beziehung auf Fichtes Wissenschaftslehre" (Explanation regarding Fichte's Science of Knowledge) (August 7, 1799), which appeared in *Allgemeine Literatur-Zeitung*, no. 109 (August 28, 1799). There Kant tried to respond to various misrepresentations of his system and separate it from Fichte's science of knowledge, by insisting that his *Critique of Pure Reason*, notwithstanding the prevailing conceits to the contrary, should "certainly be understood according to its letter" (*Gesammelte Schriften*, 13 vols. [Berlin, 1902], 12:396–97). But a more likely source is Kant's answer to a communication from Johann August Schlettwein of May 11, 1797, in which he declined to take up the challenge of explicating his system in an exchange of letters with Schlettwein, arguing that "it is absurd" to ask "a man in his 74th year" to undertake a correspondence that would take many years to complete (*Gesammelte Schriften*, 12:388–94).
5. *Wissenschaftslehre* (Science of Knowledge). "Lehre" and its etymologically related "lore" mean teaching. Cf. *CN*, 2:2442: "* * * our Language has dropt the word 'Lore' at least except in poetry—the lehre of the Germans, the Logos of the Greek * * *." While holding a professorship at Jena, Fichte wrote several works on the science of knowledge, two of which C annotated (*CM* [CC], 2:623–26).
6. Fichte preceded Schelling in grounding philosophy in an original act of the self, claiming that the self or "I" (*das Ich*) posits its own being originally and, by establishing a limitation, engenders an opposite, the "not I" (*das Nicht Ich*). Thus the "*reality of things*, (as substance)" is nothing but a product of the original activity of the "I" (*Grundlage*, 3–13; 65–80; Heath and Lachs, 93–99; 129–38).
7. For Fichte's critique of Spinoza, see *Grundlage* (16–17, 45–48; Heath and Lachs, 101–02, 118–19). There Fichte criticizes Spinoza for having attributed consciousness, as the basis of knowledge, to a substance (Spinoza's infinite God) instead of a thinking I, which Fichte himself defines as an act.
8. C has a footnote (omitted here) (*BL* [CC], 1:158–60) in which he presents a parody of Fichte's system in the form of a "dithyrambic Ode" by the presumed Querkopf von Klubstik, whose name represents a pun on the writer F. G. Klopstock (1724–1803). C met Klopstock in Germany in 1798 ("Satyrane's Letters," *BL* [CC], 2:191–206).
9. "Ordering order * * * popularly." Previous editors and critics have missed the fact that C's diatribe against Fichte is not "primarily based on a knowledge of Fichte's earlier works" (*BL* [CC], 1:160n. 3; Orsini, 190–91) but is derived from the opening two pages of commentary on Fichte in Schelling, *Darlegung*, a work in which Schelling is particularly critical of Fichte's view of nature and his disparagement of natural philosophy. Schelling summarizes Fichte's teachings as follows: "* * * *Nature is empty objectivity, mere sensory world; it consists exclusively in modifications of the self, is confined by incomprehensible boundaries within which it feels itself imprisoned. It is in essence senseless, unholy, godless; completely finite and dead throughout. The basis of all reality, of all knowledge is the personal freedom of men; one can only have belief in but no knowledge of the divine; and even this belief is of a purely moral kind. To the extent that it contains more than what can be derived from the moral concept, it is absurd and idolatrous * * *.*"

In Schelling's "NATUR-PHILOSOPHIE,"[1] and the "SYSTEM DES TRAN-SCENDENTALEN IDEALISMUS," I first found a genial coincidence with much that I had toiled out for myself, and a powerful assistance in what I had yet to do.[2]

I have introduced this statement, as appropriate to the narrative nature of this sketch; yet rather in reference to the work which I have announced in a preceding page,[3] than to my present subject. It would be but a mere act of justice to myself, were I to warn my future readers, that an identity of thought, or even similarity of phrase will not be at all times a certain proof that the passage has been borrowed from Schelling, or that the conceptions were originally learnt from him. In this instance, as in the dramatic lectures of Schlegel to which I have before alluded,[4] from the same motive of self-defence against the charge of plagiarism, many of the most striking resemblances, indeed all the main and fundamental ideas, were born and matured in my mind before I had ever seen a single page of the German Philosopher; and I might indeed affirm with truth, before the more important works of Schelling had been written, or at least made public. Nor is this coincidence at all to be wondered at. We had studied in the same school; been disciplined by the same preparatory philosophy, namely, the writings of Kant; we had both equal obligations to the polar logic and dynamic philosophy of Giordano Bruno; and Schelling has lately, and, as of recent acquisition, avowed that same affectionate reverence for the labors of Behmen, and other mystics, which I had formed at a much earlier period. The coincidence of SCHELLING's system with certain general ideas of Behmen, he declares to have been *mere* coincidence; while *my* obligations have been more direct.[5] *He* needs give to Behmen only feelings of sympathy; while I owe him a debt of gratitude. God forbid! that I should be suspected of a wish to enter into a rivalry with SCHELLING for the honors so unequivocally his right, not only as a great and original genius, but as the *founder* of the PHILOSOPHY OF NATURE, and as the most successful *improver* of the Dynamic[6] System which, begun by Bruno, was re-introduced (in a more philo-

---

1. Schelling's works on natural philosophy include *Ideen zu einer Philosophie der Natur* (Ideas for a Philosophy of Nature) (Landshut, 1797; C annotated the 1803 second revised edition), *Erster Entwurf eines Systems der Naturphilosophie* (First Outline of a System of Natural Philosophy) (Leipzig, 1799), and *Einleitung zu seinem Entwurf eines Systems der Naturphilosophie* (Introduction to his Outline of a System of Natural Philosophy) (Leipzig, 1799).
2. See CN, 2:2375 for C's sense of his predicament of finding his own thoughts expressed in the work of German philosophers. C is coyly calling attention to his plagiarisms here without actually identifying them.
3. I.e., C's "Logosophia" mentioned in chapter 8 (p. 437, n. 9 herein).
4. In chapter 2 C mentioned August Wilhelm von Schlegel, *Vorlesungen über dramatische Kunst und Literatur* (Lectures on Dramatic Art and Literature), delivered in Vienna in 1808 (*BL* [CC], 1:34n. 3).
5. In several marginal notes to Schelling, PS, C noted the "glaring" similarities between Schelling's and Böhme's views and faulted Schelling for not acknowledging his debt to Böhme (*CM* [CC], 4:424, 425, 427, 432). Although Schelling was introduced to Böhme by Johann Ludwick Tieck (1773–1853) in 1799 and subsequently had access to several editions of Böhme's works, he did not acknowledge his debt to Böhme until his *History of Modern Philosophy* (1833) (*BL* [CC], 1:161n. 4).
6. C has a footnote (omitted here) that presents a eulogy of the surgeon Richard Saumarez (1764–1835) for being the first to introduce dynamic philosophy in England without any prior acquaintance with the works of Kant or Schelling (*BL* [CC], 1:162–63).

sophical form, and freed from all its impurities and visionary accompaniments) by KANT;[7] in whom it was the native and necessary growth of his own system. KANT's followers, however, on whom (for the greater part) their master's *cloak* had fallen without, or with a very scanty portion of, his *spirit*, had adopted his dynamic ideas, only as a more refined species of mechanics. With exception of one or two fundamental ideas, which cannot be with-held from FICHTE,[8] to SCHELLING we owe the completion, and the most important victories, of this revolution in philosophy. To me it will be happiness and honor enough, should I succeed in rendering the system itself intelligible to my countrymen, and in the application of it to the most awful of subjects for the most important of purposes, Whether a work is the offspring of a man's own spirit, and the product of original thinking, will be discovered by those who are its sole legitimate judges, by better tests than the mere reference to dates. For readers in general, let whatever shall be found in this or any future work of mine, that resembles, or coincides with, the doctrines of my German predecessor, though contemporary, be wholly attributed to *him*: provided, that the absence of distinct references to his books, which I could not at all times make with truth as designating citations or thoughts actually *derived* from him; and which, I trust, would, after this general acknowledgment be superfluous; be not charged on me as an ungenerous concealment or intentional plagiarism.[9] I have not indeed (eheu! res angusta domi!)[1] been hitherto able to procure more than two of his books, viz. the 1st volume of his collected Tracts, and his System of Transcendental Idealism;[2] to which, however, I must add a small pamphlet against Fichte, the spirit of which was to *my* feelings painfully incongruous with the principles, and which (with the usual allowance afforded to an antithesis) displayed the love of wisdom rather than the wisdom of love.[3] I regard truth as a divine ventriloquist: I care not from whose mouth the sounds are supposed to proceed, if only the words are audible and intelligible.[4] "Albeit, I must confess to be half in doubt, whether I should bring it forth or no, it being so contrary to the eye of the world, and the world so potent in most men's hearts, that I shall endanger either not to be regarded or not to be understood."

MILTON: *Reason of Church Government.*[5]

*   *   *

7. C refers to Kant's system of nature based on the dyamic interaction of the forces of attraction and repulsion, as presented in his *Metaphysical Foundations of Natural Science*.
8. C may have in mind Fichte's view of the self as an original activity, which Schelling expanded in his philosophy (see p. 446, n. 6 herein).
9. This disclaimer did not protect C from charges of plagiarism (see pp. 374–75 herein).
1. "Alas! the narrow circumstances at home!" On this common expression, see *BL* (CC) 1:164 n. 2.
2. I.e., Schelling, *PS* and *System*. By 1817 C had also procured and annotated Schelling's *Darlegung, Denkmal der Schrift von den göttlichen Dingen &c des Herrn Friedrich Heinrich Jacobi* (Memorial to Mr. Friedrich Heinrich Jacobi's Work on Divine Things &c) (Tübingen, 1812) and *Ideen*.
3. C refers to Schelling, *Darlegung* (see p. 446, n. 9 herein).
4. For this habitual Coleridgean view, see *Friend* (CC), 2:127, and *EOT* (CC), 1:120.
5. C cites this passage from Thomas Birch's edition of Milton, *Works*, 2 vols. (1738), 1:62. The passage also appears in a notebook of 1810 (*CN*, 3:3678).

From Chapter X

A chapter of digression and anecdotes, as an interlude preceding that on the nature and genesis of the imagination or plastic power—On pedantry and pedantic expressions—Advice to young authors respecting publication—Various anecdotes of the author's literary life, and the progress of his opinions in religion and politics.

"*Esemplastic. The word is not in Johnson, nor have I met with it elsewhere.*" Neither have I! I constructed it myself from the Greek words, εις εν πλαττειν i. e. to shape into one;[6] because, having to convey a new sense, I thought that a new term would both aid the recollection of my meaning, and prevent its being confounded with the usual import of the word, imagination.

* * *

Thus to express in one word, all that appertains to the perception considered as passive, and merely recipient, I have adopted from our elder classics the word *sensuous*; because *sensual* is not at present used, except in a bad sense, or at least as a *moral* distinction, while *sensitive* and *sensible* would each convey a different meaning.[7] Thus too I have followed Hooker, Sanderson, Milton, &c. in designating the *immediateness* of any act or object of knowledge by the word *intuition*,[8] used sometimes subjectively, sometimes objectively, even as we use the word, thought; now as *the* thought, or act of thinking, and now as *a* thought, or the object of our reflection; and we do this without confusion or obscurity. The very words, *objective* and *subjective*, of such constant recurrence in the schools of yore, I have ventured to re-introduce, because I could not so briefly, or conveniently by any more familiar terms distinguish the percipere from

6. C coined the term "esemplastic" and its correlatives "Eisenoplacy, or esenoplastic Power," from the German *In-Eins Bildung* (formation into one), as used in Schelling, *Darlegung* (61–62) and *Vorlesungen über die Methode des akademischen Studiums* (Lectures on the Method of Academic Study) (Tübingen, 1803), 313. "How excellently," C wrote in a notebook entry of 1813, "the German Einbildungskraft expresses this prime & loftiest Faculty, the power of co-adunation, the faculty that forms the many into one, *in eins Bildung*" (*CN*, 3:4176). For an earlier representation of the imagination as a "*modifying*, and *co-adunating* Faculty," see C's letter to Sotheby of September 1802 (*CL*, 2:866). C employed this terminology in an effort to ground the distinction between the imagination as a shaping, unifying faculty and fancy as a merely "*aggregating* power" (see pp. 416–19 and 488–89 herein). For the definition of the imagination as a "plastic" power (also used by Wordsworth in the Preface to his 1815 *Poems* [*W Prose*, 3:36]), C was indebted not only to German but also to British philosophers. See, e.g., William Duff, *An Essay on Original Genius* (1767), on imagination's "plastic power of inventing new associations of ideas" (7, 20, 89), and *BL* (*CC*), 1:168n. 2.

7. The word "sensuous" was coined by Milton and used in his definition of poetry as "simple, sensuous, and passionate" (*Of Education* in *Works*, ed. Thomas Birch, 2 vols. [1738], 1:139). For C's use of this definition, see p. 324, n. 1 herein. In a notebook entry of 1805 C complained about the lack of adequate terms "of comprehensive generality" in the language, singling out "that good and necessary word 'sensuous' which we have likewise dropt, opposed to sensual, sensitive, sensible" (*CN*, 2:2442). According to Johnson's *Dictionary*, "sensuous" was no longer in use.

8. In *PGC* and the *Logic* (*CC*), 151, C refers to Hooker's definition of intuition as an "immediate beholding." The use of "intuition" in the works of Robert Sanderson (1587–1663) has not been traced. On Milton's use of "intuitive reason" in *Paradise Lost*, see C's citation (p. 450 herein) and cf. Johnson's *Dictionary* for the definition of intuition as "immediate knowledge."

the percipi.[9] Lastly, I have cautiously discriminated the terms, the
REASON, and the UNDERSTANDING, encouraged and confirmed by the
authority of our genuine divines, and philosophers, before the revolution.[1]

> ———both life, and sense,
> Fancy, and *understanding*: whence the soul
> *Reason* receives, and REASON is her *being*,
> DISCURSIVE or INTUITIVE. Discourse*
> Is oftest your's, the latter most is our's,
> Differing but in *degree*, in *kind* the same.
> PARADISE LOST, *Book V.*[3]

I say, that I was *confirmed* by authority so venerable: for I had previous
and higher motives in my own conviction of the importance, nay of
the necessity of the distinction, as both an indispensable condition
and a vital part of all sound speculation in metaphysics, ethical or theological. To establish this distinction was one main object of THE
FRIEND;[4] if even in a biography of my own literary life I can with propriety refer to a work, which was printed rather than published, or so
published that it had been well for the unfortunate author, if it had remained in manuscript![5]

*   *   *

Toward the close of the first year from the time, that in an inauspi-
cious hour I left the friendly cloysters, and the happy grove of quiet,
ever honored Jesus College, Cambridge, I was persuaded by sundry
Philanthropists and Anti-polemists[6] to set on foot a periodical work,

---

* But for sundry notes on Shakspeare, &c. which have fallen in my way, I should have deemed
it unnecessary to observe, that *discourse* here, or elsewhere does not mean what we *now* call
discoursing; but the *discursion* of the *mind*, the processes of generalization and subsumption, of deduction and conclusion. Thus, Philosophy has *hitherto* been DISCURSIVE: while
Geometry is *always* and *essentially* INTUITIVE.[2]

---

9. "To perceive . . . to be perceived." On the origin of the terms "subjective" and "objective" in
   scholastic thought and their use in 18th- and 19th-century English and German philosophy,
   see *BL* (CC), 1:172n. 3.
1. C's main source for the distinction between reason and understanding was Kant, who
   stressed the gap separating the faculty of the understanding, which offers constitutive
   knowledge of the world, and reason, whose ideas are merely regulative and do not admit of
   any sensory representation. C modifies this distinction by merging imagination with reason
   and regarding the ideas of reason as constitutive. See later in this chapter (p. 456 and n. 7
   herein). See also McFarland, "Aspects of Coleridge's Distinction between Reason and Understanding" in *Coleridge's Visionary Languages*, ed. Tim Fulford and Morton Paley, 165–80;
   The Statesman's Manual (p. 356, n. 8 herein; p. 357, n. 2 herein; p. 362, n. 2 herein); *The
   Friend* (pp. 555–60 herein).
2. The most detailed discussion of the distinction between intuitive knowledge characteristic of mathematics and discursive knowledge based on the concepts of the understanding
   appears in the *Logic* (CC), 198–261, and is drawn from several works by Kant. Cf. *Logic*
   (CC), 247: "The knowledge thus obtained by the understanding we entitled 'discursive', in
   distinction from the 'intuitive' knowledge given by the sense; the understanding itself being
   named by elder logicians the 'discursive' faculty, and * * * by our great dramatic poet
   [Shakespeare] 'discourse of reasons'. * * * The temple of Truth has two main portals, the
   first and more magnificent being the science of intuition, or MATHEMATICS, the other and
   narrower but not less necessary, the science of discourse and the discursive faculty, or
   LOGIC."
3. Milton, *Paradise Lost* 5.485–90 (var.).
4. On the distinction between reason and understanding, see n. 1 above.
5. See the headnote to *The Friend* (pp. 552–54 herein).
6. Defined as "a professed opponent of war" (*OED*, citing this example from C).

entitled THE WATCHMAN, that (according to the general motto of the work) *all might know the truth, and that the truth might make us free!*[7] In order to exempt it from the stamp-tax, and likewise to contribute as little as possible to the supposed guilt of a war against freedom, it was to be published on every eighth day, thirty-two pages, large octavo, closely printed, and price only FOUR-PENCE. Accordingly with a flaming prospectus, *"Knowledge is Power,"* &c. *to cry the state of the political atmosphere,*[8] and so forth, I set off on a tour to the North, from Bristol to Sheffield, for the purpose of procuring customers, preaching by the way in most of the great towns, as an hireless volunteer, in a blue coat and white waistcoat, that not a rag of the woman of Babylon might be seen on me. For I was at that time and long after, though a Trinitarian (i. e. ad normam Platonis)[9] in philosophy, yet a zealous Unitarian in Religion; more accurately, I was a *psilanthropist,*[1] one of those who believe our Lord to have been the real son of Joseph, and who lay the main stress on the resurrection rather than on the crucifixion.[2] O! never can I remember those days with either shame or regret. For I was most sincere, most disinterested! My opinions were indeed in many and most important points erroneous; but my heart was single. Wealth, rank, life itself then seemed cheap to me, compared with the interests of (what I believed to be) the truth, and the will of my maker. I cannot even accuse myself of having been actuated by vanity; for in the expansion of my enthusiasm I did not think of *myself* at all.

My campaign commenced at Birmingham.[3] * * * The same hospitable reception, the same dissuasion, and (that failing) the same kind exertions in my behalf, I met with at Manchester, Derby, Nottingham, Sheffield, indeed, at every place in which I took up my sojourn. I often recall with affectionate pleasure the many respectable men who interested themselves for me, a perfect stranger to them, not a few of whom I can still name among my friends. They will bear witness for me, how opposite even then my principles were to those of jacobinism or even of democracy, and can attest the strict accuracy of the statement which

7. C left Jesus College, Cambridge, in December 1794 and decided to launch *The Watchman* (1796) as a way of disseminating the views he presented in his political lectures of 1795. The motto displayed on each issue of *The Watchman* ("That all may know the Truth; and that the Truth may make us free!") was adapted from John 8.32.
8. For the Prospectus and the citation from Bacon, see p. 283, n. 2 herein.
9. "Following the pattern of Plato."
1. A term designating the belief, strongly supported by Unitarians, that Christ was merely human, rather than divine. From the Greek *psilos* ("bare" or "mere") and *anthropos* ("person"). See *LS* (CC), 176n. 4.
2. C was converted to Unitarianism by William Frend (1757–1841) at Cambridge in 1794 and later considered joining the Unitarian ministry. In *Lectures on Revealed Religion* (1795) C rejected, primarily under the influence of Priestley, the mystery of the Trinity, the doctrine of atonement and of the divinity of Christ, regarding Christ as the son of Joseph rather than of God. C began to endorse the view of Christ's divinity in late 1803 (see *CN*, 1:1445) as he became more critical of Unitarianism and ready to embrace Trinitarianism (see p. 264, n. 1 herein). Later in this chapter (p. 457 and n. 2 herein) C notes that his philosophical differences from Unitarians prepared the ground for his later adoption of Trinitarianism. See also p. 264, n. 1 and p. 265, n. 5 herein.
3. Actually at Worcester, as C indicated in a letter to Josiah Wade (*CL*, 1:175). In the following section, omitted here, C presents a lively narrative, full of good humor, of his tour of the Midlands and the North to secure support for *The Watchman*. See *BL* (CC), 1:180–84 and his letters to Wade (*CL*, 1:175–78, 180–81, 184).

I have left on record in the 10th and 11th numbers of THE FRIEND.[4]

From this rememberable tour I returned with nearly a thousand names on the subscription list of the Watchman; yet more than half convinced, that prudence dictated the abandonment of the scheme. But for this very reason I persevered in it; for I was at that period of my life so compleatly hag-ridden by the fear of being influenced by selfish motives that to know a mode of conduct to be the dictate of *prudence* was a sort of presumptive proof to my feelings, that the contrary was the dictate of *duty*. Accordingly, I commenced the work, which was announced in London by long bills in letters larger than had ever been seen before, and which (I have been informed, for I did not see them myself) eclipsed the glories even of the lottery puffs. But, alas! the publication of the very first number was delayed beyond the day announced for its appearance.[5] In the second number an essay against fast days, with a most censurable application of a text from Isaiah for its motto, lost me near five hundred of my subscribers at one blow.[6] In the two following numbers I made enemies of all my Jacobin and Democratic Patrons; for disgusted by their infidelity, and their adoption of French morals with French *psilosophy*;[7] and perhaps thinking, that charity ought to begin nearest home; instead of abusing the Government and the Aristocrats chiefly or entirely, as had been expected of me, I levelled my attacks at *"modern patriotism,"*[8] and even ventured to declare my belief that whatever the motives of ministers might have been for the sedition (or as it was then the fashion to call them, the *gagging*) bills, yet the bills themselves would produce an effect to be desired by all the true friends of freedom, as far as they should contribute to deter men from openly declaiming on subjects, the principles of which they had never bottomed,[9]

---

4. In the tenth and eleventh issues of the 1809 *The Friend*, C included a section from his essay "Once a Jacobin Always a Jacobin," originally published in *MP* in 1802, to demonstrate that he had never been at any time "a Convert to the System" of Jacobinism (*Friend* [CC], 2:144–46). Responding to this passage, Thelwall wrote in his copy of the *Biographia* that "Mr C. was indeed far from Democracy, because he was far beyond it, I well remember—for he was a downright zealous leveller & indeed in one of the worst senses of the word he was a Jacobin, a man of blood * * *" (B. R. Pollin and R. Burke, "John Thelwall's Marginalia in a Copy of Coleridge's *Biographia Literaria*," *Bulletin of the New York Public Library* 74 [1970]: 81). See also the headnote to "Once a Jacobin Always a Jacobin" (p. 299 herein).
5. The first issue announced for February 5 did not appear till March 1.
6. C used a motto from Isaiah 16.11 ("Wherefore my bowels shall sound like an harp") in his satiric "Essay on Fasts," in which, like other Dissenters, he opposed this practice. The essay appeared on March 9, 1796, a national fast-day (*Watchman* [CC], 51–55). See also the headnote to *The Watchman* (p. 281 herein).
7. A term coined by Coleridge from the Greek *psilos* (slender) and *Sophia* (Wisdom) to distinguish between genuine philosophy and a "nominal" brand "without Imagination" (*CN*, 2:3158). See *CL*, 4:922 and *The Friend* (CC), 1:94 and n. 4.
8. C refers to his essay of that title, which was directed at various reformers but especially Godwin. The essay, as Colmer assessed (49–50), alienated the sympathies of the very groups from which C had to draw subscribers. See *The Watchman* (pp. 284–86 herein).
9. For C's attack on the two repressive bills against seditious literature and political gatherings introduced by the parliament in 1795, see *The Plot Discovered* (p. 274 herein). These bills were also known as "gagging bills" after the title of an essay by Thomas Beddoes (see p. 280, n. 8 herein). In *The Watchman* C softened his stance toward these bills, by suggesting that they "yet will not have been useless if they should render the language of political publications more cool and guarded, or even confine us for a while to the teaching of first principles, or the diffusion of that general knowledge which should be the basis or substratum of politics" (*Watchman* [CC], 14). On "principles of which they had never bottomed," a phrase derived from Burke, see *A Moral and Political Lecture* (p. 240, n. 1 herein).

and from "pleading to the poor and ignorant, instead of pleading *for* them."[1]

* * *

Conscientiously an opponent of the first revolutionary war,[2] yet with my eyes thoroughly opened to the true character and impotence of the favorers of revolutionary principles in England, principles which I held in abhorrence (for it was part of my political creed, that whoever ceased to act as an *individual* by making himself a member of any *society* not sanctioned by his Government, forfeited the rights of a citizen)—a vehement anti-ministerialist,[3] but after the invasion of Switzerland a more vehement anti-gallican, and still more intensely an anti-jacobin,[4] I retired to a cottage at Stowey,[5] and provided for my scanty maintenance by writing verses for a London Morning Paper.[6] I saw plainly, that literature was not a profession, by which I could expect to live;[7] for I could not disguise from myself, that whatever my talents might or might not be in other respects, yet they were not of the sort that could enable me to become a popular writer; and that whatever my opinions might be in themselves, they were almost equi-distant from all the three prominent parties, the Pittites, the Foxites, and the Democrats.[8] Of the unsaleable nature of my writings I had an amusing memento one morning from our own servant girl. For happening to rise at an earlier hour than usual, I observed her putting an extravagant quantity of paper into the grate in order to light the fire, and mildly checked her for her wastefulness; la, Sir! (replied poor Nanny) why, it is only "WATCHMEN."

* * *

Far different were the days to which these anecdotes have carried me back. The dark guesses of some zealous Quidnunc[9] met with so congenial a soil in the grave alarm of a titled Dogberry[1] of our neigh-

<hr>

1. C quotes from the tenth issue of *The Friend* (1809), in which he made this statement (var.) (*Friend* [CC], 2:137). Earlier, in the "Introductory Address" of *Conciones ad Populum*, he had articulated the same position that a true patriot ought to "plead *for* the Oppressed, not *to* them" (*Lects 1795* [CC], 43).
2. An accurate representation of C's vehement opposition to the war with France (see *Conciones ad Populum*, p. 248 herein).
3. C's outspoken criticism of Pitt was sharply articulated in his 1795 political lectures. See p. 254, nn. 4–6 herein; p. 276, n. 1 herein; p. 278, n. 5 herein; and the essay on the character of Pitt in *MP* of March 19, 1800 (*EOT* [CC], 1:219–26).
4. The invasion of Switzerland by France in March 1798 led to C's composition of the poem "Recantation," published in *MP* (p. 129 herein).
5. C retired with his family to Nether Stowey, close to Poole's residence, on December 31, 1796. On Poole's role in securing the cottage but also his advice against settling in it, see *BL* (1907), 1:255n.
6. Namely *MP*, for which C began writing in December 1797 and to which, before his departure for Germany in 1798, he contributed the poems "Fire, Famine & Slaughter," "The Raven," "Lewti," and "Recantation," among others. On his contributions to *MP*, see p. 122 herein.
7. Cf. C's advice to authors in the next chapter not to pursue literature as a trade (pp. 461–63 herein).
8. C's attempt to dissociate himself from party politics, especially as represented by Thelwall, Godwin, and Holcroft, has been regarded as disingenuous by both his contemporaries and later critics. A contemporary granted C's claim that he was anti-Pittite and anti-Foxite, but added, "If ever a democrat existed," C undoubtedly was one (*Lects 1795* [CC], xxxi). In his 1795 lectures C articulated views that were in line with those of radicals as well as Whig politicians, such as Charles James Fox (see pp. 236–39 herein and Roe, p. 722 herein).
9. "What now." The term indentifies an intrusive, nosy person.
1. The head constable of Messina in Shakespeare's *Much Ado About Nothing* (see p. 323, n. 4 herein and p. 411 herein). C may have in mind Sir Philip Hales (d. 1824) (*BL* [CC], 1:193n. 1).

bourhood, that a SPY was actually sent down from the government
pour surveillance of myself and friend. There must have been not only
abundance, but *variety* of these "honorable men"[2] at the disposal of
Ministers: for this proved a very honest fellow. After three week's truly
Indian perseverance in tracking us (for we were commonly together)
during all which time seldom were we out of doors, but he contrived
to be within hearing (and all the while utterly unsuspected; how indeed *could* such a suspicion enter our fancies?) he not only rejected
Sir Dogberry's request that he would try yet a little longer, but declared to him his belief, that both my friend and myself were as good
subjects, for aught he could discover to the contrary, as any in His
Majesty's dominions.[3] He had repeatedly hid himself, he said, for
hours together behind a bank at the sea-side (our favorite seat) and
overheard our conversation. At first he fancied, that we were aware of
our danger; for he often heard me talk of one *Spy Nozy*,[4] which he was
inclined to interpret of himself, and of a remarkable feature belonging
to him; but he was speedily convinced that it was the name of a man
who had made a book and lived long ago. Our talk ran most upon
books, and we were perpetually desiring each other to look at *this*, and
to listen to *that*; but he could not catch a word about politics. Once he
had joined me on the road; (this occurred, as I was returning home
alone from my friend's house, which was about three miles from my
own cottage) and passing himself off as a traveller, he had entered into
conversation with me, and talked of purpose in a *democrat* way in order to draw me out. The result, it appears, not only convinced him
that I was no friend of jacobinism; but (he added) I had "plainly made
it out to be such a silly as well as wicked thing, that he felt ashamed,
though he had only *put it on.*" I distinctly remembered the occurrence, and had mentioned it immediately on my return, repeating
what the traveller with his Bardolph nose[5] had said, with my own answer; and so little did I suspect the true object of my "tempter ere accuser,"[6] that I expressed with no small pleasure my hope and belief,
that the conversation had been of some service to the poor misled
malcontent. This incident therefore prevented all doubt as to the truth
of the report, which through a friendly medium came to me from the
master of the village inn, who had been ordered to entertain the *Government Gentleman* in his best manner, but above all to be silent con-

2. A reference to Antony's speech in Shakespeare, *Julius Caesar* 3.2.80.
3. The story of how the Wordsworths and C came under suspicion of being agents for the
   French government and became subject to surveillance by government detective George
   Walsh has been often told. See Roe, 248–62, and A. J. Eaglestone, "Wordsworth, Coleridge,
   and the Spy," in *Coleridge: Studies by Several Hands,* ed. Edmund Blunden and Earl Leslie
   Griggs (London, 1934), 73–87.
4. A pun on the name of the philosopher Spinoza. Both Eaglestone (86) and McFarland
   (*Coleridge and the Pantheist Tradition,* 165n. 2) have called into question the authenticity of
   this story about "Spy Nozy."
5. An inflamed nose owing to alcoholism or syphilis. Cf. the character Bardolph in Shakespeare, *1 Henry IV* 3.3:22–25, *2 Henry IV* 2.4.300–06, and *Henry V* 2.3.34–35. Cf. C's reference to Falstaff's comparison of a flea on Bardolph's nose with a soul suffering in
   Purgatory (*Henry V*) in *Lects 1808–19* (CC), 1:294, 2:485.
6. A reference to Satan as "The Tempter ere th'Accuser of man-kind" in Milton, *Paradise Lost*
   4.10.

cerning such a person being in his house. At length, he received Sir Dogberry's commands to accompany his guest at the final interview; and after the absolving suffrage of the *gentleman honored with the confidence of Ministers* answered, as follows, to the following queries? D. Well, landlord! and what do you know of the person in question? L. I see him often pass by with maister ————, my landlord (*i.e. the owner of the house*) and sometimes with the new-comers at Holford:[7] but I never said a word to him or he to me. D. But do you not know, that he has distributed papers and hand-bills of a seditious nature among the common people! L. No, your honor! I never heard of such a thing. D. Have you not seen this Mr. Coleridge, or heard of, his haranguing and talking to knots and clusters of the inhabitants?—What are you grinning at, Sir! L. Beg your honor's pardon! but I was only thinking, how they'd have stared at him. If what I have heard be true, your honor! they would not have understood a word, he said. When our vicar was here, Dr. L. the master of the great school and canon of Windsor,[8] there was a great dinner party at maister ————'s; and one of the farmers, that was there, told us that he and the Doctor talked real Hebrew Greek at each other for an hour together after dinner. D. Answer the question, Sir! Does he ever harangue the people? L. I hope, your honor an't angry with me. I can say no more than I know. I never saw him talking with any one, but my landlord, and our curate, and the strange gentleman. D. Has he not been seen wandering on the hills towards the Channel, and along the shore, with books and papers in his hand, taking charts and maps of the country? L. Why, as to that, your honor! I own, I have heard; I am sure, I would not wish to say ill of any body; but it is certain, that I have heard—D. Speak out man! don't be afraid, you are doing your duty to your King and Government. What have you heard? L. Why, folks do say, your honor! as how that he is a *Poet*, and that he is going to put Quantock and all about here in print; and as they be so much together, I suppose that the strange gentleman has some *consarn* in the business.—So ended this formidable inquisition, the latter part of which alone requires explanation, and at the same time entitles the anecdote to a place in my literary life.

*   *   *

I retired to a cottage in Somersetshire at the foot of Quantock,[9] and devoted my thoughts and studies to the foundations of religion and morals. Here I found myself all afloat. Doubts rushed in; broke upon me *"from the fountains of the great deep,"* and fell *"from the windows of heaven."*[1] The fontal truths of natural religion and the books of Revelation alike contributed to the flood; and it was long ere my ark touched on an Ararat, and rested. The *idea* of the Supreme Being appeared to me to be as necessarily implied in all particular modes of being as the idea of infinite space in all the geometrical figures by which space is limited. I was pleased with the Cartesian opinion, that the

7. A hamlet near Alfoxden where the Wordsworths resided.
8. Dr. William Langford (1763–1814), master of Eton, the boarding school.
9. I.e., in Nether Stowey.
1. Genesis 7.11 (var.).

idea of God is distinguished from all other ideas by involving its *reality*; but I was not wholly satisfied.[2]

* * *

For a very long time indeed I could not reconcile personality with infinity; and my head was with Spinoza, though my whole heart remained with Paul and John. Yet there had dawned upon me, even before I had met with the Critique of the Pure Reason, a certain guiding light. If the mere intellect could make no certain discovery of a holy and intelligent first cause, it might yet supply a demonstration, that no legitimate argument could be drawn from the intellect *against* its truth.[3] And what is this more than St. Paul's assertion, that by wisdom (more properly translated by the powers of reasoning) no man ever arrived at the knowledge of God?[4] What more than the sublimest, and probably the oldest, book on earth has taught us.[5]

* * *

I became convinced, that religion, as both the corner-stone and the key-stone of morality, must have a *moral* origin;[6] so far at least, that the evidence of its doctrines could not, like the truths of abstract science, be wholly independent of the will. It were therefore to be expected, that its *fundamental* truth would be such as MIGHT be denied; though only, by the *fool*, and even by the fool from the madness of the *heart* alone!

The question then concerning our faith in the existence of a God, not only as the *ground* of the universe by his essence, but as its maker and judge by his wisdom and holy will, appeared to stand thus. The sciential *reason*, whose objects are purely theoretical, remains neutral, as long as its name and semblance are not usurped by the opponents of the doctrine. But it *then* becomes an effective ally by exposing the false shew of demonstration, or by evincing the equal demonstrability of the contrary from premises equally logical. The *understanding* mean time suggests, the analogy of *experience* facilitates, the belief.[7] Nature ex-

---

2. C's partial dissatisfaction with Descartes's view that the idea of God necessarily implies his existence (see *Discourse on Method*, part 4 [*Philosophical Writings*, 1:128–30]) was mainly influenced by Kant, who in *Der einzig mögliche Beweisgrund zu einer Demonstration des Daseyns Gottes* (The Only Possible Proof for a Demonstration of God's Existence) (1763) and *Pure Reason* (A592–631/B620–59), exposed the fallacy of the ontological proof for the existence of God. In his marginalia to Moses Mendelssohn (1729–1786) C pointed out that the deficiency of Descartes's view consisted in his ignoring the crucial fact that the "thing to be proved is, not that the Idea of God involves the Idea of his Existence, but that the Idea of God contains in itself the Belief in that Idea" (*CM* [CC], 3:859–60). For C's endorsement of Kant's thesis that the existence of God cannot be proven by means of speculative reason, see his entry of February 22, 1834, in *TT* (CC), 1:462–63). But cf. C's un-Kantian religious perspective on the question of the proof of the existence of God: "All we can or need say is, that the existence of a necessary Being is so transcendentally Rational, that it is Reason itself—and that there is no other form under which this Being is contemplable but that of a holy and intelligent Will" (*CM* [CC], 3:333). See also *SM* (CC), 68n. 3 and p. 365 herein.
3. For Kant's view that the existence of the God can neither be proved nor disproved by speculative reason, thus remaining "*a faultless ideal*," see p. 441, n. 6 herein.
4. 1 Corinthians 1.17–21.
5. C illustrates this view by translating Jacobi's verse paraphrase (248–49) of a passage from the Book of Job 28 (omitted here) (see *BL* [CC], 1:202 and n. 2).
6. Cf. C's statement to Poole in his letter of July 1817 that the object of the third volume of *The Friend* was to show "that Morality without Religion is as senseless a scheme as Religion without Morality" (*CL*, 4:756). C addressed this question in the 1818 *The Friend* (CC), 1:409–14.
7. Cf. C's marginal note to Mendelssohn concerning the "unspeakable importance of the Distinction between the Reason, and the Human Understanding, as the only Ground of the Cogency of the Proof a posteriori of the Existence of a God from the order of the known Universe" (*CM* [CC], 3:848). On this recurrent distinction in C, see p. 450, nn. 1, 4 herein.

cites and recalls it, as by a perpetual revelation. Our feelings almost necessitate it; and the law of conscience peremptorily commands it. The arguments, that at all apply to it, are in its favor; and there is nothing against it, but its own sublimity. It could not be intellectually more evident without becoming morally less effective; without counteracting its own end by sacrificing the *life* of faith to the cold mechanism of a worthless because compulsory assent. The belief of a God and a future state (if a passive acquiescence may be flattered with the name of *belief*) does not indeed always beget a good heart; but a good heart so naturally begets the belief, that the very few exceptions must be regarded as strange anomalies from strange and unfortunate circumstances.

From these premises I proceeded to draw the following conclusions. First, that having once fully admitted the existence of an infinite yet self-conscious Creator, we are not allowed to ground the irrationality of any other article of faith on arguments which would equally prove that to be irrational, which we had allowed to be *real*. Secondly, that whatever is deducible from the admission of a *self-comprehending* and *creative* spirit may be legitimately used in proof of the *possibility* of any further mystery concerning the divine nature. *Possibilitatem* mysteriorum, (Trinitatis, &c.) contra insultus Infidelium et Hereticorum a contradictionibus vindico; haud quidem *veritatem*, quæ revelatione solâ stabiliri possit; says LEIBNITZ in a letter to his Duke. He then adds the following just and important remark. "In vain will tradition or texts of scripture be adduced in support of a doctrine, donec clava impossibilitatis et contradictionis e manibus horum Herculum extorta fuerit.[8] For the heretic will still reply, that texts, the literal sense of which is not so much *above* as directly *against* all reason, must be understood *figuratively*, as Herod is a fox, &c."

These principles I held, *philosophically*, while in respect of revealed religion I remained a zealous Unitarian.[9] I considered the *idea* of the Trinity a fair scholastic inference from the being of God, as a creative intelligence; and that it was therefore entitled to the rank of an *esoteric* doctrine of natural religion. But seeing in the same no practical or moral bearing, I confined it to the schools of philosophy. The admission of the logos, as *hypostasized*[1] (i. e. neither a mere attribute or a personification) in no respect removed my doubts concerning the incarnation and the redemption by the cross; which I could neither reconcile *in reason* with the impassiveness of the Divine Being, nor in my moral feelings with the sacred distinction between things and persons,[2] the

8. C quotes (var.) from Leibniz's letter to Duke Johann Friedrich of Braunschweig-Luneberg (1671), which appeared in *Magazin für das Kirchenrecht die Kirchen-und Gelehrten-Geschichte*, ed. G. W. Böhmer (Göttingen, 1787), 1:142: "I am freeing the *possibility* of mysteries (of the Trinity, etc.) from the contradictions, against the attacks of Unbelievers and Heretics; not, indeed, *the truth*, which can be established only by revelation * * * until the club of impossibility and contradiction has been wrested from the hands of these Hercule-ses" (*BL* [*CC*], 1:204n. 1).

9. See p. 451, n. 2 herein.

1. To turn into a hypostasis, i.e., to confer self-sufficient substance to an entity. C was the first to use the term (*OED*; *Friend* [*CC*], 2:75).

2. On C's rejection, in line with Unitarian doctrine, of the traditional view of Christ's vicarious suffering and atonement, see p. 264, n. 1 herein; p. 265, n. 5 herein; and p. 266, n. 6 herein. On the "sacred distinction between things and persons," see *Friend* (*CC*), 2:125, 266, 280. For this distinction C was indebted to the argument in Kant, *Grundlegung* (63–77; Gregor, 36–42), that one must treat another never as a means to an end, but exclusively as an end in itself.

vicarious payment of a debt and the vicarious expiation of guilt. A more thorough revolution in my philosophic principles, and a deeper insight into my own heart, were yet wanting. Nevertheless, I cannot doubt, that the difference of my metaphysical notions from those of Unitarians in general contributed to my final re-conversion to the whole truth in Christ;[3] even as according to his own confession the books of certain Platonic philosophers (*libri quorundam Platonicorum*)[4] commenced the rescue of St. Augustine's faith from the same error aggravated by the far darker accompaniment of the Manichæan heresy.[5]

* * *

In Mr. Burke's writings indeed the germs of almost all political truths may be found.[6] But I dare assume to myself the merit of having first explicitly defined and analyzed the nature of Jacobinism; and that in distinguishing the jacobin from the republican, the democrat, and the mere demagogue, I both rescued the word from remaining a mere term of abuse, and put on their guard many honest minds, who even in their heat of zeal against jacobinism, admitted or supported principles from which the worst parts of that system may be legitimately deduced.[7] That these are not necessary *practical* results of such principles, we owe to that fortunate inconsequence of our nature, which permits the heart to rectify the errors of the understanding. The detailed examination of the consular Government and its pretended constitution, and the proof given by me, that it was a consummate despotism in masquerade, extorted a recantation even from the Morning Chronicle, which had previously extolled this constitution as the perfection of a wise and regulated liberty.[8]

* * *

To have lived in vain must be a painful thought to any man, and especially so to him who has made literature his profession. I should therefore rather condole than be angry with the mind, which could attribute to no worthier feelings, than those of vanity or self-love, the satisfaction which I acknowledge to have enjoyed from the republication of my political essays (either whole or as extracts) not only in many of our own provincial papers, but in the federal journals throughout America. I regarded it as some proof of my not having labored altogether in vain, that from the articles written by me shortly

---

3. According to McFarland, C "was pushed away from Unitarianism by its pantheistic implications" and "was initially impelled toward the Trinity by his conviction that all other systematic possibilities led to Spinozism" (*Coleridge and the Pantheist Tradition*, 226–27).
4. "Books of certain Platonists."
5. C refers to Saint Augustine, *Confessions* 7.9 and 7.10, which describe the importance of "some books of the Platonists" to Augustine's understanding of major articles of Christian faith and inner restoration (Saint Augustine, *Confessions*, trans. Henry Chadwick [Oxford, 1991], 121–23).
6. Earlier in the chapter C praised Burke as a "scientific statesman" and "seer," whose writings and speeches had exerted a more enduring influence than "those of his illustrious confederates," being based on principles and laws that determine actions and events (*BL* [CC], 1:191). On Burke, cf. p. 254 and its n. 3.
7. See headnote to "Once a Jacobin Always a Jacobin" (pp. 299–301 herein).
8. C may refer here to his articles "On the French Constitution" published in *MP* in December 1799 (see *EOT* [CC], 1:31–36; 46–57). The "recantation" by the *Morning Chronicle* refers to its article of December 26, 1799, concerning the French Constitution (*EOT* [CC], 1:51n. 6).

before and at the commencement of the late unhappy war with America,[9] not only the sentiments were adopted, but in some instances the very language, in several of the Massachussets state-papers.

But no one of these motives nor all conjointly would have impelled me to a statement so uncomfortable to my own feelings, had not my character been repeatedly attacked, by an unjustifiable intrusion on private life, as of a man incorrigibly idle, and who intrusted not only with ample talents, but favored with unusual opportunities of improving them, had nevertheless suffered them to rust away without any efficient exertion either for his own good or that of his fellow-creatures. Even if the compositions, which I have made public, and that too in a form the most certain of an extensive circulation, though the least flattering to an author's self-love, had been published in *books*, they would have filled a respectable number of volumes, though every passage of merely temporary interest were omitted. My prose writings have been charged with a disproportionate demand on the attention; with an excess of refinement in the mode of arriving at truths; with beating the ground for that which might have been run down by the eye; with the length and laborious construction of my periods; in short with obscurity and the love of paradox. But my severest critics have not pretended to have found in my compositions triviality, or traces of a mind that shrunk from the toil of thinking. No one has charged me with tricking out in other words the thoughts of others,[1] or with hashing up anew the crambe jam decies coctam[2] of English literature or philosophy. Seldom have I written that in a day, the acquisition or investigation of which had not cost me the previous labor of a month.

But are books the only channel through which the stream of intellectual usefulness can flow? Is the diffusion of truth to be estimated by publications; or publications by the truth, which they diffuse or at least contain? I speak it in the excusable warmth of a mind stung by an accusation, which has not only been advanced in reviews of the widest circulation, not only registered in the bulkiest works of periodical literature, but by frequency of repetition has become an admitted fact in private literary circles, and thoughtlessly repeated by too many who call themselves my friends, and whose own recollections ought to have suggested a contrary testimony. Would that the criterion of a scholar's utility were the number and moral value of the truths, which he has been the means of throwing into the general circulation; or the number and value of the minds, whom by his conversation or letters,

9. Aware of the threat that America would declare war on Britain (which happened on June 18, 1812), C wrote a series of articles for the *Courier* in 1811, examining the consequences of this unfortunate course of action on both countries, which were "still interlinked by more and stronger chains of mutual benefit, than ever in former ages * * *." See *EOT* (CC), 2:142, 233–37, 303–05.

1. C may have in mind the review of *The Friend* (1809) in the *Eclectic Review* attributed to the Baptist minister John Foster (1770–1843) that offers a detailed analysis of the difficulties encountered by readers in coping with C's prose style and the obscurities of his "manner of thinking," specifically "its extreme abstractness" (*CH*, 1:92–110). At the same time, the reviewer acknowledged that C was "an original thinker" and that one of the "distinguishing properties of the 'Friend's' intellectual and literary character" was "the independence and wide reach with which he thinks" (100, 110).

2. "Cabbage already ten times cooked (or warmed over)." The phrase is proverbial.

he has excited into activity, and supplied with the germs of their after-growth! A distinguished rank might not indeed, even then, be awarded to my exertions, but I should dare look forward with confidence to an honorable acquittal. I should dare appeal to the numerous and re-spectable audiences, which at different times and in different places honored my lecture-rooms with their attendance, whether the points of view from which the subjects treated of were surveyed, whether the grounds of my reasoning were such, as they had heard or read else-where, or have since found in previous publications. I can conscien-tiously declare, that the complete success of the REMORSE on the first night of its representation[3] did not give me as great or as heart-felt a pleasure, as the observation that the pit and boxes were crowded with faces familiar to me, though of individuals whose names I did not know, and of whom I knew nothing, but that they had attended one or other of my courses of lectures. It is an excellent though perhaps somewhat vulgar proverb, that there are cases where a man may be as well *"in for a pound as for a penny."* To those, who from ignorance of the serious injury I have received from this rumour of having dreamt away my life to no purpose, injuries which I unwillingly remember at all, much less am disposed to record in a sketch of my literary life; or to those, who from their own feelings, or the gratification they derive from thinking contemptuously of others, would like Job's comforters attribute these complaints, extorted from me by the sense of wrong, to self-conceit or presumptuous vanity. I have already furnished such ample materials, that I shall gain nothing by with-holding the remain-der. I will not therefore hesitate to ask the consciences of those, who from their long acquaintance with me and with the circumstances are best qualified to decide or be my judges whether the restitution of the suum cuique[4] would increase or detract from my literary reputation. In this exculpation I hope to be understood as speaking of myself com-paratively, and in proportion to the claims, which others are intitled to make on my time or my talents. By what I *have* effected, am I to be judged by my fellow men; what I *could* have done, is a question for my own conscience. On my own account I may perhaps have had suffi-cient reason to lament my deficiency in self-controul, and the neglect of concentering my powers to the realization of some permanent work. But to verse rather than to prose, if to either, belongs the ["]voice of mourning" for

> Keen pangs of love awakening as a babe
> Turbulent, with an outcry in the heart,
> And fears self-will'd that shunn'd the eye of hope,
> And hope that scarce would know itself from fear;
> Sense of past youth, and manhood come in vain
> And genius given and knowledge won in vain,
> And all which I had cull'd in wood-walks wild
> And all which patient toil had rear'd, and all

---

3. The play opened on January 23, 1813, at Drury Lane and ran for twenty nights.
4. "To each his own."

Commune with thee had open'd out—but flowers
Strew'd on my corpse, and borne upon my bier
In the same coffin, for the self-same grave!

S. T. C.[5]

These will exist, for the future, I trust only in the poetic strains, which the feelings at the time called forth. In those only, gentle reader,

Affectus animi varios, bellumque sequacis
Perlegis invidiæ; curasque revolvis inanes;
Quas humilis tenero stylus olim effudit in ævo.
Perlegis et lacrymas, et quod pharetratus acutâ
Ille puer puero fecit mihi cuspide vulnus.
OMNIA PAULATIM CONSUMIT LONGIOR ÆTAS
VIVENDOQUE SIMUL MORIMUR, RAPIMURQUE MANENDO.
Ipse mihi collatus enim non ille videbor;
Frons alia est, moresque alii, nova mentis imago,
Vox alindque sonat. Jamque observatio vitæ
Multa dedit:—lugere nihil, ferre omnia; jamque
Paulatim lacrymas rerum experientia tersit.[6]

FROM CHAPTER XI

*An affectionate exhortation to those who in early life feel
themselves disposed to become authors.*

* * *

With no other privilege than that of sympathy and sincere good wishes, I would address an affectionate exhortation to the youthful literati, grounded on my own experience. It will be but short; for the beginning, middle, and end converge to one charge: NEVER PURSUE LIT-ERATURE AS A TRADE. With the exception of one extraordinary man,[7] I have never known an individual, least of all an individual of genius, healthy or happy without a *profession*, i. e. some *regular* employment, which does not depend on the will of the moment, and which can be carried on so far *mechanically* that an average quantum only of health, spirits, and intellectual exertion are requisite to its faithful discharge. Three hours of leisure, unannoyed by any alien anxiety, and looked forward to with delight as a change and recreation, will suffice to real-ize in literature a larger product of what is truly *genial*, than weeks of compulsion. Money, and immediate reputation form only an arbitrary

5. "To a Gentleman" ("To William Wordsworth"), lines 65–75, published in *Sybilline Leaves* (1817) (p. 202 herein).
6. Petrarch, "Epistola Barbato Sulmonensi" (Letter to Barbato da Sulmona), lines 40–50 (var.) (*Opera* 3:76). This was also quoted in chapter 1 (p. 384 herein). See CN, 3:4178, for a note-book entry that records this passage: "You read of various passions of the mind, of the war-fare of persistent malice, you peruse the idle cares that once, in tender youth, my humble pen poured forth. You read too of tears, and of the wound given me, a boy, by that quivered boy with piercing barb. ADVANCING TIME DEVOURS ALL THINGS BY DEGREES, AND AS WE LIVE WE DIE, AND AS WE REST WE ARE HURRIED ONWARD. For, compared to myself, I shall not seem that self; my face is another, my ways are changed, I have a new sort of mind, my voice sounds otherwise. Already the study of life has given me much:—to grieve at nothing, to endure all things; and already experience has little by little wiped away my tears" (*BL* [CC], 1:222n. 2).
7. Possibly a reference to Robert Southey.

and accidental end of literary labor. The *hope* of increasing them by any given exertion will often prove a stimulant to industry; but the *necessity* of acquiring them will in all works of genius convert the stimulant into a *narcotic*.[8] Motives by excess reverse their very nature, and instead of exciting, stun and stupify the mind. For it is one contradistinction of genius from talent,[9] that its predominant end is always comprized in the means; and this is one of the many points, which establish an analogy between genius and virtue. Now though talents may exist without genius, yet as genius cannot exist, certainly not manifest itself, without talents, I would advise every scholar, who feels the genial power working within him, so far to make a division between the two, as that he should devote his *talents* to the acquirement of competence in some known trade or profession, and his genius to objects of his tranquil and unbiassed choice; while the consciousness of being actuated in both alike by the sincere desire to perform his duty, will alike ennoble both.[1]

* * *

But whatever be the profession or trade chosen, the advantages are many and important, compared with the state of a *mere* literary man, who in any degree depends on the sale of his works for the necessaries and comforts of life. In the former a man lives in sympathy with the world, in which he lives. At least he acquires a better and quicker tact for the knowledge of that, with which men in general can sympathize. He learns to manage his genius more prudently and efficaciously. His powers and acquirements gain him likewise more real admiration; for they surpass the legitimate expectations of others. He is something besides an author, and is not therefore considered merely as an author. The hearts of men are open to him, as to one of their own class; and whether he exerts himself or not in the conversational circles of his acquaintance, his silence is not attributed to pride, nor his communicativeness to vanity. To these advantages I will venture to add a superior chance of happiness in domestic life, were it only that it is as natural for the man to be out of the circle of his household during the day, as it is meritorious for the woman to remain for the most part within it. But this subject involves points of consideration so numerous and so delicate, and would not only permit, but require such ample documents from the biography of literary men, that I now merely allude to it *in transitu*. When the same circumstance has occurred at very different times to very different persons, all of whom have some one thing in common; there is reason to suppose that such circumstance is not merely attributable to the *persons* concerned, but is in some measure occasioned by the one point in common to them all. Instead of the vehement and almost slanderous dehortation from marriage, which the *Misogyne*, Boccaccio (*Vita e Costumi* di Dante, p. 12, 16) addresses to

8. On the conversion of stimulants into narcotics, see p. 488 herein.
9. On the distinction between genius and talent, see p. 415, n. 2 herein and p. 485, n. 9 herein.
1. In the passage omitted here C gives examples of several writers, both ancient and contemporary, who were able to combine literary pursuits with an independent profession, recommending the church as best suited in uniting "the widest schemes of literary utility with the strictest performance of professional duties" (*BL* [CC], 1:224–28).

literary men,[2] I would substitute the simple advice: be not *merely* a man of letters! Let literature be an honourable *augmentation* to your arms; but not constitute the coat, or fill the escutchion!

*   *   *

FROM CHAPTER XII

A Chapter of requests and premonitions concerning the perusal or omission of the chapter that follows.

In the perusal of philosophical works I have been greatly benefited by a resolve, which, in the antithetic form and with the allowed quaintness of an adage or maxim, I have been accustomed to word thus: "*until you understand a writer's ignorance, presume yourself ignorant of his understanding.*"[3] This *golden rule* of mine does, I own, resemble those of Pythagoras in its obscurity rather than in its depth. If however the reader will permit me to be my own Hierocles,[4] I trust, that he will find its meaning fully explained by the following instances. I have now before me a treatise of a religious fanatic, full of dreams and supernatural *experiences*. I see clearly the writer's grounds, and their hollowness. I have a complete insight into the causes, which through the medium of his body had acted on his mind; and by application of received and ascertained laws I can satisfactorily explain to my own reason all the strange incidents, which the writer records of himself. And this I can do without suspecting him of any intentional falsehood. As when in broad day-light a man tracks the steps of a traveller, who had lost his way in a fog or by treacherous moonshine, even so, and with the same tranquil sense of certainty, can I follow the traces of this bewildered visionary. I UNDERSTAND HIS IGNORANCE.

*   *   *

In lieu of the various requests which the anxiety of authorship addresses to the unknown reader, I advance but this one; that he will either pass over the following chapter altogether, or read the whole connectedly. The fairest part of the most beautiful body will appear deformed and monstrous, if dissevered from its place in the organic Whole. Nay, on delicate subjects, where a seemingly trifling difference of more or less may constitute a difference in *kind*, even a *faithful* display of the main and supporting ideas, if yet they are separated from the forms by which they are at once cloathed and modified, may perchance present a skeleton indeed; but a skeleton to alarm and deter.[5] Though I might find numerous precedents, I shall not desire the

2. C refers to Boccaccio's warning to philosophers of the dangers posed by marriage to the pursuit of "sacred studies" and poetry (*Opera*, 6 vols. [Florence, 1723–24], 4.3:12–16). For C's annotations of this edition, see *CM* (CC), 1:542–44. For this passage from Boccaccio, see *BL* (CC), 1:229n. 1.
3. For this favorite maxim of C's, see *CN*, 1:928; *CL*, 3:278.
4. Hierocles of Alexandria (fl. 430 C.E.), Neoplatonist philosopher and commentator on the neo-Pythagorean *Carmina aurea* (Golden Verses). C means that he is commenting on himself.
5. An instance of C's application of an organic model not just to poetry (see p. 389, n. 5 herein) but also to philosophy, and expressive of C's statement in chapter 13 that "There is a philosophic, no less than a poetic genius, which is differenced from the highest perfection of talent, not by degree but by kind" (p. 485 herein). On the difference between "kind" and "degree," see *BL* (CC), 1:171 and n. 2, 287 and p. 356, n. 8 herein.

reader to strip his mind of all prejudices, or to keep all prior systems out of view during his examination of the present. For in truth, such requests appear to me not much unlike the advice given to hypochondriacal patients in Dr. Buchan's domestic medicine;[6] videlicet,[7] to preserve themselves uniformly tranquil and in good spirits.

* * *

But it is time to tell the truth; though it requires some courage to avow it in an age and country, in which disquisitions on all subjects, not privileged to adopt technical terms or scientific symbols, must be addressed to the PUBLIC.[8] I say then, that it is neither possible or necessary for all men, or for many, to be PHILOSOPHERS. There is a *philosophic* (and inasmuch as it is actualized by an effort of freedom, an *artificial*) *consciousness*, which lies beneath or (as it were) *behind* the spontaneous consciousness natural to all reflecting beings.[9] As the elder Romans distinguished their northern provinces into Cis-Alpine and Trans-Alpine, so may we divide all the objects of human knowledge into those on this side, and those on the other side of the spontaneous consciousness; citra et trans conscientiam communem.[1] The latter is exclusively the domain of PURE philosophy, which is therefore properly entitled *transcendental*, in order to discriminate it at once, both from mere reflection and *re*-presentation on the one hand, and on the other from those flights of lawless speculation which abandoned by *all* distinct consciousness, because transgressing the bounds and purposes of our intellectual faculties, are justly condemned, as[2] *transcendent*.[3]

6. Dr. William Buchan (1729–1805), the author of the popular *Domestic Medicine; or the Family Physician* (1769). Buchan wrote with reference to "Hypochondriac Affections" that "Cheerfulness and serenity of mind are by all means to be cultivated" (21st ed., [1813], 449; see *CN*, 3:4268 and n.).

7. "That is."

8. Cf. C's discussion at the end of chapter 12 regarding the unsympathetic reception in England of technical terms and metaphysics in general (*BL* [*CC*], 1:290–93).

9. C draws here primarily on Schelling, *Abhandlungen* (290–92), in which he articulated the view that philosophy was not available to everyone, and was a special brand of science that required the "work of culture and education," as well as a high measure of freedom and self-reliance. Philosophy, therefore, he concluded, "cannot be *every man's possession*" and cannot derive from a universally valid *a priori* postulate. On the distinction between a "natural" and "artificial" consciousness, see Schelling, *System* (10; Heath, 9), which shows that philosophy must separate the segments "*I exist*" and "*There are things outside me*," which coexist in ordinary consciousness, to establish their identity from a transcendental perspective "which is in no way natural, but artificial [*künstliche*]."

1. "General consciousness [i.e. possessed by everyone] on this and the other side." C draws on Schelling, *Abhandlungen* (327), which refers to philosophy as resting on a spiritual principle, "that namely which lies *"on the other side* of consciousness," and "must necessarily be greatly incomprehensible to those who have not exercised or strengthened this spiritual consciousness." C uses the entire passage from Schelling later in this chapter (p. 465, n. 7 herein).

2. C has a footnote (not included here) in which, among other matters, he takes issue with the confusion of the terms "transcendental" and "transcendent" in Johnson's *Dictionary* (*BL* [*CC*], 1:237–39).

3. Schelling, *Abhandlungen* (326–27), cites passages from Kant and Karl Leonhard Reinhold (1758–1823) on the distinction between these terms. Absolute freedom, he explains, becomes transcendental "only in so far as it is at the same time empirical," whereas the "transcendent" is severed from any reference to the empirical. In *Prolegomena* Kant argues that "transcendental * * * does not mean something that surpasses all possible experience, but something that indeed precedes experience (*a priori*), but that, all the same, is destined to nothing more than solely to make cognition from experience possible. If these concepts cross beyond experience, their use is then called transcendent, which is distinguished from the immanent use (i.e. use limited to experience)" (204n.; Hatfield, 128n.).

*   *   *

They and they only can acquire the philosophic imagination, the sacred power of self-intuition,[4] who within themselves can interpret and understand the symbol, that the wings of the air-sylph are forming within the skin of the caterpillar; those only, who feel in their own spirits the same instinct, which impels the chrysalis of the horned fly to leave room in its involucrum for antennæ yet to come. They know and feel, that the *potential* works *in* them, even as the *actual* works on them! In short, all the organs of sense are framed for a corresponding world of sense; and we have it. All the organs of spirit are framed for a correspondent world of spirit: tho' the latter organs are not developed in all alike. But they exist in all, and their first appearance discloses itself in the *moral* being. How else could it be, that even worldlings, not wholly debased, will contemplate the man of simple and disinterested goodness with contradictory feelings of pity and respect? "Poor man! he is not made for *this* world." Oh! herein they utter a prophecy of universal fulfilment; for man *must* either rise or sink.[5]

It is the essential mark of the true philosopher to rest satisfied with no imperfect light, as long as the impossibility of attaining a fuller knowledge has not been demonstrated. That the common consciousness itself will furnish proofs by its own direction, that it is connected with master-currents below the surface, I shall merely assume as a postulate pro tempore.[6] This having been granted, though but in expectation of the argument, I can safely deduce from it the equal truth of my former assertion, that philosophy cannot be intelligible to all, even of the most learned and cultivated classes. A system,[7] the first principle of which it is to render the mind intuitive of the *spiritual* in man (i.e of that which lies *on the other side* of our natural consciousness) must needs have a great obscurity for those, who have never disciplined and strengthened this ulterior consciousness. It must in truth be a land of darkness, a perfect *Anti-Goshen*, for men to whom the noblest treasures of their own being are reported only through the imperfect translation of lifeless and sightless *notions*. Perhaps, in great part, through words which are but the shadows of notions; even as the notional understanding itself is but the shadowy abstraction of living and actual truth. On the IMMEDIATE, which dwells in every man, and on the original intuition, or absolute affirmation of it, (which is likewise in every man, but does not in every man rise into consciousness)

---

4. The power of self-intuition is highly prized in transcendental philosophy. Both Fichte and Schelling view it as an immediate self-consciousness that brings about the unity of subject and object. See, e.g., Schelling, *Abhandlungen* (223, 241) and *System* (11; Heath, 9).
5. This paragraph from "who within themselves" up to here is a close adaptation of part of a longer notebook entry of 1811 inspired by Jean Paul Richter (1763–1825) (see CN, 3:4088). On C's interest in the metamorphosis of the caterpillar, see p. 413, n. 2 herein.
6. "For the time being."
7. From here to the end of the paragraph C translates a passage from Schelling, *Abhandlungen* (327–28), with a number of changes and additions. For example, C renders Schelling's "spiritual consciousness" as "ulterior consciousness" and then adds "It must in truth be a land of darkness, a perfect *Anti-Goshen*" (on *Anti-Goshen*, cf. EOT [CC], 1:120n. 8). C also adds the sentence on words as "shadows of notions" ("Perhaps * * * actual truth"), the parenthesis "(were it only * * * bondage)" and the segment "or bewilders himself * * * stagnant understanding!" For other changes, see BL (CC), 1:243n. 1. C finally attributes to Schelling the last statement ("To remain * * * man"), which he paraphrases from *Abhandlungen*.

all the *certainty* of our knowledge depends; and this becomes intelligible to no man by the ministery of mere words from without. The medium, by which spirits understand each other, is not the surrounding air; but the *freedom* which they possess in common, as the common ethereal element of their being, the tremulous reciprocations of which propagate themselves even to the inmost of the soul. Where the spirit of a man is not *filled* with the consciousness of freedom (were it only from its restlessness, as of one still struggling in bondage) all spiritual intercourse is interrupted, not only with others, but even with himself. No wonder then, that he remains incomprehensible to himself as well as to others. No wonder, that in the fearful desert of his consciousness, he wearies himself out with empty words, to which no friendly echo answers, either from his own heart, or the heart of a fellow being; or bewilders himself in the pursuit of *notional* phantoms, the mere refractions from unseen and distant truths through the distorting medium of his own unenlivened and stagnant understanding! To remain unintelligible to such a mind, exclaims Schelling on a like occasion, is honor and a good name before God and man.

* * *

The postulate of philosophy and at the same time the test of philosophic capacity, is no other than the heaven-descended KNOW THYSELF! (*E cœlo descendit,* Γνῶθι σεαυτον).[8] And this at once practically and speculatively. For as philosophy is neither a science of the reason or understanding only, nor merely a science of morals, but the science of BEING altogether, its primary ground can be neither merely speculative or merely practical, but both in one.[9] All knowledge rests on the coincidence of an object with a subject.[1] (My readers have been warned in a former chapter[2] that for their convenience as well as the writer's, the term, subject is used by me in its scholastic sense as equivalent to mind or sentient being, and as the necessary correlative of object or *quicquid objicitur menti.*)[3] For we can *know* that only which is true: and the truth is universally placed in the coincidence of the thought with the thing, of the representation with the object represented.[4]

Now the sum[5] of all that is merely OBJECTIVE, we will henceforth

8. "It descended from heaven, *Know thyself*" (Juvenal 11.27). C was fond of citing this "heaven-descended precept," which he also used as a motto to his poem "—E cœlo descendit," or "Self-knowledge," according to the title given to it by JDC in 1893. See p. 226 herein. See also p. 369, n. 2; and the Preface to *Aids to Reflection* (p. 572, n. 8 herein).
9. C reproduces Schelling's argument in *Abhandlungen* (332) that "the first principle of philosophy must be *simultaneously theoretical and practical, namely a postulate.*"
1. From "All knowledge rests" through this and the next four paragraphs up to the clause "intelligence and self-consciousness" (p. 468 herein), C translates from the opening of Schelling, *System* (1–5; Heath, 5–6), rearranging some of Schelling's sentences and making a number of additions and changes. Schelling's phrase here is "coincidence of an objective with a subjective." Most of the other changes are noted herein. For more details, see *BL* (CC), 1:252–56.
2. C adds the parenthesis, referring to chapter 10 (p. 449 herein and p. 450, n. 9 herein), where he defines the terms "subjective" and "objective."
3. "Something put before the mind."
4. Schelling's phrase is "coincidence of presentations with their objects." C adds "of the thought with the thing."
5. C translates Schelling's "Inbegriff" (intrinsic notion) as "sum" and adds "confining the term * * * known to us."

call NATURE, confining the term to its passive and material sense, as comprising all the phænomena by which its existence is made known to us. On the other hand the sum of all that is SUBJECTIVE, we may comprehend in the name of the SELF or INTELLIGENCE. Both conceptions are in necessary antithesis.[6] Intelligence is conceived of as exclusively representative, nature as exclusively represented; the one as conscious, the other as without consciousness. Now in all acts of positive[7] knowledge there is required a reciprocal concurrence of both, namely of the conscious being, and of that which is in itself unconscious. Our problem is to explain this concurrence, its possibility and its necessity.

During the act of knowledge itself,[8] the objective and subjective are so instantly[9] united, that we cannot determine to which of the two the priority belongs. There is here no first, and no second; both are coinstantaneous and one. While I am attempting to explain this intimate coalition,[1] I must suppose it dissolved. I must necessarily set out from the one, to which therefore I give hypothetical antecedence, in order to arrive at the other. But as there are but two factors or elements in the problem, subject and object, and as it is left indeterminate from which of them I should commence, there are two cases equally possible.[2]

1. EITHER THE OBJECTIVE IS TAKEN AS THE FIRST, AND THEN WE HAVE TO ACCOUNT FOR THE SUPERVENTION OF THE SUBJECTIVE, WHICH COALESCES WITH IT.

The notion of the subjective is not contained in the notion of the objective. On the contrary they mutually exclude each other. The subjective therefore must supervene to the objective. The conception of nature does not apparently[3] involve the co-presence of an intelligence making an ideal duplicate of it,[4] i. e. representing it. This desk for instance would (according to our natural notions) be, though there should exist no sentient being to look at it. This then is the problem of natural philosophy. It assumes the objective or unconscious nature as the first, and has therefore to explain how intelligence can supervene to it, or how itself can grow into intelligence. If it should appear, that all enlightened naturalists without having distinctly proposed the problem to themselves have yet constantly moved in the line of its solution, it must afford a strong presumption that the problem itself is founded in nature. For if all knowledge has as it were two poles reciprocally required and presupposed, all sciences must proceed from the one or the other, and must tend toward the opposite as far as the equatorial point

6. C translates "sich entgegengesetzt" (mutually opposed) as "in necessary antithesis" and drops Schelling's "ursprünglich" (originally) before "conceived."
7. The word "positive" is not in Schelling's sentence.
8. Schelling's text here is: "In knowing as such—*in the fact of* my knowing" (Heath, 5).
9. C adds "instantly."
1. C translates Schelling's "Identität" (identity) as "intimate coalition."
2. C tightens Schelling's text here, which reads: "3. * * * To explain it, inasmuch as nothing else is given me (as explanatory principle) beyond these two factors of knowledge, I must necessarily *give priority* to one over the other, *set out* from the one, in order thence to arrive at the other; from *which* of the two I start, the problem does not specify. 4. Hence there are only two possibilities" (Heath, 5).
3. C adds "apparently."
4. C adds "making an ideal duplicate of it", and the example of the desk. From "If it should appear * * *" to "founded in nature" C paraphrases Schelling more loosely (see *BL* [CC], 1:253n. 3).

in which both are reconciled and become identical.[5] The necessary tendency therefore of all natural philosophy is from nature to intelligence; and this, and no other is the true ground and occasion of the instinctive striving to introduce theory into our views of natural phænomena. The highest perfection of natural philosophy would consist in the perfect spiritualization of all the laws of nature into laws of intuition and intellect. The phænomena (*the material*) must wholly disappear, and the laws alone (*the formal*) must remain. Thence it comes, that in nature itself the more the principle of law breaks forth, the more does the *husk* drop off, the phænomena themselves become more spiritual and at length cease altogether[6] in our consciousness. The optical phænomena are but a geometry, the lines of which are drawn by light, and the materiality of this light itself has already become matter of doubt. In the appearances of magnetism all trace of matter is lost, and of the phænomena of gravitation, which not a few among the most illustrious Newtonians[7] have declared no otherwise comprehensible than as an immediate spiritual influence, there remains nothing but its law, the execution of which on a vast scale is the mechanism of the heavenly motions. The theory of natural philosophy would then be completed, when all nature was demonstrated to be identical in essence with that, which in its highest known power exists in man as intelligence and self-consciousness; when the heavens and the earth shall declare not only the power of their maker, but the glory and the presence of their God, even as he appeared to the great prophet during the vision of the mount in the skirts of his divinity.[8]

This may suffice to show, that even natural science, which commences with the material phænomenon as the reality and substance of things existing, does yet by the necessity of theorising unconsciously, and as it were instinctively, end in nature as an intelligence; and by this tendency the science of nature becomes finally natural philosophy, the one of the two poles of fundamental science.[9]

2. OR THE SUBJECTIVE IS TAKEN AS THE FIRST, AND THE PROBLEM THEN IS, NOW THERE SUPERVENES TO IT A COINCIDENT OBJECTIVE.[1]

In the pursuit of these sciences, our success in each, depends on an austere and faithful adherence to its own principles with a careful separation and exclusion of those, which appertain to the opposite science.[2] As the natural philosopher, who directs his views to the

---

5. C condenses Schelling's text here and adds "as far as * * * identical."
6. Schelling's sentence ends here. C adds "in our consciousness."
7. C adds "not a few of * * * Newtonians."
8. From "The theory * * *" to "self-consciousness" C condenses a passage in Schelling, *System* (4–5; Heath, 6) and adds "when the heavens * * * divinity" (for which, cf. Psalms 19.1 and Exodus 24.12–18).
9. Adapted from Schelling, *System* (5; Heath, 6). C adds "which commences * * * of things existing" and "of theorizing * * * instinctively." He also changes Schelling's statement that natural philosophy is "one of the basic sciences of philosophy" to "the one of the two poles of fundamental science."
1. Translated from Schelling, *System* (5; Heath, 6).
2. From here to the end of the paragraph C draws on Schelling, *System* (8; Heath, 7–8), with several interpolations. C's sentence "This purification * * * certainty," and the last sentence after the Descartes citation ("Nor is it * * * truth"), is a significantly altered version of Schelling's text: "The means of separation lie in absolute scepticism—not the half-scepticism which merely contends against the common prejudices of mankind, while never

objective, avoids above all things the intermixture of the subjective in his knowledge, as for instance, arbitrary suppositions or rather suffictions, occult qualities, spiritual agents, and the substitution of final for efficient causes;[3] so on the other hand, the transcendental or intelligential philosopher is equally anxious to preclude all interpolation of the objective into the subjective principles of his science, as for instance the assumption of impresses or configurations in the brain, correspondent to miniature pictures on the retina painted by rays of light from supposed originals,[4] which are not the immediate and real objects of vision, but deductions from it for the purposes of explanation. This purification of the mind is effected by an absolute and scientific scepticism to which the mind voluntary determines itself for the specific purpose of future certainty. Des Cartes who (in his meditations) himself first, at least of the moderns, gave a beautiful example of this voluntary doubt, this self-determined indetermination, happily expresses its utter difference from the scepticism of vanity or irreligion: Nec tamen in eo scepticos imitabar, qui dubitant tantum ut dubitent, et preter incertitudinem ipsam nihil quærunt. Nam contra totus in eo eram ut aliquid certi reperirem. DES CARTES, de Methodo.[5] Nor is it less distinct in its motives and final aim, than in its proper objects, which are not as in ordinary scepticism the prejudices of education and circumstance, but those original and innate prejudices which nature herself has planted in all men, and which to all but the philosopher are the first principles of knowledge, and the final test of truth.

Now[6] these essential prejudices are all reducible to the one fundamental presumption, THAT THERE EXIST THINGS WITHOUT US. As this on the one hand originates, neither in grounds or arguments, and yet on the other hand remains proof against all attempts to remove it by grounds or arguments (naturam furca expellas tamen usque redibit;)[7] on the one hand lays claim to IMMEDIATE certainty as a position at once indemonstrable and irresistible, and yet on the other hand, inasmuch as it refers to something essentially different from ourselves, nay even in opposition to ourselves, leaves it inconceivable how it could possibly become a part of our immediate consciousness; (in other words how that, which ex hypothesi is and continues to be ex-

---

looking to fundamentals, but rather that thoroughgoing scepticism which is directed, not against individual prejudices, but against the basic preconception, whose rejection leads automatically to the collapse of everything else. For in addition to the artificial prejudices implanted in mankind, there are others far more fundamental, laid down in us not by art or education, but by nature herself; prejudices which, for everyone but philosophers, serve as the principles of all knowledge, and for the merely self-made thinker rank even as the touchstone of all truth" (Heath, 8).

3. On the Aristotelian distinction between efficient and final causes, see p. 427, n. 9 herein.

4. This interpolated passage on ocular images from "supposed originals" is itself indebted to Schelling, Ideen (22; Harris and Heath, 20) and Abhandlungen (254n.). See BL (CC), 1:137–38n. 6.

5. "In doing this I was not copying the sceptics, who doubt for the sake of doubting and pretend to be always undecided; on the contrary, my whole aim was to reach certainty." C used this citation from Descartes, Discourse on Method, part 3 (Philosophical Writings, 1:125) in Lecture 12 of Lects 1818–19 (CC), 2:512–13; CL, 2:688; and CN, 1:914.

6. C follows closely Schelling's next paragraph (System, 8–9; Heath, 8), adding "as a position * * * irresistible" and the parenthesis ("in other words * * * being").

7. "You may drive nature out with a pitchfork but she will always return." Horace, Epistles 1:10.24 (var.).

trinsic and alien to our being, should become a modification of our being) the philosopher therefore compels himself to treat this faith as nothing more than a prejudice, innate indeed and connatural, but still a prejudice.

The other position,[8] which not only claims but necessitates the admission of its immediate certainty, equally for the scientific reason of the philosopher as for the common sense of mankind at large, namely, I AM, cannot so properly be intitled a prejudice. It is groundless indeed; but then in the very idea it precludes all ground, and separated from the immediate consciousness loses its whole sense and import. It is groundless; but only because it is itself the ground of all other certainty. Now the apparent contradiction, that the former position, namely, the existence of things without us, which from its nature cannot be immediately certain should be received as blindly and as independently of all grounds as the existence of our own being, the transcendental philosopher can solve only by the supposition, that the former is unconsciously involved in the latter; that it is not only coherent but identical, and one and the same thing with our own immediate self-consciousness. To demonstrate this identity is the office and object of his philosophy.

If it be said, that this is Idealism, let it be remembered that it is only so far idealism, as it is at the same time, and on that very account, the truest and most binding realism. For wherein does the realism of mankind properly consist? In the assertion that there exists a something without them, what, or how, or where they know not, which occasions the objects of their perception? Oh no! This is neither connatural or universal. It is what a few have taught and learnt in the schools, and which the many repeat without asking themselves concerning their own meaning. The realism common to all mankind is far elder and lies infinitely deeper than this hypothetical explanation of the origin of our perceptions, an explanation skimmed from the mere surface of mechanical philosophy.[9] It is the table itself, which the man of common sense believes himself to see, not the phantom of a table, from which he may argumentatively deduce the reality of a table, which he does not see. If to destroy the reality of all, that we actually behold, be idealism, what can be more egregiously so, than the system of modern metaphysics, which banishes us to a land of shadows, sur-

8. This paragraph is an abridged and adapted close version of the next two paragraphs of Schelling, *System* (9–10; Heath, 8). For the German passage and its translation, see *BL* (CC), 1:259n. 1.

9. This paragraph up to here is drawn from Schelling, *Abhandlungen* (273–74), with two C additions ("This is neither connatural or universal" and the reference to "mechanical philosophy"). See *BL* (CC), 1:260–61. The specification that the system of transcendental idealism is at the same time "the most perfect realism" is also made in Schelling, *System* (148–49; Heath, 73). Schelling is following in Kant's footsteps in trying to define his own brand of idealism as grounded in realism and different from systems such as Berkeley's. Cf. Kant, *Pure Reason* (A371): "Thus the transcendental idealist is an empirical realist, and grants to matter, as appearance, a reality which need not be inferred, but is immediately perceived"; and *Prolegomena* (207 and n.): "My so-called (properly, critical) idealism is therefore of a wholly peculiar kind, namely such that it overturns ordinary idealism, and such that by means of it all cognition *a priori*, even that of geometry, first receives objective reality, which, without my proven ideality of space and time, could not be have been asserted by even the most zealous of realists" (Hatfield, 130 and n.).

rounds us with apparitions,[1] and distinguishes truth from illusion only by the majority of those who dream the same dream? "*I* asserted that the world was mad," exclaimed poor Lee, "and the world said, that I was mad, and confound them, they outvoted me."[2]

It is to the true and original realism, that I would direct the attention.[3] This believes and requires neither more nor less, than that the object which it beholds or presents to itself, is the real and very object. In this sense, however much we may strive against it, we are all collectively born idealists, and therefore and only therefore are we at the same time realists. But of this the philosophers of the schools know nothing, or despise the faith as the prejudice of the ignorant vulgar, because they live and move in a crowd of phrases and notions from which human nature has long ago vanished. Oh, ye that reverence yourselves, and walk humbly with the divinity in your own hearts, ye are worthy of a better philosophy! Let the dead bury the dead,[4] but do you preserve your human nature, the depth of which was never yet fathomed by a philosophy made up of notions and mere logical entities.

In the third treatise of my *Logosophia*, announced at the end of this volume, I shall give (deo volente) the demonstrations and constructions of the Dynamic Philosophy scientifically arranged.[5] It is, according to my conviction, no other than the system of Pythagoras and of Plato revived and purified from impure mixtures. Doctrina per tot manus tradita tandem in VAPPAM desiit.[6] The science of arithmetic furnishes instances, that a rule may be useful in practical application, and for the particular purpose may be sufficiently authenticated by the result, before it has itself been fully demonstrated. It is enough, if only it be rendered intelligible.[7]

1. This passage has affinities with a section from Schelling, *Abhandlungen* (217–18), in which Schelling criticized Kant's idealism as committing one to a world "surrounded on all sides by phantoms." C used this passage in chapter 8 in a critique of Berkeley's idealism (p. 437 herein and p. 438, nn. 1–2 herein).

2. Nathaniel Lee (c. 1653–1692), Restoration playwright, was committed to Bedlam, a lunatic asylum, from 1684 to 1689 but, as indicated by the title of a poem by William Wycherley (c. 1640–1716), thought that "He ought no more to be in Bethlem for Want of Sense than other Mad Libertines and Poets abroad, or any Sober Fools Whatever" (*BL* [*CC*], 1:262n. 2). Lee is mentioned by Joseph Priestley in *A Comparison of the Institutions of Moses with Those of the Hindoos and Other Ancient Nations* (Northumberland, 1799), 303n.: "When Lee the tragedian was in a mad house, and was asked by a stranger how he came there, he said he was outvoted. Being desired to explain himself, he replied, 'I said the world was mad, and the world said I was mad, and they outvoted me.' " C echoes this remark by Priestley in a marginal note to Kant: "The man in a fever is only *outvoted* by his Attendants—He does not see their Dream, and they do not see his" (*CM* [*CC*], 3:249 and n.). C planned to attach a note to his poem "Limbo," identifying Lee as the author who wrote this poem while in Bedlam (*CL*, 6:779).

3. This paragraph is adapted from Schelling, *Abhandlungen* (274), with several additions, the longer ones being "and therefore * * * realists"; "or despise * * * ignorant vulgar"; and "Oh, ye * * * your own hearts" (cf. Micah 6.8). See *BL* (*CC*), 1:262n. 3.

4. Matthew 8.22 (var.); Luke 9.60 (var.).

5. No printed announcement of the treatise has been found. The treatise of the *Logosophia* was to deal with the principles of "Dynamic or Constructive Philosophy" (*CL*, 4:589) or, more broadly, with "the Science of Premises, or transcendental Philosophy" (*CL*, 4:592). See p. 437, n. 9 herein; pp. 447, 487–88 herein.

6. "A Doctrine passed through so many hands ends up as *flat wine.*" Schelling used this quotation with reference to Leibniz in *Abhandlungen* (212). *BL* (1847), 1:268n. *Deo volente*: God willing.

7. In this paragraph through the ten theses of transcendental idealism, C uses a notebook entry of 1815 from which he was probably dictating to Morgan, modifying and rearranging the material as he went on, and drawing on his copy of Schelling, *PS* and *System* (*CN*, 3:4265 and n.). In the notebook entry this paragraph appears at the end of the ten theses, rather than preceding them.

This will, I trust, have been effected in the following Theses for those of my readers, who are willing to accompany me through the following Chapter, in which the results will be applied to the deduction of the imagination, and with it the principles of production and of genial criticism in the fine arts.[8]

Thesis i.

Truth is correlative to being. Knowledge without a correspondent reality is no knowledge; if we know, there must be somewhat known by us. To know is in its very essence a verb active.[9]

Thesis ii.

All truth is either mediate, that is, derived from some other truth or truths; or immediate and original. The latter is absolute, and its formula A. A.; the former is of dependent or conditional certainty, and represented in the formula B. A. The certainty, which inheres in A, is attributable to B.[1]

Scholium. A chain without a staple, from which all the links derived their stability, or a series without a first, has been not inaptly allegorized, as a string of blind men, each holding the skirt of the man before him, reaching far out of sight, but all moving without the least deviation in one strait line. It would be naturally taken for granted, that there was a guide at the head of the file: what if it were answered,

---

8. C follows here the structure of Schelling, *System*, which closes with the philosophy of art, regarded by Schelling as the "universal organon of philosophy" and as the "keystone" and completion of his system of knowledge (18–21, 452–86; Heath, 12–14, 219–36).

9. In the notebook entry (CN, 3:4265) of thesis 1, the last sentence (var.) comes first ("Know essentially a verb active") and the first (var.) is placed last ("In other words, Truth and Being are Correlatives"). As noted by W. G. T. Shedd (*Collected Works of Samuel Taylor Coleridge*, 7 vols. [New York, 1853], 3:342), C's primary source for this thesis and the next five is Schelling, Vom Ich (1–3): "Who would know something would know at the same time that his knowledge had reality. A knowledge without reality is no knowledge. * * * The ultimate ground of all reality specifically is a something * * * *by which the Principle of being and of thinking coincide.*" As this citation shows, the notebook more closely reproduces the conceptual order in Schelling's text than the version here. For other sources in Schelling, *System* and *Abhandlungen* on the coincidence of the principle of knowledge and being, see BL (CC), 1:264n. 2, and for earlier sources of this position in Aquinas, see p. 440, n. 5 herein. It is important to bear in mind, however, that in *System*, Schelling specifies that the highest principle of knowledge lies within knowledge itself (i.e., the act of self-consciousness) and cannot be anchored in being (i.e., in an ontology): "There is no question at all of an absolute principle of *being* * * *; what we seek is an absolute principle of *knowledge*" (27; Heath, 16). C himself reproduces Schelling's view that "self-consciousness is not a kind of *being*, but a kind of *knowing*" in thesis 10 (see p. 479 herein), but cf. thesis 9 (p. 478 herein) on the religious transformation of this position. On knowledge as a "verb active," cf. Schelling, *System* (45; Heath, 24–25): "Every thinking is an act, and every determinate thinking is a determinate act; yet by every such act there originates for us also a determinate *concept*. The concept is nothing else but the act of thinking itself, and abstracted from this it is nothing."

1. The closest analogue for this thesis is Schelling's distinction in *System* (37–40; Heath, 21–22) between unconditional, original knowledge which is absolutely autonomous, depending on no other principle outside itself, and conditional knowledge, which ultimately depends on "an unconditional certainty" lent by the former. This leads Schelling to differentiate between analytical propositions (A = A), which represent the unconditioned and define the pure identity of subjectivity abstracted from any relation to an object outside itself, and synthetic propositions (A = B), in which "a wholly alien objective coincides with the subjective."

No! Sir, the men are without number, and infinite blindness supplies the place of sight?[2]

Equally *inconceivable* is a cycle of equal truths without a common and central principle, which prescribes to each its proper sphere in the system of science. That the absurdity does not so immediately strike us, that it does not seem equally *unimaginable*, is owing to a surreptitious act of the imagination, which, instinctively and without our noticing the same, not only fills at the intervening spaces, and contemplates the *cycle* (of B. C. D. E. F. &c.) as a continuous *circle* (A.) giving to all collectively the unity of their common orbit; but likewise supplies by a sort of *subintelligitur*[3] the one central power, which renders the movement harmonious and cyclical.[4]

THESIS III.

We are to seek therefore for some absolute truth capable of communicating to other positions a certainty, which it has not itself borrowed; a truth self-grounded, unconditional and known by its own light. In short, we have to find a somewhat which *is*, simply because it *is*. In order to be such, it must be one which is its own predicate, so far at least that all other nominal predicates must be modes and repetitions of itself. Its existence too must be such, as to preclude the possibility of requiring a cause or antecedent without an absurdity.[5]

---

2. C draws on Schelling's description of conditioned knowledge characteristic of synthetic judgments as "an endless regress from principle to principle" and as a series "genuinely without end" unless it is linked with unconditioned knowledge as the *"absolutely true"* (*System*, 41; Heath, 23). In *Vom Ich* (3) Schelling uses the image of a "chain" of knowledge, proceeding from one conditioned knowledge to another without direction, to show the fate of knowledge in the absence of an unconditioned ultimate principle. C's reference to a string of blind men without a guide is thus an apt illustration of Schelling's view of synthetic conditioned knowledge. C had used the figure of the blind men in his indictment of the practices of the Church of England in Lecture 1 of *LRR* ("An Allegoric Vision," *Lects 1795* [CC], 92–93).

3. "Intuitive understanding."

4. Schelling, *System* (34–35; Heath, 20), uses the image of the circle as representative of a system of knowledge (see *CN*, 3:4265n.), as does Fichte in *Ueber den Begriff der Wissenschaftslehre* (Concerning the Concept of Wissenschaftslehre), (38–39; Breazeale, 119). In *Logic* (CC), 85–87, which uses thesis 2 and its "Scholium," the unifying principle is represented as the "I AM," which "is logically and scientifically affirmable of consciousness generally." C's view of the imagination here is indebted to Kant who viewed imagination as a synthetic power, "a blind though indispensable function of the soul, without which we would have no cognition at all, but of which we are seldom even conscious" (Kant, *Pure Reason*, B103).

5. Cf. Jacobi (426–27) on the unconditional as that which cannot be grasped by concepts but is given *"as fact—It is!"* See also the Preface and section 1 of Schelling, *Vom Ich* (xii, 1–3), on the unconditioned as the "unique, immediate element in our knowledge" by which we know *"that* we do know" and "of which Spinoza could say, it is the light that illuminates the darkness and itself"; and the recurrent statement in *System* (27, 48; Heath, 16, 26) that the highest principle of knowledge is self-grounded and can be found only within knowledge itself, that is, "it has no other predicate than that of self-consciousness." The notebook version of thesis 3 adds the clarification that the absolute principle of knowledge is one that presupposes the identity of being and knowledge, drawing on Schelling's view that this principle "cannot have the ground of its cognition in something higher still. Hence, for us too, its *principium essendi* and *principium cognoscendi* must be one, and coincide in a unity" (*System*, 48; Heath, 26).

THESIS IV.

That there can be but one such principle, may be proved a priori; for were there two or more, each must refer to some other, by which its equality is affirmed; consequently neither would be self-established, as the hypothesis demands. And a posteriori, it will be proved by the principle itself when it is discovered, as involving universal anticedents in its very conception.[6]

SCHOLIUM. If we affirm of a board that it is blue, the predicate (blue) is accidental, and not implied in the subject, board. If we affirm of a circle that it is equi-radial, the predicate indeed is implied in the definition of the subject; but the existence of the subject itself is contingent, and supposes both a cause and a percipient. The same reasoning will apply to the indefinite number of supposed indemonstrable truths exempted from the prophane approach of philosophic investigation by the amiable Beattie,[7] and other less eloquent and not more profound inaugurators of common sense on the throne of philosophy; a fruitless attempt, were it only that it is the two-fold function of philosophy to reconcile reason with common sense, and to elevate common sense into reason.

THESIS V.

Such a principle cannot be any THING or OBJECT. Each thing is what it is in consequence of some other thing. An infinite, independent* thing, is no less a contradiction, than an infinite circle or a sideless triangle. Besides a thing is that, which is capable of being an object of which itself is not the sole percipient.[9] But an object is inconceivable without a subject as its antithesis. Omne perceptum percipientem supponit.[1]

---

* The impossibility of an absolute thing (substantia unica) as neither genus, species, nor individuum: as well as its utter unfitness for the fundamental position of a philosophic system will be demonstrated in the critique on Spinozism in the fifth treatise of my Logosophia.[8]

---

6. C draws on Schelling, Vom Ich (3–4) and System (25–26; Heath, 15), for the view that "All possible theories of the unconditioned" principle "must be determined a priori" and that "There can only be one such principle" from which truth is derived. Thesis 4 does not appear in the notebook but reappears (including its "Scholium") in a revised version in Logic (CC), 86–87.

7. James Beattie (1735–1803), Scottish author of the popular poem "The Minstrel" (1771–74) and of the philosophical treatise An Essay on the Nature and Immutability of Truth * * * (1770), in which he attacked the system of scepticism (as advocated by Hume) from the vantage point of common sense. On Beattie's charge that Hume failed "egregiously in explaining the operations of the mind," adopted "the most illiberal prejudices against natural and revealed religion" (11), and based his system on contradictory principles, see esp. 9–13, 248–67. C was not sympathetic to the accusations against Hume launched by Beattie or the Scottish philosopher Thomas Reid (1710–1796) (see Logic [CC], 192–93n.).

8. The source of C's footnote is Vom Ich (4), where Schelling notes that the unconditioned cannot be found in a generic notion and must be sought "in an absolute object that is neither genus, nor species, nor individual—" (BL [CC], 1:271n. 1). The fifth treatise of the Logosophia was to deal with the systems of pantheists and mystics (Bruno, Böhme, George Fox [1624–1691], and Spinoza) (see p. 471, n. 5 herein).

9. The point that the unconditional "cannot be sought in any kind of thing," being the principle and not the object of knowledge, is made by Schelling in System (49; Heath, 26) and in Vom Ich (4, 7–9), where Schelling also notes that "a thing" is an object of perception and "therefore cannot embody the actual ground of all knowledge and perception." Thesis 5 here corresponds to thesis 4 in CN, 3:4265, which also includes thesis 6 (pp. 475–76 herein).

1. "Everything perceived supposes a perceiver."

But neither can the principle be found in a subject as a subject, contra-distinguished from an object: for unicuique percipienti aliquid objicitur perceptum.[2] It is to be found therefore neither in object or subject taken separately, and consequently, as no other third is conceivable, it must be found in that which is neither subject nor object exclusively, but which is the identity of both.[3]

THESIS VI.

This principle, and so characterised manifests itself in the SUM[4] or I AM; which I shall hereafter indiscriminately express by the words spirit, self, and self-consciousness. In this, and in this alone, object and subject, being and knowing, are identical, each involving and supposing the other. In other words, it is a subject which becomes a subject by the act of constructing itself objectively to itself; but which never is an object except for itself, and only so far as by the very same act it becomes a subject. It may be described therefore as a perpetual self-duplication of one and the same power into object and subject, which pre-suppose each other, and can exist only as antitheses.[5]

SCHOLIUM. If a man be asked how he *knows* that he is? he can only answer, sum quia sum.[6] But if (the absoluteness of this certainty having been admitted) he be again asked, how he, the individual person, came to be, then in relation to the ground of his *existence*, not to the ground of his *knowledge* of that existence, he might reply, sum quia deus est, or still more philosophically, sum quia in deo sum.[7]

But if we elevate our conception to the absolute self, the great eternal I AM, then the principle of being, and of knowledge, of idea, and of reality; the ground of existence, and the ground of

2. "For every perceiver there is an object perceived."
3. The point that the unconditioned consists in the identity of subject and object, which always presuppose one another, is made by Schelling in *Vom Ich* (3–7) and *System* (29–30, 42–43 and passim; Heath, 17, 23–24 and passim).
4. "I am." The "I am" is a grounding principle of German transcendentalist philosophy. In Kant it is represented by the "pure *original* apperception" of the "transcendental unity of self-consciousness" (*Pure Reason*, B131–36). See p. 444, n. 2 herein. C's immediate source here is Schelling, *Vom Ich* (7–9) and *System* (esp. 43–62; Heath, 24–33). Fichte preceded Schelling in postulating the activity of the "I Am" as the starting point and fundamental principle of all science of knowledge (see p. 446 n. 6 herein). In these, among other sources, the terms "self," "spirit," "I," and "self-consciousness" appear frequently; although, as David Ferris argues, they are not as interchangeable as C implies ("C's Ventriloquy," 57). On the "I am," see also p. 595 and its n. 1 herein.
5. In both Fichte and Schelling the self or self-consciousness, which is originally an identity of subject and object, goes through a stage of self-division, during which "*the self becomes an object to itself*" and "*is itself nothing other than this act*" (Schelling, *System*, 67, 45; Heath, 36, 25). The self, Schelling clarifies, "is indeed an object, but only *for itself*, and is thus not *originally* in the world of objects; it first *becomes* an object by making itself into an object, and does not become one for anything external, but always only for itself" (*System*, 48; Heath, 26).
6. "I am because I am"; a version of God's statement to Moses "I AM THAT I AM" (Exodus 3.14). Schelling uses it in *Vom Ich* (8, 9), and Fichte makes it the ground of his system: "*Ich bin schlechtin, weil ich bin*" (I am absolutely, because I am) (*Grundlage*, 12; Heath and Lachs, 99). Cf. also Jacobi's view, an important source in C's theistic rendering of the "I am," that God as quintessential being cannot be understood by us except as given, "that is, *as fact—It is!*" (426–27).
7. "I am because God is" . . . "I am because I exist in God."

the knowledge of existence, are absolutely identical, Sum quia sum;*
I am, because I affirm myself to be; I affirm myself to be, because I
am.[9]

Thesis vii.

If then I know myself only through myself, it is contradictory to require any other predicate of self, but that of self-consciousness. Only
in the self-consciousness of a spirit is there the required identity of
object and of representation; for herein consists the essence of a
spirit; that it is self-representative. If therefore this be the one only immediate truth, in the certainty of which the reality of our collective
knowledge is grounded, it must follow that the spirit in all the objects
which it views, views only itself. If this could be proved, the immediate
reality of all intuitive knowledge would be assured. It has been shown,
that a spirit is that, which is its own object, yet not originally an

---

*   It is most worthy of notice, that in the first revelation of himself, not confined to individuals;
indeed in the very first revelation of his absolute being, Jehovah at the same time revealed
the fundamental truth of all philosophy, which must either commence with the absolute, or
have no fixed commencement; i.e. cease to be philosophy. I cannot but express my regret,
that in the equivocal use of the word *that*, for *in that*, or *because*, our admirable version has
rendered the passage susceptible of a degraded interpretation in the mind of common readers or hearers, as if it were a mere reproof to an impertinent question, I am what I am,
which might be equally affirmed of himself by any existent being.[8]
      The Cartesian Cogito, ergo sum is objectionable, because either the Cogito is used extra
Gradum,[9] and then it is involved in the sum and is tautological, or it is taken as a particular
mode or dignity, and then it is subordinated to the sum as the species to the genus, or rather
as a particular modification to the subject modified; and not pre-ordinated as the arguments
seem to require. For Cogito is Sum Cogitans.[1] This is clear by the inevidence of the converse. Cogitat ergo est[2] is true, because it is a mere application of the logical rule: Quicquid
ingenere est, est et in specie. Est (cogitans) ergo est.[3] It is a cherry tree; therefore it is a tree.
But, est ergo cogitat,[4] is illogical: for quod est in specie, non *necessario* in genere est.[5] It may
be true. I hold it to be true, that quicquid vere est, est per veram sui affirmationem;[6] but it
is derivative, not an immediate truth. Here then we have, by anticipation the distinction between the conditional finite I (which as known in distinct consciousness by occasion of experience is called by Kant's followers the empirical I) and the absolute I AM, and likewise the
dependence or rather the inherence of the former in the latter:[7] in whom "we live, and
move, and have our being," as St. Paul divinely asserts[8] differing widely from the Theists of
the mechanic school (as Sir J. Newton, Locke, &c.) who must say from *whom* we *had* our
being, and with it life and the powers of life.

---

8. Cf. C's attempt to clarify the meaning of "that" in the biblical statement ("I AM IN THAT I AM")
   in response to Southey's comment in *Omniana* "*I am he who am*, is better than *I am that I
   am*": "No! The sense of *that* is = because, or in that—[I a]m, in [tha]t I am! [meani]ng I [af-
   fir]m myself [and], affir[min]g myself to be, I am. Causa Sua [self-cause]. My own [ac]t is
   the Ground of my existence" (*CM* [CC], 3:1065).
9. "As an additional step." On Descartes's famous "*cogito, ergo sum*" (I think, therefore I am)
   and the critical evaluations of it by Kant, Fichte, and Schelling, see p. 442, n. 3 herein.
1. "I think" is "I am thinking."
2. "He thinks, therefore he is."
3. "Whatever is in the genus is also in the species. He is (thinking), therefore he is."
4. "He is, therefore he thinks."
5. "What is in the species is not *necessarily* in the genus."
6. "Whatever truly is, exists through the true affirmation of itself."
7. On the distinction between "the empirical I" and the "absolute I am," see Fichte, *Grundlage*
   (43; Heath and Lachs, 116–17), and Schelling, *System* (59–60; Heath, 31–32).
8. Acts 17.28. The biblical passage is used by Schelling in *Philosophische Untersuchungen über
   das Wesen der menchlichen Freiheit* (Philosophical Disquisitions on the Essence of Human
   Freedom) (*PS*, 404). For a revised version of C's footnote, which also appears in *CN*,
   3:4265, see *Logic* (CC), 3:1065.
9. Thesis 6 (which in a revised version appears in *Logic* [CC], 84–85) prepares the ground for
   C's culminating position in thesis 9 that the end point of self-consciousness is God, just as
   the end point of philosophy is religion (p. 478 herein).

object, but an absolute subject for which all, itself included, may become an object. It must therefore be an ACT; for every object is, as an *object*, dead, fixed, incapable in itself of any action, and necessarily finite. Again, the spirit (originally the identity of object and subject) must in some sense dissolve this identity, in order to be conscious of it:[1] fit alter et idem.[2] But this implies an act,[3] and it follows therefore that intelligence or self-consciousness is impossible, except by and in a will. The self-conscious spirit therefore is a will; and freedom must be assumed as a *ground* of philosophy, and can never be deduced from it.[4]

THESIS VIII.

Whatever in its origin is objective, is likewise as such necessarily finite. Therefore, since the spirit is not originally an object, and as the subject exists in antithesis to an object, the spirit cannot originally be finite. But neither can it be a subject without becoming an object, and as it is originally the identity of both, it can be conceived neither as infinite or finite exclusively, but as the most original union of both.[5] In the existence, in the reconciling, and in the recurrence of this contradiction consists the process and mystery of production and life.

THESIS IX.

This principium commune essendi et cognoscendi,[6] as subsisting in a WILL, or primary ACT of self-duplication, is the mediate or indirect principle of every science; but it is the immediate and direct principle

---

1. Thesis 7 (a version of which appears as thesis 6 and 7 in *CN*, 3:4265) is derived from Schelling, *Abhandlungen* (223–29). For individual citations, see *BL* (CC), 1:278–79nn. The process whereby the self or self-consciousness as absolute subject constructs an object, dissolving the original identity of the two is also explored by Schelling in *System* and by Fichte in *Grundlage*.
2. "It is made another and the same."
3. The view that the self is an act rather than a thing, or (as in Spinoza) a substance, is a major presupposition of both Fichte's and Schelling's systems. For Fichte, see p. 446, n. 6 herein. See also, e.g., Schelling, *System* (44–45; Heath, 24–25):

    Self-consciousness is the act whereby the thinker immediately becomes an object to himself, and conversely, this act and no other is self-consciousness.—This act is an exercise of absolute freedom, to which one can certainly be directed, but not compelled. * * * Self-consciousness is an act, yet by every act something is brought about in us.— Every thinking is an act, and every determinate thinking a determinate act * * * The concept is nothing else but the act of thinking itself, and abstracted from this it is nothing. * * * The concept of the self arises through the act of self-consciousness, and thus *apart* from this act the self is nothing; * * * Thus the self can only be presented *qua act* as such, and is otherwise nothing.

4. On the importance of the will in C as an answer to associationist philosophy, see p. 427, nn. 1–2 and pp. 432–33 herein. In *Abhandlungen* Schelling defines the will as "a self-determination of the spirit" and as "*the highest condition of self-consciousness*" (262). In part 4 of *System* (322–444; Heath, 155–214) he examines in detail the process whereby the intelligence becomes an object to itself by means of the original self-determination of the will. According to Ferris, Schelling does not attribute to the will "such an explicitly causative role" as does C, and unlike C, he distinguishes the will from self-consciousness ("Coleridge's Ventriloqui, 54–56).
5. Thesis 8 is a condensed paraphrase of Schelling, *Abhandlungen* (224–25). For the relevant passages, see *BL* (CC), 1:280n. 3, 281n. 1.
6. "Common principle of being and of knowing." See Schelling, *System* (48; Heath, 26) and "Aphorismen," *Jahrbücher* (1:21), on the coincidence of being and knowledge in God.

of the ultimate science alone, i.e. of transcendental philosophy alone.[7] For it must be remembered, that all these Theses refer solely to one of the two Polar Sciences, namely, to that which commences with and rigidly confines itself within the subjective, leaving the objective (as far as it is exclusively objective) to natural philosophy, which is its opposite pole.[8] In its very idea therefore as a systematic knowledge of our collective KNOWING, (scientia scientiæ)[9] it involves the necessity of some one highest principle of knowing, as at once the source and the accompanying form in all particular acts of intellect and perception. This, it has been shown, can be found only in the act and evolution of self-consciousness. We are not investigating an absolute principium essendi; for then, I admit, many valid objections might be started against our theory; but an absolute principium cognoscendi.[1] The result of both the sciences, or their equatorial point, would be the principle of a total and undivided philosophy, as for prudential reasons, I have chosen to anticipate in the Scholium to Thesis VI. and the note subjoined.[2] In other words, philosophy would pass into religion, and religion become inclusive of philosophy. We begin with the I KNOW MYSELF, in order to end with the absolute I AM. We proceed from the SELF, in order to lose and find all self in GOD.[3]

THESIS X.[4]

The transcendental philosopher does not enquire, what ultimate ground of our knowledge there may lie out of our knowing, but what is the last in our knowing itself, beyond which *we* cannot pass. The principle of our knowing is sought within the sphere of our knowing. It must be something therefore, which can itself be known. It is asserted only, that the act of self-consciousness is for *us* the source and principle of all *our* possible knowledge. Whether abstracted from us there exists any thing higher and beyond this primary self-knowing, which is for us the form of all our knowing, must be decided by the result.

That the self-consciousness is the fixt point, to which for *us* all is morticed and annexed, needs no further proof. But that the self-consciousness may be the modification of a higher form of being, perhaps of a higher consciousness, and this again of a yet higher, and so on in an infinite regressus; in short, that self-consciousness may be itself something explicable into something, which must lie beyond the possibility of our knowledge, because the whole synthesis of our intel-

---

7. From "is the immediate" to here C draws on Schelling, *System* (26–29; Heath, 15–16).
8. See Schelling, *System* (29; Heath, 17).
9. "The science of sciences."
1. From "In its very idea * * *" to here C draws on Schelling, *System* (26–27; Heath, 15–16). There Schelling places the ultimate ground of knowledge in self-consciousness and indicates that he is seeking an absolute principle of knowledge (*principium cognoscendi*) rather than a principle of being (*principium essendi*). See also p. 473, n. 5 herein.
2. See thesis 6 (p. 475 herein).
3. On the merging of philosophy with religion, cf. *Friend* (CC), 1:463, and *Lects 1818–19* (CC), 1:339.
4. Thesis 10 up to the last two sentences of the second paragraph is a close translation and adaptation of Schelling, *System* (27–29; Heath, 16–17).

ligence is first formed in and through the self-consciousness, does not at all concern us as transcendental philosophers. For to us the self-consciousness is not a kind of *being*, but a kind of *knowing*, and that too the highest and farthest that exists for *us*. It may however be shown, and has in part already been shown in pages [467–68], that even when the Objective is assumed as the first, we yet can never pass beyond the principle of self-consciousness. Should we attempt it, we must be driven back from ground to ground, each of which would cease to be a Ground the moment we pressed on it. We must be whirl'd down the gulph of an infinite series. But this would make our reason baffle the end and purpose of all reason, namely, unity and system. Or we must break off the series arbitrarily, and affirm an absolute something that is in and of itself at once cause and effect (*causa sui*)[5] subject and object, or rather the absolute identity of both. But as this is inconceivable, except in a self-consciousness, it follows, that even as natural philosophers we must arrive at the same principle from which as transcendental philosophers we set out; that is, in a self-consciousness in which the principium essendi does not stand to the principium cognoscendi in the relation of cause to effect, but both the one and the other are co-inherent and identical. Thus the true system of natural philosophy places the sole reality of things in an AB-SOLUTE, which is at once causa sui et effectus, πατηρ αυτοπατωρ γιος εαυτου[6]—in the absolute identity of subject and object, which it calls nature, and which in its highest power is nothing else but self-conscious will or intelligence. In this sense the position of Malbranche, that we see all things in God,[7] is a strict philosophical truth; and equally true is the assertion of Hobbes, of Hartley, and of their masters in ancient Greece, that all real knowledge supposes a prior sensation. For sensation itself is but vision nascent, not the cause of intelligence, but intelligence itself revealed as an earlier power in the process of self-construction.

> Μάκαρ, ἱλαθί μοι!
> Πάτερ, ἱλαθί μοι
> Εἰ παρὰ κόσμον,
> Εἰ παρὰ μῖραν
> Τῶν σῶν ἔθιγον![8]

Bearing then this in mind, that intelligence is a self-developement, not a quality supervening to a substance, we may abstract from all *de-*

---

5. "Its own cause." Jacobi, in a passage that is close to the theistic direction of C's thought here (416–17n.), identifies God as "causa sui" (cause of himself) and "effectus sui" (effect of himself).

6. Synesius, "Hymn," 3, lines 146, 148 (var.). "Father of himself, son of himself" (*BL* [CC], 1:285n. 2).

7. Both Kant in *De Mundi sensibilis atque intelligibilis forma et principii* (On the Form and Principle of the Sensible and Intelligible World) (*Vermischte Schriften*, 2:474; Walford, 405) and Schelling in *System* (319; Heath, 153) quote this statement by Nicolas Malebranche (1638–1715), which appeared in *De la recherche de la verité* (On the Pursuit of Truth) (1674). Cf. CN, 3:3592, 3974 and nn.

8. Synesius, Hymn 3, lines 113–17: "Be full of goodness unto me, Blessed One, be full of goodness unto me, Father, if beyond what is ordered, beyond what is destined, I touch upon that which is thine" (*BL* [CC], 1:286n. 1).

gree, and for the purpose of philosophic construction reduce it to *kind*,[9] under the idea of an indestructible power with two opposite and counteracting forces, which, by a metaphor borrowed from astronomy, we may call the centrifugal and centripedal forces.[1] The intelligence in the one tends to *objectize* itself, and in the other to *know* itself in the object. It will be hereafter my business to construct by a series of intuitions the progressive schemes, that must follow from such a power with such forces, till I arrive at the fulness of the *human* intelligence.[2] For my present purpose, I *assume* such a power as my principle, in order to deduce from it a faculty, the generation, agency, and application of which form the contents of the ensuing chapter.[3]

*   *   *

I shall now proceed to the nature and genesis of the imagination; but I must first take leave to notice, that after a more accurate perusal of Mr. Wordsworth's remarks on the imagination in his preface to the new edition of his poems, I find that my conclusions are not so consentient with his, as I confess, I had taken for granted.[4] In an article contributed by me to Mr. Southey's Omniana, on the soul and its organs of sense, are the following sentences. "These (the human faculties) I would arrange under the different senses and powers; as the eye, the ear, the touch, &c.; the imitative power, voluntary and automatic; the imagination, or shaping and modifying power; the fancy, or the aggregative and associative power; the understanding, or the regulative, substantiating and realizing power; the speculative reason—vis theoretica et scientifica, or the power by which we produce, or aim to produce unity, necessity, and universality in all our knowledge by means of principles* a priori; the will, or practical reason; the faculty of choice (*Germanice*, Willkühr) and (distinct both from the moral will and the

---

*   This phase, a priori, is in common most grossly misunderstood, and an absurdity burthened on it, which does not deserve! By knowledge, a priori, we do not mean, that we can know any thing previously to experience, which would be a contradiction in terms; but that having once known it by occasion of experience (i. e. something acting upon us from without) we then know, that it must have preexisted, or the experience itself would have been impossible. By experience only I know, that I have eyes; but then my reason convinces me, that I must have had eyes in order to [have] the experience.[5]

---

9. On the distinction between "kind" and "degree," see p. 356, n. 8 herein.
1. The model of two opposite interactive forces informs C's dynamic system of nature, which was influenced in large measure by Kant's, Schelling's, and Steffens's philosophy of nature. For Kant's view of matter as constituted by the forces of attraction and repulsion and Schelling's reaction to it, see p. 433, nn. 3–4 herein. In C's system of nature the force of attraction (which is the centripetal force) represents magnetism, whereas the force of repulsion (which is the centrifugal force) represents electricity. Gravitation is conceived as a synthetic force, unifying the centripetal and centrifugal forces. See, e.g., CN, 3:4418, 4420.
2. This is, as Orsini notes (209), the general object of Schelling's *System*. See Schelling's statement in the "Foreword" that his purpose was to present "every part of philosophy in a single continuum, and the whole of philosophy as what in fact it is, namely a progressive history of self-consciousness" by means of "a *graduated sequence* of intuitions, whereby the self raises itself to the highest power of consciousness" (viii–ix; Heath, 2).
3. I.e., chapter 13 on the imagination as "esemplastic power" (see p. 481 herein).
4. I.e., the Preface to *Poems* (1815).
5. The Kantian notion of the "a priori," whether referring to intuitions or concepts, is defined as that which makes experience possible and hence cannot be derived from experience. In *Logic* (CC), 76 C also complained about the frequent misuse of this term.

choice) the *sensation* of volition, which I have found reason to include under the head of single and double touch."[6] To this, as far as it relates to the subject in question, namely the words (*the aggregative and associative power*) Mr. Wordsworth's "only objection is that the definition is too general. To aggregate and to associate, to evoke and combine, belong as well to the imagination as the fancy."[7] I reply, that if by the power of evoking and combining, Mr. W. means the same as, and no more than, I meant by the aggregative and associative, I continue to deny, that it belongs at all to the imagination; and I am disposed to conjecture, that he has mistaken the co-presence of fancy with imagination for the operation of the latter singly. A man may work with two very different tools at the same moment; each has its share in the work, but the work effected by each is distinct and different. But it will probably appear in the next Chapter, that deeming it necessary to go back much further than Mr. Wordsworth's subject required or permitted, I have attached a meaning to both fancy and imagination, which he had not in view, at least while he was writing that preface. He will judge. Would to heaven, I might meet with many such readers. I will conclude with the words of Bishop Jeremy Taylor: he to whom all things are one, who draweth all things to one, and seeth all things in one, may enjoy true peace and rest of spirit. (*J. Taylor's* VIA PACIS.)[8]

CHAPTER XIII

On the imagination, or esemplastic power.[9]

O Adam! one Almighty is, from whom
All things proceed, and up to him return
If not depraved from good: created all
Such to perfection, one first nature all
Indued with various forms, various degrees
Of substance, and in things that live, of life;
But more refin'd, more spiritous and pure,
As nearer to him plac'd or nearer tending,
Each in their several active spheres assign'd,
Till body up to spirit work, in bounds
Proportion'd to each kind. So from the root
Springs lighter the green stalk: from thence the leaves
More airy: last, the bright consummate flower
Spirits odorous breathes. Flowers and their fruit,
Man's nourishment, by gradual scale sublim'd,
To *vital* spirits aspire: to *animal*:
To *intellectual!*—give both life and sense,

6. *Omniana*, 2:13–14 (no. 174 [var.]). C explored the phenomenon of "double touch" in several notebooks entries (see CN, 1:1827 and n., 2:2399, and 3:4046). C discussed the distinction between single and double touch with the contemporary poet John Keats (1795–1821). See p. 594, n. 3 herein.
7. Wordsworth makes this complaint in his Preface to *Poems* (1815) (*W Prose*, 3:36). In chapter 4 C had similarly tried to indicate his superior conception of the distinction between fancy and imagination (see pp. 416–19 and nn. herein).
8. C copied this remark in a notebook entry (CN, 1:876 and n.), quoting from the Sunday prayer in "*Via Pacis*" (Way of Peace), a collection of prayers for each day of the week, printed in Taylor's *The Golden Grove: or a Manual of Daily Prayers and Litanies* (1655).
9. On imagination as an "esemplastic power," see p. 449, n. 6 herein.

Fancy and understanding: whence the soul
REASON receives. And reason is her *being*,
Discursive or intuitive.

PAR. LOST, b. v.[1]

"Sane si res corporales nil nisi materiale continerent, verissime dicer-
entur in fluxu consistere neque habere substantiale quicquam, quem-
admodum et Platonici olim recte agnovêre.—Hinc igitur, præter purè
mathematica et phantasiæ subjecta, collegi quædam metaphysica
solâque mente perceptibilia, esse admittenda: et massæ materiali
principium quoddam superius et, ut sic dicam, *formale* addendum:
quandoquidem omnes veritates rerum corporearum ex solis axiomati-
bus logisticis et geometricis, nempe de magno et parvo, toto et parte,
figurâ et situ, colligi non possint; sed alia de causâ et effectu, *ac-
tioneque* et *passione*, accedere debeant, quibus ordinis rerum rationes
salventur. Id principium rerum, an ἐντελεχὲιαν an vim appellemus,
non refert, modó meminerimus, per solam *Virium* notionem intelligi-
biliter explicari."

LEIBNITZ: Op. T. II. P. II. p. 53.—T. III. p. 321.[2]

Σέβομαι Νοερῶυ
Κρυφίαν τάξιν
Χωρει ΤΙ ΜΕΣΟΝ
Ου καταχυθέν.

SYNESII, *Hymn III. I.* 231.[3]

DES CARTES, speaking as a naturalist, and in imitation of Archimedes,
said, give me matter and motion and I will construct you the universe.[4] We must of course understand him to have meant; I will render
the construction of the universe intelligible. In the same sense the transcendental philosopher says; grant me a nature having two contrary
forces, the one of which tends to expand infinitely, while the other strives

1. Milton, *Paradise Lost* 5.469–88 (var.), also quoted in part in chapter 10 (p. 450 herein).
2. C combines passages from two different essays by Leibniz. The first (from *Sane* up to *agnovêre*) is from *De ipsa natura* (On Nature Itself) (section 8). The second (from "Hinc igitur"
to the end) is from *Specimen dynamicum* (Dynamic Specimen). *Opera omnia*, ed. Louis
Dutens, 6 vols. (Geneva, 1768), 2:53; 3:231. Even though C used Dutens's edition, his
source is most likely Jacobi who cites longer passages from the Dutens edition (365n.;
369–70n.). Jacobi introduced several variants in his citations from Dutens, which are reproduced by C, and C introduced new variants in relation to the text given in Jacobi, most notably "phantasiæ" for "imagination" and "rerum" for "formam" (second passage).
    Translation (from *BL* [CC], 1:296n. 1): "If indeed corporeal things contained nothing but
matter they might truly be said to consist in flux and to have no substance, as the Platonists
once rightly recognized. . . . And so, apart from the purely mathematical and what is subject
to fancy, I have come to the conclusion that certain metaphysical elements perceptible by
the mind alone should be admitted, and that some higher and, so to speak, *formal principle*
should be added to the material mass, since all the truths about corporeal things cannot be
collected from logistic and geometrical axioms alone, i.e. those concerning great and small,
whole and part, shape and position, but others must enter into it, i.e. cause and effect, *action* and *passion*, by which the reasons for the order of things are maintained. It does not
matter whether we call this principle of things an entelechy or a power so long as we remember that it is intelligibly to be explained only by the idea of *powers*."
3. Synesius, "Hymn," lines 231–34: "I venerate the hidden ordering of intellectual things, but
there is some medial element that may not be distributed" (*BL* [CC], 1:296n. 2). Cf. p. 479,
nn. 6 and 8 herein.
4. C refers to Archimedes' notorious statement "Give me somewhere to stand and I will move
the world" (see *CN*, 1:1166 and 3:3592 and nn.) and extracts the reference to Descartes's
statement from Schelling, *System* (147; Heath, 72). The whole first paragraph, with the exception of the second sentence ("We must of course * * * intelligible"), is translated and
adapted from Schelling, *System* (147; Heath, 72–73).

to apprehend or *find* itself in this infinity, and I will cause the world of intelligences with the whole system of their representations to rise up before you. Every other science pre-supposes intelligence as already existing and complete: the philosopher contemplates it in its growth, and as it were represents its history to the mind from its birth to its maturity.

The venerable Sage of Koenigsberg has preceded the march of this master-thought as an effective pioneer in his essay on the introduction of negative quantities into philosophy, published 1763.[5] In this he has shown, that instead of assailing the science of mathematics by metaphysics, as Berkley did in his Analyst,[6] or of sophisticating it, as Wolff did, by the vain attempt of deducing the first principles of geometry from supposed deeper grounds of ontology,[7] it behoved the metaphysician rather to examine whether the only province of knowledge, which man has succeeded in erecting into a pure science, might not furnish materials or at least hints for establishing and pacifying the unsettled, warring, and embroiled domain of philosophy. An imitation of the mathematical *method* had indeed been attempted with no better success than attended the essay of David to wear the armour of Saul.[8] Another use however is possible and of far greater promise, namely, the actual application of the positions which had so wonderfully enlarged the discoveries of geometry, mutatis mutandis,[9] to philosophical subjects.[1] Kant having briefly illustrated the utility of such an attempt in the questions of space, motion, and infinitely small quantities, as employed by the mathematician, proceeds to the idea of negative quanti-

5. Kant, *Versuch den Begriff der negativen Grössen in die Weltweisheit einzuführen* (Attempt to Introduce the Concept of Negative Magnitudes into Philosophy) (1763), in *Vermischte Schriften*, 1:611–76 (Walford, 203–41).
6. In *The Analyst; or a Discourse Addressed to an Infidel Mathematician * * * (Works*, 2:151–205), Berkeley exposed the arrogant assumption of modern mathematicians of being "the great masters of reason" and analyzed the errors of their doctrine of fluxions, resulting from their unwillingness to look beyond their conclusions to the principles whereby they arrived at them. "Be the principles therefore ever so abstruse and metaphysical, they must be studied by whoever would comprehend the doctrine of fluxions. Nor can any geometrician have a right to apply the rules of the great author, without first considering his metaphysical notions whence they were derived" (193). In one of the queries listed at the end of the treatise, he asked a question that has a Kantian ring: "Whether there be not really a *philosophia prima*, a certain transcendental science superior to and more extensive than mathematics, which it might behove our modern analysts rather to learn than despise?" (203). On the importance of metaphysics to mathematics, see also *Works*, 2:157–58, 161–62, 164, 171–72, 182–84, 194–95, 197, 200–01, 203.
7. Wolff, who began his career at Jena as a mathematician and wrote several treatises on mathematics, regarded this science as providing a rich and accurate source of knowledge for philosophy. In *Philosophia prima, sive ontologia * * * (First Philosophy or Ontology * * *)* (Frankfurt, 1736), Wolff makes the claim that ontology is at the basis of all branches of knowledge and that Euclid's first principles and demonstrations are based on ontological notions (see esp. the Preface; on Euclid, see, e.g., 336, 358–60). C's source, however, might have been the English translation of Wolff's *Logic* (1770), which he annotated. This features a sketch of Wolff's life and works with a summary of *First Philosophy* drawn from Wolff's Preface to this work in which the following passage appears: "But on enquiring into the nature of the evidence of Euclid's demonstrations, he [Wolff] found, that it depended * * * on ontological notions: that Euclid's first principles are nominal definitions, and axioms, most of which are ontological propositions; and that thus mathematics are indebted to ontology for all their certainty * * *" (xxvii). See also p. 434, n. 3 herein.
8. 1 Samuel 17.38–39.
9. "Changing the things that must be changed."
1. C draws on Kant's argument in the preface to *Versuch*, in which he shows that metaphysics has much to gain from mathematics, not by imitating its method but by a "genuine application of its propositions to the objects of philosophy" (*Vermischte Schriften*, 1:613; Walford, 207).

ties and the transfer of them to metaphysical investigation.[2] Opposites, he well observes, are of two kinds, either logical, i.e. such as are absolutely incompatible; or real without being contradictory. The former he denominates Nihil negativum irrepræsentabile, the connexion of which produces nonsense. A body in motion is something—Aliquid cogitabile;[3] but a body, at one and the same time in motion and not in motion, is nothing, or at most, air articulated into nonsense. But a motory force of a body in one direction, and an equal force of the same body in an opposite direction is not incompatible, and the result, namely rest, is real and representable. For the purposes of mathematical calculus it is indifferent which force we term negative, and which positive, and consequently we appropriate the latter to that, which happens to be the principal object in our thoughts.[4] Thus if a man's capital be ten and his debts eight, the subtraction will be the same, whether we call the capital negative debt, or the debt negative capital. But in as much as the latter stands practically in reference to the former, we of course represent the sum as 10–8.[5] It is equally clear that two equal forces acting in opposite directions, both being finite and each distinguished from the other by its direction only, must neutralize or reduce each other to inaction. Now the transcendental philosophy demands;[6] first, that two forces should be conceived which counteract each other by their essential nature; not only not in consequence of the accidental direction of each, but as prior to all direction, nay, as the primary forces from which the conditions of all possible directions are derivative and deducible: secondly, that these forces should be assumed to be both alike infinite, both alike indestructible. The problem will then be to discover the result or product of two such forces, as distinguished from the result of those forces which are finite, and derive their difference solely from the circumstance of their direction. When we have formed a scheme or outline of these two different kinds of force, and of their

---

2. These topics are discussed by Kant in Versuch (Vermischte Schriften, 1:614–16; Walford, 207–08). Kant specifies that the term "negative magnitudes" does not refer to a negation of quantities, but to something positive in itself that designates a relationship of real (as opposed to logical) opposition, in which two opposite predicates can be asserted simultaneously without contradiction (617 ff.; Walford, 209ff.). As he explains (625; Walford, 213), "A magnitude is, relative to another magnitude, negative, in so far as it can only be combined with it by means of opposition * * *." Thus a negative magnitude is designated as "–a" in relation to another marked as "+a," the negative and positive referring not to the inner condition of things but merely to their relationship of opposition.
3. C follows Kant closely here, translating parts of the text (Versuch, 620–21; Walford, 211). The Latin terms Nihil negativum irrepræsentabile (A negative nothing which is incapable of being represented) and cogitabile (capable of being thought) are also used by Kant. C adds aliquid (something) to cogitabile.
4. Kant, Versuch (624–25; Walford, 213).
5. The example of capital negative debt and the figures are in Kant, Versuch (626; Walford, 214).
6. From here to the end of the next paragraph C draws on numerous elaborations of the principle of polarity in transcendental philosophy, including Kant's concept of the dynamic interaction of attraction and repulsion, the original forces that constitute matter; Schelling's refinement of Kant's system of nature by showing the identity of the two forces in an original spiritual activity identical with self-consciousness (see p. 433, nn. 3–4 herein and p. 438 herein); and Fichte's and Schelling's analyses of the self or self-consciousness as creating both an opposition between an active and passive principle, subject and object, as well as enabling their synthesis (see p. 432, n. 6 herein). For Fichte's and Schelling's view of the imagination as the faculty that reconciles opposite powers, see BL (CC), 1:299 and n. 1, 300 and n. 2.

different results by the process of discursive reasoning, it will then remain for us to elevate the Thesis from notional to actual, by contemplating intuitively this one power with its two inherent indestructible yet counteracting forces, and the results or generations to which their inter-penetration gives existence, in the living principle and in the process of our own self-consciousness. By what instrument this is possible the solution itself will discover, at the same time that it will reveal, to and for whom it is possible. Non omnia possumus omnes.[7] There is a philosophic, no less than a poetic genius,[8] which is differenced from the highest perfection of talent, not by degree but by kind.[9]

The counteraction then of the two assumed forces does not depend on their meeting from opposite directions; the power which acts in them is indestructible; it is therefore inexhaustibly re-ebullient; and as something must be the result of these two forces, both alike infinite, and both alike indestructible; and as rest or neutralization cannot be this result; no other conception is possible, but that the product must be a tertium aliquid, or finite generation. Consequently this conception is necessary. Now this tertium aliquid can be no other than an inter-penetration of the counteracting powers, partaking of both.[1]

*   *   *   *   *   *   *   *   *   *   *   *   *   *   *

Thus far had the work been transcribed for the press, when I received the following letter from a friend, whose practical judgement I have had ample reason to estimate and revere, and whose taste and sensibility preclude all the excuses which my self-love might possibly have prompted me to set up in plea against the decision of advisers of equal good sense, but with less tact and feeling.[2]

---

7. Virgil, *Eclogues* 8.63; "We are not all capable of everything."
8. An important point that serves C's attempt to establish his supremacy as thinker and philosopher through the impressive intellectual biography he presents in the first volume of the *Biographia*. In chapter 15 (in volume 2), before launching his critique of Wordsworth's critical principles in the Preface to the *LB* (1800), C reinforces this standard in his representation of Shakespeare's "DEPTH, and ENERGY of THOUGHT" as a characteristic of his genius, adding that "No man was ever yet a great poet, without being at the same time a profound philosopher" (*BL* [CC], 2:25–26).
9. On C's frequent distinction between genius and talent, see, e.g., *Friend* (CC), 1:419; *CN*, 3:3453; *Lects 1808–19* (CC), 1:287; p. 415, n. 2 herein and p. 462, n. 9 herein.
1. C's discussion here has close parallels with Schelling's elaboration of the principles of a "universal theory of nature" in *Einleitung zu seinem Entwurf eines Systems der Naturphilosophy* (Introduction to his Outlines of a System of Natural Philosophy) (Jena, 1799) (61; Davidson, 211), which deals with the generation of the product from an original "perpetual" antithesis between opposing forces in nature, mediated by *a tertium quid*: "Since that *tertium quid* itself *presupposes* the primary antithesis, the antithesis itself cannot be *absolutely* removed by it; *the condition of the continuance of that tertium quid* [of that third activity, or of Nature] *is the perpetual continuance of the antithesis*, just as, conversely, *the continuance of the antithesis is conditioned by the continuance of the tertium quid*" (Davidson, 211–12). *Tertium aliquid*: some third thing. See p. 397, n. 5 herein, and cf. Fichte's reference to "the accidental encounter of the efficacy of the I and the efficacy of the not-I *in some third thing which neither is nor can be anything more than that in which the I and the not-I meet* * * *" (*Grundriss des Eigenthümlichen der Wissenschaftslehre* [Outline of the Distinctive Character of the Wissenschaftslehre], 81; Breazeale, 291). See also Schelling, *System* (100; Heath, 51): "*Inasmuch as the opposing activities of self-consciousness merge in a third, there arises a common product of them both.*"
2. The letter was written by C himself to avoid a long discussion of the imagination and to bring volume 1 to closure.

"*Dear C.*

"*You ask my opinion concerning your Chapter on the Imagination, both as to the impressions it made on myself, and as to those which I think it will make on the* PUBLIC, *i.e. that part of the public, who from the title of the work and from its forming a sort of introduction to a volume of poems, are likely to constitute the great majority of your readers.*

"*As to myself, and stating in the first place the effect on my* understanding, *your opinions and method of argument were not only so new to me, but so directly the reverse of all I had ever been accustomed to consider as truth, that even if I had comprehended your premises sufficiently to have admitted them, and had seen the necessity of your conclusions, I should still have been in that state of mind, which in your note, p. [409], you have so ingeniously evolved, as the antithesis to that in which a man is, when he makes a bull.*[3] *In your own words, I should have felt as if I had been standing on my head.*

"*The effect on my* feelings, *on the other hand, I cannot better represent, than by supposing myself to have known only our light airy modern chapels of ease, and then for the first time to have been placed, and left alone, in one of our largest Gothic cathedrals in a gusty moonlight night of autumn.* "*Now in glimmer, and now in gloom;*"[4] *often in palpable darkness not without a chilly sensation of terror; then suddenly emerging into broad yet visionary lights with coloured shadows, of fantastic shapes yet all decked with holy insignia and mystic symbols; and ever and anon coming out full upon pictures and stone-work images of great men, with whose names I was familiar, but which looked upon me with countenances and an expression, the most dissimilar to all I had been in the habit of connecting with those names. Those whom I had been taught to venerate as almost super-human in magnitude of intellect, I found perched in little fret-work niches, as grotesque dwarfs; while the grotesques, in my hitherto belief, stood guarding the high altar with all the characters of Apotheosis. In short, what I had supposed substances were thinned away into shadows, while every where shadows were deepened into substances:*

> If substance may be call'd what shadow seem'd,
> For each seem'd either!
>
>   MILTON.[5]

"*Yet after all, I could not but repeat the lines which you had quoted from a MS. poem of your own in the* FRIEND, *and applied to a work of Mr. Wordsworth's though with a few of the words altered:*

> ——An orphic tale indeed,
> A tale *obscure* of high and passionate thoughts
> To *a strange* music chaunted![6]

3. See p. 409, n. 6 herein.
4. "Christabel," line 163 (p. 167 herein).
5. From the description of death in Milton, *Paradise Lost* 2.669–70 (var.), which C also cited and analyzed in Lecture 7 of the 1811 series (*Lects 1808–19* [CC], 1:311–12).
6. "To a Gentleman" ["To William Wordsworth"], lines 45–47 (var.) (p. 201 herein). A version of these lines appeared in the 1809 *The Friend*, which differs from this citation in capitalization and the use of "a Tale divine" for "A Tale *obscure*" and "To their own music" for "To *a strange* music" (*Friend* [CC], 2:258). For the manuscript version of these lines, see *BL* (1907), 1:271n.

"*Be assured, however, that I look forward anxiously to your great book on the* CONSTRUCTIVE PHILOSOPHY, *which you have promised and announced:*[7] *and that I will do my best to understand it. Only I will not promise to descend into the dark cave of Trophonius*[8] *with you, there to rub my own eyes, in order to* make *the sparks and figured flashes, which I am required to* see.

"*So much for myself. But as for the* PUBLIC, *I do not hesitate a moment in advising and urging you to withdraw the Chapter from the present work, and to reserve it for your announced treatises on the Logos or communicative intellect in Man and Deity.*[9] *First, because imperfectly as I understand the present Chapter, I see clearly that you have done too much, and yet not enough. You have been obliged to omit so many links, from the necessity of compression, that what remains, looks (if I may recur to my former illustration) like the fragments of the winding steps of an old ruined tower. Secondly, a still stronger argument (at least one that I am sure will be more forcible with you) is, that your readers will have both right and reason to complain of you. This Chapter, which cannot, when it is printed, amount to so little as an hundred pages, will of necessity greatly increase the expense of the work; and every reader who, like myself, is neither prepared or perhaps calculated for the study of so abstruse a subject so abstrusely treated, will, as I have before hinted, be almost entitled to accuse you of a sort of imposition on him. For who, he might truly observe, could from your title-page, viz.* "𝕸𝖞 𝕷𝖎𝖙𝖊𝖗𝖆𝖗𝖞 𝕷𝖎𝖋𝖊 𝖆𝖓𝖉 𝕺𝖕𝖎𝖓𝖎𝖔𝖓𝖘," *published too as introductory to a volume of miscellaneous poems, have anticipated, or even conjectured, a long treatise on ideal Realism,*[1] *which holds the same relation in abstruseness to Plotinus, as Plotinus does to Plato. It will be well, if already you have not too much of metaphysical disquisition in your work, though as the larger part of the disquisition is historical, it will doubtless be both interesting and instructive to many to whose* unprepared *minds your speculations on the esemplastic power*[2] *would be utterly unintelligible. Be assured, if you do publish this Chapter in the present work, you will be reminded of Bishop Berkley's Siris, announced as an Essay on Tarwater, which beginning with Tar ends with the Trinity,*[3] *the omne sci-*

---

7. On *Logosophia*, see p. 437, n. 9 herein; p. 447; 471, n. 5 herein. "Constructive philosophy" refers to the grounding of a philosophical system in primary concepts that are distinguished from those employed by other sciences, especially mathematics. Cf. Schelling's work *Ueber die Construktion in der Philosophie* (On Construction in Philosophy) (1803) and C's view, drawn from Schelling, that in geometry "the primary construction is not demonstrated, but postulated" (*BL* [CC], 1:248–49, 302n. 2).

8. In Greek mythology an architect who, after robbing a treasury he had designed with his brother Agamedes, was swallowed up by the earth and became an oracular god. Since his oracle was in a cave from which suppliants emerged dejected, it became proverbial to say of people appearing melancholy that they had visited the cave of Trophonius.

9. See n. 7 on this page.

1. A concept with which both Kant and Schelling defined their particular brand of transcendental idealism (see p. 470, n. 9 herein).

2. On the esemplastic power of imagination, see p. 449, n. 6 herein.

3. In *Siris: a Chain of Philosophical Reflexions and Inquiries Concerning the Virtues of Tar Water, and Divers other Subjects * * * * (Dublin, 1744), Berkeley began with an analysis of tar water and its medicinal uses and encompassed a variety of subjects, including the theory of acids; Newton's view of aether; the limitations of mechanical philosophy; and Platonic, Pythagorean, and Egyptian views on matter, spirit, and the deity. In the closing section of the book Berkeley showed that philosophers of Greece and the East, and in particular Plato,

bile[4] *forming the interspace. I say in the* present *work. In that greater work to which you have devoted so many years, and study so intense and various, it will be in its proper place. Your prospectus will have described and announced both its contents and their nature;*[5] *and if any persons purchase it, who feel no interest in the subjects of which it treats, they will have themselves only to blame.*

"*I could add to these arguments one derived from pecuniary motives, and particularly from the probable effects on the sale of your present publication; but they would weigh little with you compared with the preceding. Besides, I have long observed, that arguments drawn from your own personal interests more often act on you as narcotics than as stimulants,*[6] *and that in money concerns you have some small portion of pig-nature in your moral idiosyncracy, and like these amiable creatures, must occasionally be pulled backward from the boat in order to make you enter it. All success attend you, for if hard thinking and hard reading are merits, you have deserved it.*

> *Your affectionate, &c.*"

In consequence of this very judicious letter, which produced complete conviction on my mind, I shall content myself for the present with stating the main result of the Chapter, which I have reserved for that future publication, a detailed prospectus of which the reader will find at the close of the second volume.

The IMAGINATION then I consider either as primary, or secondary. The primary IMAGINATION I hold to be the living Power and prime Agent of all human Perception, and as a repetition in the finite mind of the eternal act of creation in the infinite I AM.[7] The secondary I consider as an echo of the former, co-existing with the conscious will, yet still as identical with the primary in the *kind* of its agency, and differing only in *degree*, and in the *mode* of its operation. It dissolves, diffuses, dissipates, in order to re-create; or where this process is rendered impossible, yet still at all events it struggles to idealize and to unify.[8] It is essentially

---

had a developed conception of the Trinity, which they reached not through reason but "by a divine tradition from the author of all things" (*Works*, 2:617, 624–27). C drew on this work repeatedly (see e.g. *SM* [CC], 27–28; *LS* [CC], 192–94) and expressed his appreciation of it in a marginal note (*CM* [CC], 1:410).

4. "Everything knowable" (cf. *BL* [CC], 1:235 and *CN*, 3:4134).
5. I.e., the *Logosophia* (see p. 487, n. 7 herein). The prospectus was probably never written and did not appear at the end of volume 2, as C claims here.
6. See chapter 11 (p. 462 herein) for the use of the stimulant/narcotic entanglement with reference to the impact of monetary incentives on "literary labor."
7. SC noted (*BL* [1847], 1:297n.) that C deleted the last part of the sentence from "and as a repetition" to "I AM" in a copy of the *Biographia*. See also chapter 12 and the notes to theses 6 and 7 (pp. 475–77 herein).
8. Much has been written on the distinction between the primary and the secondary imagination and its various sources in British and German philosophy, even as C did not give it any prominence in subsequent works. Among the numerous sources that can be cited for this passage, beginning with the distinction between the reproductive and productive imagination, Kant, *Pure Reason* (*BL* [CC], 1:lxxxv–xcvii, 304–05, n. 4), Tetens (McFarland, *Originality and Imagination*, 100–06, 108–09, 111–18), and Schelling are the most relevant. In Schelling C found both the model of a dual activity, one unconsciously, the other consciously productive, as well as a model of the repetition in an individual consciousness of the eternal "I AM." Cf. Schelling's view that reflective philosophy is "nothing but the free imitation, the free recapitulation of the original * * * act of self-consciousness," one that is absolutely free and necessary at the same time and therefore analogous to "an action in

vital, even as all objects (*as* objects) are essentially fixed and dead.[9]

FANCY, on the contrary, has no other counters to play with, but fixities and definites. The Fancy is indeed no other than a mode of Memory emancipated from the order of time and space; and blended with, and modified by that empirical phenomenon of the will, which we express by the word CHOICE. But equally with the ordinary memory it must receive all its materials ready made from the law of association.[1]

Whatever more than this, I shall think it fit to declare concerning the powers and privileges of the imagination in the present work, will be found in the critical essay on the uses of the Supernatural in poetry and the principles that regulate its introduction: which the reader will find prefixed to the poem of 𝕿𝖍𝖊 𝕬𝖓𝖈𝖎𝖊𝖓𝖙 𝕸𝖆𝖗𝖎𝖓𝖊𝖗.[2]

END OF VOLUME FIRST.

From Volume 2

CHAPTER XIV

Occasion of the Lyrical Ballads, and the objects originally proposed—Preface to the second edition—The ensuing controversy, its causes and acrimony—Philosophic definitions of a poem and poetry with scholia.[1]

During the first year that Mr. Wordsworth and I were neighbours,[2] our conversations turned frequently on the two cardinal points of poetry, the power of exciting the sympathy of the reader by a faithful adherence to the truth of nature, and the power of giving the interest of novelty by the modifying colours of imagination.[3] The sudden charm, which accidents of light and shade, which moon-light or sun-set diffused over a known and

God" (*System*, 92–97; Heath, 47–49). C refers to the existence of an "original unific Consciousness, the primary Perception" in *CN*, 3:3295, and to the relationship between imagination, imitation and repetition in *CN* 3:3744. See also his reference to a primary and secondary consciousness in his marginalia to Schelling's *Einleitung* (*CM* [CC], 4:374). C's passage on the imagination, though stressing along Schellingean lines the fundamental unity of consciousness, shows, however, the traces of a possible tear in the consummate fabric C creates here. To the extent to which the secondary imagination remains an echo of the first, which itself is an echo of the original creativity in the divine, its sphere of activity is inherently limited. To operate in the artistic sphere, the secondary imagination must necessarily also "dissolve" and "dissipate" rather than reproduce the data provided by the primary imagination; it must offer a new creation in its struggle to "unify" what has been rent asunder.

9. Cf. Schelling's view in *Abhandlungen* (223–24), reproduced by C in chapter 12, that an object by itself, separated from the activity of self-consciousness, is "something *dead*" and "*incapable* of any action" (p. 476 herein and p. 477, nn. 1 and 3 herein).
1. On the distinction between fancy and imagination, see p. 416, n. 5 herein; p. 417, n. 6 herein; p. 419, n. 7 herein; and *BL* [CC], 1:305n. 1. See also *CN*, 3:4066 on a comparison of fancy with "the Gorgon Head, which *looked* death into every thing" and the "worth & dignity of poetic Imagination, that fixing unfixes & while it melts & bedims the Image, still leaves in the Soul its living meaning—."
2. In a letter to Byron of 1815 (*CL*, 4:561) C also mentioned his plan to write "a Particular Preface to the Ancient Mariner and the Ballads, on the employment of the Supernatural in Poetry and the Laws which regulate it," but no such work has surfaced. The advertisement for Lecture 11 of the 1818 series also includes the subject of the supernatural, but no reports of the lecture are extant. See *Lects 1808–19* (CC), 2:188–94.
1. Explanatory notes or comments, usually on an ancient author.
2. The Wordsworths moved into Alfoxden House, three miles from C's cottage at Nether Stowey, on July 16, 1797, and left at the end of June 1798.
3. See the headnote to *Lyrical Ballads* (p. 55 herein).

familiar landscape, appeared to represent the practicability of combining both. These are the poetry of nature. The thought suggested itself (to which of us I do not recollect) that a series of poems might be composed of two sorts. In the one, the incidents and agents were to be, in part at least, supernatural; and the excellence aimed at was to consist in the interesting of the affections by the dramatic truth of such emotions, as would naturally accompany such situations, supposing them real. And real in *this* sense they have been to every human being who, from whatever source of delusion, has at any time believed himself under supernatural agency. For the second class, subjects were to be chosen from ordinary life; the characters and incidents were to be such, as will be found in every village and its vicinity, where there is a meditative and feeling mind to seek after them, or to notice them, when they present themselves.

In this idea originated the plan of the "Lyrical Ballads;" in which it was agreed, that my endeavours should be directed to persons and characters supernatural, or at least romantic; yet so as to transfer from our inward nature a human interest and a semblance of truth sufficient to procure for these shadows of imagination that willing suspension of disbelief for the moment, which constitutes poetic faith.[4] Mr. Wordsworth, on the other hand, was to propose to himself as his object, to give the charm of novelty to things of every day, and to excite a feeling analogous to the supernatural, by awakening the mind's attention from the lethargy of custom, and directing it to the loveliness and the wonders of the world before us; an inexhaustible treasure, but for which in consequence of the film of familiarity and selfish solicitude we have eyes, yet see not, ears that hear not, and hearts that neither feel nor understand.[5]

With this view I wrote the "Ancient Mariner," and was preparing among other poems, the "Dark Ladie,"[6] and the "Christabel," in which I should have more nearly realized my ideal, than I had done in my first attempt. But Mr. Wordsworth's industry had proved so much more successful, and the number of his poems so much greater, that my compositions, instead of forming a balance, appeared rather an interpolation of heterogeneous matter. Mr. Wordsworth added two or three poems written in his own character, in the impassioned, lofty, and sustained diction, which is characteristic of his genius. In this form the "Lyrical Ballads" were published;[7] and were presented by

---

4. On the "willing suspension of disbelief" in dramatic illusion, see "[On Dramatic Illusion]" (p. 328 herein).
5. Jeremiah 5.21: "Hear now this, O foolish people, and without understanding; which have eyes, and see not; which have ears, and hear not." Wordsworth's Preface to *LB* (1802) reads: "The principal object, then, proposed in these Poems was to choose incidents and situations from common life, and to relate or describe them, throughout, as far as was possible in a selection of language really used by men, and, at the same time, to throw over them a certain colouring of imagination, whereby ordinary things should be presented to the mind in an unusual way; and, further, and above all, to make these incidents and situations interesting by tracing in them, truly though not ostentatiously, the primary laws of our nature: chiefly, as far as regards the manner in which we associate ideas in a state of excitement" (*W Prose*, 1:123, 125).
6. See "Love" (p. 106, n. 1 herein) and the headnote to "Christabel" (p. 158 herein).
7. For C's contributions to *Lyrical Ballads*, see p. 54 herein. Wordsworth's poems "written in his own character" include "Tintern Abbey," the final poem in the volume and the last written. C perhaps also refers to "Lines Left upon a Seat in a Yew-Tree," "Lines Written at a Small Distance from My House," "Lines Written in Early Spring," "Expostulation and Reply," and "The Tables Turned."

him, as an *experiment*, whether subjects, which from their nature rejected the usual ornaments and extra-colloquial style of poems in general, might not be so managed in the language of ordinary life as to produce the pleasureable interest, which it is the peculiar business of poetry to impart.[8] To the second edition he added a preface of considerable length; in which notwithstanding some passages of apparently a contrary import, he was understood to contend for the extension of this style to poetry of all kinds, and to reject as vicious and indefensible all phrases and forms of style that were not included in what he (unfortunately, I think, adopting an equivocal expression) called the language of *real* life.[9] From this preface, prefixed to poems in which it was impossible to deny the presence of original genius, however mistaken its direction might be deemed, arose the whole long continued controversy. For from the conjunction of perceived power with supposed heresy I explain the inveteracy and in some instances, I grieve to say, the acrimonious passions, with which the controversy has been conducted by the assailants.[1]

Had Mr. Wordsworth's poems been the silly, the childish things, which they were for a long time described as being; had they been really distinguished from the compositions of other poets merely by meanness of language and inanity of thought; had they indeed contained nothing more than what is found in the parodies and pretended imitations of them;[2] they must have sunk at once, a dead weight, into the slough of oblivion, and have dragged the preface along with them.

8. The Advertisement to *LB* (1798) said, "The majority of the following poems are to be considered as experiments. They were written chiefly with a view to ascertain how far the language of conversation in the middle and lower classes of society is adapted to the purposes of poetic pleasure" (*W Prose*, 1:116).

9. The Preface first appeared in *LB* (1800), was expanded in *LB* (1802), and then reprinted with revisions in all subsequent editions. In 1836 Wordsworth removed most of the first-person references (*W Prose*, 1:111). In both the 1800 and 1802 versions Wordsworth claimed to use a "selection of the real language of men in a state of vivid sensation" (*W Prose*, 1:118, 119).

1. The connections between poetry, religion, and politics are clear in the opening paragraphs of Francis Jeffrey's review of Southey's *Thalaba* (1801) in the *Edinburgh Review* of October 1802, which attacked the "Lake School" (i.e., C, Wordsworth, and Southey).

> Poetry has this much, at least, in common with religion, that its standards were fixed long ago, by certain inspired writers, whose authority it is no longer lawful to call in question * * * . The author who is now before us [Southey], belongs to a *sect* of poets, that has established itself in this country within these ten or twelve years, and is looked upon, we believe, as one of its chief champions and apostles. The peculiar doctrines of this sect, it would not perhaps, be very easy to explain; but, that they are *dissenters* from the established systems in poetry and criticism * * * . The greater part of [their principles] will, we apprehend, be found to be composed of the following elements: 1. The antisocial principles, and distempered sensibility of Rousseau—his discontent with the present constitution of society—his paradoxical morality, and his perpetual hankerings after some unattainable state of voluptuous virtue and perfection. 2. The simplicity and energy * * * of [August von] Kotzebue [1761–1819, German playwright] and Schiller. 3. The homeliness and harshness of some of Cowper's language and versification, interchanged occasionally with the *innocence* of Ambrose Philips [1675–1749, pastoral poet], or the quaintness of [Francis] Quarles [1592–1644, epigrammatic poet], and Dr Donne * * * . Their most distinguishing symbol, is an affectation of great simplicity and familiarity of language [which produces] absolute meanness and insipidity [63–65].

2. Wordsworth's simplicity was ridiculed in, e.g., Richard Mant, *The Simpliciad; A Satirico-Dadactic Poem* (1808), an attack on Wordsworth, C, and Southey as members of "the Anti-Classical School"; Byron, *English Bards and Scotch Reviewers* (1809), lines 235–54; and Leigh Hunt, *Feast of the Poets* (1811), reprinted in 1814 with extensive notes on C, Southey, and Wordsworth (11–14, 75–109).

But year after year increased the number of Mr. Wordsworth's admirers. They were found too not in the lower classes of the reading public, but chiefly among young men of strong sensibility and meditative minds; and their admiration (inflamed perhaps in some degree by opposition) was distinguished by its intensity, I might almost say, by its *religious* fervour. These facts, and the intellectual energy of the author, which was more or less consciously felt, where it was outwardly and even boisterously denied, meeting with sentiments of aversion to his opinions, and of alarm at their consequences, produced an eddy of criticism, which would of itself have borne up the poems by the violence, with which it whirled them round and round. With many parts of this preface in the sense attributed to them and which the words undoubtedly seem to authorise, I never concurred; but on the contrary objected to them as erroneous in principle, and as contradictory (in appearance at least) both to other parts of the same preface, and to the author's own practice in the greater number of the poems themselves. Mr. Wordsworth in his recent collection[3] has, I find, degraded this prefatory disquisition to the end of his second volume, to be read or not at the reader's choice. But he has not, as far as I can discover, announced any change in his poetic creed. At all events, considering it as the source of a controversy, in which I have been honored more, than I deserve, by the frequent conjunction of my name with his, I think it expedient to declare once for all, in what points I coincide with his opinions, and in what points I altogether differ. But in order to render myself intelligible I must previously, in as few words as possible, explain my ideas, first, of a POEM; and secondly, of POETRY itself, in *kind*, and in *essence*.

The office of philosophical *disquisition* consists in just *distinction*; while it is the priviledge of the philosopher to preserve himself constantly aware, that distinction is not division. In order to obtain adequate notions of any truth, we must intellectually separate its distinguishable parts; and this is the technical *process* of philosophy. But having so done, we must then restore them in our conceptions to the unity, in which they actually co-exist; and this is the *result* of philosophy. A poem contains the same elements as a prose composition; the difference therefore must consist in a different combination of them, in consequence of a different object proposed. According to the difference of the object will be the difference of the combination. It is possible, that the object may be merely to facilitate the recollection of any given facts or observations by artificial arrangement; and the composition will be a poem, merely because it is distinguished from prose by metre, or by rhyme, or by both conjointly. In this, the lowest sense, a man might attribute the name of a poem to the well known enumeration of the days in the several months;

---

3. *Poems by William Wordsworth: Including Lyrical Ballads, and the Miscellaneous Pieces of the Author, With Additional Poems, A New Preface, and a Supplementary Essay,* 2 vols. (1815). The first volume began with a new preface and concluded with an "Essay, Supplementary to the Preface" on poetic diction. A revised version of the Preface to *LB* (1802) concluded the second volume. In July 1802 C told William Sotheby that the Preface to *LB* derived from his conversations with Wordsworth, and was originally supposed to be written by Coleridge himself (*CL*, 2:811–12).

> Thirty days hath September,
> April, June, and November, &c.

and others of the same class and purpose. And as a particular pleasure is found in anticipating the recurrence of sounds and quantities, all compositions that have this charm superadded, whatever be their contents, *may* be entitled poems.

So much for the superficial *form*. A difference of object and contents supplies an additional ground of distinction. The immediate purpose may be the communication of truths; either of truth absolute and demonstrable, as in works of science; or of facts experienced and recorded, as in history. Pleasure, and that of the highest and most permanent kind, may *result* from the *attainment* of the end; but it is not itself the immediate end. In other works the communication of pleasure may be the immediate purpose; and though truth, either moral or intellectual, ought to be the *ultimate* end, yet this will distinguish the character of the author, not the class to which the work belongs. Blest indeed is that state of society, in which the immediate purpose would be baffled by the perversion of the proper ultimate end; in which no charm of diction or imagery could exempt the Bathyllus even of an Anacreon, or the Alexis of Virgil, from disgust and aversion![4]

But the communication of pleasure may be the immediate object of a work not metrically composed; and that object may have been in a high degree attained, as in novels and romances. Would then the mere superaddition of metre, with or without rhyme, entitle *these* to the name of poems? The answer is, that nothing can permanently please, which does not contain in itself the reason why it is so, and not otherwise. If metre be superadded, all other parts must be made consonant with it.[5] They must be such, as to justify the perpetual and distinct attention to each part, which an exact correspondent recurrence of accent and sound are calculated to excite. The final definition then, so deduced, may be thus worded. A poem is that species of composition, which is opposed to works of science, by proposing for its *immediate* object pleasure, not truth; and from all other species (having *this* object in common with it) it is discriminated by proposing to itself such delight from the *whole*, as is compatible with a distinct gratification from each component *part*.

Controversy is not seldom excited in consequence of the disputants attaching each a different meaning to the same word; and in few instances has this been more striking, than in disputes concerning the present subject. If a man chooses to call every composition a poem,

---

4. C objects to the representation of homosexual love in poetry: Virgil's second *Eclogue* is a lament by the shepherd Coridon for Alexis, and the seventeenth of the *Anacreontea* (poems written in the style of the ancient Greek poet Anacreon but no longer thought to be by him) is an ode to the poet's beloved Bathyllus.

5. Wordsworth begins a long addition, printed in 1802, to the Preface to *LB* with the comments that the poet offers a "selection of the language really spoken by men; that this selection * * * will entirely separate the composition from the vulgarity and meanness of ordinary life; and, if metre be superadded thereto, I believe that a dissimilitude will be produced altogether sufficient for the gratification of a rational mind" (*W Prose*, 1:137). Wordsworth does not argue for the unmediated imitation of the syntax of ordinary speech, as C implies in chapter 20, but he does suggest that meter is simply "superadded."

which is rhyme, or measure, or both, I must leave his opinion uncontroverted. The distinction is at least competent to characterize the writer's intention. If it were subjoined, that the whole is likewise entertaining or affecting, as a tale, or as a series of interesting reflections, I of course admit this as another fit ingredient of a poem, and an additional merit. But if the definition sought for be that of a *legitimate* poem, I answer, it must be one, the parts of which mutually support and explain each other; all in their proportion harmonizing with, and supporting the purpose and known influences of metrical arrangement. The philosophic critics of all ages coincide with the ultimate judgement of all countries, in equally denying the praises of a just poem, on the one hand, to a series of striking lines or distichs, each of which absorbing the whole attention of the reader to itself disjoins it from its context, and makes it a separate whole, instead of an harmonizing part; and on the other hand, to an unsustained composition, from which the reader collects rapidly the general result unattracted by the component parts.[6] The reader should be carried forward, not merely or chiefly by the mechanical impulse of curiosity, or by a restless desire to arrive at the final solution; but by the pleasureable activity of mind excited by the attractions of the journey itself. Like the motion of a serpent, which the Egyptians made the emblem of intellectual power; or like the path of sound through the air; at every step he pauses and half recedes, and from the retrogressive movement collects the force which again carries him onward.[7] Precipitandus est *liber* spiritus, says Petronius Arbiter most happily.[8] The epithet, *liber*, here balances the preceding verb; and it is not easy to conceive more meaning condensed in fewer words.

But if this should be admitted as a satisfactory character of a poem, we have still to seek for a definition of poetry. The writings of PLATO, and Bishop TAYLOR, and the Theoria Sacra of BURNET,[9] furnish undeniable proofs that poetry of the highest kind may exist without metre, and even without the contradistinguishing objects of a poem. The first chapter of Isaiah (indeed a very large proportion of the whole book) is poetry in the most emphatic sense; yet it would be not less irrational than strange to assert, that pleasure, and not truth, was the immediate object of the prophet. In short, whatever *specific* import we attach to

---

6. See, e.g., Aristotle, *Poetics* 8.4.1451a (trans. Ingram Bywater in *The Complete Works of Aristotle* [Princeton, 1984], 2322): "just as in the other imitative arts one imitation is always of one thing, so in poetry the story, as an imitation of action, must represent one action, a complete whole, with its several incidents so closely connected that the transposition or withdrawal of any one of them will disjoin and dislocate the whole." For C's definition of beauty as the "reduction of the many to one," see *Essays on the Principles of Genial Criticism* (p. 345 herein).

7. Cf. C's example of the water insect in chapter 7 (p. 432 herein).

8. Petronius, *Satyricon* 118 (trans. Michael Heseltine and E. H. Warmington [LCL, 1969], 297): "The free spirit of genius must plunge headlong * * * into allusions and divine interpositions, and rack itself for great thoughts coloured by mythology, so that what results seems rather the prophecies of an inspired seer than the exactitude of a statement made on oath before witnesses."

9. Jeremy Taylor (1613–1667), an Anglican bishop whose prose style C admired, is best known for his devotional works *The Rule and Exercise of Holy Living* (1650) and *The Rule and Exercise of Holy Dying* (1651). Thomas Burnet (1635–1715) wrote, first in Latin and then in English, *The Sacred Theory of the Earth* (1684–90), an account of the earth's fate after the Flood, which C thought of rewriting in blank verse (CN, 1:61).

the word, poetry, there will be found involved in it, as a necessary consequence, that a poem of any length neither can be, or ought to be, all poetry. Yet if an harmonious whole is to be produced, the remaining parts must be preserved *in keeping* with the poetry; and this can be no otherwise effected than by such a studied selection and artificial arrangement, as will partake of *one*, though not a *peculiar*, property of poetry. And this again can be no other than the property of exciting a more continuous and equal attention, than the language of prose aims at, whether colloquial or written.

My own conclusions on the nature of poetry, in the strictest use of the word, have been in part anticipated in the preceding disquisition on the fancy and imagination. What is poetry? is so nearly the same question with, what is a poet?[1] that the answer to the one is involved in the solution of the other. For it is a distinction resulting from the poetic genius itself, which sustains and modifies the images, thoughts, and emotions of the poet's own mind. The poet, described in *ideal* perfection, brings the whole soul of man into activity,[2] with the subordination of its faculties to each other, according to their relative worth and dignity. He diffuses a tone, and spirit of unity, that blends, and (as it were) *fuses*, each into each, by that synthetic and magical power, to which we have exclusively appropriated the name of imagination. This power, first put in action by the will and understanding, and retained under their irremissive, though gentle and unnoticed, controul (*laxis effertur habenis*)[3] reveals itself in the balance or reconciliation of opposite or discordant qualities:[4] of sameness, with difference; of the general, with the concrete; the idea, with the image; the individual, with the representative; the sense of novelty and freshness, with old and familiar objects; a more than usual state of emotion, with more than usual order; judgement ever awake and steady self-possession, with enthusiasm and feeling profound or vehement; and while it blends and harmonizes the natural and the artificial, still subordinates art to nature; the manner to the matter; and our admiration of the poet to our sympathy with the poetry. "Doubtless," as Sir John Davies

1. Wordsworth's 1802 addition to the Preface to *Lyrical Ballads* begins with the question:

   What is a Poet? * * * He is a man speaking to men: a man, it is true, endued with more lively sensibility, more enthusiasm and tenderness, who has a greater knowledge of human nature, and a more comprehensive soul, than are supposed to be common among mankind; a man pleased with his own passions and volitions, and who rejoices more than other men in the spirit of life that is in him; delighting to contemplate similar volitions and passions as manifested in the goings-on of the Universe, and habitually impelled to create them where he does not find them [*W Prose*, 1:138].

2. Cf. Schelling, *System*: "Art brings *the whole man*, as he is, to that point, namely to a knowledge of the highest, and this is what underlies the eternal difference and the marvel of art." Schelling refers to the difference between art and philosophy, the latter involving only "the fraction of a man" (Heath, 233).
3. "Carried on with slackened reins." Line 39 from Petrarch, "Epistle to Barbato di Sulmona," which C copied into his notebook in 1813 (*CN*, 3:4178 and n.; *BL* [*CC*], 2:16n. 6) and used to conclude chapter 10 (p. 461 herein) and as the motto for "Love Poems" in *Sibylline Leaves*.
4. C's argument here has an affinity with Friedrich Schiller's in *On the Aesthestic Education of Man* (1795), which proposes that successful poetry represents a balance of potentialities in the mind. In *The Prelude* (1805) 1.352–55 Wordsworth attributed to nature a power similar to that which C attributes to imagination: "There is a dark / Invisible workmanship that reconciles / Discordant elements, and makes them move / In one society."

observes of the soul (and his words may with slight alteration be applied, and even more appropriately to the poetic IMAGINATION.)

> Doubtless this could not be, but that she turns
> Bodies to spirit by sublimation strange,
> As fire converts to fire the things it burns,
> As we our food into our nature change.

> From their gross matter she abstracts their forms,
> And draws a kind of quintessence from things;
> Which to her proper nature she transforms
> To bear them light, on her celestial wings.

> Thus does she, when from individual states
> She doth abstract the universal kinds;
> Which then re-clothed in divers names and fates
> Steal access through our senses to our minds.[5]

Finally, GOOD SENSE is the BODY of poetic genius, FANCY its DRAPERY, MOTION its LIFE, and IMAGINATION the SOUL that is every where, and in each; and forms all into one graceful and intelligent whole.

FROM CHAPTER XVII

Examination of the tenets peculiar to Mr. Wordsworth—Rustic life (above all, low and rustic life) especially unfavorable to the formation of a human diction—The best parts of language the product of philosophers, not clowns or shepherds—Poetry essentially ideal and generic—The language of Milton as much the language of real life, yea, incomparably more so than that of the cottager.

* * *

My own differences from certain supposed parts of Mr. Wordsworth's theory ground themselves on the assumption, that his words had been rightly interpreted, as purporting that the proper diction for poetry in general consists altogether in a language taken, with due exceptions, from the mouths of men in real life, a language which actually constitutes the natural conversation of men under the influence of natural feelings. My objection is, first, that in *any* sense this rule is applicable only to *certain* classes of poetry; secondly, that even to these classes it is not applicable, except in such a sense, as hath never by any one (as far as I know or have read) been denied or doubted; and lastly, that as far as, and in that degree in which it is *practicable*, yet as a *rule* it is useless, if not injurious, and therefore either need not, or ought not to be practised. The poet informs his reader, that he had generally chosen *low and rustic* life; but not *as low*

5. Sir John Davies, *Nosce Teipsum: Of the Soule of Man and the Immortalitie Thereof* (1599), under the heading "That it cannot be a bodie," stanzas 8–10. SC, in *BL* (1847), 2:15n. 10, noted that C rewrote the last stanza, which in the original runs, "This doth she when from things *particular* / She doth abstract the *universall kinds*, / Which bodiless, and immateriall are, / And can be lodg'd but onely in our minds." He also substituted "food" for "meats" in line 4. C copied this quotation with his alterations into a notebook in 1811 with the comment, "the words & lines in the last stanza * * * added by me to apply these verses to the Poetic Genius" (*CN*, 3:4112).

and rustic, or in order to repeat that pleasure of doubtful moral effect, which persons of elevated rank and of superior refinement oftentimes derive from a happy *imitation* of the rude unpolished manners and discourse of their inferiors. For the pleasure so derived may be traced to three exciting causes. The first is the naturalness, in *fact*, of the things represented. The second is the apparent naturalness of the *representation*, as raised and qualified by an imperceptible infusion of the author's own knowledge and talent, which infusion does, indeed, constitute it an *imitation* as distinguished from a mere *copy*.[6] The third cause may be found in the reader's conscious feeling of his superiority awakened by the contrast presented to him; even as for the same purpose the kings and great barons of yore retained, sometimes *actual* clowns and fools, but more frequently shrewd and witty fellows in that *character*. These, however, were not Mr. Wordsworth's objects. *He* chose low and rustic life, "because in that condition the essential passions of the heart find a better soil, in which they can attain their maturity, are less under restraint, and speak a plainer and more emphatic language; because in that condition of life our elementary feelings co-exist in a state of greater simplicity, and consequently may be more accurately contemplated, and more forcibly communicated; because the manners of rural life germinate from those elementary feelings; and from the necessary character of rural occupations are more easily comprehended, and are more durable; and lastly, because in that condition the passions of men are incorporated with the beautiful and permanent forms of nature."[7]

Now it is clear to me, that in the most interesting of the poems, in which the author is more or less dramatic, as the "Brothers," "Michael," "Ruth," the "Mad Mother," &c.[8] the persons introduced are by no means taken *from low or rustic life* in the common acceptation of those words; and it is not less clear, that the sentiments and language, as far as they can be conceived to have been really transferred from the minds and conversation of such persons, are attributable to causes and circumstances not necessarily connected with "their occupations and abode." The thoughts, feelings, language, and manners of the shepherd-farmers in the vales of Cumberland and Westmoreland, as far as they are actually adopted in those poems, may be accounted for from causes, which will and do produce the same results in *every* state of life, whether in town or country. As the two principal I rank that INDEPENDENCE, which raises a man above servitude, or daily toil for the profit of others, yet not above the necessity of in-

---

6. See "[On Dramatic Illusion]" (p. 337, n. 5 herein).
7. C quotes the revised 1802 Preface to *LB* (*W Prose*, 1:125).
8. "The Brothers" (1800) is a dialogue between a clergyman and a shepherd who has returned to his native village "with some small wealth" after a twenty-year absence to find out that his brother is dead. In "Michael" (1800) the main character is a shepherd who is so strongly attached to his property that, in the hope of keeping it, he sends his son away to work. Wordsworth regarded Michael as representative of the class of "statesmen, men of respectable education who daily labour on their own little properties. The domestic affections will always be strong amongst men * * * if these men are placed above poverty" (*LB* [1992], 401). Ruth marries a military man, emigrates with him to America, is abandoned, and goes mad. "The Mad Mother" became "Her Eyes are Wild" in 1815.

dustry and a frugal simplicity of domestic life; and the accompanying unambitious, but solid and religious EDUCATION, which has rendered few books familiar, but the bible, and the liturgy or hymn book. To this latter cause, indeed, which is so far *accidental*, that it is the blessing of particular countries and a particular age, not the product of particular places or employments, the poet owes the shew of probability, that his personages might really feel, think, and talk with any tolerable resemblance to his representation. It is an excellent remark of Dr. Henry More's (Enthusiasmus triumphatus, Sec. xxxv) that "a man of confined education, but of good parts, by constant reading of the bible will naturally form a more winning and commanding rhetoric than those that are learned; the intermixture of tongues and of artificial phrases debasing *their* style."[9]

It is, moreover, to be considered that to the formation of healthy feelings, and a reflecting mind, *negations* involve impediments not less formidable, than sophistication and vicious intermixture. I am convinced, that for the human soul to prosper in rustic life, a certain vantage-ground is pre-requisite. It is not every man, that is likely to be improved by a country life or by country labours. Education, or original sensibility, or both, must pre-exist, if the changes, forms, and incidents of nature are to prove a sufficient stimulant. And where these are not sufficient, the mind contracts and hardens by want of stimulants; and the man becomes selfish, sensual, gross, and hard-hearted. Let the management of the POOR LAWS in Liverpool, Manchester, or Bristol be compared with the ordinary dispensation of the poor rates in agricultural villages, where the *farmers* are the overseers and guardians of the poor.[1] If my own experience have not been particularly unfortunate, as well as that of the many respectable country clergymen with whom I have conversed on the subject, the result would engender more than scepticism concerning the desirable influences of low and rustic life in and for itself. Whatever may be concluded on the other side, from the stronger local attachments and enterprizing spirit of the Swiss, and other mountaineers, applies to a particular mode of pastoral life, under forms of property, that permit and beget manners truly republican, not to rustic life in general, or to the absence of artificial cultivation. On the contrary the mountaineers, whose manners have been so often eulogized, are in general better educated and greater readers than men of equal rank elsewhere. But where this is not the case, as among the peasantry of North Wales, the ancient mountains, with all their terrors and all their glories, are pictures to the blind, and music to the deaf.

I should not have entered so much into detail upon this passage, but here seems to be the point, to which all the lines of difference converge as to their source and centre. (I mean, as far as, and in what-

9. C quotes (var.) from Henry More's *Enthusiasmus Triumphatus* (originally published 1656), an attack on imagined religious inspiration. In 1801–02 C copied out this passage from More's *Collection of Several Philosophical Writings* (1662), 2:24 (CN, 1:1000I).

1. Poor rates were taxes levied on landowners for the relief of the poor. These taxes increased dramatically between 1776 and 1820, impoverishing many landholding farmers.

ever respect, my poetic creed *does* differ from the doctrines promulged in this preface.) I adopt with full faith the principle of Aristotle, that poetry as poetry is essentially[2] *ideal*, that it avoids and excludes all *accident*; that its apparent individualities of rank, character, or occupation must be *representative* of a class; and that the *persons* of poetry must be clothed with *generic* attributes, with the *common* attributes of the class; not with such as one gifted individual might *possibly* possess, but such as from his situation it is most probable before-hand, that he *would* possess.[3] If my premises are right, and my deductions legitimate, it follows that there can be no *poetic* medium between the swains of Theocritus[4] and those of an imaginary golden age.

The characters of the vicar and the shepherd-mariner in the poem of the "BROTHERS," those of the shepherd of Green-head Gill in the "MICHAEL," have all the verisimilitude and representative quality, that the purposes of poetry can require. They are persons of a known and abiding class, and their manners and sentiments the natural product of circumstances common to the class. Take "MICHAEL" for instance:

> An old man stout of heart, and strong of limb;
> His bodily frame had been from youth to age
> Of an unusual strength: his mind was keen,
> Intense and frugal, apt for all affairs,
> And in his shepherd's calling he was prompt
> And watchful more than ordinary men.
> Hence he had learnt the meaning of all winds,
> Of blasts of every tone, and oftentimes
> When others heeded not, he heard the South
> Make subterraneous music, like the noise
> Of bagpipers on distant highland hills.
> The shepherd, at such warning, of his flock
> Bethought him, and he to himself would say,
> The winds are now devising work for me!
> And truly at all times the storm, that drives
> The traveller to a shelter, summon'd him
> Up to the mountains. He had been alone
> Amid the heart of many thousand mists,
> That came to him and left him on the heights.
> So liv'd he, till his eightieth year was pass'd.
> And grossly that man errs, who should suppose
> That the green vallies, and the streams and rocks,
> Were things indifferent to the shepherd's thoughts.
> Fields, where with chearful spirits he had breath'd
> The common air; the hills, which he so oft
> Had climb'd with vigorous steps; which had impress'd
> So many incidents upon his mind
> Of hardship, skill or courage, joy or fear;

2. A note in which C quotes from *The Friend* is omitted here.
3. Aristotle, *Poetics* 9.1451b (*The Complete Works*, 2323): "Hence poetry is something more philosophic and of graver import than history, since its statements are of the nature of universals, whereas those of history are of singulars."
4. Greek bucolic poet (early 3rd century B.C.E.).

Which like a book preserved the memory
Of the dumb animals, whom he had sav'd,
Had fed or shelter'd, linking to such acts,
So grateful in themselves, the certainty
Of honorable gains; these fields, these hills
Which were his living being, even more
Than his own blood—what could they less? had laid
Strong hold on his affections, were to him
A pleasurable feeling of blind love,
The pleasure which there is in life itself.[5]

On the other hand, in the poems which are pitched at a lower note, as the "Harry Gill," "Idiot Boy," &c. the *feelings* are those of human nature in general; though the poet has judiciously laid the *scene* in the country, in order to place *himself* in the vicinity of interesting images, without the necessity of ascribing a sentimental perception of their beauty to the persons of his drama.[6] In the "Idiot Boy," indeed, the mother's character is not so much a real and native product of a "situation where the essential passions of the heart find a better soil, in which they can attain their maturity and speak a plainer and more emphatic language,"[7] as it is an impersonation of an instinct abandoned by judgement. Hence the two following charges seem to me not wholly groundless: at least, they are the only plausible objections, which I have heard to that fine poem. The one is, that the author has not, in the poem itself, taken sufficient care to preclude from the reader's fancy the disgusting images of *ordinary*, *morbid idiocy*, which yet it was by no means his intention to represent. He has even by the "burr, burr, burr," uncounteracted by any preceding description of the boy's beauty, assisted in recalling them.[8] The other is, that the idiocy of the *boy* is so evenly balanced by the folly of the *mother*, as to present to the general reader rather a laughable burlesque on the blindness of anile dotage, than an analytic display of maternal affection in its ordinary workings.[9]

In the "Thorn," the poet himself acknowledges in a note the necessity of an introductory poem, in which he should have pourtrayed the character of the person from whom the words of the poem are supposed to proceed: a superstitious man moderately imaginative, of slow faculties and deep feelings, "a captain of a small trading vessel, for example, who being past the middle age of life, had retired upon an annuity, or small independent income, to some village or country town of

---

5. "Michael" (1800), lines 42–79 (var.).
6. "Goodly Blake and Harry Gill" displays the feelings of Harry Gill, who believes himself cursed. In the Preface to *LB* (1800) Wordsworth commented that the poem "is one of the rudest of this collection" and that the purpose of "The Idiot Boy" is to trace "the maternal passion through many of its more subtle windings" (*W Prose*, 1:150, 126).
7. C repeats (with omissions) the quotation from p. 497 herein, but here the wording is closer to the 1800 Preface, since C uses "situation" rather than the later "condition" (*W Prose*, 1:124–25).
8. Cf. "The Idiot Boy" (1798), lines 107–08, 387–88: "Burr, burr—now Johnny's lips they burr, / As loud as any mill, or near it" and "And Johnny burrs, and laughs aloud, / Whether in cunning or in joy, / I cannot tell."
9. Cf. Byron, *English Bards and Scotch Reviewers* (1809), lines 247–48: "Betty Foy / The idiot mother of 'an idiot boy.' "

which he was not a native, or in which he had not been accustomed to live. Such men having nothing to do become credulous and talkative from indolence."[1] But in a poem, still more in a lyric poem (and the NURSE in Shakespeare's Romeo and Juliet alone prevents me from extending the remark even to dramatic *poetry*, if indeed the Nurse itself can be deemed altogether a case in point)[2] it is not possible to imitate truly a dull and garrulous discourser, without repeating the effects of dulness and garrulity.[3] However this may be, I dare assert, that the parts (and these form the far larger portion of the whole) which might as well or still better have proceeded from the poet's own imagination, and have been spoken in his own character, are those which have given, and which will continue to give universal delight; and that the passages exclusively appropriate to the supposed narrator, such as the last couplet of the third stanza;[4] the seven last lines of the tenth;[5] and the five following stanzas, with the exception of the four admirable lines at the commencement of the fourteenth are felt by many unprejudiced and unsophisticated hearts, as sudden and unpleasant sinkings from the height to which the poet had previously lifted them,[6] and to which he again re-elevates both himself and his reader.

If then I am compelled to doubt the theory, by which the choice of *characters* was to be directed, not only *a priori*, from grounds of reason, but both from the few instances in which the poet himself *need* be supposed to have been governed by it, and from the comparative inferiority of those instances; still more must I hesitate in my assent to the sentence which immediately follows the former citation; and which I can neither admit as particular fact, or as general rule. "The language too of these men is adopted (purified indeed from what appears to be its real defects, from all lasting and rational causes of dislike or disgust) because such men hourly communicate with the best objects from which the best part of language is originally derived; and because, from their rank in society, and the sameness and narrow circle of their intercourse, being less under the action of social vanity,

1. C quotes (var.) from Wordsworth's note to "The Thorn," included in editions of *LB* from 1800 to 1805. In the note Wordsworth acknowledged the need for an introductory poem to illustrate "the general laws by which superstition acts upon the mind. Superstitious men are almost always men of slow faculties and deep feelings; their minds are not loose but adhesive; they have a reasonable share of imagination, by which word I mean the faculty which produces impressive effects out of simple elements; but they are utterly destitute of fancy, the power by which pleasure and surprize are excited by sudden varieties of situation and by accumulated imagery" (*LB* [1992], 351).
2. See C's comments on the nurse in "[On *Romeo and Juliet*]" (p. 313 herein).
3. Cf. Southey's judgment on "The Thorn" in his review of *LB* (1798) in the *Critical Review* (October 1798): 200: "The author should have recollected that he who personates tiresome loquacity, become tiresome himself."
4. In a footnote (omitted here) C quotes "The Thorn" (1798), lines 32–33: "I've measured it from side to side; / 'Tis three feet long, and two feet wide." When Henry Crabb Robinson slighted these lines, Wordsworth responded that "they ought to be liked" (*CRB*, 1:166); but in 1820 he changed them to "Though but of compass small, and bare / To thirsty suns and parching air" (*LB* [1992], 78; *BL* [*CC*], 2:50n. 1).
5. In a footnote (omitted here) C quotes "The Thorn" (1815), lines 104–43, 148–65. In 1820 Wordsworth extensively revised the poem, including the first eleven lines quoted in C's note (*LB* [1992], 80–82).
6. C alludes to Pope's *Peri Bathous: or, Martinus Scriblerus, His Treatise of the Art of Sinking in Poetry* (1728), which ridicules inappropriate language in poetry and contrasts it with the language of sublimity.

they convey their feelings and notions in simple and unelaborated expressions."[7] To this I reply; that a rustic's language, purified from all provincialism and grossness, and so far re-constructed as to be made consistent with the rules of grammar (which are in essence no other than the laws of universal logic, applied to Psychological materials) will not differ from the language of any other man of common-sense, however learned or refined he may be, except as far as the notions, which the rustic has to convey, are fewer and more indiscriminate. This will become still clearer, if we add the consideration (equally important though less obvious) that the rustic, from the more imperfect developement of his faculties, and from the lower state of their cultivation, aims almost solely to convey *insulated facts*, either those of his scanty experience or his traditional belief; while the educated man chiefly seeks to discover and express those *connections* of things, or those relative *bearings* of fact to fact, from which some more or less general law is deducible. For *facts* are valuable to a wise man, chiefly as they lead to the discovery of the indwelling *law*, which is the true *being* of things, the sole solution of their modes of existence, and in the knowledge of which consists our dignity and our power.

As little can I agree with the assertion, that from the objects with which the rustic hourly communicates, the best part of language is formed. For first, if to communicate with an object implies such an acquaintance with it, as renders it capable of being discriminately reflected on; the distinct knowledge of an uneducated rustic would furnish a very scanty vocabulary. The few things, and modes of action, requisite for his bodily conveniences, would alone be individualized; while all the rest of nature would be expressed by a small number of confused, general terms. Secondly, I deny that the words and combinations of words derived from the objects, with which the rustic is familiar, whether with distinct or confused knowledge, can be justly said to form the *best* part of language. It is more than probable, that many classes of the brute creation possess discriminating sounds, by which they can convey to each other notices of such objects as concern their food, shelter, or safety. Yet we hesitate to call the aggregate of such sounds a language, otherwise than metaphorically. The best part of human language, properly so called, is derived from reflection on the acts of the mind itself.[8] It is formed by a voluntary appropriation of fixed symbols to internal acts, to processes and results of imagination, the greater part of which have no place in the consciousness of uneducated man; though in civilized society, by imitation and passive remembrance of what they hear from their religious instructors and other superiors, the most uneducated share in the harvest which they neither sowed or reaped. If the history of the phrases in hourly currency among our peasants were traced, a person not previously aware of the fact would be surprised at finding so large a number, which

---

7. C quotes from the 1802 version of the Preface to *Lyrical Ballads* (*W Prose*, 1:124).
8. For further reflections on the nature of language, see the Preface to *Aids to Reflection* (p. 571 herein) and "Language" (p. 594 herein).

three or four centuries ago were the exclusive property of the universities and the schools; and at the commencement of the Reformation had been transferred from the school to the pulpit, and thus gradually passed into common life. The extreme difficulty, and often the impossibility, of finding words for the simplest moral and intellectual processes in the languages of uncivilized tribes has proved perhaps the weightiest obstacle to the progress of our most zealous and adroit missionaries. Yet these tribes are surrounded by the same nature, as our peasants are; but in still more impressive forms; and they are, moreover, obliged to *particularize* many more of them. When therefore Mr. Wordsworth adds, "accordingly such a language" (meaning, as before, the language of rustic life purified from provincialism) "arising out of repeated experience and regular feelings is a more permanent, and a far more philosophical language, than that which is frequently substituted for it by poets, who think they are conferring honor upon themselves and their art in proportion as they indulge in arbitrary and capricious habits of expression;"[9] it may be answered, that the language, which he has in view, can be attributed to rustics with no greater right, than the style of Hooker or Bacon to Tom Brown or Sir Roger L'Estrange.[1] Doubtless, if what is peculiar to each were omitted in each, the result must needs be the same. Further, that the poet, who uses an illogical diction, or a style fitted to excite only the low and changeable pleasure of wonder by means of groundless novelty, substitutes a language of *folly* and *vanity*, not for that of the *rustic*, but for that of *good sense* and *natural feeling*.

Here let me be permitted to remind the reader, that the positions, which I controvert, are contained in the sentences—"*a selection of the* REAL *language of men;*"—"*the language of these men* (i. e. men in low and rustic life) *I propose to myself to imitate, and as far as possible, to adopt the very language of men.*" "*Between the language of prose and that of metrical composition, there neither is, nor can be any essential difference.*"[2] It is against these exclusively, that my opposition is directed.

I object, in the very first instance, to an equivocation in the use of the word "real." Every man's language varies, according to the extent of his knowledge, the activity of his faculties, and the depth or quickness of his feelings. Every man's language has, first, its *individualities*; secondly, the common properties of the *class* to which he belongs; and thirdly, words and phrases of *universal* use. The language of Hooker, Bacon, Bishop Taylor, and Burke, differ from the common language of the learned class only by the superior number and novelty of the

---

9. C omits a clause after "in proportion as they": "separate themselves from the sympathies of men, and" (*W Prose*, 1:124).

1. Richard Hooker (c. 1554–1600), Anglican divine; Thomas Brown (1663–1704), satirist and Tory pamphleteer; Sir Roger L 'Estrange (1616–1704), journalist and royalist pamphleteer.

2. C cites the 1802 revisions of the Preface to *LB* (*W Prose*, 1:123, 131, 135). The actual wording of first passage is "a selection of language really used by men"; the second, "My purpose was to imitate, and, as far as is possible, to adopt the very language of men"; and the third, "that there neither is, nor can be, any *essential* difference between the language of prose and metrical composition."

thoughts and relations which they had to convey. The language of Algernon Sidney[3] differs not at all from that, which every well educated gentleman would wish to write, and (with due allowances for the undeliberateness, and less connected train, of thinking natural and proper to conversation) such as he would wish to talk. Neither one or the other differ half as much from the general language of cultivated society, as the language of Mr. Wordsworth's homeliest composition differs from that of a common peasant. For "real" therefore, we must substitute *ordinary*, or *lingua communis*.[4] And this, we have proved, is no more to be found in the phraseology of low and rustic life, than in that of any other class. Omit the peculiarities of each, and the result of course must be common to all. And assuredly the omissions and changes to be made in the language of rustics, before it could be transferred to any species of poem, except the drama or other professed imitation, are at least as numerous and weighty, as would be required in adapting to the same purpose the ordinary language of tradesmen and manufacturers. Not to mention, that the language so highly extolled by Mr. Wordsworth varies in every county, nay in every village, according to the accidental character of the clergyman, the existence or nonexistence of schools; or even, perhaps, as the exciseman, publican, or barber happen to be, or not to be, zealous politicians, and readers of the weekly newspaper *pro bono publico*.[5] Anterior to cultivation the lingua communis of every country, as Dante has well observed, exists every where in parts, and no where as a whole.[6]

Neither is the case rendered at all more tenable by the addition of the words, "*in a state of excitement*."[7] For the nature of a man's words, when he is strongly affected by joy, grief, or anger, must necessarily depend on the number and quality of the general truths, conceptions and images, and of the words expressing them, with which his mind had been previously stored. For the property of passion is not to *create*; but to set in increased activity. At least, whatever new connections of thoughts or images, or (which is equally, if not more than equally, the appropriate effect of strong excitement) whatever generalizations of truth or experience, the heat of passion may produce; yet the terms of their conveyance must have pre-existed in his former conversations, and are only collected and crowded together by the unusual stimulation. It is indeed very possible to adopt in a poem the unmeaning repetitions, habitual phrases, and other blank counters, which an unfurnished or confused understanding interposes at short intervals, in order to keep hold of his subject which is still slipping from him,

3. Algernon Sidney (1622–1683) fought for the parliamentary army during the English Civil War (1642–45) and was a member of the council of state of the Commonwealth. At the Restoration he was unjustly accused of plotting against Charles II and executed. His *Discourses Concerning Government* was published in 1698.
4. "Common language."
5. "For the public good."
6. George Watson (*BL* [1965], 199) identifies the source as Dante, *De vulgari eloquentia* (On the Eloquence of the Vernacular) (1303) 1.16: the vernacular language in Italy is "illustrious, cardinal, courtly and curial" and "belongs to all the Italian cities but not obviously to any one of them."
7. C misquotes the Preface to *LB* (1802), which reads, "a selection of the real language of men in a state of vivid sensation" (*W Prose*, 1:123). See also chapter 14 (p. 490 herein).

and to give him time for recollection; or in mere aid of vacancy, as in the scanty companies of a country stage the same player pops backwards and forwards, in order to prevent the appearance of empty spaces, in the procession of Macbeth, or Henry VIIIth.[8] But what assistance to the poet, or ornament to the poem, these can supply, I am at a loss to conjecture. Nothing assuredly can differ either in origin or in mode more widely from the *apparent* tautologies of intense and turbulent feeling, in which the passion is greater and of longer endurance, than to be exhausted or satisfied by a single representation of the image or incident exciting it. Such repetitions I admit to be a beauty of the highest kind; as illustrated by Mr. Wordsworth himself from the song of Deborah. *"At her feet he bowed, he fell, he lay down; at her feet he bowed, he fell; where he bowed, there he fell down dead."*[9]

FROM CHAPTER XVIII

Language of metrical composition, why and wherein essentially different from that of prose—Origin and elements of metre—Its necessary consequences, and the conditions thereby imposed on the metrical writer in the choice of his diction.

* * *

Now I will take the first stanza, on which I have chanced to open, in the Lyrical Ballads. It is one the most simple and the least peculiar in its language.

> In distant countries I have been,
> And yet I have not often seen
> A healthy man, a man full grown,
> Weep in the public road alone.
> But such a one, on English ground,
> And in the broad highway I met;
> Along the broad highway he came,
> His cheeks with tears were wet.
> Sturdy he seem'd, though he was sad,
> And in his arms a lamb he had.[1]

The words here are doubtless such as are current in all ranks of life; and of course not less so, in the hamlet and cottage, than in the shop,

---

8. C presumably refers to act 5, scene 9 of Shakespeare's *Macbeth*, and act 4, scene 1 of his *Henry VIII*.
9. Judges 5.27. Wordsworth makes a similar point in the manuscript of his note to "The Thorn" (*LB* [1992], 350–51):

> For the Reader cannot be too often be reminded that Poetry is passion; it is the history or science of feelings; now every man must know that an attempt is rarely made to communicate impassioned feelings without something of an accompanying consciousness of the inadequateness of our own powers, or the deficiencies of language. During such efforts there will be a craving in the mind, and as long as it is unsatisfied the Speaker will cling to the same words, or words of the same character. * * * The truth of these remarks might be shown by innumerable passages from the Bible, and from the impassioned poetry of every nation. Awake, awake, Deborah: awake, awake, utter a song: arise Barak and lead thy captivity captive, thou Son of Abinoam [Judges 5.12]. * * * Why is his Chariot so long in coming? Why tarry the Wheels of his Chariot? [Judges 5.28].

1. Wordsworth, "The Last of the Flock," lines 1–10, from *Poems* (1815), which has "roads" in line 4.

manufactory, college, or palace. But is this the *order*, in which the rustic would have placed the words? I am grievously deceived, if the following less *compact* mode of commencing the same tale be not a far more faithful copy. "I have been in a many parts far and near, and I don't know that I ever saw before a man crying by himself in the public road; a grown man I mean, that was neither sick nor hurt," &c. &c. But when I turn to the following stanza in "The Thorn:"

> At all times of the day and night
> This wretched woman thither goes,
> And she is known to every star
> And every wind that blows:
> And there beside the thorn she sits,
> When the blue day-light's in the skies;
> And when the whirlwind's on the hill,
> Or frosty air is keen and still;
> And to herself she cries,
> Oh misery! Oh misery!
> Oh woe is me! Oh misery![2]

And compare this with the language of ordinary men; or with that which I can conceive at all likely to proceed, in *real* life, from *such* a narrator, as is supposed in the note to the poem; compare it either in the succession of the images or of the sentences, I am reminded of the sublime prayer and hymn of praise, which Milton, in opposition to an established liturgy, presents as a fair *specimen* of common extemporary devotion, and such as we might expect to hear from every self-inspired minister of a conventicle![3] And I reflect with delight, how little a mere theory, though of his own workmanship, interferes with the processes of genuine imagination in a man of true poetic genius, who possesses, as Mr. Wordsworth, if ever man did, most assuredly does possess,

The Vision and the Faculty Divine.[4]

One point then alone remains, but that the most important; its examination having been, indeed, my chief inducement for the preceding inquisition. "*There neither is or can be any essential difference between the language of prose and metrical composition.*"[5] Such is Mr. Wordsworth's assertion. Now prose itself, at least, in all argumentative and consecutive works differs, and ought to differ, from the language of conversation; even as[6] reading ought to differ from talking. Unless therefore the difference denied be that of the mere *words*, as materials common to all styles of writing, and not of the *style* itself in the universally admitted sense of the term, it might be naturally presumed

---

2. "The Thorn," lines 67–77, from *Poems* (1815).
3. Shawcross (*BL* [1907], 2:276) takes C to refer to *Paradise Lost* 5.145–49: "Thir Orisons, each Morning duly paid / In various style, for neither various style / Nor holy rapture wanted they to praise / Thir Maker, in fit strains pronounc't or sung / Unmeditated."
4. Wordsworth, *The Excursion* (1814) 1.79.
5. C quotes (var.) from the 1802 Preface to *LB* (*W Prose*, 1:135).
6. A note by C on education is omitted here.

that there must exist a still greater between the ordonnance[7] of poetic composition and that of prose, than is expected to distinguish prose from ordinary conversation.

There are not, indeed, examples wanting in the history of literature, of apparent paradoxes that have summoned the public wonder as new and startling truths, but which on examination have shrunk into tame and harmless *truisms*; as the eyes of a cat, seen in the dark, have been mistaken for flames of fire. But Mr. Wordsworth is among the last men, to whom a delusion of this kind would be attributed by any one, who had enjoyed the slightest opportunity of understanding his mind and character. Where an objection has been anticipated by such an author as natural, his answer to it must needs be interpreted in some sense which either is, or has been, or is capable of being controverted. My object then must be to discover some other meaning for the term *"essential difference"* in this place, exclusive of the indistinction and community of the words themselves. For whether there ought to exist a class of words in the English, in any degree resembling the poetic dialect of the Greek and Italian, is a question of very subordinate importance. The number of such words would be small indeed, in our language; and even in the Italian and Greek, they consist not so much of different words, as of slight differences in the *forms* of declining and conjugating the same words; forms, doubtless, which having been, at some period more or less remote, the common grammatic flexions[8] of some tribe or province, had been accidentally appropriated to poetry by the general admiration of certain master intellects, the first established lights of inspiration, to whom that dialect happened to be native.

Essence, in its primary signification, means the principle of *individuation*, the inmost principle of the *possibility* of any thing, *as* that particular thing.[9] It is equivalent to the *idea* of a thing, whenever we use the word idea, with philosophic precision. Existence, on the other hand, is distinguished from essence, by the superinduction of *reality*. Thus we speak of the essence, and essential properties of a circle; but we do not therefore assert, that any thing, which really *exists*, is mathematically circular. Thus too, without any tautology we contend for the *existence* of the Supreme Being; that is, for a reality correspondent to the idea. There is, next, a *secondary* use of the word essence, in which it signifies the point or ground of contra-distinction between two modifications of the same substance or subject. Thus we should be allowed to say, that the style of architecture of Westminster Abbey is *essentially* different from that of Saint Paul, even though both had been built with blocks cut into the same form, and from the same quarry. Only in this latter sense of the term must it have been *denied* by Mr. Wordsworth (for in this sense alone is it *affirmed* by the general

---

7. A "systematic arrangement, esp. of literary material * * * a plan or method of composition" (*OED*).
8. I.e., inflections, changes in the forms of words to indicate their grammatical function.
9. In the *Theory of Life*, composed in 1816, C defined life itself as "the principle of individuation" (see p. 597 herein). On ideas, see also chapter 9 (p. 445 herein).

opinion) that the language of poetry (i. e. the formal construction, or architecture, of the words and phrases) is *essentially* different from that of prose. Now the burthen of the proof lies with the oppugner, not with the supporters of the common belief. Mr. Wordsworth, in consequence, assigns as the proof of his position, "that not only the language of a large portion of every good poem, even of the most elevated character, must necessarily, except with reference to the metre, in no respect differ from that of good prose; but likewise that some of the most interesting parts of the best poems will be found to be strictly the language of prose, when prose is well written. The truth of this assertion might be demonstrated by innumerable passages from almost all the poetical writings even of Milton himself." He then quotes Gray's sonnet—

> In vain to me the smiling mornings shine,
> And reddening Phœbus lifts his golden fire;
> The birds in vain their amorous descant join,
> Or cheerful fields resume their green attire;
> These ears alas! for other notes repine;
> *A different object do these eyes require;*
> *My lonely anguish melts no heart but mine,*
> *And in my breast the imperfect joys expire!*
> Yet morning smiles the busy race to cheer,
> And new born pleasure brings to happier men:
> The fields to all their wonted tributes bear,
> To warm their little loves the birds complain.
> *I fruitless mourn to him that cannot hear,*
> *And weep the more because I weep in vain;*[1]

and adds the following remark:—"It will easily be perceived, that the only part of this Sonnet which is of any value, is the lines printed in italics. It is equally obvious, that except in the rhyme, and in the use of the single word "fruitless" for fruitlessly, which is so far a defect, the language of these lines does in no respect differ from that of prose."[2]

An idealist defending his system by the fact, that when asleep we often believe ourselves awake, was well answered by his plain neighbour, "Ah, but when awake do we ever believe ourselves asleep?"—Things identical must be convertible. The preceding passage seems to rest on a similar sophism. For the question is not, whether there may not occur in prose an order of words, which would be equally proper in a poem; nor whether there are not beautiful lines and sentences of frequent occurrence in good poems, which would be equally becoming as well as beautiful in good prose; for neither the one or the other has ever been either denied or doubted by any one. The true question must be, whether there are not modes of expression, a *construction*, and an *order* of sentences, which are in their fit and natural place in a serious prose composition, but would be disproportionate and hetero-

---

1. Thomas Gray, "Sonnet on the Death of Mr. Richard West" (posthumously published, 1775). Gray's poem has "tribute" in line 11. The italics are Wordsworth's.
2. Preface to *LB* (1802) (*W Prose*, 1:133, 135).

geneous in metrical poetry; and, vice versa, whether in the language of a serious poem there may not be an arrangement both of words and sentences, and a use and selection of (what are called) *figures of speech*, both as to their kind, their frequency, and their occasions, which on a subject of equal weight would be vicious and alien in correct and manly prose. I contend, that in both cases this unfitness of each for the place of the other frequently will and ought to exist.

And first from the *origin* of metre. This I would trace to the balance in the mind effected by that spontaneous effort which strives to hold in check the workings of passion.[3] It might be easily explained likewise in what manner this salutary antagonism is assisted by the very state, which it counteracts; and how this balance of antagonists became organized into *metre* (in the usual acceptation of that term) by a supervening act of the will and judgement, consciously and for the foreseen purpose of pleasure.[4] Assuming these principles, as the data of our argument, we deduce from them two legitimate conditions, which the critic is entitled to expect in every metrical work. First, that as the *elements* of metre owe their existence to a state of increased excitement, so the metre itself should be accompanied by the natural language of excitement. Secondly, that as these elements are formed into metre *artificially*, by a *voluntary* act, with the design and for the purpose of blending *delight* with emotion, so the traces of present *volition* should throughout the metrical language be proportionally discernible. Now these two conditions must be reconciled and co-present. There must be not only a partnership, but a union; an interpenetration of passion and of will, of *spontaneous* impulse and of *voluntary* purpose. Again, this union can be manifested only in a frequency of forms and figures of speech (originally the offspring of passion, but now the adopted children of power) greater, than would be desired or endured, where the emotion is not voluntarily encouraged, and kept up for the sake of that pleasure, which such emotion so tempered and mastered by the will is found capable of communicating. It not only dictates, but of itself tends to produce, a more frequent employment of picturesque and vivifying language, than would be natural in any other case, in which there did not exist, as there does in the present, a previous and well understood, though tacit, *compact* between the poet and his reader, that the latter is entitled to expect, and the former bound to supply this species and degree of pleasurable excitement. We may in some

---

3. Cf. Wordsworth's 1802 Preface to *LB* (*W Prose*, 1:147): "the co-presence of something regular, something to which the mind has been accustomed in various moods and in a less excited state, cannot but have great efficacy in tempering and restraining the passion by an intermixture of ordinary feeling, and of feeling not strictly and necessarily connected with the passion. This is unquestionably true; and hence, though the opinion will at first appear paradoxical, from the tendency of metre to divest language, in a certain degree, of its reality, and thus throw a sort of half-consciousness of unsubstantial existence over the whole composition, there can be little doubt but that more pathetic situations and sentiments, that is, those which have a greater proportion of pain connected with them, may be endured in metrical composition, especially in rhyme, than in prose." Shawcross (*BL* [1907], 2:277) points out C's letter to William Sotheby of July 13, 1802: "*metre itself* implies a *passion*, i.e. a state of excitement, both in the Poet's mind, & is expected in that of the Reader—and tho' I stated this to Wordsworth, & he has in some sort stated it in his preface, yet he has [not] done justice to it, nor has he in my opinion sufficiently answered it" (*CL*, 2:812).
4. See also chapter 14 (p. 493 herein).

measure apply to this union the answer of POLIXENES, in the Winter's Tale, to PERDITA'S neglect of the streaked gilly-flowers, because she had heard it said,

> There is an art which in their piedness shares
> With great creating nature.
>   *Pol:* Say there be:
> Yet nature is made better by no mean,
> But nature makes that mean. So ev'n that art,
> Which you say adds to nature, is an art,
> That nature makes! You see, sweet maid, we marry
> *A gentler scyon to the wildest stock:*
> And make conceive a bark of ruder kind
> By bud of nobler race. This is an art,
> Which does mend nature—change it rather; but
> The art itself is nature.[5]

Secondly, I argue from the EFFECTS of metre. As far as metre acts in and for itself, it tends to increase the vivacity and susceptibility both of the general feelings and of the attention. This effect it produces by the continued excitement of surprize, and by the quick reciprocations of curiosity still gratified and still re-excited, which are too slight indeed to be at any one moment objects of distinct consciousness, yet become considerable in their aggregate influence. As a medicated atmosphere, or as wine during animated conversation; they act powerfully, though themselves unnoticed. Where, therefore, correspondent food and appropriate matter are not provided for the attention and feelings thus roused, there must needs be a disappointment felt; like that of leaping in the dark from the last step of a stair-case, when we had prepared our muscles for a leap of three or four.

The discussion on the powers of metre in the preface is highly ingenious and touches at all points on truth. But I cannot find any statement of its powers considered abstractly and separately. On the contrary Mr. Wordsworth seems always to estimate metre by the powers, which it exerts during (and, as I think, in *consequence of*) its combination with other elements of poetry. Thus the previous difficulty is left unanswered, *what* the elements are, with which it must be combined in order to produce its own effects to any pleasurable purpose. Double and tri-syllable rhymes, indeed, form a lower species of wit, and attended to exclusively for their own sake may become a source of momentary amusement; as in poor Smart's distich to the Welch 'Squire who had promised him a hare:

> Tell me thou son of great Cadwallader!
> Hast sent the hare? or hast thou swallow'd her?[6]

But for any *poetic* purposes, metre resembles (if the aptness of the simile may excuse its meanness) yeast, worthless or disagreeable by it-

---

5. Shakespeare, *The Winter's Tale* 4.4.88–97 (var.).
6. Christopher Smart, "To the Rev. Mr. Powell on the Non-Performance of a Promise He Made the Author of a Hare" (1752), lines 13–14 (var.).

self, but giving vivacity and spirit to the liquor with which it is proportionally combined.

*   *   *

Metre in itself is simply a stimulant of the attention, and therefore excites the question: Why is the attention to be thus stimulated? Now the question cannot be answered by the pleasure of the metre itself: for this we have shown to be *conditional*, and dependent on the appropriateness of the thoughts and expressions, to which the metrical form is superadded. Neither can I conceive any other answer that can be rationally given, short of this: I write in metre, because I am about to use a language different from that of prose. Besides, where the language is not such, how interesting soever the reflections are, that are capable of being drawn by a philosophic mind from the thoughts or incidents of the poem, the metre itself must often become feeble. Take the three last stanzas of the SAILOR'S MOTHER, for instance. If I could for a moment abstract from the effect produced on the author's feelings, as a man, by the incident at the time of its real occurrence, I would dare appeal to his own judgement, whether in the *metre* itself he found a sufficient reason for *their* being written *metrically*?

> And thus continuing, she said
> I had a son, who many a day
> Sailed on the seas; but he is dead;
> In Denmark he was cast away:
> And I have travelled far as Hull, to see
> What clothes he might have left, or other property.
>
> The bird and cage, they both were his;
> 'Twas my son's bird; and neat and trim
> He kept it; many voyages
> This singing bird hath gone with him;
> When last he sailed he left the bird behind;
> As it might be, perhaps, from bodings of his mind.
>
> He to a fellow-lodger's care
> Had left it, to be watched and fed,
> Till he came back again; and there
> I found it when my son was dead;
> And now, God help me for my little wit!
> I trail it with me, Sir! he took so much delight in it.[7]

If disproportioning the emphasis we read these stanzas so as to make the rhymes perceptible, even *tri-syllable* rhymes could scarcely produce an equal sense of oddity and strangeness, as we feel here in finding *rhymes at all* in sentences so exclusively colloquial. I would further ask whether, but for that visionary state, into which the figure of the woman and the susceptibility of his own genius had placed the poet's imagination (a state, which spreads its influence and coloring over all, that co-exists with the exciting cause, and in which

---

7. "The Sailor's Mother" (1807), lines 19–36. Wordsworth revised these stanzas in 1820, particularly lines 19–24 (*PTV*, 78).

The simplest, and the most familiar things
Gain a strange power of spreading awe around* them)

I would ask the poet whether he would not have felt an abrupt down-fall in these verses from the preceding stanza?

The ancient spirit is not dead;
Old times, thought I, are breathing there!
Proud was I, that my country bred
Such strength, a dignity so fair!
She begged an alms, like one in poor estate;
I looked at her again, nor did my pride abate.[9]

It must not be omitted, and is besides worthy of notice, that those stanzas furnish the only fair instance that I have been able to discover in all Mr. Wordsworth's writings, of an *actual* adoption, or true imitation, of the *real* and *very* language of *low and rustic life*, freed from provincialisms.

Thirdly, I deduce the position from all the causes elsewhere assigned, which render metre the proper form of poetry, and poetry imperfect and defective without metre. Metre therefore having been connected with *poetry* most often and by a peculiar fitness, whatever else is combined with *metre* must, though it be not itself *essentially* poetic, have nevertheless some property in common with poetry, as an inter-medium of affinity, a sort (if I may dare borrow a well-known phrase from technical chemistry) of *mordaunt*[1] between it and the super-added metre. Now poetry, Mr. Wordsworth truly affirms, does always imply PASSION; which word must be here understood in its most general sense, as an excited state of the feelings and faculties. And as every passion has its proper pulse, so will it likewise have its characteristic modes of expression.[2] But where there exists that degree of genius and talent which entitles a writer to aim at the honors of a poet, the very *act* of poetic composition *itself* is, and is *allowed* to imply and

---

* Altered from the description of Night-mair in the Remorse.

Oh Heaven! 'twas frightful! Now run-down and stared at,
By hideous shapes that cannot be remembered;
Now seeing nothing and imaging nothing;
But only being afraid—stiffled with fear!
While every goodly or familiar form
Had a strange power of spreading terror round me.[8]

N.B. Though Shakspeare has for his own *all-justifying* purposes introduced the Night-Mare with her own foals, yet Mair means a Sister or perhaps a Hag.

---

8. C quotes his own play *Remorse* 4.1.68–73 (var.). The first two lines of this passage as it appears in *Remorse* are "O sleep of horrors! Now run down and stared at / By forms so hideous that they mock remembrance," and the original has "breathing" instead of "spreading" in the final line (*PW*, 2:861). The Shakespearean passage C means is *King Lear* 3.4.107–08: "Swithin footed thrice the wold, / A met the night mare and her nine foal." C understood "foal" to mean not a horse, but a "fold," a familiar or demon. He is correct that "mare" (or "mair," as he usually spells it) in the word "nightmare" means "hag" or "spectre," not a female horse with "foals."
9. "The Sailor's Mother," lines 7–12.
1. "An instrument that bites or holds fast * * *. A substance used for fixing" colors in dyeing (*OED*).
2. In November 1801 C copied a similar sentence from Sir Kenelm Digby's *Two Treatises* (1645) into a notebook: "Every passion, say the Physicians, hath an distinct Pulse" (*CN*, 1:1005).

to produce, an unusual state of excitement, which of course justifies
and demands a correspondent difference of language, as truly, though
not perhaps in as marked a degree, as the excitement of love, fear,
rage, or jealousy. The vividness of the descriptions or declamations in
DONNE, or DRYDEN, is as much and as often derived from the force
and fervour of the describer, as from the reflections, forms, or incidents which constitute their subject and materials. The wheels take
fire from the mere rapidity of their motion.[3] To what extent, and under
what modifications, this may be admitted to act, I shall attempt to
define in an after remark on Mr. Wordsworth's reply to this objection,
or rather on his objection to this reply, as already anticipated in his
preface.

Fourthly, and as intimately connected with this, if not the same argument in a more general form, I adduce the high spiritual instinct of
the human being impelling us to seek unity by harmonious adjust-
ment, and thus establishing the principle, that *all* the parts of an organized whole must be assimilated to the more *important* and *essential*
parts.[4] This and the preceding arguments may be strengthened by the
reflection, that the composition of a poem is among the *imitative* arts;
and that imitation, as opposed to copying, consists either in the interfusion of the SAME throughout the radically DIFFERENT, or of the different throughout a base radically the same.

Lastly, I appeal to the practice of the best poets, of all countries and
in all ages, as *authorizing* the opinion, (*deduced* from all the foregoing)
that in every import of the word ESSENTIAL, which would not here involve a mere truism, there may be, is, and ought to be, an *essential* difference between the language of prose and of metrical composition.

* * *

Among the possible effects of practical adherence to a theory, that
aims to *identify* the style of prose and verse (if it does not indeed claim
for the latter a yet nearer resemblance to the average style of men in
the vivâ voce[5] intercourse of real life) we might anticipate the following
as not the least likely to occur. It will happen, as I have indeed before
observed, that the metre itself, the sole acknowledged difference, will
occasionally become metre to the eye only. The existence of *prosaisms*,
and that they detract from the merit of a poem, *must* at length be conceded, when a number of successive lines can be rendered, even to the
most delicate ear, unrecognizable as verse, or as having even been intended for verse, by simply transcribing them as prose:[6] when if the
poem be in blank verse, this can be effected without any alteration, or

3. Cf. Ezekiel 10.9–11: "And when I looked, behold the four wheels by the cherubims, one
   wheel by one cherub, and another wheel by another cherub: and the appearance of the
   wheels was as the colour of a beryl stone. And as for their appearances, they four had one
   likeness, as if a wheel had been in the midst of a wheel. When they went, they went upon
   their four sides; they turned not as they went, but to the place whither the head looked they
   followed it; they turned not as they went." See also *The Statesman's Manual* (p. 359 herein).
4. On unity as a criterion of beauty, see the *Essays on the Principles of Genial Criticism* (p. 345
   herein).
5. "Spoken."
6. Cf. the Preface to *LB* (1802): "there is a numerous class of critics, who, when they stumble
   upon these prosaisms, as they call them, imagine that they have made a notable discovery,
   and exult over the Poet as over a man ignorant of his own profession" (*W Prose*, 1:133).

at most by merely restoring one or two words to their proper places, from which they had been[7] transplanted for no assignable cause or reason but that of the author's convenience; but if it be in rhyme, by the mere exchange of the final word of each line for some other of the same meaning, equally appropriate, dignified and euphonic.

The answer or objection in the preface to the anticipated remark "that metre paves the way to other distinctions," is contained in the following words. "The distinction of rhyme and metre is voluntary and uniform, and not like that produced by (what is called) poetic diction, arbitrary and subject to infinite caprices, upon which no calculation whatever can be made. In the one case the reader is utterly at the mercy of the poet respecting what imagery or diction he may choose to connect with the passion."[8] But is this a *poet*, of whom a poet is speaking? No surely! rather of a fool or madman: or at best of a vain or ignorant phantast! And might not Brains so wild and so deficient make just the same havock with rhymes and metres, as they are supposed to effect with modes and figures of speech? How is the reader at the *mercy* of such men? If he continue to read their nonsense, is it not his own fault? The ultimate end of criticism is much more to establish the principles of writing, than to furnish *rules* how to pass judgement on what has been written by others; if indeed it were possible that the two could be separated. But if it be asked, by what principles the poet is to regulate his own style, if he do not adhere closely to the sort and order of words which he hears in the market, wake, high-road, or plough-field? I reply; by principles, the ignorance or neglect of which would convict him of being no *poet*, but a silly or presumptuous usurper of the name! By the principles of grammar, logic, psychology! In one word by such a knowledge of the facts, material and spiritual, that most appertain to his art, as if it have been governed and applied by *good sense*, and rendered instinctive by habit, becomes the representative and reward of our past conscious reasonings, insights, and conclusions, and acquires the name of TASTE.[9] By what *rule* that does not leave the reader at the poet's mercy, and the poet at his own, is the latter to distinguish between the language suitable to *suppressed*, and the language, which is characteristic of *indulged*, anger? Or between that of rage and that of jealousy? Is it obtained by wandering about in search of angry or jealous people in uncultivated society, in order to copy their words? Or not far rather by the power of imagination proceeding upon the *all in each* of human nature? By *meditation*, rather than by *observation*?[1] And by

---

7. A note by C on Wordsworth's poem "The Brothers" is omitted here.
8. From the Preface to *LB* (1802). Wordsworth actually wrote, "The distinction of metre is regular and uniform, and not, like that which is produced by what is usually called POETIC DICTION * * *" (*W Prose*, 1:145).
9. C defined "taste" in his 1808 literary lectures: "Taste implies an intellectual perception of any object blended with a distinct consciousness of pain or pleasure conceived as resulting from that Object. * * * Taste then may be defined—a distinct Perception of any arrangement conceived as external to us co-existent with some degree of Dislike or Complacency conceived as resulting from that arrangement—and this immediately, without any prospect of consequences" (*Lects 1808–19* [CC], 1:30).
1. Wordsworth's Preface to *Poems* (1815) opens with the claim that "The powers requisite for the production of poetry are: first, those of Observation and Description" (*W Prose*, 3:26).

the latter in consequence only of the former? As eyes, for which the former has pre-determined their field of vision, and to which, as to *its* organ, it communicates a microscopic power? There is not, I firmly believe, a man now living, who has from his own inward experience a clearer intuition, than Mr. Wordsworth himself, that the last mentioned are the true sources of *genial*[2] discrimination. Through the same process and by the same creative agency will the poet distinguish the degree and kind of the excitement produced by the very act of poetic composition. As intuitively will he know, what differences of style it at once inspires and justifies; what intermixture of conscious volition is natural to that state; and in what instances such figures and colors of speech degenerate into mere creatures of an arbitrary purpose, cold technical artifices of ornament or connection. For even as truth is its own light and evidence, discovering at once itself and falsehood, so is it the prerogative of poetic genius to distinguish by parental instinct its proper offspring from the changelings, which the gnomes of vanity or the fairies of fashion may have laid in its cradle or called by its names. Could a rule be given from *without*, poetry would cease to be poetry, and sink into a mechanical art.[3] It would be μορφωσις·, not ποιησις.[4] The *rules* of the IMAGINATION are themselves the very powers of growth and production. The *words*, to which they are reducible, present only the outlines and external appearance of the fruit. A deceptive counterfeit of the superficial form and colors may be elaborated; but the marble peach feels cold and heavy, and *children* only put it to their mouths. We find no difficulty in admitting as excellent, and the legitimate language of poetic fervor self-impassioned, DONNE'S apostrophe to the Sun in the second stanza of his "Progress of the Soul."

> Thee, eye of heaven! this great soul envies not:
> By thy male force is all, we have, begot.
> In the first East thou now beginn'st to shine,
> Suck'st early balm and island spices there;
> And wilt anon in thy loose-rein'd career
> At Tagus, Po, Seine, Thames, and Danow dine,
> And see at night this western world of mine:
> Yet hast thou not more nations seen, than she,
> Who before thee one day began to be,
> And, thy frail light being quenched, shall long, long out-live thee!

Or the next stanza but one:

> Great destiny, the commissary of God,
> That hast marked out a path and period
> For ev'ry thing! Who, where we offspring took,
> Our ways and ends see'st at one instant: thou
> Knot of all causes! Thou, whose changeless brow

2. For C's conception of "genial," see the headnote to the *Essays on the Principles of Genial Criticism* (p. 339 herein).
3. Cf. the distinction, derived from the German critic August Wilhelm Schlegel (1767–1845), between mechanical and organic form in "[On *The Tempest*]" (p. 325 herein).
4. A "fashioning," not a "creation."

Ne'er smiles or frowns! O vouchsafe thou to look,
And shew my story in thy eternal book, &c.[5]

*   *   *

FROM CHAPTER XIX

Continuation—Concerning the real object which, it is probable, Mr.
Wordsworth had before him, in his critical preface—Elucidation and
application of this.

It might appear from some passages in the former part of Mr.
Wordsworth's preface, that he meant to confine his theory of style, and
the necessity of a close accordance with the actual language of men, to
those particular subjects from low and rustic life, which by way of
experiment he had purposed to naturalize as a new species in our English poetry. But from the train of argument that follows; from the reference to Milton; and from the spirit of his critique on Gray's sonnet;
those sentences appear to have been rather courtesies of modesty, than
actual limitations of his system. Yet so groundless does this system appear on a close examination; and so strange and[6] over-whelming in its
consequences, that I cannot, and I do not, believe that the poet did
ever himself adopt it in the unqualified sense, in which his expressions
have been understood by others, and which indeed according to all the
common laws of interpretation they seem to bear. What then did he
mean? I apprehend, that in the clear perception, not unaccompanied
with disgust or contempt, of the gaudy affectations of a style which
passed too current with too many for poetic diction, (though in truth it
had as little pretensions to poetry, as to logic or common sense) he narrowed his view for the time; and feeling a justifiable preference for the
language of nature, and of good-sense, even in its humblest and least
ornamented forms, he suffered himself to express, in terms at once too
large and too exclusive, his predilection for a style the most remote possible from the false and showy splendor which he wished to explode. It
is possible, that this predilection, at first merely comparative, deviated
for a time into direct partiality. But the real object, which he had in
view, was, I doubt not, a species of excellence which had been long before most happily characterized by the judicious and amiable GARVE,
whose works are so justly beloved and esteemed by the Germans, in his
remarks on GELLERT (see Sammlung Einiger Abhandlungen von Christian Garve) from which the following is literally translated.[7] "The talent, that is required in order to make excellent verses, is perhaps
greater than the philosopher is ready to admit, or would find it in his
power to acquire: the talent to seek only the apt expression of the
thought, and yet to find at the same time with it the rhyme and the metre. Gellert possessed this happy gift, if ever any one of our poets pos-

---

5. John Donne, "Metempsychosis: The Progress of the Soule" (1633), lines 11–20, 31–37
(var.). On C's view of Donne, see Uncollected Poetry (p. 234 herein).
6. A note by C on the German language is omitted here.
7. Christian Garve (1742–1798), author of several books on ethics and translator of works of
British philosophy, succeeded the poet C. F. Gellert (1715–1769) as professor of moral philosophy at Leipzig University upon the latter's death.

sessed it; and nothing perhaps contributed more to the great and universal impression which his fables made on their first publication, or conduces more to their continued popularity. It was a strange and curious phenomenon, and such as in Germany had been previously unheard of, to read verses in which every thing was expressed, just as one would wish to talk, and yet all dignified, attractive, and interesting; and all at the same time perfectly correct as to the measure of the syllables and the rhyme. It is certain, that poetry when it has attained this excellence makes a far greater impression than prose. So much so indeed, that even the gratification which the very rhymes afford, becomes then no longer a contemptible or trifling gratification."[8]

*   *   *

FROM CHAPTER XX

The former subject continued—The neutral style, or that common to Prose and Poetry, exemplified by specimens from Chaucer, Herbert, &c.

I have no fear in declaring my conviction, that the excellence defined and exemplified in the preceding Chapter is not the characteristic excellence of Mr. Wordsworth's style; because I can add with equal sincerity, that it is precluded by higher powers. The praise of uniform adherence to genuine, logical English is undoubtedly his; nay, laying the main emphasis on the word *uniform* I will dare add that, of all contemporary poets, it is *his alone*. For in a less absolute sense of the word, I should certainly include MR. BOWLES, LORD BYRON,[9] and, as to all his later writings, MR. SOUTHEY, the exceptions in their works being so few and unimportant. But of the specific excellence described in the quotation from Garve,[1] I appear to find more, and more undoubted specimens in the works of others; for instance, among the minor poems of Mr. Thomas Moore, and of our illustrious Laureate.[2] To me it will always remain a singular and noticeable fact; that a theory which would establish this *lingua communis*, not only as the best, but as the only commendable style, should have proceeded from a poet, whose diction, next to that of Shakspeare and Milton, appears to me of all others the most *individualized* and characteristic. And let it be remembered too, that I am now interpreting the controverted passages of Mr. W.'s critical preface by the purpose and object, which he may be supposed to have intended, rather than by the sense which the words themselves must convey, if they are taken without this allowance.

8. C translates freely (not literally) from Garve's comments on Gellert in his *Sammlung einiger Abhandlungen* (Collection of Several Essays) (Leipzig, 1799), 233–34, a passage that C had copied into a notebook in December 1803 (*CN*, 1:1702; *BL* [CC], 2:90n. 1). As Kathleen Coburn notes, C adds "ready to admit" to the first sentence and "on their first publication, or conduces more to their continued popularity" to the second sentence, and he omits Garve's insistence that philosophy is unable "exactly to describe" poetic talent (*CN*, 1:1702n.).
9. On Bowles, see also "Effusion I" (p. 12 herein), and *Biographia* (p. 382 herein). For C's appeal to Lord Byron for assistance in publishing his poems, see the headnotes to "Christabel" (p. 159 herein) and *SL* (p. 185 herein).
1. See chapter 19.
2. Thomas Moore (1779–1852), Irish poet best known for his *Irish Melodies* (1807) and his Oriental tale *Lalla Rookh* (1817). Southey was appointed poet laureate in 1813.

A person of any taste, who had but studied three or four of Shak-speare's principal plays, would without the name affixed scarcely fail to recognize as Shakspeare's, a quotation from any other play, though but of a few lines. A similar peculiarity, though in a less degree, attends Mr. Wordsworth's style, whenever he speaks in his own person; or whenever, though under a feigned name, it is clear that he himself is still speaking, as in the different dramatis personæ of the "RECLUSE."³ Even in the other poems in which he purposes to be most dramatic, there are few in which it does not occasionally burst forth. The reader might often address the poet in his own words with reference to the persons introduced;

> It seems, as I retrace the ballad line by line
> That but half of it is theirs, and the better half is thine.⁴

Who, having been previously acquainted with any considerable por-tion of Mr. Wordsworth's publications, and having studied them with a full feeling of the author's genius, would not at once claim as Wordsworthian the little poem on the rainbow?

> The child is father of the man,⁵ &c.

Or in the "Lucy Gray"?

> No mate, no comrade Lucy knew;
> She dwelt on a wide moor;
> *The sweetest thing that ever grew*
> *Beside a human door.*⁶

Or in the "Idle Shepherd-boys"?

> Along the river's stony marge
> The sand-lark chaunts a joyous song;
> The thrush is busy in the wood,
> And carols loud and strong.
> A thousand lambs are on the rock
> All newly born! both earth and sky
> Keep jubilee, and more than all,
> Those boys with their green coronal,
> They never hear the cry,
> That plaintive cry which up the hill
> Comes from the depth of Dungeon Gill.⁷

---

3. Wordsworth planned *The Recluse* to contain his views on "Nature, Man, and Society," as he announced in March 1798 (*WL*, 1:212). It was to be in three parts. The first part, of which about a thousand lines were written, was never completed (see *Home at Grasmere*, ed. Beth Darlington [Ithaca, N.Y., 1977]); the second part, the only one that C's readers would have known, was published as *The Excursion* (1814); and the third part was never written. *The Prelude* was to be prelusive to the completed *Recluse* and was not published until 1850. In 1817 Wordsworth would have been known mainly as the author of *Lyrical Ballads, Poems in Two Volumes* (1807), and *The Excursion*.
4. "The Pet Lamb" (1800), lines 63–64: "And it seem'd as I retrac'd the ballad line by line / That but half of it was hers, and one half of it was mine" (*LB* [1992], 224).
5. "My heart leaps up when I behold," line 7, published in the category of "Moods of My Own Mind" in *PTV* (1807). In 1815 the last three lines were used as the motto of the Immortal-ity Ode: "The Child is Father of the Man; / And I could wish my days to be / Bound each to each by natural piety."
6. "Lucy Gray" (1800), lines 5–8 (with C's italics).
7. "The Idle Shepherd-Boys, or Dungeon-Gill Force, A Pastoral" (1800), lines 23–33 (var.).

Need I mention the exquisite description of the Sea Lock in the "Blind Highland Boy." Who but a poet tells a tale in such language to the little ones by the fire-side as—

> Yet had he many a restless dream
> Both when he heard the eagle's scream,
> And when he heard the torrents roar,
> And heard the water beat the shore
> Near where their cottage stood.
>
> Beside a lake their cottage stood,
> Not small like our's a peaceful flood;
> But one of mighty size, and strange
> That rough or smooth is full of change
> And stirring in its bed.
>
> For to this lake by night and day,
> The great sea-water finds its way
> Through long, long windings of the hills,
> And drinks up all the pretty rills;
> And rivers large and strong:
>
> Then hurries back the road it came—
> Returns on errand still the same;
> This did it when the earth was new;
> And this for evermore will do,
> As long as earth shall last.
>
> And with the coming of the tide,
> Come boats and ships that sweetly ride,
> Between the woods and lofty rocks;
> And to the shepherd with their flocks
> Bring tales of distant lands.[8]

I might quote almost the whole of his "RUTH," but take the following stanzas:

> But as you have before been told,
> This stripling, sportive gay and bold,
> And with his dancing crest,
> So beautiful, through savage lands
> Had roam'd about with vagrant bands
> Of Indians in the West.
>
> The wind, the tempest roaring high.
> The tumult of a tropic sky,
> Might well be dangerous food
> For him, a youth to whom was given
> So much of earth, so much of heaven,
> And such impetuous blood.

8. "The Blind Highland Boy" (1807), lines 46–70 (var.).

Whatever in those climes he found
Irregular in sight or sound,
Did to his mind impart
A kindred impulse; seem'd allied
To his own powers, and justified
    The workings of his heart.

Nor less to feed voluptuous thought
The beauteous forms of nature wrought,
Fair trees and lovely flowers;
The breezes their own langour lent,
The stars had feelings, which they sent
    Into those magic bowers.

Yet in his worst pursuits, I ween,
That sometimes there did intervene
Pure hopes of high intent:
For passions, link'd to forms so fair
And stately, needs must have their share
    Of noble sentiment.[9]

But from Mr. Wordsworth's more elevated compositions, which already form three-fourths of his works; and will, I trust, constitute hereafter a still larger proportion;—from these, whether in rhyme or blank-verse, it would be difficult and almost superfluous to select instances of a diction peculiarly his own, of a style which cannot be imitated without its being at once recognized, as originating in Mr. Wordsworth. It would not be easy to open on any one of his loftier strains, that does not contain examples of this; and more in proportion as the lines are more excellent, and most like the author. For those, who may happen to have been less familiar with his writings, I will give three specimens taken with little choice. The first from the lines on the "BOY OF WINANDER-MERE,"—who

Blew mimic hootings to the silent owls,
That they might answer him. And they would shout,
Across the watery vale and shout again
With long halloos, and screams, and echoes loud
Redoubled and redoubled, concourse wild
Of mirth and jocund din. And when it chanc'd.
That pauses of deep silence mock'd his skill,
Then sometimes in that silence, while he hung
Listening, a gentle shock of mild surprise
Has carried far into his heart the voice
Of mountain torrents; or the visible scene[1]
Would enter unawares into his mind
With all its solemn imagery, its rocks,

9. "Ruth," lines 109–38, in *Poems* (1815).
1. A note by C on the word "scene" is omitted here.

Its woods, and that uncertain heaven, received
Into the bosom of the steady lake.[2]

The second shall be that noble imitation of Drayton[3] (if it was not rather a coincidence) in the "JOANNA."

> When I had gazed perhaps two minutes space,
> Joanna, looking in my eyes, beheld
> That ravishment of mine, and laugh'd aloud.
> The rock, like something starting from a sleep,
> Took up the lady's voice, and laugh'd again!
> That ancient woman seated on *Helm-crag*
> Was ready with her cavern! *Hammar-scar*,
> And the tall steep of SILVER-HOW sent forth
> A noise of laughter: southern LOUGHRIGG heard,
> And FAIRFIELD answered with a mountain tone.
> HELVELLYN far into the clear blue sky
> Carried the lady's voice!—old SKIDDAW blew
> His speaking trumpet!—back out of the clouds
> From GLARAMARA southward came the voice:
> And KIRKSTONE tossed it from his misty head![4]

The third which is in rhyme I take from the "Song at the feast of Broughham Castle, upon the restoration of Lord Clifford the shepherd to the estates of his ancestors."

> Now another day is come
> Fitter hope, and nobler doom:
> He hath thrown aside his crook,
> And hath buried deep his book;
> *Armour rusting in the halls*
> *On the blood of Clifford calls;*
> *Quell the Scot, exclaims the lance!*
> *Bear me to the heart of France*
> *Is the longing of the shield—*

2. "There was a Boy," lines 10–25 (with C's italics). It was the second poem in volume 2 of *LB* (1800), where Wordsworth had "a wild scene" in line 15, and the first poem in the category of "Poems of Imagination" in *Poems* (1815), where the phrase was changed to "concourse wild" (a change of which C expresses approval in the omitted footnote). C omits line 13, "Responsive to his call, with quivering peals," which appears in both versions (*LB* [1992], 140). Wordsworth composed the poem in the fall of 1798 and sent a draft of it to C, who responded on December 10, 1798, "That 'Uncertain heaven received / Into the bosom of the steady lake,' I should have recognised any where; and had I met these lines running wild in the deserts of Arabia, I should have instantly screamed out 'Wordsworth'" (*CL*, 1:452–53). Wordsworth described the poem in the Preface to *Poems* (1815): "Guided by one of my own primary consciousnesses, I have represented a commutation and transfer of internal feelings, co-operating with external accidents, to plant, for immortality, images of sound and sight, in the celestial soil of the Imagination. The Boy, there introduced, is listening, with something of a feverish and restless anxiety, for the recurrence of the riotous sounds which he had previously excited; and, at the moment when the intenseness of his mind is beginning to remit, he is surprised into a perception of the solemn and tranquillizing images which the Poem describes" (*LB* [1992], 379). It was later included as book 5, lines 389–413 of the 1805 version of *The Prelude* (*The Thirteen-Book Prelude*, ed. Mark L. Reed [Ithaca, N.Y., 1991], 1:171–72).
3. In a footnote omitted here C quotes lines 155–64 of "Song XXX: Cumberland. Westmorland" from Michael Drayton, *Poly-Olbion* (1612–22).
4. "To Joanna," lines 51–65, in "Poems on the Naming of Places" both in *LB* (1800) and *Poems* (1815), with C's italics and small capitals and substituting "From" for "Of" in the penultimate line.

Tell thy name, thou trembling field!
Field of death, where'er thou be,
Groan thou with our victory!
Happy day, and mighty hour,
When our shepherd, in his power,
Mailed and horsed with lance and sword,
To his ancestors restored,
Like a re-appearing star,
Like a glory from afar,
First shall head the flock of war!
   Alas! the fervent harper did not know,
That for a tranquil soul the lay was framed,
Who, long compelled in humble walks to go
Was softened into feeling, soothed, and tamed.
Love had he found in huts where poor men lie:
His daily teachers had been woods and rills,
The silence that is in the starry sky,
The sleep that is among the lonely hills.[5]

The words themselves in the foregoing extracts, are, no doubt, sufficiently common for the greater part. (But in what poem are they not so? if we except a few misadventurous attempts to translate the arts and sciences into verse?) In the "Excursion" the number of polysyllabic (or what the common people call, *dictionary*) words is more than usually great. And so must it needs be, in proportion to the number and variety of an author's conceptions, and his solicitude to express them with precision.) But are those words *in those places* commonly employed in real life to express the same thought or outward thing? Are they the style used in the ordinary intercourse of spoken words? No! nor are the modes of connections: and still less the breaks and transitions. Would any but a poet—at least could any one without being conscious that he had expressed himself with noticeable vivacity—have described a bird singing loud by, "The thrush is *busy* in the wood?" Or have spoken of boys with a string of club-moss round their rusty hats, as the boys "*with their green coronal?*" Or have translated a beautiful May-day into "*Both earth and sky keep jubilee?*" Or have brought all the different marks and circumstances of a sea-loch before the mind, as the actions of a living and acting power? Or have represented the reflection of the sky in the water, as "*That uncertain heaven received into the bosom of the steady lake?*" Even the grammatical construction is not unfrequently peculiar; as "The wind, the tempest roaring high, the tumult of a tropic sky, might well be *dangerous food to him*, a youth to whom was given, &c."[6] There is a peculiarity in the frequent use of the ἀσυνάρτητον[7] (i. e. the omission of the connective particle before the last of several words, or several sentences used grammatically as single words, all being in the same case and

5. "Song, at the Feast of Brougham Castle" (1807), lines 142–68 (C's italics). In *Poems* (1815) it was printed with the "Poems of Imagination."
6. C quotes, respectively, "The Idle Shepherd Boys," lines 25, 30, 28–29; "There was a Boy," line 25; and "Ruth" (1815 version), lines 121–24.
7. "Unarticulated."

governing or governed by the same verb) and not less in the construction of words by apposition (*to him; a youth.*) In short, were there excluded from Mr. Wordsworth's poetic compositions all, that a literal adherence to the theory of his preface *would* exclude, two-thirds at least of the marked beauties of his poetry must be erased. For a far greater number of lines would be sacrificed, than in any other recent poet; because the pleasure received from Wordsworth's poems being less derived either from excitement of curiosity or the rapid flow of narration, the *striking* passages form a larger proportion of their value. I do not adduce it as a fair criterion of comparative excellence, nor do I even think it such; but merely as matter of fact. I affirm, that from no contemporary writer could so many lines be quoted, without reference to the poem in which they are found, for their own independent weight or beauty. From the sphere of my own experience I can bring to my recollection three persons of no every-day powers and acquirements, who had read the poems of others with more and more unallayed pleasure, and had thought more highly of their authors, as poets; who yet have confessed to me, that from no modern work had so many passages started up anew in their minds at different times, and as different occasions had awakened a meditative mood.

FROM CHAPTER XXII

The characteristic defects of Wordsworth's poetry, with the principles from which the judgement, that they are defects, is deduced—Their proportion to the beauties—For the greatest part characteristic of his theory only.

If Mr. Wordsworth have set forth principles of poetry which his arguments are insufficient to support, let him and those who have adopted his sentiments be set right by the confutation of those arguments, and by the substitution of more philosophical principles. And still let the due credit be given to the portion and importance of the truths, which are blended with his theory. truths, the too exclusive attention to which had occasioned its errors, by tempting him to carry those truths beyond their proper limits. If his mistaken theory have at all influenced his poetic compositions, let the effects be pointed out, and the instances given. But let it likewise be shewn, how far the influence has acted; whether diffusively, or only by starts; whether the number and importance of the poems and passages thus infected be great or trifling compared with the sound portion; and lastly, whether they are inwoven into the texture of his works, or are loose and separable. The result of such a trial would evince beyond a doubt, what it is high time to announce decisively and aloud, that the *supposed* characteristics of Mr. Wordsworth's poetry, whether admired or reprobated; whether they are simplicity or simpleness; faithful adherence to essential nature, or wilful selections from human nature of its meanest forms and under the least attractive associations; are as little the *real* characteristics of his poetry at large, as of his genius and the constitution of his mind.

In a comparatively small number of poems, he chose to try an experiment; and this experiment we will suppose to have failed. Yet even in these poems it is impossible not to perceive, that the natural *tendency* of the poet's mind is to great objects and elevated conceptions. The poem intitled "Fidelity" is for the greater part written in language, as unraised and naked as any perhaps in the two volumes.[8] Yet take the following stanza and compare it with the preceding stanzas of the same poem.

> There sometimes does a leaping fish
> Send through the tarn a lonely cheer;
> The crags repeat the Raven's croak
> In symphony austere;
> Thither the rainbow comes—the cloud,
> And mists that spread the flying shroud;
> And sun-beams; and the sounding blast,
> That if it could would hurry past,
> But that enormous barrier binds it fast.[9]

Or compare the four last lines of the concluding stanza with the former half:

> Yet proof was plain that since the day
> On which the traveller thus had died,
> The dog had watch'd about the spot,
> Or by his master's side:
> *How nourish'd there for such long time*
> *He knows who gave that love sublime,*
> *And gave that strength of feeling great*
> *Above all human estimate.*[1]

Can any candid and intelligent mind hesitate in determining, which of these best represents the tendency and native character of the poet's genius? Will he not decide that the one was written because the poet *would* so write, and the other because he could not so entirely repress the force and grandeur of his mind, but that he must in some part or other of *every* composition write otherwise? In short, that his only disease is the being out of his element; like the swan, that having amused himself, for a while, with crushing the weeds on the river's bank, soon returns to his own majestic movements on its reflecting and sustaining surface. Let it be observed, that I am here supposing the imagined judge, to whom I appeal, to have already decided against the poet's theory, as far as it is different from the principles of the art, generally acknowledged.

I cannot here enter into a detailed examination of Mr. Wordsworth's

8. *Poems* (1815) was published in two volumes.
9. Wordsworth, "Fidelity" (1807), lines 25–33.
1. "Fidelity," lines 58–65 with the substitution of "Yet" for "Yes" in the first line and "there for" for "here through" in line 62. On September 11, 1816, Wordsworth told Henry Crabb Robinson that he "purposely made the narrative as prosaic as possible so that no discredit might be thrown on the truth of the incident. In the description at the beginning and in the moral at the end he has alone indulged in a poetic vein—and these parts he thinks he has peculiarly succeeded in" (*PTV*, 404).

works; but I will attempt to give the main results of my own judgement, after an acquaintance of many years, and repeated perusals. And though, to appreciate the defects of a great mind it is necessary to understand previously its characteristic excellences, yet I have already expressed myself with sufficient fulness, to preclude most of the ill effects that might arise from my pursuing a contrary arrangement. I will therefore commence with what I deem the prominent *defects* of his poems hitherto published.

The first *characteristic, though only occasional* defect, which I appear to myself to find in these poems is the INCONSTANCY of the *style*. Under this name I refer to the sudden and unprepared transitions from lines or sentences of peculiar felicity (at all events striking and original) to a style, not only unimpassioned but undistinguished. He sinks too often and too abruptly to that style, which I should place in the second division of language, dividing it into the three species; *first*, that which is peculiar to poetry; *second*, that which is only proper in prose; and *third*, the neutral or common to both.

* * *

I refer the reader to the exquisite stanzas cited for another purpose from the blind Highland Boy; and then annex as being in my opinion instances of this *disharmony* in style the two following:

> And one, the rarest, was a shell,
> Which he, poor child, had studied well:
> The shell of a green turtle, thin
> And hollow;—you might sit therein,
>   It was so wide, and deep.

> Our Highland Boy oft visited
> The house which held this prize, and led
> By choice or chance did thither come
> One day, when no one was at home
>   And found the door unbarred.[2]

Or page 172, vol. I.

> 'Tis gone forgotten, *let me do*
> *My best.* There was a smile or two—
> I can remember them, I see
> The smiles worth all the world to me.
> Dear Baby, I must lay thee down:
> Thou troublest me with strange alarms!
> Smiles hast thou, sweet ones of thine own;

2. "The Blind Highland Boy," lines 116–20, 136–40 as revised for *Poems* (1815). In the first version (1807) the boy used "A Household Tub, like one of those / Which women use to wash their clothes" (lines 113–14). In January 1808 C noted, "had I written the sweet Tale of the blind Highland Boy, I would have substituted for the washing Tub, and the awkward Stanza in which it is specified the image suggested in the following Lines from [William Dampier, *A Collection of Voyages* (1729), 1:105–06]: 'I heard of a monstrous green Turtle one taken at the Port Royal in the Bay of Campeachy, that was four feet deep from the back to the belly, and the belly six feet Broad. Captn. Roch's son, of about 9 or 10 years of age, went in it as in a boat' " (CN, 3:3240). In a note to *Poems* (1815) Wordsworth admitted that "upon the suggestion of a Friend, I have substituted such a Shell for that less elegant vessel in which my blind voyager did actually intrust himself" (*PTV*, 420).

> I cannot keep thee in my arms,
> For they confound me: *as it is,*
> I have forgot those smiles of his!³

Or page 269, vol. I.

> Thou hast a nest, for thy love and thy rest,
> And though little troubled with sloth
> Drunken lark! thou would'st be loth
> To be such a traveller as I.
> Happy, happy liver
> *With a soul as strong as a mountain river*
> *Pouring out praise to th' Almighty giver!*
> Joy and jollity be with us both,
> Hearing thee or else some other,
> As merry a brother
> I on the earth will go plodding on
> By myself chearfully till the day is done.⁴

The incongruity, which I appear to find in this passage, is that of the two noble lines in italics with the preceding and following. So vol. II, page 30.

> Close by a pond, upon the further side
> He stood alone; a minute's space I guess,
> I watch'd him, he continuing motionless;
> To the pool's further margin then I drew;
> He being all the while before me full in view.⁵

Compare this with the repetition of the same image, in the next stanza but two.

> And still as I drew near with gentle pace,
> Beside the little pond or moorish flood
> Motionless as a cloud the old man stood;
> That heareth not the loud winds as they call
> And moveth altogether, if it move at all.⁶

Or lastly, the second of the three following stanzas, compared both with the first and the third.

> My former thoughts returned, the fear that kills;
> And hope that is unwilling to be fed;
> Cold, pain, and labour, and all fleshly ills;
> And mighty poets in their misery dead.

---

3. Untitled as Poem 20 in the category of "Poems Founded upon the Affections" in *Poems* (1815), and later titled "The Emigrant Mother" in 1820, when Wordsworth revised the lines in italics (*PTV*, 249–50). C quotes lines 55–64 and adds italics.
4. The third and final stanza of "To a Skylark," in *Poems* (1815), included under the category "Poems of the Fancy." Wordsworth revised the final four lines several times in later versions (*PTV*, 118).
5. "Resolution and Independence," lines 59–63, in *PTV* (1807). Wordsworth removed these lines in 1820 (*PTV*, 125).
6. "Resolution and Independence," lines 80–84 (var.), in *PTV* (1807). In the Preface to *Poems* (1815) Wordsworth compared the image of the old man to that of a "huge stone" and "sea-beast" in the preceding lines of the poem to illustrate "the conferring, the abstracting, and the modifying powers of the Imagination" (*W Prose*, 3:33).

But now, perplex'd by what the old man had said,
My question eagerly did I renew,
How is it that you live, and what is it you do?

He with a smile did then his tale repeat;
And said, that, gathering leeches far and wide
He travelled; stirring thus about his feet
The waters of the ponds where they abide.
"Once I could meet with them on every side,
But they have dwindled long by slow decay;
Yet still I persevere, and find them where I may."

While he was talking thus, the lonely place
The old man's shape, and speech, all troubled me:
In my mind's eye I seemed to see him pace
About the weary moors continually,
Wandering about alone and silently.[7]

Indeed this fine poem is *especially* characteristic of the author. There is scarce a defect or excellence in his writings of which it would not present a specimen. But it would be unjust not to repeat that this defect is only occasional. From a careful reperusal of the two volumes of poems, I doubt whether the objectionable passages would amount in the whole to one hundred lines; not the eighth part of the number of pages. In the EXCURSION[8] the feeling of incongruity is seldom excited by the diction of any passage considered in itself, but by the sudden superiority of some other passage forming the context.

The second defect I could generalize with tolerable accuracy, if the reader will pardon an uncouth and new coined word. There is, I should say, not seldom a *matter-of-factness* in certain poems.[9] This may be divided into, *first*, a laborious minuteness and fidelity in the representation of objects, and their positions, as they appeared to the poet himself; *secondly*, the insertion of accidental circumstances, in order to the full explanation of his living characters, their dispositions and actions; which circumstances might be necessary to establish the probability of a statement in real life, where nothing is taken for granted by the hearer, but appear superfluous in poetry, where the reader is willing to believe for his own sake. To this *accidentality*, I object, as contravening the essence of poetry, which Aristotle pronounces to be σπουδαιότατον καὶ φιλοσοφικώτατον γενὸς,[1] the most intense, weighty and philosophical product of human art; adding, as the *reason*, that it is the most catholic and abstract. The following passage from Davenant's prefatory letter to Hobbs well expresses this truth. "When I considered the actions which I meant to describe (those inferring the persons) I was again persuaded rather to choose those of a former age, than the present; and in a century so far removed as might preserve me

---

7. C quotes lines 78–91 of the version in *Poems* (1815).
8. On *The Excursion* (1814), see chapter 20 (p. 518, n. 3 herein).
9. In 1802 C criticized Wordsworth's shorter poems for "a daring Humbleness of Language & Versification, and a strict adherence to matter of fact, even to prolixity" (*CL*, 2:830).
1. "The noblest and most philosophical form" of writing (*Poetics* 9.1451b). See chapter 17 (p. 499, n. 3 herein).

from their improper examinations, who know not the requisites of a poem, nor how much pleasure they lose (and even the pleasures of heroic poesy are not unprofitable) who take away the liberty of a poet, and fetter his feet in the shackles of an historian. For why should a poet doubt in story to mend the intrigues of fortune by more delightful conveyances of probable fictions, because austere historians have entered into bond to truth? An obligation, which were in poets as foolish and unnecessary, as is the bondage of false martyrs, who lie in chains for a mistaken opinion. *But by this I would imply, that truth, narrative and past is the idol of historians (who worship a dead thing) and truth operative, and by effects continually alive, is the mistress of poets, who hath not her existence in matter, but in reason.*"[2]

For this minute accuracy in the painting of local imagery, the lines in the EXCURSION, p. 96, 97, and 98, may be taken, if not as a striking instance yet as an illustration of my meaning.[3] It must be some strong motive (as, for instance, that the description was necessary to the intelligibility of the tale) which could induce me to describe in a number of verses what a draftsman could present to the eye with incomparably greater satisfaction by half a dozen stokes of his pencil, or the painter with as many touches of his brush. Such descriptions too often occasion in the mind of a reader, who is determined to understand his author, a feeling of labor, not very dissimilar to that, with which he would construct a diagram, line by line, for a long geometrical proposition. It seems to be like taking the pieces of a dissected map out of its box. We first look at one part, and then at another, then join and dove-tail them; and when the successive acts of attention have been completed, there is a retrogressive effort of mind to behold it as a whole. The Poet should paint to the imagination, not to the fancy; and I know no happier case to exemplify the distinction between these two faculties.[4] Master-pieces of the former mode of poetic painting abound in the writings of Milton, ex. gr.

> The fig tree, not that kind for fruit renown'd,
> But such as at this day to Indians known
> In Malabar or Decan, spreads her arms
> Branching so broad and long, that in the ground
> The bended twigs take root, *and daughters grow*
> *About the mother-tree, a pillar'd shade*
> *High over-arched, and* ECHOING WALKS BETWEEN:
> *There oft the Indian Herdsman shunning heat*
> *Shelters in cool, and tends his pasturing herds*
> *At loop holes cut through thickest shade.*
>   MILTON, P. L. 9, 1100.[5]

This is *creation* rather than *painting*, or if painting, yet such, and with such co-presence of the whole picture flash'd at once upon the

---

2. Sir William Davenant, Preface to *Gondibert* (1651).
3. *The Excursion* (1814) 3.23–75 describes paths, waterfalls, rocks, and trees in the Lake District with minute accuracy.
4. For the distinction between fancy and imagination, see chapter 13 (p. 488 herein).
5. Milton, *Paradise Lost* 9.1101–10 (with C's italics and small capitals).

eye, as the sun paints in a camera obscura. But the poet must likewise understand and command what Bacon calls the *vestigia communia*[6] of the senses, the latency of all in each, and more especially as by a magical *penna duplex*,[7] the excitement of vision by sound and the exponents of sound. Thus, "THE ECHOING WALKS BETWEEN," may be almost said to reverse the fable in tradition of the head of Memnon, in the Egyptian statue.[8] Such may be deservedly entitled the *creative words* in the world of imagination.

The second division respects an apparent minute adherence to *matter-of-fact* in character and incidents; a *biographical* attention to probability, and an *anxiety* of explanation and retrospect. Under this head I shall deliver, with no feigned diffidence, the results of my best reflection on the great point of controversy between Mr. Wordsworth, and his objectors; namely, on THE CHOICE OF HIS CHARACTERS.[9] I have already declared, and, I trust justified, my utter dissent from the mode of argument which his critics have hitherto employed. To *their* question, why did you chuse such a character, or a character from such a rank of life? the Poet might in my opinion fairly retort: why, with the conception of my character did you make wilful choice of mean or ludicrous associations not furnished by me, but supplied from your own sickly and fastidious feelings? How was it, indeed, probable, that such arguments could have any weight with an author, whose plan, whose guiding principle, and main object it was to attack and subdue that state of association, which leads us to place the chief value on those things on which man DIFFERS from man, and to forget or disregard the high dignities, which belong to HUMAN NATURE, the sense and the feeling, which *may* be, and *ought* to be, found in *all* ranks? The feelings with which, as christians, we contemplate a mixed congregation rising or kneeling before their common maker: Mr. Wordsworth would have us entertain at *all* times as men, and as readers; and by the excitement of this lofty, yet prideless impartiality in *poetry*, he might hope to have encouraged its continuance in *real life*. The praise of good men be his! In real life, and, I trust, even in my imagination, I honor a virtuous and wise man, without reference to the presence or absence of artificial advantages. Whether in the person of an armed baron, a laurel'd bard, &c. or of an old pedlar, or still older leach-gatherer, the same

6. "Common traces." In the summer of 1809, in a notebook entry on the relation of thoughts to things, C wrote, "Refer to Lord Bacon's impressio communis—unum vestigium insensus varios" (common impression—one trace upon all the senses). The precise source in Bacon has not been identified (*CN*, 3:3587 and n.; *BL* [CC], 2:128–29n. 3).
7. "Double pen." C is perhaps thinking of the device patented by Ralph Wedgwood in 1808 to copy documents by moving two pens with one hand (*BL* [CC], 2:128n. 3).
8. One of the two colossi of Memnon, statues of the Egyptian king Amenophis III (c. 1411–1379 B.C.E.) on the west bank of the Nile, emitted a sound like a harp when the sun struck it at dawn. George Watson suggests that C's point is that as light produces sound, so sound, or literature, can produce sight, both literally and imaginatively (*BL* [1965], 253).
9. In his review of *The Excursion* in the *Edinburgh Review* (November 1814), 29–30, Francis Jeffrey asked, "Why should Mr Wordsworth have made his hero a superannuated Pedlar? What but the most wretched and provoking perversity of taste and judgment, could induce any one to place his chosen advocate of wisdom and virtue in so absurd and fantastic a condition? Did Mr Wordsworth really imagine, that his favourite doctrines were likely to gain any thing in point of effect or authority by being put into the mouth of a person accustomed to higgle about tape, or brass sleeve-buttons."

qualities of head and heart must claim the same reverence. And even in poetry I am not conscious, that I have ever suffered my feelings to be disturbed or offended by any thoughts or images, which the poet himself has not presented.

But yet I object nevertheless, and for the following reasons. First, because the object in view, as an *immediate* object, belongs to the moral philosopher, and would be pursued, not only more appropriately, but in my opinion with far greater probability of success, in sermons or moral essays, than in an elevated poem. It seems, indeed, to destroy the main fundamental distinction, not only between a *poem* and *prose*, but even between philosophy and works of fiction, inasmuch as it proposes *truth* for its immediate object, instead of *pleasure*.[1] Now till the blessed time shall come, when truth itself shall be pleasure, and both shall be so united, as to be distinguishable in words only, not in feeling, it will remain the poet's office to proceed upon that state of association, which actually exists as *general*; instead of attempting first to *make* it what it ought to be, and then to let the pleasure follow. But here is unfortunately a small *Hysteron-Proteron*.[2] For the communication of pleasure is the introductory means by which alone the poet must expect to moralize his readers. Secondly: though I were to admit, for a moment, *this* argument to be groundless: yet how is the moral effect to be produced, by merely attaching the name of some low profession to powers which are *least* likely, and to qualities which are assuredly not *more* likely, to be found in it? The poet, speaking in his own person, may at once delight and improve us by sentiments, which teach us the independence of goodness, of wisdom, and even of genius, on the favors of fortune. And having made a due reverence before the throne of Antonine, he may bow with equal awe before Epictetus[3] among his fellow-slaves—

> —————————————————— and rejoice
> In the plain presence of his dignity.[4]

Who is not at once delighted and improved, when the POET Wordsworth himself exclaims,

> O many are the poets that are sown
> By Nature; men endowed with highest gifts,
> The vision send the faculty divine,
> Yet wanting the accomplishment of verse,
> Nor having e'er, as life advanced, been led
> By circumstance to take unto the height
> The measure of themselves, these favor'd beings,
> All but a scatter'd few, live out their time
> Husbanding that which they possess within,

1. On this point, see also chapters 14 (p. 493 herein) and 18 (p. 509 herein).
2. "A figure of speech in which what should come last is put first" (*OED*).
3. Both the Roman emperor Marcus Aurelius Antonius (121–180 C.E.) and the slave Epictetus (c. 55–c. 135) were Stoic philosophers.
4. *The Excursion* (1814) 1.79–80.

And go to the grave unthought of. Strongest minds
Are often those of whom the noisy world
Hears least.
                                        EXCURSION, B. 1.[5]

To use a colloquial phrase, such sentiments, in such language, do
one's heart good; though I for my part, have not the fullest faith in the
truth of the observation. On the contrary I believe the instances to be
exceedingly rare; and should feel almost as strong an objection to introduce such a character in a poetic fiction, as a pair of black swans
on a lake, in a fancy-landscape. When I think how many, and how
much better books, than Homer, or even than Herodotus, Pindar or
Eschylus, could have read, are in the power of almost every man, in a
country where almost every man is instructed to read and write; and
how restless, how difficultly hidden, the powers of genius are; and yet
find even in situations the most favorable, according to Mr.
Wordsworth, for the formation of a pure and poetic language; in situations which ensure familiarity with the grandest objects of the imagination; but *one* BURNS, among the shepherds of *Scotland*, and not a
single poet of humble life among those of *English* lakes and mountains; I conclude, that POETIC GENIUS is not only a very delicate but a
very rare plant.

                            *   *   *

Is there one word for instance, attributed to the pedlar in the Ex-
CURSION, characteristic of a *pedlar*? One sentiment, that might not
more plausibly, even without the aid of any previous explanation, have
proceeded from any wise and beneficent old man, of a rank or profession in which the language of learning and refinement are natural and
to be expected? Need the rank have been at all particularized, where
nothing follows which the knowledge of that rank is to explain or illustrate? When on the contrary this information renders the man's
language, feelings, sentiments, and information a riddle, which must
itself be solved by episodes of anecdote? Finally when this, and this
alone, could have induced a genuine *poet* to inweave in a poem of the
loftiest style, and on subjects the loftiest and of most universal interest, such minute matters of fact, (not unlike those furnished for the
obituary of a magazine by the friends of some obscure *ornament of society lately deceased* in some obscure town,[)] as

> Among the hills of Athol he was born.
> There on a small hereditary farm,
> An unproductive slip of rugged ground,
> His Father dwelt; and died in poverty:
> While he, whose lowly fortune I retrace,
> The youngest of three sons, was yet a babe,
> A little one—unconscious of their loss.
> But 'ere he had outgrown his infant days
> His widowed mother, for a second mate,
> Espoused the teacher of the Village School;

5. *The Excursion* 1.81–84, 90–97 (with "send" for "and" in line 81).

Who on her offspring zealously bestowed
Needful instruction.

From his sixth year, the Boy of whom I speak,
In summer, tended cattle on the hills;
But through the inclement and the perilous days
Of long-continuing winter, he repaired
To his step-father's school.—&c.[6]

For all the admirable passages interposed in this narration, might, with trifling alterations, have been far more appropriately, and with far greater verisimilitude, told of a poet in the character of a poet; and without incurring another defect which I shall now mention, and a sufficient illustration of which will have been here anticipated.

Third; an undue predilection for the *dramatic* form in certain poems, from which one or other of two evils result. Either the thoughts and diction are different from that of the poet, and then there arises an incongruity of style; or they are the same and indistinguishable, and then it presents a species of ventriloquism, where two are represented as talking, while in truth one man only speaks.

The fourth class of defects is closely connected with the former; but yet are such as arise likewise from an intensity of feeling disproportionate to *such* knowledge and value of the objects described, as can be fairly anticipated of men in general, even of the most cultivated classes; and with which therefore few only, and those few particularly circumstanced, can be supposed to sympathize: In this class, I comprize occasional prolixity, repetition, and an eddying instead of progression of thought. As instances, see page 27, 28, and 62 of the Poems, Vol. I. and the first eighty lines of the Sixth Book of the Excursion.[7]

Fifth and last; thoughts and images too great for the subject. This is an approximation to what might be called *mental* bombast, as distinguished from verbal: for, as in the latter there is a disproportion of the expressions to the thoughts so in this there is a disproportion of thought to the circumstance and occasion. This, by the bye, is a fault of which none but a man of genius is capable. It is the awkwardness and strength of Hercules with the distaff of Omphale.[8]

It is a well known fact, that bright colours in motion both make and leave the strongest impressions on the eye. Nothing is more likely too, than that a vivid image or visual spectrum, thus originated, may be-

---

6. *The Excursion* 1.112–23, 134–38. Wordsworth later revised and shortened the first passage beginning with the fourth line: "His Parents, with their numerous offspring, dwelt; / A virtuous household, though exceeding poor! / Pure livers were they all, austere and grave, / And fearing God; the very children taught / Stern self-respect, a reverence for God's word / And an habitual piety, maintained / With strictness scarcely known on English ground" (*WPW,* 5:11–12)

7. *Poems* (1815), 1:27–28 contains stanzas 4–13 of "Anecdote for Fathers," which Wordsworth later revised (*LB* [1992], 71–72). Page 62 of volume 1 is blank; SC suggests that C meant page 62 of volume 2, which contains lines 80–103 of "Song at the Feast of Brougham Castle" (*BL* [1847], 2:152, n. 22). The first lines of book 6 of *The Excursion* praise "the crown by Freedom shaped" (line 1) and "the spiritual fabric of her Church" (line 8) (*WPW,* 5:186).

8. For the murder of Iphitus, Hercules was sentenced to serve Omphale, queen of Lydia, who made him wear women's clothing and spin wool.

come the link of association in recalling the feelings and images that had accompanied the original impression. But if we describe this in such lines, as

> They flash upon that inward eye,
> Which is the bliss of solitude!

in what words shall we describe the joy of retrospection, when the images and virtuous actions of a whole well-spent life, pass before that conscience which is indeed the *inward* eye: which is indeed *"the bliss of solitude?"* Assuredly we seem to sink most abruptly, not to say burlesquely, and almost as in a *medly* from this couplet to —

> And then my heart with pleasure fills,
> And dances with the *daffodils*. Vol. I. p. 329.[9]

The second instance is from Vol. II. page 12, where the poet having gone out for a day's tour of pleasure, meets early in the morning with a knot of *gypsies*, who had pitched their blanket-tents and straw-beds, together with their children and asses, in some field by the road-side. At the close of the day on his return our tourist found them in the same place. "Twelve hours," says he,

> Twelve hours, twelve bounteous hours, are gone while I
> Have been a traveller under open sky,
> Much witnessing of change and cheer,
> Yet as I left I find them here!

Whereat the poet, without seeming to reflect that the poor tawny wanderers might probably have been tramping for weeks together through road and lane, over moor and mountain, and consequently must have been right glad to rest themselves, their children and cattle, for one whole day; and overlooking the obvious truth, that such repose might be quite as necessary for *them*, as a walk of the same continuance was pleasing or healthful for the more fortunate poet; expresses his indignation in a series of lines, the diction and imagery of which would have been rather above, than below the mark, had they been applied to the immense empire of China improgressive for thirty centuries:

> The weary SUN betook himself to rest,
> —Then issued VESPER from the fulgent west,
> Outshining, like a visible God,
> The glorious path in which he trod!
> And now ascending, after one dark hour,
> And one night's diminution of her power,
> Behold the mighty MOON! this way
> She looks, as if at them—but they
> Regard not her:—oh, better wrong and strife,
> Better vain deeds or evil than such life!

9. C contrasts lines 21–22 with lines 23–24 of "I Wandered Lonely as a Cloud." In *Poems* (1815) Wordsworth included a note to lines 21–22: "The subject of these Stanzas is rather an elementary feeling and simple impression (approaching to the nature of an ocular spectrum) upon the imaginative faculty, than an *exertion* of it" (*PTV*, 419).

The silent HEAVENS have goings on:
The STARS have tasks!—but *these* have none![1]

The last instance of this defect, (for I know no other than these already cited) is from the Ode, page 351. Vol. II. where, speaking of a child, "a six year's darling of a pigmy size," he thus addresses him:

Thou best philosopher who yet dost keep
Thy heritage! Thou eye among the blind,
That, deaf and silent, read'st the eternal deep,
Haunted for ever by the Eternal Mind—
Mighty Prophet! Seer blest!
On whom those truths do rest,
Which we are toiling all our lives to find!
Thou, over whom thy immortality
Broods like the day, a master o'er the slave.
A presence that is not to be put by![2]

Now here, not to stop at the daring spirit of metaphor which connects the epithets "deaf and silent," with the apostrophized *eye*: or (if we are to refer it to the preceding word, philosopher) the faulty and equivocal syntax of the passage; and without examining the propriety of making a "master *brood* o'er a slave," or the *day* brood *at all*; we will merely ask, what does all this mean? In what sense is a child of that age a *philosopher*? In what sense does he *read* "the eternal deep?" In what sense is he declared to be "*for ever haunted*" by the Supreme Being? or so inspired as to deserve the splendid titles of a *mighty prophet*, a *blessed seer*? By reflection? by knowledge? by conscious intuition? or by *any* form or modification of consciousness? These would be tidings indeed; but such as would pre-suppose an immediate revelation to the inspired communicator, and require miracles to authenticate his inspiration. Children at this age give us no such information of themselves; and at what time were we dipt in the Lethe, which has produced such utter oblivion of a state so godlike? There are many of us that still possess some remembrances, more or less distinct, respecting themselves at six years old; pity that the worthless straws only should float, while treasures, compared with which all the mines of Golconda and Mexico were but straws, should be absorbed by some unknown gulf into some unknown abyss.

* * *

So with regard to this passage. In what sense can the magnificent attributes, above quoted, be appropriated to a *child*, which would not make them equally suitable to a *bee*, or a *dog*, or *a field of corn*; or even to a ship, or to the wind and waves that propel it? The omni-present

---

1. "Gipsies" (1807), lines 9–12, 13–24.
2. "Ode. Intimations of Immortality from Recollections of Early Childhood" (1815), lines 86 and 110–19. In January 1815 Wordsworth wrote to Catherine Clarkson, "The poem rests entirely upon two recollections of childhood, one that of a splendor in the objects of sense which is passed away, and the other an indisposition to bend the law of death as applying to our own particular case. A Reader who has not a vivid recollection of these feelings having existed in his mind cannot understand that poem" (*PTV*, 428–29).

Spirit works equally in *them*, as in the child; and the child is equally unconscious of it as they. It cannot surely be, that the four lines, immediately following, are to contain the explanation?

> To whom the grave
> Is but a lonely bed without the sense or sight
> Of day or the warm light,
> A place of thought where we in waiting lie.[3]

Surely, it cannot be that this wonder-rousing apostrophe is but a comment on the little poem of "We are Seven?"[4] that the whole meaning of the passage is reducible to the assertion, that a *child*, who by the bye at six years old would have been better instructed in most christian families, has no other notion of death than that of lying in a dark, cold place? And still, I hope, not as *in a place of thought!* not the frightful notion of lying *awake* in his grave! The analogy between death and sleep is too simple, too natural, to render so horrid a belief possible for children; even had they not been in the habit, as all christian children are, of hearing the latter term used to express the former. But if the child's belief be only, that "he is not dead, but sleepeth:"[5] wherein does it differ from that of his father and mother, or any other adult and instructed person? To form an idea of a thing's becoming nothing; or of nothing becoming a thing; is impossible to all finite beings alike, of whatever age, and however educated or uneducated. Thus it is with splendid paradoxes in general. If the words are taken in the common sense, they convey an absurdity; and if, in contempt of dictionaries and custom, they are so interpreted as to avoid the absurdity, the meaning dwindles into some bald truism. Thus you must at once understand the words *contrary* to their common import, in order to arrive at any *sense*; and *according* to their common import, if you are to receive from them any feeling of *sublimity* or *admiration*.

Though the instances of this defect in Mr. Wordsworth's poems are so few, that for themselves it would have been scarcely just to attract the reader's attention toward them; yet I have dwelt on it, and perhaps the more for this very reason. For being so very few, they cannot sensibly detract from the reputation of an author, who is even characterized by the number of profound truths in his writings, which will stand the severest analysis; and yet few as they are, they are exactly those passages which his *blind* admirers would be most likely, and best able, to imitate. But WORDSWORTH, where he is indeed Wordsworth, may be mimicked by Copyists, he may be plundered by Plagiarists; but he can not be imitated, except by those who are not born to be imitators. For without his depth of feeling and his imaginative power his *Sense*

---

3. "Ode" (1815), lines 120–23. In 1820 Wordsworth removed these lines (*PTV*, 274).
4. Published in *LB* (1798). In the 1815 version it begins, "A simple child / That lightly draws its breath, / And feels its life in every limb, / What should it know of death?" After writing the poem and reciting it to his sister and C, Wordsworth decided that "A prefatory Stanza must be added." He "mentioned in substance what [he] wished to be expressed, and Coleridge immediately threw off the stanza thus: 'A little child, dear brother Jem'" (*LB* [1992], 348). C thus criticizes a poem he helped to write.
5. Cf. Matthew 9.24: "Give place: for the maid is not dead, but sleepeth."

would want its vital warmth and peculiarity; and without his strong sense, his *mysticism* would become *sickly*—mere fog, and dimness!

To these defects which, as appears by the extracts, are only occasional, I may oppose with far less fear of encountering the dissent of any candid and intelligent reader, the following (for the most part correspondent) excellencies. First, an austere purity of language both grammatically and logically; in short a perfect appropriateness of the words to the meaning. Of how high value I deem this, and how particularly estimable I hold the example at the present day, has been already stated: and in part too the reasons on which I ground both the moral and intellectual importance of habituating ourselves to a strict accuracy of expression. It is noticeable, how limited an acquaintance with the master-pieces of art will suffice to form a correct and even a sensitive taste, where none but master-pieces have been seen and admired: while on the other hand, the most correct notions, and the widest acquaintance with the works of excellence of all ages and countries, will not perfectly secure us against the contagious familiarity with the far more numerous offspring of tastelessness or of a perverted taste. If this be the case, as it notoriously is, with the arts of music and painting, much more difficult will it be, to avoid the infection of multiplied and daily examples in the practice of an art, which uses words, and words only, as its instruments. In poetry, in which every line, every phrase, may pass the ordeal of deliberation and deliberate choice, it is possible, and barely possible, to attain that ultimatum which I have ventured to propose as the infallible test of a blameless style; namely; its *untranslatableness* in words of the same language without injury to the meaning. Be it observed, however, that I include in the *meaning* of a word not only its correspondent object, but likewise all the associations which it recalls. For language is framed to convey not the object alone, but likewise the character, mood and intentions of the person who is representing it. In poetry it *is* practicable to preserve the diction uncorrupted by the affectations and misappropriations, which promiscuous authorship, and reading not promiscuous only because it is disproportionally most conversant with the compositions of the day, have rendered general. Yet even to the poet, composing in his own province, it is an arduous work: and as the result and pledge of a watchful good sense, of fine and luminous distinction, and of complete self-possession, may justly claim all the honor which belongs to an attainment equally difficult and valuable, and the more valuable for being rare. It is at *all* times the proper food of the understanding; but in an age of corrupt eloquence it is both food and antidote.

*   *   *

The second characteristic excellence of Mr. W's works is: a correspondent weight and sanity of the Thoughts and Sentiments,— won, not from books; but—from the poet's own meditative observation. They are *fresh* and have the dew upon them. His muse, at least when in her strength of wing, and when she hovers aloft in her proper element,

Makes audible a linked lay of truth,
Of truth profound a sweet continuous lay,
Not learnt, but native, her own natural notes!
                                        S. T. C.[6]

Even throughout his smaller poems there is scarcely one, which is
not rendered valuable by some just and original reflection.

See page 25, vol. 2nd:[7] or the two following passages in one of his
humblest compositions.

O Reader! had you in your mind
Such stores as silent thought can bring,
O gentle Reader! you would find
A tale in every thing.

and

I have heard of hearts unkind, kind deeds
With coldness still returning.
Alas! the gratitude of men
Has oftener left *me* mourning.[8]

or in a still higher strain the six beautiful quatrains, page 134.

Thus fares it still in our decay:
And yet the wiser mind
Mourns less for what age takes away
That what it leaves behind.

The Blackbird in the summer trees,
The Lark upon the hill,
Let loose their carols when they please,
Are quiet when they will.

With nature never do *they* wage
A foolish strife; they see
A happy youth, and their old age
Is beautiful and free!

But we are pressed by heavy laws;
And often, glad no more,
We wear a face of joy, because
We have been glad of yore.

If there is one, who need bemoan
His kindred laid in earth,
The household hearts that were his own,
It is the man of mirth.

My days, my Friend, are almost gone,
My life has been approved,

6. "To William Wordsworth" (written 1807, published 1817), lines 58–60. See "To a Gentleman" (p. 200 herein).
7. "Star-Gazers" (1807), lines 9–26.
8. "Simon Lee" (1798), lines 73–76, 101–04 (with C's italics in the last line).

And many love me; but by none
Am I enough beloved.[9]

or the sonnet on Buonaparte, page 202, vol. 2;[1] or finally (for a volume would scarce suffice to exhaust the instances,) the last stanza of the poem on the withered Celandine, vol. 2, p. 312.[2]

To be a prodigal's favorite—then, worse truth,
A miser's pensioner—behold our lot!
Oh man! that from thy fair and shining youth
Age might but take the things, youth needed not.

Both in respect of this and of the former excellence, Mr. Wordsworth strikingly resembles Samuel Daniel, one of the golden writers of our golden Elizabethan age, now most causelessly neglected:[3] Samuel Daniel, whose diction bears no mark of time, no distinction of age, which has been, and as long as our language shall last, will be so far the language of the to-day and for ever, as that it is more intelligible to us, than the transitory fashions of our own particular age. A similar praise is due to his sentiments. No frequency of perusal can deprive them of their freshness. For though they are brought into the full day-light of every reader's comprehension; yet are they drawn up from depths which few in any age are priviledged to visit, into which few in any age have courage or inclination to descend. If Mr. Wordsworth is not equally with Daniel alike intelligible to all readers of average understanding in all passages of his works, the comparative difficulty does not arise from the greater impurity of the ore, but from the nature and uses of the metal. A poem is not necessarily obscure, because it does not aim to be popular. It is enough, if a work be perspicuous to those for whom it is written, and,

Fit audience find, though few.[4]

To the "Ode on the intimation of immortality from recollections of early childhood" the poet might have prefixed the lines which Dante addresses to one of his own Canzoni—

Canzon, io credo, che saranno radi
Che tua ragione intendan bene:
Tanto lor sei faticoso ed alto.

O lyric song, there will be few, think I,
Who may thy import understand aright:
Thou art for *them* so arduous and so high![5]

But the ode was intended for such readers only as had been accustomed to watch the flux and reflux of their inmost nature, to venture at times into the twilight realms of consciousness, and to feel a deep

9. "The Fountain" (1800), lines 33–56.
1. I.e., "I grieved for Buonparte" (1807).
2. "The Small Celandine" (1807), lines 21–24.
3. An Elizabethan poet (1563–1619) whom C admired, also mentioned in chapter 18.
4. Milton, *Paradise Lost* 7.31.
5. Dante, *Convivio* 2.1.53–55 (var.), with C's translation.

interest in modes of inmost being, to which they know that the attributes of time and space are inapplicable and alien, but which yet can not be conveyed, save in symbols of time and space. For such readers the sense is sufficiently plain, and they will be as little disposed to charge Mr. Wordsworth with believing the platonic pre-existence in the ordinary interpretation of the words, as I am to believe, that Plato himself ever meant or taught it.[6] * * *

Third (and wherein he soars far above Daniel) the sinewy strength and originality of single lines and paragraphs: the frequent curiosa felicitas[7] of his diction, of which I need not here give specimens, having anticipated them in a preceding page. This beauty, and as eminently characteristic of Wordsworth's poetry, his rudest assailants have felt themselves compelled to acknowledge and admire.

Fourth; the perfect truth of nature in his images and descriptions as taken immediately from nature, and proving a long and genial intimacy with the very spirit which gives the physiognomic expression to all the works of nature. Like a green field reflected in a calm and perfectly transparent lake, the image is distinguished from the reality only by its greater softness and lustre. Like the moisture or the polish on a pebble, genius neither distorts nor false-colours its objects; but on the contrary brings out many a vein and many a tint, which escape the eye of common observation, thus raising to the rank of gems, what had been often kicked away by the hurrying foot of the traveller on the dusty high road of custom.

Let me refer to the whole description of skating, vol. I, page 42 to 47, especially to the lines

> So through the darkness and the cold we flew,
> And not a voice was idle: with the din
> Meanwhile the precipices rang aloud;
> The leafless trees and every icy crag
> Tinkled like iron; while the distant hills
> Into the tumult sent an alien sound
> Of melancholy, not unnoticed, while the stars
> Eastward were sparkling clear, and in the west
> The orange sky of evening died away.[8]

Or to the poem on the green linnet, vol. I. p. 244. What can be more accurate yet more lovely than the two concluding stanzas?

6. Wordsworth commented to Isabella Fenwick, "To that dream-like vividness and splendour which invest objects of sight in childhood every one, I believe, if he would look back, could bear testimony, and I need not dwell upon it here—but having in the Poem regarded it as presumptive evidence of a prior state of existence, I think it right to protest against a conclusion which has given pain to some good and pious persons that I meant to inculcate such a belief. It is far too shadowy a notion to be recommended to faith as more than an element in our instincts of immortality" (*PTV*, 428).

7. "Studied felicity." From Petronius's comments on Horace in *Satyricon* 118: "one must take care that the thoughts do not stand out from the body of the speech: they must shine with a brilliancy that is woven into the material. Homer proves this, and the lyric poets, and Roman Virgil, and the studied felicity of Horace" (trans. Michael Heseltine and E. H. Warmington [LCL, 1969], 295).

8. "Growth of Genius from the Influence of Natural Objects, on the Imagination in Boyhood, and Early Youth," lines 38–46, first published in *The Friend*, December 28, 1809 (*Friend* [CC], 2:259). The passage was drafted with the early episodes of *The Prelude* and later included in the 1805 version of *The Prelude* 1.465–74. C's page reference to *Poems* (1815) should be 44, not 42.

Upon yon tuft of hazel trees,
That twinkle to the gusty breeze,
Behold him perched in ecstacies,
      Yet seeming still to hover,
There! where the flutter of his wings
Upon his back and body flings
Shadows and sunny glimmerings
      That cover him all over.

While thus before my eyes he gleams,
A brother of the leaves he seems;
When in a moment forth he teems
      His little song in gushes:
As if it pleased him to disdain
And mock the form when he did feign
While he was dancing with the train
      Of leaves among the bushes.[9]

Or the description of the blue-cap, and of the noon-tide silence, p. 284; or the poem to the cuckoo, p. 299; or, lastly, though I might multiply the references to ten times the number, to the poem so completely Wordsworth's commencing

Three years she grew in sun and shower, &c.[1]

Fifth: a meditative pathos, a union of deep and subtle thought with sensibility; a sympathy with man as man; the sympathy indeed of a contemplator, rather than a fellow-sufferer or co-mate, (spectator, haud particeps)[2] but of a contemplator, from whose view no difference of rank conceals the sameness of the nature; no injuries of wind or weather, of toil, or even of ignorance, wholly disguise the human face divine. The superscription and the image of the Creator still remain legible to *him* under the dark lines, with which guilt or calamity had cancelled or cross-barred it. Here the man and the poet lose and find themselves in each other, the one as glorified, the latter as substantiated. In this mild and philosophic pathos, Wordsworth appears to me without a compeer. Such he *is*: so he *writes*. See vol. I. page 134 to 136,[3] or that most affecting composition, the "Affliction of Margaret —— of ——," page 165 to 168, which no mother, and if I may judge by my own experience, no parent can read without a tear. Or turn to that genuine lyric, in the former edition, entitled, the "Mad Mother," page 174 to 178, of which I can not refrain from quoting two of the stanzas, both of them for their pathos, and the former for the fine transition in the two concluding lines of the stanza, so expressive of that deranged state, in which from

---

9. "The Green Linnet," lines 25–40, included among the "Poems of the Fancy" in *Poems* (1815).
1. C refers to "The Kitten and the Falling Leaves," lines 65–88; "To the Cuckoo," lines 1–16; and "Three years she grew in sun and shower," all in volume 1 of *Poems* (1815).
2. "A spectator, not at all a participant." In 1833 C commented that Wordsworth and Goethe "both have this quality of non-sympathy with the subjects of their poetry. They are always both ab extra—feeling for but never *with* their characters" (*TT* [CC], 1:342). See also p. 609 herein for a similar comment.
3. I.e., "Tis Said, that Some Have Died of Love" (1800).

the increased sensibility the sufferer's attention is abruptly drawn off by every trifle, and in the same instant plucked back again by the one despotic thought, and bringing home with it, by the blending, *fusing* power of Imagination and Passion,[4] the alien object to which it had been so abruptly diverted, no longer an alien but an ally and an inmate.

> Suck, little babe, oh suck again!
> It cools my blood; it cools my brain:
> Thy lips, I feel them, baby! they
> Draw from my heart the pain away.
> Oh! press me with thy little hand;
> It loosens something at my chest;
> About that tight and deadly band
> I feel thy little fingers prest.
> The breeze I see is in the tree!
> It comes to cool my babe and me.
>
> Thy father cares not for my breast,
> 'Tis thine, sweet baby, there to rest,
> 'Tis all thine own!—and, if its hue,
> Be changed, that was so fair to view,
> 'Tis fair enough for thee, my dove!
> My beauty, little child, is flown,
> But thou wilt live with me in love,
> And what if my poor cheek be brown?
> 'Tis well for me, thou can'st not see
> How pale and wan it else would be.[5]

Last, and pre-eminently, I challenge for this poet the gift of IMAGINATION in the highest and strictest sense of the word. In the play of *Fancy*, Wordsworth, to my feelings, is not always graceful, and sometimes *recondite*.[6] The *likeness* is occasionally too strange, or demands too peculiar a point of view, or is such as appears the creature of predetermined research, rather than spontaneous presentation. Indeed his fancy seldom displays itself, as mere and unmodified fancy. But in imaginative power, he stands nearest of all modern writers to Shakespear and Milton; and yet in a kind perfectly unborrowed and his own. To employ his own words, which are at once an instance and an illustration, he does indeed to all thoughts and to all objects—

> ——————————————add the gleam,
> The light that never was on sea or land,
> The consecration, and the poet's dream.[7]

I shall select a few examples as most obviously manifesting this faculty; but if I should ever be fortunate enough to render my analysis of

---

4. On the imagination's fusing power, see also chapter 14 (p. 495 herein).
5. "Her Eyes are wild," lines 31–40, 61–70, untitled in *Poems* (1815). In 1804 C wrote in a notebook, "of the sudden Images *seized* on from external Contingents by Passion & Imagination (which is Passion eagle-eyed)—The Breeze I see, is in the Tree—It comes to cool my Babe and me.—which is the property & prerogative of continuous minds of the highest order" (CN, 2:2112).
6. For the distinction between imagination and fancy, see chapter 13 (p. 488 herein).
7. "Elegiac Stanzas, Suggested by a Picture of Peele Castle" (1807), lines 14–16.

imagination, its origin and characters thoroughly intelligible to the reader, he will scarcely open on a page of this poet's works without recognizing, more or less, the presence and the influences of this faculty.

From the poem on the Yew Trees, vol. I. page 303, 304.

> But worthier still of note
> Are those fraternal four of Borrowdale,
> Joined in one solemn and capacious grove:
> Huge trunks!—and each particular trunk a growth
> Of intertwisted fibres serpentine
> Up-coiling, and inveterately convolved,—
> Not uninformed with phantasy, and looks
> That threaten the prophane;—a pillared shade,
> Upon whose grassless floor of red-brown hue,
> By sheddings from the pinal umbrage tinged
> Perennially—beneath whose sable roof
> Of boughs, as if for festal purpose decked
> With unrejoicing berries, ghostly shapes
> May meet at noontide—FEAR and trembling HOPE,
> SILENCE and FORESIGHT—DEATH, the skeleton,
> And TIME, the shadow—there to celebrate,
> As in a natural temple scattered o'er
> With altars undisturbed of mossy stone,
> United worship; or in mute repose
> To lie, and listen to the mountain flood
> Murmuring from Glaramora's inmost caves.[8]

The effect of the old man's figure in the poem of Resignation and Independence, vol. II. page 33.

> While he was talking thus, the lonely place
> The old man's shape, and speech, all troubled me:
> In my mind's eye I seemed to see him pace
> About the weary moors continually,
> Wandering about alone and silently.[9]

Or the 8th, 9th, 19th, 26th, 31st, and 33d, in the collection of miscellaneous sonnets—the sonnet on the subjugation of Switzerland, page 210, or the last ode from which I especially select the two following stanzas or paragraphs, page 349 to 350.[1]

> Our birth is but a sleep and a forgetting:
> The soul that rises with us, our life's star

8. "Yew-Trees" (1815), lines 13–33, with "pinal" in place of Wordsworth's "pining" (line 22) and the addition of small capitals. SC commented: "I have left my Father's substitution, as a curious instance of a possible different reading. 'Piny shade' and 'piny verdure' we read of in the poets; but 'pinal' I believe is new. *Pining*, which has a quite different sense, is doubtless still better; but perhaps my Father's ear shrunk from it after the word '*sheddings*' at the beginning of the line" (*BL* [1847], 2:177).
9. "Resolution and Independence" (1807), lines 134–38.
1. C lists "Where Lies the Land," "Even as a Dragon's Eye," "To the River Duddon," "Composed upon Westminster Bridge," "Methought I Saw the Footsteps," "It is a Beauteous Evening," and "Thought of a Briton on the Subjugation of Switzerland" in the category "Sonnets Dedicated to Liberty" in *Poems* (1815).

Hath had elsewhere its setting,
    And cometh from afar.
Not in entire forgetfulness,
And not in utter nakedness,
But trailing clouds of glory do we come
From God who is our home:
Heaven lies about us in our infancy!
Shades of the prison-house begin to close
    Upon the growing boy;
But he beholds the light, and whence it flows,
    He sees it in his joy!
The youth who daily further from the east
Must travel, still is nature's priest,
    And by the vision splendid
    Is on his way attended;
At length the man perceives it die away,
And fade into the light of common day.[2]

And page 352 to 354 of the same ode.

O joy that in our embers
Is something that doth live,
That nature yet remembers
What was so fugitive!
The thought of our past years in me doth breed
Perpetual benedictions: not indeed
For that which is most worthy to be blest
Delight and liberty the simple creed
Of childhood, whether busy or at rest,
With new-fledged hope still fluttering in his breast:—
Not for these I raise
The song of thanks and praise;
But for those obstinate questionings
Of sense and outward things,
Fallings from us, vanishings;
Blank misgivings of a creature
Moving about in worlds not realized,
High instincts, before which our mortal nature
Did tremble like a guilty thing surprised!
But for those first affections,
Those shadowy recollections,
Which, be they what they may,
Are yet the fountain light of all our day,
Are yet a master light of all our seeing;
Uphold us—cherish—and have power to make
Our noisy years seem moments in the being
Of the eternal silence; truths that wake
    To perish never:
Which neither listlessness, nor mad endeavour
Nor man nor boy

---

2. "Ode. Intimations of Immortality" (1815 version), lines 58–77 (var.).

Nor all that is at enmity with joy
Can utterly abolish or destroy!
Hence, in a season of calm weather,
Though inland far we be,
Our souls have sight of that immortal sea
Which brought us hither,
Can in a moment travel thither—
And see the children sport upon the shore,
And hear the mighty waters rolling evermore.[3]

*   *   *

The following analogy will, I am apprehensive, appear dim and fantastic, but in reading Bartram's Travels I could not help transcribing the following lines as a sort of allegory, or connected simile and metaphor of Wordsworth's intellect and genius.—"The soil is a deep, rich, dark mould, on a deep stratum of tenacious clay; and that on a foundation of rocks, which often break through both strata, lifting their back above the surface. The trees which chiefly grow here are the gigantic, black oak; magnolia magnifloria; fraximus excelsior; platane; and a few stately tulip trees."[4] What Mr. Wordsworth *will* produce, it is not for me to prophecy: but I could pronounce with the liveliest convictions what he is capable of producing. It is the FIRST GENUINE PHILOSOPHIC POEM.

*   *   *

FROM CHAPTER XXIV

CONCLUSION[5]

It sometimes happens that we are punished for our faults by incidents, in the causation of which these faults had no share: and this I have always felt the severest punishment. The wound indeed is of the same dimensions; but the edges are jagged, and there is a dull underpain that survives the smart which it had aggravated. For there is always a consolatory feeling that accompanies the sense of a proportion between antecedents and consequents. The sense of Before and After becomes both intelligible and intellectual when, and *only* when, we contemplate the succession in the relations of Cause and Effect, which like the two poles of the magnet manifest the being and unity of the one power by relative opposites, and give, as it were, a substratum of permanence, of identity, and therefore of reality, to the shadowy flux of Time. It is Eternity revealing itself in the phænomena of Time: and the perception and acknowledgement of the proportionality and ap-

---

3. "Ode. Intimations of Immortality" (1815 version), lines 130–68 (var.).
4. C condensed and copied this passage from William Bartram's *Travels through North and South Carolina* (1791) in a notebook and added, "I applied this by a fantastic analogue & similitude to Wordsworth's Mind. March 26 1801" (CN, 1:926).
5. This chapter was written between late February and mid-May 1817 and refers to events in C's literary life after he sent the earlier chapters to the printer in the fall of 1815 (CL, 4:707, 729): the rejection of his play *Zapolya* in April 1816, the harsh reviews of *Christabel* in the *Examiner* and the *Edinburgh Review*, and the similarly harsh review of *The Statesman's Manual* in the *Edinburgh Review* for December 1816, which did not reach C until February 1817.

propriateness of the Present to the Past, prove to the afflicted Soul, that it has not yet been deprived of the sight of God, that it can still recognize the effective presence of a Father, though through a darkened glass and a turbid atmosphere, though of a Father that is chastising it. And for this cause, doubtless, are we so framed in mind, and even so organized in brain and nerve, that all confusion is painful.—It is within the experience of many medical practitioners, that a patient, with strange and unusual symptoms of disease, has been more distressed in mind, more wretched, from the fact of being unintelligible to himself and others, than from the pain or danger of the disease: nay, that the patient has received the most solid comfort, and resumed a genial and enduring chearfulness, from some new symptom or product, that had at once determined the name and nature of his complaint, and rendered it an intelligible effect of an intelligible cause: even though the discovery did at the same moment preclude all hope of restoration.

*   *   *

I shall not make this an excuse, however, for troubling my Readers with any complaints or explanations, with which, as Readers, they have little or no concern. It may suffice (for the present at least) to declare that the causes that have delayed the publication of these volumes for so long a period after they had been printed off, were not connected with any neglect of my own; and that they would form an instructive comment on the Chapter concerning Authorship as a Trade, addressed to young men of genius in the first volume of this work.[6] I remember the ludicrous effect which the first sentence of an Auto-biography, which happily for the writer was as meagre in incidents as it is well possible for the Life of an Individual to be—"The *eventful* Life which I am about to record, from the hour in which I rose into exist[ence] on this Planet, &c.."[7] Yet when, notwithstand[ing] this warning example of Self-importance before me, I review my own life, I cannot refrain from applying the same epithet to it, and with more than ordinary emphasis—and no private feeling, that affected myself only, should prevent me from *publishing* the same, (for *write* it I assuredly shall, should life and leisure be granted me)[8] if continued reflection should strengthen my present belief, that my history would add its contingent to the enforcement of one important truth, viz. that we must not only love our neighbours as ourselves, but ourselves likewise as our neighbours; and that we can do neither unless we love God above both.[9]

Who lives, that's not
Depraved or depraves? Who dies, *that bears
Not one spurn to the grave—of their friends' gift?*[1]

6. A reference to chapter 11.
7. Untraced, but variations of this formula were common in 18th-century autobiographical writings.
8. C never did write such an autobiography.
9. Matthew 22.39: "Thou shalt love thy neighbor as thyself."
1. Shakespeare, *Timon of Athens* 1.2.132–34 (var.).

Strange as the delusion may appear, yet it is most true that three years ago I did not know or believe that I had an enemy in the world:[2] and now even my strongest sensations of gratitude are mingled with fear, and I reproach myself for being too often disposed to ask,—Have I one friend?—During the many years which intervened between the composition and the publication of the Christabel, it became almost as well known among literary men as if it had been on common sale, the same references were made to it, and the same liberties taken with it, even to the very names of the imaginary persons in the poem. From almost all of our most celebrated Poets, and from some with whom I had no personal acquaintance, I either received or heard of expressions of admiration that (I can truly say) appeared to myself utterly disproportionate to a work, that pretended to be nothing more than a common Faery Tale. Many, who had allowed no merit to my other poems, whether printed or manuscript, and who have frankly told me as much, uniformly made an exception in favour of the CHRISTABEL and the Poem, entitled LOVE.[3] Year after year, and in societies of the most different kinds, I had been entreated to recite it: and the result was still the same in all, and altogether different in this respect from the effect produced by the occasional recitation of any other poems I had composed.—This before the publication. And since then, with very few exceptions, I have heard nothing but abuse, and this too in a spirit of bitterness at least as disproportionate to the pretensions of the poem, had it been the most pitiably below mediocrity, as the previous eulogies, and far more inexplicable. In the Edinburgh Review it was assailed with a malignity and a spirit of personal hatred that ought to have injured only the work in which such a Tirade was suffered to appear: and this review was generally attributed (whether rightly or no I know not) to a man, who both in my presence and in my absence, has repeatedly pronounced it the finest poem of its kind in the language.[4]—This may serve as a warning to authors, that in their calculations on the probable reception of a poem, they must subtract to a large amount from the panegyric, which may have encouraged them to

---

2. Although C and Wordsworth were ridiculed for their poetic style and attacked for their radical politics from their first publications, it was not until 1813–14 that the criticisms of their writings became bitter and personal. In April 1813 Wordsworth was named to the government post of distributer of stamps for the counties of Cumberland and Westmorland, and in October 1813 Southey was named poet laureate. In January 1814 Leigh Hunt's *Examiner* began a series of attacks on Southey as a turncoat, and these articles also attacked C.

3. See "Love" (p. 106, n. 1 herein).

4. *Christabel* was reviewed in the *Edinburgh Review* in September 1816. Since Hazlitt had reviewed the poem harshly in the *Examiner* (see the headnote to *Christabel*, p. 159 herein), C thought the *Edinburgh's* review was also by Hazlitt, but Elisabeth Schneider has argued that Thomas Moore was the author ("The Unknown Reviewer of *Christabel*," *PMLA* 70 [1955]: 417–32). The authorship remains in doubt, and C's prose suggests that he himself was not sure. The reviewer remarks that "we look upon this publication as one of the most notable pieces of impertinence of which the press has lately been guilty * * *. The other productions of the Lake School have generally exhibited talents thrown away upon subjects so mean, that no power of genius could ennoble them. * * * But the thing now before us, is utterly destitute of value" (*CH*, 1:234–35).

publish it, however unsuspicious and however various the sources of
this panegyric may have been. And, first, allowances must be made for
private enmity, of the very existence of which they had perhaps entertained no suspicion—for personal enmity behind the mask of anonymous criticism:[5] secondly, for the necessity of a certain proportion of
abuse and ridicule in a Review, in order to make it saleable, in consequence of which, if they have no friends behind the scenes, the chance
must needs be against them; but lastly and chiefly, for the excitement
and temporary sympathy of feeling, which the recitation of the poem by
an admirer, especially if he be at once a warm admirer and a man of
acknowledged celebrity, calls forth in the audience. For this is really a
species of Animal Magnetism, in which the enkindling Reciter, by perpetual comment of looks and tones, lends his own will and apprehensive faculty to his Auditors.[6] They *live* for the time within the dilated
sphere of his intellectual Being. It is equally possible, though not
equally common, that a reader left to himself should sink below the
poem, as that the poem left to itself should flag beneath the feelings of
the reader.—But in my own instance, I had the additional misfortune
of having been gossipped about, as devoted to metaphysics, and worse
than all to a system incomparably nearer to the visionary flights of
Plato, and even to the jargon of the mystics, than to the established
tenets of Locke. Whatever therefore appeared with my name was condemned before hand, as predestined metaphysics. In a dramatic poem,
which had been submitted by me to a gentleman of great influence in
the Theatrical world, occurred the following passage.—

> O we are querulous creatures! Little less
> Than all things can suffice to make us happy:
> And little more than nothing is enough
> To make us wretched.[7]

Aye, here now! (exclaimed the Critic) here come Coleridge's *Metaphysics*! And the very same motive (that is, not that the lines were unfit for the present state of our immense Theatres; but that they were
Metaphysics[8]) was assigned elsewhere for the rejection of the two following passages. The first is spoken in answer to a usurper, who had
rested his plea on the circumstance, that he had been chosen by the
acclamations of the people.—

> What people? How conven'd? Or if conven'd,
> Must not that magic power that charms together
> Millions of men in council, needs have power

---

5. John Beer has argued that Hazlitt's personal attacks began when he thought that C, and perhaps Wordsworth, circulated rumors of his sexual advances to a woman in the Lake District
   in 1803 ("Coleridge, Hazlitt, and 'Christabel,' " *Review of English Studies* 37 [1986]: 40–54;
   see also C's letter of September 16, 1803, to Tom Wedgwood, p. 633 herein). But Hazlitt's
   attacks, along with Leigh Hunt's, were also prompted by the Lake poets' change of political
   opinions and acceptance of government appointments.
6. On animal magnetism, see "The Rime of the Ancient Mariner," p. 60, n. 1 herein.
7. C's play *Zapolya* was written in 1815 and rejected by Covent Garden Theatre in April 1816.
   C then sent it to Byron for the Drury Lane Theatre, but it was rejected there as well. It was
   finally produced at the Surrey Theatre in February 1818. C quotes part 2, 1.1.23–26 (var.).
8. A footnote by C on metaphysics as self-knowledge is omitted here.

To win or wield them? Rather, O far rather,
Shout forth thy titles to yon circling mountains,
And with a thousandfold reverberation
Make the rocks flatter thee, and the volleying air,
Unbribed, shout back to thee, King Emerich!
By wholesome laws to embank the Sovereign Power;
To deepen by restraint; and by prevention
Of lawless will to amass and guide the flood
In its majestic channel, is man's task
And the true patriot's glory! In all else
Men safelier trust to heaven, than to themselves
When least themselves: even in those whirling crowds
Where folly is contagious, and too oft
Even wise men leave their better sense at home
To chide and wonder at them, when return'd.

The second passage is in the mouth of an old and experienced Courtier, betrayed by the man in whom he had most trusted.

And yet Sarolta, simple, inexperienced,
Could see him as he was and oft has warn'd me.
Whence learnt she this? O she was innocent.
And to be innocent is Nature's wisdom.
The fledge dove knows the prowlers of the air
Fear'd soon as seen, and flutters back to shelter!
And the young steed recoils upon his haunches,
The never-yet-seen adder's hiss first heard!
Ah! surer than suspicion's hundred eyes
Is that fine sense, which to the pure in heart
By mere oppugnancy of their own goodness
Reveals the approach of evil![9]

As therefore my character as a writer could not easily be more injured by an overt-act than it was already in consequence of the report, I published a work, a large portion of which was professedly metaphysical. A long delay occurred between its first annunciation and its appearance; it was reviewed therefore by anticipation with a malignity, so avowedly and exclusively personal, as is, I believe, unprecedented even in the present contempt of all common humanity that disgraces and endangers the liberty of the press. After its appearance, the author of this lampoon was chosen to review it in the Edinburgh Review:[1] and under the single condition, that he should have written what he himself really thought, and have criticized the work as he would have done had its author been indifferent to him, I should have chosen that man myself both from the vigour and

9. Zapolya, prelude, 1.1.355–72 (var.) and 4.1.70–81.
1. See the headnote to The Statesman's Manual (p. 353 herein). Hazlitt "reviewed" the pamphlet in the Examiner of September 8, 1816, before it was published and before he had read it, commenting on C's failed promise, "The ingenious author, in a preface which is a masterpiece in its kind, having neither beginning, middle, nor end, apologizes for having published a work, not a line of which is written, or ever likely to be written * * *. We see no sort of difference between his published and his unpublished compositions. It is just as impossible to get at the meaning of the one as the other" (CH, 1:248–49). Hazlitt also reviewed The Statesman's Manual in the Edinburgh Review of December 1816.

the originality of his mind, and from his particular acuteness in speculative reasoning, before all others.—I remembered Catullus's lines,

> Desine de quoquam quicquam bene velle mereri,
> Aut aliquem fieri posse putare pium.
> Omnia sunt ingrata: nihil fecisse benigne est:
> Imo', etiam tædet, tædet obestque magis.
> Ut mihi, quem nemo gravius nec acerbius urget
> Quam modo qui me unum atque unicum amicum habuit.[2]

But I can truly say, that the grief with which I read this rhapsody of
predetermined insult, had the Rhapsodist himself for its whole and sole
object: and that the indignant contempt which it excited in me, was as
exclusively confined to his employer and suborner.[3] I refer to this Review at present, in consequence of information having been given me,
that the innuendo of my "potential infidelity,"[4] grounded on one passage of my first Lay Sermon, has been received and propagated with a
degree of credence, of which I can safely acquit the originator of the
calumny. I give the sentences as they stand in the sermon, premising
only that I was speaking exclusively of miracles worked for the outward
senses of men. "It was only to overthrow the usurpation exercised in
and through the senses, that the senses were miraculously appealed to.
REASON AND RELIGION ARE THEIR OWN EVIDENCE. The natural sun is in
this respect a symbol of the spiritual. Ere he is fully arisen, and while
his glories are still under veil, he calls up the breeze to chase away the
usurping vapours of the night-season, and thus converts the air itself
into the minister of its own purification: not surely in proof or elucidation of the light from heaven, but to prevent its interception.

"Wherever, therefore, similar circumstances co-exist with the same
moral causes, the principles revealed, and the examples recorded, in
the inspired writings render miracles superfluous: and if we neglect to
apply truths in expectation of wonders, or under pretext of the cessa-
tion of the latter, we tempt God and merit the same reply which our
Lord gave to the Pharisees on a like occasion."[5]

---

2. Catullus, Poem 73: "Leave off wishing to deserve any thanks from any one, or thinking that
any one can ever become grateful. All this wins no thanks; to have acted kindly is nothing,
rather it is wearisome, wearisome and harmful; so it is now with me, who am vexed and troubled by no one so bitterly as by him who but now held me for his one and only friend" (trans.
Francis Warre Cornish [LCL, 1988], 153).

3. C most likely refers to Hazlitt and to Francis Jeffrey, the editor of the *Edinburgh Review*. He
may also refer to Leigh Hunt as the editor of the *Examiner*.

4. The phrase is C's. He protested the educational "plan of poisoning the children of the poor
with a sort of *potential* infidelity under the '*liberal idea*' of teaching those points only of religious faith, in which all denominations agree" (*SM* [CC], 40). Hazlitt applied the phrase to
C's comment that "Reason and Religion are their own evidence" (*SM* [CC], 10) and to C's
writings on miracles: "He treats the miracles recorded in the Scriptures, with more than
heretical boldness, as mere appeals to 'sense and fancy,' or to 'the natural man,' to counteract the impressions of sense and fancy * * *. We might challenge Mr. Coleridge to point out
a single writer, Catholic, Protestant or Sectarian, whose principles are not regarded as *potential infidelity* by the rest, that does not consider the miraculous attestation of certain revealed doctrines as proofs of their truth, independently of their internal evidence" (*CH*,
1:270).

5. C quotes from *The Statesman's Manual* (*SM* [CC], 10) and refers to Matthew 12.38–39:
"Then certain of the scribes and of the Pharisees answered, saying, Master, we would see a
sign from thee. But he answered and said unto them, An evil and adulterous generation
seeketh after a sign; and there shall no sign be given to it, but the sign of the prophet Jonas."

In the sermon and the notes both the historical truth and the necessity of the miracles are strongly and frequently asserted. "The testimony of books of history (i.e. relatively to the signs and wonders, with which Christ came) is one of the strong and stately *pillars* of the church; but it is not the *foundation!*"[6] Instead, therefore, of defending myself, which I could easily effect by a series of passages, expressing the same opinion, from the Fathers and the most eminent Protestant Divines, from the Reformation to the Revolution, I shall merely state what my belief is, concerning the true evidences of Christianity. 1. Its consistency with right Reason, I consider as the outer Court of the Temple—the common area, within which it stands. 2. The miracles, with and through which the Religion was first revealed and attested, I regard as the steps, the vestibule, and the portal of the Temple. 3. The sense, the inward feeling, in the soul of each Believer of its exceeding *desirableness*—the experience, that he *needs* something, joined with the strong Fore-tokening, that the Redemption and the Graces propounded to us in Christ are *what* he needs—this I hold to be the true FOUNDATION of the spiritual Edifice. With the strong *a priori* probability that flows in from 1 and 3 on the correspondent historical evidence of 2, no man can refuse or neglect to make the experiment without guilt. But, 4, it is the experience derived from a practical conformity to the conditions of the Gospel—it is the opening Eye; the dawning Light; the terrors and the promises of spiritual Growth; the blessedness of loving God as God, the nascent sense of Sin hated as Sin, and of the incapability of attaining to either without Christ; it is the sorrow that still rises up from beneath and the consolation that meets it from above; the bosom treacheries of the Principal in the warfare and the exceeding faithfulness and long-suffering of the uninterested Ally;—in a word, it is the actual *Trial* of the Faith in Christ, with its accompaniments and results, that must form the arched ROOF, and the Faith itself is the completing KEY-STONE.[7] In order to an efficient belief in Christianity, a man must have been a Christian, and this is the seeming *argumentum in circulo*, incident to all spiritual Truths, to every subject not presentable under the forms of Time and Space, as long as we attempt to master by the reflex acts of the Understanding what we can only *know* by the act of *becoming*. "Do the will of my father, and ye shall KNOW whether I am of God."[8] These four evidences I believe to have been and still to be, for the world, for the whole church, all necessary, all equally necessary; but that at present, and for the majority of Christians born in christian countries, I believe the third and the fourth evidences to be the most operative, not as superseding but as involving a glad undoubting faith in the two former. Credidi, ideóque intellexi,[9] appears to me the dictate equally of Philosophy and Religion, even as I believe Redemption to be the antecedent of Sanctifica-

---

6. C quotes again from *The Statesman's Manual* (*SM* [CC], 55–56) and adds the parenthesis.
7. C elaborates on the necessity of faith in *Aids to Reflection* (see pp. 568–69 herein).
8. John 7.17: "If any man will do his will, he shall know of the doctrine, whether it be of God, or whether I speak of myself."
9. "I believed, and therefore I understood."

tion, and not its consequent. All spiritual predicates may be construed indifferently as modes of Action or as states of Being. Thus Holiness and Blessedness are the same idea, now seen in relation to act and now to existence. The ready belief which has been yielded to the slander of my "potential infidelity," I attribute in part to the openness with which I have avowed my doubts, whether the heavy interdict, under which the name of BENEDICT SPINOZA lies, is merited on the whole or to the whole extent.[1] Be this as it may, I wish, however, that I could find in the books of philosophy, theoretical or moral, which are alone recommended to the present students of Theology in our established schools, a few passages as thoroughly *Pauline*,[2] as compleatly accordant with the doctrines of the established Church, as the following sentences in the concluding page of Spinoza's Ethics. Deinde quó mens amore divino seu beatitudine magis gaudet, eó plus *intelligit*, eó majorem in affectus habet potentiam, et eó minus ab affectibus, qui mali sunt, patitur: atque adeò ex eo, quód mens hoc amore divino seu beatitudine gaudet, potestatem habet libidines coercendi, nemo beatitudine gaudet quia affectus coercuit; sed contra potestas libidines coercendi ex ipsâ beatitudine oritur.[3]

With regard to the Unitarians, it has been shamelessly asserted, that I have denied them to be Christians.[4] God forbid! For how should I know, what the piety of the Heart may be, or what Quantum of Error in the Understanding may consist with a saving Faith in the intentions and actual dispositions of the whole moral Being in any one Individual? Never will God reject a soul that sincerely loves him: be his speculative opinions what they may: and whether in any given instance certain opinions, be they Unbelief, or Misbelief, are compatible with a sincere Love of God, God only can know.—But this I have said, and shall continue to say: that if the Doctrines, the sum of which I *believe* to constitute the Truth in Christ, *be* Christianity, then Unitaria*nism* is not, and vice versâ: and that in speaking theologically and *impersonally*, i.e. of PSILANTHROPISM and THEANTHROPISM as schemes of Belief,[5] without reference to Individuals who profess either the one or the other, it will be absurd to use a different language as long as it is

---

1. C commented on Spinoza in *The Friend* (1809): "I venture to assert, that the whole first book, De Deo, might be read in a literal English Translation to any congregation in the kingdom, and that no Individual, who had not been habituated to the strictest and most laborious process of Reasoning, would even suspect its orthodoxy or piety" (*Friend* [CC], 2:48).
2. The writings and doctrines of St. Paul.
3. C quotes Spinoza's *Ethics*, part 5, proposition 42, demonstration, in the original Latin. In translation the passage reads (with C's emphasis added): "Next, the more the Mind enjoys this divine Love, or blessedness, the more it *understands*, i.e. the greater the power it has over the affects [emotions], and the less it is acted on by evil affects. So because the Mind enjoys this divine Love or blessedness, it has the power of restraining lusts * * * no one enjoys blessedness because he has restrained the affects. Instead, his power to restrain lusts arises from blessedness itself" (*The Collected Works of Spinoza*, trans. Edwin Curley [Princeton, 1985], 1:616).
4. C may be responding to criticisms such as Hazlitt's in the *Edinburgh Review*: "The senseless jargon which Mr. Coleridge has let fall on this subject, is the more extraordinary, inasmuch as he declares * * * that 'Religion and Reason are their own evidence';—a position which appears to us 'fraught with *potential infidelity*' quite as much as Unitarianism" (*CH*, 1:269).
5. C coined the word "Psilanthropism" for the belief that Christ was "the real son of Joseph, and who lay the main stress on the resurrection rather than the crucifixion" (see chapter 10, p. 451 herein). "Theanthropism" is "the doctrine of the union of the divine and human natures," especially in Christ (*OED*).

the dictate of common sense, that two opposites cannot properly be called by the same name. I should feel no offence if a Unitarian applied the same to me, any more than if he were to say, that 2 and 2 being 4, 4 and 4 must be 8.

* * *

This has been my Object, and this alone can be my Defence—and O! that with this my personal as well as my LITERARY LIFE might conclude! the unquenched desire I mean, not without the consciousness of having earnestly endeavoured to kindle young minds, and to guard them against the temptations of Scorners, by shewing that the Scheme of Christianity, as taught in the Liturgy and Homilies of our Church, though not discoverable by human Reason, is yet in accordance with it; that link follows link by necessary consequence; that Religion passes out of the ken of Reason only where the eye of Reason has reached its own Horizon; and that Faith is then but its continuation: even as the Day softens away into the sweet Twilight, and Twilight, hushed and breathless, steals into the Darkness. It is Night, sacred Night! the upraised Eye views only the starry Heaven which manifests itself alone: and the outward Beholding is fixed on the sparks twinkling in the aweful depth, though Suns of other Worlds, only to preserve the Soul steady and collected in its pure *Act* of inward Adoration to the great I AM, and to the filial WORD that re-affirmeth it from Eternity to Eternity, whose choral Echo is the Universe.
ΘΕΩ ΜΟΝΩ ΔΟΞΑ.[6]

THE FRIEND (1818)

As early as 1804 Coleridge mused about publishing a collection of essays on "the exercise and right application of the Reason, the Imagination, and the moral Feelings" (*CL*, 2:1036). This was still his purpose four years later, when he began in earnest to plan a periodical that he would call *The Friend*. Although Britain was still at war with France, as it had been in 1796 when Coleridge published *The Watchman*, this periodical was to be concerned with general intellectual questions rather than with contemporary events, and addressed to the same social classes as his two *Lay Sermons* of 1816–17: "I do not write in this Work for the *Multitude*," Coleridge explained to his friend Humphry Davy in December 1808, "but for those, who by Rank, or Fortune, or official Situation, or Talents and Habits of Reflection, are to *influence* the Multitude. I write to found true PRINCIPLES, to oppose false PRINCIPLES, in Criticism, Legislation, Philosophy, Morals, and International Law" (*CL*, 3:143). He addressed himself especially to those "afflicted in Misfortune, or Disease, or Dejection of Mind" (*Friend* [*CC*], 2:18).

The title of the periodical may have been intended to attract subscribers from the Society of Friends, or Quakers, whose members were well repre-

---

6. "Glory to God alone." Possibly C's variation on 1 Timothy 1.17 ("unto * * * the only wise God, be honour and glory"), Luke 2.14 ("Glory to God in the highest"), or the Morning Prayer in the Anglican Book of Common Prayer ("Glory be to the Father, and to the Son: and to the Holy Ghost"). In the original Greek the wording of the passage in 1 Timothy is closer to that of C's phrase than the King James translation suggests.

sented in industry, banking, and the professions. In December 1808 Coleridge wrote his Quaker friend Thomas Wilkinson that although he did not proclaim himself a Quaker in *The Friend*, "I say aloud everywhere, that in the essentials of their faith I believe as the Quakers do" (*CL*, 3:157). Founded by George Fox (1624–1691) in the mid-seventeenth century, Quakerism stressed the individual's private experience of God and, accordingly, had neither a clergy nor a liturgy; but by the end of the eighteenth century it was publicly associated most strongly with philanthropic activity and the abolitionist movement. Coleridge did succeed in attracting Quaker subscribers (see the list in *Friend* [*CC*], 2:408–67), but he later complained of their unwillingness to pay for or to keep up their subscriptions (*CL*, 3:280).

In November 1808 Coleridge published a prospectus (reprinted in *Friend* [*CC*], 2:16–20) describing his plans for the periodical, of which he expected to publish twenty weekly issues, and by the following January he had secured 180 subscribers (*CL*, 3:164), though few of his friends believed that the project would succeed. Indeed Wordsworth confided to Thomas Poole, Coleridge's former neighbor in Nether Stowey, "It is *impossible* utterly impossible—that he should carry it on; and therefore, better never begin it * * * I give it to you as my deliberate opinion * * * that he neither will nor can execute anything of important benefit either to himself his family or mankind" (*WL*, 2:352). After difficulties in finding a printer, a paper supplier, and the money to pay both, he published the first issue on June 1, 1809. By the time the fourth issue appeared on September 7, the number of recorded subscribers had reached 398. A total of twenty-eight issues appeared, but exhaustion, sickness, and the failure of numerous subscribers to pay for their subscriptions finally led Coleridge to give up the periodical in March 1810 (see *CL*, 4:737).

The first ten issues were concerned largely, as promised, with political philosophy, in particular with critiques of materialism, Jacobinism, and the Napoleonic regime. The next eleven issues were more miscellaneous in content, including reflections on education, accounts of the supernatural, travel letters, and poetry (Wordsworth's as well Coleridge's own). The last seven issues contained biographical portraits of Lord Nelson (1758–1805), the admiral who had defeated the Napoleonic fleet at Trafalgar, and Sir Alexander Ball (1757–1809), the colonial governor under whom Coleridge had served as secretary in Malta, as well as an essay by Wordsworth on epitaphs. (For more information about this 1809–10 edition, see Deirdre Coleman, *Coleridge and "The Friend."*)

Just over a year later Coleridge told an unidentified correspondent that he wanted to continue *The Friend* to a fortieth issue (*CL*, 3:317), and in October 1811 he received encouragement to do so from a long review of the original series in the *Eclectic Review* (reprinted in *CH*, 92–110). But eventually he decided to have the original issues reprinted in book form with occasional revisions to the text: this reissue of 1812 is considered the second edition. In 1816 Coleridge returned to the project, negotiating with Thomas Curtis, whose firm Gale and Curtis (later Gale and Fenner) had published the 1812 edition, for a new edition of *The Friend* as well as for *Biographia Literaria* and *Sibylline Leaves* (*CL*, 4:652–53). While these negotiations dragged on (to the publisher's advantage), Coleridge not only rewrote and expanded *The Friend* as a collection of essays, but wrote a plan and introduction for an encyclopedia that Gale and Fenner wanted to publish (see p. 560, n. 1 herein). By the summer of 1818 he had enough material to fill three volumes, and in November the three volumes were published under the title *The Friend: A Series of Essays in Three Volumes to Aid in the Formation of Fixed Principles in Politics, Morals, and Religion with Literary Amusements Interspersed.* This edition contained fifty-eight essays divided among six sections: sixteen essays of introduction, another sixteen in the section "On the Principles of Political Knowledge," eleven in the section "On the Grounds of Morals and Religion," and fifteen in three sections called "Landing-Places, or Essays Interposed for Amusement, Retrospect, and Preparation." (The first selection printed here, originally written as a digression in the 1809–10 edition and then expanded into a full-fledged essay, comes from the first "Landing-Place.") C incorporated most of the first edition of *The Friend* into the new edition, though with much rewriting and rearranging of material, and he even included a toned-down version of his 1795 lecture *Conciones ad Populum* (p. 248 herein). But he also added much newly written material, in particular the essays on method (reprinted in part here). In this revised form, which he dedicated to his Highgate hosts Anne and James Gillman, *The Friend* was to be Coleridge's longest and most thematically diverse prose publication. It was not much noticed at the time, although in 1821 a reviewer for the *Edinburgh Magazine* described it as "the only work published in modern times which breathes the same lofty and profound spirit of philosophy * * * as were ushered to the world in the brightest days of our literature" (*CH*, 1:428).

Returning the final proofs of the 1818 edition to the publisher, Coleridge remarked, "I am able to lift my head & eyes with some cheerfulness" (*CL*, 4:882). The cheerfulness did not last long, however, for only 250 copies (of 750 printed) were sold before Gale and Fenner went bankrupt, forcing Coleridge to borrow money to buy up the unsold copies and the publisher's share of the copyright: "I am now free and sole proprietor of my own works, and may adopt as my emblem 0000001—the figure one = myself, the round cyphers, symbols of eternity, a fortiori [more conclusively] therefore, of immortality, representing my books, and their market value!" (*CL*, 4:949). (He later told Thomas De Quincey that he had lost a total of £1200 through his involvement with Gale and Fenner [*CL*, 5:163].) The only other edition of *The Friend* to appear in Coleridge's lifetime was published in 1831 in Vermont by an American admirer, James Marsh (1794–1842). The first posthumous edition, which incorporated some of Coleridge's corrections to the 1818 edition, was published in 1837; and it was followed by another eight editions between 1844 and 1899. (For a full account of the publication of the first three editions and of the differences between them, see *Friend* [*CC*], 1:xxxv–cv.)

The selections included here are printed from the 1818 *Friend* and incorporate the printed errata from that edition. The notes record the holograph alterations and comments that Coleridge made in two copies of it (both examined by the editor): the first (the "Morgan copy"), which may have been Coleridge's own working copy as well as the copy-text for the 1837 edition, was formerly in the possession of his son Derwent and is now in the Pierpont Morgan Library, New York; the other (the "BL copy"), presented by Coleridge to his friend John Kenyon in 1820, is now in the British Library, London, though it was listed as unlocated in *Friend* (*CC*), 2:390–91. Where the corrections in these copies differ, as they do slightly in a few places, those in the Morgan copy are followed. (Very similar holograph corrections in further presentation copies of the 1818 edition are recorded in the notes to volume 1 of *Friend* [*CC*] and a list of the known annotated copies appears in 2:388–92.)

FROM THE FRIEND: A SERIES OF ESSAYS IN THREE
VOLUMES TO AID IN THE FORMATION OF FIXED PRINCIPLES
IN POLITICS, MORALS, AND RELIGION WITH LITERARY
AMUSEMENTS INTERSPERSED

[Reason and Understanding]¹

*   *   *

I should have no objection to define Reason with Jacobi, and with
his friend Hemsterhuis,² as an organ bearing the same relation to spiritual objects, the Universal, the Eternal, and the Necessary, as the eye
bears to material and contingent phænomena. But then it must be
added, that it is an organ identical with its appropriate objects. Thus,
God, the Soul, eternal Truth, &c. are the objects of Reason; but they
are themselves *reason*. We name God the Supreme Reason; and Milton says, "Whence the Soul *Reason* receives, and Reason is her Being."³ Whatever is conscious *Self*-knowledge is Reason; and in this
sense it may be safely defined the organ of the Supersensuous; even as
the Understanding wherever it does not possess or use the Reason, as
another and⁴ inward eye, may be defined the conception of the Sensuous, or the faculty by which we generalize and arrange the phænomena of perception: that faculty, the functions of which contain the
rules and constitute the possibility of outward Experience.⁵ In short,
the Understanding supposes something that is *understood*. This may
be merely its own acts or forms, that is, formal Logic; but *real* objects,

---

1. From Essay 5 of "The Landing-Place" in volume 1 of the 1818 *The Friend*. As the headnote
to this section explains, the text printed here incorporates C's corrections to the 1818 edition. In a letter of November 24, 1819, to the clergyman Joseph Hughes, C stated that his
philosophy was "built on the distinction between the Reason and the Understanding" and
added that "the perusal of *philosophical* writings, at least, will be a mere waste of time" to
anyone who does not comprehend this distinction as it is expounded in the present essay
(*CL*, 6:1049–50). The distinction itself is expressed most succinctly in one of C's marginalia: while understanding is "the faculty *judging according to Sense* * * * Reason on the contrary is the Power and the Substance of universal, necessary, self-evident & supersensual
Truths. The Judgements of the Understanding are binding only in relation to the objects of
the Senses * * * [but] there neither is nor can be but one Reason, one & the same in all—
even 'the Light that lighteth every *man*' [John 1.9]" (*CM*, 3:557–58).
    C adopted the distinction from Kant's *Critique of Pure Reason*, which defined understand-
ing as the mental faculty concerned with organizing sense perceptions into distinct experiences, and reason as that concerned with unifying experiences by means of ideas that
cannot themselves be derived from experience. (C's earliest mention of the distinction, in a
letter of October 13, 1806, draws on the *Critique of Pure Reason* [B744] without naming the
book or its author [*CL*, 2:1198].) But there is a crucial difference between their conceptions
of reason: for Kant reason *cannot* yield insight into metaphysical issues such as the existence
of God, because it only regulates experiences; for C it *must* do so, because it originates in
God.
2. C probably knew of the Dutch philosopher François Hemsterhuis (1721–1790) from the
quotations of his work in F. H. Jacobi, *Über die Lehre des Spinoza* (On Spinoza's System),
2nd ed. (1789), a book that C annotated heavily around 1815. Jacobi defined reason (*Vernunft*) as an "organ, the existence of which becomes known to us through feelings alone
* * * a spiritual eye for spiritual objects" (*David Hume über den Glauben, oder Idealismus
und Realismus: Ein Gespräch* [David Hume on Faith, or Idealism and Realism: A Dialogue],
in *Werke*, vol. 2 [Leipzig, 1815], 74).
3. Milton, *Paradise Lost* 5.486–87. A favorite verse of C's, quoted also in *Biographia*, chapter
10 (p. 450 herein), in connection with the distinction between reason and understanding.
4. In the Morgan and BL copies C altered "another and" to "its."
5. C's argument here follows Jacobi's in *David Hume* (*Werke*, 2:9).

the materials of *substantial* knowledge, must be furnished, we might safely say *revealed*, to it by Organs of Sense. The understanding of the higher Brutes has only organs of outward sense, and consequently material objects only; but man's understanding has likewise an organ of inward sense, and therefore the power of acquainting itself with invisible realities or spiritual objects. This organ is his Reason.

Again, the Understanding and Experience may exist[6] without Reason. But Reason cannot exist without Understanding; nor does it or can it manifest itself but in and through the understanding, which in our elder writers is often called *discourse*, or the discursive faculty, as by Hooker, Lord Bacon, and Hobbes, and an understanding enlightened by reason Shakespear gives us as the contra-distinguishing character of man, under the name *discourse of reason.*[7] In short, the human understanding possesses two distinct organs, the outward sense, and "the mind's eye" which is reason:[8] wherever we use that phrase (the mind's eye) in its proper sense, and not as a mere synonyme of the memory or the fancy. In this way we reconcile the promise of Revelation, that the blessed will see God, with the declaration of St. John, God hath no one seen at any time.[9]

We will add one other illustration to prevent any misconception, as if we were dividing the human soul into different essences, or ideal persons. In this piece of *steel* I acknowledge the properties of hardness, brittleness, high polish, and the capability of forming a mirror. I find all these likewise in the plate glass of a friend's carriage; but in *addition* to all these, I find the quality of transparency, or the power of transmitting as well as of reflecting rays of light. The application is obvious.

If the reader therefore will take the trouble of bearing in mind these and the following explanations, he will have removed before hand every possible difficulty from the Friend's political section. For there is another use of the word, Reason, arising out of the former indeed, but less definite, and more exposed to misconception. In this latter use it means the understanding considered as using the Reason, so far as by the organ of Reason only we possess the ideas of the Necessary and the Universal; and this is the more common use of the word, when it is applied with *any* attempt at clear and distinct conceptions. In this narrow and derivative sense the best definition of Reason, which I can

---

6. "Of this no one would feel inclined to doubt, who had seen the poodle dog, whom the celebrated BLUMENBACH, a name so dear to science, as a physiologist and Comparative Anatomist, and not less dear as a man, to all Englishmen who have ever resided at Gottingen in the course of their education, trained up, not only to hatch the eggs of the hen with all the mother's care and patience, but to attend the chickens afterwards, and find the food for them. I have myself known a Newfoundland dog, who watched and guarded a family of young children with all the intelligence of a nurse, during their walks." [C's note.] J. F. Blumenbach (1752–1840), a professor of medicine at Göttingen, where C had attended his lectures on physiology and natural history in 1799 (see also p. 573, n. 3 herein).

7. *Hamlet* 1.2.150. *Discourse*: in the 16th and 17th centuries, could mean "reasoning" and "the faculty of reasoning," as in Hobbes's *Leviathan* 1.2 ("Of the Ends and Resolutions of Discourse"). Richard Hooker (c. 1554–1600), Anglican theologian. C later accused Hooker of confounding the terms "reason" and "understanding" (*CM* [CC], 2:1151–52). "Shakespear" was a common spelling in C's time.

8. *Hamlet* 1.2.184.

9. See John 1.18 and especially 1 John 4.12: "No man hath seen God at any time. If we love one another, God dwelleth in us, and his love is perfected in us."

give, will be found in the third member of the following sentence, in which the understanding is described in its three-fold operation, and from each receives an appropriate name. The Sense, (vis sensitiva vel intuitiva) *perceives*: Vis regulatrix (the understanding, in its own peculiar operation) *conceives*: Vis rationales[1] (the Reason or rationalized understanding) *comprehends*. The first is impressed through the organs of sense; the second combines these multifarious impressions into individual *Notions*, and by reducing these notions to Rules, according to the analogy of all its former notices, constitutes *Experience*: the third subordinates both these notions[2] and the rules of Experience to ABSOLUTE PRINCIPLES or necessary LAWS: and thus concerning objects, which our experience has proved to have *real* existence, it demonstrates, moreover, in what way they are *possible*, and in doing this constitutes *Science*. Reason therefore, in this secondary sense, and used, *not* as a spiritual *Organ* but as a Faculty (namely, the Understanding or Soul *enlightened* by that organ)— Reason, I say, or the *scientific* Faculty, is the Intellection of the *possibility* or *essential* properties of things by means of the Laws that constitute them. Thus the *rational* idea of a Circle is that of a figure constituted by the circumvolution of a straight line with its one end fixed.

Every man must feel, that though he may not be exerting different faculties, he is exerting his faculties in a different way, when in one instance he begins with some one self-evident truth (that the radii of a circle, for instance, are all equal), and in consequence of this being true sees at once, without any actual experience, that some other thing must be true likewise, and that, this being true, some *third* thing must be equally true, and so on till he comes, we will say, to the properties of the lever, considered as the spoke of a circle; which is capable of having all its marvellous powers demonstrated even to a savage who had never seen a lever, and without supposing any other previous knowledge in his mind, but this one, that there is a conceivable figure, all possible lines from the middle to the circumference of which are of the same length: or when, in the second instance, he brings together the facts of experience, each of which has its own separate value, neither encreased nor diminished by the truth of any other fact which may have preceded it; and making these several facts bear upon some particular project, according as one or the other class of facts preponderate: as, for instance, whether it would be better to plant a particular spot of ground with larch, or with Scotch fir, or with oak in preference to either. Surely every man will acknowledge, that his mind was very differently employed in the first case from what it was in the second; and all men have agreed to call the results of the first class the truths of *science*, such as not only are true, but which it is impossible to conceive otherwise: while the results of the second class are called *facts*, or things of *experience*: and as to these latter we must often con-

1. "Rational power." Vis sensitiva vel intuitiva: "sensory or intuitive power." Vis regulatrix: "regulative power."
2. In the Morgan and BL copies C altered "these notions" to "of them, the notions namely."

tent ourselves with the greater *probability*, that they are so, or so, rather than otherwise—nay, even when we have no doubt that they are so in the particular case, we never presume to assert that they must continue so always, and under all circumstances. On the contrary, our conclusions depend altogether on contingent *circumstances*. Now when the mind is employed, as in the case first-mentioned, I call it *Reasoning*, or the use of the pure Reason; but, in the second case, the *Understanding* or *Prudence*.

This reason applied to the *motives* of our conduct, and combined with the sense of our moral responsibility, is the conditional clause of *Conscience*, which is a spiritual sense or testifying state of the coincidence or discordance of the FREE WILL with the REASON. But as the Reasoning consists wholly in a man's power of seeing, whether any two ideas,[3] which happen to be in his mind, are, or are not in contradiction with each other, it follows of necessity, not only that all men have reason, but that every man has it in the same degree. For Reasoning (or Reason, in this its *secondary* sense) does not consist in the Ideas, or in their clearness, but simply, when they *are* in the mind, in seeing whether they contradict each other or no.

And again, as in the determinations of Conscience the only knowledge required is that my own *intention*—whether in doing such a thing, instead of leaving it undone, I did what I should think right if any other person had done it; it follows that in the mere question of guilt or innocence, all men have not only Reason equally, but likewise all the materials on which the reason, considered as *Conscience*, is to work. But when we pass out of ourselves, and speak, not exclusively of the *agent as meaning* well or ill, but of the action in its consequences, then of course experience is required, judgment in making use of it, and all those other qualities of the mind which are so differently dispensed to different persons, both by nature and education. And though *the reason itself* is the same in all men, yet the means of exercising it, and the materials (i.e. the facts and ideas) on which it is exercised, being possessed in very different degrees by different persons, the *practical Result* is, of course, equally different—and the whole groundwork of Rousseau's Philosophy ends in a mere Nothingism.[4] Even in that branch of knowledge, on which the *ideas*, on the congruity of which with each other, the Reason is to decide, are all possessed alike by all men, namely, in Geometry (for all men in their senses possess all the component images, viz. *simple* curves and straight lines), yet the power of *attention* required for the perception of linked Truths, even of *such* Truths, is so very different in A and B, that Sir Isaac Newton professed that it was in this power only that he

---

3. In the Morgan and BL copies C changed "ideas" to "conceptions."
4. The word is not C's coinage, but the *OED* cites this as the first instance of its use as a synonym of "nihilism." Elsewhere in *The Friend* C elaborated on his objection to the social contract theory of Jean-Jacques Rousseau: confounding the reason actually present in individuals with reason in the abstract ("which, it is true, dwells in every man *potentially*, but actually and in perfect purity is found in no man and in no body of men"), Rousseau unjustly attributed to society as a whole the power of acting rationally and having a sovereign right to choose its form of government (*Friend* [CC], 1:191–97).

was superior to ordinary men.[5] In short, the sophism is as gross as if I should say—The *Souls* of all men have the *faculty* of sight in an *equal degree*—forgetting to add, that this faculty cannot be exercised without *eyes*, and that some men are blind and others short-sighted,[6] &c.— or of chusing the sharpest sighted men for our guides.

Having exposed this gross sophism, I must warn against an opposite error—namely, that if Reason, as distinguished from Prudence, consists merely in knowing that Black cannot be White—or when a man has a clear conception of an inclosed figure, and another equally clear conception of a straight line, his Reason teaches him that these two conceptions are incompatible in the same object, i.e., that two straight lines *cannot* include[7] a space—the said Reason must be a very *insignificant* faculty. But a moment's self-reflection will shew us, that in the simple determination "Black is not White"—or, "that two straight lines cannot include a space"—all the powers are implied, that distinguish Man from Animals—first, the power of *reflection*—2d. of *comparison*—3d. and therefore of *suspension* of the mind—4th. therefore of a controlling will, and the power of acting from *notions*, instead of mere images exciting appetites; from *motives*, and not from mere dark *instincts*. Was it an insignificant thing to weigh the Planets, to determine all their courses, and prophecy every possible relation of the Heavens a thousand years hence? Yet all this mighty chain of science is nothing but a *linking* together of truths of the same kind, as, *the whole is greater than its part*—or, if A and B = C, then A = B—or 3 + 4 = 7, therefore 7 + 5 = 12, and so forth. X is to be found either in A or B or C or D: It is not found in A, B, or C, therefore it is to be found in D. What can be simpler? Apply this to an animal—a Dog misses his master where four roads meet—he has come up one, smells to two of the others, and then with his head aloft darts forward to the third road without any examination. If this was done by a conclusion, the Dog would have *Reason*—how comes it then, that he never shews it in his *ordinary* habits? Why does this story excite either wonder or incredulity? If the story be a fact, I should say—the Breeze brought his Master's scent down the fourth Road to the Dog's nose, and that *therefore* he did not put it down to the Road, as in the former two instances. So aweful and almost miraculous does the simple act of con-

5. This attributed statement, which has not been identified, might be based on a memory of something that C had read in one of Newton's works, such as the *Opticks*, 3rd ed. (London, 1721), 380: "in Natural Philosophy, the Investigation of difficult Things by the Method of Analysis, ought ever to precede the Method of Composition. This Analysis consists in making Experiments and Observations, and in drawing general Conclusions from them by Induction. * * * For Hypotheses are not to be regarded in experimental Philosophy." It is also possible that C was recalling Kant, *Judgment*, section 47: "Thus everything that Newton expounded in his immortal work on the principles of natural philosophy, no matter how great a mind it took to discover it, can still be learned. * * * In the scientific sphere, therefore, the greatest discoverer differs only in degree from the most hard working imitator and apprentice." C did not accept the conventional English veneration of Newton as an original thinker, and repeatedly described Newton's achievement in terms like those recorded by his nephew in October 1830: "We praise Newton's clearness and steadiness; he was clear and steady when working out by the help of an admirable geometry, no doubt, the Idea brought forth by another" (*TT* [CC], 1:211).
6. I.e., near-sighted.
7. I.e., enclose.

cluding that *take* 3 *from* 4, *there remains one*, appear to us when attributed to the most sagacious of all animals.

From Essays on the Principles of Method[1]

[I]

Ὅ δὲ δίκαιον ἐστι ποιεῖν, ἄκουε πῶς χρὴ ἔχειν ἐμὲ καὶ σὲ πρὸς ἀλλήλους. Εἰ μὲν ὅλως φιλοσοφίας καταπεφρόνηκας, ἔᾱν καίπειν· ἐὶ δὲ παρ' ἑτέρου ἀκήκοας ἤ αὐτὸς βελτίονα εὕρηκας τῶν παρ' ἐμοι, ἐκεῖνα τίμα· ἐι δ' ἄρα τὰ παρ' ἡμῶν σοὶ ἀρέσκει τιμητέον καὶ ἐμὲ μάλιστα.

ΠΛΑΤΩΝ·ΔΙΩΝ: επιστ· δευτερα.

(*Translation.*)—Hear then what are the terms on which you and I ought to stand toward each other. If you hold philosophy altogether in contempt, bid it farewell. Or if you have heard from any other person, or have yourself found out a better than mine, then give honor to that, which ever it be. But if the doctrine taught in these our works please you, then it is but just that you should honor me too in the same proportion.

Plato's 2d Letter to Dion.[2]

What is that which first strikes us, and strikes us at once, in a man of education? And which, among educated men, so instantly distinguishes the man of superior mind, that (as was observed with eminent propriety of the late Edmund Burke) "we cannot stand under the same arch-way during a shower of rain, *without finding him out*"?[3] Not the weight or novelty of his remarks; not any unusual interest of facts

1. The "Essay on Method" was written as an introduction to the *Encyclopaedia Metropolitana*, the plan of which C had devised for his publisher Rest Fenner in 1817 (see SW&F [CC], 576–87). As published (in twenty-eight volumes between 1818 and 1845), the encyclopedia departed significantly from his plan, which called for the division of the work into four categories: pure sciences (including mathematics, grammar, metaphysics, and theology), applied sciences, biographical and historical sciences, and miscellaneous and lexicographical sciences. Even the introduction, which appeared in 1818, was so altered in its published form that C demanded the return of his manuscript so that he could republish it on his own (CL, 4:860). He then rewrote and expanded the essay, publishing it as Essays IV to XI in the second section (vol. 3) of the 1818 *The Friend*. The original published version of the essay is in SW&F (CC), 625–87; the selections here are from the first, second, third, seventh, and eighth of the eight "Essays on the Principles of Method."
   C conceives method as a "germinal power" of organizing facts and ideas in a "progressive transition" that reveals their underlying principles. Method cannot be founded on observation but requires what C calls an "initiative" from the mind itself, which is possible on the assumption of an inherent (if hidden) harmony between human reason and the order of the universe as created by God, a harmony to which C refers in his eighth essay and Appendix C to *The Statesman's Manual* (p. 367 herein). C opposes method to arbitrary schemes of classification, of which he considers the chief examples to be the alphabetical arrangement of encyclopedias and the system of plant classification developed by the Swedish botanist Linnaeus (Carl von Linné, 1707–1788). Among his exemplars of method are Plato, Francis Bacon, Shakespeare, the astronomer Johannes Kepler (1571–1630), and the chemist Humphry Davy. The importance of C's concept of method in his criticism is discussed by J. R. de J. Jackson, *Method and Imagination in Coleridge's Criticism*, 36–47, and by Jerome Christensen, *Coleridge's Blessed Machine of Language*, 232–65.
2. Plato, *Letters* 2.312b. This letter to Dionysius (c. 431–367 B.C.E.), tyrant of Syracuse, is no longer considered genuine.
3. C misremembers, or alters to suit his purpose, a remark made by Samuel Johnson and recorded by James Boswell in his *Life of Johnson* (1791; ed. G. B. Hill and L. F. Powell [Oxford, 1934], 4:275): "Yes, Sir; if a man were to go by chance at the same time with Burke under a shed, to shun a shower, he would say—'this is an extraordinary man.' "

communicated by him; for we may suppose both the one and the other precluded by the shortness of our intercourse, and the triviality of the subjects. The difference will be impressed and felt, though the conversation should be confined to the state of the weather or the pavement. Still less will it arise from any peculiarity in his words and phrases. For if he be, as we now assume, a *well*-educated man as well as a man of superior powers, he will not fail to follow the golden rule of Julius Caesar, *Insolens verbum, tanquam scopulum, evitare.*[4] Unless where new things necessitate new terms, he will avoid an unusual word as a rock. It must have been among the earliest lessons of his youth, that the breach of this precept, at all times hazardous, becomes ridiculous in the topics of ordinary conversation. There remains but one other point of distinction possible; and this must be, and in fact is, the true cause of the impression made on us. It is the unpremeditated and evidently habitual *arrangement* of his words, grounded on the habit of foreseeing, in each integral part, or (more plainly) in every sentence, the whole that he then intends to communicate. However irregular and desultory his talk, there is *method* in the fragments.

Listen, on the other hand, to an ignorant man, though perhaps shrewd and able in his particular calling; whether he be describing or relating. We immediately perceive, that his memory alone is called into action; and that the objects and events recur in the narration in the same order, and with the same accompaniments, however accidental or impertinent, as they had first occurred to the narrator. The necessity of taking breath, the efforts of recollection, and the abrupt rectification of its failures, produce all his pauses; and with the exception of the "*and then,*" the "*and there,*" and the still less significant, "*and so,*" they constitute likewise all his connections.

Our discussion, however, is confined to Method as employed in the formation of the understanding, and in the construction of science and literature. It would indeed be superfluous to attempt a proof of its importance in the business and economy of active or domestic life. From the cotter's hearth or the workshop of the artisan, to the palace or the arsenal, the first merit, that which admits neither substitute nor equivalent, is, that *every thing is in its place.*[5] Where this charm is wanting, every other merit either loses its name, or becomes an additional ground of accusation and regret. Of one, by whom it is eminently possessed, we say proverbially, he is like clock-work. The resemblance extends beyond the point of regularity, and yet falls short or the truth. Both do, indeed, at once divide and announce the silent and otherwise indistinguishable lapse of time. But the man of me-

---

4. "To avoid an unusual word as if it were a rock." From Caesar's *De analogia* (On Analogy) as quoted in the *Noctes Atticae* (Attic Nights) 1.10.4 of Aulus Gellus (2nd century C.E.); see also *Biographia*, chapter 1 (p. 378 herein).

5. C is reported to have defined poetry in 1827 as "the best words in the best order" (*TT* [CC], 1:90), and in a letter of 1832 he repeated Jonathan Swift's definition of literary style as "proper words in proper places" (*CL*, 6:928; cf. Swift, *A Letter to a Young Gentleman, Lately enter'd into Holy Orders* [1721], in *Prose Works*, vol. 9, ed. Herbert Davis [Oxford, 1948], 65).

thodical industry and honorable pursuits, does more: he realizes its ideal divisions, and gives a character and individuality to its moments. If the idle are described as killing time, he may be justly said to call it into life and moral being, while he makes it the distinct object not only of the consciousness, but of the conscience. He organizes the hours, and gives them a soul: and that, the very essence of which is to fleet away, and evermore *to have been*, he takes up into his own permanence, and communicates to it the imperishableness of a spiritual nature. Of the good and faithful servant, whose energies, thus directed, are thus methodized, it is less truly affirmed, that He lives in time, than that Time lives in him. His days, months, and years, as the stops and punctual marks in the records of duties performed, will survive the wreck of worlds, and remain extant when time itself shall be no more.

* * *

The difference between the products of a well-disciplined and those of an uncultivated understanding, in relation to what we will now venture to call the *Science of Method*, is often and admirably exhibited by our great Dramatist.[6] We need scarcely refer to the Clown's evidence, in the first scene of the second act of "Measure for Measure," or the Nurse in "Romeo and Juliet."[7] * * * For the absence of Method, which characterizes the uneducated, is occasioned by an habitual submission of the understanding to mere events and images as such, and independent of any power in the mind to classify or appropriate. The general accompaniments of time and place are the only relations which persons of this class appear to regard in their statements. As this constitutes *their* leading feature, the contrary excellence, as distinguishing the well-educated man, must be referred to the contrary habit. METHOD, therefore, becomes natural to the mind which has been accustomed to contemplate not *things* only, or for their own sake alone, but likewise and chiefly the *relations* of things, either their relations to each other, or to the observer, or to the state and apprehension of the hearers. To enumerate and analyze these relations, with the conditions under which alone they are discoverable, is to teach the science of Method.

* * *

Instances of the want of generalization are of no rare occurrence in real life: and the narrations of Shakespeare's Hostess and the Tapster,[8] differ from those of the ignorant and unthinking in general, by their superior humor, the poet's own gift and infusion, not by their want of Method, which is not greater than we often meet with in that class, of which they are the dramatic representatives. Instances of the opposite fault, arising from the excess of generalization and reflection in minds of the opposite class, will, like the minds themselves, occur less fre-

6. I.e., Shakespeare.
7. See p. 313 herein. *Clown's evidence*: the witty defense of Pompey (referred to as "Clown" in the First Folio speech prefixes) against the charge of running a bordello.
8. Mistress Quickly, the comic tavern hostess whose generosity is continually exploited by Sir John Falstaff in the two parts of *Henry IV*, and Pompey in *Measure for Measure*.

quently in the course of our own personal experience. Yet they will not have been wanting to our readers, nor will they have passed unobserved, though the great poet himself (ὁ τὴν ἑαυτοῦ ψυχὴν ὧδει ὑλὴν τίνα ἀσώματον μορφαῖς ποικιλαῖς μορφώσας)[9] has more conveniently supplied the illustrations. To complete, therefore, the purpose aforementioned, that of presenting each of the two components as separately as possible, we chose an instance in which, by the surplus of its own activity, Hamlet's mind disturbs the arrangement, of which that very activity had been the cause and impulse.[1]

Thus exuberance of the mind, on the one hand, interferes with the *forms* of Method; but sterility of mind, on the other, wanting the spring and impulse to mental action, is wholly destructive of Method itself. For in attending too exclusively to the relations which the past or passing events and objects bear to general truth, and the moods of his own Thought, the most intelligent man is sometimes in danger of overlooking that other relation, in which they are likewise to be placed to the apprehension and sympathies of his hearers. His discourse appears like soliloquy intermixed with dialogue.[2] But the uneducated and unreflecting talker overlooks *all* mental relations, both logical and psychological; and consequently precludes all Method, that is not purely accidental. Hence the nearer the things and incidents in time and space, the more distant, disjointed, and impertinent to each other, and to any common purpose, will they appear in his narration: and this from the want of a *staple*, or *starting-post*, in the narrator himself; from the absence of *the leading Thought*, which, borrowing a phrase from the nomenclature of legislation, we may not inaptly call the INITIATIVE.[3] On the contrary, where the habit of Method is present and effective, things the most remote and diverse in time, place, and outward circumstance, are brought into mental contiguity and succession, the more striking as the less expected. But while we would impress the necessity of this habit, the illustrations adduced give proof that in undue preponderance, and when the prerogative of the mind is stretched into despotism, the discourse may degenerate into the grotesque or the fantastical.

With what a profound insight into the constitution of the human soul is this exhibited in the character of the Prince of Denmark, where flying from the sense of reality, and seeking a reprieve from the pressure of its duties, in that ideal activity, the overbalance of which, with the consequent indisposition to action, is his disease, he compels the reluctant good sense of the high yet healthful-minded Horatio, to fol-

---

9. "*Translation.*—He that moulded his own soul, as some incorporeal material, into various forms. THEMISTIUS" [C's note]. The quotation is from the *Paraphrase of Aristotle's "On the Soul"* 3.8 by Themistius (c. 317–388 C.E.), a minor Greek philosopher and rhetorician (*Friend* [CC], 1:454n. 2). A more accurate translation would be, "For it [the soul] is that which structures matter with a complex variety of structures" (*On Aristotle on the Soul*, trans. Robert B. Todd [London, 1996], 142).

1. Cf. C's analysis of Hamlet's character in "[On *Hamlet*]" (p. 332 herein).

2. In his literary lecture of February 17, 1818, C explained that soliloquies "have no other purpose but our fear lest the person to whom we speak should not understand us" (*Lects 1808–19* [CC], 2:151).

3. The word is not in Johnson's *Dictionary*, and the OED cites no instance of its use before 1793, when William Godwin used it in his *Political Justice* in the context of legislation.

low him in his wayward meditation amid the graves? *"To what base uses we may return, Horatio! Why may not imagination trace the noble dust of Alexander, till he find it stopping a bung-hole?*[4] HOR. *It were to consider too curiously to consider so.* HAM. *No, faith, not a jot; but to follow him thither with modesty enough and likelihood to lead it. As thus: Alexander was buried, Alexander returneth to dust—the dust is earth; of earth we make loam: and why of that loam, whereto he was converted, might they not stop a beer-barrel?*

Imperial Caesar, dead and turn'd to clay,
Might stop a hole to keep the wind away!"[5]

*   *   *

It is Shakespeare's peculiar excellence, that throughout the whole of his splendid picture gallery (the reader will excuse the confest inadequacy of this metaphor),[6] we find individuality every where, mere portrait no where. In all his various characters, we still feel ourselves communing with the same human nature,[7] which is every where present as the vegetable sap in the branches, sprays, leaves, buds, blossoms, and fruits, their shapes, tastes, and odours. Speaking of the effect, i.e. his works themselves, we may define the excellence of *their* method as consisting in that just proportion, that union and interpenetration of the universal and the particular, which must ever pervade all works of decided genius and true science. For Method implies a *progressive transition*, and it is the meaning of the word in the original language. The Greek Μεθοδος,[8] is literally *a way*, or *path of Transit*. Thus we extol the Elements of Euclid, or Socrates' discourse with the slave in the Menon,[9] as *methodical*, a term which no one who holds himself bound to think or speak correctly, would apply to the alphabetical order or arrangement of a common dictionary. But as, without continuous transition, there can be no Method, so without a preconception there can be no transition without continuity. The term, Method, cannot therefore, otherwise than by abuse, be applied to a mere dead arrangement, containing in itself no principle of progression.

[II]

* * * It has been observed, in a preceding page, that the RELATIONS of object are prime *materials* of Method, and that the contemplation of relations is the indispensible condition of thinking methodically. It becomes necessary, therefore to add, that there are two kinds of relation,

---

4. The opening of a cask.
5. *Hamlet* 5.1.186–97 (var.).
6. C recalls Boydell's Shakespeare Gallery—a collection of paintings of scenes from Shakespeare's plays—opened in London in 1789 by the engraver John Boydell (1719–1804).
7. At this point C noted in the Morgan copy (and var. in the BL copy) of *The Friend*, "*muning, human*—how difficult it is in the most sensitive Ear to avoid occasional *Jingles* of sound." In *CL*, 4:881 he recommended crossing out the word "human" to remove the jingle (*Friend* [CC], 1:457n. 2).
8. Although the ancient Greek word *methodos* is derived from *hodos* (road, way), it actually means "pursuit of knowledge" and "mode of investigation."
9. Plato, *Meno* 82b–85c, in which Socrates assists a slave boy in reasoning about squares and triangles.

in which objects of mind may be contemplated. The first is that of LAW, which, in its absolute perfection, is conceivable only of the Supreme Being, whose creative IDEA not only appoints to each things its position, and in consequence of that position, gives it its qualities, yea, it gives its very existence, as *that particular* thing. Yet in whatever science the relation of the parts to each other and to the whole is predetermined by a truth originating in the *mind*, and not abstracted or generalized from observation of the parts, there we affirm the presence of a *law*, if we are speaking of the physical sciences, as of Astronomy for instance; or the presence of fundamental *ideas*, if our discourse be upon those sciences, the truths of which, as truths absolute, not merely have an independent *origin* in the mind, but continue to exist in and for the mind alone.[1] Such, for instance, is Geometry, and such are the ideas[2] of a perfect circle, of asymptotes, &c.

We have thus assigned the first place in the science of Method to LAW; and first of the first, to *Law*, as the absolute *kind* which comprehending in itself the substance of every possible degree, not by generalization but by its own plenitude. As such, therefore, and as the sufficient cause of the reality correspondent thereto, we contemplate it as exclusively an attribute of the Supreme Being, inseparable from the idea of God: adding, however, that from the contemplation of law in this, its only perfect form, must be derived all true insight into all other grounds and principles necessary to Method, as the science common to all sciences, which in each τυγχάνει ὄν ἄλλο αὐτης της ἐπιστήμης.[3] Alienated from this (intuition shall we call it? or stedfast faith?) ingenious men may produce schemes, conducive to the peculiar purposes of particular sciences, but no scientific system.

*   *   *

[III][4]

* * * The second relation is that of THEORY, in which the existing forms and qualities of objects, discovered by observation or experiment, suggest a given arrangement of many under one point of view: and this not merely or principally in order to facilitate the remembrance, recollection, or communication of the same; but for the purposes of understanding, and in most instances of controlling, them. In

1. See p. 567, n. 7 herein.
2. C commented in the Morgan copy (and var. in the BL copy): "Here I have fallen into an error. The terms, Idea and Law, are always Correlative. Instead of geometrical *Ideas* I ought to have said, *Theorems*. N.B. not Theories—but θεωρήματα [objects of contemplation, speculations], the intelligible Products of Contemplation intellectual, objects in the mind, of and for the mind exclusively. S.T.C."
3. Plato, *Charmides* 166a. C used this passage again as part of the motto to the fourth essay in the series, paraphrasing it as follows: "may prove to be something more than the mere aggregate of the knowledges in any particular science." C's point, like Socrates's in Plato's dialogue, is that the subject of a science is not the same as the science itself: computation, Socrates explains, is concerned with numbers, but does not itself consist in numbers.
4. In the 1818 *The Friend* the following paragraphs were printed as part of the preceding essay, but both a chapter break (which necessitated the renumbering of the chapters) and a motto from the Greek philosopher Theophrastus (c. 371–287 B.C.E.) were included in the errata list, as well as inserted in C's hand in the Morgan and BL copies.

other words, all THEORY supposes the general idea of cause and effect. The scientific arts of Medicine, Chemistry, and of Psychology in general, are examples of a method hitherto founded on this second sort of relation.

Between these two lies the Method in the FINE ARTS, which belongs indeed to this second or external relation, because the effect and position of the parts is always more or less influenced by the knowledge and experience of their previous qualities; but which nevertheless constitute a link connecting the second form of relation with the first. For in all, that truly merits the name of *Poetry* in its most comprehensive sense, there is a necessary predominance of the Ideas (i.e. of that which originates in the artist himself), and a comparative indifference of the materials. A true musical taste is soon dissatisfied with the Harmonica, or any similar instrument of glass or steel, because the *body* of the sound (as the Italians phrase it), or that effect which is derived from the *materials*, encroaches too far on the effect from the *proportions* of the notes, or that which is *given* to Music by the mind. To prove the high value as well as the superior dignity of the first relation; and to evince, that on this alone a *perfect* Method can be grounded, and that the Methods attainable by the second are at best but approximations to the first, or tentative exercises in the hope of discovering it, form the first object of the present disquisition.

These truths we have (as the most pleasing and popular mode of introducing the subject) hitherto illustrated from Shakespeare. But the same truths, namely the necessity of a mental Initiative to all Method, as well as a careful attention to the conduct of the mind in the exercise of Method itself, may be equally, and here perhaps more characteristically, proved from the most familiar of the SCIENCES. We may draw our elucidation even from among those which are at present fashionable among us: from BOTANY or from CHEMISTRY. In the lowest attempt at a methodical arrangement of the former science, that of artificial classification for the purpose of a nomenclature, some *antecedent* must have been contributed by the mind itself; some *purpose* must be in view; or some question at least must have been proposed to nature, grounded, as all questions are, upon *some* idea of the answer. As, for instance, the assumption,

That two great sexes animate the world.[5]

For no man can confidently conceive a fact to be *universally* true who does not with equal confidence anticipate its *necessity*, and who does not believe that necessity to be demonstrable by an insight into its nature, whenever and wherever such insight can be obtained.

*   *   *

[VII]

* * * All method supposes a union of *several* things to a common end, either by disposition, as in the works of man; or by convergence, as in

5. Milton, *Paradise Lost* 8.151 (var.).

the operations and products of nature. That we acknowledge a *method*, even in the latter, results from the religious instinct which bids us "find tongues in trees; books in the running streams; sermons in stones: and good (*that is, some useful end answering to some good purpose*) in every thing."[6] In a self-conscious and thence reflecting being, no instinct can exist, without engendering the belief of an object corresponding to it, either present or future, real or capable of being realized: much less the instinct, in which humanity itself is grounded: that by which, in every act of conscious perception, we at once identify our being with that of the world without us, and yet place ourselves in contra-distinction to that world. Least of all can this mysterious pre-disposition exist without evolving a belief that the productive power, which is in nature[7] as nature, is essentially one (i.e. of one kind) with the intelligence, which is in the human mind above nature.

* * *

[VIII]

* * * Long indeed will man strive to satisfy the inward querist with the phrase, laws of nature. But though the individual may rest content with the seemly metaphor, the race cannot. If a law of nature be a mere generalization, it is included in the above as an act of mind. But if it be other and more, and yet manifestable only in and to an intelligent spirit, it must in act and substance be itself spiritual: for things utterly heterogeneous can have no intercommunion. In order therefore to the recognition of himself in nature man must first learn to comprehend nature in himself, and its laws in the ground of his own existence. Then only can he reduce Phænomena to Principles—then only will he have achieved the METHOD, the self-unravelling clue, which alone can securely guide him to the conquest of the former— when he has discovered in the basis of their union the necessity of their differences; in the principle of their continuance the solution of their changes. It is the idea of the common centre, of the universal law, by which all power manifests itself in opposite yet interdependent forces * * * that enlightening inquiry, multiplying experiment, and at once inspiring humility and perseverance will lead him to comprehend

---

6. Shakespeare, *As You Like It* 2.1.16–17 (var.). The parenthesis is C's.
7. In the Morgan copy C altered "is in nature" to "acts in nature" and added the following note in the margin:

> Obscure from too general compression. The sense is, that the productive Power = vis natur*ans*, which in the sensible World = natur*â* natur*atâ*, is what we mean by the word, Nature, when we speak of the same as an *Agent*, is essentially &c. In other words, Idea and Law are the Subjective and Objective *Poles* of the same magnet—i.e. of the same living and energizing Reason. What is an Idea in the Subject, i.e. in the Mind, is a Law in the Object, i.e. in nature. But thoughout these Essays, the want of illustrative examples, and varied exposition, is the main Defect—and was occasioned by the haunting dread of being tedious! But O! the cold water that was thrown on me from all quarters, chiefly by those from whom I ought to have received warmth & encouragement. "Whom do you expect will read this?" &c. &c. But vanity as it may appear, it is nevertheless true & uttered with feelings the most unlike those of Self-conceit—that it has been the Author's mistake thro' life, to be looking *up* to, when he ought to have looking *at*, nay (in some instances) *down upon*. 23 June 1829.

gradually and progressively the relation of each to the other, of each to all, and of all to each.

* * *

AIDS TO REFLECTION (1825)

Aids to Reflection was originally conceived as an anthology of the writings of Archbishop Robert Leighton (1611–1684), a Scottish divine who was brought to Coleridge's attention in 1814, during a period of severe illness and profound depression related to his opium addiction. He responded strongly to Leighton as a compassionate and sober thinker: "No Shew of Learning! no appearance of Eloquence," he told his old Bristol publisher Joseph Cottle, "but a something that must be felt even as the Scriptures must be felt" (*CL*, 3:479n.). Five years later, James Gillman, in whose household Coleridge was now living, acquired a copy of Leighton's *Genuine Works* (4 vols., 1819) which his guest both read and annotated (see *CM* [*CC*], 3:514–36).

Coleridge first proposed the idea of an annotated anthology of Leighton to John Murray, the publisher of "Christabel," on January 18, 1822: "The Beauties of Archbishop Leighton selected and methodized, with a (*better*) Life of the Author, i.e. a biographical and critical Introduction or Preface, and Notes—would make not only a useful but an interesting POCKET VOLUME" (*CL*, 5:200). Leighton's value to contemporary readers, Coleridge elaborated, lay in his dissuasion of "students and the generality of Christians from all attempts at explaining the Mysteries of Faith by *notional* and metaphysical speculations, and rather by a heavenly life and temper to obtain a closer view of these Truths, the *full* Sight and Knowledge of which it is in Heaven only that we shall possess" (*CL*, 5:199–200). Murray not only responded encouragingly but sent Coleridge a copy of Leighton's *Whole Works* (4 vols., 1820) from which to select passages (*CL*, 5:205 and n. 1). But after a year Murray decided against publishing the book (*CL*, 5:282), whereupon Coleridge offered it to another publisher, Taylor and Hessey, with a new title and the following outline: "Aids to Reflection: or Beauties and Characteristics of Archbishop Leighton, extracted from his various Writings, and arranged on a principle of connection under the three Heads, of 1. Philosophical and Miscellaneous. 2. Moral and Prudential. 3. Spiritual—with a Life of Leighton & a critique on his writings and opinions—with notes throughout by the Editor" (*CL*, 5:290). This time the response was favorable (*CL*, 5:294), and Coleridge began collecting materials for the biography of Leighton.

On September 9, 1823, he reported to the publisher that he was almost finished with the biography (*CL*, 5:299–301), but if that was true, he must have abandoned it, for it was never printed. The anthology of Leighton, on the other hand, was sent to the printer section by section, so that Coleridge was able to see proofs of at least part of the book before he had completed it. It was only at this stage, after examining some proofs in November 1823 and realizing how extensive his own comments were, that he hit upon the idea of arranging the book as a series of numbered aphorisms (some in fact self-contained essays) instead of as continuous prose with intermixed quotation and commentary (*CL*, 5:306–07). (A surviving page of the early proofs, showing the original arrangement, is reproduced in *AR* [*CC*], after 456.) By the time the book was published in May 1825, it had become "an original work almost," as Coleridge conceded to a correspondent (CL, 5:336). Although he modestly referred to himself in the book as the "editor," the title-page more accurately indicated the relation between Leighton's "beauties" and Coleridge's commentary: *Aids to Reflection in the Formation of a Manly Character * * * Illustrated by Selected Passages from Our Elder Divines, Especially from Archbishop Leighton.* Charles Lamb's hope that the book would contain "more of Bishop Coleridge than Leighton" was not disappointed (*The Letters of Charles and Mary Lamb*, ed. E. V. Lucas [London, 1935], 2:416).

Addressed, as Coleridge informed a young admirer in February 1824, to "serious young men of ordinary education who are sincerely searching after moral and religious Truth but are perplexed by the common prejudice, that Faith in the peculiar Tenets of Christianity demands a sacrifice of the Reason and is at enmity with Common-Sense" (CL, 5:336–37), *Aids to Reflection* was intended at once to encourage a religious renewal in England and to secure Coleridge's reputation as a thinker. Calling on his readers to reflect on their own spiritual needs and ask themselves whether those needs could be satisfied without a Christian faith, Coleridge proceeded from moral to spiritual questions, trying to demonstrate that morality must not be considered in isolation from religion because it can only be grounded in religion.

A fundamental premise of *Aids to Reflection*, as of Coleridge's other prose writings, was that a genuine self-understanding required both a new understanding of language and a more precise use of it. (This concern with language is represented by the selections printed here from the Preface and from Aphorism VII, on the language of the Gospels, in the "Aphorisms on Spiritual Religion.") Because he also wanted to establish that reason is not incompatible with spiritual truths but the means by which they are recognized—"the Source and Substance of Truths above Sense" (*AR* [CC], 216)—Coleridge returned in *Aids to Reflection* to the distinction between reason and understanding, which he had already elaborated in *The Friend*. His claims for reason and his conception of the scale of nature are both represented in the selection from Aphorism XXXVI in "Moral and Religious Aphorisms."

At first *Aids to Reflection* received little notice in the press, but it soon found favor among young, predominantly Cambridge-educated clergymen (and future clergymen) like Julius Hare (1795–1855), John Sterling (1806–1844), and Frederick Denison Maurice (1805–1872), who promoted it as an argument against the dominant utilitarian and materialist philosophy of the time. Inspired by Coleridge, they initiated what became known as the Broad Church movement, an attempt to liberalize and revivify the Church of England (see C. R. Sanders, *Coleridge and the Broad Church Movement* [Durham, N.C., 1942]). In 1842, when Maurice published the second edition of his book *The Kingdom of Christ*, he noted that "the history of his mind, and therein the history of our time" could be read in *Aids to Reflection* (quoted in Rosemary Ashton, *The Life of Samuel Taylor Coleridge*, 365). Meanwhile, Coleridge's reputation as a religious thinker spread across the Atlantic when James Marsh (1794–1842), the president of the University of Vermont, published an American edition of *Aids to Reflection* (1829). Among its admirers in the United States were Ralph Waldo Emerson (1803–1892) and John Muir (1838–1914), the Scottish-born naturalist. (For a full account of the composition, publication, contents, and reception of the book, see the introduction to *AR* [CC].)

In 1828 Coleridge began considering a new edition of *Aids to Reflection*, "considerably improved" (*CL*, 6:773). But because he was in intermittently poor health and occupied with preparing *On the Constitution of the Church and State* for the press, he could not devote himself fully to revising *Aids to Reflection*, and he entrusted the task to Henry Nelson Coleridge (*CL*, 6:819, 848–49, 853). The revised edition appeared in 1831. Some of the revisions were unquestionably authorial, including the replacement of the original "Advertisement" with a short note "To the Reader" and the addition of a "Synoptical Summary" as an appendix. But others are of uncertain authority, notably the omission of several passages from the early part of the book and of the designations "LEIGHTON" and "EDITOR" throughout. The result of this last omission was to obscure the distinction between Coleridge's own contributions and the texts by Leighton and others. Neither the printed errata nor Coleridge's holograph annotations in various copies of the first edition were systematically incorporated into the second, and the reduced capitalization of nouns in the second edition does not conform to Coleridge's usual practice in his manuscripts. For these reasons we have preferred the readings of the 1825 edition, although in fact none of the passages included here was altered significantly in 1831.

FROM AIDS TO REFLECTION IN THE FORMATION OF A MANLY CHARACTER

From Preface

An Author has three points to settle: to what sort his Work belongs, for what Description of Readers it is intended, and the specific end or object, which it is to answer. There is indeed a preliminary Interrogative respecting the end which the Writer himself has in view, whether the Number of Purchasers, or the Benefit of the Readers. But this may be safely passed by; since where the book itself or the known principles of the writer do not supersede the question, there will seldom be sufficient strength of character for good or for evil, to afford much chance of its being either distinctly put or fairly answered.

I shall proceed therefore to state as briefly as possible the intentions of the present volume in reference to the three first-mentioned, viz. *What? For Whom?* and *For* what?

I. WHAT? The answer is contained in the Title-page. It belongs to the class of *didactic* Works. Consequently, those who neither wish instruction for themselves, nor assistance in instructing others, have no interest in its contents. *Sis Sus, sis Divus: Sum* CALTHA, *et non tibi spiro!*[1]

II. FOR WHOM?

*   *   *

---

1. "Whether you are a pig or a god, I am Caltha, and do not breathe for you." An exact source of this quotation (if it is one) has not been located, but *AR* (*CC*), 5n. 1 identifies similar sayings in Erasmus and Sir Philip Sidney.

But if I am to mention any particular class or description of Readers, that were prominent in my thought during the composition of the volume, my Reply must be: that it was *especially* designed for the studious Young at the close of their education or on their first entrance into the duties of manhood and the rights of self-government. And of these, again, in thought and wish I destined the work (the latter and larger portion, at least) yet more particularly to Students intended for the Ministry; *first*, as in duty bound, to the members of our two Universities:[2] *secondly*, (but only in respect of this mental precedency *second*) to all alike of whatever name, who have dedicated their future lives to the cultivation of their Race, as Pastors, Preachers, Missionaries, or Instructors of Youth.

III. FOR WHAT? The Worth of the Author is estimated by the ends, the attainment of which he proposed to himself by the particular work: while the Value of the Work depends on its fitness, as the Means. The Objects of the present volume are the following, arranged in the order of their comparative importance.

1. To direct the Reader's attention to the value of the Science of Words, their use and abuse * * * and the incalculable advantages attached to the habit of using them appropriately, and with a distinct knowlege of their primary, derivative, and metaphorical senses. And in furtherance of this Object I have neglected no occasion of enforcing the maxim, that to expose a sophism and to detect the equivocal or double meaning of a word is, in the great majority of cases, one and the same thing. Horne Tooke entitled his celebrated work, Επεα πτεροεντα, Winged Words: or Language, not only the *Vehicle* of Thought but the *Wheels*.[3] With my convictions and views, for επεα I should substitute λογοι, i. e. Words *select* and *determinate*,[4] and for πτεροεντα ζωοντες, i. e. *living* Words. The *Wheels* of the intellect I admit them to be; but such as Ezekiel beheld in "the visions of God" as he sate among the Captives by the river of Chebar.[5] "Whithersoever the Spirit was to go, the Wheels went, and thither was their Spirit to go: *for the Spirit of the living creature was in the wheels also.*"[6]

2. To establish the *distinct* characters of Prudence, Morality, and Religion: and to impress the conviction, that though the second re-

2. Until 1828, when the University of London was founded, the only universities in England were at Oxford and Cambridge.
3. *Winged Words*: translation of the Greek phrase (taken from Homer's *Iliad* 1.201), which was the title of a linguistic treatise better known by its subtitle, *The Diversions of Purley* (vol. 1, 1786; vol. 2, 1805). In his youth C had admired its author, John Horne Tooke, whom he met in 1799 (*CL*, 1:559), but in later years he became severely critical of Tooke's materialist philology, which reduced all words to names for sense impressions. Here C alludes to Tooke's assertion that language is "the vehicle of our thoughts" and that abbreviations are "the *wheels* of language" (ΕΠΕΑ ΠΤΕΡΟΕΝΤΑ; *or*, *The Diversions of Purley*, vol. 1, 2nd ed. [London, 1798], 24–25). See p. 595, n. 1 herein.
4. C prefers *logoi* to *epea* because, although both mean "words," the former has associations with the Logos, or Word of God in the New Testament, and with reason in Greek philosophy (*logos* also meant "reason" in ancient Greek).
5. Ezekiel 1.1.
6. Ezekiel 1.20: "Whithersoever the spirit was to go, they went, thither was their spirit to go; and the wheels were lifted up over against them: for the spirit of the living creature was in the wheels." For C's interpretation of this passage, see *The Statesman's Manual* (p. 359 herein).

quires the first, and the third contains and supposes both the former; yet still Moral Goodness is other and more than Prudence, or the Principle of Expediency; and Religion more and higher than Morality. For this distinction the better Schools even of Pagan Philosophy contended. * * *

3. To substantiate and set forth at large the momentous distinction between REASON and Understanding.[7]

*   *   *

READER!—You have been bred in a land abounding with men, able in arts, learning, and knowledges manifold, this man in one, this in another, few in many, none in all. But there is one art, of which every man should be master, the art of REFLECTION. If you are not a *thinking* man, to what purpose are you a *man* at all? In like manner, there is one knowledge, which it is every man's interest and duty to acquire, namely, SELF-KNOWLEDGE; or to what end was man alone, of all animals, indued by the Creator with the faculty of *self-consciousness?* Truly said the Pagan moralist, E cœlo descendit, Γνῶθι Σέαυτον.[8]

But you are likewise born in a CHRISTIAN land: and Revelation has provided for you new subjects for reflection, and new treasures of knowledge, never to be unlocked by him who remains self-ignorant. Self-knowledge is the key to this casket; and by reflection alone can it be obtained. Reflect on your own thoughts, actions, circumstances, and—which will be of especial aid to you in forming a *habit* of reflection,—accustom yourself to reflect on the words you use, hear, or read, their birth, derivation, and history. For if words are not THINGS, they are LIVING POWERS,[9] by which the things of most importance to mankind are actuated, combined, and humanized. Finally, by reflection you may draw from the fleeting facts of your worldly trade, art, or profession, a science permanent as your immortal soul; and make even these subsidiary and preparative to the reception of spiritual truth, "doing as the dyers do, who having first dipt their silks in colours of less value, then give them the last tincture of crimson in grain."[1]

---

7. For C's elaboration of this distinction, see *The Friend* (p. 555 herein).
8. "It descended from heaven, *Know yourself,*" a favorite line from Juvenal's *Satires* 11.27. The Greek phrase was one of the maxims inscribed in the temple of Apollo at Delphi. (See the poem on p. 226 and Appendix C to *The Statesman's Manual*, p. 369 herein.)
9. As early as 1800, discussing Horne Tooke's linguistic theory in a letter to William Godwin, C had expressed the wish to treat words not as names for things or thoughts but as "living Things" (*CL*, 1:626). Here he proposes that words and thoughts are inherently related, thinking being constituted by language.
1. Unidentified. C was interested in the process of dyeing and may have done some reading about it (*AR* [CC], 10n. 12; *CN*, 2:3606n).

From Moral and Religious Aphorisms

Aphorism XXV   EDITOR.

He, who begins by loving Christianity better than Truth, will proceed by loving his own Sect or Church better than Christianity, and end in loving himself better than all.[1]

* * *

Aphorism XXXVI   LEIGHTON.

Your blessedness is not,—no, believe it, it is not where most of you seek it, in things below you. How can that be? It must be in a higher good to make you happy.[2]

COMMENT

Every rank of Creatures, as it ascends in the scale of Creation, leaves Death behind it or under it.[3] The Metal at its height of Being seems a mute Prophecy of the coming Vegetation, into a mimic semblance of which it crystallizes. The Blossom and Flower, the Acmè of Vegetable Life, divides into correspondent Organs with reciprocal functions, and by instinctive motions and approximations seems impatient of that fixture, by which it is differenced in kind from the flower-shaped Psyche, that flutters with free wing above it.[4] And wonderfully in the insect realm doth the Irritability, the proper seat of Instinct, while yet the nascent Sensibility[5] is subordinated thereto—most wonderfully, I say, doth the muscular Life in the Insect and the musculo-arterial in the Bird, imitate and typically rehearse the adaptive

1. The utilitarian philosopher John Stuart Mill (1806–1873), who visited C at Highgate in the 1820s, cited this aphorism in support of his own defense of independent, undogmatic thought (*Mill on Bentham and Coleridge* [London, 1950], 113). It may owe something to an aphorism traditionally attributed to Aristotle: "Plato is dear to me, but dearer still is truth." *Editor*. C himself.
2. From Robert Leighton, *A Practical Commentary upon the First Epistle General of St. Peter* (1693), in *Whole Works* (1820), 2:52. C wrote the draft of his comment on this passage in the margin of his copy of Leighton, *Whole Works* (see CM [CC], 3:580–81).
3. C considered nature to be organized hierarchically in stages of increasing organization and individuation: mass (metals), crystallization (minerals), reproduction or organs (plants), irritability or sensation (insects), sensibility or understanding (animals), reflection or reason (humans). Each stage after the first incorporates the characteristics of the stages below it, and each stage before the last has characteristics (e.g., the reproductive organs of plants) anticipating those of the stages above it. In 1819 he had written, "Nature leaves nothing *behind* but still takes up the lower into the higher, still refining and ennobling what it elevates" (CN, 4:4517). *Scale of Creation*: see the *Theory of Life* in SW&F (CC), 481–557; and Trevor Levere, *Poetry Realized in Nature*, 204–12. See also "Life" (p. 596 herein).
4. A butterfly. C frequently associated butterflies with the soul. Psyche is the Greek word for "soul" as well as the name of the maiden with whom Cupid falls in love in Apuleius's Latin novel *The Golden Ass* (2nd century C.E.). See, e.g., the opening lines of a poem C published without a title in the *Biographia*: "The butterfly the ancient Grecians made / The soul's fair emblem, and its only name" (p. 413 herein).
5. "Irritability" and "sensibility" were the terms applied by the Swiss physician Albrecht Haller (1708–1777) to the responsiveness of, respectively, muscle fiber and nerve fiber to stimulation. Haller's theory found wide acceptance in the 18th century, and C would have been exposed to modified versions of it in Erasmus Darwin's *Zoonomia* (1794–96) and in the teachings of J. F. Blumenbach (1752–1840), whose lectures he had attended in Göttingen in 1799.

Understanding, yea, and the moral affections and charities, of Man.[6] Let us carry ourselves back, in spirit, to the mysterious Week, the teeming Work-days of the Creator: as they rose in vision before the eye of the inspired Historian of "the Generations of the Heaven and Earth, in the days that the Lord God made the Earth and the Heavens."[7] And who that hath watched their ways with an understanding heart, could contemplate the filial and loyal Bee; the home-building, wedded, and divorceless Swallow; and above all the manifoldly intelligent[8] Ant-tribes, with their Commonwealths and Confederacies, their Warriors and Miners, the Husbandfolk, that fold in their tiny flocks on the honeyed Leaf, and the Virgin Sisters with the holy Instincts of Maternal Love, detached and in selfless purity[9]—and not say to himself, Behold the Shadow of approaching Humanity, the Sun rising from behind, in the kindling Morn of Creation! Thus all lower Natures find their higher Good in semblances and seekings of that which is higher and better. All things strive to ascend, and ascend in their striving.[1] And shall man alone stoop? Shall his pursuits and desires, the *reflections* of his inward life, be like the reflected Image of a Tree on the edge of a Pool, that grows downward, and seeks a mock heaven in the unstable element beneath it,[2] in neighbourhood with the slim water-weeds and oozy bottom grass that are yet better than itself and more noble, in as far as Substances that appear as Shadows are preferable to Shadows mistaken for Substance![3] No! it must be a higher good to

6. On understanding in animals, see also "[Reason and Understanding]" (p. 556 herein).
7. Genesis 2.4 (var.).
8. "See Huber on Bees, and on Ants." [C's note.] C is actually referring to books by two authors (a father and son), both of whom comment on the loyalty of bees to their queen: François Huber, *New Observations on the Natural History of Bees* (Edinburgh, 1820), and Pierre Huber, *Natural History of Ants* (London, 1820). *Divorceless Swallow*: The adjective was evidently suggested by swallows' habit of returning from their winter migration to their old nests.
9. C's analogy between ant and human behavior is drawn in part from Pierre Huber, whose book included chapters on "Insects that live in Republics" and "The Wars of Ants." *Husbandfolk*: the ants that cultivate aphids as food-sources. *Virgin Sisters*: sterile female ants that feed the other ants in the colony and tend the lavae (AR [CC], 118n. 10).
1. In the *Theory of Life* (1816), referring to the possession of reason as "that wide chasm between man and the noblest animals of the brute creation, which no perceivable or conceivable difference of organization is sufficient to *overbridge*," C implicitly denied that humans could have evolved over time from less complex forms of life (SW&F [CC], 501). This denial was explicit in a letter of May 30, 1815, to Wordsworth: "I understood that you * * * have exploded the absurd notion of Pope's Essay on Man, Darwin, and all the countless Believers * * * of Man's having progressed from an Ouran Outang state—so contrary to all History, nay, to all Possibility" (CL, 4:574–57). C was perhaps thinking of the contrast between Newton and an ape in *An Essay on Man* 2.31–34, but he ignored Pope's insistence that humans differ in kind from animals by virtue of their reason (1.223–32). Erasmus Darwin had proposed that all animals developed from a single organism by means of their "animality," a God-given power of adapting to environmental challenges (with new organs and abilities) and of passing those adaptations on to their offspring (*Zoonomia*, vol. 1 [1794], 505). Although C's assumption of the possibility of self-improvement recalls Darwin's theory, his emphasis in the present passage is on moral rather than physical development.
2. AR (CC), 118n. 14 suggests a reminiscence here of lines written by Wordsworth in 1798 and eventually incorporated into *The Prelude* (1805) 5.404–13: "the visible scene / Would enter unawares into his mind / With all its solemn imagery, its rocks, / Its woods, and that uncertain heaven received / Into the bosom of the steady lake." C had written Wordsworth in 1798, "had I met these lines running wild in the deserts of Arabia, I should have instantly screamed out 'Wordsworth!' " (CL, 1:453).
3. The distinction between "Substances" and "Shadows" recalls the allegory of the cave in Plato's *Republic* 7.514–19: we are prisoners chained inside a cave, unable to see anything but shadows, which we mistake for reality; philosophical enlightenment is an escape from the cave; and reality, the realm of eternal "Forms," is the world outside the cave.

make you happy. While you labour for any thing below your proper Humanity, you must seek a happy Life in the region of Death. Well saith the moral Poet—

> Unless above himself he can
> Erect himself, how mean a thing is man![4]

From Aphorisms on Spiritual Religion

Aphorism VII

* * * The Life, we seek after, is a mystery; but so both in itself and in its origin is the Life we have. In order to meet this question, however, with minds duly prepared, there are two preliminary enquiries to be decided; the first respecting the *purport*, the second respecting the *language* of the Gospel.

First then of the *purport*, viz. what the Gospel does *not*, and what it *does* profess to be. The Gospel is not a system of Theology, nor a Syntagma[1] of theoretical propositions and conclusions for the enlargement of speculative knowledge, ethical or metaphysical. But it is a History, a series of Facts and Events related or announced. These do indeed, involve, or rather I should say they at the same time *are*, most important doctrinal Truths; but still *Facts* and Declaration of *Facts*.

Secondly of the *language*. This is a wide subject. But the point, to which I chiefly advert, is the necessity of thoroughly understanding the distinction between *analogous*, and *metaphorical* language. *Analogies* are used in aid of *Conviction: Metaphors*, as means of *Illustration*. The language is analogous, wherever a thing, power, or principle in a higher dignity is expressed by the same thing, power, or principle in a lower but more known form. Such, for instance, is the language of John iii. 6. *That which is born of the Flesh, is Flesh; that which is born of the Spirit, is Spirit.*[2] The latter half of the verse contains the fact *asserted*; the former half the *analogous* fact, by which it is rendered intelligible. If any man choose to call this *metaphorical* or figurative I ask him whether with Hobbs and Bolingbroke[3] he applies the same rule to the moral attributes of the Deity? Whether he regards the divine Justice, for instance, as a *metaphorical* term, a mere figure of speech? If he disclaims

---

4. Samuel Daniel, "To the Lady Margaret, Countess of Cumberland" (1603), lines 95–96 (var.) (*The Works of the British Poets*, vol. 4, ed. Robert Anderson [1795], 205). C was fond of these lines, having quoted them earlier in *Aids to Reflection* as well as in other writings (see *AR* [CC], 16 and n. 1).
1. "A regular or orderly collection of statements, propositions, doctrines, etc.; a systematically arranged treatise" (*OED*).
2. John 3.6 (var.).
3. Henry St. John, Viscount Bolingbroke (1678–1751), English politician, writer, and freethinker of whom C wrote, "Bolingbroke removed Love, Justice, and Choice, from Power and Intelligence, and yet pretended to have left unimpaired the conviction of a Deity" (*Friend* [CC], 1:46). *AR* (CC), 205nn. 37–38 suggests that C has in mind Thomas Hobbes's *Leviathan* 2.31 ("in the Attributes which we give to God, we are not to consider the signification of Philosophical Truth; but the signification of Pious Intention") and Bolingbroke's "Fragments, or Minutes of Essays," in *Works*, vol. 7 (1808), 387 ("a very short analyse of the excellencies of our own nature will be sufficient to show, that they cannot be applied from man to God without profaneness").

this, then I answer, neither do I regard the words, *born again*, or *spiritual life*, as figures or metaphors. I have only to add, that these analogies are the material, or (to speak chemically) the *base*, of Symbols and symbolical expressions; the nature of which as always *tau*tegorical[4] (i.e. expressing the *same* subject but with a *difference*) in contra-distinction from metaphors and similitudes, that are always *alle*gorical (i.e. expressing a *different* subject but with a resemblance) will be found explained at large in the STATESMAN'S MANUAL, p. 35–38.

Of *metaphorical* language, on the other hand, let the following be taken as an instance and illustration. I am speaking, we will suppose, of an Act, which in its own nature, and as a producing and efficient *cause*,[5] is transcendent; but which produces sundry *effects*, each of which is the same in kind with an effect produced by a Cause well known and of ordinary occurrence. Now when I characterize or designate this transcendent Act, in exclusive reference to these its *effects*, by a succession of names borrowed from their ordinary causes; not for the purpose of rendering the Act itself, or in the manner of the Agency, conceivable, but in order to show the nature and magnitude of the Benefits received from it, and thus to excite the due admiration, gratitude, and love in the Receivers;—in this case I should rightly be described as speaking *metaphorically*. And in this case to confound *the similarity* in respect of the effects relatively to the Recipients with *an identity* in respect of the causes or modes of causation relatively to the transcendent Act or the Divine Agent, is a confusion of metaphor with analogy, and of figurative with literal; and has been and continues to be a fruitful source of superstition or enthusiasm in Believers, and of objections and prejudices to Infidels and Sceptics.

*   *   *

ON THE CONSTITUTION OF THE CHURCH AND STATE (1830)

Church and State was Coleridge's last published and most influential work of political philosophy. As John Colmer notes, it "was the only one of his works that achieved anything like a popular success," leaving "a permanent mark on the thought of the nineteenth century" (165), and inspiring a re-evaluation of the function of the church among liberal Anglicans. The volume was first published in December 1829, although the date of publication on the title page is listed as 1830. Soon afterward, in January 1830, Coleridge prepared a second revised edition, which included some additions and emendations and gained greater clarity by having the material of the first half of the volume divided into twelve chapters with subject headings. Coleridge felt that the structure of the work was rather "patchy" and had planned to include a defensive advertisement, suggesting that its title

4. The English form of C's Greek coinage ταυτηγόρικον, which he applies to the symbol in the passage from *The Statesman's Manual* to which he refers here (see p. 360 and its n. 1 herein).
5. A term from Aristotelian philosophy, meaning "the force, instrument, or agency by which a thing is produced," and commonly opposed to "final cause," meaning "the end or purpose for which a thing is done" (*OED*).

should be "Epistolary Disquisitions, or Extracts from a series of Letters" on the subject of "Idea" and on the "Constitution, the State, the Church, according to the Idea" (*C&S* [CC], lvi). However, neither this nor a concluding chapter, which Coleridge had promised his publisher Thomas Hurst to give the volume "an air of completeness" (*CL*, 6:819), ever materialized.

The composition of *Church and State* began in 1825 in the form of a projected "Essay on the Church" (see *C&S* [CC], li–lv, for the uncertain status of this essay) triggered by the debate in parliament over the bill for Catholic emancipation introduced by Francis Burdett (1770–1844). The issue of Catholic emancipation (i.e., allowing Catholics to vote and hold government or military offices) dominated British politics in the late eighteenth and early nineteenth centuries and became especially acute after the union of Britain with Ireland in 1800, causing the collapse of several ministries, including Pitt's in 1801. By the time Coleridge completed *Church and State*, the issue of Catholic emancipation, which had been the original occasion for the work, had already been settled. (In 1829 the parliament passed the bill for Catholic emancipation.) This put Coleridge in the awkward position of having to lend his support to existing legislation, while being fully aware that his previous opposition to Catholic emancipation could not have gone unnoticed. In articles written for the *Morning Post* in 1800 and for the *Courier* in 1811 and 1814 (*EOT* [CC], 1:105–08, 133–34; 2:279–82, 305–13, 373–417), Coleridge had voiced grave worries about the implication of the union with Ireland and the Catholic emancipation with which it was connected, even as he did not oppose "gradually conceding the whole claim" of the Irish for emancipation (*EOT* [CC], 2:281–82).

Coleridge's main strategy in getting around the political difficulties tied to the Catholic question was to adopt a modified version of the Kantian distinction between the ideas of reason and the concepts of the understanding, a distinction that becomes the central focus of the opening chapter of *Church and State*. Throughout this work Coleridge emphasizes repeatedly that his goal is not to offer "an historical account of the legislative body" (chapter 2) or to define the constitution as a specific body of laws, such as the Bill of Rights, but to deal with the constitution and the state as "ideas." An idea is antecedent to and (unlike conceptions) can neither be abstracted from nor embodied in concrete forms of representation. Nonetheless an idea has real existence "as a *principle*" in "the minds and consciences of the persons, whose duties it prescribes, and whose rights it determines" (*C&S* [CC], 12–13, 19). Ideas thus constitute the "final criterion by which all particular frames of government" and the difference between "progressive" and degenerate developments can be judged (*C&S* [CC], 12, 20). As John Morrow observes, Coleridge's view of the constitution as idea implies that "actual constitutions ought to change in order to realise the idea more adequately" and that the demands of Catholics for emancipation could not be refused on the ground that "they would introduce a change into the constitutional structure established in 1688–9" (131–32).

For Coleridge the "*ultimate aim*" to which a constitution was answerable consisted in the balance within a state of the following three sets of opposite interests and forces: (1) permanence and progression (chapter 2); (2) institutionalized powers (e.g., the Houses of Parliament) and "the free and permeative life and energy of the Nation" (*C&S* [CC], 85–94); and

(3) actual and potential powers (C&S [CC], 95–101). The first defines the opposition between the interests of landowners and those of the mercantile and the manufacturing class. The second refers to the importance of free pockets of resistance outside institutionalized powers of government that, however, sustain rather than overwhelm these powers. (It was the overbalance of the free forces of society that, according to Coleridge, led to the demise of democracies in ancient Greece, just as an overbalance of state power at the expense of these energies led to the fall of the Republic of Venice (C&S [CC], 86). The third opposition draws attention to the existence of latent powers representing "the unific mind and energy of the nation" that are rarely manifest, existing mainly as "an *Idea* only," yet one that forcefully limits the actual powers. As David P. Calleo notes, "Potential Power cannot exist unless various groups within society enjoy a significant degree of autonomy" (100).

It was such a system of interdependent and mutually limiting forces that guaranteed the well-being of the state, by safeguarding it against an undue concentration of power in any one of its constituent parts, be it the king or the parliament (For Coleridge's "utmost horror for any doctrine concerning the omnipotence of Parliament," see Colmer, 162, Morrow, 141 and C&S [CC], 97–101.) But ultimately for Coleridge, the most essential factor in the maintenance of a proper balance within a state was the National Church. As the third estate, the National Church was crucial in counteracting the influence of the other two estates, represented by landowners and the commercial class (chapter 5) and in providing "a counterweight to the quite legitimate concentration of proprietorial interests in both Houses of Parliament" (Morrow, 145). At a time when the Catholic emancipation debates generated numerous defenses of the church and interpretations of its necessary alliance with the state (see C&S [CC], 33–40; Morrow, 128–30, 142, 146–47), Coleridge formulated a distinct theory that proposed an oppositional interdependence of these two bodies, in the way two poles of the same magnet presuppose each other (chapter 2), but also emphasized the importance of maintaining the independence of the church and of its own property, which unlike personal property—or what Coleridge called "propriety"—served national interests (C&S [CC], 35). Coleridge conferred on the National Church the vital function of creating the "clerisy" of the nation, an elite group of learned men from varied professions charged with the task of educating the population (chapter 5). While earlier Coleridge had identified the need for the enlightenment of the people by an elite, here he delegated this function to the institution of the National Church. It is for this reason that the National Church had to maintain a position of substantial independence from the state based on its own property and thus be able to fulfil its moral and educating function in society, free from influence from the rich, or "future depredations by a legislature that contained a significant number of indifferent or hostile 'Liberalists', Dissenters and Roman Catholics" (Morrow, 144–47, 154–55, 158–60; see also Calleo, 96–102).

Compared to Coleridge's denunciation of the corruption of the Church of England, his opposition to the alliance of church and state and his attack on private property in his political and religious writings of the 1790s, *Church and State* might appear to some observers as "nothing more than a conservative apology for traditional English aristocratic society" (Calleo, 102), based on a strict equation of political power with proprietal privileges. But as several critics have argued, liberalism remained a salient feature of Coleridge's political philosophy, even during his "conservative" phase (see Charles Richard Sanders, *Coleridge and the Broad Church Movement* [Durham, N.C., 1942], chapter 2) and many contemporaries as well as later writers responded to the unorthodox characteristics of Coleridge's political theory, especially his view of the National Church and the clerisy (Morrow, 163–64). For the enormous influence of *Church and State* on subsequent religious movements and nineteenth- and twentieth-century writers, including Mathew Arnold (1822–1888), John Stuart Mill (1806–1873), J. H. Newman (1801–1890), and T. S. Eliot (1888–1965), see *C&S* (*CC*), lviii–lxviii; Charles Richard Sanders, *Coleridge and the Broad Church Movement* (Durham, N.C., 1942); Basil Willey, *Nineteenth Century Studies* (London, 1949); and Anthony Harding, *Coleridge and the Inspired Word* (chapters 4 and 5).

The text printed here is from *On the Constitution of the Church and State*, 2nd. ed. (London, 1830). This edition has been chosen over the first edition of 1829 because Coleridge made structural improvements, alterations, and additions in it. Variants in the first edition and in two annotated presentation copies of the second edition (the copies owned by James Gilman [Copy G] and William Wordsworth [Copy W]) are cited selectively in the notes. For a description of the four extant annotated copies, see *C&S* (*CC*), 237–38.

From On the Constitution of the Church and State

From Chapter II

The idea of a State in the larger sense of the term, introductory to the constitution of the State in the narrower sense, as it exists in this Country.[1]

A Constitution is the attribute of a state,[2] *i. e.* of a body politic, having the principle of its unity within itself, whether by concentration of its forces, as a constitutional pure Monarchy, which, however, has hitherto continued to be *ens rationale*,[3] unknown in history (B. *Spinozæ Tract. Pol. cap. VI. De Monarchiâ ex rationis præscripto*),[4]—or—with which we are alone concerned—by equipoise and interdependency: the *lex equilibrii*,[5] the principle prescribing the means and conditions by and under which this balance is to be established and preserved, being the constitution of the state. It is the chief of many blessings derived from the insular character and circumstances of our country, that our social institutions have formed themselves out of our proper needs and

1. The first edition introduced this section with the title "CONCERNING THE RIGHT IDEA OF THE CONSTITUTION." The chapter numbers and subject headings were added in the second edition. At the end of chapter 1, C explained that the state in a larger sense includes the church, whereas in a narrower sense is understood to be its antithesis, "as in the phrase, Church and State" (*C&S* [*CC*], 22).
2. In chapter 1 C defined the constitution as "an idea arising out of the idea of a state" and distinguished, along Kantian lines, between ideas and conceptions (*C&S* [*CC*], 19–20). T. S. Eliot (*The Idea of a Christian Society* [New York, 1940], 4–5, 67n.) acknowledged using "ideas" in the exact terms defined by C in *C&S*.
3. "Rational entity."
4. Spinoza, *Tractatus politicus*, 6.3, 5 (in *Opera*, 2 vols. ed. H. E. G. Paulus [Jena, 1802–03], 2:332–34). On Spinoza, see p. 443, n. 9 herein; p. 587, n. 1 herein; p. 603, n. 8 herein.
5. "Law of balance."

interests; that long and fierce as the birth-struggle and the growing pains have been, the antagonist powers have been of our own system, and have been allowed to work out their final balance with less disturbance from external forces, than was possible in the Continental states.[6]

*   *   *

Now, in every country of civilized men, acknowledging the rights of property, and by means of determined boundaries and common laws united into one people or nation,[7] the two antagonist powers or opposite interests of the state, under which all other state interests are comprised, are those of PERMANENCE and of PROGRESSION.[8]

It will not be necessary to enumerate the several causes that combine to connect the permanence of a state with the land and the landed property.[9] To found a family, and to convert his wealth into land, are twin thoughts, births of the same moment, in the mind of the opulent merchant, when he thinks of reposing from his labours. From the class of the Novi Homines[1] he redeems himself by becoming the staple ring of the chain, by which the present will become connected with the past; and the test and evidence of permanency afforded. To the same principle appertain primogeniture and hereditary titles, and the influence which these exert in accumulating large masses of property, and in counteracting the antagonist and dispersive forces, which the follies, the vices, and misfortunes of individuals can scarcely fail to supply.[2] To this, likewise, tends the proverbial obduracy of prejudices characteristic of the humbler tillers of the soil, and their aversion even to benefits that are offered in the form of innovations. But why need I attempt to explain a fact which no thinking man will deny, and where the admission of the fact is all that my argument requires?

On the other hand, with as little chance of contradiction, I may assert, that the progression of a state, in the arts and comforts of life, in the diffusion of the information and knowledge, useful or necessary

6. In the passage omitted here C cites "Ode on the Departing Year," lines 129–40 (var.). See p. 41 herein).
7. In a note in Copy G, C distinguishes between the terms "nation," "people," and "state," claiming that while nation designates "the Unity of the successive Generations of a People," the state represents "the conservative Form (therefore, at once the Form and the Power) of the unity of a People" (C&S [CC], 24n. 2).
8. In a footnote omitted here C draws attention to the "essential difference" between opposites and contraries to show that permanence and progression are opposites and, therefore, like the poles of a magnet, presuppose each other. See also *Friend* (CC), 1:94n.; *CM* (CC), 3:1026; and *CN*, 3:4241.
9. C's view of property changed from a radical rejection of it in his 1795 political writings (see p. 269, n. 5 herein) to his assertive defense of it, as here. See also p. 306, n. 5 herein; *Friend* (CC), 2:131–32; and Morrow, passim.
1. "New men."
2. C was indebted to Edmund Burke for the view of the necessary balance of "permanence and progression" and the defense of hereditary titles. In *Reflections on the Revolution in France* (1790) Burke maintained that it "is far from impossible to reconcile * * * the use both of a fixed rule and an occasional deviation; the sacredness of an hereditary principle of succession in our government, with a power of change in its application in cases of extreme emergency." Burke called the two principles "conservation and correction," arguing that they are inextricably bound ("A state without the means of some change is without the means of its conservation" [29]), and at one point used the term "progression" to define the principle that counteracts permanence: "* * * the human race, the whole, at one time, is never old, or middle-aged, or young, but in a condition of unchangeable constancy, moves on through the varied tenour of perpetual decay, fall, renovation, and progression" (48). For Burke's view of inheritance, see esp. 34, 36, 44–50.

for all; in short, all advances in civilization, and the rights and privileges of citizens, are especially connected with, and derived from the four classes of the mercantile, the manufacturing, the distributive, and the professional.

* * *

But whether this[3] conjecture be well or ill grounded, the *principle* of the constitution remains the same. That harmonious balance of the two great correspondent, at once supporting and counterpoising, interests of the state, its permanence, and its progression: that balance of the landed and the personal interests was to be secured by a legislature of two Houses; the first consisting wholly of barons or landholders, permanent and hereditary senators; the second of the knights or minor barons, elected by, and as the representatives of, the remaining landed community, together with the burgesses, the representatives of the commercial, manufacturing, distributive, and professional classes,— the latter (the elected burgesses) constituting the major number. The king, meanwhile, in whom the executive power is vested, it will suffice at present to consider as the beam of the constitutional scales. A more comprehensive view of the kingly office must be deferred, till the remaining problem (the idea of a national church) has been solved.[4]

I must here intreat the reader to bear in mind what I have before endeavoured to impress on him, that I am not giving an historical account of the legislative body; nor can I be supposed to assert that such was the earliest mode or form in which the national council was constructed. My assertion is simply this, that its formation has advanced in this direction. The line of evolution, however sinuous, has still tended to this point, sometimes with, sometimes without, not seldom, perhaps, against, the intention of the individual actors, but always as if a power, greater, and better, than the men themselves, had intended it for them. Nor let it be forgotten that every new growth, every power and privilege, bought or extorted, has uniformly been claimed by an antecedent right; not acknowledged as a boon conferred, but both demanded and received as what had always belonged to them, though withheld by violence and the injury of the times. This too,[5] in cases, where, if documents and historical records, or even consistent traditions, had been required in evidence, the monarch would have had the better of the argument. But, in truth, it was no more than a *practical* way of saying: this or that[6] is contained in the *idea* of our government, and it is a consequence of the "Lex, Mater Legum," which, in the very first law of state ever[7] promulgated in the land, was pre-supposed as the ground of that first law.

3. The first edition has "my" instead of "this."
4. C discussed the function of the king in chapter 10 (C&S [CC], 82–94). For C the king, as head of both the state and the National Church, was "the Protector and Supreme Trustee of the NATIONALITY" (83) and a symbol of national unity. Through the royal veto, the king also owned "potential power" that limited the "actual power" of Parliament (Colmer, 162–63; Morrow, 141, 147). For a summary of C's "Constitutional Creed," which includes the balance of the forces of permanence and progression and a view of the king as "Agent and Trustee" for all estates, see *CM* (CC), 3:799–801.
5. Copy G adds "has been the language of our Parliaments even."
6. The first edition has "saying, it" instead of "saying: this or that."
7. The first edition has "State that was" instead of "state ever." *Lex, Mater Legum*: "Law, Mother of Laws."

Before I conclude this part of my subject, I must press on your attention, that the preceding is offered only as the constitutional idea of the *State*.[8] In order to correct views respecting the constitution, in the more enlarged sense of the term, viz. the constitution of the *Nation*, we must, in addition to a grounded knowledge of the *State*,[9] have the right idea of the *National Church*. These[1] are two poles of the same magnet; the magnet itself, which is constituted by them, is the CONSTITUTION of the nation.

Chapter V

Of the Church of England, or National Clergy, according to the Constitution; its characteristic ends, purposes and functions; and of the persons comprehended under the Clergy, or the Functionaries of the National Church.

After these introductory preparations,[2] I can have no difficulty in setting forth the right idea of a national church as in the language of Elizabeth the *third* great venerable estate of the realm. The first being the estate of the land-owners or possessors of fixed property, consisting of the two classes of the Barons and the Franklins; the second comprising the merchants, the manufacturers, free artizans, and the distributive class.[3] To comprehend, therefore, this third estate, in whom the reserved nationality was vested, we must first ascertain the end, or national purpose, for which it was reserved.

Now, as in the former state, the permanency of the nation was provided for; and in the second estate its progressiveness, and personal freedom; while in the king the cohesion by interdependence, and the unity of the country, were established; there remains for the third estate only that interest, which is the ground, the necessary antecedent condition, of both the former. Now[4] these depend on a continuing and progressive civilization. But[5] civilization is itself but a mixed good, if not far more a corrupting influence, the hectic of disease, not the bloom of health, and a nation so distinguished more fitly to be called a varnished than a polished people; where this civilization is not

---

8. Copy G adds "*State*, in the narrower acceptation of the Word." In a note in Jonathan Green's copy of *C&S*, C emphasized that his concern was to discuss the idea of the state rather than its representation in an actual history or "*form*" of the British Legislature." He also gives another synopsis of his view of the constitution as a balance of various powers (*C&S* [CC], 31n. 2).
9. The first edition has "*Nation* in addition to grounded knowledge of the *State*, we must" instead of "*Nation*, we must * * * of the *State*."
1. Copy G adds "These, the national *State*, and the National *Church*".
2. In chapters 3 and 4 (*C&S* [CC], 32–41) C began to explore the idea of the National Church, drawing on the example of the Hebrew commonwealth and constitution, a subject that he treated in a more radical vein in Lecture 2 of *LRR* (pp. 259–62 herein).
3. In England and France the church represented the first estate, the hereditary nobility the second, and the commons the third. C draws from Elizabethan writers the notion of the clergy as a third estate. This suits his organic model of an interdependece of opposite forces (those of permanence and progression) made possible by a common ground, the national clergy, without which, "the nation could be neither permanent nor progressive" (p. 583 herein). The clergy is thus invested with the originating power of an inherent unity that is then reflected in the figure of the king.
4. The first edition has "All" instead of "Now."
5. The first edition has "civilization, but" instead of "civilization. But."

grounded in *cultivation*, in the harmonious developement of those qualities and faculties that characterise our *humanity*.[6] We must be men in order to be citizens.[7]

The Nationalty, therefore, was reserved for the support and maintenance of a permanent class or order, with the following duties. A certain smaller number were to remain at the fountain heads of the humanities, in cultivating and enlarging the knowledge already possessed, and in watching over the interests of physical and moral science; being, likewise, the instructors of such as constituted, or were to constitute, the remaining more numerous classes of the order. This latter and far more numerous body were to be distributed throughout the country, so as not to leave even the smallest integral part or division without a resident guide, guardian, and instructor; the objects[8] and final intention of the whole order being these—to preserve the stores, to guard the treasures, of past civilization, and thus to bind the present with the past;[9] to perfect and add to the same, and thus to connect the present with the future; but especially to diffuse through the whole community, and to every native entitled to its laws and rights, that quantity and quality of knowledge which was indispensable both for the understanding of those rights, and for the performance of the duties correspondent. Finally, to secure for the nation, if not a superiority over the neighbouring states, yet an equality at least, in that character of general civilization, which equally with, or rather more than, fleets, armies, and revenue, forms the ground of its defensive and offensive power. The object of the two former estates of the realm, which conjointly form the STATE, was to reconcile the interests of permanence with that of progression—law with liberty. The object of the National Church, the third remaining estate of the realm, was to secure and improve that civilization, without which the nation could be neither permanent nor progressive.

That in all ages, individuals who have directed their meditations and their studies to the nobler characters of our nature, to the cultivation of those powers and instincts which constitute the man, at least separate him from the animal, and distinguish the nobler from the animal part of his own being, will be led by the *supernatural* in themselves to the contemplation of a power which is likewise super*human*;[1] that science, and especially moral science, will lead to religion, and remain

---

6. For the distinction between civilization and cultivation, see *Friend* (CC), 1:494, 500. On the influence in 19th-century thought of the related distinction between material wealth and cultural well-being, see *C&S* (CC), 42n. 2.

7. In the first edition the sentence began with "In short, we." In a marginal note in Copy G, C reflected on how the contradiction between this proposition and the contrary one ("We must be citizens in order to be men") could be resolved by introducing an additional pair of terms: "potential" and "actual." The formula then becomes: "We must be *potential* men in order to be made Citizens, but likewise we must be citizens in order to [be]come actual Men" (*C&S* [CC], 43n. 2).

8. The first edition has "object" instead of "objects."

9. C's view of the important continuity between the present and the past made possible by the clerisy is indebted to Burke's defense of inheritance in *Reflections on the Revolution in France*. See p. 580, n. 2 herein. The second edition has "these—to bind" instead of the first edition's "thus to bind."

1. "My great aim and object," C wrote in a notebook entry, "is to assert the *Superhuman* in order to diffuse more & more widely the faith in the *Supernatural*" (*C&S* [CC], 44n. 2).

blended with it—this, I say, will, in all ages, be the course of things. That in the earlier ages, and in the dawn of civility, there will be a twilight in which science and religion give light, but a light refracted through the dense and the dark, a superstition—this is what we learn from history, and what philosophy would have taught us to expect. But we affirm, that in the spiritual purpose of the word, and as understood in reference to a future state, and to the abiding essential interest of the individual as a person, and not as the citizen, neighbour, or subject, religion may be an indispensable ally, but is not the essential constitutive end of that national institute, which is unfortunately, at least improperly, styled a church—a name which, in its best sense is exclusively appropriate to the church of Christ.[2] If this latter be ecclesia, the communion of such as are called out of the world, *i.e.* in reference to the especial ends and purposes of that communion; this other might more expressively have been entitled *enclesia*,[3] or an order of men, chosen in and of the realm, and constituting an estate of that realm. And in fact, such was the original and proper sense of the more appropriately named CLERGY. It comprehended the learned of all names, and the CLERK was the synonyme of the man of learning. Nor can any fact more strikingly illustrate the conviction entertained by our ancestors, respecting the intimate connexion of this clergy with the peace and weal of the nation, than the privilege formerly recognized by our laws, in the well-known phrase, "benefit of clergy."[4]

Deeply do I feel, for clearly do I see, the importance of my Theme. And had I equal confidence in my ability to awaken the same interest in the minds of others, I should dismiss as affronting to my readers all apprehension of being charged with prolixity, while I am labouring to compress in two or three brief Chapters, the principal sides and aspects of a subject so large and multilateral as to require a volume for its full exposition. With what success will be seen in what follows,

2. One of the most important contributions of C&S was C's endeavor to show that the National Church was free from theological dogma and independent of Christianity. In a separate section C offered a detailed analysis of the distinguishing characteristics of the Church of Christ and its divergence from the National Church (C&S [CC], 111–28). He claimed that the Church of Christ was not a realm or a state, and, unlike the National Church, was not opposed to the state or particular institutions. Its main opponent was the world and its proper destination was "*another* world" dissociated from "all Bodies Politic" (117). The Church of Christ was, however, visible and public in counterdistinction to "the spiritual and the invisible church, known only to the Father of all Spirits" (116, 127). It was also universal rather than national and acknowledged no center of authority other than Christ, "the universal Shepherd" (118–19). C thought that a cooperative relationship between the two churches was desirable but only as long as the differences between them remained clearly in view. Cf. an entry of February 22, 1832, in *TT* (CC), 1:265–66: "Would to God that the Bishops and the Clergy in general could once fully understand that the Christian Church and the National Church ought as little to be confounded as divided! I think the fate of the Reform Bill of comparatively minor importance; the fate of the national church occupies my mind with greater intensity." See Morrow, 149–55.

3. The term *ecclesia* derived from Greek, designates an assembly of citizens and, in its Christian appropriation, an assembly of men devoted to otherwordly matters. This term commonly used with reference to the church (for contemporary examples see Morrow, 150; 194n. 111). C thought, however, that it captured the essence of the Church of Christ exclusively, and he coined the term *enclesia* to represent the National Church, which, unlike the former, is grounded in the world, the nation, and particular political institutions. For other examples of C's use of the distinction between *ecclesia* and *enclesia*, see C&S (CC), 45n. 1.

4. The clergy were exempt from arrest and trial in the king's court, a privilege finally abolished by an Act of Parliament in 1827.

commencing with the Churchmen, or (a far apter and less objection-able designation,) the National CLERISY.[5]

THE CLERISY of the nation, or[6] national church, in its primary accep-tation and original intention comprehended the learned of all denom-inations;—the sages and professors of[7] the law and jurisprudence; of medicine and physiology; of music; of military and civil architecture; of the physical sciences; with the mathematical as the common *organ* of the preceding; in short, all the so called liberal arts and sciences, the possession and application of which constitute the civilization of a country, as well as the Theological. The last was, indeed, placed at the head of all; and of good right did it claim the precedence. But why? Because under the name of Theology, or Divinity, were contained the interpretation of languages; the conservation and tradition of past events; the momentous epochs, and revolutions of the race and na-tion; the continuation of the records; logic, ethics, and the determina-tion of ethical science, in application to the rights and duties of men in all their various relations, social and civil; and lastly, the ground-knowledge, the prima scientia[8] as it was named,—PHILOSOPHY, or the doctrine and discipline* of *ideas*.

---

* That is, of knowledges immediate, yet real, and herein distinguished *in kind* from logical and mathematical truths, which express not realities, but only the necessary *forms* of conceiving and perceiving, and are therefore named the *formal* or *abstract* sciences. Ideas, on the other hand, or the truths of philosophy, properly so called, correspond to substantial beings, to ob-jects whose actual subsistence is *implied* in their idea, though only *by* the idea revealable.[9] To adopt the language of the great philosophic apostle, they are *"spiritual realities that can only spiritually be discerned,"*[1] and the inherent aptitude and moral *preconfiguration* to which constitutes what we mean by ideas, and by the presence of *ideal* truth, and of *ideal* power, in the human being. They, in fact, constitute his *humanity*. For try to conceive a *man* without the ideas of God, eternity, freedom, will, absolute truth, of the good, the true, the beautiful, the infinite.[2] An *animal* endowed with a memory of appearances and of facts might remain. But the *man* will have vanished, and you have instead a creature, "more subtile than any beast of the field, but likewise cursed above every beast of the field; upon the belly must it go and dust must it eat all the days of its life."[3] But I recal myself from a train of thoughts, little likely to find favour in this age of sense and selfishness.

---

5. In the first edition the paragraph reads: "From the narrow limits prescribed by my object in *compressing* the substance of my letters to you, I am driven to apologise for prolixity, even while I am pondering on the means of presenting, in three or four numbered paragraphs, the principal sides and aspects of a subject so large and multilateral as to require a volume for their full exposition. Regard the following, then, as the text. The commentary may be given hereafter:—PARAGRAPH THE FIRST." The term "clerisy" is C's coinage from the German *Clerisei* and Latin *clericia* (C&S [CC], 46n. 1). The germ of this view of an elite class charged with the enlightenment of the nation can be found in *A Moral and Political Lecture* (1795), where he singled out "that small but glorious band" of patriots who were meant to be the true leaders and saviors of England (p. 245, n. 6 herein). See also his reference to "an unresisting yet deeply principled Minority" in Lecture 6 of *LRR* (p. 269, n. 4 herein). The notion of the clerisy was transformed into that of the "Community of Christians" by T. S. Eliot, who thought that the content of C's formula, "had been somehow voided by time." For Eliot's view that, compared to C's clerisy, his altered version was "at once wider" (including the laity and monastic orders ignored by C) and "more restricted" (including "many but not all, of the clergy"), see *The Idea of a Christian Society*, 34–44, 75n.
6. The first edition has "nation (a far apter exponent of the thing meant, than the term which the usus norma loquendi [normal way of speaking] forces on me), the clerisy, I say, or."
7. The second edition adds "sages and professors of."
8. "First knowledge."
9. The distinction between abstractions and ideas and the corollary distinctions between con-ceptions and ideas, understanding and reason, are fundamental to C's thinking and developed through a close perusal of Kant's works. For C abstractions, unlike ideas, do not contain any reality, providing merely the forms of perception and thought. In a marginal note to Kant's *Logik* (Königsberg, 1800), C insisted that ideas and abstractions are heterogeneous entities rather than opposites that presuppose the same essence. Therefore ideas can never be trans-

Theology formed only a part of the objects, the Theologians formed only a portion of the clerks or clergy of the national church. The theological order had precedency indeed, and deservedly; but not because its members were priests, whose office was to conciliate the invisible powers, and to superintend the interests that survive the grave; not as being exclusively, or even principally, sacerdotal or templar, which, when it did occur, is to be considered as an accident of the age, a misgrowth of ignorance and oppression, a falsification of the constitutive principle, not a constituent part of the same. No! The Theologians took the lead, because the SCIENCE of Theology was the root and the trunk of the knowledges that civilized man, because it gave unity and the circulating sap of life to all other sciences, by virtue of which alone they could be contemplated as forming, collectively, the living tree of knowledge. It had the precedency, because, under the name theology, were comprised all the main aids, instruments, and materials of NATIONAL EDUCATION, the *nisus formativus*[4] of the body politic, the shaping and informing spirit, which *educing*,[5] *i.e.* eliciting, the latent *man* in all the natives of the soil, *trains them up* to citizens of the country, free subjects of the realm. And lastly, because to divinity belong those fundamental truths, which are the common ground-work of our civil and our religious duties, not less indispensable to a right view of our temporal concerns, than to a rational faith respecting our immortal well-being. (Not without celestial observations, can even terrestrial charts be accurately constructed.) And of especial importance is it to the objects here contemplated, that only by the vital warmth diffused by these truths throughout the MANY, and by the guiding light from the philosophy, which is the basis of *divinity*, possessed by the FEW, can either the community or its rulers fully comprehend, or rightly appreciate, the permanent *distinction*, and the occasional *contrast*, between cultivation and civilization; or be made to understand this most valuable of the lessons taught by history, and exemplified alike in her oldest and her most recent records—that a nation can never be a too cultivated, but may easily become an over-civilized race.

---

formed into abstractions (*CM* [CC], 3:261–62). For a detailed examination of the difference between ideas and abstractions, see *Logic* (CC), 62–4; cf. *Friend* (CC), 1:520–24.

1. St Paul. Cf. 1 Corinthians 2.14.
2. This list corresponds to what Kant in *Pure Reason* would define as supersensibile ideas that are beyond rational cognition and have a purely regulative rather than constitutive function. In *Friend* (CC), 2:72 C recapitulated this list as an index of the sublime.
3. Genesis 3.1, 14 (var.).
4. "Formative impulse." C derived the term from the German word *Bildungstrieb*, as used by Johann Friedrich Blumenbach, whose lectures he attended during his trip to Germany in 1798–99. See *CN*, 3:3744 and n.; and p. 430, n. 5 herein.
5. C used this term (see p. 359, n. 3 herein) to designate the proper goal of education as that of "*eliciting* the faculties of the Human Mind, and at the same time subordinating them to the Reason and Conscience; varying the means of this common end according to the sphere and particular mode, in which the Individual is likely to act and become useful" (*Friend* [CC], 2:288n.).

MISCELLANEOUS PROSE

Androgynous Minds[1]

I have known *strong* minds with imposing, undoubting, Cobbet-like manners,[2] but I have never met a *great* mind of this sort. The truth is, a great mind must be androgynous. Great minds—Swedenborg's[3] for instance—are never wrong but in consequence of being in the right, but imperfectly.

The Bible[1]

The Bible is the appointed conservatory, an indispensable criterion and a continual source and support of true Belief. But that the Bible is the sole source; that it not only contains, but constitutes, the Christian Religion; that it is, in short, a Creed, consisting wholly of articles of Faith;[2] that consequently we need no rule, help, or guide, spiritual or historical, to teach us what parts are and what are not articles of Faith—all being such—, and the difference between the Bible and Creed being this, that the clauses of the latter are all unconditionally necessary to salvation, but those of the former conditionally so, that is, as soon as the words are known to exist in any one of the canonical Books;[3] and that, under this limitation, the belief is of the same necessity in both, and not at all affected by the greater or lesser importance of the matter to be believed;—this scheme differs widely from

---

1. *Table Talk* (1835), 2:96 (September 1, 1832).
2. William Cobbett (1762–1835), publisher of *Cobbett's Political Register,* a radical newspaper whose format (but not content) C imitated in *The Friend.* C had long disapproved of Cobbett's politics and writing style and may have been the author of a fierce denunciation of Cobbett in the pro-government newspaper the *Courier* (see *EOT* [CC], 3:87–90).
3. Emmanuel Swedenborg (1688–1772), Swedish mystic who spent his later years in England, where the first church inspired by his teachings was established in 1787. Swedenborg's theology, which assumed a system of correspondences between the physical and spiritual worlds, affirmed Christ's perfection as a person but denied his divinity. C's interest in Swedenborg was stimulated by his friendship with the lawyer Charles Augustus Tulk (1786–1849), who helped found a society devoted to publishing Swedenborg's extensive writings.
1. From *Confessions of an Inquiring Spirit,* ed. Henry Nelson Coleridge (1840), 51–56. This posthumously published work on the interpretation of the Bible, written as a series of seven letters to an unnamed friend, was prepared by C's son-in-law from a manuscript of the 1820s. (The heavily corrected manuscript version is published in *SW&F* [CC], 1111–71.) C's basic argument was that because the various writers of the biblical books were divinely inspired but not infallible and because the texts they produced reflected their historical circumstances, the Bible had to be interpreted with the aid of the theological tradition and historical scholarship. In the 1820s C was one of the few Englishmen aware of the "higher" or historical criticism of the Bible as it had been advanced in Germany by Johann Gottfried Eichhorn (1752–1827) and others under the influence of Spinoza's *Tractatus Theologico-politicus* (Theologico-political Treatise) (1670) and Robert Lowth's *Lectures on the Sacred Poetry of the Hebrews* (1753).
2. A concise, formal statement of the basic tenets of Christian doctrine intended for recitation in religious services. The two most important creeds are the Apostles' Creed (dating from the 8th century) and the Nicene Creed (dating from 325), both of which are included in the Anglican Book of Common Prayer.
3. In the Protestant Bible, the books of the Old and New Testaments but not those of the Apocrypha.

the preceding, though its adherents often make use of the same words in expressing their belief.[4]

* * *

Every sentence found in a canonical Book, rightly interpreted, contains the *dictum* of an infallible Mind;—but what the right interpretation is,—or whether the very words now extent are corrupt or genuine—must be determined by the industry and understanding of fallible and alas! more or less prejudiced theologians.

* * *

But if—though but with the faith of a Seneca or an Antonine[5]—you admit the co-operation of a divine Spirit in souls desirous of good, even as the breath of heaven works variously in each several plant according to its kind, character, period of growth, and circumstance of soil, clime, and aspect;—on what ground can you assume that its presence is incompatible with all imperfection in the subject,—even with such imperfection as is the natural accompaniment of the unripe season? If you call your gardener or husbandman to account for the plants or crops he is raising, would you not regard the special purpose in each, and judge of each by that which it was tending to? Thorns are not flowers, nor is the husk serviceable. But it was not for its thorns, but for its sweet and medicinal flowers that the rose was cultivated; and he who cannot separate the husk from the grain, wants the power because sloth or malice has prevented the will. I demand for the Bible only the justice which you grant to other books of grave authority, and to other proved and acknowledged benefactors of mankind. Will you deny a spirit of wisdom in Lord Bacon,[6] because in particular facts he did not possess perfect science, or an entire immunity from the positive errors which result from imperfect insight?

* * *

Death[1]

* * * The con*crete* in nature nearest to the *abstract* of Death is Death by a Flash of Lightning. Repeatedly during this night's storm have I desired that I might be taken off, not knowing when or where/but a few moments past a vivid flash passed across me, my nerves thrilled,

---

4. C is criticizing the view that he labels "Bibliolatry," by which he means an excessive veneration of the text of the Bible and an excessive denigration of the tradition of biblical interpretation. The foremost of the "Bibliolaters" for him was the Protestant theologian William Chillingworth (1602–1643), who maintained that "a Writing may be so perfect a Rule, as to need neither Addition not Interpretation: But the *Scripture you acknowledge a perfect Rule* * * * therefore it needs neither Addition nor Interpretation" (*The Religion of Protestants*, in *Works*, 10th ed. [London, 1743], 1:81). C scornfully annotated two copies of Chillingworth's *Works* (*CM* [CC], 2:24–41).
5. The Roman playwright Seneca the Younger (c. 4 B.C.E.–65 C.E.) and the Roman emperor Marcus Aurelius (120–180 C.E.), both of whom espoused Stoicism, a philosophy that regards the universe as an organic whole in which God is present everywhere as a spirit. C is implicitly rebuking the Bibliolaters by insisting that even these pagan philosophers of antiquity would have recognized the justice of his argument.
6. I.e., Francis Bacon.
1. From a notebook entry of June 22, 1806 (*CN*, 2:2866). C was in Pisa, about to return to England in worse physical and mental shape than when he had left for Malta in 1804.

and I earnestly wished, so help me God! like a Love-longing, that
it would pass through me!—Death without pain, without degrees,
without the possibility of cowardly wishes, or recreant changes
of resolve/Death without deformity, or assassin-like self-disorganiza-
tion/Death, in which the mind by its *own* wish might seem to have
caused its own purpose to be performed, as instantaneously and by an
instrument almost as spiritual, as the Wish itself/!—

> Come, come, thou bleak December Wind,
> And blow the dry Leaves from the Tree!
> Flash, like a Love-thought, thro' me, Death
> And take a Life, that wearies me.

Dreams and Sleep

1[1]

October 3—Night—My Dreams uncommonly illustrative of the non-
existence of Surprize in sleep—I dreamt that I was asleep in the Cloys-
ter at Christs Hospital[2] & had awoken with a pain in my hand from
some corrosion/boys & nurses daughters peeping at me/On their implying that I was not in the School, I answered yes I am/I am only
twenty—I then recollected that I was thirty, & of course could not be in
the School—& was perplexed—but not in the least surprize[d] that I
could fall into such an error/So I dreamt of Dorothy, William & Mary[3]
& that Dorothy was altered in every feature, a fat, thick-limbed &
rather red-haired—in short, no resemblance to her at all—and I said, if
I did not *know* you to be Dorothy, I never should *suppose* it/ Why, says
she—I have not a feature the same/& yet I was not surprized—

I was followed up & down by a frightful pale woman who, I thought,
wanted to kiss me, & had the property of giving a shameful Disease by
breathing in the face/

& again I dreamt that a figure of a woman of a gigantic Height, dim
& indefinite & smokelike appeared—& that I was forced to run up toward it—& then it changed to a stool—& then appeared again in another place—& again I went up in great fright—& it changed to some
other common thing—yet I felt no surprize.

2[4]

I humbly thank God, that I have for some time past been more attentive to the regulation of my Thoughts—& the attention has been
blessed with a great measure of Success. There are few Day-dreams
that I dare allow myself at any time; and few & cautiously built as they

---

1. A notebook entry of October 3, 1802 (CN, 1:1250).
2. Christ's Hospital, the London boarding school that C attended from 1782 to 1791. C wrote
   about his experience of this school in his letter of February 19, 1798, to Thomas Poole (p.
   625 herein) and in chapter 1 of the *Biographia*.
3. The Wordsworths.
4. A notebook entry of April 1805 (CN, 2:2543).

are, it is very seldom that I can think myself entitled to make lazy Holiday with any one of them. I must have worked hard, long, and well to have earned that privilege. So akin to Reason is reality, that what I could *do* with exulting Innocence, I can not always *imagine* with perfect innocence/for Reason and Reality can stop and stand still, new Influxes from without counteracting the Impulses from within, and *poising* the Thought. But Fancy and Sleep *stream on*,[5] and (Instead of outward Forms and Sounds, the Sanctifiers, the Strengtheners!) they connect with them motions of the blood and nerves, and images forced into the mind by the feelings that arise out of the position & state of the Body and its different members. I have done innocently what afterwards in absence I have likewise day-dreamed innocently, during the being awake; but the Reality was followed in Sleep by no suspicious fancies, the Day-dream *has* been. Thank Heaven! however/Sleep has never yet desecrated the images, or supposed[6] Presences, of those whom I love and revere.[7] * * *

3[8]

*   *   *

Night-mair is, I think, always—even when it occurs in the midst of Sleep, and not as it more commonly does after a waking Interval, a state not of Sleep but of Stupor of the outward organs of Sense, not in words indeed but yet in fact distinguishable from the suspended power of the senses in true Sleep; while the volitions of *Reason* i.e. comparing &c, are awake, tho' disturbed. * * * In short, this Nightmair is not properly *a Dream*; but a species of Reverie, akin to Somnambulism, during which the Understanding and Moral Sense are awake tho' more or less confused, and over the Terrors of which Reason can exert no influence because it is not true Terror: i.e. apprehension of danger, but a sensation as much as the Tooth-ache, a Cramp—I.e. the Terror does not *arise* out of a painful Sensation, but is itself a specific sensation = terror corporeus sive materialis.[9]* * *

---

5. I.e., images are connected to one another without guidance from the reason or will. On fancy, see also chapter 13 of the *Biographia*.
6. "There is often a dim sense of the Presence of a Person in our dreams, whose form does not appear." [C's note.]
7. C's language is cryptic, but he seems to be referring to the absence of any sexual content in his nocturnal dreams—as opposed to his daydreams—about Sara Hutchinson or others. Other notebook entries from this time, when C was in Malta, reveal that Hutchinson was much on his mind, and a month or so later he recorded a dream about her that was "wholly without *desire*, or bodily Inquietude" (*CN*, 2:2600). See also "Love, Lust, and Friendship" (p. 597 herein).
8. From a notebook entry of January 1811 (*CN*, 3:4046).
9. "Bodily or material terror." C, who suffered terribly from nightmares (see his letter to Thomas Wedgwood, p. 634 herein), consistently differentiated them from ordinary dreams and sleep. On the suspension of reason in sleep, see also p. 338 herein.

Education[1]

* * * Here he observed, that he ought, perhaps, before to have noticed the word Education: it was to educe, to call forth;[2] as the blossom is educed from the bud, the vital excellencies are within; the acorn is but educed or brought forth form the bud. In proportion to the situation in which the individual is likely to be placed, all that is good and proper should be educed; for it was not merely a degradation of the word Education, but an affront of human nature, to include within its meaning, the bare attainment of reading and writing * * * its object and its end would only be pernicious, of it did not make men worthy and estimable beings.

* * *

It was a great error to cram the young mind with so much knowledge as made the child talk much and fluently: what was more ridiculous than to hear a child questioned, what it thought of the last poem of Walter Scott?[3] a child should be child-like, and possess no other idea than what was loving and admiring. A youth might devour with avidity without comprehending the excellencies of Young and Gray;[4] the Lecturer himself recollected the innocent and delightful intoxication with which he read them; the feeling was as necessary to a future Poet, as the bud to the flower, or the flower to the seed.

One good effect of children teaching each other was, that it gave the Superintendent a power of precluding every thing of a procrastinating nature—the habit of procrastinating was early acquired—the Lecturer could trace it in himself, when 3 hours were allowed at school to learn what he could attain in 15 minutes; the present moment was neglected, because the future was considered as sufficient. It was a great secret in education, that there should not be a single moment allowed a child in which it should not learn something—the moment it has done learning, it should play; the doing nothing was the great error; the time that children are rendered passive, is the time that they are led into error.

* * *

---

1. From a report in the *Bristol Gazette* (November 25, 1813) of a lecture that C gave on November 18, 1813, in Bristol (*Lects 1808–19* [CC], 1:585–86, 589). C's own fragmentary notes are reprinted in CN, 3:4181 and *Lects 1808–19* [CC], 1:581–82). The context of the lecture was an ongoing debate between supporters of rival systems of primary education, one by Andrew Bell (1753–1832) and the other by Joseph Lancaster (1778–1838). In both systems the more advanced pupils tutored the less advanced ones, thereby enabling the teacher to oversee a large class. The chief difference between the systems was that Lancaster's encouraged the teacher to maintain discipline with corporal punishment, whereas Bell's required the pupils themselves to decide when and how punishments should be administered. C, who in the *Biographia* recalled the beatings he had received in school, first proclaimed his support for Bell publicly in a lecture of May 3, 1808 (*Lects 1808–19* [CC], 1:96–104).
2. C's etymology is correct: "education" and "educe" both derive from the Latin verb *educere*, meaning "draw out."
3. C probably chose Scott as an example because he was one of the most popular poets of the time.
4. Edward Young (1683–1765) and Thomas Gray (1716–1771), English poets popular during C's youth, when he himself was an admirer of Gray in particular.

Of the difference of education between the higher and middle classes, he should speak with the deepest feeling; the ladder of privileged society in this country was not constituted of disproportionate steps, it was consistent with all order and true freedom. In the first part of education there should be no difference; all moral and religious truths were essential to all; the middle classes were not only to be useful, but the higher the same; but to render the latter so, all that was necessary was a different degree of *acquirement*, a gradation of *acquisition of language and knowledge*, proportionate to the sphere in which they were to move.

* * *

Evil[1]

I will at least make the attempt to explain to myself the Origin of moral Evil from the *streamy* Nature of Association, which Thinking = Reason, curbs & rudders/how this comes to be so difficult/Do not the bad Passions in Dreams throw light & shew proof upon this Hypothesis?—Explain those bad Passions: & I shall gain Light, I am sure—A Clue! A Clue! * * * But take in the blessedness of Innocent Children, the blessedness of sweet Sleep, &c &c &c: are these or are they not contradictions to the evil from *streamy* association?—I hope not: all is to be thought *over* and *into*—but what is the height, & ideal of mere association?—Delirium—But how far is the state produced by Pain & Denaturalization? And what are these?—In short, as far as I can see any thing in this Total Mist, Vice is imperfect yet existing Volition, giving diseased Currents of association, because it yields on all sides & *yet* is—So think of Madness:—O if I live! Grasmere, Dec. 29, 1803.

Feelings[1]

—and the deep power of Joy
We see into the *Life* of Things—[2]

i.e. By deep feeling we make our *Ideas dim*—& this is what we mean by our Life—ourselves. I think of the Wall—it is before me, a distinct Image—here. I necessarily think of the *Idea* & the Thinking I as two distinct & opposite Things. Now let me think of *myself*—of the thinking Being—the Idea becomes dim whatever it be—so dim that I know not what it is—but the Feeling is deep & steady—and this I call *I*—identifying the Percipient & the Perceived.[3]

---

1. A notebook entry of December 29, 1803 (CN, 1:1770).
1. A notebook entry of February–March 1801 (CN, 1:921).
2. Wordsworth, "Lines Composed a Few Miles above Tintern Abbey," lines 50–51. This was the final poem in *LB* (1798).
3. C is implicitly criticizing René Descartes, who maintained that "clear and distinct" ideas and a recognition of the thinking self were the basis of philosophical thought. C suggests that thinking of oneself involves feeling rather than rational cognition, since in the self the distinction between knowing subject and known object is dissolved. This point is expressed more fully in the *Biographia*, chapter 12.

The French Revolution[1]

Atrocious were the crimes of the French Revolution, and dreadful has been their punishment. Do not then let us forget or transfer the benefits which it has produced. The Revolution was not brought about, any more than it was begun, by the Terrorists—No! nor which has been so endlessly asserted, by the irreligious doctrines of philosophers whom Vanity & Experience of Popery[2] had misled into Irreligion, may have had in the complex cause of revolutionary Preparation.—The Infidels were, in numbers at least, an inconsiderable Minority in the Constitutional Assembly.[3] No! Let the truth be told! Ignorant, inexperienced, and presumptuous they were * * * But sanguinary, despisers of God and the Moral Law they were not—. Had they been so, never could they have effected what they did effect!—They broke down the Monasteries, Nunneries; restored the Lands & Domains of the Church to an independent agriculture of the Country;[4] destroyed the whole Babel of feudal Vexations; & established the equal Descent of Property by Gavelkind[5]—Were these, think you, small Blessings?—Ask of our late Travellers the state of France, at present, under all the abominations of a ferocious Despotism, & the Conscript Code[6]—If you find the empire in many respects more prosperous than a good man would wish * * * to what can you attribute these blessings but to the measures of the first Constituent Assembly.—O yet this shall be suspicious Reasoning! The snake of Jacobinism[7] in the Grass!—And our present opposition Orators, nay, some of our Ministers, choose against all possibility as well as dates & documents to attribute them to the stupendous Wisdom of Napoleon, whom Mr Ponsonby,[8] a few nights past, pronounced the greatest & wisest human Being that ever existed on Earth!! Good God! in what a state must that heart and Mind be which can find it more delightful to refer benefits to selfish Cunning, oath-trampling Usurpation, remorseless Tyranny, and thirst

1. From a notebook entry of c. June 1, 1810 (CN, 3:3845).
2. Roman Catholicism.
3. I.e., the Constituent Assembly, which was created in July 1789 by disaffected representatives of the vast majority of French people (the so-called Third Estate) who were neither aristocrats nor clergymen. In addition to instituting the reforms that C proceeds to list, the assembly issued the foundational "Declaration of the Rights of Man and the Citizen" and drew up a new constitution, which King Louis XVI was forced to sign on September 14, 1791, after which the assembly broke up.
4. In 1789 the Constituent Assembly appropriated the lands of the Roman Catholic Church and sold them to help pay off the national debt; in 1790 it dissolved the monasteries and convents and required priests to swear an oath of allegiance to the government.
5. The equal division of a deceased person's property among all the sons. On March 15, 1790, the Constituent Assembly abolished primogeniture, in which only the eldest son inherits the property.
6. The French Civil Code, popularly known as the Code Napoléon, was introduced by Napoleon in 1804 and briefly imposed on all areas under French control (hence "conscript"). Establishing personal and property rights, the Code Napoléon, which C read in an Italian translation of 1806 (see CM [CC], 3:932–33), still forms the basis of French law.
7. For C's view of Jacobins, see "Once a Jacobin Always a Jacobin" (p. 299 herein).
8. George Ponsonby (1755–1817), leader of the Whig opposition in the House of Commons, had praised Napoleon (against whom Britain was at war) in a speech of May 25, 1810: "As a military—as a political man; as a man of general activity, Bonaparte was unquestionably the greatest man that had ever lived on the face of the earth" (quoted in CN, 3:3845n).

of War & Rapine unquenchable, than to enthusiastic and mistaken, yet sincere & disinterested Love of Freedom and of Humanity! * * *

John Keats[1]

A loose, not well-dressed youth, met Mr. ———[2] and myself in a lane near Highgate. ——— knew him, and spoke. It was Keats. He was introduced to me, and staid a minute or so. After he had left us a little way, he came back, and said: "Let me carry away the memory, Coleridge, of having pressed your hand!"[3]—"There is death in that hand." I said to ———, when Keats was gone; yet this was, I believe, before the consumption showed itself distinctly.[4]

Language

1[1]

It seems to elucidate the Theory of Language, Hartley, just able to speak a few words,[2] making a fire-place of stones, with stones for fire,—four stones—fire-place—two stones—fire—/arbitrary symbols in Imagination/Hartley walked remarkably soon/& *therefore* learnt to talk rem[arkably] late.[3]

2[4]

Language & all *symbols* give *outness*[5] to Thoughts/& this the philosophical essence & purpose of Language/

1. From *Table Talk* (1835), 2:89–90 (August 14, 1832).
2. The person meant is C's friend Joseph Henry Green, who taught anatomy at Guy's Hospital, Southwark (now part of London), where Keats studied medicine in 1815–16.
3. Keats's own account of the meeting, written to his brother George on April 15, 1819, differs considerably from C's: "Last Sunday [April 11] I took a Walk towards highgate and * * * I met Mr Green our Demonstrator at Guy's in conversation with Coleridge—I joined them * * * I walked with him a[t] his alderman-after dinner pace for near two miles I suppose In those two Miles he broaches a thousand things—let me see if I can give you a list—Nightingales, Poetry—on Poetical sensation—Metaphysics—Different genera and species of Dreams—Nightmare—a dream accompanied by a sense of touch—single and double touch—A dream related—First and second consciousness—the difference explained between will and Volition—so m[an]y metaphysicians from a want of smoking the second consciousness—Monsters—the Kraken—Mermaids—southey believes in them—southeys belief too much diluted—A Ghost story—Good morning—I heard his voice as he came towards me—I heard it as he moved away—I had heard it all the interval—if it may be called so. He was civil enough to ask me to call on him at Highgate Good Night!" (*The Letters of John Keats*, ed. Hyder Edward Rollins [Cambridge, Mass., 1958], 2:88–89).
4. Keats evidently did not know that he had tuberculosis until he coughed up blood on the morning of February 3, 1820 (see Walter Jackson Bate, *John Keats* [Cambridge, Mass., 1963], 636). He died just over a year later, in Rome.
1. A notebook entry of February–March 1801 (CN, 1:918).
2. C's son Hartley was four and a half years old.
3. It was an important proposition in book 3 of Locke's extremely influential *Essay concerning Human Understanding* (1690), and widely accepted in 18th-century British and French linguistics, that language consisted of arbitrary signs of ideas.
4. A notebook entry of c. April 1803 (CN, 1:1387).
5. External form. C appropriated the term from George Berkeley, who used it in his *Essays towards a New Theory of Vision* (1709) and *Treatise concerning the Principles of Human Knowledge* (1710) as a synonym for "distance." C used the term again in a similar context in a notebook entry of May 1808 (see "Symbol," p. 609 herein).

3[6]

* * *For all words express either being or action, or the predominance of the one over the other. In philosophical grammar, they are either substantives, or verbs, or as adnouns[7] and adverbs express the modification of the one by the other. But the verb substantive ("am," *sum*, εἰμι)[8] expresses the identity or coinherence of being and act. It is the act of being. All other words therefore may be considered as tending from this point, or more truly from the mid-point of the line, the *punctum indifferentiae* representing the *punctum identitatis*,[9] even as the whole line represents the same point as produced or polarised.[1]

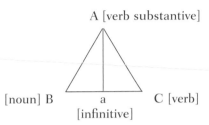

A [verb substantive]

[noun] B   a   C [verb]
[infinitive]

In this simple diagram A (= the point of identity) is supposed to generate by perpetual eradiation the line *BC*, the pole *B* representing being in its greatest predominance, and the pole *C* action in like manner: while the point *a*, expressing the indifference of being and action, of substantive and verb, is the more especial representative or analogon of the *point A*, *as* a point. A, the the point of identity, is verb and substantive in one and as one; *a*, the point of indifference, is *either* verb *or* substantive, or even both at the same time, but *not* in the same *relation*. Such in grammar is the *infinitive*: and though instances of its functions as indifferently verb or substantive are far more frequent and idiomatic in the Greek, Italian, French, and German languages, they are not wanting in our own. Take, for example, the two following lines from Spenser:

> For not to dip the hero in the lake
> Could save the son of Thetis from *to die*.[2]

6. From the *Logic* (CC), 16–17. The date of composition is uncertain but probably falls between 1819 and 1823.
7. Adjectives. *Substantives*: nouns.
8. "I am" (Latin and Greek).
9. "Point of indifference" (i.e., lack of differentiation) and "point of identity," corresponding to point *a* (the infinitive) in the diagram.
1. In deriving all words from the utterance "I am," in which he considers verb and noun to be united, C rejects both sides of an ancient controversy (revived in the 18th century) about the priority of nouns and verbs. In a notebook entry of March 1820 he explicitly identifies the "verb substantive" as the "grammatical correspondent" of "the absolute I AM" (a reference to God's self-affirmation in Exodus 3.14: "I am that I am"), thus implying that language derives ultimately from God. C's linguistic theory is opposed to the Lockean theory (represented by John Horne Tooke) that words originated as names for things perceived by the senses. On the "I am" as a first principle in philosophy, see the *Biographia* (pp. 475, 488 herein); on C's place in the noun–verb controversy, see James McKusick, *Coleridge's Philosophy of Language*, 33–52, 134–37.
2. Edmund Spenser, "The Ruins of Time" (1591), lines 428–89 (var.). The example and its explanation are taken from James Harris, *Hermes: or, A Philosophical Inquiry concerning Language and Universal Grammar* (London, 1751), 164n (*Logic* [CC], 17n. 3). Harris (1709–1780) also applied the term "verb substantive" to verbs expressing existence (88–93).

Here the infinitive, "to dip," is a substantive as the nominative case of the verb, "could save"; and at the *same* time but in a different relation, it is a verb active, governing "the hero" as its accusative case or object. So too the verb neuter is governed as a substantive in "from to die"; and in Greek the preceding article would have been declined in the case required by the preposition.[3]

Life[1]

*   *   *

To *account* for Life is one thing; to explain Life another. In the first we are supposed to state something prior (if not in time, yet in the order of Nature) to the thing accounted for, as the ground or cause of that thing, or (what comprises the meaning and force of both words) as its *sufficient cause, quae et facit, et subest.*[2] And to this, in the question of Life, I know of no possible answer, but GOD. To account for a thing is to see into the principle of its possibility, and from that principle to evolve its being. * * * To explain a power, on the other hand, is * * * to unfold it or spread it out: *ex implicito planum facere.*[3] In the present instance, such an explanation would consist in the reduction of the idea of Life to its simplest and most comprehensive form or mode of action; that is, to some characteristic *instinct* or *tendency*, evident in all its manifestations, and involved in the idea itself. * * *

From the preceding it should appear that the most comprehensive formula to which life is reducible, would be that of the internal copula[4] of bodies, or (if we may venture to borrow a phrase from the Platonic school) the *power* which discloses itself from within as a principle of *unity* in the *many.* * * * I should at the same time have borrowed a scholastic *term*, and defined life *absolutely*, as the principle of unity in *multeity*,[5]

---

3. I.e., in ancient Greek "to die" would have been treated as a verbal noun, the gender of which would have been neuter and the grammatical case of which would have been determined by the equivalent of the English preposition "from." In Greek the number, gender, and case of a noun are indicated by a preceding definite article.

1. From *Hints towards the Formation of a More Comprehensive Theory of Life,* ed. Seth B. Watson (London, 1848), 35–36, 41–42. This essay was written by C, probably in November–December 1816, for James Gillman to present as the theoretical section of his submission for an essay prize awarded annually by the Royal College of Surgeons. The subject was the glandular disease known as scrofula, but C digressed into a long reflection on the nature of life, and the essay was not finished in time for the deadline of December 25, 1816 (*SW&F* [CC], 454). Gillman made no submission, and C's contribution remained unpublished until after Gillman's death, when his son James Gillman Jr. showed the manuscript (which is now lost) to the physician Seth Watson, who published it on his own without permission from the Gillman family or from C's literary executors. For further details of this essay and a review of its scientific context, see *SW&F* (CC), 454–56, 481–84; and Trevor Levere, *Poetry Realized in Nature,* 42–46, 161–66, 206–09. See also p. 573, n. 3 herein.

2. "Which both makes [a thing] and lies behind it."

3. "To make something plain from something confused." Literally, "to make something flat from something folded up."

4. Link or connection.

5. "The quality or condition of being many or consisting of many parts" (*OED*). A favorite phrase of C's, which he also used as a definition of beauty, although in the sense of "the many seen as one" (*Lects 1808–19* [CC], 2:220; see also p. 345, n. 5 herein).

as far as the former, the unity to wit, is produced *ab intra;*[6] but *emi-nently* * * * I define life as *the principle of individuation*, or the power which unites a given *all* into a *whole* that is presupposed by all its parts.[7] The link which combines the two,[8] and acts throughout both, will, of course, be defined by the *tendency* to *individuation.* * * *

Love, Lust, and Friendship

1[1]

I have loved—& still do love—*truly* i.e. not in a fanciful attribution of certain ideal perfections to an existing Being, who possesses perhaps no one of them; but in a true & palpable sympathy of manners, senti-ments, & affections. So have I loved *one* Woman; & believe that such a love of such a Woman is the highest Friendship—for we cannot love a Friend as a Woman, but we can love a Woman as a Friend.[2]

2[3]

Unhappy I!—I have loved many more than ever I loved myself, & one beyond myself, & beyond all things, & all persons[4]—but never, never, have I met with any Being who did not love many better than they loved me—Several Women that would have married me because no one whom they better loved, was in their power; but never any one, who would have married me, because they loved *me* better than any one. This seems the complaint of Selfishness; yet it is in truth the pang most felt by such as have the least selfishness & most constancy of nature, such as would revolt from the very thought, that they could cease to love, or love less A to whom they had given their love, because they had found in B or C. greater Beauty, or Wit.—O mercy! O mercy!—In the Anger of Agony I could almost bid ;κϑγ[5] look at her-

---

6. "From within."
7. In a footnote C distinguished this power, which comes from within a being itself, from me-chanical formation, which is imposed on something from outside it: "Thus we may say that whatever is organized from without, is a product of mechanism; whatever is mechanized from within, is a production of organization." C's conception of life as the power of self-organization was indebted to the writings of the Norwegian-born German geologist and philosopher Henrik Steffens (1773–1845), in particular his *Beyträge zur innern Naturgeschichte der Erde* (Contributions to the Inner Natural History of the Earth) (1801) and *Grundzüge der philosophischen Naturwissenschaft* (Fundamentals of Philosophical Nat-ural Science) (1806). For C's marginalia on these works, see *CM* (CC), 5:255–67, 352–60.
8. I.e., the whole and the parts.
1. An annotation of 1802 on Sir Thomas Browne, *Religio Medici*, 6th ed. (1669): *CM* (CC), 1:751.
2. C is referring to his unrequited love for Sara Hutchinson (see also p. 590, n. 7 herein).
3. A notebook entry of c. 1808–09 (CN, 3:3442). In 1809 C was living with the Wordsworths and dictating essays for his periodical *The Friend* to Sara Hutchinson.
4. Sara Hutchinson.
5. "Asra," C's name for Sara Hutchinson, who never married. Kathleen Coburn argues that the sentiments expressed in this entry suggest a date before C's falling out with Wordsworth in October 1810, after which he and Asra ceased corresponding with each other and seldom saw each other (CN, 3:3442n). Immediately after the quarrel C wrote bitterly about Hutchinson in his notebook: "Not *Loved* but one whose Love is what has given pleasure/ O this is a sad mistake! How perceptibly has ———'s love for poor C lessened since he has procured other enthusiastic admirers!" (CN, 3:3991).

self, & into herself, & then ask whether *she* beloved constantly has a right to compare others with me, & love them better because they are more vigorous, or more this thing or the other—Love *more!*—O blasphemy! As if in the Love, I am speaking of, there were any *degrees*—as if more than *one* COULD in this sense be LOVED.

<h2 style="text-align:center">3⁶</h2>

Among many other proofs, which I have noted elsewhere, this may be added, of the difference in kind between Friendship and Love: and in confutation of the debasing but alas! the common opinion, that the purest love is no more than Friendship + Lust. Were this the truth, a woman might be in love with half a dozen Persons. But all, who are capable of Love, know that it must be exclusive—and the reason is evident, where it is seen that Friendship is Sympathy, but Love Correspondence—not a juxta-position of homonimous pole (gleichnämigen Polen)[7] but the Union of opposite Poles. Hence too the more intensive the Individuality in a man, the more necessarily is his Love exclusive.

Madness[1]

Madness is not simply a bodily disease. It is the sleep of the spirit with certain conditions of wakefulness; that is to say, lucid intervals. During this sleep, or recession of the spirit, the lower or bestial states of life rise up into action and prominence. It is an awful thing to be eternally tempted by the perverted senses. The reason may resist—it does resist—for a long time; but too often, at length, it yields for a moment, and the man is mad for ever. An act of the will is, in many instances, precedent to complete insanity. I think it was Bishop Butler, who said, that he was all his life struggling against the devilish suggestions of his senses, which would have maddened him, if he had relaxed the stern wakefulness of his reason for a single moment.[2]

6. An annotation of c. 1826 on Wilhem De Wette, *Theodor oder des Zweiflers Weihe* (Theodor, or The Skeptic's Consecration) (1822) (*CM* [CC], 2:196–97). De Wette equates friendship with love and insists that "the more one loves, the more capable one becomes of love, and the more of it one can bestow on one's friends."
7. An error for *gleichnamigen Polen*, "poles with the same name"—which is also the meaning of "homonimous" (as C spells the word "homonymous").
1. *Table Talk* (1835), 1:109–10 (May 1, 1830).
2. C probably means Joseph Butler (1692–1752), bishop of Durham and author of *The Analogy of Religion Natural and Revealed to the Constitution and Course of Nature* (1736), although the anecdote is apparently apocryphal (see *TT* [CC], 1:108n. 4).

Nature

1[1]

Nature, the πολυμηχανος Εγρανια,[2] an ever industrious Penelope[3] for ever unravelling what she had woven, for ever weaving what she had unravelled.

2[4]

Contemplate the Plants & the lower species of animal Life, [such] as Insects—then we may find at once an instance & an illustration of the poetic process. In them we find united the conquest of all the circumstances of place, soil, climate, element &c over the living power, & at the same time the victory of the living Power over these circumstances—every living object in nature exists as the reconciliation of contradictions, by the law of Balance.—The vital principle of the Plant can make itself manifest only by embodying itself in the materials that immediately surround it, and in the very elements, into which it may be decomposed, bears witness of its birth place & the conditions of its outward growth.—On the other hand, it takes them up into itself, forces them into parts of its own Life, modifies & transmutes every power by which it is itself modified: & the result is, a living whole, in which we may in thought & by artificial Abstraction distinguish the material Body from the indwelling Spirit, the contingent or accidental from the universal & essential, but in reality, in the thing itself, we cannot separate them.[5]

*   *   *

3[6]

* * * I say, that all the primary Powers of Nature may be reduced to Two, each of which produces two others, and a third as the Union of both.—

For in the first place, all Power is either that, the nature of which is to *manifest*; or that, the nature of which is to hide or keep hidden—. It either tends to draw *out* and to *distinguish*; or to draw *back* & to bring into one *mass*, *without* distinction of parts.—Let us call the latter the

1. Notebook entry of December 1804 (*CN*, 2:2351).
2. "Resourceful worker" (the second word should be *erganē*, not *egrania*). C would have encountered the adjective *polymēchanos* in Homer's *Iliad* and *Odyssey*, where it is frequently applied to Odysseus (e.g., *Iliad* 2.173).
3. Odysseus's wife in the *Odyssey*. Awaiting her husband's return from the Trojan War, she puts off suitors by promising to choose one of them after she has finished weaving a shroud for Odysseus's father; but every night she unravels what she has woven during the day.
4. From C's notes for a lecture of May 26, 1812, on Greek drama (*Lects 1808–19* [CC], 1:447).
5. I.e., a plant's growth is the result of the harmonious interaction between the properties of the plant itself and those of its environment, the plant and the environment each being to some degree transformed by the other in the process.
6. From a manuscript fragment of c. 1820, perhaps intended for Joseph Henry Green (*SW&F* [CC], 849–51).

Agglomerative Power; the former the Distinctive Power: or (to avoid repeating such long-tailed words) A and D.[7]

A tends *inward* and *to* the centre, and is therefore *intro*-active or what is called centri*petal*.

D. tends *outward, from* the center; or *to* the periphery (i.e. circumference.) D. is therefore *extröitive*,[8] or what is called centri*fugal*.

Or for the sake of brevity we may name A. the central, D. the peripheric Power. But it would be better still to copy Moses,[9] and call the Distinctive Power LIGHT, and the agglomerative or *amassive* Power, DARKNESS—N.b. the *power* of Darkness, that is, Opacity, or what causes *opaqueness; not* Darkness, considered as the mere Absence of Light:—You are likewise to keep in mind with regard to the Power, LIGHT, that the word in Gen. I. v. 3 does not mean visual Light solar Light, which was not yet in existence;[1] but that [it] *goes forth to declare*, like a word spoken; or *remains* on the surface (or *outside*) to *distinguish*, like a word *written*; and in both cases, makes the thing *outw*ard, and *outers* (now spelt, utters) its nature. P.S. Hence the Son of God is called indifferently The Light, that lighteth; and the Word.[2]

But as A. is the principle of *Weight*, (in Latin, Gravitas), the most expedient way of all will be to call the Distinctive Power, Light, and the Aggl. Power Gravity or Gravitation.

Well then, I say that all Powers may be reduced, in the first instance, into

Light & Gravity.

But each of these beget two other powers. Under Gravity we place Attraction and Repulsion: and under Light the Powers of Contraction and Dilation. But in each instance there was to be a third power, as the union of the Two:—And so we shall find it./ For from the union of the Attractive & repulsive Powers there results Solidity or the solidific Power: and from the union of Contraction and Dilation results Fluidity, or the fluidific Power.—

Now these are the *Constituent* Powers—that is, all things are constituted by them, and of course *pre*-suppose them. But after the Things are made, the same Powers re-appear *in* the things, but differently modified—and may be called the *Real* Powers, (from Res,[3] a thing) and the former *Ideal* Powers.—Thus the Ideal Power of Gravity re-appears in the *Real* Power of Magnetism: the I.P. of Light in the

---

7. In other writings, e.g., the *Theory of Life,* C referred to the agglomerative and distinctive powers "as unifying and individualising powers, or as connection with and separation from the universal life of nature" (SW&F [CC], 850n. 1).
8. *OED* defines this word as "directed to external objects" and cites a different passage from C as its only example of usage.
9. Moses as the supposed author of Genesis (which is known as the "first book of Moses").
1. In Genesis 1.3–4 God first creates light, then divides it from darkness: "And God said, Let there be light: and there was light. And God saw the light, that it was good: and God divided the light from the darkness."
2. In Middle English the verb "utter" could also be spelled "outer," and the adjective "outer" could be spelled "utter." But C's implication that the verb derives from the adjective is incorrect. *The Light, that lighteth*: in John 1.1, 9 Christ is called the Word of God and "the true Light, which lighteth every man that cometh into the world."
3. "Thing" (Latin).

R.P. of Electricity: while the union of the two is the Real Power of Galvanism.[4] And so the I.P. of Attraction is the R.P. of Negative Magnetism; the I.P. of Repulsion re-appears in the R.P. of positive Magnetism—& so

Contraction = Neg. Electricity
Dilation = Pos. Electricity.[5]

*   *   *

Opium[1]

An Ode to Pleasure—not sought for herself, but as a the conditio sine qua non[2] of virtuous activity—I not deprecating Pain, but Weight, Langor, & the soul-sickening Necessity of attending to barren bodily functions, in bowels, in stomach, or organ of Taste. Pain without gloom & anxious Horror, & from causes communicable openly to all, rheumatism, &c[3] O it is a sport!—but the Obscure, or the disgustful— the dull quasi-finger pressure on the liver, the endless Flatulence, the frightful constipation when the dead Filth *impales* the lower Gut—to weep & sweat & moan & scream for the parturience of an excrement with such pangs & such convulsions as a woman with an Infant heir of Immortality[4]/for Sleep a pandemonium of all the shames & miseries of the past Life from early childhood all huddled together, & bronzed with stormy Light of Terror & Self-torture/ O this is hard, hard, hard!—O dear God, give me strength of Soul to make one thorough Trial—if I land at Malta/ spite of all horrors to go through one month of unstimulated Nature[5]—yielding to nothing but manifest Danger of

4. Electricity produced by a chemical action, a phenomenon originally named after the Italian physiologist Luigi Galvani (1737–1798) and now known as electrochemistry. C's friend Humphry Davy conducted galvanic experiments, and galvanism occupied a central place in the *Naturphilosophie* of Schelling and his followers.

5. C, like Schelling and Henrik Steffens (see p. 597, n. 7 herein), was fond of schematizing the polar forces of nature as the points of a compass. In this instance the north pole is occupied by attraction and negative magnetism, the south by repulsion and positive magnetism, the east by contraction and negative electrical charge, and the west by dilation and positive electrical charge. At the midpoint are solidity (as the union of attraction and repulsion) and fluidity (or water, as the union of contraction and dilation). Between 1815 and 1830 C made numerous diagrams of this "compass of nature" (with occasional variations in its explanation), most notably in a notebook entry of c. 1815 (CN, 3:4226), in the *Theory of Life* (SW&F [CC], 523), in a manuscript of late 1817 (SW&F [CC], 602–03), and in annotations on Steffens (CM [CC], 5:334–35, 343–44). The appeal of the compass scheme was that it suggested the relatedness, and hence the underlying harmony, of the different forces of nature. For detailed discussion of the compass, see Trevor Levere, *Poetry Realized in Nature,* 114–19; and Raimonda Modiano, *Coleridge and the Concept of Nature,* 173–86.

1. From a notebook entry of May 13, 1804 (CN, 2:2091). C was aboard a ship bound for Malta when he wrote this entry.

2. "Indispensable condition."

3. I.e., the pain of constipation, which in C's case was especially shameful because it was a consequence of his opium use and could not be discussed openly with others, unlike the pains caused by rheumatism or other afflictions.

4. Four days earlier, in what C described in his notebook as "a day of Horror," his constipation had become so painful that he submitted to the humiliation of receiving an enema from the ship's surgeon (CN, 2:2085).

5. Without using opium. C's view of his dependence on opium as a moral failing was characteristic of his time. See also the letters C wrote to James Morgan in 1814, when his addiction had become so debilitating that he had himself confined in a friend's home and kept under constant watch (pp. 637–40 herein).

Life!—O great God! Grant me grace truly to look into myself, & to begin the serious work of Self-amendment.

* * *

Pantheism

1[1]

* * * In strict accordance with Reason, therefore, the Bible begins the History of Mankind with declaring the first state of Religion—namely, that there is but one Being worthy the name of God—and that he is a *living* God, all-good, all-wise, and Almighty: the Maker of all things and the *Father* of all Men. Now this is of high importance as an historical fact no less than as a religious truth: as you will hereafter find.—Now a Watch-maker[2] is not the same as a Watch; nor is a Father the same as his Children. In the first Religion, therefore, God was reverently distinguished from the World and the Life spread throughout the World.

Secondly, we learn that God delegated a portion of his Authority to the Father in each Family. The Family was the Representative of God to his Family, and of his Family to God. In other words, the Father was both the first human Sovereign, and the first Priest. The original Government was patriarchal: and the patriarchal Government united in itself the Kingly and the Sacredotal.[3] Thirdly, men became corrupt—yet not so entirely but that those men, who most faithfully followed the maxims and retained possession of the Knowledge and the Wisdom of the first Fathers, were allowed an Authority over the rest—and thus the Second Government was Sacerdotal or theocratic. Fourthly, the Corruption increased, and there took place a dreadful falling-off in the first great and fundamental Truth of Religion itself. God was confounded with his Works. The World was worshipped as God, and the Elements, the Heavenly Bodies and the real or supposed starry influences were adored, at first as Divine Attributes (= the Numina Dei) and then as themselves Divinities or Dei Minores.[4] And so general was

1. From a lesson on the origin of human society and religion that C wrote out, possibly in October 1826, for James Gillman's son James Jr. (*SW&F* [CC], 1355–56). C here repeats the historical survey that he presented in more detail in "On the Prometheus of Aeschylus," a lecture he gave to the Royal Society of Literature on May 18, 1825 (*SW&F* [CC], 1251–1301). His theory of pantheism and polytheism as corruptions of an originally monotheistic religion rejected the well-known arguments of David Hume (*Natural History of Religion*, 1757) and William Warburton (*The Divine Legation of Moses*, 1737–41) that polytheism had preceded monotheism. C's theory had more in common with that of the classical philologist Friedrich Creuzer (1771–1858), whose massive study in comparative religion, *Symbolik und Mythologie der alten Völker* (Symbolism and Mythology of Ancient Peoples) (1810–12), he read in 1821; but he rejected Creuzer's assertion that monotheism had originated in India (see *CN*, 4:4831–32, 4839).
2. An image associated with William Paley (1743–1805), who used it at the beginning of his *Natural Theology* (1802) as a metaphor for God as creator. C strongly disapproved of "the watch-making scheme that knows nothing of the Maker but what can be proved out of the Watch" (*CM* [CC], 2:324) and probably used the metaphor here simply because it would have been easy for his pupil to understand.
3. C's identification of the earliest government with the structure of the patriarchal family represents his alternative to the social-contract theories of Hobbes and Rousseau, both of which postulated an arrangement willingly entered into by individuals as the origin of government.
4. "Lesser gods." *Numina Dei*: "powers of God."

this Apostacy that it would doubtless have become universal, if God had not graciously selected one particular Family,[5] and in this, by a series of providential and miraculous Acts, kept alive the knowledge and the practice of the true Religion: which we will henceforward name Monotheism, while the Corrupt Belief we will distinguish by the name of Pantheism, of which Polytheism and Idolatry were the inevitable and speedy Consequences.

* * *

2[6]

* * * Now that the *personëity* of God, the idea of God as the I AM,[7] is presented more prominently in Scripture, than the (so called) physical attributes, is most true; and forms one of the distinctive characters of its superior worth and value. It was by dwelling too exclusively on the Infinities, that the ancient Greek Philosophers, Plato excepted, fell into Pantheism, as in later times did Spinosa.[8] *I forbid you*, says Plato, *to call God the Infinite! If you dare name him at all, say rather the Measure of Infinity.*[9]

* * *

Parliamentary Reform[1]

I could not help smiling, in reading the report of Lord Grey's speech in the House of Lords, the other night, when he asked Lord Wicklow whether he seriously believed that he, Lord Grey, or any of the ministers, intended to subvert the institutions of the country.[2] Had I been in

5. The Jews.
6. From *On the Constitution of the Church and State* (1830), 201–02 (an annotation on Isaac Taylor, *Natural History of Enthusiasm* [1829]). C is responding to Taylor's observation on the relative lack of comment in the Bible on God's nature: "By some naked affirmations we are indeed secured against false and grovelling notions of the Divine nature; but these hints are incidental, and so scanty, that every excursive mind goes far beyond them in its conceptions of the infinite attributes" (26).
7. On God as the "I am," see pp. 475–78 and p. 595, n. 1 herein. *Personëity*: C's coinage, meaning "personhood" or "essence as a person."
8. C probably means the Neoplatonists in particular (see "Neoplatonism" in the Glossary). Elsewhere he accused Plotinus of conceiving the world as continuous with its creator (see *AR* [CC], 169). Baruch de Spinoza's *Ethics* (1677) proceeds from a definition of God as "a being absolutely infinite, i.e. a substance consisting of an infinity of attributes, each of which expresses an eternal and infinite essence" (*Collected Works*, trans. Edwin Curley [Princeton, N.J., 1988], 1:409). Since Spinoza considered all things to be attributes or modes of God, he made no distinction between God and the world. C's criticism of Spinoza's pantheism was usually tempered by praise for his character and religious feeling (see *SW&F* [CC], 607–24; *CM* [CC], 5:199–220). On C's general ambivalence about pantheism, see Thomas McFarland, *Coleridge and the Pantheist Tradition*.
9. A paraphrase of Plato's insistence in *Laws* 4.716c that God has no measure but is "the measure of all things." *C&S* (CC), 168n. 6 suggests that C's source was not the Platonic passage itself but a paraphrase of it in F. H. Jacobi's *Von den göttlichen Dingen* (On the Divine Things) (1811) or in a quotation of Jacobi's paraphrase by Schelling in his own *Denkmal der Schrift von den göttlichen Dingen* (Memorial to the Work on the Divine Things) (Tübingen, 1812), 96–97.
1. *Table Talk* (1835), 2:23–25 (February 22, 1832).
2. C refers to a debate in the House of Lords on February 17, 1832, in which the prime minister, Charles Grey, second Earl Grey (1764–1845), challenged William Howard, fourth earl

Lord Wicklow's place, I should have been tempted to answer this question something in the following way:—"Waiving the charge in an offensive sense of personal consciousness against the noble earl, and all but one or two of his colleagues, upon my honour, and in the presence of Almighty God, I answer, Yes! You have destroyed the freedom of parliament; you have done your best to shut the door of the House of Commons to the property, the birth, the rank, the wisdom of the people, and have flung it open to their passions and their follies. You have agitated the mob, and thrown the balance of political power into the hands of that class (the shopkeepers) which, in all countries and in all ages, has been, is now, and ever will be, the least patriotic and the least conservative of any.[3] You are now preparing to destroy for ever the constitutional independence of the House of Lords; you are for ever displacing it from its supremacy as a co-ordinate estate of the realm; and whether you succeed in passing your bill by actually swamping our votes by a batch of new peers, or by frightening a sufficient number of us out of our opinions by the threat of one,—equally you will have superseded the triple assent which the constitution requires to the enactment of a valid law, and have left the king alone with the delegates of the populace!"[4]

Philosophy[1]

The pith of my system is to make the senses out of the mind—not the mind of the senses, as Locke did.[2]

---

of Wicklow (1877–1869), "Could that Noble Earl believe they [the prime minister and his cabinet] were persons likely to shake the foundations of the laws, and to subvert the institutions of the Country?" (quoted in *TT* [*CC*], 1:266n. 4). Grey's Whig government had introduced the third version of its controversial parliamentary reform bill in the House of Commons on December 21, 1831, in response to the public unrest that had followed the rejection of the second version by the House of Lords on October 8. The bill was still being debated in the Commons when C made these anti-reform comments two months later.

3. C's fear that the Reform Act would shift power from the landed gentry to the mercantile middle classes was unfounded: although it abolished fifty-six parliamentary constituencies and created forty-six new ones in previously unrepresented or underrepresented areas (including Manchester, Birmingham, and Leeds), the act also increased the number of rural constituencies, so that its net effect was to favor the interests of the gentry.

4. An extreme exaggeration, since the Reform Act neither diminished the powers of the House of Lords nor satisfied popular demands for universal manhood suffrage and secret ballots. Although it extended the franchise geographically and nearly doubled the size of the electorate, the act still restricted the vote to land-owning or lease-holding men, so that the number of registered voters in 1833 (roughly 808,000) amounted to just over 3.3% of the total population of the United Kingdom (Michael Brock, *The Great Reform Act* [London, 1973], 312–13). It is unlikely that C himself would have been eligible to vote before or after the implementation of the Reform Act. *New peers*: to get his bill through the Lords (after its passage by the Commons on March 23, 1832), Lord Grey sought William IV's permission to increase the number of peers (i.e., lords) by as much as sixty. The king at first refused, but was forced to relent and recall Grey to power after the opposition Tories proved unable to form a government. The threat of new peers was sufficient to overcome the opposition to the Reform Bill, which was passed on June 4, 1832, and became law on June 7. *Triple assent*: C means approval by both houses of Parliament and the monarch.

1. *Table Talk* (1835), 2:76 (July 25, 1832).

2. An elaboration of a Latin maxim of which C was fond (see *Biographia*, chapter 9, p. 440 herein): *nihil in intellectus quod non prius in sensu, praeter intellectum ipsum* ("There is nothing in the mind that was not previously in the senses, except the mind itself"). He is criticizing the empiricist philosophy of Locke. The basis of C's criticism, which follows that of Kant, *Pure Reason*, is the objection that the mind itself conditions the operations of the senses.

Platonists and Aristotelians[1]

Every man is born an Aristotelian, or a Platonist. I do not think it possible that any one born an Aristotelian can become a Platonist; and I am sure that no born Platonist can ever change into an Aristotelian. They are the two classes of men, beside which it is impossible to conceive a third. The one considers a reason a quality, or attribute; the other considers it a power.[2] I believe Aristotle never could get to understand what Plato meant by an idea.[3] * * * With Plato ideas are constitutive in themselves.

Aristotle was, and still is, the sovereign lord of the understanding;— the faculty judging by the senses.[4] He was a conceptualist, and never could raise himself into that higher state, which was natural to Plato, and has been so to others, in which the understanding is distinctly contemplated, and, as it were, looked down upon from the throne of actual ideas, or living, inborn, essential truths. * * *

Poetry[1]

* * * Poetry a rationalized dream dealing [?out][2] to manifold Forms our own Feelings, that never perhaps were attached by us consciously to our own personal Selves.—What is the Lear, the Othello, but a divine Dream/all Shakespeare, & nothing Shakespeare.[3]—O there are Truths below the Surface in the subject of Sympathy, & how we *become* that which we understandly behold & hear, having, how much God perhaps only knows, created part even of the Form.—[?and so] good night.

Prayer

My Nightly Prayer[1]

Almighty God, by thy eternal Word my Creator, Redeemer & Preserver! who hast in thy free communicative goodness glorified me with the capability of knowing thee, the only one Absolute Good, the eternal I AM,[2] as the Author of my Being, & of desiring & seeking thee as its ultimate end—Who, when I fell from thee into the Misery of the

---

1. From *Table Talk* (1835), 1:182–83 (July 2, 1830).
2. The first clause refers to the Aristotelian; the second, to the Platonist.
3. Aristotle criticized Plato's theory of Forms or Ideas, rejecting the transcendence of the Forms (*Metaphysics* 987a–988a, 990a–993a, 1078b–1080a). C encountered the distinction between Platonists and Aristotelians in Goethe's *Zur Farbenlehre* (On the Theory of Colors) (1810) sometime before 1819, when he mentioned it to Joseph Henry Green (*CL*, 4:911).
4. See "[Reason and Understanding]" (p. 555, herein).
1. From a notebook entry of May 1804 (*CN*, 2:2086).
2. Kathleen Coburn's uncertain reading is "[?about]," but "out" makes more sense.
3. Later, in his literary lectures, C presented Shakespeare as a playwright who subordinated his own personality to the personalities of the characters he created (see "[On Romeo and Juliet]," p. 309 herein).
1. From a transcript of 1830 (*SW&F* [CC], 1486–88).
2. Compare C's discussion of "the great eternal I AM" in the *Biographia* (p. 475 herein).

false & evil Will, didst not abandon the poor self lost Creature, but in thy condescending Mercy didst provide an access & a return to thyself, even to thee the Holy One, in thine only begotten Son, the Way & the Truth from Everlasting, & who took on himself Humanity, Yea, became flesh, even the Man Christ Jesus, that for the Man he might be the Life & the Resurrection. O Giver of all good Gifts, who art thyself the one only Absolute Good, from whom I have received whatever good I have, whatever capability of good there is in me, and from thee Good alone,—from myself & my own corrupted Will all Evil & the consequents of Evil—with inward prostration of Will, Mind, & Affections, I adore thy infinite Majesty, I aspire to love thy transcendent Goodness * * * Thy mercies have followed me through all the hours & moments of my Life, and now I lift up my heart in awe & thankfulness for the perseveration of my Life tho' the past day, for the alleviation of my bodily sufferings & languors, for the manifold comforts, which thou hast reserved for me, yea, in thy fatherly compassion hast rescued me from the wreck of my own Sins, or sinful infirmities, for the kind & affectionate Friends thou hast raised up for me, especially for them of this Household, for the Mother & Mistress of this Family, whose love to me hath been great & faithful, & for the dear Friend, the supporter & sharer of my studies & researches,[3] but above all, for the heavenly Friend, the crucified Saviour, the glorified Mediator, Christ Jesus, and for the heavenly Comforter, source of all abiding comforts, thy Holy Spirit! * * * To Thee, great omnipresent Spirit, whose Mercy is over all thy Works, who now beholdest me, who hearest me, who hast framed my heart to seek & to trust in thee, in the name of my Lord & Saviour Christ Jesus, I humbly commit and commend my Body, Soul, & Spirit!

Glory be to thee, O God!

Religion[1]

Tuesday, an hour and ½ after Noon (½ after 1.) Feb. 12, 1805.—Thinking during my perusal of Horsley's Letters in Rep. to D[r] P. objections to the Trinity on the part of Jews, Mahometans, and Infidels,[2] it burst upon me at once as an awful Truth what 7 or 8 years ago I thought of proving with a *hollow Faith* and for an *ambiguous purpose*, my mind then wavering in its necessary passage from Unitarianism

---

3. C is referring to James Gillman and his wife, Anne.
1. A notebook entry of February 12, 1805 (CN, 2:2448). This notebook entry, which Coleridge dated with unusual precision, reveals his dissatisfaction with his Unitarianism of the 1790s and his growing acceptance of Trinitarianism.
2. *Letters from the Archdeacon of Saint Albans in Reply to Dr. Priestley* (1784), written by Samuel Horsley (1733–1806) to defend the orthodox Anglican view that the early Christian Church had asserted the consubstantiality of the Father and Son in the Trinity and hence the divinity of Christ. Horsley's opponent was Joseph Priestley, who in *An History of the Corruptions of Christianity* (1782) claimed that the early Church had been Unitarian, rejecting the divinity of Christ. Horsley's Letter 11 was headed, "The Unitarian doctrine not well calculated for the conversion of Jews, Mahometans, or Infidels of any description [to Christianity]" (CN, 2:2448n). See also the *Lectures on Revealed Religion* (p. 267 herein). *Mahometans*: Muslims.

(which I have often said is the Religion of a man, whose Reason would make him an Atheist but whose Heart and Common sense will not permit him to be so) thro' Spinosism into Plato and St John/No Christ, No God!^{3}—This I now feel with all its needful evidence, of the Understanding: would to God, my spirit were made conform thereto—that No Trinity, no God.—That Unitarianism in all its Forms is Idolatry— * * * truly the trick of Mahomet, who finding that the Mountain would not come to *him* went to the Mountain.^{4} O that this Conviction may work upon me and in me/and that my mind may be made up as to the character of Jesus, and of historical Christianity, as clearly as it is of the Logos and intellectual or spiritual Christianity—that I may be made to know either their especial and peculiar Union, or the absolute disunion in any peculiar Sense.^{5}

Self-Analysis

1^1

There are two sorts of talkative fellows whom it would be injurious to confound/& I, S. T. Coleridge, am the latter. The first sort is of those who use five hundred more words than needs to express an idea—that is not my case * * *. The second sort is of those who use five hundred more ideas, images, reasons &c than there is any need of to arrive at their object/till the only object arrived at is that the mind's eye of the bye-stander is dazzled with colours succeeding so rapidly as to leave one vague impression that there has been a great Blaze of colours all about something. Now this is my case—& a grievous fault it is/my illustrations swallow up my thesis—I feel too intensely the omnipresence of all in each, platonically speaking—or psychologically my brain-fibres, or the spiritual Light which abides in the brain marrow as visible Light appears to do in sundry rotten mackerel & other *smashy* matters, is of too general an affinity with all things/ & tho' it perceives the *difference* of things, yet is eternally pursuing the likeness, or rather that which is common/ * * *

2^2

It is a most instructive part of my Life the fact, that I have been always preyed on by some Dread, and perhaps all my faulty actions have been

3. This summary of the development of C's religious thought anticipates the one presented in chapter 10 of the *Biographia*. *Spinosism*: the pantheistic philosophy of Spinoza, to which C was attracted, despite his objections to it on moral grounds (see p. 603, n. 8 herein). C prized Plato as a philosopher who maintained the transcendence of God and, therefore, avoided identifying God with nature (*AR* [CC], 251–52n.). The Gospel according to St. John begins with the assertion that Christ is the incarnated Word of God (John 1.1–4, 14–18). C now believes that to deny Christ's divinity is tantamount to being an atheist.

4. At the age of forty, Muhammad (c. 570–c. 632) went to Mt. Hira, near Mecca, where he had a vision of the angel Gabriel, who commanded him to preach the religion that came to be called Islam.

5. C's lingering doubts about the Trinity at this point in his life seem to derive from his uncertainty about how to interpret the relation between Jesus the man and Christ the Son and Word (or Logos) of God.

1. From a notebook entry of December 1804 (CN, 2:2372).

2. From a notebook entry of January 11, 1805 (CN, 2:2398).

the consequence of some Dread or other on my mind/from fear of
Pain, or Shame, not from prospect of Pleasure/ * * *

Symbol

1[1]

Hard to express that sense of the analogy or likeness of a Thing which
enables a Symbol to represent it, so that we think of the Thing itself—
& yet knowing that the Thing is not present to us.—Surely, on this
universal fact of words & images depends by more or less meditations
the *imitation* instead of *copy* which is illustrated in very nature *shake-
spearianized/*[2]—that Proteus Essence that could assume the very
form,[3] but yet known & felt not to be the Thing by that very difference
of the Substance which made every atom of the Form another thing/—
that likeness not identity—an exact web, every line of direction miraculously the same, but the one worsted, the other silk.

2[4]

Saturday Night, April 14, 1805—In looking at objects of Nature while
I am thinking, as at yonder moon dim-glimmering thro' the dewy
window-pane, I seem rather to be seeking, as it were *asking*, a symbolical language for something within me that already and forever exists,
than observing any thing new. Even when that latter is the case, yet
still I have always an obscure feeling as if that new phænomenon were
the dim Awaking of a forgotten or hidden Truth of my inner Nature/It
is still interesting as a Word, a Symbol! It is Λογος,[5] the Creator! and
the Evolver!

* * *

3[6]

Ah! dear Book! Sole Confidant of a breaking Heart, whose social nature
compels *some* Outlet. I write more unconscious that I am writing, than
in my most earnest modes I *talk*—I am not then so unconscious of

---

1. A notebook entry of uncertain date, probably October–December 1804 but possibly as late
   as 1808 (*CN*, 2:2274).
2. C's coinage, referring to Shakespeare's subordination of his own personality to those of the
   characters in his plays, as discussed in "[On *Romeo and Juliet*]" (p. 309 herein). Just as we
   can recognize something distinctively Shakespearean in plays from which the personality of
   the playwright himself is absent, so we can recognize the absent idea or object in a symbol
   from the one that is present, even when the symbolizing object is entirely different in nature
   from what it represents. Later, e.g., in *The Statesman's Manual*, C insisted that symbols are
   inherently related to what they represent. On C's distinction between imitation and copy,
   see, e.g., "[On Dramatic Illusion]" (p. 337 herein).
3. Proteus, in Homer's *Odyssey* 4.349–70, is a sea god with the ability to change his shape
   (whence the adjective "Protean" in English).
4. From a notebook entry of April 14, 1805 (*CN*, 2:2546). C was in Malta at this time.
5. *Logos* (Greek for "word" and "reason"), specifically Christ as the Word of God (as in John
   1.1–5). In *The Statesman's Manual* C argued that the divinely instituted power of reason was
   present both in the human mind and in the organization of nature. See also "Language" (p.
   595 herein).
6. From a notebook entry of May 1808 (*CN*, 3:3325).

talking, as when I write in these dear, and only once profaned, Books,[7] I am of the act of writing—So much so, that even in the last minute or two that I have been writing on my writing, I detected that the former Habit was predominant—that I was only *thinking*. All minds must think by some *symbols*—the strongest minds possess the most vivid Symbols in the Imagination—yet this ingenerates a want, ποθον, *desiderium*,[8] for vividness of Symbol: which something that is without, that has the property of *Outness* (a word that Berkeley preferred to "Externality")[9] can alone fully gratify/even that indeed not fully—for the utmost is only an approximation to that absolute *Union*, which the soul sensible of its imperfection in itself, of its *Halfness*, yearns after, whenever it exists free from meaner passions, as Lust, Avarice, love of worldly power, passion for distinction in all its forms * * * I say, every generous mind not already filled by some one of these passions feels its *Halfness*—it cannot *think* without a symbol—neither can it *live* without something that is to be at once its Symbol, & its *Other half*.[1]

* * *

Women[1]

"Most women have no character at all," said Pope,[2] and meant it for satire. Shakespeare, who knew men and women much better, saw that it, in fact, was the perfection of women to be characterless. Every one wishes a Desdemona or Ophelia for a wife,—creatures who, though they may not always understand you, do always feel you, and feel with you.[3]

William Wordsworth[1]

I think Wordsworth possessed more of the genius of a true poet than any man I ever knew, or, as I believe, has existed in England since Milton; but it seems to me that he ought never to have abandoned the contemplative position which is peculiarly—perhaps I might say exclusively—fitted for him. His proper title is *Spectator ab extra*.[2]

7. It is not known what incident C is referring to here. In May 1808, intensely lonely and seriously ill, he was living in rooms above the noisy printing shop of the *Courier*, a newspaper for which he wrote, and lecturing on literature and education at the Royal Institution.
8. Greek and Latin for "longing" (the Greek should be πόθος, however).
9. In fact Berkeley used the term in a different sense from C (see p. 594, n. 5 herein).
1. Cf. C's notion of love as "the Union of opposite Poles," (see p. 598 herein) as well as his later definition, in *The Statesman's Manual*, of the symbol as being "consubstantial" with what it refers to (p. 359 herein).
1. *Table Talk* (1835), 1:212–13 (September 27, 1830).
2. Alexander Pope, *Moral Essays*, Epistle 2, "To a Lady" (1735), lines 1–2: "Nothing so true as what you once let fall, / 'Most women have no characters at all.' " In a note Pope explained, "their particular Characters are not so strongly mark'd as those of Men, seldom so fixed, and still more inconsistent with themselves" (*Poems*, ed. John Butt [London, 1963], 561).
3. Desdemona, married to and eventually smothered by Othello after being unjustly accused of adultery, remains unwaveringly loyal to her husband. Ophelia, devoted to Hamlet yet obedient to her father, goes insane after Hamlet rejects her and murders her father.
1. *Table Talk* (1835), 2:71–72 (July 21, 1832).
2. "Observer from the outside." For an earlier opinion of Wordsworth, see C's letter of October, 14, 1803, to Tom Poole (p. 636 herein).

THE LETTERS (1796–1820)

In an age of junk mail and electronic mail, when the sender need not trouble to establish any meaningful relationship with the recipient, it is difficult to appreciate the set of expectations that attended letter writing in Coleridge's time. Before the introduction of the adhesive postage stamp in Britain in 1840, the addressees of letters had to pay for the postage, unless they chose not to accept a letter. This arrangement had several important consequences. First, it promoted the exchange of occasional long letters, since the greater cost of frequent short letters made them less welcome to the recipient. (Someone in the habit of writing his friends three-line letters four times a day—a practice that e-mail has made both common and acceptable—would quickly have lost his friends.) Second, it encouraged recipients to treat letters as objects of value, to be preserved and passed down from one generation to the next. Third, it fostered in senders a sense of obligation to write letters that would justify their cost. The understanding that letter writing not only had its own conventions but constituted a kind of literary activity was both reflected in and reinforced by the popular epistolary novels of the eighteenth century (e.g., Samuel Richardson's *Pamela* and *Clarissa*) and the common practice of publishing prose tracts and even poems in epistolary form.

But if letter writing was no less convention-bound than any other kind of writing, Coleridge seems to have found its demands less onerous than those of writing for publication. The difference, of course, was that his letters were usually intended for a private audience and, therefore, did not have the same implications for his public reputation that his publications (or lack of them) did. Since the public would not judge him as a writer or as a man by his correspondence, neither did he have to do so. In letters, freed by the nature of the genre and by the restrictedness of the audience from the pressure to please a reviewer, meet a deadline, or sustain a logical argument, Coleridge could be more unbuttoned and spontaneous—not to mention self-indulgent. Thus we may find him ingratiating himself with his addressee, displaying his erudition, losing himself in digressions, telling jokes, dispensing advice, offering sympathy, rehearsing grievances, confessing weaknesses, begging for help. The seventeen letters chosen for inclusion here—from nearly 1,800 published in the six volumes of Coleridge's *Collected Letters*—are addressed to nine different recipients and range in date from 1796, when Coleridge was active in radical politics and beginning his poetical career, to 1820, when he had become the "sage of Highgate" and was devoting his attention to theology and conservative politics. The subjects in these letters include, to give the broadest indication, Coleridge's childhood, politics, poetry, literary projects, literary contemporaries, philosophy, marital difficulties, nightmares and stomach complaints, and opium dependence. The letters were chosen both for their biographical interest and for their relatedness to other writings in this volume.

The texts of nine letters are taken from *CL*; the remaining texts (identified in the notes) offer new transcriptions of the original manuscripts.

To John Thelwall (November 19, 1796)[1]

Saturday Nov. 19th
Oxford Street, Bristol

My dear Thelwall

Ah me! literary *Adventure* is but bread and cheese *by chance!* I keenly sympathize with you—sympathy, the only poor consolation I can offer you. Can no plan be suggested? I mention one not as myself approving it; but because it was mentioned to me—Briefly thus—If the Lovers of Freedom[2] in the principal towns would join together by eights or tens, to send for what *books* they want directly to you, & if you could place yourself in such a line that you might have books from the different Publishers at Booksellers' price.—Suppose now, that 12 or 14 people should agree together that a little order book should be kept in the *Shop* of one of them—& when any one of these wanted a book, to write it down. And as soon as enough were ordered, to make it worth the carriage, to write up to you for them?——I repeat, that I mention the plan merely because it was mentioned to me. Shame fall on the friends of Freedom if they will do nothing better! If they will do nothing better, they will not do even this!—And the plan would disgust the Country Booksellers, who ought not to be alienated.

Have you any connection with the Corresponding Society Magazine[3]—I have not seen it yet—Robert Southey is one of its benefactors—Of course, you have read the Joan of Arc.[4] Homer is the Poet for the Warrior—Milton for the Religionist—Tasso[5] for Women—Robert Southey for the Patriot. The first & fourth books of the Joan of Arc are to me more interesting than the same number of Lines in any poem whatsoever.—But you, & I, my dear Thelwall hold different *creeds* in poetry as well as religion. N'importe.[6]—By the bye, of your works I have now all, except your essay on animal vitality which I never had, & your *poems* which I bought on their first publication, & lost them.[7]

---

1. C became acquainted with Thelwall in 1796 and two years later attempted unsuccessfully, with Wordsworth, to find him accomodation in their part of Somerset. Thelwall, whose political activities had made his staying in London dangerous, went instead to Wales.
2. I.e., supporters of political reform in Britain.
3. Founded in 1792 by Thomas Hardy (1752–1832), a Scottish shoemaker, the London Corresponding Society was the first of a network of associations of tradesmen and artisans established in English and Scottish cities for the purpose of promoting parliamentary reform. In 1793–94 the corresponding societies elected delegates to a national convention on the French model, prompting a government crackdown; within three years these societies had been almost entirely suppressed. Hardy, along with Thelwall and John Horne Tooke, was tried for treason and acquitted in 1794. Thelwall was a contributor to the London Corresponding Society's *Moral and Political Reformer,* which was published for a few months in 1796.
4. *Joan of Arc: An Epic* (1796), a poem by C's brother-in-law Robert Southey, contained several hundred lines by C himself, the majority in parts 1 and 2. A reworked version of some of these lines was published separately in 1817 with additional material as "The Destiny of Nations" (see *PW*, 1:131–48, 2:1027–30; *CM* [CC], 5:108–19; and p. 125, n. 1 herein).
5. Torquato Tasso (1544–1595), an Italian poet best known for *Gerusalemme liberata* (Jerusalem Delivered) (1581), an epic poem about the capture of Jerusalem by Christians during the First Crusade (1095–99).
6. "It doesn't matter."
7. C refers to Thelwall's *Poems on Various Subjects,* 2 vols. (1787) and *An Essay towards a Definition of Animal Vitality* (1793).

From those poems I should have supposed our poetical *tastes* more nearly alike, than I find, they are.—The poem on the So[u]ls flashes Genius thro' Strophe I. Antistrophe I. & Epode I.[8]—the rest I do not perhaps understand——only I *love* these two lines—

> Yet sure the Verse that shews the friendly mind
> To Friendship's ear not harshly flows.—[9]

Your larger *Narrative* affected me greatly. It is admirably written—& displays strong Sense animated by Feeling, & illumined by Imagination—& neither in the thoughts or rhythm does it encroach on poetry.——

*   *   *

Your portrait of yourself interested me—As to me, my face, unless when animated by immediate eloquence, expresses great Sloth, & great, indeed almost ideotic, good nature. 'Tis a mere carcase of a face: fat, flabby, & expressive chiefly of inexpression.—Yet, I am told, that my eyes, eyebrows, & forehead are physiognomically good—; but of this the Deponent knoweth not. As to my shape, 'tis a good shape enough, if measured—but my gait is awkward, & the walk, & the *Whole man* indicates *indolence capable of energies.*—I am, & ever have been, a great reader—& have read almost every thing—a library-cormorant—I am *deep* in all out of the way books, whether of the monkish times, or of the puritanical aera—I have read & digested most of the Historical Writers—; but I do not *like* History. Metaphysics, & Poetry, & 'Facts of mind'—(i.e. Accounts of all the strange phantasms that ever possessed your philosophy-dreamers from Tauth, the Egyptian to Taylor, the English Pagan,[1]) are my darling Studies.—In short, I seldom read except to amuse myself—& I am almost always reading.——Of useful knowlege, I am a so-so chemist, & I love chemistry——all else is *blank*,——but I *will* be (please God) an Horticulturist & a Farmer. I compose very little—& I absolutely hate composition. Such is my dislike, that even a sense of Duty is sometimes too weak to overpower it.

I cannot breathe thro' my nose—so my mouth, with sensual thick lips, is almost always open. In conversation I am impassioned, and oppose what I deem [error] with an eagerness, which is often mistaken for personal asperity——but I am ever so swallowed up in the *thing*, that I perfectly forget my *opponent.* Such am I. I am just about to read Dupuis' 12 octavos,[2] which I have got from London. I shall read only one Octavo a week—for I cannot *speak* French at all, & I read it slowly.——

*   *   *

8. The strophe, antistrophe, and epode are the three parts of the Pindaric ode, a poetic form named after the Greek poet who established it, Pindar (c. 518–438 B.C.E.).
9. These lines have not been traced in Thelwall's *Poems on Various Subjects, Ode to Science* (1791), or *The Peripatetic* (1793). The *Ode to Science* does, however, refer to friendship.
1. Thomas Taylor (1758–1835), an English translator of Plato and Neoplatonic authors. *Tauth*: i.e., Thoth, an ancient Egyptian god traditionally identified with Hermes Trismegistus ("Thrice-great Hermes"), the supposed author of a body of theological and astrological writings actually composed in the first three centuries C.E.
2. Books of the most frequently used format, printed on sheets of paper folded three times to make eight leaves. C refers to Charles François Dupuis, *Origine de tous les cultes, ou Religion universelle* (Origin of All Faiths, or Universal Religion), 7 vols. in 12 (Paris, 1795).

To Thomas Poole (February 6, 1797)[1]

Feb. 6, 1797 Monday.

My dear Poole

I could inform the dullest author how he might write an interesting book—let him relate the events of his own Life with honesty, not disguising the feelings that accompanied them.—I never yet read even a Methodist's "Experience" in the Gospel Magazine without receiving instruction & amusement: & I should almost despair of that Man, who could peruse the Life of John Woolman[2] without an amelioration of Heart—As to my Life, it has all the charms of variety: high Life, & low Life, Vices & Virtues, great Folly & some Wisdom. However what I am depends on what I have been; and you, MY BEST FRIEND! have a right to the narration.—To me the task will be a useful one; it will renew and deepen *my* reflections on the past; and it will perhaps make you behold with no unforgiving or impatient eye those weaknesses and defects in my character, which so many untoward circumstances have concurred to plant there.——

My family on my Mother's side can be traced up, I know not, how far—The Bowdens inherited a house-stye & a pig-stye in the Exmore[3] Country, in the reign of Elizabeth, as I have been told—& to my own knowlege, they have inherited nothing better since that time.—On my father's side I can rise no higher than my Grandfather, who was dropped, when a child, in the Hundred of Coleridge in the County of Devon; christened, educated, & apprenticed by the parish.—He afterwards became a respectable Woolen-draper in the town of South Molton. / I have mentioned these particulars, as the time may come in which it will be useful to be able to prove myself a genuine Sans culotte,[4] my veins uncontaminated with one drop of Gentility. My father received a better education than the others of his Family in consequence of his own exertions, not of his superior advantages. When he was not quite 16 years old, my Grandfather became bankrupt; and by a series of misfortunes was reduced to extreme poverty. My father re-

---

1. This letter and the following four letters to Poole were written over the course of a year at Poole's request. C had first met Poole on a visit to Nether Stowey in 1794, and he became Poole's neighbor there at the latter's invitation in December 1796. These letters, which C originally agreed to write at weekly intervals, provide the fullest firsthand account of his early childhood and its emotional traumas and are less guarded and polished than the autobiographical notes he wrote much later for James Gillman (Gillman quotes from those notes in his *Life of Samuel Taylor Coleridge,* 1836). The texts of these letters have been transcribed from the manuscripts in the Victoria College Library, University of Toronto (S MS F3.58).
2. John Woolman (1729–1772), an American Quaker, known for his opposition to the slave trade and for his *Journal,* a spiritual autobiography, published in 1774. *The Gospel Magazine,* a Methodist monthly begun in 1766 and continued, with interruptions and slight changes in the title, until 1839, published short autobiographies by converts to Methodism, usually titled simply "Experience."
3. I.e., Exmoor, a hilly region on the boundary between Somerset and Devon in southwest England.
4. I.e., Sansculotte (literally "without knee-breeches"), the popular designation of a lower-class republican in the French Revolution or more generally of a supporter of the republican cause. C was not averse to suggesting a certain gentility, however, by identifying himself in some early publications as a student of Jesus College, Cambridge, and in later ones as an "Esquire."

ceived the half of his last crown & his blessing; and walked off to seek his fortune. After he had proceeded a few miles, he sate him down on the side of the road, so overwhelmed with painful thoughts that he wept audibly. A Gentleman passed by, who knew him: & enquiring into his distresses took my father with him, & settled him in a neighb'ring town as a schoolmaster. His school increased; and he got money & knowlege: for he commenced a severe & ardent student. Here too he married his first wife, by whom he had three daughters;[5] all now alive. While his first wife lived, having scraped up money enough, at the age of 20 he walked to Cambridge, entered at Sidney College, distinguished himself for Hebrew & Mathematics, & might have had a fellowship: if he had not been married.—He returned—his wife died—Judge Buller's Father gave him the living of Ottery St Mary, & put the present Judge to school with him—he married my Mother, by whom he had ten children of whom I am the youngest, born October 20,[6] 1772.

These sketches I received from my mother & Aunt; but I am utterly unable to fill them up by any particularity of times, or places, or names. Here I shall conclude my first Letter, because I cannot pledge myself for the accuracy of the accounts, & I will not therefore mingle them with those, for the accuracy of which in the minutest parts I shall hold myself amenable to the Tribunal of Truth.—You must regard this Letter, as the first chapter of an history; which is devoted to dim traditions of times too remote to be pierced by the eye of investigation.——

Yours affectionately
S. T. Coleridge

To Thomas Poole (March 1797)

Sunday March 1797

My dear Poole

My Father, (Vicar of, and Schoolmaster at, Ottery St. Mary, Devon) was a profound Mathematician, and well-versed in the Latin, Greek, & Oriental Languages. He published, or rather attempted to publish, several works: 1st, Miscellaneous Dissertations arising from the 17th and 18th Chapters of the Book of Judges; II. Sententiae excerptae,[1] for the use of his own School; 3rd (& his best work) a Critical Latin Grammar; in the preface to which he proposes a bold Innovation in the names of the Cases. My father's new nomenclature was not likely to become popular, altho' it must be allowed to be both sonorous and

---

5. Actually four.
6. Actually October 21. C's father, the Reverend John Coleridge (1719–1781), was ordained in 1750 and appointed vicar of Ottery St. Mary ten years later; his first wife, Mary Lendon, died in 1751 and in 1754 he married Ann Bowden (1727–1809), who bore him ten children between 1754 and 1772.
1. "Excerpted sentences."

expressive—exempli gratiâ—he calls the ablative the Quippe-quare-quale-quia-quidditive Case![2]—My Father made the world his confidant with respect to his Learning & ingenuity: & the world seems to have kept the secret very faithfully.—His various works, uncut, unthumbed, have been preserved free from all pollution, except that of his Family's Tails.—This piece of good-luck promises to be hereditary: for all *my* compositions have the same amiable *homestaying* propensity.—The truth is, My Father was not a first-rate Genius—he was however a first-rate Christian. I need not detain you with his Character—in learning, good-heartedness, absentness of mind, & excessive ignorance of the world, he was a perfect *Parson Adams*.[3]—My Mother was an admirable Economist, and managed exclusively.—My eldest Brother's name was John: he went over to the East Indies in the Company's Service; he was a successful Officer, & a brave one, I have heard: he died of a consumption[4] there about 8 years ago. My second Brother was called William—he went to Pembroke College, Oxford; and afterwards was assistant to Mr Newcome's School, at Hackney. He died of a putrid fever the year before my Father's death, & just as he was on the eve of marriage with Miss Jane Hart, the eldest Daughter of a very wealthy Druggist in Exeter.—My third Brother, James, has been in the army since the age of sixteen—has married a woman of fortune—and now lives at Ottery St Mary, a respectable Man. My Brother Edward, the wit of the Family, went to Pembroke College; & afterwards, to Salisbury, as assistant to Dr Skinner: he married a woman 20 years older than his Mother. She is dead: & he now lives at Ottery St Mary, an idle Parson. My fifth Brother, George, was educated at Pembroke College, Oxford; and from thence went to Mr Newcome's, Hackney, on the death of William. He stayed there fourteen years: when the living of Ottery St Mary[5] was given him—there he now has a fine school, and has lately married Miss Jane Hart; who with beauty, & wealth, had remained a faithful Widow to the memory of William for 16 years.—My Brother George[6] is a man of reflective mind & elegant Genius. He possesses Learning in a greater degree than any of the Family, excepting myself. His manners are grave, & hued over with a tender sadness. In his moral character he approaches every way nearer to Perfection than any man I ever yet knew—indeed, he is worth the whole family in a Lump. My sixth Brother, Luke (indeed the seventh, for one Brother, the second, died in his Infancy, & I had forgot to mention him) was bred as a medical Man—he married

2. A compound adjective formed from the Latin words meaning, respectively, "for indeed," "by what means," "of what kind," "because," and "who/which/what"—examples of the kinds of questions answered by the ablative case, which is used to express direction, cause, agency, manner, time, place, etc.
3. The learned but unworldly clergyman in Henry Fielding's novel *Joseph Andrews* (1742).
4. The family correspondence concerning John contains hints that his death was a suicide, although C himself may have been unaware of this (see James Engell, *Coleridge: The Early Family Letters*, 85–88, 94n.).
5. In 1794 George Coleridge was appointed headmaster of the King Henry VIII Grammar School in Ottery St. Mary, a position once held by his father, but he did not follow his father as vicar of St. Mary's.
6. C dedicated his *Poems* of 1797 to George (see "To the Rev. George Coleridge," p. 44 herein).

Miss Sara Hart: and died at the age of 22,[7] leaving one child, a lovely Boy, still alive. My Brother Luke was a man of uncommon Genius,—a severe student, & a good man.——The 8th Child was a Sister, Anne— she died a little after my Brother Luke—aged 21.

> Rest, gentle Shade! & wait thy Maker's will;
> Then rise *unchang'd*, and be an Angel still![8]

The 9th Child was called Francis: he went out as a Midshipman, under Admiral Graves—his Ship lay on the Bengal Coast—& he accidentally met his Brother John—who took him to Land, & procured him a Commission in the Army.—He shot himself (having been left carelessly by his attendant) in a delirious fever brought on by his excessive exertions at the siege of Seringapatam: at which his conduct had been so gallant, that Lord Cornwallis payed him a high compliment in the presence of the army, & presented him with a valuable gold Watch, which my Mother now has.—All my Brothers are remarkably handsome; but they were as inferior to Francis as I am to them. He went by the name of 'the handsome Coleridge.' The tenth & last Child was S. T. Coleridge, the subject of these Epistles: born (as I told you in my last) October 20th, 1772.

From October 20th, 1772 to October 20th, 1773.——Christened Samuel Taylor Coleridge—my Godfather's name being Samuel Taylor Esq. I had another Godfather, his name was Evans: & two Godmothers; both called "Monday"—[9]

From October 20th, 1773 to October 20th 1774.——In this year I was carelessly left by my Nurse—ran to the Fire, and pulled out a live coal—burnt myself dreadfully—while my hand was being Drest by a Mr Young, I spoke for the first time (so my Mother informs me) & said—"Nasty Doctor Young"!—The snatching at fire, & the circumstance of my first words expressing hatred to professional men, are they at all *ominous*? This Year, I went to School—My Schoolmistress, the very image of Shenstone's, was named, Old Dame Key—she was nearly related to Sir Joshua Renyolds.—[1]

From October 20th 1774 to October 1775. I was inoculated; which I mention, because I distinctly remember it: & that my eyes were bound—at which I manifested so much obstinate indignation, that at last they removed the bandage—and unaffrighted I looked at the lancet & suffered the scratch.—At the close of this Year I could read a Chapter in the Bible.

Here I shall end; because the remaining years of my Life *all* assisted to form *my particular mind*—the three first years had nothing in them that seems to relate to it.

---

7. Actually twenty-five.
8. Source untraced.
9. Actually Mundy.
1. Sir Joshua Reynolds (1723–1793), leading portrait painter of his age and (from 1768) the first president of the Royal Academy. William Shenstone (1714–1763), poet and landscape gardener whose most popular work, the mock-Spenserian poem *The Schoolmistress*, was first published in 1737.

To Joseph Cottle (April 1797)

My dearest Cottle

I love & respect you as a Brother, and my memory deceives me woe-fully, if I have not evidenced by the animated turn of my conversation, when we have been tête à tête, how much your company interested me.—But when last in Bristol the day I meant to have devoted to you, was such a day of sadness, that I could *do nothing*—On the Saturday, the Sunday, & the ten days after my arrival at Stowey[1] I felt a depression too dreadful to be described—

> So much I felt my genial spirits droop!
> My Hopes all flat, Nature within me seem'd
> In all her functions weary of herself.[2]

Wordsworth's conversation &c rous'd me somewhat; but even now I am not the man I have been—& I think, never shall.—A sort of calm hopelessness diffuses itself over my heart.—Indeed every mode of life which has promised me bread & cheese, has been, one after another torn away from me—but God remains! I have no immediate pressing distress, having received ten pounds from Lloyd's Father[3] at Birmingham.—I employ myself now on a book of Morals in answer to Godwin, and on my Tragedy.[4] . . . David Hartley is well & grows.—Sara[5] is well and desires a sister's love to you—

Tom Poole desires to be kindly remembered to you. I see they have reviewed Southey's Poems and my Ode[6] in the Monthly Review. Notwithstanding the Reviews, I, who in the sincerity of my heart am *jealous* for Robert Southey's fame, regret the publication of that volume. Wordsworth complains, with justice, that Southey writes *too much at his ease*—that he seldom "feels his burthen'd breast

> Heaving beneath th' incumbent Deity."[7]

He certainly will make literature more *profitable to him* from the fluency with which he writes, & the facility, with which he pleases himself. But I fear, that to Posterity his Wreath will look unseemly—here

---

1. Nether Stowey, where C lived in 1797–98, thirty miles southwest of Bristol.
2. Milton, *Samson Agonistes*, lines 594–96 (substituting the past tense for the present).
3. Charles Lloyd senior, father of the poet Charles Lloyd (1775–1839), thirty-nine of whose poems C published in the 1797 edition of his own *Poems* (see the headnote, p. 43 herein). In February 1797 the younger Lloyd had moved in with the Coleridges at Nether Stowey, but within a month he had suffered five seizures and had to be put under the care of the physician Erasmus Darwin. After recovering he antagonized C by publishing the satirical novel *Edmund Oliver* (1798), which included a thinly disguised caricature of C.
4. In March 1797 C had been commissioned by the playwright and theater manager Richard Brinsley Sheridan (1751–1816) to write a tragedy for the Drury Lane Theatre. The completed play, *Osorio*, was rejected in December 1797; but in January 1813 a revised version of it, *Remorse*, had a successful run at Drury Lane. The plan to write a reply to William Godwin's *Political Justice* (1793), which proposed the perfectibility of humanity on the basis of reason and benevolent action, was not realized.
5. C's son Hartley and his wife, Sara.
6. "Ode on the Departing Year" (p. 37 herein) and Southey's *Poems* (1797) were reviewed in the March 1797 issue of the *Monthly Review*.
7. Southey, *Joan of Arc* (1796) 1.463–64 (var.). Southey himself was alluding to Virgil's description of the Cumaean Sibyl in the *Aeneid* 6.79–80.

an ever living Amaranth, & close by its side some Weed of an hour, sere, yellow, & shapeless—his exquisite Beauties will lose half their effect from the bad company they keep.—Besides I am fearful that he will begin to rely too much on *story* & *event* in his poems to the neglect of those *lofty imaginings*, that are peculiar to, & definitive of, *the* POET. The *story* of Milton might be told in *two pages*—it is this which distinguishes an EPIC *Poem* from a *Romance in metre.* Observe the march of Milton—his severe application, his laborious polish, his deep metaphysical researches, his *prayers to God* before he began his great poem—all, that could lift & swell his intellect, became his daily food. —I should not think of devoting less than 20 years to an Epic Poem. Ten to collect materials, & warm my mind with universal Science—I would be a tolerable Mathematician, I would thoroughly know mechanics, hydrostatics, optics, & astronomy—Botany, Metallurgy, fossilism, chemistry, geology, Anatomy, Medicine—then *the mind of man*—then the *minds of men*—in *all* Travels, Voyages & Histories. So I would spend ten years—the next five in the composition of the poem—& the five last to the correction of it. So I would write, haply not unhearing of that divine and nightly-whispering Voice, which speaks to Mighty minds of predestinated Garlands starry & unwithering!

God love you, & S. T. Coleridge

To Thomas Poole (October 9, 1797)

October 9th, 1797

My dearest Poole

From March to October—a long silence! but [as] it is possible, that I may have been preparing materials for future letters, the time cannot be considered as altogether subtracted from you.

From October 1775 to October 1778.

These three years I continued at the reading-school—because I was too little to be trusted among my Father's School-boys—. After breakfast I had a halfpenny given me, with which I bought three cakes at the Baker's close by the school of my old mistress—& these were my dinner on every day except Saturday & Sunday—when I used to dine at home, and wallowed in a beef & pudding dinner.—I am remarkably fond of Beans & Bacon—and this fondness I attribute to my father's having given me a penny for having eat a large quantity of beans, one Saturday—for the other boys did not like them, and as it was an economic food, my father thought, that my attachment & penchant for it ought to be encouraged.——My Father was very fond of me, and I was my mother's darling—in consequence, I was very miserable. For Molly, who had nursed my Brother Francis, and was immoderately fond of him, hated me because my mother took more notice of me than of Frank—and Frank hated me, because my mother gave me now & then a bit of cake, when he had none—quite forgetting that for one bit of cake which I had & he had not, he had twenty sops in the pan & pieces of bread & butter with sugar on them from Molly, from whom I received only thumps & ill names.—So I became fretful, & timorous, & a tell-tale—& the School-boys drove me from play, & were always tormenting me—& hence I took no pleasure in boyish sports—but read incessantly. My Father's Sister kept an *every-thing* Shop at Crediton—and there I read thro' all the gilt-cover little books that could be had at that time, & likewise all the uncovered tales of Tom Hickathrift, Jack the Giant-killer, &c & &c &c—/—and I used to lie by the wall, and *mope*—and my spirits used to come upon me suddenly, & in a flood—& then I was accustomed to run up and down the church-yard, and act over all I had been reading on the docks, the nettles, and the rank-grass.—At six years old I remember to have read Belisarius, Robinson Crusoe, & Philip Quarle[1]—and then I found the Arabian Nights' entertainments—one tale of which (the tale of a man who was compelled to seek for a pure virgin) made so deep an impression on me (I had read it in the evening while my mother was mending stockings) that I was haunted by spectres, whenever I was in the dark—and I distinctly remember the anxious & fearful eagerness, with which I used to watch the window, in which the books lay—& whenever the Sun lay upon them, I would seize it, carry it by the wall, & bask, & read—. My Father found out the effect, which these books had produced—and burnt them.—So I became a *dreamer*—and acquired an indisposition to all bodily activity—and I was fretful, and inordinately passionate, and as I could not play at any thing, and was slothful, I was despised & hated by the boys; and because I could read & spell, & had, I may truly say, a memory & understanding forced into almost an unnatural ripeness, I was flattered & wondered at by all the old women—& so I became very vain, and despised most of the boys, that were at all near my own age—and before I was eight years old, I was a *character*—sensibility, imagination, vanity, sloth, & feelings of deep & bitter contempt for almost all who traversed the orbit of my understanding, were even then prominent & manifest.

From October 1778 to 1779.—That which I began to be from 3 to 6, I continued from 6 to 9.—In this year I was admitted into the grammer school,[2] and soon outstripped all of my age.—I had a dangerous putrid fever this year—My Brother George lay ill of the same fever in the next room.——My poor Brother Francis, I remember, stole up in spite of orders to the contrary, & sate by my bedside, & read Pope's Homer to me—Frank had a violent love of beating me—but whenever that was superseded by any humour or circumstance, he was always very fond of me—& used to regard me with a strange mixture of admiration & contempt—strange it was not—: for he hated books, and

---

1. Daniel Defoe's *Robinson Crusoe* (1719), Peter Longueville's *Adventures of Philip Quarll* (1727), and *The Arabian Nights Entertainments* (first translated from the French in 1705–08) were popular children's reading in C's day. Belisarius (505–565), a Byzantine general who served under the Roman emperor Justinian I, was the subject of an historical romance translated in 1767 from the French of Jean François Marmontel (1723–1799).
2. I.e., the King's Grammar School, of which his father was headmaster.

loved climbing, fighting, playing, & robbing orchards, to distraction.—
My mother relates a story of me, which I repeat here—because it
must be regarded as my first piece of wit.—During my fever I asked
why Lady Northcote (our neighbour) did not come & see me.—My
mother said, She was afraid of catching the fever—I was piqued & answered—Ah—Mamma! the four Angels round my bed an't afraid of
catching it.—I suppose, you know the old prayer—

> Matthew! Mark! Luke! & John!
> God bless the bed which I lie on.
> Four Angels round me spread,
> Two at my foot & two at my bed.[3]

This prayer I said nightly—& most firmly believed the truth of it.—
Frequently have I, half-awake & half-asleep, my body diseased &
fevered by my imagination, seen armies of ugly Things bursting in
upon me, & these four angels keeping them off.—In my next I shall
carry on my life to my Father's Death.—

> God bless you, my dear Poole! & your affectionate
> > S. T. Coleridge.

To Thomas Poole (October 16, 1797)

Dear Poole

From October 1779 to Oct. 1781.——I had asked my mother one
evening to cut my cheese *entire*, so that I might toast it: this was no
easy matter, it being a *crumbly* cheese—My mother however did it— /
I went into the garden for some thing or other, and in the mean time
my Brother Frank *minced* my cheese, "to disappoint the favorite." I returned, saw the exploit, and in an agony of passion flew at Frank—he
pretended to have been seriously hurt by my blow, flung himself on
the ground, and there lay with outstretched limbs——I hung over him
moaning & in a great fright—he leaped up, & with a horse-laugh gave
me a severe blow in the face—I seized a knife, and was running at
him, when my Mother came in & took me by the arm— / I expected a
flogging—& struggling from her I ran away, to a hill at the bottom of
which the Otter flows—about one mile from Ottery.—There I stayed;
my rage died away; but my obstinacy vanquished my fears—& taking
out a little shilling book which had, at the end, morning & evening
prayers, I very devoutly repeated them—thinking *at the same time* with
inward & gloomy satisfaction, how miserable my Mother must be!—I
distinctly remember my feelings when I saw a Mr Vaughan pass over
the Bridge, at about a furlong's distance—and how I watched the
Calves in the fields beyond the river. It grew dark—& I fell asleep—it
was towards the latter end of October—& it proved a dreadful stormy
night— / I felt the cold in my sleep, and dreamt that I was pulling the
blanket over me, & actually pulled over me a dry thorn bush, which lay

---

3. The last word should be "head."

Dear Poole

From October 1779 to Oct. 1781. — I had asked my mother one evening to cut my cheese entire, so that I might toast it. This was no easy matter, it being a crumbly cheese— my mother however did it—/ I went into the garden for some thing or other, and in the mean time my Brother Frank minced my cheese, "to disappoint the favorite". I returned, saw the exploit, and in an agony of passion flew at Frank — he pretended to have been seriously hurt by my blow, flung himself on the ground, and there lay with outstretched limbs —. I hung over him moaning & in a great fright — he leaped up, & with a horse-laugh gave me a severe blow in the face — I seized a knife, and was running at him, when my mother came in & took me by the arm —/ I expected a flogging — & struggling from her I ran away, to a hill, at the bottom of which the Otter flows — about one mile from Ottery. — There I stayed; my rage died away; but my obstinacy vanquished my fears — & taking out a little Shilling book which had, at the end, morning & evening prayers, I very devoutly repeated them — thinking at the same time with inward & gloomy satisfaction, how miserable my mother must be! — I distinctly remember my feelings when I saw a Mr Vaughan pass over the Bridge, at about a furlong's distance — and how I watched the Calves in the fields beyond the river. It grew dark — & I fell asleep — it was towards the latter end of October — & it proved a dreadful stormy night —/ I felt the cold in my sleep, and dreamt that I was pulling the blanket over me, & actually pulled over me a dry thorn bush, which lay on the hill — in my sleep I had rolled from the top of the hill to within three yards of the River, which flowed by the unfenced edge of the bottom. — I awoke several times, and finding myself wet & stiff, and cold, closed my eyes again that I might forget it. — In the mean time my mother waited about half an hour, expecting my return, when the Sulks had evaporated — I not returning, she sent into the church-yard, & round the town — not found! — Several men

First page of letter to Thomas Poole, October 16, 1797.

on the hill—in my sleep I had rolled from the top of the hill to within three yards of the River, which flowed by the unfenced edge of the bottom.—I awoke several times, and finding myself wet & stiff, and cold, closed my eyes again that I might forget it.——In the mean time my Mother waited about half an hour, expecting my return, when the *Sulks* had evaporated—I not returning, she sent into the Church-yard, & round the town—not found!—Several men & all the boys were sent to ramble about & seek me—in vain! My Mother was almost distracted—and at ten o'clock at night I was *cry'd* by the crier in Ottery,[1] and in two villages near it—with a reward offered for me.—No one went to bed—indeed, I believe, half the town were up all one night! To return to myself—About five in the morning or a little after, I was broad awake; and attempted to get up & walk—but I could not move—I saw the Shepherds & Workmen at a distance—& cryed but so faintly, that it was impossible to hear me 30 yards off——and there I might have lain & died—for I was now almost given over, the ponds & even the river near which I was lying, having been dragged.—But by good luck Sir Stafford Northcote[2] who had been out all night, resolved to make one other trial, and came so near that he heard my crying— He carried me in his arms, for near a quarter of a mile; when we met my father & Sir Stafford's Servants.—I remember, & never shall forget, my father's face as he looked upon me while I lay in the servant's arms—so calm, and the tears stealing down his face: for I was the child of his old age.——My Mother, as you may suppose, was outrageous with joy—in rushed a *young Lady*, crying out—"I hope, you'll whip him, Mrs Coleridge!"—This woman still lives at Ottery—& neither Philosophy or Religion have been able to conquer the antipathy which I *feel* towards her, whenever I see her.—I was put to bed—& recovered in a day or so—but I was certainly injured—For I was weakly, & subject to the ague for many years after—.—

My Father (who had so little of parental ambition in him, that he had destined his children to be Blacksmiths &c, & had accomplished his intention but for my Mother's pride & spirit of aggrandizing her family) my father had however resolved, that I should be a Parson. I read every book that came in my way without distinction—and my father was fond of me, & used to take me on his knee, and hold long conversations with me. I remember, that at eight years old I walked with him one winter evening from a farmer's house, a mile from Ottery——& he told me the names of the stars—and how Jupiter was a thousand times larger than our world—and that the other twinkling stars were Suns that had worlds rolling round them—& when I came home, he shewed me how they rolled round— /. I heard him with a profound delight & admiration; but without the least mixture of wonder or incredulity. For from my early reading of Faery Tales, & Genii &c &c—my mind had been habituated *to the Vast*——& I never regarded *my senses* in any way as the criteria of my belief. I regulated all

---

1. I.e., the town criers called out his name in the streets.
2. A neighbor (1762–1851) whose daughter, Maria, C's brother Frank hoped to marry.

my creeds by my conceptions not by my *sight*—even at that age. Should children be permitted to read Romances, & Relations of Giants & Magicians, & Genii?——I know all that has been said against it; but I have formed my faith in the affirmative.—I know no other way of giving the mind a love of "the Great," & "the Whole."—Those who have been led to the same truths step by step thro' the constant testimony of their senses, seem to me to want a sense which I possess— They contemplate nothing but *parts*—and all *parts* are necessarily little—and the Universe to them is but a mass of *little things*.[3]—It is true, that the mind *may* become credulous & prone to superstition by the former method—but are not the Experimentalists credulous even to madness in believing any absurdity, rather than believe the grandest truths, if they have not the testimony of their own senses in their favor?—I have known some who have been *rationally* educated, as it is styled. They were marked by a microscopic acuteness; but when they looked at great things, all became a blank & they saw nothing—and denied (very illogically) that any thing could be seen; and uniformly put the negation of a power for the possession of a power—& called the want of imagination Judgment, & the never being moved to Rapture Philosophy!——

Towards the latter end of September 1781 my Father went to Plymouth with my Brother Francis, who was to go as Midshipman under Admiral Graves; the Admiral was a friend of my Father's.—My Father settled my Brother; & returned Oct. 4th, 1781—. He arrived at Exeter about six o'clock—& was pressed to take a bed there by the Harts— but he refused—and to avoid their intreaties he told them—that he had never been superstitious—but that the night before he had had a dream which had made a deep impression. He dreamt that Death had appeared to him, as he is commonly painted, & touched him with his Dart.[4] Well he returned home—& all his family, I excepted, were up. He told my mother his dream—; but he was in high health & good spirits—& there was a bowl of Punch made—& my Father gave a long & particular account of his Travel, and that he had placed Frank under a religious Captain &c—/ At length, he went to bed, very well, & in high Spirits.—A short time after he had lain down he complained of a pain in his bowells, which he was subject to, from the wind—my mother got him some peppermint water—and after a pause, he said— "I am much better now, my dear!"—and lay down again. In a minute my mother heard a noise in his throat—and spoke to him—but he did not answer—and she spoke repeatedly in vain. Her *shriek* awaked me—& I said, "Papa is dead"—I did not know [of] my Father's return, but I knew that he was expected. How I came to think of his Death, I

---

3. In a letter written two days earlier to John Thelwall, C had lamented, "I can contemplate nothing but parts, & parts are all *little*—!—My mind feels as if it ached to behold & know something *great*—something *one & indivisible*—and it is only in the faith of this that rocks or waterfalls, mountains or caverns give me the sense of sublimity or majesty!" (*CL*, 1:349).

4. C referred to this dream frequently in later years, regarding it as a premonition not only of his father's death but of his own: "It is strongly impressed on my mind, that I shall imitate my dear Father in this as faithfully as Nature imitates or repeats him in me in so many other points—viz. that I shall die in sleep" (*CN*, 4:5360; cf. *CN*, 3:4396).

cannot tell; but so it was.—Dead he was—some said it was the Gout in the Heart—probably, it was a fit of Apoplexy / —He was an Israelite without guile; simple, generous, and, taking some scripture texts in their literal sense, he was conscientiously indifferent to the good & the evil of this world.—

God love you & S. T. Coleridge

To Thomas Poole (February 19, 1798)

From October 1781 to October 1782.

After the death of my father we, of course, changed houses, & I remained with my mother till the spring of 1782, and was a day-scholar to Parson Warren, my Father's successor— / He was a booby, I believe; and I used to delight my poor mother by relating little instances of his deficiency in grammar knowlege—every detraction from his merits seemed an oblation to the memory of my Father, especially as Parson Warren did certainly *pulpitize* much better.—Somewhere, I think, about April 1792, Judge Buller, who had been educated by my Father, sent for me, having procured a Christ's Hospital Presentation.[1]—I accordingly went to London, and was received by my mother's Brother, Mr Bowden, a Tobacconist & (at the same [time]) clerk to an Underwriter. My Uncle lived at the corner of the Stock exchange, & carried on his shop by means of a confidential Servant, who, I suppose, fleeced him most unmercifully.—He was a widower, & had one daughter who lived with a Miss Cabriere, an old Maid of great sensibilities & a taste for literature——Betsy Bowden had obtained an unlimited influence over her mind, which she still retains—Mrs Holt (for this is her name now) was, when I knew her, an ugly & an artful woman & not the kindest of Daughters—but indeed, my poor Uncle would have wearied the patience & affection of an Euphrasia.—He was generous as the air & a man of very considerable talents—but he was a Sot.— He received me with great affection, and I stayed ten weeks at his house, during which time I went occasionally to Judge Buller's. My Uncle was very proud of me, & used to carry me from Coffee-house to Coffee-house, and Tavern to Tavern, where I drank, & talked & disputed, as if I had been a man—— /. Nothing was more common than for a large party to exclaim in my hearing, that I *was a prodigy*, &c &c &c—so that, while I remained at my Uncle's, I was most completely spoilt & pampered, both mind & body. At length the time came, & I donned the *Blue* coat & yellow stockings, & was sent down to Hertford, a town 20 miles from London, where there are about 300 of the

---

1. In March 1782 (C miswrote the year) C's godfather, Samuel Taylor, petitioned Christ's Hospital, a London boarding school for clergymen's sons, to accept C as a pupil. The petition was accepted the following month, and C was immediately sent to stay with his maternal uncle John Bowden in London until his enrollment at the Christ's Hospital junior school in Hertford on July 8. Six weeks later he was transferred to Christ's Hospital proper, where he remained until 1791. C refers to this period elsewhere too, recalling his loneliness in "Frost at Midnight," lines 26–48 (1817), and the harsh schoolmaster James Boyer in the *Biographia*, chapter 1.

younger Blue coat boys—At Hertford I was very happy, on the whole; for I had plenty to eat & drink, & pudding & vegetables almost every day. I stayed there six weeks; and then was drafted up to the great school at London, where I arrived in September, 1792—and was placed in the second ward, then called Jefferies's ward; & in the under Grammar School. There are twelve Wards, or dormitories, of unequal sizes, beside the Sick Ward, in the great School—& they contained, all together, 700 boys; of whom I think nearly one third were the Sons of Clergymen. There are 5 Schools, a Mathematical, a Grammar, a drawing, a reading, & a writing School—all very large Buildings.—When a boy is admitted, if he read very badly, he is either sent to Hertford or to the Reading-School—(N.B. Boys are admissible from 7 to 12 years old)—If he learn to read tolerably well before 9, he is drafted into the lower Grammar-school—if not, into the writing-school, as having given proof of unfitness for classical attainment.—If before he is eleven he climbs up to the first form of the lower Grammar-school, he is drafted into the head Grammar School—if not, at 11 years old he is sent into the writing School, where he continues till 14 or 15—and is then either apprenticed, & articled as clerk, or whatever else his turn of mind, or of fortune shall have provided for him. Two or three times a year the Mathematical Master beats up for recruits for the King's boys, as they are called—and all, who like the navy, are drafted into the Mathematical & Drawing Schools—where they continue till 16 or 17, & go out as Midshipmen & Schoolmasters in the Navy.—The Boys, who are drafted into the head Grammar School, remain there till 13—& then if not chosen for the university, go into the writing school. Each dormitory has a Nurse, or Matron—& there is a head Matron to superintend all these Nurses.—The boys were, when I was admitted, under excessive subordination to each other, according to rank in School—& every ward was governed by four Monitors, (appointed by the *Steward*, who was the supreme Governor out of School—our Temporal Lord) and by four *Markers*, who wore silver medals, & were appointed by the head Grammar Master, who was our supreme Spiritual Lord. The same boys were commonly both Monitors & Markers—We read in classes on Sundays to our *Markers*, & were catechized by them, & under their sole authority during prayers, &c—all other authority was in the monitors; but, as I said, the same boys were ordinarily both the one & the other.—Our diet was very scanty—Every morning a bit of dry bread & some bad small beer—every evening a larger piece of bread, & cheese or butter, whichever we liked—For dinner—on Sunday, boiled beef & broth—Monday, Bread & butter, & milk & water—on Tuesday, roast mutton, Wednesday, bread & butter & rice milk, Thurday, boiled beef & broth—Friday, boiled mutton & broth—Saturday, bread & butter, & pease porritch—Our food was portioned—& excepting on Wednesdays I never had a belly full. Our appetites were *damped* never satisfied—and we had no vegetables.—

S. T. Coleridge

To George Coleridge (c. March 10, 1798)

My dear Brother

*   *   *

You think, my Brother! that there can be but two *parties* at present, for the Government & against the Government.—It may be so—I am of no party. It is true, I think the present ministry weak & perhaps unprincipled men; but I could not with a safe conscience vote for their removal; for I could point out no substitutes. I think very seldom on the subject; but as far as I have thought, I am inclined to consider the Aristocrats as the more respectable of our three factions, because they are more decorous. The Opposition & the Democrats are not only vicious—they wear the *filthy garments* of vice.

> He that takes
> Deep in his soft credulity the stamp
> Design'd by loud Declaimers on the part
> Of Liberty, themselves the slaves of Lust,
> Incurs derision for his easy faith
> And lack of Knowledge—& with cause enough.
> For when was public Virtue to be found
> Where private was not? Can he love the whole
> Who loves no part? He be a *nation's* friend
> Who is, in truth, the friend of no man there?
> Can he be strenuous in his country's cause
> Who slights the charities, for whose dear sake
> That country, if at all, must be belov'd?
>   Cowper.—[1]

I am prepared to suffer without discontent the consequences of my follies & mistakes—: and unable to conceive how that which I am, of Good could have been without that which I have been of Evil, it is withheld from me to regret any thing: I therefore consent to be deemed a Democrat & a Seditionist. A man's character follows him long after he has ceased to deserve it—but I have snapped my squeaking baby-trumpet of Sedition & the fragments lie scattered in the lumber-room of Penitence.

*   *   *

1. William Cowper, *The Task* (1785) 5.496–508 (var.).

To Thomas Poole (March 16, 1801)[1]

Monday Night.

My Dear Friend

The interval since my last Letter has been filled up by me in the most intense Study. If I do not greatly delude myself, I have not only completely extricated the notions of Time, and Space; but have overthrown the doctrine of Association, as taught by Hartley, and with it all the irreligious metaphysics of modern Infidels—especially, the Doctrine of Necessity.[2] This I have *done*; but I trust, that I am about to do more—namely, that I shall be able to evolve all the five senses, that is, to deduce them from *one sense*, & to state their growth, & the cause of their difference—& in this evolvement to solve the process of Life & Consciousness.—I write this to *you only*; & I pray you, mention what I have written to no one.—At Wordsworth's advice, or rather fervent Intreaty, I have intermitted the pursuit—the intensity of thought, & the multitude of minute experiments with Light & Figure, have made me so nervous & feverish, that I cannot sleep as long as I ought & have been used to: & the Sleep, which I have, is made up of Ideas so connected, & so little different from the operations of Reason, that it does not afford me the due Refreshment. I shall therefore take a week's respite: & make Christabel ready for the Press—in order to get rid of all my engagements with Longman[3]—My German Book I have suffered to remain suspended, chiefly because the thoughts which had employed my sleepless nights during my illness were *imperious* over me, and tho' Poverty was staring me in the face, yet I dared behold my Image miniatured in the pupil of her hollow eye, so steadily did I look her in the Face!—for it seemed to me a Suicide of my very soul to divert my attention from Truths so important, which came to me almost as a Revelation / Likewise, I cannot express to you, dear Friend of my heart!—the loathing, which I once or twice felt, when I attempted to write, merely for the Bookseller, without any sense of the moral utility of what I was writing.—I shall therefore, as I said, immediately publish my CHRISTABEL, with two Essays annexed to it, on the Præternatural—and on Metre.[4] This done I shall propose to Longman instead of my Travels (which tho' nearly done I am exceedingly anxious not to publish, because it brings me forward in a *personal* way, as a man who

1. Transcribed from the manuscript in the British Library (Add. MS 35,343 f. 177). The passage in brackets at the end of the letter is missing from the manuscript, and has been supplied from a transcript reprinted in CL, 2:707.
2. I.e., necessitarianism.
3. Thomas Longman, the publisher of C's translations of Friedrich Schiller's Wallenstein plays in 1800, had given C a £30 advance for a biography of the German playwright, critic, and controversialist Gotthold Ephraim Lessing (1729–1781). Wordsworth repaid the advance on March 25, 1801 (CL, 2:715–18; WL, 1:321), at which time C also proposed that Longman publish an illustrated edition of "Christabel." But the biography, which grew in C's mind to incorporate a history of German literature (CL, 1:455, 484), was never completed.
4. In fact "Christabel" remained unpublished until 1816, when John Murray published it in a small volume with "Kubla Khan" and "The Pains of Sleep." C did not write the essays he refers to here, but he did include a paragraph on the meter of "Christabel" in his brief preface to the published poem (see p. 162 herein).

relates little adventures of himself to *amuse* people—& thereby exposes me to sarcasm & the malignity of anonymous Critics, & is besides *beneath me*—I say, *beneath me* / for to whom should a young man utter the pride of his Heart if not to the man whom he loves more than all others?) I shall propose to Longman to accept instead of these Travels a work on the originality & merits of Locke, Hobbes, & Hume[5] / which work I mean as a *Pioneer* to my greater work, and as exhibiting a proof that I have not formed opinions without an attentive Perusal of the works of my Predecessors from Aristotle to Kant.—I am *confident*, that I can prove that the Reputation of these three men has been wholly unmerited, & that I have in [what I have already written traced the whole history of the causes that effected this reputation entirely to Wordsworth's satisfaction.

You have seen, I hope, the lyrical Ballads * * *.] The character of the Lyrical Ballads is very great, and will increase daily. They have *extolled* them in the British Critic.[6]

*   *   *

To Thomas Poole (March 23, 1801)[1]

* * * Be not afraid, that I shall join the party of the *Little-ists*.[2]—I believe, that I shall delight you by the detection of their artifices—Now Mr Locke was the founder of this sect, himself a perfect Little-ist. My opinion is this—that deep Thinking is attainable only by a man of deep Feeling, and that all Truth is a species of Revelation. The more I understand of Sir Isaac Newton's works, the more boldly I dare utter to my own mind & therefore to *you*, that I believe the souls of 500 Sir Isaac Newtons would go to the making up of a Shakespeare or a Milton. But if it please the Almighty to grant me health, hope, and a steady mind, (always the 3 clauses of my hourly prayers) Before my 30th year I will thoroughly understand the whole of Newton's Works— At present, I must content myself with endeavouring to make myself entire master of his easier work, that on Optics. I am exceedingly delighted with the beauty & neatness of his experiments, & with the accuracy of his *immediate* Deductions from them—but the opinions founded on these Deductions, and indeed his whole Theory is, I am persuaded, so exceedingly superficial as without impropriety to be deemed false. Newton was a mere materialist—*Mind* in his system is

---

5. Although C did not write the book he envisioned here, he did devote parts of the *Biographia* and *The Friend* to criticizing the empiricist philosophies of Locke, Hobbes, and Hume.
6. An anonymous review of the *LB* (1800) in the *British Critic* in February 1801 praised Wordsworth, under whose name the book had appeared, for having "thought for himself; he has deeply studied human nature * * * and he has adopted his language from the same sources as his sources as his feelings" (*The Romantics Reviewed*, part A, vol. 1, ed. Donald Reiman, 131).
1. Transcribed from the manuscript in the British Library (Add. MS 35,343 ff. 265–66).
2. A term used by Poole in a letter of March 14, 1801, to C in response to a critique of Locke that C had sent to both Poole and Josiah Wedgwood (see *CL*, 2:678–85): "Think before you join the herd of *Little-ists*, who, without knowing in what Locke is defective, wish to strip the *popular mind* of him, leaving nothing in his place *nothing—darkness, total darkness*" (quoted in *CL*, 2:708n. 5).

always passive—a lazy Looker-on on an external World. If the mind be not *passive*, if it be indeed made in God's Image, & that too in the sublimest sense—the Image of the *Creator*—there is ground for suspicion, that any system built on the passiveness of the mind must be false, as a system. / I need not observe, My dear Friend, how unutterably silly & contemptible these Opinions would be, if written to any but to another Self. I assure you, solemnly assure you, that you & Wordsworth are the only men on Earth to whom I would have uttered a word on this subject—.[3] It is a rule, by which I hope to direct all my literary efforts, to let my Opinions & my Proofs go together. It is *insolent* to *differ* from the public *opinion* in *opinion*, if it be only *opinion*. It is sticking up little *i by itself i* against the whole alphabet. But one *word* with *meaning* in it is worth the whole alphabet together—such is sound Argument, an incontrovertible Fact.—

O for a lodge in a Land, where human Life was an end, to which Labor was only a Means, instead of being, as it [is] here, a mere means of carrying on Labor.—I am oppressed at times with a true heart-gnawing melancholy when I contemplate the state of my poor oppressed Country.—God knows, it is as much as I can do to put meat & bread on my own table; & hourly some poor starving wretch comes to my door, to put in his claim for part of it.—It fills me with indignation to hear the *croaking* accounts, which the English Emigrants send home of America. The society is so bad—the manners so vulgar—the servants so insolent.—Why then do they not seek out one another, & make a society—? It is arrant ingratitude to talk so of a Land in which there is no Poverty but as a consequence of absolute Idleness—and to talk of it too with abuse comparatively with England, with a place where the laborious Poor are dying with Grass with[in] their Bellies?—It is idle to talk of the Seasons—as if that country must not needs be miserably misgoverned in which an unfavorable Season introduces a famine.[4] No! No! dear Poole! it is our pestilent Commerce, our unnatural crowding together of men in Cities, & our Government by Rich Men, that are bringing about the manifestations of offended Deity.—I am assumed that such is the depravity of the public mind, that no literary man can find bread in England except by misemploying & debasing his Talents—that nothing of real excellence would be either felt or understood.* * *

---

3. Although C later begged Poole to destroy this letter "respecting Sir Isaac Newton's Optics * * * a Letter which if I were to die & it should ever see the *Light* would damn me forever, as a man mad with Presumption" (p. 637 herein), he remained fond of equations belittling Newton: see also *TT* (CC), 1:210 ("two or three Galileos and Newtons to make one Kepler"). His critique of materialism is developed more fully in *The Friend*, where Newton is again mentioned (p. 559 herein).

4. C was not exaggerating: a bad harvest in 1799–1800, combined with a sharp rise in food prices, led, particularly in rural areas, to famine among the English poor between 1799 and 1801.

To William Sotheby[1] (September 10, 1802)

* * * It is my Faith, that the "Genus irritabile" is a phrase applicable only to *bad* poets[2]—Men of great Genius have indeed, as an essential of their composition, great sensibility, but they have likewise great confidence in their own powers—and Fear must always precede anger, in the human mind. I can with truth say, that from those, I love, mere general praise of any thing, I have written, is as far from giving me pleasure, as mere general censure—in any thing, I mean, to which I have devoted much time or effort. "Be minute, & assign your Reasons often, & your first impressions always—& then blame or praise—I care not which—I shall be gratified"—These are *my* sentiments, & I assuredly believe, that they are the sentiments of all, who have indeed felt *a true Call* to the Ministry of *Song*. Of course, I too "will act on the golden rule of doing to others, what I wish others to do unto me."—[3] * * *—Bowles's Stanzas on Navigation are among the best in that second Volume / but the whole volume is woefully inferior to its Predecessor.[4] There reigns thro' all the blank verse poems such a perpetual trick of *moralizing* every thing—which is very well, occasionally—but never to see or describe any interesting appearance in nature, without connecting it by dim analogies with the moral world, proves faintness of Impression. Nature has her proper interest; & he will know what it is, who believes & feels, that every Thing has a Life of its own, & that we are all *one Life*.[5] A Poet's *Heart & Intellect* should be *combined*, *intimately* combined & *unified*, with the great appearances in Nature—& not merely held in solution & loose mixture with them, in the shape of formal Similies. I do not mean to *exclude* these formal Similies—there are moods of mind, in which they are natural—pleasing moods of mind, & such as a Poet will often have, & sometimes express; but they are not his highest, & most appropriate moods. They are "Sermoni propiora" which I once translated—"*Properer for a Sermon.*"[6] The truth is—Bowles has indeed the *sensibility* of a poet; but he has not the *Passion* of a great Poet. His latter Writings all want *native* Passion—Milton here & there supplies him with an appearance of it—but he has no native Passion, because he is not a Thinker—& has probably weakened his Intellect by the

1. Translator (chiefly from the classics) and minor poet (1757–1833) to whom C gave advice on poetical matters.
2. "Irritable race [of poets]," a phrase from Horace, *Epistles* 2.2.102, used also in the *Biographia* (see p. 393, n. 7 herein).
3. Cf. Matthew 7.12: "All things whatsoever ye would that men should do to you, do ye even so to them."
4. C refers to an unfinished poem, "The Spirit of Navigation and Discovery," in the second volume of *Poems* (1801) by William Lisle Bowles. The first volume contained Bowles's sonnets. This letter marks a cooling of C's early enthusiasm for Bowles, which was reflected in a sonnet ("Effusion I," p. 12 herein) and discussed in the *Biographia* (see chapter 1, pp. 328–29 herein).
5. Cf. the lines on "the one Life, within us and abroad" added in 1817 to "The Eolian Harp," originally called "Effusion XXXV" (see p. 18, n. 6 herein).
6. The Latin phrase, which actually means "nearer to prose," is from Horace's *Satires* 1.4.42, where it refers to bad poetry. C had used it before as the motto to his "Reflections on Having Left a Place of Retirement" (see p. 52, n. 2 herein).

haunting Fear of becoming extravagant / Young somewhere in one of his prose works remarks that there is as profound a Logic in the most daring & dithyrambic parts of Pindar, as in the ʹΌργανον[7] of Aristotle—the remark is a valuable one /

> Poetic Feelings, like the flexuous Boughs
> Of mighty Oaks, yield homage to the Gale,
> Toss in the strong winds, drive before the Gust,
> Themselves one giddy storm of fluttering Leaves;
> Yet all the while, self-limited, remain
> Equally near the fix'd and parent Trunk
> Of Truth & Nature, in the howling Blast
> As in the Calm that stills the Aspen Grove.—[8]

That this is deep in our Nature, I felt when I was on Sca' fell—.[9] I involuntarily poured forth a Hymn in the manner of the *Psalms*, tho' afterwards I thought the Ideas &c disproportionate to our humble mountains—& accidentally lighting on a short Note in some swiss Poems, concerning the Vale of Chamouny, & its Mountain, I transferred myself thither, in the Spirit, & adapted my former feelings to these grander external objects. You will soon see it in the Morning Post—& I should be glad to know whether & how far it pleased you.[1]—It has struck [me] with great force lately, that the Psalms afford a most compleat answer to those, who state the Jehovah of the Jews, as a personal & national God—& the Jews, as differing from the Greeks, only in calling the minor Gods, Cherubim & Seraphim[2]—& confining the word God to their Jupiter. It must occur to every Reader that the Greeks in their religious poems address always the Numina Loci, the Genii, the Dryads, the Naiads,[3] &c &c—All natural Objects were *dead*—mere hollow Statues—but there was a Godkin or Goddessling *included* in each—In the Hebrew Poetry you find nothing of this poor Stuff—as poor in genuine Imagination, as it is mean in Intellect— / At best, it is but Fancy, or the aggregating Faculty of the mind—not *Imagination*[4] or the *modifying*, and *co-adunating* Faculty. This the Hebrew Poets appear to me to have possessed beyond all others—& next to them the English. In the Hebrew Poets each Thing has a Life of its own, & yet they are all one Life. In God they move & live, & *have* their

---

7. *Logic*. Edward Young remarks in "On Lyric Poetry" (1728) that "Pindar * * * has as much logic at the bottom as Aristotle or Euclid" (see p. 380, n. 5 herein). *Dithyrambic parts*: choral songs in honor of the god Dionysus. For Pindar, see p. 612, n. 8 herein.
8. "To Mathilda Betham from a Stranger," lines 34–41 (*PW*, 1:374).
9. I.e., Scafell Pike, the highest mountain in the Lake District (3205 feet), which C had climbed on August 5, 1802.
1. C refers to his "Hymn before Sun-Rise, in the Vale of Chamouni," which incorporates an unacknowledged translation of a poem by German poet Friederika Brun (see p. 195, n. 1 herein). *CL*, 2:865n suggests that C's "Hymn" and his reflection on the Greeks in the following sentences were also influenced by lines 16–24 of Bowles's "Coombe-Ellen," which refer to nature as a divine power worshiped by the ancient Greeks.
2. In the Old Testament, orders of angels near the throne of God (Isaiah 6.2–3, Ezekiel 10).
3. Sea-dwelling nymphs. *Numina Loci*: deities associated with specific places. *Genii*: supernatural spirits. *Dryads*: tree-dwelling nymphs.
4. This distinction between fancy and imagination is elaborated in chapter 13 of the *Biographia* (p. 488 herein).

Being[5]—not *had*, as the cold System of Newtonian Theology represents / but *have*. Great pleasure indeed, my dear Sir! did I receive from the latter part of your Letter. If there be any two subjects which have in the very depth of my Nature interested me, it has been the Hebrew & Christian Theology, & the Theology of Plato. Last winter I read the Parmenides & the Timaeus[6] with great care—and O! that you were here, even in this howling Rain-Storm that dashes itself against my windows, on the other side of my blazing Fire, in that great Arm Chair there—I guess, we should encroach on the morning before we parted. How little the Commentators of Milton have availed themselves of the writings of Plato / Milton's Darling! But alas! commentators only hunt out verbal Parallelisms—*numen abest.*[7]

* * *

To Sara Coleridge (November 23, 1802)[1]

* * * My dear Love! let me in the spirit of love say two things / I. I owe duties, & solemn ones, to you, as my wife; but I owe equally solemn ones to Myself, to my Children, to my Friends, and to Society. Where Duties are at variance, dreadful as the case may be, there must be a Choice. I can neither retain my Happiness nor my Faculties, unless I move, live, & love, in perfect Freedom, limited only by my own purity & self-respect, & by my incapability of loving any person, man or woman, unless I at the same time honor & esteem them. My Love is made up %oths of fervent wishes for the permanent *Peace* of mind of those, whom I love, be it man or woman; & for their Progression in purity, goodness, & true Knowledge. Such being the nature of my Love, no human Being can have a right to be jealous. My nature is quick to love, & retentive. Of those, who are within the immediate sphere of my daily agency, & bound to me by bonds of Nature or Neighbourhood, I shall love each, as they appear to me to deserve my Love, & to be capable of returning it. More is not in my power. If I would do it, I could not. That we can love but one person, is a miserable mistake, & the cause of abundant unhappiness. I can & do love many people, dearly—so dearly, that I really scarcely know, which I love the best. Is it not so with every good mother who has a large number of Children—& with many, many Brothers & Sisters in large & af-

---

5. An allusion to Acts 17.28: "In him [God] we live, and move, and have our being." C's view of the Hebrew Bible may have been influenced by Robert Lowth's commentary on the Book of Isaiah (1778) and in *Lectures on the Sacred Poetry of the Hebrews*, the original Latin edition of which (1753) he had borrowed from the Bristol Library in 1796 (*Borrowings*, 123).
6. Platonic dialogues, the first concerned with logic, the second with cosmology.
7. "The spirit is wanting."
1. On November 4, 1802, C had angered his wife, Sara, who was expecting a baby in January, by suddenly leaving their home in Keswick to join his ailing friend Tom Wedgwood in the West Country. He spent the rest of November traveling with Wedgwood, mostly in Wales. Although the surviving correspondence between C and Sara Coleridge from this period is incomplete, it can be inferred from the surviving letters (*CL*, 2:879–94) that he angered her further by revealing that he had spent November 5 with Sara Hutchinson in Penrith, fourteen miles east of Keswick. In this letter C recounts his travels through Wales, gives details of his opium use, and demands that Sara Coleridge be more tolerant of his friends.

fectionate Families?—Why should it be otherwise with Friends? Would any good & wise man, any warm & wide hearted man marry at all, if it were part of the Contract—Hence-forth this Woman is your only friend, your sole beloved! all the rest of mankind, however amiable & akin to you, must be only your *acquaintance*!—? It were well, if every woman wrote down before her marriage all, she thought, she had a *right* to, from her Husband—& to examine each in this form— By what *Law* of God, of Man, or of general reason, do I claim *this* Right?—I suspect, that this Process would make a ludicrous Quantity of Blots and Erasures in most of the first rude Draughts of these Rights of Wives—infinitely however to their own Advantage, & to the security of their true & genuine Rights. 2.—Permit me, my dear Sara! without offence to you, as Heaven knows! it is without any feeling of Pride in myself, to say—that in sex, acquirements, and in the quantity and quality of natural endowments whether of Feeling, or of Intellect, you are the Inferior. Therefore it would be preposterous to expect that I should see with your eyes, & dismiss my Friends from *my* heart, only because you have not chosen to give them any Share of *your* Heart; but it is not preposterous, in me, on the contrary I have a *right* to expect & demand, that you should to a certain degree love, & act kindly to, those whom I deem worthy of my Love.—If you read this Letter with half the Tenderness, with which it is written, it will do you & both of us, GOOD; & contribute its share to the turning of a mere Cat-hole into a Dove's nest! You know, Sally Pally! I must have a Joke—or it would not be me!—

* * *

To Thomas Wedgwood (September 16, 1803)

Greta Hall, Keswick. Sept. 16. Friday
My dear Wedgwood

I reached home on yesterday noon; & it was not a Post Day.— William Hazlitt[1] is a thinking, observant, original man, of great power as a Painter of Character Portraits, & far more in the manner of the old Painters, than any living Artist, but the Object must be *before* him / he has no imaginative memory. So much for his Intellectuals.—His manners are to 99 in 100 singularly repulsive—: brow-hanging, shoe-contemplative, *strange* / Sharp seemed to like him / but Sharp saw him only for half an hour, & that walking—he is, I verily believe, kindly-natured—is very fond of, attentive to, & patient with, children / but he is jealous, gloomy, & of an irritable Pride—& addicted to women, as objects of sexual Indulgence.[2] With all this, there is much good in

1. Hazlitt had first encountered C when the latter was preaching at a Unitarian service in 1798 (an event memorialized in Hazlitt's essay "On My First Acquaintance with Poets"). Initially on friendly terms with C and Wordsworth, he was estranged from them after the incident described next.
2. This assessment was confirmed in October 1803, when Hazlitt, visiting C and Wordsworth in the Lake District, "narrowly escaped being ducked by the populace, and probably sent to prison for some gross attacks on women" (*CRB*, 1:169).

him—he is disinterested, an enthusiastic Lover of the great men, who have been before us—he says things that are his own in a way of his own—& tho' from habitual Shyness & the Outside & bearskin at least of misanthropy, he is strangely confused & dark in his conversation & delivers himself of almost all his conceptions with a Forceps, yet he says more than any man, I ever knew, yourself only excepted, that is his own in a way of his own—& the oftentimes when he has warmed his mind, & the synovial juice has come out & spread over his joints he will gallop for half an hour together with real Eloquence. He sends well-headed & well-feathered Thoughts straight forwards to the mark with a Twang of the Bow-string.—If you could recommend him, as a Portrait-painter, I should be glad. To be your Companion he is, in my opinion, utterly unfit. His own Health is fitful—I have written, as I ought to do, to you most freely imo ex corde[3] / you know me, both head & heart, & will make what deductions, your reason will dictate to you. I can think of no other person. What wonder? For the last years I have been shy of all mere acquaintances—

> To live belov'd is all, I need,
> And whom I love, I love indeed.[4]

I never had any ambition; & now, I trust, I have almost as little Vanity.—

For 5 months past my mind has been strangely shut up. I have taken the paper with an intention to write to you many times / but it has been all one blank Feeling, one blank idealess Feeling. I had nothing to say, I could say nothing. How deeply I love you, my very Dreams make known to me.—I will not trouble you with the gloomy Tale of my Health. While I am awake, by patience, employment, effort of mind, & walking I can keep the fiend at Arm's length; but the Night is my Hell,[5] Sleep my tormenting Angel. Three Nights out of four I fall asleep, struggling to lie awake—& my frequent Night-screams have almost made me a nuisance in my own House. Dreams with me are no Shadows, but the very Substances & foot-thick Calamities of my Life. Beddoes,[6] who has been to me ever a very kind man, suspects that my Stomach "brews Vinegar"—it may be so—but I have no other symptom but that of Flatulence / shewing itself by an asthmatic Puffing, & transient paralytic Affections / this Flatulence has never any acid Taste in my mouth / I have now no bowel-rumblings. I am too careful of my Diet—the supercarbonated Kali[7] does me no service, nor magnesia— neither have I any headach. But I am grown hysterical.—Meantime my Looks & Strength have improved. I myself fully believe it to be either atonic, hypochondriacal Gout, or a scrophulous affection of the

3. "Truly from the heart."
4. The concluding lines (var.) of "The Pains of Sleep."
5. C's nightmares seem to have been worst during periods of withdrawal from opium.
6. C had met the eminent physician Thomas Beddoes (1760–1808) in Bristol in 1796, when both were agitating for political reform. Three years later Beddoes, with Tom Wedgwood's financial help, opened his Pneumatic Institute for treating respiratory illnesses.
7. Soda ash, an antacid.

mesenteric Glands.[8] In the hope of driving the Gout, if Gout it should be, into the feet, I walked, previously to my getting into the Coach at Perth, 263 miles in eight Days, with no unpleasant fatigue: & if I could do you any service by coming to town, & there were no Coaches, I would undertake to be with you, on foot, in 7 days.—I must have strength somewhere / My head is indefatigably strong, my limbs too are strong—but acid or not acid, Gout or Scrofula. Something there is [in] my stomach or Guts that transubstantiates my Bread & Wine into the Body & Blood of the Devil[9]—Meat & Drink I should say—for I eat but little bread, & take nothing, in any form, spirituous or narcotic, stronger than Table Beer.—I am about to try the new Gout Medicine / & if it cures me, I will turn Preacher, form a new Sect in honor of the Discoverer, & make a greater clamour *in his Favor*, as the Antipodagra, "that was to come & is already in the world,"[1] than ever the Puritans did *against* the poor Pope, as Anti-christ.—All my Family are well. Southey, his Wife & Mrs Lovell are with us. He has lost his little Girl,[2] the unexpected Gift of a long marriage, & stricken to the very Heart is come hither for such poor comforts as my society can afford him.——— To diversify this dusky Letter I will write in a Post-script an Epitaph, which I composed in my Sleep for myself, while dreaming that I was dying. To the best of my recollection I have not altered a word—Yours, dear Wedgwood, and of all, that are dear to you at Gunville,[3] gratefully & most affectionately, S. T. Coleridge

Epitaph

Here sleeps at length poor Col, & without Screaming,
Who died, as he had always liv'd, a dreaming:
Shot dead, while sleeping, by the Gout within,
Alone, and all unknown, at E'nbro' in an Inn.

It was on Tuesday Night last at the Black Bull, Edinburgh—

8. Folds of tissue that hold the intestines to the abdominal walls. C may have dwelt on his illness to show his empathy with Wedgwood, whose own illness (possibly stomach cancer) was to prove fatal by 1805. *Atonic gout*: condition recognized in 18th-century medicine: "The atonic state is when the gouty diathesis [predisposition] prevails in the system, but * * * does not produce the inflammatory affection [malady] of the joints. In this case, the morbid symptoms which appear are chiefly affections of of the stomach; such as loss of appetite, nausea, vomiting, flatulency" (William Cullen, *First Lines of the Practice of Physic*, vol. 2 [Edinburgh, 1796], 78). Cullen's description was repeated almost verbatim in the article "Medicine" in the *Encyclopaedia Britannica* (1797), which C consulted in search of a diagnosis (CL, 2:974). *Scrophulous affection*: In the 17th and 18th centuries scrofula was usually defined as a disease involving glandular swelling, especially in the neck. It was commonly known as "the king's evil," presumably on account of the traditional belief that a king's touch would cure it, although C speculated in a treatise on the subject that the name derived from Psalm 38.3–8, where King David is described as having a scrofula-like condition (SW&F [CC], 462–63).
9. A playful allusion to the Roman Catholic doctrine of transubstantiation, according to which the bread and wine of the Eucharist are transformed in substance into the body and blood of Christ.
1. 1 John 4.3. *Anti-podagra*: anti-gout (a neologism formed by analogy to "Antichrist").
2. C had just returned to the Lake District from Perth, Scotland, to be with Southey, whose only child, Margaret, had died. Mary Lovell (née Fricker, c. 1772–1862), sister-in-law of both C and Robert Southey and widow of their friend Robert Lovell (c. 1770–1796), with whom they had planned the Pantisocracy scheme.
3. Josiah Wedgwood's home in Dorset, southwest England, where C had spent February 1803 with Tom Wedgwood.

To Thomas Poole (October 14, 1803)[1]

* * * Wordsworth is in good health, & all his family. He has one LARGE Boy, christened John. He has made a Beginning to his Recluse.[2] He was here on Sunday: his Wife's Sister,[3] who is on a visit at Grasmere, was in a bad hysterical way, & he rode in to consult our excellent medical men. I now see very little of Wordsworth: my own Health makes it inconvenient & unfit for me to go thither one third as often, as I used to do—and Wordsworth's Indolence, &c keeps him at home. Indeed, were I an irritable man, and an unthinking one, I should probably have considered myself as having been very unkindly used by him in this respect—for I was at one time confined for two months, & he never came in to see me/ me, who had ever payed such unremitting attentions to him. But we must take the good & the ill together; & by seriously & habitually reflecting on our own faults & endeavouring to amend them we shall then find little difficulty in confining our attention as far as it acts on our Friends' characters, to their good Qualities.—Indeed, I owe it to Truth & Justice as well as to myself to say, that the concern, which I have felt in this instance, and one or two other more *crying* instances, of Self-involution in Wordsworth, has been almost wholly a Feeling of friendly Regret, & disinterested Apprehension—I saw him more & more benetted in hypochondriacal Fancies, living wholly among *Devotees*—having every the minutest Thing, almost his very Eating & Drinking, done for him by his Sister, or Wife—& I trembled, lest a Film should arise, and thicken on his moral Eye.—The habit too of writing such a multitude of small Poems was in this instance hurtful to him—such Things as that Sonnet of his in Monday's Morning Post, about Simonides & the Ghost—[4] I rejoice therefore with a deep & true Joy, that he has at length yielded to my urgent & repeated—almost unremitting—requests & remonstrances—& will go on with the Recluse exclusively.—A Great Work, in which he will sail; on an open Ocean, & a steady wind; unfretted by short tacks, reefing, & hawling & disentangling the ropes—great work necessarily comprehending his attention & Feelings within the circle of great objects & elevated Conceptions—this is his natural Element!—the having been out of it has been his Disease—to return into it is the specific Remedy, both Remedy & Health. It is what Food is to Famine. I have seen enough, positively to give me feelings of hostility towards the plan of several of the Poems in the L. Ballads: & I really consider it as

1. Transcribed from the manuscript in the British Library (Add. Ms. 35,343 ff. 339–40).
2. Conceived in conversation with C in 1798, it was to be an epic poem on "Nature, Man, and Society" (WL, 1:212). When *The Excursion* was published in 1814 (the only part of *The Recluse* published in Wordsworth's lifetime), C expressed disappointment that Wordsworth had not fulfilled his expectation of a philosophical poem (CL, 4:564, 570–76). See also p. 518, n. 3 herein and p. 544 herein.
3. Joanna Hutchinson (1780–1843), the youngest of the Hutchinson sisters.
4. Wordsworth's untitled sonnet beginning "I find it written of Simonides," published in *MP* on October 10, 1803, and not reprinted in Wordsworth's lifetime (WPW, 3:408). The poem relates how the Greek poet Simonides (?556–466 B.C.E.), having arranged the burial of a corpse he discovered, is dissuaded by its ghost from boarding a boat that is then wrecked at sea. For another view, see "William Wordsworth" (p. 609 herein).

a misfortune, that Wordsworth has ever deserted his former mountain Track to wander in Lanes & allies;[5] tho' in the event it may prove to have been a great Benefit to him. He will steer, I trust, the middle course.—But he found himself to be, or rather to be called, the Head & founder of a *Sect* of Poetry: & assuredly he has written—& published in the M. Post, as W.L.D. & sometimes with no signature—poems written with a *sectarian* spirit, & in a sort of Bravado.[6]—I know, my dear Poole, that you are in the habit of keeping my Letters; but I must request of you, & do *rely* on it, that you will be so good as to destroy this Letter—& likewise, if it be not already done, that Letter which in the ebulliency of indistinct Conceptions I wrote to you respecting Sir Isaac Newton's Optics—& which to my *Horror* & Shame I saw that Ward had transcribed—a Letter which if I were to die & it should ever see the *Light* would damn me forever, as a man mad with Presumption.[7] * * * O that I could but be in London with you. It seems to me you are entering on the Porch of a Temple, for which Nature has made & destined you to be the Priest.[8] But more of this hereafter.—

I have been, to use a mild word, agitated by two INFAMOUS atrocious Paragraphs in the Morning Post of Thursday & Friday last—I believe them to be Mackintosh's[9]—*O that they were!* I would hunt him into Infamy.—I am now exerting myself to the utmost on this Subject. Do write me *instantly what* you think of them / or rather, what you thought, what you felt, what you said!—

S. T. Coleridge

*   *   *

To J. J. Morgan (May 14, 1814)[1]

14 May, Saturday
2. Queen's Square—

My dear Morgan

If it could be said with as little *appearance* of profaneness, as there is feeling or intention in my mind, I might affirm; that I had been crucified, dead, and buried, descended into *Hell*, and am now, I humbly

---

5. I.e., alleys.

6. In 1803 Wordsworth published seven sonnets (later gathered with others under the group title "Poems Dedicated to National Independence and Liberty") in *MP* (see *WPW*, 3:109–14, 117–18).

7. A reference to the letter of March 23, 1801 (p. 628 herein).

8. C's language here recalls the titles of two books by George Herbert (1593–1632): *The Temple* (which includes a section called "The Church-Porch") and *A Priest to the Temple*. C admired Herbert's poetry and annotated a copy of *The Temple* (see *CM* [CC], 2:1032–41).

9. C refers to anonymous editorials recommending the severe treatment of French prisoners of war in the event of a French invasion, England and France having resumed war in May 1803 after a peace lasting fourteen months (*Selected Letters*, ed. H. J. Jackson [Oxford, 1987], 287). Sir James Mackintosh (1765–1832), Scottish philosopher and politician, was notorious for having embraced Burke's conservatism and renounced his initial support of the French Revolution, which had been expressed in an attack on Burke called *Vindiciae Gallicae* (1791). In 1798 Mackintosh had helped secure C work contributing articles to *MP*.

1. This and the following letter were written from the house of C's longtime friend Josiah Wade, a Bristol businessman, where C stayed from December 1813 to September 1814.

trust, rising again, tho' slowly and gradually.[2] I thank you from my heart for your far too kind Letter to Mr Hood[3]—so much of it is true that such as you described I always wished to be. I know, it will be vain to attempt to persuade Mrs Morgan or Charlotte, that a man, whose moral feelings, reason, understanding, and senses are perfectly sane and vigorous, may yet have been *mad*—And yet nothing is more true. By the long long Habit of the accursed Poison my Volition (by which I mean the faculty *instrumental* to the Will, and by which alone the Will can realize itself—its Hands, Legs, & Feet, as it were) was compleatly deranged, at times frenzied, dissevered itself from the Will, & became an independent faculty: so that I was perpetually in the state, in which you may have seen paralytic Persons, who attempting to push a step forward in one direction are violently forced round to the opposite. I was sure that no ease, much less pleasure, would ensue: nay, was certain of an accumulation of pain. But tho' there was no prospect, no gleam of Light before, an indefinite indescribable Terror as with a scourge of ever restless, ever coiling and uncoiling Serpents, drove me on from behind.—The worst was, that in *exact proportion* to the *importance* and *urgency* of any Duty was it, as of a fatal necessity, sure to be neglected: because it added to the Terror above described. In exact proportion, as I *loved* any person or persons more than others, & would have sacrificed my Life for them, were *they* sure to be the most barbarously mistreated by silence, absence, or breach of promise.—I used to think St James's Text,"He who offendeth in one point of the Law, offendeth in all,"[4] very harsh; but my own sad experience has taught me its aweful, dreadful Truth.—What crime is there scarcely which has not been included in or followed from the one guilt of taking opium? Not to speak of ingratitude to my maker for the wasted Talents; of ingratitude to so many friends who have loved me I know not why; of barbarous neglect of my family; excess of cruelty to Mary & Charlotte, when at Box, and both ill—(a vision of Hell to me when I think of it!) I have in this one dirty business of Laudanum an hundred times deceived, tricked, nay, actually & consciously LIED.— And yet *all* these vices are so opposite to my nature, that but for this *free-agency-annihilating* Poison, I verily believe that I should have suffered myself to have been cut to pieces rather than have committed any one of them.

At length, it became too bad. I used to take [from] 4 to 5 ounces a day of Laudanum, once . . .[5] [ou]nces, i.e. near a Pint—besides great

---

2. C recalls the words of the Apostles' Creed in the Book of Common Prayer: "Jesus Christ * * * Was crucified, dead, and buried, He descended into hell; The third day he rose again from the dead * * *."
3. William Hood, one of the Bristol friends who, with Wade and Joseph Cottle, had arranged for the physician Henry Daniel to care for C.
4. James 2.10 (var.).
5. The manuscript is torn here (*CL*, 3:490n. 1). Because pharmaceuticals were unregulated in Britain until the mid-1800s and the strengths of preparations varied widely, it is impossible to know how much morphine C was actually ingesting, even if his figure of four to five ounces of laudanum per day was accurate (Cottle later claimed that C was consuming as much as two pints per day at this time [*ER*, 2:169]). See also "Opium" (p. 601 herein) and, on the medical context of C's opium use, Molly Lefebure, *Samuel Taylor Coleridge: The Bondage of Opium*, 51–68.

quantities [of liquo]r. From the Sole of my foot to the Crown of [my h]eart there was not an Inch in which I was not [contin]ually in torture: for more than a fortnight no [sleep] ever visited my Eye lids—but the agonies of [remor]se were far worse than all!—Letters past between Cottle, Hood, & myself—& our kind Friend, Hood, sent Mr Daniel to me. At his second Call I told him plainly (for I had sculked out the night before & got Laudanum) that while I was in my own power, all would be in vain—I should inevitably cheat & trick *him*, just as I had done Dr Tuthill[6]—that I must either be removed to a place of confinement, or at all events have a Keeper.—Daniel saw the truth of my observations, & my most faithful excellent friend, Wade, procured a strong-bodied, but decent, meek, elderly man, to superintend me, under the name of my Valet—All in the House were forbidden to fetch any thing but by the Doctor's order.—Daniel generally spends two or three hours a day with me—and already from 4 & 5 ounces has brought me down to four tea spoonfuls in the 24 Hours—The terror & the indefinite craving are gone—& he expects to drop it altogether by the middle of next week—Till a day or two after that I would rather not see you.

To J. J. Morgan (May 15, 1814)

Sunday, 15 May, 1814.
2. Queen's Square.

My dear Morgan

To continue from my last—Such was the direful state of my mind, that (I tell it you with horror) the razors, penknife, & every possible instrument of Suicide it was found necessary to remove from my room! My faithful, my *inexhaustibly patient* Friend, WADE, has caused a person to sleep by my bed side, on a bed on the floor: so that I might never be altogether alone—O Good God! why do such good men love me! At times, it would be more delightful to me to lie in the Kennel,[1] & (as Southey said) "unfit to be pulled out by any honest man except with a pair of Tongs."—What *he* then said (perhaps) rather unkindly of me, was prophetically true! Often have I wished to have been thus trodden & spit upon, if by any means it might be an atonement for the direful guilt, that (like all others) first *smiled* on me, like Innocence! then crept closer, & yet closer, till it had thrown its serpent folds round & round me,[2] and I was no longer in my own power! *Something* even the most wretched of Beings (*human* Beings at least) owes to himself—& this I *will* say & *dare* with truth say—that never was I led to this wicked direful practice of taking Opium or Laudanum by any

6. Sir George Leman Tuthill (1772–1835) had cared for Mary Lamb in 1810 and for Washington Allston (p. 339 herein) in 1813, but it is not certain when he had cared for C. Since C himself had arranged for Tuthill to treat Allston, however, he must have known him by the summer of 1813 (*CL*, 3:490n. 2).
1. I.e., the gutter.
2. Cf. the "viper thoughts, that coil about my mind" in "Dejection: An Ode," line 94.

desire or expectation of exciting *pleasurable* sensations; but purely by *terror*, by cowardice of pain, first of mental pain, & afterwards as my System became weakened, even of bodily Pain.

My Prayers have been fervent, in agony of Spirit, and for hours together, incessant! still ending, O! only for the merits, for the agonies, for the cross of my blessed Redeemer! For I am nothing, but evil—I can do nothing, but evil! Help, Help!—I believe! help thou my unbelief!—[3]

Mr Daniel has been the wisest of physicians to me. I cannot say, how much I am indebted both to his Skill and Kindness. But he is one of the few rare men, who can make even their Kindness Skill, & the best and most unaffected Virtues of their Hearts *professionally* useful.

Anxious as I am to see you, yet I would wish to delay it till some 3 days after the total abandonment of the Poison. I expect, that this will commence on Tuesday next.—[4]

*   *   *

To Thomas Allsop (March 30, 1820)[1]

Thursday Afternoon

*   *   *

There never was a time, in which the *complaint* would be so little wise, tho' perhaps none in which the *fact* is more *prominent*. Neither Philosophy or Poetry ever did, nor as long as they are terms of comparative excellence & contradistinction, ever can be *popular*, nor honored with the praise and favor of Contemporaries. But on the other hand, there never was a time, in which either books, that were *held* for excellent as poetic or philosophic, had so extensive and rapid a sale, or men reputed Poets and Philosophers of a high rank were so much *looked up* to in Society or so munificently, almost profusely, rewarded.—Walter Scott's Poems & Novels (except only the two wretched Abortions, Ivanhoe & the Bride of Ravensmuir[2] or whatever its name be) supply both instance & solution of the *present* conditions & components of popular-

---

3. Cf. Mark 9.24: "And straightaway the father of the child cried out, and said with tears, Lord, I believe; help thou my unbelief."
4. In fact C was never able to give up taking laudanum; and even after his daily dosage had been reduced and regularized by James Gillman, he would secretly procure additional doses from a local chemist (see Richard Holmes, *Coleridge: Darker Reflections*, 521–22, 541–42).
1. Thomas Allsop (1795–1880), a wealthy businessman, met C in 1818 after attending one of his literary lectures and became a close friend.
2. C had never admired Scott's poetry, and thought that Scott had insufficiently acknowledged the indebtedness of his "Lay of the Last Minstrel" (1805) to C's own (then unpublished) "Christabel" (*CL*, 3:290–96, 854–58). But he did admire Scott's anonymously published novels, and he told Allsop on April 8, 1820, that he had read most of them "twice, & several three times, over with undiminished pleasure and interest; and that in my reprobation of the Bride of Lammar Muir * * * and of the Ivanhoe, I meant to imply the grounds of my admiration of the others" (*CL*, 5:33). Ivanhoe (1819), historical fiction, is about a 12th-century Saxon nobleman, Wilfred of Ivanhoe, who supports the Norman king Richard I against the Saxons and is eventually united with his beloved, Rowenna. *The Bride of Lammermore* (1819), set in Scotland in the 1690s, concerns the frustrated love of the temperamental Master of Ravenswood and his enemy's daughter, Lucy Ashton, who descends into madness. What C does not mention here, though he would complain about it later, is that chapter 9 of *Ivanhoe* contained an unacknowledged quotation from his unpublished poem "The Knight's Tomb" (*CL*, 5:24n. 2; 379–81; *PW*, 1:432 and n.). For C's extensive annotations on Scott's works, see *CM* (*CC*), 4:574–614.

ity—viz—to amuse without requiring any effort of thought, & without exciting any deep emotion. The age seems *sore* from excess of stimulation, just as a day or two after a thorough Debauch & long sustained Drinking-match a man feels all over like a Bruise. Even to *admire* otherwise than *on the whole* and where "I admire" is but a synonyme for "I remember, I *liked* it very much *when I was reading it*," is too much an effort, would be too disquieting an emotion!

* * *

—Of my poetic works I would fain finish the Christabel—Alas! for the proud times when I planned, when I had present to my mind the materials as well as the Scheme of the Hymns, entitled Spirit, Sun, Earth, Air, Water, Fire, and Man: and the Epic Poem on what still appears to me the one only fit subject remaining for an Epic Poem, Jerusalem besieged & destroyed by Titus.[3]

And here comes, my dear Allsop!—here comes my sorrow and my weakness, my grievance and my confession. Anxious to perform the duties of the day arising out of the wants of the day, these wants too presenting themselves in the most painful of all forms, that of a debt owing to those who will not exact and yet need its payment—and the delay, the long (not live-long but *death*-long) BEHIND-HAND of my accounts to Friends whose utmost care and frugality on the one side and industry on the other, the wife's Management & the Husband's assiduity, are put in requisition to make both ends meet, I am at once forbidden to attempt and too perplext effectually to pursue, the *accomplishment* of the works worthy of me, those I mean above enumerated—even if, savagely as I have been injured by one of the two influencive Reviews & with more effective enmity undermined by the utter silence or occasional detractive compliments of the other,[4] I had the probable chance of disposing of them to the Booksellers so as even to liquidate my mere *Boarding* accounts during the time expended in the transcription, arrangement, and Proof-correction—and yet on the other hand my Heart & Mind are for ever recurring to them—Yes! my Conscience forces me to plead guilty—I have only by fits and starts even prayed, I have not even prevailed on myself to pray to God in sincerity and entireness, for the fortitude that might enable me to resign myself to the abandonment of all my Life's best Hopes—to say boldly to myself—"Gifted with powers confessedly above mediocrity, aided by an Education of which no less from almost unexampled Hardships & Sufferings than from manifold & peculiar advantages I have never yet found a Parallel, I have devoted myself to a Life of unintermitted Reading, Thinking, Meditating and Observing—I have not only sacrificed all wor[l]dly prospects of wealth & advancement but have in my

---

3. C neither "finished" "Christabel" nor began the epic on the capture of Jerusalem in 70 C.E. by the Roman general (and later emperor) Titus (39–71). On the place of this unwritten epic in C's thought, see E. S. Shaffer, *"Kubla Khan" and "The Fall of Jerusalem,"* 17–61. The hymns, conceived as early as 1796, also remained unwritten (*CL*, 5:28n. 1).

4. "Neither my Literary Life (2 Vol.) [*Biographia Literaria*] nor Sibylline Leaves (1 Vol.) nor Friend (3 Vol.) nor Lay-Sermons [*The Statesman's Manual* and *A Lay Sermon*], nor Zapolya, nor Christabel, have ever been noticed by the Quarterly Review, of which Southey is yet the main support." [C's note.]

inmost soul stood aloof even from temporary Reputation—in consequence of these toils & this self-dedication I possess a calm & clear
consciousness that in many & most important departments of Truth &
Beauty I have outstrode my Contemporaries, those at least of highest
name—that the number of my printed works bears witness that I have
not been idle, and the seldom acknowledged but yet strictly *proveable*
effects of my labors appropriated to the immediate welfare of my Age,
in the Morning Post before, and during the Peace of Amiens, in the
Courier afterwards, and in the series & various subjects of my Lectures, at Bristol, and at the Royal, & Surry Institutions; in Fetter Lane;
in Willis's Rooms; at the Crown & Anchor[5] &c (add to which the unlimited freedom of my communications in colloquial life) may surely
be allowed as evidence that I have not been useless in my generation,
but from circumstances the *main* portion of my Harvest is still on the
ground, ripe indeed and only waiting, a few for the sickle, but a large
part only for the *sheaving*, and carting and housing—but from all this
I must turn away, must let them rot as they lie, & be as tho' they never
had been: for I must go to gather Blackberries, and Earth Nuts, or
pick mushrooms & gild Oak-Apples for the Palates & Fancies of
chance Customers.—I must abrogate the name of Philosopher, and
Poet, and scribble as fast as I can & with as little thought as I can for
Blackwood's Magazine,[6] or as I have been employed for the last days,
in writing MSS sermons for lazy Clergymen who stipulate that the
composition must not be *more* than respectable, for fear they should
be desired to publish the Visitation Sermon!"—This I have not yet had
courage to do—My soul sickens & my Heart sinks—& thus oscillating
between both I do neither—neither as it ought to be done, or to any
profitable end. If I were to detail only the various, I might say, capricious interruptions that have prevented the finishing of this very
scrawl, begun on the very day I received your last kind letter with the
Hare, you would need no other illustrations—

*   *   *

5. C gave a series of philosophical lectures at the Crown and Anchor Tavern in London in
   1818–19. He wrote articles for *MP* from 1798 to 1803 and for the *Courier* from 1804 to
   1818. *Peace of Amiens*: a fourteenth-month hiatus, from March 1802 to May 1803, in the
   war between Britain and France. For the lectures in London and Bristol see the headnote,
   p. 307 herein.
6. C was to contribute a series of literary letters and an article, "The Historie and Gests of
   Maxilian," to *Blackwood's Edinburgh Magazine* in 1821–22 (*SW&F* [CC], 915–53, 963–85).

CRITICISM

Nineteenth Century: Britain

WILLIAM WORDSWORTH

The Prelude (1805), book 6, lines 249–331†

Far art thou wandered now in search of health,[1]
And milder breezes—melancholy lot—   250
But thou art with us, with us in the past,
The present, with us in the times to come.
There is no grief, no sorrow, no despair,
No languor, no dejection, no dismay,
No absence scarcely can there be, for those   255
Who love as we do. Speed thee well! divide
Thy pleasure with us; thy returning strength,
Receive it daily as a joy of ours;
Share with us thy fresh spirits, whether gift
Of gales Etesian[2] or of loving thoughts.   260

    I too have been a wanderer, but, alas,
How different is the fate of different men,
Though twins almost in genius and in mind.
Unknown unto each other, yea, and breathing
As if in different elements, we were framed   265
To bend at last to the same discipline,
Predestined, if two beings ever were,
To seek the same delights, and have one health,
One happiness. Throughout this narrative,
Else sooner ended, I have known full well   270
For whom I thus record the birth and growth
Of gentleness, simplicity, and truth,
And joyous loves that hallow innocent days
Of peace and self-command. Of rivers, fields,
And groves, I speak to thee, my friend—to thee   275
Who, yet a liveried schoolboy in the depths
Of the huge city, on the leaded roof
Of that wide edifice, thy home and school,
Wast used to lie and gaze upon the clouds
Moving in heaven, or haply, tired of this,   280

---

† *The Prelude: 1799, 1805, 1850*, ed. Jonathan Wordsworth, M. H. Abrams, and Stephen Gill (New York: W. W. Norton, 1979), 198–202. Reprinted by permission of the publisher.
1. Composed in March 1804, these lines refer to C's trip to Malta (1804–06), which he undertook to seek a reprieve from his deteriorating health caused by opium addiction.
2. Mediterranean summer winds.

To shut thine eyes and by internal light
See trees, and meadows, and thy native stream[3]
Far distant—thus beheld from year to year
Of thy long exile.[4] Nor could I forget
In this late portion of my argument   285
That scarcely had I finally resigned
My rights among those academic bowers
When thou wert thither guided. From the heart
Of London, and from cloisters there, thou cam'st
And didst sit down in temperance and peace,   290
A rigorous student. What a stormy course
Then followed[5]—oh, it is a pang that calls
For utterance, to think how small a change
Of circumstances might to thee have spared
A world of pain, ripened ten thousand hopes   295
For ever withered. Through this retrospect
Of my own college life I still have had
Thy after-sojourn in the self-same place
Present before my eyes, have played with times
(I speak of private business of the thought)   300
And accidents as children do with cards,
Or as a man, who, when his house is built,
A frame locked up in wood and stone, doth still
In impotence of mind by his fireside
Rebuild it to his liking. I have thought   305
Of thee, thy learning, gorgeous eloquence,
And all the strength and plumage of thy youth,
Thy subtle speculations, toils abstruse[6]
Among the schoolmen, and Platonic forms
Of wild ideal pageantry, shaped out   310
From things well-matched, or ill, and words for things—
The self-created sustenance of a mind
Debarred from Nature's living images,
Compelled to be a life unto itself,
And unrelentingly possessed by thirst   315
Of greatness, love, and beauty. Not alone,
Ah, surely not in singleness of heart
Should I have seen the light of evening fade
Upon the silent Cam, if we had met,
Even at that early time: I needs must hope,   320
Must feel, must trust, that my maturer age
And temperature less willing to be moved,

3. The river Otter, to which C dedicated the sonnet "To the River Otter" (p. 50 herein).
4. Wordsworth alludes to C's depiction in "Frost at Midnight" (lines 56–58) of his lonely time
   at Christ's Hospital in London, in "the great city, pent mid cloisters dim" (see p. 121 herein
   and p. 385, n. 6 herein).
5. The "stormy" events that followed C's stay at Christ's Hospital include his years at Cambridge University, during which he became involved in radical politics and Unitarian religion, as well as his brief career in the army, which, as a result of incurring large debts, he
   joined in 1793.
6. Cf. Lamb's description of C's absorption in metaphysics and Neoplatonic philosophy at
   Christ's Hospital (see p. 647 herein). Wordsworth alludes here to stanza 6 of C's "Dejection:
   An Ode," in which C attributes the loss of his creative powers to "abstruse research."

My calmer habits, and more steady voice,
Would with an influence benign have soothed
Or chased away the airy wretchedness   325
That battened on thy youth. But thou hast trod,
In watchful meditation thou hast trod,
A march of glory, which doth put to shame[7]
These vain regrets; health suffers in thee, else
Such grief for thee would be the weakest thought   330
That ever harboured in the breast of man.

CHARLES LAMB

From Christ's Hospital Five and Thirty Years Ago
(1820)†

* * * Come back into memory, like as thou wert in the day-spring of thy fancies, with hope like a fiery column before thee—the dark pillar not yet turned—Samuel Taylor Coleridge—Logician, Metaphysician, Bard!—How have I seen the casual passer through the Cloisters stand still, intranced with admiration (while he weighed the disproportion between the *speech* and the *garb* of the young Mirandula),[1] to hear thee unfold, in thy deep and sweet intonations, the mysteries of Jamblichus, or Plotinus[2] (for even in years though waxedst not pale at such philosophic draughts), or reciting Homer in his Greek, or Pindar—while the walls of the old Grey Friars[3] re-echoed to the accents of the *inspired charity-boy!*—Many were the "wit-combats," (to dally awhile with the words of old Fuller), between him and C. V. Le G[rice],[4] "which two I behold like a Spanish great galleon, and an English man of war; Master Coleridge, like the former, was built far higher in learning, solid, but slow in his performances. C. V. L[e Grice], with the English man of war, lesser in bulk, but lighter in sailing, could turn with all tides, tack about, and take advantage of all winds, by the quickness of his wit and invention."

7. An allusion to Milton, *Samson Agonistes*, line 597: "My race of glory run, and race of shame." On this passage by Wordsworth and the significance of this Miltonic allusion, see Lucy Newlyn, *Coleridge, Wordsworth and the Language of Allusion*, 176–77.
† *Elia and the Last Essays of Elia*, ed. Jonathan Bate (Oxford: Oxford University Press, 1997), 24–25.
1. Giovanni Pico della Mirandola (1463–1494), Italian Neoplatonic philosopher.
2. Iamblichus (c. 250–c. 325) and Plotinus (c. 205–270), Neoplatonic philosophers.
3. Christ's Hospital, the London charity institution where C went to school from 1781 to 1791, previously belonged to the Grey Friars (i.e., Franciscans). See also p. 624, n. 1 herein.
4. Charles Valentine Le Grice (1773–1858), fellow student and friend of C's at Christ's Hospital and later at Cambridge. In 1834 he published "Reminiscences of Mr. Coleridge" in *The Gentleman's Magazine*, to which he was a frequent contributor. *Wit-combats*: battles of wit between Shakespeare and Ben Jonson as described by Thomas Fuller in *Worthies of England* (1662).

From Letters†

* * * I am sorry that Coleridge has christened his Ancient Marinere "a poet's reverie"—it is as bad as Bottom the Weaver's declaration that he is not a Lion but only the scenical representation of a Lion.[1] What new idea is gained by this Title, but one subversive of all credit, which the Tale should force upon us, of its truth?—For me, I was never so affected with any human Tale. After first reading it, I was totally possessed with it for many days.—I dislike all the miraculous part of it, but the feelings of the man under the operation of such scenery dragged me along like Tom Piper's magic Whistle.—I totally differ from your idea that the Marinere should have had a character and a profession.—[2] This is a Beauty in Gulliver's Travels,[3] where the mind is kept in a placid state of little wonderments; but the Ancient Marinere undergoes such Trials, as overwhelm and bury all individuality or memory of what he was.—Like the state of a man in a Bad dream, one terrible peculiarity of which is, that all consciousness of personality is gone.—Your other observation is I think as well a little unfounded: the Marinere from being conversant in supernatural events has acquired a supernatural and strange cast of *phrase*, eye, appearance &c. which frighten the wedding guest.—[4] You will excuse my remarks, because I am hurt and vexed that you should think it necessary, with a prose apology, to open they[5] eyes of dead men that cannot see.——. To sum up a general opinion of the second vol.—I do not feel any one poem in it so forcibly as the Ancient Marinere, the Mad mother, and the Lines at Tintern Abbey in the first.[6]——I could, too, have wished that The Critical preface had appeared in a separate treatise.—All its dogmas are true and just and most of them new, *as* criticism.—But they associate a *diminishing* idea with the Poems which follow, as having been written for Experiments on the public taste, more than having sprung (as they must have done) from living and daily circumstances.[7] * * *

---

† Letter to William Wordsworth of January 30, 1801 (*LL*, 1:266–67). Reprinted by permission of the Harry Ranson Humanities Research Center, University of Texas at Austin.
1. Shakespeare, *A Midsummer Night's Dream* 3.1.32–40. C added the subtitle "A Poet's Reverie" to "The Rhyme of the Ancient Mariner" in *LB* (1800); it was finally omitted after the fourth edition (1805).
2. Lamb refers to Wordsworth's apologetic note attached to "The Ancient Mariner" in *LB* (1800), in which he complained that the mariner had no "distinct character" or profession. See headnote to *Lyrical Ballads* (p. 56 herein).
3. The popular work by Jonathan Swift.
4. In the note appended to "The Ancient Mariner," Wordsworth also complained that the Mariner, by being too much under the influence of the supernatural, partook of its character.
5. Error in the manuscript for "the."
6. C's poem "The Mad Mother" and Wordsworth's "Tintern Abbey" appeared in the first edition of the *LB* (1798) and were included in volume 1 of the second edition (1800).
7. Cf. C's attack on Wordsworth's critical preface and his sense that the principles of the Preface are contradicted by Wordsworth's poems (see chapters 4 and 14 of the *Biographia*).

From [The Album of a London Bookseller]†

When I heard of the death of Coleridge, it was without grief. It seemed to me that he long had been on the confines of the next world,—that he had a hunger for eternity. I grieved then that I could not grieve. But since, I feel how great a part he was of me. His great and dear spirit haunts me. I cannot think a thought, I cannot make a criticism on men or books, without an ineffectual turning and reference to him. He was the proof and touchstone of all my cogitations. * * * Great in his writings, he was greatest in his conversation. In him was disproved that old maxim, that we should allow every one his share of talk. He would talk from morn to dewy eve, nor cease till far midnight, yet who ever would interrupt him,—who would obstruct that continuous flow of converse, fetched from Helicon or Zion? He had the tact of making the unintelligible seem plain. Many who read the abstruser parts of his "Friend" would complain that his works did not answer to his spoken wisdom. They were identical. But he had a tone in oral delivery, which seemed to convey sense to those who were otherwise imperfect recipients. He was my fifty years old friend without a dissension. Never saw I likeness, nor probably the world can see again. * * *

WILLIAM HAZLITT

From Lectures on the English Poets (1818)‡

* * * It remains that I should say a few words of Mr Coleridge; and there is no one who has a better right to say what he thinks of him than I have. "Is there here any dear friend of Cæsar? To him I say, that Brutus's love to Cæsar was no less than his."[1] But no matter.—His Ancient Mariner is his most remarkable performance, and the only one that I could point out to any one as giving an adequate idea of his great natural powers. It is high German, however, and in it he seems to "conceive of poetry but as a drunken dream, reckless, careless, and heedless, of past, present, and to come."[2] His tragedies (for he has written two) are not answerable to it; they are, except a few poetical passages, drawling sentiment / and metaphysical jargon. He has no genuine dramatic talent. There is one fine passage in his Christobel, that which contains the description of the quarrel between Sir Leoline and Sir Roland de Vaux of Tryermaine, who had been friends in youth.[3]

*   *   *

† *Coleridge the Talker*, ed. R. W. Armour and R. F. Howes (Ithaca, N.Y., 1940), 280–81.
‡ *The Selected Writings of William Hazlitt*, ed. Duncan Wu, 9 vols. (London: Pickering & Chatto, 1998), 2:318–20. Reprinted by permission of the publisher.
1. Shakespeare, *Julius Caesar* 3.2.17–19 (var.).
2. Shakespeare, *Measure for Measure* 4.2.132–34 (var.).
3. Hazlitt proceeds to cite a passage (omitted here) from "Christabel," lines 396–418.

It might seem insidious if I were to praise his ode entitled Fire, Famine, and Slaughter, as an effusion of high poetical enthusiasm, and strong political feeling. His Sonnet to Schiller conveys a fine compliment to the author of the Robbers, and an equally fine idea of the state of youthful enthusiasm in which he composed it.[4]

* * *

His *Conciones ad Populum,* Watchman, &c. are dreary trash. Of his Friend, I have spoken the truth elsewhere. But I may say of him here, that he is the only person I ever knew who answered to the idea of a man of genius. He is the only person from whom I ever learnt any thing. There is only one thing he could learn from me in return, but *that* he has not. He was the first poet I ever knew. His genius at that time had angelic wings, and fed on manna. He talked on for ever; and you wished him to talk on for ever. His thoughts did not seem to come with labour and effort; but as if borne on the gusts of genius, and as if the wings of his imagination lifted him from off his feet. His voice rolled on the ear like the pealing organ, and its sound alone was the music of thought. His mind was clothed with wings; and raised on them, he lifted philosophy to heaven. In his descriptions, you then saw the progress of human happiness and liberty in bright and never-ending succession, like the steps of Jacob's ladder, with airy shapes ascending and descending, and with the voice of God at the top of the ladder. And shall I, who heard him then, listen to him now? Not I! . . . That spell is broke; that time is gone for ever; that voice is heard no more: but still the recollection comes rushing by with thoughts of long-past years, and rings in my ears with never-dying sound.[5]

* * *

From The Spirit of the Age (1825)†

Mr Coleridge

The present is an age of talkers, and not of doers; and the reason is, that the world is growing old. We are so far advanced in the Arts and Sciences, that we live in retrospect, and doat on past achievements.

* * *

If Mr Coleridge had not been the most impressive talker of his age, he would probably have been the finest writer; but he lays down his pen to make sure of an auditor, and mortgages the admiration of posterity for the stare of an idler. If he had not been a poet, he would have been a powerful logician; if he had not dipped his wing in the Unitarian controversy, he might have soared to the very summit of fancy. But in writing verse, he is trying to subject the Muse to *transcendental* theories: in his abstract reasoning, he misses his way by

---

4. Hazlitt cites C's sonnet to Schiller ("Effusion XX," p. 16 herein).
5. Hazlitt continues with a passage (omitted here) from Wordsworth, "Ode (Intimations of Immortality)," lines 178–87, 189.
† "The Spirit of the Age," *Selected Writings,* 4:98–105. Reprinted by permission of the publisher.

strewing it with flowers. All that he has done of moment, he had done twenty years ago: since then, he may be said to have lived on the sound of his own voice. Mr Coleridge is too rich in intellectual wealth, to need to task himself to any drudgery: he has only to draw the sliders of his imagination, and a thousand subjects expand before him, startling him with their brilliancy, or losing themselves in endless obscurity—

> And by the force of blear illusion,
> They draw him on to his confusion.[1]

What is the little he could add to the stock, compared with the countless stores that lie about him, that he should stoop to pick up a name, or to polish an idle fancy? He walks abroad in the majesty of an universal understanding, eyeing the "rich strond,"[2] or golden sky above him, and "goes sounding on his way,"[3] in eloquent accents, uncompelled and free!

*　*　*

Mr Coleridge talks of himself, without being an egotist, for in him the individual is always merged in the abstract and general. He distinguished himself at school and at the University by his knowledge of the classics, and gained several prizes for Greek epigrams.[4] How many men are there (great scholars, celebrated names in literature) who having done the same thing in their youth, have no other idea all the rest of their lives but of this achievement, of a fellowship and dinner, and who, installed in academic honours, would look down on our author as a mere strolling bard! At Christ's Hospital, where he was brought up, he was the idol of those among his schoolfellows, who mingled with their bookish studies the music of thought and of humanity;[5] and he was usually attended round the cloisters by a group of these (inspiring and inspired) whose hearts, even then, burnt within them as he talked, and where the sounds yet linger to mock ELIA on his way, still turning pensive to the past![6] One of the finest and rarest parts of Mr Coleridge's conversation, is when he expatiates / on the Greek tragedians (not that he is not well acquainted, when he pleases, with the epic poets, or the philosophers, or orators, or historians of antiquity)—on the subtle reasonings and melting pathos of Euripides, on the harmonious gracefulness of Sophocles, tuning his love-laboured song, like sweetest warblings from a sacred grove; on the high-wrought trumpet-tongued eloquence of Æschylus, whose Prometheus, above all, is like an Ode to Fate, and a pleading with Providence, his thoughts being let loose as his body is chained on his solitary rock, and his afflicted will (the emblem of mortality)

---

1. Shakespeare, *Macbeth* 3.5.28–29 (var.).
2. Spenser, *The Faerie Queene* 3.4.34.
3. This line from Wordsworth, *The Excursion* (1814), 3.701, was also used by C in chapter 5 of the *Biographia* (see p. 423, n. 3 herein).
4. In 1792, while a student at Jesus College, Cambridge, C won the Browne medal for his Greek ode on the slave trade.
5. An echo of Wordsworth, "Tintern Abbey," line 92: "The still, sad music of humanity." *Christ's Hospital*: see p. 380, n. 2 herein and p. 647 herein.
6. Luke 24.32.

Struggling in vain with ruthless destiny.[7]

As the impassioned critic speaks and rises in his theme, you would think you heard the voice of the Man hated by the Gods, contending with the wild winds as they roar, and his eye glitters with the spirit of Antiquity!

*   *   *

Of all Mr Coleridge's productions, the *Ancient Mariner* is the only one that we could with confidence put into any person's hands, on whom we wished to impress a favourable idea of his extraordinary powers. Let whatever other objections be made to it, it is unquestionably a work of genius—of wild, irregular, overwhelming imagination, and has that rich, varied movement in the verse, which gives a distant idea of the lofty or changeful tones of Mr Coleridge's voice. In the *Christobel*, there is one splendid passage on divided friendship.[8] The *Translation of Schiller's Wallenstein*[9] is also a masterly production in its kind, faithful and spirited. Among his smaller pieces there are occasional bursts of pathos and fancy, equal to what we might expect from him; but these form / the exception, and not the rule. Such, for instance, is his affecting Sonnet to the author of the Robbers.[1]

*   *   *

His Tragedy, entitled *Remorse*,[2] is full of beautiful and striking passages, but it does not place the author in the first rank of dramatic writers. But if Mr Coleridge's works do not place him in that rank, they injure instead of conveying a just idea of the man, for he himself is certainly in the first class of general intellect.

If our author's poetry is inferior to his conversation, his prose is utterly abortive. Hardly a gleam is to be found in it of the brilliancy and richness of those stores of thought and language that he pours out incessantly, when they / are lost like drops of water in the ground. The principal work, in which he has attempted to embody his general views of things, is the FRIEND, of which, though it contains some noble passages and fine trains of thought, prolixity and obscurity are the most frequent characteristics. * * *

---

7. Wordsworth, *The Excursion* (1814), 6.557.
8. I.e., lines 396–418. See also p. 173, n. 1 herein.
9. C's translation was published in 1800.
1. "Effusion XX" (p. 16 herein).
2. See *BL* (CC), 1:26n.1.

ANNE JACKSON MATHEWS[1]

From The Life and Correspondence of Charles Mathews the Elder, Comedian†

Many, many delightful hours did Mr. Coleridge's splendid conversation give us and our friends. From his kind-heartedness, his beautiful simplicity of manner (for his familiar thoughts and expressions were as admirable as the higher attributes of his vast mind) we really loved, as much as we admired him.

* * *

The simplicity of Mr. Coleridge's character on familiar occasions gave us infinite amusement, which, on his perceiving it, he allowed, with a smile against himself, while some charming remark would increase our enjoyment, and he would leave us with his benevolent features beaming with good-humour and kindness. One invariable result of his earnestly engaging in a long subject of discourse was a total abstraction of mind succeeding to it. In our drawing-room we had placed a large mirror, which reached from the ceiling to the floor, so inserted (without any visible frame) as to seem a continuation of the apartment. On taking leave, morning or night, he generally made an effort to pass through this glass; and it was our custom always to watch his first movement of departure, in order to be ready to guard against the consequences of an attempt to make his way out through this palpable impediment, and guide him to the door. To all this he would submit, talking and laughing upon the point which prevented his knowledge of outward things, until the entrance-gate was closed upon him. * * *

During the first part of our acquaintance with him, Mr. Coleridge talked much to us of his friend "Charles Lamb," and expressed a strong desire that we should know him. * * * At last Mr. and Miss Lamb appeared, and Mr. Coleridge led his friend up to my husband with a look which seemed to say, "I pray you, like this fellow." Mr. Lamb's first approach was not prepossessing. * * * Guessing that he had been extolled, he mischievously resolved to thwart his panegyrist, disappoint the strangers, and altogether to upset the suspected plan of showing him off. The lamb, in fact, would not consent to be made a lion of, and it followed that he became puerile and annoying all the day, to Mr. Coleridge's visible mortification. Before dinner he was suspicious and silent, as if he was taking measure of the man he came to meet, and about whom he seemed very curious. Dinner, however, opened his lips for more than one purpose; and the first glass of wine set his spirit free, and he became quite impracticable. He made the

---

1. Anne Jackson (1782?–1869), an actor, married the celebrated comic actor and mimic Charles Mathews (1776–1835) in 1803 and frequently performed with him before her retirement from the stage in 1810. From 1819 to 1833 the Mathews lived near C, of whom Charles Mathews did private impersonations.

† *The Life and Correspondence of Charles Mathews the Elder, Comedian,* ed. Edmund Yates (London, 1860), 243–46.

most absurd puns and ridiculous jokes, and almost harassed Coleridge
out of his self-complacency, though he managed to maintain a tolerable degree of evenness with his tormentor, now and then only rebuking him mildly for what he termed "such unworthy trifling." * * *

Mr. Lamb's last fire, however, was at length expended, and Mr. Coleridge took advantage of a pause to introduce some topic that might divert the party from his friend's determined foolery. He chose a subject
which he deemed unlikely, if not impossible, for Lamb to interrupt
with a jest. Mr. Coleridge stated that he had originally been intended
for the pulpit, and had taken orders—nay, had actually preached several times. At this moment, fancying he saw something in Lamb's face
that denoted a lucid interval, and wishing to turn him back from the
nonsense which had so "spoiled the pleasure of the time," with a desire also to conciliate the "pouting boy," as he seemed (who, to our observation, was only waiting for an opportunity to revenge himself upon
his friend for all the grave checks he had given to his jocular vein during dinner), Coleridge turned benignly towards him, and observed—
"Charles Lamb, I believe you never heard me preach?" As if
concentrating his pent-up resentment into one focus, and with less of
his wonted hesitation, Lamb replied, with great emphasis, "I ne-ever
heard you do anything else!"

THOMAS DE QUINCEY

From Samuel Taylor Coleridge†

CHAPTER II[1]

It was, I think, in the month of August, but certainly in the summer
season, and certainly in the year 1807, that I first saw this illustrious
man. My knowledge of him as a man of most original genius began
about the year 1799. A little before that time Wordsworth had published the first edition (in a single volume) of the "Lyrical Ballads,"[2]
and into this had been introduced Mr. Coleridge's poem of the "Ancient Mariner," as the contribution of an anonymous friend. It would
be directing the reader's attention too much to myself if I were to linger
upon this, the greatest event in the unfolding of my own mind. Let me
say, in one word, that, at a period when neither the one nor the other
writer was valued by the public—both having a long warfare to accomplish of contumely and ridicule before they could rise into their present

---

† "Samuel Taylor Coleridge" in *The Collected Writings of Thomas De Quincey*, ed. David Masson, 14 vols. (Edinburgh, 1889–90), 2:138–39, 152–57.
1. This essay is a revised version of a series of four articles published originally in *Tait's Magazine*, September, October, and November 1834 and January 1835. De Quincey was the first
to reveal C's plagiarisms. Himself an opium addict (see his *Confessions of an English Opium
Eater*, 1822) and interested in German philosophy, De Quincey desired a close relationship
with C but felt overshadowed by his stature; after C's death, in the articles in *Tait's Magazine*, he exposed C's weaknesses, his failed marriage, and his antipathies to certain celebrated contemporaries, such as the theologian William Paley.
2. See pp. 54–57 herein.

estimation—I found in these poems "the ray of a new morning," and an absolute revelation of untrodden worlds teeming with power and beauty as yet unsuspected amongst men.

* * *

Coleridge led me to a drawing-room, rang the bell for refreshments, and omitted no point of a courteous reception. He told me that there would be a very large dinner party on that day, which, perhaps, might be disagreeable to a perfect stranger; but, if not, he could assure me of a most hospitable welcome from the family. I was too anxious to see him under all aspects to think of declining this invitation. That point being settled, Coleridge, like some great river, the Orellana, or the St. Lawrence, that, having been checked and fretted by rocks or thwarting islands, suddenly recovers its volume of waters and its mighty music, swept at once, as if returning to his natural business, into a continuous strain of eloquent dissertation, certainly the most novel, the most finely illustrated, and traversing the most spacious fields of thought by transitions the most just and logical, that it was possible to conceive. What I mean by saying that his transitions were "just" is by way of contradistinction to that mode of conversation which courts variety through links of *verbal* connexions. Coleridge, to many people, and often I have heard the complaint, seemed to wander; and he seemed then to wander the most when, in fact, his resistance to the wandering instinct was greatest—viz., when the compass and huge circuit by which his illustrations moved travelled farthest into remote regions before they began to revolve. Long before this coming round commenced most people had lost him, and naturally enough supposed that he had lost himself. They continued to admire the separate beauty of the thoughts, but did not see their relations to the dominant theme. Had the conversation been thrown upon paper, it might have been easy to trace the continuity of the links; just as in Bishop Berkeley's "Siris,"[3] from a pedestal so low and abject, so culinary, as Tar Water, the method of preparing it, and its medicinal effects, the dissertation ascends, like Jacob's ladder, by just graduations, into the Heaven of Heavens and the thrones of the Trinity. But Heaven is there connected with earth by the Homeric chain of gold; and, being subject to steady examination, it is easy to trace the links; whereas, in conversation, the loss of a single word may cause the whole cohesion to disappear from view. However, I can assert, upon my long and intimate knowledge of Coleridge's mind, that logic the most severe was as inalienable from his modes of thinking as grammar from his language.

On the present occasion, the original theme, started by myself, was Hartley and the Hartleian theory. * * * It is known to most literary people that Coleridge was, in early life, so passionate an admirer of the Hartleian philosophy that "Hartley" was the sole baptismal name which he gave to his eldest child; and in an early poem, entitled "Religious Musings," he has characterized Hartley as

---

3. Published in 1744, it begins by considering the medicinal uses of tar water and concludes by considering the Trinity (see p. 487, n. 3 herein).

> Him of mortal kind
> Wisest, him first who mark'd the ideal tribes
> Up the fine fibres through the sentient brain
> Pass in fine surges.[4]

But at present (August 1807) all this was a forgotten thing. Coleridge was so profoundly ashamed of the shallow Unitarianism of Hartley, and so disgusted to think that he could at any time have countenanced that creed, that he would scarcely allow to Hartley the reverence which is undoubtedly his due; for I must contend that, waiving all question of the extent to which Hartley would have pushed it (as though the law of association accounted not only for our complex pleasures and pains, but also might be made to explain the act of ratiocination),—waiving also the physical substratum of nervous vibrations and miniature vibrations to which he has chosen to marry his theory of association;—all this apart, I must contend that the "Essay on Man, his Frame, his Duty, and his Expectations" stands forward as a specimen almost unique of elaborate theorizing, and a monument of absolute beauty in the impression left of its architectural grace. In this respect it has, to my mind, the spotless beauty and the ideal proportions of some Grecian statue. However, I confess that, being myself, from my earliest years, a reverential believer in the doctrine of the Trinity, simply because I never attempted to bring all things within the mechanic understanding, and because, like Sir Thomas Browne, my mind almost demanded mysteries in so mysterious a system of relations as those which connect us with another world, and also because the farther my understanding opened the more I perceived of dim analogies to strengthen my creed, and because nature herself, mere physical nature, has mysteries no less profound; for these, and for many other "*becauses*," I could not reconcile with my general reverence for Mr. Coleridge the fact, so often reported to me, that he was a Unitarian. But, said some Bristol people to me, not only is he a Unitarian—he is also a Socinian. In that case, I replied, I cannot hold him a Christian. I am a liberal man, and have no bigotry or hostile feelings towards a Socinian; but I can never think that man a Christian who has blotted out of his scheme the very powers by which only the great offices and functions of Christianity can be sustained.[5]

* * *

Coleridge told me that it had cost him a painful effort, but not a moment's hesitation, to abjure his Unitarianism, from the circumstance that he had amongst the Unitarians many friends, to some of whom he was greatly indebted for great kindness. In particular, he mentioned Mr. Estlin of Bristol, a distinguished Dissenting clergyman,[6] as one whom it grieved him to grieve. But he would not dissem-

---

4. "Religious Musings," lines 383–86 (p. 32 herein).
5. On C's conversion to Unitarianism at Cambridge and his later rejection of it in favor of Trinitarianism, see p. 264, n. 1 herein; p. 265, n. 5 herein; p. 266, n. 6 herein; p. 457, n. 2 herein; and "Religion" (pp. 606–07 herein).
6. John Prior Estlin (1747–1817), a Unitarian friend and supporter of C until 1814, when C's attack on Unitarians and description of Milton's Satan as a "sceptical Socinian," in a literary lecture of April 7, 1814, strained their relationship. See CL, 3:471–72, 477–78.

ble his altered views. I will add, at the risk of appearing to dwell too long on religious topics, that, on this my first introduction to Coleridge, he reverted with strong compunction to a sentiment which he had expressed in earlier days upon prayer. In one of his youthful poems, speaking of God, he had said—

> Of whose omniscient and all-spreading love
> Aught to implore were impotence of mind.[7]

This sentiment he now so utterly condemned that, on the contrary, he told me, as his own peculiar opinion, that the act of praying was the very highest energy of which the human heart was capable; praying, that is, with the total concentration of the faculties; and the great mass of worldly men, and of learned men, he pronounced absolutely incapable of prayer.

For about three hours he had continued to talk, and in the course of this performance he had delivered many most striking aphorisms, embalming more weight of truth, and separately more deserving to be themselves embalmed, than would easily be found in a month's course of select reading.

* * *

HARRIET MARTINEAU[1]

From Autobiography†

* * * If Coleridge should be remembered, it will be as a warning,—as much in his philosophical as his moral character.—Such is my view of him now. Twenty years ago I regarded him as poet,—in his "Friend" as much as his verse. He was, to be sure, a most remarkable looking personage, as he entered the room, and slowly approached and greeted me. He looked very old, with his rounded shoulders and drooping head, and excessively thin limbs. His eyes were as wonderful as they were ever represented to be;—light grey, extremely prominent, and actually glittering: an appearance I am told common among opium eaters. His onset amused me not a little. He told me that he (the last person whom I should have suspected) read my tales as they came out on the first of the month; and, after paying some compliments, he avowed that there were points on which we differed: (I was full of wonder that there were any on which we agreed:) "for instance," said he, "you appear to consider that society is an aggregate of individuals!" I replied that I certainly did: whereupon he went off on one of the several metaphysical interpretations which may be put upon the many-

---

7. "Effusion XXII. To a Friend together with an Unfinished Poem," lines 27–28 (p. 17 herein).
1. Martineau (1802–1876) was a Unitarian writer best known for her collection of short stories, *Illustrations of Political Economy* (1832–34), which advocated utilitarianism. She met C near the end of his life, and in 1845 she settled in the Lake District and befriended the Wordsworths.
† *Autobiography*, 3 vols. (London, 1877), 1:396–99.

sided fact of an organised human society, subject to natural laws in virtue of its aggregate character and organisation together. After a long flight in survey of society from his own balloon in his own current, he came down again to some considerations of individuals, and at length to some special biographical topics, ending with criticisms on old biographers, whose venerable works he brought down from the shelf. No one else spoke, of course, except when I once or twice put a question; and when his monologue came to what seemed a natural stop, I rose to go. * * * Coleridge appears to me to have been constitutionally defective in will, in conscientiousness and in apprehension of the real and true, while gifted or cursed with inordinate reflective and analogical faculties, as well as prodigious word power. Hence his success as an instigator of thought in others, and as a talker and writer; while utterly failing in his apprehension of truth, and in the conduct of his life.

*   *   *

THOMAS CARLYLE[1]

From The Life of John Sterling†

Coleridge sat on the brow of Highgate Hill, in those years, looking down on London and its smoke-tumult, like a sage escaped from the inanity of life's battle; attracting towards him the thoughts of innumerable brave souls still engaged there. His express contributions to poetry, philosophy, or any specific province of human literature or enlightenment, had been small and sadly intermittent, but he had, especially among young inquiring men, a higher than literary, a kind of prophetic or magician character. He was thought to hold, he alone in England, the key of German and other Transcendentalisms; knew the sublime secret of believing by "the reason" what "the understanding" had been obliged to fling out as incredible; and could still, after Hume and Voltaire had done their best and worst with him, profess himself an orthodox Christian, and say and print to the Church of England, with its singular old rubrics and surplices at Allhallowtide, Esto perpetua.[2] A sublime man; who, alone in those dark days, had saved his crown of spiritual manhood; escaping from the black materialisms, and revolutionary deluges, with "God, Freedom, Immortality" still his:

---

1. John Sterling (1806–1844), a novelist and contributor of essays to many journals, was introduced to C around 1828 and became one of his fervent admirers. Carlyle (1795–1881), the Scottish historian and novelist who shared C's interest in German literature, had a more ambivalent relationship with C, whom he first visited in 1824. In addition to the biography of his friend Sterling, Carlyle wrote the novel Sartor Resartus (1833–34), The French Revolution (1837), On Heroes, Hero-Worship, and the Heroic in History (1841), and Past and Present (1843).
† The Life of John Sterling (London, 1851), 46–54.
2. "Be constant."

a king of men. The practical intellects of the world did not much heed him, or carelessly reckoned him a metaphysical dreamer: but to the rising spirits of the young generation he had this dusky sublime character; and sat there as a kind of *Magus*, girt in mystery and enigma; his Dodona oak-grove (Mr. Gillman's house at Highgate) whispering strange things, uncertain whether oracles or jargon.

*   *   *

The good man, he was now getting old, towards sixty perhaps; and gave you the idea of a life that had been full of sufferings; a life heavy-laden, half-vanquished, still swimming painfully in seas of manifold physical and other bewilderment. Brow and head were round, and of massive weight, but the face was flabby and irresolute. The deep eyes, of a light hazel, were as full of sorrow as of inspiration; confused pain looked mildly from them, as in a kind of mild astonishment. The whole figure and air, good and amiable otherwise, might be called flabby and irresolute; expressive of weakness under possibility of strength. He hung loosely on his limbs, with knees bent, and stooping attitude; in walking, he rather shuffled than decisively stept; and a lady once remarked, he never could fix which side of the garden walk would suit him best, but continually shifted, in corkscrew fashion, and kept trying both. A heavy-laden, high-aspiring and surely much-suffering man. His voice, naturally soft and good, had contracted itself into a plaintive snuffle and singsong; he spoke as if preaching,—you would have said, preaching earnestly and also hopelessly the weightiest things. I still recollect his "object" and "subject," terms of continual recurrence in the Kantean province; and how he sang and snuffled them into "om-m-mject" and "sum-m-mject," with a kind of solemn shake or quaver, as he rolled along. No talk, in his century or in any other, could be more surprising.

*   *   *

Nothing could be more copious than his talk; and furthermore it was always, virtually or literally, of the nature of a monologue; suffering no interruption, however reverent; hastily putting aside all foreign additions, annotations, or most ingenuous desires for elucidation, as well-meant superfluities which would never do. Besides, it was talk not flowing anywhither like a river, but spreading everywhither in intricable currents and regurgitations like a lake or sea; terribly deficient in definite goal or aim, nay often in logical intelligibility; *what* you were to believe or do, on any earthly or heavenly thing, obstinately refusing to appear from it. So that, most times, you felt logically lost; swamped near to drowning in this tide of ingenious vocables, spreading out boundless as if to submerge the world.

To sit as a passive bucket and be pumped into, whether you consent or not, can in the long-run be exhilarating to no creature; how eloquent soever the flood of utterance that is descending. But if it be withal a confused unintelligible flood of utterance, threatening to submerge all known landmarks of thought, and drown the world and you!—I have heard Coleridge talk, with eager musical energy, two stricken hours, his face radiant and moist, and communicate no meaning whatsoever to any individual of his hearers,—certain of whom, I for one, still kept eagerly listening in hope; the most had long before given up, and formed (if the room were large enough) secondary humming groups of their own. He began anywhere: you put some question to him, made some suggestive observation: instead of answering this, or decidedly setting out towards answer of it, he would accumulate formidable apparatus, logical swim-bladders, transcendental life-preservers and other precautionary and vehiculatory gear, for setting out; perhaps did at last get under way,—but was swiftly solicited, turned aside by the glance of some radiant new game on this hand or that, into new courses; and ever into new; and before long into all the Universe, where it was uncertain what game you would catch, or whether any.

His talk, alas, was distinguished, like himself, by irresolution: it disliked to be troubled with conditions, abstinences, definite fulfilments;—loved to wander at its own sweet will, and make its auditor and his claims and humble wishes a mere passive bucket for itself! He had knowledge about many things and topics, much curious reading; but generally all topics led him, after a pass or two, into the high seas of theosophic philosophy, the hazy infinitude of Kantean transcendentalism, with its "sum-m-mjects" and "om-m-mjects." Sad enough; for with such indolent impatience of the claims and ignorances of others, he had not the least talent for explaining this or anything unknown to them; and you swam and fluttered in the mistiest wide unintelligible deluge of things, for most part in a rather profitless uncomfortable manner.

*   *   *

In close colloquy, flowing within narrower banks, I suppose he was more definite and apprehensible; Sterling in aftertimes did not complain of his unintelligibility, or imputed it only to the abstruse high nature of the topics handled. Let us hope so, let us try to believe so! There is no doubt but Coleridge could speak plain words on things plain: his observations and responses on the trivial matters that occurred were as simple as the commonest man's, or were even distinguished by superior simplicity as well as pertinency. "Ah, your tea is too cold, Mr. Coleridge!" mourned the good Mrs. Gillman once, in her kind, reverential and yet protective manner, handling him a very tolerable though belated cup.—"It's better than I deserve!" snuffled he, in a low hoarse murmur, partly courteous, chiefly pious, the tone of which still abides with me: "It's better than I deserve!"

But indeed, to the young ardent mind, instinct with pious nobleness, yet driven to the grim deserts of Radicalism for a faith, his speculations had a charm much more than literary, a charm almost religious and prophetic. The constant gist of his discourse was lamentation over the sunk condition of the world; which he recognised to be given-up to Atheism and Materialism, full of mere sordid misbeliefs, mispursuits and misresults. All Science had become mechanical; the science not of men, but of a kind of human beavers. Churches themselves had died away into a godless mechanical condition; and stood there as mere Cases of Articles, mere Forms of Churches; like the dried carcasses of once-swift camels, which you find left withering in the thirst of the universal desert,—ghastly portents for the present, beneficent ships of the desert no more. Men's souls were blinded, hebetated; and sunk under the influence of Atheism and Materialism, and Hume and Voltaire: the world for the present was as an extinct world, deserted of God, and incapable of welldoing till it changed its heart and spirit. This, expressed I think with less of indignation and with more of long-drawn querulousness, was always recognisable as the ground-tone:—in which truly a pious young heart, driven into Radicalism and the opposition party, could not but recognise a too sorrowful truth; and ask of the Oracle, with all earnestness, What remedy, then?

* * *

The truth is, I now see, Coleridge's talk and speculation was the emblem of himself: in it as in him, a ray of heavenly inspiration struggled, in a tragically ineffectual degree, with the weakness of flesh and blood. He says once, he "had skirted the howling deserts of Infidelity"; this was evident enough: but he had not had the courage, in defiance of pain and terror, to press resolutely across said deserts to the new firm lands of Faith beyond; he preferred to create logical fatamorganas for himself on this hither side, and laboriously solace himself with these.

To the man himself Nature had given, in high measure, the seeds of a noble endowment; and to unfold it had been forbidden him. A subtle lynx-eyed intellect, tremulous pious sensibility to all good and all beautiful; truly a ray of empyrean light;—but imbedded in such weak laxity of character, in such indolences and esuriences as had made strange work with it. Once more, the tragic story of a high endowment with an insufficient will. An eye to discern the divineness of the Heaven's splendours and lightnings, the insatiable wish to revel in their godlike radiances and brilliances; but no heart to front the scathing terrors of them, which is the first condition of your conquering an abiding place there. The courage necessary for him, above all things, had been denied this man. His life, with such ray of the empyrean in it, was great and terrible to him; and he had not valiantly grappled with it, he had fled from it; sought refuge in vague daydreams, hollow compromises, in opium, in theosophic metaphysics.

* * *

JOHN STUART MILL[1]

From Coleridge (1840)†

The name of Coleridge is one of the few English names of our time which are likely to be oftener pronounced, and to become symbolical of more important things, in proportion as the inward workings of the age manifest themselves more and more in outward facts. Bentham excepted, no Englishman of recent date has left his impress so deeply in the opinions and mental tendencies of those among us who attempt to enlighten their practice by philosophical meditation. If it be true, as Lord Bacon affirms, that a knowledge of the speculative opinions of the men between twenty and thirty years of age is the great source of political prophecy, the existence of Coleridge will show itself by no slight or ambiguous traces in the coming history of our country; for no one has contributed more to shape the opinions of those among its younger men, who can be said to have opinions at all.

The influence of Coleridge, like that of Bentham, extends far beyond those who share in the peculiarities of his religious or philosophical creed. He has been the great awakener in this country of the spirit of philosophy, within the bounds of traditional opinions. He has been, almost as truly as Bentham, "the great questioner of things established;" for a questioner needs not necessarily be an enemy. By Bentham, beyond all others, men have been led to ask themselves, in regard to any ancient or received opinion, Is it true? and by Coleridge, What is the meaning of it? The one took his stand outside the received opinion, and surveyed it as an entire stranger to it: the other looked at it from within, and endeavoured to see it with the eyes of a believer in it; to discover by what apparent facts it was at first suggested, and by what appearances it has ever since been rendered continually credible—has seemed, to a succession of persons, to be a faithful interpretation of their experience. Bentham judged a proposition true or false as it accorded or not with the result of his own inquiries; and did not search very curiously into what might be meant by the proposition, when it obviously did not mean what he thought true. With Coleridge, on the contrary, the very fact that any doctrine had been believed by thoughtful men, and received by whole nations or generations of mankind, was part of the problem to be solved, was one of the phenomena to be accounted for. * * * From this difference in the points of view of the two philosophers, and from the too rigid adherence of each of his own, it was to be expected that Bentham should continu-

---

1. This essay, which compares C to the utilitarian philosopher Jeremy Bentham (1748–1832), was originally published in the *London and Westminster Review* (March 1840). Mill (1806–1873), who was introduced to C in the 1820s by John Sterling, wrote widely on social philosophy and political and economic theory, publishing *Principles of Political Economy* (1848), *Utilitarianism* (1861), *Considerations on Representative Government* (1861), *The Subjection of Women* (1869), and an *Autobiography* (1873). See p. 573, n. 1 herein.

† *Essays on Ethics, Religion and Society*, ed. J. M. Robson (London: Routledge & Kegan Paul, 1969), 119–22, 162–63. Copyright by the University of Toronto Press 1969. Reprinted by permission of the publisher.

ally miss the truth which is in the traditional opinions, and Coleridge that which is out of them, and at variance with them. But it was also likely that each would find, or show the way to finding, much of what the other missed.

*   *   *

In every respect the two men are each other's "completing counterpart:" the strong points of each correspond to the weak points of the other. Whoever could master the premises and combine the methods of both, would possess the entire English philosophy of their age. Coleridge used to say that every one is born either a Platonist or an Aristotelian:[2] it may be similarly affirmed, that every Englishman of the present day is by implication either a Benthamite or a Coleridgian; holds views of human affairs which can only be proved true on the principles either of Bentham or of Coleridge. In one respect, indeed, the parallel fails. Bentham so improved and added to the system of philosophy he adopted, that for his successors he may almost be accounted its founder; while Coleridge, though he has left on the system he inculcated, such traces of himself as cannot fail to be left by any mind of original powers, was anticipated in all the essentials of his doctrine by the great Germans of the latter half of the last century, and was accompanied in it by the remarkable series of their French expositors and followers. Hence, although Coleridge is to Englishmen the type and the main source of that doctrine, he is the creator rather of the shape in which it has appeared among us, than of the doctrine itself.

The time is yet far distant when, in the estimation of Coleridge, and of his influence upon the intellect of our time, anything like unanimity can be looked for. As a poet, Coleridge has taken his place. The healthier taste, and more intelligent canons of poetic criticism, which he was himself mainly instrumental in diffusing, have at length assigned to him his proper rank, as one among the great, and (if we look to the powers shown rather than to the amount of actual achievement) among the greatest, names in our literature. But as a philosopher, the class of thinkers has scarcely yet arisen by whom he is to be judged. The limited philosophical public of this country is as yet too exclusively divided between those to whom Coleridge and the views which he promulgated or defended are everything, and those to whom they are nothing. A true thinker can only be justly estimated when his thoughts have worked their way into minds formed in a different school; have been wrought and moulded into consistency with all other true and relevant thoughts; when the noisy conflict of half-truths, angrily denying one another, has subsided, and ideas which seemed mutually incompatible, have been found only to require mutual limitations. This time has not yet come for Coleridge. The spirit of philosophy in England, like that of religion, is still rootedly sectarian. Conservative thinkers and Liberals, transcendentalists and admirers of Hobbes and Locke, regard each other as out of the pale of

2. See "Platonists and Aristotelians" (p. 605 herein).

philosophical intercourse; look upon each other's speculations as vitiated by an original taint, which makes all study of them, except for purposes of attack, useless if not mischievous.

* * *

Theological discussion is beyond our province, and it is not for us, in this place, to judge these sentiments of Coleridge; but it is clear enough that they are not the sentiments of a bigot, or of one who is to be dreaded by Liberals, lest he should illiberalize the minds of the rising generation of Tories and High-Churchmen. We think the danger is rather lest they should find him vastly too liberal. And yet, now when the most orthodox divines, both in the Church and out of it, find it necessary to explain away the obvious sense of the whole first chapter of Genesis, or failing to do that, consent to disbelieve it provisionally, on the speculation that there may hereafter be discovered a sense in which it can be believed, one would think the time gone by for expecting to learn from the Bible what it never could have been intended to communicate, and to find in all its statements a literal truth neither necessary nor conducive to what the volume itself declares to be the ends of revelation. Such at least was Coleridge's opinion: and whatever influence such an opinion may have over Conservatives, it cannot do other than make them less bigots, and better philosophers.

* * * We do not pretend to have given any sufficient account of Coleridge; but we hope we may have proved to some, not previously aware of it, that there is something both in him, and in the school to which he belongs, not unworthy of their better knowledge. We may have done something to show that a Tory philosopher cannot be wholly a Tory, but must often be a better Liberal than Liberals themselves; while he is the natural means of rescuing from oblivion truths which Tories have forgotten, and which the prevailing schools of Liberalism never knew.

* * *

RALPH WALDO EMERSON[1]

From Letters†

To Mary Moody Emerson (December 10, 1829)

* * * I am reading Coleridge's Friend[2] with great interest. You don't speak of it with respect. He has a tone a little lower than greatness— but what a living Soul what a universal knowledge. I like to encounter these citizens of the Universe that be[le]ive the mind was made to be spectator of all, inquisitor of all, & whose philosophy compares with others much as astronomy with other sciences—taking post at the centre & as from a specular mount sending sovereign glances to the circumferences of things. * * *

To William and Edward Emerson (January 4, 1830)

* * * Did not somebody ask me what books I read? I heard it in my sleep or waking. Coleridge's Friend—with great interest; Coleridge's "Aids to reflection" with yet deeper. * * *

To Ellis Gray Loring (March 27, 1858)

* * * I found yesterday at Phillips & Sampson's the engraved head of Coleridge,[3] which, I believe, had been waiting for me some days. I brought it home with due care, & unrolled it with hope, which was more than fulfilled[.] Tis a noble copy of a master's picture of a master. I wonder that I see it for the first time: so many lovers of Coleridge as are in this country, tis strange this excellent print should not be known & multiplied here. I heartily thank you for giving this trusted treasure a direction to me. I shall have it properly mounted & hung in my library, as a perpetual memorial of the English seer, and also of yourself. * * *

1. Emerson (1803–1882), American Transcendentalist writer and lecturer, briefly a Unitarian minister; author of *Nature* (1836), *The American Scholar* (1837), *Essays* (1837), and *English Traits* (1856). Emerson met C during a European tour of 1832–33, and through him became acquainted with German idealist thought.
† *The Letters of Ralph Waldo Emerson*, ed. Ralph L. Rusk and Elinor M. Tilton, 10 vols. (New York: Columbia University Press, 1939–95), 7:188–89, 1:291, 8:559.
2. Emerson owned the three-volume edition of the 1818 *Friend*.
3. This engraving of 1854 by Samuel Cousins is from Washington Allston's painting of C (1814).

From Journals and Miscellaneous Notebooks†

Coleridge is one of those who save England from the reproach of no longer possessing in the land of appreciation of what highest wit the land has yielded, as Shakespeare, Spenser, Herbert, &c. But for Coleridge, and a lurking taciturn or rarely-speaking minority, one would say that, in Germany, & in America, is the best mind of England rightly respected. * * *

From First Visit to England‡

From London, on the 5th August, I went to Highgate, and wrote a note to Mr. Coleridge, requesting leave to pay my respects to him. It was near noon. Mr. Coleridge sent a verbal message, that he was in bed, but if I would call after one o'clock, he would see me. I returned at one, and he appeared, a short, thick old man, with bright blue eyes and fine clear complexion, leaning on his cane. He took snuff freely, which presently soiled his cravat and neat black suit. He asked whether I knew Allston, and spoke warmly of his merits and doings when he knew him in Rome; what a master of the Titianesque he was, &c., &c. He spoke of Dr. Channing.[1] It was an unspeakable misfortune that he should have turned out a Unitarian after all. On this, he burst into a declamation on the folly and ignorance of Unitarianism,— its high unreasonableness; and taking up Bishop Waterland's[2] book, which lay on the table, he read with vehemence two or three pages written by himself in the fly-leaves,—passages, too, which, I believe, are printed in the "Aids to Reflection." When he stopped to take breath, I interposed, that, "whilst I highly valued all his explanations, I was bound to tell him that I was born and bred a Unitarian." "Yes," he said, "I supposed so;" and continued as before. "It was a wonder, that after so many ages of unquestioning acquiescence in the doctrine of St. Paul,—the doctrine of the Trinity, which was also, according to Philo Judæus, the doctrine of the Jews before Christ,—this handful of Priestleians should take on themselves to deny it, &c., &c. He was very sorry that Dr. Channing,—a man to whom he looked up,—no, to say that he looked *up* to him would be to speak falsely; but a man whom he looked *at* with so much interest,—should embrace such views. When he saw Dr. Channing, he had hinted to him that he was

---

† *Journals and Miscellaneous Notebooks*, ed. William H. Gilman et al., 16 vols. (Cambridge, Mass.: Belknap Press of Harvard University Press, 1960–82), 14:12.
‡ *English Traits* (orig. published 1856), in Emerson, *Collected Works*, ed. D. E. Wilson, 5 vols. (Cambridge, Mass.: Harvard University Press, 1971–1994), 5:5–7. Copyright © 1994 by the President and Fellows of Harvard College. Reprinted by permission of the publisher.
1. William Ellery Channing (1780–1842), Unitarian minister who visited C in 1823. See *TT* (CC), 1: 280n. 6.
2. Daniel Waterland (1683–1740), Anglican theologian who defended the doctrines of the Trinity and Christ's divinity in controversies with the Deists. C admired Waterland and annotated extensively his *Vindication of Christ's Divinity* (1719) and *Importance of the Doctrine of the Holy Trinity Asserted* (1734) (CM [CC], 6:54–93).

afraid he loved Christianity for what was lovely and excellent,—he loved the good in it, and not the true; and I tell you, sir, that I have known ten persons who loved the good, for one person who loved the true; but it is a far greater virtue to love the true for itself alone, than to love the good for itself alone. He (Coleridge) knew all about Unitarianism perfectly well, because he had once been a Unitarian, and knew what quackery it was. He had been called 'the rising star of Unitarianism.' " He went on defining, or rather refining: "The Trinitarian doctrine was realism; the idea of God was not essential, but superessential; talked of *trinism* and *tetrakism*, and much more, of which I only caught this, that the will was that by which a person is a person; because, if one should push me in the street, and so I should force the man next me into the kennel, I should at once exclaim, 'I did not do it, sir,' meaning it was not my will." And this also, "that if you should insist on your faith here in England, and I on mine, mine would be the hotter side of the fagot."

I took advantage of a pause to say, that he had many readers of all religious opinions in America, and I proceeded to inquire if the "extract" from the Independent's pamphlet, in the third volume of the Friend, were a veritable quotation. He replied, that it was really taken from a pamphlet in his possession, entitled "A Protest of one of the Independents," or something to that effect. I told him how excellent I thought it, and how much I wished to see the entire work. "Yes," he said, "the man was a chaos of truths, but lacked the knowledge that God was a God of order. Yet the passage would no doubt strike you more in the quotation than in the original, for I have filtered it."

When I rose to go, he said, "I do not know whether you care about poetry, but I will repeat some verses I lately made on my baptismal anniversary," and he recited with strong emphasis, standing, ten or twelve lines, beginning,

Born unto God in Christ———[3]

He inquired where I had been travelling; and on learning that I had been in Malta and Sicily, he compared one island with the other, "repeating what he had said to the Bishop of London when he returned from that country, that Sicily was an excellent school of political economy; for, in any town there, it only needed to ask what the government enacted, and reverse that to know what ought to be done; it was the most felicitously opposite legislation to any thing good and wise. There were only three things which the government had brought into that garden of delights, namely, itch, pox, and famine. Whereas, in Malta, the force of law and mind was seen, in making that barren rock of semi-Saracen inhabitants the seat of population and plenty." Going out, he showed me in the next apartment a picture of Allston's, and told me "that Montague, a picture-dealer, once came to see him, and, glancing towards this, said, 'Well, you have got a picture!' thinking it the work of an old master; afterwards, Montague, still talking with his

3. See "My Baptismal Birth-day," *PW* (CC), 2.1341–44.

back to the canvas, put up his hand and touched it, and exclaimed, 'By Heaven! this picture is not ten years old:'—so delicate and skilful was that man's touch."

I was in his company for about an hour, but find it impossible to recall the largest part of his discourse, which was often like so many printed paragraphs in his book,—perhaps the same,—so readily did he fall into certain commonplaces. As I might have foreseen, the visit was rather a spectacle than a conversation, of no use beyond the satisfaction of my curiosity. He was old and preoccupied, and could not bend to a new companion and think with him.

EDGAR ALLAN POE[1]

From Letter to B——†

* * * Of Coleridge I cannot speak but with reverence. His towering intellect! his gigantic power! * * * He has imprisoned his own conceptions by the barrier he has erected against those of others. It is lamentable to think that such a mind should be buried in metaphysics, and, like Nyctanthes, waste its perfume upon the night alone. In reading his poetry I tremble—like one who stands upon a volcano, conscious, from the very darkness bursting from the crater, of the fire and the light that are weltering below.

From a Review of Letters, Conversations and Recollections‡

We feel even a deeper interest in this book than in the late Table-Talk.[1] But with us (we are not ashamed to confess it) the most trivial memorial of Coleridge is a treasure of inestimable price. He was indeed a "myriad-minded man," and ah, how little understood, and how pitifully villified! How merely nominal was the difference (and this too in his own land) between what he himself calls the "broad, predetermined abuse" of the Edinburgh Review,[2] and the cold and brief compliments with the warm *regrets* of the Quarterly. If there be any one thing more than another which stirs within us a deep spirit of indigna-

1. Poe (1809–1849), American short story writer, poet, and journalist; author of *Tales of the Grotesque and Arabesque* (1840), *Tales* (1845), *The Raven and Other Poems* (1846), and *Eureka* (1848).
† "Letter to B——," in Poe, *Essays and Reviews*, ed. G.R. Thompson (New York: Library of America, 1984), 10–11. Originally published as the Preface to Poe's *Poems* (1831), then reprinted in the *Southern Literary Messenger* (July 1836).
‡ From Poe's review of *Letters, Conversations and Recollections of S. T. Coleridge*, ed. Thomas Allsop (1836), in *Essays and Reviews*, 181. Originally published in the *Southern Literary Messenger* (June 1836).
1. An American edition of *Specimens of the Table Talk of the Late Samuel Taylor Coleridge* was published in 1835, the same year as the original British edition.
2. Poe quotes from C's letter to Allsop of December 2, 1818 (see *CL*, 4:889). C frequently complained that while the Whig *Edinburgh Review* attacked his works, the Tory *Quarterly Review* (of which Southey was a supporter) simply ignored them.

tion and disgust, it is that damnation of faint praise which so many of the Narcissi of critical literature have had the infinite presumption to breathe against the majesty of Coleridge—of Coleridge—the man to whose gigantic mind the proudest intellects of Europe found it impossible not to succumb. And as no man was more richly-gifted with all the elements of mental renown, so none was more fully worthy of the love and veneration of every truly good man. Even through the exertion of his great powers he sought no immediate worldly advantages. To use his own words, he not only sacrificed all present prospects of wealth and advancement, but, in his inmost soul, stood aloof from temporary reputation.[3]

*   *   *

MARGARET FULLER[1]

From Art, Literature and the Drama†

* * * Such are Southey, Coleridge, Wordsworth. * * * To them poetry was, must be, the expression of what is eternal in man's nature, through illustrations drawn from his temporal state; a representation in letters of fire, on life's dark curtain, of that which lies beyond; philosophy dressed in the robes of Taste and Imagination; the voice of Nature and of God, humanized by being echoed back from the understanding hearts of Priests and Seers! Of course this could not be the popular poetry of the day. Being eminently the product of reflection and experience, it could only be appreciated by those who had thought and felt to some depth. I confess that it is not the best possible poetry, since so exclusively adapted to the meditative few.

*   *   *

This fault which I have admitted, this want of universality is not surprising, since it was necessary for these three poets to stand apart from the tide of opinion, and disregard the popular tastes, in order to attain firmness, depth, or permanent beauty. And they being, as I have said, the pilot-minds of their time, their works enjoy a growing, though not a rapidly growing, popularity.

Coleridge, in particular, is now very much read, nor, withstanding his was but occasional homage to the shrine of poesy, was he the least valuable votary of the three, since, if he has done least, if his works form a less perfect whole, and are therefore less satisfactory than those of the other two, he is far more suggestive, more filled with the divine magnetism of intuition, than they.

*   *   *

3. On the distinction between fame and reputation, see p. 394, n. 8 herein.
1. Fuller (1810–1850), an American Unitarian and feminist acquainted with Harriet Martineau, Ralph Waldo Emerson, and William Ellery Channing. In 1845 Fuller published her study *Woman in the Nineteenth Century*, and the following year she traveled to England, where she met C, Wordsworth, Thomas Carlyle, and Matthew Arnold.
† *Art, Literature and the Drama* (Boston, 1889), 91–92, 96–99.

Of Coleridge I shall say little. Few minds are capable of fathoming his by their own sympathies, and he has left us no adequate manifestation of himself as a poet by which to judge him. For his dramas,[2] I consider them complete failures, and more like visions than dramas. For a metaphysical mind like his to attempt that walk, was scarcely more judicious than it would be for a blind man to essay painting the bay of Naples. Many of his smaller pieces are perfect in their way, indeed no writer could excell him in depicting a single mood of mind, as Dejection, for instance. Could Shakespeare have surpassed these lines?[3]

*   *   *

Give Coleridge a canvass, and he will paint a single mood as if his colors were made of the mind's own atoms. Here he is very unlike Southey. There is nothing of the spectator about Coleridge; he is all life; not impassioned, not vehement, but searching, intellectual life, which seems "listening through the frame" to its own pulses.

I have little more to say at present except to express a great, though not fanatical veneration for Coleridge, and a conviction that the benefits conferred by him on this and future ages are as yet incalculable. Every mind will praise him for what it can best receive from him. He can suggest to an infinite degree; he can *in*form, but he cannot *re*form and renovate. To the unprepared he is nothing, to the prepared, every thing. Of him, may be said what he said of Nature,

> We receive but what we give,
> In kind though not in measure.[4]

I was once requested, by a very sensible and excellent personage to explain what is meant by "Christabel" and "The Ancient Mariner." I declined the task. I had not then seen Coleridge's answer to a question of similar tenor from Mrs. Barbauld,[5] or I should have referred to that as an expression, not altogether unintelligible, of the discrepancy which must ever exist between those minds which are commonly styled *rational*, (as the received definition of *common* sense is insensibility to *uncommon* sense,) and that of Coleridge. As to myself, if I understand nothing beyond the execution of those "singularly wild and original poems,"[6] I could not tell my gratitude for the degree of refinement which Taste has received from them. To those who cannot understand the voice of Nature or Poetry, unless it speak in apothegms, and tag each story with a moral, I have nothing to say. My own greatest obligation to Coleridge I have already mentioned. It is for his suggestive power that I thank him.

---

2. Presumably a reference to C's plays *Remorse* (1813) and *Zapolya* (1817).
3. Fuller cites stanzas 2 and 3 of "Dejection: An Ode" (see pp. 155–56 herein).
4. A misquotation or adaptation of "Dejection," lines 47–48: "O Lady! we receive but what we give, / And in our life alone does nature live."
5. Presumably a reference to the poet Anna Laetitia Barbauld's view that "The Rime of the Ancient Mariner" had no moral (see p. 98, n. 7 herein).
6. Adapted from Byron's description of "Christabel" in a note to his *Siege of Corinth* (p. 159 herein).

Twentieth Century

ROBERT PENN WARREN

From A Poem of Pure Imagination: An Experiment in Reading†

II

*   *   *

If *The Ancient Mariner* has a meaning, what is that meaning?

*   *   *

In *The Ancient Mariner,* I wish to distinguish two basic themes, both of them very rich and provocative, and I shall, in the course of my discussion, attempt to establish their interrelation.

One theme I shall call *primary,* the other *secondary.* I do not mean to imply that one is more important than the other. But the one which I shall call primary is more obviously presented to us, is, as it were, at the threshold of the poem. The primary theme may be defined as the issue of the fable (or of the situation or discourse if we are applying this kind of analysis to a poem which does not present a fable). The primary theme does not necessarily receive a full statement. In fact, in *The Ancient Mariner* it receives only a kind of coy and dramatically naïve understatement which serves merely as a clue—"He prayeth best, etc." But the theme thus hinted at is the outcome of the fable taken at its face value as a story of crime and punishment and reconciliation. I shall label the primary theme in this poem as the theme of sacramental vision, or the theme of the "One Life." The operation of this theme in the poem I shall presently explore.

As the primary theme may be taken as the issue of the fable, so the secondary theme may be taken as concerned with the context of values in which the fable is presented and which the fable may be found ultimately to embody, just as more obviously it embodies the primary theme. I shall label the secondary theme in this poem as the theme of the imagination. After having explored the operation of the theme of sacramental unity in the poem, I shall explore the operation of the

† From *New and Selected Essays* (New York: Random House, 1989), 346–99. © by Robert Penn Warren. Reprinted by permission of the William Morris Agency Inc. on behalf of the author.

theme of the imagination, and shall then attempt to define the significance of their final symbolic fusion in the poem.

*   *   *

III

* * * The fable, in broadest and simplest terms, is a story of crime and
punishment and repentance and reconciliation (I have refrained from
using the word *sin*, because one school of interpretation would
scarcely accept the full burden of the implications of the word). It is
an example, to adopt for the moment Maud Bodkin's term, without
necessarily adopting the full implications of her theory, of the archetypal story of Rebirth or the Night Journey. The Mariner shoots the
bird; suffers various pains, the greatest of which is loneliness and spiritual anguish; upon recognizing the beauty of the foul sea snakes, experiences a gush of love for them and is able to pray; is returned
miraculously to his home port, where he discovers the joy of human
communion in God, and utters the moral "He prayeth best who loveth
best, etc." We arrive at the notion of a universal charity, which even
[Irving] Babbitt admits to be "unexceptionable" in itself, the sense of
the "One Life" in which all creation participates and which Coleridge
perhaps derived from his neo-Platonic studies and which he had already celebrated, and was to celebrate, in other and more discursive
poems.

Such an account as the above, however, leaves certain questions
unanswered, and perhaps the best way to get at those questions is to
consider the nature of the Mariner's transgression. Many critics, even
Lowes, for example, dismiss the matter with such words as *wanton,
trivial,* or *unthinking.* They are concerned with the act at the literal
level only. In substance, they ask: Did the Mariner as a man have a
good practical reason for killing the bird? This literal-mindedness
leads to the view that there is a monstrous and illogical discrepancy
between the crime and the punishment, a view shared by persons as
diverse in critical principles as Lowes with his aestheticism and Babbitt with his neo-humanistic moralism. But we have to ask ourselves
what is the symbolic reading of the act. In asking ourselves this question, we have to remember that the symbol, in Coleridge's view, is not
arbitrary, but *must contain in itself, literally considered, the seeds of the
logic of its extension—that is, it must participate in the unity of which it
is representative* [p. 360 herein]. And, more importantly, in asking ourselves this question, we must be prepared to answer quite candidly to
ourselves what our own experience of poetry, and life, tells us about
the nature of symbolic import; and we must be prepared to abide the
risks of the answer. It would be nicer, in fact, if we could forget Coleridge's own theory and stick simply to our own innocent experience.
But that, at this date, is scarcely possible.

*   *   *

[I]n the period just before the composition of *The Ancient Mariner*—
before he had struck upon that fable to embody his idea—the poet

was meditating a long poem on the theme of the origin of evil. Early in 1797, Lamb wrote him: "I have a dim recollection that, when in town, you were talking of the Origin of Evil as a most prolific subject for a long poem." As a matter of fact, Coleridge never did "solve" his problem: he found peace simply by accepting the idea of Original Sin as a mystery.

In the *Table Talk* he says: "A Fall of some sort or other—the creation, as it were, of the nonabsolute—is the fundamental postulate of the moral history of Man. Without this hypothesis, Man is unintelligible; with it, every phenomenon is explicable. The mystery itself is too profound for human insight."

In his more elaborate and systematic treatment of the subject Coleridge adds another point which is of significance for the poem. Original Sin is not hereditary sin; it is original with the sinner and is of his will. There is no previous determination of the will, because the will exists outside the chain of cause and effect, which is of Nature and not of Spirit. And as for the time of this act of sin, he says that the "subject stands in no relation to time, can neither be in time nor out of time." The bolt whizzes from the crossbow and the bird falls and all comment that the Mariner has no proper dramatic motive or is the child of necessity or is innocent of everything except a little wantonness is completely irrelevant, for we are confronting the mystery of the corruption of the will, the mystery which is the beginning of the "moral history of Man."

The fact that the act is unmotivated in any practical sense, that it appears merely perverse, has offended literalists and Aristotelians alike, and, for that matter, Wordsworth, who held that the Mariner had no "character" (and we may elaborate by saying that having no character, he could exhibit no motive) and did not act but was acted upon. The lack of motivation, the perversity, which flies in the face of the Aristotelian doctrine of *hamartia* [tragic flaw], is exactly the significant thing about the Mariner's act. The act re-enacts the Fall, and the Fall has two qualities important here: it is a condition of will, as Coleridge says, "out of time," and it is the result of no single human motive.

One more comment, even though I have belabored this point. What is the nature of this sin, what is its content? Though the act which re-enacts the mystery of the Fall is appropriately without motive, the sin of the will must be the appropriate expression of the essence of the will. And we shall turn to a passage in *The Statesman's Manual.* Having just said that, in its "state of immanence or indwelling in reason and religion," the will appears indifferently as wisdom or love, Coleridge proceeds: "But in its utmost abstraction and consequent state of reprobation, the will becomes Satanic pride and rebellious self-idolatry in the relations of the spirit to itself, and remorseless despotism relatively to others . . . by the fearful resolve to find in itself alone the one absolute motive of action." Then he sketches the portrait of the will in abstraction, concluding with the observation that "these are the marks, that have characterized the masters of mischief, the lib-

erticides, the mighty hunters of mankind, from Nimrod to Bonaparte"
[p. 364 herein].

We may observe a peculiar phrase, the "mighty hunters of mankind,
from Nimrod to Bonaparte," and in this blending of the hunting of
beasts and the hunting of man—for Nimrod was himself both the
mighty hunter and the founder of the first military state—we have an
identification that takes us straight to the crime of the Mariner. The
Mariner did not kill a man but a bird, and the literal-minded readers
have echoed Mrs. Barbauld and Leslie Stephen: what a lot of pother
about a bird. But they forget that this bird is more than a bird. I do not
intend, however, to rest my case on the phrase just quoted from *The
Statesman's Manual*, for the phrase itself I take to be but an echo from
the poem at the time when the author was revising and reliving his favorite poem. Let us go to the poem itself to learn the significance of
the bird.

In the poem itself the same identification occurs: the hunting of the
bird becomes the hunting of man. When the bird first appears,

> As if it had been a Christian soul,
> We hailed it in God's name.

It ate food "it ne'er had eat," and every day "came to the mariner's
hollo," and then later perched on the mast or shroud for "vespers
nine." It partakes of the human food and pleasure and devotions. To
make matters more explicit, Coleridge adds in the Gloss the statement
that the bird was received with "hospitality" and adds, after the crime,
that the Mariner "inhospitably killeth the pious bird of good omen."
The crime is, symbolically, a murder, and a particularly heinous murder, for it involves the violation of hospitality and of gratitude (*pious*
equals *faithful* and the bird is "of good omen") and of sanctity (the religious connotations of *pious*, etc.). This factor of betrayal in the crime
is re-emphasized in Part V when one of the Spirits says that the bird
had "loved the man" who killed it.

But why did the poet not give us a literal murder in the first place?
By way of answering this question, we must remember that the crime,
to maintain its symbolic reference to the Fall, must be motiveless. But
the motiveless murder of a man would truly raise the issue of probability. Furthermore, the literal shock of such an act, especially if perverse and unmotivated, would be so great that it would distract from
the symbolic significance. The poet's problem, then, was to provide an
act which, on one hand, would not accent the issue of probability or
shockingly distract from the symbolic significance, but which, on the
other hand, would be adequately criminal to justify the consequences.
And the necessary criminality is established, we have seen, in two
ways: (1) by making the gravity of the act depend on the state of the
will which prompts it, and (2) by symbolically defining the bird as a
"Christian soul," as "pious," etc.

There is, however, a third way in which the criminality is established. We can get at it by considering the observation that if a man
had been killed, we could not have the "lesson of humanitarianism,"

which some critics have taken to be the point of the poem. But we must remember that the humanitarianism itself is a manifestation of a deeper concern, a sacramental conception of the universe, for the bird is hailed "in God's name," both literally and symbolically, and in the end we have, therefore, in the crime against Nature a crime against God. If a man had been killed, the secular nature of the crime—a crime then against man—would have overshadowed the ultimate religious significance involved. The idea of the crime against God rather than man is further emphasized by the fact that the cross is removed from the Mariner's neck to make place for the dead bird, and here we get a symbolic transference from Christ to the Albatross, from the slain Son of God to the slain creature of God. And the death of the creature of God, like the death of the Son of God, will, in its own way, work for vision and salvation.

*   *   *

To return to the problems raised by the poem: We have not yet done with the matter of crime and punishment. There is the question of the fellow mariners, who suffer death. Here we encounter not infrequently the objection that they do not merit their fate. The tragic *hamartia*, we are told, is not adequate. The Gloss, however, flatly defines the nature of the crime of the fellow mariners: they have made themselves "accomplices." But apparently the Gloss needs a gloss. The fellow mariners have, in a kind of structural counterpoint (and such a counterpoint is, as we shall see, a characteristic of the poem), duplicated the Mariner's own crime of pride, of "will in abstraction." That is, they make their desire the measure of the act: they first condemn the act, when they think the bird had brought the favorable breeze; then applaud the act when the fog clears and the breeze springs back up, now saying that the bird had brought the fog; then in the dead calm, again condemn the act. Their crime has another aspect: they have violated the sacramental conception of the universe, by making man's convenience the measure of an act, by isolating him from Nature and the "One Life." This point is picked up later in Part IV:

> The many men, so beautiful!
> And they all dead did lie:
> And a thousand thousand slimy things
> Lived on; and so did I.

The stanza is important for the reading of the poem. The usual statement for the poem is that the Mariner moves from love of the sea snakes to a love of men (and in the broad sense this is true), but here we see that long before he blesses the snakes he is aware, in his guilt, of the beauty of the dead men, and protests against the fact that the slimy things should live while the beautiful men lie dead. In other words, we have here, even in his remorse, a repetition of the original crime against the sacramental view of the universe: man is still set over, in pride, against Nature. The Gloss points to the important thing here: "He despiseth the creatures of the calm."

There is one other aspect of the guilt of the fellow mariners worthy of notice. They judge the moral content of an act by its consequence; in other words, they would make good disciples of Bishop Paley, who, according to Coleridge, in *Aids to Reflection,* was no moralist because he would judge the morality of an act by consequence and not "contemplate the same in its original spiritual source," the state of the will. The will of the fellow mariners is corrupt. And this re-emphasizes the fact that what is at stake throughout is not the objective magnitude of the act performed—the bird is, literally, a trivial creature—but the spirit in which the act is performed, the condition of the will.

So much for the crime of the Mariner and the crime of his fellows. And we know the sequel, the regeneration of the Mariner. In the end, he accepts the sacramental view of the universe, and his will is released from its state of "utmost abstraction" and gains the state of "immanence" in wisdom and love. We shall observe the stages whereby this process is consummated—this primary theme of the "One Life" is developed—as we investigate the secondary theme, the theme of the imagination.

IV

If in the poem one follows the obvious theme of the "One Life" as presented by the Mariner's crime, punishment, and reconciliation, one is struck by the fact that large areas of the poem seem to be irrelevant to this business: for instance, the special atmosphere of the poem, and certain images which, because of the insistence with which they are presented, seem to be endowed with a special import. Perhaps the best approach to the problem of the secondary theme is to consider the importance of light, or rather, of the different kinds of light.

There is a constant contrast between moonlight and sunlight, and the main events of the poem can be sorted out according to the kinds of light in which they occur. Coleridge underscores the importance of the distinction between the two kinds of light by introducing the poem by the motto from Burnet, added in the last revision of 1817 (in fact, the general significance of the motto has, so far as I know, never been explored). The motto ends: "But meanwhile we must earnestly seek after truth, maintaining measure, that we may distinguish things certain from those uncertain, day from night." The motto ends on the day-night contrast, and points to this contrast as a central fact of the poem. We may get some clue to the content of the distinction by remembering that in the poem the good events take place under the aegis of the moon, the bad events under that of the sun. This, it may be objected, reverses the order of Burnet, who obviously wishes to equate the "certain" or the good with day and the "uncertain" or bad with night. Coleridge's reversal is, I take it, quite deliberate—an ironical reversal which, in effect, says that the rational and conventional view expressed by Burnet seeks truth by the wrong light. In other words, Burnet becomes the spokesman of what we shall presently find Coleridge calling the "mere reflective faculty" which partakes of "Death."

*   *   *

I have already indicated how the bird-man fusion is set up, how the bird is hailed in God's name, etc., how, in other words, the theme of the "One Life" and the sacramental vision is presented. Now, as a moment of great significance in the poem, I wish to indicate how the primary theme of the sacramental vision is for the first time assimilated to the secondary theme of the imagination. The Albatross, the sacramental bird, is also, as it were, a moon-bird. For here, with the bird, the moon first enters the poem, and the two are intimately associated:

> In mist or cloud, on mast or shroud,
> It perched for vespers nine;
> Whiles all the night, through fog-smoke white,
> Glimmered the white Moon-shine.

The sun is kept entirely out of the matter. The lighting is always indirect, for even in the day we have only "mist or cloud"—the luminous haze, the symbolic equivalent of moonlight. Not only is the moon associated with the bird, but the wind also. Upon the bird's advent a "good south wind sprung up behind." And so we have the creative wind, the friendly bird, the moonlight of imagination, all together in one symbolic cluster.

As soon as the cluster is established, the crime, with shocking suddenness, is announced. We have seen how the crime is to be read at the level of the primary theme. At the level of the secondary theme it is, of course, a crime against the imagination. Here, in the crime, the two themes are fused. (As a sidelight on this fact, we may recall that in "Dejection: An Ode," Coleridge gives us the same fusion of the moral and the aesthetic. In bewailing his own loss of creative power he hints, at the same time, at a moral taint. The "Pure of heart" do not lose the imaginative power, "this strong music in the soul.")

With the announcement of the crime, comes one of the most effective turns in the poem. As the Wedding Guest recoils from his glittering eye, the Mariner announces:

> . . . With my cross-bow
> I shot the Albatross.

And then the next line of the poem:

> The Sun now rose upon the right.

The crime, as it were, brings the sun. Ostensibly, the line simply describes a change in the ship's direction, but it suddenly, with dramatic violence, supplants moon with sun in association with the unexpected revelation of the crime, and with the fact, indicates not only the change of the direction of the ship but the change of the direction of the Mariner's life. The same device is repeated with the second murder of the Albatross—the acceptance of the crime by the fellow mariners. They first condemn the Mariner for having killed the bird "that made the breeze to blow," but immediately upon the rising of the sun, they accept the crime:

> Nor dim nor red, like God's own head,
> The glorious Sun uprist:
> Then all averred, I had killed the bird
> That brought the fog and mist.

As has been pointed out earlier, the mariners act in the arrogance of their own convenience. So even their condemnation of the crime has been based on error: they have not understood the nature of the breeze they think the bird had brought. But here we must observe a peculiar and cunningly contrived circumstance: the mariners do not accept the crime until the sun rises, and rises gloriously "like God's own head." The sun is, symbolically speaking, the cause of their acceptance of the crime—they read God as justifying the act on the ground of practical consequence, just as, shall we say, Bishop Paley would have done. They justify the crime because the bird had, they say, brought the fog and mist. In other words, they repudiate the luminous haze, the other light, and consider it an evil, though we know that the fog and mist are associated with the moon in the wind-bird-moon cluster at the end of Part I.

At this point where the sun has been introduced into the poem, it is time to ask how we shall regard it. It is the light which shows the familiar as familiar, it is the light of practical convenience, it is the light in which pride preens itself, it is, to adopt Coleridge's later terminology, the light of the "understanding," it is the light of that "mere reflective faculty" that "partook of Death." And within a few lines, its acceptance by the mariners has taken them to the sea of death, wherein the sun itself, which had risen so promisingly and so gloriously like "God's own head," is suddenly the "bloody sun," the sun of death—as though we had implied here a fable of the Enlightenment and the Age of Reason, whose fair promises had wound up in the bloodbath of the end of the century.

*   *   *

Part III consists of two scenes, one of the sun, one of the moon, in even balance. The first is the appearance of the specter-bark, which is in close association with the sun. There is the elaborate description of the sun, but in addition there is the constant repetition of the word, five times within twelve lines:

> 1. Rested the broad bright Sun
> 2. Betwixt us and the Sun
> 3. And straight the Sun was flecked with bars
> 4. Are those *her* sails that glance in the Sun
> 5. Are those *her* ribs through which the Sun

The whole passage, by means of the iteration, is devoted to the emotional equating of the sun and the death-bark.

Then the "Sun's rim dips," and we have the full and beautiful description of the rising of the "star-dogged Moon." But the moon does not bring relief; instead "At the rising of the Moon," as specified by the placement of the Gloss,

> Fear at my heart, as at a cup,
> My life-blood seemed to sip!

And immediately after, in the moonlight, the fellow mariners curse the Mariner with a look, and, one after another, fall down dead. The fact of these unhappy events under the aegis of the supposedly beneficent moon raises a question: Does this violate the symbolism of the moon? I do not feel that the poem is inconsistent here. First, if we accept the interpretation that the Polar Spirit belongs to the imagination cluster and yet exacts vengeance, then the fact that horror comes in the moonlight here is simply an extension of the same principle: violated and despised, the imagination yet persists and exacts vengeance. Second, we find a substantial piece of evidence supporting this view, in the parallel scene in Part VI, another scene of the curse by the eye in moonlight:

> All fixed on me their stony eyes,
> That in the Moon did glitter.

But this parallelism gives us a repetition with a difference. This event occurs after the Mariner has had his change of heart, and so now when the curse by the eye is placed upon him in moonlight, it does not avail; in moonlight now "this spell was snapt," and the creative wind rose again to breathe on the Mariner. In other words, the passage in Part VI interprets by contrast that in Part III. The moonlight, when the heart is unregenerate, shows horror; when the heart has changed, it shows joy.

In Part IV the penance of loneliness and horror, both associated with the crime against the imagination (loneliness by denial of the imagination, horror by the perversion of it), is aggravated with the despising of the creatures of the calm and with the curse in the eyes of the dead. Then, suddenly, we have the second moonrise:

> The moving Moon went up the sky,
> And no where did abide:
> Softly she was going up,
> And a star or two beside—

The Gloss here tells us all we need to know, defining the Mariner's relation to the Moon:

> In his loneliness and fixedness he yearneth towards the journeying Moon, and the stars that still sojourn, yet still move onward; and every where the blue sky belongs to them, and is their appointed rest, and their native country and their own natural homes, which they enter unnannounced, as lords that are certainly expected and yet there is a silent joy at their arrival.

Life, order, universal communion and process, joy—all these things from which the Mariner is alienated are involved here in the description of the moon and stars. And immediately the description of the water snakes picks up and extends the sense of the stars. The snakes become creatures of light to give us another symbolic cluster:

They moved in tracks of shining white,
And when they reared, the elfish light
Fell off in hoary flakes.

For the Gloss says here: "By the light of the Moon he beholdeth God's creatures of the great calm." And in the light of the moon we have the stages of the redeeming process: first, the recognition of happiness and beauty; second, love; third, the blessing of the creatures; fourth, freedom from the spell. The sequence is important, and we shall return to it. In it the theme of the sacramental vision and the theme of imagination are fused.

Part V, in carrying forward the next period of development consequent upon the Mariner's restored imaginative view of the world, continues, in new combinations, the sun-moon contrast, but here we move toward it by the refreshing rain and then the storm. In the Mariner's dream, which comes in the first heaven-sent sleep, we have the presentiment of the rain and storm, a dream which corresponds to the dream of the Polar Spirit which had hinted to the fellow mariners the nature of the crime: in both cases, at this instinctive, subrational level, the truth is darkly shadowed forth before it is realized in the waking world. In the Mariner's dream, before the real rain comes, the "silly buckets" are filled with dew. Upon waking and drinking the rain, the Mariner, in his light and blessed condition, hears a roaring wind; then, as the Gloss puts it, there are "strange sights and commotions in the sky and the elements," presided over by the moon, which hangs at the edge of the black cloud. The moon of imagination and the storm of creative vitality here join triumphantly to celebrate the Mariner's salvation.

But here let us pause to observe a peculiar fact. The wind does not reach the ship, and the Polar Spirit, who had originally set forth on an errand of vengeance, provides the power of locomotion for the ship. Though he has been functioning as the sinister aspect of the imagination, he, too, is now drawn, in "obedience to the angelic troop," into the new beneficent activity. Not that he is to lose entirely his sinister aspect; we shall see that his vengeance persists, for the Mariner, in his role as the *poète maudit,* will show that the imagination is a curse as well as a blessing. But for the moment, though grudgingly, the Spirit joins the forces of salvation.

* * *

As we have seen, the poem is shot through with religious associations. On the other hand, the theme of imagination is essentially aesthetic—it presents us with the "great forms" of nature, but those forms as actively seized upon by the human mind and loved *not merely as vehicles for transcendental meaning but in themselves as participating in the reality which they "render intelligible"* [p. 360 herein]. The theme is essentially aesthetic, but it is also "natural" in the sense just defined as contrasted with the sense in which nature is regarded as the neutral material worked on by the mere "understanding." The Hermit, who kneels in the woods, embodies both views, both themes.

The Hermit, however, has another aspect. He is also the priest of Society, for it is by the Hermit, who urges the Pilot on despite his fears, that the Mariner is received back into the world of men. This re-joining of the world of men is not, we observe, accomplished simply by the welcoming committee. There is the terrific sound which sinks the ship and flings the stunned Mariner into the Pilot's boat. In the logic of the symbolic structure this would be, I presume, a repetition of the wind or storm motif: the creative storm has a part in re-establishing the Mariner's relation to other men.[24] Even if the destruction of the ship is regarded, as some readers regard it, as a final act of the Polar Spirit, to show, as it were, what he could do if he had a mind to, the symbolic import is not altered, for the Spirit belongs to the cluster of imagination which has the terrifying and cataclysmic as well as benign aspect. As a matter of fact, since the Gloss has earlier dismissed the Polar Spirit at the end of Part V, saying that he "returneth southward," it seems more reasonable to me to interpret the destruction of the ship as the work of the angelic troop, whose capacity to work marvels has already been amply demonstrated. And this reading gives us a fuller symbolic burden, too, and is consistent with the final fusion of themes which we observe in this general episode. At the level of the primary theme, the angelic troop wipe out the crime (i.e., the "criminal" ship and the dead bodies); at the level of the secondary theme, they do so by means of the "storm," which belongs to the symbolic cluster of the imagination.

*   *   *

VII

*   *   *

One last word: In this essay I have not attempted to "explain" how poetry appeals, or why. I have been primarily concerned to give a discursive reading of the symbol which is the poem, in so far as I can project the import of the symbol in such a fashion. I humbly trust that I am not more insensitive than most to the "magical lines," but at the same time I cannot admit that our experience, even our aesthetic experience, is ineluctably and vindictively divided into the "magical" and the rational, with an abyss between. If poetry does anything for us, it reconciles, by its symbolical reading of experience (for by its very nature it is in itself a myth of the unity of being), the self-devisive internecine malices which arise at the superficial level on which we conduct most of our living.

And *The Ancient Mariner* is a poem on this subject.

M. H. ABRAMS

From Structure and Style in the Greater Romantic Lyric†

There is no accepted name for the kind of poem I want to talk about, even though it was a distinctive and widely practiced variety of the longer Romantic lyric and includes some of the greatest Romantic achievements in any form. Coleridge's *The Eolian Harp, Frost at Midnight, Fears in Solitude,* and *Dejection: An Ode* exemplify the type, as does Wordsworth's *Tintern Abbey,* his *Ode: Intimations of Immortality,* and (with a change in initial reference from scene to painting) his *Elegiac Stanzas Suggested by a Picture of Peele Castle, in a Storm.* Shelley's *Stanzas Written in Dejection* follows the formula exactly, and his *Ode to the West Wind* is a variant on it. Of Keats's odes, that to a nightingale is the one which approximates the pattern most closely. Only Byron, among the major poets, did not write in this mode at all.

These instances yield a paradigm for the type. Some of the poems are called odes, while the others approach the ode in having lyric magnitude and a serious subject, feelingfully meditated. They present a determinate speaker in a particularized, and usually a localized, outdoor setting, whom we overhear as he carries on, in a fluent vernacular which rises easily to a more formal speech, a sustained colloquy, sometimes with himself or with the outer scene, but more frequently with a silent human auditor, present or absent. The speaker begins with a description of the landscape; an aspect or change of aspect in the landscape evokes a varied but integral process of memory, thought, anticipation, and feeling which remains closely intervolved with the outer scene. In the course of this meditation the lyric speaker achieves an insight, faces up to a tragic loss, comes to a moral decision, or resolves an emotional problem. Often the poem rounds upon itself to end where it began, at the outer scene, but with an altered mood and deepened understanding which is the result of the intervening meditation.

What shall we call this Romantic genre? To label these poems simply nature lyrics is not only inadequate, but radically misleading. We have not yet entirely recovered from the earlier critical stress on Wordsworth's statement that "I have at all times endeavoured to look steadily at my subject," to the neglect of his repeated warnings that accurate natural description, though a necessary, is an inadequate condition for poetry. Like Blake and Coleridge, Wordsworth manifested wariness, almost terror, at the threat of the corporeal eye and material object to tyrannize over the mind and imagination, in opposition to that normative experience in which

† "Structure and Style in the Greater Romantic Lyric," in *The Correspondent Breeze* (New York: Norton, 1984), 76–108, 268–71. Reprinted by permission of the publisher. [All footnotes are the author's.]

> The mind is lord and master—outward sense
> The obedient servant of her will.[1]

In the extended lyrics we are considering, the visual report is invariably the occasion for a meditation which turns out to constitute the *raison d'être* of the poem. Romantic writers, though nature poets, were humanists above all, for they dealt with the nonhuman only insofar as it is the occasion for the activity which defines man: thought, the process of intellection.

"The descriptive-meditative poem" is a possible, but a clumsy term. *Faute de mieux,* I shall call this poetic type "the greater Romantic lyric," intending to suggest, not that it is a higher achievement than other Romantic lyrics, but that it displaced what neoclassical critics had called "the greater ode"—the elevated Pindaric, in distinction to "the lesser ode" modeled chiefly on Horace—as the favored form for the long lyric poem.

The repeated out-in-out process, in which mind confronts nature and their interplay constitutes the poem, is a remarkable phenomenon in literary history. If we don't find it strange, it is because our responses have been dulled by long familiarity with such a procedure not only in the Romantic poets, but in their many successors who played variations on the mode, from Matthew Arnold and Walt Whitman—both *Dover Beach* and *Crossing Brooklyn Ferry,* for example, closely follow the pattern of the greater Romantic lyric—to Wallace Stevens and W. H. Auden. But at the beginning of the nineteenth century this procedure in the lyric was part of a new and exciting poetic strategy, no less epidemic than Donne's in his day, or T. S. Eliot's in the period after the First World War. For several decades poets did not often talk about the great issues of life, death, love, joy, dejection, or God without talking at the same time about the landscape. Wordsworth's narrative of Michael emerges from a description of the scene around/"the tumultuous brook of Green-head Ghyll," to which in the end it returns:

> and the remains
> Of the unfinished Sheep-fold may be seen
> Beside the boisterous brook of Green-head Ghyll.

Coleridge's great, neglected love poem, *Recollections of Love,* opens with a Quantock scene revisited after eight years have passed, and adverts suddenly to the river Greta at the close:

> But when those meek eyes first did seem
> To tell me, Love within you wrought—
> O Greta, dear domestic stream!
>
> Has not, since then, Love's prompture deep,
> Has not Love's whisper evermore

---

1. *The Prelude* (1850 text), XII, 222–23. Even Keats, though he sometimes longed for a life of sensations rather than of thought, objected to the poems of John Clare that too often "the Description overlaid and stifled that which ought to be the prevailing Idea" (letter to John Clare from John Taylor, 27 September 1820, quoted by Edmund Blunden, *Keats's Publisher*, London, 1936, p. 80).

Been ceaseless, as thy gentle roar?
Sole voice, when other voices sleep,
Dear under-song in clamor's hour.

Keats's first long poem of consequence, though it is his introduction to
an *ars poetica*, represents what he saw, then what he thought, while he
"stood tip-toe upon a little hill." Shelley treats the theme of permanence in change by describing the mutations of a cloud, defines the
pure Idea of joy in a meditation on the flight and song of a skylark,
and presents his ultimate concept of the secret and impersonal power
behind all process in a description of Mont Blanc and the Vale of
Chamouni. Wordsworth's *The Prelude* can be viewed as an epic expansion of the mode of *Tintern Abbey*, in both overall design and local tactics. It begins with the description of a landscape visited in maturity,
evokes the entire life of the poet as a protracted meditation on things
past, and presents the growth of the poet's mind as an interaction with
the natural milieu by which it is fostered, from which it is tragically
alienated, and to which in the resolution it is restored, with a difference attributable to the intervening experiences; the poem ends at the
time of its beginning.

What I have called "the greater lyric," then, is only a special instance of a very widespread manner of proceeding in Romantic poetry;
but it is of great interest because it was the earliest Romantic formal
invention, and at once demonstrated the stability of organization and
the capacity to engender successors which define a distinct lyric
species. New lyric forms are not as plentiful as blackberries, and when
one turns up, it is worth critical attention. Suppose, therefore, that we
ask some questions about this one: about its genesis, its nearest literary antecedents, and the reasons why this way of proceeding, out of
the alternatives in common lyric practice, should have appealed so
powerfully to the Romantic sensibility. Inquiry into some probable
causes of the structure and style of the greater lyric will take us not
only to the evolution of certain descriptive genres in the seventeenth
and eighteenth centuries, but also to contemporary developments in
philosophy and in theology, and to the spiritual posture in which many
poets, as well as philosophers, found themselves at the end of the Enlightenment.

I. COLERIDGE AND WORDSWORTH

In this investigation Coleridge must be our central reference, not only
because he had the most to say about these matters in prose, but because it was he, not Wordsworth, who inaugurated the greater Romantic lyric, firmly established its pattern, and wrote the largest
number of instances. Wordsworth's first trial in the extended lyric was
Tintern Abbey, which he composed in July 1798. Up to that time his
only efforts in the long descriptive and reflective mode were the
schoolboy effort, *The Vale of Esthwaite*, and the two tour-poems of
1793, *An Evening Walk* and *Descriptive Sketches*. The first of these
was written in octosyllabic and the latter two in heroic couplets, and

all differ in little but merit and the detail of single passages from hundreds of eighteenth-century predecessors.[2] Coleridge, however, as early as 20 August 1795, composed a short first version of *The Eolian Harp*, and in 1796—two years before *Tintern Abbey*—expanded it to fifty-six lines which established, in epitome, the ordonnance, materials, and style of the greater lyric.[3] It is in the dramatic mode of intimate talk to an unanswering auditor in easy blank-verse paragraphs. It begins with a description of the peaceful outer scene; this, in parallel with the vagrant sounds evoked from a wind-harp, calls forth a recollection in tranquillity of earlier experiences in the same setting and leads to a sequence of reflections which are suggested by, and also incorporate, perceptual qualities of the scene. The poem closes with a summary reprise of the opening description of "Peace, and this Cot, and Thee, heart-honour'd Maid!"

Between the autumn of 1796 and the spring of 1798 Coleridge composed a number of variations on this lyric type, including *Reflections on Having Left a Place of Retirement*, *This Lime-Tree Bower*, *Fears in Solitude*, and *The Nightingale*. To these writings G. M. Harper applied the term which Coleridge himself used for *The Nightingale*, "conversation poems"; very aptly, because they are written (though some of them only intermittently) in a blank verse which at its best captures remarkably the qualities of the intimate speaking voice, yet remains capable of adapting without strain to the varying levels of the subject-matter and feeling. And within this period, in February of 1798, Coleridge produced one of the masterpieces of the greater lyric, perfectly modulated and proportioned, but so successful in the quiet way that it hides its art that it has only recently attracted its meed of critical admiration. The poem is *Frost at Midnight*, and it follows, but greatly enlarges and subtilizes, the pattern of *The Eolian Harp*. What seems at first impression to be the free association of its central meditation turns out to have been called forth, qualified, and controlled by the opening description, which evokes the strangeness in the familiar surroundings of the solitary and wakeful speaker: the "secret ministry" of the frost, the "strange / And extreme silentness" of "sea, and hill, and wood," the life of the sleeping village "inaudible as dreams," and the film that flutters on the grate "the sole unquiet thing." In consonance with these elements, and directed especially by the rhythm of the seemingly unnoticed breathing of a sleeping infant, the meditative mind disengages itself from the physical locale, moves back in time to

2. *Descriptive Sketches* (1793) drew from a contemporary reviewer the cry: "More descriptive poetry! Have we not yet enough? . . . Yes; more, and yet more: so it is decreed" (*Monthly Review*, 2nd ser., 12 [1793], cited by Robert A. Aubin, *Topographical Poetry in XVIII-Century England*, New York, 1936, p. 255; see also pp. 217–19).

3. Perhaps that is the reason for Coleridge's later judgment that *The Eolian Harp* was "the most perfect poem I ever wrote" (quoted by James D. Campbell, ed., *The Poetical Works of Samuel Taylor Coleridge*, London, 1893, p. 578). The first version of the poem and a MS version of 1797 (Coleridge then entitled it "Effusion") are reproduced in *The Complete Poetical Works*, ed. E. H. Coleridge (Oxford, 1912), II, 1021–23. For accounts of the revisions of the poem, see J. H. W. Milley, "Some Notes on Coleridge's 'Eolian Harp,' " *Modern Philology*, 36 (1938–39), 359–75, and M. H. Abrams, "Coleridge's 'A Light in Sound': Science, Metascience, and Poetic Imagination," pp. 158–91 in the present volume [*The Correspondent Breeze*].

the speaker's childhood, still farther back, to his own infancy, then forward to express, in the intonation of a blessing, the hope that his son shall have the life in nature that his father lacked; until, in anticipating the future, it incorporates both the present scene and the results of the remembered past in the enchanting close—

> whether the eave-drops fall
> Heard only in the trances of the blast,
> Or if the secret ministry of frost
> Shall hang them up in silent icicles,
> Quietly shining to the quiet Moon.

In the original version this concluding sentence trailed off in six more verse-lines, which Coleridge, in order to emphasize the lyric rondure, later excised. Plainly, Coleridge worked out the lyric device of the return-upon-itself—which he used in *Reflections on Having Left a Place of Retirement* and *Fears in Solitude*, as well as in *The Eolian Harp* and *Frost at Midnight*—in a deliberate endeavor to transform a segment of experience broken out of time into a sufficient aesthetic whole. "The common end of all *narrative*, nay, of *all*, Poems," he wrote to Joseph Cottle in 1815, "is to convert a *series* into a *Whole*: to make those events, which in real or imagined History move on in a *strait* Line, assume to our Understandings a *circular* motion—the snake with its Tail in its Mouth."[4] From the time of the early Greek philosophers, the circle had been the shape of perfection; and in occult philosophy the *ouroboros*, the tail-eating snake, had become the symbol for eternity and for the divine process of creation, since it is complete, self-sufficient, and endless. For Coleridge the perfect shape for the descriptive-meditative-descriptive poem was precisely the one described and exemplified in T. S. Eliot's *East Coker*, which begins, "In my beginning is my end," and ends, "In my end is my beginning"; another modern writer who knew esoteric lore designed *Finnegans Wake* so that the headless sentence which begins the book completes the tailless sentence with which it ends.

Five months after the composition of *Frost at Midnight*, Wordsworth set out on a walking tour with his sister. Reposing on a high bank of the River Wye, he remembered this among others of Coleridge's conversation poems—the dramatic mode of address to an unanswering listener in flexible blank verse; the opening description which evolves into a sustained meditation assimilating perceptual, personal, and philosophical elements; the free movement of thought from the present scene to recollection in tranquillity, to prayer-like prediction, and back to the scene; even some of Coleridge's specific concepts and phrases—and in the next four or five days' walk, worked out *Lines Composed a Few Miles above Tintern Abbey* and appended it forthwith to *Lyrical Ballads*, which was already in press.

To claim that it was Coleridge who deflected Wordsworth's poetry into a channel so entirely congenial to him is in no way to derogate

---

4. *Collected Letters of Samuel Taylor Coleridge*, ed. E. L. Griggs (Oxford, 1956–71), IV, 545.

Wordsworth's achievement, nor his powers of invention. *Tintern Abbey* has greater dimension and intricacy and a more various verbal orchestration than *Frost at Midnight*. In its conclusion Wordsworth managed Coleridge's specialty, the return-upon-itself, with a mastery of involuted reference without match in the poems of its begetter. *Tintern Abbey* also inaugurated the wonderfully functional device Wordsworth later called the "two consciousness": a scene is revisited, and the remembered landscape ("the picture of the mind") is superimposed on the picture before the eye; the two landscapes fail to match, and so set a problem ("a sad perplexity") which compels the meditation. Wordsworth played variations on this stratagem in all his later trials in the greater lyric, and in *The Prelude* he expanded it into a persisting double awareness of things as they are and as they were, and so anticipated the structural principle of the most influential masterpiece of our own century, Proust's *À la recherche du temps perdu*.

II. THE LOCAL POEM

What was the closest poetic antecedent of this controlled and shapely lyric genre? It was not the ancient lyric formula, going back to the spring-songs of the troubadours, which set forth an ideal spring scene (the *Natureingang*) and then presented a human experience in harmony or contrast—a formula which survived in Burns's

> Ye flowery banks o' bonnie Doon,
>   How can ye blume sae fair?
> How can ye chant, ye little birds,
>   And I sae fu' o' care?

Nor was it Thomson's *Seasons*, that omnibus of unlocalized description, episodic narration, and general reflection, in which the pious observer moves from Nature to Nature's God with the help of Isaac Newton's *Principia*. And certainly it was not the formal descriptive poem such as Collins' *Ode to Evening*, which adapted Pindar's ceremonial panegyric to landscape mainly by the device of transforming descriptive and meditative propositions into a sequence of tableaux and brief allegories—a mode which Keats revitalized in his ode *To Autumn*.[5] The clue to the provenience of the greater Romantic lyric is to be found in the attributes of the opening description. This landscape is not only particularized; it is in most cases precisely localized, in place, and sometimes in time as well. Critics have often remarked on Wordsworth's scrupulosity about specifying the circumstances for his poems, but his fellow poets were often no less meticulous in giving their greater lyrics an exact locality. We have "The Eolian Harp, Composed at Clevedon, Somersetshire" (the first versions also appended to

5. Keats used a different figure for the poetic return. In a letter of December 1818–January 1819 he transcribed *Fancy* and *Bards of passion and of mirth*, in which the last lines are variants of the opening lines, and said, "These are specimens of a sort of rondeau which I think I shall become partial to" (*The Letters of John Keats*, ed. H. E. Rollins, Cambridge, Mass., 1958, II, 21–26). In the next few months he exemplified the rondeau form in *The Eve of St. Agnes* and *La Belle Dame sans Merci*, as well as in the descriptive-meditative lyric *Ode to a Nightingale*.

the title a date, 20 August 1795); "This Lime-Tree Bower My Prison," with the headnote: "In the June of 1797 . . . the author's cottage . . . composed . . . in the garden-bower"; "Fears in Solitude written April, 1798. . . . The Scene, the Hills near Stowey";[6] "Lines Composed a Few Miles above Tintern Abbey . . . July 13, 1798"; "Elegiac Stanzas Suggested by a Picture of Peele Castle, in a Storm"; "Stanzas Written in Dejection, near Naples." Even when its setting is not named in the title, the poem usually has an identifiable local habitation, such as the milieu of Coleridge's cottage at Nether Stowey for *Frost at Midnight*, or the view from Coleridge's study at Keswick in *Dejection: An Ode*. To his *Ode to the West Wind*, Shelley was careful to add the note: "Written in a wood that skirts the Arno, near Florence. . . ."

There existed in the eighteenth century a well defined and immensely popular poetic type, in which the title named a geographical location, and which combined a description of that scene with the thoughts that the scene suggested. This was known as the "local" or "loco-descriptive" poem; Robert A. Aubin, in his compendious and amusing survey of *Topographical Poetry in XVIII-Century England*, lists almost two thousand instances of the form. "Local poetry," as Dr. Johnson concisely defined it in his life of John Denham, was

> a species of composition . . . of which the fundamental subject is some particular landscape to be poetically described, with the addition of such embellishments as may be supplied by historical retrospection or incidental meditation.[7]

The evidence, I think, makes it clear that the most characteristic Romantic lyric developed directly out of one of the most stable and widely employed of all the neoclassic kinds.

By general consent Denham, as Dr. Johnson said, was the "author" of the genre, in that excellent poem *Cooper's Hill*, of which the first version was written in 1642. In it the poet inventories the prospect of the Thames valley visible from the hilltop, with distant London on one side and Windsor Castle on the other. As Earl Wasserman has shown, the poem is a complex construction, in which the topographical elements are selected and managed so as to yield concepts which support a Royalist viewpoint on the eve of the civil wars.[8] But if, like Dr. Johnson, we abstract and classify Denham's incidental meditations, we find that some are historical and political, but that others are broadly sententious, and are achieved by the device of adducing to a natural object a correspondent moral idea. Thus the "aery Mountain" (lines 217–22), forced to endure the onslaught of winds and storms, instances "the common fate of all that's high or great," while the Thames (lines 163–64) hastens "to pay tribute to the Sea, / Like mortal life to meet Eternity."

This latter procedure is worth dwelling on for a moment, because

---

6. So titled in the Dowden MS in the Morgan Library; see Carl R. Woodring, *Politics in the Poetry of Coleridge* (Madison, 1961), p. 255, n. 16.
7. *Lives of the English Poets*, ed. G. B. Hill (Oxford, 1905), I, 77.
8. *The Subtler Language* (Baltimore, 1959), chap. 3.

for many of Denham's successors it displaced history and politics to become the sole meditative component in local poems, and it later evolved into the extended meditation of the Romantic lyric. The *paysage moralisé* was not invented as a rhetorical device by poets, but was grounded on two collateral and pervasive concepts in medieval and Renaissance philosophy. One of these was the doctrine that God has supplemented the Holy Scriptures with the *liber creaturarum*, so that objects of nature, as Sir Thomas Browne said, carry "in Stenography and short Characters, something of Divinity"[9] and show forth the attributes and providence of their Author. The second concept, of independent philosophic origin but often fused with the first, is that the divine Architect has designed the universe analogically, relating the physical, moral, and spiritual realms by an elaborate system of correspondences. A landscape, accordingly, consists of *verba visibilia* which enable pious interpreters such as Shakespeare's Duke in *As You Like It* to find "books in the running brooks, / Sermons in stones, and good in everything."

The metaphysic of a symbolic and analogical universe underlay the figurative tactics of the seventeenth-century metaphysical poets who were John Denham's predecessors and contemporaries. The secular and amatory poems exploited unexpected correspondences mainly as display rhetoric, positing the analogue in order to show the author's wit in supporting an argument and to evoke in the reader the shock of delightful discovery. In their devotional poems, however, the poets put forward their figures as grounded in the divine plan underlying the universe. Thus Henry Vaughan, musing over a waterfall, was enabled by the guidance of its Creator to discover its built-in correspondences with the life and destiny of man:

> What sublime truths and wholesome themes,
> Lodge in thy mystical deep streams!
> Such as dull man can never find
> Unless that spirit lead his mind
> Which first upon thy face did move,
> And hatched all with his quick'ning love.

In 1655, the year in which Vaughan published *The Waterfall*, Denham added to his enlarged edition of *Cooper's Hill* the famous pair of couplets on the Thames which link description to concepts by a sustained parallel between the flow of the stream and the ideal conduct of life and art:

> O could I flow like thee, and make thy stream
> My great example, as it is my theme!
> Though deep, yet clear, though gentle, yet not dull,
> Strong without rage, without o'erflowing, full.

The metaphysical device and ingenuity are still apparent, but we can see why this became the best known and most influential passage in the poetry of neoclassicism—a model not only for its versification, but

9. *The Works of Sir Thomas Browne*, ed. Geoffrey Keynes (London, 1928–31), I, 17.

also for some of its most characteristic ideas and rhetorical devices. In these lines the metaphysical wit has been tamed and ordered into the "true wit" which became the eighteenth-century ideal; Denham's "strength" (which Dr. Johnson defined as "much meaning in few words"), so universally admired, has replaced the "strong lines" (the compressed and hyperbolic ingeniousness) of John Donne; while the startling revelation of *discordia concors* between object and idea has been smoothed to a neoclassic decency, moulded to the deft play of antitheses around the caesura, and adapted to the presentation of the cardinal neoclassic ideal of a mean between extremes.[1]

In the enormous number of eighteenth-century local poems the organization of *Cooper's Hill* around a controlling political motif was soon reduced mainly to the procedure of setting up parallels between landscape and moral commonplaces. The subtitle of Richard Jago's long *Edge Hill* (1767) neatly defines the double function: "The Rural Prospect Delineated and Moralized"; while the title of an anonymous poem of 1790 reveals how monstrous this development could be: *An Evening's Reflection on the Universe, in a Walk on the Seashore*. The literal belief in a universe of divine types and correspondences, which had originally supported this structural trope, faded,[2] and the coupling of sensuous phenomena with moral statements came to be regarded as a rhetorical device particularly apt to the descriptive poet's double aim of combining instruction with delight. John Dyer's *Grongar Hill* (1726) was justly esteemed as one of the most deft and agreeable of prospect-poems. Mounting the hill, the poet describes the widening prospect with a particularity beyond the call of the moralist's duty. Yet the details of the scene are duly equated with *sententiae*; and when he comes to moralize the river (always, after Denham's passage on the Thames, the favorite item in the topographic inventory), Dyer echoes the great theological concept of a typological universe lightly, as a pleasant conceit:

1. The opening eight lines of *Cooper's Hill*, despite some approximation to neoclassic neatness and dispatch, are much closer to Donne's couplets, in the cramped syntax of their run-on lines, which deploy a tortuous analogical argument to demonstrate a paradox that inverts and explodes a mythological cliché:

> Sure there are Poets which did never dream
> Upon *Parnassus*, nor did taste the stream
> Of *Helicon*, we therefore may suppose
> Those made no Poets, but the Poets those.
> And as Courts make not Kings, but Kings the Court,
> So where the Muses and their train resort,
> *Parnassus* stands; if I can be to thee
> A Poet, thou Parnassus are to me.

Compare the opening of Andrew Marvell's *Upon the Hill and Grove at Billborow* (probably written in the early 1650s) for the jolting movement, the doughty hyperbole, and witty shock tactics of the thoroughly metaphysical management of a local hill-poem.

2. See Earl R. Wasserman, "Nature Moralized: The Divine Analogy in the Eighteenth Century," *ELH*, 20 (1953), 39–76. For commentators on the local poem, the chief structural problem was how to establish easy, just, yet varied connections between its two components, the *visibilia* and the *moralia*. Joseph Warton's observation is typical, that "it is one of the greatest and most pleasing arts of descriptive poetry, to introduce moral sentences and instructions in an oblique and indirect manner" (An *Essay on the Genius and Writings of Pope* [1756], London, 1806, I, 29).

And see the rivers how they run . . .
Wave succeeding wave, they go
A various journey to the deep,
Like human life to endless sleep!
Thus is nature's vesture wrought,
To instruct our wand'ring thought;
Thus she dresses green and gay,
To disperse our cares away.

Thomas Gray's *Ode on a Distant Prospect of Eton College* (1747) provides significant evidence that the local poem evolved into the greater Romantic lyric. It is a hill-poem, and its setting—Windsor heights and the Thames valley—is part of the very prospect which Denham had described. The topographical form, however, has been adapted to the Horatian ode, so that the focus of interest is no longer in the analogical inventory of scenic detail, but in the mental and emotional experience of a specific lyric speaker. The meditation becomes a coherent and dramatic sequence of thought, triggered by what was to become Wordsworth's favorite device of *déjà vu*: the scene is a scene revisited, and it evokes in memory the lost self of the speaker's youth:

I feel the gales that from ye blow
A momentary bliss bestow,
As, waving fresh their gladsome wing,
My weary soul they seem to soothe,
And, redolent of joy and youth,
To breathe a second spring.

As he watches the heedless schoolboys at their games, the speaker's first impulse is to warn them of the ambuscades which the "ministers of human fate" are even now laying for them: "Ah, tell them they are men!" But a new thought leads to a reversal of intention, for he suddenly realizes that since life's horrors are inescapable, forewarning is a needless cruelty.

We are a long way, however, from the free flow of consciousness, the interweaving of thought, feeling, and perceptual detail, and the easy naturalness of the speaking voice which characterize the Romantic lyric. Gray deliberately rendered both his observations and reflections in the hieratic style of a formal odic *oratio*. The poet's recollection of times past, for example, is managed through an invocation to Father Thames to tell him "who foremost now delight to cleave / With pliant arm thy glassy wave," and the language throughout is heightened and stylized by the apostrophe, exclamation, rhetorical question, and studied periphrasis which Wordsworth decried in Gray—"more than any other man curiously elaborate in the structure of his . . . poetic diction."[3] Both reminiscence and reflection are depersonalized, and occur mainly as general propositions which are sometimes expressed as *sententiae* ("where ignorance is bliss / 'Tis folly

3. Preface to *Lyrical Ballads*, in *The Prose Works of William Wordsworth*, ed. W. J. B. Owen and Jane W. Smyser (Oxford, 1974), I, 133.

to be wise"), and at other times as propositions which, in the standard
artifice of the contemporary ode, are converted into the tableau-and-
allegory form that Coleridge derogated as Gray's "translations of prose
thoughts into poetic language."[4] Gray's poem is structurally inventive,
and excellent in its kind, but it remains distinctly a mid-century period
piece. We need to look elsewhere for the immediate occasion of Coleridge's invention of the greater Romantic lyric.

* * *

IV. THE COALESCENCE OF SUBJECT AND OBJECT

* * * The shift in Coleridge's theory of descriptive poetry corre-
sponded with a change in his practice of the form; and in the sequence of sonnets and conversation poems that he wrote under
Bowles's influence we can observe him in the process of converting
the conjunction of parts, in which nature stays on one side and
thought on the other, into the Romantic interfusion of subject and object. W. K. Wimsatt has acutely remarked that Coleridge's sonnet *To
the River Otter*—though written in express imitation of Bowles's *To the
River Itchin,* perhaps so early as 1793—has begun to diverge from
Bowles's "simple association . . . simply asserted" by involving the
thought in the descriptive details so that the design "is latent in the
multiform sensuous picture."[5] *The Eolian Harp* (1795–96) set the expanded pattern of the greater lyric, but in it the meditative flight is a
short one, while the thought is still at times expressed in the mode of
sententiae which are joined to the details of the scene by formal similes. We sit

> beside our Cot, our Cot o'ergrown
> With white-flower'd Jasmin, and the broad-leav'd Myrtle,
> (Meet emblems they of Innocence and Love!)
> And watch the clouds, that late were rich with light,
> Slow saddening round, and mark the star of eve
> Serenely brilliant (such should Wisdom be)
> Shine opposite!

In *Frost at Midnight,* however, written two years later, the images in
the initial description are already suffused with an unstated significance which, in Coleridge's terms, is merely "elicited" and expanded
by the subsequent reflection, which in turn "superinduces" a richer
meaning upon the scene to which it reverts. *Fears in Solitude,* a few
months after that, exemplifies the sustained dialogue between mind
and landscape which Coleridge describes in lines 215–20 of the
poem: the prospect of sea and fields

> seems like society—
> Conversing with the mind, and giving it
> A livelier impulse and a dance of thought!

4. *Biographia Literaria,* ed. J. Shawcross (Oxford, 1907), I, 13.
5. "The Structure of Romantic Nature Imagery," in *The Verbal Icon* (Lexington, Ky., 1954), pp. 106, 111.

And *Dejection: An Ode,* on which Coleridge was working in 1802 just as he got Bowles's poems into critical perspective, is a triumph of the "co-adunating" imagination, in the very poem which laments the severance of his community with nature and the suspension of his shaping spirit of imagination. In unspoken consonance with the change of the outer scene and of the responsive wind-harp from ominous quiet to violent storm to momentary calm, the poet's mind, momentarily revitalized by a correspondent inner breeze, moves from torpor through violence to calm, by a process in which the properties earlier specified of the landscape—the spring rebirth, the radiated light of moon and stars, the clouds and rain, the voice of the harp—reappear as the metaphors of the evolving meditation on the relation of mind to nature; these culminate in the figure of the one life as an eddy between antitheses:

> To her may all things live, from pole to pole,
> Their life the eddying of her living soul!

On Coleridge's philosophical premises, in this poem nature is made thought and thought nature, both by their sustained interaction and by their seamless metaphoric continuity.

The best Romantic meditations on a landscape, following Coleridge's examples, all manifest a transaction between subject and object in which the thought incorporates and makes explicit what was already implicit in the outer scene. And all the poets testify independently to a fact of consciousness which underlay these poems, and was the experiential source and warrant for the philosophy of cognition as an interfusion of mind and nature. When the Romantic poet confronted a landscape, the distinction between self and not-self tended to dissolve. Coleridge asserted that from childhood he had been accustomed to "unrealize . . . and then by a sort of transfusion and transmission of my consciousness to identify myself with the Object"; also that

> in looking at objects of Nature while I am thinking . . . I seem rather to be seeking, as it were *asking,* a symbolical language for something within me that already and forever exists, than observing any thing new.

So with Wordsworth: "I was often unable to think of external things as having external existence, and I communed with all that I saw as something not apart from, but inherent in, my own immaterial nature." Shelley witnessed to "the state called reverie," when men "feel as if their nature were dissolved into the surrounding universe, or as if the surrounding universe were absorbed into their being. They are conscious of no distinction." Even Byron's Childe Harold claimed that "I live not in myself," but that mountains, waves, and skies become "a part / Of me, and of my soul, as I of them." Keats's experience differs, but only in the conditions that, instead of assimilating the other to the self, the self goes out into the other, and that the boundary of self is "annihilated" when he contemplates, not a broad prospect, but a solid particular endowed with outline, mass, and posture or motion. That type of poet of which "I am a Member . . . has no self" but "is continually [informing] and filling some other Body"—a moving billiard ball, a breaking wave, a human form in arrested motion, a sparrow, an urn, or a nightingale.[6]

V. THE ROMANTIC MEDITATION

The greater Romantic lyric, then, as established by Coleridge, evolved from the descriptive-meditative structure of the eighteenth-century local poem, primarily through the intermediate stage of Bowles's sequence of sonnets. There remains, however, a wide disparity between the Romantic lyric and its predecessors, a disparity in the organization and nature of the meditation proper. In local poetry the order of the thoughts is the sequence in which the natural objects are observed; the poet surveys a prospect, or climbs a hill, or undertakes a tour, or follows the course of a stream, and he introduces memories and ideas intermittently, as the descriptive occasion offers. In Bowles's sonnets, the meditation, while more continuous, is severely limited by the straitness of the form, and consists mainly of the pensive commonplaces of the typical late-century man of feeling. In the fully developed Romantic lyric, on the other hand, the description is structurally subordinate to the meditation, and the meditation is sustained, continuous, and highly serious. Even when the initial impression is of the casual movement of a relaxed mind, retrospect reveals the whole to have been firmly organized around an emotional issue pressing for resolution. And in a number of the greatest lyrics—including Coleridge's *Dejection*, Wordsworth's *Intimations*, Shelley's *Stanzas Written in Dejection* and *West Wind*, Keats's *Nightingale*—the issue is one of a recurrent state often called by the specialized term "dejection." This is not the pleasing melancholy of the eighteenth-century poet of sensibility, nor Bowles's muted self-pity, but a profound sadness, sometimes bordering on the anguish of terror or despair, at the sense of loss, dereliction, isolation, or inner death, which is presented as inherent in the conditions of the speaker's existence.

*   *   *

The Romantic meditations, then, though secular meditations, often turn on crises—alienation, dejection, the loss of a "celestial light" or "glory" in experiencing the created world—which are closely akin to the spiritual crises of the earlier religious poets. And at times Romantic lyrics become overtly theological in expression. Some of them include not only colloquies with a human auditor, real or imagined, and with what de Sales called "insensible creatures," but also with God or with a Spirit of Nature, in the mode of a formal prayer (*Reflections on Having Left a Place of Retirement*, *Ode to the West Wind*), or else of a terminal benediction. Thus Coleridge's *Frost at Midnight* falls into the ritual language of a blessing ("Therefore all seasons shall be sweet to

6. Coleridge, *Collected Letters*, IV, 974–75, and *Notebooks*, II, entry 2546; Wordsworth, *Poetical Works*, IV, 463; *Shelley's Prose*, ed. D. L. Clark (Albuquerque, 1954), p. 174; Byron, *Childe Harold*, III, lxxii, lxxv; Keats, *Letters*, I, 387.

thee")—a tactic which Wordsworth at once picked up in *Tintern Abbey* ("and this prayer I make. . . . Therefore let the moon / Shine on thee in thy solitary walk") and which Coleridge himself repeated in *Dejection* ("Visit her, gentle Sleep! with wings of healing. . . . To her may all things live, from pole to pole").

We must not drive the parallel too hard. There is little external evidence of the direct influence of the metaphysical poem upon the greater Romantic lyric; the similarity between them may well be the result of a common tradition of meditations on the creatures—a tradition which continued in the eighteenth century in so prodigiously popular a work as James Hervey's *Meditations and Contemplations* (1746–47).[7] And there is a very conspicuous and significant difference between the Romantic lyric and the seventeenth-century meditation on created nature—a difference in the description which initiates and directs the process of mind. The "composition of place" was not a specific locality, nor did it need to be present to the eyes of the speaker, but was a typical scene or object, usually called up, as Saint Ignatius and other preceptors said, before "the eyes of the imagination,"[8] in order to set off and guide the thought by means of correspondences whose interpretation was firmly controlled by an inherited typology. The landscape set forth in Vaughan's *Regeneration*, for example, is not a particular geographical location, nor even a literal setting, but the allegorical landscape common to the genre of spiritual pilgrimages, from the *Divine Comedy* to *Pilgrim's Progress*. And Herbert's flower is not a specified plant, described by the poet with his eye on the object, but a generic one; it is simply the class of all perennials, in which God has inscribed the invariable signatures of His providential plan. In the Romantic poem, on the other hand, the speaker merely happens upon a natural scene which is present, particular, and almost always precisely located; and though Coleridge occasionally alludes to it still as "that eternal language, which thy God / Utters,"[9] the primary meanings educed from the scene are not governed by a public symbolism, but have been brought to it by the private mind which perceives it. But we know already that these attributes also had a seventeenth-century origin, in a poet who inherited the metaphysical tradition yet went on, as Dryden and many of his successors commented,[1] to alter it in such a way as to establish the typical meter, rhetoric, and formal devices of neoclassic poetry. The crucial event in the development of the most distinctive of the Romantic lyric forms occurred when John Denham climbed Cooper's Hill and undertook to describe, in balanced cou-

---

7. In the *Meditations and Contemplations*, 7th ed. (London, 1750), II, xv–xvii, Hervey describes his aim to "exhibit a Prospect of still *Life*, and grand *Operation*" in order "to *open* the *Door* of Meditation," and show how we may "*gather up* the unstable, fluctuating *Train* of Fancy; and collect her fickle Powers into a consistent, regular, and useful Habit of Thinking."

8. See Louis L. Martz, *The Poetry of Meditation* (New Haven, 1954), pp. 27–28.

9. *Frost at Midnight*, lines 58–62; cf. *This Lime-Tree Bower*, lines 39–43, and *Fears in Solitude*, lines 22–24. In Coleridge's *Hymn before Sunrise* (1802), unlike his greater lyrics, the meditation moves from the creatures to the Creator by a hereditary symbolism as old as Psalm 19: "The heavens declare the glory of God; and the firmament sheweth his handywork."

1. Dr. Johnson listed Denham among the metaphysical poets, then added, in the great commonplace of neoclassical literary history, that he "and Waller sought another way to fame, by improving the harmony of our numbers" ("Cowley," in *Lives of the English Poets*, I, 22).

plets, the landscape before his eyes, and to embellish the description with incidental reminiscence and meditation.

FRANCES FERGUSON

Coleridge and the Deluded Reader: "The Rime of the Ancient Mariner"†

The criticism of "The Rime of the Ancient Mariner" reflects a craving for causes. Opium, or Coleridge's guilt-obsessed personality, or (as Robert Penn Warren would have it) his convergent beliefs in the "One Life within us all" and in the Imagination caused the poem to come into being in its own peculiar form. A "teaching text" like *The Norton Anthology of English Literature* sets out to explicate the lines:

> The Wedding-Guest stood still,
> And listens like a three years' child:
> The Mariner hath his will (ll. 14–16)[1]

—and sets up a nice causal connection by asserting that "the Mariner has gained control of the will of the Wedding Guest by hypnosis—or, as it was called in Coleridge's time—by 'mesmerism' " (2:331). There may be some form of hypnosis—or mesmerism—in the rather monotonous rhythms of the lines, but the annotation converts hypnosis into a misguidedly "scientific" explanation of why the Wedding Guest couldn't or didn't bother to get away.

This construction of causes—for the poem as a whole or for individual passages—is particularly striking because it appears as a series of belated rejoinders to the many complaints that greeted the poem's first public appearance. The "Rime" was quite widely censured for extravagance, unconnectedness, and improbability. Even Wordsworth in his Note to the "Rime" in the 1800 edition of *Lyrical Ballads* registered various objections that amounted to the assertion that the poem was deficient in connections and causes:

> The Poem of my Friend has indeed great defects; first, that the principal person has no distinct character, either in his profession of Mariner, or as a human being who having been long under the controul of supernatural impressions might be supposed himself to partake of something supernatural: secondly, that he does not act, but is continually acted upon: thirdly, that the events having no necessary connection do not produce each other; and lastly, that the imagery is somewhat too laboriously accumulated. (Wordsworth, pp. 270–71)

---

† From *Samuel Taylor Coleridge: The Rime of the Ancient Mariner*, ed. Paul Fry (Boston & New York: Bedford St. Martin's, 1999), 113–30. Reprinted by permission of the author. [The footnote is the author's.]
1. All direct quotations from the "Rime" follow the text of *The Complete Poetical Works of Samuel Taylor Coleridge*, ed. Ernest Hartley Coleridge, Oxford, 1968.

Wordsworth's account of the poem's "defects" in a note that is a manifesto for its being reprinted may well be of a piece with the simultaneously published Preface to *Lyrical Ballads*, in which he sought to avoid the appearance of *"reasoning* [the reader] into an approbation of these particular Poems" (Wordsworth, pp. 236–37). Everywhere in his account of defects Wordsworth cites formal features (albeit in the extended sense)—character, plot, motive, and imagery; and it is hard to believe that Wordsworth was doing anything more than repeating—and thereby acknowledging—the categories of poetic appreciation that he and Coleridge were explicitly attacking in *Lyrical Ballads*. But if the author of "The Thorn," "We are seven," and *The Prelude* seems improbable in the role of someone wedded to clearly delineated character, plot, motive, and imagery, Coleridge's own remarks about the poem are even more difficult to assimilate to the critical search for causes and consequences. For example, Coleridge's famous account of Mrs. Barbauld's opinion of the "Rime" figures in almost every article on the poem, but to diverse ends:

> MRS. BARBAULD once told me that she admired the Ancient Mariner very much, but that there were two faults in it,—it was improbable, and had no moral. As for the probability, I owned that that might admit some question; but as to the want of a moral, I told her that in my own judgment the poem had too much; and that the only or chief fault, if I might say so, was the obtrusion of the moral sentiment so openly on the reader as a principle or cause of action in a work of such pure imagination. It ought to have had no more moral than the Arabian Nights' tale of the merchant's sitting down to eat dates by the side of a well, and throwing the shells aside, and lo! a geni starts up, and says he *must* kill the aforesaid merchant, *because* one of the date-shells had, it seems, put out the eye of the geni's son. (*Table Talk*, 2:100)

On the one hand, critics have harnessed this passage to an attempt to eschew interpretation; the poem as a "work of . . . pure imagination" has no discursively translatable meaning. (This is the "What-do-you-think-when-you-think-nothing?" school of criticism.) On the other hand, perhaps the most influential modern critic of the poem, Warren, confesses that he is "inclined to sympathize with the lady's desire that poetry have some significant relation to the world, some meaning" (p. 199). Thus, his reading of the passage from *Table Talk* about Mrs. Barbauld is this: "If the passage affirms anything, it affirms that Coleridge intended the poem to have a 'moral sentiment,' but felt that he had been a trifle unsubtle in fulfilling his intention" (p. 200).

The no-moral position seems patently unconvincing because it becomes an excuse for hanging in one's confusions; but even though Warren's essay remains the most provocative interpretation, it also seems progressively to overspecify the "moral sentiment." What Warren calls the sacramental vision, the theme of the "One Life" that is expressed in the poem's conclusion ("He prayeth best. . . .") and what he calls the imagination (the symbols of the poem) are both models of unity and fusion. And since unity and coherence are poetry for Warren, this poem must be both unified and unifying by definition; images must be symbols, and the symbols must speak of the Mariner's—and the reader's—"expressive integration" (p. 262) with the universe and "with other men, with society" (p. 255). Warren's interpretation suggests not merely that the sin of pride is involved in the "Rime" but also that the poem in some sense involves teaching one—all of us—to avoid that sin. But while I agree with Warren that morals are at issue in the poem, Coleridgean morality seems to me consistently more problematic than he suggests. For the difficulty of the poem is that the possibility of learning from the Mariner's experience depends upon sorting that experience into a more linear and complete pattern than the poem ever agrees to do. For the poem seems almost as thorough a work of backwardness—or hysteron proteron [basic error]—as we have.

One aspect of this backwardness led a contemporary reviewer (Charles Burney) to fulminate in 1799 against *Lyrical Ballads* in general and against the "Rime" in particular:

> Though we have been extremely entertained with the fancy, the facility, and (in general) the sentiments, of these pieces, we cannot regard them as *poetry*, of a class to be cultivated at the expence of a higher species of versification, unknown in our language at the time when our elder writers, whom this author condescends to imitate, wrote their ballads. Would it not be degrading poetry, as well as the English language, to go back to the barbarous and uncouth numbers of Chaucer? . . . Should we be gainers by the retrogradation? . . . None but savages have submitted to eat acorns after·corn was found. (Jackson, p. 55)

But the archaistic diction is only one aspect of the poem's "retrogradation." For Coleridge not only reverses linguistic and poetic *progress* in the "Rime," he so thoroughly compounds the past with the present tense that the action or progress of the poem hovers in a temporal limbo:

> The Wedding-Guest he beat his breast,
> Yet he cannot choose but hear;
> And thus spake on that ancient man,
> The bright-eyed Mariner. (ll. 37–40)

And even such a basic question as that of the Mariner's motive for killing the bird is given a tardy (and insufficient) answer. The event of the killing is recounted in the first section of the poem; and the suggestion that the Mariner may have been trying to confute his shipmates' superstitious connections between the Albatross and the weather emerges only in the second section. The possibility that the Mariner may have hoped—scientifically—to disprove their superstition is the closest thing to an hypothesis we are offered, and it appears only when we desire a motive so strongly that we must mistrust our own efforts to reestablish a cause-and-effect sequence.

But how does any reader, any critic sort out the action that presumably points the moral of the poem? Or, in other words, how does one sort out the moral value of the agents of the poem? The Mariner concludes his story to the Wedding Guest with the following "good" words:

> He prayeth well, who loveth well
> Both man and bird and beast.
>
> He prayeth best, who loveth best
> All things both great and small;
> For the dear God who loveth us,
> He made and loveth all. (ll. 616–21)

But the Mariner has a decidedly malignant effect on the persons who save his body after his spiritual redemption on the ship: the Pilot collapses in a fit, and the Pilot's boy goes mad. Likewise, the Albatross seems good, then bad, then good, because the death of the Albatross causes first fog and mist (bad), then clearing (good), and finally the failure of the breeze (bad). Our difficulty is that all the evidences of moral value are mutually contradictory.

There is, however, one element of the poem that leads us. In 1815–16 Coleridge added the Gloss along the left margin as he was readying his work for the 1817 edition of *Sibylline Leaves*. And the critical "advances" that have been made in the last century and a half pay tribute to Coleridge's sagacity in having supplied this helpful commentary. John Livingston Lowes notes the literary elegance of the Gloss's prose (pp. 297–98). B. R. McElderry, Jr., sees the Gloss as an "artistic restatement and ornament of what is obvious in the text," and as a chance for Coleridge to relive the pleasure of writing his "one completed masterpiece" (p. 91). And Robert Penn Warren peppers his long essay on the "Rime" with statements like this: "The Gloss here tells us all we need to know, defining the Mariner's relation to the moon" (p. 243). The almost universal opinion seems to be that Coleridge wrote the Gloss (either as Coleridge or in the role of a fictitious editor) because he was attempting to clarify and unify the poem after entertaining the legion of hostile comments upon its confusions and inconsequence.

But the Gloss provides a strange kind of clarity and unity. Consider some examples. As the Wedding Guest speaks for the first time about anything except the wedding he wishes he could attend, this is what the text offers:

> "God save thee, ancient Mariner!
> From the fiends, that plague thee thus!—
> Why look'st thou so?"—With my cross-bow
> I shot the ALBATROSS. (ll. 79–82)

And the Gloss comments—"The ancient Mariner inhospitably killeth the pious bird of good omen." "Inhospitably," "pious," and "good omen" bespeak conclusions that do not echo the main text because the main text never reaches such value judgments.

The Argument that Coleridge deleted from the poem after 1800 recounted that "the Ancient Mariner cruelly and in contempt of the laws of hospitality killed a Sea-bird," but the Gloss here seems even stronger than the Argument had been. However forceful the ancient laws of hospitality, the notion of a man's hospitality toward a bird contains a rather anomalous and itself prideful assumption—that the bird is a visitor in the Mariner's domain. If the Mariner commits a sin of pride in killing the Albatross and thereby asserting his power over it, even the Mariner's refusal to kill the bird would in this context involve the pride-laden assurance that man's domain measures the universe. But the even more striking feature of the Gloss is the attribution of unambiguous moral qualities to the bird—"the pious bird of good omen." And while the text of the poem proper registers only the sailors' vacillations on the moral standing of the bird, the Gloss is conspicuously conclusive on that point. The main text offers the sailors' contradictory opinions:

> And I had done a hellish thing,
> And it would work 'em woe:
> For all averred, I had killed the bird
> That made the breeze to blow.
> Ah wretch! said they, the bird to slay,
> That made the breeze to blow!
>
> Nor dim nor red, like God's own head,
> The glorious Sun uprist:
> Then all averred, I had killed the bird
> That brought the fog and mist.
> 'Twas right, said they, such birds to slay,
> That brought the fog and mist. (ll. 91–102)

And the Gloss seems merely to scorn the sailors' confusions: first "His shipmates cry out against the ancient Mariner, for killing the bird of good luck"; then, "But when the fog cleared off, they justify the same, and thus make themselves accomplices in the crime."

When the ship is stalled, and everyone aboard is desperately searching the horizon in hope of rescue, the text recounts things this way:

> A weary time! a weary time!
> How glazed each weary eye,
> When looking westward, I beheld
> A something in the sky.
>
> At first it seemed a little speck,
> And then it seemed a mist;
> It moved and moved, and took at last
> A certain shape, I wist. (ll. 145–52)

And the Gloss makes this remark: "The Ancient Mariner beholdeth a sign in the element afar off." Nothing is ever really "afar off" for the Gloss. What for the main text is merely "a something" and "a certain shape" is already categorized for the Gloss as a sign, a symbol. The Gloss, in assuming that things must be significant and interpretable, finds significance and interpretability, but only by reading ahead of— or beyond—the main text.

Now the only portion of the Gloss that has been cited as an editorializing incursion upon the main text is the scholarly comment that supports the dreams which some of the sailors have about an avenging spirit: "A Spirit had followed them; one of the invisible inhabitants of this planet, neither departed souls nor angels; concerning whom the learned Jew, Josephus, and the Platonic Constantinopolitan, Michael Psellus, may be consulted. They are very numerous, and there is no climate or element without one or more." But both the entire Gloss and the bulk of critical opinion of the poem may well be editorializing, in that they mold contradictory evidences into a cause-and-effect pattern that the main text never quite offers: the Albatross was a good bird, the Mariner killed it, the Mariner was punished for his crime, the Mariner learned to acknowledge the beauty of all natural creatures and was saved to proselytize for this eminently noble moral position.

But let us return to the remarks on the poem in the *Specimens of the Table Talk of the Late Samuel Taylor Coleridge*; in Coleridge's account of the first tale from the *Arabian Nights* the geni "says he *must* kill the aforesaid merchant, *because* one of the date-shells had, it seems, put out the eye of the geni's son" (2:100, emphasis Coleridge's). If the poem should have had no more moral than this, we may ask, what kind of moral is it? The merchant, presumably, would not have thrown his date-shells into the well if he had dreamed that he would do harm to the geni's son; and by the same logic, the Mariner would, presumably, not have killed the Albatross if he had recognized its goodness and significance. As is common in Coleridge's work generally, intention and effect are absolutely discontinuous, and the moral is that morality appears to involve certainty only if you can already know the full outcome of every action before you commit it.

Coleridge's recounting his conversation with Mrs. Barbauld about the poem seems to me particularly striking in the context of this moral problem. A rather sizable collection of reviewers had complained about the poem's improbability and lack of moral, but Mrs. Barbauld became his most significant interlocutor on the poem's moral import. A brief excursus on Anna Laetitia Barbauld may suggest why she in particular would be an appropriate real or fictitious disputant of record. Mrs. Barbauld was firmly committed to the education of children, and she demonstrated her commitment by authoring *Lessons for Children* (1780) and *Hymns in Prose for Children* (1781). *Lessons for Children* was divided into four parts—*Lessons* . . . 1) For Children from Two to Three Years Old; 2) and 3) For Children of Three Years Old; and 4) For Children from Three to Four Years Old, so that the readings moved from simple to more complex in a gradual scale. As Mrs. Barbauld stated in her Preface to *Hymns in Prose*, this was her purpose:

> to impress devotional feelings as early as possible on the infant mind . . . to impress them by connecting religion with a variety of sensible objects; with all that he sees, all that he hears, all that affects his young mind with wonder or delight; and thus by deep, strong, and permanent associations to lay the best foundation for practical devotion in future life. (vi)

Reading was thus not merely a neutral exercise; reading and religion were to be taught simultaneously. Now in this respect Mrs. Barbauld's project was not exactly unheard of. Such a linkage was explicit in the practice of using the Bible as the textbook for reading; and from the sixteenth century, when people began to be concerned about the heretical interpretations of the Bible that neophyte readers produced, the primer had been seen as a temporary substitute for the Bible or as a preparation for the Bible itself. Additionally the primer was supposed to supply relevance; it would not merely link reading with religion, it would also prepare the child to recognize the moral dilemmas of his everyday life.

Thus, the child learning to read in the late eighteenth and early nineteenth centuries was given (by Mrs. Barbauld, Mrs. Trimmer, Thomas Day, Maria Edgeworth, and others) texts that endowed nature with particular significance for the child, and as a religious child, he was to behave with particular moral probity towards nature. In fact, the most frequently recurrent theme in primer literature of the time was the sinfulness of cruelty to animals—particularly birds. Mrs. Barbauld's *Lessons for Children of Three Years Old*, Part I, in fact, concludes with two short stories, the first of which enforces the moral of kindness to birds:

> A naughty boy will not feed a starving and freezing robin; in fact he even pulls the poor bird's tail! It dies. Shortly after that, the boy's parents leave him because he is cruel, and he is forced to beg for food. He goes into a forest, sits down and cries, and is never heard of again; it is believed that bears ate him. (Patterson, p. 44)

No wonder Wordsworth recounts in Book I of *The Prelude* (ll. 333–50) that his childish act of stealing eggs from a bird's nest produced a major crisis of guilt.

Now I obviously don't mean to suggest either that Coleridge wrote "The Rime of the Ancient Mariner" or that Wordsworth wrote that passage from *The Prelude* as a direct attack on Mrs. Barbauld or primers generally. But I do want to suggest that the moral causality that most critics discern in the "Rime" sounds less appropriate to Coleridge's poem than to the conclusion of Mrs. Barbauld's "Epitaph on a Goldfinch":

> Reader,
> if suffering innocence can hope for retribution,
> deny not to the gentle shade
> of this unfortunate captive
> the natural though uncertain hope
> of animating some happier form,
> or trying his new-fledged pinions
> in some humble Elysium,
> beyond the reach of Man,
> the tyrant
> of this lower universe. (*Works*, Vol. 2, p. 323)

The primary difference between Mrs. Barbauld's literary morals and Coleridge's seems to lie in her emphasis upon acts and his agonizing explorations of the difficulties of recognizing the full implications of an action before it is committed, put in the context of the full range of human history (particularly the context of the Bible), and interpreted. Mrs. Barbauld's story of the little boy who was cruel to the starving and freezing robin is, one might assert, no less improbable than the "Rime," no less committed to what we might see as excessive punishment for the crime perpetrated. But while the critics of the "Rime" almost invariably mock Mrs. Barbauld as an obtuse and simplistic moralist, they also subscribe to the moral line of the Gloss, which leads them to a Barbauldian moral.

We must return to a rather simple-minded question: How bad was the Mariner to kill the bird? The act was certainly one of "motiveless malignity," for the Albatross had done nothing to him. But the crucial point is that he "didn't know any better"; it's merely the kind of explanation that enlightened parents of our own century employ to exonerate a child who has just destroyed the drapes in order to "play dress-up" or who has pulled the cat's tail. And while Mrs. Barbauld could be said to regard the learning of reading and morals as *technical* skills, Coleridge recognizes reading as moral because one's *techné* can never suffice. One acts, Coleridge would say, on the basis of one's reading or interpretation, but if reading and interpretation are the genesis of moral action, they may be infinitely divorced for moral outcome—may, in fact, reverse one's interpretation of the moral value of the act. Reading as a *techné* and morals as techniques of behavior thus become suspect for Coleridge because they imply that experience—and one's interpretation of it—are both stable and repetitive—that once can learn what one needs to know.

In this context, Coleridge's Gloss to the "Rime" recalls not merely the archetypal glosses—those in the margins of early printed editions of the Bible; it also raises the question of the ways in which such glosses and the primer tradition made the Bible more accessible and comprehensible while also domesticating that main text. For if glosses and primers came to be felt necessary because readers "couldn't understand" the Bible properly, Coleridge's addition of his Gloss to the "Rime" seems to have answered the critics who called his poem incomprehensible, largely by a domestication. Think back to the main text of the poem. The Wedding Guest, in the first stanza, asks, "Now wherefore stopp'st thou me?" Nowhere in the poem is the Wedding Guest's question answered, not even at the end, although we know then:

> He went like one that hath been stunned,
> And is of sense forlorn:
> A sadder and a wiser man,
> He rose the morrow morn. (ll. 626–29)

The Mariner's stopping the Wedding Guest is probably the most arbitrary event in a poem filled with arbitrary events, and any explanation

that asserts that he was chosen because his callowness needed correction seems farfetched. The main interest of the Wedding Guest is that
he has something to do. He has the intention of going to a wedding; in
Part I of the poem he alternately pays attention to the Mariner and to
the sounds of the wedding; but then, at the end of the poem he turns
"from the bridegroom's door." Most importantly, neither his personality nor his intentions matter; he becomes what he reads (or hears).
But if this account seems a fabulous escalation of the power of the
word, think of the fate of the other sailors on the Mariner's ship. Nothing happens to them when they denounce the Mariner's act of murder,
but then they reverse themselves when the fog clears and the fair
breeze continues. The Gloss informs us that they thus become accomplices in the Mariner's crime. But in Part III of the poem, the Mariner
is awarded to Life-in-Death while all the rest of the crew become the
property of Death. We never know whether this eventuality is a delayed
punishment for their first opinion or a more immediate punishment for
their second. Since the Mariner did the killing when they only expressed opinions about it, their fate seems cruel indeed. But the implication seems to be that every interpretation involves a moral
commitment with consequences that are inevitably more far-reaching
and unpredictable than one could have imagined. And neither the
sailor's paucity of information (which necessarily produces a limited
perspective) nor their intentions (to praise the good and denounce the
bad) are any exoneration for them (because most human interpretations are similarly limited, well-intentioned, and unexonerated).

Some of the major revisions of the poem, at least in retrospect,
seem designed to make not the moral but the process of arriving at
morals the major issue. In 1798 the poem was published under the title, "The Rime of the Ancient Mariner," and its Argument preceding
the text provided rather neutral information, primarily geographical—
"How a Ship having passed the Line was driven by storms to the Cold
Country towards the South Pole; . . . and of the strange things that befell. . . ." But in keeping with Coleridge's rather persistent practice of
giving with one hand while taking away with the other, the 1800 version was titled "The Ancient Mariner. A Poet's Reverie," as if to emphasize the unreality of the piece, while the Argument was far more
morally directive—"how the Ancient Mariner cruelly and in contempt
of the laws of hospitality killed a Sea-bird and how he was followed by
many and strange Judgements." And a similar doubleness or confusion
arises with the introduction of the Gloss in 1817. For while the Gloss
sorts out a moral line for the poem, it is accompanied by an epigraph
that Coleridge excerpted from Thomas Burnet:

> I believe easily that there are more invisible than visible beings in
> the universe. But of them all, who will tell us the race? and the
> ranks and relationships and differences and functions of each
> one? What do they do? What places do they inhabit? The human
> mind has always circled about the knowledge of these things but
> has never reached it. Still, it is undeniably desirable to contem-
> plate in the mind, as it were in a picture, the image of a greater

and better world: lest the mind, accustomed to the small details of daily life, become contracted and sink entirely into trivial thoughts. But meanwhile we must be watchful of truth and must keep within suitable limits, in order that we may distinguish the certain from the uncertain, day from night.

(Translation of Burnet in Coleridge, *Selected Poetry and Prose*, ed. Schneider, pp. 634–35)

Although a number of critics have taken the epigraph as an ironic foil to the progress of the poem, its waverings between belief and self-cautionary gestures are closer to the pattern of the main text than has been acknowledged. For here an assertion of belief dissolves into a discourse on the lack of information, while an assertion of the necessity of belief even from limited information dwindles into the necessity of accepting limitation. But the most interesting feature of the epigraph is not primarily what it says but what it refuses to say. For the main text of the "Rime" is written in imitation of medieval ballads; and while the persona of the Gloss is that of a seventeenth-century-editor who lays claim to sorting out the medieval tale, the author of the epigraph, his contemporary, merely provides us with a record of his lack of certainty. Thus, for the "Rime," a mini-epic of progress that moves largely by retrogradation, we have a Gloss of progress and an epigraph that sees the progress of knowledge only in terms of circling—or, perhaps, hanging on the line. Even Coleridge's revisions not only maintain but also intensify the contradictory interpretations that the main text keeps throwing up to us.

As Coleridge would (and did) say, "I would be understood." Although I have criticized (and perhaps even derided) the Gloss and Gloss-bound criticism, I do not mean to suggest simply that the position of the Gloss is wrong and that uncertainty (or no position) is right. That would be to plunge the poem back into the criticism that maintains that the poem doesn't mean anything because it is a "poem . . . of pure imagination." Coleridge vented his spleen against common schemes of the progress of knowledge—the "general conceit that states and governments might be and ought to be constructed as machines, every movement of which might be foreseen and taken into previous calculation" (*Lay Sermons*, p. 34) and against education infected by "the vile sophistications and mutilations of ignorant mountebanks" (*The Friend*, Essay XIV, 1:102). But he was equally virulent on the subject of indolence (especially his own) as an attempt to avoid commitment. Commitment—or belief—is inevitable for Coleridge, but it does not issue in certainty or as a guide to future action.

So what is "The Rime of the Ancient Mariner" then? Some have maintained that it is an attempt to befuddle the reader with a welter of strange evidence and contradictory interpretations, that it is an elaborate *tour de force* of mystification. This account of the poem casts Coleridge in the role of Milton's Satan, who continually changes shape to lure men to their doom. But it might be said that perhaps no other writer in English worries more concertedly than Coleridge about deluding his readers. One almost hears him saying, "My intentions are good,

how can I be misunderstood?" And this discomfort at the possibility of
being misunderstood perhaps accounts for the peculiar procedure of
stratifying his lay sermons for preselected audiences (*The Statesman's
Manual* was "addressed to the higher classes of society"; *A Lay Sermon*
was to "the higher and middle classes"; and a projected third lay sermon was to have been directed to "the lower and labouring classes of
society"). Even his critique (in *Biographia Literaria*, Chap. XVII) of the
theories of poetic diction that Wordsworth expounded in the two Prefaces to *Lyrical Ballads* (and in the Appendix of 1802) involves primarily
an argument against the confusions that might arise from importing a
"natural" language that would appear strikingly "unnatural" to the audience for poetry. Wordsworth did not really mean what he said about
imitating the language of the lower and rustic classes of society,
Coleridge insists, because a rustic's language, "purified from all provincialism and grossness, and so far reconstructed as to be made
consistent with the rules of grammar" is really a version of the philosophic and ideal language to which all poets and all readers of poetry
are accustomed. Coleridge, as he says repeatedly, would be understood.

Why is it, then, that Coleridge is so monumentally difficult to understand? Not only poems like the "Rime," "Kubla Khan," and
"Christabel," but also Coleridge's various prose works continually frus-
trate many readers who struggle to understand what, exactly, he is saying. And this is a particular problem because Coleridge is continually
presented to us as important primarily because of his distinctions—
between virtue and vice, symbol and allegory, imagination and fancy.
Barbauld-like critics of the "Rime" separate good from evil, and I. A.
Richards separates the good (the imagination) from the not-so-good
(the fancy). What is it that they know that we don't know?

It may be useful here to turn to the *Biographia Literaria* because it
provides the most explicit account of Coleridge's experience and views
of reading (and of the ways in which reading involves one's entire set
of beliefs about the world). Chapter XII is named "A Chapter of requests and premonitions concerning the perusal or omission of the
chapter that follows." And Coleridge begins it with the following remarks on his reading:

> [In reading philosophical works, I have made the following re-
> solve] "*until you understand a writer's ignorance, presume yourself
> ignorant of his understanding.*" This *golden rule* of mine does, I
> own, resemble those of Pythagoras in its obscurity rather than its
> depth . . . [But the reader] will find its meaning fully explained by
> the following instances. I have now before me a treatise of a reli-
> gious fanatic, full of dreams and supernatural *experiences*. I see
> clearly the writer's grounds, and their hollowness. I have a com-
> plete insight into the causes, which through the medium of his
> body has [sic] acted on his mind; and by application of received
> and ascertained laws I can satisfactorily explain to my own reason
> all the strange incidents, which the writer records of himself. And

this I can do without suspecting him of any intentional falsehood. . . . I UNDERSTAND HIS IGNORANCE.

On the other hand, I have been re-perusing with the best energies of my mind the Timaeus of PLATO. Whatever I comprehend, impresses me with a reverential sense of the author's genius; but there is a considerable portion of the work, to which I can attach no consistent meaning. . . . I have no insight into the possibility of a man so eminently wise using words with such half meanings to himself, as must perforce pass into no-meaning to his readers. . . . Therefore, utterly baffled in all my attempts to understand the ignorance of Plato, I CONCLUDE MYSELF IGNORANT OF HIS UNDERSTANDING. (Vol. I, pp. 160–61)

Although Coleridge later speaks of the "organic unity" of this chapter, that "golden rule" of his turns the problem of reading from the text (or the writer) to the reader. For Coleridge's "tolerance" for the ignorant writer—in refusing to suspect him of "any intentional falsehood"—exculpates that writer by turning the reader's own prejudices into a self-reinforcing standard of judgment. No knowledge or virtue or imagination on the part of the author, from this perspective, is susceptible of revealing itself to a reader who does not already believe that such qualities inhere in the work. And the curiosity of the piece is that explanation is fullest (even including physiological causation) when Coleridge describes himself reading a book that he had dismissed before he ever began to read. "Understanding ignorance" and being "ignorant of an author's understanding" are merely techniques through which a reader adjusts his demands to accord with his beliefs.

Such beliefs or prejudices are inevitable, unless, as Coleridge says, we discover "the art of destroying the memory *a parte post*, without injury to its future operations, and without detriment to the judgment" (*Ibid.*, p. 162). Now Coleridge described his project in *Lyrical Ballads* as that of writing on "supernatural" subjects "so as to transfer from our inward nature a human interest and a semblance of truth sufficient to . . . [produce] that willing suspension of disbelief for the moment, which constitutes poetic faith" (*Biographia Literaria*, Vol. II, p. 6). But, after all that we have been saying Coleridge said, how is such a "suspension of disbelief" possible? Disbelief is merely a subset of belief, a kind of belief that a thing is not (to paraphrase Gulliver). And the most famous chapter of the *Biographia Literaria*, Chapter XIII, "On the imagination, or esemplastic power," reveals this process as well as anything in Coleridge's work. Let us start from the end—the distinction between imagination and fancy—to which Coleridge has, he says, been building through the entire book. The secondary imagination idealizes and unifies in its processes of *vital* understanding. The fancy is merely a mechanical and associationist operation that can only rearrange fixities and definites. At some moments Coleridge uses these terms as classficatory (see *Shakespearean Criticism*, 1:203–20); and for I. A. Richards they seem to be universally applicable categories. Richards, for instance, quotes four lines of *Annus Mirabilis* and remarks, "To attempt to read this in the mode of Imagination would be to experiment in mania. . . ." And then he generalizes that in "prose fiction, the detective novel is a type of Fancy, but any presentation of an integral view of life will take the structure of Imagination" (pp. 94–95).

But various other elements of Coleridge's chapter would seem to cast doubt on projects like Richards' *Coleridge on Imagination* and *Practical Criticism* and their assumption that one man's "imagination" is the same as another's. For the letter that Coleridge inserts immediately before the famous distinction is (fictitiously) a letter from a friend "whose practical judgment [Coleridge had] had ample reason to estimate and revere" (*Biographia Literaria*, Vol. I, pp. 198–99). And although the friend admits that he may not fully understand Coleridge's chapter on imagination, he continually suggests that Coleridge is guilty of breach of promise—for instance, he cites the *Biographia Literaria*'s subtitle, "Biographical Sketches of My Literary Life and Opinions," to argue that it does not lead the reader to anticipate Coleridge's arcane speculations in the *Biographia Literaria*. But the rather major difficulty here is that Coleridge's chapter must do battle with the accumulated expectations of the friend's lifetime: "Your opinions and method of argument were not only so new to me, but so directly the reverse of all I had ever been accustomed to consider as truth . . ." (*Ibid.*, p. 199). Once again, we are left with a question about the nature of the text (in this case, a deleted or unwritten text): Is the "deficiency" in the text or in the reader?

It seems that a reader can only read the texts that say what he already knows. Thus, the editor of the Gloss reads a text that he knows, while the no-moral critics read a text that they know. And the difficulty is that for Coleridge what you know and what you read are part of a moral dilemma, because one can only act on the basis of what one knows (i. e., believes) and vice is merely the result of incomplete information. Coleridge says in *The Friend* (Essay XIV, p. 104) that "virtue would not be virtue, could it be *given* by one fellow-creature to another" (italics his). In other words, a man must be virtuous to understand the understanding of anyone else's knowledge—and thus to be virtuous.

And if this situation seems to present us with an impasse, it may perhaps explain why Coleridge so desperately wanted to write a summa or *Omniana*, a book of universal knowledge. He continually quotes from an incredibly diverse collection of texts, makes one statement only to confound it with the next, and he even plagiarizes. Many readers feel imposed upon by what they take to be Coleridge's efforts to delude them with airy nothings and falsehoods; and Norman Fruman is merely the latest in the line of critics who "expose" the "scandal" of Coleridge's plagiarisms. But both the plagiarism and the voracious reading perhaps point to related ends: If you are what you read, plagiarism (in a more or less obvious form) becomes inevitable; and if insufficient knowledge or reading is the cause of moral inadequacy, then nothing less than all knowledge—everything—will suffice. Coleridge, like Leibnitz, would "explain and collect the fragments of truth scattered through systems apparently the most incongruous" (*Biographia Literaria*, Vol. I, p. 169). But like so many of Coleridge's projects, the summa was never completed because incomplete information (as Coleridge recognized) was not the problem. The problem, rather, was that he could sort information from knowledge, delusion from truth, with no more certainty than anyone else who has lived long enough to have a memory and, thus, prejudice. Robert Penn Warren aptly summarizes him as saying, in the *Aids to Reflection*, that "original sin is not hereditary sin; it is original with the sinner and is of his will" (p. 227). And for Coleridge this original sin was interpretation from a limited perspective that had disproportionate consequences, for the peril was that any apparent extension or reversal might, always, be merely a disguised entrenchment of that particular limitation or prejudice. The Ancient Mariner's redemption or conversion, we are told, occurs when he blesses the sea-snakes. But if it seems like a conversion for a man who killed a rather appealing bird to see beauty in snakes, there is also room for a different interpretation. The bird is spoken of in Part V of the poem as something of a Christ figure, and we all know about the spiritual connotations of snakes. The Mariner's conversion, then, may be a redemption, or, merely a deluded capitulation to the devil. For Coleridge, as for the Ancient Mariner, the problem is that one cannot know better even about whether or not one is knowing better.

Works Cited

Abrams, M. H., ed. *The Norton Anthology of English Literature*. 6th ed. Vol. 2. New York: Norton, 1996.

Barbauld, Mrs. (Anna Laetitia). Foreword. *Hymns in Prose for Children*. By Barbauld. London: Murray, 1866.

Barbauld, Anna Laetitia. *The Works of Anna Laetitia Barbauld*. (Memoir by Lucy Aikin). Vol. 2. New York: Carvill, 1826.

Coleridge, S. T. (Samuel Taylor). *Aids to Reflection*. Ed. Thomas Fenby. New York: Dutton, 1905.

———. *Biographia Literaria*. Ed. J. Shawcross. 2 Vols. Oxford: Clarendon, 1907.

———. *The Friend*. Ed. Barbara E. Rooke. 2 Vols. Bollingen Ser. 75: *The Collected Works of Samuel Taylor Coleridge*. 4. Princeton: Princeton UP, 1969.

———. *Lay Sermons*. Ed. R. J. White. Bollingen Ser. 75: *The Collected Works of Samuel Taylor Coleridge*. 6. Princeton: Princeton UP, 1972.

———. *Selected Poetry and Prose*. Ed. Elisabeth Schneider. San Francisco: Rinehart, 1971.

———. *Shakespearean Criticism*. Ed. Thomas Middleton Raysor. 2 Vols. London: Dent, 1960.

———. *Table Talk*. Ed. Carl Woodring. 2 Vols. Bollingen Ser. 75: *The Collected Works of Samuel Taylor Coleridge*. Princeton: Princeton UP, 1990.

Jackson, J. R. de J., ed., *Coleridge: The Critical Heritage*. Critical Heritage Ser. London: Routledge, 1970.

Lowes, John Livingston. *The Road to Xanadu: A Study in the Ways of the Imagination*. 1927. Boston: Houghton, 1955.

McElderry, B. R., Jr. "Coleridge's Revision of 'The Ancient Mariner.'" *Studies in Philology*, 29 (1932): 69–94.

Patterson, Sylvia W. *Rousseau's Emile and Early Children's Literature*. Metuchen: Scarecrow, 1971.

Richards, I. A. *Coleridge on Imagination*. 1934. 3rd Ed. London: Routledge, 1962.

Warren, Robert Penn. *Selected Essays*. New York: Random, 1958.

Wordsworth, William, and Samuel Taylor Coleridge. *Lyrical Ballads*. Ed. R. L. Brett and A. R. Jones. Cambridge: Cambridge UP, 1963.

KAREN SWANN

From "Christabel": The Wandering Mother and the Enigma of Form†

The first questions Christabel asks Geraldine refer to identity and origins: "who art thou?" and "how camest thou here?" Geraldine's response is oblique; in effect she replies, "I am like you, and my story is like your own":

> My sire is of a noble line,
> And my name is Geraldine:
> Five warriors seized me yestermorn,
> Me, even me, a maid forlorn: . . .
>
> They spurred amain, their steeds were white:
> And once we crossed the shade of night.
> As sure as Heaven shall rescue me,
> I have no thought what men they be;
> Nor do I know how long it is
> (For I have lain entranced I wis)
> Since one, the tallest of the five,
> Took me from the palfrey's back,
> A weary woman, scarce alive. . . .
>
> Whither they went I cannot tell—
> I thought I heard, some minutes past,
> Sounds as of a castle bell.
> Stretch forth thy hand (thus ended she),
> And help a wretched maid to flee.
>
> (ll. 79–104)[1]

Geraldine's tale echoes and anticipates Christabel's. Christabel is also first introduced as the daughter of a "noble" father; she, too, experiences things she "cannot tell," calls on Heaven to rescue her, crosses threshholds and falls into trances. But in contrast to the story "Christabel," often criticized for its ambiguities, Geraldine's tale presents sexual and moral categories as unambiguous and distinct: villainous male force appropriates and silences an innocent female victim. This difference effects a corresponding clarification of genre. Geraldine translates "Christabel" into the familiar terms of the tale of terror.

Geraldine's translation would appear to establish the identity of the woman. Ultimately, however, her story complicates the issue of feminine identity by suggesting its entanglement, at the origin, with genre. How one takes Geraldine depends on one's sense of the "line" of representations she comes from. For Christabel, but also, for any ab-

---

† *Studies in Romanticism* 23 (1984): 533–47. Reprinted by courtesy of the Trustees of Boston University. [All footnotes are the author's.]
1. Quotations from "Christabel" and its preface are taken from *Coleridge's Poetical Works*, ed. Ernest Hartley Coleridge (1912; rpt. Oxford: Oxford U. Press, 1969).

sorbed reader of circulating library romances, Geraldine's story of abduction works as a seduction—Christabel recognizes Geraldine as a
certain type of heroine and embraces her.[2] More guarded readers appropriate Geraldine as confidently as Christabel does, but they see her
quite differently. Charles Tomlinson, for example, reads "Christabel"
as "a tale of terror," but in contrast to Geraldine's own story casts her
in the role of villain, while for Patricia Adair, Geraldine is betrayed by
her very conventionality: she tells her story in "rather unconvincing
and second-rate verse which was, no doubt, deliberately meant to
sound false."[3] Geraldine is "false" because she comes from an ignoble
line of Gothic temptresses, or, in the case of other critics, because she
can be traced back to the ignoble Duessa and to a host of other preda-
tory figures. Tellingly these sophisticated readers, who employ literary
history to read Geraldine as a figure of untruth, are the worst ruffi-
ans—they either refuse to hear the woman's story of her own abduction, or assume that her protests are really a come-on.

  Geraldine may be Christabel's ghost or projection as many critics
have suggested, but only if we acknowledge that Christabel produces
herself as a received representation—a feminine character who in turn
raises the ghosts of different subtexts, each dictating a reading of her
as victim or seductress, good or evil, genuine or affected. I will be arguing in this essay that "Christabel" both dramatizes and provokes
hysteria. The poem explores the possessing force of certain bodies—
Geraldine's, of course, but also bodies of literary convention, which I
am calling "genres." Particularly in Coleridge's day, debates on literary
decorum allowed the gendering of structure in a way that seemed to
assuage anxiety about the subject's relation to cultural forms. Questions involving the subject's autonomy could be framed as an opposition between authentic, contained "manly" speech and "feminine"
bodies—the utterly conventional yet licentiously imaginative female
characters, readers, and genres of the circulating libraries. In
"Christabel," Coleridge both capitalizes on and exposes culture's tactical gendering of formal questions. The poem invites us to link the displacing movement of cultural forms through subjects to the
"feminine" malady of hysteria and the "feminine" genres of the circulating library; at the same time, it mockingly and dreamily informs us
that hysteria is the condition of all subjects in discourse, and that the
attribution of this condition to feminine bodies is a conventional, hysterical response.

I

If Coleridge were thinking of dramatizing hysteria in a poem, he might
have turned to Burton's account of "Maids', Nuns', and Widows'

---

2. See Susan Luther, " 'Christabel' as Dream Reverie," *Romantic Reassessments* 61, ed. Dr.
   James Hogg (Salzburg: Institut für englische Sprache und Literatur, Univ. Salzburg A5020,
   1976), for the argument that Christabel is a reader of romances.
3. " 'Christabel' " (1955), rpt. in *The Ancient Mariner and Other Poems: A Casebook*, eds. Alun
   R. Jones and William Tydemann (London and Basingstoke: Macmillan, 1973), p. 235; *The
   Waking Dream: A Study of Coleridge's Poetry* (London: Edward Arnold, 1967), p. 146.

Melancholy" in *The Anatomy of Melancholy*, a book he knew well. According to Burton, hysterics "think themselves bewitched":

> Some think they see visions, confer with spirits and devils, they shall surely be damned, are afraid of some treachery, imminent danger, and the like, they will not speak, make answer to any question, but are almost distracted, mad, or stupid for the time, and by fits. . . .[4]

The malady befalls barren or celibate women; among these, Catholic noblewomen who are forced to remain idle are particularly susceptible. Most of the symptoms Burton catalogues are touched on in the passage quoted above. Hysterics have visions and are afraid "by fits"— the "fits of the mother" or womb ("the heart itself beats, is sore grieved, and faints . . . like fits of the mother" [p. 415]). The symptom which most interests Burton, though, is the inability of hysterics to communicate their troubles: they "cannot tell" what ails them. This fact becomes a refrain of his own exposition: "and yet will not, cannot again tell how, where, or what offends them"; "many of them cannot tell how to express themselves in words, or how it holds them, what ails them; you cannot understand them, or well tell what to make of their sayings" (p. 416).

They "cannot tell," and *you* cannot "well tell" what to make of them: the phenomenon of their blocked or incomprehensible speech seems to produce similar effects in the writer. And indeed, Burton's impetous and fitful prose in many respects resembles the discourse of the hysteric, into whose point of view he regularly tumbles ("Some *think* they see visions," but "they *shall* surely be damned" [my italics]). Far from resisting this identification, Burton makes narrative capital from the slippage, as here, when he allows himself to become "carried away" by sympathy for the Christabel-like afflicted:

> I do not so much pity them that may otherwise be cased, but those alone that out of a strong temperament, innate constitution, are violently carried away with this torrent of inward humours, and though very modest of themselves, sober, religious, virtuous, and well given (as many so distressed maids are), yet cannot make resistance . . .

and then, as if shaking off a "fit," comically pauses to reflect on his own indecorous "torrents":

> But where am I? Into what subject have I rushed? What have I to do with nuns, maids, virgins, widows? I am a bachelor myself, and lead a monastic life in a college: *nae ego sane ineptus qui haec dixerim* [what I said was truly improper], I confess 'tis an indecorum, and as Pallas, a virgin, blushed when Jupiter by chance spake of love matters in her presence, and turned away her face, *me reprimam* [I shall restrain myself]; though my subject necessarily require it, I will say no more. (p. 417)

4. *The Anatomy of Melancholy*, ed. Holbrook Jackson (New York: Random House-Vintage Books, 1977), p. 416. Future references to this edition appear in the text.

Protesting all the while his ignorance of women, the "old bachelor" coyly figures himself as a virgin whose body betrays her when desire takes her unawares. He also takes the part of the apparently more knowing and self-controlled Jupiter, but only to suggest that the latter's fatherly indifference is an act. For whether he is an artful or artless seducer, Jupiter himself appears only to rush into speech "by chance"—the "chance," we suspect, of finding himself in such close proximity to his virginal daughter. The woman whose desire is written on her body is like the man who makes love the "matter" of his discourse: both attempt to disguise desire, and become the more seductive when desire is revealed in the context of their attempts to suppress it.

The story of Pallas and Jupiter is placed at a strategic point in Burton's chapter. It punctuates his resolve to check the torrents of his narrative, a resolve immediately and engagingly broken when, more "by chance" than design, he finds he has to say something more ("And yet I must and will say something more"). This time he is prompted by his commiseration with all distressed women to launch an attack on "them that are in fault,"

> . . . those tyrannizing pseudo-politicians, superstitious orders, rash vows, hard-hearted parents, guardians, unnatural friends, allies (call them how you will), those careless and stupid overseers . . .

those fathers and parental substitutes (particularly the Church), who "suppress the vigour of youth" and ensure the orderly descent of their estates through the enforced celibacy of their daughters (p. 418). An "old bachelor" who leads a monastic life in a college; whose own discourse, like the discourse of the hysteric, seems to be the product of a strained compromise between lawless impulses and the claims of order; who might himself be said to be possessed by spirits and the dead language in which they wrote, ends his discussion of "maids', nuns', and widows' melancholy" by championing those who "cannot tell" against the ungenerous legislators of the world.

There are suggestive correspondences between Burton's chapter on hysteria and "Christabel." Christabel is a virtuous Catholic gentlewoman whose lover is away, possibly at the behest of her father, out of whose castle she "steals" at the beginning of the poem. Whether or not he is responsible for blighting love affairs,[5] Sir Leoline has affinities with both of Burton's father-figures: like the "pseudopoliticians" he is intimately linked with repressive law; like Jupiter, his relation to his daughter is somewhat suspect. Moreover, the poem's descriptions of Christabel's experiences—first with the possibly supernatural Geraldine and later, with a traumatic memory or scene which comes over her by fits and bars her from telling—and its insistent references to a "mother" who at one point threatens to block Geraldine's speech ("Off, wandering mother!" [l. 205]), follow Burton's account of the

---

5. In "Sir Cauline," the ballad from which Coleridge took the name Christabel, this is the case; that Christabel's lover is dismissed by her father.

characteristic symptoms of hysteria. But Coleridge may have appreciated most the comic slippages in Burton's narrative between the
slightly hysterical scholar whose business it is to "tell" and the women
who are the matter of his discourse. When he came to write "Christabel," Coleridge told the story through narrators who are as enigmatic
as the women they tell about—we cannot "well tell" if they are one
voice or two. More than any detail of the plot, the participation of
these narrators in the "feminine" exchanges they describe, and the
poem's playful suggestion that hysteria cannot be restricted to *feminine* bodies, marks the kinship of "Christabel" and Burton's text.

II

Who is Geraldine and where does she come from? Possibly, from
Christabel. In the opening of the poem Christabel has gone into the
woods to pray for her absent lover after having had uneasy dreams "all
yesternight"—"Dreams, that made her moan and leap, / As on her bed
she lay in sleep," we are told in the 1816 version of the poem. In the
woods *two* ladies perform the actions of moaning and leaping which,
yesternight, *one* lady had performed alone:

> The lady leaps up suddenly,
> The lovely lady, Christabel!
> It moaned as near, as near can be,
> But what it is she cannot tell—
> On the other side it seems to be,
> Of the huge, broad-breasted, old oak tree.
>   (1816: ll. 37–42)

For a moment we, too, are in the woods, particularly if, like the poem's
"first" readers, we already know something of the plot. Does "the lady"
refer to Christabel or Geraldine? Is her leaping up the cause or effect
of fright? The next lines supply answers to these questions, and as the
scene proceeds "it" resolves into the distinct, articulate character
Geraldine. For a moment's space, however, we entertain the notion
that an uneasy lady leaped up suddenly and terrified herself.

Burton says of hysterics, "some think they see visions, confer with
spirits and devils, they shall surely be damned." Geraldine is such a
"vision." She appears in response to what Burton implies and psycho-
analysis declares are the wishes of hysterics—to get around patriarchal
law, which legislates desire. In the beginning of the poem Christabel
"cannot tell" what ails her, but critics have theorized from her sighs
that she is suffering from romance, from frustrated love for the "lover
that's far away," for the Baron, or even, for the mother.[6] Geraldine,
who appears as if in answer to Christabel's prayer, "steals" with her

---

6. See for example Roy Basler, *Sex, Symbolism, and Psychology in Literature* (New Brunswick:
Rutgers U. Press, 1948), p. 41; Gerald Enscoe, *Eros and the Romantics* (The Hague and
Paris: Mouton, 1967), pp. 44–45; Jonas Spatz. "The Mystery of Eros: Sexual Initiation in
Coleridge's 'Christabel,' " *PMLA* 90 (1975), 112–13; Barbara A. Schapiro, *The Romantic
Mother: Narcissistic Patterns in Romantic Poetry* (Baltimore and London: Johns Hopkins U.
Press, 1983), 61–85.

back into the castle, sleeps with her "as a mother with her child," and then meets the Baron's embrace, allows the performance of these wishes. Moreover, like an hysterical symptom, which figures both desire and its repression, Geraldine also fulfills the last clause of Burton's formula: although much is ambiguous *before* she appears, it is not until she appears that Christabel feels "damned," and that we are invited to moralize ambiguity as duplicity, the cause of "sorrow and shame" (ll. 270, 296, 674).

As well as answering *Christabel's* desires, however, Geraldine answers the indeterminacy of the narrative and the reader's expectancy. The wood outside the Baron's castle is not the "natural" world, as is often declared,[7] but a world stocked with cultural artifacts. Before Geraldine ever appears it is haunted by the ghosts of old stories: familiar settings and props function as portents, both for the superstitious and the well-read. The wood and the midnight hour are the "moment's space" where innocence is traditionally put to the test, or when spirits walk abroad; other details—the cock's crow at midnight, the mastiff's unrest, the contracted moon—we know to be art's way of signifying nature's response to human disorder. These so-called "Gothic trappings" ensnare us because they mean nothing ("Tu-whit, tu-whoo") and too much: like the sighs we seize on as evidence of Christabel's inner life, they gesture to an enigma, something as yet hidden from view. Geraldine makes "answer meet" to these suspensions of the narrative, not by providing closure, but by representing indeterminacy:

> There she sees a damsel bright,
> Drest in a silken robe of white,
> That shadowy in the moonlight shone:
> The neck that made that white robe wan,
> Her stately neck, and arms were bare;
> Her blue-veined feet unsandal'd were,
> And wildly glittered here and there
> The gems entangled in her hair.
>
> (ll. 58–65)

Precipitating out of the Gothic atmosphere, Geraldine promises to contain in herself an entrapping play of surfaces and shadows; with her appearance suspense resolves into a familiar sign of ambiguity.

Geraldine is a fantasy, produced by the psychic operations of condensation and displacement. On the one hand, her function is to objectify: she intervenes in moments of interpretive crisis as a legible representation—a "vision," a story, and a plot. At the same time, though, she, the story she tells, and the plot she seems to set in motion are all displacing performances of ambiguities she might at first promise to "answer" more decisively. After she pops up, two women dramatize the implied doubleness of the daughter who "stole" along

---

7. See for example Enscoe, p. 43; John Beer, *Coleridge's Poetic Intelligence* (London and Basingstoke: Macmillan, 1977), p. 187; and H. W. Piper, "The Disunity of *Christabel* and the Fall of Nature," *Essays in Criticism* 28 (1978), 216–27.

the forest keeping her thoughts to herself (l. 31). Very little else changes. Prompted by an uneasy dream one woman "stole" out of her father's castle; two women return to it "as if in stealth" (l. 120), and by the end of Part I Christabel has simply resumed "fearfully dreaming," at least according to the narrator (l. 294). The spell that becomes "lord of her utterance" (l. 268) that night does no more than render explicit the inhibition of her "telling" already operative in the opening scene of the poem, where her silence was obscurely connected to the brooding, dreaming "lord" of the castle, the father who loved the daughter "so well." By the end of the poem we have simply returned to where we began: Christabel is "inly praying" once again, this time at the "old" Baron's feet, and once again Geraldine is on "the other side" (l. 614).

While it proposes an answer to the question "who art thou?" this reading only makes Christabel's second question to Geraldine more problematic: Geraldine is a fantasy, but she does not seem to "come from" any locatable place. The many source studies of the poem have shown that her origins are as much in literature as in Christabel: she first appears to the latter as a highly aestheticized object, and first speaks, many readers think to her discredit, in a highly encoded discourse. A material, communally available representation, she could have been dreamed up by any of the characters to whom she appears in the course of the poem—by the uneasy dreamer Christabel, but also by the Baron, into whose castle she steals while he is asleep, and, Christabel suggests, dreaming uneasily (l. 165), or by Bracy, whose dream of her seems to "live upon [his] eye" the next day (l. 559). She could even be part of *our* dream. For in "Christabel" as in all of his poems of the supernatural, Coleridge plots to turn us into dreamers—to "procure" our "willing suspension of disbelief," our happy relinquishment of the reality principle. In "Christabel" as in dreams there is no version of the negative: questions raise possibilities that are neither confirmed nor wholly dismissed ("Is it the wind . . . ? / There is not wind enough . . ." [ll. 44–45]). Tags drift from one "lady" to another, suggesting the affinity of apparent adversaries; signs are familiar yet unreadable, laden with associations which neither exclude each other nor resolve into univocality.

Geraldine intervenes into these several dreamlike states as a figure of the imaginary itself—a figure whose legibility derives from its status within the symbolic order. She obeys the laws which structure all psychic phenomena, including dreams, jokes, and hysteria, the malady which allowed Freud to "discover" these very laws. The latter, however, do not explain why *particular* representations become collectively privileged. Why, at moments when they brush with the (il-)logic of the unconscious, do subjects automatically, even hysterically, produce certain *gendered* sights and stories?—produce the image of a radically divided woman, or of two women in each other's arms; and produce the story of a woman who seduces, and/or is seduced, abducted, and silenced by a father, a seducer, and/or a ruffian? This story, including all the ambiguities that make it hard to "tell," is of course the story of hysteria as told by Burton, and later, painstakingly reconstructed by Freud from its plural, displacing performances on the bodies of women. Even the common reader would know it, however, for it describes all the permutations of the romance plot—a form largely, but not exclusively, associated with a body of popular, "feminine" literature.

If a body like Geraldine's pops up from behind a tree when all the witnesses are in the woods, it is no accident: everyone thinks feminine forms appropriately represent the dangers and attractions of fantasy life. Coleridge, who dramatized the highly overdetermined romance/hysteria plot in "Christabel" and happily flaunted feminine bodies when it suited him, was no exception. But I want to argue, first by looking at his generic play, and then by examining his treatment of the family romance, that in "Christabel" he was also mockingly obtruding a conspiracy to view, allowing us to see "feminine" genre and gender alike as cultural fantasy.

III

"Christabel's" narrators are themselves hysterics. The poem's interlocutor and respondent mime the entanglement of Geraldine and Christabel—I call them "they," but it is not clear if we hear two voices or one. Like the women they describe, they are overmastered by "visions." Repeatedly, they abandon an authoritative point of view to fall into the story's present; or they engage in transferential exchanges with the characters whose plot they are narrating. In the opening scene, for example, one of them plunges into the tale to plead to and for Christabel: "Hush, beating heart of Christabel! / Jesu, Maria, shield her well!" As if she hears, a stanza later Christabel cries out, "Mary mother, save me now!" (ll. 53–54, 69). Further on, the sequence is reversed when the speaker seems to take up Christabel's speech. She has just assured Geraldine that Sir Leoline will "guide and guard [her] safe and free" (l. 110); although the narrators generally are not as trusting as Christabel, one seems inspired by her confidence to echo her, twice: "So free from danger, free from fear / They crossed the court: right glad they were" (ll. 135–36, 143–44).

These narrators create the conditions and logic of dream: like them, and because of them, the reader is impotent to decide the poem's ambiguities from a position outside its fictions. Furthermore, the poem's "fictions" seem to be about little else than these formal slippages. The repressed of "Christabel's" dreamwork is almost too visible to be seen—not a particular psychic content but literary conventions themselves, like those which demand that narrators speak from privileged points of view, and important for this argument, bodies of conventions or "genres." "Christabel" obtrudes genre to our notice. The Gothic atmosphere of the first stanza, with its enumerations of ominously coincident bird and clock noises, goes slightly bad in the second—partly because of the very presence of the shocking "mastiff bitch," but also because both mastiff and narrator become heady with coincidence:

making answer to the clock, "Four for the quarters, and twelve for the hour . . . Sixteen short howls, not over loud," she becomes an obvious piece of Gothic machinery (ll. 10–13). A similar generic disturbance occurs between Part 1, told more or less in the "tale of terror" convention, and its conclusion, which recapitulates the story in a new convention, that of sentimental fiction. Suddenly Christabel "means" "a bourgeois lady of delicate, even saccharine, sensibility": "Her face, oh call it fair not pale, / And both blue eyes more bright than clear, / Each about to have a tear" (ll. 289–91). As suddenly, the narrators are exposed in a desperate act of wielding genre, using convention to force legibility on a sight that won't be explained.

Once we become aware of these instabilities, no stretch of the poem is exempt. In life women might faint, dogs might moan, and fires might flare up without anyone remarking it; if these coincide in story, they mean something. When they coincide in the overloaded, tonally unsettling Part 1 of "Christabel" they simultaneously draw attention to themselves as elements of a code. Although we may think of genres as vessels which successive authors infuse with original content, "Christabel's" "originality" is to expose them as the means by which significance is produced and contained.

This analysis raises the issue of the generic status of "Christabel." What is its literary genre? But also, what genre of psychic phenomenon does the poem aspire to—is it like a dream, as we first proposed, or like a joke? The latter question may not immediately seem important, since jokes and dreams have so much in common: like hysteria, they work by condensation and displacement to bring the repressed to light.[8] But for the poem's first readers, at least, it clearly mattered which was which. The reviewers of 1816 fiercely protested the poem's "licentious" mixing of joke and dream, categories of psychic phenomena which they translated into literary categories: was "Christabel" a bit of "doggrel," a wild, weird tale of terror, or a fantastic combination of the two? (Modern readers, less tuned to genre play, have decided the question by not hearing the jokes.)[9] Coleridge's contemporaries recognized that jokes and dreams demand different attitudes: if one responds to "Christabel" as though it were just a wild weird tale, and it turns out to be a joke, then the joke is on oneself. "Christabel" frightened its reviewers, not because it was such a successful tale of terror, but because they couldn't decide what sort of tale it was.

"Christabel" made its first readers hysterical because it is not one genre or another but a joke on our desire to decide genre. As such, it turned a "merely" formal question into a matter of one upsmanship.

---

8. Or so Freud claims in *Jokes and their Relation to the Unconscious*, chapter VI ("Jokes, Dreams, and the Unconscious"), trans. James Strachey (New York: Norton, 1963), pp. 159–80.

9. For examples of the reviews, see *The Romantic Reviewed*, ed. Donald H. Reiman (New York and London: Garland, 1977), II, 666, 239. Modern critics sometimes notice tonal or generic instability as "falls" into Gothic trickery, into caricature of the Gothic, or into sentimentality; see for example Max Schulz, *The Poetic Voices of Coleridge* (Detroit: Wayne State U. Press, 1963), pp. 66–71; and Paul Edwards and MacDonald Emslie, " 'Thoughts all so unlike each other': The Paradoxical in *Christabel*," *English Studies* 52 (1971), 328. The latter suggest these discrepancies are intended to shock.

Most of the critics responded by redirecting the joke, giving the impression that it was on the poem and the author. Coleridge, they claimed, mixed the genres of joke and dream, not as a joke, but in a dream. What is telling is their almost universal decision to recast these issues of literary and formal mastery into the more obviously charged and manageable terms of sexual difference. According to them, the poem was, after all, just one of those tales of terror which ladies like to read ("For what woman of fashion would not purchase a book recommended by Lord Byron?" asks the AntiJacobin[1]); the author, variously described as an "enchanted virgin," an "old nurse," a "dreamer"—by implication, a hysteric—simply could not control the discourses that spoke through him like so many "lords" of his utterance.[2]

Gendering the formal question, the reviewers reenact the scene of Geraldine's first appearance: then, too, a variety of characters responded to indeterminacy by producing a feminine body at once utterly conventional and too full of significance. In critical discourse as in fantasy life, it seems, feminine forms—the derogated genres of the circulating library, the feminized body of the author, or the body of Geraldine—represent the enigma of form itself. Female bodies "naturally" seem to figure an ungraspable truth: that form, habitually viewed as the arbitrary, contingent vessel of more enduring meanings, is yet the source and determinant of all meanings, whether the subject's or the world's.

Displacing what is problematic about form onto the feminine gender ultimately serves the hypothetical authenticity and integrity of masculine gender and "manly" language. Look, for example, at the opening lines of the passage Hazlitt selects as the only "genuine burst of humanity" "worthy of the author" in the whole poem—the only place where "no dream oppresses him, no spell binds him"[3]:

> Alas! they had been friends in youth;
> But whispering tongues can poison truth;
> And constancy lives in realms above;
> And life is thorny; and youth is vain;
> And to be wroth with one we love
> Doth work like madness in the brain.
> And thus it chanced, as I divine,
> With Roland and Sir Leoline.
>
> (ll. 408–15)

Hazlitt was not alone in his approbation: many reviewers of the poem quoted this passage with approval, and Coleridge himself called them "the best & sweetest Lines [he] ever wrote."[4] They are indeed out-

1. Romantics Reviewed I, 23.
2. Romantics Reviewed I, 373; II, 866; II, 531. I discuss these reviews more fully in my essay "Literary Gentlemen and Lovely Ladies: The Debate on the Character of 'Christabel,'" forthcoming in ELH.
3. Romantics Reviewed II, 531.
4. Collected Letters of Samuel Taylor Coleridge, ed. Earl Leslie Griggs (Oxford: Clarendon Press, 1956–71), III, 435.

standing—the only moment, in this tale about mysterious exchanges among women, when an already-past, already-interpreted, fully-breached male friendship is encountered. For those of us who don't equate "manliness" with universality and authenticity, this unremarked confluence of masculine subject-matter and "genuine" discourse is of course suspicious: it's not *simply* purity of style that made this passage the standard against which all other Christabellian discourse could be measured and found "licentious," "indecorous," "affected"—in short, effeminate.

But here, we are anticipated by the passage itself, which exposes "manliness" as a gendered convention. When the narrator begins this impassioned flight, we assume he speaks from privileged knowledge: why else such drama? Several lines later, though, he betrays that this is all something he has "divined," something that may have chanced. "Chancing" on a situation that really spoke to him—a ruined manly friendship—the narrator has constructed a "divination" based on what he knows—about constancy (it isn't to be found on earth), life (it's thorny), and youth (it's vain). Although he is more caught up in his speech than she, his voice is as "hollow" as Geraldine's. His flight or "genuine burst of humanity" is a fit of the mother, and a mocking treatment of manly discourse on the part of Coleridge, whose later accession to the going opinion was either a private joke or a guilty, revisionary reading of his licentious youth. If this tonal instability was lost on "Christabel's" reviewers, it can only be because, like the narrator himself, they were reading hysterically: a "vision" of autonomous male identities caused them automatically to produce a set of received ideas about manly discourse.

"Christabel" exposes the conventionality of manly authenticity and the giddiness of manly decorum; in the same move, it suggests that attributing hysteria to feminine forms is a hysterical response to a more general condition. In the poem as elsewhere, "the feminine" is the locus of erotic and generic license: this can have the exciting charge of perversity or madness, or can seem absolutely conventional, affected. "Christabel" contrives to have these alternatives redound on the reader, who continually feels mad or just stupid, unable to "tell" how to characterize the verse at any given point. Here is Christabel "imprisoned" in the arms of Geraldine:

> With open eyes (ah woe is me!)
> Asleep, and dreaming fearfully,
> Fearfully dreaming, yet, I wis,
> Dreaming that alone, which is—
> O sorrow and shame! Can this be she,
> The lady, who knelt at the old oak tree?
> And lo! the worker of these harms,
> That holds the maiden in her arms,
> Seems to slumber still and mild,
> As a mother with her child.
>   (ll. 292–301)

Geraldine's arms, the scene of the close embrace, and the conclusion as a whole, which recasts part I as a sentimental narrative—all in some sense work to imprison the significances of the text. Yet the scenario only imperfectly traps, and closes not at all, the questions which circulated through part I. Identity is still a matter of debate, and still hangs on a suggestively ambiguous "she" ("Can this be she?"). Even the women's gender identities and roles are undecidable, their single embrace "read" by multiple, superimposed relationships. Geraldine, a "lady" like Christabel, is also sleeping with Christabel; a "worker of harms," a ruffian-like assaultor of unspecified gender, she is also like a "mild," protective mother. If in keeping with the sentimentality of this section of the poem, the mother/child analogy is introduced to clean up the post-coital embrace of the women, it redounds to suggest the eroticism of maternal attention. These ghostly stories, all already raised in the text of Part I, work to create the compellingly charged erotic ambivalence of "Christabel"—ambivalence about becoming absorbed into a body which may be "the same" as one's own, or may belong to an adversary, a "worker of harms," and which is associated with, or represented by, the maternal body.

Christabel's situation, including, perhaps her feminine situation, is contagious. The narrator, who seems overmastered by the very spell he is describing, can only direct us to a "sight" ("And lo!"), the significance of which he "cannot tell." His speech breaks down before the woman who is "dreaming fearfully, / Fearfully dreaming," before the form that may conceal "that alone, which is."

The narrator circles round but cannot tell the enigma of form, of the body or sign that is at once meaningless and too full of significance. His own discourse repeats the paradox of the "sight," and becomes a locus of the reader's interpretive breakdown. His lament strikes us as coming from "genuine" distress at the remembrance of Christabel's horrible predicament. But particularly in context, the lines—

> With open eyes (ah woe is me!)
> Asleep and dreaming fearfully,
> Fearfully dreaming, yet, I wis,
> Dreaming that alone which is—

raise the ghost of a sentimental style that as a matter of course suppresses all distressing sights and implications, while coyly directing the reader to what's not being said. To decide the narrator's credibility—is he bewildered or merely "affected," effeminate; could he even be camping it up?—it is necessary to bring genre to bear, to decide whether Gothic or sentimental romance is a determining convention. This is simultaneously to recognize that the voice we have been hearing cannot be authentic—if mad, it speaks in the tale of terror's legislated mad discourse; that genres are constructs which produce meaning for the subject; and that genres, like fantasy, reproduce the indeterminacies they at first appear to limit or control. Our relation to

Christabel's narrators is like theirs to Christabel: the enigmatic form
of their discourse turns us into hysterical readers, subject to the possessing, conventional bodies that that discourse raises in us.

                              *   *   *

NICHOLAS ROE

From Wordsworth and Coleridge: The Radical Years†

Twelve years after the fall of the Bastille, William Godwin recollected
the response to that event in Britain. "Where was the ingenuous heart
which did not beat with exultation", he enquired, "at seeing a great
and cultivated people shake off the chains of one of the most oppressive political systems in the world, the most replenished with abuses,
the least mollified and relieved by any infusion of liberty? Thus far we
were all of us disinterested and generous."[1] Coleridge disagreed. In
the margin of his own copy of Godwin's pamphlet *Thoughts Occasioned by the Perusal of Dr Parr's Spital Sermon*, Coleridge wrote beside this passage:

> Had this been the fact, which the whole History of the French
> Revolution in its first workings disproves *a posteriori*, it would
> have been *a priori* impossible that such a revolution could have
> taken place. No! it was the discord & contradictory ferment of old
> abuses & recent indulgences or connivances—the heat & light of
> Freedom let in on a half-cleared, rank soil, made twilight by the
> black fierce Reek, which this Dawn did itself draw up.—Still,
> however, taking the sentence dramatically, i.e. as the then notion
> of good men in general, it is well—and just.[2]

While conceding that Godwin's immaculate revolution was true to
"the then notion of good men in general" in 1789, Coleridge emphasized that with hindsight it was not "the fact". When seen "a posteriori" it appeared flawed from the outset, an abortive and "contradictory
ferment" that had deceived a generation of liberals and radicals
throughout Europe and America. However, Coleridge's early poem
"The Destruction of the Bastille" reveals that he too had shared Godwin's "disinterested" exultation,

> I see, I see! glad Liberty succeed
> With every patriot virtue in her train!
>   (ll. 23–4)

---

† *Wordsworth and Coleridge: The Radical Years* (Oxford: Clarendon Press, 1988), 1–14.
Reprinted by permission of the publisher. [All footnotes are the author's.]
1. William Godwin, *Thoughts Occasioned by the Perusal of Dr. Parr's Spital Sermon* (London,
1801), pp. 2–3, reproduced in William Godwin, *Uncollected Writings, 1785–1822*
(Gainesville, Florida, 1968) (cited hereafter as Godwin, *Thoughts*, and Godwin, *Uncollected
Writings*).
2. Coleridge's manuscript marginalia appear in Godwin, *Uncollected Writings*, pp. 285–7.

—and although they appear to differ in their later ideas of revolution, Godwin's pamphlet and Coleridge's note had a common purpose. Each was concerned to justify his former support for the French Revolution in the aftermath of its failure.

Godwin's immediate motive had been to rebuff recent criticism of *Political Justice* by invoking the generous spirit with which it had originally been written: "My book, as was announced by me in the preface, was the child of the French revolution," he claimed.[3] William Hazlitt remembered that when *Political Justice* first appeared in February 1793 it was treated as "the oracles of thought", its author "talked of . . . looked up to . . . sought after" (Howe, xi. 16). Eight years later the popularity of Godwin's book had diminished, and he was at pains to explain why. "If the temper and tone in which this publication has been treated have undergone a change," Godwin wrote in his pamphlet, 'it has been only that I was destined to suffer a part, in the great revolution which has operated in nations, parties, political creeds, and the views and interests of ambitious men. I have fallen (if I have fallen) in one common grave with the cause and love of liberty. . .".[4] Godwin's "great revolution" in public opinion was conditioned by the demise of revolutionary idealism and subsequent imperial expansion of France, and by repressive hostility to political and social reform in Britain during the 1790s and throughout the Napoleonic wars. In *The Prelude* Wordsworth dates his own experience of betrayal precisely to February 1793, and the outbreak of war between France and Britain:

> Not in my single self alone I found,
> But in the minds of all ingenuous youth,
> Change and subversion from this hour.
>
> (x. 231–3)

That drawn-out and disenchanting process of "change and subversion" is Wordsworth's subject in *The Prelude*, Books Ten and Eleven, where it appears as the immediate context for his emergence as poet and friend of Coleridge. For Coleridge, on the other hand, the "hour" of final disappointment did not come until February 1798 when France attacked Switzerland and threatened to invade Britain. That moment of disillusion is recorded in two poems, "France, an Ode" and "Fears in Solitude"; it stands at the threshold to Coleridge's declining creativity in the years following, and is bound up with opium dependence in the larger anguish of his family life and relation to Wordsworth and Sara Hutchinson. For Wordsworth as writer of *The Prelude* revolutionary disappointment was compensated in his power and calling as a poet; for Coleridge it issued as breakdown and creative paralysis. These differing experiences inevitably coloured the ways in which each looked back upon his earlier radical self.

"[J]uvenile errors are my theme", Wordsworth announces a little over half-way through *The Prelude*, Book Ten (x. 637). In *Newspapers Thirty-Five Years Ago* Charles Lamb similarly recalled his first "boyish

3. Godwin, *Thoughts*, p. 2.
4. Godwin, *Thoughts*, p. 2.

heats" of political awareness "kindled by the French Revolution, when if we were misled, we erred in the company of some, who are accounted very good men now".[5] But of course it only appeared that those good men had "erred" in retrospect; there was no sense of being "misled" at the time. Coleridge's note in Godwin's pamphlet registered this double perspective by allowing the generous welcome for revolution in 1789 but also pointing out that, "a posteriori", another view might be possible. Elsewhere, Coleridge was less candid about his own politics during the revolutionary decade. In his letter to Sir George and Lady Beaumont of 1 October 1803, for instance, Coleridge announced that during the 1790s he had been

> utterly unconnected with any party or club or society—(& this praise I must take to myself, that I disclaimed all these Societies, these Imperia in Imperio, these Ascarides in the Bowels of the State, subsisting on the weakness & diseasedness, & having for their final Object the Death of that State, whose Life had been their Birth & growth, & continued to be their sole nourishment—. All such Societies, under whatever name, I abhorred as wicked Conspiracies—and to this principle I adhered immoveably, simply because it was a principle . . . (*CL* ii. 1001)

Not so: Coleridge never adhered 'immoveably' to a principle "simply because it was a principle". The grotesque and laboured disgust with which Coleridge emphasizes his distance from the popular reform movement betrays his own uneasiness at vindicating a position no one would have thought to challenge in 1803; rather than confirming his independence from such "wicked Conspiracies", his letter to the Beaumonts is a memorial of personal complicity. Coleridge was ill, unhappy, and sleepless when writing it; granted, but he was also misrepresenting his former self to his "dear Friends". He repeated his claim to have been "utterly unconnected" with other reformists in his essay "Enthusiasm for an Ideal World" in *The Friend*. "I was a sharer in the general vortex," he concedes there, "though my little world described the path of its revolution in an orbit of its own" (*Friend*, i. 223). A little later in this essay Coleridge says that, while he rescued himself from "the pitfalls of sedition, . . . there were thousands as young and as innocent as myself who, not like me, sheltered in the tranquil nook or inland cove of a particular fancy, were driven along with the general current!" (*Friend*, i. 224).

By representing his then beliefs as "a particular fancy" of his "innocent" youth, Coleridge blurred and sentimentalized that period of his life. In 1817 he used an identical strategy to defend Southey's authorship of the recently pirated *Wat Tyler*, arguing in the *Courier* for Southey's "lofty, imaginative, and *innocent* spirit" in writing the play while still "a very young man" (*ET* ii. 459).[6] By so doing Coleridge contrived to hide the past, but at a cost. He was deliberately betraying

5. *The Works of Charles and Mary Lamb*, ed. E. V. Lucas (7 vols; London and New York, 1903–5), ii. 225.
6. Mr. Southey', *Courier* (18 Mar. 1817).

ideals and opinions once fundamental to his own identity and career, the disappointment of which had inevitably proved damaging and disabling. If Coleridge had indeed been "sheltered" from the mainstream of British radicalism in the 1790s, there was no need for his later elaborate justifications of that position (why all the pother, if he had *not* been involved?). But this had never been the case. It was Coleridge's self-implication in that cause and its ultimate defeat which provided the motive for his subsequent evasiveness and falsification.

Coleridge's letter to George Dyer in February 1795 indicates that he was very much "connected with a party" at Bristol, and by no means sheltered from the "general current" of radical politics. "The Democrats are . . . sturdy in the support of me," he says, "but their number is comparatively small," and then goes on to tell Dyer about the "scarcely restrained" threats of attack at his lectures (*CL* i. 152). If one allows a little exaggeration for Dyer's benefit, it is nevertheless clear that Coleridge was a popular figure among the Bristol opposition; equally, his political concerns were not confined to a merely local "orbit" as he later pretended in *The Friend*. In December 1795 one of his "chief objects" announced in the Prospectus to the *Watchman* was explicity "to co-operate . . . with the PATRIOTIC SOCIETIES" in opposing Pitt's and Grenville's Two Acts, and in pressing for "a Right of Suffrage general and frequent" (*Watchman*, p. 5). At this moment "PATRIOTIC SOCIETIES" meant the London Corresponding Society and its provincial associates in the campaign for parliamentary reform—precisely those societies he later told the Beaumonts he had "abhorred as wicked Conspiracies"—and, to underline the extent of his co-operation and commitment, he set out on 9 January 1796 on an extensive tour through the Midlands canvassing subscriptions for his journal.

Fourteen years after Coleridge's 1803 letter to the Beaumonts, reformists were once again active following the end of the Napoleonic wars. Coleridge's concern to distance himself from this revival was one encouragement to the misconstructions in Chapter ten of *Biographia Literaria* where, for example, he claimed that his opinions had been "opposite . . . to those of jacobinism or even of democracy" (*BL* i. 184). John Thelwall's memory did not coincide with this version of the past. In the margin of his own copy of *Biographia*, Thelwall replied:

> that Mr C. was indeed far from Democracy, because he was far beyond it, I well remember—for he was a downright zealous leveller & indeed in one of the worst senses of the word he was a Jacobin, a man of blood—Does he forget the letters he wrote to me (& which I believe I yet have) acknowledging the justice of my castigation of him for the violence, and sanguinary tendency of some of his doctrines . . .[7]

The point at issue here is not whether Coleridge's opinions had been democratic, levelling, "Jacobin", or "sanguinary", although I shall return to these matters later on. Thelwall's note is most salutary for

7. B. Pollin and R. Burke, 'John Thelwall's Marginalia in a Copy of Coleridge's *Biographia Literaria*,' *Bulletin of the New York Public Library*, lxxiv (1970), 81.

identifying the reality of Coleridge's letters, lectures, and poems during the radical years that his later accounts in *Biographia* and elsewhere contrive to suppress or forget.

* * *

Delineating Our Present Oppositionists

> To delineate with a free hand the different Classes of our present Op-
> positionists to "Things as they are,"—may be a delicate, but it is a
> necessary Task . . .
>
> (*Lects. 1795*, pp. 7–8)

In his *Moral and Political Lecture* Coleridge differentiates four categories among the "present Oppositionists". The first he describes as
"indolent" and inconsistent, depending "with weather-cock uncertainty on the winds of Rumor, that blow from France" (*Lects. 1795*, p.
8). His "second class" are "wild" and potentially violent, while the
"third class among the friends of Freedom" appear "steadily" but self-
ishly interested, "with narrow and self-centering views" (*Lects. 1795*,
pp. 9, II). It was with the fourth category of oppositionists, "that small
but glorious band, whom we may truly distinguish by the name of
thinking and disinterested Patriots", that Coleridge identified himself,
along with four others: Joseph Gerrald, Maurice Margarot, Thomas
Muir, and Thomas Fysshe Palmer (*Lects. 1795*, pp. 12, 14).

All of these men welcomed the French Revolution in 1789, and
agreed on the need for parliamentary reform and liberty of conscience
in Britain. Nevertheless, Coleridge's "small but glorious band" also
represented three subsections of contemporary opposition. Gerrald
and Margarot were leaders of the popular reform movement in the
London Corresponding Society, and both were delegates to the first
British Convention at Edinburgh where they were arrested on 5 December 1793 (Goodwin, p. 303). Thomas Muir was a lawyer and
founder of the relatively moderate whig Friends of the People in Edinburgh. Thomas Fysshe Palmer was a Cambridge graduate and unitarian minister at Dundee where he also belonged to the Friends of the
People, thereby representing the political radicalism of religious dissent. All four of Coleridge's patriots were tried for sedition between
August 1793 and March 1794. They were found guilty and transported to Botany Bay; Margarot was the only one of the four who lived
to return to Britain.

In Southey's poem "To the Exiled Patriots", Gerrald, Margarot,
Muir, and Palmer are hailed as

> Martyrs of Freedom—ye who firmly good
> Stept forth the champions in her glorious cause,
> Ye who against Corruption nobly stood
> For Justice, Liberty, and equal Laws.
>
> (*Lects. 1795*, p. 16)

—and for Coleridge too they were men of vision, perseverance, and
patience, qualities that he later associated with his "elect" in "Reli-

gious Musings". Coleridge's own position in 1795 was close to Thomas Fysshe Palmer in that both were Cambridge men, unitarians, reformists. But, while he shared Palmer's academic and religious background, Coleridge's political lecturing was more akin to John Thelwall's activities in London as a leader of the London Corresponding Society, and their opinions frequently and strikingly coincided between 1794 and 1797. Differentiating opposition in the 1790s remains a "delicate task". Superficially distinct groupings of radicals and reformists tended to overlap. The Friends of the People, the Society for Constitutional Information, and the London Corresponding Society all shared common interests and aims, and members concerted their efforts for reform in petitions, subscriptions, dinners, meetings, and so on. Godwin's circle of friends, to which Wordsworth belonged in 1795, also included the leaders of the London Corresponding Society and others actively involved in metropolitan opposition. Among them can be found John Thelwall, political lecturer; John Binns, plumber's labourer; William Frend, unitarian; Felix Vaughan and James Losh, radical barristers; Thomas Holcroft, atheist member of the Constitutional Society, acquitted of treason in December 1794. Not only does this suggest that Wordsworth was moving close to—and very probably within—the popular reform movement while in London during 1795, it should give pause to those who still cherish the image of Godwin holding himself discretely aloof from active political affairs.[8]

It is essential to unravel the complexities of Wordsworth's and Coleridge's radical years, not simply to identify where they agreed or disagreed, but because in a longer perspective those similarities and differences were to form the basis of their creative interaction in later years. The problem can be focused in their crucial early meetings at Bristol and Racedown in 1795 and 1797. The poets' first acquaintance at Bristol in August and September 1795 was apparently encouraged by sympathetic political opinions, subsequently reflected in Coleridge's admiration of "Salisbury Plain" and Wordsworth's reciprocal esteem for "Religious Musings" (CL i. 215–16).[9] Each had opposed the war since 1793, and they would have agreed on the urgent need for reform. Looking back to the period of their first meetings in The Prelude, though, Wordsworth reminds Coleridge of a significant difference between them: "Ah, then it was", he says,

> That thou, most precious friend, about this time
> First known to me, didst lend a living help
> To regulate my soul.
>
> (x. 904–7)

Wordsworth's chronology is vague—"about this time"—because his concern here was to emphasize his need for the intellectual and philosophic guidance Coleridge was able to offer him over a period of years. The Prelude does not recall the coincidence of two like minds, but the

---

8. See Chapter 5 [of Wordsworth and Coleridge: The Radical Years] for a full discussion of this.
9. In R. Woof, 'Wordsworth and Coleridge: Some Early Matters', BWS, 82–3.

dynamic potential released through disparity. While their political opinions were superficially identical and with their shared literary ambitions would have warmed each to each, it was the philosophic divergences within otherwise compatible politics that proved decisive in their emergent creative relationship. In *The Prelude*, Book Ten, Coleridge and Dorothy are presented as redeeming figures who sustained Wordsworth in the moral "despair" to which Godwinian rationalism had brought him. When Wordsworth remembered that time, he did so in the knowledge that Coleridge's power to "lend a living help" was related to his earlier rejection of *Political Justice* at a time when Wordsworth himself had been a worshipper at "the oracles of thought".

Coleridge's earliest recorded reference to Godwin occurs in his letter to Southey of 11 September 1794: "Godwin *thinks* himself *inclined* to *Atheism*—acknowledges there are arguments *for* deity, he cannot answer—but not so many, as *against* his Existence—He is writing a book about it. I set him at Defiance—tho' if he convinces me, I will acknowledge it in a letter in the newspapers—" (*CL* i. 102). In mid-1794 Wordsworth did not share Coleridge's desire to set Godwin "at Defiance". Three months before Coleridge's letter to Southey, Wordsworth had told William Mathews that "every enlightened friend of mankind" had a duty to "diffuse by every method a knowledge of those rules of political justice", and elaborated plans for their journal the *Philanthropist* in terms that demonstrate his familiarity with Godwin's book (*EY*, p. 124). Just over a year before they met, therefore, Wordsworth was drawing encouragement from *Political Justice* while Coleridge was in conflict with its author. The major issue on which Wordsworth and Coleridge would have differed was the question of Godwin's atheism. For Wordsworth it was not an obstacle; as Britain appeared to be following France towards a violent repression in 1793–4, *Political Justice* offered a philosophic justification for progress that eliminated recourse to revolutionary action. But for Coleridge Godwin's system threatened a moral and spiritual breakdown, in that it neglected the reconciling love of God which was vital to Coleridge's idea of human society. While Wordsworth and Coleridge would have agreed on any number of day-to-day issues in contemporary opposition, Coleridge's radicalism was inseparable from religious principles Wordsworth did not hold. This set their different bearings towards Godwin, and is perhaps well enough known. But the wider implications of their respective attitudes to Godwin have been misunderstood.

In the Introduction to their excellent edition of Coleridge's *Lectures 1795 on Politics and Religion*, Lewis Patton and Peter Mann allege that Coleridge's defiance of Godwin "affected his attitude to the whole radical movement", and that it is "the key to much of his social and religious thinking in 1795" (*Lects. 1795*, lxvii). They elaborate this argument in some detail:

> Coleridge's complex and critical feelings about Godwin, Paine, Holcroft, Thelwall, and other radical figures, the majority of whom were "infidels" of some sort, made it additionally difficult for him to sustain a strong and consistent attitude during the

1790's, when events in France, combined with repression and re-action at home, made political agitation difficult, dangerous, and dispiriting. In addition, his distrust of the political methods of the Corresponding Societies . . . necessarily isolated him to some extent from the most important active forces for reform . . . (*Lects. 1795*, pp. lxxvii–lxxviii)

The precise extent of Coleridge's "necessary isolation" is not defined, nor are his "complex and critical feelings" about other leading political and intellectual radicals explained. Nevertheless, Patton and Mann acknowledge that their account is substantially what Coleridge wished the Beaumonts to believe in 1803, when he told them he had been "insulated" from other reformists. It is unfortunate that the editors' final words on Coleridge's position in 1795 reiterate his later version of this year without question: "By reason of his Christian, moral, and philosophical principles, which he attempted to clarify and justify in his lectures, Coleridge found himself in a state of 'insulation' (to use his own expressive word) from the democratic movement and its ideas" (*Lects. 1795*, p. lxxix). This would have delighted the author of *The Friend*, but it seriously misrepresents Coleridge as an active political figure in Cambridge, London, Bristol, and the Midlands between 1792 and 1796. Yes, his religion did mean that his attitude to Godwin, Holcroft, and other radical leaders was complex and sometimes critical, but the corollary is not that he should have been "necessarily isolated". To differ with Godwin was not to reject the ideas and aspirations of other friends of liberty, as the Prospectus to the *Watchman* demonstrates. Nor is it the only "key" to Coleridge's social and religious thinking, his relation to other radicals and to Wordsworth in particular. This must be sought in the "Christian, moral, and philosophical principles" that influenced his response to Godwin in the first place and which, contrary to Patton's and Mann's argument, enabled Coleridge to maintain a remarkable stability in opposition through years when Wordsworth experienced

> sorrow, disappointment, vexing thoughts,
> Confusion of the judgement, zeal decayed—
> And lastly, utter loss of hope itself
> And things to hope for.
>
> (*P*. xi. 4–7)

Wordsworth's radicalism was the product of his own experiences in France and was responsive to the changing course of the Revolution thereafter. As peaceful progress was succeeded by terrorism and war in 1793, he turned to *Political Justice* to sustain his "solicitude for man", eventually to discover that Godwin's philosophy was inadequate to the practicalities of social change, and to his own experience of human nature. With that realization, Coleridge's critique of Godwin became relevant and accessible to Wordsworth as the "regulating" and inspiring influence recollected in *The Prelude*, Book Ten. Coleridge was not forced to shift his political and philosophic allegiances to the same extent and there were, I think, two principal reasons for this. The first was Coleridge's consistent effort to reconcile "all the affairs of man as a process" within God's providence; the second reason was that the religious principles on which he based his idea of political progress belonged in a tradition of radical dissent that was encouraged by the French Revolution, but not inextricably dependent upon its course from day to day. As late as January 1798, when other friends of liberty had been exiled, emigrated, gone underground, or withdrawn from politics, Coleridge was still preaching against war and the political and religious establishment to the unitarian congregation at Shrewsbury (Howe, xvii. 108).

In this perspective Coleridge was not "isolated" or "insulated" at all. He relished the thought of himself as successor to such eminent dissenters as Richard Price, Joseph Priestley, Thomas Fysshe Palmer, and, most importantly, William Frend. Each of these men had welcomed the French Revolution in 1789 as the advent of political and religious liberty elsewhere in Europe; all of them had delivered political sermons and lectures, and published controversial pamphlets too. Not one of them was "isolated" from the general current of radical affairs by his faith; on the contrary, their dissent urged them to the forefront of controversy in calling for the removal of Test Acts and an extension of the suffrage. Price's exultant welcome for revolution—"Tremble all ye oppressors of the world! Take warning all ye supporters of slavish governments, and slavish hierarchies!"—alarmed Burke into composing his *Reflections* as a counter to "this spiritual doctor of politics" (*R.*, p. 97).[1] Priestley's unitarianism offered no "insulation" from the church-and-king mob at Birmingham in 1791; his radical dissent was precisely the reason for the attack on his home and laboratory. Two years later William Frend's "Christian, moral, and philosophical principles" afforded no defence before the university court at Cambridge in May 1793, nor did Fysshe Palmer's dissent serve to mitigate his seven years" exile at Botany Bay in September of that year. When Joseph Gerrald protested to Braxfield that Christ himself had been a reformist, the judge chuckled in reply, "Muckle he made o' that; *he* was hanget" (*M W C*, pp. 139–40). There is no reason to suppose that Coleridge's religious or philosophic thinking made him any less exposed than Priestley, Frend, and Fysshe Palmer, or that his opposition was in any way separate from the wider democratic reform movement as he later tried to claim. The anonymous *TLS* reviewer (E. P. Thompson?) of Patton's and Mann's volume puts the matter succinctly: "the curve of Coleridge's commitment, in 1795–6, took him very close indeed to the popular societies—or towards their more intellectual component . . . and such a trajectory, if it had not been arrested by the retirement at Stowey, would almost certainly have led him to prison."[2]

On Sunday, 21 December 1794 Coleridge met Godwin for the first time at Thomas Holcroft's house. Godwin noted in his diary "talk of

1. Richard Price, *A Discourse on the Love of Our Country* (2nd edn; London, 1789), p. 50 (cited hereafter as Price, *Discourse*).
2. See "Bliss was it in that Dawn: The Matter of Coleridge's Revolutionary Youth," *TLS* (6 Aug. 1971), 929–32.

self love & God", which suggests that Coleridge fulfilled his promise to challenge Godwin's atheism. A little over two months later, on 27 February 1795, Wordsworth also met Godwin over tea at William Frend's house—but as disciple rather than critic and in company with some of the most prominent radicals in London. By this time Coleridge had already written and delivered three political lectures at Bristol. His meeting with Godwin and his wish to counter Godwin's intellectual influence among other reformists served to accelerate his emergence as an active political figure, drawing him into contemporary controversy rather than pushing him off into an orbit of his own. The near coincidence of Wordsworth's and Coleridge's first meetings with Godwin reveal both of them in much the same company, at the epicentre of British radical life.

* * *

PETER HOHEISEL

Coleridge on Shakespeare: Method Amid the Rhetoric†

When Henry Crabb Robinson wrote that Coleridge's "pretended lectures are immethodical rhapsodies, moral, metaphysical, and literary, abounding in brilliant thoughts, fine flashes of rhetoric, ingenious paradoxes, occasionally profound and salutary truths," but not "an instructive course of readings on any one subject a man can wish to fix his attention on," he described a manner of presentation which continues to vex Coleridge's readers as it did at least one of his auditors.[1]

Far from developing a full body of Shakespearean criticism, Coleridge did not even give a detailed critique of any one play. But, contrary to Robinson, there is a method amid the rhetoric, and that method, to put it in a Coleridgean way, is to illuminate certain central principles which contain endless potentiality for development because they are a unique and vital way of looking at the plays.

To explain his vision of the plays, Coleridge found it important to establish their genre, because classical criticism, though admitting the genius behind them, could not explain *how* they succeeded in blatant violation of classical rules. Thus they are what Coleridge calls "Romantic dramas, or dramatic romances," appealing not primarily to the senses, but to the imagination and to "reason as contemplating our inward nature." And since this contemplation involves "eternal" truths of human nature, the dramatist is liberated from strict chronological time and the limitations of space; in effect he creates his own time and space. External rules, convention, and materialistic probability are

---

† *Studies in Romanticism* 13 (1979): 15–23. Reprinted by courtesy of the Trustees of Boston University. [All footnotes are the author's.]

1. *Coleridge's Shakespearean Criticism* (Cambridge, Mass.: Harvard U. Press, 1930), Thomas M. Raysor, ed., Vol. II, 227. Coleridge quotations from this work will subsequently be indicated in the body of the article; other sources will be individually noted.

therefore unimportant; the only exigency to be obeyed is that created by the vision which is being dramatized. A Shakespeare play then is "romantic poetry revealing itself in the drama" (I, 197–98) and its structure develops from an internal logic. External rules, such as the classical unities, cannot be imposed on it like a grid. Put in another way, the vision itself contains the potentiality for its incarnation into a structured, unified drama and it must proceed according to its own logic.

The Tempest is the best example of what Coleridge means by romantic drama. Its interests, he says, are "independent of all historical facts and associations, and arise from their fitness to that faculty of our nature, the Imagination I mean, which owes no allegiances to time and place,—a species of drama, therefore, in which errors in chronology and geography, no mortal sins in any species, are venial, or count for nothing" (I, 131). Categories such as temporal and geographical consistency are therefore unimportant in romantic drama, because the point of such drama is not literal realism but contemplation of an eternal truth which transcends these categories. While classical norms may fit other plays, the romantic drama creates its own categories—those in which we willingly suspend what W. H. Auden calls the "wearily historic, the dingily geographic, the dully sensible."[2]

Shattering the classical lens through which Shakespeare's plays had been seen, by establishing that they are a unique genre, Coleridge can then show that "the judgement of Shakespeare is commensurate with his genius—nay, that his genius reveals itself in his judgement, as in its most exalted form" (I, 126). Incensed at the idea, common in his time, that Shakespeare was a wild unconscious genius who inexplicably created great plays even though he violated all the rules, Coleridge was concerned in the lectures to show that Shakespeare was as much a genius in his dramatic and artistic judgement as he was in his poetic vision. But of course if Shakespeare's craft is judged according to classical craft he remains a dramatic surd. But judged, as Coleridge would have it, by how successfully each play incarnates the idea in mind for that play, the skill is manifest.

The dramatic judgement of Shakespeare is evidenced in his skillful use of language and imagery, and above all in the profound grasp of eternal human truth which that language and imagery embody. Coleridge praises the language of the plays because it is natural. Not natural simply in the sense that it is plausible and realistic, but natural because it coheres with the seminal idea which Shakespeare has of that character and is in perfect harmony with the dramatic presentation of that character (II, 137). Thus Hamlet, locked in a private intellectual and imaginative world insufficiently related to the world of objective events, speaks with too much method, too much internal ordering of reality, while Mrs. Quickley speaks with too little method, a total inability to control intellectually the reality which she experiences—

---

2. Collected Longer Poems (New York: Random House, 1965), "The Sea and the Mirror," p. 227.

both speaking faithfully according to Shakespeare's idea of each character (II, 346). This Coleridgean sense of naturalness of language and character is to be understood not simply as the ability to reproduce the characters and language he observed, but as the god-like power genuinely to create those characters, not copy them, and thus their naturalness is not praised because they are like people who exist, but because they are faithful artistic renderings, adequate incarnations, of the idea of them which exists in Shakespeare.

Likewise the images of Shakespeare prove his genius not primarily because they are striking or beautiful or faithfully copy nature, but because they are modified by a predominant passion and because they reduce multitude to unity or succession to an instant (II, 330). They are the work of genius because they are adequate symbols of the vision. The dramatist creates his images according to his idea; their virtue, again, lies in how well they make us see that idea, not the images for their own sake. Prospero's speech to Miranda is an example Coleridge gives:

> . . . One midnight,
> Fated to the purpose, did Antonio open
> The gates of Milan; and i' the dead of darkness,
> The ministers for the purpose hurried thence
> Me, and thy crying self.

The word "crying," says Coleridge, presents a complete picture to the mind (II, 174). The simple image "crying self" telescopes time, reduces succession to an instant, and relates the present Miranda to an instant consciousness of her historical self; through it we participate in the idea of Miranda's history.

Shakespeare's judgement, therefore, in the use of language and imagery to embody adequately his artistic idea makes him a "master of himself and his subject—a genuine Proteus; we see all things in him, as images in a calm lake, most distinct, most accurate—only more splendid, more glorified. This is correctness in the only philosophical sense" (I, 79). Shakespeare's mind, contemplating the idea (the eternal human truth), is like a mirror and a lamp, to use Abrams' well-known images, in which and through whose energy and genius we see that eternal reality because the playwright has embedded it in a concrete play which becomes a symbol of the idea. Thus we do not see Shakespeare. We see what he sees. And his craftsmanship and judgement as an artist resides in his ability to make us see what he sees.

What do we see? What is the specifically Shakespearean vision of human life? That human existence is fundamentally moral existence. In essence Coleridge admires Shakespeare for his grasp of moral reality in human reality. Shakespeare is not a moralist in the sense of someone who moralizes, gives an opinion on the rightness or wrongness of an action; rather he grasps the consequences of any distortion in what it means to be a whole human being. To Coleridge, Shakespeare had virtually surveyed all the great component powers and impulses of human nature,—had seen that their different combinations and subordinations were in fact the individualizers of men, and showed how their harmony was produced by reciprocal disproportions of excess or deficiency. The language in which each of these truths are expressed was not drawn from any set fashion, but from the profoundest depths of his moral being, and is therefore for all ages. (I, 137)

Throughout his critical work on other writers, Coleridge constantly searches the man's ability to grasp principles—in science, in philosophy, in poetry, in theology—in whatever field the mind exerts itself; and to him Shakespeare's triumph is to have grasped basic moral principles at work in human life and to be able to delineate with artistic fidelity the consequences of those principles: whether they are in harmony, such as in Banquo, or disharmony, such as in Macbeth.

A principle, to Coleridge, as Walter Jackson Bate explains, has separate, objective existence and is therefore a universal.[3] The process by which Shakespeare embodies in each play the moral vision which he is contemplating is the process of union between that universal and the particular: a universal, moral principle finding its way into the particular stuff of human life. Just as an individual character corresponds to, and is the result of, the union between that specific character and the idea of that character in Shakespeare's mind, so the individual play flows from the process of the union between the idea of a universal, moral principle wedded to the concrete reality of human life. Thus, in its totality, the individual play becomes a symbol of moral truth. And because it is an eternal moral truth, it has validity "for all ages." To Coleridge, then, a Shakespeare play is admired for its language and imagery, which ultimately serve to symbolize the moral value which the play embodies.

Art as an end in itself, divorced from consideration of the truth symbolized and brought into being by the artistic act, would be deficient to Coleridge, because to him art is a servant of the truth not an autonomous lord. This attitude explains how Coleridge can approve both personality and impersonality in art. He finds Milton a highly personal artist in the sense that in no line of his work is Milton ever absent; he is the all-pervasive, not hidden god. Shakespeare however is the supreme *Deus Absconditus*, the highest example of negative capability, leading us to see not himself, but what he sees (II, 353). Coleridge admires both because he is convinced that both serve the truth. Style, whether personal or impersonal, is secondary; and while the modern arguments about personality and impersonality in art would be interesting to him, Coleridge would find any definition of art deficient if it did not include reference to what art symbolizes and says. This same impulse, not simply weakness of character, as so many of his friends and subsequent critics have felt, led him to enormous efforts to establish Wordsworth's reputation—because of what

3. *Coleridge* (New York: Macmillan, 1968), p. 152.

Wordsworth was saying and because Wordsworth created a poetic form which was the perfect symbolization of that truth.

The process, then, of artistic creation behind a Shakespeare play is the embodiment of an eternal moral truth in a living work of art: the universal, the objectively existing principle becoming particular. This actualization takes place through an *idea* in the mind of Shakespeare. The idea is both the contemplation of the universal and the impulse to embody it in a drama. To Coleridge, the idea is at the core of the human creative act, just as it is of the divine. In a theological letter, which we may here use for insight into what Coleridge means by "idea," Coleridge says that God's ideas, through which He created the world, are archetypal, anterior, and adequate.[4] That is, they are more real than the reality created through them; they are prior to and constitutive of creation and, in the deepest sense, effective. Since the human creative act is participation in the divine creative act,[5] insofar as it is capable through analogy of being, the creative idea of the artist (in this case Shakespeare) is archetypal, anterior, and adequate. It is greater than its type (the play), prior to it in time, and contains in itself all the potentiality which is actualized in the specific play which Shakespeare writes. And when that idea is incarnated in the drama, it functions as form to the matter of the play, becoming itself by becoming constitutive of the play, which releases the potentiality inherent in

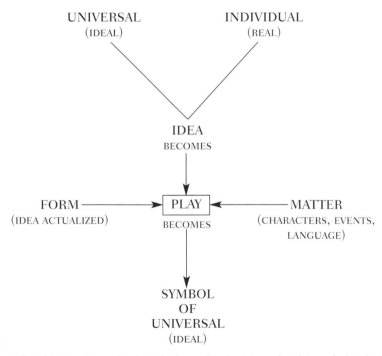

UNIVERSAL   INDIVIDUAL
(IDEAL)   (REAL)

IDEA
BECOMES

FORM ——————▶ PLAY ◀—————— MATTER
(IDEA ACTUALIZED)   BECOMES   (CHARACTERS, EVENTS,
                                                            LANGUAGE)

SYMBOL
OF
UNIVERSAL
(IDEAL)

4. *Collected Letters of Samuel Taylor Coleridge*, Earl Leslie Griggs, ed., Vol. II (Oxford: Oxford U. Press, 1959), 1195.
5. *Coleridge's Biographia Literaria* (Oxford: Oxford U. Press, 1907), J. Shawcross ed., Vol. I, 202.

the idea. In contrast to the universal, or the principle, which has objective and independent existence, the idea is actualized, becomes idea, when concretely joined with the matter—the specific play—which it forms. Thus to Coleridge the idea is the universal in the individual, having been given, by the creative act, a "local habitation." And like a principle, it is "prospective," carrying knowledge within itself (II, 352), and therefore, contains "conditions and consequences *ad infinitum*" (II, 347), the specific play of course being only one of its infinite consequences. According to Coleridge, therefore, when the idea becomes itself through incarnation in the art work, "a sphere of *actual* operations" is given to the ideal and the real is "elevated and refined" (II, 129). In short the play becomes symbol of the ideal. The particular genius of a Shakespeare play, then, is that through contemplation of a universal moral truth, Shakespeare's mind educes an idea which becomes actualized in a specific art work, which in turn becomes a living symbol of that universal. And we, who experience the play, participate in Shakespeare's contemplation through the symbol he has created. The diagram on the opposite page may help clarify this.

With this view of the creative act, one can see why Coleridge was so intent on ridding criticism of a fossilized approach to dramatic structure. In realizing itself in a play, the idea behind it must educe its own internal potential, creating the structures which accord with its own law of being as it actualizes itself. Coleridge is not so interested in the dramatic structure of the play itself, but in the structure of the idea behind it. Typically, and infuriatingly to many, he continually transcends the play to speculate on the idea in the mind of the creator.

He finds that idea most often in a character or characters in relation to one another. To Coleridge a character is a living incarnation of the moral idea symbolized in the play. He calls characters "ideal realities," naturalized by the concept of the artist (II, 162). They become living symbols, artistic renderings of a human moral truth, reflecting either a balance or a distortion in the human mind itself.

Thus when Coleridge is called a psychological critic, it is important to see the kind of psychological critic he is, just as he felt it important to see the kind of plays Shakespeare wrote. Defending himself against an implied criticism of plagiarism from Schlegel, Coleridge says that both Schlegel and himself

> studied deeply and perseverantly the philosophy of Kant, the distinguishing feature of which is to treat every subject in reference to the operation of the mental faculties to which it specially appertains, and to commence by the cautious discrimination of what is essential, i.e., explicable by mere consideration of the faculties in themselves, from what is empirical, i.e., the modifying or disturbing forces of time, place, and circumstances. (II, 237)

In the Shakespeare plays, therefore, Coleridge finds the dramatic impulse in a controlling idea related to a mental faculty in the characters. Usually he finds a moral imbalance, some psychological distortion, in the mind of the main character. And this imbalance symbolizes an eternal truth about a fault in human nature. As a psychological critic, Coleridge is not primarily concerned about interaction between characters, or an analysis of their motivations and desires for its own sake, but with the permanent psychological truth about the eternal condition of human nature which each character portrays. To the core Coleridge is a metaphysician who believes in an eternal human nature expressed in varying conditions, not an empirical psychological critic who is concerned with describing the dynamics of human interaction in Shakespeare's plays. He sees Shakespeare as not essentially concerned with simply showing how people react to different situations and people, but with creating types whose basic interest and artistic viability consist in how well they incarnate the permanent moral condition of mankind. Just as Kant treated each subject in relation to the mental faculty to which it pertained, so Coleridge sees each play in relation to the mental state of the characters, representing either a moral balance or imbalance.

Thus Coleridge finds Shakespeare often creating characters in which an intellectual or moral faculty is in "morbid excess." For example he sees Hamlet as showing the need to maintain a healthy balance between "outward objects" and "inward thoughts—a due balance between the real and the imaginary world." Failing to maintain this balance, Hamlet's immediate perceptions are distorted by his imagination and contemplation (I, 37). While Hamlet has enormous intellectual activity, exaggerated method, he shrinks from action, reaching the point only of knowing what to do, dramatizing the need to act, and deciding to act. Polonius, likewise, illustrates another moral, mental distortion: fossilized memory. He is a man of dead maxims which summarize dead facts, devoid of future value (II, 352). A "Skeleton of his own former skill and statecraft," he "hunts the trail of policy at a dead scent" (I, 26). Macbeth is another moral aberration; in him Shakespeare presents the idea of a man lusting after the kingship at the very opening of the play, while the play develops through Macbeth progressively cutting himself off from his conscience and from nature until he becomes a mere shell of a man living "in a preternatural state," inclined to superstition and disorder in order to satisfy that lust for power (I, 76). Coleridge contrasts Banquo's unsullied mind at the opening of the play with the already tainted mind of Macbeth. Banquo typifies an unpossessed mind, one which is "wholly present to the present object" (I, 68), with the result that his encounter with the witches shows that he has only a natural and disinterested curiosity in contrast to the morbid and self-seeking interest of Macbeth. *Macbeth*, therefore, works out the idea of the effects of ambition cut off from moral concerns. Likewise the characters in *The Tempest* symbolize various mental conditions, with Prospero and Miranda showing the moral and humane union of the head and the heart, or intelligence and feeling, while Caliban illustrates the dawning of understanding combined with the lack of reason and a moral sense (I, 133–34).

The drama and development of the plays, therefore, is simply the working out, the consequences, the incarnation in event, dialogue, and characterization, of the seminal moral idea which Shakespeare is meditating upon and to which he gives dramatic and artistic expression. Thus because of his conviction that the idea contains the consequences, Coleridge devotes most of his attention to the opening of the play where the idea is established, and practically ignores the rest of the play, to the chagrin of the Henry Crabb Robinsons among his auditors and those subsequent critics who have muttered "incomplete" (though none more critical than S.T.C. himself) in judgement of his effort at analysis.

To summarize the method amid the rhetoric, Coleridge sees the plays of Shakespeare as romantic dramas, imaginative incarnations of moral ideas, which, "shaping their rapid flight in forms always regular,"[4] create a unity dependent not on external criteria, but on the inherent logical dynamism of that specific idea embodied in concrete characters living in specific circumstances. His critical technique is to search for the controlling idea which both transcends the play and is incarnated in it. His focus is indeed psychological, but in the sense of trying to discover how the mental state of each character symbolizes the necessary and permanent consequences in human life of a moral state of being. He is indeed a character critic, but one who looks upon characters not for their own sakes, but rather as a kind of lens through which we contemplate a permanent mental characteristic of mankind. In this sense, Coleridge does not see the plays as structured by characters, but on the ideas which those characters symbolize and represent.

Coleridge has not left us a fully developed body of Shakespearean criticism, but he has left us a way of looking at Shakespeare's work, which, to use some Coleridgean terms, is energetic, prospective, and consequential, with the result that he has given to criticism living principles and ideas, not dead maxims.

JEROME J. McGANN

From The *Biographia Literaria* and the Contentions of English Romanticism†

The *Biographia Literaria* is one of the chief documents of English Romantic theory, and in recent years, thanks to the work of various critics, we have also begun to see the book as a more coherently developed text than it was earlier thought to be. This new scholarship has proved eminently Coleridgean in character, for out of it has emerged a reconciliation of much material in the *Biographia* which had before seemed rather opposite and discordant in its qualities. To-

---

4. An image which Coleridge uses to describe the movement of poetry, *Letters*, n. 814.
† From *Coleridge and the "Biographia Literaria,"* ed. Frederick Burwick (Columbus, Ohio: Ohio State University Press, 1989), 233–46, 306–07. Reprinted by permission of the author. [All footnotes are the author's.]

day we see the book more clearly, I think, than we have ever seen it before; and the consequence of this new clarity is that we may also begin to see in exactly what ways the *Biographia* is crucial to an understanding of English Romanticism.

First of all, it is not crucial because it is the *central* theoretical document—not, at any rate, if by "central" we mean the one that incorporates all the major lines of thought associated with English Romanticism. Indeed, my present inquiry will try to *decenter* the *Biographia* in precisely this respect, to contrast it with two other important theoretical approaches that emerged in the Romantic movement. But in decentering Coleridge's book, I shall also be arguing its seminal importance for the development of the original strands of English Romanticism, as well as for our understanding of the movement as a whole. A careful look at the *Biographia* in its contemporary setting, even in the restricted terms I am proposing for this essay, brings the variety and richness of Romantic thought and practice into sharp relief.

The first thing we need to see is what Coleridge himself thought about the form and purpose of his book. It is the author of the "Essays on Method" who glanced intramurally at the *Biographia* as an "immethodical . . . miscellany,"[1] yet the same author was to say a bit later, and extramurally, that the work "cannot justly be regarded as a motley Patchwork, or Farrago of heterogeneous Effusions."[2] Following the recent work of McFarland, Jackson, Christensen, Wheeler, and Wallace, however, we have learned to see the kind of order that underlies Coleridge's often wayward and digressive procedures—indeed, to see that Coleridge's "mosaic" or "marginal" or "miscellaneous" manner of composition is precisely what is needed, in his view, if one is to execute a truly methodical and theoretically sound critical operation.[3]

None of this is to say, of course, that the *Biographia* is a formal masterpiece, or even that all of the interlaced topics are equally interesting, or handled with equal skill. What we are bound to see, however, if we want to read the book profitably, is the truth in Coleridge's own account of what he had written. "Let the following words," he said, "be prefixed as the Common Heading" of the work:

> An attempt to fix the true meaning of the Terms, Reason, Understanding, Sense, Imagination, Conscience & Ideas, with reflections on the theoretical & practical Consequences of their perversion from the Revolution (1688) to the present day, 1816—the moral of the whole being that the Man who gives to the Understanding the primacy due to the Reason, and lets the motives of Expedience usurp the place of the prescripts of the Conscience, in both cases loses the one and spoils the other. . . .[4]

---

1. *Biographia Literaria*, ed. James Engell and W. Jackson Bate (Princeton: Princeton University Press, 1983) 1:88. This edition is used throughout and page references are given in the text.
2. See *Lay Sermons*, ed. R. J. White (Princeton: Princeton University Press, 1972), 114n.
3. For Coleridge's "marginal" method of proceeding in *Biographia* see Thomas McFarland, *Coleridge and the Pantheist Tradition* (Oxford: Clarendon Press, 1969), 27; and Jerome Christensen, *Coleridge's Blessed Machine of Language* (Ithaca: Cornell University Press, 1981), ch. 3.
4. *Lay Sermons*, 114n.

This is a fair enough description, generally speaking, but trouble-some because Coleridge said that it applied just as well to *The States-man's Manual, A Lay Sermon,* and the three-volume *Friend* (1818). Yet this general application by Coleridge was both shrewd and correct. On the one hand, it called attention to the coherence of his purposes and preoccupations in these different works, and on the other it implied that the differences between them involved shifts in emphasis and in the relations established between the several topics. We need only glance at the "Essays on Method" to be clear about Coleridge's mean-ing. The *Biographia* moves by a process that Coleridge called "*progres-sive transition.*" This is no "mere dead arrangement"[5] but an accumulating set of interrelations which develop gradually (with refer-ences backward and anticipations forward) under the guidance and di-rection of a leading Idea, or what Coleridge called a "preconception" and "Initiative":

> Lord Bacon equally with ourselves, demands what we have ven-tured to call the intellectual or mental initiative, as the motive and guide of every philosophical experiment; some well-grounded purposes, some distinct impression of the probable results, some self-consistent anticipation as the grounds of the "*prudens quaes-tio*" (the fore-thoughtful query), which he affirms to be the prior *half* of the knowledge sought. . . .[6]

The *Biographia* takes up all of the same topics handled in *The Lay Sermons* and *The Friend* but disposes of them in a biographical field of relations. The emphasis of the work is therefore "literary," although lit-erary in the broadest sense because Coleridge's literary life encom-passed (besides poetry and plays) journalism, political pamphleteering, and philosophy. The *Biographia* is no different from Coleridge's other works in being committed to a critical procedure based upon what he liked to call "principles." Thus, when he speaks of an investigation or a discourse of "well-grounded purposes," the term "well-grounded" glances at the need for an initiative established on *a priori* "principles" rather than on *a posteriori* generalizations arrived at and refined through cumulative observation.

What then—to come to *my* leading idea—are Coleridge's "purposes" in the *Biographia,* what is his "distinct impression of the probable re-sults" of this most famous of English literary lives? They are generally the same as those he specified for the Appendix to *The Stateman's Manual:* "The Object was to rouse and stimulate the mind—to set the reader a thinking—and at least to obtain entrance for the question, whether the [truth of the] Opinions in fashion . . . is quite so certain as he had hitherto taken for granted."[7] Coleridge set this attitude as the motto of most of his work, and it plainly applies to the whole thrust of the *Biographia*—in its critique of the reigning empirical

5. *The Friend,* ed. Barbara E. Rooke (Princeton: Princeton University Press, 1969) 1:457.
6. *The Collected Letters of Samuel Taylor Coleridge,* ed. Earl Leslie Griggs (Oxford: Clarendon Press, 1956–71) 2:812.
7. *Lay Sermons,* 114n.

school of philosophy; reviews and ideas about poetry; and gossip about Coleridge, Wordsworth, and the so-called Lake School of poetry. The *Biographia* opposed the "Opinions in fashion" on all these matters— indeed, opposes the idea that any truth at all could ever be found in fashion or grounded in opinion.

More particularly, Coleridge's purpose was to set forth a theory of poetry grounded in the distinction between imagination and fancy, for

> were it once fully ascertained, that this division is . . . grounded in nature . . . the theory of the fine arts, and of poetry in particular, could not, I thought, but derive some additional and important light. It would in its immediate effects furnish a torch of guidance to the philosophical critic; and ultimately to the poet himself. In energetic minds, truth soon changes by domestication into power; and from directing in the discrimination and appraisal of the product, becomes influencive in the production. To admire on principle, is the only way to imitate without loss of originality. (1:85)

This passage, which culminates the introductory four chapters of the *Biographia*, sets forth the "well-grounded purposes" and hoped-for "results" that Coleridge anticipated for his book. On the one hand, the *Biographia* was to be a model of literary criticism that would be *represented* in the practical discussions of Shakespeare, Wordsworth, and Maturin; and that would be *polemicized* in the critique of Jeffrey and the reviewing institution of the period. On the other hand, the *Biographia* was to establish guidelines for the writing of poetry. Both of these practical aims were to succeed because Coleridge's was a work of "philosophical" criticism which could be a model for critics, on the one hand, and which could show poets, on the other, how "to imitate without loss of originality" the work of other poets and of nature itself.

Coleridge's "well-grounded purposes" would be, finally, set forth as a man of letters' intellectual biography. The significance of the biographical frame for Coleridge's work cannot be too greatly emphasized, for the story he tells reveals a person whose work was steadfast in its principles—more, was steadfast *in principles* as such, was steadfast (that is to say) in God——from the beginning, but who only *grew* into his developing self-conscious grasp of the operation of these principles in his own life's work and practice. Like every human being in a world made by God, Coleridge was born a child of truth, but only gradually did he raise himself from an ignorance of what that meant to a methodical and active assent to its reality. In the *Biographia* he comes forth as the person he calls in *The Friend* the "*well*-educated man," of whom he goes on to say: "However irregular and desultory his talk, there is *method* in the fragments."[8] The ultimate myth, or faith, of the *Biographia* is, therefore, that the "principles" of all things, including the principles of a benevolently dynamic human self-consciousness, are "grounded in nature." Coleridge's life and its narrative are important because together they "furnish a torch of guidance" to others. Ac-

8. *The Friend*, 1:449.

cording to Coleridge, the intellectual dynamic that has been his life is the birthright of every human being—every Christian human being, at any rate.

We need to be clear about Coleridge's explicit aims and purposes in the *Biographia* if we are to begin an accurate assessment of its achievements. The accusations of incoherence and disorganization, installed with the early reviews, have grown to seem much less important, and in certain respects misguided, as readers have tended to favor an aesthetic or hermeneutical method of reading the work over a positive and critical approach. To the degree that scholars have been interested in judging the correctness of Coleridge's various ideas and positions in philosophy, politics, and literary criticism, the consensus seems to be that (a) his critique of the empirical tradition and of materialism, and his correlative defense of Idealist positions, leaves that old debate more or less where it has always been (undecided, exactly where his German mentors in philosophy had left it); (b) his political views are independent and conservative, with both characteristics deriving ultimately from his religious and theological convictions; (c) the representation of his views on all matters, *in order to be objectively understood,* have to pass through the filter of Coleridge's subjectivity, and Coleridge himself must be the vehicle but not the master of that subjectivity (that is to say, Coleridge is not always candid, even with himself); (d) the literary criticism, both practical and theoretical, is the great achievement of the work.

For the remainder of this essay I shall be concentrating on Coleridge's literary criticism in the *Biographia.* I have spent some time on the general structure and method because the literary theory and criticism is of a piece with the rest of the book. Thus, Coleridge's argument that poetry is essentially ideal relates directly to his account of Idealist philosophy. Similarly, his critique of associationism and empirical philosophy connects just as directly with his critique of Wordsworth's poetry, and especially the principles which underly that poetry. Finally, the history of his own life from his early radicalism to his achieved religious conservatism—and culminating in the *Biographia* itself—argues the social and political importance of a correct view of poetry and criticism. Coleridge repeatedly associates radical political thought with the philosophic positions he attacks directly and at length. Indeed, much of this kind of "philosophical" political commentary in the *Biographia* is simply jingoism, as we see very clearly in his discussion of associationism. "Opinions fundamentally false" on these academic matters are not, he says, "harmless" at the political and social level:

> the sting of the adder remains venemous. . . . Some indeed there
> seem to have been, in an unfortunate neighbour-nation at least,
> who have embraced this system with a full view of all its moral
> and religious consequences; some
>
> who deem themselves most free,
> When they within this gross and visible sphere

Chain down the winged thought, scoffing assent,
Proud in their meanness; and themselves they cheat
With noisy emptiness of learned phrase,
    Their subtle fluids, impacts, essences,
    Self-working tools, uncaus'd effects, and all
    Those blind omniscients, those Almighty slaves,
    Untenanting Creation of its God!

Such men need discipline, not argument; they must be made better men, before they can become wiser. (1:122–23)

These are the contexts in which Coleridge engages the question of
poetry and of literary criticism—to his credit, let it be said that whatever one may think of his reactionary cultural and social views, he
struggled to maintain a holistic approach to all human studies. The
question of the excellences and defects of Wordsworth's poetry, and of
Wordsworth's theoretical justification of that poetry, was important for
Coleridge not simply for personal reasons, but because he felt that the
poetry (in particular, the *Lyrical Ballads*) occupied a nexus of great importance for English, and even for European, society. Today we take it
for granted that Coleridge won the argument with Wordsworth.[9] I
want to reconsider this question again by examining Coleridge's position for what it is, a polemical set of ideas about the nature and function of poetry. * * *

II

Coleridge said that, although the "Preface" to *Lyrical Ballads* was half
the product of his own brain, and although he and Wordsworth shared
many of the same ideas about poetry, a fundamental difference of
opinion about poetry separated them. He was right. Both men talked
equally about the interchanges of mind and nature, but in each the
emphasis was different; and this difference of emphasis, in the end,
proved radical. In the *Biographia* Coleridge traced the source of this
difference to eighteenth-century theories of association and sensation,
which he came to reject but which Wordsworth—if one is to judge by
the "preface" to *Lyrical Ballads*—remained committed to. Chapters
17–22 of the *Biographia* argue that the defects of Wordsworth's poetry
are the consequence of a defective, ultimately an associationist, theory
of mind.[1]

One of the root problems with associationist thought, in Coleridge's
view, was that it based itself not on "principles," or *a priori* categories,
or "innate ideas," but on observation. A poetry founded on such a the-

---

9. Even John Crowe Ransom, in his excellent discussion of Wordsworth's position, grudgingly
agrees that Coleridge's views have been—in contrast to Wordsworth's—a "permanent influence on poetic theory" (see Ransom's "William Wordsworth: Notes Toward an Understanding of Poetry," in *Wordsworth. Centenary Studies*, ed. Gilbert T. Dunklin (Princeton:
Princeton University Press, 1951), 92. A strong case for Wordsworth's theoretical importance has been made by Gene Ruoff, "Wordsworth on Language: Towards a Radical Poetics
of English Romanticism," *The Wordsworth Circle* (1972), 204–11.
1. Compare *Blake, Complete Writings*, ed. Geoffrey Keynes (London: Oxford University Press,
1966), 782–84.

ory would therefore have to be in error, for "poetry as poetry is essentially *ideal*, [and] avoids and excludes all *accident*; . . . its apparent individualities . . . must be *representative* . . . and . . . thc *persons* of poetry must be clothed with *generic* attributes" (2:45–46). Again and again Coleridge returns to this theme in his critique of Wordsworth's theoretical and practical defects. Laying so much stress on the language of people in low and rustic life as a model for poetic language, Wordsworth "leads us to place the chief value on those things on which man DIFFERS from man and to forget or disregard the high dignities, which . . . *may* be, and *ought* to be, found in all ranks" (2:130). Wordsworth's is a *levelling* poetry, perhaps even a democratic or Jacobinical poetry: a poetry which proposes that a "rustic's" mode of experience and discourse is a more appropriate norm for poetical experience and discourse than is the experience and discourse of "the educated man" (2:52–53). Coleridge vigorously opposes such an idea. In actual fact, Coleridge says,

> the rustic, from the more imperfect development of his faculties, and from the lower state of their cultivation, aims almost solely to convey *insulated facts*, either those of his scanty experience or his traditional belief; while the educated man seeks to discover and express those *connections* of things, or those relative *bearings* of fact to fact, from which some more or less general law is deducible. For *facts* are valuable to a wise man, chiefly as they lead to the discovery of the indwelling *law*, which is the true *being* of things. . . . (2:52–53)

The rustic is here used as a figure of what Coleridge called elsewhere "the ignorant man," the man who lacks the requisite self-consciousness to raise up out of his experience an image or reflex of subsistent harmony. For Coleridge, that image or reflex is the ground of imagination, and hence the essential feature of poetry; and it comes, he says, from "*meditation*, rather than . . . *observation*" (2:82). Wordsworth's views not only place entirely too much emphasis upon details and particulars, on what Coleridge calls "matters-of-fact"; they suggest that the subject of poetry lies outside the mind, somehow in "reality" or "the world." On the contrary, Coleridge insists that the poet's eye is not the observer's eye but the mind's eye, and further, that the mind's eye is directed inward, to the ideal world created and revealed through the imagination (both primary and secondary). This aspect of Coleridge's views has been insisted upon by all of his best readers: "The reality that poems 'imitate,' " as Catherine Wallace has recently put it, "is not the objective world as such but, rather, the consciousness of the poet himself *in his encounters with* the objective world. . . . the poet's only genuine subject matter is himself, and the only ideas he presents will be ideas about the activity of consciousness in the world around him."[2]

Finally, by emphasizing observation rather than meditation, and

2. C. M. Wallace, *The Design of Biographia Literaria* (London: George Allen & Unwin, 1983), 113.

matters-of-fact rather than the ideal, Wordsworth suggests that his theory of imagination is mechanistic and associationist rather than creative and idealist. This difference which Coleridge observes leads him to stress the volitional character of poetic imagination. The whole point of chapters 5–8 of the *Biographia* is to insist upon the primacy of conscious will in the human being, and to attack associationist thought as a "mechanist" philosophy which undermines the concept of the will. Poetry is and must always be a product of what he calls "the conscious will" (1:304). When the poet "brings the whole soul of man into activity," the power of imagination is "first put in action by the will and understanding, and retained under their irremissive, though gentle and unnoticed, controul" (2:15–16).

In his best practice, and recurrently in his theory as set forth in the "Preface" to the *Lyrical Ballads*, Wordsworth (according to Coleridge) illustrates Coleridge's own ideas about the ideal, the conscious, and the volitional character of poetry and imagination. The defects in Wordsworth's poetic work are traceable to certain defects in his principles, in his theory of poetry as set forth in his famous preface. Coleridge scrutinizes the preface for residual traces of Wordsworth's associationist ideas, and he then argues that the faults in the poems in the *Lyrical Ballads* are the consequence of these residual—and, so far as Wordsworth's true genius as a poet is concerned—inessential ideas. This is the method of Coleridge's critique of Wordsworth in the *Biographia*.

And in point of fact he was right; Wordsworth's poetic theory and practice remained committed to certain associationist positions as Coleridge's did not. Where Coleridge would always stress the poet's will and self-consciousness—indeed, where Coleridge would suggest that the poet's (or at least the modern poet's) central subject ought to be the act of the conscious will itself—Wordsworth's poetic impulses drove him toward insights and revelations that stood beyond the limits of the conscious will. In contemporary terms, Coleridge's is a theory of poetry as a process of revelation via mediations—indeed, a poetry whose subject is the acts and processes of mediation. Wordsworth, on the other hand, sets out in quest of an unmediated poetry, and in the preface to the *Lyrical Ballads* he offers a theoretical sketch of what such a project involves.

Briefly, what Wordsworth aspires to is a direct perception of what he calls "the subject." This is his primary aim as a poet: "I have at all times endeavoured to look steadily at my subject; consequently, there is I hope in these poems little falsehood of description. . . ."[3] This purpose, apparently so simple, is reiterated in more emphatic and explicit terms in 1815: "The powers requisite for the production of poetry are: first, those of Observation and Description,—*i.e.*, the ability to observe with accuracy things as they are in themselves, and with fidelity to describe them, unmodified by any passion or feeling existing in the mind

---

3. *The Prose Works of William Wordsworth*, ed. W. J. B. Owen and J. W. Smyser (Oxford: Clarendon, 1974), 1:133. References hereafter will be cited in the text to this edition.

of the describer" (*Prose Works* 3:26). Coleridge, however, in his distinction between "copy" and "imitation," vigorously opposes Wordsworth's ideas on this matter, and later commentators—particularly 20th century critics and academics—have sided with Coleridge, and have even come to believe that his is the more innovative view. The most influential contemporary scholarship of Wordsworth's poetry— the line established through the work of Geoffrey Hartman—has armed itself with Coleridge's vision in order to save Wordsworth's poetry from the poet himself. Wordsworth, we are now urged to think, was no mystic, and least of all was he a poet of nature. He is the poet of the mind, the revealer of the operations of the consciousness. He is, in short, what Coleridge said he was and ought to be.

In trying to understand the importance of the differences that separate Wordsworth's and Coleridge's ideas about poetry, we must not abandon what we have come to learn about Wordsworth's poetry of consciousness. What we have to see, however, is that *all* his poetry— "The Idiot Boy" as much as *The Prelude*—is a poetry based in a committment to unmediated perception, on the one hand, and to a theory of nonconscious awareness on the other (what Wordsworth calls "habits"). Both aspects of his ideas about poetry are intimately related to each other. In his critique of Wordsworth, Coleridge argued that Wordsworth's attack on poetic diction in the Preface to the *Lyrical Ballads* was not, (could not have been), fundamental, but was rather directed to peculiar circumstances which had developed in English poetry in the eighteenth century (2:40–42). This is a very conservative reading of Wordsworth's ideas, and in the end it is wrong. Wordsworth's whole argument that there neither is nor can be any real or essential difference between poetry and prose is grounded in an impulse to avert altogether the grids, the Kantian "categories," and all the complex mediations which stand between the act of perception and the objects perceived. It did not matter to Wordsworth whether the "subject" of the poet was an idiot boy, a broken pot, an abstract reality (nature, social classes or conventions, psychological events like "fidelity"), God, or even "the mind of man" itself and all its complex states of consciousness. The ideal was to set these matters free of the mediations which necessarily conveyed them, either to one's self or to others.

This could be done, Wordsworth believed, by grounding poetry not in "the conscious will" but in "spontaneous" and "powerful feelings," on the one hand, and "habits of meditation" on the other (1:127):

> Poems to which any value can be attached were never produced on any variety of subjects but by a man who, being possessed of more than usual organic sensibility, had also thought long and deeply. For our continued influxes of feeling are modified and directed by our thoughts, which are indeed the representatives of all our past feelings; and, as by contemplating the relation of these general representatives to each other, we discover what is really important to men, so, by the repetition and continuance of this act, our feelings will be connected with important subjects,

till at length . . . such habits of mind will be produced, that, by obeying blindly and mechanically the impulses of those habits, we shall describe objects, and utter sentiments . . . that the understanding of the Reader must necessarily be in some degree enlightened, and his affections strengthened and purified. (1:127)

This is a highly pragmatic, even a tactical, way of stating his position. Not until Shelley would reformulate Wordsworth's ideas more than twenty years later would the theory insinuated by Wordsworth receive a comprehensive and adequate formulation. This would happen when Shelley provided Wordsworth's ideas with a broad social and political dimension, a comprehensive theory of culture in which poetry was revealed as a set of various related, and imaginatively grounded, social practices.

That subject is, however, beyond the scope of my present concerns. Here I want only to indicate how consciousness and the structure of all forms of mediation are viewed by Wordsworth. Simply, they are impediments to clear vision. For Wordsworth, to show (in practice) or argue (in theory) that the mediations are themselves the subject of the poet is to abandon the ground of any nonsubjective experience, and hence to abandon the ground of all human intercourse and social life, which involve sympathetic relationships between persons distinct and different. To Wordsworth, Coleridge's position also involves a theoretical contradiction: for we cannot have knowledge of anything, not even knowledge of the mediations, unless an unmediated consciousness is at some point admitted to acts of knowledge and perception. In effect, Coleridge's Kantian position, by resituating the problem of knowledge, has merely reopened it at the level of epistemology. Coleridge's position stands under threat to the critique of an infinite regress: what will mediate the mediations? Coleridge's eventual response to this question, developed out of Schelling, was to argue for a continuous and self-developing process of mediated knowledge—that is to say, it was to make a virtue of necessity and turn the infinite regress into an organic process. It was also, needless to say, to have literally postponed both the problem and the answer to the problem. The move was a brilliant finesse.

Wordsworth took a different course—less spectacular and intellectually brilliant but in the end perhaps more daring and profound, at least so far as poetry is concerned. Observing and describing without the intervention of consciousness or subjective mediations, following blindly and mechanically the unselfconsciously meditated directions of unselfconscious feeling and thought: these are Wordsworth's remarkable procedures. Their object, as he says in various ways, is to avoid the veils of familiarity—the mediations—through which we experience the world. Unlike Coleridge, Wordsworth is seeking for a poetry, and a mode of perception, which will lay the mortal mind asleep in order that it may see into the life of things—in order that it may transcend the limits of experience laid down by Coleridge's self-conscious will and Kant's categorical imperatives. This program, needless to say, is anything but supernaturalist; it is in fact a deeply materialist and mundane program. What it seeks to transcend is not this world or concrete experience but the ideologies of this world and our modes of perceiving it. Coleridge was quite right to oppose this program on principle, for Wordsworth's ideal, in principle, is toward a poetry in which the mind transcends its own volitions and categories; in which the mind, following not consciousness but "feelings," "impulses," and "sensations," is suddenly confronted with the unknown, the revelation of what is miraculous. Wordsworth calls his ideal "sympathy," an experience in which

> passions and thoughts and feelings are . . . connected with our
> moral sentiments and animal sensations, and with the causes
> which excite these; with the operations of the elements, and the
> appearances of the visible universe; with storm and sunshine,
> with the revolutions of the seasons, with cold and heat, with loss
> of friends and kindred, with injuries and resentments, gratitude
> and hope, with fear and sorrow. (1:142)

At such moments—glimpsing a hedgehog or a flower, observing a peculiar encounter between two people, being wrapped in a specific atmospheric moment, perhaps of wind and humidity—the mind will be led to feel that it suddenly *understands*, that it has been brought to some moment of ultimate knowledge. In Wordsworth we are gently led on to these moments by the affections; it is not the conscious will that controls experiences of primary or secondary imagination, it is "habit," "impulse," and "feeling." Consciousness follows experience, not the other way round.

When Coleridge linked Wordsworth's poetry to materialist and associationist principles, then, his insight was acute. Equally acute was the way he attacked Wordsworth's "matter-of-factness." The "laborious minuteness and fidelity in the representation of objects, and . . . the insertion of accidental circumstances" (2:126) infects the poetry with what Coleridge sees as a sort of misplaced concreteness. Wordsworth's insistence upon treating *peculiar* experiences puts at risk the Coleridgean ideal of poetic harmony and the reconciliation of opposite and discordant qualities. In Wordsworth, Coleridge is constantly being brought up against resistant particulars, details that somehow evade— or rather, details that seem *determined* to evade—the necessary poetic harmony and reconciliation. Coleridge calls this Wordsworth's "*accidentality*," and he says that it contravenes "the essence of poetry," which must be, he adds, "catholic and abstract" (2:126). "Accidentality" works against Coleridge's idea that poetry is the most philosophical of discourses because it alone can reveal the general in the especial, the sameness in the differences.

To Wordsworth, however, accidentality was precisely the means by which feelings and impulses outwitted the mind's catholic and abstracting censors. "I am sensible," he says,

> that my associations must have sometimes been particular instead
> of general, and that, consequently, giving to things a false impor-

tance, I may have sometimes written on unworthy subjects; but I am less apprehensive on this account, than that my language may frequently have suffered from those arbitrary connections of feelings and ideas with particular words and phrases, from which no man can altogether protect himself. . . . Such faulty expressions . . . I would willingly take all reasonable pains to correct. But it is dangerous to make these alterations on the simple authority of a few individuals, or even of certain classes of men; for where the understanding of an Author is not convinced, or his feelings altered, this cannot be done without great injury to himself: for his own feelings are his stay and support. . . . To this may be added, that the critic ought never to forget that he is himself exposed to the same errors as the Poet, and, perhaps, in a much greater degree. . . . (1:153)

Once again the ground of Wordsworth's decisions, both as regards his subject matter and his choice of words, is determined by "feelings." He means to act, as Blake said of Jesus, by impulse, and not by rules. The critical mind—even the poet's own conscious and critical operations—may suspect accidentality and arbitrariness in the poem's subject matter or language, but if the feelings which led the poet to his choices cannot be shown to be factitious, then the choices must be maintained. It is not merely that the heart has its reasons; the choice must be maintained because *the consciousness has its reasons. The mind* directs itself to the ordering of experience, to the establishment of harmonies; *the feelings* direct themselves to the enlarging of experience itself. Wordsworth's "feeling" is what Blake called "the Prolific": judge and censor of the judgmental and censorious consciousness, the feelings and their concomitant train of accidentalities refuse to let the mind settle into its *a priori* harmonies.

Coleridge is an ideologue, and his theory of poetry is not merely an ideology of poetry; it finally argues that poetry is the perfect form of Ideology (more philosophical than philosophy, more concrete than history). Poetry is the revelation and expression of the Ideal, of the idea and what is ideational, of the world as a play of the mediations of consciousness. It is the product of the conscious will. But to Wordsworth, the true human will is not located in the ego or the superego, it lies in the unconscious; it is a form of desire, an eros, not a form of thought, an eidolon. A poetry of sympathy rather than a poetry of consciousness, it covets irrelevant detail and "accidentality" as the limit and test of its own imaginative reach.

Insofar as it is a poetry of the mind and consciousness, Wordsworth's work is strongest and most characteristic when it represents mind at the moment of its dawning and self-discovery, consciousness falling upon itself in its instants of wonder and surprise. In such poetry—*The Prelude* is the preeminent example—consciousness is rendered as an experience rather than as a knowledge or form of thought. The difference between Coleridge's and Wordsworth's theorizing on these matters reflects, then, a small but in the end crucial difference of emphasis: for Coleridge, poetry is an idea and is to be

understood via the networks of intellectual mediations which are poetry's ultimate ground and "principles"; for Wordsworth poetry is an
experience and is to be understood primarily in the event itself, but in
any case only through the rhetorical and sympathetic networks which
the poems set in motion. It is a matter, as Wordsworth's "Preface"
says, of contracts and arrangements, not—as Coleridge insists—of *a
priori* ideas and "principles."

Ultimately, Coleridge's theory of poetry sees it as a continuous play
of signifiers and signifieds, and its object is to provide, in the traces
left by this play, glimpses of the ordering process which is the ground
of the play. For Wordsworth, however, the semiotic dance traces a ref-
erential system back into the material world. In the play of language,
the dance of the signifiers and the signifieds, we glimpse the structure
in which the system of symbols and the order of references hold themselves together. Coleridge, too, says that poetry affords a glimpse of a
superior reality lying behind the appearances of things. But for Coleridge this superior reality is nonmaterial, in the order of platonic or
ideal forms. For Wordsworth, by contrast, the order is emphatically
concrete and material, an order of actual sympathies and arrangements which we have, in our getting and spending, only neglected or
forgotten. In Wordsworth, the play of the signifiers and the signifieds,
the spectacle of the mediations, lies under judgment to a superior reality, the order of the referents. Wordsworth's poetry is a symbolic system which aims to disappear, but with a flash that reveals the invisible
world—which is to say, *this* material and human world, the very world
of all of us that has too regularly "been disappeared" (so to speak) in
the symbols and ideas we have made of it.

*   *   *

THOMAS McFARLAND

[Coleridge's Theory of the Imagination]†

Coleridge—together with other Romantics, and indeed with virtually
all who have thought on the matter—saw that "imagination" (*a*) bears
witness to the indispensability of nature—that is to say, an image must
have as its content the representation of an external object (an 'it
is')—and (*b*) that it simultaneously bears witness to the mind's independence of nature—that is to say, one can "imagine" an image of nature even though the object itself is not present in space or time: I can
babble of non-existent green fields or think of non-existent perfect islands; I can even make play with Berkeley's trees in the park—I can
imagine them as oaks, and then I can imagine them as beeches, I can
imagine them in the autumn, or budding in the spring, as saplings or
full-grown, and when I am tired of imagining them, I can simply dis-

† From *Coleridge and the Pantheist Tradition* (Oxford: Clarendon Press, 1969), 306–310.
Reprinted by permission of the publisher.

miss them from my mind. And in this possibility I realize that the imagination is intimately connected with the will—for in "imagination", as distinct from that which we call "reality", I change or alter the existence of images simply by willing to do so.

Now the Scylla and Charybdis that guard the approach to a true understanding of Coleridge's theory of imagination consist, on the one hand, in the error of Richards that takes "imagination" out of its historical context in Romanticism and Coleridgean thought, and, on the other hand—and this is both a more common and a less noble error than the first—in the attempt to make the conception *merely* historical, and even merely quirkily and idiosyncratically Coleridgean. What in fact does Coleridge mean by "imagination"? To this the answer is clear: *he means exactly what we all mean in ordinary language by the word imagination.* By "imagination" Coleridge means what Descartes means by "imaginatio"; what Kant means by "Einbildungskraft"; what Wordsworth means by "imagination"; what Fichte, and Schelling, and Herder, and the Schlegels, and all others, mean wherever they refer to the imaging faculty. For "imagination" is a given in experience, not the property, nor the terminological construct, of a special philosopher. "Imagination", as Spinoza says, is precisely "the idea wherewith the mind contemplates a thing as present" (*Ethica* v. 24. Demonstratio.) The differences in the formulations of the nature of imagination are dictated by differing conceptions of the faculty's *function* in a systematic view of reality.

The resurgence of interest in the nature of the imagination during the Romantic era was a corollary of the resurgence of interest in the external world. The decline of trust in externally given forms that, for whatever reason, characterized Baroque and Neoclassic activity in the seventeenth and eighteenth centuries, led to a diminution in the importance attached to imagination by poetic theory and philosophical schematism. Thus the great Descartes makes *imaginatio* a faculty inferior to *intellectio* (which needs no images). Hobbes thinks of "IMAGINATION" as "nothing but *decaying sense.* . . . *Imagination* and *Memory*, are but one thing. . . . *Reason* is the pace" (*Leviathan* [London, 1651], pp. 5, 22). Conversely, the great revival of interest in external nature that became one of the hallmarks of Romanticism was necessarily accompanied by renewed interest in the scope and function of the previously despised *imaginatio*. Imagination now became this "wonderful faculty" (Schelling, *Werke* [1856–61], i. 332 n.), or that "awful Power" (Wordsworth, *The Prelude*, Book VI, line 594), and was hailed with reverence—as, for instance, in Baader's musing about "imagination" as "a wonder of wonders", which is "no mere word, but a microcosmos of secret forces within us" (Baader, *Werke* [1850–60], xi. 85).

In this new assertion of the importance of imagination, however, Schelling's emphasis does not coincide with that of Coleridge. For Schelling, imagination was involved in the creation of reality itself. Since "the system of Nature is at the same time the system of our Spirit" (*Werke*, ii. 39), it would follow that the imagination recognizes no essential difference between object and image. "One might explain imagination as the power of transposing itself through complete self-activity into complete passivity" (*Werke*, i. 332 n.). The function of imagination in a system of absolute idealism is always constitutive and regulative, therefore, never, as with Coleridge, truly mediating and reconciling—for indeed, there is no need to mediate between "nature" and "spirit" when they are really the same. Thus Friedrich Schlegel can say that "in der Einbildungskraft ist es die Natur, die in uns denkt"[1] (*Philosophische Vorlesungen* [1836–37], ii. 461)—a pantheist emphasis quite different from Coleridge's conception. Again, Fichte says that "Alle Realität . . . blos durch die Einbildungskraft hervorgebracht werde"[2] (*Grundlage der gesammten Wissenschaftslehre* (Leipzig, 1794), p. 195). And Schelling says that "Einbildungskraft" is the "only faculty" that can "comprehend negative and positive activity and represent them in one common product". But his context is an assertion that "the object is not something which is given to us from outside, but only a product of the original spiritual self-activation, which by opposed activities creates and produces a third in common" (*Werke*, i. 357). For Schelling, therefore, as for Fichte, imagination was the coordinator of the reciprocal energies by which (in the words of Schelling's youthful poem) "Eine Kraft, Ein Pulsschlag nur, Ein Leben/Ein Wechselspiel von Hemmen und von Streben"[3] poured out all reality (Plitt, *Aus Schellings Leben* [1869], i. 287). Indeed a recent commentator, noting that Schelling's imagination "can be formulated as participation of man in the creation of the world", goes so far as to term "Schellings Philosophie eine *Mystik der Einbildungskraft*"[4] (Rudolf Hablürzel, *Dialektik und Einbildungskraft; F. W. J. Schellings Lehre von der menschlichen Erkenntniss* (Basel, 1954), pp. 81, 82). In Coleridge's view, on the contrary, imagination mediates between a nature of *real* objects and a *real* "I am", creates poetry, not the world, and maintains the priority of the "I am" over the "it is". Coleridge was closer to Kant than he was to Schelling, and closer to Kant than Schelling was to Kant, who maintains that "die Einbildungskraft nach dem Assoziationsgesetz macht unseren Zustand der Zufriedenheit physisch abhängig", on the one hand, but on the other "ist Werkzeug der Vernunft und ihrer Ideen" and therefore "asserts our independence of the influences of nature"[5] (Kant, *Werke*, v. 341). Yet Coleridge differed from Kant also by his practical emphasis on poetry, and by his active faith in religion. The function of imagination accordingly takes on in his thought a religious coloration which it does not have in the Kantian scheme.

Though an emphasis on imagination always means an emphasis on external nature, imagination itself is the exclusive faculty for mental *poiesis* or *fiction*—is, as Baader says, "die Mutter der Poesie".[6] In his

1. "In the imagination it is nature that thinks in us." [Editors' note.]
2. "All reality . . . is brought forth merely by the imagination." [Editors' note.]
3. "One force, one pulsation, one life / An interplay of ceasing and striving" [Editors' note.]
4. "Schelling's philosophy a *mysticism of the imagination*." [Editors' note.]
5. "For the imagination, in accordance with the law of association, makes our state of contentment physically dependent"; "is an instrument of reason and its ideas" (Kant, *Judgment*, 152). [Editors' note.]
6. "The Mother of poetry." [Editors' note.]

own poetry Coleridge, both in theory and in practice, conceived the imagination as a bulwark for the primacy of the "I am". Thus *The Ancient Mariner*, a poem of "pure imagination", depends as little as possible upon the memory or reproduction of actual scenes or objects experienced in the external world, but is rather a willed creation and coordination of images by the "I am". Wordsworth's poetic practice, on the other hand, tended towards actual recollection of the real presence of external nature, or even present description of that nature, and hence it was that Coleridge was "disposed to conjecture" that Wordsworth "has mistaken the co-presence of fancy with imagination for the operation of the latter singly" (*Biographia* [1907], i. 194). Compare Hartman: "An unresolved opposition between Imagination and Nature prevents [Wordsworth] from becoming a visionary poet. It is a paradox, though not an unfruitful one, that he should scrupulously record nature's workmanship, which prepares the soul for its independence from sense-experience, yet refrain to use that independence out of respect of nature. His greatest verse *still takes its origin* in the memory of given experiences to which he is often pedantically faithful" (Geoffrey Hartman, *Wordsworth's Poetry 1787–1814* (New Haven and London, 1964), p. 39). Certainly one of the reasons why Coleridge divided the imaginative function into "imagination" and "fancy", the latter taking upon itself the inferior functional status of Descartes' *imaginatio* or Hobbes's equation of Imagination and Memory, was that he wanted to emphasize as much as possible the freedom of the poetic imagination from slavish dependence on the "it is". "Fancy is indeed no other than a mode of Memory" (*Biographia*, i. 202), while "Imagination" is "essentially *vital*, even as all objects (*as* objects) are essentially fixed and dead" (*Biographia*, i. 202). In short, for Coleridge the theory of imagination allowed the recognition and use of the "it is" while strongly insisting on the primacy and control of the "I am", and in this sense was a "reconciling and mediatory power" (*Works* [1853], i. 436).

Though Coleridge's later definitions of imagination are more carefully elaborated than his early statements, they seem to elucidate rather than contradict them. In his full statement in the *Biographia Literaria* the "primary IMAGINATION" is the "living Power and prime Agent of all human Perception", a "repetition in the finite mind of the eternal act of creation in the infinite I AM" (i. 202). Though this definition might well owe something to Fichte or Boehme * * *, it is also, and at least, an expansion of that definition of 1804 in which "Imagination" in the "highest sense of the word" is a "dim Analogue of Creation, not all that we can *believe* but all that we can *conceive* of creation" (*Letters*, ii. 1034). And this in its turn is a restatement of a formulation of 1796, where (though at that time without the term "imagination") Coleridge enunciates the Platonism that "Man . . . is urged to develop the powers of the creator, and by new combinations of these powers to imitate his creativeness" (*The Watchman*, p. 101). Again, the secondary imagination in the *Biographia Literaria* "dissolves, diffuses, dissipates, in order to recreate" and "at all events it

struggles to idealize and to unify" (i. 202). And this emphasis is her-
alded by the definition in 1804 of "Imagination" as the "*modifying*
Power" (*Letters*, ii. 1034); still earlier by the "shaping spirit of imagination" of the *Dejection* ode; again still earlier by the "*Imagination*"
which in 1802 is the "*modifying, and co-adunating* Faculty" (*Letters*, ii.
866). These early flowerings open from still earlier buds—though not
as yet named "imagination". Thus in December 1796 Coleridge speaks
of "my own shaping and disquisitive mind" (*Letters*, i. 271); in March
1796 of "the catenating Faculty . . . the silk thread that ought to run
through the Pearl-chain of Ratiocination" (*Letters*, i. 193). Likewise
for Fancy. "Fancy", in 1817, "has no other counters to play with, but
fixities and definites. The Fancy is indeed no other than a mode of
Memory emancipated from the order of time and space." In 1804
"Fancy" is "the *aggregating* power" (*Letters*, ii. 1034); in 1802 "Fancy"
is "the aggregating Faculty" (*Letters*, ii. 865).

In his earliest statements Coleridge does not differentiate between
"Imagination" and "Fancy"—using them (as indeed *Phantasie* and *Einbildungskraft* are customarily used in German) as synonyms. Thus in
June 1796 he says that Thelwall's poetry lacks "the *light* of Fancy"
(*Letters*, i. 221), while in May of that year he says that Godwin lacks
"strength of intellect" and "the powers of imagination". None the less,
though not fully schematized, the "imagination" is, from early in his
career, clearly important to Coleridge as a central and vital power of
his poetic being. In 1799, for instance, he speaks of "my Imagination"
as "tired, down, flat and powerless" (*Letters*, i. 470). Again, in December 1796 he says that Southey "does not possess opulence of Imagination, lofty-paced Harmony, or that *toil* of thinking, which is necessary
in order to plan a *Whole*" (*Letters*, i. 293–4)—and it is evident here
that we see the beginnings of the theory by which "imagination" struggles "to idealize and to unify" (*Biographia*, i. 202). The later differentiation between the two terms actually puts the "I am" more firmly in
control of "imagination" than when that faculty had also to bear the
burden of Hobbes's equation of "*Imagination* and *Memory*". Imagination, as it were, remains in the sled while the baby of "fancy" is sacrificed to the "it is". By allowing "fancy" to discharge one necessary
function of the imaging faculty—that is, to image external reality by
aggregation and memory—Coleridge is able to emphasize the free creativity of the imagination, to co-ordinate it with "the eternal act of creation in the infinite I AM" (*Biographia*, i. 202).

Furthermore, Coleridge's distinction of imagination and fancy (despite his own explicit claims, e.g. *Biographia*, i. 60–61) does not really
divide the imaging faculty, but only distinguishes its modes. Thus in a
marginal note on the flyleaf of Maass's *Versuch über die Einbildungskraft, verbesserte Ausgabe* (Halle und Leipzig, 1797), Coleridge
speaks of "the sensuous Einbildungskraft . . . which we call Imagination, Fancy &c. all poor & inadequate Terms. . .". Coleridge's feeling
that he improves these poor & inadequate Terms' by fixing special significances for the synonymous "Imagination, Fancy" is actually li-
censed by an ambiguity in the meaning of imagination in ordinary

language. If we examine our common understanding of the word "imagination" we see that the single term is used in two ways, one somewhat denigrative and one honorific: (1) a child cries out in the night that a monster is in its room; its parents assure the child that "it's only your imagination"; while (2) the highest praise that can crown recognition of capability is to say that a man has "imagination". It is the existence of the unbidden mental phantoms of the first order that sanctions Coleridge's "fancy", and it is the unified, consciously willed, creative control of the potential ramifications of a situation, signalized by the second use, that sanctions Coleridge's "imagination".

So too the distinction between primary and secondary imagination. To perceive any object we must have an image—the chair we perceive remains in the room, and another chair, made up of impulses in our brains, occurs in our consciousnesses. We could perceive nothing without such images, and hence their faculty, the "primary" imagination is "the living Power and prime Agent of all human Perception". But we can "imagine" the chair in another way: we can leave the room, and then, by willing to do so, bring to mind the "image" of that same chair. This "secondary" imagination, accordingly, is "an echo of the former, co-existing with the conscious will . . ." and can "dissolve" and "recreate" images into a poetic whole.

*　　*　　*

BEN KNIGHTS

From The Idea of the Clerisy: Samuel Taylor Coleridge†

> I hold it the disgrace and calamity of a professed statesman not to know and acknowledge, that a permanent, nationalized, learned order, a national clerisy or Church is an essential element of a rightly constituted nation, without which it wants the best security alike for its permanence and its progression; and for which neither tract societies nor conventicles, nor Lancasterian schools, nor mechanics' institutions, nor lecture bazaars under the absurd name of universities, nor all these collectively can be a substitute.
>
> Coleridge, *On the Constitution of the Church and State*
> *according to the Idea of Each*

It is not merely because he gave us the word that Coleridge figures first in a study of the idea of the clerisy in nineteenth-century England. In his last completed work, *On the Constitution of the Church and State according to the Idea of Each*, he gave a wide-ranging account of the clerisy and its relations to society. But the idea was germane to his most central thinking, and in his work, his aspirations,

† From *The Idea of the Clerisy in the Nineteenth Century* (Cambridge: Cambridge University Press, 1978), 37–42, 63–71, 237, 240–41. Reprinted by permission of the publisher. [All footnotes are the author's.]

and dilemmas we can watch the theory growing, and sense what needs it was supposed to answer. Individual as his theory is, its study is an essential preliminary to the study of the clerisy theme in the nineteenth century, for his response to problems which in fact survived him was in a sense paradigmatic. Above all, Coleridge's argument on behalf of the clerisy must make us aware of the interconnection of philosophy, theology, and social theory within educational politics. Let us not forget his own words: "Of this however we may be certain . . . that our minds are in a state unsusceptible of Knowledge when we feel an eagerness to detect the falsehood of an adversary's reasonings, not a sincere wish to discover if there be Truth in them."[1] While asking questions about the nature of Coleridge's projected order, we must be aware of the fertility of his insights, and even, paradoxically, of the dependence of those insights on the very theory which we wish to criticise.

HARMONY OR DISSOLUTION?

In June 1817, the Prime Minister, Lord Liverpool, received a letter from Coleridge, by then domiciled with the Gillmans at Highgate. Social tensions, following the end of the Napoleonic Wars and the subsequent economic depression, were increasing: sterner measures were in train for the control of the radical press, the army was standing by to put down insurrections, and Cobbett had fled to the United States. Coleridge wrote to strip down the affairs of the nation to their essential principles. As R. J. White pointed out, the letter is a classic instance of Coleridge's sense of the interconnectedness of things. His science, his philosophy, and his sociology are inextricable from each other.

> As long as the principles of our Gentry and Clergy are grounded on a false Philosophy, which retains but the name of *Logic*, and has succeeded in rendering Metaphysics a term of opprobrium, all the Sunday and National schools in the world will not preclude Schism in the middle & lower classes. The predominant philosophy is the keynote.[2]

The national health required the acceptance of what Coleridge was beginning to call the "dynamic philosophy"—that system of thought which he had been working towards with the help of the writings of Kant, Fichte, and Schelling, since his German visit in 1799, and which he saw as a continuation of the great Platonic tradition. The mechanical philosophy which it should replace was, he argued, inimical to social life because it located life not in the whole but in the parts, and viewed institutions as artificial contrivances of convenience. The consequence was the disaster of natural rights theory, of which Coleridge shared Burke's opinion:

1. *The Friend*, CW, IV, pp. i, 336–7.
2. CL, IV, p. 762; and see R. J. White, *Waterloo to Peterloo* (Harmondsworth, 1968), pp. 58–9; *Political Thought of Coleridge*, ed. R. J. White (Cambridge, 1938), p. 210.

The independent atoms of the state of nature cluster round a
common centre and make a convention; that convention becomes
a constitution of government; then the makers and the made
make a contract, which ensures to the former the right of breaking it whenever it shall seem good to them, and assigns to the
governed an indefeasible right of sovereignty over their governors,
which being withstood, this one-sided compact is dissolved, the
compages fall abroad into the independent atoms aforesaid,
which are then to dance the Hayes until a new constitution is
made for them. For, as Mr. Locke and Major Cartwright saga-
ciously observe, an atom is an atom, neither more nor less, and by
the pure attribute of his atom has an equal claim with every other
atom to be constituent and demiurgic on all occasions.[3]

Amusing, after the second *Treatise of Civil Government*, but not exactly open to what a Cartwright might be trying to achieve. "The
predominant philosophy is the keynote." Coleridge linked the mechanistic nature of enlightenment thought with its individualism and its
materialism, and saw these blooms as rooted in the common soil of associationist psychology. But enlightenment thought had had its day,
and one had now to work one's way back to the recognition that life
was not to be predicated of parts, but of wholes. The thesis of the primacy of speculative philosophy, with its implied correlative—the importance of the speculative philosopher—must be seen in the context
of what Alfred Cobban rather misleadingly called the "revolt against
the eighteenth century."[4] Cobban's simplification of both eighteenth
century and revolt, as well as the implied chronological watershed, is
nevertheless well grounded in the self-images of those whom he studied. For Coleridge, as for Burke, the age of reason (so called) ended
quite logically in the excesses of the French Revolution.

The primacy of speculative philosophy runs through Coleridge's
work, and is the premise upon which his own practice as a prophetic
social commentator is based. Two examples may clarify the point. The
breakdown of Roman politics in the era of the triumvirates and civil
wars was one with the dearth of philosophy:

The eye which was the light of the body had become filmed and
jaundiced. The only two nations which possessed intellect, and
with that intellect the power of communicating order and civilisation were corrupted and became the vilest of the vile.[5]

Or again, he asserted that:

the history of all civilised nations . . . the recorded experience of
Mankind [attests] the important fact—that the Taste and Character, the whole tone of Manners and Feeling, and above all the Religious (at least the Theological) and the Political tendencies of

---

3. *CL*, IV, p. 761.
4. *Edmund Burke and the Revolt against the Eighteenth Century* (1929); and cf. David
   Cameron's *The Social Thought of Rousseau and Burke* (1973)—an effective antidote to some
   of the glibber generalisations about "eighteenth-century thought".
5. *Philosophical Lectures*, ed. Kathleen Coburn (1949), p. 221.

the public mind, have ever borne such a close correspondence, so
distinct and evident an Analogy to the predominant system of
speculative Philosophy . . . as must remain inexplicable, unless
we admit not only a reaction and interdependence on both sides,
but a powerful, tho' most often indirect influence of the latter on
the former.[6]

It would be a travesty of Coleridge's thought to say that he anachro-
nistically asserted a kind of philosophical determinism at a time when
the political economists had already drawn attention to the importance of material wealth in creating the national life. The Coleridge
who involved himself in the struggle for the passage of Sir Robert
Peel's child labour bill, or whose letters show him concerned in the
debate over the Corn Laws, was not one to overlook the economic
foundations of society. But his very awareness of the importance of
economic activity seems to have bred a correspondingly great emphasis on the intellectual activity that was to keep economic life in its
proper, subordinate place. The formation of a just understanding of
the parts of the national life in relation to one another depended on
the currency of a life-giving philosophy among the higher classes.

Characteristic of the imbalance between elements of the national
life was the development of civilisation at the expense of cultivation.
Coleridge's distinction between the two must be seen in the context of
other complementary pairs of terms to which the dialectical nature of
his thought gave rise. Like other pairs of opposites (Coleridge was at
pains to distinguish between opposites, which were complementary,
and contraries, which were essentially different from each other)—
reason and understanding, genius and talent, imagination and fancy—
it represents another aspect of that *Entzweiung* which Kant's
successors strove to overcome. The "permanent distinction and the
occasional contrast, between cultivation and civilisation," between
material progress and moral culture, was one which all Coleridge's
successors retained.[7] The distinction served not only in criticising the
contemporary world but as an aid to reflection on history, since periods could be characterised in terms of the predominance of civilisation or culture. We must remember the

> momentous fact, fearfully as it has been, and even now is exem-
> plified in a neighbour country, that a nation can never be too cul-
> tivated, but may easily become an over-civilised, race.[8]

First publicly made in 1808, the distinction remained central to
Church and State over twenty years later. Civilisation

> is in itself but a mixed good, if not far more a corrupting influ-
> ence, the hectic of disease, not the bloom of health, and a nation
> so distinguished more fitly to be called a varnished than a pol-
> ished people; where this civilisation is not grounded in *cultiva-*

---

6. *CL*, IV, p. 759.
7. *The Friend, CW*, I, p. 494; see the discussion in Raymond Williams' *Culture and Society*
   (Harmondsworth, 1963), Introduction and pt I.
8. *The Friend, CW*, I, p. 494.

tion, in the harmonious development of those qualities and faculties that characterize our *humanity*.[9]

England was in danger of becoming permanently enamoured of civilisation, and hence wasting in disease. Yet to represent the threat thus was to take the actual course of material development as the only possible type of such development; thus the corrective to existing civilisation was envisaged not as an alternative form of civilisation but as cultivation.

In the place of the philosophy of the enlightenment we should put the "dynamic philosophy," whose acceptance would be—the musical image is insistent—a return to harmony, to a recognition of the essential interconnectedness of things. Towards the end of his life Coleridge once said, as reported by his nephew:

> All harmony is founded on a relation to rest—a relative rest. Take a metallic plate and strew sand on it; sound an harmonic chord over the sand, and the grains will whirl about in circles and other geometrical figures, all, as it were, depending on some point of sand relatively at rest. Sound a discord, and every grain will whisk about without any order at all, in no figures and with no points of rest.
>
> The clerisy of a nation, that is, its learned men, whether poets, or philosophers, or scholars, are these points of relative rest. There could be no order, no harmony of the whole without them.[1]

The development of the idea of the clerisy is inseparable from the war against mechanist philosophy and associationist psychology, a campaign which Coleridge found prefigured in Plato's confrontation with the sophists. For Plato

> taught the idea, namely the possibility, and the duty of all who would arrive at the greatest perfection of the human mind, of striving to contemplate things not in their phenomenon, not in their superficies, but in their essential powers, first as they exist in relation to the other powers, then as they exist in relation to the other powers co-existing with them, but lastly and chiefly as they exist in the Supreme Mind, independent of all material division, distinct and yet indivisible.[2]

We shall return to the image of Plato and his reinstatement of universals. Here I must insist on the political dimension of Coleridge's thought. Continued adherence to a false philosophy threatens society with dissolution in asserting the state as an artificial contrivance for meeting the needs of an aggregate of individuals. But the state, asserts Coleridge, is no such thing:

> It is high time, My Lord, that the subjects of Christian Governments should be taught that neither historically nor morally, in

9. CCS, pp. 33–4.
1. *The Table Talk and Omniana of Samuel Taylor Coleridge*, ed. H. N. Coleridge (1917), *sub* 10 April 1832.
2. *Philosophical Lectures*, p. 166.

fact or by right, have men made the state; but that the state, and that alone makes them men.

Depend upon it, whatever is grand, whatever is truly organic and living, the whole is prior to the parts.

> Who does not know what a poor worthless creature man would be if it were not for the unity of human nature being preserved from age to age through the godlike form of the state?[3]

The state is defined in terms of its ultimate end. There is, however, a corollary, though one on which Coleridge was chary of insisting. If the state fails in its moral and educational duty towards its citizens, it absolves them of their obligation to the state. Thus, in speaking of Henry VIII's alienation of the church lands (in Coleridge's terms, the "Nationality"), he speaks of them as dedicated to "the potential divinity in every man, which is the ground and condition of his *civil* existence, that without which a man can be neither free nor obliged, and by which alone, therefore, he is capable of being a free subject—a citizen."[4] The theory of the minimal state is therefore self-destructive. The alternative to a recognition of the state's ethical role to humanise its citizens is the continuance of a state of affairs which will lead straight to social dissolution and the naked struggle of particular interests.

*   *   *

The burden of this chapter has been the argument that Coleridge's idea of the clerisy—although not fully developed until his last years—was active in his thinking all along. From an early age he looked to an elite to purify and revivify society, hoped that he himself might play such a mediating part, and developed a theory in which speculative philosophy was essential to the cultivation, ultimately even the existence, of the nation. His struggles with epistemology forced his attention to pedagogical issues. It would indeed have been possible for him to develop a theory of an intellectual elite without recourse to other than German materials. But in fact there were two other important stimuli. One was his high regard for the Hebrew prophets ("protectors of the Nation and privileged state moralists")[5] and his conviction that the Bible should be expounded prophetically. The other was his growing commitment to the Anglican Church, in which, he believed, despite the historical conflation of the national church and the church of Christ, certain essentials had been maintained. Historically, the church had provided a home for the national clerisy. This held advantages for men of letters, and even by the time of the *Biographia* he was observing that "the church presents to every man of learning and genius a profession in which he may cherish a rational hope of being able to unite the widest schemes of literary utility with the strictest performance of professional duties."[6] But the chief advantages were

---

3. Letter to Lord Liverpool, *CL*, IV, p. 762; *Philosophical Lectures*, p. 196.
4. CCS, p. 41; as John Barrell notes in his introduction, this is a "remarkable contribution to the theory of political obligation".
5. CCS, p. 29.
6. *Biographia*, I, p. 154.

for society as a whole, and in a passage which he reproduced in *Church and State* he wrote as follows:

> That to every parish throughout the kingdom there is transplanted a germ of civilisation; that in the remotes villages there is a nucleus round which the capabilities of the place may crystallize and brighten; a model sufficiently superior to excite, yet sufficiently near to encourage and facilitate imitation; this, the unobtrusive, continuous agency of a Protestant church establishment, this it is which the patriot and the philanthropist, who would fain unite the love of peace with the faith in the progressive amelioration of mankind, cannot estimate at too high a price.[7]

Memories of Ottery St Mary haunt Coleridge's intellectual odyssey. The church provided a model for an intellectual establishment upon whose value to society he had long brooded in terms which he could find among the common stock of Renaissance humanism.[8] But more than that, it provided a model for diffusion, for the means of spreading the benefits accrued through speculative and scholarly activity. The history of education "has been this: from the schools to the pulpit, not by any long circuit but directly, to the common people."[9] The existence of a national clerisy had been one of the characteristic features of the period of English cultural efflorescence of the sixteenth and seventeenth centuries to which he looked back so fondly, and the style of whose Anglican divines he had attempted to adopt. The clerisy as an audience for the intellectual achievements of its own members was contrasted with the "public"—usually a derogatory term—and its disappearance was shown to be a feature of that dead time that began in 1688: "After the Revolution, the spirit of the nation became more commercial than it had been before; a learned body, or clerisy, as such, gradually disappeared, and literature in general then began to be addressed to the common miscellaneous public."[1] We might profitably compare the argument, with its embryonic sociology of literature, with Arnold's account of the functions of criticism and of academies. The appeal of the church to Coleridge was strong; one more attraction, and another overlap with the idea of the elite, was the very separateness of its ministers: while serving the world, their eyes were not fixed exclusively upon it. He felt that the purity of the few must be safeguarded; the accommodations demanded by popular education could be dangerous:

7. *Ibid.*, I, pp. 155–6; CCS, pp. 59–61.
8. See the epigraph to the ninth essay in the revised *Friend*, which was taken from Erasmus' letters: "Hoc potissimum pacto felicem ac magnum regem se fore judicans: non si quam plurimis sed si quam optimis imperit. Proinde parum esse putat justis praesidiis regnum suum muniisse, nisi idem viris cruditione juxta ac vitae integritate praecellentibus ditet atque honestet. Nimirum intelligit haec demum esse vera regni decora, has veras opes: hanc veram et nullis unquam seculis cessuram gloriam" (*Friend*, I, p. 251).
9. *Philosophical Lectures*, p. 201; cf. *Biographia*, II, 31, 40.
1. Literary Lectures, 1818, in *Literary Remains*, ed. H. N. Coleridge (4 vols., 1836), I, pp. 238–9. This is the earliest occasion known to me on which Coleridge makes use of this word, though he is obviously near it in adverting to the *clerum* to which the *Statesman's Manual* was addressed in 1816 (*Statesman's Manual*, p. 36).

There are, in every country, times when the few who know the truth have clothed it for the vulgar, and addressed the vulgar in the vulgar language and modes of conception, in order to convey any part of the truth. This, however, could not be done with safety, even to the *illuminati* themselves in the first instance; but to their successors habit gradually turned lie into belief, partial and *stagnate* truth into ignorance, and the teachers of the vulgar (like the Franciscan friars in the South of Europe) became a part of the vulgar.[2]

The search for truth must be carried on free from contamination, but at the same time, in order that the purifying consequences of that search might be nationally effective, they must be presented in terms of morality and religion to the nation at large. The Church of England provided the requisite model. But Coleridge now had to discriminate between the church of Christ—the "*sustaining, correcting, befriending* Opposite of the world"[3]—and the national church, and we can observe him doing this, both in his letters and other writings, from around 1820.[4] The matured theory of the clerisy which we find in *Church and State* arose from the accommodation of his development of German idealist philosophy to English cultural conditions. As such it is specifically English and Coleridgean, and even the industry of Professor Fruman can find no immediate German source for it.[5] Coleridge's relative security and stability after settling at Highgate did not, it is true, permit him to finish his *Magnum Opus*. But they did permit him to precipitate, to make public in the form of a social theory, an idea of the intellectual life in its social and moral bearing that had sustained him throughout his career as a consolatory and reassuring vision.

The ostensible reason for writing and publishing *Church and State* was to intervene in the debate on Catholic emancipation. However, the Test Act had been repealed in 1829, the year before the book was published, and it is clear that the debate provided Coleridge with the occasion to say something he was wanting to say in any case. There was also a concern with the growing Reform crisis which—although it does not appear on the surface of Coleridge's work—means that we can usefully compare *Church and State* to Arnold's *Culture and Anarchy*. As the "last relic of our nationality," the Church of England retained an essential role in preventing social dissolution, and the *Table Talk* shows Coleridge horrified by reports that the church was to suffer despoliation.[6] Social dissolution, beginning as philosophical and moral blindness, became political in the accepted sense. "What," he

2. *Anima Poetae* (1895), p. 228. I have been unable to trace this in NB.
3. CCS, p. 98.
4. CL, IV, pp. 51, 455; Snyder, *On Logic and Learning*, pp. 7–8; R. F. Brinkley, *Coleridge on the Seventeenth Century* (New York, 1968), gives the text of a manuscript note (unfortunately undatable) on Donne's sermons (*Literary Remains*, III, pp. 119–20; Brinkley, pp. 181–2) in which Coleridge exclaims over the consequences of conflating the Christian with the national church, and actually uses the word "clerisy." When Kathleen Coburn's edition of the NB reaches the 1820s it will undoubtedly provide much information on the development of the argument of CCS.
5. *Coleridge, the Damaged Archangel*—to judge at least by the paucity of his references to that work.
6. *Table Talk*, pp. 167, 214.

had once demanded in a letter about the "Anti-magnet of social Disorganization and *Dissoluteness*," "are the clergy doing?"[7] Since society
was not—could not be—a mere conglomeration of self-fulfilling individuals, the dissolution of the body politic (a "constituted realm, kingdom, commonwealth, or nation . . . where the integral parts, classes or
orders are so balanced or interdependent, as to constitute more or
less, a moral unit, an organic whole"[8]) would in itself terminate the
progressive humanisation of its erstwhile members. The reconstitution
of the clerisy was the only hope.

The social model within which the clerisy was to act was in essence
the dialectical one which had long appealed to Coleridge. He invoked
one of his favourite images, the bar magnet, to illustrate it. The agricultural interest and the possessors of land constituted one pole, the
mercantile, professional, and personal interests the other.[9] The interaction of these forces of permanence and progression constituted the
state. In the absence of either, the state would cease to exist. We must,
however, remember that he is talking about the idea of the state, not
about realised actuality. While his philosophy of history asserts that it
is towards the realisation of this idea that national history has been
moving ("sometimes with, sometimes without, not seldom, perhaps,
against, the intention of the individual actors, but always as if a power,
greater, and better than the men themselves, had intended it for
them"—the cunning of reason is an inescapable feature of philosophies of history), there is no inevitability about the final realisation.
Imbalance between the two forces is a distinct possibility, and had indeed, according to Coleridge, been a factor in the social condition into
which England fell after 1688. The point needs to be emphasised,
since it is the clerisy that creates a possibility of continued balance
and interaction. This is what I mean when I claim that in his theory,
the members of the clerisy act as horizontal mediators; their activity is
a precondition of the healthful opposition of powers.

The existence of imbalance was a problem to which Coleridge had
addressed himself, in the *Second Lay Sermon,* as early as 1817. There
he had asserted that the underlying causes of the present distress were
"resolvable into the overbalance of the commercial spirit in consequence of the absence or weakness of the counterweights."[1] Then, he
had hurried through the "natural counterforces" in order to concen-
trate on the influence of religion. But on the way he enunciated a pro-
gramme which he was to fulfil in *Church and State.* An excess in our
"attachment to temporal and personal objects can be counteracted
only by a pre-occupation of the intellect and the affections with permanent, universal, and eternal truths." The ascendancy of unchecked
commercialism, in other words, shares a fundamental identity with
the ascendancy of the unleavened understanding, for he had left himself no means of discriminating between the effects of commercialism

7. *CL*, IV, p. 711.
8. *CCS*, p. 91.
9. *Ibid.* pp. 16, 22, and ch. 2 in general; cf. *Philosophical Lectures*, pp. 86–7.
1. *Second Lay Sermon*, p. 169.

in particular, and those of attachment to material objects in general. Coleridge's epistemology and his social theory are inseparable. The subject led him on, but he explained: "I must not permit myself to any more on this subject, desirous as I am of shewing the importance of a philosophic class, and of evincing that it is of vital utility, and even an essential element in the composition of a civilised community."[2] This desire he achieved in *Church and State*.

Without the clerisy, the dialectic would fall apart. Coleridge used the example of the ancient Greek democracies which fell into dissolution from an excess of the "permeative" over the organised powers, "the permeative powers deranging the functions, and by explosions shattering the organic structures, they should have enlivened."[3] Basic to his theory was the notion of the "nationalty" the national heritage of land, set aside for the good of the nation, illegitimately possessed in the middle ages by the church, and much of it later, and wrongfully, alienated. This nationalty was intended in the idea for the maintenance of the national church, a body different from the church of Christ, which he discussed later on. The national church was the "third estate of the realm," and its object was "to secure and improve that civilization, without which the nation could be neither permanent nor progressive."[4] The order which was to carry on this civilising and mediating work was to be divided into a larger and a smaller body. The smaller was to

> remain at the fountain heads of the humanities, in cultivating and enlarging the knowledge already possessed, and in watching over the interests of physical and moral science; being likewise, the instructors of such as constituted, or were to constitute, the remaining more numerous classes of the order.

The latter were to be distributed throughout the nation

> so as not to leave the smallest integral part or division without a resident guide, guardian and instructor; the objects and final intention of the whole order being these—to preserve the stores, to guard the treasures, of past civilisation, and thus to bind the present with the past; to perfect and add to the same, and thus to connect the present with the future; but especially to diffuse through the whole community . . . that quantity and quality of knowledge which was indispensable both for the understanding of [their] rights, and for the performance of the duties correspondent.

In such fashion the clerisy was to irradiate the body politic much as the reason was held to irradiate the understanding. Higher education did not pertain to the mass of the people, but the civilising effects of the speculation and scholarship carried on by the inner clerisy—so to speak—were to be mediated to society at large by the distributed

2. *Ibid.* pp. 173–4.
3. CCS, p. 70.
4. *Ibid.* ch. 5, which, with ch. 6, contains the central account of the national church, and on which the following account is based.

clerisy. The learning which they represented was fundamental to the national vitality.

> THE CLERISY of the nation, or national church, in its primary acceptation and original intention comprehended the learned of all denominations;—the sages and professors of the law and jurisprudence; of medicine and physiology; of music; of military and civil architecture; of the physical sciences; with the mathematical as the common *organ* of the preceding; in short, all the so called liberal arts and sciences, the possession and application of which constitute the civilization of a country, as well as the Theological. The last was, indeed, placed at the head of all; and of good right did it claim the precedence. But why? Because under the name of Theology . . . were contained the interpretation of languages; the conservation and tradition of past events; the momentous epochs, and revolutions of the race and nation; the continuation of the records; logic, ethics, and the determination of ethical science, in application to the rights and duties of men in all their various relations, social and civil; and lastly, the ground-knowledge, the prima scientia as it was named,—PHILOSOPHY, or the doctrine and discipline of *ideas*.

Many of Coleridge's perennial concerns have crystallised here, in a forcible statement of the relevance to national well-being of the kind of intellectual work to which he was himself devoted. Only instead of being scattered and divided, out on the edge of things, and limited in its influence, the clerisy has come home. The sociological dimension of his thought insisted that the clerisy be provided for: in a rightly constituted society, the clerks would not be driven from temporary shelter to temporary shelter and from financial expedient to financial depen-dence. His readers were left to decide how best the lesson might be applied in the nineteenth century in the light of Coleridge's account of Henry VIII's failure. For Henry had had the opportunity of restoring the lands wrongfully—sacrilegiously indeed—alienated from the nationalty, but had failed to take it. If he had, the land should have been distributed for the maintenance (1) of the universities and "great schools of liberal learning"; (2) of a pastor in each parish; (3) of a school-master in each parish who should assist the pastor, and in due course succeed him. It is this practical element in his thought that sets Coleridge's idea of the clerisy apart from, say, Arnold's idea of the critics. The former wanted to know in detail how his elite was to work upon society and how it was itself to be maintained.

From the description of how the clerisy ought to have been organised, Coleridge turned (as should not surprise us) back to the reason and the understanding. The "commanding knowledge, the *power* of truth, given or obtained by contemplating the subject in the fontal mirror of the Idea, is in Scripture ordinarily expressed by Vision." And, he repeated, "Where no vision is, the people perisheth." Yet ordinary people, we have seen, were incapable of vision in this sense. The absence of a functional clerisy therefore deprived the nation of that leavening of reason that alone could bring about the humanisation of its members, and we lived "under the dynasty of the understanding." In such a condition—and the terms in which he speaks of it parallel Arnold's distrust of "machinery"—true freedom was impossible, for the understanding pandered merely to material need. Coleridge's model of the mind underwrites and sustains his model of society. The French Revolution had failed, he long ago claimed, because the French were "too sensual to be free." "The Sensual and the Dark rebel in vain, Slaves by their own compulsion."[5] The "New Heaven and the New Earth" consists in an interior condition, "Undreamt of by the sensual and the proud." The clerisy, mediating reason, is the *sine qua non* of genuine society.

In a recent lecture, Donald MacKinnon has spoken of the irony of Coleridge's descent into a "complacent Anglicanism," and, more broadly, of his falling for a kind of sectarianism in arrogating to himself absolute moral judgment. He sought the triumph of the ideas with which he had identified himself at the expense of their corruption.[6] Where his educational and social thought is concerned, we may, I believe, speak of another irony. That is that we have a theory of mind and of education of a wonderful fruitful sort, a psychological intelligence of enormous power which becomes committed to a limiting desire to separate the faculties of mind. In weighting the proposed dialectic in favour of the so-called "higher" faculty, it impoverishes intellect, and (while appropriating the higher form of intellectual health for the few) sustains class society by proposing a merely partial and dutiful notion of intellectual health for the many. Dialectical interplay resolves into the subordination of one faculty to another, and the dynamic philosophy ends up supporting an organic and largely static idea of the state.

The pathos of unity and infallibility had absorbed Coleridge. The clerisy represented unity in a divided and divisive world by reason of its foothold in the noumenal world, and he invested it with those attributes which he apparently desired for himself. The cultivation, of which it was to be the agent, represented the passage beyond striving to a state of communication with a world of surety, a condition which permitted interpretation of the multitudinousness of the real world within the framework of the ideas firmly anchored in the changeless. Back in about 1797 he had copied into his Notebook a quotation from Jeremy Taylor; he used it again in the philosophical twelfth chapter of the *Biographia*, and it might serve almost as a motto to his thought: "he to whom all things are one, who draweth all things to one, and seeth all things in one, may enjoy true peace and rest of spirit."[7] The pursuit of the synthesis in which all the details might be safely subsumed became all-absorbing; Coleridge's thought on the subject of the clerisy is the precipitation of a mind that had ceased to regard the essential unity—whether of knowledge, or of the transcendent world, or of the idea of church and state—as merely provisional. The theory of

5. Respectively "Fears in Solitude" and "'France, an Ode," *Poetical Works*, pp. 256, 243.
6. MacKinnon, "Coleridge and Kant," p. 198.
7. *Biographia*, I, p. 194; Beer, *Coleridge the Visionary*, ch. 9.

the clerisy in nineteenth-century England thus starts with an inheritance of idealism in both the everyday and the philosophic senses. And at a purely practical level this inheritance could lead to some remarkable oversights.

In describing his own philosophic progress, Coleridge spoke of his indebtedness to the mystical tradition which he saw represented by George Fox, Jakob Boehme, and William Law. In doing so, and in a passage whose relevance is in no way diminished by Fruman's observation that it is lifted from Schelling's *Natur-Philosophie,* he made some interesting admissions:

> Whoever is acquainted with the history of philosophy during the last two or three centuries cannot but admit that there appears to have existed a sort of secret and tacit compact among the learned not to pass beyond a certain limit in speculative science. . . . Therefore the true depth of science, and the penetration to the inmost centre, from which all the lines of knowledge diverge to their ever distant circumference, was abandoned to the illiterate and the simple, whom unstilled learning and an original ebulliency of spirit had urged to the investigation of the indwelling and living ground of things. These then, because their names had never been inrolled in the guilds of the learned, were persecuted by the registered livery-men as interlopers on their rights and privileges. All without distinction were branded as fanatics and phantasts. . . . And this for no other reason but because they were the *unlearned*, men of humble and obscure occupations. When, and from whom among the literati by profession, have we ever heard the divine doxology repeated, "I thank Thee O Father . . . because Thou hast hid these things from the wise and prudent, and has revealed them unto babes"? No! the haughty priests of learning not only banished from the schools and marts of science all who had dared draw living waters from the fountain, but drove them out of the very Temple, which meantime the "buyers, and sellers and money-changers" were suffered to make "a den of thieves."[8]

When he came to formulate the idea of the clerisy, Coleridge would have done well to reflect on this very danger. For he gives no reason to think that his own clerisy would not be capable of a similar, or even greater treason.

---

8. *Biographia*, I, pp. 95–6; Fruman, *Coleridge, the Damaged Archangel*, p. 81.

Biographical Register

Aristotle (384–322 B.C.E.), Greek philosopher and tutor of Alexander the Great, rivaled only by his teacher Plato in his influence on Western thought; author of treatises on logic, metaphysics, ethics, politics, rhetoric, poetics, zoology, physics, and other subjects.

Francis Bacon, Baron Verulam and Viscount St. Albans (1561–1626), English philosopher and politician, author of *The Advancement of Learning* (1605) and the *New Organon* (1620); celebrated for his writings on scientific method and admired by Coleridge for both his thought and his prose style.

George Berkeley (1685–1753), Irish-born Anglican bishop and idealist philosopher; denied the existence of matter and maintained that reality consists in ideas in the mind; author of *A Treatise concerning the Principles of Human Knowledge* (1710), *Alciphron* (1732), and *Siris* (1744).

William Lisle Bowles (1762–1850), poet and Anglican priest; author of *Fourteen Sonnets* (1789), *Elegiac Stanzas* (1796), and other volumes. The youthful Coleridge admired Bowles's poetry and dedicated a sonnet to him, but he later strained their relationship by suggesting revisions of some of Bowles's poems.

Edmund Burke (1729–1797), Irish-born Whig Party politician and philosopher; formulated an influential distinction between the sublime and beautiful in *A Philosophical Enquiry into the Origin of Our Ideas of the Sublime and Beautiful* (1757); in 1765 entered parliament, where he supported American independence, Irish emancipation, and reform of the colonial administration in India; fiercely attacked the French Revolution in *Reflections on the Revolution in France* (1790).

George Gordon, Lord Byron (1788–1824), the most widely read English poet in the Romantic period, notorious for his tempestuous personal life. An admirer of Coleridge's poetry, he was instrumental in getting the play *Remorse* performed in 1813 and the poem "Christabel" published in 1816; but he also satirized Coleridge (along with Wordsworth and Southey) in *Don Juan* (1819–24).

Berkeley Coleridge (1798–1799), Coleridge's second son, who was born and died while his father was in Germany.

Derwent Coleridge (1800–1883), Coleridge's third son, named after the River Derwent in the English Lake District; attended St. John's College, Cambridge, and eventually became an Anglican priest. He edited three volumes of his father's theological writings (1853).

Ernest Hartley Coleridge (1846–1920), son of Derwent Coleridge, editor of his grandfather's *Complete Poetical Works* (1912).

George Coleridge (1764–1828), one of Coleridge's older brothers, a kind of surrogate father to him after their father's death in 1781; assumed his father's old position as headmaster of the Grammar School in Ottery St. Mary, Devonshire, in 1794; fell out with Coleridge in 1807 over the latter's separation from his wife.

Hartley Coleridge (1796–1849), Coleridge's first child, named after David Hartley; attended Merton College, Oxford, but was deprived of a fellowship at Oriel College on grounds of drunkenness; settled in the Lake District as a poet and essayist.

Henry Nelson Coleridge (1798–1843), Coleridge's nephew and (from 1829) son-in-law; editor of his uncle's *Table Talk* (1835), *Literary Remains* (1836–39), and other works.

Sara Coleridge, née Fricker (1770–1845), Coleridge's wife and Robert Southey's sister in-law; engaged to Coleridge in Bristol in August 1794 and married in October 1795. After years of discord Coleridge separated from her in 1807, and she continued living with their children in the Lake District in the house they shared with the Southeys.

Sara Coleridge (1802–1852), Coleridge's daughter; married her first cousin Henry Nelson Coleridge in 1829; edited or co-edited her father's *Confessions of an Inquiring Spirit* (1841), *Biographia Literaria* (1847), *Notes and Lectures upon Shakespeare* (1849), and *Essays on His Own Times* (1850).

Joseph Cottle (1770–1853), Bristol bookseller, publisher of Coleridge's *Poems* (1797) and the *Lyrical Ballads* of Wordsworth and Coleridge (1798); wrote a controversial memoir, *Early Recollections, Chiefly Relating to Samuel Taylor Coleridge* (1837), which included a frank and unsympathetic account of Coleridge's opium addiction.

Erasmus Darwin (1731–1802), physician, botanist, inventor, and poet, known for his verse popularizations of contemporary scientific thought (e.g., *The Botanic Garden*, 1791); formulated a theory of evolution (in *Zoonomia*, 1794–96) which in some respects anticipated that of his grandson Charles.

Sir Humphry Davy (1778–1829), chemist and lecturer, president of the Royal Society from 1820; experimented with nitrous oxide (laughing gas) and discovered potassium, sodium, calcium, and other elements by decomposing chemical compounds with electricity. He met Coleridge in 1799 and arranged for his first literary lectures in 1808, but they grew more distant after Davy was knighted in 1812.

Thomas De Quincey (1785–1859), essayist and journalist, friend of Coleridge and Wordsworth from 1807; revealed Coleridge's plagiarisms from German authors after Coleridge's death. An opium addict like Coleridge, he recounted his experience of opium use in *Confessions of an English Opium-Eater* (1822).

René Descartes (1596–1650), French rationalist philosopher and mathematician, one of the founding figures of modern philosophical and scientific thought; sought to establish a rational and nonsensory basis of knowledge; author of *Discourse on the Method of Rightly Conducting One's Reason* (1637), *Meditations on First Philosophy* (1641), and *Principles of Philosophy* (1644).

Johann Gottlieb Fichte (1762–1814), German idealist philosopher, follower of Kant; defined existence in terms of the ego's positing of itself, and the world in terms of the ego's positing of a nonego; wrote several volumes of *Wissenschaftslehre* (Science of Knowledge) (1794–96) and the nationalistic *Speeches to the German Nation* (1807–08).

Charles James Fox (1749–1806), Whig Party politician and (from 1783) leader of the opposition in parliament against William Pitt; campaigned for religious liberty, American and Irish independence, the abolition of the slave trade, and peace with France; was revered by liberal Whigs, but hampered as party leader by divisions among the Whigs.

Anne Gillman, née Harding (c. 1799–1860), wife of James Gillman; looked after Coleridge from 1816 to his death.

James Gillman (1782–1839), surgeon in Highgate (then a northern suburb of London) who took Coleridge into his house in 1816 as a patient and nonpaying guest, an arrangement that continued for the rest of Coleridge's life. While Gillman regulated Coleridge's opium use, Coleridge assisted Gillman with his researches and tutored his sons.

William Godwin (1756–1836), political philosopher, novelist, and historian, husband of Mary Wollstonecraft and father of Mary Wollstonecraft Godwin (later Shelley); befriended Coleridge in 1799; author of *Caleb Williams* (1794) and five later novels; was celebrated in radical circles for *An Enquiry concerning Political Justice* (1793), which opposed all forms of government force and argued that individuals can be motivated solely by reason to act benevolently toward others.

Johann Wolfgang Goethe (1749–1832), German poet, playwright, novelist, scientific writer, and government official; author of *The Sorrows of Young Werther* (1774), *Faust* (part 1, 1808; part 2, 1832), and *Zur Farbenlehre* (On the Theory of Colors) (1810).

Joseph Henry Green (1791–1863), surgeon and anatomy instructor with an interest in German philosophy; met Coleridge in 1817 and become his friend and amanuensis; eventually became one of Coleridge's literary executors and the president of the Royal College of Surgeons.

David Hartley (1705–57), English associationist philosopher and physician; author of *Observations on Man, His Frame, His Duty, and His Expectations* (1749), a physiological explanation of the formation and association of ideas.

William Hazlitt (1778–1830), literary and art critic, essayist, lecturer, and painter; became a friend of Coleridge and Wordsworth after hearing Coleridge preach at a Unitarian service in 1798, but alienated them during a visit to the Lake District in 1803 and later became severely critical of Coleridge, whose philosophical interests and political conservatism he rejected.

Thomas Hobbes (1588–1679), English political and natural philosopher, generally regarded as the founder of British political philosophy; author of *Leviathan* (1651), a materialist account of human behavior and a justification of absolutist government.

David Hume (1711–1776), Scottish empiricist philosopher and historian; emphasized the roles of instinct and habit, as opposed to reason, in human thought, especially in causal inferences (*Treatise of Human Nature*, 1739–40); attacked the rationality of religious belief in his controversial *Natural History of Religion* (1757); also wrote the immensely popular *History of Great Britain* (1754–62).

Sara Hutchinson (1775–1835), whom Coleridge called "Asra," was William Wordsworth's sister-in-law (from 1802) and the object of Coleridge's unrequited love for many years after their first meeting in 1799. Coleridge dictated his periodical *The Friend* to her in 1809–10, but his estrangement from Wordsworth in October 1810 effectively ended contact between him and Hutchinson.

Friedrich Heinrich Jacobi (1743–1819), German philosopher and novelist, critic of Spinoza and Kant; insisted on the insufficiency of abstract reasoning and on the necessity of religious belief (*David Hume über den Glaube* (David Hume on Faith), 1787), and ignited a decade-long controversy about Spinoza and pantheism with his *Über die Lehre des Spinozas* (On Spinoza's Doctrine) (1785; rev. 1789).

Samuel Johnson (1709–1784), poet, lexicographer, essayist, and one of the foremost critics of English literature; author of *Rasselas* (1759) and *Lives of the English Poets* (1778–81), compiler of the *Dictionary of the English Language* (1755), and editor of Shakespeare (1765).

Immanuel Kant (1724–1805), the most influential German philosopher of the eighteenth century; particularly concerned with epistemology and the limits of human reason (*Critique of Pure Reason*, 1781; rev. 1787), ethics (*Critique of Practical Reason*, 1788), and aesthetics (*Critique of Judgment*, 1790).

Charles Lamb (1775–1834), essayist, poet, critic; worked as a clerk for the East India Company and cared for his sister Mary, who killed their mother in 1796 in a bout of insanity; author of *Essays from Elia* (1823), co-author (with Mary) of *Tales from Shakespeare* (1807). He and Coleridge were schoolmates at Christ's Hospital, and they remained friends for the rest of their lives.

Gottfried Wilhelm Leibniz (1646–1716), German philosopher and mathematician who asserted that this world is best of all the ones God could have created, that there is a sufficient reason for everything in the world, and that the world is composed of mind-like entities ("monads"); developed calculus; author of *Theodicy* (1710), *Monadology* (1714), and *New Essays on Human Understanding* (1765).

John Locke (1632–1704), English philosopher whose *Essay concerning Human Understanding* (1690) is generally regarded as the founding-text of British empiricism; also wrote on political philosophy (*Treatises of Government,* 1690).

John James Morgan (c. 1775–1820), a lawyer whose household included his wife, Mary, and sister Charlotte, gave Coleridge refuge in Bristol in 1807 and again in London in 1810. Coleridge lived with the Morgans on and off from October 1810 to April 1816, through repeated changes of address, Morgan's bankruptcy, and the worst period of Coleridge's opium addiction.

Napoléon Bonaparte (1769–1821), Corsican-born soldier and politician, emperor of France (as Napoleon I, 1804–15); joined the French revolutionary army in 1792, commanded it in Italy in 1796; led an unsuccessful campaign in Egypt in 1798; became First Consul in 1799, Consul for Life in 1802, and emperor in 1804, by which time he controlled much of western Europe; after a disastrous assault on Russia (1812) he was defeated at Leipzig (1813) and forced into exile on Elba (1814), but he returned to France in 1815 (the "Hundred Days") and raised another army; was defeated by the Duke of Wellington at Waterloo and permanently exiled to the Atlantic island of St. Helena. Napoleon was endlessly demonized and caricatured in the British press, not least by Coleridge.

Thomas Paine (1737–1809), revolutionary pamphleteer and orator; sailed to America in 1774 and wrote *Common Sense* (1776) in support of American independence, then returned to England in 1787 and published a refutation of Burke and defense of natural rights, *The Rights of Man* (1791), which prompted the government to charge him with libel; fled to France, where he was elected a member of the National Convention and wrote *The Age of Reason* (1793); fell out with the Jacobins, was arrested and imprisoned in December 1793. Released in 1796, he returned in 1803 to America, where he died in obscurity.

William Pitt the younger (1759–1806), Tory Party politician, twice prime minister (1783–1801, 1804–06); supported abolition and electoral reform, but during the war with France (1793–1815) ruthlessly suppressed dissent with anti-sedition laws, treason trials, and a network of domestic spies.

Plato (c. 428–347 B.C.E.), Greek philosopher, student of Socrates, founder of the Athenian Academy; author of some thirty dialogues on such subjects as love (*Symposium*), beauty (*Phaedrus*), the nature of the Good and the ideal state (*Republic*), and cosmology (*Timaeus*).

Plotinus (205–270), Greek philosopher, founder of Neoplatonism; studied in Alexandria and settled in Rome, where he taught philosophy and wrote fifty-four tracts edited by his student Porphyry as the *Enneads*.

Thomas Poole (1765–1837), wealthy tanner and philanthropist well known in the Bristol region for his democratic views; Coleridge's close friend and neighbor in Nether Stowey, Somerset, from December 1796.

Joseph Priestley (1733–1804), English Presbyterian (later Unitarian) minister, religious controversialist, chemist, and political activist, notorious for his support of the American and French Revolutions; emigrated to Pennsylvania in 1794 because his life was in danger. One of England's most important chemists, he isolated numerous gases and discovered photosynthesis.

Henry Crabb Robinson (1775–1867), lawyer, journalist, and diarist; acquaintance of numerous English and German writers, including Wordsworth, Goethe, and Schelling; became a friend of Coleridge's in 1810, and helped reconcile him and Wordsworth in 1812.

Jean-Jacques Rousseau (1712–1778), Genevan political philosopher and novelist, advocate of republican government and educational reform, an inspiration for the eighteenth-century cult of "sensibility" and the French Revolution; author of *The Social Contract* (1762), the novels *La Nouvelle Héloïse* (1761) and *Émile* (1762), and the posthumously published *Confessions* (1782–89).

Friedrich Wilhelm Joseph Schelling (1775–1854), German idealist philosopher, follower of Fichte and exponent of *"Naturphilosophie"*; identified the source of the self and nature as absolute reason, which manifests itself most fully in art; author of the *System of Transcendental Idealism* (1800) and other works, from which Coleridge translated without acknowledgment in *Biographia Literaria* and elsewhere.

Sir Walter Scott (1771–1832), immensely popular Scottish poet and novelist, trained as a lawyer; author of *Waverley* (1814), *Rob Roy* (1817), *Ivanhoe* (1819), and two dozen more historical novels. The indebtedness of his poem *The Lay of the Last Minstrel* (1805) to the then-unpublished "Christabel" was a sore point for Coleridge.

Robert Southey (1774–1843), poet and biographer, poet laureate from 1813; met Coleridge at Oxford in 1794, and with him planned to establish a communal farming society ("Pantisocracy") in Pennsylvania. The failure of this scheme temporarily alienated Coleridge and Southey, who had become brothers-in-law by marrying the Fricker sisters of Bristol in 1795, but in 1801 the Southeys joined the Coleridges at Greta Hall, Keswick. Southey oversaw the education of the Coleridge children after their parents' separation.

Baruch (or Benedictus) de Spinoza (1632–1677), Dutch Jewish philosopher, widely reviled by his contemporaries as irreligious but admired by the German Romantics as a pantheist; author of the *Tractatus Theologico-politicus* (1670), a historical examination of the Bible, and of the posthumously published *Ethics* (1677), a treatise on God (whom he identified with nature) and humanity.

John Thelwall (1764–1834), radical political lecturer and poet, tried for treason (with John Horne Tooke) and acquitted in 1794; met Coleridge in 1796 and visited him and Wordsworth in Somerset in 1797; retired to Wales in 1798, but eventually returned to London and the public eye as a teacher of elocution.

John Horne Tooke (1736–1812), radical political activist and philologist; founded the Constitutional Society in support of American independence in 1771; agitated for political and economic reform in Britain until he was tried for and acquitted of treason in 1794; author of *The Diversions of Purley* (1786–1805), a materialist theory of the origin of language.

Voltaire, originally François Marie Arouet (1694–1778), French Enlightenment writer, renowned for his satirical skills and detested by Coleridge as an embodiment of French superficiality; author of *Micromégas* (1752), *Candide* (1759), and a *Philosophical Dictionary* (1762).

Thomas Wedgwood (1777–1805), philanthropist and amateur scientist, younger son of the famous potter Josiah Wedgwood (1730–1795); together with his brother Josiah

(1769–1843) provided Coleridge with a £150 annuity from 1798 to enable him to devote himself fully to poetry and philosophy.

Dorothy Wordsworth (1771–1853), diarist and travel writer, devoted sister of William Wordsworth, with whom she lived permanently from 1795; she also traveled to Germany with her brother and Coleridge in 1798–99.

Mary Wordsworth, née Hutchinson (1770–1859), sister of Sara Hutchinson and (from 1802) wife of William Wordsworth.

William Wordsworth (1770–1850), poet from the English Lake District and brother of Dorothy Wordsworth, successor to Southey as poet laureate; met Coleridge in 1795 and moved to Somerset in 1797 to be nearer to him, becoming his close friend and collaborator on *Lyrical Ballads* (1798); traveled to Germany with Coleridge in 1798–99 and began writing his autobiographical masterpiece *The Prelude,* which he always called the "poem to Coleridge"; married Mary Hutchinson, Sara's sister, in 1802. In October 1810 a series of misunderstandings led to a two-year rupture in his friendship with Coleridge, which never regained its previous closeness. Coleridge had long acknowledged Wordsworth's importance as a poet, but widespread public recognition only followed the publication of *The Excursion* (1814) and the two-volume *Poems* (1815).

Glossary

abolitionism: a term covering two movements in Britain, the first—which had wide-spread popular support, especially in the 1780s and 1790s—for the abolition of the slave *trade*, and the second for the abolition of slavery itself in British colonies (it was not practiced within Britain). The most prominent abolitionists were the philanthropist Thomas Clarkson (1760–1846) and the parliamentarian William Wilberforce (1759–1833), who succeeded in 1807 in pressuring parliament to ban the slave trade. The movement to abolish slavery gathered force in the 1820s, but it was not until 1834–37 that the slaves were finally emancipated.

associationism: a form of empiricist philosophy concerned with the process by which ideas are formed out of sense-data and other ideas ("association of ideas"). Hartley, the first systematic associationist, sought to identify regular patterns of idea-formation, while David Hume and John Stuart Mill rejected such "laws of association."

empiricism: a philosophical tradition (represented in Britain by Locke and his successors) that maintains that knowledge is derived from sensory experience and that the function of the mind is to organize the sense-data it receives into ideas. Empiricism is opposed to rationalism, which postulates *a priori* knowledge or innate ideas.

Gnosticism: a religious movement, consisting of various sects, that flourished in the second and following centuries C.E. and was vigorously opposed by both orthodox Christian theologians and pagan Neoplatonic philosophers. Although few Gnostic texts were available in Coleridge's time, certain crucial tenets of Gnosticism were known, including its radical dualism, manifested in the distinction between an evil creator god (who forms and rules the physical world) and a good but utterly remote supreme god (who implants a dim knowledge of himself, or *gnosis*, in the minds of select persons).

idealism: a term designating philosophies that identify reality with the contents of the mind. Examples include Berkeley's "subjective idealism," which maintains that existence consists in being perceived by the mind; Kant's "transcendental idealism," which maintains that objects can be known not as they are in themselves but only as they conform to the subjective conditions of human perception, e.g., by appearing in time and space; and the "absolute idealism" of Fichte and Schelling, which explains the world as the contents of an absolute mind.

Jacobins: a term originally applied to the members of a political society convened in 1789 at the Dominican monastery of St. Jacques in Paris to promote democratic reform, but soon used more broadly—and, in Britain, chiefly as a term of abuse—to designate any sympathizers of the French Revolution or supporters of democratic government.

mechanical philosophy: a philosophy of nature (of which Descartes's is the foremost example) postulating that all natural phenomena can be explained in terms of matter and motion.

Naturphilosophie: "philosophy of nature" (German), mostly closely associated with

Schelling and his followers, who conceived nature as a vast organism ordered according to the same principles as human thought and governed by opposing forces (positive and negative charge in electricity, north and south poles in magnetism, etc.) that derived from a single original polarity (*Urpolarität*). German Romantic *Naturphilosophie* was strongly opposed to the mechanical philosophy.

necessitarianism: a deterministic philosophy rooted in the associationist psychology of Locke and most fully developed by Hartley. The necessitarians, who included radical thinkers like Priestley and Godwin, explained all events as effects determined by prior events in a causal chain.

Neoplatonism: a philosophical movement inaugurated by Plotinus and continued by Porphyry (c. 232–304), Proclus (c. 410–485), and their successors through the sixth century C.E. It conceives the universe as emanating from an unchanging, transcendent, and absolutely good One in a series of degradations, beginning with the emergence of the mind and ending with the emergence of matter. At the farthest remove from the One, the process is reversed and all things return to the One. Though anti-Christian in origin, Neoplatonism exerted considerable influence on medieval Christian thought, as well as on Renaissance humanism and Romantic idealism.

opium: a narcotic prepared from the juice of the opium poppy (*Papaver somniferum*) and known since antiquity for its analgesic and euphoric effects. Unregulated in Britain until 1868, it was readily available in the eighteenth and nineteenth centuries in numerous forms and strengths—to be drunk, eaten, or smoked—and was widely used as a painkiller, without an understanding of its addictive properties. Laudanum, the form that Coleridge used, was an alcoholic solution of the opium derivative morphine.

pantheism: a doctrine asserting that everything existing constitutes a divine unity, so that there is no distinction between God and the world. The best-known example of pantheism in Coleridge's time was the philosophy of Spinoza's *Ethics*, which derived all finite things from a single substance that Spinoza called "God or nature" (*Deus sive natura*). Many eighteenth- and nineteenth-century German intellectuals (e.g., Goethe and Schelling) embraced some form of pantheism.

Pantisocracy: Coleridge's name (meaning "government by all") for the plan he and Robert Southey formed in 1794 of emigrating to Pennsylvania with their wives and a handful of friends to establish on the banks of the Susquehanna River a democratic farming community in which all property would be owned communally and labors shared equally. By September 1795 the plan had collapsed as a result of its impracticability and the temperamental differences between Coleridge and Southey.

patriotism: In its eighteenth-century usage, this term designated not merely a love of one's country but a more comprehensive ideology developed out of disgust with government corruption, a celebration of traditional English liberties, Protestant notions of an elect people, nostalgia for an idealized Saxon past, anti-Catholic sentiment, and virulent xenophobia (especially Francophobia). This ideology was represented iconographically in the figures of John Bull (somewhat analogous to the American Uncle Sam) and the goddess Britannia. During the American and French Revolutions, however, the label of "patriot" was claimed by both opponents and supporters of the revolutionary causes.

Plato's theory of Forms: Plato taught (e.g., in the *Phaedo*) that the general qualities of things in the immanent world of our experience (redness, roundness, similarity, beauty, goodness, etc.) either imitate or somehow participate in eternal, immutable Forms or Ideas of those qualities in a transcendent world (thus Socrates's wisdom is an imperfect reflection of the Form of wisdom). We are born with a dim recollection of the Forms, which is the basis of true knowledge; the goal of philosophy is to improve that knowledge.

polarity: the interaction of two opposed forces. *Naturphilosophie* postulated the operation of polar forces throughout nature, and Coleridge found even wider applications (in law, religion, and government, as well as in nature) for the so-called law of polarity, according to which every power manifests itself in the opposition of forces that seek to be reunited with each other.

sensibility: a term defined by Samuel Johnson as "quickness of sensation [or] perception," but often used in the eighteenth and early nineteenth centuries more specifically to describe an extreme sensitivity to sensory or emotional stimuli, or an unrestrained power of emotional sympathy. The trait was much celebrated in eighteenth-century fiction, but by the end of the century was being criticized by some social reformers and novelists as anti-rational and unmanly.

Trinitarianism: adherence to the central Christian doctrine of the Trinity, according to which God exists in three Persons (Father, Son, and Holy Spirit) with one substance. Although the precise nature of the relationship of the Persons has been much disputed since the doctrine's introduction in the second century, the basic principles of their co-equality and the unity of their substance were established at the Councils of Nicaea (325) and Constantinople (381).

Unitarianism: a form of Christian belief that, claiming the authority of scripture and reason, rejects the doctrines of the Trinity and of Christ's divinity. Although certain Unitarian views were in circulation as early as the second and third centuries, the organized Unitarian movement dates from the sixteenth and seventeenth centuries, when congregations were established in Poland, Hungary, and England. In the eighteenth century Unitarianism attracted many English Presbyterians (like Joseph Priestley) and liberal Anglicans, including, for a time, Coleridge. Two important anti-Trinitarian sects associated with Unitarianism were the Arians and the Socinians: the former were followers of the north African priest Arius (d. 336), who maintained that Christ was divine but not coeternal with God the Father; the latter were followers (concentrated in Poland until 1638) of the Italian-born teacher Faustus Socinus (1539–1604), who maintained that Christ was divinely inspired but not divine.

Coleridge: A Chronology

1772   Born October 21 at Ottery St. Mary, Devonshire, the youngest of ten children of the Reverend John and Ann Bowdon Coleridge.

1778   Ottery Grammar School.

1781   Death of father (October 4).

1782   School at Christ's Hospital, London, a charity school (until September 1791). Pupil of the Reverend James Boyer. School friend of Charles Lamb.

1791   Enters Jesus College, Cambridge (October). Takes opium for rheumatic fever (November).

1792   Wins medal for Greek ode on the slave trade (July).

1793   At Cambridge supports the Reverend William Frend, a Fellow of Jesus College, at his trial for holding heretical views (May). Deeply in debt and depressed, enlists in His Majesty's Fifteenth Light Dragoons under the name of Silas Tomkyn Comberbache (December). With the influence of his brothers George and James, a colonel in the army, he is discharged by April 1794 on the grounds of insanity.

1794   Returns to Cambridge (April); begins a walking tour of Wales (June). At Oxford meets Robert Southey. They walk to Nether Stowey and meet Thomas Poole.

At Bristol meets and becomes engaged to Sara Fricker, the sister of Southey's fiancée.

In the summer Southey and Coleridge think of emigration to America and conceive of pantisocracy, an idealistic community with shared property. They jointly write *The Fall of Robespierre*, a drama published in Cambridge (September).

Leaves Cambridge without a degree (December). Publishes "Sonnets on Eminent Characters" in the *Morning Chronicle*.

1795   In Bristol delivers radical political lectures to earn money for emigration (January–February).

Reads Hartley's *Observations on Man*, Priestley's *History of the Corruptions of Christianity*, and Cudworth's *True Intellectual System* (late winter into spring).

Falls out with Southey, pantisocracy abandoned (August). Meets Wordsworth in Bristol (August).

Marries Sara Fricker (October 4) and moves to Clevedon on the Bristol Channel.

Conciones ad Populum and *The Plot Discovered* published (December).

1796   Travels to the Midlands (January–February) to collect sub-
        scribers for *The Watchman*, a political journal, which runs to
        from March 1 to May 13.
        Reads Bishop Berkeley's works (March).
        Publishes *Poems on Various Subjects* on April 16.
        Birth of first son, David Hartley (September 19).
        Publishes *Ode on the Departing Year* (December). With Poole's
        assistance moves to Nether Stowey.

1797   Visits with Wordsworth in Stowey (March) and at Racedown,
        the Wordsworths' home (June). The Wordsworths move to Al-
        foxden House, near Stowey (July).
        *Poems, to Which Are Now Added, Poems by Charles Lamb and
        Charles Lloyd* published (October).
        Summer visits from Charles Lamb, John Thelwall, and Joseph
        Cottle. Walking tour with Wordsworths (November). They be-
        gan "The Ancient Mariner."

1798   Delivers sermons at Unitarian Chapel at Shrewsbury with
        William Hazlitt in the audience (January). Accepts an annuity
        of £150 from the Wedgwoods.
        Writes "Frost at Midnight" (February). Finishes "The Ancient
        Mariner" (March), and writes "Fears in Solitude" and "France:
        An Ode" (April), which turn away from his most radical polit-
        ical positions.
        Writes the first part of "Christabel" (spring).
        Birth of second son, Berkeley (May 14).
        The Wordsworths leave Alfoxden in late spring, since their
        lease is not renewed.
        Lyrical Ballads and *Fears in Solitude* published (September).
        William Wordsworth, Dorothy Wordsworth, and Coleridge
        travel to Germany, leaving Sara and two children at home.
        Wordsworth settles in Goslar. Coleridge attends lectures at
        the University of Göttingen on natural history by J. F. Blu-
        menbach and divinity by J. G. Eichhorn.

1799   Death of Berkeley Coleridge (February 10). Coleridge learns of
        death in early April. Arrives back in Stowey at the end of July.
        Reads Spinoza (September). Tours the Lake District with
        Wordsworth and Cottle (October–November). Meets Sara
        Hutchinson (late October).
        Moves to London (November) to write for the *Morning Post*
        (until April 16, 1800).

1800   Visits Wordsworth at Grasmere (April). Translates Schiller's
        Wallenstein (spring).
        Moves his family to Greta Hall, Keswick, in the Lake District
        to be near Wordsworth (July).
        Birth of third son, Derwent (September 14).
        Writes the second part of "Christabel" (summer) for the sec-
        ond edition of *Lyrical Ballads*, but Wordsworth rejects the
        poem. Assists Wordsworth in preparation of copy for *Lyrical
        Ballads* (1800).

1801   Second edition of *Lyrical Ballads* published (January).
        Writes letters on Descartes and Locke to Josiah Wedgwood
        (February). Writes to Poole that he has rejected Hartley's asso-
        ciationism and materialism (March). Reads Leibniz and Kant.

1802   In London writing for *Morning Post* (January–February).
        Travels north, visiting Sara Hutchinson on the way to
        Wordsworths (March).
        April 4 writes "A Letter to ———," the first version of "Dejec-
        tion: An Ode." Severe discord with wife.
        "Dejection: An Ode" printed in the *Morning Post* (October 4).
        Birth of fourth child, Sara (December 23).

1803   Publishes *Poems*, third edition (June), supervised through the
        press by Lamb. Visits at Keswick from the Beaumonts, Hazlitt,
        and Samuel Rogers.
        Tours Scotland with the Wordsworths (August 15–29), contin-
        ues tour alone (until September 15).
        The *Morning Post* sold, ending Coleridge's writing for it (Sep-
        tember).

1804   Leaves the Lake District for London (January).
        Sails for Malta (April). Becomes secretary to Alexander Ball,
        British High Commissioner to Malta (July). Visits Sicily (Au-
        gust–November).

1805   Notebook entries accepting Trinitarian Christianity and reject-
        ing Unitarianism.
        Leaves for Naples and Rome (December).

1806   In Rome (January). Meets Washington Allston and Ludwig Tieck.

1807   Lands in England (August).
        Returns to the Lake District (October).
        Separates from his wife (December). Goes to Coleorton,
        owned by the Beaumonts, with Wordsworth, Dorothy
        Wordsworth, and Sara Hutchinson.

1807   Hears Wordsworth read *The Prelude* and writes "To a Gentle-
        man" (January). At Coleorton until April.
        Last visit to Stowey (June).
        Meets Thomas De Quincey (August).

1808   In London (January–June). About twenty lectures at the Royal
        Institution on the principles of poetry, not completed because
        of illness and opium addiction.
        Arrives in Grasmere (September) and lives with the Words-
        worths at Allan Bank.

1809   Publishes *The Friend* (June 1–March 15, 1810).

1810   Sara Hutchinson leaves the Wordsworths to live in Wales
        (March), ending her assistance in production of *The Friend*
        and Coleridge's hope for her sympathy.
        Travels to London with Basil Montague, who tells Coleridge
        of Wordsworth's loss of hope for him (October). Serious split
        with the Wordsworths. Depressed by illness and opium.
        Lives with John Morgan, consults doctors on illness and
        opium use (November).

1811   Writes for the *Courier* (April–September), signed articles sup-
         porting government, patronage, and empire. Attacked by
         Leigh Hunt in the *Examiner*.
         Seventeen lectures on Shakespeare and Milton at the London
         Philosophical Society (November–January 1812) attended by
         Byron and Henry Crabb Robinson. In the ninth lecture begins
         to borrow from A. W. Schlegel's *Lectures on Dramatic Art and
         Literature* (1809–11).
1812   Writes essays for the *Courier* (January–May).
         Visits the Lake District (February–March); avoids the Words-
         worths.
         Reconciles with Wordsworth through mediation of Lamb and
         Henry Crabb Robinson (March).
         Six lectures on drama at Willis's Rooms, London (May–
         August).
         Reads Schelling (August).
         Twelve lectures on Shakespeare at the Surrey Institution (No-
         vember 3–January 26, 1813). Half the Wedgwood annuity
         withdrawn (November).
1813   *Remorse* opens at Drury Lane Theater for successful run of
         twenty nights (January 23).
         Eight lectures in Bristol on Shakespeare and education to
         raise money for the bankrupt Morgan (October–November).
         Living with Morgans near Bristol.
         Ill, addicted, and suicidal (December–January 1814).
1814   Six lectures at Bristol on Milton and Cervantes (April).
         Publishes "Essays on the Principles of Genial Criticism" in *Fe-
         lix Farley's Bristol Journal* (August–September).
         Moves to Calne, Wiltshire, with Morgans (December).
1815   Lives at Calne and dictates the *Biographia* to John Morgan.
         Sends *Biographia Literaria* and *Sibylline Leaves* to printer in
         Bristol (September); printing begins in October.
1816   Travels to London (April); meets with Byron. *Zapolya* rejected
         for stage.
         Accepted as patient and house guest by the surgeon James
         Gillman, Highgate, where he lives for the rest of his life (April
         15).
         Publishes of *Christabel, Kubla Khan, and The Pains of Sleep*
         (May 25), which goes through three editions in 1816.
         Publishes *The Statesman's Manual* (December).
1817   Publishes second *Lay Sermon* (March).
         Adds material for second volume and writes final chapter of
         Biographia Literaria (February–May).
         Biographia Literaria and *Sibylline Leaves* published (July).
1818   "Treatise on Method" printed in the *Encyclopedia Metropoli-
         tana* (January).
         Fourteen lectures on European literature at the London Philo-
         sophical Society (January–March).
         Publishes revised edition of *The Friend* (November).

Lectures on alternate days on the history of philosophy and on literature, London (December).

1819   Seven lectures on Shakespeare, Milton, Dante, Spenser, and Cervantes (February–March).

1820   Preoccupied with son Hartley's expulsion from Oxford.

1824   Elected Fellow of the Royal Society of Literature, with an annuity (March).

1825   Lectures on Aeschylus to the Royal Society of Literature (May 18).
        Publishes *Aids to Reflection* (May).

1828   Tours Netherlands and Rhine with William and Dora Wordsworth (June 21–August 7).
        Publishes *Poetical Works*, 3 volumes (August).

1829   Publishes second edition of *Poetical Works* (May), and *On the Constitution of the Church and State* (December).

1830   Publishes second edition of *On the Constitution of the Church and State* (April).

1831   Publishes second edition of *Aids to Reflection*.
        Annuity from the Royal Society of Literature ended (May).

1833   Attends meeting of the British Association for the Advancement of Science, Cambridge (June).

1834   Publishes third edition of *Poetical Works* (March–August).
        Dies July 25. Funeral and burial in Highgate (August 2).

Selected Bibliography

BIBLIOGRAPHIES AND REFERENCES

Coffman, Ralph. *Coleridge's Library: A Bibliography of Books Owned or Read by Samuel Taylor Coleridge.* Boston, 1987.

Crawford, Walter, and Ann Crawford. *Samuel Taylor Coleridge: A Bibliography of Criticism and Scholarship [1940–65].* Vol. 3. Boston, 1996.

Crawford, Walter, Ann Crawford, and Edward Lauterbach. *Samuel Taylor Coleridge: A Bibliography of Criticism and Scholarship [1900–39].* Vol. 2. Boston, 1983.

Erdman, David V. *The Romantic Movement: A Selective and Critical Bibliography.* New York, 1980–87; West Cornwall, Conn., 1988–. An annual bibliography covering 1979 to the present.

Haven, Richard, Josephine Haven, and Maurianne Adams. *Samuel Taylor Coleridge: A Bibliography of Criticism and Scholarship [1793–1899].* Vol. 1. Boston, 1976.

Logan, Sister Eugenia, ed. *A Concordance to the Poetry of Samuel Taylor Coleridge.* St. Mary-of-the-Woods, Ind., 1940. Reprint, Gloucester, Mass., 1967.

Mays, J. C. C. "Samuel Taylor Coleridge." In *The Cambridge Bibliography of English Literature.* 3rd ed. Vol. 4. Ed. Joanne Shattock. Cambridge, 1999, 298–324. A listing of primary sources.

The MLA International Bibliography of Books and Articles on the Modern Languages and Literatures. New York, 1963–. An annual bibliography, available in printed and electronic formats.

Purton, Valerie. *A Coleridge Chronology.* Basingstoke, 1993.

Schulz, Max. "Samuel Taylor Coleridge." In *The English Romantic Poets: A Review of Research and Criticism.* 4th ed. Ed. Frank Jordan. New York, 1985, 341–463. A survey of scholarship and criticism up to about 1982.

Trott, Nicola. "Samuel Taylor Coleridge." In *Literature of the Romantic Period: A Bibliographical Guide.* Ed. Michael O'Neill. Oxford, 1998, 65–89. A supplement to Schulz's article.

Whalley, George. "Samuel Taylor Coleridge." In *The New Cambridge Bibliography of English Literature.* Vol. 3. Cambridge, 1969, 211–54. A listing of primary and secondary sources.

Wise, Thomas J. *A Bibliography of the Writings in Prose and Verse of Samuel Taylor Coleridge.* London, 1913. Supplemented by *Coleridgeiana*, London, 1919. Reprint (in one volume), London, 1970. The standard descriptive bibliography of Coleridge's works.

FIRST PUBLICATIONS IN BOOKS OF COLERIDGE'S MAJOR POETRY AND PROSE

Chronological List of Books and Periodicals Published in Coleridge's Lifetime

The Fall of Robespierre. An Historic Drama. Cambridge, 1794. Facsimile reprint, Oxford, 1991. Acts 2 and 3 are by Robert Southey.

A Moral and Political Lecture Delivered at Bristol. Bristol, 1795.

Conciones ad Populum. Or Addresses to the People. [Bristol,] 1795. Facsimile reprint, Oxford, 1992.

The Plot Discovered: or An Address to the People, Against Ministerial Treason. Bristol, 1795.

The Watchman. Bristol, 1796. A periodical published in ten numbers from March 1 to May 13, 1796. Facsimile reprint, Oxford, 1998.

Poems on Various Subjects. London and Bristol, 1796. Facsimile reprint, Oxford, 1990.

Ode on the Departing Year. Bristol, 1796.

*Poems * * * Second Edition. To which are now added Poems by Charles Lamb and Charles Lloyd.* Bristol, 1797. Facsimile reprint, Oxford, 1997.

Lyrical Ballads, with a Few Other Poems. London, 1798. Facsimile reprint, Oxford, 1990. Published anonymously by Wordsworth and Coleridge.

*Fears in Solitude * * * To which are added, France, an Ode; and Frost at Midnight.* London, 1798. Facsimile reprint, Oxford, 1989.

The Piccolomini, or the First Part of Wallenstein, A Drama in Five Acts. London, 1800. A translation of the play by the German poet Friedrich Schiller.

The Death of Wallenstein. A Tragedy in Five Acts. London, 1800. A translation of the play by Schiller.

Poems. London, 1803.

The Friend; A Literary, Moral and Political Weekly Paper. [Penrith,] 1809–10. A periodical published in twenty-eight issues from June 1, 1809, to March 15, 1810. Reprinted in book form, London, 1812. Revised and expanded, 3 vols., London, 1818.

Remorse. A Tragedy, in Five Acts. London, 1813. Facsimile reprint, Oxford, 1989.

Christabel: Kubla Khan, A Vision; The Pains of Sleep. London, 1816. Facsimile reprint, Oxford, 1991.

The Statesman's Manual; or The Bible the Best Guide to Political Skill and Foresight. London, 1816.

A Lay Sermon, Addressed to the Higher and Middle Classes, on the Existing Distresses and Discontents. London, 1817.

Biographia Literaria; or Biographical Sketches of My Literary Life and Opinions. 2 vols. London, 1817. Facsimile reprint, Menston, 1970.

Sibylline Leaves: A Collection of Poems. London, 1817. Facsimile reprint, Oxford, 1990. Includes the first publication of the revised and expanded "Rime of the Ancient Mariner."

Zapolya: A Christmas Tale, in Two Parts. London, 1817.

Aids to Reflection in the Formation of a Manly Character on the Several Grounds of Prudence, Morality, and Religion. London, 1825. Revised edition, London, 1831.

*The Poetical Works * * * Including the Dramas of Wallenstein, Remorse, and Zapolya.* 3 vols. London, 1828. Reprinted with three additional poems, 1828.

*On the Constitution of the Church and State * * * with Aids toward a Right Judgment on the Late Catholic Bill.* London, 1830. Revised edition, 1830.

The Poetical Works. 3 vols. London, 1834.

Chronological List of Posthumously Published Collections

Specimens of the Table Talk of the Late Samuel Taylor Coleridge. [Ed. Henry Nelson Coleridge.] 2 vols. London, 1835. Revised edition, 1836.

Letters, Conversations, and Recollections. [Ed. Thomas Allsop.] 2 vols. London, 1836.

Literary Remains in Prose and Verse. 4 vols. Ed. Henry Nelson Coleridge. London, 1836–39.

Confessions of an Inquiring Spirit. Ed. Henry Nelson Coleridge. London, 1840.

Hints towards the Formation of a More Comprehensive Theory of Life. Ed. Seth B. Watson. London, 1848. Facsimile reprint, Westmead, Hants., 1970.

Notes and Lectures upon Shakespeare, and Some of the Old Poets and Dramatists. Ed. Sara Coleridge. 2 vols. London, 1849.

Essays on His Own Times. Ed. Sara Coleridge. 3 vols. London, 1850.

Notes on English Divines. Ed. Derwent Coleridge. 2 vols. London, 1853.

Notes, Theological, Political, and Miscellaneous. Ed. Derwent Coleridge. London, 1853.

Complete Works. Ed. W. G. T. Shedd. 7 vols. New York, 1853.

Seven Lectures on Shakespeare and Milton. Ed. John Payne Collier. London, 1856.

Osorio, A Tragedy. [Ed. R. H. Shepherd.] London, 1873. The first publication of a play written in 1797.

Letters. Ed. Ernest Hartley Coleridge. 2 vols. London, 1895.

Anima Poetæ. Ed. Ernest Hartley Coleridge. London, 1895. Selections from the notebooks.

Coleridge on the Seventeenth Century. Ed. Roberta Florence Brinkley. Durham, N.C., 1955.

CRITICAL EDITIONS AND TEXTUAL STUDIES

Older critical editions now superseded by *The Collected Works* are omitted.

Beer, John, gen. ed. *Coleridge's Writings.* 3 vols. to date. Basingstoke, 1990–. A selected edition comprising the following titles: vol. 1, *On Politics and Society*; vol. 2, *On Humanity*; vol. 3, *On Language.*

Coburn, Kathleen, gen. ed. *The Collected Works of Samuel Taylor Coleridge.* 16 vols. (in 34). Princeton, N.J., 1969–2002. The standard edition of all the writings except the notebooks and letters, comprising the following titles: vol. 1, *Lectures 1795: On Politics and Religion*; vol. 2, *The Watchman*; vol. 3, *Essays on His Times* (3 parts); vol. 4, *The Friend* (2 parts); vol. 5, *Lectures 1808–1819: On Literature* (2 parts); vol. 6, *Lay Sermons*; vol. 7, *Biographia Literaria* (2 parts); vol. 8, *Lectures 1818–1819: On the History of Philosophy* (2 parts); vol. 9, *Aids to Reflection*; vol. 10, *On the Constitution of the Church and State*; vol. 11, *Shorter Works and Fragments* (2 parts); vol. 12, *Marginalia* (6 parts); vol. 13, *Logic*; vol. 14, *Table Talk* (2 parts); vol. 15, *Opus Maximum*; vol. 16, *Poetical Works* (6 parts).

Coburn, Kathleen, ed. *The Notebooks of Samuel Taylor Coleridge.* 5 vols. (in 10). New York, London, and Princeton, N. J., 1957–2002.

Coleridge, Ernest Hartley, ed. *The Complete Poetical Works of Samuel Taylor Coleridge.* 2 vols. Oxford, 1912.

Griggs, Earl Leslie, ed. *The Collected Letters of Samuel Taylor Coleridge.* 6 vols. Oxford, 1956–71.

Halmi, Nicholas. "The Norton Critical Edition of *Coleridge's Poetry and Prose.*" *Romanticism on the Net* 19 (August 2000) (www-sul.stanford.edu/mirrors/romnet/19halmi.html)

Mays, J. C. C. "Reflections on Having Edited Coleridge's Poems." In *Romantic Revisions.* Ed. Robert Brinkley and Keith Henley. Cambridge, 1992, 136–53.

Parrish, Stephen Maxfield, ed. *Coleridge's "Dejection": The Earliest Manuscript and the Earliest Printings.* Ithaca, N.Y., 1988.
Stillinger, Jack. *Coleridge and Textual Instability: The Multiple Versions of the Major Poems.* New York, 1994.
Wallen, Martin, ed. *Coleridge's "Ancient Mariner": An Experimental Edition of Texts and Revisions, 1798–1828.* Barrytown, N.Y., 1993.
Whalley, George. "Coleridge and the Self-Unravelling Clue." In *Editing Polymaths: Erasmus to Russell.* Ed. H. J. Jackson. Toronto, 1983, 17–40.
———."On Editing Coleridge's Marginalia." In *Editing Texts of the Romantic Period.* Ed. John D. Baird. Toronto, 1972, 89–118.

BIOGRAPHICAL WORKS

Armour, R. W., and R. F. Howe, eds. *Coleridge the Talker.* Ithaca, N.Y., 1940. Revised edition, New York, 1969.
Ashton, Rosemary. *The Life of Samuel Taylor Coleridge: A Critical Biography.* Oxford, 1996.
Bate, Walter Jackson. *Coleridge.* New York, 1968.
Campbell, James Dykes. *Samuel Taylor Coleridge: A Narrative of the Events of His Life.* London, 1894.
Coburn, Kathleen. *In Pursuit of Coleridge.* London, 1977.
Cottle, Joseph. *Early Recollections, Chiefly Relating to the Late Samuel Taylor Coleridge during His Long Residence in Bristol.* 2 vols. London, 1837.
———.*Reminiscences of Samuel Taylor Coleridge and Robert Southey.* London, 1848. Facsimile reprint, Westmead, Hants., 1970.
De Quincey, Thomas. "Coleridge and Opium-Eating." *Blackwood's Edinburgh Magazine,* January 1845. Reprinted in *The Collected Writings of Thomas De Quincey.* Vol. 5. Ed. David Masson. Edinburgh, 1890, 179–214.
———."The Lake Poets: Southey, Wordsworth, and Coleridge." *Tait's Magazine,* August 1839. Reprinted in *The Collected Writings of Thomas De Quincey.* Vol. 2. Ed. David Masson. Edinburgh, 1889, 335–47.
———."Samuel Taylor Coleridge." *Tait's Magazine,* September, October, November 1834; January 1835. Reprinted (as one chapter) in *The Collected Writings of Thomas De Quincey.* Vol. 2. Ed. David Masson. Edinburgh, 1889, 138–228.
Engell, James, ed. *Coleridge: The Early Family Letters.* Oxford, 1994.
Holmes, Richard. *Coleridge: Darker Reflections.* London, 1998.
———.*Coleridge: Early Visions.* London, 1989.
Lamb, Charles. "Christ's Hospital Five and Thirty Years Ago." In *Elia: Essays which have appeared under that signature in the London Magazine.* London, 1823, 27–50. Reprinted in *Elia and the Last Essays of Elia.* Ed. Jonathan Bate. Oxford, 1987, 14–26.
Lefebure, Molly. *Samuel Taylor Coleridge: A Bondage of Opium.* London, 1974.
Perry, Seamus, ed. *S. T. Coleridge: Interviews and Recollections.* Basingstoke, 2000.
Sultana, Donald. *Samuel Taylor Coleridge in Malta and Italy.* Oxford, 1969.

CRITICISM

The headings used in the following section are intended merely to guide readers through the large body of Coleridgean scholarship, and the classification of titles has sometimes been fairly arbitrary. Thus, for example, the fact that a book is listed with studies of Coleridge's poetry does not necessarily mean that it has nothing to say about his philosophical thought. Articles included in the collections listed in the "Collections of Criticism" section are generally not listed separately.
• indicates items included or excerpted in this Norton Critical Edition.

Introductions

In addition to the books listed below, see Bate's biography (listed above).

Cooke, Katherine. *Coleridge.* London, 1979.
Hill, John Spenser. *A Coleridge Companion: An Introduction to the Major Poems and the "Biographia Literaria."* London, 1983.
House, Humphrey. *Coleridge: The Clark Lectures, 1951–1952.* London, 1953.
Holmes, Richard. *Coleridge.* Oxford, 1982.
Willey, Basil. *Samuel Taylor Coleridge.* New York, 1971.

Collections of Criticism

The Coleridge Bulletin (1992–) is a scholarly journal devoted to Coleridge and his circle.
Beer, John, ed. *Coleridge's Variety: Bicentenary Studies.* London, 1974.
Bloom, Harold, ed. *Samuel Taylor Coleridge.* New York, 1986.
Burwick, Frederick, ed. *Coleridge's "Biographia Literaria": Text and Meaning.* Columbus, Ohio, 1989.

Coburn, Kathleen, ed. *Coleridge: A Collection of Critical Essays*. Englewood Cliffs, N.J., 1967.

Crawford, Walter, ed. *Reading Coleridge: Approaches and Applications*. Ithaca, N.Y., 1979.

Fry, Paul, ed. *Samuel Taylor Coleridge: The Rime of the Ancient Mariner*. New York, 1999.

Fulford, Tim, and Morton Paley, eds. *Coleridge's Visionary Languages: Essays in Honour of J. B. Beer*. Cambridge, 1993.

Gallant, Christine, ed. *Coleridge's Theory of Imagination Today*. New York, 1989.

Gravil, Richard, and Molly Lefeburc, eds. *The Coleridge Connection: Essays for Thomas McFarland*. Basingstoke, 1990.

Gravil, Richard, Lucy Newlyn, and Nicholas Roe, eds. *Coleridge's Imagination: Essays in Memory of Pete Laver*. Cambridge, 1985.

Hartman, Geoffrey, ed. *New Perspectives on Coleridge and Wordsworth: Selected Papers from the English Institute*. New York, 1972.

Kroeber, Karl, and Gene Ruoff, eds. *Romantic Poetry: Recent Revisionary Criticism*. New Brunswick, N.J., 1993.

Jackson, J. R. de J., ed. *Coleridge: The Critical Heritage*. 2 vols. London, 1970–91.

Miall, David, and Don Kuiken, eds. "Coleridge and Dreams." Special double-issue of *Dreaming: Journal of the Association for the Study of Dreams* 7, nos. 1–2 (1997).

Orr, Leonard, ed. *Critical Essays on Samuel Taylor Coleridge*. New York, 1994.

Roe, Nicholas, ed. *Samuel Taylor Coleridge and the Sciences of Life*. Oxford, 2001.

Reiman, Donald, ed. *The Romantics Reviewed: Contemporary Reviews of British Romantic Writers*. Part A: *The Lake Poets*. 2 vols. New York, 1972.

Woodring, Carl, ed. "Coleridge: The Politics of Imagination." Special section of *Studies in Romanticism* 21, no. 3 (Fall 1982): 447–74.

General Works

•Abrams, M. H. *The Correspondent Breeze: Essays on English Romanticism*. New York, 1984.

Ashton, Rosemary. *The German Idea: Four English Writers and the Reception of German Thought, 1800–1860*. Cambridge, 1980.

Beer, John. *Coleridge's Poetic Intelligence*. London, 1977.

———. *Coleridge the Visionary*. London, 1959.

Bygrave, Stephen. *Coleridge and the Self: Romantic Egotism*. Basingstoke, 1986.

Davidson, Graham. *Coleridge's Career*. Basingstoke, 1990.

Fruman, Norman. *Coleridge: The Damaged Archangel*. New York, 1971.

Fulford, Tim. *Coleridge's Figurative Language*. Basingstoke, 1991.

———. *Romanticism and Masculinity: Gender, Politics, and Poetics in the Writings of Burke, Coleridge, Cobbett, Wordsworth, De Quincey, and Hazlitt*. New York, 1999.

Havens, Richard. *Patterns of Consciousness: An Essay on Coleridge*. Amherst, Mass., 1969.

Hazlitt, William. "Coleridge's Literary Life." *Edinburgh Review*, August 1817. Reprinted in *The Complete Works of William Hazlitt*. Vol. 16. Ed. P. P. Howe. London, 1933, 115–39.

•———. *Lectures on the English Poets*. London, 1818, 327–31. Reprinted in *The Selected Writings of William Hazlitt*. Vol. 2. Ed. Duncan Wu. London, 1998, 318–20.

•———. "Mr. Coleridge." *The Spirit of the Age: or Contemporary Portraits*. London, 1825, 59–79. Reprinted in *The Selected Works of William Hazlitt*. Vol. 7. Ed. Duncan Wu. London, 1998, 98–105.

———. "On My First Acquaintance with Poets." *The Liberal*, April 1823. Reprinted in *The Selected Works of William Hazlitt*. Vol. 9. Ed. Duncan Wu. London, 1998, 95–110.

McFarland, Thomas. *Romanticism and the Forms of Ruin: Wordsworth, Coleridge, and Modalities of Fragmentation*. Princeton, N.J., 1981.

Perry, Seamus. *Coleridge and the Uses of Division*. Oxford, 1999.

Shaffer, E. S. *"Kubla Khan" and "The Fall of Jerusalem": The Mythological School in Biblical Criticism and Secular Literature, 1770–1880*. Cambridge, 1975.

Studies of Coleridge's Poetry

Adair, Patricia. *The Waking Dream: A Study of Coleridge's Poetry*. London, 1967.

Bloom, Harold. *The Visionary Company: A Reading of English Romantic Poetry*. Garden City, N.Y., 1961. Revised edition, Ithaca, N.Y., 1971.

Bostetter, Edward E. *The Romantic Ventriloquists: Wordsworth, Coleridge, Keats, Shelley, Byron*. Seattle, 1963.

Dekker, George. *Coleridge and the Literature of Sensibility*. New York, 1978.

Durham, Margery. "The Mother Tongue: Christabel and the Language of Love." In *The (M)other Tongue: Essays in Feminist Psychoanalytic Criticism*. Ed. Shirley Garner, Claire Kahane, and Madelon Sprengnether. Ithaca, N.Y., 1986, 169–93.

Ebbatson, J. R. "Coleridge's Mariner and the Rights of Man." *Studies in Romanticism* 11 (1972): 171–206.

Eilenberg, Susan. *Strange Power of Speech: Wordsworth, Coleridge, and Literary Possession*. New York, 1992.

Empson, William. "The Ancient Mariner." *Critical Quarterly* 6 (1964): 298–319. Reprinted in Empson, *Argufying: Essays on Literature and Culture*. London, 1987, 297–319.

————. "The Ancient Mariner: An Answer to [Robert Penn] Warren." *Kenyon Review* 15 (1953): 155–77.

————. "Introduction." *Coleridge's Verse: A Selection.* Ed. William Empson and David Pirie. London, 1972, 13–100.

Everest, Kelvin. *Coleridge's Secret Ministry: The Context of the Conversation Poems, 1795–1798.* New York, 1979.

•Ferguson, Frances. "Coleridge and the Deluded Reader." *Georgia Review* 31 (1977): 617–35.

Jones, Steven E. " 'Supernatural, or at Least Romantic': The Ancient Mariner and Parody." *Romanticism on the Net* 15 (August 1999) (www-sul.stanford.edu/mirrors/romnet/sejstc.html).

Kessler, Edward. *Coleridge's Metaphors of Being.* Princeton, N.J., 1979.

Koenig-Woodyard, Chris. "sex—text: 'Christabel' and the Christabelliads." *Romanticism on the Net* 15 (August 1999) (www-sul.stanford.edu/mirrors/romnet/parodyxtabel.html).

Lowes, John Livingston. *The Road to Xanadu: A Study in the Ways of the Imagination.* Boston, 1927. Revised edition, 1930.

Magnuson, Paul. *Coleridge and Wordsworth: A Lyrical Dialogue.* Princeton, N.J., 1988.

————. *Coleridge's Nightmare Poetry.* Charlottesville, Va., 1974.

————. *Reading Public Romanticism.* Princeton, N.J. 1998.

McGann, Jerome. "The Meaning of 'The Ancient Mariner.' " *English Romantic Writers and Contemporary Historical Methods.* Ed. G. A. Rosso and Daniel Watkins. Rutherford, N.J., 1990, 208–39.

Mileur, Jean-Pierre. *Vision and Revision: Coleridge's Art of Immanence.* Berkeley, 1982.

Nethercot, Arthur Hobart. *The Road to Tryermaine: A Study of the History, Background, and Purposes of Coleridge's "Christabel."* Chicago, 1939.

Newlyn, Lucy. *Coleridge, Wordsworth, and the Language of Allusion.* Oxford, 1986.

————. *"Paradise Lost" and the Romantic Reader.* Oxford, 1994.

Paglia, Camille. "The Daemon as Lesbian Vampire: Coleridge." In *Sexual Personae: Art and Decadence from Nefertiti to Emily Dickinson.* New Haven, Conn., 1989, 317–46.

Paley, Morton. *Coleridge's Later Poetry.* Oxford, 1996.

Parker, Reeve. *Coleridge's Meditative Art.* Ithaca, N.Y., 1975.

Parrish, Stephen Maxfield. *The Art of the "Lyrical Ballads."* Cambridge, Mass., 1973.

Piper, H. W. *The Active Universe: Pantheism and the Concept of Imagination in the English Romantic Poets.* London, 1962.

Prickett, Stephen. *Coleridge and Wordsworth: The Poetry of Growth.* Cambridge, 1970.

Richardson, Alan. *A Mental Theater: Poetic Drama and Consciousness in the Romantic Age.* University Park, Pa., 1988.

Ruoff, Gene. *Wordsworth and Coleridge: The Making of the Major Lyrics, 1802–1804.* New Brunswick, N.J., 1989.

Schneider, Elisabeth W. *Coleridge, Opium, and "Kubla Khan."* Chicago, 1953.

Schulz, Max. *The Poetic Voices of Coleridge: A Study of His Desire for Spontaneity and Passion for Order.* Detroit, 1963.

Spatz, Jonas. "The Mystery of Eros: Sexual Initiation in Coleridge's 'Christabel.' " *PMLA* 90 (1975): 107–16.

Suther, Marshall. *Visions of Xanadu.* New York, 1965.

•Swann, Karen. " 'Christabel': The Wandering Mother and the Enigma of Form." *Studies in Romanticism* 23 (1984): 533–53

Taylor, Anya. "Coleridge on Persons in Dialogue." *Modern Language Quarterly* 50 (1989): 357–74.

•Warren, Robert Penn. "A Poem of Pure Imagination: An Experiment in Reading." *Kenyon Review* 8 (1946): 391–427. Reprinted in Warren, *New and Selected Essays.* New York: Random House, 1989, 335–423.

Watson, George. *Coleridge the Poet.* London, 1966.

Watson, Jeanie. *Risking Enchantment: Coleridge's Symbolic World of Faery.* Lincoln, Nebr., 1990.

Whalley, George. *Coleridge and Sara Hutchinson and the Asra Poems.* London, 1955.

Woodring, Carl. *Politics in the Poetry of Coleridge.* Madison, Wis., 1961.

Studies of Coleridge's Criticism

Abrams, M. H. *The Mirror and the Lamp: Romantic Theory and the Critical Tradition.* New York, 1953.

Appleyard, J. A. *Coleridge's Philosophy of Literature: The Development of a Concept of Poetry, 1791–1819.* Cambridge, Mass., 1965.

Baker, James Vollant. *The Sacred River: Coleridge's Theory of the Imagination.* Baton Rouge, La., 1957.

Engell, James. *The Creative Imagination: Enlightenment to Romanticism.* Cambridge, Mass., 1981.

Ferguson, Frances. "Coleridge on Language and Delusion." *Genre* 2 (1978): 191–207.

Ferrier, James Frederick. "The Plagiarisms of S. T. Coleridge." *Blackwood's Edinburgh Magazine* 47 (March 1840): 287–99.

Ferris, David. "Coleridge's Ventriloquy: The Abduction from the *Biographia.*" *Studies of Romanticism* 24 (1985): 41–84.

Fogle, Richard Harter. *The Idea of Coleridge's Criticism.* Berkeley, 1962.
Gatta, John. "Coleridge and Allegory." *Modern Language Quarterly* 38 (1977): 62–77.
Goodson, A. C. *Verbal Imagination: Coleridge and the Language of Modern Criticism.* New York, 1988.
Hamilton, Paul. *Coleridge's Poetics.* Oxford, 1983.
Hardy, Barbara. "Distinction without Difference: Coleridge's Fancy and Imagination." *Essays in Criticism* 1 (1951): 336–44.
•Hoheisel, Peter. "Coleridge on Shakespeare: Method amid the Rhetoric." *Studies in Romanticism* 13 (1974): 15–23.
Jackson, H. J. "Coleridge's *Biographia*: When Is an Autobiography Not an Autobiography?" *Biographia* 20 (1997): 54–71.
———. "Johnson's Milton and Coleridge's Wordsworth." *Studies in Romanticism* 28 (1989): 29–47.
Jackson, J. R. de J. *Method and Imagination in Coleridge's Criticism.* London, 1969.
Leask, Nigel. *The Politics of Imagination in Coleridge's Critical Thought.* Basingstoke, 1988.
Marks, Emerson. *Coleridge on the Language of Verse.* Princeton, N.J., 1981.
•McGann, Jerome. "The *Biographia Literaria* and the Contentions of English Romanticism." In *Coleridge's "Biographia Literaria": Text and Meaning.* Ed. Frederick Burwick. Columbus, Ohio, 1989, 233–46.
Modiano, Raimonda. "Coleridge and Wordsworth: The Ethics of Gift Exchange and Literary Ownership." *The Wordsworth Circle* 20 (1989): 113–20.
Read, Herbert. *Coleridge as Critic.* London, 1949.
Reiman, Donald. "Coleridge and the Art of Equivocation." *Studies in Romanticism* 25 (1996): 325–50.
Richards, I. A. *Coleridge on Imagination.* London, 1934. Revised edition, 1962.
Shaffer, Elinor S. "Coleridge's Revolution in the Standard of Taste." *Journal of Aesthetics and Art Criticism* 28 (1969): 213–21.
Wallace, Catherine Miles. *The Design of the "Biographia Literaria."* London, 1983.
Wheeler, Kathleen. *Sources, Processes, and Methods in Coleridge's "Biographia Literaria."* Cambridge, 1980.
Wellek, René. "Coleridge." *A History of Modern Criticism, 1750–1950.* Vol. 2. New Haven, Conn., 1955, 151–87.

Studies of Coleridge's Philosophical and Religious Thought

Abrams, M. H. *Natural Supernaturalism: Tradition and Revolution in Romantic Literature.* New York, 1971.
Barth, J. Robert. *Coleridge and Christian Doctrine.* Cambridge, Mass., 1969.
Benziger, James. "Organic Unity: Leibniz to Coleridge." *PMLA* 66 (1951): 24–48.
Boulger, James. *Coleridge as Religious Thinker.* New Haven, Conn., 1961.
Christensen, Jerome. *Coleridge's Blessed Machine of Language.* Ithaca, N.Y., 1981.
Coleman, Deirde. *Coleridge and "The Friend" (1809–1810).* Oxford, 1988.
Ford, Jennifer. *Coleridge on Dreaming: Romanticism, Dreams and the Medical Imagination.* Cambridge, 1998.
Halmi, Nicholas. "How Christian Is the Coleridgean Symbol?" *The Wordsworth Circle* 26 (1995): 26–31.
Harding, Anthony John. *Coleridge and the Idea of Love.* Cambridge, 1974.
———. *Coleridge and the Inspired Word.* Montreal, 1985.
———. "Coleridge, the Afterlife, and the Meaning of 'Hades.' " *Studies in Philology* 96 (1999): 204–23.
Hedley, Douglas. *Coleridge, Philosophy, and Religion.* Cambridge, 1999.
Jasper, David. *Coleridge, Schleiermacher, and Romanticism.* London, 1986.
•Knights, Ben. *The Idea of the Clerisy in the Nineteenth Century.* Cambridge, 1978.
Levere, Trevor H. *Poetry Realized in Nature: Samuel Taylor Coleridge and Early Nineteenth-Century Science.* Cambridge, 1981.
Lockridge, Lawrence. *Coleridge the Moralist.* Ithaca, N.Y., 1977.
•McFarland, Thomas. *Coleridge and the Pantheist Tradition.* Oxford, 1969.
———. *Originality and Imagination.* Baltimore, 1985.
McKusick, James. *Coleridge's Philosophy of Language.* New Haven, Conn., 1986.
Miall, David. "The Meaning of Dreams: Coleridge's Ambivalence." *Studies in Romanticism* 21 (1982): 57–71.
Mill, John Stuart. *Mill on Bentham and Coleridge.* Ed. F. R. Leavis. London, 1950.
Muirhead, John. *Coleridge as Philosopher.* London, 1930.
Modiano, Raimonda. *Coleridge and the Concept of Nature.* London, 1985.
Orsini, G. N. G. *Coleridge and German Idealism.* Carbondale, Ill., 1969.
Perkins, Mary Anne. *Coleridge's Philosophy: The Logos as Unifying Principle.* Oxford, 1994.
Sanders, Charles Richard. *Coleridge and the Broad Church Movement.* Durham, N.C., 1942.
Taylor, Anya. *Coleridge's Defense of the Human.* Columbus, Ohio, 1986.
Vallins, David. *Coleridge and the Psychology of Romanticism.* Basingstoke, 1999.
Wellek, René. *Immanuel Kant in England, 1793–1838.* Princeton, N.J., 1931.
Wylie, Ian. *Young Coleridge and the Philosophers of Nature.* Oxford, 1989.

Studies of Coleridge's Political Thought

Calleo, David. *Coleridge and the Idea of the Modern State.* New Haven, Conn., 1966.
Colmer, John. *Coleridge, Critic of Society.* Oxford, 1959.
De Paolo, Charles. *Coleridge's Philosophy of Social Reform.* New York, 1987.
Keane, Patrick. *Coleridge's Submerged Politics: The "Ancient Mariner" and "Robinson Crusoe."* Columbus, Ohio, 1994.
Kooy, Michael John. "Coleridge's Francophobia." *Modern Language Review* 95 (2000): 924–41.
McFarland, Thomas. *Romanticism and the Heritage of Rousseau.* Oxford, 1995.
Morrow, John. *Coleridge's Political Thought: Property, Morality, and the Limits of Traditional Discourse.* Basingstoke, 1990.
•Roe, Nicholas. *Wordsworth and Coleridge: The Radical Years.* Oxford, 1988.
Thompson, E. P. *The Romantics: England in a Revolutionary Age.* New York, 1997.

Index of Poem Titles and First Lines